USA TODAY SPORTS RON SHANDLER'S **2013**

BASEBALL FORECASTER

AND ENCYCLOPEDIA OF FANALYTICS

TRIUMPH
BOOKS

Triumph Books and colophon are registered trademarks of Random House, Inc.

This book is available in quantity at special discounts for your group or organization. For further information, contact:

Triumph Books
542 South Dearborn Street
Suite 750
Chicago, Illinois 60605
(312) 939-3330
Fax (312) 663-3557

Printed in U.S.A.
ISBN: 978-1-60078-740-9

Rotisserie League Baseball is a registered trademark of the Rotisserie League Baseball Association, Inc.

Statistics provided by Baseball Info Solutions

Cover design by Brent Hershey
Front cover photograph by Charles LeClaire/US Presswire
Author photograph by Kevin Hurley

Ron Shandler's
BASEBALL FORECASTER

Editors
Ray Murphy
Brent Hershey

Associate Editor
Rod Truesdell

· · · · · ·

Technical Wizard
Rob Rosenfeld

Design
Brent Hershey

Data and Charts
Matt Cederholm

Player Commentaries
Dave Adler
Dan Becker
Rob Carroll
Matt Cederholm
Matt Gelfand
Brent Hershey
Ray Murphy
Stephen Nickrand
Kristopher Olson
Josh Paley
Brian Rudd
Jock Thompson
Rod Truesdell

Research and Articles
Bob Berger
Matt Cederholm
Patrick Davitt
Bill Macey
Ray Murphy

Prospects
Rob Gordon
Jeremy Deloney
Tom Mulhall

Injuries
Rick Wilton

Acknowledgments

Twenty-seven years. I thought I might be done by now, but the song of the Sirens keeps calling me back.

These days, I am just the captain of a ship with an amazing crew. The ones who do the heavy lifting for the S.S. Forecaster are the names that appear to your left. Their hard work is what makes this book so valuable and keeps us delivering these treasures, year after year. A special thanks to Ray, Brent and Rod for leading the charge.

A big thank you to the rest of the BaseballHQ.com staff, who do the yeoman's work in populating the website with 12 months of incredible online content: Andy Andres, Matt Baic, Matt Beagle, Alex Beckey, Brian Brickley, Ryan Bloomfield, Ed DeCaria, Doug Dennis, Pat DiCaprio, Matt Dodge, Neil FitzGerald, Colby Garrapy, Scott Gellman, Phil Hertz, Joe Hoffer, Tom Kephart, Chris Lee, Chris Mallonee, Troy Martell, Scott Monroe, Craig Neuman, Harold Nichols, Frank Noto, Greg Pyron, Nick Richards, Brian Rudd, Mike Shears, Peter Sheridan, Skip Snow, Jeffrey Tomich, Michael Weddell and Joshua Weller.

Thank you to BaseballHQ.com's tech team: Mike Krebs and Rob Rosenfeld.

Thank you to Lynda Knezovich, the Queen of Qustomer Service.

Thank you to all my industry colleagues. Most people don't realize how incredible these people are. Despite many of them being competitors, we function as a community for the better of the industry. It's an amazing group and I am proud to be included among them.

Thank you for all the support from the folks at Triumph Books and Action Printing.

I am honored to now be a part of the USA TODAY Sports Media Group. Great things are coming. Keep watching.

As always, thank you to my ladies. Darielle is wrapping up her senior year as president of the drama society, has done light design for several plays and made a brief, ad hoc appearance on a Broadway stage. After a summer living in Manhattan, the odds of her returning to Southwest Virginia have now dropped to 0%.

Justina's sophomore year has been highlighted by the release of her first EP and winning an international songwriting competition. After 18 months living in Florida, the odds of her returning to Southwest Virginia have now dropped to 0%. It's all simple math.

If there is one person in the world who is the reason for this book making it to age 27, it is my wonderful wife, Sue, and her unending support during the entirety of our 27-year marriage. As parents of two kids pursuing the arts, retirement is no longer an option, so I think we're going to be around for awhile longer.

Finally, thank *you*… for continuing to support our effort and following us on this journey. I remain forever grateful.

Ron Shandler
November 2012

2009 was the very first year I drafted at team in the **National Fantasy Baseball Championship.** I just was starting to get serious about fantasy baseball around that time. I had no clue how to look for skills to find bargain or breakout players; my draft list was based mostly on surface stats.

Since then, I've read the **Baseball Forecaster** cover to cover every December as my first look at the upcoming fantasy baseball season. My knowledge of fantasy baseball statistical analysis has improved dramatically from the insights included in this book and at **BaseballHQ.com**.

The best thing about the **Baseball Forecaster** is the different ways you can use it:

- You want great projections? You can get them here.
- You want an insightful comment on each player? Check.
- Or, if you want to learn how to dig in and make your own projections, the **Baseball Forecaster** and **BaseballHQ.com** gives you all the stats, teaches you what they mean and how to apply them to building a winning fantasy team.

I also love the strategy articles, which have given me new ideas for planning my draft and making in-season decisions. The statistical research in the **Baseball Forecaster**, when coupled with the player projections and stats, has taught me how to better value and rank players.

I have probably visited **BaseballHQ.com** pretty close to every single day since 2009; reading and learning and improving my process. Obviously, it has paid off for me.

To compete in the **National Fantasy Baseball Championship**, you need to be a step ahead in predicting breakout players, as well as overrated players likely to fall off. **Ron Shandler's Baseball Forecaster** and **BaseballHQ.com** gives you every tool necessary to look beyond the obvious in player evaluation on your road to a fantasy championship.

—Dave Potts, $100,000 winner
2012 National Fantasy Baseball Championship

TABLE OF CONTENTS

Gravity

It has been a year of great achievements and great anomalies.

Trout

We just spent the 2012 baseball season marveling at an extreme performance from a player who, as late as August, could not legally drink. He finished the season as the #1 ranked fantasy commodity in all of baseball, posting the best Rotisserie line we've seen in 14 years.

These were the amazing numbers he put up at age 20, in about five months of play:

AB	R	H	HR	RBI	SB	BA
559	129	182	30	83	49	.326

No other player in major league history had ever compiled the trifecta of 125 runs, 30 home runs and 45 steals in a rookie season. There are 60 members of the 30-30 club, only four members of 40-40, but the 30-50 club is even more exclusive:

Player	Year	Age	AB	R	H	HR	RBI	SB	BA
Davis, Eric	1987	25	474	120	139	37	100	50	.293
Bonds,Barry	1990	25	519	104	156	33	114	52	.301

Trout fell short by one bag. Here are other seasons that fell just short of achieving the 30-50 milestone:

Player	Year	Age	AB	R	H	HR	RBI	SB	BA
Henderson,R	1986	27	608	130	160	28	74	87	.263
Davis, Eric	1986	24	415	97	115	27	71	80	.277
Henderson,R	1990	31	489	119	159	28	61	65	.325
Rodriguez,A	1998	22	686	123	213	42	124	46	.310

Pretty elite company.

But all the players on these lists were at least a few years older than Trout, and in some cases, much older. All of them had established a multi-year performance baseline. We don't have any such baseline for Trout so we don't know what direction his future may take. Rookies are unpredictable; sophomores only slightly less.

Of course, he might put up better numbers just by virtue of playing a full six months in 2013. If anything, that extra month provides a buffer against any major pullback in raw numbers.

And at age 21 now (and of legal age to drink but not to rent a car), he's a good 5-7 years from his physical peak. Could he get better? Sure, though it seems tough to imagine given the lofty perch from which he's made his debut.

Obviously, the percentage play is to expect *some* regression. But how much? Some folks like to toss around the 20% figure as a reasonable expectation of volatility. Well, 20% regression barely touches his standing as one of the game's elite. (We'll temper his batting average over a .250 base.)

AB	R	H	HR	RBI	SB	BA
559	103	174	24	66	39	.311

That still makes him a candidate for a first round Average Draft Position (ADP) in 2013. That's still potentially a $40 player.

The amazing thing is that even a 50% regression would keep him in the discussion for the first two rounds and a $25-$30 value:

AB	R	H	HR	RBI	SB	BA
559	65	161	15	42	25	.288

That's essentially Andrew McCutchen's line from 2010.

This all looks wonderful, but there is one problem with it. Using the past season as a point of reference is wrong. This is one of the biggest mistakes that analysts often make. Every season starts as a clean slate. We take that blank panel and then build a new projection from the ground up, using the past merely as a rough guide.

Anyway, that's the way we *should* be doing it.

But come Draft Day, the recency bias will drive our expectations. All we'll see are his 2012 numbers as that fixed point of reference, carved in concrete.

The word on the street is that Trout will definitely go in the first round of most 2013 fantasy drafts, perhaps even at #1. According to the street, this is not even debatable:

"Trout is the second coming of Mickey Mantle....minus the switch hitting. I get the regression, but everyone has made adjustments and it has not worked. Dude is special."

"The key with Trout is that unless he gets hurt, he will still steal tons of bases for you. I am betting on something like .280 / 25 / 85 / 105 / 45 from him for next season which surely would put him in the top couple rounds. It's one thing to bet on regression, but another to ignore things like his supreme confidence and speed."

"I think I remember the year Albert Pujols and Alfonso Soriano were impact rookies, they continued to perform well for at least the next couple of years. That Braun guy was pretty good on a consistent basis since his rookie year too."

"As someone who is currently #1 overall out of 1050 teams in a high stakes NFBC league, I put my credibility on the line with this statement: Mike Trout will be the #1 player in fantasy baseball next year by any reasonable measure. My conservative projection: .285-125-20-70-60. (This assumes he leads off all year.) I actually expect more like .290-130-25-80-65. No one else will even sniff these numbers."

Sure, I get it. You look at 2012 and think, "How can he *not* be a top 5 pick?" How could he *not* go for more than $40? At minimum, he has to return first round value, right?

Maybe not.

If history can be used as a guide at all, it does not provide much optimism. Rookie stars don't always sustain their early success over an entire career. Just look at the last 10 years' worth of Rookie of the Year award winners:

2002: Eric Hinske and Jason Jennings
2003: Angel Berroa and Dontrelle Willis
2004: Bobby Crosby and Jason Bay
2005: Huston Street and Ryan Howard
2006: Justin Verlander and Hanley Ramirez
2007: Dustin Pedroia and Ryan Braun
2008: Evan Longoria and Geovany Soto
2009: Andrew Bailey and Chris Coghlan
2010: Neftali Feliz and Buster Posey
2011: Jeremy Hellickson and Craig Kimbrel

Granted, none of these players had the type of rookie season Trout posted. Still, the number of sustained superstars makes up less than half the list. Some of these players were, in fact, one year wonders.

And as talented as baseball's best players are, it's also not just about skill. It's also about *skill relative to the rest of a volatile player pool.*

ADP research has shown that the first round (top 15) has a whopping 66% turnover rate each year. Players who hit the top 15 for the first time are only a 14% bet to repeat the feat the following year. And #1 finishers plummet easily from that tall pedestal.

In 2005, Derrek Lee hit 46 HR and batted .335, making him the #1 player that year. This was an 8-year veteran who had never hit more than 32 HRs or batted higher than .282. The next spring, he was being drafted at an ADP of 7. But after that one season, he never came close to cracking the first round.

In 2006, Ryan Howard hit 58 HRs and batted .313 in his first full major league season, ranking him 4th among all players. Howard opened the next *four seasons* with a first round ADP, but he *never* finished among the game's top 15 players after that first year.

In 2009, Joe Mauer hit 28 HRs and batted a career high .365, boosting him to a first round ADP the following spring. He hasn't finished anywhere in the top four *rounds* since. In 2010, Carlos Gonzalez finished #1 by posting a 34 HR, 26 SB, .336 line in his first full season. He's fallen short of the first round in the two seasons since, yet is *still* being ranked that high in early 2013 drafts.

In 2011, Matt Kemp, Jacoby Ellsbury, Adrian Gonzalez and Curtis Granderson used breakout performances as a springboard to a 2012 first round ADP. All four finished nowhere near the first round last year.

In each of these years, we could not conceive of those players failing. But statistical volatility, injury and the ever-changing composition of the player pool scattered them throughout the subsequent rankings.

Trout faces a similarly daunting task.

As amazing as his season was, it was not without a few vulnerabilities. (You can be sure that opposing teams will be looking to exploit these in 2013.)

His hit rate—or batting average on balls in play—was a high 39%. This is not a sustainable level, which means his batting average is likely to head south. In fact, his hit rate could easily drop 5-10%, yielding a batting average as low as .260.

A drop in batting average doesn't happen in a vacuum. If his BA heads south, so will his home run total and his stolen base opportunities. Projecting him to drop 40 points in BA while maintaining his output simply does not add up. Math.

His performance was already starting to wane as the season wore on. His second half monthly BAs were .392 in July, .284 in August and .257 in September. He wrapped the season with a nice 7 for 13 performance on October 1-3, but that was against the lowly Mariners.

And while Trout paced the field in raw stats and Rotisserie value, his peripherals were consistently behind more established players. He ranked fifth in OPS, third in Runs Created per Game,

third in Runs Above Replacement and eighth in Base Performance Value. By all these measures, players like Braun, Miguel Cabrera and even Buster Posey and Giancarlo Stanton ranked higher. With more at-bats, Joey Votto might have lapped him as well.

And… he could get hurt. Sure, it is impossible to predict what players are going to hit the disabled list at any time, but the odds are not good.

We've already seen that 45%-50% of each year's top 300 players spend time on the DL. The Top 30 are no less immune:

Year	Number of Top 30 ADP Who Spent Time on the DL
2009	14 (47%)
2010	12 (40%)
2011	16 (53%)
2012	14 (47%)

And Trout is an all-in, max-effort defensive player.

Yes, there have been players who hit the ground running and never let up, like Pujols, Soriano and Braun. Note, however, that Pujols made his debut at age 22 (allegedly), Soriano at 26 and Braun at 24. They were somewhat more formed entities; Soriano could even rent a car. Trout is a mere embryo by comparison; his forecast error bar is potentially huge.

In late October, I was on Sirius/XM Radio's Rotowire Fantasy Sports show. Chris Liss asked me the following question:

Chris: Off the top of your head, Ron, give me a percent chance that last year was the best fantasy year of Mike Trout's career.

Me: Like 99%.

Regression and gravity are the two strongest forces known to man. They are unforgiving.

Maybe.

Miggy

There was quite a discussion among fans and analysts this fall regarding the race for the American League Most Valuable Player award. Some said that Trout was a no-brainer. Some said that Miguel Cabrera's Triple Crown season—the 16th ever recorded in major league history—combined with the Detroit Tigers' division title made him the more worthy candidate.

Regardless of the result, Cabrera's Triple Crown—44 HRs, 139 RBIs, .330 BA—is still noteworthy. The last player to pull off the feat was Carl Yazstrzemski.

That was 45 years ago.

Long stretches between major feats and milestones are not uncommon.

It took Pete Rose 62 years to eclipse Ty Cobb's lifetime hits record. It took Roger Maris 34 years to edge out Babe Ruth's single season home run record. And another 37 years for Mark McGwire to lay waste to that again.

But given today's game, will it take another multi-decade stretch for the next Triple Crown winner?

Joe Sheehan of JoeSheehan.com suggested that "Cabrera achieved the greatest Triple Crown ever. Forget the raw numbers or any single-number evaluation of his season, and consider that he beat out the largest field of any winner. No one had won the Triple Crown since 1967, and that's not a coincidence; it has nothing to do with specialization, the idea that there are more hitters for power and more for average. There are simply more hitters. It's a math problem."

Then the math solution would suggest that it will be a very long time until the next Triple Crown winner. That player will have to produce not only an extraordinary season on its own but also relative to the rest of a volatile—and large—player pool. If nothing else, regression and gravity will likely suppress a repeat performance by Cabrera.

But maybe not.

Dickey

Hall-of-Famer Willie Stargell once said, "Throwing a knuckleball for a strike is like throwing a butterfly with hiccups across the street into your neighbor's mailbox."

Knuckleballers are a different breed. We often say that a "young knuckleballer is 31" and that they "don't follow any of our rules." The history of some of the best knuckleball pitchers is characterized by lots of low-stress innings, productivity well into their 40s and no Cy Young Awards. At least until now.

Now, the lack of Cys was not necessarily an indictment of the pitch or bias against knuckleballers. According to Bill James in his Historical Baseball Abstract: "The Cy Young award usually goes to the pitcher with the best won-loss record and most knuckleball pitchers pitch for bad teams." Good teams can get better pitchers; bad teams have to settle for the uncertainty of the knuckleball.

But among the fellowship of the knuckle, Dickey is different still.

For one, he's broken through with a Cy Young Award.

Most knuckleballs are thrown at about 60-65 mph. Jim Bouton says he pitched his at 70 mph. Dickey can ramp his up over 80.

SBNation's Rob Neyer wrote, "R.A. Dickey is probably throwing a pitch that no professional batter had ever seen before he started throwing it."

The results are tangible. Dickey arguably had the best season ever for a knuckleball pitcher. He struck out 230 batters in 234 innings (8.9 Dom), walked only 54 (2.1 Ctl) with a 2.73 ERA and 1.05 WHIP. His Base Performance Value (BPV) was 127. And all this at 37 years old.

Neyer again: "If you were 29 years old and threw 85-90 miles an hour but your career seemed to be stalled in the high minors, what would you do? Keep plugging along and hope for a miracle? There might be another way, though. Lots of guys have tried to reinvent themselves as knuckleballers, and very few of them have succeeded. Maybe they *were doing it wrong.* Maybe instead of learning to throw it 65 miles an hour like Wilbur Wood and Phil Niekro and Tim Wakefield, they should have been learning to throw it like R.A. Dickey."

Maybe. But the real test will be to see if Dickey can repeat. Is the level of success demonstrated by this pitch a repeatable skill?

Regression and gravity remain powerful forces. But it's possible that an 80-plus mph floater could defy gravity.

Rodney

In the early days of our Base Performance Value (BPV) gauge, Dennis Eckersley set the bar pretty high. In fact, the original version of the formula made him the only player ever to post four consecutive seasons with BPV levels more than 200. We've taken to calling that "Vintage Eck Territory."

It is tougher to achieve a BPV of 200 with the new formula introduced a few years ago. You'll find a few pitchers in this book that achieved it over short periods of time. The new formula is a little less appreciative of Eckersley's feat:

Year	Age	ERA	Dom	Ctl	BPV Old	BPV New
1989	34	1.56	8.6	0.5	345	159
1990	35	0.61	9.0	0.5	347	167
1991	36	2.96	10.3	1.1	226	174
1992	37	1.91	10.5	1.2	210	175

Compare that to Fernando Rodney, the pitcher who broke Eck's 0.61 ERA record (for all pitchers with minimum 60 IP):

Year	Age	ERA	Dom	Ctl	BPV
2008	31	4.91	10.9	6.7	34
2009	32	4.40	7.3	4.9	35
2010	33	4.24	7.0	4.6	29
2011	34	4.50	7.3	7.9	-45
2012	35	0.60	9.2	1.8	152

Rodney's season is extraordinary not so much because of the infinitesimal ERA but because of the huge improvement in underlying skill. (Still, his 152 BPV falls just short of the levels posted by Eckersley.) Tampa coaches did make some adjustments to his approach and delivery, but it is tough to imagine this level of turnaround from someone who was a non-entity a year ago.

This was a player who went undrafted in virtually every 2012 fantasy league.

But in a season that saw the highest rate of closer *failure* in at least the last 14 years (since we began recording that rate), it is antithetic that we'd see not one, but two closers break records for *positive* achievement, and a third fall just short. Rodney was one. The others:

Craig Kimbrel

Year	Age	ERA	Dom	Ctl	BPV
2011	23	2.10	14.8	3.7	189
2012	24	1.01	16.7	2.0	273

Aroldis Chapman

Year	Age	ERA	Dom	Ctl	BPV
2011	23	3.60	12.8	7.4	62
2012	24	1.51	15.3	2.9	213

Kimbrel's 273 BPV and Chapman's 213 both leave Eckersley in the dust. Kimbrel's 16.7 strikeout rate breaks the record for a single season (min. 60 IP). Behind him on the list now:

Pitcher	Year	Dom
Marmol, Carlos	2010	15.99
Chapman, Aroldis	2012	15.32
Gagne, Eric	2003	14.98
Wagner, Billy	1999	14.95
Lidge, Brad	2004	14.93
Kimbrel, Craig	2011	14.84
Benitez, Armando	1999	14.77

In the entire list of the top 30, there is only one pre-1997 pitcher: Rob Dibble. Over the past 15 years, Ks are king.

What can we expect for 2013? What do you think? Regression and gravity. Regression and gravity. But with so many achievements and anomalies this year, can we still count on natural forces and planetary alignment to direct our expectations? You have to wonder.

At minimum, it seems short-sighted to think that these extraordinary performances are all isolated, unrelated events. We made that mistake once before.

Melky

The May 29, 2012 issue of *Sports Illustrated* contained a story about Dan Naulty, a fringe relief pitcher in the late 1990s. It described how Naulty's use of performance-enhancing drugs added 40-plus pounds to his thin frame, 10 mph to his fastball and won him a spot on a Major League roster. It told how he came up through the Minnesota system with three other pitchers of similar skill and how the others all fell short of reaching the majors because they played it clean.

Naulty credited PEDs with having given him an MLB career.

The reason that this story was published this year is that it's the 10th anniversary of the late Ken Caminiti coming forward about his own PED use. That was the watershed event that led to the lynch mobs over the subsequent years, ending (temporarily, at least) with the Mitchell Report.

Of course, everyone would like to put this all behind us already.

But we can't. Even now, we have been alternately entertained and disgusted by the legal issues of Barry Bonds and Roger Clemens. We have been reminded by the periodic headlines made by superstars like Alex Rodriguez, Manny Ramirez and Ryan Braun. We are still taken in by the proclamations that the sport has been cleaned up, only to be reawakened by the suspensions to players like Melky Cabrera and Bartolo Colon.

Oh, and Yasmani Grandal. That makes six players nailed this year, the most since 2007.

Year	# Players Suspended
2005	12
2006	3
2007	8
2008	1
2009	4
2010	2
2011	2
2012	6

Yeah, well... it's obviously not over. It's far from being over. We are going to be hearing the subtle quacking for a very long time. In fact, it may never be over.

Those who have read all I had to say about the issue over the past decade know that I do not have any moral, ethical, legal or political agenda when it comes to players using illegal performance enhancers. My interest is solely the impact PEDs have on my ability to project player performance. As long as PEDs may or may not be a factor, it makes my job as a prognosticator very difficult. It adds another unpredictable variable to an already-difficult

process. It messes with my ability to do my job well. That's the only reason why it is important to me. It's personal.

And I still think about it a lot. Why? Because there is one piece of information that I can't get past. One little sticking point. It was almost a throwaway comment back when this was front page news, yet it seems that current discussion about PEDs sidesteps the one ever-present reality:

The laboratories are always going to be one step ahead of the testers.

It was true 10 years ago and it's still true now. MLB's stricter drug policies don't affect the laboratories; they only affect the testing and the penalties. As long as millionaires have their livelihoods on the line, someone is going to pay for the development of new performance enhancing drugs, and that development will also include new masking agents.

So that immediately puts to question those who defend MLB's testing policy as being effective. Perhaps it is working to catch some transgressors, but its success as a deterrent is dubious because players are still getting caught. The fact that *anyone* is still getting caught is evidence that, at minimum, it is perhaps not nearly enough of a deterrent. And of course, it's naïve to think that the only ones getting caught are the only ones using.

But Melky Cabrera got nailed big time, and even pushed the envelope of guilt. The amount of effort put into the attempted cover-up—from fabricating a product to acquiring a website to legitimize that product—was far more damning than anything that had happened previously in the steroids era. It was an overt confirmation of intentional wrongdoing, not just a canned P.R. statement of "Oops!" contrition.

Some industry writers reasonably asked, "What about all the tests that Melky passed?" He must have passed about 18 tests prior to the one he failed.

Well, players typically don't take steroids all the time; they cycle on and then cycle off. Those currently taking testosterone know that it only stays in the body for 48-72 hours. So Cabrera could easily have eluded detection for a good many of those tests.

But the better response may be, simply, "The laboratories are always going to be one step ahead of the testers." It's a constantly moving target and Melky got outpaced.

Then the next obvious question has to be... In all the thousands of players, is he the only one who would ever stoop to that level?

Probably not, and here's why...

Players are always going to look for an edge to create, protect or prolong their careers.

See Dan Naulty above. Re-read Rob Neyer's comment. Mastersball.com's Lawr Michaels always reminds us, "Playing baseball is *hard*." And given the great wealth that awaits a successful Major Leaguer, ethics will be compromised. The temptation is too great.

Heck, we all do this. If there was ever a threat to our livelihood, we'd do anything we could to protect ourselves. The decision to cross the line is sometimes less an issue of ethics than one of survival. Imagine if some hotshot brown-noser at work was making points with the boss, putting your job in jeopardy. Tell me you wouldn't consider every possible option in order to save your position.

Now imagine you're a poor kid in the Dominican Republic whose only path out is with a pro baseball contract. It's not a stretch to think that you'd put anything into your body to get *even one* MLB paycheck. One check and a lifetime suspension is a very equitable trade-off for someone living in abject poverty.

So it is also not beyond the realm of possibility that a player, whose performance trend is putting him on the brink of extinction, will similarly try to find a way back. Like perhaps, Melky and Colon?

Melky Cabrera

Year	AB	HR	SB	BA	bb%	ct%	h%	PX	Spd
2006	460	7	12	280	11%	87%	31%	66	103
2007	545	8	13	273	7%	88%	30%	66	119
2008	414	8	9	249	7%	86%	27%	54	95
2009	485	13	10	274	8%	88%	29%	84	74
2010	458	4	7	255	8%	86%	29%	70	90
2011	658	18	20	305	5%	86%	34%	104	113
2012	459	11	13	346	7%	86%	38%	99	148

There are those who insist that we cannot detect PED use in a stat line. That may well be true. Cabrera's scan above is tough to analyze. His underlying skill has not changed appreciably over the past few years. Power and speed were slightly elevated but the one stat that significantly changed—batting average—seems to be driven by hit rate (BABIP), which can be random. Still, after all the years of sub-30% levels, why did the same skills suddenly produce two seasons' worth of extraordinary results?

Joe Sheehan asked, "Bonds: HR/FB-enhancing drugs. Clemens: K-enhancing drugs. Melky: BABIP-enhancing drugs. What did Alex Sanchez take? Grandal? Byrd?"

Reasonable questions. Perhaps the easy response might be just to ask, "Why would players take them and risk their careers if they didn't think these substances did *something* to help their performance?"

Bartolo Colon

Year	IP	K	ERA	XERA	CTL	DOM	CMD	BPV
2002	233	149	2.93	4.25	2.7	5.7	2.1	55
2003	242	173	3.87	4.25	2.5	6.4	2.6	64
2004	208	158	5.01	4.50	3.1	6.8	2.2	56
2005	223	157	3.48	4.01	1.7	6.3	3.7	86
2006	56	31	5.11	4.60	1.8	5.0	2.8	61
2007	99	76	6.34	4.55	2.6	6.9	2.6	73
2008	39	27	3.92	4.44	2.3	6.2	2.7	68
2009	62	38	4.19	4.74	3.0	5.5	1.8	39
2011	164	135	4.00	3.58	2.2	7.4	3.4	96
2012	152	91	3.43	4.09	1.4	5.4	4.0	84

Here, the rebirth over the past two years seems a little more noticeable, at ages 38 and 39. But who knows?

So are 2012's extraordinary performances a product of Steroids Era 2.0? Maybe, maybe not. But we should at least consider where we are as we enter 2013.

2013

One of the admonishments made during Steroids Era 1.0 was that everyone turned a blind eye to the problem. I'm not sure we all deliberately buried our heads in the sand; I think we just did not realize that something bigger was going on. All we saw was a marginally-related group of isolated events. Like now.

Back in 1998-2002, we went day by day, commenting on the home runs and run-scoring with interest and wonder. We did some cursory analysis, attributing the offensive barrage to juiced balls, smaller ballparks and expansion-depleted pitching staffs. But we rarely asked tough questions or demanded answers. Why would we? We were never faced with these *particular* types of events. There was no reason for us to see beyond their face value, try to string them together and recognize the gravity of the issue. But after it was all over, we were forced to look back. Only then did we put the pieces together and realize, "Wow, how could we have missed that?"

It seems that we are being lulled into a false sense of complacency—again. Since baseball did implement an outwardly strict testing policy, we are led to believe that the problem, if not completely solved, is at least under control. And with declining offense over the past few years, it seems to reinforce the fact that PEDs are no longer an issue.

But there's bigger stuff still going on. Last time, we watched blindly as home runs were flying out of stadiums with amazing frequency. Today, we seem to be exhibiting similarly apathetic wonder at an equal, if not greater, stream of anomalous performances. It's not just home runs any more. It's strikeouts, and no-hitters, and miniscule ERAs and all flavors of record-breakers.

Are we going to just ignore this?

Years	No-hitters
1992-94	7
1995-97	6
1998-00	4
2001-03	6
2004-06	2
2007-09	7
2010-12	16

Or this?

Years	# Hitters 35+ HRs	# Pitchers < 3.50 ERA (120+ IP)
2001-02	39	54
2003-04	39	46
2005-06	37	39
2007-08	20	47
2009-10	19	61
2011-12	17	80

The June 11, 2012 edition of *ESPN The Magazine* included an article about the rise in strikeouts: "Through May 22, the major league strikeout rate was 19.5%, on pace to shatter the record of 18.6% set... last year. By comparison, in 1973... big leaguers struck out just 13.7% of the time."

That was in May. The rate rose even more by season's end to finish at 19.8%.

The article attributed *this* phenomenon to:

- hitters facing fresh relievers more often than fatigued starters
- umpires calling more strikes due to the threat of PITCHf/x
- teams more willing to let their sluggers swing away as long as the HRs still come
- the rise of the cutter

All of these are adequate explanations, just like juiced balls, smaller ballparks and expansion-depleted pitching staffs were adequate ten years ago. Another reason—a passing comment in the article—is the fact that average fastball velocities have risen over the past four years. That doesn't come from nowhere, and while we can't directly attribute it to PEDs, we can't dismiss the possibility either. From FanGraphs:

Number of Pitchers with with an average fastball velocity of 95+ mph (min 30 IP)	
2003-04	24
2005-06	29
2007-08	27
2009-10	53
2011-12	68

We're still seeing outlying performances, just different outlying performances with different types of players.

Several 30something hitters who had been following the career path of those with classic "old player skills" suddenly found new life the past few seasons. In many cases, these were not just little rebounds; these were skills not seen in years, if ever. Granted, these could just be anomalies. Or these could be players doing everything they can to stay gainfully employed.

Whenever there is a player who has put up a level of performance ridiculously out of line with every other player of his era—especially at an advanced age—the question has to be asked. Back in 2006, it had to be asked with Barry Bonds. In that fall's *Baseball Forecaster*—more than a year before the Mitchell Report came out—I took a lot of heat for writing this:

"No player in the history of Major League Baseball has ever posted the type of performance numbers that Barry Bonds has at his age. The same can be said for Roger Clemens. Neither has ever failed a drug test. Yet, grand jury leaks, circumstantial evidence and best-selling books have already convicted Bonds in the court of public opinion. Apparently, Clemens holds more iconic status so nobody would dare investigate him. But his performance at age 44 is no less remarkable or worthy of question."

And if we're talking about icons, there are a few still out there now who have put up numbers far beyond their age and skills progression. You don't often find players hovering around 40 putting up triple-digit BPVs and performance levels they were unable to achieve 10 years earlier. But there are still some.

Let's at least ask the question.

And maybe it's not PEDs. Maybe it's something else that we haven't considered because it's not on our radar, just like PEDs were outside our line of sight 15 years ago. I don't know what that

something is. Maybe it is a legitimate new conditioning program that teams are reluctant to share with the public. Maybe it's the next Moneyball variable. I don't know.

Since accurate information about PED use is not available, I have always approached the issue with some combination of analysis, speculation and cynicism. Sometimes you have to string together observations to paint a picture, but these are still just observations.

It's sort of like climate change. We might notice slight shifts in weather patterns—a particularly warm March or a rainy November. But it's the increasing number of *unusual* events that really gets our attention. The increased frequency of tornados, earthquakes and tsunamis. The increased severity of hurricanes and floods. The increased frequency of no-hitters. The increased number of sub-3.00 ERAs. The individual performances that are far outside the range of expectation. The quantity of unusual events is often more telling of an underlying change than the silent drone of daily performance.

At some point, you have to ask the obvious questions—Is something else going on? Do all these isolated events paint a bigger picture? If the laboratories are always one step ahead of the testers, could it be PEDs? Could it be something else?

And so, when you start scanning the players in this book and come across someone who put up a season that is out of context with his career or his contemporaries, *you* have to be the one to ask these questions.

Why? Because, in this book, we are just going to project regression and gravity. It is the only analytically sound approach. If the odds are 80%-20%, we will always go with the 80% percentage play. If the comfort zone for a projection is between 25 and 35 HRs, we will be hard-pressed to step over the line at either extreme.

So we will be projecting regression for Mike Trout, Miguel Cabrera, R.A. Dickey, Fernando Rodney, Craig Kimbrel, Aroldis Chapman, Melky Cabrera, Bartolo Colon and Yasmani Grandal. We'll be projecting gravity for the 40somethings parading around with statistics only 20somethings used to produce. We'll be regressing the players on the brink of irrelevance who suddenly start posting star-level performances. And we'll be pulling back our projections for the fringe prospects who suddenly create careers with newfound skills beyond anything in a scouting report.

But the truth is, we just don't know. We've seen far too many gravity-defying performances the past few years. So you have to be the one to exercise a little cynicism and think, "Maybe I should venture out of the comfort zone. Maybe this time I should speculate on the 20% play, whether it's Mike Trout maintaining his numbers, or maybe even taking the next step…

Consider: 36 HRs, 100 RBIs, 155 Runs, 60 SB and a .340 batting average.

Impossible?

Perhaps not. That's just his 2012 pace pro-rated to a full season.

Welcome to the 27th Edition

If you are new to the *Forecaster*, this book may seem a bit overwhelming. Granted, there is 3.5 tons of information here, divided up into about 300 pages of just over 23 pounds each (yay, math!). But unless you're reading this note on the night before your fantasy draft, you have time to get into the weight room, strap on the gear and ascend the learning curve. It's not that steep (or heavy, really), you don't have to memorize anything and there will be no pop quiz. All you have to do is focus and visualize the goal —*fantasy league domination.*

No sweat.

Do approach this methodically, however. The best place to start is with the Encyclopedia of Fanalytics, which provides the foundation concepts for everything else that appears in these pages. Take a cursory read-through, stopping at any section that looks interesting. You'll keep coming back here frequently.

Then just jump in. Close your eyes, flip to a random page, and put your finger down anywhere. Oh, look—Dayan Viceido… Despite his 25-HR breakout season, his ratio of dominating to disaster weeks was a feast-or-famine 41% to 52%—deadly numbers for head-to-head gamers who rely on consistency.

See, you've learned something already!

What's New in 2013?

New LIMA benchmarks: On the 15th anniversary of the introduction of the LIMA Plan, we acknowledge that the world is changing and we need to change along with it.

Mayberry Method 3.0 Update: We fix the deficiency in how we evaluate stolen base potential.

Pitching type: We bring back the indicators that identify power versus contact pitchers, and ground ball versus fly ball pitchers.

Answers to questions, such as: Do doubles turn into home runs? Does ERA regress to xERA during the season? Is there a spring training stat that matters? How can we get better control of our fantasy bullpens? Can you really lose your draft in the first round? How can we introduce trading into non-trading leagues? Is there a way to increase forecasting accuracy for fantasy gaming purposes? And much more.

Updates

The Baseball Forecaster page at BaseballHQ.com is at http://www.baseballhq.com/content/ron-shandlers-baseball-forecaster-2013. This is your headquarters for all information and updates regarding this book. Here you will find links to the following:

Content Updates: In a project of this magnitude, there are occasionally items that need clarification or correction. You can find them here.

Free Projections Update: As a buyer of this book, you get one free 2013 projections update. This is a set of Excel spreadsheet files that will be posted on or about March 1, 2013. Remember to keep the book handy when you visit as the access codes are hidden within these pages.

Electronic book: The complete PDF version of the Forecaster —plus Excel versions of most key charts—is available free to those who bought the book directly through the BaseballHQ.com website. These files will be available in January 2013; contact us if you do not receive information via e-mail about accessing them. If you purchased the book through an online vendor or bookstore, or would like these files earlier, you can purchase them from us for $9.95. Call 1-800-422-7820 for more information.

Beyond the Forecaster

The *Baseball Forecaster* is just the beginning. The following companion products and services are described in more detail in the back of the book.

BaseballHQ.com is our newly designed home website. It provides regular updates to everything in this book, including daily updated statistics and projections. A subscription to BHQ gets you more than 1,000 articles over the course of a year, customized tools, access to data going back over a decade, plus several tons more. If this book is 3.5 tons, BaseballHQ.com is probably closer to 20.

First Pitch Forums are a series of conferences we run all over the country, where you can meet some of the top industry analysts and network with fellow fantasy leaguers in your area. We'll be in cities from coast to coast in February and March. Our big annual symposium at the Arizona Fall League is the first weekend in November.

The 8th edition of the *Minor League Baseball Analyst,* by Rob Gordon and Jeremy Deloney, is the minor league companion to this book, with stat boxes for 1,000-plus prospects, and more. It weighs about 2.75 tons and is available in January.

We still have copies available of *How to Value Players for Rotisserie Baseball,* Art McGee's ground-breaking book on valuation theory. They are still on closeout at 50% off. A ton and a half, at least.

RotoLab is the best draft software on the market and comes pre-loaded with our projections.

Visit us on *Facebook* at http://www.facebook.com/baseballhq. "Like" the Baseball HQ page for updates, photos from First Pitch events and links to other important stuff. I have my own personal page as well, but I reserve that for personal stuff so I do not accept friend requests from folks I don't know personally. I will accept requests from those on LinkedIn, though.

Follow us on Twitter. Some of the BaseballHQ.com analysts are tweeting all over the place @BaseballHQ. I also have a personal account (@RonShandler) where I share random brain flakes and 140-character mini-rants. It's embarrassing, frankly.

And there you have it. We are a large, and very heavy multiplatform information service. And we're now owned by USA TODAY, which puts a 1,000-ton behemoth in our corner. That means we can guarantee you the most comprehensive information for your fanalytic needs available anywhere.

Girth is good.

—Ron Shandler (0.09 tons)

CONSUMER ADVISORY

AN IMPORTANT MESSAGE FOR FANTASY LEAGUERS
REGARDING PROPER USAGE OF THE *BASEBALL FORECASTER*

This document is provided in compliance with authorities to outline the prospective risks and hazards possible in the event that the Baseball Forecaster is used incorrectly. Please be aware of these potentially dangerous situations and avoid them. The publisher assumes no risk related to any financial loss or stress-induced illnesses caused by ignoring the items as described below.

1. The statistical projections in this book are intended as general guidelines, not as gospel. It is highly dangerous to use the projected statistics alone, and then live and die by them. That's like going to a ballgame, being given a choice of any seat in the park, and deliberately choosing the last row in the right field corner with an obstructed view. The projections are there, you can look at them, but there are so many better places to sit.

We have to publish those numbers, but they are stagnant, inert pieces of data. This book focuses on a live forecasting process that provides the tools so that you can understand the leading indicators and draw your own conclusions. If you at least attempt your own analyses of the data, and enhance them with the player commentaries, you can paint more robust, colorful pictures of the future.

In other words...

If you bought this book purely for the projected statistics and do not intend to spend at least some time learning about the process, then you might as well just buy an $8 magazine.

2. The player commentaries in this book are written by humans, just like you. These commentaries provide an overall evaluation of performance and likely future direction, but 60-word capsules cannot capture everything. Your greatest value will be to use these as a springboard to your own analysis of the data. Odds are, if you take the time, you'll find hidden indicators that we might have missed. Forecaster veterans say that this self-guided excursion is the best part of owning the book.

3. This book does not attempt to tackle playing time. Rather than making arbitrary decisions about how roles will shake out, the focus is on performance. The playing time projections presented here are merely to help you better evaluate each player's talent. Our online preseason projections update provides more current AB and IP expectations based on how roles are being assigned.

4. The dollar values in this book are intended solely for player-to-player comparisons. They are not driven by a finite pool of playing time—which is required for valuation systems to work properly—so they cannot be used for bid values to be used in your own draft.

There are two reasons for this:

a. The finite pool of players that will generate the finite pool of playing time will not be determined until much closer to Opening Day. And, if we are to be brutally honest, there is really no such thing as a finite pool of players.

b. Your particular league's construction will drive the values; a $10 player in a 10-team mixed league will not be the same as a $10 player in a 13-team NL-only league.

Note that book dollar values also cannot be compared to those published at BaseballHQ.com as the online values are generated by a more finite player pool.

5. Do not pass judgment on the effectiveness of this book based on the performance of a few individual players. The test, rather, is on the collective predictive value of the book's methods. Are players with better base skills more likely to produce good results than bad ones? Years of research suggest that the answer is "yes." Does that mean that every high skilled player will do well? No. But many more of them will perform well than will the average low-skilled player. You should always side with the better percentage plays, but recognize that there are factors we cannot predict. Good decisions that beget bad outcomes do not invalidate the methods.

6. If your copy of this book is not marked up and dog-eared by Draft Day, you probably did not get as much value out of it as you might have.

7. This edition of the Forecaster is not intended to provide absorbency for spills of more than 7.5 ounces.

8. This edition is not intended to provide stabilizing weight for more than 18 sheets of 20 lb. paper in winds of more than 45 mph.

9. The pages of this book are not recommended for avian waste collection. In independent laboratory studies, 87% of migratory water fowl refused to excrete on interior pages, even when coaxed.

10. This book, when rolled into a cylindrical shape, is not intended to be used as a weapon for any purpose, including but not limited to insect extermination, canine training or to influence bidding behavior at a fantasy draft.

For new readers...

Everything begins here. The information in the following pages represents the foundation that powers everything we do.

You'll learn about the underlying concepts for our unique mode of analysis. You'll find answers to long-asked questions, interesting insights into what makes players tick, and innovative applications for all this newfound knowledge.

This Encyclopedia is organized into several logical sections:

1. Fundamentals
2. Batters
3. Pitchers
4. Prospects
5. Gaming

Enough talking. Jump in.

Remember to breathe.

For veteran readers...

As we do in each edition, this year's ever-expanding Encyclopedia includes relevant research results we've published over the past year. We've added some of the essays from the Research Abstracts and Gaming Abstracts sections in the 2012 *Forecaster* as well as some other essays from BaseballHQ.com.

And we continue to mold the content to best fit how fantasy leaguers use their information. Many readers consider this their fantasy information bible.

Okay, time to jump-start the analytical process for 2013. Remember to breathe—it's always good advice.

Abbreviations

Fundamentals

What is Fanalytics?

Fanalytics is the scientific approach to fantasy baseball analysis. A contraction of "fantasy" and "analytics," fanalytic gaming might be considered a mode of play that requires a more strategic and quantitative approach to player analysis and game decisions.

The three key elements of fanalytics are:

1. **Performance analysis**
2. **Performance forecasting**
3. **Gaming analysis**

For performance analysis, we tap into the vast knowledge of the sabermetric community. Founded by Bill James, this area of study provides objective and progressive new ways to assess skill. What we do in this book is called "component skills analysis." We break down performance into its component parts, then reverse-engineer it back into the traditional measures with which we are more familiar.

Our forecasting methodology is one part science and one part art. We start with a computer-generated baseline for each player. We then make subjective adjustments based on a variety of factors, such as discrepancies in skills indicators and historical guidelines gleaned from more than 20 years of research. We don't rely on a rigid model; our method forces us to get our hands dirty.

You might say that our brand of forecasting is more about finding logical journeys than blind destinations.

Gaming analysis is an integrated approach designed to help us win our fantasy leagues. It takes the knowledge gleaned from the first two elements and adds the strategic and tactical aspect of each specific fantasy game format.

Definitions

Base Performance Indicator (BPI): A statistical formula that measures an isolated aspect of a player's situation-independent raw skill or a gauge that helps capture the effects that random chance has on skill.

Leading Indicator: A statistical formula that can be used to project potential future performance.

Noise: Irrelevant or meaningless pieces of information that can distort the results of an analysis. In news, this is opinion or rumor that can invalidate valuable information. In forecasting, these are unimportant elements of statistical data that can artificially inflate or depress a set of numbers.

Situation Independent: Describing performance that is separate from the context of team, ballpark, or other outside variables. Strikeouts and walks, as they are unaffected by the performance of a batter's team, are often considered situation independent stats. Conversely, RBIs are situation dependent because individual performance varies greatly by the performance of other batters on the team (you can't drive in runs if there is nobody on base). Situation independent gauges are important for us to be able to isolate and judge performance on its own merits.

Soft Skills: BPIs with levels below established minimums for acceptable performance.

Surface Stats: Traditional gauges that the mainstream media uses to measure performance. Stats like batting average, wins, and ERA only touch the surface of a player's skill and often distort the truth. To uncover a player's true skill, you have to look at component skills statistics.

Component Skills Analysis

Familiar gauges like HR and ERA have long been used to measure skill. In fact, these gauges only measure the outcome of an individual event, or series of events. They represent statistical output. They are "surface stats."

Raw skill is the talent beneath the stats, the individual elements of a player's makeup. Players use these skills to create the individual events, or components, that we record using measures like HR and ERA. Our approach:

1. **It's not about batting average; it's about seeing the ball and making contact.** We target hitters based on elements such as their batting eye (walks to strikeouts ratio), how often they make contact and the type of contact they make. We then combine these components into an "expected batting average." By comparing each hitter's actual BA to how he should be performing, we can draw conclusions about the future.

2. **It's not about home runs; it's about power.** From the perspective of a round bat meeting a round ball, it may be only a fraction of an inch at the point of contact that makes the difference between a HR or a long foul ball. When a ball is hit safely, often it is only a few inches that separate a HR from a double. We tend to neglect these facts in our analyses, although the outcomes—the doubles, triples, long fly balls—may be no less a measure of that batter's raw power skill. We must incorporate all these components to paint a complete picture.

3. **It's not about ERA; it's about getting the ball over the plate and keeping it in the park.** Forget ERA. You want to draft pitchers who walk few batters (Control), strike out many (Dominance) and succeed at both in tandem (Command). You also want pitchers who keep the ball on the ground (because home runs are bad). All of this translates into an "expected ERA" that you can use to compare to a pitcher's actual performance.

4. **It's never about wins.** For pitchers, winning ballgames is less about skill than it is about offensive support. As such, projecting wins is a very high-risk exercise and valuing hurlers based on their win history is dangerous. Target skill; wins will come.

5. **It's not about saves; it's about opportunity first and skills second.** While the highest skilled pitchers have the best potential to succeed as closers, they still have to be given the ball with the game on the line in the 9th inning, and that is a decision left to others. Over the past 10 years, about 40% of relievers drafted for saves failed to hold the role for the entire season. The lesson: Don't take chances on draft day. There will always be saves in the free agent pool.

Accounting for "luck"

Luck has been used as a catch-all term to describe random chance. When we use the term here, we're talking about unexplained variances that shape the statistics. While these variances may be random, they are also often measurable and projectable.

To get a better read on "luck," we use formulas that capture the external variability of the data.

Through our research and the work of others, we have learned that when raw skill is separated from statistical output, what's remaining is often unexplained variance. The aggregate totals of many of these variances, for all players, is often a constant. For instance, while a pitcher's ERA might fluctuate, the rate at which his opposition's batted balls fall for hits will tend towards 30%. Large variances can be expected to regress towards 30%.

Why is all this important? Analysts complain about the lack of predictability of many traditional statistical gauges. The reason they find it difficult is that they are trying to project performance using gauges that are loaded with external noise. Raw skills gauges are more pure and follow better defined trends during a player's career. Then, as we get a better handle on the variances—explained and unexplained—we can construct a complete picture of what a player's statistics really mean.

Baseball Forecasting

Forecasting in perspective

Forecasts. Projections. Predictions. Prognostications. The crystal ball aura of this process conceals the fact it is a process. We might define it as "the systematic process of determining likely end results." At its core, it's scientific.

However, the *outcomes* of forecasted events are what is most closely scrutinized, and are used to judge the success or failure of the forecast. That said, as long as the process is sound, the forecast has done the best job it can do. *In the end, forecasting is about analysis, not prophecy.*

Baseball performance forecasting is inherently a high-risk exercise with a very modest accuracy rate. This is because the process involves not only statistics, but also unscientific elements, from random chance to human volatility. And even from within the statistical aspect there are multiple elements that need to be evaluated, from skill to playing time to a host of external variables.

Every system is comprised of the same core elements:

- Players will tend to perform within the framework of past history and/or trends.
- Skills will develop and decline according to age.
- Statistics will be shaped by a player's health, expected role and venue.

While all systems are built from these same elements, they also are constrained by the same limitations. We are all still trying to project a bunch of human beings, each one...

- with his own individual skill set
- with his own rate of growth and decline
- with his own ability to resist and recover from injury
- limited to opportunities determined by other people
- generating a group of statistics largely affected by external noise.

Research has shown that the best accuracy rate that can be attained by any system is about 70%. In fact, a simple system that uses three-year averages adjusted for age ("Marcel") can attain

a success rate of 65%. This means all the advanced systems are fighting for occupation of the remaining 5%.

But there is a bigger question… *what exactly are we measuring?* When we search for accuracy, what does that mean? In fact, any quest for accuracy is going to run into a brick wall of paradoxes:

- If a slugging average projection is dead on, but the player hits 10 fewer HRs than expected (and likely, 20 more doubles), is that a success or a failure?
- If a projection of hits and walks allowed by a pitcher is on the mark, but the bullpen and defense implodes, and inflates his ERA by a run, is that a success or a failure?
- If the projection of a speedster's rate of stolen base success is perfect, but his team replaces the manager with one that doesn't run, and the player ends up with half as many SBs as expected, is that a success or a failure?
- If a batter is traded to a hitters' ballpark and all the touts project an increase in production, but he posts a statistical line exactly what would have been projected had he not been traded to that park, is that a success or a failure?
- If the projection for a bullpen closer's ERA, WHIP and peripheral numbers is perfect, but he saves 20 games instead of 40 because the GM decided to bring in a high-priced free agent at the trading deadline, is that a success or a failure?
- If a player is projected to hit .272 in 550 AB and only hits .249, is that a success or failure? Most will say "failure." But wait a minute! The real difference is only two hits per month. That shortfall of 23 points in batting average is because a fielder might have made a spectacular play, or a screaming liner might have been hit right at someone, or a long shot to the outfield might have been held up by the wind... once every 14 games. Does that constitute "failure"?

Even if we were to isolate a single statistic that measures "overall performance" and run our accuracy tests on it, the results will still be inconclusive.

According to OPS, these players are virtually identical:

BATTER	HR	RBI	SB	BA	OBA	SLG	OPS
Choo,S	16	37	21	.283	.361	.441	.802
Dunn,A	40	96	2	.204	.334	.468	.802

If I projected Shin Soo Choo-caliber stats and ended up with Adam Dunn numbers, I'd hardly call that an accurate projection, especially if my fantasy team was in dire need of batting average and stolen bases.

According to Roto dollars, these players are also dead-on:

BATTER	HR	RBI	Runs	SB	BA	R$
Molina,Y	22	76	65	12	.315	$20
Jackson,A	16	66	103	12	.300	$20
Willingham,J	35	110	85	3	.260	$20
Upton,BJ	28	78	79	31	.246	$20

It's not so simple for someone to claim they have accurate projections. And so, it is best to focus on the bigger picture, especially when it comes to winning at fantasy baseball.

More on this: "The Great Myths of Projective Accuracy"

http://www.baseballhq.com/great-myths-projective-accuracy

Baseball Forecaster's forecasting process

We are all about component skills. Our approach is to assemble these evaluators in such a way that they can be used to validate our observations, analyze their relevance and project a likely future direction.

In a perfect world, if a player's raw skills improve, then so should his surface stats. If his skills decline, then his stats should follow as well. But, sometimes a player's skill indicators increase while his surface stats decline. These variances may be due to a variety of factors.

Our forecasting process is based on the expectation that events tend to move towards universal order. Surface stats will eventually approach their skill levels. Unexplained variances will regress to a mean. And from this, we can identify players whose performance may potentially change.

For most of us, this process begins with the previous year's numbers. Last season provides us with a point of reference, so it's a natural way to begin the process of looking at the future. Component skills analysis allows us to validate those numbers. A batter with few HRs but a high linear weighted power level has a good probability of improving his future HR output. A pitcher whose ERA was poor while his command ratio was solid is a good bet for ERA improvement.

Of course, these leading indicators do not always follow the rules. There are more shades of grey than blacks and whites. When indicators are in conflict—for instance, a pitcher who is displaying both a rising strikeout rate and a rising walk rate—then we have to find ways to sort out what these indicators might be saying.

It is often helpful to look at leading indicators in a hierarchy, of sorts. In fact, a hierarchy of the most important pitching base performance indicators might look like this: Command (k/bb), Dominance (k/9), Control (bb/9) and GB/FB rate. For batters, contact rate might top the list, followed by power, walk rate and speed.

Assimilating additional research

Once we've painted the statistical picture of a player's potential, we then use additional criteria and research results to help us add some color to the analysis. These other criteria include the player's health, age, changes in role, ballpark and a variety of other factors. We also use the research results described in the following pages. This research looks at things like traditional periods of peak performance and breakout profiles.

The final element of the process is assimilating the news into the forecast. This is the element that many fantasy leaguers tend to rely on most since it is the most accessible. However, it is also the element that provides the most noise. Players, management and the media have absolute control over what we are allowed to know. Factors such as hidden injuries, messy divorces and clubhouse unrest are routinely kept from us, while we are fed red herrings and media spam. *We will never know the entire truth.*

Quite often, all you are reading is just other people's opinions... a manager who believes that a player has what it takes to be a regular or a team physician whose diagnosis is that a player is healthy enough to play. These words from experts have some element of truth, but cannot be wholly relied upon to provide an accurate expectation of future events. As such, it is often helpful to develop an appropriate cynicism for what you read.

For instance, if a player is struggling for no apparent reason and there are denials about health issues, don't dismiss the possibility that an injury does exist. There are often motives for such news to be withheld from the public.

And so, as long as we do not know all the facts, we cannot dismiss the possibility that any one fact is true, no matter how often the media assures it, deplores it, or ignores it. Don't believe everything you read; use your own judgment. If your observations conflict with what is being reported, that's powerful insight that should not be ignored.

Also remember that nothing lasts forever in major league baseball. *Reality is fluid.* One decision begets a series of events that lead to other decisions. Any reported action can easily be reversed based on subsequent events. My favorite examples are announcements of a team's new bullpen closer. Those are about the shortest realities known to man.

We need the media to provide us with context for our analyses, and the real news they provide is valuable intelligence. But separating the news from the noise is difficult. In most cases, the only thing you can trust is how that player actually performs.

Embracing imprecision

Precision in baseball prognosticating is a fool's quest. There are far too many unexpected variables and noise that can render our projections useless. The truth is, the best we can ever hope for is to accurately forecast general tendencies and percentage plays.

However, even when you follow an 80% percentage play, for instance, you will still lose 20% of the time. That 20% is what skeptics use as justification to dismiss prognosticators; they conveniently ignore the more prevalent 80%. The paradox, of course, is that fantasy league titles are often won or lost by those exceptions. Still, long-term success dictates that you always chase the 80% and accept the fact that you will be wrong 20% of the time. Or, whatever that percentage play happens to be.

For fantasy purposes, playing the percentages can take on an even less precise spin. The best projections are often the ones that are just far enough away from the field of expectation to alter decision-making. In other words, it doesn't matter if I project Player X to bat .320 and he only bats .295; it matters that I project .320 and everyone else projects .280. Those who follow my less-accurate projection will go the extra dollar to acquire him in their draft.

Or, perhaps we should evaluate the projections based upon their intrinsic value. For instance, coming into 2012, would it have been more important for me to tell you that Albert Pujols was going to hit 32 HRs or that Edwin Encarnacion would hit 32 HRs? By season's end, the Pujols projection would have been more accurate, but the Encarnacion projection—even though it was off by 10 HRs—would have been far more *valuable*.

And that has to be enough. Any tout who projects a player's statistics dead-on will have just been lucky with his dart throws that day.

Perpetuity

Forecasting is not an exercise that produces a single set of numbers. It is dynamic, cyclical and ongoing. Conditions are constantly changing and we must react to those changes by adjusting our expectations. A pre-season projection is just a snapshot in time. Once the first batter steps to the plate on Opening Day, that projection has become obsolete. Its value is merely to provide a starting point, a baseline for what is about to occur.

During the season, if a projection appears to have been invalidated by current performance, the process continues. It is then that we need to ask... What went wrong? What conditions have changed? In fact, has *anything* changed? We need to analyze the situation and revise our expectation, if necessary. This process must be ongoing.

When good projections go bad

We cannot predict the future; all we can do is provide a sound process for constructing a "most likely expectation for future performance." All we can control is the process.

As such, there is a limit to how much blame we can shoulder for each year's misses. If we've captured as much information as is available, used the best methodology and analyzed the results correctly, that's about the best we can do. We simply can't control outcomes.

What we *can* do is analyze all the misses to see *why* they occurred. This is always a valuable exercise each year. It puts a proper focus on the variables that were out of our control as well as providing perspective on those players that we might have done a better job with.

In general, we can organize our forecasting misses into several categories. To demonstrate, here are the players whose 2012 Rotisserie earnings varied from projections by at least $10:

The performances that exceeded expectation

Development beyond the growth trend: These are young players for whom we knew there was skill. Some of them were prized prospects in the past who have taken their time ascending the growth curve. Others were a surprise only because their performance spike arrived sooner than anyone anticipated... Jose Altuve, Pedro Alvarez, Ian Desmond, Alcides Escobar, Carlos Gomez, Bryce Harper, Chase Headley, Jason Heyward, Austin Jackson, Andrew McCutchen, Josh Reddick, Ben Revere, Wilin Rosario, Mike Trout, Ryan Cook, Ross Detwiler, Gio Gonzalez, Kris Medlen, Wade Miley, Chris Sale.

While I include Trout in this group, it is clear nobody would have ever expected these types of numbers, even at his peak. So he does remain in a class by himself.

Skilled players who just had big years: We knew these guys were good too; we just didn't anticipate they'd be *this* good... Edwin Encarnacion, Aaron Hill, Carlos Ruiz, A.J. Burnett, Matt Cain, Ryan Dempster.

Unexpected health: We knew these players had the goods; we just didn't think they'd be healthy... Adam LaRoche, Buster Posey.

Unexpected playing time: These players had the skills—and may have even displayed them at some time in the past—but had questionable playing time potential coming into this season.

Some benefited from another player's injury, a rookie who didn't pan out or leveraged a short streak into a regular gig... Norichika Aoki, Tyler Colvin, Todd Frazier, Chris Johnson, Juan Pierre, Michael Saunders, Kyle Seager.

Unexpected return to form: These players had the skills, having displayed them at some point in the past. But those skills had been M.I.A. long enough that we began to doubt that they'd ever return; our projections model got sick of waiting. Or previous skills displays were so inconsistent that projecting an "up year" would have been a shot in the dark; our projections model got sick of guessing. Yes, "once you display a skill, you own it" but still... Adam Dunn, Ryan Ludwick, Angel Pagan, Alex Rios.

Unexpected role: Every year, there are relief pitchers who are on nobody's radar to become a frontline closer but are suddenly thrust into the role with great success... Aroldis Chapman, Ernesto Frieri, Kenley Jansen, Casey Janssen, Jim Johnson, Rafael Soriano, Tom Wilhelmsen.

The anti-regressions: After 2011, some players had regression written all over them. Sometimes it was statistical regression; sometimes a change of venue should have been foreboding. In the end, they somehow performed just like they did in 2011... Mark Trumbo, Matt Harrison, Hiroki Kuroda.

Melky Cabrera would have been a part of this group had we not found out the real reason for his exciting, new skill set.

The unexplained: How these players put up the numbers they did is a mystery, but, the odds of a comparable follow-up —particularly those with soft peripherals—will be small: Garrett Jones' breakout at age 31, A.J. Pierzynski's power, Alfonso Soriano's career year at age 36, R.A. Dickey, Kyle Lohse's breakout at age 33, and the Eckersely-record-breaking Fernando Rodney.

The performances that fell short of expectation

The DL denizens: These are players who got hurt, may not have returned fully healthy, or may have never been fully healthy (whether they'd admit it or not)... Jose Bautista, Jason Bay, Lance Berkman, Carl Crawford, Michael Cuddyer, Jacoby Ellsbury, Brett Gardner, Matt Kemp, Adam Lind, Evan Longoria, Michael Morse, Mike Napoli, Pablo Sandoval, Mark Teixeira, Troy Tulowitzki, Joey Votto, Jayson Werth, Chris Young, Josh Beckett, Chris Carpenter, John Danks, Neftali Feliz, Jaime Garcia, Matt Garza, Roy Halladay, Dan Haren, Daniel Hudson, Jon Lester, Ted Lilly, Cory Luebke, Mariano Rivera, Drew Storen.

Note that some of these players seemed to be putting up sub-par numbers before they actually hit the DL. Many were likely playing through the hurt before breaking down.

Accelerated skills erosion: These are players who we knew were on the downside of their careers but who we did not think would plummet so quickly. In some cases, there were injuries involved, but all in all, 2012 may be the beginning of the end... Marlon Byrd, Dan Uggla, Kevin Youkilis, Michael Young, Heath Bell.

Inflated expectations: Here are players who we really should not have expected much more than what they produced. Some had short or spotty track records, others had soft peripherals coming into 2012, and still others were inflated by media hype...

Jeff Francoeur, Eric Hosmer, Howie Kendrick, Brett Lawrie, John Mayberry, Gavin Floyd, Josh Johnson, Ian Kennedy, Matt Moore.

Misplaced regression: Sometimes, we're so bullish on a player that we ignore the potential for regression within the bounds of random variance... Robinson Cano, Mike Adams, Cliff Lee, C.C. Sabathia, C.J. Wilson.

Unexpected loss of role: This category is usually composed of closers who lost their job through no fault of their own. But this year, we can thank Mike Trout for putting Peter Bourjos on the list. Oh, and Kyle Farnsworth.

The unexplained: These are the players for whom we have no rational explanation for what happened. We can speculate that they hid an injury, went off of PEDs, or just didn't have their head on right in 2012: Albert Pujols' first six weeks, John Axford despite his 33 saves, Daniel Bard's implosion, Tim Lincecum's rollercoaster season, and Ricky Romero.

About fantasy baseball touts

As a group, there is a strong tendency for all pundits to provide numbers that are publicly palatable, often at the expense of realism. That's because committing to either end of the range of expectation poses a high risk. Few touts will put their credibility on the line like that, even though we all know that those outliers are inevitable. Among our projections, you will find few .350 hitters and 70-steal speedsters. *Someone* is going to post a 2.50 ERA next year, but damned if any of us will commit to that. So we take an easier road. We'll hedge our numbers or split the difference between two equally possible outcomes.

In the world of prognosticating, this is called the *comfort zone*. This represents the outer tolerances for the public acceptability of a set of numbers. In most circumstances, even if the evidence is outstanding, prognosticators will not stray from within the comfort zone.

As for this book, occasionally we do commit to outlying numbers when we feel the data support it. But on the whole, most of the numbers here can be nearly as cowardly as everyone else's. We get around this by providing "color" to the projections in the capsule commentaries. That is where you will find the players whose projection has the best potential to stray beyond the limits of the comfort zone.

As analyst John Burnson once wrote: "The issue is not the success rate for one player, but the success rate for all players. No system is 100% reliable, and in trying to capture the outliers, you weaken the middle and thereby lose more predictive pull than you gain. At some level, everyone is an exception!"

Formula for consistent success

Anyone can win a league in any given season. Winning once proves very little, especially in redraft leagues. True success has to be defined as the ability to win consistently. It is a feat in itself to reach the mountaintop, but the battle isn't truly won unless you can stay atop that peak while others keep trying to knock you off.

What does it take to win that battle? We surveyed 12 of the most prolific fantasy champions in national experts league play. Here is how they rated six variables:

	Percent ranked			
	1-2	3-4	5-6	Score
Better in-draft strategy/tactics	77%	15%	7%	5.00
Better sense of player value	46%	46%	7%	4.15
Better luck	46%	23%	31%	3.85
Better grasp of contextual elements that affect players	31%	38%	31%	3.62
Better in-season roster management	31%	38%	31%	3.54
Better player projections	12%	31%	54%	2.62

Validating Performance

Performance validation criteria

The following is a set of support variables that helps determine whether a player's statistical output is an accurate reflection of his skills. From this we can validate or refute stats that vary from expectation, essentially asking, is this performance "fact or fluke?"

1. Age: Is the player at the stage of development when we might expect a change in performance?

2. Health: Is he coming off an injury, reconditioned and healthy for the first time in years, or a habitual resident of the disabled list?

3. Minor league performance: Has he shown the potential for greater things at some level of the minors? Or does his minor league history show a poor skill set that might indicate a lower ceiling?

4. Historical trends: Have his skill levels over time been on an upswing or downswing?

5. Component skills indicators: Looking beyond batting averages and ERAs, what do his support ratios look like?

6. Ballpark, team, league: Pitchers going to Texas will see their ERA spike. Pitchers going to PETCO Park will see their ERA improve.

7. Team performance: Has a player's performance been affected by overall team chemistry or the environment fostered by a winning or losing club?

8. Batting stance, pitching style: Has a change in performance been due to a mechanical adjustment?

9. Usage pattern, lineup position, role: Has a change in RBI opportunities been a result of moving further up or down in the batting order? Has pitching effectiveness been impacted by moving from the bullpen to the rotation?

10. Coaching effects: Has the coaching staff changed the way a player approaches his conditioning, or how he approaches the game itself?

11. Off-season activity: Has the player spent the winter frequenting workout rooms or banquet tables?

12. Personal factors: Has the player undergone a family crisis? Experienced spiritual rebirth? Given up red meat? Taken up testosterone?

Skills ownership

Once a player displays a skill, he owns it. That display could occur at any time—earlier in his career, back in the minors, or even in winter ball play. And while that skill may lie dormant after its initial display, the potential is always there for him to tap back into that skill at some point, barring injury or age. That dormant skill can reappear at any time given the right set of circumstances.

Caveats:

1. The initial display of skill must have occurred over an extended period of time. An isolated 1-hit shut-out in Single-A ball amidst a 5.00 ERA season is not enough. The shorter the display of skill in the past, the more likely it can be attributed to random chance. The longer the display, the more likely that any re-emergence is for real.

2. If a player has been suspected of using performance enhancing drugs at any time, all bets are off.

Corollaries:

1. Once a player displays a vulnerability or skills deficiency, he owns that as well. That vulnerability could be an old injury problem, an inability to hit breaking pitches, or just a tendency to go into prolonged slumps.

2. The probability of a player correcting a skills deficiency declines with each year that deficiency exists.

Contract year performance *(Tom Mullooly)*

There is a contention that players step up their game when they are playing for a contract. Research looked at contract year players and their performance during that year as compared to career levels. Of the batters and pitchers studied, 53% of the batters performed as if they were on a salary drive, while only 15% of the pitchers exhibited some level of contract year behavior.

How do players fare *after* signing a large contract (minimum $4M per year)? Research from 2005-2008 revealed that only 30% of pitchers and 22% of hitters exhibited an increase of more than 15% in BPV after signing a large deal either with their new team, or re-signing with the previous team. But nearly half of the pitchers (49%) and nearly half of the hitters (47%) saw a drop in BPV of more than 15% in the year after signing.

Risk management and reliability grades

Forecasts are constructed with the best data available, but there are factors that can impact the variability. One way we manage this risk is to assign each player Reliability Grades. The more certainty we see in a data set, the higher the reliability grades assigned to that player. The following variables are evaluated:

Health: Players with a history of staying healthy and off the DL are valuable to own. Unfortunately, while the ability to stay healthy can be considered skill, it is not very projectable. We can track the number of days spent on the disabled list and draw rough conclusions. The grades in the player boxes also include an adjustment for older players, who have a higher likelihood of getting hurt. That is the only forward-looking element of the grade.

"A" level players would have accumulated fewer than 30 days on the major league DL over the past five years. "F" grades go to those who've spent more than 120 days on the DL. Recent DL stays are given a heavier weight in the calculation.

Playing Time and Experience (PT/Exp): The greater the pool of MLB history to draw from, the greater our ability to construct a viable forecast. Length of service—and consistent service—is important. So players who bounce up and down from the majors to the minors are higher risk players. And rookies are all high risk.

For batters, we simply track plate appearances. Major league PAs have greater weight than minor league PAs. "A" level players would have averaged at least 550 major league PAs per year over the past three years. "F" graded players averaged fewer than 250 major league PA per year.

For pitchers, workload can be a double-edged sword. On one hand, small IP samples are deceptive in providing a read on a pitcher's true potential. Even a consistent 65-inning reliever can be considered higher risk since it would take just one bad outing to skew an entire season's work.

On the flipside, high workload levels also need to be monitored, especially in the formative years of a pitcher's career. Exceeding those levels elevates the risk of injury, burnout, or breakdown. So, tracking workload must be done within a range of innings. The grades capture this.

Consistency: Consistent performers are easier to project and garner higher reliability grades. Players that mix mediocrity with occasional flashes of brilliance or badness generate higher risk projections. Even those who exhibit a consistent upward or downward trend cannot be considered truly consistent as we do not know whether those trends will continue. Typically, they don't.

"A" level players are those whose runs created per game level (xERA for pitchers) has fluctuated by less than half a run during each of the past three years. "F" grades go to those whose RC/G or xERA has fluctuated by two runs or more.

Remember that these grades have nothing to do with quality of performance; they strictly refer to confidence in our expectations. So a grade of **AAA** for Joe Saunders, for instance, only means that there is a high probability he will perform as poorly as we've projected.

Reliability and age

Peak batting reliability occurs at ages 29 and 30, followed by a minor decline for four years. So, to draft the most reliable batters, and maximize the odds of returning at least par value on your investments, you should target the age range of 28-34.

The most reliable age range for pitchers is 29-34. While we are forever looking for "sleepers" and hot prospects, it is very risky to draft any pitcher under 27 or over 35.

Using 3-year trends as leading indicators *(Ed DeCaria)*

It is almost irresistibly tempting to look at three numbers moving in one direction and expect that the fourth will continue that progression. However, for both hitters and pitchers riding positive trends over any consecutive three-year period, not only do most players not continue their positive trend into a fourth year, their Year 4 performance usually regresses significantly. This is true for every metric tested (whether related to playing time, batting skills, pitching skills, running skills, luck indicators, or valuation). Negative trends show similar reversals, but tend to be more "sticky," meaning that rebounds are neither as frequent nor as strong as positive trend regressions. Challenge any analysis that hints at a player's demise coming off of a negative trend or that suggests an imminent breakout following a positive trend; more often than not, such predictions do not pan out.

Health Analysis

Disabled list statistics

Year	#Players	3yr Avg	DL Days	3yr Avg
2002	337	-	23,724	-
2003	351	-	22,118	-
2004	382	357	25,423	23,755
2005	356	363	24,016	23,852
2006	347	362	22,472	23,970
2007	404	369	28,524	25,004
2008	422	391	28,187	26,394
2009	408	411	26,252	27,654
2010	393	408	22,911	25,783
2011	422	408	25,610	24,924
2012	409	408	30,408	27,038

D.L. days as a leading indicator *(Bill Macey)*

Players who are injured in one year are likely to be injured in a subsequent year:

% DL batters in Year 1 who are also DL in year 2	38%
Under age 30	36%
Age 30 and older	41%
% DL batters in Year 1 and 2 who are also DL in year 3	54%
% DL pitchers in Year 1 who are also DL in year 2	43%
Under age 30	45%
Age 30 and older	41%
% DL pitchers in Yr 1 and 2 who are also DL in year 3	41%

Previously injured players also tend to spend a longer time on the DL. The average number of days on the DL was 51 days for batters and 73 days for pitchers. For the subset of these players who get hurt again the following year, the average number of days on the DL was 58 days for batters and 88 days for pitchers.

Spring training spin *(Dave Adler)*

Spring training sound bites raise expectations among fantasy leaguers, but how much of that "news" is really "noise"? Thanks to a summary listed at RotoAuthority.com, we were able to compile the stats for 2009. Verdict: Noise.

BATTERS	No.	IMPROVED	DECLINED
Weight change	30	33%	30%
Fitness program	3	0%	67%
Eye surgery	6	50%	33%
Plans more SB	6	17%	33%

PITCHERS	No.	IMPROVED	DECLINED
Weight change	18	44%	44%
Fitness program	4	50%	50%
Eye surgery	2	0%	50%
New pitch	5	60%	40%

In-Season Analysis

April performance as a leading indicator

We isolated all players who earned at least $10 more or $10 less than we had projected in March. Then we looked at the April stats of these players to see if we could have picked out the $10 outliers after just one month.

	Identifiable in April
Earned $10+ more than projected	
BATTERS	39%
PITCHERS	44%
Earned -$10 less than projected	
BATTERS	56%
PITCHERS	74%

Nearly three out of every four pitchers who earned at least $10 less than projected also struggled in April. For all the other surprises—batters or pitchers—April was not a strong leading indicator. Another look:

	Pct.
Batters who finished +$25	45%
Pitchers who finished +$20	44%
Batters who finished under $0	60%
Pitchers who finished under -$5	78%

April surgers are less than a 50/50 proposition to maintain that level all season. Those who finished April at the bottom of the roto rankings were more likely to continue struggling, especially pitchers. In fact, of those pitchers who finished April with a value *under -$10*, 91% finished the season in the red. Holes are tough to dig out of.

The weight of early season numbers

Early season strugglers who surge later in the year get no respect because they have to live with the weight of their early number all season long. Conversely, quick starters who fade late get far more accolades than they deserve.

For instance, take Max Scherzer's month-by-month ERAs. Based solely on his final 3.74 ERA, the perception is that he had a moderately successful year, but nothing out of the ordinary. Reality is different. If not for a truly horrible April, 2012 might have been considered Scherzer's career year. How many people know that, from May 1 on, he had an ERA of 3.14?

Month	ERA	Cum ERA
April	7.77	7.77
May	4.04	5.55
June	3.86	4.98
July	3.62	4.62
August	2.25	4.13
Sept-Oct	1.91	3.74

Courtship period

Any time a player is put into a new situation, he enters into what we might call a courtship period. This period might occur when a player switches leagues, or switches teams. It could be the first few games when a minor leaguer is called up. It could occur when a reliever moves into the rotation, or when a lead-off hitter is moved to another spot in the lineup. There is a team-wide courtship period when a manager is replaced. Any external situation that could affect a player's performance sets off a new decision point in evaluating that performance.

During this period, it is difficult to get a true read on how a player is going to ultimately perform. He is adjusting to the new situation. Things could be volatile during this time. For instance, a role change that doesn't work could spur other moves. A rookie hurler might buy himself a few extra starts with a solid debut, even if he has questionable skills.

It is best not to make a decision on a player who is going through a courtship period. Wait until his stats stabilize. Don't cut a struggling pitcher in his first few starts after a managerial change. Don't pick up a hitter who smacks a pair of HRs in his first game after having been traded. Unless, of course, talent and track record say otherwise.

Half-season fallacies

A popular exercise at the midpoint of each season is to analyze those players who are consistent first half to second half surgers or faders. There are several fallacies with this analytical approach.

1. Half-season consistency is rare. There are very few players who show consistent changes in performance from one half of the season to the other.

Research results from a three-year study conducted in the late-1990s: The test groups... batters with min. 300 AB full season, 150 AB first half, and pitchers with min. 100 IP full season, 50 IP first half. Of those groups (size noted):

3-year consistency in	BATTERS (98)	PITCHERS (42)
1 stat category	40%	57%
2 stat categories	18%	21%
3 stat categories	3%	5%

When the analysis was stretched to a fourth year, only 1% of all players showed consistency in even one category.

2. Analysts often use false indicators. Situational statistics provide us with tools that can be misused. Several sources offer up 3- and 5-year stats intended to paint a picture of a long-term performance. Some analysts look at a player's half-season swing over that multi-year period and conclude that he is demonstrating consistent performance.

The fallacy is that those multi-year scans may not show any consistency at all. They are not individual season performances but *aggregate* performances. A player whose 5-year batting average shows a 15-point rise in the 2nd half, for instance, may actually have experienced a BA decline in several of those years, a fact that might have been offset by a huge BA rise in one of the years.

3. It's arbitrary. The season's midpoint is an arbitrary delineator of performance swings. Some players are slow starters and might be more appropriately evaluated as pre-May 1 and post-May 1. Others bring their game up a notch with a pennant chase and might see a performance swing with August 15 as the cut-off. Each player has his own individual tendency, if, in fact, one exists at all. There's nothing magical about mid-season as the break point, and certainly not over a multi-year period.

Half-season tendencies

Despite the above, it stands to reason logically that there might be some underlying tendencies on a more global scale, first half to second half. In fact, one would think that the player population as a whole might decline in performance as the season drones on.

There are many variables that might contribute to a player wearing down—workload, weather, boredom—and the longer a player is on the field, the higher the likelihood that he is going to get hurt. A recent 5-year study uncovered the following tendencies:

Batting

Overall, batting skills held up pretty well, half to half. There was a 5% erosion of playing time, likely due, in part, to September roster expansion.

Power: First half power studs (20 HRs in 1H) saw a 10% drop-off in the second half. 34% of first half 20+ HR hitters hit 15 or fewer in the second half and only 27% were able to improve on their first half output.

Speed: Second half speed waned as well. About 26% of the 20+ SB speedsters stole *at least 10 fewer bases* in the second half. Only 26% increased their second half SB output at all.

Batting average: 60% of first half .300 hitters failed to hit .300 in the second half. Only 20% showed any second half improvement at all. As for 1H strugglers, managers tended to stick with their full-timers despite poor starts. Nearly one in five of the sub-.250 1H hitters managed to hit *more than* .300 in the second half.

Pitching

Overall, there was some slight erosion in innings and ERA despite marginal improvement in some peripherals.

ERA: For those who pitched at least 100 innings in the first half, ERAs rose an average of 0.40 runs in the 2H. Of those with first half ERAs less than 4.00, only 49% were able to maintain a sub-4.00 ERA in the second half.

Wins: Pitchers who won 18 or more games in a season tended to pitch *more* innings in the 2H and had slightly better peripherals.

Saves: Of those closers who saved 20 or more games in the first half, only 39% were able to post 20 or more saves in the 2H, and 26% posted fewer than 15 saves. Aggregate ERAs of these pitchers rose from 2.45 to 3.17, half to half.

Teams

Johnson Effect *(Bryan Johnson)*: Teams whose actual won/loss record exceeds or falls short of their statistically projected record in one season will tend to revert to the level of their projection in the following season.

Law of Competitive Balance *(Bill James)*: The level at which a team (or player) will address its problems is inversely related to its current level of success. Low performers will tend to make changes to improve; high performers will not. This law explains the existence of the Plexiglass and Whirlpool Principles.

Plexiglass Principle *(Bill James)*: If a player or team improves markedly in one season, it will likely decline in the next. The opposite is true but not as often (because a poor performer gets fewer opportunities to rebound).

Whirlpool Principle *(Bill James)*: All team and player performances are forcefully drawn to the center. For teams, that center is a .500 record. For players, it represents their career average level of performance.

Other Diamonds

The Fanalytic Fundamentals

1. This is not a game of accuracy or precision. It is a game of human beings and tendencies.
2. This is not a game of projections. It is a game of market value versus real value.
3. Draft skills, not stats. Draft skills, not roles.
4. A player's ability to post acceptable stats despite lousy BPIs will eventually run out.
5. Once you display a skill, you own it.
6. Virtually every player is vulnerable to a month of aberrant performance. Or a year.
7. Exercise excruciating patience.

Aging Axioms

1. Age is the only variable for which we can project a rising trend with 100% accuracy. (Or, age never regresses.)
2. The aging process slows down for those who maintain a firm grasp on the strike zone. Plate patience and pitching command can preserve any waning skill they have left.
3. Negatives tend to snowball as you age.

Steve Avery List

Players who hang onto MLB rosters for six years searching for a skill level they only had for three.

Bylaws of Badness

1. Some players are better than an open roster spot, but not by much.
2. Some players have bad years because they are unlucky. Others have *many* bad years because they are bad... and lucky.

George Brett Path to Retirement

Get out while you're still putting up good numbers and the public perception of you is favorable. Like Mike Mussina and Billy Wagner. And Chipper Jones.

Steve Carlton Path to Retirement

Hang around the majors long enough for your numbers to become so wretched that people begin to forget your past successes.

Classic cases include Jose Mesa, Doc Gooden, Nomar Garciaparra and of course, Steve Carlton. Recent players who have taken this path include Ivan Rodriguez, Mike Cameron and Miguel Tejada. Current players who could be on a similar course include Jason Bay, Chone Figgins, Carlos Pena, Andruw Jones, Johnny Damon and Jason Giambi.

Christie Brinkley Law of Statistical Analysis

Never get married to the model.

Employment Standards

1. If you are right-brain dominant, own a catcher's mitt and are under 40, you will always be gainfully employed.
2. Some teams believe that it is better to employ a player with any experience because it has to be better than the devil they don't know.
3. It's not so good to go *pffft* in a contract year.

Laws of Prognosticating Perspective

- *Berkeley's 17th Law:* A great many problems do not have accurate answers, but do have approximate answers, from which sensible decisions can be made.
- *Ashley-Perry Statistical Axiom #4:* A complex system that works is invariably found to have evolved from a simple system that works.
- *Baseball Variation of Harvard Law:* Under the most rigorously observed conditions of skill, age, environment, statistical rules and other variables, a ballplayer will perform as he damn well pleases.

Brad Fullmer List

Players whose leading indicators indicate upside potential, year after year, but consistently fail to reach that full potential. Players like Jake Arrieta, Phil Hughes, Nick Markakis, Ricky Nolasco, Bud Norris and Carlos Quentin are on the list right now.

Ceiling

The highest professional level at which a player maintains acceptable BPIs. Also, the peak performance level that a player will likely reach, given his BPIs.

Good Luck Truism

Good luck is rare and everyone has more of it than you do. That's the law.

The Gravity Principles

1. It is easier to be crappy than it is to be good.
2. All performance starts at zero, ends at zero and can drop to zero at any time.
3. The odds of a good performer slumping are far greater than the odds of a poor performer surging.
4. Once a player is in a slump, it takes several 3-for-5 days to get out of it. Once he is on a streak, it takes a single 0-for-4 day to begin the downward spiral. *Corollary:* Once a player is in a slump, not only does it take several 3-for-5 days to get out of it, but he also has to get his name back on the lineup card.
5. Eventually all performance comes down to earth. It may take a week, or a month, or may not happen until he's 45, but eventually it's going to happen.

Health Homilies

1. Staying healthy is a skill (and "DL Days" should be a Rotisserie category).
2. A $40 player can get hurt just as easily as a $5 player but is eight times tougher to replace.
3. Chronically injured players never suddenly get healthy.
4. There are two kinds of pitchers: those that are hurt and those that are not hurt... yet.
5. Players with back problems are always worth $10 less.
6. "Opting out of surgery" usually means it's coming anyway, just later.

The Health Hush

Players get hurt and potentially have a lot to lose, so there is an incentive for them to hide injuries. HIPAA laws restrict the disclosure of health information. Team doctors and trainers have been instructed not to talk with the media. So, when it comes to information on a player's health status, we're all pretty much in the dark.

Hidden Injury Progression

1. Player's skills implode.
2. Team and player deny injury.
3. More unexplained struggles.
4. Injury revealed; surgery follows.

Law of Injury Estimation (Westheimer's Rule)

To calculate an accurate projection of the amount of time a player will be out of action due to injury, first take the published time estimate, double it and change the unit of measure to the next highest unit. Thus, a player estimated to be out two weeks will actually be out four months.

The Livan Level

The point when a player's career Runs Above Replacement level has dropped so far below zero that he has effectively cancelled out any possible remaining future value. (Similarly, the Dontrelle Demarcation.)

Monocarp

A player whose career consists of only one productive season.

Paradoxes and Conundrums

1. Is a player's improvement in performance from one year to the next a point in a growth trend, an isolated outlier or a complete anomaly?
2. A player can play through an injury, post rotten numbers and put his job at risk… or… he can admit that he can't play through an injury, allow himself to be taken out of the lineup/rotation, and put his job at risk.
3. Did irregular playing time take its toll on the player's performance or did poor performance force a reduction in his playing time?
4. Is a player only in the game versus right-handers because he has a true skills deficiency versus left-handers? Or is his poor performance versus left-handers because he's never given a chance to face them?
5. The problem with stockpiling bench players in the hope that one pans out is that you end up evaluating performance using data sets that are too small to be reliable.
6. There are players who could give you 20 stolen bases if they got 400 AB. But if they got 400 AB, they would likely be on a bad team that wouldn't let them steal.

Process-Outcome Matrix *(Russo and Schoemaker)*

	Good Outcome	Bad Outcome
Good Process	Deserved Success	Bad Break
Bad Process	Dumb Luck	Poetic Justice

Quack!

An exclamation in response to the educated speculation that a player has used performance enhancing drugs. While it is rare to have absolute proof, there is often enough information to suggest that, "if it looks like a duck and quacks like a duck, then odds are it's a duck."

Tenets of Optimal Timing

1. If a second half fader had put up his second half stats in the first half and his first half stats in the second half, then he probably wouldn't even have had a second half.
2. Fast starters can often buy six months of playing time out of one month of productivity.
3. Poor 2nd halves don't get recognized until it's too late.
4. "Baseball is like this. Have one good year and you can fool them for five more, because for five more years they expect you to have another good one." — Frankie Frisch

The Three True Outcomes

1. Strikeouts
2. Walks
3. Home runs

The Three True Handicaps

1. Has power but can't make contact.
2. Has speed but can't hit safely.
3. Has potential but is too old.

UGLY (Unreasonable Good Luck Year)

The driving force behind every winning team. It's what they really mean when they say "winning ugly."

Walbeckian

Possessing below replacement level stats, as in "Ryan Raburn's season was downright Walbeckian." Alternate usage: "Ryan Raburn's stats were so bad that I might as well have had Walbeck in there."

Wasted talent

A player with a high level skill that is negated by a deficiency in another skill. For instance, base path speed can be negated by poor on base ability. Pitchers with strong arms can be wasted because home plate is an elusive concept to them.

Zombie

A player who is indestructible, continuing to get work, year-after-year, no matter how dead his BPIs are. Like Jeff Suppan, Derek Lowe or Livan Hernandez.

Batters

Batting Eye, Contact and Batting Average

Batting average (BA, or Avg)

This is where it starts. BA is a grand old nugget that has long outgrown its usefulness. We revere .300 hitting superstars and scoff at .250 hitters, yet the difference between the two is one hit every 20 ABs. This one hit every five games is not nearly the wide variance that exists in our perceptions of what it means to be a .300 or .250 hitter. BA is a poor evaluator of performance in that it neglects the offensive value of the base on balls and assumes that all hits are created equal.

Walk rate (bb%)
(BB / (AB + BB))

A measure of a batter's plate patience. **BENCHMARKS:** The best batters will have levels more than 10%. Those with poor plate patience will have levels of 5% or less.

On base average (OB)
(H + BB) / (AB + BB)

Addressing a key deficiency with BA, OB gives value to events that get batters on base, but are not hits. An OB of .350 can be read as "this batter gets on base 35% of the time." When a run is scored, there is no distinction made as to how that runner reached base. So, two-thirds of the time—about how often a batter comes to the plate with the bases empty—a walk really is as good as a hit.

The official version of this formula includes hit batsmen. We do not include it because our focus is on skills-based gauges; research has shown that HBP is not a measure of batting skill but of pitching deficiency. **BENCHMARKS:** We know what a .300 hitter is, but what represents "good" for OB? That comparable level would likely be .400, with .275 representing the comparable level of futility.

Ground ball, line drive, fly ball percentages (G/L/F)

The percentage of all balls in play that are hit on the ground, as line drives and in the air. For batters, increased fly ball tendency may foretell a rise in power skills; increased line drive tendency may foretell an improvement in batting average. For a pitcher, the ability to keep the ball on the ground can contribute to his statistical output exceeding his demonstrated skill level.

*BIP Type	Total%	Out%
Ground ball	45%	72%
Line drive	20%	28%
Fly ball	35%	85%
TOTAL	*100%*	*69%*

*Data only includes fieldable balls and is net of HRs.

Line drives and luck *(Patrick Davitt)*

Given that each individual batter's hit rate sets its own baseline, and that line drives (LD) are the most productive type of batted ball, a study looked at the relationship between the two. Among the findings were that hit rates on LDs are much higher than on FBs or GBs, and are generally stable in a range from 70% to 74%.

Among individual batters, LDh% has been relatively consistent around 72-73%, with 95% of all batters falling into an LDh% range of 60%-86%. Batters outside this range regress very quickly, often within the season.

Note that batters' BAs did not always follow their LD% up or down, because some of them enjoyed higher hit rates on other batted balls, improved their contact rates, or both. Still, it's justifiable to bet that players hitting the ball with authority but getting fewer hits than they should will correct over time.

Batting eye (Eye)
(Walks / Strikeouts)

A measure of a player's strike zone judgment. **BENCHMARKS:** The best hitters have Eye ratios more than 1.00 (indicating more walks than strikeouts) and are the most likely to be among a league's .300 hitters. Ratios less than 0.50 represent batters who likely also have lower BAs.

Batting eye as a leading indicator

There is a strong correlation between strike zone judgment and batting average. However, research shows that this is more descriptive than predictive:

	Batting Average				
Batting Eye	2008	2009	2010	2011	2012
0.00 - 0.25	.242	.239	.235	.232	.243
0.26 - 0.50	.261	.259	.260	.254	.255
0.51 - 0.75	.273	.272	.264	.267	.268
0.76 - 1.00	.280	.274	.272	.276	.276
1.01 and over	.285	.292	.280	.298	.292

We can create percentage plays for the different levels:

For Eye	Pct who bat	
Levels of	.300+	.250-
0.00 - 0.25	7%	39%
0.26 - 0.50	14%	26%
0.51 - 0.75	18%	17%
0.76 - 1.00	32%	14%
1.01 - 1.50	51%	9%
1.51 +	59%	4%

Any batter with an eye ratio more than 1.50 has about a 4% chance of hitting less than .250 over 500 at bats.

Of all .300 hitters, those with ratios of at least 1.00 have a 65% chance of repeating as .300 hitters. Those with ratios less than 1.00 have less than a 50% chance of repeating.

Only 4% of sub-.250 hitters with ratios less than 0.50 will mature into .300 hitters the following year.

In a 1995-2000 study, only 37 batters hit .300-plus with a sub-0.50 eye ratio over at least 300 AB in a season. Of this group, 30% were able to accomplish this feat on a consistent basis. For the other 70%, this was a short-term aberration.

Contact rate (ct%)
((AB - K) / AB)

Measures a batter's ability to get wood on the ball and hit it into the field of play. **BENCHMARKS:** Those batters with the best contact skill will have levels of 90% or better. The hackers of society will have levels of 75% or less.

Contact rate as a leading indicator

The more often a batter makes contact with the ball, the higher the likelihood that he will hit safely.

	Batting Average				
Contact Rate	2008	2009	2010	2011	2012
0% - 60%	.210	.189	.187	.171	.197
61% - 65%	.226	.229	.235	.199	.226
66% - 70%	.235	.241	.236	.229	.231
71% - 75%	.250	.247	.254	.243	.252
76% - 80%	.262	.263	.256	.260	.255
81% - 85%	.273	.275	.271	.268	.268
86% - 90%	.284	.281	.273	.272	.278
Over 90%	.285	.287	.270	.290	.282

Contact rate and walk rate as leading indicators

A matrix of contact rates and walk rates can provide expectation benchmarks for a player's batting average:

	Walk rate (bb%)			
Contact rate (ct%)	0-5	6-10	11-15	16+
65-	.179	.195	.229	.237
66-75	.190	.248	.254	.272
76-85	.265	.267	.276	.283
86+	.269	.279	.301	.309

A contact rate of 65% or lower offers virtually no chance for a player to hit even .250, no matter how high a walk rate he has. The .300 hitters most often come from the group with a minimum 86% contact and 11% walk rate.

HCt and HctX *(Patrick Davitt)*

HCt= hard hit ball rate x contact rate

HctX= Player Hct divided by league average Hct, normalized to 100

The combination of making contact and hitting the ball hard might be the most important skills for a batter. HctX correlates very strongly with BA, and at higher BA levels often does so with high accuracy. Its success with HR was somewhat limited, probably due to GB/FB differences. **BENCHMARKS:** The average major-leaguer in a given year has a HctX of 100. Elite batters have an HctX of 135 or above; weakest batters have HctX of 55 or below.

Balls in play (BIP)

(AB – K)

The total number of batted balls that are hit fair, both hits and outs. An analysis of how these balls are hit—on the ground, in the air, hits, outs, etc.—can provide analytical insight, from player skill levels to the impact of luck on statistical output.

Batting average on balls in play *(Voros McCracken)*

(H – HR) / (AB – HR – K)

Also called hit rate (h%). The percent of balls hit into the field of play that fall for hits. **BENCHMARK:** Every hitter establishes his own individual hit rate that stabilizes over time. A batter whose seasonal hit rate varies significantly from the h% he has established over the preceding three seasons (variance of at least +/- 3%) is likely to improve or regress to his individual h% mean (with over-performer declines more likely and sharper than under-performer recoveries). Three-year h% levels strongly predict a player's h% the following year.

P/PA as a leading indicator for BA *(Paul Petera)*

The art of working the count has long been considered one of the more crucial aspects of good hitting. It is common knowledge that the more pitches a hitter sees, the greater opportunity he has to reach base safely.

P/PA	OBA	BA
4.00+	.360	.264
3.75-3.99	.347	.271
3.50-3.74	.334	.274
Under 3.50	.321	.276

Generally speaking, the more pitches seen, the lower the BA, but the higher the OBA. But what about the outliers, those players that bucked the trend in year #1?

	YEAR TWO	
	BA Improved	BA Declined
Low P/PA and Low BA	77%	23%
High P/PA and High BA	21%	79%

In these scenarios, there was a strong tendency for performance to normalize in year #2.

Expected batting average *(John Burnson)*

$xCT\% * [xH1\% + xH2\%]$

where

$xH1\% = GB\% \times [0.0004\ PX + 0.062\ ln(SX)]$
$\quad + LD\% \times [0.93 - 0.086\ ln(SX)]$
$\quad + FB\% \times 0.12$

and

$xH2\% = FB\% \times [0.0013\ PX - 0.0002\ SX - 0.057]$
$\quad + GB\% \times [0.0006\ PX]$

A hitter's batting average as calculated by multiplying the percentage of balls put in play (contact rate) by the chance that a ball in play falls for a hit. The likelihood that a ball in play falls for a hit is a product of the speed of the ball and distance it is hit (PX), the speed of the batter (SX), and distribution of ground balls, fly balls, and line drives. We further split it out by non-homerun hit rate (xH1%) and homerun hit rate (xH2%). **BENCHMARKS:** In general, xBA should approximate batting average fairly closely. Those hitters who have large variances between the two gauges are candidates for further analysis. **LIMITATION:** xBA tends to understate a batter's true value if he is an extreme ground ball hitter (G/F ratio over 3.0) with a low PX. These players are not inherently weak, but choose to take safe singles rather than swing for the fences.

Expected batting average variance

xBA – BA

The variance between a batter's BA and his xBA is a measure of over- or under-achievement. A positive variance indicates the potential for a batter's BA to rise. A negative variance indicates the potential for BA to decline. **BENCHMARK:** Discount variances that are less than 20 points. Any variance more than 30 points is regarded as a strong indicator of future change.

Power

Slugging average (Slg)
(Singles + (2 x Doubles) + (3 x Triples) + (4 x HR)) / AB

A measure of the total number of bases accumulated (or the minimum number of runners' bases advanced) per at bat. It is a misnomer; it is not a true measure of a batter's slugging ability because it includes singles. Slg also assumes that each type of hit has proportionately increasing value (i.e. a double is twice as valuable as a single, etc.) which is not true. For instance, with the bases loaded, a HR always scores four runs, a triple always scores three, but a double could score two or three and a single could score one, or two, or even three. **BENCHMARKS:** Top batters will have levels over .500. The bottom batters will have levels less than .300.

Fly ball tendency and power *(Mat Olkin)*
There is a proven connection between a hitter's ground ball/fly ball tendencies and his power production.

1. *Extreme ground ball hitters generally do not hit for much power.* It's almost impossible for a hitter with a ground/fly ratio over 1.80 to hit enough fly balls to produce even 25 HRs in a season. However, this does not mean that a low G/F ratio necessarily guarantees power production. Some players have no problem getting the ball into the air, but lack the strength to reach the fences consistently.

2. *Most batters' ground/fly ratios stay pretty steady over time.* Most year-to-year changes are small and random, as they are in any other statistical category. A large, sudden change in G/F, on the other hand, can signal a conscious change in plate approach. And so...

3. *If a player posts high G/F ratios in his first few years, he probably isn't ever going to hit for all that much power.*

4. *When a batter's power suddenly jumps, his G/F ratio often drops at the same time.*

5. *Every so often, a hitter's ratio will drop significantly even as his power production remains level.* In these rare cases, impending power development is likely, since the two factors almost always follow each other.

Home runs to fly ball rate (hr/f)
The percent of fly balls that are hit for HRs.

hr/f rate as a leading indicator *(Joshua Randall)*
Each batter establishes an individual home run to fly ball rate that stabilizes over rolling three-year periods; those levels strongly predict the hr/f in the subsequent year. A batter who varies significantly from his hr/f is likely to regress toward his individual hr/f mean, with over-performance decline more likely and more severe than under-performance recovery.

Linear weighted power (LWPwr)
((Doubles x .8) + (Triples x .8) + (HR x 1.4)) / (At bats- K) x 100

A variation of the linear weights formula that considers only events that are measures of a batter's pure power. **BENCHMARKS:** Top sluggers typically top the 17 mark. Weak hitters will have a LWPwr level of less than 10.

Linear weighted power index (PX)
(Batter's LWPwr / League LWPwr) x 100

LWPwr is presented in this book in its normalized form to get a better read on a batter's accomplishment in each year. For instance, a 30-HR season today is much more of an accomplishment than 30 HRs hit in a higher offense year like 2003. **BENCHMARKS:** A level of 100 equals league average power skills. Any player with a value more than 100 has above average power skills, and those more than 150 are the Slugging Elite.

Expected LW power index (xPX) *(Bill Macey)*
2.6 + 269*HHLD% + 724*HHFB%

Previous research has shown that hard-hit balls are more likely to result in hits and hard-hit fly balls are more likely to end up as HRs. As such, we can use hard-hit ball data to calculate an expected skills-based power index. This metric starts with hard-hit ball data, which measures a player's fundamental skill of making solid contact, and then places it on the same scale as PX (xPX). In the above formula, HHLD% is calculated as the number of hard hit-line drives divided by the total number of balls put in play. HHFB% is similarly calculated for fly balls.

P/PA as a leading indicator for PX *(Paul Petera)*
Working the count has a positive effect on power.

P/PA	PX
4.00+	123
3.75-3.99	108
3.50-3.74	96
Under 3.50	84

As for the year #1 outliers:

	YEAR TWO	
	PX Improved	PX Declined
Low P/PA and High PX	11%	89%
High P/PA and Low PX	70%	30%

In these scenarios, there was a strong tendency for performance to normalize in year #2

Opposite field home runs *(Ed DeCaria)*
From 2001-2008, nearly 75% of all HRs were hit to the batter's pull field, with the remaining 25% distributed roughly evenly between straight away and opposite field. Left-handers accomplished the feat slightly more often than right-handers (including switch-hitters hitting each way), and younger hitters did it significantly more often than older hitters. The trend toward pulled home runs was especially strong after age 36.

Power Quartile	AB/HR	Opp. Field	Straight Away	Pull Field
Top 25%	17.2	15.8%	16.0%	68.2%
2nd 25%	28.0	10.7%	12.2%	77.0%
3rd 25%	44.1	8.9%	10.0%	81.1%
Bot 25%	94.7	5.4%	5.9%	88.7%

Opposite field HRs serve as a strong indicator of overall home run power (AB/HR). Power hitters (smaller AB/HR rates) hit a far higher percentage of their HR to the opposite field or straight away (over 30%). Conversely, non-power hitters hit almost 90% of their home runs to their pull field.

Performance in Y2-Y4 (% of Group)			
Y1 Trigger	<=30 AB/HR	5.5+ RC/G	$16+ R$
2+ OppHR	69%	46%	33%
<2 OppHR	29%	13%	12%

Players who hit just two or more OppHR in one season were 2-3 times as likely as those who hit zero or one OppHR to sustain strong AB/HR rates, RC/G levels, or R$ values over the following three seasons.

Y2-Y4 Breakout Performance		
(% Breakout by Group, Age <=26 Only)		
	AB/HR	RC/G	R$
Y1 Trigger	>35 to <=30	<4.5 to 5.5+	<$8 to $16+
2+ OppHR	32%	21%	30%
<2 OppHR	23%	12%	10%

Roughly one of every 3-4 batters age 26 or younger experiences a *sustained three-year breakout* in AB/HR, RC/G or R$ after a season in which they hit 2+ OppHR, far better odds than the one in 8-10 batters who experience a breakout without the 2+ OppHR trigger.

Power breakout profile

It is not easy to predict which batters will experience a power spike. We can categorize power breakouts to determine the likelihood of a player taking a step up or of a surprise performer repeating his feat. Possibilities:

- Increase in playing time
- History of power skills at some time in the past
- Redistribution of already demonstrated extra base hit power
- Normal skills growth
- Situational breakouts, particularly in hitter-friendly venues
- Increased fly ball tendency
- Use of illegal performance-enhancing substances
- Miscellaneous unexplained variables

Speed

Wasted talent on the base paths

We refer to some players as having "wasted talent," a high level skill that is negated by a deficiency in another skill. Among these types are players who have blazing speed that is negated by a sub-.300 on base average.

These players can have short-term value. However, their stolen base totals are tied so tightly to their "green light" that any change in managerial strategy could completely erase that value. A higher OB mitigates that downside; the good news is that plate patience can be taught.

Players in 2012 who had at least 20 SBs with an OBP less than .300, and whose SB output could be at risk, are Carlos Gomez (37 SB, .294 OBP), Dee Gordon (32, .276), Drew Stubbs (30, .275), Jordan Schafer (27, .292), Alexi Casilla (21, .279) and Alexei Ramirez (20, .284).

Speed score *(Bill James)*

A measure of the various elements that comprise a runner's speed skills. Although this formula (a variation of James' original

version) may be used as a leading indicator for stolen base output, SB attempts are controlled by managerial strategy which makes speed score somewhat less valuable.

Speed score is calculated as the mean value of the following four elements:

1. Stolen base efficiency = $(((SB + 3)/(SB + CS + 7)) - .4) \times 20$
2. Stolen base freq. = *Square root of $((SB + CS)/(Singles + BB))/.07$*
3. Triples rating = $(3B / (AB - HR - K))$ and the result assigned a value based on the following chart:

< 0.001	0	0.0105	6
0.001	1	0.013	7
0.0023	2	0.0158	8
0.0039	3	0.0189	9
0.0058	4	0.0223+	10
0.008	5		

4. Runs scored as a percentage of times on base = $(((R - HR) / (H + BB - HR)) - .1) / .04$

Speed score index (SX)

(Batter's speed score / League speed score) x 100

Normalized speed scores get a better read on a runner's accomplishment in context. A level of 100 equals league average speed skill. Values more than 100 indicate above average skill, more than 200 represent the Fleet of Feet Elite.

Statistically scouted speed (Spd) *(Ed DeCaria)*

$(104 + \{[(Runs-HR+10*age\_wt)/(RBI-HR+10)]/lg\_av*100\} / 5$
$+ \{[(3B+5*age\_wt)/(2B+3B+5)]/lg\_av*100\} / 5$
$+ \{[(SoftMedGBhits+25*age\_wt)/(SoftMedGB+25)]/lg\_av*100\} / 2$
$- \{[Weight (Lbs)/Height (In)^2 * 703]/lg\_av*100\}$

A skills-based gauge that measures speed without relying on stolen bases. Its components are:

- *(Runs − HR) / (RBI − HR)*: This metric aims to minimize the influence of extra base hit power and team run-scoring rates on perceived speed.
- *3B / (2B + 3B)*: No one can deny that triples are a fast runner's stat; dividing them by 2B+3B instead of all balls in play dampens the power aspect of extra base hits.
- *(Soft + Medium Ground Ball Hits) / (Soft + Medium Ground Balls)*: Faster runners are more likely than slower runners to beat out routine grounders. Hard hit balls are excluded from numerator and denominator.
- *Body Mass Index (BMI)*: Calculated as *Weight (lbs) / Height (in)2 * 703*. All other factors considered, leaner players run faster than heavier ones.

In this book, the formula is scaled as an index with a midpoint of 100.

Stolen base opportunity percent (SBO)

(SB + CS) / (BB + Singles)

A rough approximation of how often a baserunner attempts a stolen base. Provides a comparative measure for players on a given team and, as a team measure, the propensity of a manager to give a "green light" to his runners.

Overall Performance Analysis

On base plus slugging average (OPS)

A simple sum of the two gauges, it is considered one of the better evaluators of overall performance. OPS combines the two basic elements of offensive production—the ability to get on base (OB) and the ability to advance baserunners (Slg). **BENCHMARKS:** The game's top batters will have OPS levels more than .900. The worst batters will have levels less than .600.

Base Performance Value (BPV)

(Walk rate - 5) x 2)

+ ((Contact rate - 75) x 4)

+ ((Power Index - 80) x 0.8)

+ ((Spd - 80) x 0.3)

A single value that describes a player's overall raw skill level. This is more useful than traditional statistical gauges to track player performance trends and project future statistical output. The BPV formula combines and weights several BPIs.

This formula combines the individual raw skills of batting eye, contact rate, power and speed. **BENCHMARKS:** The best hitters will have a BPV of 50 or greater.

Base Performance Index (BPX)

BPV scaled to league average to account for year-to-year fluctuations in league-wide statistical performance. It's a snapshot of a player's overall skills compared to an average player. **BENCHMARK:** A level of 100 means a player had a league-average BPV in that given season.

Linear weights   *(Pete Palmer)*

((Singles x .46) + (Doubles x .8) + (Triples x 1.02)

+ (Home runs x 1.4) + (Walks x .33) + (Stolen Bases x .3)

- (Caught Stealing x .6) - ((At bats - Hits) x Normalizing Factor)

(Also referred to as Batting Runs.) Formula whose premise is that all events in baseball are linear; that is, the output (runs) is directly proportional to the input (offensive events). Each of these events is then weighted according to its relative value in producing runs. Positive events—hits, walks, stolen bases—have positive values. Negative events—outs, caught stealing—have negative values.

The normalizing factor, representing the value of an out, is an offset to the level of offense in a given year. It changes every season, growing larger in high offense years and smaller in low offense years. The value is about .26 and varies by league.

LW is not included in the player forecast boxes, but the LW concept is used with the linear weighted power gauge.

Runs above replacement (RAR)

An estimate of the number of runs a player contributes above a "replacement level" player. "Replacement" is defined as the level of performance at which another player can easily be found at little or no cost to a team. What constitutes replacement level is a topic that is hotly debated. There are a variety of formulas and rules of thumb used to determine this level for each position (replacement level for a shortstop will be very different from replacement level for an outfielder). Our estimates appear below.

One of the major values of RAR for fantasy applications is that it can be used to assemble an integrated ranking of batters and pitchers for drafting purposes.

To calculate RAR for batters:

- Start with a batter's runs created per game (RC/G).
- Subtract his position's replacement level RC/G.
- Multiply by number of games played: (AB - H + CS) / 25.5.

Replacement levels used in this book:

POS	AL	NL
C	4.14	4.29
1B	5.29	5.43
2B	4.17	4.35
3B	4.55	4.61
SS	3.91	4.11
LF	4.57	4.73
CF	4.86	4.69
RF	4.86	5.15
DH	4.89	

RAR can also be used to calculate rough projected team won-loss records. *(Roger Miller)* Total the RAR levels for all the players on a team, divide by 10 and add to 53 wins.

Runs created   *(Bill James)*

(H + BB – CS) x (Total bases + (.55 x SB)) / (AB + BB)

A formula that converts all offensive events into a total of runs scored. As calculated for individual teams, the result approximates a club's actual run total with great accuracy.

Runs created per game   (RC/G)

Bill James version: *Runs Created / ((AB - H + CS) / 25.5)*

RC expressed on a per-game basis might be considered the hypothetical ERA compiled against a particular batter. Another way to look at it: A batter with a RC/G of 7.00 would be expected to score 7 runs per game if he were cloned nine times and faced an average pitcher in every at bat. Cloning batters is not a practice we recommend. **BENCHMARKS:** Few players surpass the level of a 10.00 RC/G, but any level more than 7.50 can still be considered very good. At the bottom are levels less than 3.00.

Plate Appearances as a leading indicator   *(Patrick Davitt)*

While targeting players "age 26 with experience" as potential breakout candidates has become a commonly accepted concept, a study has found that cumulative plate appearances, especially during the first two years of a young player's career, can also have predictive value in assessing a coming spike in production. Three main conclusions:

- When projecting players, MLB experience is more important than age.
- Players who amass 800+ PAs in their first two seasons are highly likely to have double-digit value in Year 3.
- Also target young players in the season where they attain 400 PAs, as they are twice as likely as other players to grow significantly in value.

Handedness

1. While pure southpaws account for about 27% of total ABs (RHers about 55% and switch-hitters about 18%), they hit 31% of the triples and take 30% of the walks.

2. The average lefty posts a batting average about 10 points higher than the average RHer. The on base averages of pure LHers are nearly 20 points higher than RHers, but only 10 points higher than switch-hitters.

3. LHers tend to have a better batting eye ratio than RHers, but about the same as switch-hitters.

4. Pure righties and lefties have virtually identical power skills. Switch-hitters tend to have less power, on average.

5. Switch-hitters tend to have the best speed, followed by LHers, and then RHers.

6. On an overall production basis, LHers have an 8% advantage over RHers and a 14% edge over switch-hitters.

Skill-specific aging patterns for batters *(Ed DeCaria)*

Baseball forecasters obsess over "peak age" of player performance because we must understand player ascent toward and decline from that peak to predict future value. Most published aging analyses are done using composite estimates of value such as OPS or linear weights. By contrast, fantasy GMs are typically more concerned with category-specific player value (HR, SB, AVG, etc.). We can better forecast what matters most by analyzing peak age of individual baseball skills rather than overall player value.

For batters, recognized peak age for overall batting value is a player's late 20s. But individual skills do not peak uniformly at the same time:

Contact rate (ct%): Ascends modestly by about a half point of contact per year from age 22 to 26, then holds steady within a half point of peak until age 35, after which players lose a half point of contact per year.

Walk rate (bb%): Trends the opposite way with age compared to contact rate, as batters tend to peak at age 30 and largely remain there until they turn 38.

Stolen Base Opportunity (SBO): Typically, players maintain their SBO through age 27, but then reduce their attempts steadily in each remaining year of their careers.

Stolen base success rate (SB%): Aggressive runners (>14% SBO) tend to lose about 2 points per year as they age. However, less aggressive runners (<=14% SBO) actually improve their SB% by about 2 points per year until age 28, after which they reverse course and give back 1-2 pts every year as they age.

GB%/LD%/FB%: Both GB% and LD% peak at the start of a player's career and then decline as many hitters seemingly learn to elevate the ball more. But at about age 30, hitter GB% ascends toward a second late-career peak while LD% continues to plummet and FB% continues to rise through age 38.

Hit rate (h%): Declines linearly with age. This is a natural result of a loss of speed and change in batted ball trajectory.

Isolated Power (ISO): Typically peaks from age 24-26. Similarly, home runs per fly ball, opposite field HR %, and Hard Hit % all peak by age 25 and decline somewhat linearly from that point on.

Catchers and late-career performance spikes *(Ed Spaulding)*

Many catchers—particularly second line catchers—have their best seasons late in their careers. Some possible reasons why:

1. Catchers, like shortstops, often get to the big leagues for defensive reasons and not their offensive skills. These skills take longer to develop.

2. The heavy emphasis on learning the catching/ defense/ pitching side of the game detracts from their time to learn about, and practice, hitting.

3. Injuries often curtail their ability to show offensive skills, though these injuries (typically jammed fingers, bruises on the arms, rib injuries from collisions) often don't lead to time on the disabled list.

4. The time spent behind the plate has to impact the ability to recognize, and eventually hit, all kinds of pitches.

Spring training Slg as leading indicator *(John Dewan)*

A hitter's spring training Slg .200 or more above his lifetime Slg is a leading indicator for a better than normal season.

Overall batting breakout profile *(Brandon Kruse)*

We define a breakout performance as one where a player posts a Roto value of $20+ after having never posted a value of $10. These criteria are used to validate an apparent breakout in the current season but may also be used carefully to project a potential upcoming breakout:

- Age 27 or younger
- An increase in at least two of: h%, PX or Spd
- Minimum league average PX or Spd (100)
- Minimum contact rate of 75%
- Minimum xBA of .270

In-Season Analysis

Batting order facts *(Ed DeCaria)*

Eighty-eight percent of today's leadoff hitters bat leadoff again in their next game, 78% still bat leadoff 10 games later, and 68% still bat leadoff 50 games later. Despite this level of turnover after 50 games, leadoff hitters have the best chance of retaining their role over time. After leadoff, #3 and #4 hitters are the next most likely to retain their lineup slots.

On a season-to-season basis, leadoff hitters are again the most stable, with 69% of last year's primary leadoff hitters retaining the #1 slot next year.

Plate appearances decline linearly by lineup slot. Leadoff batters receive 10-12% more PAs than when batting lower in the lineup. AL #9 batters and NL #8 batters get 9-10% fewer PAs. These results mirror play-by-play data showing a 15-20 PA drop by lineup slot over a full season.

Walk rate is largely unaffected by lineup slot in the AL. Beware strong walk rates by NL #8 hitters, as much of this "skill" will disappear if ever moved from the #8 slot.

Batting order has no discernable effect on contact rate.

Hit rate slopes gently upward as hitters are slotted deeper in the lineup.

As expected, the #3-4-5 slots are ideal for non-HR RBIs, at the expense of #6 hitters. RBIs are worst for players in the #1-2 slots. Batting atop the order sharply increases the probability of scoring runs, especially in the NL.

The leadoff slot easily has the highest stolen base attempt rate. #4-5-6 hitters attempt steals more often when batting out of those slots than they do batting elsewhere. The NL #8 hitter is a SB attempt sink hole. A change in batting order from #8 to #1 in the NL could nearly double a player's SB output due to lineup slot alone.

DOMination and DISaster rates

Week-to-week consistency is measured using a batter's BPV compiled in each week. A player earns a DOMinant week if his BPV was greater or equal to 50 for that week. A player registers a DISaster if his BPV was less than 0 for that week. The percentage of Dominant weeks, DOM%, is simply calculated as the number of DOM weeks divided by the total number of weeks played.

Is week-to-week consistency a repeatable skill? *(Bill Macey)*

To test whether consistent performance is a repeatable skill for batters, we examined how closely related a player's DOM% was from year to year.

YR1 DOM%	AVG YR2 DOM%
< 35%	37%
35%–45%	40%
46%–55%	45%
56%+	56%

Quality/consistency score (QC)

$(DOM\% - (2 \times DIS\%)) \times 2$

Using the DOM/DIS percentages, this score measures both the quality of performance as well as week–to-week consistency.

Sample size reliability *(Russell Carleton)*

At what point during the season do statistics become reliable indicators of skill? Measured in plate appearances:

- 100: Contact rate
- 150: Strikeout rate, line drive rate, pitches/PA
- 200: Walk rate, ground ball rate, GB/FB
- 250: Fly ball rate
- 300: HR rate, hr/f
- 500: OBP, Slg, OPS
- 550: Isolated power

Unlisted stats did not stabilize over a full season of play.

Projecting RBIs *(Patrick Davitt)*

Evaluating players in-season for RBI potential is a function of the interplay among four factors:

- Teammates' ability to reach base ahead of him and to run the bases efficiently
- His own ability to drive them in by hitting, especially XBH
- Number of Games Played
- Place in the batting order

3-4-5 Hitters:

$(0.69 \times GP \times TOB) + (0.30 \times ITB) + (0.275 \times HR) - (.191 \times GP)$

6-7-8 Hitters:

$(0.63 \times GP \times TOB) + (0.27 \times ITB) + (0.250 \times HR) - (.191 \times GP)$

9-1-2 Hitters:

$(0.57 \times GP \times TOB) + (0.24 \times ITB) + (0.225 \times HR) - (.191 \times GP)$

...where GP = games played, TOB = team on-base pct. and ITB = individual total bases (ITB).

Apply this pRBI formula after 70 games played or so (to reduce the variation from small sample size) to find players more than 9 RBIs over or under their projected RBI. There could be a correction coming.

You should also consider other factors, like injury or trade (involving the player or a top-of-the-order speedster) or team SB philosophy and success rate.

Remember: the player himself has an impact on his TOB. When we first did this study, we excluded the player from his TOB and got better results. The formula overestimates projected RBI for players with high OBP who skew his teams' OBP but can't benefit in RBI from that effect.

Other Diamonds

It's a Busy World Shortcut

For marginal utility-type players, scan their PX and Spd history to see if there's anything to mine for. If you see triple digits anywhere, stop and look further. If not, move on.

Chronology of the Classic Free-Swinger with Pop

1. Gets off to a good start.
2. Thinks he's in a groove.
3. Gets lax, careless.
4. Pitchers begin to catch on.
5. Fades down the stretch.

Errant Gust of Wind

A unit of measure used to describe the difference between your home run projection and mine.

Hannahan Concession

Players with a .218 BA rarely get 500 plate appearances, but when they do, it's usually once.

Mendoza Line

Named for Mario Mendoza, it represents the benchmark for batting futility. Usually refers to a .200 batting average, but can also be used for low levels of other statistical categories. Note that Mendoza's lifetime batting average was actually a much more robust .215.

Small Sample Certitude

If players' careers were judged based what they did in a single game performance, then Tuffy Rhodes and Mark Whiten would be in the Hall of Fame.

Esix Snead List

Players with excellent speed and sub-.300 on base averages who get a lot of practice running down the line to first base, and then back to the dugout. Also used as an adjective, as in "Esix-Sneadian."

Pitchers

Strikeouts and Walks

Fundamental skills

Unreliable pitching performance is a fallacy driven by the practice of attempting to project pitching stats using gauges that are poor evaluators of skill.

How can we better evaluate pitching skill? We can start with the three statistical categories that are generally unaffected by external factors. These three stats capture the outcome of an individual pitcher versus batter match-up without regard to supporting offense, defense or bullpen:

Walks Allowed, Strikeouts and Ground Balls

Even with only these stats to observe, there is a wealth of insight that these measures can provide.

Control rate (Ctl, bb/9), or opposition walks per game
BB allowed x 9 / IP

Measures how many walks a pitcher allows per game equivalent. BENCHMARK: The best pitchers will have bb/9 levels of 2.8 or less.

Dominance rate (Dom, k/9), or opposition strikeouts/game
Strikeouts recorded x 9 / IP

Measures how many strikeouts a pitcher allows per game equivalent. BENCHMARK: The best pitchers will have k/9 levels of 7.0 or higher.

Command ratio (Cmd)
(Strikeouts / Walks)

A measure of a pitcher's ability to get the ball over the plate. There is no more fundamental a skill than this, and so it is used as a leading indicator to project future rises and falls in other gauges, such as ERA. BENCHMARKS: Baseball's best pitchers will have ratios in excess of 3.0. Pitchers with ratios less than 1.0—indicating that they walk more batters than they strike out—have virtually no potential for long-term success. If you make no other changes in your approach to drafting pitchers, limiting your focus to only pitchers with a command ratio of 2.5 or better will substantially improve your odds of success.

Command ratio as a leading indicator

The ability to get the ball over the plate—command of the strike zone—is one of the best leading indicators for future performance. Command ratio (K/BB) can be used to project potential in ERA as well as other skills gauges.

1. Research indicates that there is a high correlation between a pitcher's Cmd ratio and his ERA.

	Earned Run Average				
Command	2008	2009	2010	2011	2012
0.0 - 1.0	7.00	6.43	5.86	5.45	6.22
1.1 - 1.5	5.07	5.10	5.14	4.84	5.03
1.6 - 2.0	4.60	4.41	4.34	4.35	4.48
2.1 - 2.5	3.96	4.19	3.95	3.89	4.09
2.6 - 3.0	3.89	3.70	3.71	3.66	3.88
3.1 +	3.35	3.40	3.25	3.28	3.39

We can create percentage plays for the different levels:

For Cmd	% with ERA of	
Levels of	3.50-	4.50+
0.0 - 1.0	0%	87%
1.1 - 1.5	7%	67%
1.6 - 2.0	7%	57%
2.1 - 2.5	19%	35%
2.6 - 3.0	26%	25%
3.1 +	53%	5%

Pitchers who maintain a Cmd over 2.5 have a high probability of long-term success. For fantasy drafting purposes, it is best to avoid pitchers with sub-2.0 ratios. Avoid bullpen closers if they have a ratio less than 2.5.

2. A pitcher's Command in tandem with Dominance (strikeout rate) provides even greater predictive abilities.

	Earned Run Average	
Command	-5.6 Dom	5.6+ Dom
0.0-0.9	5.36	5.99
1.0-1.4	4.94	5.03
1.5-1.9	4.67	4.47
2.0-2.4	4.32	4.08
2.5-2.9	4.21	3.88
3.0-3.9	4.04	3.46
4.0+	4.12	2.96

This helps to highlight the limited upside potential of soft-tossers with pinpoint control. The extra dominance makes a huge difference.

3. Research also suggests that there is a strong correlation between a pitcher's command ratio and his propensity to win ballgames. Over three quarters of those with ratios over 3.0 post winning records, and the collective W/L record of those command artists is nearly .600.

The command/winning correlation holds up in both leagues, although the effect was more pronounced in the NL. Over four times more NL hurlers than AL hurlers had Cmd over 3.0, and higher ratios were required in the NL to maintain good winning percentages. A ratio between 2.0 and 2.9 was good enough for a winning record for over 70% of AL pitchers, but that level in the NL generated an above-.500 mark slightly more than half the time.

In short, in order to have at least a 70% chance of drafting a pitcher with a winning record, you must target NL pitchers with at least a 3.0 command ratio. To achieve the same odds in the AL, a 2.0 command ratio will suffice.

Power/contact rating
(BB + K) / IP

Measures the level by which a pitcher allows balls to be put into play. In general, extreme power pitchers can be successful even with poor defensive teams. Power pitchers tend to have greater longevity in the game. Contact pitchers with poor defenses behind them are high-risks to have poor W-L records and ERA. BENCHMARKS: A level of 1.13+ describes pure throwers. A level of .93 or less describes high contact pitchers.

Balls in Play

Balls in play (BIP)
(Batters faced – (BB + HBP + SAC)) + H – K

The total number of batted balls that are hit fair, both hits and outs. An analysis of how these balls are hit—on the ground, in the air, hits, outs, etc.—can provide analytical insight, from player skill levels to the impact of luck on statistical output.

Batting average on balls in play *(Voros McCracken)*
(H – HR) / (Batters faced – (BB + HBP + SAC)) + H – K – HR

Abbreviated as BABIP; also called hit rate (H%). The percent of balls hit into the field of play that fall for hits. BENCHMARK: The league average is 30%, which is also the level that individual performances will regress to on a year to year basis. Any +/- variance of 3% or more can affect a pitcher's ERA.

BABIP as a leading indicator *(Voros McCracken)*
In 2000, Voros McCracken published a study that concluded that "there is little if any difference among major league pitchers in their ability to prevent hits on balls hit in the field of play." His assertion was that, while a Johan Santana would have a better ability to prevent a batter from getting wood on a ball, or perhaps keeping the ball in the park, once that ball was hit in the field of play, the probability of it falling for a hit was virtually no different than for any other pitcher.

Among the findings in his study were:

- There is little correlation between what a pitcher does one year in the stat and what he will do the next. This is not true with other significant stats (BB, K, HR).
- You can better predict a pitcher's hits per balls in play from the rate of the rest of the pitcher's team than from the pitcher's own rate.

This last point brings a team's defense into the picture. It begs the question, when a batter gets a hit, is it because the pitcher made a bad pitch, the batter took a good swing, or the defense was not positioned correctly?

Pitchers will often post hit rates per balls-in-play that are far off from the league average, but then revert to the mean the following year. As such, we can use that mean to project the direction of a pitcher's ERA.

Subsequent research has shown that ground ball or fly ball propensity has some impact on this rate.

Hit rate *(See Batting average on balls in play)*

Opposition batting average (OBA)
Hits allowed / (Batters faced – (BB + HBP + SAC))

The batting average achieved by opposing batters against a pitcher. BENCHMARKS: The best pitchers will have levels less than .250; the worst pitchers levels more than .300.

Opposition on base average (OOB)
(Hits allowed + BB) / ((Batters faced – (BB + HBP + SAC)) + Hits allowed + BB)

The on base average achieved by opposing batters against a pitcher. BENCHMARK: The best pitchers will have levels less than .300; the worst pitchers levels more than .375.

Walks plus hits divided by innings pitched (WHIP)
Essentially the same measure as opposition on base average, but used for Rotisserie purposes. BENCHMARKS: A WHIP of less than 1.20 is considered top level; more than 1.50 indicative of poor performance. Levels less than 1.00—allowing fewer runners than IP—represent extraordinary performance and are rarely maintained over time.

Ground ball, line drive, fly ball percentage (G/L/F)
The percentage of all balls-in-play that are hit on the ground, in the air and as line drives. For a pitcher, the ability to keep the ball on the ground can contribute to his statistical output exceeding his demonstrated skill level.

Ground ball tendency as a leading indicator *(John Burnson)*
Ground ball pitchers tend to give up fewer HRs than do fly ball pitchers. There is also evidence that GB pitchers have higher hit rates. In other words, a ground ball has a higher chance of being a hit than does a fly ball that is not out of the park.

GB pitchers have lower strikeout rates. We should be more forgiving of a low strikeout rate (under 5.5 K/9) if it belongs to an extreme ground ball pitcher.

GB pitchers have a lower ERA but a higher WHIP than do fly ball pitchers. On balance, GB pitchers come out ahead, even when considering strikeouts, because a lower ERA also leads to more wins.

Groundball and strikeout tendencies as indicators
(Mike Dranchak)

Pitchers were assembled into 9 groups based on the following profiles (minimum 23 starts in 2005):

Profile	Ground Ball Rate
Ground Ball	higher than 47%
Neutral	42% to 47%
Fly Ball	less than 42%

Profile	Strikeout Rate (k/9)
Strikeout	higher than 6.6 k/9
Average	5.4 to 6.6 k/9
Soft-Tosser	less than 5.4 k/9

Findings: Pitchers with higher strikeout rates had better ERAs and WHIPs than pitchers with lower strikeout rates, regardless of ground ball profile. However, for pitchers with similar strikeout rates, those with higher ground ball rates had better ERAs and WHIPs than those with lower ground ball rates.

Pitchers with higher strikeout rates tended to strand more baserunners than those with lower K rates. Fly ball pitchers tended to strand fewer runners than their GB or neutral counterparts within their strikeout profile.

Ground ball pitchers (especially those who lacked high-dominance) yielded more home runs per fly ball than did fly ball pitchers. However, the ERA risk was mitigated by the fact that ground ball pitchers (by definition) gave up fewer fly balls to begin with.

Line drive percentage as a leading indicator *(Seth Samuels)*

Also beyond a pitcher's control is the percentage of balls-in-play that are line drives. Line drives do the most damage; from 1994-2003, here were the expected hit rates and number of total bases per type of BIP.

	Type of BIP		
	GB	FB	LD
H%	26%	23%	56%
Total bases	0.29	0.57	0.80

Despite the damage done by LDs, pitchers do not have any innate skill to avoid them. There is little relationship between a pitcher's LD% one year and his rate the next year. All rates tend to regress towards a mean of 22.6%.

However, GB pitchers do have a slight ability to prevent LDs (21.7%) and extreme GB hurlers even moreso (18.5%). Extreme FB pitchers have a slight ability to prevent LDs (21.1%) as well.

Home run to fly ball rate (hr/f)

HR / FB

The percent of fly balls that are hit for home runs.

hr/f as a leading indicator *(John Burnson)*

McCracken's work focused on "balls in play," omitting home runs from the study. However, pitchers also do not have much control over the percentage of fly balls that turn into HR. Research shows that there is an underlying rate of HR as a percentage of fly balls of about 10%. A pitcher's HR/FB rate will vary each year but always tends to regress to that 10%. The element that pitchers do have control over is the number of fly balls they allow. That is the underlying skill or deficiency that controls their HR rate.

Pitchers who keep the ball out of the air more often correlate well with Roto value.

Opposition home runs per game (hr/9)

(HR Allowed x 9 / IP)

Also, expected opposition HR rate = (FB x 0.10) x 9 / IP

Measures how many HR a pitcher allows per game equivalent. Since FB tend to go yard at about a 10% rate, we can also estimate this rate off of fly balls. BENCHMARK: The best pitchers will have hr/9 levels of less than 1.0.

Runs

Expected earned run average

Gill and Reeve version: *(.575 x H [per 9 IP]) + (.94 x HR [per 9 IP]) + (.28 x BB [per 9 IP]) – (.01 x K [per 9 IP]) – Normalizing Factor*

John Burnson version (used in this book):
(xER x 9)/IP, where xER is defined as
xER% x (FB/10) + (1-xS%) x [0.3 x (BIP – FB/10) + BB]
where xER% = 0.96 – (0.0284 x (GB/FB))
and
xS% = (64.5 + (K/9 x 1.2) – (BB/9 x (BB/9 + 1)) / 20)
+ ((0.0012 x (GB%^2)) – (0.001 x GB%) - 2.4)

xERA represents the an equivalent of what a pitcher's real ERA might be, calculated solely with skills-based measures. It is not influenced by situation-dependent factors.

Expected ERA variance

xERA – ERA

The variance between a pitcher's ERA and his xERA is a measure of over or underachievement. A positive variance indicates the potential for a pitcher's ERA to rise. A negative variance indicates the potential for ERA improvement. BENCHMARK: Discount variances that are less than 0.50. Any variance more than 1.00 (one run per game) is regarded as a indicator of future change.

Projected xERA or projected ERA?

Which should we be using to forecast a pitcher's ERA? Projected xERA is more accurate for looking ahead on a purely skills basis. Projected ERA includes *situation-dependent* events—bullpen support, park factors, etc.—which are reflected better by ERA. The optimal approach is to use both gauges as *a range of expectation* for forecasting purposes.

Strand rate (S%)

(H + BB – ER) / (H + BB – HR)

Measures the percentage of allowed runners a pitcher strands (earned runs only), which incorporates both individual pitcher skill and bullpen effectiveness. BENCHMARKS: The most adept at stranding runners will have S% levels over 75%. Those with rates over 80% will have artificially low ERAs which will be prone to relapse. Levels below 65% will inflate ERA but have a high probability of regression.

Expected strand rate *(Michael Weddell)*

*73.935 + K/9 - 0.116 * (BB/9*(BB/9+1))*
*+ (0.0047 * GB%^2 - 0.3385 * GB%)*
+ (MAX(2,MIN(4,IP/G))/2-1)
+ (0.82 if left-handed)

This formula is based on three core skills: strikeouts per nine innings, walks per nine innings, and groundballs per balls in play, with adjustments for whether the pitcher is a starter or reliever (measured by IP/G), and his handedness.

Strand rate as a leading indicator *(Ed DeCaria)*

Strand rate often regresses/rebounds toward past rates (usually 69-74%), resulting in Year 2 ERA changes:

% of Pitchers with Year 2 Regression/Rebound

Y1 S%	RP	SP	LR
<60%	100%	94%	94%
65	81%	74%	88%
70	53%	48%	65%
75	55%	85%	100%
80	80%	100%	100%
85	100%	100%	100%

Typical ERA Regression/Rebound in Year 2

Y1 S%	RP	SP	LR
<60%	-2.54	-2.03	-2.79
65	-1.00	-0.64	-0.93
70	-0.10	-0.05	-0.44
75	0.24	0.54	0.75
80	1.15	1.36	2.29
85	1.71	2.21	n/a

Starting pitchers (SP) have a narrower range of strand rate outcomes than do relievers (RP) or swingmen/long relievers (LR).

Relief pitchers with Y1 strand rates of <=67% or >=78% are likely to experience a +/- ERA regression in Y2. **Starters and swingmen/long relievers** with Y1 strand rates of <=65% or >=75% are likely to experience a +/- ERA regression in Y2. Pitchers with strand rates that deviate more than a few points off of their individual expected strand rates are likely to experience some degree of ERA regression in Y2. Over-performing (or "lucky") pitchers are more likely than underperforming (or "unlucky") pitchers to see such a correction.

Wins

Projecting/chasing wins

There are five events that need to occur in order for a pitcher to post a single win...

1. He must pitch well, allowing few runs.
2. The offense must score enough runs.
3. The defense must successfully field all batted balls.
4. The bullpen must hold the lead.
5. The manager must leave the pitcher in for 5 innings, and not remove him if the team is still behind.

Of these five events, only one is within the control of the pitcher. As such, projecting or chasing wins based on skills alone can be an exercise in futility.

Home field advantage *(John Burnson)*

A 2006 study found that home starting pitchers get credited with a win in 38% of their outings. Visiting team starters are credited with a win in 33% of their outings.

Usage

Batters faced per game *(Craig Wright)*

$((Batters\ faced - (BB + HBP + SAC)) + H + BB) / G$

A measure of pitcher usage and one of the leading indicators for potential pitcher burnout.

Workload

Research suggests that there is a finite number of innings in a pitcher's arm. This number varies by pitcher, by development cycle, and by pitching style and repertoire. We can measure a pitcher's potential for future arm problems and/or reduced effectiveness (burnout):

Sharp increases in usage from one year to the next. Common wisdom has suggested that pitchers who significantly increase their workload from one year to the next are candidates for burnout symptoms. This has often been called the Verducci Effect, after writer Tom Verducci. BaseballHQ.com analyst Michael Weddell tested pitchers with sharp workload increases during the period 1988-2008 and found that no such effect exists.

Starters' overuse. Consistent "batters faced per game" (BF/G) levels of 28.0 or higher, combined with consistent seasonal IP totals of 200 or more may indicate burnout potential. Within a season, a BF/G of more than 30.0 with a projected IP total of 200 may indicate a late season fade.

Relievers' overuse. Warning flags should be up for relievers who post in excess of 100 IP in a season, while averaging fewer than 2 IP per outing.

When focusing solely on minor league pitchers, research results are striking:

Stamina: Virtually every minor league pitcher who had a BF/G of 28.5 or more in one season experienced a drop-off in BF/G the following year. Many were unable to ever duplicate that previous level of durability.

Performance: Most pitchers experienced an associated drop-off in their BPVs in the years following the 28.5 BF/G season. Some were able to salvage their effectiveness later on by moving to the bullpen.

Protecting young pitchers *(Craig Wright)*

There is a link between some degree of eventual arm trouble and a history of heavy workloads in a pitcher's formative years. Some recommendations from this research:

Teenagers (A-ball): No 200 IP seasons and no BF/G over 28.5 in any 150 IP span. No starts on three days rest.

Ages 20-22: Average no more than 105 pitches per start with a single game ceiling of 130 pitches.

Ages 23-24: Average no more than 110 pitches per start with a single game ceiling of 140 pitches.

When possible, a young starter should be introduced to the majors in long relief before he goes into the rotation.

Overall Performance Analysis

Base Performance Value (BPV)

$((Dominance\ Rate - 5.0)\ x\ 18)$
$+ ((4.0 - Walk\ Rate)\ x\ 27))$
$+ (Ground\ ball\ rate\ as\ a\ whole\ number - 40\%)$

A single value that describes a player's overall raw skill level. This is more useful than traditional statistical gauges to track player performance trends and project future statistical output. The formula combines the individual raw skills of power, control and the ability to keep the ball down in the zone, all characteristics that are unaffected by most external factors. In tandem with a pitcher's strand rate, it provides a more complete picture of the elements that contribute to ERA, and therefore serves as an accurate tool to project likely changes in ERA. **BENCHMARKS:** A BPV of 50 is the minimum level required for long-term success. The elite of the bullpen aces will have BPVs in excess of 100 and it is rare for these stoppers to enjoy long term success with consistent levels under 75.

Base Performance Index (BPX)

BPV scaled to league average to account for year-to-year fluctuations in league-wide statistical performance. It's a snapshot of a player's overall skills compared to an average player. **BENCHMARK:** A level of 100 means a player had a league-average BPV in that given season.

Runs above replacement (RAR)

An estimate of the number of runs a player contributes above a "replacement level" player.

Batters create runs; pitchers save runs. But are batters and pitchers who have comparable RAR levels truly equal in value? Pitchers might be considered to have higher value. Saving an additional run is more important than producing an additional run. A pitcher who throws a shutout is guaranteed to win that game, whereas no matter how many runs a batter produces, his team can still lose given poor pitching support.

To calculate RAR for pitchers:

1. Start with the replacement level league ERA.
2. Subtract the pitcher's ERA. (To calculate projected RAR, use the pitcher's xERA.)
3. Multiply by number of games played, calculated as plate appearances (IP x 4.34) divided by 38.
4. Multiply the resulting RAR level by 1.08 to account for the variance between earned runs and total runs.

Handedness

1. LHers tend to peak about a year after RHers.
2. LHers post only 15% of the total saves. Typically, LHers are reserved for specialist roles so few are frontline closers.
3. RHers have slightly better command and HR rate.
4. There is no significant variance in ERA.
5. On an overall skills basis, RHers have about a 6% advantage.

Skill-Specific Aging Patterns for Pitchers *(Ed DeCaria)*

Baseball forecasters obsess over "peak age" of player performance because we must understand player ascent toward and decline from that peak to predict future value. Most published aging analyses are done using composite estimates of value such as OPS or linear weights. By contrast, fantasy GMs are typically more concerned with category-specific player value (K, ERA, WHIP, etc.). We can better forecast what matters most by analyzing peak age of individual baseball skills rather than overall player value.

For pitchers, prior research has shown that pitcher value peaks somewhere in the late 20s to early 30s. But how does aging affect each demonstrable pitching skill?

Strikeout rate (k/9): Declines fairly linearly beginning at age 25.

Walk rate (bb/9): Improves until age 25 and holds somewhat steady until age 29, at which point it begins to steadily worsen. Deteriorating k/9 and bb/9 rates result in inefficiency, as it requires far more pitches to get an out. For starting pitchers, this affects the ability to pitch deep into games.

Innings Pitched per game (IP/G): Among starters, it improves slightly until age 27 and then tails off considerably with age, costing pitchers nearly one full IP/G by age 33 and one more by age 39.

Hit rate (H%): Among pitchers, H% appears to increase slowly but steadily as pitchers age, to the tune of .002-.003 points per year.

Strand rate (S%): Very similar to hit rate, except strand rate decreases with age rather than increasing. GB%/LD%/FB%: Line drives increase steadily from age 24 onward, and outfield flies increase beginning at age 31. Because 70%+ of line drives fall for hits, and 10%+ of fly balls become home runs, this spells trouble for aging pitchers.

Home runs per fly ball (hr/f): As each year passes, a higher percentage of a pitcher's fly balls become home runs allowed increases with age.

Catchers' effect on pitching *(Thomas Hanrahan)*

A typical catcher handles a pitching staff better after having been with a club for a few years. Research has shown that there is an improvement in team ERA of approximately 0.37 runs from a catcher's rookie season to his prime years with a club. Expect a pitcher's ERA to be higher than expected if he is throwing to a rookie backstop.

First productive season *(Michael Weddell)*

To find those starting pitchers who are about to post their first productive season in the majors (10 wins, 150 IP, ERA of 4.00 or less), look for:

- Pitchers entering their age 23-26 seasons, especially those about to pitch their age 25 season.
- Pitchers who already have good skills, shown by an xERA in the prior year of 4.25 or less.
- Pitchers coming off of at least a partial season in the majors without a major health problem.
- To the extent that one speculates on pitchers who are one skill away, look for pitchers who only need to improve their control (bb/9).

Overall pitching breakout profile *(Brandon Kruse)*

A breakout performance is defined here as one where a player posts a Rotisserie value of $20 or higher after having never posted a value of $10 previously. These criteria are primarily used to validate an apparent breakout in the current season but may also be used carefully to project a potential breakout for an upcoming season.

- Age 27 or younger
- Minimum 5.6 Dom, 2.0 Cmd, 1.1 hr/9 and 50 BPV
- Maximum 30% hit rate
- Minimum 71% strand rate
- Starters should have a hit rate no greater than the previous year's hit rate. Relievers should show improved command
- Maximum xERA of 4.00

Career year drop-off *(Rick Wilton)*

Research shows that a pitcher's post-career year drop-off, on average, looks like this:

- ERA increases by 1.00
- WHIP increases by 0.14.
- Nearly 6 fewer wins

Closers

Saves

There are six events that need to occur in order for a relief pitcher to post a single save:

1. The starting pitcher and middle relievers must pitch well.
2. The offense must score enough runs.
3. It must be a reasonably close game.
4. The manager must put the pitcher in for a save opportunity.
5. The pitcher must pitch well and hold the lead.
6. The manager must let him finish the game.

Of these six events, only one is within the control of the relief pitcher. As such, projecting saves for a reliever has little to do with skill and a lot to do with opportunity. However, pitchers with excellent skills may create opportunity for themselves.

Saves conversion rate (Sv%)

Saves / Save Opportunities

The percentage of save opportunities that are successfully converted. **BENCHMARK:** We look for a minimum 80% for long-term success.

Leverage index (LI) *(Tom Tango)*

Leverage index measures the amount of swing in the possible change in win probability indexed against an average value of 1.00. Thus, relievers who come into games in various situations create a composite score and if that average score is higher than 1.00, then their manager is showing enough confidence in them to try to win games with them. If the average score is below 1.00, then the manager is using them, but not showing nearly as much confidence that they can win games.

Saves chances and wins *(Craig Neuman)*

Should the quality of a pitcher's MLB team be a consideration in drafting a closer? One school of thought says that more wins means more save opportunities. The flipside is that when poor teams win they do so by a small margin, which means more save opportunities.

A six-season correlation yielded these results for saves, save opportunities, save percentage, wins, quality starts and run differential. (Any value above .50 suggests at least a moderate correlation.)

	Sv	SvO	W	Sv%	RD	QS
SV	1					
SVO	.78	1				
W	.66	.41	1			
S%	.66	.05	.56	1		
RD	.48	.26	.92	.44	1	
QS	.41	.24	.58	.34	.60	1

Saves do correlate with wins. As for the theory that teams who play in close games would accumulate more saves, the low correlation between saves and run differential seems to dispel that a bit.

On average, teams registered one save for every two wins. However, there is a relationship between wins and the number of saves per win a team achieves:

Win Total	Saves/Win
>90	.494
80-89	.492
70-79	.505
<69	.525

Teams with fewer wins end up with more saves per win. So, when poor teams win, they are more likely to have a save chance.

Origin of closers

History has long maintained that ace closers are not easily recognizable early on in their careers, so that every season does see its share of the unexpected. Fernando Rodney, Casey Janssen, Tom Wilhelmsen, Tyler Clippard, Santiago Casilla, Alfredo Aceves, Ernesto Frieri, Greg Holland, Steve Cishek… who would have thought it a year ago?

Accepted facts, all of which have some element of truth:

- You cannot find major league closers from pitchers who were closers in the minors.
- Closers begin their careers as starters.
- Closers are converted set-up men.
- Closers are pitchers who were unable to develop a third effective pitch.

More simply, closers are a product of circumstance.

Are the minor leagues a place to look at all?

From 1990-2004, there were 280 twenty-save seasons in Double-A and Triple-A, accomplished by 254 pitchers.

Of those 254, only 46 ever made it to the majors at all.

Of those 46, only 13 ever saved 20 games in a season.

Of those 13, only 5 ever posted more than one 20-save season in the majors: John Wetteland, Mark Wohlers, Ricky Bottalico, Braden Looper and Francisco Cordero.

Five out of 254 pitchers, over 15 years—a rate of 2%.

One of the reasons that minor league closers rarely become major league closers is because, in general, they do not get enough innings in the minors to sufficiently develop their arms into big-league caliber.

In fact, organizations do not look at minor league closing performance seriously, assigning that role to pitchers who they do not see as legitimate prospects. The average age of minor league closers over the past decade has been 27.5.

Elements of saves success

The task of finding future closing potential comes down to looking at two elements:

Talent: The raw skills to mow down hitters for short periods of time. Optimal BPVs over 100, but not under 75.

Opportunity: The more important element, yet the one that pitchers have no control over.

There are pitchers that have Talent, but not Opportunity. These pitchers are not given a chance to close for a variety of reasons (e.g. being blocked by a solid front-liner in the pen, being left-handed, etc.), but are good to own because they will not likely hurt your pitching staff. You just can't count on them for saves, at least not in the near term.

There are pitchers that have Opportunity, but not Talent. MLB managers decide who to give the ball to in the 9th inning based on their own perceptions about what skills are required to succeed, even if those perceived "skills" don't translate into acceptable BPI levels.

Those pitchers without the BPIs may have some initial short-term success, but their long-term prognosis is poor and they are high risks to your roster. Classic examples of the short life span of these types of pitchers include Matt Karchner, Heath Slocumb, Ryan Kohlmeier, Dan Miceli, Joe Borowski and Danny Kolb. More recent examples include Brian Fuentes and Javy Guerra.

Closers' job retention *(Michael Weddell)*
Of pitchers with 20 or more saves in one year, only 67.5% of these closers earned 20 or more saves the following year. The variables that best predicted whether a closer would avoid this attrition:

- *Saves history:* Career saves was the most important factor.
- *Age:* Closers are most likely to keep their jobs at age 27. For long-time closers, their growing career saves totals more than offset the negative impact of their advanced ages. Older closers without a long history of racking up saves tend to be bad candidates for retaining their roles.
- *Performance:* Actual performance, measured by ERA+, was of only minor importance.
- *Being right-handed:* Increased the odds of retaining the closer's role by 9% over left-handers.

How well can we predict which closers will keep their jobs? Of the 10 best closers during 1989-2007, 90% saved at least 20 games during the following season. Of the 10 worst bets, only 20% saved at least 20 games the next year.

Closer volatility history

			Number of Closers		
Year	Drafted	Avg R$	Failed	%	New Sources
1999	23	$25	5	22%	7
2000	27	$25	10	37%	9
2001	25	$26	7	28%	7
2002	28	$22	8	29%	12
2003	29	$21.97	17	59%	14
2004	29	$19.78	11	38%	15
2005	28	$20.79	12	43%	15
2006	30	$17.80	10	33%	12
2007	28	$17.67	10	36%	11
2008	32	$17.78	10	31%	11
2009	28	$17.56	9	32%	13
2010	28	$16.96	7	25%	13
2011	30	$15.47	11	37%	8
2012	29	$15.28	19	66%	18

Drafted refers to the number of saves sources purchased in both LABR and Tout Wars experts leagues each year. These only include relievers drafted for at least $10, specifically for saves speculation. *Avg R$* refers to the average purchase price of these pitchers in the AL-only and NL-only leagues. *Failed* is the number (and percentage) of saves sources drafted that did not return at least 50% of their value that year. The failures include those that lost their value due to ineffectiveness, injury or managerial decision. *New Sources* are arms that were drafted for less than $10 (if drafted at all) but finished with at least double-digit saves.

The failed saves investments in 2012 were John Axford, Andrew Bailey, Heath Bell, Rafael Betancourt, Matt Capps, Kyle Farnsworth, Frank Francisco, Javy Guerra, Brandon League, Carlos Marmol, Sean Marshall, Brett Myers, Mariano Rivera, Sergio Santos, Drew Storen, Matt Thornton, Jose Valverde, Jordan Walden and Brian Wilson. (Not included: Ryan Madson and Joakim Soria, injured in pre-season.) The new sources in 2012 were Alfredo Aceves, Jonathan Broxton, Santiago Casilla, Steve Cishek, Aroldis Chapman, Tyler Clippard, Ryan Cook, Ernesto Frieri, Greg Holland, Casey Janssen, Jim Johnson, Wilton Lopez, Glen Perkins, Addison Reed, Fernando Rodney, Sergio Romo, Rafael Soriano and Tom Wilhelmsen.

BPV as a leading indicator *(Doug Dennis)*
Research has shown that base performance value (BPV) is an excellent indicator of long-term success as a closer. Here are 20-plus saves seasons, by year:

		|------------------BPV------------------|	
Year	No.	100+	75+	<75
1999	26	27%	54%	46%
2000	24	25%	54%	46%
2001	25	56%	80%	20%
2002	25	60%	72%	28%
2003	25	36%	64%	36%
2004	23	61%	61%	39%
2005	25	36%	64%	36%
2006	25	52%	72%	28%
2007	23	52%	74%	26%
MEAN	*25*	*45%*	*66%*	*34%*

Though 20-saves success with a 75+ BPV is only a 66% percentage play in any given year, the below-75 group is composed of closers who are rarely able to repeat the feat in the following season:

Year	No. with BPV < 75	No. who followed up 20+ saves <75 BPV
1999	12	2
2000	11	2
2001	5	2
2002	7	3
2003	9	3
2004	9	2
2005	9	1
2006	7	3
2007	6	0

Other Relievers

Projecting holds *(Doug Dennis)*
Here are some general rules of thumb for identifying pitchers who might be in line to accumulate holds. The percentages represent the portion of 2003's top holds leaders who fell into the category noted.

1. Left-handed set-up men with excellent BPIs. (43%)
2. A "go-to" right-handed set-up man with excellent BPIs. This is the one set-up RHer that a manager turns to with a small lead in the 7th or 8th innings. These pitchers also tend to vulture wins. (43%, but 6 of the top 9)
3. Excellent BPIs, but not a firm role as the main LHed or RHed set-up man. Roles change during the season; cream rises to the top. Relievers projected to post great BPIs often overtake lesser set-up men in-season. (14%)

Reliever efficiency percent (REff%)

(Wins + Saves + Holds) / (Wins + Losses + SaveOpps + Holds)

This is a measure of how often a reliever contributes positively to the outcome of a game. A record of consistent, positive impact on game outcomes breeds managerial confidence, and that confidence could pave the way to save opportunities. For those pitchers suddenly thrust into a closer's role, this formula helps gauge their potential to succeed based on past successes in similar roles. BENCHMARK: Minimum of 80%.

Vulture

A pitcher, typically a middle reliever, who accumulates an unusually high number of wins by preying on other pitchers' misfortunes. More accurately, this is a pitcher typically brought into a game after a starting pitcher has put his team behind, and then pitches well enough and long enough to allow his offense to take the lead, thereby "vulturing" a win from the starter.

In-Season Analysis

Pure Quality Starts

We've always approached performance measures on an aggregate basis. Each individual event that our statistics chronicle gets dumped into a huge pool of data. We then use our formulas to try to sort and slice and manipulate the data into more usable information.

Pure Quality Starts (PQS) take a different approach. It says that the smallest unit of measure should not be the "event" but instead be the "game." Within that game, we can accumulate all the strikeouts, hits and walks, and evaluate that outing as a whole. After all, when a pitcher takes the mound, he is either "on" or "off" his game; he is either dominant or struggling, or somewhere in between.

In PQS, we give a starting pitcher credit for exhibiting certain skills in each of his starts. Then by tracking his "PQS Score" over time, we can follow his progress. A starter earns one point for each of the following criteria:

1. *The pitcher must go a minimum of 6 innings.* This measures stamina. If he goes less than 5 innings, he automatically gets a total PQS score of zero, no matter what other stats he produces.

2. *He must allow no more than an equal number of hits to the number of innings pitched.* This measures hit prevention.

3. *His number of strikeouts must be no fewer than two less than his innings pitched.* This measures dominance.

4. *He must strike out at least twice as many batters as he walks.* This measures command.

5. *He must allow no more than one home run.* This measures his ability to keep the ball in the park.

A perfect PQS score is 5. Any pitcher who averages 3 or more over the course of the season is probably performing admirably. The nice thing about PQS is it allows you to approach each start as more than an all-or-nothing event.

Note the absence of earned runs. No matter how many runs a pitcher allows, if he scores high on the PQS scale, he has hurled a good game in terms of his base skills. The number of runs allowed—a function of not only the pitcher's ability but that of his bullpen and defense—will tend to even out over time.

It doesn't matter if a few extra balls got through the infield, or the pitcher was given the hook in the fourth or sixth inning, or the bullpen was able to strand their inherited baserunners. When we look at performance in the aggregate, those events do matter, and will affect a pitcher's BPIs and ERA. But with PQS, the minutia is less relevant than the overall performance.

In the end, a dominating performance is a dominating performance, whether Stephen Strasburg is hurling a 2-hit shutout or giving up three runs while striking out 8 in 6 IP. And a disaster is still a disaster, whether Francisco Liriano gets a 3rd inning hook after giving up 5 runs, or "takes one for the team" and gets shelled for seven runs in 2.2 IP.

Skill versus consistency

Two pitchers have identical 4.50 ERAs and identical 3.0 PQS averages. Their PQS logs look like this:

PITCHER A:	3	3	3	3	3
PITCHER B:	5	0	5	0	5

Which pitcher would you rather have on your team? The risk-averse manager would choose Pitcher A as he represents the perfectly known commodity. Many fantasy leaguers might opt for Pitcher B because his occasional dominating starts show that there is an upside. His Achilles Heel is inconsistency—he is unable to sustain that high level. Is there any hope for Pitcher B?

- If a pitcher's inconsistency is characterized by more poor starts than good starts, his upside is limited.
- Pitchers with extreme inconsistency rarely get a full season of starts.
- However, inconsistency is neither chronic nor fatal.

The outlook for Pitcher A is actually worse. Disaster avoidance might buy these pitchers more starts, but history shows that the lack of dominating outings is more telling of future potential. In short, consistent mediocrity is bad.

PQS DOMination and DISaster rates *(Gene McCaffrey)*

DOM% is the percentage of a starting pitcher's outings that rate as a PQS-4 or PQS-5. DIS% is the percentage that rate as a PQS-0 or PQS-1.

DOM/DIS percentages open up a new perspective, providing us with two separate scales of performance. In tandem, they measure consistency.

PQS ERA (qERA)

A pitcher's DOM/DIS split can be converted back to an equivalent ERA. By creating a grid of individual DOM% and DIS% levels, we can determine the average ERA at each cross point. The result is an ERA based purely on PQS.

Quality/consistency score (QC)

(DOM% – (2 x DIS%)) x 2

Using PQS and DOM/DIS percentages, this score measures both the quality of performance as well as start-to-start consistency.

PQS correlation with Quality Starts *(Paul Petera)*

PQS	QS%
0	0%
1	3%
2	21%
3	51%
4	75%
5	95%

Forward-looking PQS *(John Burnson)*

PQS says whether a pitcher performed ably in a *past* start—it doesn't say anything about how he'll do in the *next* start. We built a version of PQS that attempts to do that. For each series of five starts for a pitcher, we looked at his average IP, K/9, HR/9, H/9, and K/BB, and then whether the pitcher won his next start. We catalogued the results by indicator and calculated the observed future winning percentage for each data point.

This research suggested that a forward-looking version of PQS should have these criteria:

- The pitcher must have lasted at least 6.2 innings.
- He must have recorded at least IP – 1 strikeouts.
- He must have allowed zero home runs.
- He must have allowed no more hits than IP+2.
- He must have had a Command (K/BB) of at least 2.5.

Pure Quality Relief *(Patrick Davitt)*

A system for evaluating reliever outings. The scoring :

1. Two points for the first out, and one point for each subsequent out, to a maximum of four points.
2. One point for having at least one strikeout for every four full outs (one K for 1-4 outs, two Ks for 5-8 outs, etc.).
3. One point for zero baserunners, minus one point for each baserunner, though allowing the pitcher one unpenalized runner for each three full outs (one baserunner for 3-5 outs, two for 6-8 outs, three for nine outs)
4. Minus one point for each earned run, though allowing one ER for 8– or 9-out appearances.
5. An automatic PQR-0 for allowing a home run.

Avoiding relief disasters *(Ed DeCaria)*

Relief disasters (defined as ER>=3 and IP<=3), occur in 5%+ of all appearances. The chance of a disaster exceeds 13% in any 7-day period. To minimize the odds of a disaster, we created a model that produced the following list of factors, in order of influence:

1. Strength of opposing offense
2. Park factor of home stadium
3. BB/9 over latest 31 days (more walks is bad)
4. Pitch count over previous 7 days (more pitches is bad)
5. Latest 31 Days ERA>xERA (recent bad luck continues)

Daily league owners who can slot relievers by individual game should also pay attention to days of rest: pitching on less rest than one is accustomed to increases disaster risk.

Sample size reliability *(Russell Carleton)*

At what point during the season do statistics become reliable indicators of skill? Measured in batters faced:

150: K/PA, ground ball rate, line drive rate
200: Fly ball rate, GB/FB
500: K/BB
550: BB/PA

Unlisted stats did not stabilize over a full season of play. *(Note that 150 BF is roughly equivalent to six outings for a starting pitcher; 550 BF would be 22 starts, etc.)*

Pitching streaks

It is possible to find predictive value in strings of DOMinating (PQS 4/5) or DISaster (PQS 0/1) starts:

Once a pitcher enters into a DOM streak of any length, the probability is that his next start is going to be better than average. The further a player is into a DOM streak, the higher the likelihood that the subsequent performance will be high quality. In fact, once a pitcher has posted six DOM starts in a row, there is greater than a 70% probability that the streak will continue. When it does end, there is less than a 10% probability that the streak-breaker is going to be a DISaster.

Once a pitcher enters into a DIS streak of any length, the probability is that his next start is going to be below average, even if it breaks the streak. However, DIS streaks end quickly. Once a pitcher hits the skids, odds are low that he will post a good start in the short term, though the duration itself should be brief.

5-game PQS predictability *(Bill Macey)*

5-Game avg PQS	Avg PQS	DOM%	DIS%
Less than 1	2.1	27%	40%
Between 1 and 2	2.4	32%	32%
Between 2 and 3	2.6	36%	26%
Between 3 and 4	3.0	47%	19%
4 or greater	3.5	61%	12%

Pitchers with higher PQS scores in their previous 5 starts tended to pitch better in their next start. But the relative parity of subsequent DOM and DIS starts for all but the hottest of streaks warn us not to put too much effort into predicting any given start. That more than a quarter of pitchers who had been awful over their previous 5 starts still put up a dominating start next shows that anything can happen in a single game.

Pitch counts as a leading indicator

Workload analysis is an ongoing science. However, can we draw any conclusions from short-term trends? For this analysis, GS from 2005-2006 were isolated—looking at pitch counts and PQS scores—and compared with each pitcher's subsequent outing. We examined two-start trends, the immediate impact that the length of one performance would have on the next start.

		Next Start			
Pitch Ct	Pct.	PQS	DOM	DIS	qERA
< 80	13%	2.5	33%	28%	4.90
80-89	14%	2.6	35%	29%	4.82
90-99	28%	2.7	37%	26%	4.82
100-109	30%	2.9	41%	23%	4.56
110-119	13%	3.1	46%	18%	4.40
120+	3%	3.0	43%	20%	4.56

There does appear to be merit to the concern over limiting hurlers to 120 pitches per start. The research shows a slight drop-off in performance in those starts following a 120+ pitch outing. However, the impact does not appear to be all that great and the fallout might just affect those pitchers who have no business going that deep into games anyway. Additional detail to this research (not displayed) showed that higher-skilled pitchers were more successful throwing over 120 pitches but less-skilled pitchers were not.

Days of rest as a leading indicator

Workload is only part of the equation. The other part is how often a pitcher is sent out to the mound. For instance, it's possible that a hurler might see no erosion in skill after a 120+ pitch outing if he had enough rest between starts:

PITCH COUNTS		NEXT START			
Three days rest	Pct.	PQS	DOM	DIS	qERA
< 100	72%	2.8	35%	17%	4.60
100-119	28%	2.3	44%	44%	5.21
Four Days rest					
< 100	52%	2.7	36%	27%	4.82
100-119	45%	2.9	42%	22%	4.56
120+	3%	3.0	42%	20%	4.44
Five Days rest					
< 100	54%	2.7	38%	25%	4.79
100-119	43%	3.0	44%	19%	4.44
120+	3%	3.2	48%	14%	4.28
Six Days rest					
< 100	58%	2.7	39%	30%	5.00
100-119	40%	2.8	40%	26%	4.82
120+	3%	1.8	20%	60%	7.98
20+ Days rest					
< 100	85%	1.8	20%	46%	6.12
100-119	15%	2.3	33%	33%	5.08

Managers are reluctant to put a starter on the mound with any fewer than four days rest, and the results for those who pitched deeper into games shows why. Four days rest is the most common usage pattern and even appears to mitigate the drop-off at 120+ pitches.

Perhaps most surprising is that an extra day of rest improves performance across the board and squeezes even more productivity out of the 120+ pitch outings.

Performance begins to erode at six days (and continues at 7-20 days, though those are not displayed). The 20+ Days chart represents pitchers who were primarily injury rehabs and failed call-ups, and the length of the "days rest" was occasionally well over 100 days. This chart shows the result of their performance in their first start back. The good news is that the workload was limited for 85% of these returnees. The bad news is that these are not pitchers you want active. So for those who obsess over getting your DL returnees activated in time to catch every start, the better percentage play is to avoid that first outing.

Post-DL Pitching Performance *(Bill Macey)*

One question that fantasy baseball managers frequently struggle with is whether or not to start a pitcher when he first returns from the disabled list. A 2011 study compared each pitcher's PQS score in their first post-DL start against his average PQS score for that year (limited to pitchers who had at least 15 starts during the year and whose first post-DL appearance was as a starter). The findings:

- In general, exercise caution with immediate activations. Pitchers performed worse than their yearly average in the first post-DL start, with a high rate of PQS-DIS starts.
- Avoid pitchers returning from the DL due to an arm injury, as they perform significantly worse than average.
- If there are no better options available, feel comfortable activating pitchers who spent near the minimum amount of time on the DL and/or suffered a leg injury, as they typically perform at a level consistent with their yearly average.

Other Diamonds

The Pitching Postulates

1. Never sign a soft-tosser to a long-term contract.
2. Right-brain dominance has a very long shelf life.
3. A fly ball pitcher who gives up many HRs is expected. A GB pitcher who gives up many HRs is making mistakes.
4. Never draft a contact fly ball pitcher who plays in a hitter's park.
5. Only bad teams ever have a need for an inning-eater.
6. Never chase wins.

Dontrelle Willis List

Pitchers with BPIs so incredibly horrible that you have to wonder how they can possibly draw a major league paycheck year after year.

Chaconian

Having the ability to post many saves despite sub-Mendoza BPIs and an ERA in the stratosphere.

Vintage Eck Territory

A BPV greater than 200, a level achieved by Dennis Eckersley for four consecutive years.

Edwhitsonitis

A dreaded malady marked by the sudden and unexplained loss of pitching ability upon a trade to the New York Yankees.

ERA Benchmark

A half run of ERA over 200 innings comes out to just one earned run every four starts.

Gopheritis (also, Acute Gopheritis and Chronic Gopheritis)

The dreaded malady in which a pitcher is unable to keep the ball in the park. Pitchers with gopheritis have a FB rate of at least 40%. More severe cases have a FB% over 45%.

The Knuckleballers Rule: Knuckleballers don't follow no stinkin' rules.

Brad Lidge Lament

When a closer posts a 62% strand rate, he has nobody to blame but himself.

LOOGY (Lefty One Out GuY)

A left-handed reliever whose job it is to get one out in important situations.

Vin Mazzaro Vindication
Occasional nightmares (2.1 innings, 14 ER) are just a part of the game.

Meltdown
Any game in which a starting pitcher allows more runs than innings pitched.

Lance Painter Lesson
Six months of solid performance can be screwed up by one bad outing. (In 2000, Painter finished with an ERA of 4.76. However, prior to his final appearance of the year—in which he pitched 1 inning and gave up 8 earned runs—his ERA was 3.70.)

The Five Saves Certainties
1. On every team, there will be save opportunities and someone will get them. At a bare minimum, there will be at least 30 saves to go around, and not unlikely more than 45.

2. Any pitcher could end up being the chief beneficiary. Bullpen management is a fickle endeavor.

3. Relief pitchers are often the ones that require the most time at the start of the season to find a groove. The weather is cold, the schedule is sparse and their usage is erratic.

4. Despite the talk about "bullpens by committee," managers prefer a go-to guy. It makes their job easier.

5. As many as 50% of the saves in any year will come from pitchers who are unselected at the end of Draft Day.

Soft-tosser
A pitcher with a strikeout rate of 5.5 or less.

Soft-tosser land
The place where feebler arms leave their fortunes in the hands of the defense, variable hit and strand rates, and park dimensions. It's a place where many live, but few survive.

Prospects

General

Minor league prospecting in perspective

In our perpetual quest to be the genius who uncovers the next Mike Trout when he's still in high school, there is an obsessive fascination with minor league prospects. That's not to say that prospecting is not important. The issue is perspective:

1. During the 10 year period of 1996 to 2005, only 8% of players selected in the first round of the Major League Baseball First Year Player Draft went on to become stars.

2. Some prospects are going to hit the ground running (Ryan Braun) and some are going to immediately struggle (Alex Gordon), no matter what level of hype follows them.

3. Some prospects are going to start fast (since the league is unfamiliar with them) and then fade (as the league figures them out). Others will start slow (since they are unfamiliar with the opposition) and then improve (as they adjust to the competition). So if you make your free agent and roster decisions based on small early samples sizes, you are just as likely to be an idiot as a genius.

4. How any individual player will perform relative to his talent is largely unknown because there is a psychological element that is vastly unexplored. Some make the transition to the majors seamlessly, some not, completely regardless of how talented they are.

5. Still, talent is the best predictor of future success, so major league equivalent base performance indicators still have a valuable role in the process. As do scouting reports, carefully filtered.

6. Follow the player's path to the majors. Did he have to repeat certain levels? Was he allowed to stay at a level long enough to learn how to adjust to the level of competition? A player with only two great months at Double-A is a good bet to struggle if promoted directly to the majors because he was never fully tested at Double-A, let alone Triple-A.

7. Younger players holding their own against older competition is a good thing. Older players reaching their physical peak, regardless of their current address, can be a good thing too. The R.A. Dickeys and Ryan Ludwicks can have some very profitable years.

8. Remember team context. A prospect with superior potential often will not unseat a steady but unspectacular incumbent, especially one with a large contract.

9. Don't try to anticipate how a team is going to manage their talent, both at the major and minor league level. You might think it's time to promote Billy Hamilton and give him an everyday role. You are not running the Reds.

10. Those who play in shallow, one-year leagues should have little cause to be looking at the minors at all. The risk versus reward is so skewed against you, and there is so much talent available with a track record, that taking a chance on an unproven commodity makes little sense.

11. Decide where your priorities really are. If your goal is to win, prospect analysis is just a *part* of the process, not the entire process.

Factors affecting minor league stats *(Terry Linhart)*

1. Often, there is an exaggerated emphasis on short-term performance in an environment that is supposed to focus on the long-term. Two poor outings don't mean a 21-year-old pitcher is washed up.

2. Ballpark dimensions and altitude create hitters parks and pitchers parks, but a factor rarely mentioned is that many parks in the lower minors are inconsistent in their field quality. Minor league clubs have limited resources to maintain field conditions, and this can artificially depress defensive statistics while inflating stats like batting average.

3. Some players' skills are so superior to the competition at their level that you can't get a true picture of what they're going to do from their stats alone.

4. Many pitchers are told to work on secondary pitches in unorthodox situations just to gain confidence in the pitch. The result is an artificially increased number of walks.

5. The #3, #4, and #5 pitchers in the lower minors are truly longshots to make the majors. They often possess only two pitches and are unable to disguise the off-speed offerings. Hitters can see inflated statistics in these leagues.

Minor league level versus age

When evaluating minor leaguers, look at the age of the prospect in relation to the median age of the league he is in:

Low level A	*Between 19-20*
Upper level A	*Around 20*
Double-A	*21*
Triple-A	*22*

These are the ideal ages for prospects at the particular level. If a prospect is younger than most and holds his own against older and more experienced players, elevate his status. If he is older than the median, reduce his status.

Triple-A experience as a leading indicator

The probability that a minor leaguer will immediately succeed in the majors can vary depending upon the level of Triple-A experience he has amassed at the time of call-up.

	BATTERS		PITCHERS	
	< 1 Yr	Full	< 1 Yr	Full
Performed well	57%	56%	16%	56%
Performed poorly	21%	38%	77%	33%
2nd half drop-off	21%	7%	6%	10%

The odds of a batter achieving immediate MLB success was slightly more than 50-50. More than 80% of all pitchers promoted with less than a full year at Triple-A struggled in their first year in the majors. Those pitchers with a year in Triple-A succeeded at a level equal to that of batters.

Major League Equivalency (MLE) *(Bill James)*

A formula that converts a player's minor or foreign league statistics into a comparable performance in the major leagues. These are not projections, but conversions of current performance. MLEs contain adjustments for the level of play in individual leagues and teams. They work best with Triple-A stats, not quite as well with Double-A stats, and hardly at all with the lower levels. Foreign conversions are still a work in process. James' original formula only addressed batting. Our research has devised conversion formulas for pitchers, however, their best use comes when looking at BPIs, not traditional stats.

Adjusting to the competition

All players must "adjust to the competition" at every level of professional play. Players often get off to fast or slow starts. During their second tour at that level is when we get to see whether the slow starters have caught up or whether the league has figured out the fast starters. That second half "adjustment" period is a good baseline for projecting the subsequent season, in the majors or minors.

Premature major league call-ups often negate the ability for us to accurately evaluate a player due to the lack of this adjustment period. For instance, a hotshot Double-A player might open the season in Triple-A. After putting up solid numbers for a month, he gets a call to the bigs, and struggles. The fact is, we don't have enough evidence that the player has mastered the Triple-A level. We don't know whether the rest of the league would have caught up to him during his second tour of the league. But now he's labeled as an underperformer in the bigs when in fact he has never truly proven his skills at the lower levels.

Rookie playing time

Weaker-performing teams have historically (1976-2009) been far more dependent on debut rookies than stronger-performing teams. This makes sense, as non-contenders have greater incentive and flexibility to allow young players to gain experience at the MLB level. Additionally, individual player characteristics can provide clues as to which debut rookies will earn significant PA or IP:

- Rookies who can play up-the-middle (CF, 2B, SS) or on the left side (LF, 3B) are likely to see more debut playing time than those at 1B, RF, C, or DH.
- LH batters and pitchers are slightly more likely than righties to earn significant PA or IP in their debuts.
- Rookies under age 22 earn nearly twice the PAs of those aged 25-26 in their debut season. Pitchers under age 23 earn twice the innings of those aged 26-27.

Bull Durham prospects

There is some potential talent in older players—age 26, 27 or higher—who, for many reasons (untimely injury, circumstance, bad luck, etc.), don't reach the majors until they have already been downgraded from prospect to suspect. Equating potential with age is an economic reality for major league clubs, but not necessarily a skills reality.

Skills growth and decline is universal, whether it occurs at the major league level or in the minors. So a high-skills journeyman

in Triple-A is just as likely to peak at age 27 as a major leaguer of the same age. The question becomes one of opportunity—will the parent club see fit to reap the benefits of that peak performance?

Prospecting these players for your fantasy team is, admittedly, a high risk endeavor, though there are some criteria you can use. Look for a player who is/has:

- Optimally, age 27-28 for overall peak skills, age 30-31 for power skills, or age 28-31 for pitchers.
- At least two seasons of experience at Triple-A. Career Double-A players are generally not good picks.
- Solid base skills levels.
- Shallow organizational depth at their position.
- Notable winter league or spring training performance.

Players who meet these conditions are not typically draftable players, but worthwhile reserve or FAAB picks.

Batters

MLE PX as a leading indicator *(Bill Macey)*

Looking at minor league performance (as MLE) in one year and the corresponding MLB performance the subsequent year:

	Year 1 MLE	Year 2 MLB
Observations	496	496
Median PX	95	96
Percent PX > 100	43%	46%

In addition, 53% of the players had a MLB PX in year 2 that exceeded their MLE PX in year 1. A slight bias towards improved performance in year 2 is consistent with general career trajectories.

Year 1 MLE PX	Year 2 MLB PX	Pct. Incr	Pct. MLB PX > 100
<= 50	61	70.3%	5.4%
51-75	85	69.6%	29.4%
76-100	93	55.2%	39.9%
101-125	111	47.4%	62.0%
126-150	119	32.1%	66.1%
> 150	142	28.6%	76.2%

Slicing the numbers by performance level, there is a good amount of regression to the mean.

Players rarely suddenly develop power at the MLB level if they didn't previously display that skill at the minor league level. However, the relatively large gap between the median MLE PX and MLB PX for these players, 125 to 110, confirms the notion that the best players continue to improve once they reach the major leagues.

MLE contact rate as a leading indicator *(Bill Macey)*

There is a strong positive correlation (0.63) between a player's MLE ct% in Year 1 and his actual ct% at the MLB level in Year 2.

MLE ct%	Year 1 MLE ct%	Year 2 MLB ct%
< 70%	69%	68%
70% - 74%	73%	72%
75% - 79%	77%	75%
80% - 84%	82%	77%
85% - 89%	87%	82%
90% +	91%	86%
TOTAL	**84%**	**79%**

There is very little difference between the median MLE BA in Year 1 and the median MLB BA in Year 2:

MLE ct%	Year 1 MLE BA	Year 2 MLB BA
< 70%	.230	.270
70% - 74%	.257	.248
75% - 79%	.248	.255
80% - 84%	.257	.255
85% - 89%	.266	.270
90% +	.282	.273
TOTAL	.261	.262

Excluding the <70% cohort (which was a tiny sample size), there is a positive relationship between MLE ct% and MLB BA.

Pitchers

BPIs as a leading indicator for pitching success
The percentage of hurlers that were good investments in the year that they were called up varied by the level of their historical minor league BPIs prior to that year.

Pitchers who had:	Fared well	Fared poorly
Good indicators	79%	21%
Marginal or poor indicators	18%	82%

The data used here were MLE levels from the previous two years, not the season in which they were called up. The significance? Solid current performance is what merits a call-up, but this is not a good indicator of short-term MLB success, because a) the performance data set is too small, typically just a few month's worth of statistics, and b) for those putting up good numbers at a new minor league level, there has typically not been enough time for the scouting reports to make their rounds.

Minor league BPV as a leading indicator (Al Melchior)
There is a link between minor league skill and how a pitching prospect will fare in his first 5 starts upon call-up.

PQS Avg	MLE BPV < 50	50-99	100+
0.0-1.9	60%	28%	19%
2.0-2.9	32%	40%	29%
3.0-5.0	8%	33%	52%

Pitchers who demonstrate sub-par skills in the minors (sub-50 BPV) tend to fare poorly in their first big league starts. Three-fifths of these pitchers register a PQS average below 2.0, while only 8% average over 3.0.

Fewer than 1 out of 5 minor leaguers with a 100+ MLE BPV go on to post a sub-2.0 PQS average in their initial major league starts, but more than half average 3.0 or better.

Late season performance of rookie starting pitchers (Ray Murphy)
Given that a rookie's second tour of the league provides insight as to future success, do rookie pitchers typically run out of gas? We studied 2002-2005, identified 56 rookies who threw at least 75 IP and analyzed their PQS logs. The group:

All rookies	#	#GS/P	DOM%	DIS%	qERA
before 7/31	56	13.3	42%	21%	4.56
after 7/31	56	9.3	37%	29%	4.82

There is some erosion, but a 0.26 run rise in qERA is hardly cause for panic. If we re-focus our study class, the qERA variance increased to 4.44-5.08 for those who made at least 16 starts before July 31. The variance also was larger (3.97-4.56) for those who had a PQS-3 average prior to July 31. The pitchers who intersected these two sub-groups:

PQS>3+GS>15	#	#GS/P	DOM%	DIS%	qERA
before 7/31	8	19.1	51%	12%	4.23
after 7/31	8	9.6	34%	30%	5.08

While the sample size is small, the degree of flameout by these guys (0.85 runs) is more significant.

Japanese Baseball (Tom Mulhall)

Comparing MLB and Japanese Baseball
The Japanese major leagues are generally considered to be equivalent to very good Triple-A ball and the pitching may be even better. However, statistics are difficult to convert due to differences in the way the game is played in Japan.

1. While strong on fundamentals, Japanese baseball's guiding philosophy is risk avoidance. Mistakes are not tolerated. Runners rarely take extra bases, batters focus on making contact rather than driving the ball, and managers play for one run at a time. As a result, offenses score fewer runs than they should given the number of hits. Pitching stats tend to look better than the talent behind them.

2. Stadiums in Japan usually have shorter fences. Normally this would mean more HRs, but given #1 above, it is the American players who make up the majority of Japan's power elite. Power hitters do not make an equivalent transition to the MLB.

3. There are more artificial turf fields, which increases the number of ground ball singles. Only a few stadiums have infield grass and some still use dirt infields.

4. The quality of umpiring is questionable; there are no sanctioned umpiring schools in Japan. Fewer errors are called, reflecting the cultural philosophy of low tolerance for mistakes and the desire to avoid publicly embarrassing a player. Moreover, umpires are routinely intimidated.

5. Teams have smaller pitching staffs and use a six-man rotation. Starters usually pitch once a week, typically on the same day since Monday is an off-day for the entire league. Many starters will also occasionally pitch in relief between starts. Moreover, managers push for complete games, no matter what the score or situation. Despite superior conditioning, Japanese pitchers tend to burn out early due to overuse.

6. In 2011, a standardized ball was required for the first time. The new ball has an adverse affect on offense by using lower-elasticity rubber surrounding the cork. Pitching stats are conversely inflated and must be viewed with some skepticism.

7. Tie games are allowed. If the score remains even after 12 innings, the game goes into the books as a tie.

Japanese players as fantasy farm selections

Many fantasy leagues have large reserve or farm teams with rules allowing them to draft foreign players before they sign with a MLB team. With increased coverage by fantasy experts, the internet, and exposure from the World Baseball Classic, anyone willing to do a modicum of research can compile an adequate list of good players.

However, the key is not to identify the best Japanese players—the key is to identify impact players who have the desire and opportunity to sign with a MLB team. It is easy to overestimate the value of drafting these players. Since 1995, only about three dozen Japanese players have made a big league roster, and about half of them were middle relievers. But for owners who are allowed to carry a large reserve or farm team at reduced salaries, these players could be a real windfall, especially if your competitors do not do their homework.

A list of Japanese League players who could jump to the majors appears in the Prospects section.

Other Diamonds

Age 26 Paradox

Age 26 is when a player begins to reach his peak skill, no matter what his address is. If circumstances have him celebrating that birthday in the majors, he is a breakout candidate. If circumstances have him celebrating that birthday in the minors, he is washed up.

A-Rod 10-Step Path to Stardom

Not all well-hyped prospects hit the ground running. More often they follow an alternative path:

1. Prospect puts up phenomenal minor league numbers.
2. The media machine gets oiled up.
3. Prospect gets called up, but struggles, Year 1.
4. Prospect gets demoted.
5. Prospect tears it up in the minors, Year 2.
6. Prospect gets called up, but struggles, Year 2.
7. Prospect gets demoted.
8. The media turns their backs. Fantasy leaguers reduce their expectations.
9. Prospect tears it up in the minors, Year 3. The public shrugs its collective shoulders.
10. Prospect is promoted in Year 3 and explodes. Some lucky fantasy leaguer lands a franchise player for under $5.

Some players that are currently stuck at one of the interim steps, and may or may not ever reach Step 10, include Julio Teheran, Devin Mesoraco, and Zach Britton.

Developmental Dogmata

1. Defense is what gets a minor league prospect to the majors; offense is what keeps him there. *(Deric McKamey)*
2. The reason why rapidly promoted minor leaguers often fail is that they are never given the opportunity to master the skill of "adjusting to the competition."
3. Rookies who are promoted in-season often perform better than those that make the club out of spring training. Inferior March competition can inflate the latter group's perceived talent level.
4. Young players rarely lose their inherent skills. Pitchers may uncover weaknesses and the players may have difficulty adjusting. These are bumps along the growth curve, but they do not reflect a loss of skill.
5. Late bloomers have smaller windows of opportunity and much less chance for forgiveness.
6. The greatest risk in this game is to pay for performance that a player has never achieved.
7. Some outwardly talented prospects simply have a ceiling that's spelled "A-A-A."

Rule 5 Reminder

Don't ignore the Rule 5 draft lest you ignore the possibility of players like Jose Bautista, Josh Hamilton, Johan Santana, Joakim Soria, Dan Uggla, Shane Victorino and Jayson Werth. All were Rule 5 draftees.

Trout Inflation

The tendency for rookies to go for exorbitant draft prices following a year when there was a very good rookie crop.

Gaming

Standard Rules and Variations

Rotisserie Baseball was invented as an elegant confluence of baseball and economics. Whether by design or accident, the result has lasted for three decades. But what would Rotisserie and fantasy have been like if the Founding Fathers knew then what we know now about statistical analysis and game design? You can be sure things would be different.

The world has changed since the original game was introduced yet many leagues use the same rules today. New technologies have opened up opportunities to improve elements of the game that might have been limited by the capabilities of the 1980s. New analytical approaches have revealed areas where the original game falls short.

As such, there are good reasons to tinker and experiment; to find ways to enhance the experience.

Following are the basic elements of fantasy competition, those that provide opportunities for alternative rules and experimentation. This is by no means an exhaustive list, but at minimum provides some interesting food-for-thought.

Player pool

Standard: American League-only, National League-only or Mixed League. With the new MLB alignment of 15 teams per league, there has been discussion about what would constitute a new standard for the single-league fantasy player pool. The cleanest solution is to maintain the numbers of teams in AL-only leagues and to reduce the size of NL-only league by one team.

AL/NL-only typically drafts 8-12 teams (pool penetration of 49% to 74%). Mixed leagues draft 10-18 teams (31% to 55% penetration), though 15 teams (46%) is a common number.

Drafting of reserve players will increase the penetration percentages. A 12-team AL/NL-only league adding six reserves onto 23-man rosters would draft 93% of the available pool of players on all teams' 25-man rosters.

The draft penetration level determines which fantasy management skills are most important to your league. The higher the penetration, the more important it is to draft a good team. The lower the penetration, the greater the availability of free agents and the more important in-season roster management becomes.

There is no generally-accepted optimal penetration level, but we have often suggested that 75% (including reserves) provides a good balance between the skills required for both draft prep and in-season management.

Alternative pools: There is a wide variety of options here. Certain leagues draft from within a small group of major league divisions or teams. Some competitions, like home run leagues, only draft batters.

Bottom-tier pool: Drafting from the entire major league population, the only players available are those who posted a Rotisserie dollar value of $5 or less in the previous season. Intended as a test of an owner's ability to identify talent with upside. Best used as a pick-a-player contest with any number of teams participating.

Positional structure

Standard: 23 players. One at each defensive position (though three outfielders may be from any of LF, CF or RF), plus one additional catcher, one middle infielder (2B or SS), one corner infielder (1B or 3B), two additional outfielders and a utility player/designated hitter (which often can be a batter who qualifies anywhere). Nine pitchers, typically holding any starting or relief role.

Open: 25 players. One at each defensive position (plus DH), 5-man starting rotation and two relief pitchers. Nine additional players at any position, which may be a part of the active roster or constitute a reserve list.

40-man: Standard 23 plus 17 reserves. Used in many keeper and dynasty leagues.

Reapportioned: In recent years, new obstacles are being faced by 12-team AL/NL-only leagues thanks to changes in the real game. The 14/9 split between batters and pitchers no longer reflects how MLB teams structure their rosters. Of the 30 teams, each with 25-man rosters, not one contains 14 batters for any length of time. In fact, many spend a good part of the season with only 12 batters, which means teams often have more pitchers than hitters.

For fantasy purposes in AL/NL-only leagues, that leaves a disproportionate draft penetration into the batter and pitcher pools:

	BATTERS	PITCHERS
On all MLB rosters	195	180
Players drafted	168	108
Pct.	86%	60%

These drafts are depleting 26% more batters out of the pool than pitchers. Add in those leagues with reserve lists—perhaps an additional six players per team removing another 72 players—and post-draft free agent pools are very thin, especially on the batting side.

The impact is less in 15-team mixed leagues, though the FA pitching pool is still disproportionately deep.

	BATTERS	PITCHERS
On all rosters	381	369
Drafted	210	135
Pct.	55%	37%

One solution is to reapportion the number of batters and pitchers that are rostered. Adding one pitcher slot and eliminating one batter slot may be enough to provide better balance. The batting slot most often removed is the second catcher, since it is the position with the least depth.

Beginning in the 2012 season, the Tout Wars AL/NL-only experts leagues opted to eliminate one of the outfield slots and replace it with a "swingman" position. This position could be any batter or pitcher, depending upon the owner's needs at any given time. At the end of the 2012 season, 10 of 12 AL owners had batters in the swingman slot; seven of 13 NL owners had batters in that slot.

Selecting players

Standard: The three most prevalent methods for stocking fantasy rosters are:

Snake/Straight/Serpentine draft: Players are selected in order with seeds reversed in alternating rounds. This method has become the most popular due to its speed, ease of implementation and ease of automation.

In these drafts, the underlying assumption is that value can be ranked relative to a linear baseline. Pick #1 is better than pick #2, which is better than pick #3, and the difference between each pick is assumed to be somewhat equivalent. While a faulty assumption, we must believe in it to assume a level playing field.

Auction: Players are sold to the highest bidder from a fixed budget, typically $260. Auctions provide the team owner with the most control over which players will be on his team, but can take twice as long as snake drafts.

The baseline is $0 at the beginning of each player put up for bid. The final purchase price for each player is shaped by many wildly variable factors, from roster need to geographic location of the draft. A $30 player can mean different things to different drafters.

One option that can help reduce the time commitment of auctions is to force minimum bids at each hour mark. You could mandate $15 openers in hour #1; $10 openers in hour #2, etc.

Pick-a-player / Salary cap: Players are assigned fixed dollar values and owners assemble their roster within a fixed cap. This type of roster-stocking is an individual exercise which results in teams typically having some of the same players.

In these leagues, the "value" decision is taken out of the hands of the owners. Each player has a fixed value, pre-assigned based on past season performance.

Hybrid snake-auction: Each draft begins as an auction. Each team has to fill its first seven roster slots from a budget of $154. Opening bid for any player is $15. This assures that player values will be close to reality. After each team has filled seven slots, it becomes a snake draft.

If you like, you can assign fixed salaries to the snake-drafted players in such a way that rosters will still add up to about $260.

Round	Salary		Round	Salary
8	$14		16	$6
9	$13		17	$5
10	$12		18	$4
11	$11		19	$3
12	$10		20	$2
13	$9		21	$1
14	$8		22	$1
15	$7		23	$1

You can also use this chart to decide how deep you want to auction. If you want to auction the first 15 players, for instance, you'd use a budget of $238. Though not shown, if you only wanted to auction the first 5 players, your budget would be $121.

This method is intended to reduce draft time while still providing an economic component for selecting players.

Stat categories

Standard: The standard statistical categories for Rotisserie leagues are:

4x4: HR, RBI, SB, BA, W, Sv, ERA, WHIP

5x5: HR, R, RBI, SB, BA, W, Sv, K, ERA, WHIP

6x6: Categories typically added are Holds and OPS.

7x7, etc.: Any number of categories may be added.

In general, the more categories you add, the more complicated it is to isolate individual performance and manage the categorical impact on your roster. There is also the danger of redundancy; with multiple categories measuring like stats, certain skills can get over-valued. For instance, home runs are double-counted when using the categories of both HR and slugging average. (Though note that HRs are actually already triple-counted in standard 5x5—HRs, runs, and RBIs)

If the goal is to have categories that create a more encompassing picture of player performance, it is actually possible to accomplish more with less:

Modified 4x4: HR, (R+RBI-HR), SB, OBA, W, (Sv+Hld-BSv), K, ERA

This provides a better balance between batting and pitching in that each has three counting categories and one ratio category. In fact, the balance is shown to be even more notable here:

	BATTING	PITCHING
Pure skill counting stat	HR	K
Ratio category	OBA	ERA
Dependent upon managerial decision	SB	(Sv+Hold-BSv)
Dependent upon team support	R+RBI-HR	W

Keeping score

Standard: These are the most common scoring methods:

Rotisserie: Players are evaluated in several statistical categories. Totals of these statistics are ranked by team. The winner is the team with the highest cumulative ranking.

Points: Players receive points for events that they contribute to in each game. Points are totaled for each team and teams are then ranked.

Head-to-Head (H2H): Using Rotisserie or points scoring, teams are scheduled in daily or weekly matchups. The winner of each matchup is the team that finishes higher in more categories (Rotisserie) or scores the most points.

Hybrid H2H-Rotisserie: Rotisserie's category ranking system can be converted into a weekly won-loss record. Depending upon where your team finishes for that week's statistics determines how many games you win for that week. Each week, your team will play seven games.

*Place	Record		*Place	Record
1st	7-0		7th	3-4
2nd	6-1		8th	2-5
3rd	6-1		9th	2-5
4th	5-2		10th	1-6
5th	5-2		11th	1-6
6th	4-3		12th	0-7

* Based on overall Rotisserie category ranking for the week.

At the end of each week, all the statistics revert to zero and you start over. You never dig a hole in any category that you can't climb out of, because all categories themselves are incidental to the standings.

The regular season lasts for 23 weeks, which equals 161 games. Weeks 24, 25 and 26 are for play-offs.

Free agent acquisition

Standard: Three methods are the most common for acquiring free agent players during the season.

First to the phone: Free agents are awarded to the first owner who claims them.

Reverse order of standings: Access to the free agent pool is typically in a snake draft fashion with the last place team getting the first pick, and each successive team higher in the standings picking afterwards.

Free agent acquisition budget (FAAB): Teams are given a set budget at the beginning of the season (typically, $100 or $1000) from which they bid on free agents in a closed auction process.

Vickrey FAAB: Research has shown that more than 50% of FAAB dollars are lost via overbid on an annual basis. Given that this is a scarce commodity, one would think that a system to better manage these dollars might be desirable. The Vickrey system conducts a closed auction in the same way as standard FAAB, but the price of the winning bid is set at the amount of the second highest bid, plus $1. In some cases, gross overbids (at least $10 over) are reduced to the second highest bid plus $5.

This method was designed by William Vickrey, a Professor of Economics at Columbia University. His theory was that this process reveals the true value of the commodity. For his work, Vickrey was awarded the Nobel Prize for Economics (and $1.2 million) in 1996.

Double-Bid FAAB: One of the inherent difficulties in the current FAAB system is that we have so many options for setting a bid amount. You can bid $47, or $51, or $23. You might agonize over whether to go $38 or $39. With a $100 budget, there are 100 decision points. And while you may come up with a rough guesstimate of the range in which your opponents might bid, the results for any individual player bidding are typically random within that range.

The first part of this process reduces the number of decision points. Owners must categorize their interest by bidding a fixed number of pre-set dollar amounts for each player. In a $100 FAAB league, for instance, those levels might be $1, $5, $10, $15, $20, $30, $40 or $50. All owners would set the general market value for free agents in these eight levels of interest. (This system sets a $50 maximum, but that is not absolutely necessary.)

The initial stage of the bidding process serves to screen out those who are not interested in a player at the appropriate market level. That leaves a high potential for tied owners, those who share the same level of interest.

The tied owners must then submit a second bid of equal or greater value than their first bid. These bids can be in $1 increments. The winning owner gets the player; if there is still a tie, then the player would go to the owner lower in the standings.

An advantage of this second bid is that it gives owners an opportunity to see who they are going up against, and adjust. If you are bidding against an owner close to you in the standings,

you may need to be more aggressive in that second bid. If you see that the tied owner(s) wouldn't hurt you by acquiring that player, then maybe you resubmit the original bid and be content to potentially lose out on the player. If you're ahead in the standings, it's actually a way to potentially opt out on that player completely by resubmitting your original bid and forcing another owner to spend his FAAB.

Some leagues will balk at adding another layer to the weekly deadline process; it's a trade-off to having more control over managing your FAAB.

Fixed price free agents: In the same way as salary cap games have pre-assigned prices for players at the draft, free agents can be assigned a fixed price as well. For a player who has been in the free agent pool and available for at least two weeks, his price would be his current Rotisserie dollar value. For a player who is a recent call-up or in the pool for less than two weeks, he would be assigned a baseline (e.g. $5 in a $100 FAAB league) augmented by a pre-determined amount based on contextual factors.

For instance, claiming a current minor league call-up would cost an owner the $5 baseline, plus an additional $5 for each month the player is expected to be a full-timer, plus perhaps another $5 if he is on a .500 or better ballclub, in a favorable ballpark, etc. The final pre-set price will serve to screen out only the most interested owners. Multiple like claims would be awarded to the team lower in the standings.

The season

Standard: Leagues are played out during the course of the entire Major League Baseball season.

Split-season: Leagues are conducted from Opening Day through the All-Star break, then re-drafted to play from the All-Star break through the end of the season.

50-game split-season: Leagues are divided into three 50-game split-seasons. There would be a one-week break in between each segment. The advantages:

- With dwindling attention spans over the long 162-game season, 50 games is a more accessible time frame to maintain interest. There would be fewer abandoned teams.
- There would be four shots at a title each year; the first place team from each split, plus the team with the best overall record for the entire year.
- Given that drafting is considered the most fun aspect of the game, these splits triple the opportunities to participate in some type of draft. Leagues may choose to do complete re-drafts and treat the year as three distinct mini-seasons. Or, leagues might allow teams to drop their five worst players and conduct a restocking draft at each break.

Monthly leagues: See page 72.

Single game (Quint-Inning Lite format): Played with five owners drafting from the active rosters of two major league teams in a single game. Prior to the game, 5-player rosters are snake-drafted (no positional requirements). Points are awarded based on how players perform during the game. Batters accumulate points for bases gained:

Single	+1
Double	+2
Triple	+3
HR	+4
BB	+1
HBP	+1
SB	+1

Pitchers get +1 point for each full inning completed (3 outs) and lose 1 point for each run allowed (both earned and unearned).

A deck of standard playing cards may be used as an aid for scorekeeping and to break ties.

Players may be dropped, added or traded after the first inning. However, an owner must always have 5 players by the beginning of each half inning. Any player can be cut from an owner's roster. Free agents (players not rostered by any of the owners) can be claimed by any owner, between half-innings, in reverse order of the current standings. If two owners are tied and both want to place a claim, the tie is broken by drawing high card from the scorekeeping deck. Trades can be consummated at any time, between any two or more owners.

At the beginning of the 5th inning, each owner has the option of doubling the points (positive and negative) for any one player on his roster for the remainder of the game (the "Quint"). Should that player be traded, or dropped and then re-acquired, his "Quint" status remains for the game.

Beginning in the 9th inning, all batting points are doubled.

Quint-Inning can be played as a low stakes, moderate or higher stakes competition.

- It costs ($1/$5/$55) to get in the game.
- It costs (25 cents/$1/$5) per inning to stay in the game for the first four innings.
- Beginning with the 5th inning, the stakes go up to (50 cents/$2/$10) per inning to stay in the game.
- Should the game go into extra innings, the stakes rise to ($1/$5/$25) to stay in the game until its conclusion.

Each owner has to decide whether he is still in the game at the end of each full inning. Owners can drop out at the end of any inning, thus forfeiting any monies they've already contributed to the pot. When an owner drops, his players go back into the pool and can be acquired as free agents by the other owners.

The winner is the owner who finishes the game with the most points.

Post-season league: Some leagues re-draft teams from among the MLB post-season contenders and play out a separate competition. It is possible, however, to make a post-season competition that is an extension of the regular season.

Start by designating a set number of regular season finishers as qualifying for the post-season. The top four teams in a league is a good number.

These four teams would designate a fixed 23-man roster for all post-season games. First, they would freeze all of their currently-owned players who are on MLB post-season teams.

In order to fill the roster holes that will likely exist, these four teams would then pick players from their league's non-playoff teams (for the sake of the post-season only). This would be in the form of a snake draft done on the day following the end of the regular season. Draft order would be regular season finish, so the play-off team with the most regular season points would get first pick. Picks would continue until all four rosters are filled with 23 men.

Regular scoring would be used for all games during October. The team with the best play-off stats at the end of the World Series is the overall champ.

Snake Drafting

Snake draft first round history

The following tables record the comparison between pre-season projected player rankings (using Average Draft Position data from Mock Draft Central) and actual end-of-season results. The nine-year success rate of identifying each season's top talent is only 36.3%.

2004	ADP		ACTUAL = 6
1	Alex Rodriguez	1	Ichiro Suzuki
2	Albert Pujols	2	Vlad Guerrero (5)
3	Carlos Beltran	3	Randy Johnson
4	Todd Helton	4	Albert Pujols (2)
5	Vlad Guerrero	5	Johan Santana
6	Alfonso Soriano	6	Bobby Abreu
7	N. Garciaparra	7	Adrian Beltre
8	Barry Bonds	8	Barry Bonds (8)
9	Pedro Martinez	9	Carlos Beltran (3)
10	Mark Prior	10	Ben Sheets
11	Manny Ramirez	11	Melvin Mora
12	Roy Halladay	12	Carl Crawford
13	Magglio Ordonez	13	Manny Ramirez (11)
14	Edgar Renteria	14	Miguel Tejada
15	Sammy Sosa	15	Todd Helton (4)

2005	ADP		ACTUAL = 7
1	Alex Rodriguez	1	Derrek Lee
2	Carlos Beltran	2	Alex Rodriguez (1)
3	Albert Pujols	3	Albert Pujols (3)
4	Vlad Guerrero	4	David Ortiz
5	Manny Ramirez	5	Mark Teixeira
6	Bobby Abreu	6	Carl Crawford (12)
7	Miguel Tejada	7	Chone Figgins
8	Johan Santana	8	Jason Bay
9	Todd Helton	9	Miguel Cabrera
10	Jason Schmidt	10	Manny Ramirez (5)
11	Randy Johnson	11	Michael Young
12	Carl Crawford	12	Vlad Guerrero (4)
13	Alfonso Soriano	13	Ichiro Suzuki
14	Ben Sheets	14	Bobby Abreu (6)
15	Curt Schilling	15	Johan Santana (8)

2006	ADP		ACTUAL = 4
1	Albert Pujols	1	Jose Reyes
2	Alex Rodriguez	2	Derek Jeter
3	Vlad Guerrero	3	Albert Pujols (1)
4	Mark Teixeira	4	Ryan Howard
5	Manny Ramirez	5	Johan Santana
6	Miguel Cabrera	6	Alfonso Soriano
7	Derrek Lee	7	Carl Crawford (10)
8	Bobby Abreu	8	Matt Holliday
9	Miguel Tejada	9	Vlad Guerrero (3)
10	Carl Crawford	10	Miguel Cabrera (6)
11	Michael Young	11	Ichiro Suzuki
12	Carlos Beltran	12	Chase Utley
13	Jason Bay	13	Garrett Atkins
14	David Ortiz	14	Jermaine Dye
15	David Wright	15	Lance Berkman

2007	ADP		ACTUAL = 5
1	Albert Pujols	1	Alex Rodriguez (4)
2	Alfonso Soriano	2	Hanley Ramirez
3	Jose Reyes	3	Matt Holliday
4	Alex Rodriguez	4	Magglio Ordonez
5	Ryan Howard	5	David Wright (12)
6	Johan Santana	6	Jimmy Rollins
7	Carl Crawford	7	Ichiro Suzuki
8	Chase Utley	8	Jose Reyes (3)
9	Carlos Beltran	9	Jake Peavy
10	David Ortiz	10	David Ortiz (10)
11	Vlad Guerrero	11	Carl Crawford (7)
12	David Wright	12	Eric Byrnes
13	Miguel Cabrera	13	Brandon Phillips
14	Lance Berkman	14	Chipper Jones
15	Carlos Lee	15	Prince Fielder

2008	ADP		ACTUAL = 7
1	Alex Rodriguez	1	Albert Pujols (10)
2	Hanley Ramirez	2	Jose Reyes (4)
3	David Wright	3	Hanley Ramirez (2)
4	Jose Reyes	4	Manny Ramirez
5	Matt Holliday	5	Matt Holliday (5)
6	Jimmy Rollins	6	David Wright (3)
7	Miguel Cabrera	7	Lance Berkman
8	Chase Utley	8	Dustin Pedroia
9	Ryan Howard	9	Roy Halladay
10	Albert Pujols	10	Josh Hamilton
11	Prince Fielder	11	Alex Rodriguez (1)
12	Ryan Braun	12	C.C. Sabathia
13	Johan Santana	13	Carlos Beltran
14	Carl Crawford	14	Grady Sizemore
15	Alfonso Soriano	15	Chase Utley (8)

2009	ADP		ACTUAL = 5
1	Hanley Ramirez	1	Albert Pujols (2)
2	Albert Pujols	2	Hanley Ramirez (1)
3	Jose Reyes	3	Tim Lincecum
4	David Wright	4	Dan Haren
5	Grady Sizemore	5	Carl Crawford
6	Miguel Cabrera	6	Matt Kemp
7	Ryan Braun	7	Joe Mauer
8	Jimmy Rollins	8	Derek Jeter
9	Ian Kinsler	9	Zach Greinke
10	Josh Hamilton	10	Ryan Braun (7)
11	Ryan Howard	11	Jacoby Ellsbury
12	Mark Teixeira	12	Mark Reynolds
13	Alex Rodriguez	13	Prince Fielder
14	Matt Holliday	14	Chase Utley (15)
15	Chase Utley	15	Miguel Cabrera (6)

2010	ADP		ACTUAL = 5
1	Albert Pujols	1	Carlos Gonzalez
2	Hanley Ramirez	2	Albert Pujols (1)
3	Alex Rodriguez	3	Joey Votto
4	Chase Utley	4	Roy Halladay
5	Ryan Braun	5	Carl Crawford (15)
6	Mark Teixeira	6	Miguel Cabrera (9)
7	Matt Kemp	7	Josh Hamilton
8	Prince Fielder	8	Adam Wainwright
9	Miguel Cabrera	9	Felix Hernandez
10	Ryan Howard	10	Robinson Cano
11	Evan Longoria	11	Jose Bautista
12	Tom Lincecum	12	Paul Konerko
13	Joe Mauer	13	Matt Holliday
14	David Wright	14	Ryan Braun (5)
15	Carl Crawford	15	Hanley Ramirez (2)

2011	ADP		ACTUAL = 6
1	Albert Pujols	1	Matt Kemp
2	Hanley Ramirez	2	Jacoby Ellsbury
3	Miguel Cabrera	3	Ryan Braun (10)
4	Troy Tulowitzki	4	Justin Verlander
5	Evan Longoria	5	Clayton Kershaw
6	Carlos Gonzalez	6	Curtis Granderson
7	Joey Votto	7	Adrian Gonzalez (8)
8	Adrian Gonzalez	8	Miguel Cabrera (3)
9	Robinson Cano	9	Roy Halladay (15)
10	Ryan Braun	10	Cliff Lee
11	David Wright	11	Jose Bautista
12	Mark Teixeira	12	Dustin Pedroia
13	Carl Crawford	13	Jered Weaver
14	Josh Hamilton	14	Albert Pujols (1)
15	Roy Halladay	15	Robinson Cano (9)

2012	ADP		ACTUAL = 4
1	Matt Kemp	1	Mike Trout
2	Ryan Braun	2	Ryan Braun (2)
3	Albert Pujols	3	Miguel Cabrera (4)
4	Miguel Cabrera	4	Andrew McCutchen
5	Troy Tulowitzki	5	R.A. Dickey
6	Jose Bautista	6	Clayton Kershaw
7	Jacoby Ellsbury	7	Justin Verlander (8)
8	Justin Verlander	8	Josh Hamilton
9	Adrian Gonzalez	9	Fernando Rodney
10	Justin Upton	10	Adrian Beltre
11	Robinson Cano	11	Alex Rios
12	Joey Votto	12	David Price
13	Evan Longoria	13	Chase Headley
14	Carlos Gonzalez	14	Robinson Cano (11)
15	Prince Fielder	15	Edwin Encarnacion

ADP attrition

Why is our success rate so low in identifying what should be the most easy-to-project players each year? We rank and draft players based on the expectation that those ranked higher will return greater value in terms of productivity and playing time, as well as being the safest investments. However, there are many variables affecting where players finish.

Earlier, it was shown that players spend an inordinate number of days on the disabled list. In fact, of the players projected to finish in the top 300 coming into each of the past four seasons, the number who lost playing time due to injuries, demotions and suspensions has been extreme:

Year	Pct. of top-ranked 300 players who lost PT
2009	51%
2010	44%
2011	49%
2012	45%

When you consider that about half of each season's very best players had fewer at-bats or innings pitched than we projected, it shows how tough it is to rank players each year.

The fallout? Consider: It is nearly a foregone conclusion that Mike Trout and Andrew McCutchen—players who finished in the top 15 for the first time last year—will rank as first round picks in 2013. The above data provide a strong argument against them returning first-round value.

Yes, they are excellent players, two of the best in the game, in 2012 anyway. But the issue is not their skills profile. The issue is the profile of what makes a worthy first rounder. Note:

- From 2004-2011, two-thirds of players finishing in the Top 15 were not in the Top 15 the previous year. There is a great deal of turnover in the first round, year-to-year.

- Of those who were first-timers, only 14% repeated in the first round the following year.

- Established superstars who finished in the Top 15 were no guarantee to repeat but occasionally reappear in a later year. These were players like David Ortiz (twice in 1st round, twice unable to repeat), Mark Teixeira (#5, 2005), Ryan Howard (#4, 2006) and Chase Utley (3 times in 1st round, only repeated once). First-time stars like Josh Hamilton (2008), Joe Mauer (2009) and Carlos Gonzalez (2010) are even less likely to repeat.

- From 2005 to 2007, 14 of the top 15 players were batters. In 2008, that dropped to 13. In 2009 and 2010, it dropped again to 12. The past two years, only 10 of 15 were batters. As player value shifts toward pitching, more arms are appearing in the first round, leaving fewer spots for the top batters.

As such, the odds are against Trout and McCutchen repeating in the first round, as counter-intuitive as it may seem. But we said the same thing last year about Jacoby Ellsbury and Curtis Granderson, and the year before that for Carlos Gonzalez. As talented as these players are, it's not just about skill; it's also about skill relative to the rest of a volatile player pool.

What is the best seed to draft from?

Most drafters like mid-round so they never have to wait too long for their next player. Some like the swing pick, suggesting that getting two players at 15 and 16 is better than a 1 and a 30. Many drafters assume that the swing pick means you'd be getting something like two $30 players instead of a $40 and $20.

Equivalent auction dollar values reveal the following facts about the first two snake draft rounds:

In an AL/NL-only league, the top seed would get a $44 player (at #1) and a $24 player (at #24) for a total of $68; the 12th seed would get two $29s (at #12 and #13) for $58.

In a mixed league, the top seed would get a $47 and a $24 ($71); the 15th seed would get two $28s ($56).

Since the talent level flattens out after the 2nd round, low seeds never get a chance to catch up:

Dollar value difference between first player selected and last player selected

Round	12-team	15-team
1	$15	$19
2	$7	$8
3	$5	$4
4	$3	$3
5	$2	$2
6	$2	$1
7-17	$1	$1
18-23	$0	$0

The total value each seed accumulates at the end of the draft is hardly equitable:

Seed	Mixed	AL/NL-only
1	$266	$273
2	$264	$269
3	$263	$261
4	$262	$262
5	$259	$260
6	$261	$260
7	$260	$260
8	$261	$260
9	$261	$258
10	$257	$260
11	$257	$257
12	$258	$257
13	$254	
14	$255	
15	$256	

Of course, the draft is just the starting point for managing your roster and player values are variable. Still, it's tough to imagine a scenario where the top seed wouldn't have an advantage over the bottom seed.

Using ADPs to determine when to select players *(Bill Macey)*

Although average draft position (ADP) data gives us a good idea of where in the draft each player is selected, it can be misleading when trying to determine how early to target a player. This chart summarizes the percentage of players drafted within 15 picks of his ADP as well as the average standard deviation by grouping of players.

ADP Rank	% within 15 picks	Standard Deviation
1-25	100%	2.5
26-50	97%	6.1
51-100	87%	9.6
100-150	72%	14.0
150-200	61%	17.4
200-250	53%	20.9

As the draft progresses, the picks for each player become more widely dispersed and less clustered around the average. Most top 100 players will go within one round of their ADP-converted round. However, as you reach the mid-to-late rounds, there is much more uncertainty as to when a player will be selected. Pitchers have slightly smaller standard deviations than do batters (i.e. they tend to be drafted in a narrower range). This suggests that drafters may be more likely to reach for a batter than for a pitcher.

Using the ADP and corresponding standard deviation, we can to estimate the likelihood that a given player will be available at a certain draft pick. We estimate the predicted standard deviation for each player as follows:

Stdev = -0.42 + 0.42*(ADP - Earliest Pick)

(That the figure 0.42 appears twice is pure coincidence; the numbers are not equal past two decimal points.)

If we assume that the picks are normally distributed, we can use a player's ADP and estimated standard deviation to estimate the likelihood that the player is available with a certain pick (MS Excel formula):

=1-normdist(x,ADP,Standard Deviation,True)

where «x» represents the pick number to be evaluated.

We can use this information to prepare for a snake draft by determining how early we may need to reach in order to roster a player. Suppose you have the 8th pick in a 15-team league draft and your target is 2009 sleeper candidate Nelson Cruz. His ADP is 128.9 and his earliest selection was with the 94th pick. This yields an estimated standard deviation of 14.2. You can then enter these values into the formula above to estimate the likelihood that he is still available at each of the following picks:

Likelihood	
Pick	Available
83	100%
98	99%
113	87%
128	53%
143	16%
158	2%

ADPs and scarcity *(Bill Macey)*

Most players are selected within a round or two of their ADP with tight clustering around the average. But every draft is unique and every pick in the draft seemingly affects the ordering of subsequent picks. In fact, deviations from "expected" sequences can sometimes start a chain reaction at that position. This is most often seen in runs at scarce positions such as the closer; once the first one goes, the next seems sure to closely follow.

Research also suggests that within each position, there is a correlation within tiers of players. The sooner players within a generally accepted tier are selected, the sooner other players within the same tier will be taken. However, once that tier is exhausted, draft order reverts to normal.

How can we use this information? If you notice a reach pick, you can expect that other drafters may follow suit. If your draft plan is to get a similar player within that tier, you'll need to adjust your picks accordingly.

Mapping ADPs to auction value *(Bill Macey)*

Reliable average auction values (AAV) are often tougher to come by than ADP data for snake drafts. However, we can estimate predicted auction prices as a function of ADP, arriving at the following equation:

y = -9.8ln(x) + 57.8
where ln(x) is the natural log function, x represents the actual ADP, and y represents the predicted AAV.

This equation does an excellent job estimating auction prices (r2=0.93), though deviations are unavoidable. The asymptotic nature of the logarithmic function, however, causes the model to predict overly high prices for the top players. So be aware of that, and adjust.

Auction Value Analysis

Auction values (R$) in perspective

R$ is the dollar value placed on a player's statistical performance in a Rotisserie league, and designed to measure the impact that player has on the standings.

There are several methods to calculate a player's value from his projected (or actual) statistics.

One method is Standings Gain Points, described in the book, *How to Value Players for Rotisserie Baseball*, by Art McGee (2nd edition available at BaseballHQ.com). SGP converts a player's statistics in each Rotisserie category into the number of points those stats will allow you to gain in the standings. These are then converted back into dollars.

Another popular method is the Percentage Valuation Method. In PVM, a least valuable, or replacement performance level is set for each category (in a given league size) and then values are calculated representing the incremental improvement from that base. A player is then awarded value in direct proportion to the level he contributes to each category.

As much as these methods serve to attach a firm number to projected performance, the winning bid for any player is still highly variable depending upon many factors:

- the salary cap limit
- the number of teams in the league
- each team's roster size
- the impact of any protected players
- each team's positional demands at the time of bidding
- the statistical category demands at the time of bidding
- external factors, e.g. media inflation or deflation of value

In other words, a $30 player is only a $30 player if someone in your draft pays $30 for him.

Roster slot valuation *(John Burnson)*

Tenets of player valuation say that the number of ballplayers with positive value—either positive projected value (before the season) or positive actual value (after the season)—must equal the total number of roster spots, and that, before the season, the value of a player must match his expected production. These propositions are wrong.

The unit of production in Rotisserie is not "the player" or "the statistic" but the player-week. If you own a player, you must own him for at least one week, and if you own him for more than one week, you must own him for multiples of one week. Moreover, you cannot break down his production—everything that a player does in a given week, you earn. (In leagues that allow daily transactions, the unit is the player-day. The point stays.)

When you draft a player, what have you bought?

"You have bought the stats generated by this player."

No. You have bought the stats generated by his slot. Initially, the drafted player fills the slot, but he need not fill the slot for the season, and he need not contribute from Day One. If you trade the player during the season, then your bid on Draft Day paid for the stats of the original player plus the stats of the new player. If the player misses time due to injury or demotion, then you bought the stats of whomever fills the weeks while the drafted player is missing. At season's end, there will be more players providing positive value than there are roster slots.

Before the season, the number of players projected for positive value has to equal the total number of roster slots—after all, we can't order owners to draft more players than can fit on their rosters. However, the projected productivity should be adjusted by the potential to capture extra value in the slot. This is especially important for injury-rehab cases and late-season call-ups. For example, if we think that a player will miss half the season, then we would augment his projected stats with a half-year of stats from a replacement-level player at his position. Only then would we calculate prices. Essentially, we want to apportion $260 per team among the slots, not the players.

Average player value by draft round

Rd	AL/NL	Mxd
1	$34	$34
2	$26	$26
3	$23	$23
4	$20	$20
5	$18	$18
6	$17	$16
7	$16	$15
8	$15	$13
9	$13	$12
10	$12	$11
11	$11	$10
12	$10	$9
13	$9	$8
14	$8	$8
15	$7	$7
16	$6	$6
17	$5	$5
18	$4	$4
19	$3	$3
20	$2	$2
21	$1	$2
22	$1	$1
23	$1	$1

Benchmarks for auction players:
- All $30 players will go in the first round.
- All $20-plus players will go in the first four rounds.
- Double-digit value ends pretty much after Round 11.
- The $1 end game starts at about Round 21.

Dollar values by lineup position *(Michael Roy)*
How much value is derived from batting order position?

Pos	PA	R	RBI	R$
#1	747	107	72	$18.75
#2	728	102	84	$19.00
#3	715	95	100	$19.45
#4	698	93	104	$19.36
#5	682	86	94	$18.18
#6	665	85	82	$17.19
#7	645	81	80	$16.60
#8	623	78	80	$16.19
#9	600	78	73	$15.50

So, a batter moving from the bottom of the order to the clean-up spot, with no change in performance, would gain nearly $4 in value from runs and RBIs alone.

Dollar values: expected projective accuracy
There is a 65% chance that a player projected for a certain dollar value will finish the season with a final value within plus-or-minus $5 of that projection. That means, if you value a player at $25, you only have about a 2-in-3 shot of him finishing between $20 and $30.

If you want to get your odds up to 80%, the range now becomes +/- $9. You have an 80% shot that your $25 player will finish somewhere between $16 and $34.

How likely is it that a $30 player will repeat? *(Matt Cederholm)*
From 2003-2008, there were 205 players who earned $30 or more (using single-league 5x5 values). Only 70 of them (34%) earned $30 or more in the next season.

In fact, the odds of repeating a $30 season aren't good. As seen below, the best odds during that period were 42%. And as we would expect, pitchers fare far worse than hitters.

	Total>$30	# Repeat	% Repeat
Hitters	167	64	38%
Pitchers	38	6	16%
Total	205	70	34%
High-Reliability*			
Hitters	42	16	38%
Pitchers	7	0	0%
Total	49	16	33%
100+ BPV			
Hitters	60	25	42%
Pitchers	31	6	19%
Total	91	31	19%
High-Reliability and 100+ BPV*			
Hitters	12	5	42%
Pitchers	6	0	0%
Total	18	5	28%

*Reliability figures are from 2006-2008

For players with multiple seasons of $30 or more, the numbers get better. Players with consecutive $30 seasons, 2003-2008:

	Total>$30	# Repeat	% Repeat
Two Years	62	29	55%
Three+ Years	29	19	66%

Still, a player with two consecutive seasons at $30 in value is barely a 50/50 proposition. And three consecutive seasons is only a 2/3 shot. Small sample sizes aside, this does illustrate the nature of the beast. Even the most consistent, reliable players fail 1/3 of the time. Of course, this is true whether they are kept or drafted anew, so this alone shouldn't prevent you from keeping a player.

How well do elite pitchers retain their value? *(Michael Weddell)*
An elite pitcher (one who earns at least $24 in a season) on average keeps 80% of his R$ value from year 1 to year 2. This compares to the baseline case of only 52%.

Historically, 36% of elite pitchers improve, returning a greater R$ in the second year than they did the first year. That is an impressive performance considering they already were at an elite level. 17% collapse, returning less than a third of their R$ in the second year. The remaining 47% experience a middling outcome, keeping more than a third but less than all of their R$ from one year to the next.

Valuing closers

Given the high risk associated with the closer's role, it is difficult to determine a fair draft value. Typically, those who have successfully held the role for several seasons will earn the highest draft price, but valuing less stable commodities is troublesome.

A rough rule of thumb is to start by paying $10 for the role alone. Any pitcher tagged the closer on draft day should merit at least $10. Then add anywhere from $0 to $15 for support skills.

In this way, the top level talents will draw upwards of $20-$25. Those with moderate skill will draw $15-$20, and those with more questionable skill in the $10-$15 range.

Profiling the end game

What types of players are typically the most profitable in the end-game? First, our overall track record on $1 picks:

Avg Return	%Profitable	Avg Prof	Avg. Loss
$1.89	51%	$10.37	($7.17)

On aggregate, the hundreds of players drafted in the end-game earned $1.89 on our $1 investments. While they were profitable overall, only 51% of them actually turned a profit. Those that did cleared more than $10 on average. Those that didn't—the other 49%—lost about $7 apiece.

Pos	Pct.of tot	Avg Val	%Profit	Avg Prof	Avg Loss
CA	12%	($1.68)	41%	$7.11	($7.77)
CO	9%	$6.12	71%	$10.97	($3.80)
MI	9%	$3.59	53%	$10.33	($4.84)
OF	22%	$2.61	46%	$12.06	($5.90)
SP	29%	$1.96	52%	$8.19	($7.06)
RP	19%	$0.35	50%	$11.33	($10.10)

These results bear out the danger of leaving catchers to the end; only catchers returned negative value. Corner infielder returns say leaving a 1B or 3B open until late.

Age	Pct.of tot	Avg Val	%Profit	Avg Prof	Avg Loss
< 25	15%	($0.88)	33%	$8.25	($8.71)
25-29	48%	$2.59	56%	$11.10	($8.38)
30-35	28%	$2.06	44%	$10.39	($5.04)
35+	9%	$2.15	41%	$8.86	($5.67)

The practice of speculating on younger players—mostly rookies—in the end game was a washout. Part of the reason was that those that even made it to the end game were often the long-term or fringe type. Better prospects were typically drafted earlier.

	Pct.of tot	Avg Val	%Profit	Avg Prof	Avg Loss
Injury rehabs	20%	$3.63	36%	$15.07	($5.65)

One in five end-gamers were players coming back from injury. While only 36% of them were profitable, the healthy ones returned a healthy profit. The group's losses were small, likely because they weren't healthy enough to play.

Realistic expectations of $1 endgamers *(Patrick Davitt)*

Many fantasy articles insist leagues are won or lost with $1 batters, because "that's where the profits are." But are they?

A 2011 analysis showed that when considering $1 players in deep leagues, managing $1 endgamers should be more about minimizing losses than fishing for profit. In the cohort of batters projected $0 to -$5, 82% returned losses, based on a $1 bid. Two-thirds of the projected $1 cohort returned losses. In addition, when considering $1 players, speculate on speed.

Advanced Draft Strategies

Stars & Scrubs v. Spread the Risk

Stars & Scrubs (S&S): A Rotisserie auction strategy in which a roster is anchored by a core of high priced stars and the remaining positions filled with low-cost players.

Spread the Risk (STR): An auction strategy in which available dollars are spread evenly among all roster slots.

Both approaches have benefits and risks. An experiment was conducted in 2004 whereby a league was stocked with four teams assembled as S&S, four as STR and four as a control group. Rosters were then frozen for the season.

The Stars & Scrubs teams won all three ratio categories. Those deep investments ensured stability in the categories that are typically most difficult to manage. On the batting side, however, S&S teams amassed the least amount of playing time, which in turn led to bottom-rung finishes in HRs, RBIs and Runs.

One of the arguments for the S&S approach is that it is easier to replace end-game losers (which, in turn, may help resolve the playing time issues). Not only is this true, but the results of this experiment show that replacing those bottom players is critical to success.

The Spread the Risk teams stockpiled playing time, which in turn led to strong finishes in many of the counting stats, including clear victories in RBIs, wins and strikeouts. This is a key tenet in drafting philosophy; we often say that the team that compiles the most ABs will undoubtedly be among the top teams in RBI and Runs.

The danger is on the pitching side. More innings did yield more wins and Ks, but also destroyed ERA/WHIP.

So, what approach makes the most sense? **The optimal strategy might be to STR on offense and go S&S with your pitching staff.** STR buys more ABs, so you immediately position yourself well in four of the five batting categories. On pitching, it might be more advisable to roster a few core arms, though that immediately elevates your risk exposure. Admittedly, it's a balancing act, which is why we need to pay more attention to risk analysis and look closer at strategies like the RIMA Plan and Portfolio3.

The LIMA Plan

The LIMA Plan is a strategy for Rotisserie leagues (though the underlying concept can be used in other formats) that allows you to target high skills pitchers at very low cost, thereby freeing up dollars for offense. LIMA is an acronym for Low Investment Mound Aces, and also pays tribute to Jose Lima, a $1 pitcher in 1998 who exemplified the power of the strategy. In a $260 league:

1. Budget a maximum of $60 for your pitching staff.
2. Allot no more than $30 of that budget for acquiring saves. In 5x5 leagues, it is reasonable to forego saves at the draft (and acquire them during the season) and re-allocate this $30 to starters ($20) and offense ($10).
3. Ignore ERA. Draft only pitchers with:
   - Command ratio (K/BB) of 2.5 or better.
   - Strikeout rate of 7.0 or better.
   - Expected home run rate of 1.0 or less.

4. Draft as few innings as your league rules will allow. This is intended to manage risk. For some game formats, this should be a secondary consideration.

5. Maximize your batting slots. Target batters with:
   • Contact rate of at least 80%
   • Walk rate of at least 10%
   • PX or Spd level of at least 100

Spend no more than $29 for any player and try to keep the $1 picks to a minimum.

The goal is to ace the batting categories and carefully pick your pitching staff so that it will finish in the upper third in ERA, WHIP and saves (and Ks in 5x5), and an upside of perhaps 9th in wins. In a competitive league, that should be enough to win, and definitely enough to finish in the money. Worst case, you should have an excess of offense available that you can deal for pitching.

The strategy works because it better allocates resources. Fantasy leaguers who spend a lot for pitching are not only paying for expected performance, they are also paying for better defined roles—#1 and #2 rotation starters, ace closers, etc.—which are expected to translate into more IP, wins and saves. But roles are highly variable. A pitcher's role will usually come down to his skill and performance; if he doesn't perform, he'll lose the role.

The LIMA Plan says, let's invest in skill and let the roles fall where they may. In the long run, better skills should translate into more innings, wins and saves. And as it turns out, pitching skill costs less than pitching roles do.

In *snake draft leagues,* don't start drafting starting pitchers until Round 10. In *shallow mixed leagues,* the LIMA Plan may not be necessary; just focus on the BPI benchmarks. In *simulation leagues,* build your staff around BPI benchmarks.

Variations on the LIMA Plan

LIMA Extrema: Limit your total pitching budget to only $30, or less. This can be particularly effective in shallow leagues where LIMA-caliber starting pitcher free agents are plentiful during the season.

SANTANA Plan: Instead of spending $30 on saves, you spend it on a starting pitcher anchor. In 5x5 leagues where you can reasonably punt saves at the draft table, allocating those dollars to a high-end LIMA-caliber starting pitcher can work well as long as you pick the right anchor.

One way to approach that selection is...

RIMA Plan: LIMA is based on optimal resource allocation. These days, however, no matter how good of a team you draft, player inconsistency, injuries and unexpected risk factors can wreak havoc with your season. The RIMA Plan adds the element of **RI**sk **MA**nagement.

Players are not risks by virtue of their price tags alone. A $35 Justin Verlander, for example, might be a very good buy since he is a healthy, stable commodity. But most LIMA drafters would not consider him because of the price.

The RIMA Plan involves setting up two pools of players. The first pool consists of those who meet the LIMA criteria. The second pool includes players with high Reliability grades. The set of players who appear in both pools are our prime draft targets.

We then evaluate the two pools further, integrating different levels of skill and risk.

RIMA was introduced in 2004; the specifics of the plan have since been assimilated into Portfolio3.

Total Control Drafting (TCD)

Part of the reason we play this game is the aura of "control," our ability to create a team of players we want and manage them to a title. We make every effort to control as many elements as possible, but in reality, the players that end up on our teams are largely controlled by the other owners. Their bidding affects your ability to roster the players you want. In a snake draft, the other owners control your roster even more. We are really only able to get the players we want within the limitations set by others.

However, an optimal roster can be constructed from a fanalytic assessment of skill and risk. We can create our teams from that "perfect player pool" and not be forced to roster players that don't fit our criteria. It's now possible. It's just a matter of taking Total Control.

Why this makes sense

1. Our obsession with projected player values is holding us back. If a player on your draft list is valued at $20 and you agonize when the bidding hits $23, odds are about two chances in three that he could really earn anywhere from $15 to $25. What this means is, in some cases, and within reason, you should just pay what it takes to get the players you want.

2. There is no such thing as a bargain. Most of us *don't* just pay what it takes because we are always on the lookout for players who go under value. But we really don't know which players will cost less than they will earn because prices are still driven by the draft table. The concept of "bargain" assumes that we even know what a player's true value is. To wit: If we target a player at $23 and land him for $20, we might *think* we got a bargain. In reality, this player might earn anywhere from $19 to $26, making that $3 in perceived savings virtually irrelevant.

The point is, a "bargain" is defined by your particular marketplace at the time of your particular draft, not by any list of canned values, or an "expectation" of what the market value of any player might be. So any contention that TCD forces you to overpay for your players is false.

3. "Control" is there for the taking. Most owners are so focused on their own team that they really don't pay much attention to what you're doing. There are some exceptions, and bidding wars do happen, but in general, other owners will not provide that much resistance.

How it's done

1. Create your optimal draft pool.
2. Get those players.

Start by identifying which players will be draftable based on the LIMA or Portfolio3 criteria. Then, at the draft, your focus has to be on your roster only. When it's your bid opener, toss a player you need at about 50%-75% of your projected value. Bid aggressively. Forget about bargain-hunting; just pay what you need to pay. Of course, don't spend $40 for a $25 player, but it's okay to exceed your projected value within reason.

Mix up the caliber of openers. Instead of tossing out a Miguel Cabrera at $35 in the first round, toss out a Kyle Seager at $8. *Wise Guy Baseball*'s Gene McCaffrey suggests tossing all lower-end players early, which makes sense. It helps you bottom-fill your roster with players most others won't chase early, and you can always build the top end of your roster with players others toss out.

Another good early tactic is to gauge the market value of scarce commodities with a $19 opener for Craig Kimbrell (saves) or a $29 opener for Ben Revere (stolen bases).

At the end of the draft, you may have rostered 23 players who could have been purchased at somewhat lower cost. It's tough to say. Those extra dollars likely won't mean much anyway; in fact, you might have just left them on the table. TCD almost ensures that you spend all your money.

In the end, it's okay to pay a slight premium to make sure you get the players with the highest potential to provide a good return on your investment. It's no different than the premium you'd pay to get the last valuable shortstop, or for the position flexibility a player like Emilio Bonafacio provides. With TCD, you're just spending those extra dollars up front on players with high skill and low risk.

The best part is that you take more control of your destiny. You build your roster with what you consider are the best assemblage of players. You keep the focus on your team. And you don't just roster whatever bargains the rest of the table leaves for you, because a bargain is just a fleeting perception of value we have in March.

The Portfolio3 Plan

The previously discussed strategies have had important roles in furthering our potential for success. The problem is that they all take a broad-stroke approach to the draft. The $35 first round player is evaluated and integrated into the plan in the same way that the end-gamer is. But each player has a different role on your team by virtue of his skill set, dollar value, position and risk profile. When it comes to a strategy for how to approach a specific player, one size does not fit all.

We need some players to return fair value more than others. When you spend $40 on a player, you are buying the promise of putting more than 15% of your budget in the hands of 4% of your roster. By contrast, the $1 players are easily replaceable. If you're in a snake draft league, you know that a first-rounder going belly-up is going to hurt you far more than a 23rd round bust.

We rely on some players for profit more than others. Those first-rounders are not where we are likely going to see the most profit potential. The $10-$20 players are likely to return more pure dollar profit; the end-gamers are most likely to return the highest profit percentage.

We can afford to weather more risk with some players than with others. Since those high-priced early-rounders need to return at least fair value, we cannot afford to take on excessive risk. Since we need more profit potential from the lower priced, later-round picks, that means opening up our tolerance for risk more with those players.

Players have different risk profiles based solely on what roster spot they are going to fill. Catchers are more injury prone. A closer's value is highly dependent on fickle managerial whim. These types of players are high risk even if they have the best skills on the planet. That needs to affect their draft price or draft round.

For some players, the promise of providing a scarce skill, or productivity at a scarce position, may trump risk. Not always, but sometimes. At minimum, we need to be open to the possibility. The determining factor is usually price. A late round, below value player is not something you pass up, even with a horrible Reliability Grade.

In the end, we need a way to integrate all these different types of players, roles and needs. We need to put some form to the concept of a diversified draft approach. Thus:

The **Portfolio3 Plan** provides a three-tiered approach to the draft. Just like most folks prefer to diversify their stock portfolio, P3 advises to diversify your roster with three different types of players. Depending upon the stage of the draft (and budget constraints in auction leagues), P3 uses a different set of rules for each tier that you'll draft from. The three tiers are:

1. Core Players
2. Mid-Game Players
3. End-Game Players

TIER 1: CORE PLAYERS

Roster			BATTERS		PITCHERS	
Slots	Budget	Rel	Ct	PX or Spd	Rel	BPV
5-8	Max $160	BBB	80%	100 / 100	BBB	75

These are the players who will provide the foundation to your roster. These are your prime stat contributors and where you will invest the largest percentage of your budget. In snake drafts, these are the names you pick in the early rounds. There is no room for risk here. Given their price tags, there is usually little potential for profit. The majority of your core players should be batters.

The above chart shows general roster goals. In a snake draft, you need to select core-caliber players in the first 5-8 rounds. In an auction, any player purchased for $20 or more should meet the Tier 1 filters.

The filters are not strict, but they are important, so you should stick to them as best as possible. An 80% contact rate ensures that your batting average category is covered. PX and Spd ensure that you draft players with a minimum league average power or speed. On the pitching side, a BPV of 75 ensures that, if you must draft a pitcher in your core, it will be one with high-level skill. For both batters and pitchers, minimum reliability grades of BBB cover risk.

Since these are going to be the most important players on your roster, the above guidelines help provide a report card, of sorts, for your draft. For instance, if you leave the table with only three Tier 1 players, then you know you have likely rostered too much risk or not enough skill. If you manage to draft nine Tier 1 players, that doesn't necessarily mean you've got a better roster, just a better core. There still may be more work to do in the other tiers.

Tier 1 remains the most important group of players as they are the blue chips that allow you to take chances elsewhere. However, there can be some play within this group on the batting side.

The 80% contact rate is important to help protect the batting average category. However, with some care, you can roster a few BA studs to allow you the flexibility to take on some low-contact hitters who excel in other areas (typically power). The tactic would work like this... If you are short on Tier 1 players and have exhausted the pool of those who meet all the filters, you can work your way down the following list...

TIER 1 BATTERS

	Rel	Ct%	PX	or	Spd
Primary group	BBB	80%	100		100
Secondary	BBB	75%	110		110
Tertiary	BBB	70%	120		120

...knowing full well that, for every player you roster from these lower groups, you are putting your batting average at greater risk. You should only do this if you think the power/speed gains will sufficiently offset any BA shortfalls.

These two sub-groups are not fixed filters; they form a continuum. So if you have a player with a 78% contact rate, your PX/Spd requirement would probably be somewhere around 105. I would not go anywhere near a player with a contact rate less than 70%.

TIER 2: MID-GAME PLAYERS

Roster			BATTERS		PITCHERS	
Slots	Budget	Rel	Ct% or	PX or Spd	Rel	BPV
7-13	$50-$100	BBB	80%	100 100	BBB	50

All players must be less than $20
Batters must be projected for at least 500 AB

In an early 2008 column, I noted how fellow Tout combatant, Jason Grey, was consistently able to assemble offensive juggernauts by the singular tactic of accumulating massive amounts of often-cheap playing time. Intrinsic skill was irrelevant. On the offensive side, this makes sense.

Runs and RBI are only tangentially related to skill. If a player is getting 500 AB, he is likely going to provide positive value in those categories just from opportunity alone. And given that his team is seeing fit to give him those AB, he is probably also contributing somewhere else.

These players have value to us. And we can further filter this pool of full-timers who miss the P3 skills criteria by skimming off those with high REL grades.

There are two dangers in this line of thinking. First, it potentially puts the batting average category at risk. You don't want to accumulate bad AB; when you dig yourself into a hole in BA, it is the one category that is nearly impossible to dig out of. However, this just means we need to approach it tactically; if we decide to roster a Mark Reynolds, we must also roster a Martin Prado.

Second, this line of thinking assumes we can accurately project playing time. But if we focus on those players who are locked into firm roles, there is still a decent-sized pool to draw from.

Tier 2 is often where the biggest auction bargains tend to be found as the blue-chippers are already gone and owners are reassessing their finances. It is in that mid-draft lull where you can scoop up tons of profit. In a snake draft, these players should take you down to about round 16-18.

TIER 3: END-GAME PLAYERS

Roster			BATTERS			PITCHERS	
Slots	Budget	Rel	Ct%	PX or Spd		Rel	BPV
5-10	Up to $50	n/a	80%	100 100		n/a	75

All players must be less than $10

For some fantasy leaguers, the end game is when the beer is gone and you have to complete your roster with any warm body. In P3, these are gambling chips, but every end-gamer must provide the promise of upside. For that reason, the focus must remain on skill and conditional opportunity. P3 drafters should fill the majority of their pitching slots from this group.

By definition, end-gamers are typically high risk players, but risk is something you'll want to embrace here. You probably don't want a Yunel Escobar-type player at the end of the draft. His hight Reliability Grade would provide stability, but there is no upside, so there is little profit potential. This is where you need to look for profit so it is better here to ignore reliability; instead, take a few chances in your quest for those pockets of possible profit. If the player does not pan out, he can be easily replaced.

As such, a Tier 3 end-gamer should possess the BPI skill levels noted above, and...

- playing time upside as a back-up to a risky front-liner
- an injury history that has depressed his value
- solid skills demonstrated at some point in the past
- minor league potential even if he has been more recently a major league bust

Notes on draft implementation...

Auction leagues: Tier 1 player acquisition should be via the Total Control Drafting method. Simply, pay whatever it takes, within reason. Be willing to pay a small premium for the low risk and high skills combination.

Snake drafters will have choices in the first six rounds or so. There are no guarantees—a swing-pick seed might negate any chance for rostering some players—but at least there are options. If you miss out on the cream, you can either drop down and select a lower round player early, or relax the filters a bit to grab someone who might have higher value but perhaps greater risk.

Position scarcity: While we still promote the use of position scarcity in snake drafts, it may be more important to have solid foundation players in the early rounds.

Drafting pitchers early is still something we advise against. However, if you are going to grab a pitcher in the first six rounds, at least make sure it's a Tier 1 name. It is still a viable strategy to hold off on starting pitchers until as late as Round 10 or 11; however, if it's Round 7 and Cole Hamels is still sitting out there, by all means jump.

LIMA Plan: Although LIMA says no starting pitchers over $20, Tier 1 provides a few options where it would be okay to break the rules. You can adjust your $60 pitching budget up to accommodate, or downgrade saves targets.

Punting saves: Still viable, unless a Tier 1 closer falls into your lap. These are extremely rare commodities anyway.

Keeper leagues: When you decide upon your freeze list, you should be looking for two types of keepers—the best values and the most valuable players. Freezing a $15 James Shields is a no-brainer; where some drafters struggle is with the $25 Corey

Hart. Given that TCD says that we should be willing to pay a premium for Tier 1 players, any name on that list should be a freeze consideration.

Adding in the variable of potential draft inflation, you should be more flexible with the prices you'd be willing to freeze players at. For instance, if you currently own a $40 Miguel Cabrera, you might be tempted to throw him back. However, between draft inflation and the premium you should be willing to pay for a Tier 1 commodity, his real value could be well over $50.

The Mayberry Method

The Mayberry Method—named after the fictional TV village where life was simpler—is a player evaluation method that embraces the imprecision of the forecasting process and projects performance in broad strokes rather than with precise statistics.

MM reduces every player to a 7-character code. The format of the code is 5555AAA, where the first four characters describe elements of a player's skill on a scale of 0 to 5. The three alpha characters are our reliability grades (health, experience and consistency). The skills numerics are forward-looking; the alpha characters grade reliability based on past history.

Batting

The first character in the MM code measures a batter's power skills. It is assigned using the following table:

PX	MM	Rough HR Approx
0 - 49	0	0
50 - 79	1	up to 10
80 - 99	2	up to 20
100 - 119	3	up to 30
120 - 159	4	up to 40
160+	5	up to 50+

The second character measures a batter's speed skills.

RSpd*	MM	Rough SB Approx
0-39	0	0
40-59	1	up to 10
60-79	2	up to 20
80-99	3	up to 30
100-119	4	up to 40
120+	5	up to 50+

Note change: RSpd = Spd x (SBO + SB%). See essay on page 67.

The third character measures expected batting average.

xBA	MM
.000 - .239	0
.240 - .254	1
.255 - .269	2
.270 - .284	3
.285 - .299	4
.300+	5

The fourth character measures playing time.

Role	PA	MM
Potential full-timers	450+	5
Mid-timers	250-449	3
Fringe/bench	100-249	1
Non-factors	0-99	0

An overall MM batting score is calculated as:

MM Score = (PX score + Spd score + xBA score + PA score)
x PA score

The highest score you can get is 100, so this becomes an easy scale to evaluate.

Pitching

The first character in the pitching MM code measures xERA, which captures a pitcher's overall ability and is a proxy for ERA, and even WHIP.

xERA	MM
4.81+	0
4.41 - 4.80	1
4.01 - 4.40	2
3.61 - 4.00	3
3.21 - 3.60	4
3.20-	5

The second character measures strikeout ability.

K/9	MM
0.0 - 4.9	0
5.0 - 5.9	1
6.0 - 6.9	2
7.0 - 7.9	3
8.0 - 8.9	4
9.0+	5

The third character measures saves potential.

Description	Saves est.	MM
No hope for saves; starting pitchers	0	0
Speculative closer	1-9	1
Closer in a pen with alternatives	10-24	2
Frontline closer with firm bullpen role	25+	3

The fourth character measures playing time.

Role	IP	MM
Potential #1-2 starters	180+	5
Potential #3-4 starters	130-179	3
#5 starters/swingmen	70-129	1
Relievers	0-69	0

An overall MM pitching score is calculated as:

MM Score =
((xERA score x 2) + K/9 score + Saves score + IP score)
x (IP score + Saves score)

Integrating Mayberry and Portfolio3

Mayberry scores can be used as a proxy for the BPI filters in the Portfolio3 chart. Pretty much all you need to remember is the number "3."

Roster			BATTERS					PITCHERS	
Tr	Slots	Budget	Rel	PA	xBA	PX or RSpd		Rel	xERA
1	5-8	Max $160	BBB	n/a	3	3	3	BBB	3
2	7-13	$50-$100	BBB	5	3 or	3	3	BBB	2
3	5-10	Up to $50	n/a	n/a	3	3	3	n/a	3

The conversion to Mayberry is pretty straightforward. On the batting side, xBA provides a good proxy for contact rate (since ct% drives xBA), and PX and Spd stay. For pitching, xERA easily replaces BPV.

Mayberry's broad-stroke approach significantly opens up the draftable player pool, particularly for Tier 3 sleeper types. About 25% more players will be draft-worthy using these filters.

Targets

For roster budgeting purposes, here are targets for several standard leagues:

BATTING	PX	RSpd	xBA	PA	MM
12-team mixed	41	28	40	66	840
15-team mixed	41	26	39	64	790
12-team AL/NL	37	23	32	54	600
PITCHING	**ERA**	**K***	**Sv**	**IP**	**MM**
12-team mixed	23	33	7	29	460
15-team mixed	20	30	6	30	430
12-team AL/NL	17	27	5	25	320

* Make sure the majority of these points come from starting pitchers.

In-Season Analyses

The efficacy of streaming *(John Burnson)*

In leagues that allow weekly or daily transactions, many owners flit from hot player to hot player. But published dollar values don't capture this traffic—they assume that players are owned from April to October. For many leagues, this may be unrealistic.

We decided to calculate these "investor returns." For each week, we identified the top players by one statistic—BA for hitters, ERA for pitchers—and took the top 100 hitters and top 50 pitchers. We then said that, at the end of the week, the #1 player was picked up (or already owned) by 100% of teams, the #2 player was picked up or owned by 99% of teams, and so on, down to the 100th player, who was on 1% of teams. (For pitchers, we stepped by 2%.) Last, we tracked each player's performance in the next week, when ownership matters.

We ran this process anew for every week of the season, tabulating each player's "investor returns" along the way. If a player was owned by 100% of teams, then we awarded him 100% of his performance. If the player was owned by half the teams, we gave him half his performance. If he was owned by no one (that is, he was not among the top players in the prior week), his performance was ignored. A player's cumulative stats over the season was his investor return.

The results...

- 60% of pitchers had poorer investor returns, with an aggregate ERA 0.40 higher than their true ERA.
- 55% of batters had poorer investor returns, but with an aggregate batting average virtually identical to the true BA.

Sitting stars and starting scrubs *(Ed DeCaria)*

In setting your pitching rotation, conventional wisdom suggests sticking with trusted stars despite difficult matchups. But does this hold up? And can you carefully start inferior pitchers against weaker opponents? Here are the ERA's posted by varying skilled pitchers facing a range of different strength offenses:

	OPPOSING OFFENSE (RC/G)				
Pitcher (ERA)	5.25+	5.00	4.25	4.00	<4.00
3.00-	3.46	3.04	3.04	2.50	2.20
3.50	3.98	3.94	3.44	3.17	2.87
4.00	4.72	4.57	3.96	3.66	3.24
4.50	5.37	4.92	4.47	4.07	3.66
5.00+	6.02	5.41	5.15	4.94	4.42

Recommendations:

1. Never start below replacement-level pitchers.
2. Always start elite pitchers.
3. Other than that, never say never or always.

Playing matchups can pay off when the difference in opposing offense is severe.

Two-start pitcher weeks *(Ed DeCaria)*

A two-start pitcher is a prized possession. But those starts can mean two DOMinant outings, two DISasters, or anything else in between, as shown by these results:

PQS Pair	% Weeks	ERA	WHIP	Win/Wk	K/Wk
DOM-DOM	20%	2.53	1.02	1.1	12.0
DOM-AVG	28%	3.60	1.25	0.8	9.2
AVG-AVG	14%	4.44	1.45	0.7	6.8
DOM-DIS	15%	5.24	1.48	0.6	7.9
AVG-DIS	17%	6.58	1.74	0.5	5.7
DIS-DIS	6%	8.85	2.07	0.3	5.0

Weeks that include even one DISaster start produce terrible results. Unfortunately, avoiding such disasters is much easier in hindsight. But what is the actual impact of this decision on the stat categories?

ERA and WHIP: When the difference between opponents is extreme, inferior pitchers can actually be a better percentage play. This is true both for one-start pitchers and two-start pitchers, and for choosing inferior one-start pitchers over superior two-start pitchers.

Strikeouts per Week: Unlike the two rate stats, there is a massive shift in the balance of power between one-start and two-start pitchers in the strikeout category. Even stars with easy one-start matchups can only barely keep pace with two-start replacement-level arms in strikeouts per week.

Wins per week are also dominated by the two-start pitchers. Even the very worst two-start pitchers will earn a half of a win on average, which is the same rate as the very best one-start pitchers.

The bottom line: If strikeouts and wins are the strategic priority, use as many two-start weeks as the rules allow, even if it means using a replacement-level pitcher with two tough starts instead of a mid-level arm with a single easy start. But if ERA and/or WHIP management are the priority, two-start pitchers can be very powerful, as a single week might impact the standings by over 1.5 points in ERA/WHIP, positively or negatively.

Consistency *(Dylan Hedges)*

Few things are as valuable to head-to-head league success as filling your roster with players who can produce a solid baseline of stats, week in and week out. In traditional leagues, while consistency is not as important—all we care about are aggregate numbers—filling your team with consistent players can make roster management easier.

Consistent batters have good plate discipline, walk rates and on base percentages. These are foundation skills. Those who add power to the mix are obviously more valuable, however, the ability to hit home runs consistently is rare.

Consistent pitchers demonstrate similar skills in each outing; if they also produce similar results, they are even more valuable.

We can track consistency but predicting it is difficult. Many fantasy leaguers try to predict a batter's hot or cold streaks, or individual pitcher starts, but that is typically a fool's errand. The best we can do is find players who demonstrate seasonal consistency over time; in-season, we want to manage players and consistency tactically.

Consistency in points leagues *(Bill Macey)*
Previous research has demonstrated that week-to-week statistical consistency is important for Rotisserie-based head-to-head play. But one can use the same foundation in points-based games. A study showed that not only do players with better skills post more overall points in this format, but that the format caters to consistent performances on a week-to-week basis, even after accounting for differences in total points scored and playing-time.

Therefore, when drafting your batters in points-based head-to-head leagues, ct% and bb% make excellent tiebreakers if you are having trouble deciding between two players with similarly projected point totals. Likewise, when rostering pitchers, favor those who tend not to give up home runs.

Other Diamonds

Cellar value
The dollar value at which a player cannot help but earn more than he costs. Always profit here.

Crickets
The sound heard when someone's opening draft bid on a player is also the only bid.

Scott Elarton List
Players you drop out on when the bidding reaches $1.

End-game wasteland
Home for players undraftable in the deepest of leagues, who stay in the free agent pool all year. It's the place where even crickets keep quiet when a name is called at the draft.

FAAB Forewarnings
1. Spend early and often.
2. Emptying your budget for one prime league-crosser is a tactic that should be reserved for the desperate.
3. If you chase two rabbits, you will lose them both.

Fantasy Economics 101
The market value for a player is generally based on the aura of past performance, not the promise of future potential. Your greatest advantage is to leverage the variance between market value and real value.

Fantasy Economics 102
The variance between market value and real value is far more important than the absolute accuracy of any individual player projection.

Hope
A commodity that routinely goes for $5 over value at the draft table.

JA$G
Just Another Dollar Guy.

Professional Free Agent (PFA)
Player whose name will never come up on draft day but will always end up on a roster at some point during the season as an injury replacement.

RUM pick
A player who is rosterable only as a Reserve, Ultra or Minors pick.

Standings Vantage Points
First Place: It's lonely at the top, but it's comforting to look down upon everyone else.
Sixth Place: The toughest position to be in is mid-pack at dump time.
Last Place in April: The sooner you fall behind, the more time you will have to catch up.
Last Place, Yet Again: If you can't learn to do something well, learn to enjoy doing it badly.

Mike Timlin List
Players who you are unable to resist drafting even though they have burned you multiple times in the past.

Seasonal Assessment Standard
If you still have reason to be reading the boxscores during the last weekend of the season, then your year has to be considered a success.

The Three Cardinal Rules for Winners
If you cherish this hobby, you will live by them or die by them...
1. Revel in your success; fame is fleeting.
2. Exercise excruciating humility.
3. 100% of winnings must be spent on significant others.

"Normal" Production Variance

by Patrick Davitt

Early each season, we are consistently warned to wait until we have enough trials—a big enough sample of ABs or IP—to "understand" what is *really* happening with player performance. Unfortunately, nobody ever says how many trials provide a big enough sample to make decisions.

We're told, for instance, that we should wait until mid-May or even late May to start making decisions—presumably because the samples are big enough by then. But they're not.

At the end of May, a full-time player will have 200 or so AB or 70 or so IP—still short of a sample large enough to feel confident that we understand a player's "normal" performance level.

And there's a second problem, caused by the arbitrariness of what we call a "season." Even when we *do* have enough trials to feel confident we understand the player's normal performance in a 150-game span, there is still variation among the player's many 150-game spans. That is, we can be very sure a player's "normal" BA is .300, but in any particular 150-game span, his actual BA could be far better—or far worse. Similarly, even if we are very confident a batter will hit 30 HR per 150-game season, his actual performance in any particular 150-game period will be sometimes far better —or, again, far worse.

To understand the range of "normal" performance, we looked at two active players with 10,000 or more ABs, Derek Jeter and Alex Rodriguez of the Yankees, and a pitcher with more than 10,000 batters faced, Mark Buehrle. Ten thousand trials is a number often cited in probability lessons as the level at which we can be confident that the "noise" in a study has been worked out.

(Using 10,000 ABs introduces other issues, chiefly aging effects, but bear with us.)

We compiled these players' game-by-game results from the starts of their careers through the end of 2011, ignoring the handful of ABs/IP in their first seasons in MLB.

Batting Average: We calculated each batter's career BA from his first AB to the AB at any point in his career. We also calculated his BA on a rolling 150-game basis, so at any point in his career, we knew his BA for the previous 150 games including that game. Then we plotted the two results on graphs. Jeter's career BA graph:

After some large variations early on, Jeter's career BA (the dark line) settles into a relatively narrow range. Trials pile up, and his "true" or "normal" BA level is established between .310 and .320.

But observe Jeter's BA over the past 150 games at every point in his career (gray line). Even in the latter half of the time period, when his career BA has settled into the relatively narrow range ~.315, his 150-game BA still swings wildly from lows around .255 to highs around .350! And in fact, when we review Jeter's seasonal BAs from the midpoint of his career in 2004, we see a low of .270 in 2010, and a high of .343 in 2006.

The important idea is that *all of these results are valid* for Jeter's ability. To paraphrase Ron Shandler, in a 600-AB season, the difference between .343 and .270 is less than two hits a week. Because a "season" is an arbitrarily chosen set of 150 games containing relatively few ABs, a "season" has the wide range of outcomes we see above.

Repeating the exercise for Alex Rodriguez, we found a similar pattern. Even as his career BA settled into a relatively narrow range around .310, his rolling 150-game BAs swung back and forth from around .260 to as high as .330. Again, any of these performances must be considered "normal" for Rodriguez.

Home Runs: We also looked at Rodriguez, a noted power hitter, for his HR performance over his career, using HR/150 games as our career metric and actual HR per previous 150 games as the performance metric.

His shapes are different than with BA. Rodriguez starts his career at a relatively low HR/150 level, then brings it up into the low 40s for many years before settling into a slow decline that has pulled his career rate back to barely over 40.

As with Jeter, there were variations over rolling 150-game periods. After his big, probably steroid-aided 50+ peaks near mid-career, his HR/150 bounces back and forth between the mid-30s and the high 40s. And his actual seasonal levels fall into about that same range. Owners of A-Rod in the low-30-HR seasons bemoaned his "subpar" performance in those years, but they shouldn't have—all those results were within Rodriguez's "normal" range of HR performance.

Pitching: We also adapted this research method to examine the career track of an established "quality" pitcher, looking at his career performance on a game-by-game basis, while

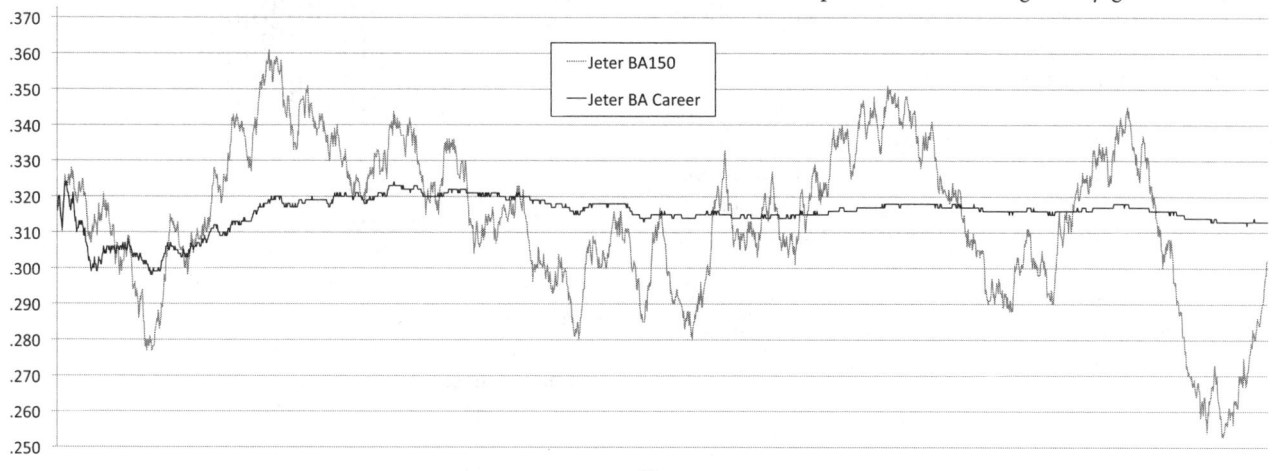

simultaneously looking at the variation in that performance over a shorter 24-start period. We chose Mark Buehrle, a consistent SP whose career ERA/WHIP marks through 2011 were 3.82/1.28.

But those career marks were amassed over 11 years and 362 starts, which has given ratios a chance to settle and lock in. Over shorter terms, his ERA and WHIP have been subject to wide swings.

Buehrle's ERA over his career, from his 24th start through to the end of 2011, settled quite quickly at his career level and varied minimally, from 2.96 to 3.86, with two-thirds of his ERA in a 0.36-run range from 3.57 to 3.93.

But his ERA for all the 24-start periods during his career showed much greater variation, from a low of 2.60 to a high of 6.08, with two-thirds of his results in a 1.24-run range from 3.20-4.44. You can't really expect a career-level ERA in 24 starts; you can only expect a result in that 24-start range (and even then, outliers are possible in both directions).

Similarly, Buehrle's career WHIP ranged from 1.00 to 1.28, with two-thirds of his results between 1.18 and 1.30. But again, his 24-start range was much wider, from 0.94-1.56, with two-thirds in the range 1.18-1.40.

Conclusion

Given this analysis, it seems truly pointless to make player moves based on two weeks' worth of stats at the start of a season. Jeter's 12-game BAs have ranged from .098 to .548. It's probably fairly near to pointless to make decisions based on two months' worth as well. Jeter's 50-game BAs have been as low as .202 and as high as .411. Rodriguez' BA and HR rate show similar wide variance.

On the other hand, later in the year, it might be worth a calculated risk to bet on catching the good side of the variance. You might not want to acquire a Buehrle when you know you might get a 6.08/1.40 that is still within the greater part of both ranges.

But don't be fooled by career marks, for good or ill. As the number of games decreases, the range of possibilities grows. If you were to acquire Buehrle with only 11 starts left, his 11-start ERA has been as low as 1.74 and his WHIP as low as 1.00. That's the good outcome. You could also get a 7.49/1.75, the worst totals for 11-start runs.

Short-term performance is necessarily a crapshoot. As we work on these data, we hope to be able to figure out what makes a pitcher (or a batter) a better bet to finish within a more defined range.

Until then, be willing to play the range.

Of course, as owners, we need to be aware of external circumstances that could have legitimate effects on performance—injury being the main one, but also age-related change, personal circumstance (divorce, family illness, and so on), park change, mechanical change through coaching, etc. And younger, less experienced players are even more prone to wide outcome swings!

Absent those external influences, though, be very cautious about jumping to conclusions about roster moves. Especially with players who have long track records, remember that "normal" performance includes a wide range of outcomes.

Do Doubles Turn into HR?

by Bill Macey

Whether it was Brady Anderson's 50 HR in 1996 or Jose Bautista's 54 HR in 2010, these types of breakout home run seasons make many a fantasy championship. As such, we search long and hard for these black swans, squinting as needed, for some sign that a player is poised to enjoy a power breakout the following year.

A statistic frequently used to fuel speculation is the number of doubles a player hits. There is often conjecture that a player with a lot of doubles in one year might turn them some of them into HR the next. But does this actually happen with reliable frequency?

Before we delve directly into this question, let's begin by looking at the frequency of both doubles and home runs over the ten year period, 2002-2011. The analysis in this article examines rates on a per-AB basis rather than using raw totals so as to adjust for differences in playing time. As shown below, we see that the rates were quite stable for both 2B/AB and HR/AB on a league-wide basis over this time frame:

Year	2B/AB	HR/AB
2002	5.3%	3.1%
2003	5.4%	3.2%
2004	5.4%	3.3%
2005	5.4%	3.1%
2006	5.6%	3.3%
2007	5.6%	3.0%
2008	5.5%	3.0%
2009	5.4%	3.1%
2010	5.2%	2.9%
2011	5.2%	2.8%
Average	*5.4%*	*3.1%*

The distribution of 2B/AB over the ten-year period approximated a normal distribution, with most of the observations centered around the median, but the distribution of HR/AB was skewed towards lower rates:

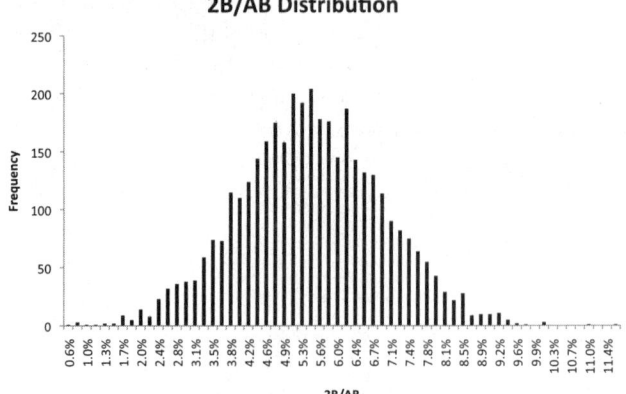

To examine whether players with high rates of doubles in Year One hit more HR in Year Two, we looked at the players in the highest quartile of observations—those with 2B/AB rates greater or equal to 6.4% (which is approximately 35 doubles in a full 550 AB season)—to see how they performed in the following year. For this, and all subsequent analysis, we only considered seasons with at least 150 AB.

	2B/AB	HR/AB
Year 1 Avg	7.1%	3.6%
Year 2 Avg	5.9%	3.5%
Change	*-1.2%*	*-0.1%*

On average for this sample of players, we see that their high rate of doubles regressed substantially in the second year, albeit remaining above the long-term league average of 5.4%. Their average HR rate remained virtually unchanged, at a rate also above the long-term league average rate.

We next looked at the sample of players who had both a high doubles rate and a low HR rate (less than 1.6% HR/AB)—were these players more likely to enjoy a HR bounce in the subsequent year?

	2B/AB	HR/AB
Year 1 Avg	7.1%	1.1%
Year 2 Avg	5.3%	1.8%
Change	*-1.8%*	*0.7%*

When you look at the high doubles, low-HR outliers, they gave back even more of their doubles as compared to the larger sample; their 2B/AB rate regressed to just below the league average rate. However, some of these doubles did seem to turn into HR as their HR/AB rate increased by a noticeable amount. Note, however, that their improved HR/AB rate still trailed the league average by more than one HR per 100 AB.

(It's worth noting that we analyzed the above scenarios at more extreme 2B/AB rates but found no appreciable difference in the results.)

As an alternative means of looking at 2B/AB as a leading indicator of HR power, we expanded our analysis to consider players whose 2B/AB rates improved markedly from one year to the next, regardless of whether the first year rate was high or not. Specifically, we examined players whose 2B/AB rate increased by one percentage point or more.

We identified a sample of 483 players whose 2B/AB rate increased by at least 1% from Year 1 to Year 2 and measured their performance in Year 3. Because we're restricting ourselves to outliers, the average increase in 2B/AB for this cohort from Year 1 to Year 2 was high at 2.1 percentage points.

Consistent with the results presented above, most (78% of the 483) gave back some of those gains; the average decline in 2B/AB in Year 3 was 1.1%. Unfortunately, it does not appear that these extra doubles in Year 2 develop into HR in the third year - the average HR/AB rate dropped by 0.3% from Year 2 to Year 3. There was also a negative correlation between the rate changes between the years: the greater the gain in 2B/AB from Year 1 to Year 2, the greater the drop in 2B/AB from Year 2 to Year 3.

All taken together, it seems that a reversion to the mean is driving these results more than any power growth augured by high 2B/AB rates. Let's take one last cut of the data to verify: for those batters whose 2B/AB rate increased and their HR/AB rate decreased between Years 1 and 2, does their HR/AB rate bounce back again Year 3?

There were 185 players in the subsample above whose HR/AB rate decreased by 0.5 percentage points or more from Year 1 to Year 2. Amongst that sample, 104 (56%) posted higher HR/AB rates in Year 3, but the average increase for the sample of 185 was a negligible 0.1%. It appears that the gravity principle is strong at work here and that it is much easier for a player's performance to decline than improve.

Conclusion

Our search to see whether doubles turn into HR found little support for the theory. However, we did learn:

- Batters with high doubles rates also tend to hit more HR/AB than the league average; oddly, they are unable to sustain the high 2B/AB rate but do sustain their higher HR/AB rates.
- Batters with high 2B/AB rates and low HR/AB rates are more likely to see HR gains in the following year, but those rates will still typically trail the league average.
- Batters who experience a surge in 2B/AB typically give back most of those gains in the following year without any corresponding gain in HR.

ERA/xERA Variance

by Matt Cederholm

This study asks two questions: How much can you rely on ERA/xERA variance in making roster decisions? And, can we expect a pitcher's luck to reverse over the second half of a season?

Over a five-year period (2007-11), we compared the first-half performances of pitchers with large ERA/xERA variances to their second-half performance. Starters needed to have 65 IP or more in both halves and relievers needed 25 IP or more to be included. We analyzed starters and relievers independently, as relief pitchers' ERA tends to be more volatile.

Starters and relievers fit into very unlucky, unlucky, lucky, and very lucky. The first thing that stood out is how many more pitchers fall on the "lucky" side of things: 141 "unlucky" pitchers versus 528 "lucky." This could be an artifact of the break points used, but one very likely explanation is implied by juxtaposing the Whirlpool and Plexiglass Principles: while all players will regress to their career average level performance eventually, those who are underperforming may not be given the opportunity to do so.

The overall results were pretty much what we expected. Remember, "regression" in this piece means "results closer to expectations" and not simply "got worse," as it is often used.

Starting Pitchers

Very Unlucky (ERA 1.5 or more greater than xERA; 15 total)

Average Improvement (lower ERA)	1.82	
Improved by 2 or more points	7	
Improved by 1 to 2 points	0	
Improved by 0.5 to 1 point	3	
Declined (ERA was higher)	2	
DNQ (not enough 2H innings to qualify)	3	(20%)

Unlucky (ERA 0.75-1.5 greater than xERA; 29 total)

Average Improvement (lower ERA)	1.20	
Improved by 2 or more points	4	
Improved by 1 to 2 points	4	
Improved by 0.5 to 1 point	3	
Declined (ERA was higher)	1	
DNQ (not enough 2H innings to qualify)	17	(59%)

Very Lucky (ERA 1.5 or more lower than xERA; 28 total)

Average Decline (higher ERA)	1.39	
Declined by 2 or more points	8	
Declined by 1 to 2 points	7	
Declined by 0.5 to 1 point	5	
Improved (ERA was lower)	4	
DNQ (not enough 2H innings to qualify)	4	(14%)

Lucky (ERA 0.75 to 1.5 lower than xERA; 120 total)

Average Decline (higher ERA)	0.98	
Declined by 2 or more points	19	
Declined by 1 to 2 points	33	
Declined by 0.5 to 1 point	24	
Improved (ERA was lower)	12	
DNQ (not enough 2H innings to qualify)	32	(27%)

Relievers

Very Unlucky (ERA 1.5 or more greater than xERA; 42 total)

Average Improvement (lower ERA)	2.34	
Improved by 2 or more points	9	
Improved by 1 to 2 points	0	
Improved by 0.5 to 1 point	5	
Declined (ERA was higher)	2	
DNQ (not enough 2H innings to qualify)	26	(62%)

Unlucky (ERA 0.75-1.5 greater than xERA; 55 total)

Average Improvement (lower ERA)	1.74	
Improved by 2 or more points	13	
Improved by 1 to 2 points	2	
Improved by 0.5 to 1 point	6	
Declined (ERA was higher)	8	
DNQ (not enough 2H innings to qualify)	26	(47%)

Very Lucky (ERA 1.5 or more lower than xERA; 192 total)

Average Decline (higher ERA)	1.55	
Declined by 2 or more points	57	
Declined by 1 to 2 points	38	
Declined by 0.5 to 1 point	11	
Improved (ERA was lower)	43	
DNQ (not enough 2H innings to qualify)	43	(22%)

Lucky (ERA 0.75 to 1.5 lower than xERA; 188 total)

Average Decline (higher ERA)	0.57	
Declined by 2 or more points	21	
Declined by 1 to 2 points	22	
Declined by 0.5 to 1 point	20	
Improved (ERA was lower)	66	
DNQ (not enough 2H innings to qualify)	59	(31%)

These results are pretty clear and every group performed as expected: the "lucky" pitchers had higher second-half ERAs, on average, and the "unlucky" had lower second-half ERAs, and the "very" unlucky/lucky pitchers showed greater regression than the moderately lucky/unlucky. Overall, there was a -0.56 correlation between pitcher's variances and the amount by which they regressed, and that was virtually identical for starters and relievers.

	% of "survivors" that regressed		
Group	Starters	Relievers	Overall
Very Lucky	83%	71%	73%
Lucky	86%	49%	64%
Unlucky	92%	72%	78%
Very Unlucky	83%	88%	86%
All "Very"	83%	73%	75%
All Moderate	87%	53%	66%

We can see that starters are more likely to turn things around than relievers, and that pitchers with extreme variances are more likely to turn things around than those with moderate variances. It's all worked out rather neatly, in fact.

Conclusions

First, we know that most pitchers with large first-half ERA/xERA variances will see regression towards their xERA in the second half, if they are allowed (and are able) to finish out the season. Starters seem to have a stronger regression tendency, which we would expect to see given the larger sample sizes (e.g., more innings pitched) relative to relievers.

We've also seen that there is substantial attrition among all types of pitchers, but those who are "unlucky" have a much higher rate. So while you can be confident that a pitcher underperforming his xERA will rebound in the second half, you need to be careful to analyze each situation and assess that pitcher's ability to hold on to his job long enough to see that regression come to fruition. Certainly, a string of strong appearances where a pitcher is demonstrating both health and competence should go a long way to helping you make those decisions. In those cases, the odds should be in your favor.

Predicting Stolen Base Breakouts

By Bob Berger

Teams that win fantasy titles often have players on their rosters who deliver more value than either their draft round or their auction price would predict. Often these are players who have breakouts in one or more scoring categories that were not anticipated. This research examines whether we can target players in drafts who have a possibility of returning significant profit in the SB category by developing a profile of players who have demonstrated a SB breakout in the past.

From 1990 to 2012 there were 424 player-seasons of 30 or more SBs. A total of 150 different players stole 30+ bases at least once during that time. This research focuses on the 40 players who had four or more 30+ SB seasons during this time because of their demonstrated consistency. These 40 players accounted for 54% of all 30+ seasons. Ichiro Suzuki was eliminated from the study because all of his experience before his first 30+ SB season was in Japan. By examining the pattern of performance of these players before they stole 30+ bases in a season, we may be able to develop a profile of what to look for in targeting potential SB breakout candidates.

For the purposes of this study, a SB breakout is defined as the first season a player steals 30 or more bases in the major leagues. This approach may be particularly valuable to those in deep keeper or dynasty leagues because the profile is based on players who consistently stole 30+ bases after their first time. Understanding the resulting profile also can provide a "watch list" for players who may be called up during the season, or who may take on increased playing time to target as a free agent pickup.

From 1990 to 2012 there were an average of eighteen 30+ SB performances per season in the majors, showing that a 30+ SB season is a scarce commodity. Of those 18, only six (on average each year) were contributed by players who stole 30+ for the first time. It would be particularly valuable if we could increase our chances of identifying the first-time 30+ performers, because it is likely that those with previous 30+ SB season histories will be fairly valued in a draft. Unanticipated sources of 30+ steals are potential profit.

Another reason 30 SBs is a good benchmark to define a breakout is that of the 40 players on our list, nine had no MLB SBs in the year before their first 30+ SB season, and less than a third had even 20 MLB SBs in the prior season. Usually, the first time a player steals 30+ bases it is a significant change in performance at the major league level.

The profile of our SB breakout candidates will include their age, professional experience, previous demonstrated ability to steal at the major league level (defined as having accumulated at least one steal at the major league level prior to the breakout season), previous three years' (combined major and minor league) stolen base averages, and a history of stealing at least 30 bases in one or more professional seasons. Examining these characteristics of the 40 players who have had four or more 30+ SB seasons from 1990 to 2012 shows the following:

- The first part of our profile is the age at which we can expect a breakout. The mean (and median) age of our 40 players is 24 years old, and 75% of them had their first 30+ SB season between the ages of 22 and 27.

- The next part of the profile is professional experience. The mean (and median) professional experience is five years, and 75% of them had between three and seven years of experience when they had their first 30+ SB season.

- Of the 40 players, 34 had stolen bases at the major league level before their first 30+ SB season, although as we've seen, less than a third of them had as many as 20 SBs in an MLB season before their first 30+ steal season.

- Another important factor in our profile is that the breakout candidate should have demonstrated the ability to steal 30+ bases in a year. All but one of the players (Derek Jeter) in our group stole 30+ at least once (and most multiple times) in the minors, or in their combined minor plus major league season totals. Fifty-nine per cent of the players on this list averaged 30+ steals (combined majors and minors) for the three years before they first reached the 30 steal plateau in the majors and 89% averaged at least 20+ steals combined during the three years prior.

Profile of the 30+ steal breakout candidate based on historical data

Age (22-27 yrs old)	75%
Professional experience (3-7 yrs)	75%
Previous steals at major league level	85%
Averaged 30+ steals previous 3 yrs (majors & minors combined)	59%
Averaged 20+ steals previous 3 yrs (majors & minor combined)	89%
Had at least one professional season with 30+ steals	98%

One way to use this steal breakout profile is to scan for players who meet all six criteria. Players who meet the 30+ steal average should be rated higher than those who only meet the 20+ average criterion. This list (this scan has resulted in about 8-10 players as breakout candidates each season) can then be compared to SB pre-season projections to see if any of the players are undervalued. A second scan could identify players who meet all but one of the criteria to assemble a lower priority list of players to acquire. This list can be used during the draft to target potential breakout steal sources, but also can be used throughout the season as roles change and minor leaguers who meet the criteria are called up.

Conclusion

By screening for players who have profiles similar to historical SB breakout candidates, we can increase our chances of identifying potential breakout candidates in future seasons. The stolen base breakout profile outlined in this article can be used for the draft and in-season for possible free agent acquisitions.

HctX for Pitchers

by Patrick Davitt

After BaseballHQ.com developed a new HctX metric for batters, combining their ability to put the ball into play and to hit the ball hard, it occurred to us that a similar measure might be useful for looking at pitchers.

So we calculated pitchers' HctX calculation, using Baseball Info Solutions' (BIS) hard-hit ball data from 2008-2011.

First, we calculated each pitcher's balls-in-play (BIP) percentage by subtracting his strikeouts and walks from his Total Batters Faced (TBF), then dividing the result by TBF minus walks.

Then we calculated each pitcher's individual hard-hit percentage (HH%), by summing his hard-hit GB, FB and LD and dividing by BIP.

Then we multiplied the two results, giving each pitcher's Hard-Hit Contact percentage (HCt%). Note that since we want pitchers to minimize BIP by getting strikeouts and to minimize hard contact, a lower HCt% is better than a higher one.

We repeated for all pitchers to get a game-wide HCt%.

And finally, we divided each player's HCt% into the MLB HCt%, to compare each individual with the game. We multiplied that result by 100 to normalize (like PX, a level of 100 is exactly average), and called the result Hard Contact Index, or HctX.

For this last part of the study, we looked only at 2011 pitchers, but included their results from previous seasons back to 2008.

Results: Overall

First, here are the MLB-wide results, capturing all pitchers in all years 2008-2011:

Year	HH%	BIP%	HCt%
2011	26%	81%	.214
2010	31%	82%	.257
2009	29%	82%	.236
2008	29%	82%	.236

The BIP% remained very stable, but we were surprised to see how widely the HH% fluctuated.

We also tested correlations of HctX with ERA and WHIP. We were expecting negative correlation—higher HctX scores tied to lower ERAs and WHIPs. And we did:

Year	ERA	WHIP
2011	-0.45	-0.37
2010	-0.04	-0.04
2009	-0.42	-0.29
2008	-0.32	-0.38

Not the strongest correlations you'll ever see, but enough to suggest that HctX is connected to these fundamental fantasy scoring units.

Results: Starters

When we sorted 2011 starting pitchers (100+ TBF) by 2011 HctX, we saw many of the usual suspects—Kershaw, Halladay, Verlander, Lincecum, Hernandez and Lee. But we were also surprised to see such names as Dana Eveland, Scott Feldman, Jonathon Niese and Matt Harrison. And we were positively shocked to note Dontrelle Willis and Kevin Millwood!

At the bottom were such starters as Kevins Correia and Slowey, Vin Mazzaro, and Andy Sonnanstine.

We also looked at the consistency of pitcher HctX over time, to see if HctX is a "skill" that a pitcher can own. Since the BIP% is the inverse of Dom, which we already accept is a skill, we are asking if the HH% component is stable.

It really wasn't among the starters. Their median percentage gap between high HctX and low was 25%, and only 20 had a high-low gap less than 10%. Even Halladay, widely and rightly regarded as a paragon of consistency, was above the median with a 26-point high-low difference.

That said, several starters were very consistent, with HctX scores near or above 100 throughout the period and high-low gaps under 10%. Those pitchers included Bud Norris, Josh Beckett, Tommy Hanson, Lee and Ricky Romero.

Results: Relievers

Not surprisingly, we saw a far wider range of HctX in relievers, with the top guy, Randy Choate, scoring a 302 and the bottom guy, J.P. Howell, a 68. Few RPs qualified because of the 100-BF minimum.

But many top RPs have strong track records over several years. Of the 61 pitcher-seasons among the top 22 relievers, only 16 were below 100, and 15 were above 160. And many pitchers with wide high-low variance have the gaps because they went from being great to being other-worldly, like Rivera's 89-point gap between his "low" of 146 and his high of 235.

Among the entire RP cohort, 26 had four years out of four with HctX scores over 100. That group included not only established closers like Rivera, Papelbon and Heath Bell, but potential closers like Jim Johnson, Grant Balfour and Brian Fuentes, and quality LIMA guys like George Sherrill, Darren Oliver, Evan Meek and Sean Marshall.

Conclusion

It stands to reason that we should be interested in pitchers who combine the ability to keep balls out of play via strikeouts with the ability get weaker contact when the ball is hit. The names on the high-HctX list (and the low) provide anecdotal evidence, while the solid correlation figures provide more scientific support.

Still, the correlation numbers show much more than HctX going on in pitchers' ERAs and WHIPs. And there's enough year-over-year inconsistency, especially among starters, to make us suspect that HctX will be of limited predictive use.

As one last quick investigation, we found 26 pitchers who had shown steady HctX improvement from 2008-11 and at least a 95 HctX in 2011. This identified pitchers getting stronger at it. Drafting from this list could have landed a savvy BHQ subscriber such gems as Oliver, Joel Hanrahan, Gio Gonzalez, Madison Bumgarner, Mat Latos, Doug Fister and R.A. Dickey.

Mind you, it could also have got that owner Philip Humber and Mark Melancon.

In future, we'll be looking at how pitchers' hard-hit FB percentages affect HR/FB ratio on the theory that we might be painting with too broad a brush to say that any pitcher with x amount of FB should have 0.1x HRs, because the FB count doesn't differentiate among hard-, soft- and medium-hit FBs.

Can Hitters Get Hot?
The Predictive Value of Ten-Game Hitting Streaks

By Bob Berger

Readers of the *Baseball Forecaster* are familiar with the guidance to be careful of coming to conclusions about a player's potential statistical output based on small sample sizes. We consistently caution owners not to make significant moves early in the season because we know that over-performers and under-performers tend to return to their documented baseline skill levels. Despite this counsel, how many fantasy team managers look at a player's recent performance to decide whom to bid on at FAAB time, or who to target in a trade? We examined hitting streaks of 10 games or longer in 2011 and 2012 and asked the question: "Can a 10-game hitting streak forecast improved longer-term BA performance?"

The research began with all 2011 and all 2012 hitting streaks of at least 10 games that started with more than 20 games left in the season. This allowed us to evaluate at least 10 games of performance after the initial 10-game streak.

We eliminated the following streaks:

- Those that began during April, reasoning that a streak that started in April did not have enough of a "pre-streak" baseline to fairly evaluate a player's BA performance.

- We kept only a player's first 10-game or higher streak of the season for those who had multiple streaks. For example, Starlin Castro (SS, CHC) had four streaks of 10 or more games in 2011 and we only used his first streak for the analysis.

This left a sample of 111 streaks from 2011 and 97 streaks from 2012 for analysis.

We divided each player's season into 3 groups:

1) BA before the 10-game streak started.
2) BA during the 10-game streak (or the first 10 games of a longer streak).
3) BA after the 10-game streak (or after the first 10 games of a longer streak).

The table below summarizes the results:

Comparison of BAs before and after 10-game hitting streaks (2011 and 2012 combined)

	Players	%
Players with ten game (or higher) streaks	208	100%
Players with higher BA after 10-game streak	127	61%
Players with lower BA after 10-game streak	81	39%

Cumulative BA statistics before and after 10-game hitting streaks

	AB	H	BA
Before streak began	45,973	12,195	.265
After first ten games of streak	51,671	14,834	.287

These results suggest that if we are seeking BA improvements for our team we should consider targeting players who have had a minimum of a 10-game hitting streak because 61% of them improved their BA after hitting safely in 10 consecutive games. Even more striking is the overall BA difference before and after the 10-game streak. When all 208 players' statistics are combined, they batted .265 before starting their 10-game streak, but .287 after!

A potential problem with this analysis might be that the longer hitting streaks, like Dan Uggla's (2B, ATL) 33-game streak in 2011, may have biased the results. Because all games after the initial ten games of the streak were part of the "After" data set, the "After" BAs may have been inflated by including the games of the longer streaks. However, for this finding to be of practical use we need to be confident that the effect holds for shorter streaks (10-11 game streaks) as well as longer streaks. That way we can target players when they have hit safely in 10 straight games without worrying whether the streak will eventually turn into a longer one.

To check this concern we looked at only the 10 and 11 game streaks from the 2011 data set (67 total streaks) and found that 42 of the players (63%) had higher BAs after the 10 games than before the 10 games. This percentage is consistent with the complete data set where 61% of players had higher BAs after the 10 games than before. When all 67 players' stats were combined they batted .259 before the streak began, and .303 after the first 10 games of the streak. See the table below.

Comparison of BAs before and after 10 and 11 game hitting streaks

	Players	%
Number players with 10- or 11-game streaks	67	100%
Players with higher BA after 10- or 11-game streak	42	63%
Players with lower BA sfter 10- or 11-game streak	25	37%

Cumulative BA statistics before / after 10- or 11-game hitting streaks

	AB	H	BA
Before streak started	14,126	3,655	.259
After 10- or 11-game streak started	16,314	4,951	.303

Conclusions

A 10-game hitting streak can reliably predict improved longer-term BA performance during the season. A player who has put together a hitting streak of at least 10 games will improve his BA for the remainder of the season about 60% of the time. This improvement can be significant, on average as much as .020 of BA. If we are attempting to improve our team's BA we should consider targeting players who have recently put together a 10-game or longer hitting streak.

xGB and xFB Pitchers

by Patrick Davitt

We've long been told to seek groundball (GB) pitchers and avoid flyball (FB) pitchers. But some argue that high-FB pitchers are just as valuable as high-GB ones, but in a different way.

In particular, FBers should tend to have higher ERAs because of HR and XBH increases, but lower WHIPs because of cans o' corn, while GBers should have lower ERAs because of fewer HRs and XBH and more GIDPs but higher WHIPs because of grounders sneaking through the infield.

Our research shows we should target high-K pitchers with either extreme GB% or FB%, but not because one helps ERA while the other helps WHIP.

First, we looked at MLB-wide rates for all main categories of outcomes per Batter Faced (BF), in the individual years 2008-11 and the combined period 2008-11. The rates were very stable, within and across seasons: 18% K%, 9% BB%, 31/14/26 G/L/F.

We next checked for correlations between GB and FB rates and ERA and WHIP, ignoring K rates. The only correlation (+0.21, still not strong) was between FB% and ERA—ERA rises with FB rate per our expectations. Since K rate obviously affects ERA and WHIP, we repeated the correlation check using only the two-thirds of pitchers clustered around the 18% K-rate median. Rising GB% again correlated with ERA declines, but, surprisingly, also with declining WHIP.

But because our interest is in extreme GB and FB pitchers, we now looked at pitchers who were normal-range K% and outside the GB% and FB% norms, which were roughly six percentage points higher than the 31% GB% median or the 26% FB median:

2008-2011	ERA	WHIP
Normal	4.19	1.35
Extreme GB	3.73	1.32
Extreme FB	4.24	1.30

While WHIP differences are minimal, GBers enjoyed almost half a run of ERA improvement.

Finally, we brought back the high-K pitchers we had excluded to isolate the GB/FB variables.

2008-2011	ERA	WHIP
Normal	4.19	1.35
High-K	3.08	1.17
High-K Extreme GB	2.55	1.11
High-K Extreme FB	2.90	1.08

In general, the overall high-K pitcher cohort (>=24% K/BF) had very good ERA and WHIP results. Extreme GB and FB pitchers were quite few, but did demonstrate improved ERA (and, to a lesser extent, WHIP) versus their normal Hi-K colleagues, with Extreme GBers showing greater ERA gains.

Conclusion

Across all pitchers, extreme-GBers offer some ERA help, but neither GB nor FB pitchers help WHIP. In the High-K cohort, extreme GBers and FBers do offer significant ERA and WHIP gains. Target pitchers with Dom and GB% or FB% in the top 15% or so.

(NOTE: The FB% and GB% used here differ from BHQ (balls in play, excluding walks, HBPs and Ks) and use Batters Faced (BF). GB and FB percentages therefore appear lower than in BHQ stats, because the denominators are larger.)

Expected Home Run per Fly Ball Rates

by Matt Cederholm

Home runs are a function of playing time (AB), total fly balls, (FB% and ct%), and the rate at which fly balls leave the park (hr/f). Of these, hr/f is subject to the most random variation. Often, the biggest change in a player's home runs, aside from changes in playing time, can be seen in hr/f.

We looked at several options to predict hr/f—hard-hit ball rate (HH%), hard-hit fly ball rate (HHFB%), ratio of hard-hit fly balls to total fly balls (HHFB/FB%), ratio of hard-hit balls to soft-hit balls (HH/SH), and ratio of hard-hit fly balls to soft-hit fly balls (HHFB/SHFB)—and their correlations to hr/f:

Correlation to hr/f	r
HHFB/SHFB	0.44
HH/SH	0.53
HH%	0.68
HHFB%	0.71
HHFB/FB%	0.71
PX	0.89

It's not surprising that PX is highly correlated with hr/f, since home runs are a big part of the formula that determines PX. But that didn't automatically stop us from using it.

We then used regression analysis to find a model that worked (using player-seasons with 250+ AB from 2003-2011). Both HHFB% and PX yielded significant results (R2-Adjusted was 0.88 for HHFB% and 0.94 for PX). We would prefer to use HHFB% since it does not include home runs in its formula. But we first needed to dig a little further.

Avg. percentage-point change in hr/f, following season		
hr/f - xhr/f	PX	HHFB%
>5%	−4.9	−3.4
0% to 5%	−1.9	−1.3
−5% to 0%	0.5	0.4
<−5%	2.7	1.9

Players with larger-than-predicted hr/f saw their rates fall, on average, and vice versa. And players at the extremes saw much larger changes. Across the board, the "rebound" in subsequent seasons was more pronounced with PX. So PX looks like the winner.

Percentage of players with a change in hr/f, following season					
hr/f - xhr/f	#	%Gain	%Drop	%Gain 3%+	%Drop 3%+
>5%	79	14%	86%	8%	63%
0% to 5%	639	32%	68%	13%	41%
−5% to 0%	1,001	53%	47%	23%	15%
<−5%	33	82%	18%	39%	3%
>0%	718	30%	70%	12%	43%
<0%	1,034	54%	46%	23%	14%

Another beauty of the PX model is the equation:

*xhr/f = .1091 * PX/100 + e; Thus: xHR = AB * ct% * FB% * (.1091 * PX/100)*

An average 100 PX yields a nearly average 10.9% hr/f (the average for players with 250+ AB from 2003-2011 was 10.6%). And you can roughly approximate xhr/f% as PX/9. The table above shows the odds of a regression in hr/f. These are actionable results.

These results focus on one skill—a player will not definitely see a drop in home runs because of an unusually high hr/f, as he could easily increase PX or FB%. And this would not have predicted Jose Bautista's 2010 breakout. But knowing a player is likely to see a correction in a particular skill can help better identify the breakouts and collapses in coming seasons.

HR, Pop-ups, and Hard-hit Flies

by Patrick Davitt

It is an article of faith that 10% of batted flyballs leave the yard. Batters establish individual levels for hr/f over time, but by definition all hitters aggregate around that 10% level.

The theory is sound based on aggregated data, but it had two possible flaws. First, it includes Infield Flyballs (IFFB), which cannot become HRs. Second, it does not consider Hard-Hit Flyballs (HHFB), which make up essentially all HRs. These two issues combine to a third: By using aggregate data to make assumptions about each batter as an individual, the theory ignores the fact that different batters have different IFFB/FB and HHFB/FB mixes.

Our theory is that batters with fewer pop-ups and/or higher HHFB rates should have higher hr/f rates, which could provide additional supporting evidence for a batter who posts a hr/f rate significantly removed from the 10% midline.

Our research found that avoiding pop-ups is a skill. We looked at all batters with at least 150 AB in each season 2009-11. Of batters below the 10% gamewide IFFB rate in 2009, 86% had at least one more low-IFFB season in 2010-11, and 60% stayed below 10% in both subsequent seasons.

Meanwhile, individual HHFB correlated with individual hr/f at 0.67, a solid connection. And while gamewide HHFB% was steady at ~12% of balls in play, the ability to generate HHFBs, which ranged from 0% to 68%, also proved a sustainable individual skill.

We looked at batters (>=150AB) with HHFB rates above 12% in 2009. Of them, 82% had one other season above the norm, and half were above the mark all three seasons. Of the highest HFFB% (>15%) batters in 2009, 92% stayed above 12% in all seasons, with 59% above 15% at least once.

Instead of looking for luck-related regressions in a standard 10% hr/f, we can look for it HR/ HHFB. Overall HR/HHFBs from 2007-2011 were as stable as regular hr/f rates, around 33% (with a 39% outlier in 2008).

So we looked again at batters >=150AB in 2009-11, and all of those with at least 35 HR/600AB had HR/HHFB rates above the gamewide norm—more than half were at 50% or higher!

We again checked for sustainability, and found:

- 86% of batters whose HR/HHFB was over 33% in 2009 had at least one more such season;
- 92% of batters with HHFB%s over 10% in 2009 overperformed the mark in at least one other year; and
- More importantly, 60% overperformed in all three seasons.

Conclusion

- Avoiding pop-ups and hitting HHFBs are sustainable core power skills.
- Consistent HHFB% performance marks batters with power potential.
- When looking for candidates to regress, we should look at individual past levels of HR/HFFB, perhaps using a three-year rolling average.

This study assumed only HHFBs can be HRs and ignored park effects. Small sample sizes reduce the predictive value of any in-season performance variations, so we'll be wise to look at players only from season to season, rather than in-season.

SB: A Spring Training Stat that Matters

by Bill Macey

One of the pleasant surprises of the 2011 season was Jeff Francoeur. He earned a career high roto value of $27, which was driven by 20 HR and a career high 22 SB. While the 20 HR weren't completely out of line for him (he had hit 29 HR in 2006), the SB seemingly came out of nowhere, after posting a previous high of just eight SB in 2011. Even in hindsight, there's no way we could have seen this outburst coming.

Right?

Well, maybe there was a hint, if only we had known where to look.

Each spring training, we're greeted with stories about players reporting "in the best shape of their lives" or we see fringe players put up gaudy stats playing against competition destined for the low minors. We've correctly learned to discount these feel-good stories and understand that even the most active batters in spring may only see 50-80 AB, which is far too few from which to draw a meaningful conclusion.

But while the ABs that each individual player gets are limited, each team in total will post upwards of 1000 AB during spring training. Now that is a meaningful sample size—perhaps enough to reveal changes in managerial tendencies. One such tendency that affects fantasy league play is the frequency at which players attempt a stolen base, also referred to as their stolen base opportunity percent (SBO).

Our first observation is that there are significant league-wide differences between spring training and the regular season. Each and every year in recent history, teams attempt to steal bases more frequently during spring training than they do during the regular season:

Year	Spring	Season
2006	10.7%	8.5%
2007	10.1%	8.5%
2008	10.8%	8.4%
2009	10.7%	9.0%
2010	10.7%	9.2%
2011	11.5%	10.5%

On average across all of MLB, SBO is approximately 1.7 percentage points higher during spring training than during the regular season. The chart above also illustrates the rising trend in stolen base attempts, perhaps as managers react to the decline in home runs.

For the six-year period 2006-2011, we compared each team's SBO during spring training with their SBO during the three preceding regular seasons and examined whether large differences were indicative of similar changes in the upcoming season. We identified 40 teams whose spring training SBO was at least five percentage points greater than their average SBO over the preceding three regular seasons. During the subsequent regular season, 32 of the 40 teams attempted more stolen bases than they had previously with an average increase of 1.9 percentage points over their prior 3-year average.

The magnitude of the increase appears to matter, as the larger the increase during spring training, the larger the subsequent increase during the subsequent regular season. There were 19 teams whose SBO during spring training increased by eight or more percentage point; 18 of those teams attempted steals more frequently during the following regular season, with their SBO increasing an average of 2.8 percentage points.

Conversely, we looked at teams whose SBO during spring training was more than one percentage point less than their prior three year regular season average. Given the general difference between SBO rates during spring training and the regular season, a SBO during spring training a full percentage point less than prior seasons is rather substantial. Thirty-one teams met this criteria, 22 of which attempted fewer stolen bases in the subsequent regular season with an average decrease of 1.0 percentage points.

Once again, the magnitude of the decrease was telling; the greater the decline during spring training, the less frequently the team ran during the subsequent regular season.

So let's return to the example of Jeff Francoeur and the 2011 Kansas City Royals. The SBO for the entire Royals team during 2011 spring training was 23.1%, which was more than double their 2008-2010 regular season average of 8.9%. But a fair question is: was this change due to a shift in team philosophy or simply a change in personnel? After all, it's reasonable to think that a team's willingness to run is at least partially dependent on the skills of its players.

To examine this, we compared the SBO of each player that earned more than 100 AB on the Royals in both 2010 and 2011. Looking at players who didn't change teams allows us to isolate managerial tendencies. This analysis also helps us address whether a change in SBO is shared across the team or isolated to just a few players.

There were only six players who met this criteria. Here's how their SBO compared in 2011 and 2010:

Name	2011 AB	2010 AB	2011 SBO	2010 SBO
Alex Gordon	611	242	13.9%	8.8%
Billy Butler	597	595	1.7%	0.0%
Chris Getz	380	224	23.7%	27.0%
Bryan Pena	222	158	0.0%	4.9%
Wilson Betemit	203	276	6.9%	0.0%
Mike Aviles	185	424	38.7%	15.6%
KC Subtotal	2198	1919	12.3%	8.9%

For completeness, here are the results for Melky Cabrera and Jeff Francoeur who were new additions to the Royals in 2011:

Name	2011 AB	2010 AB	2011 SBO	2010 SBO
Melky Cabrera	658	458	17.8%	6.4%
Jeff Francoeur	601	454	23.4%	10.0%

While the sample size of a single team in a single season is far too low from which to draw any statistically significant results, this analysis supports the hypothesis that significant differences in spring training SBO may reflect a shift in managerial tendencies that will carry to the regular season. Likewise, it also appears that the difference isn't necessarily concentrated in the results of a single player but that the additional opportunities are spread across the team.

GAMING RESEARCH ABSTRACTS

Mayberry 3.0

by Ron Shandler

For the previous three seasons, we've been using the Mayberry Method to evaluate and project Rotisserie skills. For those willing to abandon the faux precision of player projections and embrace wide error bars, Mayberry has turned out to be a very "accurate" method for judging talent.

Here are a few excerpts from our 2012 pre-season analysis on BaseballHQ.com:

- "The first big surprise is Dexter Fowler, who has been going in the 17th round. Well-hyped for three years, Fowler has disappointed each time, though taking baby steps with his skill set. Mayberry thinks his profile merits earlier notice."

- "You can pass on 3rd-rounder Carlos Santana (4125 ABA) and hold your own quite nicely with a 12th round Yadier Molina (3155 ABC)."

- "Particularly interesting are those that are not showing up in the ADP Top 300 at all but have solid MM ratings: Allen Craig (4145 CDC), Kelly Johnson (4315 ABF), Nolan Reimold (3415 ACF), Alejandro De Aza (2425 ADC), Omar Infante (1525 CCA), Johnny Giovatella (1525 ACB), Alcides Escobar (1525 ABA), Denard Span (1425 DBB)."

- "Intriguing speculations among MM's top ~50 pitchers but being drafted outside the ADP Top 300 are Ryan Dempster (3405 BAA), Brett Myers (3305 CAA), Chris Capuano (3305 ACA), Daniel Hudson (3305 ABA) and Chad Billingsley (3305 AAA)."

They weren't all winners, but the tool provides enough valuable insight that it merits notice.

Still, there is always room for improvement. There is one area that has not proven to be as "accurate" as I would like.

We have been using our Statistically Scouted Speed (Spd) score as a measure a runner's potential to amass stolen bases. The Spd formula looks at elements like beating out hits on softly hit balls, triples, runs scored and body mass index. It is essentially a measure of raw speed.

However, raw speed does not necessarily translate to the stolen bases that we play our game with. In fact, there are many "speedy" players who do not rack up mega-bags yet still score high in the Mayberry system.

There are two disconnects. The first is "opportunity." No matter how fast a runner is, he will not steal many bases if he is not given a green light. The second is a runner's ability to read a pitcher and get an adequate jump. You could be the fastest man on the planet but you will not steal many bases if you don't have those skills.

So we need to somehow incorporate our Stolen Base Opportunity rating (SBO) and stolen base success rate (SB%) into the process.

I have toyed with several advanced formulas that combine these two elements with Spd to create a new gauge. However, in the spirit of the simplicity of Mayberry, there is a much more basic formula that yields perfectly acceptable results while sacrificing little accuracy.

Roto Speed (RSpd) = Spd x (SBO + SB%)

The (SBO + SB%) adjustment ranges from zero to more than 1.5. It stratifies the pool of fast versus slow players into much more realistic groups. For those players who have a perpetual green light, the adjustment elevates their raw Spd score by as much as 50% or more. For those who never run at all, they are more appropriately valued at or close to zero.

For all players with at least 250 plate appearances this year, SB% naturally ranges from 0% to 100%, though the spread is much narrower for those who run more. SBO ranges from 0% to 91%. The sum of the two stats ranges from 0% to 170%, with 98 of 264 (37%) players having adjustments that will increase their Spd score.

The current Spd score ranges from 34 to 182. With the adjustment, the new RSpd now ranges from 0 to 260.

Let's look at a few players at the extremes.

Rajai Davis pretty much runs all the time. His SBO is 54% and he has a success rate of 78%. Adding those two together yields a 132% adjustment to his Spd score. That elevates his previous 113 level (and a Mayberry rating of 3) to 149 (and a more appropriate Mayberry rating of 5).

At the other end of the spectrum is Miguel Montero, a player who did not attempt even one steal all year. His Spd score (91) gives him Mayberry rating of 2. With an SBO of 0% and SB% of 0%, his RSpd score is now 0, yielding a more appropriate Mayberry rating of 0.

To accommodate the new scores and ranges, we also have to make an adjustment to the lookup tables that generate the Mayberry codes.

Here is the current table and the percentage of players who've achieved these levels over the past three years:

Spd	MM	Pct.
0 – 49	0	3%
50 – 79	1	35%
80 – 99	2	23%
100 – 119	3	22%
120 – 139	4	9%
140+	5	8%

As you can see, the majority of players congregate in the middle with very few achieving the highest or lowest scores. But now...

RSpd	MM	Pct.
0 – 39	0	18%
40 – 59	1	21%
60 – 79	2	22%
80 – 99	3	15%
100 – 119	4	14%
120+	5	10%

The new table flattens things out just enough. It still takes good skill to merit a 4 or 5, but now 24% of players can achieve that level as compared to 17% before. And the split between the lower three and upper three Mayberry ratings is still about 60-40.

Adjusting Mayberry for Reliability

by Patrick Davitt

Ron Shandler introduced the "Mayberry Method" in 2010 to "embrace imprecision" in forecasting by letting owners slot players into ranges of likely outcomes for Power, Speed, xBA and Playing Time, each on a scale of 0-5. Mayberry let us sort players by totalling the four component scores and multiplying by PA, creating an easy top-to-bottom list. Shandler had also been interested in reliability, especially in top player tiers. So Mayberry also included letter grades (A,B,C,D, and F) for Health, Experience and Consistency.

A pre-season sort of 2012 players by Mayberry score had anomalies like Albert Pujols behind Brett Lawrie and Carlos Beltran because of their higher Spd scores. We instinctively knew Pujols was a likelier first-rounder, because we perceived him as a much less risky than Lawrie, a rookie, and Beltran, a longtime injury bug. They were very risky, with "F" reliability ratings for Consistency and Health, respectively.

Our research showed that:

- Higher-Rel players met their Mayberry targets slightly more often than their lower-Rel counterparts;
- Players with top Rel bonuses and top bonus-adjusted Mayberry scores improved in three of four MM categories, having to meet higher targets; and
- Players with all "D" or "F" Rel scores underperformed Mayberry projections significantly more often than others.

(We didn't find any big differences among the three Rel categories, so a low Health score was no better or worse than a low Experience score.)

Adjusting for Reliability

So what if instead of separating Reliability letter-grades, we used them to adjust the overall scores? We broke the Rel scores out into separate digits and assigned bonuses or penalties:

Grade	Bonus	Grade	Bonus
A	+10%	D	−10%
B	+ 5%	F	−20%
C	0%		

Bonuses were multiplied together, so "AAA" would give a +33% bonus (1.1 x 1.1 x 1.1), while "FFF" would mean a −49% penalty.

When we recalculated the player pool, Pujols moved up a spot. Miguel Cabrera, Robinson Cano, Troy Tulowitzki and Joey Votto all stepped up, and Dexter Fowler, Matt Holliday and Andrew McCutchen climbed into the top 10. Other reliable players, like Matt Wieters, Billy Butler and Garret Jones, also climbed significantly.

Lawrie fell from 13th to 123rd and Beltran from 14th to 149th. Other big droppers included 2012 duds like Mike Napoli, Jacoby Ellsbury, and Sta-Puft Marshmallow Man lookalike Pablo Sandoval. And while the adjustment also put big drops onto some 2012 standouts like Jose Altuve, Adrian Beltre and Josh Hamilton, they often moved down to where they made more risk-management sense.

Conclusion

Writing about 2012 Mayberry targets, Shandler said: "The reliability grades of both Lawrie (lack of experience) and Beltran (health history) would make me reluctant to draft them too high." The natural next step is to formally adjust those scores, to quantify player reliability.

Rebooting LIMA

by Ray Murphy

Ron Shandler first introduced the LIMA Plan back in 1998, and it quickly became the dominant roto strategy for the early part of the 2000s. LIMA remains quite relevant as it approaches its 15th birthday, but recent shifts in MLB's scoring environment have necessitated a "LIMA reboot."

Veteran readers will quickly recognize these LIMA skill thresholds:

Ctl	<= 3.0
Dom	>= 6.0 (eventually lowered to 5.6)
Cmd	>= 2.0
hr/9	<= 1.0

The simplicity of those thresholds, all set at easy-to-remember whole-number values, made those cutoffs "sticky" in our heads. But sometimes "sticky" things are a double-edged sword: as the MLB environment has changed over the years, those thresholds are now obsolete.

To evaluate how the LIMA filters have performed over the past 15 years, we compiled the aggregate stats lines of the pitchers who worked at least 100 IP in a season and met all of the Ctl, Dom, and Cmd filters. (We left the hr/9 component out of this exercise, for reasons explained below.) The results are rather consistent:

Year	Qualifiers	Cohort IP	Cohort ERA
1998	37	7641	3.67
1999	22	4309	3.75
2000	21	4388	4.02
2001	36	6719	3.70
2002	35	6358	3.64
2003	34	6385	3.51
2004	36	6459	3.90
2005	33	6727	3.48
2006	42	7496	3.95
2007	39	7259	3.87
2008	38	7221	3.59
2009	38	7525	3.62
2010	45	8494	3.56
2011	62	11829	3.50
2012	75	13023	3.73

Over the sample size of 15 years, the performance of full LIMA qualifying pitchers has fluctuated within a narrow range. Other than a couple of outliers on either side of the bell curve, we can observe a normal range of 3.60-3.75 ERA from the qualifying cohort in any given year.

As one might expect, with overall offensive production somewhat muted in recent years, the number of qualifying pitchers per year has been rising. But that isn't necessarily good news.

Context is everything

We have established that the performance of our cohort is fairly stable over a 15-year study period. However, the performance of the league as a whole is anything but stable. Here is the performance of LIMA qualifiers measured against league average:

Year	Cohort ERA	MLB ERA	Cohort gap	% gap
1998	3.67	4.43	-0.760	-21%
1999	3.75	4.71	-0.965	-26%
2000	4.02	4.77	-0.755	-19%
2001	3.70	4.42	-0.723	-20%
2002	3.64	4.28	-0.638	-18%
2003	3.51	4.40	-0.888	-25%
2004	3.90	4.46	-0.565	-15%
2005	3.48	4.29	-0.808	-23%
2006	3.95	4.53	-0.578	-15%
2007	3.87	4.47	-0.601	-16%
2008	3.59	4.32	-0.731	-20%
2009	3.62	4.32	-0.700	-19%
2010	3.56	4.08	-0.517	-15%
2011	3.50	3.94	-0.445	-13%
2012	3.73	4.01	-0.277	-7%

The right-most column tells the tale here. That percentage is measuring the inherent advantage held by the pool of full LIMA qualifiers, as compared to the MLB pitching population at large. Especially when you consider that fantasy leaguers are not rostering 100% of the pool of MLB pitchers, the "LIMA edge" has suffered some significant erosion due to the recent reduction in run-scoring across MLB.

Resetting our filters

To look at how our filters need to be adjusted, we need to look at the league context for those metrics. Here is an abbreviated look at where they were in LIMA's early days, and where they are now:

Year	Ctl	Dom	Cmd	hr/9
1998	3.4	6.6	1.9	1.0
1999	3.7	6.5	1.7	1.2
2000	3.8	6.5	1.7	1.2
2010	3.3	7.1	2.2	1.0
2011	3.1	7.1	2.3	0.9
2012	3.1	7.5	2.4	1.0

Relative to the current league context, a traditional LIMA-qualifying pitcher could now simply be exhibiting barely-average Control, and subpar Dominance and Command!

We took a trial-and-error approach to finding a new set of filters that would restore LIMA's advantage over the league-wide player pool, and cut the pool of qualifiers back down to a similar level of selectivity as the LIMA distinction used to carry. We also wanted to retain some of the convenience of round-number levels. We found that the following levels best met these objectives:

- 2.8 Ctl
- 7.0 Dom
- 2.5 Cmd

In the following table, we compare traditional LIMA's first five years to these new levels :

Year	Qualifiers	Cohort ERA	MLB ERA	Cohort gap	% gap
traditional LIMA: 3.0 Ctl, 6.0 Dom, 2.0 Cmd					
1998	37	3.67	4.43	-0.760	-21%
1999	22	3.75	4.71	-0.965	-26%
2000	21	4.02	4.77	-0.755	-19%
2001	36	3.70	4.42	-0.723	-20%
2002	35	3.64	4.28	-0.638	-18%
«rebooted» LIMA: 2.8 Ctl, 7.0 Dom, 2.5 Cmd					
2010	25	3.40	4.08	-0.679	-20%
2011	33	3.37	3.94	-0.569	-17%
2012	46	3.55	4.01	-0.457	-13%

These new filters largely meet our goals:

- The population selectivity is right in line with original LIMA;
- The % gap is also back in line, although 2012 still lags a bit (2012 fell to the high side for cohort ERA in both the original and new formulas. We don't want to correct any further and shrink the population too far).
- 2.5 Cmd becomes the new "magic" level. Setting the new Dom threshold at 7.0 is about convenience as much as anything; you can wiggle the Ctl/Dom filters a bit as long as you stay locked on the 2.5 Cmd. For instance, if you want to really emphasize strikeouts, you can go to 3.0 Ctl/7.5 Dom as your baseline.

A word about hr/9

There are two reasons that we have ignored LIMA's original hr/9 filter in this analysis:

First, HR rates haven't moved as much as Ctl, Dom, and Cmd have in the past 15 years. After a brief spike to 1.2 hr/9 league-wide in LIMA's early years, HR rates have stayed at a consistent 1.0 hr/9 or 0.9 hr/9 in recent years. There was no sea change here; if you want to retain a hr/9 < 1.0 filter, feel free.

Second, the best argument for dropping the hr/9 requirement is that we have learned a lot over the years about where HR come from. Since HR are basically a function of fly balls allowed, we could just as easily set our filter based on FB%, for example FB% < 40%. You could even tighten or loosen that requirement a little bit based on a pitcher's home ballpark, and whether it favors hitters or pitchers. Basically, in original LIMA, the hr/9 component was a concession to the fact that we didn't understand much about how pitchers influence their HR allowed. We don't have that problem anymore.

Conclusion

To regain the advantage that LIMA offered in the late 1990s, re-train your LIMA eye to look for these levels:

Ctl	<= 2.8
Dom	>= 7.0
Cmd	>= 2.5
FB%	< approx 40% (optional)

Happy 15th birthday, LIMA! Here's to your next 15....

Navigating our Short Attention Spans

by Ron Shandler

The Daily Game Explosion

The fastest growing game in the industry right now is the daily fantasy competition. These are games where you set your roster before the first pitch of the day and collect your winnings before they turn out the stadium lights that night.

These contests feed into our ever-shortening attention spans and need for immediate gratification. This is not so much a diss as a reality check. We have become a society with limited patience and highly splintered focus. Major League Baseball continues to have the longest season and has seen its popularity wane in comparison to other sports over the years. The interminable six-month marathon is anathema to the way we function these days.

So it makes sense that daily games would become so popular.

BaseballHQ.com Managing Director Ray Murphy wrote about his first foray into the format last spring. He said: "I don't see how you could play these every day if you take them at all seriously... On the continuum of skill versus luck, this slides further down the 'luck' side than a full-season league; and any one night is probably a crapshoot. But I have to admit, it is sucking me in at least a little bit."

But there is the obvious problem. For our mode of analysis here, the shorter the time span, the less the analytical tools have utility. The variability of statistics during short time frames is huge.

Still, I think a case can be made for these short games, or at least finding the right balance between analytical relevance and short attention spans.

It's all about sample size.

In full season leagues, the critical mass of MLB games provides a sufficient sample of events. But the "game" is still the unit of measure. In these shorter contests, we need to amass as many games as possible to maintain that critical mass. So, instead of one league comprised of 162 games, we'd need some huge amount of daily games.

Basically, more samples. Whatever the configuration, as many samples as possible.

Ray noted: "While anything can happen on any given night, if you played regularly and applied sound principles, I would think your results would eventually reflect it." The shorter contests provide for a greater number of trials, which can be nearly equivalent in statistical significance to the larger sample of games in full-season leagues.

So, if you're playing a daily game, you can't just play it once or twice and abandon the concept. You have to play it consistently and it will eventually pay off.

Still, this is a game requiring a completely different mindset to play. For those of us who have been reared on the full-season league, is there any place for such a contest?

Optimal Time Horizons

The length of a competition is a question of both time and commitment.

"One day" and "six months" not only represent how much you are willing to commit to a competition but also represent how long a period in which you need to forecast player performance. And if we break up player performance into its two high-level component parts—skill and playing time—then time becomes an important decision-making factor.

Fact: It is extremely difficult to forecast playing time over six months. That's why our traditional full-season leagues are so challenging to play. Coming into 2012, given variables like injuries, skills development and managerial decisions, it would have been entirely possible for Paul Goldschmidt to end up with a 116-AB season and Lyle Overbay to amass 514 AB. Over the course of six months, anything can happen.

Fact: It is extremely difficult to forecast skill for a one game. That's why daily games are so challenging to play. On any given day, given variables like the opposing pitcher, defensive alignments and wind currents, it would be entirely possible for Mike Trout to go 0 for 4 and Bobby Wilson to go 3 for 4. In a single game match-up, anything can happen.

We have become wedded to the full-season format, but in many ways it is as tough to play as the one-day format.

On average over the past five years, about 1,275 players get at least one at-bat or inning each season. Our pre-season fantasy draft lists are not nearly that long. Every time a manager changes his closer, or a player takes longer than expected to come off the DL, or gets pushed to the bench by a rookie putting up 40 aberrant at-bats... large blocks of playing time shift around. And with more than 400 players hitting the DL annually, we're faced with a daunting task when it comes to projecting playing time.

But those precious AB and IP are still the core driver of success.

Projecting playing time for one game? Give me the lineup cards and I can pretty much nail it.

Consider, in sum:

Optimal accuracy for projecting skill requires the longest time period possible. Six months is all we get, even though it often takes longer for a full assessment. One game provides virtually no accuracy when it comes to projecting skill.

Optimal accuracy for projecting playing time requires the shortest time period possible. With one game, we know who is

> *The interminable six-month marathon is anathema to the way we function these days. So it makes sense that daily games would become so popular.*

going to play. Six months provides significantly diminished accuracy when it comes to projecting playing time.

So, is there a middle ground? I think there is, but it will force you to reassess how you approach this game.

The Search for Prognosticating Equilibrium

Ten years ago, a closer might get four or five blown saves before he is removed; today, he could lose the job after one or two bad outings. Ten years ago, young hitters might be allowed to work through their struggles; today, patience is thin.

Consider... about 70% of a season's surprise performances can be attributed to players backing into unexpected playing time. Our inability to see these changes is huge.

What can we do? We could just continue to muddle along, trying to navigate the less-projectable baseball environment. But the less we can project, the more this fantasy "game of skill" (let's call it "proficiency") becomes a gambling "game of chance." That's a tough pill to swallow because the entire fantasy concept was founded on the perception that a certain level of proficiency is required to play this game well.

So I think we need to reposition the fantasy game so it better fits into how the real game has changed over time. We need to find a way to restore more managerial control, to make our proficiency matter more. And I think that control has to come from a better balance between the projectability of skill and the projectability of playing time. More of a prognosticating equilibrium, if you will.

Or basically, playing the game in more projectable chunks of time.

Is there an optimal time period for this? I don't know. Extensive research might pin that time span at 37 days, or six-and-a-half weeks, or two months. But I played a one-month game several times this year; I think this is a time span worth exploring.

Here are some of the many benefits of a monthly league:

More drafts. Drafting is the funnest part of playing fantasy anyway. In these leagues, you get to do it six times. Not too much (as in a daily game); not too little (as in a full season league). Don't think of it as burdensome to assemble your owners that often; with this Internet thing, it's actually quite easy.

The decrease in our ability to project skill is not as bad as it seems. Player projections are still going to be grounded in full-season expectations. The variability around those projections is going to be larger for a one-month time period, but to be honest, the variability over a full season is pretty wide anyway.

The stats may seem volatile on a player-by-player basis, but they do tend to stabilize over a roster of players, even in as little as one month's time. There will be players who have great months and those who have poor months, but in aggregate, you can still get a good sense of an overall strength of your team.

What we lose in projecting skill we gain in projecting playing time and roles. There is a high volatility in these variables over six months. One month is more manageable because MLB teams will typically give their players about that long to establish themselves, adjust to a role or retain a job.

Of course, change can happen at any time, but one month limits the damage. Worst case, the effort you would ordinarily make to react to that change (i.e. trades, free agent dart-throwing, prayer, etc.) could be put into preparing for next month's draft.

You can invest more confidently in injury situations. The finite time span of one month fits much better into the shifting playing time from DL stints. For instance, had you drafted this past June, players like Roy Halladay and Evan Longoria would not have been on your draft list at all. Their replacements were easier to value because you knew they would be playing full-time for the month. In a full-season league, you really don't know how long these players are going to be out so free agent bidding for their replacements is much less precise.

The impact from extraordinary luck is minimized. Consider Fernando Rodney, a full-season game-changer who didn't even make most March draft lists. Or A.J. Pierzynski, who posted a career year at age 35. Owners who backed into surprise players like these won't be able to ride their dumb luck to a 6-month title. The benefit of those lucky picks will last no more than a month. The challenge will be to figure out if that luck will last long enough to overrate these players in subsequent drafts.

You can draft to the schedule. With the smaller time frame, you can look for players on teams that might have a particularly heavy home or road schedule, or are playing more games in hitter- or pitcher-friendly venues. Carlos Gonzalez playing 18 of 27 games at home (.368/.437/.609) is different from Gonzalez spending 18 games on the road (.234/.301/.405).

You can also steal a bunch of additional innings if you draft pitchers who have starts at the very beginning of the month. Considering that you'll only get 5-6 outings from each starter, squeezing in an additional game potentially bumps up your innings by 15-20%.

Following the standings is more fun. There is a lot more movement, day to day. Think about how the standings move in April each year and consider that each month's contest will look like that. When it comes to the enjoyment of the game, this is a good thing. Why?

Categories tend to stagnate in full-season leagues. As the rankings stratify, it sets ceilings and floors on how many points you can conceivably gain or lose. By time summer rolls around, it's often near-impossible to make major moves.

All that is different in a monthly league. The first week or so will seem like standings anarchy, but the categories will start to stabilize as the month progresses. Still, a few big games from key players can effectively net you a handful of quick points, even in the ratio categories. When your team has a 4-HR day in a seasonal league, it is gratifying; in a monthly league, it's points in the standings.

And think about all that excitement you have with close races during the last week of September each year... Six times.

A Season, by Months

The monthly league is more of a tactical game. While full-season projections provide a baseline, each individual month provides its own unique set of draft decisions.

Your April Team... For your first monthly draft, you are likely going to look at some of the exceptional March performances to see if there are players worth elevating on your ranking list. You won't be looking so much at skill as playing time. The March job-winners will open the season with regular AB/IP that they could hold with good early performances. This is regardless of whether they'll fade as the league catches up to them or their long-term skill.

Still, you might opt to avoid some players who have been historically slow-starters. You might also depress the ranking of those playing most of their games in cold weather cities.

Your May Team... If we trust our full-season player projections, then we have to conclude that particularly good or bad months are going to normalize in subsequent months. That is insight we can use to our advantage to play off of April's aberrant performances.

Poor April pitching numbers do tend to linger for those arms that don't have a long-term track record. Arms with solid skills but high early ERAs might be good targets. Hitters are more resilient; a lifetime .290 hitter who opens the season at .220 has good odds of rebounding in May.

Your June Team... Interleague play used to be centered in June, forcing tactical decisions regarding DHs losing at-bats in NL cities and NL bats gaining playing time as DHs in AL parks. Now it's spread out, though some teams will see clumps of interleague games in certain months.

Your July Team... July is a short month due to the All Star Break so decisions have to be a bit more careful. As the July 31 non-waiver deadline approaches, good players on bad teams might be on the block and moved early. Park effects and changing roles add to the risk of rostering these players.

And don't forget about the potential for workhorse players in hot weather cities to start fading a bit.

Your August Team... The trading deadline holds a huge impact for August leagues. As you draft this month, there will be a clearer demarcation between the MLB contenders and non-contenders; that will affect draft decisions.

For instance, Phillies players might have lost some value in August after the trades of Shane Victorino and Hunter Pence. Tom Milone could have been drafted for a song back in April; with the A's a contender in August, his potential value likely spiked.

Your September Team... This may be one of the more difficult months to play. With the MLB expansion to 40-man rosters, roles and playing time will be more fluid. Decisions will have to be made about the rosterability of prospects. The dividing line between MLB contenders and those playing out the string will have even more impact this month. But all of this just amps up the challenge.

Each month is its own micro-game.

Playing a Monthly League

Here is a proposal for the rules of a monthly league:

Most of the standards can remain the same. Rosters can be stocked via snake draft, auction or salary cap; that variable is immaterial. Similarly, the stat categories you choose will not affect the mode of play. Go with standard 5x5, or the hybrid 4x4 we use for the Rotisserie500 and Rotisserie350 leagues (HR, SB, BA, R+RBI-HR, W, K, ERA, SV+Hld-BSv).

This format can be played as an AL-only, NL-only or mixed league. Ten-twelve teams is probably an optimal size for AL/NL-only leagues; mixed leagues should be able to comfortably go to 15.

Roster size should be 21 players: 9 hitters, one at each defensive position, plus a utility/DH, 7 pitchers and 5 reserves. The 16 active players are the only ones that accumulate stats. You play the month within those 21 players. Intra-roster moves can be made twice-weekly, on Sunday and Thursday nights (or Monday noon and Friday noon). So you'll be setting your roster for each MLB series, more or less.

Why the smaller roster size? Since you'd be playing with smaller chunks of AB and IP, marginal players have significantly less value. It's best to pass on them rather than trying to incorporate their 5-10 weekly ABs into your draft planning. Plus, we want to make each month's draft a somewhat less grueling affair.

Allowing free agent access presents a myriad of problems with the short one-month time span. It's best to play the month out from the 21 players alone. If your team is hit with an extraordinary rash of injuries, you might have to just look ahead to the next draft. Or, you could allow trading.

The April draft should be conducted during the weekend before Opening Day. Each month's league would conclude on the first Sunday of the next month with the subsequent draft conducted that same evening. Draft order would be based on the previous month's final standings. First place gets first seed.

Teams can carry over five players each month. No more, no less. So each month's draft would be for 16 players per team. Keepers would be announced by the Friday prior to the Sunday draft in order to allow owners the weekend to prepare.

None of these drafts should take more than a couple of hours. The monthly drafts I participated in ran about two hours apiece and that was without any time limit between picks.

Six winners and six separate prize pots. If you want, you can add a chunk of change for the season's overall champ too.

If you have a tough time coming to terms with managing a team for less than a full season, consider this reality... Major League teams don't manage for a full season either. It is common wisdom that teams play three seasons: 54 games to see what they have, 54 games to make adjustments and 54 games to play it out. Each July's trading deadline results in several teams completely changing their focus for the rest of the year. Early strugglers almost always shake up their roster at some point.

A monthly league removes much of the random guessing that goes into our March expectations. This is a tough enough game to play without having to read six months' worth of tea leaves, particularly when it comes to ever-shifting roles and playing time.

Importance of the Early Rounds

by Bill Macey

Each spring as fantasy baseball drafts draw near, a popular theme in pre-season advice will invariably include some version of the popular adage "you can't win your draft in the first round, but you can lose it." It seems a reasonable proposition, but is it accurate?

To analyze this question, we examined the results of the 26 individual leagues in the 2011 National Fantasy Baseball Championship Main Event. The NFBC serves as an interesting laboratory as the format (15 team mixed, 5x5) is relatively standard, allowing us to apply the results more generally. Also, the NFBC doesn't allow trading, removing a potentially complicating factor.

Here are the top 15 players drafted in 2011 and how the teams that drafted those players finished their seasons.

Name	ADP Rank	2011 Rank	Avg Lg Finish	# 1st Place	# of Top 3
Albert Pujols	1	14	7.3	3	8
Hanley Ramirez	2	217	9.1	0	5
Troy Tulowitzki	3	25	6.8	1	7
Miguel Cabrera	4	6	7.9	2	5
Joey Votto	5	17	8.2	2	6
Carlos Gonzalez	6	25	9.3	2	2
Carl Crawford	7	167	10.0	1	3
Evan Longoria	8	90	8.5	1	2
Ryan Braun	9	3	7.4	1	8
Adrian Gonzalez	10	6	8.4	2	5
Robinson Cano	11	14	7.8	3	5
Alex Rodriguez	12	143	7.0	2	5
David Wright	13	181	7.1	1	4
Mark Teixeira	14	51	6.7	4	6
Matt Holliday	15	72	7.2	2	6

To provide context for the results, in a 15-team league, the average finish is 8th. So any average league finish better than 8.0 is better than average. Similarly, there were 28 first-place finishes in the 26 leagues (two leagues had co-champions) and 79 top 3 finishes. Thus, any number of first place finishes above 1.9 (28/15) or top 3 finishes above 5.3 (79/15) represents a better than average result.

Of the four first-round players who didn't return top-100 value, in aggregate they appeared on the roster of a league champion just four times, and appeared 17 times on the roster of a team that finished in the top three. But in 2011, the first round busts were generally mild; some of the biggest busts were drafted in the 2nd–4th rounds:

Name	ADP Rank	2011 Rank	Avg Lg Finish	# 1st Place	# of Top 3
Joe Mauer	29	389	9.1	0	2
Buster Posey	32	483	9.4	0	3
Adam Dunn	35	1244	10.2	0	1
Alex Rios	44	333	10.4	0	1
Jason Heyward	47	333	9.6	0	0

Here, we see more concrete evidence that poor performance by early round pick makes a league championship much less likely.

Similarly, drafting the best player that went among the top 15—Ryan Braun—was no guarantee of success either. Only one of the 26 teams that drafted him won its league. In fact, rostering

even some of the most profitable players was only a step in the right direction:

Name	ADP Rank	2011 Rank	Avg Lg Finish	# 1st Place	# of Top 3
Matt Kemp	18	1	5.4	6	12
Clayton Kershaw	40	5	5.8	6	13
Justin Verlander	42	4	5.0	6	10
Curtis Granderson	95	8	5.8	4	10
Asdrubal Cabrera	227	42	5.4	5	8
Alex Gordon	266	23	6.3	4	9

These results are quite illuminating: Each of these players had amazing seasons and performed at a level far exceeding his cost, yet among the teams that owned at least one of these highly profitable players, more than half still didn't finish even in the top three.

What about pitchers?

The concept of being risk-averse in the early rounds of your draft is hardly new; there have been a number of articles in previous editions of the *Baseball Forecaster* espousing such a strategy. One way that tenet has been frequently applied is by not drafting pitchers early, with the logic being that pitchers are inherently more risky than batters.

So let's use this data to see how teams that drafted pitchers early fared.

First SP Rd	Count	Avg Lg Finish
1	10	10.4
2	52	7.9
3	99	6.8
4	89	8.3
5	72	8.0
6	35	9.1
7	11	8.8
8	8	11.0
9	5	10.0
10	3	5.7
11	2	7.5
12	1	7.0
13	1	3.0
14	0	N/A
15	1	15.0
16	1	4.0

At least in 2011, drafting your first pitcher in the 3rd round seemed to offer the most success; this is partially explained by the fact that Justin Verlander and Clayton Kershaw were frequently selected in these rounds.

However, note that of the 10 instances in which a pitcher was selected in the first round, in nine times the pitcher was Roy Halladay and in the other it was Clayton Kershaw; as both had excellent seasons, poor performance by the first round pick therefore doesn't explain the poor average league results (nobody finished higher than 6th in their league). This shows that the case against selecting a pitcher early isn't extended beyond the assumption of additional performance risk. Drafting an early pitcher also carries the opportunity cost of passing up on a foundation level batter, a deficit that's not easily recovered.

Only nine teams waited until round 10 or later to select their first pitcher, but those that did fared generally well, with an average finish of 6.8 and one league champion (and an additional top-three finish) among them.

Value Drafting

The one league champion who waited on starting pitching selected Shaun Marcum in round 10, a full round later than his ADP. This inspires us to ask if "value drafting" is a viable strategy. Put another way, do teams that consistently select players that others discredit finish higher in the standings?

To answer this, we calculated for each team an average ADP+; the average difference between the spot at which they selected each player and those players' ADPs. A positive ADP means that the player "fell" to the team—the team selected the player later than he ordinarily was drafted.

Average ADP+	Count	Avg Lg Finish	# 1st Place	# of Top 3
greater than 5	100	7.2	11	25
from 0 to 5	110	8.0	8	23
from -5 to 0	85	7.4	7	22
less than -5	95	9.4	2	9

The small differences among the first three cohorts suggests there's not much advantage to getting "value." But that data does seem to tell us that if you're consistently reaching or overpaying for players, you might struggle to win. It's perfectly fine to grab your biggest targets a round or two or even more before they most often are drafted, but if you're doing this each and every round, you're probably forgoing too many opportunities to draft your targets at a better price.

Conclusion

The adage "you can't win your draft in the first round, but you can lose it" might be a bit strong—a first round bust doesn't necessarily end your title hopes—but it's grounded in truth. A poor performance, not just by your first round player but by any of player drafted in the first several rounds, significantly decreases the likelihood of a championship. Likewise, nailing your first round pick is a big step in the right direction, but it's still just the first of many steps on a long journey to your title.

Fixing the Bullpen Problem

by Ron Shandler

Since the end of the 2011 season, 23 of the 30 major league teams have turned over the closer's role to a new pitcher. Twenty of those bullpens—66%—made the change after Opening Day. The turnover was unprecedented.

In the Closer Volatility chart that we've been publishing here since 1999, the only year that comes close is 2003. That year, the in-season turnover rate was 59%, 7% less than this year.

Historically, excessive closer failures in one year tend to take a toll on closer prices the following year. Sometimes, the few "stable" closers might demand disproportionately higher prices. But you can already predict the fantasy advice that will trumpet from the rooftops next spring: "Don't Draft Closers!"

It's good advice... until you realize that it is antithetic to the goals of the game. Aren't we supposed to be accumulating positive stats, not avoiding them? The advice is telling you not to pay for a commodity that represents at least 10% of your scoring categories. Why? Because the risk far exceeds the potential value.

The problem is that we have a scarce commodity—saves—that is centered on a small group of players, thereby creating inflated demand for those players. As the risk of loss increases, the incentive to pay full value for the commodity decreases. The higher the risk, the lower the prices. If you take this to its natural, albeit absurd, extreme, our future closer investments might cost next to nothing but yield incredibly huge profits for a random group of pitchers. It would be like playing the lottery. In a game that was founded on the perception of control, "random" is the devil.

One would hope we never get to that point, and this year's experience could represent a one-year anomaly. But the funny thing about this game is that, well, it is a game. That means it has rules that can be changed as the playing environment changes.

So to fix this, we need to find a way to increase the value of the commodity by reducing the risk. We might do this by increasing the pool of players that contribute to that category, thereby spreading the risk around. The fix is so simple that many leagues are already doing it.

It's time to move from "*saves*" to "*saves plus holds.*"

Go ahead and roll your eyes, but an analysis of the numbers bears out how this largely fixes the problem.

Yes, holds are not perfect. The typical argument against them is that they are random and arbitrary. But after this year, you can say the same thing about saves. In fact, many of the pitchers who record holds are far more skilled and valuable than closers; they are often called to the mound in much higher leverage situations.

Here are two pieces of evidence showing why we might want to value closers and set-up men a little more equitably:

In 2012, Vinnie Pestano's leverage index (1.54) was greater than Chris Perez's (1.23). Antonio Bastardo's (1.37) was greater than Jonathan Papelbon's (1.24). Matt Belisle's (1.42) was greater than Rafael Betancourt's (1.22). Jake McGee's (1.39) was greater than Fernando Rodney's (1.24). Joaquin Benoit's (1.05) was greater than Jose Valverde's (0.98) for the second consecutive year. Remember that Valverde led the majors in saves in 2011.

This year, managers have been opting to skip their eighth inning reliever when naming new closers. Pitchers like Matt Thornton and Jared Burton were passed over because they were too important to move from their current middle inning role.

Neither stat is perfect, but together they form a reasonable proxy for overall bullpen performance.

And together they effectively double the player pool of draftable relievers while also flattening their values.

Check it out. The following is a list of all relievers who amassed a combination of at least 30 saves and/or holds in 2011.

				ROTO VALUE	
2011 Reliever	**Sv**	**Hld**	**LI**	**Sv**	**Sv+Hld**
Kimbrel,Craig	46	0	1.32	$27	$19
Valverde,Jose	49	0	1.10	$25	$15
Rivera,Mariano	44	0	1.44	$25	$16
Axford,John	46	0	1.15	$23	$15
Storen,Drew	43	3	1.42	$23	$16
Putz,J.J.	45	0	1.37	$22	$15
Hanrahan,Joel	40	0	1.27	$21	$14
Papelbon,Jonathan	31	0	1.27	$20	$14
Cordero,Francisco	37	0	1.20	$20	$13
Bell,Heath	43	0	1.45	$19	$11
League,Brandon	37	0	1.20	$18	$10
Salas,Fernando	24	6	1.45	$18	$16
Walden,Jordan	32	2	1.70	$17	$10
Perez,Chris	36	0	1.68	$17	$9
Santos,Sergio	30	2	1.31	$17	$11
Feliz,Neftali	32	0	1.10	$16	$10
Madson,Ryan	32	3	1.18	$16	$11
Clippard,Tyler	0	38	1.49	$15	$22
Adams,Mike	2	32	1.20	$14	$20
Venters,Jonny	5	35	1.28	$14	$19
Rodriguez,Francisco	23	17	1.37	$13	$11
Wilson,Brian	36	0	1.54	$13	$6
Marmol,Carlos	34	2	1.40	$11	$4
Robertson,David	1	34	1.38	$11	$17
Nunez,Leo	36	0	1.30	$11	$4
Marshall,Sean	5	34	1.36	$11	$16
O'Flaherty,Eric	0	32	1.23	$10	$16
Betancourt,Rafael	8	22	1.08	$10	$12
Street,Huston	29	4	1.18	$9	$4
Hernandez,David	11	23	1.17	$8	$10
Bard,Daniel	1	34	1.53	$7	$13
Benoit,Joaquin	2	29	1.26	$7	$11
total	840	352		*$508*	*$410*

This list is sorted by roto value using saves only. See how those values change when we go to saves+holds. Some key observations:

- The aggregate leverage indices for the closers on this list is 1.38. For the non-closers, 1.30. Reasonably close.
- Saves are still the dominant statistic; there are more than twice as many saves as holds. So closers would continue to drive the value in this category.
- Still, Tyler Clippard and Mike Adams become the top ranked players on the revised list. Given the seasons they had, I don't think anyone would find fault in that.
- These 32 pitchers earned nearly $100 less in total roto value when using saves+holds. The flattening of these values across all pitchers effectively spreads their risk.

And the more players around which we spread the risk, the more control we have in managing our pitching staffs.

Here is that same list for 2012:

				ROTO VALUE	
2012 Reliever	**Sv**	**Hld**	**LI**	**Sv**	**Sv+Hld**
Rodney,Fernando	48	0	1.24	$36	$26
Kimbrel,Craig	42	0	1.29	$31	$25
Chapman,Aroldis	38	6	1.42	$29	$24
Johnson,Jim	51	0	1.29	$26	$15
Motte,Jason	42	0	1.43	$24	$17
Papelbon,Jon	38	0	1.24	$22	$15
Soriano,Rafael	42	4	1.27	$22	$13
Nathan,Joe	37	0	1.10	$21	$13
Jansen,Kenley	25	8	1.31	$20	$17
Wilhelmsen,Tom	29	7	1.38	$20	$15
Frieri,Ernesto	23	7	1.03	$19	$16
Balfour,Grant	24	15	1.33	$19	$17
Cook,Ryan	14	21	1.41	$18	$19
Hanrahan,Joel	36	0	1.17	$16	$9
Perez,Chris	39	0	1.23	$16	$7
Putz,J.J.	32	0	1.07	$15	$9
Romo,Sergio	14	23	1.43	$14	$16
Casilla,Santiago	25	12	1.37	$14	$11
Betancourt,Rafael	31	1	1.24	$14	$8
Valverde,Jose	35	0	0.98	$14	$5
Clippard,Tyler	32	13	1.25	$14	$9
Broxton,Jonathan	27	10	1.33	$13	$9
Axford,John	35	3	1.22	$10	$3
Gregerson,Luke	9	24	1.19	$10	$12
Marshall,Sean	9	22	1.20	$9	$11
Reed,Addison	29	4	1.53	$8	$1
Pestano,Vinnie	2	36	1.54	$7	$13
Peralta,Joel	2	37	1.15	$6	$12
Benoit,Joaquin	2	30	1.05	$5	$10
Robertson,David	2	30	1.15	$5	$10
Grilli,Jason	2	32	1.20	$5	$9
Mujica,Edward	2	30	1.21	$4	$8
Burnett,Sean	2	31	1.02	$4	$8
Downs,Scott	9	25	1.26	$2	$4
Bell,Heath	19	13	1.09	$1	($2)
Rodriguez,Francisco	3	32	1.15	($1)	$2
total	851	476		*$512*	*$416*

- The aggregate leverage indices for all the closers on this list is 1.25. For all the non-closers, 1.23. The gap is closing, as we'd expect given the turnover in roles all season.
- Saves are still the more plentiful statistic though their dominance is greatly diminished. We would expect it to be that way this year. The fallout is that the pure closers lose a lot more value when going to Sv+Hld.
- The top three relievers on the revised list remain the top three closers, though Ryan Cook jumps from 14th to 4th.
- These top pitchers once again earn nearly $100 less in total roto value when using saves+holds.

If we are going to change a roto category, some might consider going to (Saves + Holds – Blown Saves). This is not an unreasonable approach. However, once you open the door to a "net" category, then you also have to consider (Stolen Bases – Caught Stealing) and even (Wins – Losses), which have other implications. It's a door I don't think we necessarily have to open yet.

Imagine a world where you wouldn't be kicking yourself (as much) over losing your frontline closer for the season. Maybe you would have lucked out and grabbed a set-up man with speculative saves upside from the free agent pool. Maybe you would have missed out. But consider... in the new world of saves+holds, both frontliner and set-up man would have likely been listed on your Draft Day cheat sheet at identical prices. Time for change.

Seasonal Trends in Hitting and Pitching

by Bob Berger

We all "know" that hitters perform better in warm weather and pitchers perform better in cold weather. But is this really true? Can these effects be demonstrated by examining how stats vary over the course of a season? And if it is true, what are the implications for managing our fantasy rosters?

To assess these questions, we examined monthly trends in typical statistical categories used in the 5x5 Rotisserie format: BA, SB/game, HR/game, RBI/game, ERA, WHIP, saves/game, and K/9 during the last six MLB seasons (2007-2012).

Hitting: The analysis of hitting stats showed two trends:

- First, BA tends to rise month by month until falling in Sep/Oct (HR/game and RBI/game, unsurprisingly, follow similar trends).

- But SB/game shows a significant decline in July and August before recovering somewhat in Sep/Oct.

6 Year Averages of Hitting Stats by Month (2007-2012)

	Mar/Apr	May	June	July	Aug	Sep/Oct
Batting Average	.256	.259	.260	.262	.264	.260
HR/game	0.94	0.96	1.00	1.01	1.06	1.00
RBI/game	4.27	4.25	4.23	4.36	4.38	4.34
SB/game	0.631	0.634	0.640	0.626	0.585	0.624

Pitching: ERA tends to rise in July and August and improves slightly in September. WHIP also rises in July and August. These results are consistent with the improvements we saw in the offensive stats—if hitting stats are better, pitching stats should suffer, and vice-versa. But K/9 does not follow the ERA /WHIP trend, rising steadily from May through the end of the season. The Saves/game rate remained constant throughout each season (.24-.26 Saves/game) and are therefore not included in the following tables.

6 Year Averages of Pitching Stats by Month (2007-2012)

	Mar/Apr	May	June	July	Aug	Sep/Oct
ERA	4.13	4.15	4.12	4.26	4.28	4.23
WHIP	1.390	1.386	1.378	1.389	1.392	1.397
K/9	6.92	6.92	6.97	7.05	7.10	7.33

The final table indexes the stats by normalizing each stat, using April as the baseline. The table shows the percentage change in each statistic by month relative to the April performance. For example, HR/game are 11.9% higher in August than April and there are 7.4% fewer SB/game in August than in April. ERA and WHIP have been "reverse indexed," so an ERA or WHIP higher than in than April is depicted as below 1.0, to be consistent with the other statistics (where higher is better).

Hitting and Pitching Stats Indexed to April

	May	June	July	Aug	Sep/Oct
Batting Average	+1.4%	+1.8%	+2.7%	+3.3%	+1.8%
HR/game	+1.5%	+5.9%	+7.3%	+11.9%	+6.2%
RBI/game	−0.3%	−1.0%	+2.1%	+2.7%	+1.6%
SB/game	+0.5%	+1.4%	−0.8%	−7.4%	−1.1%
ERA	0.4%	−0.2%	+3.1%	+3.6%	+2.3%
WHIP	−0.3%	−0.9%	−0.1%	+0.2%	+0.5%
K/9	−0.1%	+0.6%	+1.8%	+2.6%	+5.9%

The indexed table shows that the stats with the biggest deviations (from April) in percentage terms are HR/game, which increase significantly throughout the season relative to April and May; and SB/game, which decreases significantly after June. ERA increases (depicted by increasing ERAs on the table) after June, and K/9 increases steadily from May on.

Conclusion

How might we use this information in managing our rosters throughout the season? First, a caveat: These data don't necessarily predict individual performance, because they're based on an analysis of all players' statistics. But we might be able to exploit the revealed trends in the context of managing our roster for an incremental competitive advantage.

How to use this knowledge depends on the context of your team and your league. For example, if the six-year trend holds, HR/game will increase and SB/game will decrease from May through the end of the season. We should expect relatively more HRs for our teams to harvest, but fewer SBs, compared to the rates at which these stats accumulate during the first two months of the season. This means gaps in the SB category will be more difficult to close as the season progresses, but that standings differences in HRs may be easier to close (in relative terms).

For example, if you have a comfortable lead in SBs in June, you might consider trading some of your speed for power, because it will be relatively more difficult for your competitors to catch you in the SB category as fewer SB/game are accumulated for the remainder of the season. On the other hand, a similar lead HRs in June is more at risk than a lead in SBs because the rate of HR/game tends to increase as the season continues. In fact, in July and August the HR/game rates increase over April by 7.3% and 11.9% respectively. A leader in HRs in early June should consider carefully before trading away power.

In the pitching categories, a strategic decision based on the six-year trend in ERA, might be to implement strategies to protect your ERA and WHIP as the season progresses by shifting your roster to pitchers who will accumulate fewer innings, but with strong peripheral stats, like middle relievers. Remember, though, you will also be limiting your chances of amassing Ks as the K/9 rate steadily increases during that same time.

These are only a few examples of the possible uses of these seasonal trends. Understanding these seasonal trends in common statistical categories—within the context of your league and your team—can inform better roster management decisions. The data could influence other strategic or tactical decisions in your roster management, depending on your team's specific situation. The final table strongly suggests that there will be significant changes in the rate of accumulation of commonly used stats from April/May through the remainder of the season.

Do hitters perform better in warm weather and are pitchers better in cold weather? As a very broad statement this seems to be directionally true—BA increases throughout the summer, as does HR/game. For pitchers, ERA trends upward as the weather warms, but when we look at individual statistical categories we can see there is more to the story (K/9 steadily increases all season) and understanding the complete story will help us make strategic decisions about our fantasy rosters.

One Man's Treasure

by Ron Shandler

This past July, I owned a fairly valuable player in one of my experts leagues. I drafted him in the 9th round and had no complaints about the value he had been returning. He went for $19 in Tout Wars and was earning exactly $19 at that time. In the real game, he signed a huge contract during the off-season and his team probably felt that they'd gotten their money's worth.

But Rotisserie Baseball is all about the categories, and so I was faced with a decision of questionable ethics. This player had virtually no value for me because the category he most contributed to would not help my team. And this particular league did not allow trading, so it was not like I could deal him for something I needed.

Simply, he represented a dead roster spot. I could have better used that spot for another starting pitcher, or even some bench help for my offense. But no, he was just dead wood.

So I was seriously considering cutting... Jonathan Papelbon.

Here was the deal: I was in next to last place in saves, with 22. The team in last place didn't draft any closers and had no saves at all, so I had no downside. Above me, the next closest team had 30 saves, and the team above him had 36, so I'd need 15 additional saves over the last two months just to gain two points. That was essentially the equivalent of adding a full-time closer. And I was not going to find that in the free agent pool.

So Papelbon was useless to me.

I checked with the league commissioner and there was no rule against me cutting him. I know some leagues prevent this sort of thing, and frankly, it did pose that ethical dilemma. But I was not going to tie up a valuable roster spot with dead wood. He'd hit the free agent pool, and the following week, I'm sure there would be a mad dash to claim him. Odds are he would go for several hundred dollars in FAAB.

Someone else's FAAB spending had only marginal benefit to me.

But this situation was not the problem. It was only an unfortunate symptom of a bigger issue.

The real problem for me is the entire idea of leagues that prohibit trading. Many public competitions—especially those that are high-stakes—just take that option off the table. With so much money involved, they don't want to have to administrate this human element of fantasy play. Everyone has their own perception of value, and league operators don't want to have to play policeman for every perceived lopsided trade or accusation of collusion.

You know, I get that.

But to use an old cliche, it's like throwing the baby out with the bath water. Trading is an important tactical element of game play, and taking it completely away forces ridiculous moves... like me cutting Jonathan Papelbon.

Is there no middle ground?

I think there is. What if these no-trade leagues were to reinstate limited trades? What if you were allowed to deal one player for one player, and only one of these trades per week per team? That would eliminate all the mega-deals where massive amounts of talent are moved at one time, often disproportionately. And it would open up more options for teams to manage their rosters and roto categories.

Consider that it becomes an interesting exercise in assessing value when you are restricted by the narrow walls of a one-for-one deal. It would force owners to at least try to focus on players of comparable value, because pulling off a Carlos Gonzalez for Ryan Raburn deal just won't cut it. But that's what makes this game more fun, and challenging.

Yes, there might still need to be some fail-safes put into place, but these trades would be far easier to administrate. And at least I could have tried to get something of value back for Jonathan Papelbon instead of just tossing an elite player back into the free agent pool.

In the end, I did cut the Phillies reliever, who was then FAABed for $175 the following week. As it turned out, he was purchased by the commissioner himself, who apparently was one of the only ones paying attention to my unfortunate cut.

The following section contains player boxes for every batter who had significant playing time in 2012 and/or is expected to get fantasy roster-worthy plate appearances in 2013. In most cases, high-end prospects who have yet to make their major league debuts will not appear here; you can find scouting reports for them in the Prospects section.

Snapshot Section

The top band of each player box contains the following information:

Age as of Opening Day 2013.

Bats shows which side of the plate he bats from — (L)eft, (R)ight or (B)oth.

Positions: Up to three defensive positions are listed and represent those for which he appeared a minimum of 20 games in 2012.

Ht/Wt: Each batter's height and weight.

Reliability Grades analyze each batter's forecast risk, on an A-F scale. High grades go to those who have accumulated few disabled list days (Health), have a history of substantial and regular major league playing time (PT/Exp) and have displayed consistent performance over the past three years, using RC/G (Consist).

LIMA Plan Grade evaluates how well a batter would fit into a team using the LIMA Plan draft strategy. Best grades go to batters who have excellent base skills, are expected to see regular playing time, and are in the $10-$30 Rotisserie dollar range. Lowest grades will go to poor skills, few AB and values less than $5 or more than $30.

Random Variance Score (Rand Var) measures the impact random variance had on the batter's 2012 stats and the probability that his 2013 performance will exceed or fall short of 2012. The variables tracked are those prone to regression—h%, hr/f and xBA to BA variance. Players are rated on a scale of –5 to +5 with positive scores indicating rebounds and negative scores indicating corrections. Note that this score is computer-generated and the projections will override it on occasion.

Mayberry Method (MM) acknowledges the imprecision of the forecasting process by projecting player performance in broad strokes. The four digits of MM each represent a fantasy-relevant skill—power, speed, batting average and playing time (PA)—and are all on a scale of 0 to 5.

Commentaries for each batter provide a brief analysis of BPIs and the potential impact on performance in 2013. MLB statistics are listed first for those who played only a portion of 2012 at the major league level. Note that these commentaries generally look at performance related issues only. Role and playing time expectations may impact these analyses, so you will have to adjust accordingly. Upside (UP) and downside (DN) statistical potential appears for some players; these are less grounded in hard data and more speculative of skills potential.

Player Stat Section

The past five years' statistics represent the total accumulated in the majors as well as in Triple-A, Double-A ball and various foreign leagues during each year. All non-major league stats have been converted to a major league equivalent (MLE) performance level. Minor league levels below Double-A are not included.

Nearly all baseball publications separate a player's statistical experiences in the major leagues from the minor leagues and outside leagues. While this may be appropriate for official record-keeping purposes, it is not an easy-to-analyze snapshot of a player's complete performance for a given year.

Bill James has proven that minor league statistics (converted to MLEs), at Double-A level or above, provide as accurate a record of a player's performance as major league statistics. Other researchers have also devised conversion factors for foreign leagues. Since these are adequate barometers, we include them in the pool of historical data for each year.

Team designations: An asterisk (*) appearing with a team name means that Triple-A and/or Double-A numbers are included in that year's stat line. Any stints of less than 20 AB are not included (to screen out most rehab appearances). A designation of "a/a" means the stats were accumulated at both AA and AAA levels that year. "for" represents a foreign or independent league. The designation "2TM" appears whenever a player was on more than one major league team, crossing leagues, in a season. "2AL" and "2NL" represent more than one team in the same league. Players who were cut during the season and finished 2012 as a free agent are designated as FAA (Free agent, AL) and FAN (Free agent, NL).

Stats: Descriptions of all the categories appear in the Encyclopedia.

- The leading decimal point has been suppressed on some categories to conserve space.
- Data for platoons (vL, vR), balls-in-play (G/L/F) and consistency (Wk#, DOM, DIS) are for major league performance only.
- Formulas that use BIP data, like xBA and xPX, only appear for years in which G/L/F data is available.

Batting average is presented alongside skills-based xBA, and versus left-handed and right-handed pitchers. On base average and slugging average appear next, and the combined On Base Plus Slugging (OPS).

Batting eye and contact skill are measured with walk rate (bb%), contact rate (ct%) and hit rate (h%), the latter often referred to as batting average on balls-in-play (BABIP). Eye is the ratio of walks to strikeouts.

Once the ball leaves the bat, it will either be a (G)round ball, (L)ine drive or (F)ly ball. Looking at the ratio of fly balls is a good springboard to the Power gauges. Linear weighted power index (PX) measures a batter's skill at hitting extra base hits as compared to overall league levels. xPX measures power by assessing how hard the ball is being hit (rather than the outcomes of those hits). And the ratio of home runs to fly balls shows the results of those hits.

To assess speed, first look at on base average (does he get on base?), then Spd (is he fast enough to steal bases?), then SBO (how often is he attempting to steal bases?) and finally, SB% (when he attempts, what is his rate of success?).

In looking at consistency, we use weekly Base Performance Value (BPV) levels. Starting with the total number of weeks the batter accumulated stats (#Wk), the percentage of DOMinating weeks (BPV over 50) and DISaster weeks (BPV under 0) is shown. The larger the variance between DOM and DIS, the greater the consistency.

The final section includes several overall performance measures: runs created per game (RC/G). runs above replacement (RAR), Base performance value (BPV), Base performance index (BPX, which is BPV indexed to each year's league average) and the Rotisserie value (R$).

2013 Projections

Forecasts are computed from a player's trends over the past five years. Adjustments were made for leading indicators and variances between skill and statistical output. After reviewing the leading indicators, you might opt to make further adjustments.

Although each year's numbers include all playing time at the Double-A level or above, the 2013 forecast only represents potential playing time at the major league level, and again is highly preliminary.

Note that the projected Rotisserie values in this book will not necessarily align with each player's historical actuals. Since we currently have no idea who is going to close games for the Tigers, or whether Jurickson Profar is going to break camp with Texas, it is impossible to create a finite pool of playing time, something which is required for valuation. So the projections are roughly based on a 12-team AL/NL league, and include an inflated number of plate appearances, league-wide. This serves to flatten the spread of values and depress individual player dollar projections. In truth, a $25 player in this book might actually be worth $21, or $28. This level of precision is irrelevant in a process that is driven by market forces anyway. So, don't obsess over it.

Be aware of other sources that publish perfectly calibrated Rotisserie values over the winter. They are likely making arbitrary decisions as to where free agents are going to sign and who is going to land jobs in the spring. We do not make those leaps of faith here.

Bottom line… It is far too early to be making definitive projections for 2013, especially on playing time. Focus on the skill levels and trends, then consult BaseballHQ.com for playing time revisions as players change teams and roles become more defined. A free projections update will be available online in March.

Do-it-yourself analysis

Here are some data points you can look at in doing your own player analysis:

- Variance between vLH and vRH batting averages
- Growth or decline in walk rate (bb%)
- Growth or decline in contact rate (ct%)
- Growth or decline in G/L/F individually, or concurrent shifts
- Variance in 2012 hit rate (h%) to 2009-2011 three-year average
- Variance between Avg and xBA each year
- Growth or decline in power index (PX) rate
- Variance between PX and xPX each year
- Variance in 2012 hr/f rate to 2009-2011 three-year average
- Growth or decline in statistically scouted speed (Spd) score
- Concurrent growth/decline of gauges like ct%, FB, PX, xPX, hr/f
- Concurrent growth/decline of gauges like OB, Spd, SBO, SB%
- Trends in DOM/DIS splits

Abreu,Bobby

Age 39	Bats L	Pos LF	Health	A	LIMA Plan	F
Ht 6' 0"	Wt 210		PT/Exp	B	Rand Var	0
			Consist	B	MM	2211

Can he hang on another year? Most signs point to "no." OPS continued its now-four-year slide; power not coming back; ct% slipping as well. He can still work a base on balls, but chances are GMs will continue to tell him to take a walk (as both LA ones did in 2012), rather than umpires.

Yr	Tm	AB	R	HR	RBI	SB	BA	xBA	vL	vR	OB	Slg	OPS	bb%	ct%	h%	Eye	G	L	F	PX	xPX	hr/f	Spd	SBO	SB%	#Wk	DOM	DIS	RC/G	RAR	BPV	BPX	R$
08	NYY	609	100	20	100	22	296	292	315	287	371	471	842	11	82	33	0.67	48	23	30	113	100	13%	81	17%	67%	27	56%	22%	6.15	24.5	74	145	$30
09	LAA	563	96	15	103	30	293	267	267	305	394	435	829	14	80	34	0.83	48	19	33	92	124	10%	93	18%	79%	27	44%	33%	6.27	24.6	58	118	$30
10	LAA	573	88	20	78	24	255	272	228	267	353	435	788	13	77	30	0.66	47	17	36	131	136	12%	83	20%	71%	27	59%	19%	5.17	7.5	70	152	$22
11	LAA	502	54	8	60	21	253	249	238	259	353	365	718	13	77	31	0.69	47	21	32	88	97	6%	73	16%	81%	27	44%	41%	4.50	-3.3	35	78	$14
12	2 TM	219	29	3	24	6	242	243	267	236	352	342	694	14	74	31	0.66	48	25	27	76	93	7%	78	11%	75%	23	26%	43%	4.09	-4.1	15	38	$3
1st Half		155	20	2	19	2	252	254	278	244	356	368	723	14	74	33	0.61	45	28	27	92	102	6%	80	6%	67%	13	38%	31%	4.43	-1.0	20	50	$4
2nd Half		64	9	1	5	4	219	214	222	218	342	281	623	16	77	27	0.80	56	17	27	41	72	8%	74	21%	80%	10	10%	60%	3.32	-2.7	-5	-13	$0
13	Proj	**150**	**20**	**3**	**17**	**6**	**247**	**242**	**248**	**247**	**354**	**358**	**712**	**14**	**77**	**30**	**0.71**	**50**	**20**	**30**	**80**	**98**	**8%**	**74**	**16%**	**77%**				**4.35**	**-1.3**	**26**	**64**	**$3**

Ackley,Dustin

Age 25	Bats L	Pos 2B	Health	A	LIMA Plan	C+
Ht 6' 1"	Wt 190		PT/Exp	A	Rand Var	+1
			Consist	C	MM	2415

Not the sophomore season many were hoping for. "Latent power" highlighted in last year's Forecaster went into deep hibernation. Spd, SB% hint at room for SB growth. Perhaps removal of long-nagging ankle bone spur in October will help. BA growth will require more, and harder, contact. He's an unfinished work.

Yr	Tm	AB	R	HR	RBI	SB	BA	xBA	vL	vR	OB	Slg	OPS	bb%	ct%	h%	Eye	G	L	F	PX	xPX	hr/f	Spd	SBO	SB%	#Wk	DOM	DIS	RC/G	RAR	BPV	BPX	R$
08																																		
09																																		
10	a/a	501	61	5	39	8	231	255			312	340	652	10	82	27	0.65				79			118	8%	70%				3.51		45	0	$4
11	SEA *	604	75	11	58	10	256	249	224	290	339	389	727	11	79	31	0.60	40	22	38	92	110	6%	144	8%	75%	16	44%	44%	4.51	6.1	46	102	$13
12	SEA	607	84	12	50	13	226	234	246	215	294	328	622	9	80	27	0.48	45	19	35	67	74	7%	119	10%	81%	28	21%	43%	3.22	-17.5	22	55	$8
1st Half		290	42	4	23	7	241	231	231	246	321	331	652	10	77	30	0.51	46	21	33	65	69	5%	119	9%	88%	14	21%	43%	3.66	-5.2	11	28	$9
2nd Half		317	42	8	27	6	211	236	258	183	269	325	594	7	82	23	0.44	45	18	37	69	79	8%	114	11%	75%	14	21%	43%	2.83	-14.1	28	70	$8
13	Proj	**601**	**78**	**14**	**52**	**11**	**244**	**245**	**231**	**250**	**316**	**372**	**688**	**10**	**80**	**29**	**0.53**	**43**	**20**	**36**	**82**	**89**	**8%**	**130**	**9%**	**76%**				**3.98**	**-5.1**	**37**	**94**	**$12**

Adams,Matt

Age 24	Bats L	Pos 1B	Health	A	LIMA Plan	F
Ht 6' 3"	Wt 230		PT/Exp	D	Rand Var	0
			Consist	C	MM	3103

2-13-.244 in 86 AB at STL. Hot start upon May callup, but soon, impatience, subpar ct% got exploited, leading to MLB OPS 300 points lower than at AAA. Surgery to remove bone spur in elbow ended season in mid-August. MLEs show far better skills, so be patient with this one.

Yr	Tm	AB	R	HR	RBI	SB	BA	xBA	vL	vR	OB	Slg	OPS	bb%	ct%	h%	Eye	G	L	F	PX	xPX	hr/f	Spd	SBO	SB%	#Wk	DOM	DIS	RC/G	RAR	BPV	BPX	R$
08																																		
09																																		
10																																		
11	aa	463	51	18	64	0	234	252			276	398	674	5	78	26	0.26				109			80	1%	0%				3.61		21	0	$8
12	STL *	344	38	14	50	2	265	253	150	273	299	458	757	5	74	32	0.18	44	18	39	140	126	8%	67	5%	66%	5	20%	60%	4.71	-7.1	32	80	$9
1st Half		256	29	11	40	1	276	257	150	273	309	468	777	4	76	32	0.20	44	18	39	132	126	8%	68	5%	56%	5	20%	60%	5.02	-2.5	35	88	$13
2nd Half		88	10	3	10	1	232	247			270	430	699	5	66	31	0.15				165			74	5%	100%				3.89		22	55	-$4
13	Proj	**300**	**34**	**9**	**40**	**1**	**250**	**234**	**153**	**279**	**287**	**401**	**687**	**5**	**73**	**31**	**0.19**	**44**	**18**	**39**	**112**	**113**	**10%**	**72**	**3%**	**73%**				**3.90**	**-12.9**	**9**	**23**	**$7**

Alonso,Yonder

Age 26	Bats L	Pos 1B	Health	A	LIMA Plan	C+
Ht 6' 2"	Wt 240		PT/Exp	B	Rand Var	0
			Consist	A	MM	3035

Not surprisingly, 2011's late-season barrage was proven to be a bit of a fluke. Nonetheless, 2nd-half growth in ct%, PX pretty darn encouraging, as was the lack of a PETCO drag on his stats. Only knock on the 2H is the backslide against LHP. Still, well on his way to being a low-risk contributor with a shot at a higher ceiling.

Yr	Tm	AB	R	HR	RBI	SB	BA	xBA	vL	vR	OB	Slg	OPS	bb%	ct%	h%	Eye	G	L	F	PX	xPX	hr/f	Spd	SBO	SB%	#Wk	DOM	DIS	RC/G	RAR	BPV	BPX	R$
08																																		
09	aa	105	10	2	12	1	275	286			351	431	782	10	84	31	0.74				112			82	3%	100%				5.38		60	0	$1
10	CIN *	536	55	13	56	10	253	254	111	250	310	393	703	8	79	30	0.39	47	16	37	103	139	0%	68	10%	75%	6	17%	50%	4.15	-20.1	38	83	$11
11	CIN *	446	43	15	56	4	268	268	154	360	334	435	768	9	80	31	0.48	42	22	36	113	98	21%	76	8%	44%	10	40%	50%	4.85	-7.4	46	102	$12
12	SD	549	47	9	62	3	273	264	261	278	347	393	740	10	82	32	0.61	45	24	31	88	106	6%	49	2%	100%	27	30%	30%	4.83	-9.3	31	78	$11
1st Half		266	23	2	18	2	259	254	297	245	330	346	676	10	80	32	0.54	45	26	30	69	94	3%	71	3%	100%	13	23%	46%	3.98	-10.7	10	25	$6
2nd Half		283	24	7	44	1	286	272	228	309	363	438	801	11	83	33	0.69	45	22	33	106	117	9%	40	1%	100%	14	36%	14%	5.70	2.7	46	115	$17
13	Proj	**569**	**52**	**17**	**77**	**5**	**271**	**275**	**180**	**303**	**342**	**436**	**777**	**10**	**81**	**31**	**0.57**	**44**	**23**	**33**	**112**	**104**	**11%**	**52**	**5%**	**67%**				**5.17**	**-3.0**	**49**	**123**	**$16**

Altuve,Jose

Age 23	Bats R	Pos 2B	Health	A	LIMA Plan	C+
Ht 5' 5"	Wt 170		PT/Exp	D	Rand Var	-1
			Consist	A	MM	1535

Very nice growth year for diminutive dynamo, especially with plate skills, Spd. Maintained ct% and improved Eye and bb%, particularly in 2H, which bodes well. High SBO, increasing SB% suggests he should be good, or even great, SB source, and GB/LD approach should help prop up BA. With a little more OBP... UP: 45 SB

Yr	Tm	AB	R	HR	RBI	SB	BA	xBA	vL	vR	OB	Slg	OPS	bb%	ct%	h%	Eye	G	L	F	PX	xPX	hr/f	Spd	SBO	SB%	#Wk	DOM	DIS	RC/G	RAR	BPV	BPX	R$
08																																		
09																																		
10																																		
11	HOU *	365	41	6	30	11	293	276	321	262	313	409	722	3	88	32	0.23	50	20	30	75	54	4%	114	21%	55%	11	18%	27%	4.30	-0.4	47	104	$12
12	HOU	576	80	7	37	33	290	277	359	264	336	399	735	6	87	32	0.54	53	20	27	72	73	5%	134	27%	75%	27	37%	15%	4.79	7.3	58	145	$24
1st Half		285	45	5	23	12	309	281	370	284	343	453	796	5	86	35	0.37	52	19	29	91	81	7%	149	22%	71%	13	46%	23%	5.59	10.6	67	168	$27
2nd Half		291	35	2	14	21	271	274	347	245	329	347	676	8	89	30	0.76	53	22	25	55	64	3%	102	31%	78%	14	29%	7%	4.08	-1.5	45	113	$22
13	Proj	**564**	**71**	**6**	**39**	**37**	**289**	**272**	**347**	**269**	**326**	**389**	**715**	**5**	**88**	**32**	**0.43**	**52**	**20**	**28**	**66**	**64**	**4%**	**122**	**32%**	**75%**				**4.53**	**4.3**	**51**	**127**	**$26**

Alvarez,Pedro

Age 26	Bats L	Pos 3B	Health	B	LIMA Plan	C
Ht 6' 3"	Wt 235		PT/Exp	B	Rand Var	-1
			Consist	F	MM	4105

Power returned and then some, but stagnant ct% leaves much to be desired. Until that improves, expect more sub-.250 BAs. FB% recovery is what brought the power back, but still hits a lot of GBs for a slugger. That, plus expected regression of hr/f, makes a return to 30-HR plateau questionable at best.

Yr	Tm	AB	R	HR	RBI	SB	BA	xBA	vL	vR	OB	Slg	OPS	bb%	ct%	h%	Eye	G	L	F	PX	xPX	hr/f	Spd	SBO	SB%	#Wk	DOM	DIS	RC/G	RAR	BPV	BPX	R$
08																																		
09	aa	222	35	11	34	1	306	275			384	526	909	11	72	38	0.45				158			82	1%	100%				7.44		51	0	$8
10	PIT *	589	74	25	104	3	250	246	228	270	320	450	770	9	67	33	0.32	46	15	40	156	135	18%	75	5%	40%	16	38%	50%	4.77	2.8	36	78	$16
11	PIT *	360	30	8	33	1	201	214	158	198	281	311	592	10	65	28	0.32	55	19	25	92	89	10%	69	2%	47%	16	13%	75%	2.76	-20.9	-27	-60	-$2
12	PIT	525	64	30	85	1	244	244	207	257	318	467	785	10	66	31	0.32	47	19	34	164	144	25%	66	1%	100%	27	41%	52%	5.01	6.3	28	70	$14
1st Half		235	34	15	44	0	226	250	194	237	297	477	774	9	65	28	0.29	42	18	40	190	165	24%	53	0%	0%	13	54%	46%	4.67	0.6	41	103	$13
2nd Half		290	30	15	41	1	259	238	218	274	334	459	793	10	66	34	0.34	51	19	30	144	127	26%	83	1%	100%	14	29%	57%	5.30	6.0	14	35	$15
13	Proj	**568**	**66**	**24**	**82**	**2**	**241**	**231**	**207**	**252**	**315**	**424**	**739**	**10**	**67**	**32**	**0.33**	**49**	**17**	**34**	**137**	**123**	**19%**	**66**	**2%**	**63%**				**4.47**	**-1.8**	**12**	**31**	**$13**

Amarista,Alexi

Age 24	Bats L	Pos 2B LF	Health	A	LIMA Plan	D
Ht 5' 7"	Wt 150		PT/Exp	D	Rand Var	+4
			Consist	B	MM	1413

5-32-.240 with 8 SB in 275 AB at LAA and SD. Despite little plate patience, profile of decent ct%, good Spd and GB tilt should yield better BA if h% turns. SB% (8-for-12 at SD) suggests that skill is a work in progress. Low OBP also tamps down hopes he'll be a sleeper SB source. Check back in a year.

Yr	Tm	AB	R	HR	RBI	SB	BA	xBA	vL	vR	OB	Slg	OPS	bb%	ct%	h%	Eye	G	L	F	PX	xPX	hr/f	Spd	SBO	SB%	#Wk	DOM	DIS	RC/G	RAR	BPV	BPX	R$
08																																		
09																																		
10	a/a	256	29	1	22	6	277	250			305	333	638	4	92	30	0.49				34			123	13%	65%				3.50		35	0	$5
11	LAA *	415	35	3	39	10	227	223	0	174	258	318	576	4	83	27	0.24	43	14	43	68	53	0%	105	23%	53%	10	10%	30%	2.52	-23.6	25	56	$3
12	2 TM *	401	48	6	44	11	234	270	266	232	270	359	629	5	86	26	0.35	50	19	30	77	78	7%	130	18%	73%	22	32%	23%	3.20	-14.0	56	140	$6
1st Half		205	23	4	24	4	233	270	261	250	258	371	628	3	88	25	0.27	51	16	33	82	82	14%	117	16%	65%	8	38%	38%	3.10	-7.2	59	148	$6
2nd Half		196	25	2	20	7	235	265	268	226	282	347	629	6	84	27	0.42	50	21	29	72	77	4%	134	20%	78%	14	29%	14%	3.29	-5.8	47	118	$7
13	Proj	**335**	**36**	**5**	**33**	**9**	**241**	**251**	**209**	**250**	**274**	**357**	**632**	**4**	**86**	**27**	**0.31**	**48**	**17**	**36**	**73**	**69**	**5%**	**123**	**19%**	**65%**				**3.19**	**-10.8**	**44**	**110**	**$7**

KRIS OLSON

Andino,Robert

Age 29	Bats R	Pos 2B		Health	A	LIMA Plan	F
Ht 6' 0"	Wt 195			PT/Exp	B	Rand Var	+1
				Consist	C	MM	1203

Second half output was limited by a shoulder injury, but it's not like his numbers were grandiose before that. Growth of bb% is mitigated by poor ct% for a non-slugger; xBA is not impressed with the combo. This is the profile of a reserve infielder, and without plus speed there's no path to positive value.

Yr	Tm	AB	R	HR	RBI	SB	BA	xBA	vL	vR	OB	Slg	OPS	bb%	ct%	h%	Eye	G	L	F	PX	xPX	hr/f	Spd	SBO	SB%	#Wk	DOM	DIS	RC/G	RAR	BPV	BPX	R$
08	FLA *	244	25	6	26	6	224	279	250	186	273	369	641	6	75	28	0.26	51	28	21	102	88	25%	96	24%	50%	19	21%	63%	3.04	-9.9	25	49	$1
09	BAL	198	31	2	10	3	222	224	226	221	277	288	565	7	76	28	0.32	53	17	30	50	59	4%	114	12%	50%	26	19%	69%	2.50	-10.2	-14	-29	$0
10	BAL *	607	60	13	63	13	230	227	300	293	259	349	608	4	77	28	0.17	43	14	43	87	112	10%	118	15%	74%	5	40%	60%	2.98	-22.0	15	33	$8
11	BAL	457	63	5	36	13	263	244	306	243	323	344	667	8	82	31	0.49	46	21	33	62	70	4%	100	12%	81%	26	19%	50%	3.91	-3.4	22	49	$11
12	BAL	384	41	7	28	5	211	216	216	208	280	305	585	9	74	27	0.37	47	19	34	67	91	7%	96	10%	50%	26	12%	54%	2.66	-18.1	-11	-28	$0
1st Half		235	24	3	17	4	234	210	224	238	300	315	615	9	72	31	0.34	50	18	32	61	68	6%	103	9%	67%	13	8%	62%	3.12	-8.2	-20	-50	$3
2nd Half		149	17	4	11	1	174	227	207	154	250	289	539	9	77	20	0.43	43	20	37	76	126	10%	84	13%	25%	13	15%	46%	2.04	-11.0	2	5	-$3
13	Proj	258	30	5	21	5	222	231	240	212	282	329	612	8	77	27	0.37	46	19	35	75	93	8%	93	13%	58%				2.96	-10.4	7	18	$1

Andrus,Elvis

Age 24	Bats R	Pos SS		Health	A	LIMA Plan	C
Ht 6' 0"	Wt 200			PT/Exp	A	Rand Var	-1
				Consist	B	MM	1435

SB total suffered due to dip in SBO, not OBP: TEX attempted 53 fewer SB as a team than a year ago, with a chunk of that decline in his box. 2H was an across-the-board mess, perhaps injury or fatigue related? Lots of questions, but still owns the skills for a strong BA/Runs/SB profile, so... UP: 40 SB, 100 Runs.

Yr	Tm	AB	R	HR	RBI	SB	BA	xBA	vL	vR	OB	Slg	OPS	bb%	ct%	h%	Eye	G	L	F	PX	xPX	hr/f	Spd	SBO	SB%	#Wk	DOM	DIS	RC/G	RAR	BPV	BPX	R$
08	aa	482	65	3	52	43	271	225			314	337	651	6	80	33	0.31				48			99	44%	72%				3.62		9	0	$23
09	TEX	480	72	6	40	33	267	284	279	262	323	373	696	8	84	31	0.52	55	22	23	63	50	7%	156	28%	85%	27	37%	37%	4.37	6.5	51	104	$18
10	TEX	588	88	0	35	32	265	256	268	264	337	301	638	10	84	32	0.67	61	19	20	28	34	0%	149	23%	68%	27	7%	48%	3.49	-7.3	14	30	$18
11	TEX	587	96	5	60	37	279	284	282	279	342	361	703	9	87	31	0.76	56	23	21	57	51	5%	107	26%	76%	27	44%	15%	4.41	8.5	53	118	$26
12	TEX	629	85	3	62	21	286	275	265	294	345	378	724	8	85	33	0.59	57	22	21	61	76	3%	134	16%	68%	27	30%	26%	4.59	12.2	42	105	$21
1st Half		302	51	1	31	16	305	287	290	311	379	411	789	11	87	35	0.90	51	25	24	71	90	2%	133	20%	76%	13	54%	8%	5.73	14.5	69	173	$28
2nd Half		327	34	2	31	5	269	262	234	280	313	349	662	6	83	32	0.38	63	19	18	52	62	4%	129	11%	50%	14	7%	43%	3.65	-3.5	14	35	$15
13	Proj	610	87	4	57	29	278	271	269	282	338	359	697	8	85	32	0.60	58	22	21	54	59	3%	125	21%	71%				4.25	4.2	37	93	$23

Ankiel,Rick

Age 33	Bats L	Pos CF		Health	D	LIMA Plan	F
Ht 6' 1"	Wt 210			PT/Exp	D	Rand Var	-2
				Consist	A	MM	4101

Was early season quad injury responsible for descent into the void? K rate of 37% is impressive for a pitcher, which he once was, but no longer is. Four years of poor BA vR creates doubt that he has any remaining value, xPX says the pop is gone too. July release from WAS may have been end of the line...

Yr	Tm	AB	R	HR	RBI	SB	BA	xBA	vL	vR	OB	Slg	OPS	bb%	ct%	h%	Eye	G	L	F	PX	xPX	hr/f	Spd	SBO	SB%	#Wk	DOM	DIS	RC/G	RAR	BPV	BPX	R$
08	STL	413	65	25	71	2	264	273	224	279	332	506	838	9	76	29	0.42	36	19	45	155	136	18%	94	3%	67%	24	42%	33%	5.79	12.2	68	133	$13
09	STL	372	50	11	38	4	231	234	234	230	281	387	669	7	73	29	0.26	40	15	45	111	98	9%	89	9%	57%	25	20%	56%	3.53	-14.0	24	49	$4
10	2 TM *	278	36	8	30	3	222	238	164	256	290	383	673	9	66	30	0.28	53	14	33	137	105	13%	85	7%	75%	17	35%	59%	3.64	-10.3	17	37	$2
11	WAS	380	46	9	37	10	239	228	228	243	293	363	657	7	75	30	0.30	45	16	39	96	101	8%	87	14%	77%	24	29%	46%	3.58	-13.5	16	36	$7
12	WAS	158	15	5	15	1	228	221	174	237	282	411	694	7	63	33	0.20	41	18	41	152	107	13%	94	13%	25%	15	27%	47%	3.54	-6.0	13	33	$0
1st Half		152	14	4	13	1	224	219	174	233	280	395	675	7	63	33	0.21	43	17	40	143	103	11%	95	13%	25%	12	25%	42%	3.35	-6.8	8	20	$0
2nd Half		6	1	1	2	0	333	340		333	333	833	1167	0	50	50	0.00	0	33	67	421	238	50%	80	0%	0%	3	33%	67%	10.63	0.9	136	340	-$4
13	Proj	129	16	4	14	2	232	228	199	241	290	395	685	8	69	31	0.27	45	16	39	125	106	11%	85	10%	55%				3.70	-4.2	17	42	$2

Aoki,Norichika

Age 31	Bats L	Pos RF		Health	A	LIMA Plan	B
Ht 5' 9"	Wt 182			PT/Exp	B	Rand Var	0
				Consist	F	MM	2545

Entire skill set transferred very nicely in first MLB campaign. SB came from high SBO% rather than pure Spd skill; that and age hint at SB regression. Near-elite ct% sets a nice BA floor, SB will depend on continued green light. Even with 2H xPX "gains," high GB% says 10-15 HR is probably a ceiling.

Yr	Tm	AB	R	HR	RBI	SB	BA	xBA	vL	vR	OB	Slg	OPS	bb%	ct%	h%	Eye	G	L	F	PX	xPX	hr/f	Spd	SBO	SB%	#Wk	DOM	DIS	RC/G	RAR	BPV	BPX	R$
08	for *	444	83	8	62	28	323	290			371	480	851	7	90	35	0.76				93	5	0%	118	29%	74%				6.57	20.5	96	0	$29
09	for *	531	85	10	64	16	283	268			356	392	747	10	88	31	0.98				65	-5	0%	100	16%	59%				4.75	-2.0	57	0	$18
10	for *	583	90	8	61	17	334	286			387	457	844	8	90	36	0.88				85	-5	0%	94	11%	79%				6.81	29.6	75	0	$30
11	for *	583	71	2	43	7	272	249			320	342	661	7	91	30	0.79				43	2	0%	128	6%	68%				3.80	-18.1	44	0	$11
12	MIL	520	81	10	50	30	288	294	270	299	343	433	775	8	89	31	0.78	55	17	28	91	81	8%	122	27%	79%	27	56%	22%	5.35	9.8	86	215	$24
1st Half		199	30	4	14	10	286	296	271	295	340	437	777	7	88	31	0.70	60	15	24	90	64	10%	137	24%	77%	13	54%	38%	5.30	3.0	82	205	$14
2nd Half		321	51	6	36	20	290	292	270	301	345	430	775	8	90	31	0.84	52	18	30	91	91	7%	107	28%	80%	14	57%	7%	5.39	5.6	84	210	$31
13	Proj	583	87	12	55	24	284	289	266	294	338	422	760	8	90	30	0.80	56	17	28	84	80	8%	127	19%	77%				5.08	1.3	79	197	$25

Arencibia,J.P.

Age 27	Bats R	Pos CA		Health	B	LIMA Plan	C
Ht 6' 0"	Wt 205			PT/Exp	C	Rand Var	-1
				Consist	A	MM	4105

His power is very real and his batting Eye is genuinely atrocious. He had a hot July (.345 OBP, 1.081 OPS in 53 AB—an admittedly small sample) and then broke his hand. If July was more than a blip... UP: .250 BA, 30 HR. If not, and his bb% and OBP don't improve... DN: Backup catcher.

Yr	Tm	AB	R	HR	RBI	SB	BA	xBA	vL	vR	OB	Slg	OPS	bb%	ct%	h%	Eye	G	L	F	PX	xPX	hr/f	Spd	SBO	SB%	#Wk	DOM	DIS	RC/G	RAR	BPV	BPX	R$
08	aa	262	26	12	34	0	255	257			271	443	714	2	76	29	0.09				125			77	0%	0%				4.11		15	0	$4
09	aaa	466	49	16	55	0	200	249			232	366	597	4	71	25	0.14				123			81	2%	0%				2.66		6	0	-$1
10	TOR *	447	48	22	54	0	225	242	0	217	265	438	703	5	74	25	0.21	29	13	58	153	161	14%	77	0%	0%	8	13%	75%	3.81	-4.3	40	87	$5
11	TOR	443	47	23	78	1	219	240	259	206	278	438	716	8	70	26	0.27	35	16	50	158	153	15%	96	2%	50%	27	37%	37%	3.94	-2.6	43	96	$8
12	TOR	347	45	18	56	1	233	233	244	230	271	435	706	5	69	29	0.17	37	18	45	144	128	17%	67	2%	100%	22	41%	45%	3.94	-2.0	17	43	$7
1st Half		228	28	10	37	1	224	230	222	224	259	404	663	5	68	28	0.15	40	19	41	133	122	16%	62	2%	100%	13	31%	46%	3.46	-5.2	5	13	$9
2nd Half		119	17	8	19	0	252	240	296	239	294	496	789	6	71	29	0.20	32	15	53	163	139	18%	87	0%	0%	9	56%	44%	4.96	2.6	34	85	$4
13	Proj	462	56	25	72	1	231	239	260	222	276	451	727	6	71	27	0.21	35	16	49	151	140	16%	77	1%	68%				4.12	-1.3	32	81	$11

Arias,Joaquin

Age 28	Bats R	Pos 3B SS		Health	A	LIMA Plan	D
Ht 6' 1"	Wt 170			PT/Exp	F	Rand Var	-4
				Consist	D	MM	1523

5-34-.270 in 319 AB at SF. Power is trending in the right direction, but at this rate is a few more years from league average. Makes enough contact to prop up BA, but lack of BB keeps OBP down, and low SBO combined with that OBP stifles SB totals. Now 28 and full of skill warts, this may have been his peak.

Yr	Tm	AB	R	HR	RBI	SB	BA	xBA	vL	vR	OB	Slg	OPS	bb%	ct%	h%	Eye	G	L	F	PX	xPX	hr/f	Spd	SBO	SB%	#Wk	DOM	DIS	RC/G	RAR	BPV	BPX	R$
08	TEX *	542	59	5	46	21	266	267	417	256	294	375	669	4	87	30	0.29	48	20	32	64	41	0%	204	22%	76%	7	57%	43%	3.82	-4.5	49	96	$13
09	TEX *	512	51	4	42	20	234	164	0	0	257	298	555	3	89	26	0.29	40	0	60	38	-5	0%	137	20%	85%	2	0%	50%	2.64	-22.7	30	61	$7
10	2 TM *	159	26	0	14	1	240	215	333	232	269	290	559	4	81	30	0.20	43	18	39	41	49	0%	150	3%	100%	23	13%	57%	2.65	-6.8	-4	-9	$0
11	aaa	241	24	2	16	5	186	249			216	276	492	4	87	21	0.28				59			115	15%	79%				1.88		40	0	-$3
12	SF *	389	39	6	45	5	276	263	303	240	303	393	695	4	85	31	0.25	47	22	32	72	84	6%	140	8%	68%	24	42%	46%	4.14	0.4	34	85	$9
1st Half		232	23	2	24	4	264	259	304	204	294	352	647	4	86	30	0.30	50	21	29	57	74	2%	122	9%	75%	10	40%	50%	3.60	-2.8	26	65	$9
2nd Half		157	16	4	21	1	293	269	301	284	315	452	767	3	83	33	0.19	43	23	35	94	94	9%	149	5%	50%	14	43%	43%	5.03	4.5	44	110	$9
13	Proj	270	30	6	27	4	248	259	286	223	275	377	652	4	85	27	0.24	45	20	35	77	66	7%	145	10%	76%				3.51	-8.6	40	101	$5

Avila,Alex

Age 26	Bats L	Pos CA		Health	A	LIMA Plan	D
Ht 5' 11"	Wt 210			PT/Exp	C	Rand Var	+1
				Consist	F	MM	4113

2011 xBA and unsustainable h% warned us that gaudy 2011 would not repeat. Giving back 2011's progress vL didn't help matters. Drop in FB% suppressed HR, tanking real and fanalytic value in the process. xPX says HR more likely to return than BA. Verdict: split the difference between 2011 and 2012.

Yr	Tm	AB	R	HR	RBI	SB	BA	xBA	vL	vR	OB	Slg	OPS	bb%	ct%	h%	Eye	G	L	F	PX	xPX	hr/f	Spd	SBO	SB%	#Wk	DOM	DIS	RC/G	RAR	BPV	BPX	R$
08																																		
09	DET *	390	52	15	60	2	248	248	400	255	338	435	773	12	74	30	0.53	43	14	43	130	193	26%	83	3%	61%	9	56%	33%	4.95	9.4	43	88	$8
10	DET	294	28	7	31	2	228	239	182	234	312	340	652	11	76	28	0.51	43	22	35	82	127	9%	55	5%	50%	27	19%	52%	3.45	-6.1	4	9	$2
11	DET	464	63	19	82	3	295	264	273	304	391	506	898	14	72	38	0.56	38	22	40	160	154	14%	85	3%	75%	27	33%	41%	7.16	38.9	66	147	$20
12	DET	367	42	9	48	2	243	245	176	262	350	384	735	14	72	31	0.59	46	24	30	106	130	11%	73	2%	100%	26	35%	46%	4.57	4.7	20	50	$5
1st Half		170	20	5	22	2	241	256	244	240	335	400	735	12	72	31	0.51	47	24	29	116	138	14%	71	4%	100%	12	42%	50%	4.58	1.8	31	78	$5
2nd Half		197	22	4	26	0	244	236	114	281	363	371	734	16	71	32	0.65	46	23	31	98	123	9%	81	0%	0%	14	29%	43%	4.54	1.9	7	18	$5
13	Proj	364	43	12	51	2	254	249	207	268	354	421	776	13	73	32	0.56	43	22	35	121	141	13%	72	2%	75%				5.11	9.5	33	82	$9

JOSH PALEY

Aviles,Mike

Age	32	Bats	R	Pos	SS	Health	C	LIMA Plan	D
Ht	5' 10"	Wt	205			PT/Exp	C	Rand Var	0
						Consist	A	MM	1213

Plate skills are eerily stable, so BA fluctuations are primarily h% driven, and he took short end of that in 2H. What's more troubling is the drastic Spd decline, which calls into question whether he has any more double-digit SB seasons in him. Take that away, and there's little redeeming value here.

Yr	Tm	AB	R	HR	RBI	SB	BA	xBA	vL	vR	OB	Slg	OPS	bb%	ct%	h%	Eye	G	L	F	PX	xPX	hr/f	Spd	SBO	SB%	#Wk	DOM	DIS	RC/G	RAR	BPV	BPX	R$
08	KC *	633	98	17	81	10	310	298	348	313	337	488	826	4	87	34	0.31	46	20	33	111	83	8%	124	9%	77%	19	47%	21%	6.07	37.3	82	161	$27
09	KC	120	10	1	8	1	183	221	195	177	210	250	460	3	78	23	0.15	45	19	36	44	50	3%	101	5%	100%	7	14%	86%	1.67	-8.5	-16	-33	-$3
10	KC *	494	68	9	37	14	291	257	263	319	322	396	718	4	88	32	0.37	43	19	38	65	70	6%	144	14%	74%	24	33%	33%	4.56	9.0	47	102	$17
11	2 AL *	426	44	12	55	18	247	260	318	229	276	408	683	4	85	27	0.26	42	16	43	103	93	7%	104	33%	66%	22	50%	41%	3.61	-3.8	67	149	$12
12	BOS	512	57	13	60	14	250	254	286	236	282	381	663	4	85	27	0.30	41	19	40	84	90	7%	62	18%	70%	26	31%	35%	3.59	-4.8	41	103	$13
1st Half		305	39	9	43	9	266	273	308	248	289	420	709	3	85	29	0.22	41	22	38	99	100	9%	61	21%	69%	13	38%	15%	4.11	0.9	53	133	$20
2nd Half		207	18	4	17	5	227	224	250	219	273	324	596	6	85	25	0.41	41	16	43	62	74	5%	69	15%	71%	13	23%	54%	2.89	-7.1	20	50	$2
13	Proj	368	41	8	39	9	251	247	278	240	284	377	661	4	85	28	0.30	42	18	40	79	83	7%	85	16%	65%				3.55	-5.1	41	103	$7

Aybar,Erick

Age	29	Bats	B	Pos	SS	Health	B	LIMA Plan	C+
Ht	5' 10"	Wt	180			PT/Exp	A	Rand Var	-1
						Consist	B	MM	1435

A tale of two halves, although 2nd half explosion was one giant mirage. PX, SB and BA were all driven by variance of luck factors, which resulted in an overall flat year-long skill level. Gains vs. LHP might stick (92% ct%, 0.62 Eye vLHP), but stagnant plate approach ultimately limits further growth.

Yr	Tm	AB	R	HR	RBI	SB	BA	xBA	vL	vR	OB	Slg	OPS	bb%	ct%	h%	Eye	G	L	F	PX	xPX	hr/f	Spd	SBO	SB%	#Wk	DOM	DIS	RC/G	RAR	BPV	BPX	R$
08	LAA	346	53	3	39	7	277	272	286	274	306	384	690	4	87	31	0.31	52	18	30	68	67	4%	134	11%	78%	22	41%	27%	4.15	2.4	51	100	$9
09	LAA	504	70	5	58	14	312	278	325	305	350	423	773	6	89	34	0.56	46	21	33	65	62	4%	133	14%	67%	27	37%	30%	5.36	20.1	60	122	$20
10	LAA	534	69	5	29	22	253	237	252	253	299	330	628	6	85	29	0.43	49	15	36	51	54	3%	140	21%	73%	26	27%	42%	3.36	-8.8	31	67	$12
11	LAA	556	71	10	59	30	279	287	216	308	317	421	738	5	88	30	0.46	48	21	31	91	66	7%	118	27%	83%	25	60%	20%	4.81	14.4	79	176	$23
12	LAA	517	67	8	45	20	290	279	336	274	319	416	735	4	88	32	0.36	52	19	29	79	63	6%	110	19%	83%	25	52%	32%	4.84	13.6	63	158	$19
1st Half		267	23	1	20	5	255	253	295	238	284	341	625	4	87	29	0.32	55	16	30	58	65	2%	99	10%	83%	13	31%	54%	3.35	-5.1	34	85	$9
2nd Half		250	44	7	25	15	328	303	390	309	356	496	852	4	89	35	0.41	50	21	29	101	61	11%	118	27%	83%	12	75%	8%	6.80	18.7	87	218	$30
13	Proj	567	77	10	52	25	286	276	291	285	320	416	736	5	88	31	0.40	50	19	31	80	62	6%	116	21%	81%				4.81	12.8	64	160	$24

Baker,Jeff

Age	32	Bats	R	Pos	RF 1B	Health	B	LIMA Plan	F
Ht	6' 2"	Wt	210			PT/Exp	F	Rand Var	+2
						Consist	B	MM	3321

ABs in free fall, perhaps because his only real plus skill—ability to hit LHers—disappeared. xPX suggests whatever power he did have is waning as well. Sure, both could be sample size abberations, but he hasn't had any real fanalytic value since 2008.

Yr	Tm	AB	R	HR	RBI	SB	BA	xBA	vL	vR	OB	Slg	OPS	bb%	ct%	h%	Eye	G	L	F	PX	xPX	hr/f	Spd	SBO	SB%	#Wk	DOM	DIS	RC/G	RAR	BPV	BPX	R$
08	COL	299	55	12	48	4	268	273	290	256	326	468	794	8	72	34	0.31	43	24	33	149	141	17%	98	6%	100%	26	46%	50%	5.40	-0.2	53	104	$9
09	2 NL *	249	29	5	25	1	277	257	279	291	331	416	747	8	77	34	0.36	45	19	35	99	105	6%	117	2%	100%	19	32%	47%	4.88	-3.8	27	55	$4
10	CHC	206	29	4	21	1	272	256	350	106	324	413	737	7	76	34	0.32	42	22	36	106	92	7%	112	2%	100%	27	41%	41%	4.72	-4.1	31	67	$4
11	CHC	201	20	3	23	0	269	255	314	200	303	383	686	5	77	34	0.22	48	24	28	89	94	7%	107	0%	0%	25	32%	52%	4.05	-7.8	5	11	$2
12	3 TM	188	18	4	25	4	239	264	240	237	281	378	659	6	74	30	0.23	48	27	25	103	63	11%	88	13%	80%	27	22%	44%	3.58	-10.3	18	45	$2
1st Half		88	7	1	10	1	239	267	228	258	295	341	636	7	80	29	0.39	58	24	18	80	44	8%	78	10%	50%	13	23%	38%	3.26	-5.6	11	28	-$1
2nd Half		100	11	3	15	3	240	253	250	214	269	410	679	4	70	31	0.13	37	30	33	126	82	13%	96	17%	100%	14	21%	50%	3.85	-4.5	23	58	$4
13	Proj	198	22	4	25	3	250	258	273	211	292	387	680	6	75	31	0.24	46	25	29	102	83	9%	93	7%	85%				3.88	-6.6	19	49	$4

Baker,John

Age	32	Bats	L	Pos	CA	Health	F	LIMA Plan	F
Ht	6' 1"	Wt	220			PT/Exp	F	Rand Var	-1
						Consist	D	MM	1001

Recovery from multi-year arm troubles finally allowed him to register enough ABs to qualify for inclusion in this book for first time since 2009, but negative BPV says we are probably wasting the ink. Before he got hurt, he was a slow-footed catcher who hit too many GBs. Three years later he's still the same guy. Pass.

Yr	Tm	AB	R	HR	RBI	SB	BA	xBA	vL	vR	OB	Slg	OPS	bb%	ct%	h%	Eye	G	L	F	PX	xPX	hr/f	Spd	SBO	SB%	#Wk	DOM	DIS	RC/G	RAR	BPV	BPX	R$
08	FLA *	390	53	8	51	1	271	266	213	327	347	404	750	10	76	34	0.49	49	25	26	99	85	13%	88	3%	19%	13	46%	31%	4.78	5.5	19	37	$8
09	FLA	373	59	9	50	0	271	257	171	281	343	410	753	10	76	33	0.46	49	20	31	103	91	10%	71	0%	0%	27	33%	41%	4.92	6.7	20	41	$8
10	FLA	78	7	0	6	0	218	238	125	229	299	282	581	10	77	28	0.50	53	22	25	50	37	0%	97	0%	0%	6	0%	50%	2.75	-3.6	-9	-20	-$2
11	FLA	13	0	0	1	0	154	73		154	267	154	421	13	77	20	0.67	80	10	10	0	2	0%	82	0%	0%	4	0%	75%	1.24	-1.2	-65	-144	-$3
12	SD	193	17	0	14	2	238	223	229	241	310	280	590	9	79	30	0.49	52	21	26	38	75	0%	80	5%	67%	25	12%	64%	2.90	-8.0	-19	-48	-$1
1st Half		98	7	0	9	2	255	227	250	256	330	316	647	10	76	34	0.46	47	23	30	59	78	0%	76	7%	100%	12	8%	67%	3.70	-1.5	-15	-38	$0
2nd Half		95	10	0	5	0	221	217	217	222	288	242	531	9	82	27	0.53	58	19	23	19	72	0%	86	4%	0%	13	15%	62%	2.18	-6.0	-25	-63	-$1
13	Proj	158	19	1	16	1	253	233	213	260	326	323	648	10	78	32	0.49	52	21	27	58	69	3%	73	3%	51%				3.55	-3.1	-8	-20	$2

Barajas,Rod

Age	37	Bats	R	Pos	CA	Health	B	LIMA Plan	F
Ht	6' 2"	Wt	250			PT/Exp	D	Rand Var	+1
						Consist	B	MM	3103

What looks like the continuing decline was really just a h%-induced down year. Long-term xBA trend says you can ink in sub-.250 BA, but xPX suggests you can still count on some pop. BA should rebound some and one more double-digit HR season is a good bet, but the cliff is coming.

Yr	Tm	AB	R	HR	RBI	SB	BA	xBA	vL	vR	OB	Slg	OPS	bb%	ct%	h%	Eye	G	L	F	PX	xPX	hr/f	Spd	SBO	SB%	#Wk	DOM	DIS	RC/G	RAR	BPV	BPX	R$
08	TOR	349	44	11	49	0	249	254	204	270	284	410	694	5	83	27	0.28	37	17	46	106	111	8%	53	0%	0%	24	42%	29%	3.95	-3.3	36	71	$4
09	TOR	429	43	19	71	1	226	238	267	213	261	403	664	4	82	23	0.26	29	14	57	106	134	9%	41	1%	100%	27	41%	37%	3.47	-10.5	36	73	$5
10	2 NL	313	39	17	47	0	240	246	190	256	270	447	717	4	83	24	0.24	19	14	66	127	131	10%	56	0%	0%	23	39%	48%	4.05	-2.1	51	111	$6
11	LA	305	29	16	47	0	230	243	267	214	281	430	711	7	77	25	0.31	21	18	61	133	125	11%	47	0%	0%	23	35%	35%	4.00	-2.6	32	71	$5
12	PIT	321	29	11	31	0	206	218	167	217	271	343	614	8	79	23	0.42	24	19	57	87	129	8%	62	0%	0%	27	30%	52%	2.99	-12.9	7	18	$0
1st Half		170	17	7	18	0	218	232	133	248	277	382	660	8	79	23	0.40	21	20	59	103	143	9%	54	0%	0%	13	31%	38%	3.45	-4.0	23	58	$1
2nd Half		151	12	4	13	0	192	202	222	185	265	298	563	9	77	22	0.44	27	19	54	68	114	6%	70	0%	0%	14	29%	64%	2.49	-8.2	-11	-28	-$3
13	Proj	260	25	10	32	0	226	223	220	228	280	385	666	7	79	25	0.36	24	18	58	100	126	9%	55	0%	100%				3.56	-5.2	18	44	$3

Barmes,Clint

Age	34	Bats	R	Pos	SS	Health	B	LIMA Plan	D
Ht	6' 1"	Wt	205			PT/Exp	B	Rand Var	-1
						Consist	B	MM	1103

Only redeeming value since '09 has been lots of FBs and the hope that some might clear a fence somewhere. But even those skills cratered in 2012... leaving nothing. 2H BA "rebound" was driven by increased h%, as xBA painfully points out. Will be hard-pressed for PT, or positive value in '13.

Yr	Tm	AB	R	HR	RBI	SB	BA	xBA	vL	vR	OB	Slg	OPS	bb%	ct%	h%	Eye	G	L	F	PX	xPX	hr/f	Spd	SBO	SB%	#Wk	DOM	DIS	RC/G	RAR	BPV	BPX	R$
08	COL	393	47	11	44	13	290	259	307	283	320	468	788	4	82	33	0.25	29	22	49	113	96	7%	125	19%	76%	23	52%	17%	5.34	13.6	68	133	$14
09	COL	550	69	23	76	12	245	259	245	246	286	440	726	5	78	28	0.26	31	20	49	125	108	11%	95	20%	55%	26	50%	31%	4.00	-1.7	52	106	$14
10	COL	387	43	8	50	3	235	243	280	214	299	351	650	8	83	27	0.53	30	21	49	82	95	5%	70	5%	60%	27	37%	52%	3.46	-7.5	31	67	$4
11	HOU	446	47	12	39	3	244	247	226	251	304	386	689	8	80	28	0.43	31	22	47	102	85	7%	72	4%	75%	23	52%	30%	3.95	-2.0	35	78	$6
12	PIT	455	34	8	45	0	229	210	274	217	261	321	582	4	77	28	0.19	37	20	43	64	62	5%	88	2%	0%	27	15%	70%	2.71	-19.3	-22	-55	$1
1st Half		222	13	4	18	0	198	214	245	185	212	302	514	2	75	25	0.07	36	20	44	78	61	5%	68	6%	0%	13	23%	62%	1.93	-14.7	-24	-60	-$4
2nd Half		233	21	4	27	0	258	208	304	246	305	339	644	6	78	31	0.31	38	20	42	52	62	5%	109	0%	0%	14	7%	79%	3.55	-3.1	-21	-53	$6
13	Proj	329	31	6	34	2	240	223	265	232	285	346	630	6	79	29	0.30	34	21	45	73	77	5%	83	4%	55%				3.26	-7.4	4	9	$4

Barney,Darwin

Age	27	Bats	R	Pos	2B	Health	A	LIMA Plan	C+
Ht	5' 10"	Wt	185			PT/Exp	B	Rand Var	+2
						Consist	B	MM	1325

Minor uptick in HR was a nice complement to solid plate approach, but GB tilt will force him to rely heavily on hr/f to maintain those gains, as he depends on Wrigley winds for those HR (all 7 at home). Spd and SBO declines really sink his value, which means you're just bidding on an empty average come draft day.

Yr	Tm	AB	R	HR	RBI	SB	BA	xBA	vL	vR	OB	Slg	OPS	bb%	ct%	h%	Eye	G	L	F	PX	xPX	hr/f	Spd	SBO	SB%	#Wk	DOM	DIS	RC/G	RAR	BPV	BPX	R$
08																																		
09	a/a	464	44	3	39	7	262	243			306	330	636	6	84	31	0.40				50			85	8%	76%				3.50		11	0	$6
10	CHC *	558	60	1	35	7	244	249	280	222	272	304	576	4	87	28	0.29	54	16	30	45	40	0%	108	8%	67%	9	22%	33%	2.77	-26.2	20	43	$4
11	CHC	529	66	2	43	9	276	267	290	273	305	353	658	4	87	31	0.33	49	23	28	53	36	2%	137	8%	82%	26	23%	42%	3.83	-7.7	37	82	$12
12	CHC	548	73	7	44	6	254	273	257	252	296	354	650	6	89	27	0.57	48	22	30	62	58	5%	118	5%	86%	27	33%	30%	3.61	-11.8	51	128	$9
1st Half		266	33	3	23	5	267	282	243	276	309	376	684	6	91	29	0.64	44	24	32	70	70	4%	114	8%	100%	13	38%	38%	4.15	-0.9	62	155	$11
2nd Half		282	40	4	21	1	241	263	271	231	284	333	618	6	88	26	0.52	52	20	28	55	47	6%	117	3%	50%	14	29%	21%	3.15	-9.4	35	88	$8
13	Proj	564	70	4	44	7	258	263	266	255	296	341	636	5	88	29	0.45	49	21	29	54	47	3%	118	6%	78%				3.47	-13.0	37	92	$10

MATT GELFAND

Barton,Daric				Health	B	LIMA Plan	F
Age 27	Bats L	Pos 1B		PT/Exp	C	Rand Var	+2
Ht 6' 0"	Wt 205			Consist	D	MM	1201

1-6-.204 in 113 AB at OAK. Started the year with shoulder injury, but total power outage is not a new development. Moneyball taught us that walks are good, but he cannot channel Mario Mendoza and succeed. OAK teammates succeeded by swinging for the fences; his only plus skill involves not swinging at all.

Yr	Tm	AB	R	HR	RBI	SB	BA	xBA	vL	vR	OB	Slg	OPS	bb%	ct%	h%	Eye	G	L	F	PX	xPX	hr/f	Spd	SBO	SB%	#Wk	DOM	DIS	RC/G	RAR	BPV	BPX	R$
08	OAK *	477	62	10	49	2	222	226	273	208	317	340	657	12	79	26	0.67	35	19	46	75	94	6%	111	2%	67%	27	26%	48%	3.53	-25.6	28	55	$1
09	OAK *	413	68	10	61	1	237	258	333	257	335	386	721	13	82	27	0.83	31	20	48	101	113	5%	86	2%	28%	13	62%	23%	4.25	-12.8	55	112	$6
10	OAK	556	79	10	57	7	273	261	310	259	393	405	798	17	82	32	1.08	39	21	39	92	91	6%	113	5%	70%	27	44%	26%	5.58	4.6	61	133	$15
11	OAK *	297	33	0	24	2	199	203	253	193	311	248	558	14	78	26	0.72	38	19	43	48	103	0%	66	3%	67%	13	15%	38%	2.45	-26.5	-6	-13	-$3
12	OAK *	372	40	6	29	6	196	215	188	210	317	302	619	15	73	25	0.67	42	19	40	79	81	3%	85	6%	82%	11	9%	55%	3.08	-25.9	12	30	-$1
1st Half		193	19	3	12	2	191	215	194	200	317	310	626	16	72	25	0.66	45	16	39	93	84	3%	80	4%	100%	8	0%	50%	3.16	-13.5	14	35	-$3
2nd Half		179	21	2	16	3	202	271	0	333	318	294	612	14	75	26	0.68	0	60	40	65	39	0%	98	8%	73%	3	33%	67%	3.00	-13.3	8	20	$1
13	**Proj**	**179**	**21**	**2**	**16**	**2**	**212**	**215**	**234**	**204**	**327**	**306**	**633**	**15**	**77**	**27**	**0.73**	**39**	**19**	**42**	**70**	**95**	**4%**	**85**	**5%**	**75%**				**3.26**	**-11.7**	**14**	**35**	**-$1**

Bautista,Jose				Health	C	LIMA Plan	B+
Age 32	Bats R	Pos RF		PT/Exp	A	Rand Var	+5
Ht 6' 0"	Wt 190			Consist	F	MM	4225

Exhibit A: Skills trump surface numbers. BA dip gives facade of lost ability, but xBA and h% describe a still-fine hitter done in by poor luck after contact. FB% and PX are still excellent, dip in PX/xPX could be wrist-related. Wrist surgery is a red flag entering 2013. If healthy... UP: 40-100-.280.

Yr	Tm	AB	R	HR	RBI	SB	BA	xBA	vL	vR	OB	Slg	OPS	bb%	ct%	h%	Eye	G	L	F	PX	xPX	hr/f	Spd	SBO	SB%	#Wk	DOM	DIS	RC/G	RAR	BPV	BPX	R$
08	2 TM	370	45	15	54	1	238	238	250	233	312	405	718	10	75	28	0.44	46	15	39	113	99	14%	91	2%	50%	27	30%	59%	4.20	-7.2	24	47	$5
09	TOR	336	54	13	40	4	235	244	293	202	344	408	752	14	75	28	0.66	41	17	42	110	114	12%	123	4%	100%	27	30%	48%	4.76	-0.9	46	94	$5
10	TOR	569	109	54	124	9	260	322	222	269	371	617	988	15	80	24	0.86	31	14	54	220	173	22%	99	7%	82%	27	81%	15%	7.89	50.3	153	333	$31
11	TOR	513	105	43	103	9	302	297	336	292	445	608	1053	20	78	31	1.19	37	16	47	191	158	23%	106	6%	64%	27	70%	15%	9.73	69.4	130	289	$35
12	TOR	332	64	27	65	5	241	280	200	255	355	527	883	15	81	22	0.94	37	14	49	165	145	20%	77	7%	71%	17	71%	12%	6.25	13.9	107	268	$14
1st Half		284	56	26	62	4	239	290	203	252	355	549	905	15	82	20	0.98	36	14	50	173	146	22%	75	6%	80%	13	77%	8%	6.55	13.1	116	290	$19
2nd Half		48	8	1	3	1	250	220	182	270	357	396	753	14	77	31	0.73	43	8	49	112	137	6%	90	13%	50%	4	50%	25%	4.57	-0.6	47	118	-$17
13	**Proj**	**531**	**97**	**33**	**84**	**9**	**261**	**265**	**241**	**267**	**378**	**509**	**886**	**16**	**79**	**28**	**0.87**	**38**	**13**	**48**	**155**	**146**	**16%**	**91**	**8%**	**62%**				**6.51**	**23.4**	**93**	**231**	**$24**

Baxter,Mike				Health	F	LIMA Plan	F
Age 28	Bats L	Pos RF		PT/Exp	F	Rand Var	-4
Ht 6' 0"	Wt 195			Consist	D	MM	2203

3-17-.263 in 179 AB at NYM. Cute little 60-AB run in 1st half got derailed by collarbone injury. Lacks a true plus skill, but roughly-average power/speed skills should allow him to fill the boxscore a bit. He's in his prime already, so platoon/bench role is likely his ceiling.

Yr	Tm	AB	R	HR	RBI	SB	BA	xBA	vL	vR	OB	Slg	OPS	bb%	ct%	h%	Eye	G	L	F	PX	xPX	hr/f	Spd	SBO	SB%	#Wk	DOM	DIS	RC/G	RAR	BPV	BPX	R$
08	aa	324	34	6	40	2	228	258			298	349	647	9	85	25	0.65				75			104	5%	42%				3.36		40	0	$0
09	a/a	505	60	6	62	11	255	244			321	368	690	9	76	32	0.41				85			93	14%	57%				3.90		20	0	$10
10	SD *	490	64	11	53	16	230	241		125	294	375	669	8	79	27	0.43	43	14	43	96	137	0%	121	24%	56%	4	0%	75%	3.42	-19.9	48	104	$9
11	NYM *	98	9	2	9	1	173	163	0	250	239	292	531	8	68	23	0.27	32	8	60	83	141	7%	127	4%	100%	7	43%	43%	2.18	-8.0	-14	-31	-$3
12	NYM *	213	28	3	20	5	262	241	53	288	345	392	738	11	74	34	0.48	39	24	36	101	102	6%	88	13%	63%	19	37%	42%	4.57	-0.9	29	73	$4
1st Half		65	14	0	10	2	323	292	0	375	389	523	912	10	71	46	0.37	36	34	30	188	106	0%	82	13%	100%	9	44%	44%	7.91	5.6	95	238	$3
2nd Half		148	14	3	10	3	235	210	100	240	327	335	661	12	75	30	0.54	41	19	40	65	99	5%	99	13%	50%	10	30%	40%	3.47	-5.4	-2	-5	$4
13	**Proj**	**253**	**32**	**3**	**26**	**5**	**238**	**239**	**37**	**263**	**312**	**364**	**676**	**10**	**74**	**31**	**0.41**	**39**	**25**	**36**	**94**	**102**	**5%**	**92**	**12%**	**66%**				**3.74**	**-9.7**	**23**	**59**	**$5**

Bay,Jason				Health	F	LIMA Plan	D
Age 34	Bats R	Pos LF		PT/Exp	C	Rand Var	+5
Ht 6' 2"	Wt 210			Consist	C	MM	2303

Why He Missed Games Scoreboard: jammed finger, nondisplaced rib fracture, flu, concussion (the wall won), stiff back. Beyond the DL stints, his skills were already eroding across the board before 2012 and age is creating a headwind. There's a little pop left, but we'll probably only see it in flashes from here on.

Yr	Tm	AB	R	HR	RBI	SB	BA	xBA	vL	vR	OB	Slg	OPS	bb%	ct%	h%	Eye	G	L	F	PX	xPX	hr/f	Spd	SBO	SB%	#Wk	DOM	DIS	RC/G	RAR	BPV	BPX	R$
08	2 TM	577	111	31	101	10	286	270	252	296	374	522	896	12	76	33	0.59	38	17	46	154	158	15%	130	6%	100%	27	63%	30%	7.09	38.2	88	173	$27
09	BOS	531	103	36	119	13	267	267	292	257	378	537	914	15	69	32	0.58	33	18	49	184	176	20%	95	10%	81%	27	67%	26%	7.08	36.2	89	182	$26
10	NYM	348	48	6	47	10	259	233	259	258	342	402	744	11	74	33	0.48	36	19	45	107	152	5%	150	10%	100%	17	41%	47%	4.92	1.9	47	102	$9
11	NYM	444	59	12	57	11	245	230	300	228	330	374	704	11	75	30	0.51	43	17	40	93	102	9%	101	9%	92%	24	25%	46%	4.28	-5.8	28	62	$11
12	NYM	194	21	8	20	5	165	204	172	158	239	299	538	9	70	19	0.33	43	16	41	85	139	14%	80	15%	83%	18	17%	67%	2.23	-15.9	-9	-23	-$1
1st Half		75	10	4	6	2	187	218	182	189	256	373	629	9	69	21	0.30	45	11	43	125	111	17%	85	20%	67%	6	17%	67%	2.92	-4.2	18	45	-$2
2nd Half		119	11	4	14	3	151	196	169	125	229	252	481	9	71	18	0.34	42	19	39	60	156	12%	81	12%	100%	12	17%	67%	1.83	-11.2	-30	-75	-$1
13	**Proj**	**314**	**40**	**9**	**39**	**6**	**236**	**211**	**235**	**236**	**315**	**363**	**678**	**10**	**72**	**30**	**0.42**	**41**	**17**	**42**	**86**	**134**	**10%**	**98**	**8%**	**84%**				**3.87**	**-7.3**	**5**	**13**	**$7**

Beckham,Gordon				Health	A	LIMA Plan	D+
Age 26	Bats R	Pos 2B		PT/Exp	B	Rand Var	+2
Ht 6' 0"	Wt 190			Consist	B	MM	2115

PRO: Contact improved, h% figures to regress upward, and 2H bb% and Eye had upticks.
CON: PX and Spd are generic; OBP, OPS, and xBA are consistently poor.
VERDICT: Time running out for him to prove he's even worthy of being an MLB regular.

Yr	Tm	AB	R	HR	RBI	SB	BA	xBA	vL	vR	OB	Slg	OPS	bb%	ct%	h%	Eye	G	L	F	PX	xPX	hr/f	Spd	SBO	SB%	#Wk	DOM	DIS	RC/G	RAR	BPV	BPX	R$
08																																		
09	CHW *	553	84	18	85	9	279	282	318	250	343	469	811	9	83	31	0.57	40	17	43	127	131	10%	83	9%	69%	19	58%	32%	5.61	22.8	76	155	$19
10	CHW	444	58	9	49	4	252	249	224	261	310	378	688	8	79	30	0.40	46	17	37	91	90	7%	103	9%	40%	26	42%	46%	3.82	-4.6	29	63	$8
11	CHW	499	60	10	44	5	230	230	195	242	281	337	618	7	78	28	0.32	39	20	40	79	66	6%	101	7%	63%	27	22%	48%	3.10	-16.2	8	18	$5
12	CHW	525	62	16	60	5	234	245	225	236	288	371	660	7	83	25	0.45	38	20	42	86	90	9%	86	7%	56%	27	33%	44%	3.50	-10.6	33	83	$8
1st Half		279	38	9	34	3	244	250	209	255	287	384	671	6	84	26	0.37	39	20	41	86	87	9%	81	8%	60%	13	31%	38%	3.65	-5.1	35	88	$12
2nd Half		246	24	7	26	2	224	241	245	216	290	358	648	9	83	24	0.53	37	19	44	86	94	8%	97	7%	50%	14	36%	50%	3.33	-7.1	30	75	$4
13	**Proj**	**485**	**59**	**13**	**53**	**5**	**239**	**242**	**229**	**242**	**297**	**372**	**669**	**8**	**81**	**27**	**0.43**	**40**	**19**	**41**	**89**	**89**	**8%**	**90**	**8%**	**55%**				**3.63**	**-9.3**	**30**	**76**	**$9**

Belt,Brandon				Health	B	LIMA Plan	C
Age 25	Bats L	Pos 1B		PT/Exp	D	Rand Var	-3
Ht 6' 5"	Wt 220			Consist	F	MM	3315

Mashed RHPs when he finally got an extended opportunity in 2nd half, though xBA remains skeptical. More power to come? .906 OPS at home, so AT&T is not killing him. xPX says power still there, just waiting for more FB. Add in some hr/f regression, and.... UP: 20 HR.

Yr	Tm	AB	R	HR	RBI	SB	BA	xBA	vL	vR	OB	Slg	OPS	bb%	ct%	h%	Eye	G	L	F	PX	xPX	hr/f	Spd	SBO	SB%	#Wk	DOM	DIS	RC/G	RAR	BPV	BPX	R$
08																																		
09																																		
10	a/a	223	30	10	40	3	288	296			367	536	904	11	76	34	0.53				165			118	7%	75%				7.03		92	0	$9
11	SF *	352	42	14	39	6	236	220	348	184	325	405	730	12	68	31	0.42	42	14	44	130	111	16%	96	12%	46%	15	47%	47%	4.16	-13.6	21	47	$7
12	SF	411	47	7	56	12	275	247	242	290	359	421	780	12	74	36	0.51	38	26	37	107	112	6%	104	11%	86%	27	33%	48%	5.42	-0.1	42	105	$13
1st Half		171	18	4	29	4	257	246	300	244	371	433	804	15	72	34	0.65	43	19	38	129	106	8%	102	9%	80%	13	31%	54%	5.56	1.0	53	133	$9
2nd Half		240	29	3	27	8	288	249	216	329	350	413	762	9	76	37	0.40	34	30	36	92	116	5%	105	13%	89%	14	36%	43%	5.30	-0.4	31	78	$16
13	**Proj**	**496**	**59**	**14**	**66**	**11**	**263**	**241**	**267**	**262**	**348**	**431**	**778**	**11**	**72**	**34**	**0.47**	**40**	**21**	**39**	**120**	**112**	**10%**	**103**	**11%**	**69%**				**5.13**	**-3.4**	**41**	**101**	**$16**

Beltran,Carlos				Health	D	LIMA Plan	B
Age 36	Bats B	Pos RF		PT/Exp	B	Rand Var	0
Ht 6' 1"	Wt 215			Consist	D	MM	4135

Fantastic 1H driven by unsustainable hr/f. Then 2H showed possible cracks in the armor, whether due to age, fatigue, or knee issues. 2H across-the-board skills drop raises red flags; note how righties figured him out. This was a sweet stat line for age 35, but don't pay for anything resembling a repeat.

Yr	Tm	AB	R	HR	RBI	SB	BA	xBA	vL	vR	OB	Slg	OPS	bb%	ct%	h%	Eye	G	L	F	PX	xPX	hr/f	Spd	SBO	SB%	#Wk	DOM	DIS	RC/G	RAR	BPV	BPX	R$
08	NYM	606	116	27	112	25	284	306	326	266	378	500	878	13	84	30	0.96	45	22	33	131	107	16%	91	15%	89%	27	78%	11%	6.91	30.2	107	210	$32
09	NYM	308	50	10	48	11	325	296	326	324	414	500	914	13	86	35	1.09	45	20	35	109	102	11%	99	11%	92%	17	47%	6%	8.03	23.6	88	180	$16
10	NYM	220	21	7	27	3	255	271	292	244	344	427	771	12	82	28	0.77	42	19	39	109	131	10%	92	6%	75%	12	42%	17%	5.03	-0.7	67	146	$4
11	2 NL	520	78	22	84	4	300	298	286	306	384	525	909	12	83	33	0.81	40	21	39	147	147	13%	89	4%	67%	26	73%	12%	7.30	30.9	101	224	$24
12	STL	547	83	32	97	13	269	274	276	266	346	495	842	11	77	29	0.52	42	20	38	142	124	20%	66	12%	68%	27	52%	26%	5.88	11.6	69	173	$25
1st Half		271	48	20	61	7	310	285	275	322	395	576	970	12	79	33	0.68	41	19	40	154	130	23%	82	11%	70%	13	69%	8%	8.26	24.3	90	225	$36
2nd Half		276	35	12	36	6	228	262	276	210	297	417	714	9	75	26	0.40	42	22	36	128	118	16%	56	15%	67%	14	36%	43%	4.01	-8.4	43	108	$14
13	**Proj**	**503**	**72**	**24**	**81**	**7**	**274**	**277**	**286**	**270**	**356**	**485**	**840**	**11**	**80**	**30**	**0.64**	**42**	**21**	**38**	**132**	**128**	**15%**	**76**	**7%**	**64%**				**5.97**	**14.0**	**74**	**185**	**$21**

JOSH PALEY

Beltre,Adrian

Age 34	Bats R	Pos 3B DH	Health	C	LIMA Plan	B+
Ht 5' 11"	Wt 220		PT/Exp	A	Rand Var	-3
			Consist	B	MM	4145

Couldn't quite hold 2011's peak skills, but still improved R$ by staying healthy. That health will be tougher to maintain given his age. Make no mistake, he's terrific, and he should have a year or two more of really nice production, barring injury. But his track record for even 550 AB per year is not projectable.

Yr	Tm	AB	R	HR	RBI	SB	BA	xBA	vL	vR	OB	Slg	OPS	bb%	ct%	h%	Eye	G	L	F	PX	xPX	hr/f	Spd	SBO	SB%	#Wk	DOM	DIS	RC/G	RAR	BPV	BPX	R$
08	SEA	556	74	25	77	8	266	285	340	239	327	457	784	8	84	28	0.56	40	22	38	115	134	14%	63	7%	80%	25	64%	8%	5.20	10.4	67	131	$16
09	SEA	449	54	8	44	13	265	254	298	253	295	379	673	4	84	30	0.26	46	16	38	78	100	6%	79	15%	87%	21	33%	29%	3.95	-7.7	34	69	$11
10	BOS	589	84	28	102	2	321	312	328	318	364	553	918	6	86	34	0.49	40	19	40	148	137	13%	58	2%	67%	26	65%	8%	7.54	47.0	95	207	$31
11	TEX	487	82	32	105	1	296	315	315	290	330	561	891	5	89	28	0.47	38	18	44	156	160	16%	57	2%	50%	22	73%	9%	6.65	28.4	107	238	$27
12	TEX	604	95	36	102	1	321	299	269	339	359	561	921	6	86	33	0.44	39	21	40	136	139	17%	73	1%	100%	27	70%	11%	7.59	48.9	84	210	$33
1st Half		290	45	14	52	1	328	298	259	356	365	534	899	6	87	34	0.46	42	22	36	121	144	15%	61	1%	100%	13	69%	8%	7.42	21.7	72	180	$32
2nd Half		314	50	22	50	0	315	299	282	325	354	586	940	6	86	31	0.42	36	20	44	149	134	18%	84	0%	0%	14	71%	14%	7.73	26.6	90	225	$35
13	**Proj**	**514**	**80**	**29**	**90**	**2**	**309**	**296**	**296**	**313**	**349**	**543**	**892**	**6**	**87**	**31**	**0.46**	**39**	**20**	**41**	**135**	**141**	**16%**	**64**	**2%**	**77%**				**6.98**	**33.6**	**86**	**215**	**$26**

Berkman,Lance

Age 37	Bats B	Pos 1B	Health	F	LIMA Plan	C
Ht 6' 1"	Wt 220		PT/Exp	C	Rand Var	+1
			Consist	F	MM	4123

Year lost due to a knee injury that may mean the end of his career. If so, he would retire with 360 HR, 1200 RBI, a .296 BA, and one of the most clutch hits in World Series history. If he can play, there is still plenty of power to go with awesome plate discipline, and he could be a fine DH or premier bench player.

Yr	Tm	AB	R	HR	RBI	SB	BA	xBA	vL	vR	OB	Slg	OPS	bb%	ct%	h%	Eye	G	L	F	PX	xPX	hr/f	Spd	SBO	SB%	#Wk	DOM	DIS	RC/G	RAR	BPV	BPX	R$
08	HOU	554	114	29	106	18	312	304	276	327	417	567	983	15	81	35	0.92	43	18	39	164	135	17%	88	11%	82%	27	59%	11%	8.80	51.0	119	233	$35
09	HOU	460	73	25	80	7	274	290	231	291	400	509	909	17	79	30	0.99	43	18	39	150	142	17%	66	7%	64%	25	72%	8%	7.06	21.5	90	184	$18
10	2 TM	404	48	14	58	3	248	260	171	267	368	413	781	16	79	28	0.91	48	16	36	114	114	12%	71	4%	60%	23	39%	52%	5.11	-3.7	55	120	$8
11	STL	488	90	31	94	2	301	295	277	307	412	547	959	16	81	32	0.99	39	22	39	153	146	20%	87	4%	25%	27	63%	30%	7.91	33.8	94	209	$27
12	STL	81	12	2	7	2	259	272	176	281	368	444	813	15	77	32	0.74	45	21	34	134	90	10%	89	8%	100%	10	50%	30%	5.81	0.9	74	185	$0
1st Half		42	8	1	4	1	333	312	111	394	417	571	988	13	76	42	0.60	50	25	25	175	75	13%	87	8%	100%	4	75%	25%	9.32	4.3	105	263	$1
2nd Half		39	4	1	3	1	179	223	250	161	319	308	627	17	77	21	0.89	40	17	43	90	105	8%	78	8%	100%	6	33%	33%	3.19	-2.7	29	73	-$1
13	**Proj**	**234**	**39**	**9**	**41**	**3**	**283**	**268**	**235**	**296**	**400**	**469**	**869**	**16**	**80**	**32**	**0.96**	**43**	**20**	**37**	**122**	**114**	**13%**	**76**	**6%**	**59%**				**6.56**	**8.0**	**70**	**175**	**$10**

Bernadina,Roger

Age 29	Bats L	Pos LF CF	Health	C	LIMA Plan	F
Ht 6' 2"	Wt 215		PT/Exp	D	Rand Var	-5
			Consist	D	MM	1411

Gained 62 pts of BA over 2011, but xBA didn't budge at all. Now has an established hsitory of aggression on the bases that lets him outperform his Spd skill. Growth of bb% and Eye are encouraging; but 2H xBA, generic power, age, all limit him to fourth OF role and end-game speedster status.

Yr	Tm	AB	R	HR	RBI	SB	BA	xBA	vL	vR	OB	Slg	OPS	bb%	ct%	h%	Eye	G	L	F	PX	xPX	hr/f	Spd	SBO	SB%	#Wk	DOM	DIS	RC/G	RAR	BPV	BPX	R$
08	WAS *	533	74	7	45	37	285	264	300	197	342	401	744	8	75	37	0.35	67	15	17	79	44	0%	128	33%	70%	7	43%	43%	4.75	0.9	26	51	$24
09	WAS	4	1	0	0	1	250	345		250	400	500	900	20	75	33	1.00	33	33	33	238	78	0%	97	100%	100%	1	100%	0%	8.67	0.5	171	349	-$1
10	WAS *	475	58	13	53	22	256	243	250	246	314	393	707	8	79	30	0.40	47	13	39	91	108	9%	105	21%	83%	25	44%	32%	4.32	-5.0	42	91	$16
11	WAS *	473	59	11	37	27	229	249	191	257	281	351	633	7	75	28	0.29	52	20	28	89	91	11%	111	33%	75%	19	42%	42%	3.26	-20.9	24	53	$11
12	WAS	227	25	5	25	15	291	249	417	276	369	405	774	11	77	36	0.53	43	26	31	82	97	10%	91	23%	83%	27	33%	41%	5.56	5.6	20	50	$10
1st Half		108	8	2	13	5	241	258	222	242	322	380	702	11	71	32	0.42	44	28	28	117	110	10%	74	21%	83%	13	31%	54%	4.22	-1.8	21	53	$4
2nd Half		119	17	3	12	10	336	239	533	308	410	429	839	11	82	39	0.68	41	24	34	54	86	10%	109	24%	83%	14	36%	29%	7.04	7.2	18	45	$15
13	**Proj**	**223**	**27**	**5**	**22**	**14**	**273**	**243**	**320**	**266**	**340**	**387**	**726**	**9**	**77**	**34**	**0.44**	**48**	**21**	**31**	**78**	**91**	**9%**	**99**	**26%**	**80%**				**4.70**	**0.3**	**20**	**51**	**$10**

Berry,Quintin

Age 28	Bats L	Pos LF CF	Health	A	LIMA Plan	F
Ht 6' 1"	Wt 175		PT/Exp	C	Rand Var	-3
			Consist	B	MM	1501

2-29-.258 with 21 SB in 291 AB at DET. Very fast, terrific base stealer, gets lots of opportunities to run. Unfortunately, that is the extent of his skills, with ct% limiting ability to beat out hits. Negative BPVs for four years running tell the story. Minor league pedigree questions if can keep a job, but if he does... UP: 40 SB.

Yr	Tm	AB	R	HR	RBI	SB	BA	xBA	vL	vR	OB	Slg	OPS	bb%	ct%	h%	Eye	G	L	F	PX	xPX	hr/f	Spd	SBO	SB%	#Wk	DOM	DIS	RC/G	RAR	BPV	BPX	R$
08																																		
09	aa	516	69	4	22	37	229	209			296	288	584	9	73	30	0.35				44			124	37%	70%				2.79		-16	0	$12
10	aa	348	36	2	26	21	167	202			245	223	468	9	72	23	0.37				43			119	38%	69%				1.68		-18	0	-$1
11	a/a	338	43	4	27	27	220	200			292	299	590	9	68	31	0.31				68			92	40%	76%				2.92		-18	0	$8
12	DET *	450	57	2	37	35	243	228	214	268	306	320	625	8	70	34	0.30	60	20	20	59	64	5%	138	31%	90%	20	15%	55%	3.60	-13.0	-6	-15	$14
1st Half		280	37	1	21	26	255	224	233	330	324	324	648	9	68	37	0.32	54	25	21	58	104	6%	145	34%	87%	6	17%	33%	3.93	-6.0	-16	-40	$20
2nd Half		170	20	1	16	9	224	239	192	229	275	312	586	7	74	30	0.27	64	16	20	62	40	4%	127	23%	100%	14	14%	64%	3.08	-8.2	4	10	$5
13	**Proj**	**224**	**27**	**2**	**18**	**16**	**221**	**227**	**188**	**228**	**287**	**294**	**581**	**8**	**71**	**31**	**0.32**	**60**	**20**	**20**	**56**	**66**	**5%**	**123**	**33%**	**81%**				**2.90**	**-12.2**	**-12**	**-31**	**$6**

Betancourt,Yuniesky

Age 31	Bats R	Pos 2B	Health	B	LIMA Plan	D
Ht 5' 11"	Wt 205		PT/Exp	C	Rand Var	+2
			Consist	A	MM	2021

7-36-.228 in 215 AB at KC. The Royals signed him to a $2M contract. He responded with 3.54 pitches per plate appearance, ranking #296 in the AL. Adam Jones was at #293, Alex Rios #297, Robinson Cano #302. Heck, Tommy Milone was #281. If you're gonna hack at everything, either crush the ball or be a pitcher.

Yr	Tm	AB	R	HR	RBI	SB	BA	xBA	vL	vR	OB	Slg	OPS	bb%	ct%	h%	Eye	G	L	F	PX	xPX	hr/f	Spd	SBO	SB%	#Wk	DOM	DIS	RC/G	RAR	BPV	BPX	R$
08	SEA	559	66	7	51	4	279	273	275	281	300	392	692	3	92	29	0.40	40	20	40	72	75	3%	104	6%	50%	27	48%	15%	4.07	-3.0	58	114	$11
09	2 AL	470	40	6	49	3	245	255	283	231	277	351	628	4	91	26	0.48	42	17	41	61	67	3%	122	6%	50%	24	21%	13%	3.22	-14.6	45	92	$3
10	KC	556	60	16	78	2	259	268	289	250	288	405	693	4	88	27	0.36	40	18	42	90	85	8%	77	4%	40%	27	44%	26%	3.94	-5.2	52	113	$12
11	MIL	556	51	13	68	4	252	258	229	258	273	381	654	3	89	26	0.25	41	18	41	81	97	6%	84	7%	50%	27	44%	19%	3.46	-13.1	47	104	$10
12	KC *	238	22	8	40	0	238	266	247	215	266	412	677	4	88	24	0.31	38	18	44	104	91	8%	78	2%	0%	16	50%	25%	3.59	-4.1	56	140	$3
1st Half		155	17	6	31	0	262	276	227	261	294	452	746	4	88	26	0.39	37	19	44	109	80	9%	91	3%	0%	10	60%	20%	4.46	0.9	67	168	$7
2nd Half		83	5	2	9	0	193	240	268	119	212	337	549	2	87	20	0.18	41	15	44	95	108	6%	64	0%	0%	6	33%	33%	2.26	-5.3	34	85	-$4
13	**Proj**	**238**	**21**	**6**	**32**	**1**	**243**	**257**	**266**	**232**	**266**	**387**	**653**	**3**	**88**	**25**	**0.27**	**40**	**17**	**43**	**88**	**93**	**7%**	**73**	**4%**	**40%**				**3.40**	**-6.1**	**47**	**117**	**$4**

Betemit,Wilson

Age 31	Bats B	Pos 3B	Health	B	LIMA Plan	D
Ht 6' 2"	Wt 222		PT/Exp	C	Rand Var	-2
			Consist	B	MM	4103

Has long track record of plus power, but flails vLHPs and insufficient ct% creates BA downside. 2H numbers suffered while playing through wrist injury. Can be somewhat useful fanalytically in leagues where you can start him against RHP only, but overall, a repeat of 2012 is best-case scenario going forward.

Yr	Tm	AB	R	HR	RBI	SB	BA	xBA	vL	vR	OB	Slg	OPS	bb%	ct%	h%	Eye	G	L	F	PX	xPX	hr/f	Spd	SBO	SB%	#Wk	DOM	DIS	RC/G	RAR	BPV	BPX	R$
08	NYY *	216	28	7	29	0	267	260	233	274	301	437	739	5	70	35	0.17	43	25	33	136	154	14%	82	2%	0%	22	32%	45%	4.49	-0.3	12	24	$4
09	CHW *	306	31	10	42	2	201	231	200	200	255	365	619	7	66	27	0.21	47	16	38	133	50	0%	61	3%	100%	9	44%	33%	2.99	-14.9	1	2	$0
10	KC *	389	42	14	54	1	271	244	312	291	349	452	801	11	74	33	0.46	40	15	45	134	159	14%	88	2%	34%	19	42%	37%	5.47	10.2	37	80	$10
11	2 AL	323	40	8	46	4	285	238	236	303	347	452	799	9	67	40	0.30	43	19	37	139	109	10%	102	6%	80%	25	28%	40%	5.61	9.7	31	69	$10
12	BAL	341	41	12	40	0	261	244	140	302	323	422	745	8	70	34	0.30	40	25	34	121	124	14%	70	1%	0%	22	32%	55%	4.64	0.9	2	5	$7
1st Half		211	29	10	31	0	275	251	164	314	343	464	808	9	73	33	0.39	43	22	36	129	137	18%	78	2%	0%	13	38%	54%	5.50	5.6	24	60	$12
2nd Half		130	12	2	9	0	238	235	97	283	288	354	642	6	65	35	0.20	36	32	32	107	102	7%	62	0%	0%	9	22%	56%	3.41	-4.5	-34	-85	-$2
13	**Proj**	**354**	**40**	**10**	**43**	**1**	**270**	**239**	**190**	**298**	**328**	**429**	**757**	**8**	**69**	**37**	**0.28**	**40**	**23**	**36**	**125**	**125**	**12%**	**76**	**2%**	**62%**				**4.90**	**3.2**	**10**	**25**	**$10**

Blackmon,Charlie

Age 27	Bats L	Pos RF	Health	F	LIMA Plan	F
Ht 6' 3"	Wt 210		PT/Exp	D	Rand Var	0
			Consist	B	MM	1311

2-9-.283 in 113 AB at COL. His only plus skills in evidence are an odd reverse-platoon split vLHPs (almost certainly a fluke, since its a 43-AB sample over two years) and playing at Coors, which is not actually a skill. Worth a pickup when he's getting some short-term playing time, but that's about it.

Yr	Tm	AB	R	HR	RBI	SB	BA	xBA	vL	vR	OB	Slg	OPS	bb%	ct%	h%	Eye	G	L	F	PX	xPX	hr/f	Spd	SBO	SB%	#Wk	DOM	DIS	RC/G	RAR	BPV	BPX	R$
08																																		
09																																		
10	aa	337	40	9	42	15	273	291			320	441	761	7	87	29	0.52				106			106	27%	65%				4.71		81	0	$13
11	COL *	341	34	7	33	11	260	256	400	218	286	380	666	4	86	28	0.27	47	16	37	79	53	3%	97	24%	61%	5	20%	40%	3.54	-11.6	47	104	$8
12	COL *	341	47	5	29	7	259	265	348	267	301	390	691	6	81	31	0.32	49	21	30	92	86	7%	104	11%	77%	8	50%	25%	4.05	-6.3	45	113	$7
1st Half		64	7	1	3	1	163	221			212	241	453	6	79	20	0.30	44	20	36	50			113	10%	100%				1.62		3	8	-$12
2nd Half		277	40	5	26	6	281	274	348	267	322	425	747	6	82	33	0.33	49	21	30	102	86	7%	100	12%	74%	8	50%	25%	4.84	0.5	52	130	$11
13	**Proj**	**199**	**23**	**2**	**18**	**5**	**247**	**250**	**339**	**224**	**286**	**352**	**638**	**5**	**84**	**29**	**0.34**	**48**	**18**	**34**	**71**	**51**	**4%**	**100**	**18%**	**68%**				**3.35**	**-9.9**	**36**	**90**	**$4**

JOSH PALEY

Blanco,Gregor

Age 29	Bats L	Pos RF LF CF	Health	A	LIMA Plan	D
Ht 5' 11"	Wt 185		PT/Exp	D	Rand Var	-4
			Consist	D	MM	1503

PRO: Draws walks, plus Spd, good SB%, and enough of a glove to be a fourth OF.
CON: Little power, mediocre ct%, poor BA/xBA, poor 2H all limit him to being a fourth OF.
GO FIGURE: He's a fourth outfielder! And a decent $1 end play.

Yr	Tm	AB	R	HR	RBI	SB	BA	xBA	vL	vR	OB	Slg	OPS	bb%	ct%	h%	Eye	G	L	F	PX	xPX	hr/f	Spd	SBO	SB%	#Wk	DOM	DIS	RC/G	RAR	BPV	BPX	R$
08	ATL	430	52	1	38	13	251	237	248	252	361	309	670	15	77	32	0.75	50	24	26	43	42	1%	119	11%	72%	26	12%	54%	3.84	-16.7	3	6	$6
09	ATL *	376	47	2	24	10	188	243	83	226	274	229	503	11	75	25	0.48	69	19	13	29	-5	0%	115	13%	73%	6	17%	67%	2.01	-37.9	-20	-41	-$2
10	2 TM *	391	50	2	22	18	262	246	179	315	340	336	676	11	78	33	0.55	54	20	26	55	66	2%	134	18%	77%	19	26%	47%	4.02	-12.9	17	37	$10
11	aaa	199	29	2	10	17	159	215			268	254	522	13	70	22	0.50				81			111	40%	87%				2.32		18	0	$0
12	SF	393	56	5	34	26	244	227	248	242	331	344	675	11	74	32	0.49	44	24	32	69	73	6%	134	26%	81%	27	19%	52%	3.99	-13.7	16	40	$12
1st Half		224	38	4	19	14	254	246	289	234	340	388	728	11	76	32	0.54	43	25	33	89	65	7%	138	25%	82%	13	31%	31%	4.66	-2.3	45	113	$16
2nd Half		169	18	1	15	12	231	201	180	252	319	284	603	12	70	32	0.44	47	22	31	41	84	3%	111	27%	80%	14	7%	71%	3.18	-9.5	-28	-70	$7
13	Proj	308	41	2	22	20	232	223	196	246	323	307	630	12	73	31	0.50	49	22	29	57	68	3%	120	25%	83%				3.48	-14.4	3	7	$6

Bloomquist,Willie

Age 35	Bats R	Pos SS	Health	C	LIMA Plan	D+
Ht 5' 11"	Wt 185		PT/Exp	D	Rand Var	-4
			Consist	A	MM	1423

Every year he seems to do something to tantalize management into giving him lots of AB. But neither 2011 SB nor 2012 BA will repeat and other than Spd and hitting lefties, he lacks plus skills. 2H back injury cost him two months and age is not on his side. If healthy, split the difference between 2011 and 2012.

Yr	Tm	AB	R	HR	RBI	SB	BA	xBA	vL	vR	OB	Slg	OPS	bb%	ct%	h%	Eye	G	L	F	PX	xPX	hr/f	Spd	SBO	SB%	#Wk	DOM	DIS	RC/G	RAR	BPV	BPX	R$
08	SEA	165	32	0	9	14	279	225	351	220	374	285	659	13	82	34	0.86	56	20	24	5	20	0%	147	24%	82%	18	17%	61%	4.09	0.0	-4	-8	$7
09	KC	434	52	4	29	25	265	250	248	275	308	355	663	6	83	31	0.37	46	21	33	51	42	3%	199	26%	81%	27	15%	48%	3.88	-2.8	32	65	$13
10	2 TM	187	31	3	17	8	267	267	289	250	301	380	681	5	85	30	0.32	44	21	35	77	74	5%	102	29%	62%	27	26%	56%	3.73	-2.0	50	109	$5
11	ARI	350	44	4	26	20	266	265	303	249	311	340	651	6	85	30	0.45	49	25	26	48	43	5%	123	30%	67%	24	25%	46%	3.53	-6.0	28	62	$11
12	ARI	324	47	0	23	7	302	263	317	295	327	398	725	4	83	36	0.22	50	22	28	70	81	0%	151	20%	41%	20	30%	30%	4.27	1.5	31	78	$10
1st Half		236	36	0	12	5	297	265	319	287	328	407	735	4	81	36	0.25	47	25	29	79	87	0%	162	20%	42%	13	38%	23%	4.36	2.4	36	90	$12
2nd Half		88	11	0	11	2	318	250	313	321	326	375	701	1	88	36	0.09	57	17	26	47	67	0%	98	21%	40%	7	14%	43%	4.03	0.1	12	30	$4
13	Proj	335	47	2	29	13	289	257	306	279	319	367	686	4	85	34	0.30	50	21	28	55	62	2%	124	25%	57%				3.90	-1.1	27	67	$13

Boesch,Brennan

Age 28	Bats L	Pos RF	Health	A	LIMA Plan	C
Ht 6' 5"	Wt 235		PT/Exp	B	Rand Var	0
			Consist	C	MM	3215

What happened to his power and batting average? Across-the-board skills crater rooted in horrific plate discipline (both Eye and bb%) which resulted in lots of ground balls. Players can have inexplicable off-years, but he is still at a prime age and owns the pre-2012 skills. Bet on some rebound.

Yr	Tm	AB	R	HR	RBI	SB	BA	xBA	vL	vR	OB	Slg	OPS	bb%	ct%	h%	Eye	G	L	F	PX	xPX	hr/f	Spd	SBO	SB%	#Wk	DOM	DIS	RC/G	RAR	BPV	BPX	R$
08																																		
09	aa	527	71	23	74	9	245	264			280	443	723	5	73	29	0.19				128			109	11%	80%				4.19		44	0	$13
10	DET *	522	54	16	80	9	265	254	337	233	321	428	748	8	77	31	0.36	45	15	40	114	97	10%	93	8%	80%	25	36%	40%	4.77	-1.3	44	96	$15
11	DET	428	75	16	54	5	283	266	302	276	337	458	795	8	81	32	0.42	43	18	39	119	110	12%	97	7%	63%	23	43%	30%	5.40	6.6	59	131	$17
12	DET	470	52	12	54	6	240	239	230	244	280	372	653	5	78	29	0.25	50	16	34	89	92	10%	81	9%	67%	27	22%	48%	3.46	-19.6	18	45	$8
1st Half		284	33	7	27	3	232	230	244	228	264	349	612	4	81	27	0.22	45	16	39	76	97	8%	63	7%	75%	13	23%	38%	3.05	-16.8	13	33	$8
2nd Half		186	19	5	27	3	253	250	208	268	305	409	714	7	74	32	0.29	58	15	26	109	84	14%	103	11%	60%	14	21%	57%	4.14	-4.8	23	58	$7
13	Proj	426	54	13	56	6	257	248	261	256	305	414	718	6	77	30	0.30	48	17	35	105	98	11%	91	9%	68%				4.28	-9.1	34	86	$12

Bogusevic,Brian

Age 29	Bats L	Pos RF CF	Health	A	LIMA Plan	F
Ht 6' 3"	Wt 220		PT/Exp	C	Rand Var	+3
			Consist	B	MM	1301

Archetype for the 2012 Houston Astros. He was simply overmatched, particularly in 2H, when his league average power disappeared. Uptick in Eye and bb% would be nice if it were accompanied by some other sign of skills growth. No history of plus skills leaves him without any paths to fanalytic value.

Yr	Tm	AB	R	HR	RBI	SB	BA	xBA	vL	vR	OB	Slg	OPS	bb%	ct%	h%	Eye	G	L	F	PX	xPX	hr/f	Spd	SBO	SB%	#Wk	DOM	DIS	RC/G	RAR	BPV	BPX	R$
08	aa	124	15	2	15	6	319	259			378	471	849	9	77	40	0.41				109			103	18%	83%				6.77		48	0	$5
09	aaa	520	55	5	43	18	237	220			295	318	613	8	73	32	0.30				62			98	16%	84%				3.23		-8	0	$7
10	HOU *	530	68	9	43	17	222	266	0	192	288	327	615	8	73	29	0.34	69	19	13	82	73	0%	90	15%	89%	6	33%	67%	3.19	-31.7	9	20	$7
11	HOU *	382	40	6	38	17	241	254	154	298	305	372	676	8	74	31	0.35	52	21	27	102	104	12%	106	25%	75%	18	39%	44%	3.81	-15.5	32	71	$8
12	HOU	355	39	7	28	15	203	229	156	213	285	299	584	10	73	26	0.43	55	20	25	65	79	11%	97	20%	79%	27	19%	67%	2.79	-26.4	-2	-5	$3
1st Half		221	31	6	20	7	222	249	174	234	289	353	642	9	77	26	0.41	53	19	28	83	85	13%	104	18%	70%	13	31%	46%	3.30	-11.7	27	68	$7
2nd Half		134	8	1	8	8	172	197	111	181	279	209	488	13	66	25	0.44	59	22	19	30	65	6%	77	23%	89%	14	7%	86%	2.01	-13.1	-62	-155	-$3
13	Proj	158	16	3	13	7	217	234	148	229	295	321	615	10	72	28	0.39	55	21	25	76	86	10%	90	21%	81%				3.17	-9.0	1	2	$3

Bonifacio,Emilio

Age 28	Bats B	Pos CF	Health	D	LIMA Plan	D+
Ht 5' 11"	Wt 205		PT/Exp	C	Rand Var	-1
			Consist	D	MM	0505

Basestealing machine in 1H until he tore a ligament in his left thumb, requiring surgery, after which he experienced across-the-board skills drop. Then a knee injury ended his season. LD% will regress upward and drive some OBP recovery, so check on the status of his knee come spring. If healthy, UP: 50 SB.

Yr	Tm	AB	R	HR	RBI	SB	BA	xBA	vL	vR	OB	Slg	OPS	bb%	ct%	h%	Eye	G	L	F	PX	xPX	hr/f	Spd	SBO	SB%	#Wk	DOM	DIS	RC/G	RAR	BPV	BPX	R$
08	2 NL *	567	78	1	41	25	274	256	163	270	322	355	677	7	79	35	0.34	55	21	23	57	40	0%	141	25%	62%	14	29%	57%	3.82	-14.4	17	33	$16
09	FLA	461	72	1	27	21	252	237	315	223	303	308	611	7	79	32	0.36	53	19	28	37	23	1%	152	23%	70%	27	19%	70%	3.15	-21.3	6	12	$10
10	FLA *	344	43	0	18	18	244	239	348	231	303	310	613	8	76	32	0.35	52	22	26	51	52	0%	157	23%	79%	20	20%	55%	3.25	-14.8	5	11	$6
11	FLA	565	78	5	36	40	296	259	333	282	362	393	755	9	77	38	0.46	53	24	23	73	53	5%	140	27%	78%	27	19%	41%	5.24	8.8	29	64	$26
12	MIA	244	30	1	11	30	258	225	210	282	327	316	643	9	79	32	0.48	58	17	26	33	56	2%	169	41%	91%	12	17%	58%	4.09	-4.2	9	23	$11
1st Half		149	19	0	6	20	268	217	208	297	347	315	663	11	77	35	0.51	56	18	25	25	52	0%	169	39%	95%	7	14%	71%	4.59	-0.8	-2	-5	$13
2nd Half		95	11	1	5	10	242	236	212	258	294	316	610	7	82	29	0.41	60	14	26	44	62	5%	121	46%	83%	5	20%	40%	3.36	-4.1	19	48	$7
13	Proj	512	66	3	28	45	263	238	253	268	326	337	662	8	79	33	0.43	56	19	25	48	53	3%	154	34%	84%				4.04	-11.1	16	40	$22

Bourjos,Peter

Age 26	Bats R	Pos CF	Health	A	LIMA Plan	C
Ht 6' 1"	Wt 185		PT/Exp	C	Rand Var	0
			Consist	C	MM	2505

3-19-.220 in 168 AB at LAA. During spring, said hip pain was "bone-on-bone" but only hurt when he played off-season golf. Are there any baseball activities that are similar to swinging a golf club? Hmmm... Hip still a problem this offseason, but so much rebound potential... UP: 15 HR, 25 SB.

Yr	Tm	AB	R	HR	RBI	SB	BA	xBA	vL	vR	OB	Slg	OPS	bb%	ct%	h%	Eye	G	L	F	PX	xPX	hr/f	Spd	SBO	SB%	#Wk	DOM	DIS	RC/G	RAR	BPV	BPX	R$
08																																		
09	aa	437	65	5	46	29	269	253			335	392	726	9	82	32	0.54				72			145	32%	69%				4.42		49	0	$17
10	LAA *	595	77	15	50	29	242	237	182	214	269	382	651	4	78	29	0.17	51	10	39	86	96	12%	189	30%	77%	10	50%	20%	3.43	-25.6	39	85	$17
11	LAA	502	72	12	43	22	271	252	289	261	315	438	753	6	75	34	0.26	47	17	36	117	88	9%	185	26%	71%	26	38%	38%	4.70	-2.3	53	118	$18
12	LAA *	197	30	3	21	3	223	214	232	212	284	324	608	8	74	29	0.33	52	13	35	72	64	7%	130	8%	75%	25	8%	72%	3.03	-11.0	3	8	$1
1st Half		118	16	3	17	2	237	222	255	224	286	364	650	6	74	30	0.26	52	13	35	93	65	10%	103	11%	67%	13	15%	54%	3.43	-4.8	4	10	$3
2nd Half		79	14	0	4	1	202	198	167	188	283	263	546	10	74	27	0.44	51	14	34	41	60	0%	150	5%	100%	12	0%	92%	2.44	-5.8	-9	-23	-$2
13	Proj	455	68	9	40	15	239	231	247	234	293	372	666	7	76	30	0.32	50	14	36	87	76	7%	171	18%	74%				3.64	-15.7	32	81	$11

Bourn,Michael

Age 30	Bats L	Pos CF	Health	A	LIMA Plan	C
Ht 5' 11"	Wt 180		PT/Exp	A	Rand Var	-2
			Consist	A	MM	1515

Didn't run as much as in previous years, but the speed is still there. Struck out 155 times (88 Ks after June); perhaps 2H bb% and ct% meant he was too selective at the plate. xBA says he is a two-trick pony: SB and Runs, but not BA. Don't bet on 1H HR returning, but 50 SB still within reach.

Yr	Tm	AB	R	HR	RBI	SB	BA	xBA	vL	vR	OB	Slg	OPS	bb%	ct%	h%	Eye	G	L	F	PX	xPX	hr/f	Spd	SBO	SB%	#Wk	DOM	DIS	RC/G	RAR	BPV	BPX	R$
08	HOU	467	57	5	29	41	229	223	190	242	286	300	586	7	76	29	0.33	54	17	29	46	61	5%	153	41%	80%	27	7%	63%	2.98	-24.7	2	4	$13
09	HOU	606	97	3	35	61	285	266	287	285	353	384	737	9	77	37	0.45	58	21	21	68	49	3%	172	38%	84%	27	30%	37%	5.11	7.4	34	69	$32
10	HOU	535	84	2	38	52	265	260	229	276	338	346	684	10	80	33	0.54	59	17	23	61	54	2%	139	38%	81%	25	28%	52%	4.28	-6.4	36	78	$25
11	2 NL	656	94	2	50	61	294	265	254	312	347	386	733	7	79	37	0.38	51	27	23	70	56	2%	143	38%	81%	27	33%	52%	5.01	6.0	35	78	$35
12	ATL	624	96	9	57	42	274	251	273	275	347	391	738	10	75	35	0.45	54	22	25	80	86	8%	142	28%	76%	26	23%	46%	4.80	2.0	30	75	$28
1st Half		326	52	7	29	22	307	273	271	327	358	442	800	7	79	37	0.39	53	23	23	87	91	12%	130	29%	76%	13	31%	23%	5.78	9.1	46	115	$35
2nd Half		298	44	2	28	20	238	226	275	217	336	336	672	13	70	33	0.50	54	20	26	70	78	4%	153	27%	77%	13	15%	69%	3.87	-8.3	9	23	$20
13	Proj	602	90	5	49	49	272	250	261	277	341	372	713	9	76	35	0.44	54	22	24	70	69	5%	141	33%	79%				4.57	-3.7	28	70	$29

JOSH PALEY

Brantley,Michael

Age	26	Bats	L	Pos CF	Health	A	LIMA Plan	B
Ht	6' 2"	Wt	200		PT/Exp	B	Rand Var	-1
					Consist	B	MM	1235

Elite contact will always mitigate a BA disaster, though that's no reason to draft him. It's the promise of some speed. But while his speed skills remain slightly above average, his green light has been dimming for some time. Why? Could it be his brutal success rate? That 57% debacle could turn his light permanently red.

Yr	Tm	AB	R	HR	RBI	SB	BA	xBA	vL	vR	OB	Slg	OPS	bb%	ct%	h%	Eye	G	L	F	PX	xPX	hr/f	Spd	SBO	SB%	#Wk	DOM	DIS	RC/G	RAR	BPV	BPX	R$
08	aa	420	65	3	32	23	287	258			353	355	708	9	93	30	1.39				43			109	22%	72%				4.47		58	0	$16
09	CLE *	569	76	5	41	42	254	278	462	267	323	323	646	9	87	28	0.80	47	26	27	47	22	0%	114	30%	82%	6	0%	67%	3.74	-14.0	42	86	$19
10	CLE *	570	79	6	44	20	260	263	172	266	318	342	659	8	88	29	0.69	48	20	32	53	57	4%	108	17%	72%	17	35%	47%	3.73	-14.1	46	100	$15
11	CLE	451	63	7	46	13	266	264	214	289	318	384	701	7	83	31	0.45	49	20	31	82	82	6%	105	15%	72%	22	41%	14%	4.20	-4.8	49	109	$13
12	CLE	552	63	6	60	12	288	286	265	299	350	402	753	9	90	31	0.95	49	23	29	75	76	4%	102	13%	57%	27	44%	7%	4.87	4.7	64	160	$17
1st Half		296	33	1	35	9	280	289	281	280	326	385	711	6	90	31	0.65	53	22	25	73	57	1%	102	18%	64%	13	46%	8%	4.32	-2.9	61	153	$18
2nd Half		256	30	5	25	3	297	283	247	322	377	422	799	11	90	31	1.32	44	24	32	77	98	7%	101	8%	43%	14	43%	7%	5.52	6.3	64	160	$16
13	**Proj**	**545**	**70**	**9**	**53**	**10**	**278**	**277**	**253**	**288**	**338**	**397**	**735**	**8**	**88**	**30**	**0.75**	**48**	**22**	**30**	**75**	**72**	**6%**	**103**	**10%**	**61%**				**4.63**	**-2.2**	**55**	**138**	**$15**

Brantly,Rob

Age	23	Bats	L	Pos CA	Health	A	LIMA Plan	D
Ht	6' 2"	Wt	205		PT/Exp	F	Rand Var	0
					Consist	F	MM	2023

3-8-.290 in 100 AB at MIA. After watching John Buck and Brett Hayes, it is easy to see why MIA would want a hitter who can put the ball in play. The problem is that ct% is his lone plus skill. He won't kill you in BA and will hit a handful of homers. Perhaps he'll add more power as he develops.

Yr	Tm	AB	R	HR	RBI	SB	BA	xBA	vL	vR	OB	Slg	OPS	bb%	ct%	h%	Eye	G	L	F	PX	xPX	hr/f	Spd	SBO	SB%	#Wk	DOM	DIS	RC/G	RAR	BPV	BPX	R$
08																																		
09																																		
10																																		
11																																		
12	MIA *	462	41	7	41	1	267	260	200	313	311	375	686	6	84	31	0.41	41	24	35	76	103	10%	82	5%	19%	8	38%	25%	3.90	-5.1	20	50	$7
1st Half		258	19	2	23	0	268	244			306	359	665	5	86	30	0.39	44	20	36	65			84	5%	0%				3.60		17	43	$6
2nd Half		204	22	4	18	1	266	262	200	313	317	395	713	7	82	31	0.42	41	24	35	90	103	10%	85	4%	50%	8	38%	25%	4.29	0.5	26	65	$7
13	**Proj**	**328**	**31**	**6**	**29**	**1**	**266**	**263**	**220**	**280**	**311**	**385**	**696**	**6**	**84**	**30**	**0.40**	**41**	**24**	**35**	**82**	**62**	**6%**	**83**	**4%**	**28%**				**4.04**	**-1.7**	**24**	**61**	**$6**

Braun,Ryan

Age	29	Bats	R	Pos LF	Health	A	LIMA Plan	C
Ht	6' 1"	Wt	210		PT/Exp	A	Rand Var	-3
					Consist	C	MM	4445

First MLB player to win case on PEDs; MLB fired arbiter. Lesson learned: shoot the messenger when you lose in court. As for Braun, he responded by being almost as dominant; ct% dip is only skill blemish. Repeatability of 40 HRs hinges on maintaining 2012's hr/f gains, so best to bet against that. Still plenty of value, though.

Yr	Tm	AB	R	HR	RBI	SB	BA	xBA	vL	vR	OB	Slg	OPS	bb%	ct%	h%	Eye	G	L	F	PX	xPX	hr/f	Spd	SBO	SB%	#Wk	DOM	DIS	RC/G	RAR	BPV	BPX	R$
08	MIL	611	92	37	106	14	285	292	287	284	331	553	884	6	79	31	0.33	39	17	44	167	152	17%	128	14%	78%	27	67%	11%	6.49	30.4	98	192	$29
09	MIL	635	113	32	114	20	320	303	395	302	376	551	927	8	81	35	0.47	47	20	34	140	117	18%	117	14%	77%	27	59%	22%	7.71	51.3	90	184	$38
10	MIL	619	101	25	103	14	304	295	271	315	361	501	862	8	83	33	0.53	48	17	35	131	112	14%	94	10%	82%	27	52%	15%	6.66	32.9	82	178	$32
11	MIL	563	109	33	111	33	332	314	350	327	395	597	991	9	83	35	0.62	42	21	37	165	154	19%	108	23%	85%	26	81%	8%	9.10	65.4	128	284	$47
12	MIL	598	108	41	112	30	319	296	363	305	384	595	980	10	79	35	0.49	44	18	38	170	153	23%	99	21%	81%	27	70%	19%	8.57	62.4	105	263	$45
1st Half		275	49	22	55	13	313	294	313	313	382	611	993	10	78	33	0.52	40	19	42	176	171	24%	101	22%	72%	13	69%	8%	8.43	28.7	107	268	$43
2nd Half		323	59	19	57	17	325	299	405	299	386	582	968	9	79	36	0.47	47	18	35	165	137	21%	96	20%	89%	14	71%	29%	8.70	34.9	101	253	$47
13	**Proj**	**605**	**109**	**36**	**112**	**28**	**319**	**297**	**345**	**311**	**380**	**575**	**956**	**9**	**81**	**35**	**0.51**	**44**	**19**	**37**	**158**	**144**	**20%**	**99**	**19%**	**83%**				**8.24**	**58.8**	**104**	**260**	**$45**

Brown,Domonic

Age	25	Bats	L	Pos RF LF	Health	A	LIMA Plan	C+
Ht	6' 5"	Wt	205		PT/Exp	D	Rand Var	+2
					Consist	B	MM	2115

5-26-.235 in 187 AB at PHI. Former uber-prospect is still young enough to do something, but the luster is fading and the clock is ticking. 4 HR and 12 BB in Sept are tempered by .210 BA that month. Contact trending in the right direction, but has yet to show plus skills required of a starter, let alone a star.

Yr	Tm	AB	R	HR	RBI	SB	BA	xBA	vL	vR	OB	Slg	OPS	bb%	ct%	h%	Eye	G	L	F	PX	xPX	hr/f	Spd	SBO	SB%	#Wk	DOM	DIS	RC/G	RAR	BPV	BPX	R$
08																																		
09	aa	147	17	3	17	7	258	247			311	410	721	7	72	34	0.28				107			115	22%	86%				4.50		32	0	$3
10	PHI *	405	60	18	67	16	279	274	77	245	335	485	820	8	74	34	0.32	41	22	37	145	159	13%	107	24%	64%	9	33%	56%	5.47	3.8	61	133	$19
11	PHI *	322	46	7	31	13	238	242	281	237	336	362	698	13	77	29	0.66	47	18	35	90	90	9%	109	18%	70%	13	38%	46%	4.03	-10.9	38	84	$7
12	PHI *	407	48	9	49	3	244	256	196	250	303	384	688	8	80	29	0.42	46	21	33	94	90	10%	86	10%	32%	10	50%	40%	3.69	-17.9	34	85	$6
1st Half		173	21	3	18	3	232	237			277	360	637	6	76	29	0.26	44	20	36	90			108	27%	32%				2.80		18	45	$3
2nd Half		234	27	6	31	0	252	266	196	250	322	403	725	9	82	28	0.59	46	21	33	97	90	10%	83	0%	0%	10	50%	40%	4.42	-4.0	44	110	$9
13	**Proj**	**509**	**65**	**11**	**62**	**7**	**249**	**247**	**250**	**241**	**317**	**387**	**704**	**9**	**78**	**30**	**0.44**	**46**	**20**	**35**	**95**	**82**	**8%**	**99**	**12%**	**46%**				**3.97**	**-15.9**	**31**	**79**	**$12**

Bruce,Jay

Age	26	Bats	L	Pos RF	Health	A	LIMA Plan	B
Ht	6' 3"	Wt	225		PT/Exp	A	Rand Var	0
					Consist	B	MM	5225

PX/xPX and hr/f all jumped, but HR stayed stable. Why? Fewer FBs. Other skills stable, elevating him to minor star. Could make jump to superstar if he could grow another skill, but stagnant ct% is not helping. If he can move that needle, or lift a few more FBs... UP: 40 HR. If not, a repeat of 2012 is a good bet.

Yr	Tm	AB	R	HR	RBI	SB	BA	xBA	vL	vR	OB	Slg	OPS	bb%	ct%	h%	Eye	G	L	F	PX	xPX	hr/f	Spd	SBO	SB%	#Wk	DOM	DIS	RC/G	RAR	BPV	BPX	R$
08	CIN *	597	91	31	83	11	281	268	190	286	330	493	823	7	73	34	0.27	45	21	34	138	110	20%	102	12%	60%	19	47%	42%	5.59	7.6	49	96	$24
09	CIN	345	47	22	58	3	223	269	210	229	300	470	770	10	78	22	0.51	39	13	49	147	150	17%	91	8%	50%	18	56%	33%	4.50	-6.8	74	151	$7
10	CIN	509	80	25	70	5	281	261	277	283	354	493	848	10	73	34	0.43	36	20	44	145	139	15%	122	6%	56%	26	50%	46%	6.08	13.4	58	126	$20
11	CIN	585	84	32	97	8	256	251	240	263	337	474	810	11	73	30	0.45	36	17	47	151	150	16%	85	9%	53%	27	44%	33%	5.30	2.5	57	127	$22
12	CIN	560	89	34	99	9	252	270	225	263	326	514	841	10	72	29	0.40	35	20	44	178	162	19%	83	9%	75%	27	59%	33%	5.69	9.0	85	213	$22
1st Half		268	41	17	54	4	257	280	253	259	330	526	856	10	75	28	0.43	31	23	46	180	164	18%	68	7%	100%	13	69%	23%	6.05	8.2	88	220	$23
2nd Half		292	48	17	45	5	247	262	202	268	323	503	827	10	70	29	0.38	40	18	42	175	160	20%	102	12%	63%	14	50%	43%	5.37	3.2	76	190	$21
13	**Proj**	**579**	**89**	**36**	**102**	**8**	**266**	**264**	**241**	**276**	**340**	**523**	**862**	**10**	**73**	**30**	**0.41**	**35**	**19**	**46**	**170**	**152**	**19%**	**87**	**9%**	**63%**				**6.05**	**17.7**	**76**	**190**	**$26**

Buck,John

Age	32	Bats	R	Pos CA	Health	A	LIMA Plan	F
Ht	6' 2"	Wt	230		PT/Exp	C	Rand Var	+4
					Consist	C	MM	3003

Looks like he may have traded plate discipline in 2H to offset loss of power for the previous season and a half. He achieved that, but to what end? Sub-70% ct% is a ticket to bench or retirement, and age is working against him. Power was his plus skill and 2010 numbers won't come back. UP: 2011, but the end draws nigh.

Yr	Tm	AB	R	HR	RBI	SB	BA	xBA	vL	vR	OB	Slg	OPS	bb%	ct%	h%	Eye	G	L	F	PX	xPX	hr/f	Spd	SBO	SB%	#Wk	DOM	DIS	RC/G	RAR	BPV	BPX	R$
08	KC	370	48	9	48	0	224	231	236	219	297	365	661	9	74	28	0.40	43	16	41	105	91	8%	77	3%	0%	27	30%	48%	3.43	-9.6	14	27	$1
09	KC *	213	18	9	39	1	242	259	213	259	286	472	758	6	70	30	0.21	37	18	45	159	120	14%	92	5%	50%	22	32%	59%	4.47	1.1	45	92	$3
10	TOR	409	53	20	66	0	281	254	409	246	308	489	797	4	73	34	0.14	39	16	45	151	138	15%	73	0%	0%	25	36%	56%	5.35	12.2	30	65	$14
11	FLA	466	41	16	57	0	227	224	189	241	308	367	675	10	75	27	0.47	41	18	41	95	133	11%	65	1%	0%	27	26%	48%	3.69	-8.3	7	16	$5
12	MIA	343	29	12	41	0	192	217	162	206	293	347	640	13	70	24	0.48	43	17	40	111	123	13%	57	0%	0%	27	30%	63%	3.21	-11.6	3	8	-$1
1st Half		184	15	7	21	0	179	197	143	195	307	321	628	16	72	21	0.65	47	16	38	94	103	14%	55	0%	0%	13	31%	62%	3.06	-6.8	-3	-8	-$2
2nd Half		159	14	5	20	0	208	227	184	218	276	377	653	9	68	27	0.29	38	19	43	132	148	11%	61	0%	0%	14	29%	64%	3.35	-4.3	9	23	$0
13	**Proj**	**253**	**24**	**9**	**33**	**0**	**221**	**226**	**206**	**226**	**297**	**384**	**681**	**10**	**72**	**27**	**0.38**	**41**	**18**	**42**	**115**	**130**	**12%**	**62**	**1%**	**17%**				**3.71**	**-3.9**	**11**	**27**	**$3**

Burriss,Emmanuel

Age	28	Bats	B	Pos 2B	Health	A	LIMA Plan	F
Ht	6' 0"	Wt	205		PT/Exp	F	Rand Var	+3
					Consist	A	MM	0301

0-7-.213 in 136 AB at SF. Classic example of a player who cannot steal first base. The speed is real, but so is his demonstrated inability to translate that into baseball skills. Sometimes, it really is as simple as looking at a player's BPV and how his team has chosen to use him.

Yr	Tm	AB	R	HR	RBI	SB	BA	xBA	vL	vR	OB	Slg	OPS	bb%	ct%	h%	Eye	G	L	F	PX	xPX	hr/f	Spd	SBO	SB%	#Wk	DOM	DIS	RC/G	RAR	BPV	BPX	R$
08	SF *	302	41	1	22	14	271	259	292	278	325	316	641	7	90	30	0.80	65	14	21	28	31	2%	121	22%	67%	22	36%	45%	3.51	-5.3	32	63	$8
09	SF *	273	24	1	18	15	235	247	333	208	277	276	553	6	86	27	0.42	56	17	27	30	21	0%	100	30%	71%	11	0%	64%	2.53	-13.2	10	20	$4
10	SF *	278	25	0	15	8	236	317	0	500	270	280	550	4	88	27	0.38	75	25	0	34	57	0%	115	20%	56%	3	0%	67%	2.39	-14.6	16	35	$1
11	SF *	312	33	1	10	26	216	231	143	220	261	254	516	6	87	25	0.47	61	12	28	28	34	0%	114	45%	74%	16	0%	50%	2.20	-18.9	18	40	$4
12	SF *	242	23	0	9	8	212	244	94	250	263	249	512	6	83	25	0.42	63	18	19	28	13	0%	109	19%	73%	21	0%	81%	2.14	-14.9	1	3	-$1
1st Half		114	13	0	5	4	211	228	103	247	268	219	488	7	82	26	0.43	64	19	17	8	9	0%	94	19%	67%	13	0%	85%	1.90	-7.6	-27	-68	-$1
2nd Half		128	10	0	4	4	213	232	0	263	258	275	533	6	85	25	0.41	59	12	29	45	33	0%	114	18%	81%	8	0%	75%	2.35	-6.6	20	50	-$1
13	**Proj**	**99**	**10**	**0**	**4**	**5**	**219**	**239**	**211**	**222**	**266**	**258**	**524**	**6**	**85**	**26**	**0.44**	**60**	**16**	**23**	**28**	**22**	**0%**	**98**	**26%**	**72%**				**2.25**	**-6.2**	**6**	**16**	**$1**

JOSH PALEY

Butera,Drew

Butera,Drew				Health	A	LIMA Plan	F
Age 29	Bats R	Pos CA		PT/Exp	F	Rand Var	0
Ht 6' 1"	Wt 201			Consist	B	MM	1001

1-5-.198 in 111 AB at MIN. Plus defender busted out by almost conquering THE MENDOZA LINE! Let's see... Positives kinda sorta include 1H vR, LD%, and Spd and um... infinite 2H/1H vL ratio. We appreciate you purchasing this book and we hope our incisive analysis brings you many fantasy championships.

Yr	Tm	AB	R	HR	RBI	SB	BA	xBA	vL	vR	OB	Slg	OPS	bb%	ct%	h%	Eye	G	L	F	PX	xPX	hr/f	Spd	SBO	SB%	#Wk	DOM	DIS	RC/G	RAR	BPV	BPX	R$
08	aa	302	30	5	30	0	182	238			247	289	535	8	79	22	0.40				76			87	2%	0%				2.18		6	0	-$6
09	aaa	298	18	2	20	0	176	229			220	242	462	5	81	21	0.29				51			87	2%	0%				1.61		-13	0	-$8
10	MIN	142	12	2	13	0	197	236	183	207	219	296	515	3	82	23	0.16	40	19	41	67	52	4%	95	0%	0%	26	23%	58%	2.06	-9.2	8	17	-$2
11	MIN	234	19	2	23	0	167	203	215	148	204	239	443	4	82	19	0.26	40	15	46	53	63	2%	84	0%	0%	27	19%	63%	1.49	-20.1	-3	-7	-$6
12	MIN *	154	11	2	9	0	205	224	118	234	259	292	551	7	76	26	0.30	34	24	42	70	37	3%	88	0%	0%	20	15%	70%	2.43	-8.1	-18	-45	-$3
1st Half		97	7	1	5	0	232	254	0	302	279	330	609	6	76	30	0.27	33	30	38	84	26	0%	101	0%	0%	9	22%	67%	3.05	-3.4	-8	-20	-$3
2nd Half		57	4	1	4	0	158	187	174	147	226	228	454	8	75	19	0.36	35	19	47	46	47	5%	76	0%	0%	11	9%	73%	1.56	-5.0	-38	-95	-$3
13	Proj	99	8	1	8	0	184	209	167	192	231	259	491	6	79	22	0.29	37	19	44	56	49	3%	80	0%	0%				1.87	-7.4	-16	-40	-$3

Butler,Billy

Butler,Billy				Health	A	LIMA Plan	C+
Age 27	Bats R	Pos DH 1B		PT/Exp	A	Rand Var	-3
Ht 6' 1"	Wt 240			Consist	B	MM	4045

Announcers overuse the term "Professional Hitter;" it should be reserved for the likes of him. Took a bit of a more free-swinging approach, which BPV didn't like but yielded good results. More LDs drove BA growth, but resulting loss of FBs, plus outlying hr/f, say that the HR gains likely at their ceiling.

Yr	Tm	AB	R	HR	RBI	SB	BA	xBA	vL	vR	OB	Slg	OPS	bb%	ct%	h%	Eye	G	L	F	PX	xPX	hr/f	Spd	SBO	SB%	#Wk	DOM	DIS	RC/G	RAR	BPV	BPX	R$
08	KC *	544	58	15	65	0	282	259	340	244	336	418	754	8	88	30	0.69	49	17	35	83	86	8%	70	1%	0%	23	30%	39%	4.94	0.8	44	86	$12
09	KC	608	78	21	93	1	301	291	330	289	362	492	854	9	83	33	0.56	47	18	34	126	117	12%	59	1%	100%	27	48%	26%	6.50	26.9	64	131	$21
10	KC	595	77	15	78	0	318	278	267	330	389	469	857	10	87	35	0.88	48	18	34	104	112	8%	59	0%	0%	27	52%	19%	6.81	30.6	60	130	$24
11	KC	597	74	19	95	2	291	277	306	287	362	461	823	10	84	32	0.69	46	19	36	117	131	10%	50	2%	67%	27	52%	19%	5.99	18.2	63	140	$23
12	KC	614	72	29	107	2	313	288	333	306	368	510	878	8	82	34	0.49	47	24	29	120	118	20%	51	2%	67%	27	44%	41%	6.94	34.1	52	130	$29
1st Half		279	29	16	48	1	297	287	370	272	355	516	871	8	83	31	0.53	48	21	31	128	112	22%	50	3%	50%	13	46%	46%	6.59	13.1	59	148	$25
2nd Half		335	43	13	59	1	325	288	302	335	379	504	884	8	81	37	0.45	47	26	27	114	124	18%	56	1%	100%	14	43%	36%	7.25	20.9	46	115	$32
13	Proj	606	74	27	102	2	307	287	318	303	368	504	872	9	84	33	0.59	47	21	32	122	119	17%	49	1%	67%				6.81	31.7	62	155	$28

Cabrera,Asdrubal

Cabrera,Asdrubal				Health	B	LIMA Plan	C+
Age 27	Bats B	Pos SS		PT/Exp	A	Rand Var	0
Ht 6' 0"	Wt 180			Consist	B	MM	3225

2H marred by leg and wrist injuries. He was actually improving on his 2011 breakout with across the board skills growth (except for Spd) in 1H, with noticeably improved plate discipline and BA results that came with it. Just entering his prime; if he's healthy, treat this projection as a baseline. UP: 2011, minus the SB.

Yr	Tm	AB	R	HR	RBI	SB	BA	xBA	vL	vR	OB	Slg	OPS	bb%	ct%	h%	Eye	G	L	F	PX	xPX	hr/f	Spd	SBO	SB%	#Wk	DOM	DIS	RC/G	RAR	BPV	BPX	R$
08	CLE *	493	71	10	59	6	272	249	349	230	342	387	729	10	79	33	0.50	46	21	34	82	90	7%	85	8%	48%	23	17%	57%	4.48	8.2	20	39	$12
09	CLE	523	81	6	68	17	308	286	306	309	362	438	799	8	83	36	0.49	48	22	30	93	89	5%	115	14%	81%	23	52%	26%	5.89	28.4	59	120	$22
10	CLE	381	39	3	29	6	276	242	264	281	320	346	667	6	84	32	0.42	52	17	31	52	57	3%	102	9%	60%	18	11%	44%	3.82	-0.8	13	28	$7
11	CLE	604	87	25	92	17	273	269	291	265	323	460	783	7	80	30	0.37	44	17	39	123	115	13%	102	15%	77%	27	56%	33%	5.20	22.4	67	149	$26
12	CLE	555	70	16	68	9	270	269	286	263	333	423	756	9	82	30	0.53	41	23	36	101	105	10%	73	9%	69%	27	41%	33%	4.88	15.6	49	123	$17
1st Half		272	40	11	40	2	298	298	311	291	372	493	864	11	86	31	0.84	42	24	34	118	98	14%	86	6%	40%	13	62%	23%	6.43	18.4	78	195	$22
2nd Half		283	30	5	28	7	244	242	261	236	294	357	651	7	78	29	0.33	40	22	37	84	111	6%	66	12%	88%	14	21%	43%	3.61	-3.4	18	45	$11
13	Proj	581	74	19	70	12	271	265	284	265	328	433	761	8	82	30	0.46	43	21	37	104	99	11%	84	11%	72%				4.93	15.4	51	127	$20

Cabrera,Everth

Cabrera,Everth				Health	B	LIMA Plan	D+
Age 26	Bats B	Pos SS		PT/Exp	D	Rand Var	-3
Ht 5' 10"	Wt 175			Consist	B	MM	1505

2-24-.246 with 44 SB in 398 AB at SD. With utter lack of power, it's all about OBP and SBO, the latter being no problem. Healthy bb% is a good start toward a healthy OBP, but unacceptable ct%, especially for a noodle bat, is a red flag. Max value might be in a platoon role. With as few as 450 AB... UP: 50 SB.

Yr	Tm	AB	R	HR	RBI	SB	BA	xBA	vL	vR	OB	Slg	OPS	bb%	ct%	h%	Eye	G	L	F	PX	xPX	hr/f	Spd	SBO	SB%	#Wk	DOM	DIS	RC/G	RAR	BPV	BPX	R$
08																																		
09	SD *	404	63	2	31	26	256	259	239	261	334	360	693	10	76	33	0.49	63	15	23	72	57	3%	162	28%	76%	20	30%	40%	4.17	0.7	33	67	$13
10	SD *	243	27	1	24	12	207	229	214	206	278	272	550	9	71	29	0.34	54	22	23	50	70	3%	109	29%	67%	22	18%	55%	2.39	-13.3	-15	-33	$2
11	SD *	254	31	1	9	19	209	264	500	0	264	274	538	7	78	26	0.34	100	0	0	48	2	0%	155	48%	65%	1	0%	100%	2.20	-15.7	10	22	$2
12	SD *	542	67	2	34	54	247	237	195	267	312	319	632	9	73	34	0.35	61	19	20	60	47	4%	124	38%	93%	21	14%	57%	3.84	-4.3	2	5	$21
1st Half		278	32	2	20	22	248	237	150	287	307	342	649	8	72	34	0.30	64	14	23	79	57	10%	113	30%	100%	7	29%	57%	4.01	0.0	11	28	$19
2nd Half		264	35	0	14	32	246	232	219	257	318	295	614	10	73	34	0.40	59	22	19	41	42	0%	131	44%	89%	14	7%	57%	3.66	-2.8	-9	-23	$23
13	Proj	415	52	2	26	35	232	237	206	241	299	308	607	9	74	31	0.37	59	19	22	57	57	4%	123	38%	81%				3.22	-10.1	5	12	$13

Cabrera,Melky

Cabrera,Melky				Health	A	LIMA Plan	B
Age 28	Bats B	Pos LF		PT/Exp	A	Rand Var	-5
Ht 6' 0"	Wt 200			Consist	D	MM	2435

Things that went up: Eye, Spd (big time), GB%, BA (especially vL), xBA (does not support BA), wacky h%, and detected banned substances. Things that went down: power (new home park hurt), games played after suspension and credibility. If his numbers depended on chemicals, DN: 2010

Yr	Tm	AB	R	HR	RBI	SB	BA	xBA	vL	vR	OB	Slg	OPS	bb%	ct%	h%	Eye	G	L	F	PX	xPX	hr/f	Spd	SBO	SB%	#Wk	DOM	DIS	RC/G	RAR	BPV	BPX	R$
08	NYY *	471	49	8	41	10	255	243	213	265	308	339	647	7	86	28	0.52	46	19	35	52	66	6%	97	11%	65%	24	17%	42%	3.51	-16.9	22	43	$7
09	NYY	485	66	13	68	10	274	296	268	277	333	416	750	8	88	29	0.73	50	21	30	87	75	10%	77	9%	83%	27	56%	30%	4.93	2.7	65	133	$15
10	ATL	458	50	4	42	7	255	267	233	266	318	354	672	8	86	29	0.66	49	19	32	71	60	3%	92	6%	88%	26	35%	27%	3.91	-10.9	46	100	$7
11	KC	658	102	18	87	20	305	289	304	306	341	470	810	5	86	34	0.37	47	20	33	108	88	10%	113	18%	67%	27	56%	19%	5.70	17.7	75	167	$33
12	SF	459	84	11	60	13	346	298	395	327	394	516	910	7	86	38	0.57	52	22	26	99	80	11%	148	12%	72%	20	60%	20%	7.84	37.1	80	200	$28
1st Half		311	53	7	38	10	350	297	420	323	395	514	910	7	86	39	0.55	53	22	25	95	80	10%	149	15%	67%	13	69%	23%	7.75	25.2	76	190	$35
2nd Half		148	31	4	22	3	338	299	341	336	391	520	912	8	86	37	0.62	51	21	28	108	79	11%	127	6%	100%	7	43%	14%	8.01	12.9	86	215	$14
13	Proj	553	86	12	65	9	285	283	291	283	336	434	770	7	86	32	0.55	50	21	30	92	78	8%	122	7%	78%				5.21	8.8	69	171	$20

Cabrera,Miguel

Cabrera,Miguel				Health	A	LIMA Plan	C
Age 30	Bats R	Pos 3B		PT/Exp	A	Rand Var	-1
Ht 6' 4"	Wt 240			Consist	B	MM	4155

Does lineup protection matter? Discuss. Triple Crown numbers included BB drop from 108 to 66 (IBB from 22 to 17), as opponents worked around him less with Fielder on deck. Gloriously unsustainable 2H hr/f won't repeat, but remarkable, stable skills say that 2012, as a whole, will.

Yr	Tm	AB	R	HR	RBI	SB	BA	xBA	vL	vR	OB	Slg	OPS	bb%	ct%	h%	Eye	G	L	F	PX	xPX	hr/f	Spd	SBO	SB%	#Wk	DOM	DIS	RC/G	RAR	BPV	BPX	R$
08	DET	616	85	37	127	1	292	291	311	286	351	537	889	8	80	32	0.44	41	20	39	152	125	19%	73	1%	100%	27	59%	30%	6.81	38.6	73	143	$27
09	DET	611	96	34	103	6	324	297	315	328	392	547	938	10	82	35	0.64	43	20	37	133	140	18%	71	4%	75%	27	59%	11%	8.06	57.1	75	153	$32
10	DET	548	111	38	126	3	328	327	313	333	422	622	1045	14	83	34	0.94	39	19	42	187	169	20%	60	3%	50%	26	73%	12%	9.83	76.9	127	276	$38
11	DET	572	111	30	105	2	344	317	319	353	449	586	1034	16	84	37	1.21	44	22	34	158	140	18%	70	1%	67%	27	78%	7%	10.19	83.2	111	247	$39
12	DET	622	109	44	139	4	330	315	314	335	394	606	1000	10	84	34	0.67	42	22	36	161	161	23%	69	3%	80%	27	74%	7%	9.08	74.2	103	258	$42
1st Half		314	45	16	62	3	315	298	329	311	373	541	915	8	85	33	0.62	43	20	37	138	141	16%	67	4%	75%	13	69%	15%	7.50	24.8	84	210	$36
2nd Half		308	64	28	77	1	344	331	300	360	414	672	1087	11	83	34	0.73	41	23	35	185	181	30%	72	1%	100%	14	79%	0%	10.86	49.7	118	295	$49
13	Proj	617	114	37	132	3	332	305	314	339	412	584	995	12	84	35	0.82	42	21	36	152	156	20%	66	2%	71%				9.16	74.1	96	241	$42

Cain,Lorenzo

Cain,Lorenzo				Health	C	LIMA Plan	C
Age 27	Bats R	Pos CF		PT/Exp	D	Rand Var	-2
Ht 6' 2"	Wt 200			Consist	B	MM	2515

7-31-.266 in 222 AB at KC. Strong 2011 campaign at AAA made him a spring 2012 sleeper, but April groin injury and May torn hip flexor wrecked that. Poor plate approach limits upside, but he's in his prime and 2H Spd, PX indicate there is fanalytic value to be milked. If he can stay healthy, see 2H... UP: 15 HR, 20 SB.

Yr	Tm	AB	R	HR	RBI	SB	BA	xBA	vL	vR	OB	Slg	OPS	bb%	ct%	h%	Eye	G	L	F	PX	xPX	hr/f	Spd	SBO	SB%	#Wk	DOM	DIS	RC/G	RAR	BPV	BPX	R$
08	a/a	167	16	3	15	5	234	230			309	385	695	10	68	33	0.34				112			126	16%	68%				3.90		16	0	$1
09	aa	145	14	3	12	2	187	224			232	293	525	6	72	24	0.21				77			89	21%	42%				1.94		-18	0	-$2
10	MIL *	478	61	3	33	27	283	233	289	314	343	379	722	8	77	36	0.40	43	21	37	70	104	2%	178	21%	86%	12	42%	33%	4.81	1.6	25	54	$18
11	KC *	509	62	10	57	11	262	260	0	353	301	393	695	5	77	32	0.24	50	22	28	95	57	0%	144	15%	61%	2	50%	50%	3.96	-13.4	29	64	$13
12	KC *	274	33	8	36	10	257	252	306	247	299	407	705	6	75	31	0.24	47	22	31	101	92	13%	115	16%	100%	12	42%	42%	4.37	-3.8	29	73	$8
1st Half		46	4	1	3	0	146	199	0	200	164	244	408	2	72	17	0.08	18	27	55	65	102	0%	102	0%	0%	2	0%	100%	1.19	-5.5	-39	-98	-$13
2nd Half		228	28	7	33	10	279	261	328	250	325	440	765	6	76	34	0.28	49	21	30	107	91	15%	114	17%	100%	10	50%	30%	5.33	3.6	40	100	$12
13	Proj	457	54	11	48	17	265	246	285	255	315	406	721	7	75	33	0.29	47	21	32	97	96	10%	131	18%	80%				4.48	-4.0	29	73	$16

JOSH PALEY

Cairo,Miguel

Age 39 · Bats R · Pos 1B · Ht 6' 1" · Wt 225
Health B · PT/Exp F · Consist D · LIMA Plan F · Rand Var +5 · MM 1311

Recipe for a Cairo: Give Yuniesky Betancourt a glove made of leather instead of iron, take away all of his power and makee him eight years older. He puts the ball in play where the fielders identify it, collect it, and put him out. A fantasy RUM pick, but carved himself a nice career as a reserve.

Yr	Tm	AB	R	HR	RBI	SB	BA	xBA	vL	vR	OB	Slg	OPS	bb%	ct%	h%	Eye	G	L	F	PX	xPX	hr/f	Spd	SBO	SB%	#Wk	DOM	DIS	RC/G	RAR	BPV	BPX	R$
08	SEA	221	34	0	23	5	249	262	270	235	305	330	636	8	86	29	0.56	49	20	31	61	61	0%	113	12%	71%	26	23%	38%	3.42	-7.8	43	84	$2
09	PHI *	341	38	5	26	6	234	219	0	286	257	324	582	3	84	27	0.20	43	13	45	56	89	6%	119	10%	82%	12	25%	50%	2.80	-18.5	20	41	$2
10	CIN	200	30	4	28	4	290	284	262	304	346	410	756	8	85	33	0.57	44	25	31	84	75	7%	78	7%	100%	26	31%	42%	5.23	3.4	47	102	$7
11	CIN	245	33	8	33	3	265	262	319	253	316	412	728	7	85	28	0.50	45	19	36	87	76	10%	103	11%	43%	26	38%	38%	4.27	-2.3	50	111	$6
12	CIN	150	9	1	13	4	187	229	239	163	208	280	488	3	87	21	0.20	42	15	43	60	73	2%	91	18%	100%	23	30%	39%	1.92	-12.8	34	85	-$3
1st Half		57	4	0	4	1	140	227	214	116	169	228	398	3	93	15	0.50	45	9	45	54	36	0%	83	17%	100%	9	33%	44%	1.20	-6.5	58	145	-$6
2nd Half		93	5	1	9	3	215	229	250	197	232	312	543	2	83	25	0.13	39	19	42	63	99	3%	89	19%	100%	14	29%	36%	2.48	-6.0	16	40	$0
13	Proj	**134**	**13**	**2**	**14**	**3**	**227**	**246**	**259**	**213**	**262**	**337**	**599**	**5**	**86**	**25**	**0.35**	**43**	**18**	**38**	**69**	**73**	**5%**	**88**	**13%**	**82%**				**2.95**	**-9.8**	**39**	**98**	**$0**

Callaspo,Alberto

Age 30 · Bats B · Pos 3B · Ht 5' 9" · Wt 200
Health A · PT/Exp B · Consist C · LIMA Plan C · Rand Var +1 · MM 1125

Elite ct% and Eye have been his calling card for years; 2H suggests that both remain strong. His problem in '12 was RHP, which now point to the wrong side of a platoon. Subpar PX, Spd leave BA as his lone value generator, but the xBA trend is clear and says .300 ain't coming back. DN: Utility role sooner than later.

Yr	Tm	AB	R	HR	RBI	SB	BA	xBA	vL	vR	OB	Slg	OPS	bb%	ct%	h%	Eye	G	L	F	PX	xPX	hr/f	Spd	SBO	SB%	#Wk	DOM	DIS	RC/G	RAR	BPV	BPX	R$
08	KC	213	21	0	16	2	305	286	333	291	362	371	733	8	93	33	1.36	47	26	28	40	51	0%	103	4%	67%	20	35%	40%	4.90	2.1	47	92	$4
09	KC	576	79	11	73	2	300	283	361	273	358	457	815	8	91	32	1.02	41	17	42	93	93	5%	98	2%	67%	27	59%	11%	5.95	22.1	82	167	$17
10	2 AL	562	61	10	56	5	265	270	233	274	304	374	677	5	93	27	0.74	45	18	38	67	64	5%	81	6%	63%	27	48%	11%	3.89	-10.6	57	124	$11
11	LAA	475	54	6	46	8	288	262	306	280	366	375	741	11	90	31	1.21	41	22	37	60	64	4%	76	5%	89%	27	37%	30%	4.99	5.9	51	113	$14
12	LAA	457	55	10	53	4	252	255	306	229	333	361	694	11	87	27	0.95	44	21	36	68	77	7%	63	5%	57%	27	44%	30%	4.05	-6.7	41	103	$8
1st Half		193	21	5	21	0	259	248	310	237	329	373	702	9	87	28	0.77	44	20	36	68	81	8%	71	0%	0%	13	38%	38%	4.22	-2.0	27	68	$5
2nd Half		264	34	5	32	4	246	257	303	223	337	352	689	12	88	27	1.09	43	21	36	68	74	6%	63	8%	57%	14	50%	21%	3.93	-5.2	47	118	$11
13	Proj	**411**	**48**	**7**	**44**	**4**	**268**	**259**	**303**	**254**	**339**	**371**	**710**	**10**	**89**	**29**	**0.99**	**43**	**21**	**36**	**64**	**71**	**5%**	**71**	**5%**	**68%**				**4.36**	**-2.6**	**46**	**116**	**$10**

Campana,Tony

Age 27 · Bats L · Pos CF · Ht 5' 8" · Wt 165
Health A · PT/Exp D · Consist B · LIMA Plan D · Rand Var 0 · MM 0511

0-5-.264 with 30 SB in 174 AB at CHC. Keeps ball on the ground to utilize Spd, but can't create real baseball value if he doesn't get on base more. Not enough ct%, not enough bb%. Those kill OBP. For now, best value proposition is as a short-term pickup when he's getting some ABs.

Yr	Tm	AB	R	HR	RBI	SB	BA	xBA	vL	vR	OB	Slg	OPS	bb%	ct%	h%	Eye	G	L	F	PX	xPX	hr/f	Spd	SBO	SB%	#Wk	DOM	DIS	RC/G	RAR	BPV	BPX	R$
08																																		
09																																		
10	aa	489	55	0	28	34	274	227			318	327	645	6	81	34	0.34				43			119	40%	59%				3.30		7	0	$17
11	CHC *	263	41	1	12	29	264	248	231	265	296	321	617	4	78	34	0.20	67	16	18	46	2	6%	145	46%	90%	20	15%	60%	3.69	-7.6	6	13	$11
12	CHC *	317	43	1	8	42	248	243	229	273	291	283	575	6	74	33	0.23	69	21	9	30	-6	0%	146	60%	79%	22	14%	68%	2.98	-16.7	-26	-65	$14
1st Half		202	26	1	7	31	267	253	241	282	306	306	612	5	76	35	0.24	65	24	11	33	-6	0%	124	63%	82%	11	9%	73%	3.57	-7.3	-18	-45	$20
2nd Half		115	16	0	1	12	215	224	167	227	266	244	510	6	69	31	0.22	94	6	0	23	-11	0%	140	55%	71%	11	18%	64%	2.11	-9.9	-47	-118	$5
13	Proj	**199**	**28**	**0**	**7**	**26**	**252**	**244**	**222**	**259**	**291**	**298**	**588**	**5**	**75**	**33**	**0.22**	**66**	**21**	**14**	**37**		**2%**	**139**	**62%**	**78%**				**3.08**	**-10.4**	**-13**	**-32**	**$10**

Cano,Robinson

Age 30 · Bats L · Pos 2B · Ht 6' 0" · Wt 212
Health A · PT/Exp A · Consist B · LIMA Plan D+ · Rand Var 0 · MM 4155

PRO: Took some more walks, resumed annihilating RHPs, owns wonderfully reliable Health. (Four straight years of 623+ AB? Amazing.) CON: looming hr/f regression amid FB% decline make 30 HR repeat doubtful; suddenly has issues vLHP. NET: Remains a highly valuable and incredibly stable asset.

Yr	Tm	AB	R	HR	RBI	SB	BA	xBA	vL	vR	OB	Slg	OPS	bb%	ct%	h%	Eye	G	L	F	PX	xPX	hr/f	Spd	SBO	SB%	#Wk	DOM	DIS	RC/G	RAR	BPV	BPX	R$
08	NYY	597	70	14	72	2	271	282	292	263	302	410	712	4	89	29	0.40	47	20	33	85	89	8%	87	4%	33%	27	48%	30%	4.22	0.9	52	102	$12
09	NYY	637	103	25	85	5	320	317	309	326	351	520	870	4	90	33	0.48	47	20	33	117	90	13%	82	8%	42%	27	63%	19%	6.58	41.6	85	173	$29
10	NYY	626	103	29	109	3	319	310	285	337	376	534	910	8	88	33	0.74	44	19	36	130	125	14%	84	3%	60%	27	59%	19%	7.47	55.3	93	202	$33
11	NYY	623	104	28	118	8	302	318	314	296	342	533	875	6	85	32	0.40	47	22	31	147	116	17%	83	7%	80%	27	67%	11%	6.65	42.5	103	229	$33
12	NYY	627	105	33	94	3	313	324	239	359	374	550	924	9	85	33	0.64	49	26	26	145	115	24%	73	3%	60%	27	52%	7%	7.57	57.7	90	225	$32
1st Half		299	54	19	44	1	308	331	220	358	369	582	951	9	85	31	0.63	49	23	28	163	116	27%	77	3%	50%	13	62%	15%	7.83	29.1	106	265	$33
2nd Half		328	51	14	50	2	317	319	254	361	378	521	899	9	85	34	0.64	48	28	24	129	115	21%	71	3%	67%	14	43%	0%	7.31	26.9	76	190	$32
13	Proj	**614**	**100**	**29**	**100**	**4**	**310**	**315**	**269**	**332**	**362**	**536**	**898**	**8**	**86**	**32**	**0.57**	**47**	**23**	**29**	**137**	**114**	**19%**	**75**	**4%**	**65%**				**7.12**	**47.7**	**90**	**225**	**$32**

Canzler,Russ

Age 27 · Bats R · Pos LF · Ht 6' 2" · Wt 220
Health A · PT/Exp C · Consist C · LIMA Plan F · Rand Var 0 · MM 3101

3-11-.269 in 93 AB at CLE. Minors pedigree suggests a player with power as his one plus skill. That's not a bad one to own if you have to pick just one, but his isn't elite enough to overcome lack of plate discipline. vL looks impressive, but it's based on 30 AB over two years, and minors history doesn't support it.

Yr	Tm	AB	R	HR	RBI	SB	BA	xBA	vL	vR	OB	Slg	OPS	bb%	ct%	h%	Eye	G	L	F	PX	xPX	hr/f	Spd	SBO	SB%	#Wk	DOM	DIS	RC/G	RAR	BPV	BPX	R$
08																																		
09	aa	233	22	5	30	2	237	258			314	367	681	10	81	27	0.58				90			78	12%	23%				3.53		27	0	$1
10	aa	356	49	16	47	4	246	271			310	463	773	8	70	31	0.31				166			99	11%	44%				4.64		56	0	$9
11	TAM *	477	60	14	65	4	264	218	500	0	337	433	770	10	67	37	0.34	0	33	67	143	334	0%	89	5%	62%	3	0%	100%	5.01	-3.8	30	67	$13
12	CLE *	580	58	18	68	1	224	220	393	215	270	382	652	6	70	29	0.21	49	13	38	120	77	11%	108	6%	23%	6	17%	67%	3.27	-36.0	3	8	$5
1st Half		285	25	7	31	1	222	218			267	357	624	6	67	31	0.18				108			82	8%	17%				2.95		-18	-45	$2
2nd Half		295	33	11	37	1	225	236	393	215	273	405	679	6	73	27	0.25	49	13	38	130	77	11%	107	3%	38%	6	17%	67%	3.59	-16.0	24	60	$8
13	Proj	**194**	**22**	**5**	**24**	**1**	**238**	**224**	**348**	**191**	**297**	**390**	**688**	**8**	**71**	**31**	**0.29**	**49**	**13**	**38**	**117**	**69**	**10%**	**105**	**7%**	**41%**				**3.76**	**-5.2**	**12**	**31**	**$3**

Carp,Mike

Age 27 · Bats L · Pos LF 1B · Ht 6' 2" · Wt 210
Health D · PT/Exp D · Consist F · LIMA Plan D · Rand Var +2 · MM 3013

5-20-.213 in 164 AB at SEA. Shoulder, hip, and groin injuries wiped out his season, so give him a mulligan. 2011 minors+majors power outburst remains his upside. That power is very real, but his dubious plate approach casts doubt he'll ever consistently harness it. UP: 20 HR, DN: Back to the minors.

Yr	Tm	AB	R	HR	RBI	SB	BA	xBA	vL	vR	OB	Slg	OPS	bb%	ct%	h%	Eye	G	L	F	PX	xPX	hr/f	Spd	SBO	SB%	#Wk	DOM	DIS	RC/G	RAR	BPV	BPX	R$
08	aa	478	58	14	62	1	271	257			363	421	784	13	80	31	0.71				101			81	2%	28%				5.26		36	0	$10
09	SEA *	467	56	12	52	0	238	238	286	319	314	372	686	10	73	30	0.41	44	20	36	97	95	6%	99	1%	0%	8	50%	38%	3.87	-19.8	3	6	$4
10	SEA *	446	50	19	56	1	207	229	222	179	264	377	642	7	73	24	0.29	31	17	52	117	124	0%	87	3%	24%	4	0%	75%	3.14	-30.0	14	30	$3
11	SEA *	541	61	24	85	4	267	267	306	266	314	455	769	6	73	32	0.25	43	25	32	136	152	18%	71	6%	45%	15	40%	33%	4.83	-7.1	30	67	$18
12	SEA *	303	26	6	31	2	193	220	310	180	264	294	558	9	72	25	0.34	50	21	29	76	94	14%	68	8%	32%	16	13%	50%	2.34	-28.6	-21	-53	-$2
1st Half		134	10	4	15	2	136	196	154	157	224	259	483	10	68	16	0.36	41	16	43	90	127	16%	66	7%	100%	8	13%	50%	1.76	-16.4	-19	-48	-$6
2nd Half		169	16	2	17	0	239	247	379	212	296	324	620	8	75	31	0.33	57	26	16	66	63	10%	82	8%	0%	8	13%	50%	2.91	-12.7	-23	-58	$0
13	Proj	**386**	**39**	**14**	**47**	**2**	**247**	**245**	**295**	**230**	**308**	**400**	**708**	**8**	**73**	**30**	**0.33**	**47**	**23**	**30**	**106**	**112**	**16%**	**70**	**6%**	**35%**				**4.03**	**-7.2**	**6**	**14**	**$8**

Carpenter,Matt

Age 27 · Bats L · Pos 1B 3B · Ht 6' 3" · Wt 200
Health B · PT/Exp C · Consist D · LIMA Plan D · Rand Var -4 · MM 2123

Arrived in bigs with a nice, broad-based skill profile; then showed off his power potential in 1H, albeit in a shaky sample size. Fun stats: 3% bb% vL, 14% bb% vR; 5 HR in 98 AB vL, 1 HR in 198 AB vR... but OPS was higher vR. xBA warns of BA regression, but there's room for further growth here too. Take a flyer.

Yr	Tm	AB	R	HR	RBI	SB	BA	xBA	vL	vR	OB	Slg	OPS	bb%	ct%	h%	Eye	G	L	F	PX	xPX	hr/f	Spd	SBO	SB%	#Wk	DOM	DIS	RC/G	RAR	BPV	BPX	R$
08																																		
09																																		
10	aa	396	55	8	39	8	259	242			338	385	723	11	74	33	0.46				97			104	9%	77%				4.50		25	0	$9
11	STL *	449	41	7	48	3	228	178	0	71	323	338	661	12	81	27	0.74	45	0	55	80	2	0%	84	6%	41%	3	33%	67%	3.49	-26.6	29	64	$2
12	STL	296	44	6	46	1	294	268	265	308	367	463	830	10	79	36	0.54	40	24	36	116	114	7%	104	2%	50%	24	46%	25%	6.07	5.3	56	140	$9
1st Half		124	19	3	21	0	290	272	244	313	348	508	856	8	77	35	0.39	40	19	40	145	115	8%	112	0%	0%	10	60%	10%	6.36	3.4	69	173	$7
2nd Half		172	25	3	25	1	297	268	281	304	379	430	810	12	80	36	0.66	40	27	33	96	114	7%	94	3%	50%	14	36%	36%	5.83	2.3	40	100	$11
13	Proj	**249**	**32**	**5**	**32**	**2**	**266**	**258**	**240**	**278**	**347**	**409**	**756**	**11**	**79**	**32**	**0.59**	**40**	**24**	**36**	**100**	**114**	**7%**	**98**	**5%**	**53%**				**4.86**	**-3.7**	**42**	**106**	**$6**

JOSH PALEY

Carrera,Ezequiel

Carrera,Ezequiel		Health	A	LIMA Plan	D
Age 26	Bats L Pos LF	PT/Exp	C	Rand Var	+1
Ht 5' 10"	Wt 185	Consist	A	MM	1413

2-11-8-.272 in 147 AB in CLE. Contact rate only 76% in MLB, but 35% h% saved BA. His bb% is headed in the wrong direction, but at least LD+GB profile plays well with his speed. Has shown SB ability (8-for-9 at CLE), and team green-lighted him. If he finds 450 AB... UP: 30 SB

Yr	Tm	AB	R	HR	RBI	SB	BA	xBA	vL	vR	OB	Slg	OPS	bb%	ct%	h%	Eye	G	L	F	PX	xPX	hr/f	Spd	SBO	SB%	#Wk	DOM	DIS	RC/G	RAR	BPV	BPX	R$
08																																		
09	aa	329	61	2	34	24	314	226			411	382	793	14	78	40	0.76				48			121	27%	63%				5.52		19	0	$18
10	aaa	374	32	1	26	15	236	223			284	291	574	6	80	29	0.33				41			119	25%	63%				2.64		0	0	$4
11	CLE *	530	75	1	33	37	244	242	191	269	304	299	603	8	82	30	0.48	55	19	26	40	72	0%	132	30%	79%	14	7%	43%	3.19	-22.1	21	47	$14
12	CLE *	541	68	6	42	27	253	258	333	245	291	354	646	5	81	30	0.28	47	26	28	67	89	7%	110	28%	75%	9	33%	44%	3.51	-17.1	30	75	$15
1st Half		281	30	3	18	10	218	224			255	293	548	5	80	26	0.25				50			110	26%	64%				2.34		6	15	$8
2nd Half		260	39	3	25	17	290	270	333	245	330	422	752	6	81	35	0.31	47	26	28	86	89	7%	111	30%	83%	9	33%	44%	5.14	3.6	51	128	$23
13	**Proj**	**325**	**43**	**3**	**25**	**19**	**259**	**252**	**271**	**253**	**311**	**347**	**658**	**7**	**81**	**31**	**0.40**	**50**	**23**	**27**	**58**	**82**	**4%**	**112**	**28%**	**74%**				**3.70**	**-9.2**	**25**	**62**	**$9**

Carroll,Jamey

Carroll,Jamey		Health	A	LIMA Plan	D
Age 39	Bats R Pos 2B 3B SS	PT/Exp	B	Rand Var	+1
Ht 5' 9"	Wt 175	Consist	A	MM	0323

Perhaps the most fascinating thing you need to know about him is that the 522 plate appearances he received this year was his career high. So were his 40 RBI. So was his 56% GB rate. Career lows? 20% FB rate, 112 Spd. It was a season of extremes, all at the tender age of 39. It's all downhill from here.

Yr	Tm	AB	R	HR	RBI	SB	BA	xBA	vL	vR	OB	Slg	OPS	bb%	ct%	h%	Eye	G	L	F	PX	xPX	hr/f	Spd	SBO	SB%	#Wk	DOM	DIS	RC/G	RAR	BPV	BPX	R$
08	CLE	347	60	1	36	7	277	257	261	284	341	346	687	9	81	34	0.52	45	27	27	48	77	1%	155	9%	70%	26	15%	46%	4.14	-0.2	19	37	$8
09	CLE	315	53	2	26	4	276	245	271	278	350	340	690	10	80	34	0.57	46	24	30	44	54	3%	116	6%	67%	21	33%	57%	4.17	0.0	6	12	$6
10	LA	351	48	0	23	12	291	246	295	289	381	339	720	13	82	36	0.80	53	21	26	42	37	0%	125	12%	75%	27	22%	44%	4.69	5.2	14	30	$11
11	LA	452	52	0	17	10	290	260	304	284	357	347	704	9	87	33	0.81	50	24	27	39	28	0%	170	6%	100%	27	15%	30%	4.60	5.5	34	76	$10
12	MIN	470	65	1	40	9	268	265	338	240	341	317	658	10	86	31	0.80	56	24	20	37	17	1%	112	9%	64%	27	26%	30%	3.73	-6.0	20	50	$10
1st Half		251	31	0	25	6	251	263	323	228	329	295	623	10	87	29	0.88	61	21	18	33	10	0%	104	11%	67%	13	23%	38%	3.28	-7.3	21	53	$9
2nd Half		219	34	1	15	3	288	266	351	255	355	342	698	10	85	33	0.72	51	26	22	42	25	2%	118	7%	60%	14	29%	21%	4.29	0.2	15	38	$10
13	**Proj**	**377**	**52**	**1**	**26**	**6**	**272**	**257**	**309**	**257**	**347**	**326**	**672**	**10**	**85**	**32**	**0.76**	**53**	**24**	**24**	**39**	**29**	**1%**	**126**	**7%**	**68%**				**3.94**	**-3.5**	**19**	**48**	**$9**

Carter,Chris

Carter,Chris		Health	A	LIMA Plan	C
Age 26	Bats R Pos 1B	PT/Exp	C	Rand Var	-3
Ht 6' 4"	Wt 245	Consist	B	MM	5105

16-39-.239 in 218 AB at OAK. Just as he was shedding AAAA label, brutal September (9-for-60, 48% ct%) brought back the dark clouds. BA liability offsets tempting power, but in OAK, passable bb%-enabled OBP may keep the AB coming. If so... UP: 30 HR

Yr	Tm	AB	R	HR	RBI	SB	BA	xBA	vL	vR	OB	Slg	OPS	bb%	ct%	h%	Eye	G	L	F	PX	xPX	hr/f	Spd	SBO	SB%	#Wk	DOM	DIS	RC/G	RAR	BPV	BPX	R$
08																																		
09	a/a	544	87	20	87	10	278	263			355	463	817	11	73	35	0.44				133			84	11%	59%				5.63		44	0	$20
10	OAK *	535	70	22	70	2	201	213	200	180	276	377	653	9	66	26	0.30	32	14	54	139	70	11%	71	2%	59%	6	17%	67%	3.30	-33.3	14	30	$3
11	OAK *	340	39	11	48	3	204	224	50	208	269	352	621	8	64	28	0.25	17	38	46	123	33	0%	78	6%	74%	6	0%	83%	3.03	-24.0	-4	-9	$2
12	OAK *	494	70	23	75	3	226	228	241	237	316	426	741	12	65	30	0.37	34	20	46	156	126	25%	62	4%	73%	15	47%	40%	4.42	-13.0	27	68	$10
1st Half		283	36	9	38	3	221	209	400	500	289	382	671	9	67	29	0.29	0	33	67	126	238	50%	73	7%	73%	1	100%	0%	3.61	-15.2	12	30	$9
2nd Half		211	34	14	37	0	232	239	231	233	349	483	833	15	61	30	0.46	36	20	45	199	121	24%	60	0%	0%	14	43%	43%	5.61	1.6	43	108	$11
13	**Proj**	**468**	**65**	**25**	**70**	**3**	**233**	**227**	**223**	**239**	**317**	**445**	**761**	**11**	**65**	**30**	**0.35**	**34**	**17**	**48**	**161**	**101**	**17%**	**61**	**4%**	**69%**				**4.66**	**-9.8**	**29**	**73**	**$12**

Casilla,Alexi

Casilla,Alexi		Health	C	LIMA Plan	D
Age 28	Bats B Pos 2B	PT/Exp	D	Rand Var	+1
Ht 5' 10"	Wt 179	Consist	B	MM	1423

Ran as much as he could with .279 OBP, and why not? Caught only once in 22 attempts despite below-average Spd. Seemed to be putting it all together with .300, 5 SB April, but lost his way by mid-season, posting twin 7-for 48 months in July and August. May be hard for him to reopen window to full-time duty.

Yr	Tm	AB	R	HR	RBI	SB	BA	xBA	vL	vR	OB	Slg	OPS	bb%	ct%	h%	Eye	G	L	F	PX	xPX	hr/f	Spd	SBO	SB%	#Wk	DOM	DIS	RC/G	RAR	BPV	BPX	R$
08	MIN *	485	68	7	52	10	265	240	264	289	327	345	672	8	86	29	0.68	52	15	34	52	50	6%	98	10%	65%	19	42%	37%	3.86	-4.3	28	55	$11
09	MIN *	384	42	2	31	18	240	226	182	210	296	310	606	7	84	28	0.49	52	12	36	42	38	0%	149	24%	72%	21	24%	57%	3.08	-12.7	25	51	$6
10	MIN	152	26	1	20	6	276	261	364	252	333	395	728	8	89	31	0.76	50	13	37	71	40	2%	133	16%	86%	20	30%	55%	4.76	2.6	74	161	$5
11	MIN	323	52	2	21	15	260	267	236	272	319	368	688	8	86	30	0.62	57	13	30	78	65	3%	113	22%	79%	19	42%	16%	4.11	-0.5	67	149	$8
12	MIN	299	33	1	30	21	241	256	296	224	279	321	600	5	83	29	0.31	55	19	26	61	59	2%	90	32%	95%	27	26%	48%	3.32	-7.5	33	83	$8
1st Half		164	16	0	14	10	250	244	368	214	289	323	612	5	82	31	0.30	52	18	29	59	50	0%	90	28%	91%	13	23%	46%	3.41	-4.1	21	53	$7
2nd Half		135	17	1	16	11	230	268	212	235	268	319	586	5	84	27	0.32	57	19	23	62	70	4%	93	38%	100%	14	29%	50%	3.22	-4.2	39	98	$9
13	**Proj**	**262**	**36**	**2**	**26**	**15**	**251**	**257**	**269**	**244**	**299**	**346**	**645**	**6**	**85**	**29**	**0.45**	**54**	**16**	**29**	**65**	**58**	**2%**	**102**	**26%**	**90%**				**3.73**	**-4.1**	**49**	**122**	**$9**

Castellanos,Nick

Castellanos,Nick		Health	A	LIMA Plan	F
Age 21	Bats R Pos 3B	PT/Exp	F	Rand Var	-1
Ht 6' 4"	Wt 210	Consist	F	MM	1101

Move from 3B to OF fueled talk of a late-season callup, which never came. That may be just as well, as AA-Erie presented plenty of a challenge, dousing enthusiasm generated by 1.014 OPS over 215 AB at Single-A. Plate skills need work. Still a bright future, but may spend much of 2013 honing his craft away from DET.

Yr	Tm	AB	R	HR	RBI	SB	BA	xBA	vL	vR	OB	Slg	OPS	bb%	ct%	h%	Eye	G	L	F	PX	xPX	hr/f	Spd	SBO	SB%	#Wk	DOM	DIS	RC/G	RAR	BPV	BPX	R$
08																																		
09																																		
10																																		
11																																		
12	aa	322	29	6	21	4	244	224			269	344	614	3	76	30	0.15				71			91	12%	50%				2.99		-9	0	$2
1st Half		89	9	2	10	0	286	265			292	455	747	1	81	33	0.05				110			106	12%	0%				4.23		36	90	$0
2nd Half		233	20	3	11	4	228	209			261	302	563	4	74	29	0.18				55			96	12%	67%				2.57		-30	-75	$3
13	**Proj**	**204**	**19**	**3**	**15**	**2**	**249**	**235**			**270**	**342**	**612**	**3**	**77**	**31**	**0.12**	**42**	**24**	**34**	**68**		**5%**	**102**	**11%**	**42%**				**2.97**	**-9.9**	**-10**	**-24**	**$3**

Castillo,Welington

Castillo,Welington		Health	C	LIMA Plan	D
Age 26	Bats R Pos CA	PT/Exp	F	Rand Var	-4
Ht 5' 10"	Wt 210	Consist	B	MM	3003

5-22-.265 in 170 AB at CHC. Held his own in first extended MLB exposure, but 35% h% helped. Does show some power potential, and walk rate took a nice step up. Those two skills make him worth a follow, despite the associated BA liability.

Yr	Tm	AB	R	HR	RBI	SB	BA	xBA	vL	vR	OB	Slg	OPS	bb%	ct%	h%	Eye	G	L	F	PX	xPX	hr/f	Spd	SBO	SB%	#Wk	DOM	DIS	RC/G	RAR	BPV	BPX	R$
08	a/a	203	19	3	19	0	265	216			301	364	665	5	72	35	0.18				80			84	0%	0%				3.81		-30	0	$1
09	aa	319	23	10	32	1	218	247			248	361	609	4	76	26	0.17				97			76	1%	100%				2.93		0	0	$0
10	CHC *	259	27	11	46	0	224	218	250	333	264	423	687	5	72	27	0.20	23	8	69	151	187	11%	83	5%	0%	5	60%	20%	3.51	-6.1	35	76	$3
11	CHC *	240	24	10	22	0	224	205	0	200	263	373	636	5	71	28	0.18	50	13	38	107	2	0%	77	0%	0%	3	0%	100%	3.22	-7.7	-13	-29	$1
12	CHC *	327	34	11	42	0	246	225	476	194	324	396	720	10	70	32	0.39	46	20	34	111	99	12%	64	0%	0%	16	31%	50%	4.34	0.5	-2	-5	$5
1st Half		115	11	4	15	0	230	208	500	115	326	381	707	13	73	28	0.53	60	12	28	107	79	14%	64	0%	0%	6	33%	50%	4.11	-0.4	8	20	-$1
2nd Half		212	23	7	27	0	255	227	471	214	323	404	727	9	69	34	0.32	42	22	36	114	104	12%	69	0%	0%	10	30%	50%	4.46	1.5	-8	-20	$8
13	**Proj**	**387**	**39**	**12**	**48**	**0**	**243**	**221**	**467**	**171**	**302**	**381**	**683**	**8**	**71**	**31**	**0.29**	**49**	**18**	**33**	**102**	**94**	**13%**	**65**	**1%**	**12%**				**3.86**	**-4.0**	**-10**	**-24**	**$6**

Castro,Jason

Castro,Jason		Health	F	LIMA Plan	D
Age 26	Bats L Pos CA	PT/Exp	F	Rand Var	-2
Ht 6' 3"	Wt 215	Consist	D	MM	2123

Hopes to pick up where he left off, given that four of six HR came after Sept. 21. Nice walk rate, and league-average power were good signs after full year on shelf. Lingering concerns? Another five weeks missed with knee issues; struggles mightily against LHP. Still, wears "#2 CA with upside" tag well.

Yr	Tm	AB	R	HR	RBI	SB	BA	xBA	vL	vR	OB	Slg	OPS	bb%	ct%	h%	Eye	G	L	F	PX	xPX	hr/f	Spd	SBO	SB%	#Wk	DOM	DIS	RC/G	RAR	BPV	BPX	R$
08																																		
09	aa	239	29	2	22	2	261	242			315	338	654	7	83	30	0.48				53			96	4%	58%				3.65		13	0	$2
10	HOU *	406	49	5	27	1	217	235	70	243	296	294	591	10	80	26	0.57	41	22	37	55	62	4%	87	2%	40%	15	20%	33%	2.82	-18.3	3	7	-$1
11																																		
12	HOU	257	29	6	29	0	257	264	148	286	337	401	738	11	76	32	0.51	43	28	30	101	107	10%	84	0%	0%	22	45%	41%	4.63	2.6	24	60	$3
1st Half		154	17	2	16	0	253	262	176	275	335	383	718	11	79	31	0.59	50	22	28	92	92	6%	92	0%	0%	13	38%	46%	4.39	0.8	33	83	$3
2nd Half		103	12	4	13	0	262	278	100	301	339	427	766	10	72	33	0.41	30	36	34	117	131	15%	79	0%	0%	9	56%	33%	5.01	2.4	9	23	$4
13	**Proj**	**379**	**44**	**9**	**36**	**1**	**244**	**256**	**167**	**264**	**318**	**371**	**689**	**10**	**78**	**29**	**0.50**	**39**	**27**	**33**	**86**	**94**	**9%**	**80**	**1%**	**59%**				**3.97**	**-2.8**	**17**	**43**	**$6**

KRIS OLSON

Castro,Starlin

Age 23 · Bats R · Pos SS · Ht 6' 0" · Wt 190

Health A · PT/Exp A · Consist A · LIMA Plan C+ · Rand Var 0 · MM 2535

xBA cautioned not to expect .300 repeat, and sure enough, as h% fell, so did BA. SB% took a slight step back, negating SBO jump. Outwardly, it looks like little growth going on. But take a closer look at that 2H. Eye took a nice step up, and PX/xPX came with it. Skills consolidation? If so... UP: 15 HR, 30 SB.

Yr	Tm	AB	R	HR	RBI	SB	BA	xBA	vL	vR	OB	Slg	OPS	bb%	ct%	h%	Eye	G	L	F	PX	xPX	hr/f	Spd	SBO	SB%	#Wk	DOM	DIS	RC/G	RAR	BPV	BPX	R$
08																																		
09	aa	111	10	0	13	5	285	267			339	384	722	8	89	32	0.73				62			113	17%	100%				4.95		59	0	$2
10	CHC *	572	69	4	57	13	310	282	339	286	351	428	779	6	86	36	0.43	51	20	29	83	78	3%	146	16%	49%	22	32%	45%	5.17	17.0	53	115	$21
11	CHC	674	91	10	66	22	307	273	342	297	341	432	773	5	86	35	0.36	49	20	31	82	79	5%	143	17%	71%	27	56%	19%	5.34	22.9	58	129	$29
12	CHC	646	78	14	78	25	283	271	293	280	321	430	751	5	85	32	0.36	47	21	32	87	100	8%	152	23%	66%	27	56%	30%	4.72	11.4	59	148	$26
1st Half		315	36	6	40	16	298	265	337	284	320	432	752	3	83	35	0.18	48	23	29	76	82	8%	172	31%	64%	13	46%	46%	4.69	6.2	38	95	$29
2nd Half		331	42	8	38	9	269	275	234	277	322	429	751	7	86	29	0.58	47	19	35	96	115	8%	127	16%	69%	14	64%	14%	4.74	7.0	73	183	$23
13	**Proj**	**628**	**76**	**12**	**70**	**22**	**292**	**275**	**313**	**286**	**332**	**437**	**769**	**6**	**86**	**33**	**0.41**	**48**	**20**	**32**	**87**	**90**	**7%**	**140**	**19%**	**68%**				**5.08**	**19.1**	**62**	**155**	**$24**

Cedeno,Ronny

Age 30 · Bats R · Pos 2B SS · Ht 6' 0" · Wt 195

Health C · PT/Exp C · Consist A · LIMA Plan F · Rand Var 0 · MM 2111

4-22-.259 in 166 AB at NYM. What a marginal middle infielder looks like at "peak." A slight bump in bb%, ct%. PX approaching league average. A few more of those infrequent FB clearing fences (though 12% hr/f may be hard to repeat). Peak? More of a molehill, really.

Yr	Tm	AB	R	HR	RBI	SB	BA	xBA	vL	vR	OB	Slg	OPS	bb%	ct%	h%	Eye	G	L	F	PX	xPX	hr/f	Spd	SBO	SB%	#Wk	DOM	DIS	RC/G	RAR	BPV	BPX	R$
08	CHC	216	36	2	28	4	269	247	257	282	325	352	677	8	81	32	0.44	52	18	30	64	59	4%	90	8%	80%	27	30%	41%	4.02	-0.5	18	35	$4
09	2 TM	341	32	10	38	5	208	226	193	213	250	337	587	5	77	24	0.24	51	11	38	78	101	10%	136	10%	71%	24	29%	63%	2.70	-15.0	10	20	$1
10	PIT	468	42	8	38	12	256	251	291	246	291	382	674	5	77	32	0.22	49	16	35	96	77	7%	125	15%	80%	27	33%	37%	3.84	-3.6	27	59	$9
11	PIT	413	43	2	32	2	249	241	220	258	300	339	639	7	77	32	0.32	43	23	33	75	55	2%	106	7%	29%	25	16%	44%	3.30	-9.9	5	11	$3
12	NYM *	195	19	4	23	0	238	258	277	236	301	366	668	8	78	29	0.42	52	22	26	90	94	12%	85	2%	0%	22	32%	45%	3.61	-2.8	17	43	$0
1st Half		106	9	1	8	0	230	232	370	220	307	287	594	10	77	29	0.48	54	25	20	42	40	8%	80	0%	0%	8	0%	75%	2.92	-3.5	-31	-78	-$2
2nd Half		89	10	3	15	0	247	293	239	273	295	461	755	6	80	28	0.33	49	20	31	145	140	14%	89	6%	0%	14	50%	29%	4.37	1.0	71	178	$3
13	**Proj**	**196**	**20**	**4**	**21**	**1**	**244**	**255**	**250**	**240**	**296**	**375**	**670**	**7**	**78**	**29**	**0.34**	**49**	**21**	**30**	**93**	**83**	**8%**	**93**	**6%**	**46%**				**3.64**	**-3.6**	**23**	**58**	**$3**

Cespedes,Yoenis

Age 27 · Bats R · Pos LF CF DH · Ht 5' 10" · Wt 210

Health A · PT/Exp C · Consist B · LIMA Plan B+ · Rand Var -4 · MM 4335

Battled variety of minor injuries (hand, hamstring, wrist), perhaps no surprise, given violent swing. Otherwise, a highly successful MLB debut. Swung and missed more often in U.S., but on the flip side, found base stealing easier, particularly in 2H. Power's peaking, so 20+ HR should be a given. 20 SB could be next.

Yr	Tm	AB	R	HR	RBI	SB	BA	xBA	vL	vR	OB	Slg	OPS	bb%	ct%	h%	Eye	G	L	F	PX	xPX	hr/f	Spd	SBO	SB%	#Wk	DOM	DIS	RC/G	RAR	BPV	BPX	R$
08	for *	366	80	16	76	4	265	290			313	454	767	7	87	27	0.54				105	5	0%	105	9%	45%				4.73	-1.6	81	0	$13
09	for *	328	81	14	74	4	301	302			368	491	858	10	88	31	0.91				108	-5	0%	81	8%	45%				6.32	13.1	86	0	$17
10	for *	342	85	13	65	5	322	306			383	529	912	9	88	34	0.79				121	-5	0%	126	7%	57%				7.43	23.5	106	0	$21
11	for *	354	87	20	97	10	311	310			380	536	915	10	89	30	1.04				128	2	0%	86	12%	75%				7.47	25.0	116	0	$26
12	OAK	487	70	23	82	16	292	269	298	289	349	505	854	8	79	33	0.42	40	20	40	132	114	15%	106	15%	80%	26	50%	23%	6.36	24.5	74	185	$25
1st Half		173	19	9	35	4	283	271	264	292	337	509	846	7	76	33	0.33	34	24	42	147	134	16%	70	14%	67%	12	33%	25%	5.95	6.4	60	150	$13
2nd Half		314	51	14	47	12	296	270	316	287	356	503	859	8	81	33	0.48	44	17	39	124	104	14%	125	16%	86%	14	64%	21%	6.58	16.9	79	198	$32
13	**Proj**	**513**	**99**	**25**	**105**	**14**	**284**	**277**	**289**	**282**	**345**	**501**	**846**	**8**	**82**	**31**	**0.50**	**40**	**20**	**40**	**130**	**116**	**15%**	**105**	**13%**	**75%**				**6.11**	**21.3**	**86**	**214**	**$29**

Chavez,Endy

Age 35 · Bats L · Pos LF RF · Ht 6' 0" · Wt 170

Health C · PT/Exp F · Consist F · LIMA Plan F · Rand Var +5 · MM 1321

2-12-.203 with 3 SB in 158 AB at BAL. Batting average cratered, in part due to an unlucky hit rate, in larger part due to him being a weak hitter. Used to have value with high contact and end-game steals, but that was six years and four teams ago.

Yr	Tm	AB	R	HR	RBI	SB	BA	xBA	vL	vR	OB	Slg	OPS	bb%	ct%	h%	Eye	G	L	F	PX	xPX	hr/f	Spd	SBO	SB%	#Wk	DOM	DIS	RC/G	RAR	BPV	BPX	R$
08	NYM	270	30	1	12	6	267	266	194	278	310	330	640	6	92	29	0.77	53	19	29	40	55	1%	140	9%	86%	27	33%	30%	3.63	-7.3	43	84	$3
09	SEA	161	17	2	13	9	273	256	258	277	331	342	673	8	86	31	0.64	53	19	28	39	46	5%	131	19%	90%	11	18%	45%	4.22	-1.5	25	51	$4
10	a/a																																	
11	TEX *	384	46	6	37	13	276	280	357	290	305	392	697	4	90	29	0.42	50	20	30	71	74	8%	135	20%	73%	21	43%	52%	4.16	-4.5	62	138	$12
12	BAL *	215	19	2	15	3	181	246	185	206	214	248	462	4	85	20	0.28	55	19	27	47	32	6%	87	13%	60%	16	13%	56%	1.61	-20.5	9	23	-$4
1st Half		105	11	1	4	1	162	222	200	156	185	210	395	3	82	19	0.16	52	19	30	31	17	4%	98	18%	33%	8	0%	63%	1.06	-12.7	-16	-40	-$6
2nd Half		100	5	1	11	2	204	272	167	317	238	298	536	4	88	22	0.35	60	19	21	67	58	10%	83	11%	100%	8	25%	50%	2.35	-7.2	29	73	-$2
13	**Proj**	**134**	**12**	**2**	**11**	**4**	**229**	**264**	**212**	**233**	**264**	**324**	**589**	**5**	**87**	**25**	**0.38**	**54**	**19**	**27**	**59**	**52**	**7%**	**103**	**16%**	**76%**				**2.85**	**-7.4**	**33**	**82**	**$2**

Chavez,Eric

Age 35 · Bats L · Pos 3B · Ht 6' 1" · Wt 215

Health F · PT/Exp F · Consist C · LIMA Plan F · Rand Var -5 · MM 3013

Once you display a skill, you own it... even if it's locked away in a dark attic corner for 8 years. It was nearly impossible to see resurrection coming. Almost as hard? Forecasting how long health will allow it to last. A free agent, would be well served to stay in NY (+43% LHB HR). Elsewhere, continued production less certain.

Yr	Tm	AB	R	HR	RBI	SB	BA	xBA	vL	vR	OB	Slg	OPS	bb%	ct%	h%	Eye	G	L	F	PX	xPX	hr/f	Spd	SBO	SB%	#Wk	DOM	DIS	RC/G	RAR	BPV	BPX	R$
08	OAK *	119	15	3	16	0	254	250	333	215	301	414	714	6	77	30	0.30	42	17	41	118	121	7%	65	0%	0%	6	33%	50%	4.25	-0.9	28	55	$0
09	OAK	30	0	0	1	0	100	137	111	83	129	133	262	3	77	13	0.14	43	13	43	31	114	0%	70	0%	0%	3	0%	100%	0.49	-4.2	-62	-127	-$3
10	OAK	111	10	1	10	0	234	227	111	245	286	333	619	7	72	32	0.26	49	19	32	92	108	4%	66	0%	0%	7	14%	43%	3.17	-4.5	-14	-30	-$1
11	NYY	160	16	2	26	0	263	226	304	255	322	356	678	8	79	32	0.41	46	18	36	69	78	4%	79	0%	0%	16	25%	44%	3.96	-2.6	2	4	$2
12	NYY	278	36	16	37	0	281	276	152	299	351	496	847	10	79	31	0.51	42	23	35	132	137	21%	57	0%	0%	27	48%	33%	6.17	12.7	47	118	$9
1st Half		117	13	5	13	0	265	277	125	278	323	462	784	8	82	29	0.48	42	21	37	126	152	14%	64	0%	0%	13	38%	23%	5.17	2.0	52	130	$3
2nd Half		161	23	11	24	0	292	275	160	316	370	522	892	11	76	32	0.53	42	25	33	136	125	27%	60	0%	0%	14	57%	43%	6.96	10.6	44	110	$13
13	**Proj**	**256**	**30**	**9**	**34**	**0**	**267**	**251**	**231**	**272**	**329**	**428**	**757**	**9**	**78**	**31**	**0.42**	**44**	**21**	**35**	**107**	**116**	**13%**	**60**	**0%**	**0%**				**4.90**	**2.3**	**23**	**56**	**$7**

Chisenhall,Lonnie

Age 24 · Bats L · Pos 3B · Ht 6' 2" · Wt 190

Health C · PT/Exp C · Consist A · LIMA Plan D+ · Rand Var -2 · MM 3225

5-16-.268 in 142 AB at CLE. Broken arm cost him almost three months. On a positive note, hit 2 HR and showed more patience (11% bb%) in Sept. return. Nonetheless, Eye is still subpar, and hasn't shown much more than league-average power. 20 HR may have to wait yet another year. But he's just 24. There's time.

Yr	Tm	AB	R	HR	RBI	SB	BA	xBA	vL	vR	OB	Slg	OPS	bb%	ct%	h%	Eye	G	L	F	PX	xPX	hr/f	Spd	SBO	SB%	#Wk	DOM	DIS	RC/G	RAR	BPV	BPX	R$
08																																		
09	aa	93	12	3	12	1	170	279			225	348	573	7	81	17	0.38				109			99	7%	100%				2.44		57	0	-$2
10	aa	460	64	12	66	2	245	260			301	378	679	7	82	28	0.44				88			97	2%	100%				3.87		37	0	$9
11	CLE *	467	62	12	57	1	242	246	260	253	287	388	675	6	78	29	0.29	38	20	42	106	117	10%	101	2%	47%	14	43%	43%	3.72	-11.4	31	69	$8
12	CLE *	260	28	8	29	2	268	275	184	298	298	431	729	4	80	31	0.21	43	25	32	110	67	14%	89	5%	67%	9	33%	33%	4.43	-0.8	36	90	$5
1st Half		183	22	6	22	2	278	286	0	330	293	455	749	2	83	31	0.13	47	22	31	114	63	15%	96	9%	67%	5	40%	20%	4.66	0.4	53	133	$8
2nd Half		70	6	2	7	0	257	258	269	250	325	400	725	9	73	33	0.37	37	29	33	106	72	12%	87	0%	0%	4	25%	50%	4.46	-0.2	0	0	-$2
13	**Proj**	**459**	**54**	**16**	**55**	**2**	**247**	**264**	**188**	**273**	**295**	**415**	**711**	**6**	**78**	**28**	**0.32**	**40**	**24**	**36**	**112**	**88**	**12%**	**87**	**3%**	**73%**				**4.15**	**-5.8**	**36**	**91**	**$10**

Choo,Shin-Soo

Age 30 · Bats L · Pos RF · Ht 5' 11" · Wt 205

Health C · PT/Exp A · Consist D · LIMA Plan C+ · Rand Var -1 · MM 4225

On the surface, a return to 2009-10 production levels. Still, a couple lingering concerns: newfound struggles vs. LHP and PX dip in Aug/Sept. A hidden injury, perhaps? Spd suggests he doesn't warrant SBO, but success rate still OK. Overall, a fairly stable skill set. With health, 2012 serves as a good baseline.

Yr	Tm	AB	R	HR	RBI	SB	BA	xBA	vL	vR	OB	Slg	OPS	bb%	ct%	h%	Eye	G	L	F	PX	xPX	hr/f	Spd	SBO	SB%	#Wk	DOM	DIS	RC/G	RAR	BPV	BPX	R$
08	CLE *	359	69	15	69	5	300	283	286	317	383	523	906	12	74	37	0.51	41	23	36	161	142	16%	103	10%	43%	18	61%	22%	6.92	20.8	76	149	$17
09	CLE	583	87	20	86	21	300	270	275	312	383	489	872	12	74	38	0.52	42	22	36	131	130	13%	95	12%	91%	26	58%	23%	7.00	34.5	63	129	$28
10	CLE	550	81	22	90	22	300	277	264	319	392	484	875	13	79	35	0.70	45	20	35	124	136	15%	72	15%	76%	24	63%	25%	6.89	31.2	69	150	$30
11	CLE	313	37	8	36	12	259	245	269	254	335	390	725	10	75	32	0.46	45	22	32	91	128	10%	91	18%	71%	17	24%	53%	4.44	-3.8	28	62	$9
12	CLE	598	88	16	67	21	283	268	199	327	361	441	802	11	75	35	0.49	50	23	27	118	107	13%	75	15%	75%	27	44%	37%	5.64	13.4	47	118	$24
1st Half		278	51	8	30	9	291	277	211	330	369	471	840	11	74	37	0.48	46	25	29	136	109	14%	86	12%	90%	13	38%	23%	6.40	10.8	62	155	$25
2nd Half		320	37	8	37	12	275	259	190	324	354	416	769	11	75	34	0.49	53	21	26	102	104	13%	68	18%	67%	14	50%	50%	5.04	0.3	31	78	$24
13	**Proj**	**559**	**78**	**20**	**71**	**19**	**281**	**265**	**232**	**306**	**361**	**460**	**821**	**11**	**75**	**34**	**0.51**	**45**	**22**	**32**	**123**	**119**	**15%**	**76**	**15%**	**72%**				**5.82**	**13.2**	**53**	**132**	**$25**

KRIS OLSON

Ciriaco,Pedro

Age 27	Bats R	Pos 3B	Health	A	LIMA Plan	D+
Ht 6' 0"	Wt 170		PT/Exp	D	Rand Var	-4
			Consist	C	MM	1515

2-19-.293 with 16 SB in 259 AB at BOS. Sparkplug started hot after July callup, bolstered by 40% h%, but extreme lack of patience (check those awful Eye ratios!) caught up to him in Sept. (.217 in 92 AB). Not as successful running in high minors as in BOS (16-for-19). BA will regress, but with PT, SBs should come.

Yr	Tm	AB	R	HR	RBI	SB	BA	xBA	vL	vR	OB	Slg	OPS	bb%	ct%	h%	Eye	G	L	F	PX	xPX	hr/f	Spd	SBO	SB%	#Wk	DOM	DIS	RC/G	RAR	BPV	BPX	R$
08																																		
09	aa	469	45	3	44	32	272	238			292	339	631	3	84	32	0.17				44			105	36%	74%				3.43		14	0	$17
10	PIT *	482	49	4	42	14	224	269	0	500	238	321	559	2	82	26	0.10	33	33	33	67	244	0%	155	22%	75%	4	50%	50%	2.50	-23.9	29	63	$4
11	PIT *	310	26	1	23	11	201	262	222	333	213	259	472	1	81	25	0.07	60	24	16	40	2	0%	150	38%	55%	13	23%	38%	1.58	-25.4	-4	-9	-$1
12	BOS *	535	65	5	35	27	276	256	304	289	293	369	662	2	80	34	0.12	50	23	27	67	39	4%	152	32%	68%	14	36%	29%	3.65	-3.9	18	45	$17
1st Half		259	29	3	16	10	267	231			280	358	638	2	80	33	0.09				64			120	34%	51%				3.07		5	13	$13
2nd Half		259	33	2	19	16	293	263	304	289	315	390	705	3	82	35	0.17	50	23	27	70	39	4%	149	29%	84%	14	36%	29%	4.57	4.1	30	75	$21
13	**Proj**	**435**	**46**	**3**	**33**	**25**	**252**	**252**	**261**	**248**	**285**	**333**	**618**	**4**	**81**	**30**	**0.25**	**50**	**23**	**27**	**57**	**35**	**3%**	**156**	**34%**	**70%**				**3.15**	**-18.8**	**17**	**43**	**$11**

Clevenger,Steve

Age 27	Bats L	Pos CA	Health	B	LIMA Plan	F
Ht 6' 0"	Wt 195		PT/Exp	D	Rand Var	+5
			Consist	B	MM	1021

.500 (11-for-22) in April and then... nothing. Missed a month with strained oblique, then hit .164 over rest of season upon return. Hit rate, which never exceeded 22% June-Sept., was part to blame. xBA says it shouldn't have been THAT bad. But with no power in evidence, no sense chasing that possible BA recovery.

Yr	Tm	AB	R	HR	RBI	SB	BA	xBA	vL	vR	OB	Slg	OPS	bb%	ct%	h%	Eye	G	L	F	PX	xPX	hr/f	Spd	SBO	SB%	#Wk	DOM	DIS	RC/G	RAR	BPV	BPX	R$
08	aa	89	4	1	11	0	222	253			283	319	601	8	87	25	0.68				64			94	0%	0%				2.95		27	0	-$2
09	a/a	307	27	1	30	3	265	250			311	342	654	6	86	31	0.48				53			101	8%	50%				3.58		24	0	$3
10	aa	271	27	4	34	0	272	274			309	391	700	5	88	30	0.45				87			81	11%	0%				3.77		42	0	$5
11	CHC *	402	34	5	35	1	258	253	1000	0	308	374	683	7	86	29	0.53	25	25	50	82	2	0%	91	1%	100%				3.98	-3.5	45	100	$4
12	CHC	199	16	1	16	0	201	253	69	225	260	276	537	7	80	25	0.41	52	25	23	62	76	3%	60	2%	0%	21	29%	52%	2.24	-12.7	-2	-5	-$3
1st Half		96	12	1	13	0	271	293	105	312	293	396	689	3	83	32	0.19	49	28	24	97	95	5%	74	0%	0%	8	63%	13%	4.05	-0.4	30	75	$1
2nd Half		103	4	0	3	0	136	211	0	152	233	165	398	11	78	18	0.57	56	22	22	27	57	0%	66	4%	0%	13	8%	77%	1.08	-11.1	-38	-95	-$7
13	**Proj**	**228**	**19**	**1**	**20**	**0**	**227**	**263**	**72**	**252**	**281**	**304**	**585**	**7**	**83**	**27**	**0.45**	**53**	**24**	**23**	**60**	**72**	**2%**	**61**	**4%**	**17%**				**2.73**	**-10.4**	**10**	**24**	**$0**

Colvin,Tyler

Age 27	Bats L	Pos RF CF 1B	Health	A	LIMA Plan	C+
Ht 6' 3"	Wt 210		PT/Exp	C	Rand Var	-5
			Consist	F	MM	4315

After lost 2011, power returned to 2010 levels. However, low ct%, appalling Eye say not to count on .290 BA... or anything close. Still, he also has always displayed slightly above-average speed, and in 2H showed signs of channeling it into SBs (rising SBO, SB%). With 500 AB... UP: 25 HR, double-digit SB.

Yr	Tm	AB	R	HR	RBI	SB	BA	xBA	vL	vR	OB	Slg	OPS	bb%	ct%	h%	Eye	G	L	F	PX	xPX	hr/f	Spd	SBO	SB%	#Wk	DOM	DIS	RC/G	RAR	BPV	BPX	R$
08	aa	540	51	11	60	5	226	251			270	365	635	6	79	27	0.28				90			115	9%	54%				3.16		29	0	$2
09	CHC *	324	43	12	43	4	267	315	0	214	300	450	750	4	79	31	0.22	54	31	15	109	34	0%	116	7%	78%	2	0%	100%	4.70	-6.8	46	94	$8
10	CHC	358	60	20	56	6	254	276	250	256	312	500	812	8	72	30	0.30	43	17	40	169	147	19%	112	9%	86%	25	64%	28%	5.36	-0.6	79	172	$13
11	CHC *	409	36	10	39	1	173	212	57	170	206	323	529	4	70	22	0.14	38	15	47	112	127	9%	103	3%	33%	20	15%	65%	2.03	-45.2	5	11	-$5
12	COL	420	62	18	72	7	290	267	270	297	324	531	855	5	72	36	0.18	39	21	39	163	114	15%	118	11%	70%	27	44%	37%	6.10	7.9	67	168	$19
1st Half		157	21	8	30	1	306	276	341	292	335	580	915	4	73	38	0.16	37	22	41	177	141	17%	111	9%	33%	13	38%	38%	6.80	6.3	70	175	$12
2nd Half		263	41	10	42	6	281	263	214	300	318	502	820	5	72	36	0.19	41	21	38	155	98	14%	119	13%	86%	14	50%	36%	5.70	2.6	63	158	$22
13	**Proj**	**459**	**61**	**20**	**67**	**6**	**252**	**255**	**214**	**263**	**300**	**474**	**774**	**6**	**72**	**31**	**0.24**	**41**	**18**	**41**	**149**	**124**	**14%**	**111**	**9%**	**70%**				**4.80**	**-2.8**	**57**	**141**	**$14**

Conger,Hank

Age 25	Bats B	Pos CA	Health	A	LIMA Plan	F
Ht 6' 1"	Wt 220		PT/Exp	D	Rand Var	-1
			Consist	A	MM	2101

0-1-.167 in 18 AB at LAA. Once-bright prospect became forgotten man for Angels. When opportunity arose, was unable to answer call due to injury of his own. Eye, bb% trending in wrong direction. Nonetheless, he is a career .297 hitter in minors with double-digit pop. Clock ticking, but still a chance.

Yr	Tm	AB	R	HR	RBI	SB	BA	xBA	vL	vR	OB	Slg	OPS	bb%	ct%	h%	Eye	G	L	F	PX	xPX	hr/f	Spd	SBO	SB%	#Wk	DOM	DIS	RC/G	RAR	BPV	BPX	R$
08																																		
09	aa	459	56	10	62	3	284	261			353	403	756	10	85	32	0.70				73			92	3%	56%				5.02		37	0	$12
10	LAA *	416	41	8	39	0	245	252	0	185	315	365	680	9	82	28	0.57	55	15	30	84	82	0%	79	2%	0%	5	40%	60%	3.79	-4.2	29	63	$4
11	LAA *	277	23	9	36	0	221	230	182	211	285	361	646	8	79	25	0.43	39	18	44	95	92	10%	62	0%	0%	21	33%	43%	3.37	-6.5	15	33	$1
12	LAA *	282	32	6	29	1	229	191		167	264	344	607	5	80	27	0.23	58	0	42	79	28	0%	80	2%	100%	4	0%	25%	3.02	-9.5	8	20	$2
1st Half		124	14	1	12	1	248	186		231	291	329	620	6	82	29	0.34	64	0	36	60	-11	0%	86	2%	100%	3	0%	33%	3.28	-3.4	3	8	$0
2nd Half		158	18	5	16	1	214	177		0	242	355	597	4	78	24	0.17	40	0	60	94	139	0%	73	2%	100%	1	0%	0%	2.80	-6.9	10	25	$3
13	**Proj**	**163**	**17**	**5**	**18**	**1**	**235**	**235**	**204**	**237**	**287**	**375**	**662**	**7**	**80**	**26**	**0.37**	**39**	**18**	**44**	**91**	**83**	**9%**	**72**	**2%**	**78%**				**3.59**	**-3.1**	**22**	**55**	**$2**

Cooper,David

Age 26	Bats L	Pos 1B	Health	B	LIMA Plan	D
Ht 6' 0"	Wt 200		PT/Exp	C	Rand Var	+1
			Consist	B	MM	4031

4-11-.300 in 140 AB at TOR. Made most of brief big-league chances before back injury ended season in early Sept. Perhaps trying to impress, hacked away in TOR (3% bb%). Approach far different in minors (1.00+ Eye, 12%+ bb% in 2011-12), yielding high OBPs. With opportunity, that tack and rising power could intrigue.

Yr	Tm	AB	R	HR	RBI	SB	BA	xBA	vL	vR	OB	Slg	OPS	bb%	ct%	h%	Eye	G	L	F	PX	xPX	hr/f	Spd	SBO	SB%	#Wk	DOM	DIS	RC/G	RAR	BPV	BPX	R$
08																																		
09	aa	473	60	10	64	0	248	252			329	379	709	11	78	30	0.55				96			77	0%	0%				4.24		21	0	$6
10	aa	498	44	15	58	0	219	264			275	368	643	7	83	24	0.45				98			83	0%	0%				3.30		33	0	$2
11	TOR *	538	56	8	71	1	280	246	286	193	339	419	758	8	88	31	0.72	29	15	56	103	158	6%	61	3%	15%	8	50%	38%	4.90	-5.9	60	133	$13
12	TOR *	401	46	11	45	0	271	295	294	302	319	441	760	7	84	30	0.45	31	30	40	115	112	9%	74	2%	0%	10	40%	40%	4.81	-5.5	55	138	$8
1st Half		238	25	7	30	0	250	272	308	288	304	398	702	7	86	27	0.56	34	25	41	91	114	9%	83	2%	0%	6	33%	50%	4.04	-9.3	44	110	$9
2nd Half		163	21	4	16	0	302	319	286	315	341	505	846	6	82	35	0.32	27	34	39	152	110	8%	74	4%	0%	4	50%	25%	6.10	3.4	71	178	$8
13	**Proj**	**130**	**14**	**4**	**15**	**0**	**267**	**278**	**272**	**266**	**322**	**445**	**767**	**7**	**84**	**29**	**0.49**	**30**	**24**	**46**	**121**	**130**	**8%**	**76**	**2%**	**9%**				**4.90**	**-1.7**	**59**	**147**	**$3**

Cowgill,Collin

Age 27	Bats R	Pos LF	Health	A	LIMA Plan	F
Ht 5' 9"	Wt 185		PT/Exp	C	Rand Var	+3
			Consist	C	MM	1311

1-9-.269 with 3 SB in 104 AB at OAK. Took a step back with Eye, PX at inopportune time to avoid getting lost in OF crowd. Now 27, future may be as "spare part" and not even a particularly useful one except vs. LHP, given league-average Spd, subpar base-stealing skills (3-for-7 at OAK). Tough to recommend.

Yr	Tm	AB	R	HR	RBI	SB	BA	xBA	vL	vR	OB	Slg	OPS	bb%	ct%	h%	Eye	G	L	F	PX	xPX	hr/f	Spd	SBO	SB%	#Wk	DOM	DIS	RC/G	RAR	BPV	BPX	R$
08																																		
09																																		
10	aa	502	73	13	68	20	263	284			325	427	752	8	84	29	0.58				108			101	24%	67%				4.64		78	0	$18
11	ARI *	487	60	8	48	21	270	248	275	212	319	391	710	7	79	33	0.34	48	19	33	85	115	5%	150	20%	78%	10	20%	80%	4.39	-4.8	35	78	$16
12	OAK *	364	32	3	34	8	217	240	318	233	267	292	558	6	76	28	0.28	55	23	22	58	30	6%	102	18%	57%	11	0%	82%	2.42	-24.4	-13	-33	$1
1st Half		174	19	2	20	6	247	236	333	233	310	314	624	8	76	31	0.38	55	23	22	48	33	6%	99	19%	59%	9	0%	78%	3.16	-7.9	-18	-45	$5
2nd Half		190	13	1	14	3	189	241	250		225	271	496	4	75	25	0.19	60	20	20	67	-11	0%	90	16%	53%	2	0%	100%	1.84	-17.2	-14	-35	-$3
13	**Proj**	**131**	**14**	**2**	**13**	**4**	**240**	**248**	**296**	**205**	**289**	**337**	**625**	**6**	**78**	**30**	**0.31**	**52**	**21**	**26**	**70**	**66**	**6%**	**112**	**20%**	**68%**				**3.20**	**-5.8**	**12**	**29**	**$3**

Cozart,Zack

Age 27	Bats R	Pos SS	Health	B	LIMA Plan	C+
Ht 6' 0"	Wt 195		PT/Exp	B	Rand Var	0
			Consist	A	MM	3425

Subpar plate skills ensure that he'll continue to be a BA/OBP liability; woefully miscast as leadoff hitter. Home field (+32% RHB HR) helped prop up HR total. And yet, not the worst investment. Latent SB potential is best path to growth. With a little more OBP or more green lights... UP: 15 SB to go with those 15+ HR

Yr	Tm	AB	R	HR	RBI	SB	BA	xBA	vL	vR	OB	Slg	OPS	bb%	ct%	h%	Eye	G	L	F	PX	xPX	hr/f	Spd	SBO	SB%	#Wk	DOM	DIS	RC/G	RAR	BPV	BPX	R$
08																																		
09	aa	463	59	9	48	8	234	252			312	358	670	10	78	28	0.52				87			91	8%	78%				3.74		31	0	$5
10	aaa	553	68	14	50	22	216	251			257	349	606	5	77	26	0.24				93			106	25%	83%				2.98		34	0	$9
11	CIN *	360	47	8	26	6	260	248	333	320	292	389	681	4	81	30	0.24	58	10	32	92	163	20%	121	11%	73%	3	33%	67%	3.89	-2.2	36	80	$7
12	CIN	561	72	15	35	4	246	254	265	240	285	399	685	5	80	28	0.27	42	20	38	102	86	9%	128	3%	100%	26	31%	31%	3.89	-3.5	41	103	$8
1st Half		297	44	8	16	2	249	250	279	240	292	407	699	6	78	29	0.28	43	18	39	109	89	9%	134	3%	100%	13	31%	23%	4.08	0.6	41	103	$10
2nd Half		264	28	7	19	2	242	259	250	240	278	390	668	5	82	27	0.27	41	22	37	94	83	9%	111	4%	100%	13	31%	38%	3.69	-2.5	37	93	$6
13	**Proj**	**562**	**70**	**17**	**42**	**9**	**244**	**256**	**260**	**239**	**286**	**400**	**686**	**6**	**80**	**28**	**0.29**	**41**	**21**	**38**	**103**	**85**	**10%**	**116**	**9%**	**83%**				**3.88**	**-2.2**	**43**	**109**	**$11**

KRIS OLSON

Craig,Allen			Health	C	LIMA Plan	B
Age 28	Bats R	Pos 1B RF	PT/Exp	D	Rand Var	-2
Ht 6' 2"	Wt 210		Consist	C	MM	4245

Missed April while recovering from knee surgery, then spent rest of year re-establishing himself as one of MLB's top late bloomers. He's short on FB, and lack of xPX support is a bit concerning, but strong line-drive rate helps lock in BA. 1B/OF eligibility just icing on a tasty cake.

Yr	Tm	AB	R	HR	RBI	SB	BA	xBA	vL	vR	OB	Slg	OPS	bb%	ct%	h%	Eye	G	L	F	PX	xPX	hr/f	Spd	SBO	SB%	#Wk	DOM	DIS	RC/G	RAR	BPV	BPX	R$
08	aa	506	65	16	66	2	257	258			308	400	708	7	81	29	0.38				94			78	2%	57%				4.21		27	0	$9
09	aaa	472	61	18	65	2	272	261			314	439	753	6	77	32	0.26				108			82	2%	100%				4.85		25	0	$12
10	STL *	420	50	13	72	1	249	262	208	273	302	407	710	7	77	30	0.33	38	22	39	115	141	11%	80	2%	40%	13	38%	46%	4.15	-15.8	31	67	$9
11	STL *	241	39	12	44	5	292	291	313	316	340	508	848	7	81	32	0.39	44	19	37	144	111	18%	93	8%	100%	17	47%	47%	6.36	6.2	83	184	$11
12	STL	469	76	22	92	2	307	293	354	289	358	522	880	7	81	34	0.42	44	23	33	140	112	17%	76	2%	67%	22	59%	14%	6.85	18.1	68	170	$23
1st Half		144	25	10	38	1	319	299	395	292	395	604	999	11	76	36	0.51	44	21	36	189	138	25%	83	2%	100%	8	75%	0%	9.00	14.0	91	228	$15
2nd Half		325	51	12	54	1	302	291	337	288	340	486	826	6	83	33	0.35	44	24	32	120	101	13%	74	2%	50%	14	50%	21%	5.98	5.5	57	143	$27
13	**Proj**	**551**	**84**	**27**	**103**	**5**	**291**	**285**	**301**	**286**	**343**	**509**	**852**	**7**	**80**	**32**	**0.40**	**43**	**21**	**36**	**141**	**118**	**17%**	**82**	**4%**	**86%**				**6.30**	**14.5**	**69**	**172**	**$24**

Crawford,Brandon			Health	A	LIMA Plan	D
Age 26	Bats L	Pos SS	PT/Exp	D	Rand Var	-1
Ht 6' 2"	Wt 215		Consist	C	MM	1115

Gainfully employed for reasons other than his bat. Still, 2nd half gives tiny, infinitesimal hint of a spark. Not enough for us to hope for league average power, speed or contact ability. But just enough for him to get near-regular playing time, which means his fanalytic value rests in runs and RBIs, and nothing else.

Yr	Tm	AB	R	HR	RBI	SB	BA	xBA	vL	vR	OB	Slg	OPS	bb%	ct%	h%	Eye	G	L	F	PX	xPX	hr/f	Spd	SBO	SB%	#Wk	DOM	DIS	RC/G	RAR	BPV	BPX	R$
08																																		
09	aa	392	33	3	27	11	245	232			277	344	620	4	73	33	0.16				80			94	22%	58%				3.05		-5	0	$4
10	aa	291	37	6	19	3	223	229			303	342	645	10	71	29	0.40				89			127	6%	76%				3.41		9	0	$1
11	SF *	303	30	4	27	4	197	224	133	217	266	279	545	9	82	23	0.52	51	14	35	55	79	5%	103	13%	44%	14	36%	50%	2.22	-18.3	17	38	-$2
12	SF	435	44	4	45	1	248	246	254	246	301	349	651	7	78	31	0.35	47	23	30	77	85	4%	82	5%	20%	27	26%	59%	3.44	-8.6	7	18	$4
1st Half		237	19	1	21	1	232	244	179	253	275	329	604	6	78	30	0.26	46	23	31	78	78	2%	89	6%	33%	13	23%	54%	2.91	-8.0	6	15	$1
2nd Half		198	25	3	24	0	268	249	362	238	332	374	706	9	79	33	0.45	48	23	29	75	92	7%	77	3%	0%	14	29%	64%	4.14	0.8	10	25	$7
13	**Proj**	**451**	**48**	**6**	**42**	**4**	**252**	**240**	**244**	**254**	**312**	**352**	**664**	**8**	**80**	**30**	**0.43**	**49**	**19**	**32**	**70**	**83**	**5%**	**88**	**7%**	**43%**				**3.62**	**-5.3**	**14**	**36**	**$7**

Crawford,Carl			Health	F	LIMA Plan	C+
Age 31	Bats L	Pos LF	PT/Exp	C	Rand Var	0
Ht 6' 2"	Wt 215		Consist	F	MM	3535

3-19-.282 with 5 SB in 117 AB at BOS. Missed start of season with wrist issue; then developed elbow injury that required TJ surgery, the timing of which clouds ST availability. In cameo, showed there is still some life in bat, legs. Out of BOS spotlight, resurgence possible, but as "F" Health score indicates, hardly a given.

Yr	Tm	AB	R	HR	RBI	SB	BA	xBA	vL	vR	OB	Slg	OPS	bb%	ct%	h%	Eye	G	L	F	PX	xPX	hr/f	Spd	SBO	SB%	#Wk	DOM	DIS	RC/G	RAR	BPV	BPX	R$
08	TAM	443	69	8	57	25	273	274	248	285	319	400	719	6	86	30	0.50	49	21	30	68	65	7%	143	26%	78%	21	43%	33%	4.50	-2.9	62	122	$18
09	TAM	606	96	15	68	60	305	286	269	322	359	452	811	8	84	35	0.52	52	19	29	88	77	10%	137	41%	79%	26	50%	27%	6.00	21.7	69	141	$40
10	TAM	600	110	19	90	47	307	284	256	332	356	495	851	7	83	35	0.44	47	16	36	116	98	11%	156	34%	82%	27	56%	19%	6.58	30.9	91	198	$42
11	BOS	506	65	11	56	18	255	261	195	284	287	405	692	4	79	30	0.22	48	18	34	104	112	8%	110	23%	75%	23	30%	30%	3.95	-11.6	52	116	$14
12	BOS *	139	26	3	20	6	284	291	282	282	310	460	770	4	82	33	0.21	54	19	27	113	95	12%	112	22%	100%	6	50%	50%	5.36	2.5	79	198	$5
1st Half																																		
2nd Half		139	26	3	20	6	284	291	282	282	310	460	770	4	82	33	0.21	54	19	27	113	95	12%	112	22%	100%	6	50%	50%	5.36	2.8	79	198	$5
13	**Proj**	**462**	**77**	**12**	**61**	**28**	**287**	**277**	**255**	**303**	**327**	**457**	**784**	**6**	**82**	**33**	**0.34**	**50**	**18**	**31**	**104**	**93**	**10%**	**124**	**29%**	**83%**				**5.44**	**10.4**	**75**	**187**	**$26**

Crisp,Coco			Health	F	LIMA Plan	B
Age 33	Bats B	Pos CF	PT/Exp	C	Rand Var	+1
Ht 5' 10"	Wt 185		Consist	C	MM	2535

He was creative in earning his "F" Health score: missed games with the flu, inner ear problem, shoulder, hamstring and pink eye. 2nd half rebound retrenched him as top SB threat with some pop, but xPX skeptical of the latter. More SB, injuries likely in store, and the latter is apt to eat into the former sooner or later.

Yr	Tm	AB	R	HR	RBI	SB	BA	xBA	vL	vR	OB	Slg	OPS	bb%	ct%	h%	Eye	G	L	F	PX	xPX	hr/f	Spd	SBO	SB%	#Wk	DOM	DIS	RC/G	RAR	BPV	BPX	R$
08	BOS	361	55	7	41	20	283	253	295	278	346	407	753	9	84	32	0.59	41	20	39	80	91	6%	103	25%	74%	28	46%	36%	4.97	1.2	55	108	$15
09	KC	180	30	3	14	13	228	281	222	231	335	378	713	14	87	25	1.26	48	18	34	83	90	6%	146	28%	87%	10	50%	30%	4.42	-2.3	92	188	$4
10	OAK *	312	55	8	41	33	291	270	329	261	356	448	804	9	83	33	0.59	47	17	37	99	98	9%	130	40%	88%	14	64%	21%	6.13	11.3	81	176	$21
11	OAK	531	69	8	54	49	264	273	211	289	316	379	695	7	88	29	0.63	42	24	34	75	83	5%	102	41%	84%	26	54%	15%	4.37	-7.6	71	158	$25
12	OAK	455	68	11	46	39	259	274	248	265	326	418	744	9	86	28	0.70	44	20	36	95	76	8%	119	36%	91%	26	42%	27%	5.03	2.3	87	218	$22
1st Half		192	20	2	16	16	219	231	182	234	286	286	572	9	86	25	0.67	49	16	35	42	64	4%	103	33%	94%	12	25%	42%	3.03	-10.4	33	83	$8
2nd Half		263	48	9	30	23	289	301	284	292	355	513	868	9	86	31	0.73	41	23	36	133	84	11%	118	38%	88%	14	57%	14%	6.83	15.3	121	303	$31
13	**Proj**	**511**	**77**	**11**	**54**	**45**	**273**	**270**	**259**	**280**	**337**	**421**	**759**	**9**	**86**	**30**	**0.68**	**44**	**20**	**35**	**89**	**83**	**7%**	**115**	**36%**	**88%**				**5.29**	**7.7**	**81**	**202**	**$29**

Cruz,Luis			Health	A	LIMA Plan	F
Age 29	Bats R	Pos 3B SS	PT/Exp	C	Rand Var	-1
Ht 6' 2"	Wt 220		Consist	B	MM	1001

6-40-.297 in 283 AB at LA. Minor-league FA fell into a long look, put the ball in play (88% ct% with LA) and decent things happened. Given demonstrated inability to stay on MLB roster for long-term and lousy plate approach, another run at .300 unlikely. Could fade back into obscurity as quickly as he arrived.

Yr	Tm	AB	R	HR	RBI	SB	BA	xBA	vL	vR	OB	Slg	OPS	bb%	ct%	h%	Eye	G	L	F	PX	xPX	hr/f	Spd	SBO	SB%	#Wk	DOM	DIS	RC/G	RAR	BPV	BPX	R$
08	PIT *	562	56	7	54	5	248	253	0	259	274	350	625	4	90	26	0.38	37	18	45	69	51	0%	79	12%	37%	5	40%	20%	3.06	-26.1	43	84	$4
09	PIT *	299	27	2	20	2	218	224	172	244	245	289	535	3	88	24	0.30	38	16	47	50	22	0%	79	10%	41%	14	7%	43%	2.21	-22.2	17	35	-$2
10	MIL *	505	41	8	50	0	228	244	91	500	244	332	576	2	86	25	0.15	53	13	33	70	-5	0%	112	0%	0%	3	33%	67%	2.67	-29.5	19	41	$1
11	aaa	275	21	6	21	1	213	249			230	329	559	2	83	24	0.13				78			83	5%	50%				2.40		15	0	-$2
12	LA *	572	52	10	66	3	261	274	302	294	282	395	677	3	86	29	0.21	39	24	37	91	116	6%	74	6%	42%	14	29%	21%	3.75	-14.2	40	100	$10
1st Half		289	26	4	26	1	227	266			245	360	606	2	85	25	0.16				94			79	7%	18%				2.79		37	93	$4
2nd Half		283	26	6	40	2	297	277	302	294	318	431	750	3	88	32	0.26	39	24	37	88	116	6%	68	4%	67%	14	29%	21%	4.95	2.9	43	108	$16
13	**Proj**	**239**	**21**	**2**	**24**	**1**	**245**	**238**	**165**	**279**	**264**	**335**	**599**	**3**	**86**	**28**	**0.18**	**38**	**20**	**43**	**65**	**67**	**2%**	**76**	**5%**	**46%**				**2.93**	**-11.8**	**19**	**46**	**$3**

Cruz,Nelson			Health	C	LIMA Plan	B
Age 33	Bats R	Pos RF	PT/Exp	B	Rand Var	+1
Ht 6' 2"	Wt 240		Consist	C	MM	4135

Finally reached 500 AB, so where was the huge season? Slow first three months marked by low ct%, Eye. Picked up skills pace in 2H, raising hopes for a bit of a surge in '13. No longer a major SB threat, as running has been hazardous to his health. But if he manages another 500 AB and hr/f rebounds.... UP: 35 HR, still.

Yr	Tm	AB	R	HR	RBI	SB	BA	xBA	vL	vR	OB	Slg	OPS	bb%	ct%	h%	Eye	G	L	F	PX	xPX	hr/f	Spd	SBO	SB%	#Wk	DOM	DIS	RC/G	RAR	BPV	BPX	R$
08	TEX *	498	83	34	95	20	288	283	419	298	359	553	912	10	72	34	0.40	40	22	38	174	137	21%	115	22%	64%	6	83%	0%	6.77	27.4	83	163	$29
09	TEX	462	75	33	76	20	260	277	235	270	331	524	855	10	74	28	0.42	38	16	46	166	154	21%	79	21%	83%	25	48%	20%	6.02	15.7	82	167	$22
10	TEX *	429	61	22	81	18	311	293	330	314	369	554	924	9	80	35	0.46	37	18	45	163	149	15%	96	19%	82%	21	52%	24%	7.60	32.2	101	220	$27
11	TEX *	497	66	31	90	9	262	278	340	243	311	512	823	7	76	28	0.30	41	16	43	168	144	19%	64	13%	64%	24	58%	21%	5.36	7.3	77	171	$21
12	TEX	585	86	24	90	8	260	262	309	244	316	460	776	8	76	30	0.34	41	18	41	141	151	13%	73	9%	67%	27	41%	26%	4.94	1.4	55	138	$20
1st Half		290	46	11	49	6	255	237	305	236	310	428	737	7	72	32	0.28	40	18	41	126	133	13%	82	14%	60%	13	23%	46%	4.38	-5.4	27	68	$21
2nd Half		295	40	13	41	2	264	287	316	252	322	492	813	8	80	29	0.43	41	19	40	155	166	13%	63	3%	100%	14	57%	7%	5.53	4.4	79	198	$18
13	**Proj**	**517**	**74**	**26**	**86**	**8**	**266**	**271**	**315**	**251**	**322**	**492**	**815**	**8**	**77**	**30**	**0.36**	**40**	**18**	**42**	**152**	**149**	**16%**	**70**	**10%**	**65%**				**5.41**	**6.1**	**69**	**171**	**$21**

Cruz,Tony			Health	A	LIMA Plan	F
Age 26	Bats R	Pos CA	PT/Exp	F	Rand Var	-2
Ht 5' 11"	Wt 205		Consist	B	MM	1001

One good path to fanalytic irrelevance: Back up one of the most potent offensive catchers in the game and bring little to the table in the way of your own skills. BA was less offensive than many second catchers, though xBA says that may not last. Likely won't see enough AB for that to matter, though.

Yr	Tm	AB	R	HR	RBI	SB	BA	xBA	vL	vR	OB	Slg	OPS	bb%	ct%	h%	Eye	G	L	F	PX	xPX	hr/f	Spd	SBO	SB%	#Wk	DOM	DIS	RC/G	RAR	BPV	BPX	R$
08																																		
09	aa	405	34	7	37	1	187	242			236	299	535	6	77	23	0.28				80			87	1%	100%				2.22		3	0	-$5
10	a/a	163	20	5	15	0	231	251			288	367	655	7	78	27	0.37				97			94	0%	0%				3.51		17	0	$0
11	STL *	214	17	2	23	0	223	206	269	256	271	306	577	6	77	28	0.28	46	15	38	64	69	0%	100	4%	0%	15	27%	47%	2.59	-11.1	-15	-33	-$1
12	STL	126	11	1	11	0	254	237	195	282	271	365	636	2	85	29	0.16	46	14	40	79	92	2%	97	4%	0%	25	28%	40%	3.25	-3.8	28	70	-$1
1st Half		56	5	1	1	0	196	215	158	216	196	304	500	0	88	21	0.00	45	8	47	70	101	4%	90	14%	0%	11	18%	45%	1.68	-4.6	26	65	-$4
2nd Half		70	6	0	10	0	300	254	227	333	329	414	743	4	83	36	0.25	47	18	35	87	85	0%	101	0%	0%	14	36%	36%	4.96	1.4	29	73	$2
13	**Proj**	**134**	**12**	**0**	**13**	**0**	**239**	**217**	**223**	**247**	**273**	**320**	**593**	**4**	**81**	**29**	**0.25**	**46**	**15**	**39**	**64**	**83**	**1%**	**96**	**3%**	**4%**				**2.85**	**-5.5**	**2**	**6**	**$1**

KRIS OLSON

Cuddyer,Michael

Age 34	Bats R	Pos RF 1B	Health	C	LIMA Plan	B+
Ht 6' 2"	Wt 220		PT/Exp	B	Rand Var	+2
			Consist	B	MM	4245

Limited to just 8 AB after Aug. 1 due to oblique injury, which was a shame, because strong PX, thin air were proving to be a lethal combo. BA down a bit, but xBA says not to worry about that too much. Slip of ct%, Eye a bit concerning, especially given age. But with return to health, a stable investment.

Yr	Tm	AB	R	HR	RBI	SB	BA	xBA	vL	vR	OB	Slg	OPS	bb%	ct%	h%	Eye	G	L	F	PX	xPX	hr/f	Spd	SBO	SB%	#Wk	DOM	DIS	RC/G	RAR	BPV	BPX	R$
08	MIN	249	30	3	36	5	249	264	250	249	318	369	687	9	84	29	0.63	46	21	33	77	84	4%	131	9%	83%	15	40%	27%	4.03	-10.2	52	102	$3
09	MIN	588	93	32	94	6	276	293	307	263	336	520	857	8	80	30	0.46	44	17	40	147	122	17%	111	5%	86%	27	63%	30%	6.19	12.7	89	182	$22
10	MIN	609	93	14	81	7	271	280	285	265	334	417	751	9	85	30	0.62	50	17	33	97	90	8%	110	6%	70%	27	56%	19%	4.85	-10.0	65	141	$18
11	MIN	529	70	20	70	11	284	277	311	272	343	459	803	8	82	31	0.51	49	18	34	116	108	14%	93	8%	92%	26	46%	31%	5.71	4.1	67	149	$21
12	COL	358	53	16	58	8	260	296	258	261	321	489	809	8	78	29	0.41	49	20	31	155	125	18%	84	14%	73%	19	58%	21%	5.34	-0.8	84	210	$13
1st Half		269	41	12	49	8	257	292	247	260	315	487	802	8	77	29	0.38	49	18	33	160	133	17%	74	16%	89%	13	46%	23%	5.35	-0.1	86	215	$18
2nd Half		89	12	4	9	0	270	308	300	261	337	494	831	9	81	29	0.53	48	26	26	140	102	21%	105	9%	0%	6	83%	17%	5.30	-0.2	77	193	-$4
13	**Proj**	**544**	**77**	**23**	**83**	**8**	**270**	**290**	**287**	**264**	**332**	**478**	**810**	**9**	**81**	**30**	**0.50**	**48**	**20**	**31**	**131**	**108**	**16%**	**96**	**9%**	**62%**				**5.43**	**6.7**	**74**	**186**	**$19**

D Arnaud,Travis

Age 24	Bats R	Pos CA	Health	A	LIMA Plan	F
Ht 6' 2"	Wt 195		PT/Exp	F	Rand Var	-1
			Consist	B	MM	4121

One of game's top CA prospects, season ended in late June due to torn PCL. Put up nearly a full season's worth of stats before that, however (.333, 16 HR, 52 RBI in 62 games). Eye could stand some refinement, and TOR will likely return him to AAA for more experience. But with that power, it won't be long.

Yr	Tm	AB	R	HR	RBI	SB	BA	xBA	vL	vR	OB	Slg	OPS	bb%	ct%	h%	Eye	G	L	F	PX	xPX	hr/f	Spd	SBO	SB%	#Wk	DOM	DIS	RC/G	RAR	BPV	BPX	R$
08																																		
09																																		
10																																		
11	aa	424	61	19	66	3	290	275			334	504	838	6	74	35	0.25				160			77	6%	61%				5.97		57	0	$18
12	aaa	279	31	12	36	1	284	265			316	489	805	4	75	34	0.19				140			83	3%	38%				5.41		39	0	$8
1st Half		279	31	12	36	1	284	266			316	489	805	4	75	34	0.19				140			95	3%	38%				5.41		39	98	$8
2nd Half																																		
13	**Proj**	**133**	**17**	**5**	**19**	**1**	**286**	**270**			**321**	**486**	**807**	**5**	**75**	**35**	**0.20**	**40**	**24**	**36**	**140**		**15%**	**95**	**4%**	**55%**				**5.50**	**4.8**	**41**	**101**	**$5**

Damon,Johnny

Age 39	Bats L	Pos LF	Health	A	LIMA Plan	F
Ht 6' 2"	Wt 205		PT/Exp	B	Rand Var	+5
			Consist	B	MM	1411

Gradually-eroding skill set finally collapsed. Couldn't find home to start season. CLE then cut him loose after three impotent months. After that, phone never rang. Expected stint playing for Thailand in WBC qualifier may be last we see of him. (No, those hits don't count towards your quest for 3,000, Johnny.)

Yr	Tm	AB	R	HR	RBI	SB	BA	xBA	vL	vR	OB	Slg	OPS	bb%	ct%	h%	Eye	G	L	F	PX	xPX	hr/f	Spd	SBO	SB%	#Wk	DOM	DIS	RC/G	RAR	BPV	BPX	R$
08	NYY	555	95	17	71	29	303	282	258	321	375	461	836	10	85	33	0.78	44	22	34	95	70	10%	123	20%	78%	25	60%	16%	6.35	22.7	77	151	$30
09	NYY	550	107	24	82	12	282	282	269	288	364	489	853	11	82	31	0.72	41	16	42	128	92	13%	116	7%	100%	27	67%	15%	6.47	24.6	91	186	$23
10	DET	539	81	8	51	11	271	266	275	270	354	401	754	11	83	31	0.77	44	19	37	92	67	5%	123	7%	92%	27	44%	30%	5.06	2.6	66	143	$15
11	TAM	582	79	16	73	19	261	267	277	255	321	418	738	8	84	29	0.55	41	20	38	99	74	8%	108	17%	76%	27	56%	30%	4.61	-4.6	70	156	$20
12	CLE	207	25	4	19	4	222	245	205	227	281	329	610	8	87	24	0.63	44	19	37	60	51	6%	107	8%	100%	14	50%	43%	3.13	-11.0	44	110	$1
1st Half		145	19	4	17	2	207	245	216	204	286	338	624	10	86	22	0.76	41	18	41	76	61	8%	91	6%	100%	9	67%	33%	3.17	-7.7	51	128	$2
2nd Half		62	6	0	2	2	258	251	143	273	270	306	576	2	90	29	0.17	50	21	29	26	29	0%	116	13%	100%	5	20%	60%	3.01	-3.4	20	50	-$2
13	**Proj**	**130**	**17**	**2**	**12**	**4**	**254**	**254**	**240**	**258**	**309**	**368**	**677**	**7**	**86**	**28**	**0.58**	**44**	**20**	**36**	**68**	**58**	**6%**	**106**	**12%**	**88%**				**3.98**	**-2.5**	**48**	**120**	**$3**

Darnell,James

Age 26	Bats R	Pos LF	Health	F	LIMA Plan	F
Ht 6' 2"	Wt 195		PT/Exp	D	Rand Var	0
			Consist	B	MM	3201

1-1-.235 in 17 AB at SD. Another season, another injury. This time: a subluxation of left shoulder, the one with the surgically repaired labrum but not the one that ended his 2011 season (we know it's hard to keep track). Will health will ever allow him to tap his potential? At 26, he's entering into Bull Durham territory.

Yr	Tm	AB	R	HR	RBI	SB	BA	xBA	vL	vR	OB	Slg	OPS	bb%	ct%	h%	Eye	G	L	F	PX	xPX	hr/f	Spd	SBO	SB%	#Wk	DOM	DIS	RC/G	RAR	BPV	BPX	R$
08																																		
09																																		
10	aa	373	39	8	42	2	226	247			300	337	637	10	80	26	0.52				80			90	2%	100%				3.35		21	0	$2
11	SD *	467	55	15	58	2	233	235	143	292	310	380	690	10	77	27	0.49	49	13	38	105	66	7%	76	3%	66%	5	40%	60%	3.90	-11.6	30	67	$7
12	SD *	133	16	5	15	1	204	197	111	375	276	362	638	9	75	23	0.39	40	7	53	106	89	13%	91	6%	36%	2	50%	50%	3.10	-6.8	16	40	-$1
1st Half		133	16	5	15	1	204	197	111	375	276	362	638	9	75	23	0.39	40	7	53	106	89	13%	91	6%	36%	2	50%	50%	3.10	-6.5	16	40	-$1
2nd Half																																		
13	**Proj**	**127**	**14**	**5**	**15**	**1**	**259**	**235**			**329**	**434**	**764**	**9**	**77**	**30**	**0.46**	**38**	**16**	**46**	**113**		**12%**	**92**	**3%**	**65%**				**4.89**	**0.9**	**32**	**79**	**$3**

Davis,Chris

Age 27	Bats L	Pos DH 1B RF	Health	A	LIMA Plan	C+
Ht 6' 3"	Wt 232		PT/Exp	C	Rand Var	-2
			Consist	D	MM	5115

Finally, the power he had long displayed in the minors manifested itself over full MLB season. Unlikely to repeat hr/f, which could cut into HR total. Continued ct%, Eye issues put BA at risk and contribute to streakiness. But when he does hit the ball, he hits it far. Thus, good things should continue to happen.

Yr	Tm	AB	R	HR	RBI	SB	BA	xBA	vL	vR	OB	Slg	OPS	bb%	ct%	h%	Eye	G	L	F	PX	xPX	hr/f	Spd	SBO	SB%	#Wk	DOM	DIS	RC/G	RAR	BPV	BPX	R$
08	TEX *	592	104	36	112	6	293	286	279	287	338	556	894	6	71	36	0.24	35	25	40	185	149	20%	75	7%	68%	15	67%	27%	6.71	30.1	76	149	$29
09	TEX *	556	71	26	85	0	258	237	189	260	314	456	770	8	65	35	0.23	35	21	44	147	162	20%	88	1%	0%	21	19%	52%	4.88	-0.1	9	18	$13
10	TEX *	518	56	12	63	5	264	247	148	204	320	413	732	8	70	36	0.27	42	22	36	125	75	3%	67	6%	69%	11	9%	64%	4.55	-5.0	16	35	$12
11	2 AL *	398	58	26	71	2	299	278	350	245	333	559	892	5	67	39	0.16	38	25	37	202	137	10%	79	2%	100%	16	25%	69%	6.80	20.9	59	131	$20
12	BAL	515	75	33	85	2	270	252	265	271	319	501	820	7	67	34	0.22	39	23	38	162	150	25%	67	4%	40%	27	33%	37%	5.46	8.5	25	63	$20
1st Half		243	36	13	35	0	276	256	327	262	315	481	797	5	71	34	0.20	41	23	36	141	134	21%	75	5%	0%	13	38%	38%	5.06	1.2	21	53	$17
2nd Half		272	39	20	50	2	265	249	213	280	322	518	840	8	64	34	0.23	38	23	39	184	167	29%	67	3%	100%	14	29%	36%	5.83	7.4	33	83	$24
13	**Proj**	**524**	**74**	**29**	**91**	**3**	**257**	**253**	**260**	**257**	**305**	**479**	**784**	**6**	**67**	**33**	**0.21**	**39**	**23**	**38**	**161**	**138**	**22%**	**69**	**4%**	**61%**				**4.98**	**1.4**	**31**	**78**	**$19**

Davis,Ike

Age 26	Bats L	Pos 1B	Health	D	LIMA Plan	B
Ht 6' 4"	Wt 231		PT/Exp	C	Rand Var	+5
			Consist	F	MM	4025

Bout of Valley Fever may have contributed to slow start, rumors of demotion. From June 9 on, hit .265 with 27 HR. Contact rate likely to continue to depress BA, but xBA verifies that owners shouldn't have to endure .227 again. Already a solid power source entering his prime, if he could solve LHP, stay healthy... UP: 40 HR

Yr	Tm	AB	R	HR	RBI	SB	BA	xBA	vL	vR	OB	Slg	OPS	bb%	ct%	h%	Eye	G	L	F	PX	xPX	hr/f	Spd	SBO	SB%	#Wk	DOM	DIS	RC/G	RAR	BPV	BPX	R$
08																																		
09	aa	207	24	11	35	0	276	252			341	494	835	9	66	37	0.29				164			76	0%	0%				5.94		22	0	$5
10	NYM *	556	79	20	74	3	267	254	295	254	358	445	802	12	74	33	0.55	43	16	41	132	129	12%	85	3%	60%	25	36%	28%	5.49	1.0	45	98	$16
11	NYM	129	20	7	25	0	302	277	163	372	384	543	926	12	76	35	0.55	42	17	41	165	126	17%	97	0%	0%	7	57%	29%	7.61	7.7	77	171	$5
12	NYM	519	66	32	90	0	227	262	174	253	309	462	771	11	73	25	0.43	39	21	40	157	166	21%	50	2%	0%	27	44%	37%	4.63	-12.5	45	113	$12
1st Half		246	29	11	45	0	203	239	171	220	279	390	670	10	71	24	0.36	44	18	37	134	145	17%	52	2%	0%	13	38%	62%	3.43	-14.9	20	50	$6
2nd Half		273	37	21	45	0	249	286	176	282	334	527	862	11	75	26	0.51	34	23	42	176	184	24%	60	1%	0%	14	50%	14%	5.90	4.4	70	175	$17
13	**Proj**	**505**	**69**	**29**	**86**	**0**	**268**	**262**	**188**	**305**	**349**	**502**	**851**	**11**	**73**	**31**	**0.46**	**40**	**19**	**41**	**157**	**148**	**19%**	**69**	**1%**	**25%**				**6.05**	**10.0**	**53**	**133**	**$19**

Davis,Rajai

Age 32	Bats R	Pos LF RF	Health	B	LIMA Plan	D+
Ht 5' 9"	Wt 195		PT/Exp	B	Rand Var	-1
			Consist	C	MM	2513

Sometimes, speed is wasted on the OBP-challenged... or it least it would be, without such obscene SBO rates. Struggles vs. RHP resurfaced in 2H, increasing doubts as to whether AB will be as plentiful in '13. He did start '12 as a reserve, after all. Also, will next skipper be as generous with green light? DN: 250 AB, 25 SB

Yr	Tm	AB	R	HR	RBI	SB	BA	xBA	vL	vR	OB	Slg	OPS	bb%	ct%	h%	Eye	G	L	F	PX	xPX	hr/f	Spd	SBO	SB%	#Wk	DOM	DIS	RC/G	RAR	BPV	BPX	R$
08	2 TM	214	30	3	19	29	243	253	232	250	270	346	616	4	81	29	0.20	48	22	30	59	56	6%	180	73%	83%	25	28%	56%	3.32	-8.1	39	76	$11
09	OAK	390	65	3	48	41	305	266	316	299	353	423	776	7	82	37	0.41	46	20	34	83	72	3%	126	47%	77%	27	41%	30%	5.49	10.2	58	118	$25
10	OAK	525	66	5	52	50	284	250	304	276	318	377	695	5	85	33	0.33	48	16	37	67	58	3%	125	44%	82%	27	41%	30%	4.42	-2.1	47	102	$28
11	TOR	320	44	1	29	34	238	238	288	221	272	350	622	4	80	29	0.24	44	16	40	85	50	1%	145	71%	76%	20	35%	45%	3.12	-14.4	56	124	$11
12	TOR	447	64	8	43	46	257	248	285	243	303	378	681	6	77	32	0.28	45	23	32	86	75	7%	113	54%	78%	27	33%	41%	3.95	-8.3	36	90	$22
1st Half		154	25	4	20	20	273	252	231	303	325	422	747	7	79	32	0.36	42	22	36	95	95	10%	121	61%	80%	13	38%	38%	4.89	1.1	56	140	$18
2nd Half		293	39	4	23	26	249	247	326	217	290	355	645	5	76	31	0.25	46	23	30	81	65	6%	100	50%	76%	14	29%	43%	3.50	-10.3	23	58	$24
13	**Proj**	**398**	**56**	**5**	**39**	**37**	**259**	**246**	**283**	**248**	**298**	**376**	**674**	**5**	**80**	**31**	**0.27**	**45**	**20**	**35**	**82**	**66**	**5%**	**122**	**50%**	**79%**				**3.91**	**-8.9**	**43**	**108**	**$20**

KRIS OLSON

De Aza,Alejandro

Age	29	Bats	L	Pos	CF	Health	A	LIMA Plan	C
Ht	6' 0"	Wt	190			PT/Exp	C	Rand Var	-2
						Consist	B	MM	3425

PRO: Finally translated Spd to MLB SBs; 2H xPX/FB% hints at double-digit power. CON: Shaky ct% for a non-slugger holds down xBA; struggles vs. LHP; wobbly SB%. Healthy SBO still makes him a lock for 20+ SBs, but 2H sample hasn't fully convinced us power is coming. Bid for a repeat rather than growth.

Yr	Tm	AB	R	HR	RBI	SB	BA	xBA	vL	vR	OB	Slg	OPS	bb%	ct%	h%	Eye	G	L	F	PX	xPX	hr/f	Spd	SBO	SB%	#Wk	DOM	DIS	RC/G	RAR	BPV	BPX	R$
08																																		
09	FLA *	287	40	6	28	8	254	250	0	294	316	409	726	8	75	32	0.37	50	13	38	110	-5	0%	116	20%	58%	7	43%	57%	4.21	-4.0	44	90	$6
10	CHW*	348	46	4	38	14	252	245	250	308	300	362	662	6	78	31	0.30	56	12	32	85	45	0%	118	22%	75%	6	17%	17%	3.70	-11.9	29	63	$9
11	CHW*	537	78	12	51	29	285	266	263	338	340	440	780	8	77	35	0.36	49	20	31	115	81	11%	135	33%	61%	10	60%	20%	4.92	1.0	55	122	$24
12	CHW	524	81	9	50	26	281	259	248	291	340	410	750	8	79	34	0.43	42	26	32	88	96	7%	119	25%	68%	24	42%	33%	4.79	-1.0	44	110	$22
1st Half		302	51	5	32	14	295	261	260	307	356	411	767	9	79	36	0.45	41	30	29	78	82	7%	127	22%	67%	13	23%	46%	5.12	3.0	33	83	$27
2nd Half		222	30	4	18	12	261	259	231	271	317	410	727	8	80	31	0.40	43	21	36	102	114	6%	102	31%	71%	11	64%	18%	4.36	-2.8	57	143	$14
13	**Proj**	**548**	**79**	**12**	**52**	**26**	**272**	**261**	**228**	**283**	**329**	**421**	**750**	**8**	**78**	**33**	**0.39**	**45**	**23**	**32**	**102**	**93**	**9%**	**117**	**27%**	**67%**				**4.66**	**-1.9**	**49**	**123**	**$20**

DeJesus,David

Age	33	Bats	L	Pos	RF CF	Health	B	LIMA Plan	C+
Ht	5' 11"	Wt	190			PT/Exp	B	Rand Var	0
						Consist	D	MM	2225

Another respectable season, yes, but leave it to CHC to give someone with such ineptitude vs. LHPs more than 500 ABs. Surprising PX/xPX differential has our attention (esp. 2nd half), but he'll need to maintain low-40s GB for gains to stick. At 33, the better play is not to hope for miracles.

Yr	Tm	AB	R	HR	RBI	SB	BA	xBA	vL	vR	OB	Slg	OPS	bb%	ct%	h%	Eye	G	L	F	PX	xPX	hr/f	Spd	SBO	SB%	#Wk	DOM	DIS	RC/G	RAR	BPV	BPX	R$
08	KC	518	70	12	73	11	307	291	302	310	363	452	815	8	86	34	0.65	46	25	29	86	82	9%	106	12%	58%	25	48%	28%	5.83	9.7	63	124	$22
09	KC	558	74	13	71	4	281	277	290	277	342	434	775	8	84	31	0.59	46	20	34	91	95	8%	110	8%	31%	25	56%	12%	4.96	-2.9	55	112	$15
10	KC	352	46	5	37	3	318	282	258	340	378	443	821	9	87	36	0.72	47	21	32	86	95	5%	112	5%	50%	16	38%	19%	6.13	9.3	56	122	$13
11	OAK	442	60	10	46	4	240	252	174	265	310	376	686	9	81	28	0.52	43	20	37	91	100	8%	104	6%	57%	27	30%	33%	3.85	-17.2	43	96	$7
12	CHC	506	76	9	50	7	263	263	149	289	342	403	745	11	82	30	0.69	41	24	35	90	131	6%	115	10%	47%	27	33%	30%	4.56	-8.7	56	140	$12
1st Half		253	37	2	21	2	269	252	131	313	346	391	738	11	81	33	0.61	41	23	36	83	107	3%	117	9%	29%	13	15%	46%	4.41	-4.4	41	103	$10
2nd Half		253	39	7	29	5	257	274	182	268	338	415	753	11	84	28	0.78	41	24	35	96	154	9%	105	11%	63%	14	50%	14%	4.71	-2.2	68	170	$15
13	**Proj**	**473**	**67**	**9**	**50**	**6**	**268**	**263**	**200**	**288**	**341**	**408**	**748**	**10**	**83**	**31**	**0.65**	**43**	**22**	**35**	**88**	**116**	**7%**	**107**	**8%**	**51%**				**4.69**	**-4.4**	**54**	**134**	**$13**

Denorfia,Chris

Age	32	Bats	R	Pos	RF LF	Health	B	LIMA Plan	C
Ht	6' 0"	Wt	195			PT/Exp	D	Rand Var	-2
						Consist	B	MM	2433

Late-blooming OF was sneaky-good in part-time role, though GB% is ominous harbinger toward further relevancy. Chronic problems vRHP plus stagnant xPX typecast him as a bad-side platoon guy. Nice Spd make him a worthy end-game risk in deep formats, though.

Yr	Tm	AB	R	HR	RBI	SB	BA	xBA	vL	vR	OB	Slg	OPS	bb%	ct%	h%	Eye	G	L	F	PX	xPX	hr/f	Spd	SBO	SB%	#Wk	DOM	DIS	RC/G	RAR	BPV	BPX	R$
08	OAK *	251	33	2	23	5	245	256	241	333	285	330	615	5	79	30	0.26	61	18	20	65	85	11%	113	18%	52%	10	20%	50%	2.99	-16.4	6	12	$2
09	OAK *	434	44	6	35	10	202	285		0	240	289	529	5	85	23	0.33	100	0	0	53	-5	0%	130	21%	57%	2	0%	0%	2.10	-42.2	24	49	-$1
10	SD *	405	52	10	44	13	256	287	295	257	316	408	723	8	81	29	0.47	59	17	24	101	68	16%	126	18%	70%	21	29%	38%	4.34	-9.6	58	126	$11
11	SD	307	38	5	19	11	277	263	328	245	337	381	718	8	84	32	0.57	59	16	25	70	61	8%	126	18%	65%	23	35%	52%	4.40	-6.6	39	87	$8
12	SD	348	56	8	36	13	293	296	337	247	344	451	795	7	85	33	0.52	60	18	22	95	69	13%	140	19%	72%	27	52%	22%	5.51	3.6	73	183	$14
1st Half		173	22	2	11	4	289	300	318	259	349	428	777	8	88	32	0.76	59	20	21	88	69	6%	118	14%	57%	13	54%	23%	5.14	0.7	72	180	$9
2nd Half		175	34	6	25	9	297	292	356	235	339	474	813	6	82	33	0.35	62	16	22	103	69	19%	147	23%	82%	14	50%	21%	5.88	4.3	70	175	$20
13	**Proj**	**325**	**47**	**7**	**31**	**12**	**277**	**280**	**310**	**249**	**329**	**416**	**745**	**7**	**84**	**31**	**0.47**	**60**	**17**	**23**	**86**	**68**	**11%**	**130**	**19%**	**70%**				**4.73**	**-2.6**	**55**	**137**	**$13**

Descalso,Daniel

Age	26	Bats	L	Pos	2B SS 3B	Health	A	LIMA Plan	D
Ht	5' 10"	Wt	190			PT/Exp	C	Rand Var	0
						Consist	B	MM	1313

Speedy utilityman rarely saw green light batting out of No. 8 hole (although miserable OBP and SB% say he belonged there), and struggles vR may stymie his value even if he does escape bottom of the order. That leaves us with positional eligibility as his only redeeming quality. Pass.

Yr	Tm	AB	R	HR	RBI	SB	BA	xBA	vL	vR	OB	Slg	OPS	bb%	ct%	h%	Eye	G	L	F	PX	xPX	hr/f	Spd	SBO	SB%	#Wk	DOM	DIS	RC/G	RAR	BPV	BPX	R$
08	aa	37	5	0	3	1	317	248			358	382	740	6	91	35	0.75				36			119	15%	42%				4.65		41	0	$0
09	a/a	438	55	7	54	2	262	268			319	388	707	8	84	30	0.54				82			97	3%	68%				4.27		44	0	$7
10	STL *	502	66	6	53	7	231	276	429	222	282	329	611	7	88	25	0.58	61	14	25	69	30	0%	111	10%	58%	4	25%	75%	3.01	-20.4	48	104	$5
11	STL	326	35	1	28	2	264	241	190	280	331	353	684	9	80	33	0.51	47	20	33	72	61	1%	124	4%	50%	27	30%	52%	3.99	-3.3	20	44	$4
12	STL	374	41	4	26	6	227	235	309	200	297	324	620	9	78	28	0.45	45	23	32	60	100	4%	137	9%	67%	27	15%	52%	3.14	-13.7	13	33	$2
1st Half		169	20	3	11	2	225	229	290	210	311	343	654	11	73	29	0.47	48	21	31	77	75	8%	124	8%	50%	13	15%	46%	3.40	-4.5	9	23	$1
2nd Half		205	21	1	15	4	229	238	317	190	285	307	592	7	81	28	0.42	43	25	32	46	119	2%	134	9%	80%	14	14%	57%	2.93	-8.3	14	35	$3
13	**Proj**	**353**	**40**	**3**	**30**	**4**	**241**	**242**	**270**	**232**	**304**	**334**	**638**	**8**	**81**	**29**	**0.47**	**46**	**22**	**33**	**63**	**85**	**3%**	**122**	**7%**	**63%**				**3.37**	**-9.4**	**21**	**53**	**$4**

Desmond,Ian

Age	27	Bats	R	Pos	SS	Health	A	LIMA Plan	C
Ht	6' 2"	Wt	205			PT/Exp	A	Rand Var	-2
						Consist	D	MM	3425

Displayed unprecedented power in breakout year, but he can thank hr/f for doing most of the work. Missed a month in 2H with torn oblique, and h%, hr/f, SBO all clicked in unison upon his return. While he's moved into upper echelon of SS, that second half looks awfully unrepeatable, so ... DN: .260, 15 HR.

Yr	Tm	AB	R	HR	RBI	SB	BA	xBA	vL	vR	OB	Slg	OPS	bb%	ct%	h%	Eye	G	L	F	PX	xPX	hr/f	Spd	SBO	SB%	#Wk	DOM	DIS	RC/G	RAR	BPV	BPX	R$
08	aa	323	33	9	34	9	219	232			274	342	615	7	74	27	0.29				86			82	25%	51%				2.80		0	0	$2
09	WAS *	430	55	10	40	19	295	266	300	278	349	453	802	8	79	36	0.39	54	12	34	108	138	17%	118	21%	77%	5	40%	60%	5.70	19.3	55	112	$17
10	WAS	525	59	10	65	17	269	257	300	257	306	392	698	5	79	32	0.26	53	16	32	88	84	8%	122	17%	77%	27	30%	48%	4.19	1.2	32	70	$16
11	WAS	584	65	8	49	25	253	239	216	264	296	358	654	6	76	32	0.25	52	18	31	79	75	6%	128	24%	71%	27	22%	56%	3.56	-9.5	17	38	$15
12	WAS	513	72	25	73	21	292	279	303	289	331	511	842	6	78	33	0.27	48	18	35	142	115	18%	112	23%	78%	24	50%	38%	6.06	28.2	69	173	$27
1st Half		319	39	13	43	8	276	284	276	276	306	483	789	4	80	31	0.22	48	19	33	136	111	15%	112	17%	73%	13	46%	38%	5.13	10.3	67	168	$27
2nd Half		194	33	12	30	13	320	272	349	311	371	557	928	8	75	37	0.33	47	17	37	153	122	23%	106	29%	81%	11	55%	36%	7.77	19.9	68	170	$27
13	**Proj**	**559**	**74**	**20**	**69**	**25**	**280**	**256**	**276**	**282**	**324**	**451**	**775**	**6**	**77**	**33**	**0.28**	**49**	**17**	**34**	**114**	**104**	**13%**	**112**	**23%**	**76%**				**5.13**	**18.1**	**46**	**114**	**$26**

Diaz,Matt

Age	35	Bats	R	Pos	LF	Health	F	LIMA Plan	F
Ht	6' 0"	Wt	215			PT/Exp	F	Rand Var	+3
						Consist	B	MM	2221

Thumb surgery ended his season in August, but not before he cemented his futility vs. RHPs. Ironic how his only non-"F" mini box category is consistency (see left), considering how consistently useless he is to fantasy rosters ... DN: Retirement.

Yr	Tm	AB	R	HR	RBI	SB	BA	xBA	vL	vR	OB	Slg	OPS	bb%	ct%	h%	Eye	G	L	F	PX	xPX	hr/f	Spd	SBO	SB%	#Wk	DOM	DIS	RC/G	RAR	BPV	BPX	R$
08	ATL *	173	13	3	18	5	227	232	319	159	249	285	534	3	76	29	0.12	52	25	24	37	64	8%	77	17%	70%	10	0%	80%	2.32	-12.8	-41	-80	$0
09	ATL	371	56	13	58	12	313	281	412	255	372	488	860	9	76	38	0.39	48	25	27	114	105	17%	112	15%	71%	26	38%	38%	6.62	19.2	46	94	$18
10	ATL	224	27	7	31	3	250	296	273	223	291	438	729	5	80	28	0.30	44	23	33	131	106	12%	86	9%	75%	21	33%	38%	4.31	-2.7	67	146	$4
11	2 NL	251	16	0	20	5	263	240	295	227	297	323	619	5	79	33	0.23	53	21	26	53	51	0%	82	11%	71%	27	15%	59%	3.30	-10.4	-8	-18	$2
12	ATL	108	10	2	13	0	222	225	269	100	282	333	615	8	81	26	0.43	53	15	32	79	122	7%	75	0%	0%	16	38%	44%	3.08	-5.3	9	23	-$1
1st Half		95	8	2	13	0	232	228	284	107	291	347	639	8	81	27	0.44	50	17	33	80	120	8%	76	0%	0%	13	31%	46%	3.36	-3.7	11	28	-$1
2nd Half		13	2	0	0	0	154	217	182	0	214	231	445	7	77	20	0.33	80	0	20	72	139	0%	75	0%	0%	3	67%	33%	1.49	-1.4	3	8	-$4
13	**Proj**	**230**	**23**	**5**	**29**	**3**	**254**	**255**	**297**	**200**	**301**	**378**	**679**	**6**	**79**	**30**	**0.32**	**49**	**21**	**30**	**86**	**95**	**9%**	**79**	**9%**	**72%**				**3.87**	**-5.3**	**22**	**55**	**$5**

Dirks,Andy

Age	27	Bats	L	Pos	LF RF	Health	C	LIMA Plan	C+
Ht	6' 0"	Wt	195			PT/Exp	C	Rand Var	-5
						Consist	C	MM	2425

8-35-.322 in 314 AB at DET. Missed two months with Achilles issue, and that probably stifled his SBO, despite intriguing Spd. xBA, h% spike undermine chances of a .300 BA repeat. At age 27, it's getting to be now-or-never time. But if he gets an extended opportunity... UP: 15 HR, 15 SB.

Yr	Tm	AB	R	HR	RBI	SB	BA	xBA	vL	vR	OB	Slg	OPS	bb%	ct%	h%	Eye	G	L	F	PX	xPX	hr/f	Spd	SBO	SB%	#Wk	DOM	DIS	RC/G	RAR	BPV	BPX	R$
08																																		
09	aa	361	37	5	36	9	229	239			286	311	597	7	82	27	0.44				54			91	16%	62%				2.86		11	0	$3
10	a/a	476	60	12	49	17	257	270			299	395	693	6	83	29	0.36				92			100	19%	79%				4.06		54	0	$14
11	DET *	376	58	13	47	15	265	249	323	239	302	423	725	5	82	29	0.30	34	19	47	105	89	8%	89	22%	77%	19	42%	42%	4.42	-1.6	58	129	$14
12	DET *	351	59	9	39	3	307	268	274	336	354	470	824	7	82	35	0.42	38	24	37	101	102	8%	134	3%	71%	19	53%	21%	6.10	14.7	56	140	$14
1st Half		134	24	4	16	1	328	295	208	355	371	515	886	6	87	36	0.50	38	26	36	112	97	10%	115	3%	100%	9	56%	22%	7.30	9.4	80	200	$11
2nd Half		217	35	5	23	2	293	251	306	321	344	442	786	7	80	35	0.38	38	23	39	94	105	7%	139	4%	60%	10	50%	20%	5.43	4.7	39	98	$15
13	**Proj**	**460**	**70**	**13**	**52**	**10**	**282**	**256**	**269**	**285**	**326**	**436**	**762**	**6**	**82**	**32**	**0.37**	**37**	**22**	**41**	**97**	**97**	**8%**	**116**	**11%**	**75%**				**5.04**	**5.1**	**55**	**137**	**$18**

MATT GELFAND

Dobbs,Greg

Dobbs,Greg		Health	A	LIMA Plan	D
Age 34	Bats L Pos 3B LF	PT/Exp	D	Rand Var	-3
Ht 6' 1"	Wt 210	Consist	B	MM	1123

Additional ABs post-Hanley Ramirez trade didn't result in any significant skill spikes of note—but at age 34 we weren't holding out much hope anyway. Downward FB% trend is discouraging, and xBA doesn't buy the BA despite ct% uptick. Do we need to spell it out for you? W-A-I-V-E-R F-O-D-D-E-R.

Yr	Tm	AB	R	HR	RBI	SB	BA	xBA	vL	vR	OB	Slg	OPS	bb%	ct%	h%	Eye	G	L	F	PX	xPX	hr/f	Spd	SBO	SB%	#Wk	DOM	DIS	RC/G	RAR	BPV	BPX	R$
08	PHI	226	30	9	40	3	301	277	111	309	333	491	824	5	82	33	0.28	30	25	45	120	129	11%	71	7%	75%	26	54%	35%	5.95	8.3	58	114	$9
09	PHI	154	15	5	20	1	247	239	429	238	297	383	680	7	81	28	0.38	29	20	51	84	85	8%	72	3%	100%	24	21%	63%	3.89	-3.2	18	37	$1
10	PHI *	225	20	7	22	2	188	213	188	197	245	322	567	7	76	22	0.32	33	14	53	94	126	8%	77	8%	71%	25	40%	56%	2.47	-15.3	16	35	-$2
11	FLA	411	38	8	49	0	275	260	216	281	312	389	701	5	80	33	0.27	42	26	32	86	62	8%	65	0%	0%	27	33%	56%	4.27	-3.9	6	13	$8
12	MIA	319	26	5	39	4	285	264	279	286	315	386	701	4	83	33	0.26	43	27	30	65	64	6%	87	7%	67%	27	33%	52%	4.29	-2.8	15	38	$8
1st Half		114	11	1	18	2	289	243	333	286	325	360	685	5	84	34	0.33	42	25	33	43	56	3%	96	9%	67%	13	31%	62%	4.15	-1.4	7	18	$5
2nd Half		205	15	4	21	2	283	275	265	287	310	400	710	4	83	33	0.23	44	28	28	76	69	8%	80	6%	67%	14	36%	43%	4.37	-1.2	19	48	$9
13	**Proj**	**365**	**33**	**7**	**45**	**3**	**267**	**258**	**253**	**269**	**304**	**375**	**679**	**5**	**81**	**31**	**0.29**	**44**	**25**	**32**	**72**	**77**	**7%**	**77**	**5%**	**68%**				**3.94**	**-6.7**	**12**	**31**	**$7**

Dominguez,Matt

Dominguez,Matt		Health	A	LIMA Plan	D+
Age 23	Bats R Pos 3B	PT/Exp	C	Rand Var	+2
Ht 6' 1"	Wt 215	Consist	A	MM	2025

5-16-.284 in 109 AB at HOU. Defensive standout makes good contact but little else. Surpassed .260 only once in six minor league seasons, and poor patience (4% bb%) in MLB suggests BA regression to come. High GB% paired with inflated hr/f calls power into question too. His non-glove skills don't hold much value.

Yr	Tm	AB	R	HR	RBI	SB	BA	xBA	vL	vR	OB	Slg	OPS	bb%	ct%	h%	Eye	G	L	F	PX	xPX	hr/f	Spd	SBO	SB%	#Wk	DOM	DIS	RC/G	RAR	BPV	BPX	R$
08																																		
09	aa	97	9	2	8	0	178	238			277	304	582	12	73	23	0.50				102			87	0%	0%				2.62		5	0	-$3
10	aa	504	51	11	68	0	231	255			300	368	667	9	78	27	0.45				102			85	2%	0%				3.58		25	0	$4
11	FLA *	385	36	8	42	0	215	250	389	148	258	328	586	5	83	24	0.34	49	19	32	79	96	0%	67	1%	0%	4	25%	50%	2.71	-22.5	20	44	$0
12	HOU *	556	46	11	62	0	225	253	250	294	260	332	592	5	86	24	0.34	54	18	27	66	89	20%	94	1%	0%	8	38%	38%	2.81	-30.4	19	48	$2
1st Half		277	16	5	30	0	188	238			230	279	509	5	87	20	0.42				57			67	2%	0%				1.97		12	30	-$4
2nd Half		279	29	6	32	0	262	261	250	294	290	385	675	4	85	29	0.27	54	18	27	74	89	20%	110	0%	0%	8	38%	38%	3.86	-5.8	25	63	$8
13	**Proj**	**427**	**39**	**12**	**48**	**0**	**222**	**260**	**195**	**230**	**270**	**365**	**635**	**6**	**83**	**24**	**0.38**	**54**	**18**	**27**	**90**	**80**	**13%**	**94**	**1%**	**0%**				**3.20**	**-18.1**	**28**	**70**	**$3**

Donald,Jason

Donald,Jason		Health	A	LIMA Plan	F
Age 28	Bats R Pos 3B	PT/Exp	D	Rand Var	+3
Ht 6' 1"	Wt 195	Consist	B	MM	2311

2-11-.202 in 124 AB at CLE. Can't hit for power or contact, and rarely takes a free pass. They say you should never trust anyone with two first names. Babe Ruth is the exception...Jason Donald is the rule.

Yr	Tm	AB	R	HR	RBI	SB	BA	xBA	vL	vR	OB	Slg	OPS	bb%	ct%	h%	Eye	G	L	F	PX	xPX	hr/f	Spd	SBO	SB%	#Wk	DOM	DIS	RC/G	RAR	BPV	BPX	R$
08	aa	362	41	11	39	8	261	241			323	413	736	8	72	33	0.33				106			101	10%	78%				4.61		20	0	$8
09	aaa	243	28	1	13	5	201	215			243	283	526	5	69	29	0.18				75			99	12%	100%				2.28		-20	0	-$2
10	CLE *	433	58	5	36	12	244	256	286	243	304	364	667	8	75	32	0.34	49	22	30	95	77	6%	138	15%	78%	17	29%	59%	3.75	-10.3	30	65	$8
11	CLE *	335	40	4	21	9	274	256	377	268	320	362	682	6	75	35	0.27	52	27	21	72	83	5%	125	16%	61%	9	22%	78%	3.93	-5.9	0	0	$8
12	CLE *	380	50	6	33	7	211	237	175	224	261	319	581	6	70	28	0.23	52	24	25	83	62	10%	107	17%	55%	15	20%	73%	2.57	-23.6	-4	-10	$2
1st Half		196	23	1	16	5	191	208	95	250	253	263	516	8	72	26	0.29	47	20	33	54	39	0%	122	17%	67%	6	0%	83%	2.07	-15.8	-18	-45	$0
2nd Half		184	27	5	16	2	233	256	222	209	271	380	650	5	69	31	0.16	55	25	20	115	75	18%	94	17%	39%	9	33%	67%	3.15	-8.1	8	20	$5
13	**Proj**	**196**	**25**	**3**	**15**	**4**	**237**	**242**	**259**	**222**	**287**	**344**	**631**	**7**	**72**	**32**	**0.25**	**51**	**24**	**25**	**82**	**71**	**8%**	**110**	**15%**	**60%**				**3.20**	**-8.3**	**-2**	**-4**	**$3**

Donaldson,Josh

Donaldson,Josh		Health	A	LIMA Plan	D+
Age 27	Bats R Pos 3B	PT/Exp	C	Rand Var	0
Ht 6' 0"	Wt 220	Consist	B	MM	2115

9-33-.241 in 271 AB at OAK. Injuries propelled him into everyday role late in season, and he responded with promising power (8 HRs in Aug/Sept). Encouraging ct% growth offers a path to continued fanalytic relevance. Keep an eye on this one... UP: 20 HR, .270 BA.

Yr	Tm	AB	R	HR	RBI	SB	BA	xBA	vL	vR	OB	Slg	OPS	bb%	ct%	h%	Eye	G	L	F	PX	xPX	hr/f	Spd	SBO	SB%	#Wk	DOM	DIS	RC/G	RAR	BPV	BPX	R$
08																																		
09	aa	455	47	6	64	5	217	245			303	325	628	11	77	27	0.54				84			76	6%	68%				3.20		17	0	$2
10	OAK *	326	35	12	48	2	180	199	250	0	252	331	583	9	67	22	0.29	50	5	45	115	70	11%	69	5%	62%	6	17%	67%	2.57	-20.7	-1	-2	-$1
11	aaa	444	52	10	46	8	199	228			256	317	573	7	72	25	0.27				94			78	15%	64%				2.52		3	0	$1
12	OAK *	483	59	17	62	7	248	258	229	246	291	411	703	6	78	28	0.28	40	23	38	108	107	11%	62	10%	68%	17	24%	47%	4.01	-7.7	38	95	$12
1st Half		170	15	5	20	2	231	249	147	156	254	367	621	3	81	26	0.16	49	18	33	86	85	4%	55	16%	48%	9	11%	78%	2.91	-8.7	19	48	$0
2nd Half		313	45	12	42	5	257	261	286	291	311	437	748	7	77	30	0.34	35	25	40	120	119	14%	76	8%	83%	8	38%	13%	4.69	1.0	45	113	$18
13	**Proj**	**456**	**53**	**13**	**57**	**6**	**244**	**241**	**241**	**245**	**296**	**385**	**681**	**7**	**75**	**30**	**0.30**	**41**	**22**	**37**	**99**	**105**	**10%**	**60**	**9%**	**62%**				**3.78**	**-11.0**	**16**	**40**	**$10**

Doumit,Ryan

Doumit,Ryan		Health	D	LIMA Plan	C
Age 32	Bats B Pos CA DH	PT/Exp	C	Rand Var	-1
Ht 6' 1"	Wt 220	Consist	B	MM	3025

Amassed most AB of his career and - Voila! - has most productive season since... the last time he amassed 400 AB. Maintained acceptable BA thanks to PX, ct%—although the latter's dip is a minor concern. One healthy year doesn't absolve chronic injury history, but move to DH should be beneficial... UP: full repeat.

Yr	Tm	AB	R	HR	RBI	SB	BA	xBA	vL	vR	OB	Slg	OPS	bb%	ct%	h%	Eye	G	L	F	PX	xPX	hr/f	Spd	SBO	SB%	#Wk	DOM	DIS	RC/G	RAR	BPV	BPX	R$
08	PIT	431	71	15	69	2	318	304	330	314	352	501	854	5	87	34	0.42	41	23	35	116	117	11%	55	4%	50%	25	44%	16%	6.51	18.8	70	137	$19
09	PIT	280	31	10	38	4	250	268	266	244	300	414	714	7	83	27	0.41	42	18	40	104	103	11%	72	6%	100%	16	44%	31%	4.31	-4.7	47	96	$5
10	PIT	406	42	13	45	1	251	246	186	282	320	406	726	9	79	29	0.47	41	16	43	108	117	9%	69	1%	100%	26	38%	42%	4.44	-5.2	34	74	$7
11	PIT *	244	20	8	32	0	289	272	315	299	340	453	793	7	84	32	0.47	44	21	36	106	112	12%	80	1%	0%	19	42%	21%	5.43	3.7	47	104	$6
12	MIN	484	56	18	75	0	275	274	247	288	316	461	777	6	80	31	0.30	42	22	36	125	110	13%	59	0%	0%	27	37%	37%	5.12	3.1	42	105	$14
1st Half		210	23	7	34	0	276	267	250	288	336	448	784	8	80	32	0.44	42	23	35	113	114	11%	72	0%	0%	13	38%	31%	5.30	2.5	38	95	$11
2nd Half		274	33	11	41	0	274	279	244	288	299	471	770	4	80	31	0.18	41	22	36	133	107	14%	54	0%	0%	14	36%	43%	4.95	0.4	43	108	$17
13	**Proj**	**458**	**49**	**17**	**65**	**1**	**276**	**269**	**252**	**287**	**323**	**455**	**778**	**7**	**81**	**31**	**0.37**	**42**	**21**	**37**	**116**	**111**	**12%**	**63**	**1%**	**51%**				**5.16**	**12.3**	**45**	**112**	**$14**

Downs,Matt

Downs,Matt		Health	A	LIMA Plan	F
Age 29	Bats R Pos 1B	PT/Exp	F	Rand Var	+1
Ht 6' 1"	Wt 190	Consist	F	MM	3101

8-16-.202 in 178 AB at HOU. There's useful power lurking somewhere in this skill set, but too many obstacles in the way to extract it. For instance, subterranean BA is a bad start. Also, six of eight HR came vL, pegging him to bad-side platoon role. He's a fringe end-gamer for now.

Yr	Tm	AB	R	HR	RBI	SB	BA	xBA	vL	vR	OB	Slg	OPS	bb%	ct%	h%	Eye	G	L	F	PX	xPX	hr/f	Spd	SBO	SB%	#Wk	DOM	DIS	RC/G	RAR	BPV	BPX	R$
08	aaa	86	7	2	5	1	202	263			227	318	545	3	87	21	0.25				75			92	5%	100%				2.34		30	0	-$2
09	SF *	477	52	10	52	6	239	234	100	186	273	375	649	5	83	27	0.28	50	5	45	90	132	6%	90	9%	73%	4	25%	50%	3.42	-28.7	43	88	$5
10	2 NL *	313	34	6	28	3	201	230	256	185	264	312	576	8	79	24	0.41	37	18	45	80	126	3%	105	13%	32%	13	15%	46%	2.44	-29.9	17	37	-$1
11	HOU	199	29	10	41	0	276	279	340	257	333	518	851	8	76	32	0.36	36	17	47	178	148	14%	88	0%	0%	26	58%	35%	6.08	3.7	74	164	$7
12	HOU *	268	23	10	25	4	200	201	184	225	237	339	575	5	76	23	0.20	42	10	48	84	132	12%	98	21%	37%	25	36%	56%	2.29	-27.1	2	5	$0
1st Half		100	9	5	9	1	180	233	156	200	212	370	582	4	82	17	0.22	44	9	47	103	149	13%	107	29%	25%	13	38%	46%	2.06	-11.0	44	110	-$4
2nd Half		154	13	5	16	3	223	191	208	280	259	341	600	5	74	27	0.19	38	13	49	76	107	11%	91	19%	44%	12	33%	67%	2.65	-13.1	-16	-40	$2
13	**Proj**	**198**	**21**	**8**	**25**	**2**	**225**	**229**	**230**	**222**	**271**	**392**	**663**	**6**	**78**	**25**	**0.29**	**40**	**13**	**47**	**107**	**131**	**10%**	**89**	**14%**	**38%**				**3.27**	**-12.8**	**31**	**77**	**$3**

Dozier,Brian

Dozier,Brian		Health	A	LIMA Plan	D
Age 26	Bats R Pos SS	PT/Exp	F	Rand Var	0
Ht 5' 11"	Wt 190	Consist	C	MM	2413

6-33-.234 and 9 SBs in 316 AB at MIN. Some promising seeds here, most notably on the basepaths where Spd kicked into high gear in 2H. Power is a work in progress, but 2H xPX—and corresponding GB%/FB% flip—are steps in the right direction. Sad OBP tempers expectations, but he should be on your SS radar.

Yr	Tm	AB	R	HR	RBI	SB	BA	xBA	vL	vR	OB	Slg	OPS	bb%	ct%	h%	Eye	G	L	F	PX	xPX	hr/f	Spd	SBO	SB%	#Wk	DOM	DIS	RC/G	RAR	BPV	BPX	R$
08																																		
09																																		
10																																		
11	aa	311	43	4	25	8	269	264			314	407	721	6	83	31	0.39				94			118	21%	49%				4.11		58	0	$7
12	MIN *	497	45	7	47	11	222	231	256	227	263	317	580	5	81	26	0.28	42	21	38	64	80	6%	101	15%	73%	15	20%	53%	2.72	-18.1	12	30	$4
1st Half		288	23	4	30	5	234	240	270	219	274	322	596	5	81	28	0.29	45	22	33	65	53	6%	81	14%	52%	8	13%	63%	2.81	-10.6	2	5	$5
2nd Half		209	22	4	17	7	207	217	244	239	248	309	558	5	80	24	0.28	37	19	44	64	116	6%	127	16%	100%	7	29%	43%	2.61	-9.1	21	53	$2
13	**Proj**	**397**	**45**	**8**	**34**	**10**	**238**	**244**	**254**	**232**	**280**	**367**	**647**	**5**	**81**	**27**	**0.31**	**40**	**20**	**40**	**83**	**91**	**6%**	**124**	**18%**	**66%**				**3.35**	**-8.0**	**37**	**92**	**$8**

MATT GELFAND

Drew,Stephen

Age	30	Bats	L	Pos	SS	Health	F	LIMA Plan	D+
Ht	6' 0"	Wt	190			PT/Exp	C	Rand Var	+2
						Consist	C	MM	3215

7-28-.223 in 287 AB at ARI/OAK. Sure, ankle injury was bad, but in typical Drew family fashion, it took him far longer than expected to fully recover. Plate patience came back intact; resurgent Sept. (5 HRs, 45% FB%) along with aggregate xPX all suggest that a return of 2010 power is in play.

Yr	Tm	AB	R	HR	RBI	SB	BA	xBA	vL	vR	OB	Slg	OPS	bb%	ct%	h%	Eye	G	L	F	PX	xPX	hr/f	Spd	SBO	SB%	#Wk	DOM	DIS	RC/G	RAR	BPV	BPX	R$
08	ARI	611	91	21	67	3	291	285	267	300	336	502	838	6	82	33	0.38	35	23	43	133	133	10%	124	4%	50%	27	59%	26%	5.98	35.4	80	157	$20
09	ARI	533	71	12	65	5	261	267	200	282	323	428	751	8	84	29	0.56	39	19	42	99	106	6%	134	4%	83%	25	44%	24%	4.79	13.6	67	137	$11
10	ARI	565	83	15	61	10	278	271	255	287	349	458	808	10	81	32	0.57	40	19	41	117	108	8%	143	9%	67%	26	58%	31%	5.57	26.9	75	163	$18
11	ARI	321	44	5	45	4	252	247	224	263	316	396	712	9	77	31	0.41	39	21	40	107	109	5%	108	10%	50%	16	25%	31%	4.12	2.0	44	98	$6
12	2 TM *	328	42	8	31	1	218	237	198	234	307	347	653	11	74	27	0.49	32	28	40	89	122	8%	104	3%	33%	15	13%	47%	3.40	-7.1	10	25	$1
1st Half		53	5	1	3	0	182	233	0	182	261	297	557	10	78	21	0.48	44	22	33	65	155	0%	117	0%	0%	1	0%	100%	2.41	-2.7	3	8	-$11
2nd Half		275	37	7	28	1	225	238	200	237	315	356	671	12	73	28	0.49	32	28	40	94	120	8%	97	4%	33%	14	14%	43%	3.61	-3.4	11	28	$4
13	Proj	**504**	**65**	**14**	**53**	**4**	**250**	**245**	**219**	**262**	**324**	**407**	**732**	**10**	**77**	**30**	**0.48**	**37**	**22**	**41**	**103**	**114**	**8%**	**117**	**5%**	**52%**				**4.41**	**5.9**	**39**	**99**	**$9**

Duda,Lucas

Age	27	Bats	L	Pos	RF LF	Health	A	LIMA Plan	D
Ht	6' 4"	Wt	254			PT/Exp	C	Rand Var	0
						Consist	D	MM	3103

15-57-.239 in 401 AB at NYM. Frustrating sophomore campaign marred by ct% issues culminated in one-month demotion to AAA. While xPX suggests there's still plenty of juice in his bat, the power isn't so elite that it can overcome the strikeouts. But he owns better ct% skills in recent past, so... UP: 25 HR.

Yr	Tm	AB	R	HR	RBI	SB	BA	xBA	vL	vR	OB	Slg	OPS	bb%	ct%	h%	Eye	G	L	F	PX	xPX	hr/f	Spd	SBO	SB%	#Wk	DOM	DIS	RC/G	RAR	BPV	BPX	R$
08																																		
09	aa	395	39	7	42	2	244	238			325	369	694	11	73	32	0.44				97			82	3%	41%				3.97		5	0	$3
10	NYM *	509	63	19	75	1	240	267	158	215	308	438	746	9	76	28	0.41	35	19	46	145	129	14%	52	1%	100%	6	50%	50%	4.54	-9.2	56	122	$9
11	NYM *	430	55	18	68	1	276	274	274	297	352	476	828	10	79	31	0.57	34	22	43	136	116	9%	84	1%	100%	20	55%	35%	5.92	9.3	67	149	$15
12	NYM *	497	52	17	63	1	231	223	239	240	311	371	682	10	71	29	0.40	35	23	42	99	134	13%	44	1%	100%	23	22%	65%	3.84	-19.5	-4	-10	$6
1st Half		264	32	11	43	0	258	230	228	273	344	417	761	12	70	33	0.45	38	23	40	110	139	15%	51	0%	0%	13	23%	62%	4.93	-0.6	1	3	$13
2nd Half		233	20	6	20	1	201	211	262	179	273	319	592	9	71	25	0.35	31	22	47	86	123	9%	51	2%	100%	10	20%	70%	2.80	-16.1	-16	-40	-$1
13	Proj	**346**	**38**	**12**	**45**	**1**	**242**	**239**	**230**	**246**	**318**	**406**	**725**	**10**	**74**	**29**	**0.43**	**34**	**22**	**44**	**115**	**125**	**11%**	**60**	**1%**	**84%**				**4.36**	**-6.7**	**23**	**57**	**$7**

Duncan,Shelley

Age	33	Bats	R	Pos	LF	Health	A	LIMA Plan	F
Ht	6' 5"	Wt	225			PT/Exp	D	Rand Var	+3
						Consist	A	MM	4001

A slew of warts suggest this AB dip was well-deserved. Success vR in '11 proved to be fleeting, and while h% shoulders some of the blame, xPX suggests PX—his greatest/only asset—may be waning as well. Still lofts the ball with the best of them, but clearing that pesky fence could be an issue going forward.

Yr	Tm	AB	R	HR	RBI	SB	BA	xBA	vL	vR	OB	Slg	OPS	bb%	ct%	h%	Eye	G	L	F	PX	xPX	hr/f	Spd	SBO	SB%	#Wk	DOM	DIS	RC/G	RAR	BPV	BPX	R$
08	NYY *	262	36	11	39	5	188	234	225	59	291	363	653	13	69	23	0.46	31	22	47	131	111	5%	90	9%	78%	8	25%	63%	3.33	-10.3	28	55	$0
09	NYY *	467	69	27	80	2	225	261	250	143	306	452	758	10	74	25	0.44	30	20	50	148	95	0%	80	1%	100%	5	0%	100%	4.57	0.0	52	106	$9
10	CLE *	375	43	15	58	1	229	219	264	211	299	395	694	9	70	29	0.33	29	16	56	127	103	13%	74	1%	100%	21	33%	48%	3.91	-7.3	13	28	$5
11	CLE *	332	42	14	60	1	224	242	245	273	298	410	708	10	74	26	0.40	34	17	49	137	137	13%	70	2%	40%	21	52%	48%	3.97	-6.0	37	82	$6
12	CLE	232	29	11	31	1	203	223	212	193	288	388	676	11	75	22	0.47	31	15	54	122	77	12%	70	6%	33%	22	32%	45%	3.47	-8.0	31	78	$1
1st Half		146	19	5	15	1	205	211	206	205	310	349	659	13	72	25	0.54	30	19	51	101	70	9%	81	7%	33%	13	38%	38%	3.32	-6.2	10	25	$1
2nd Half		86	10	6	16	0	198	241	220	167	250	453	703	7	79	18	0.33	33	9	58	154	86	15%	64	0%	0%	9	22%	56%	3.60	-2.8	60	150	$1
13	Proj	**190**	**24**	**8**	**31**	**1**	**211**	**224**	**225**	**198**	**287**	**391**	**677**	**10**	**74**	**24**	**0.41**	**32**	**15**	**53**	**122**	**101**	**11%**	**68**	**3%**	**50%**				**3.58**	**-6.3**	**28**	**69**	**$3**

Dunn,Adam

Age	33	Bats	L	Pos	DH 1B	Health	A	LIMA Plan	C+
Ht	6' 6"	Wt	285			PT/Exp	A	Rand Var	+2
						Consist	F	MM	5005

We expected some correction but...wow, this was vintage. Or was it? Majestic power returned, but porous ct% from catastrophic 2011 remained. A tale of two 2Hs: xBA, ct% offer glimmers of BA recovery, but FB%, xPX dips create power pessimism. Now creeping up in age, 2H is the more appropriate baseline.

Yr	Tm	AB	R	HR	RBI	SB	BA	xBA	vL	vR	OB	Slg	OPS	bb%	ct%	h%	Eye	G	L	F	PX	xPX	hr/f	Spd	SBO	SB%	#Wk	DOM	DIS	RC/G	RAR	BPV	BPX	R$
08	2 NL	517	79	40	100	2	236	264	195	253	382	513	894	19	68	26	0.74	36	18	46	191	178	24%	54	2%	67%	27	67%	19%	6.52	25.3	75	147	$14
09	WAS	546	81	38	105	0	267	266	268	267	396	529	925	18	68	33	0.66	31	20	49	185	158	21%	49	1%	0%	27	52%	22%	7.25	37.0	60	122	$20
10	WAS	558	85	38	103	0	260	266	199	286	350	536	885	12	64	33	0.39	33	18	49	219	195	21%	63	1%	0%	27	52%	30%	6.41	24.7	72	157	$21
11	CHW	415	36	11	42	0	159	180	64	187	288	277	565	15	57	24	0.42	33	20	48	113	134	10%	38	1%	0%	27	15%	78%	2.39	-34.2	-42	-93	-$7
12	CHW	539	87	41	96	2	204	238	191	211	334	468	801	16	59	25	0.47	34	22	44	207	172	29%	39	2%	67%	27	48%	33%	4.99	1.6	47	118	$13
1st Half		272	44	24	58	0	213	243	165	238	363	515	878	19	54	28	0.51	30	24	46	255	208	35%	36	1%	0%	13	46%	31%	5.98	9.2	66	165	$18
2nd Half		267	43	17	38	2	195	235	217	183	302	419	721	13	64	23	0.42	38	21	41	165	140	24%	51	3%	100%	14	50%	36%	4.05	-7.1	32	80	$8
13	Proj	**534**	**75**	**33**	**84**	**1**	**211**	**227**	**180**	**224**	**330**	**436**	**767**	**15**	**61**	**27**	**0.46**	**34**	**21**	**46**	**177**	**163**	**22%**	**41**	**1%**	**58%**				**4.64**	**-4.2**	**27**	**66**	**$11**

Dyson,Jarrod

Age	28	Bats	L	Pos	CF	Health	A	LIMA Plan	D+
Ht	5' 9"	Wt	165			PT/Exp	D	Rand Var	-2
						Consist	B	MM	1503

0-9-.260 with 30 SB in 292 AB at KC. Decent bb% + good enough ct% + lots of GBs + green light = perfect storm of base-swiping skills. Unfortunately, LHPs own him, which drags down OBP and could ultimately cap SB potential. He's one skill away though, and if 2H OBP gains hold... UP: 50 SBs.

Yr	Tm	AB	R	HR	RBI	SB	BA	xBA	vL	vR	OB	Slg	OPS	bb%	ct%	h%	Eye	G	L	F	PX	xPX	hr/f	Spd	SBO	SB%	#Wk	DOM	DIS	RC/G	RAR	BPV	BPX	R$
08																																		
09	aa	248	28	0	10	27	223	211			282	275	556	7	76	29	0.34				36			137	52%	80%				2.72		-1	0	$6
10	KC *	277	38	2	22	20	219	238	91	239	273	302	575	7	80	27	0.37	67	5	28	61	116	9%	126	44%	71%	5	60%	40%	2.64	-19.4	30	65	$6
11	KC *	363	54	2	20	36	221	256	0	214	280	275	555	8	81	27	0.44	68	16	16	38	12	0%	148	41%	91%	11	18%	82%	2.89	-22.0	20	44	$10
12	KC *	355	60	0	12	34	262	250	206	275	324	333	657	8	83	32	0.52	57	19	24	44	56	0%	192	38%	85%	25	16%	48%	4.01	-8.8	36	90	$14
1st Half		253	39	0	10	17	253	268	216	259	309	317	626	8	84	30	0.51	62	21	17	37	45	0%	177	29%	80%	11	9%	45%	3.47	-9.9	31	78	$15
2nd Half		102	21	0	2	17	284	221	167	300	360	373	732	11	78	36	0.55	49	14	37	63	75	0%	164	56%	89%	14	21%	50%	5.51	2.2	43	108	$12
13	Proj	**320**	**52**	**3**	**14**	**35**	**246**	**237**	**164**	**263**	**311**	**335**	**646**	**9**	**80**	**30**	**0.48**	**59**	**12**	**29**	**57**	**84**	**4%**	**170**	**45%**	**86%**				**3.84**	**-9.1**	**36**	**90**	**$15**

Eaton,Adam

Age	24	Bats	L	Pos	CF	Health	A	LIMA Plan	C+
Ht	5' 8"	Wt	184			PT/Exp	F	Rand Var	-3
						Consist	D	MM	2435

2-5-.259 in 85 AB at ARI. Suffered broken hand during final week of season, but surpassed expectations in trial run. Advanced plate approach carried over from minors (14% bb, 82% ct%, 0.93 Eye in ARI), while nice GB/Spd combo suggests h% could sustain. Definite keeper league stash, with quick impact potential.

Yr	Tm	AB	R	HR	RBI	SB	BA	xBA	vL	vR	OB	Slg	OPS	bb%	ct%	h%	Eye	G	L	F	PX	xPX	hr/f	Spd	SBO	SB%	#Wk	DOM	DIS	RC/G	RAR	BPV	BPX	R$
08																																		
09																																		
10																																		
11	aa	212	22	3	20	7	268	241			333	375	709	9	82	32	0.54				68			124	22%	52%				4.00		34	0	$4
12	ARI *	613	108	7	38	32	314	276	313	226	369	443	812	8	83	37	0.52	64	12	24	91	91	13%	134	26%	67%	4	50%	50%	5.83	19.5	63	158	$31
1st Half		326	64	1	19	20	317	254			364	427	790	7	83	38	0.43				81			120	29%	71%				5.64		56	140	$35
2nd Half		287	44	6	19	12	310	281	313	226	374	462	836	9	83	36	0.62	64	12	24	101	91	13%	122	22%	62%	4	50%	50%	6.05	10.3	68	170	$27
13	Proj	**481**	**64**	**9**	**36**	**21**	**281**	**277**	**285**	**278**	**341**	**420**	**761**	**8**	**83**	**32**	**0.53**	**59**	**17**	**24**	**89**	**82**	**9%**	**130**	**23%**	**65%**				**4.89**	**1.6**	**57**	**143**	**$19**

Ellis,A.J.

Age	32	Bats	R	Pos	CA	Health	A	LIMA Plan	D
Ht	6' 3"	Wt	215			PT/Exp	D	Rand Var	-5
						Consist	C	MM	2005

PRO: patient approach; xPX validates power gains and reached new level in 2H. CON: still too many GBs to support power; mediocre ct% plus looming h% regression plus xBA all question BA gains. VERDICT: A modest investment with more value in OBP leagues.

Yr	Tm	AB	R	HR	RBI	SB	BA	xBA	vL	vR	OB	Slg	OPS	bb%	ct%	h%	Eye	G	L	F	PX	xPX	hr/f	Spd	SBO	SB%	#Wk	DOM	DIS	RC/G	RAR	BPV	BPX	R$
08	LA *	277	28	3	37	0	239	232		0	318	327	644	10	78	30	0.53	100	0	0	64	5	0%	104	3%	0%	3	0%	100%	3.35	-7.8	2	4	$0
09	LA *	293	32	0	27	1	234	199	0	125	326	274	601	12	80	29	0.68	56	11	33	33	78	0%	93	4%	34%	7	0%	43%	2.90	-12.3	-11	-22	-$1
10	LA *	169	12	0	20	1	240	215	250	284	323	295	617	11	80	30	0.60	52	16	32	49	59	0%	90	1%	100%	22	14%	68%	3.21	-5.3	-7	-15	$0
11	LA *	269	26	3	25	0	224	224	360	233	322	307	628	13	82	26	0.82	49	16	35	60	99	8%	84	3%	0%	13	46%	38%	3.13	-9.5	16	36	-$1
12	LA	423	44	13	52	0	270	243	224	285	367	414	781	13	75	33	0.61	45	23	33	100	102	13%	98	0%	0%	27	41%	48%	5.30	12.2	14	35	$9
1st Half		199	23	6	26	0	286	241	280	289	408	422	830	17	72	37	0.75	44	26	31	93	70	14%	107	0%	0%	13	46%	54%	6.16	10.8	10	25	$10
2nd Half		224	21	7	26	0	254	244	175	281	327	406	733	10	77	30	0.46	45	21	34	106	129	12%	89	0%	0%	14	36%	43%	4.54	2.1	17	43	$8
13	Proj	**399**	**39**	**10**	**45**	**0**	**249**	**235**	**264**	**245**	**342**	**372**	**713**	**12**	**78**	**30**	**0.64**	**47**	**19**	**33**	**83**	**96**	**9%**	**90**	**1%**	**27%**				**4.27**	**0.6**	**14**	**36**	**$7**

MATT GELFAND

Ellis,Mark

Age 36	Bats R	Pos 2B	Health D	LIMA Plan D
Ht 5' 10"	Wt 190		PT/Exp B	Rand Var 0
			Consist C	MM 1213

Remembered how to take a walk, started spraying LDs all over the place... and still ended up with an OPS that started with a '6'. There's just no skill in this arsenal that adds fantasy value. Even his ability to scratch out double-digit SBs from almost-average Spd is in question now. There are better end game options.

Yr	Tm	AB	R	HR	RBI	SB	BA	xBA	vL	vR	OB	Slg	OPS	bb%	ct%	h%	Eye	G	L	F	PX	xPX	hr/f	Spd	SBO	SB%	#Wk	DOM	DIS	RC/G	RAR	BPV	BPX	R$
08	OAK	442	55	12	41	14	233	250	176	256	315	373	688	11	85	25	0.82	34	20	46	85	79	7%	116	13%	88%	23	48%	17%	4.02	-4.3	65	127	$7
09	OAK *	410	53	10	63	10	252	270	260	264	292	383	675	5	86	27	0.41	40	20	39	83	69	8%	72	14%	77%	19	37%	21%	3.81	-6.4	49	100	$10
10	OAK	436	45	5	49	7	291	258	330	279	351	381	732	8	87	33	0.71	42	21	37	65	65	4%	82	9%	54%	24	33%	29%	4.65	3.7	34	74	$13
11	2 TM	480	55	7	41	14	248	245	268	241	281	346	627	4	84	28	0.29	46	17	37	70	66	5%	87	17%	74%	26	35%	42%	3.28	-15.3	33	73	$9
12	LA	415	62	7	31	5	258	260	321	228	323	364	687	9	83	30	0.57	39	27	34	72	80	6%	90	4%	100%	21	33%	24%	4.11	-2.8	35	88	$8
1st Half		132	27	2	9	3	273	271	360	220	360	364	724	12	86	30	1.00	39	31	30	54	77	6%	110	6%	100%	7	43%	29%	4.75	1.8	47	118	$5
2nd Half		283	35	5	22	2	251	255	298	231	305	364	669	7	82	29	0.42	39	24	36	80	81	6%	76	3%	100%	14	29%	21%	3.82	-3.7	24	60	$9
13	**Proj**	**388**	**52**	**6**	**34**	**5**	**260**	**254**	**303**	**242**	**316**	**364**	**680**	**8**	**84**	**29**	**0.53**	**41**	**23**	**36**	**70**	**73**	**5%**	**85**	**7%**	**73%**				**3.96**	**-3.4**	**34**	**86**	**$7**

Ellsbury,Jacoby

Age 29	Bats L	Pos CF	Health F	LIMA Plan B
Ht 6' 1"	Wt 195		PT/Exp C	Rand Var 0
			Consist F	MM 2435

Now two injury-decimated seasons in three years, with a complete breakout/outlier sandwiched in the middle; this may be the toughest 2013 projection out there. We know the speed is legit, but xPX doubted the 2011 power when it happened, so discount that until we see it again. 50 SB more likely than 20 HR.

Yr	Tm	AB	R	HR	RBI	SB	BA	xBA	vL	vR	OB	Slg	OPS	bb%	ct%	h%	Eye	G	L	F	PX	xPX	hr/f	Spd	SBO	SB%	#Wk	DOM	DIS	RC/G	RAR	BPV	BPX	R$
08	BOS	554	98	9	47	50	280	276	295	275	329	394	723	7	86	31	0.51	52	20	28	69	59	7%	148	39%	82%	28	39%	39%	4.75	-1.7	62	122	$30
09	BOS	624	94	8	60	70	301	275	318	294	352	415	767	7	88	33	0.66	50	18	32	66	84	5%	145	43%	85%	27	56%	11%	5.66	14.1	71	145	$41
10	BOS *	102	15	0	6	8	239	256	235	180	277	297	575	5	91	26	0.60	49	16	35	48	35	0%	97	37%	89%	6	17%	17%	3.00	-5.6	52	113	$2
11	BOS	660	119	32	105	39	321	313	284	337	371	552	922	7	85	34	0.53	43	23	34	145	115	17%	103	30%	72%	27	78%	4%	7.42	46.6	111	247	$49
12	BOS	303	43	4	26	14	271	259	292	259	314	370	683	6	86	30	0.44	47	20	33	70	91	5%	96	22%	82%	15	33%	27%	4.15	-6.2	43	108	$9
1st Half		26	4	0	3	0	192	294	250	167	300	269	569	13	88	22	1.33	57	26	17	63	43	0%	82	0%	0%	2	50%	0%	2.55	-1.8	46	115	-$14
2nd Half		277	39	4	23	14	278	255	296	268	315	379	694	5	86	31	0.38	46	20	34	70	96	5%	101	24%	82%	13	31%	31%	4.31	-3.7	41	103	$12
13	**Proj**	**559**	**87**	**11**	**53**	**41**	**280**	**274**	**296**	**272**	**323**	**408**	**731**	**6**	**87**	**30**	**0.50**	**47**	**20**	**33**	**81**	**79**	**7%**	**100**	**33%**	**83%**				**4.79**	**0.3**	**68**	**170**	**$29**

Encarnacion,Edwin

Age 30	Bats R	Pos DH 1B	Health C	LIMA Plan A
Ht 6' 2"	Wt 230		PT/Exp B	Rand Var 0
			Consist C	MM 4135

This monster season was just a case of sewing together skills he'd owned all along: solid plate approach/contact ('10-'11) for a slugger, plenty of FBs ('08, '10), established power ('08, '10), good health ('08, '11). Mild regression will preclude a full repeat, but this was no one-year wonder.

Yr	Tm	AB	R	HR	RBI	SB	BA	xBA	vL	vR	OB	Slg	OPS	bb%	ct%	h%	Eye	G	L	F	PX	xPX	hr/f	Spd	SBO	SB%	#Wk	DOM	DIS	RC/G	RAR	BPV	BPX	R$
08	CIN	506	75	26	68	1	251	262	292	235	332	466	798	11	80	27	0.60	34	16	50	136	94	13%	85	1%	100%	27	48%	15%	5.28	5.8	67	131	$11
09	2 TM *	330	39	15	45	2	226	248	250	219	316	409	725	12	78	25	0.59	37	17	46	111	107	12%	76	3%	67%	18	44%	33%	4.24	-6.4	43	88	$4
10	TOR *	364	52	23	58	1	251	281	234	246	309	487	796	8	83	25	0.48	32	17	51	143	133	15%	62	1%	100%	21	48%	29%	5.14	2.6	75	163	$11
11	TOR	481	70	17	55	8	272	275	276	271	332	453	785	8	84	29	0.56	36	19	44	124	124	9%	69	8%	80%	27	59%	22%	5.29	5.5	76	169	$16
12	TOR	542	93	42	110	13	280	285	301	273	377	557	934	13	83	27	0.89	33	18	49	157	153	19%	73	9%	81%	27	81%	7%	7.47	39.7	106	265	$31
1st Half		284	50	22	55	8	289	279	315	280	357	570	927	10	81	29	0.56	34	14	52	165	157	18%	83	13%	80%	13	85%	8%	7.29	19.2	100	250	$35
2nd Half		258	43	20	55	5	271	293	286	267	397	543	940	17	84	25	1.35	32	21	47	149	148	19%	63	6%	83%	14	79%	7%	7.59	20.0	110	275	$27
13	**Proj**	**527**	**82**	**36**	**97**	**9**	**278**	**284**	**292**	**274**	**361**	**537**	**897**	**11**	**83**	**28**	**0.75**	**34**	**18**	**48**	**151**	**137**	**17%**	**63**	**7%**	**81%**				**6.85**	**29.4**	**96**	**239**	**$27**

Escobar,Alcides

Age 26	Bats R	Pos SS	Health A	LIMA Plan C
Ht 6' 1"	Wt 190		PT/Exp A	Rand Var -3
			Consist B	MM 1525

Here's a chicken-or-egg problem: BA growth was driven by h% spike amidst otherwise-flat plate skills. Our research says that h% should regress. But he also turned FBs into LDs, if that was a conscious choice, he can hold the BA gains. xBA cops out and says "split the difference." Listen to xBA, he knows of what he speaks.

Yr	Tm	AB	R	HR	RBI	SB	BA	xBA	vL	vR	OB	Slg	OPS	bb%	ct%	h%	Eye	G	L	F	PX	xPX	hr/f	Spd	SBO	SB%	#Wk	DOM	DIS	RC/G	RAR	BPV	BPX	R$
08	MIL *	551	78	7	61	28	296	265	667	0	328	387	714	5	83	35	0.28	33	33	33	61	5	0%	126	24%	76%	4	0%	75%	4.58	7.4	28	55	$24
09	MIL *	555	80	4	38	37	270	254	480	260	308	357	664	5	83	32	0.32	52	17	31	58	37	3%	172	35%	74%	9	22%	56%	3.79	-5.1	33	67	$20
10	MIL	506	57	4	41	10	235	255	236	235	286	326	612	7	86	27	0.51	44	21	34	53	77	3%	184	11%	71%	27	30%	41%	3.10	-12.4	40	87	$5
11	KC	548	69	4	46	26	254	262	244	257	286	343	629	4	87	29	0.34	53	18	29	58	46	3%	162	27%	74%	27	37%	30%	3.34	-9.3	46	102	$14
12	KC	605	68	5	52	35	293	271	277	299	323	390	713	4	83	34	0.27	53	23	24	65	51	4%	134	25%	88%	27	33%	41%	4.73	14.0	37	93	$25
1st Half		268	29	2	20	12	313	281	333	306	338	422	760	4	83	37	0.22	55	23	22	79	42	4%	114	20%	86%	13	38%	46%	5.43	10.3	38	95	$21
2nd Half		337	39	3	32	23	276	262	238	292	311	365	676	5	84	32	0.31	52	23	25	54	58	4%	151	29%	88%	14	29%	36%	4.23	2.2	32	80	$29
13	**Proj**	**579**	**69**	**5**	**50**	**29**	**272**	**262**	**269**	**274**	**308**	**367**	**675**	**5**	**85**	**32**	**0.33**	**52**	**21**	**27**	**60**	**53**	**4%**	**144**	**24%**	**81%**				**4.04**	**0.5**	**39**	**98**	**$21**

Escobar,Eduardo

Age 24	Bats B	Pos 3B	Health A	LIMA Plan F
Ht 5' 10"	Wt 165		PT/Exp D	Rand Var +3
			Consist A	MM 0401

0-9-.214 with 3 SB in 131 AB at CHW/MIN. Glove-first infielder was part of the mid-season Francisco Liriano trade. PRO: Above-average Spd (though it hasn't translated to SBs yet); has some clue against LHPs. CON: Too many Ks; not enough walks; non-existent power; no clue vs. RHPs. At this point, the CONs have it.

Yr	Tm	AB	R	HR	RBI	SB	BA	xBA	vL	vR	OB	Slg	OPS	bb%	ct%	h%	Eye	G	L	F	PX	xPX	hr/f	Spd	SBO	SB%	#Wk	DOM	DIS	RC/G	RAR	BPV	BPX	R$
08																																		
09																																		
10	aa	202	19	3	19	3	241	244			270	343	613	4	81	29	0.21				68			115	6%	100%				3.18		16	0	$1
11	CHW *	496	46	4	41	11	243	296	333	250	279	321	601	5	76	31	0.21	67	33	0	62	2	0%	111	17%	56%	5	0%	80%	2.88	-25.0	-8	-18	$6
12	2 AL *	269	34	1	17	6	206	226	351	160	255	266	522	6	78	26	0.30	51	21	28	40	42	0%	146	11%	83%	19	26%	74%	2.23	-19.4	-2	-5	-$1
1st Half		68	12	0	2	2	206	195	333	170	299	250	549	12	72	29	0.47	53	17	30	29	26	0%	148	10%	100%	11	27%	73%	2.55	-4.3	-24	-60	-$5
2nd Half		201	22	1	15	4	206	242	364	146	240	272	512	4	80	25	0.22	48	25	27	43	56	0%	128	11%	76%	8	25%	75%	2.11	-15.6	0	0	$0
13	**Proj**	**231**	**26**	**0**	**16**	**5**	**224**	**225**	**419**	**155**	**270**	**278**	**548**	**6**	**77**	**29**	**0.27**	**50**	**22**	**28**	**40**	**44**	**0%**	**132**	**12%**	**74%**				**2.48**	**-14.9**	**-12**	**-29**	**$2**

Escobar,Yunel

Age 30	Bats R	Pos SS	Health A	LIMA Plan C
Ht 6' 2"	Wt 210		PT/Exp A	Rand Var +1
			Consist D	MM 1225

Hit rate continued to oscillate in a way that goes against him in even-numbered years. Combined with bb% collapse, he lost 150 points of OPS and probably triggered some questions about whether he should be a starter. Even with another 500 AB and a BA rebound, the lack of power or speed sets a low value ceiling.

Yr	Tm	AB	R	HR	RBI	SB	BA	xBA	vL	vR	OB	Slg	OPS	bb%	ct%	h%	Eye	G	L	F	PX	xPX	hr/f	Spd	SBO	SB%	#Wk	DOM	DIS	RC/G	RAR	BPV	BPX	R$
08	ATL	514	71	10	60	2	288	272	262	299	361	401	762	10	88	31	0.95	58	17	25	70	89	9%	105	4%	29%	25	44%	32%	5.02	16.1	46	90	$13
09	ATL	528	89	14	76	5	299	289	232	327	368	436	803	10	88	32	0.92	50	20	30	81	87	10%	86	5%	56%	27	52%	15%	5.72	26.6	62	127	$19
10	2 TM	497	60	4	35	6	256	255	274	251	331	318	649	10	89	28	0.98	54	18	28	44	64	3%	81	5%	75%	24	21%	29%	3.62	-4.1	30	65	$7
11	TOR	513	77	11	48	3	290	276	330	279	366	413	779	11	86	32	0.87	57	18	25	79	79	10%	126	3%	50%	24	46%	17%	5.35	20.8	52	116	$16
12	TOR	558	58	9	51	5	253	261	258	251	297	344	641	6	87	28	0.50	56	19	25	57	69	7%	88	4%	83%	27	26%	33%	3.51	-6.5	28	70	$8
1st Half		302	40	5	27	2	255	277	272	249	303	341	644	7	89	27	0.66	61	21	19	50	54	10%	103	4%	67%	13	31%	23%	3.53	-4.3	32	80	$11
2nd Half		256	18	4	24	3	250	241	243	253	289	348	637	5	85	28	0.37	51	16	33	66	88	6%	75	5%	100%	14	21%	43%	3.48	-4.0	20	50	$5
13	**Proj**	**483**	**57**	**8**	**45**	**4**	**266**	**261**	**273**	**264**	**326**	**365**	**690**	**8**	**87**	**29**	**0.68**	**55**	**18**	**27**	**62**	**75**	**7%**	**93**	**4%**	**71%**				**4.12**	**1.5**	**36**	**89**	**$11**

Espinosa,Danny

Age 26	Bats B	Pos 2B SS	Health A	LIMA Plan C+
Ht 6' 0"	Wt 195		PT/Exp A	Rand Var -2
			Consist A	MM 4405

Compelling power/speed profile comes with warning signs galore: ct% erosion reaching dangerous levels, xPX doesn't fully back HR, SBs stem from a shaky cocktail of average Spd and liberal green light. 2nd half showed positive face value, though unsupported growth. Lots of ways this can go wrong.

Yr	Tm	AB	R	HR	RBI	SB	BA	xBA	vL	vR	OB	Slg	OPS	bb%	ct%	h%	Eye	G	L	F	PX	xPX	hr/f	Spd	SBO	SB%	#Wk	DOM	DIS	RC/G	RAR	BPV	BPX	R$
08																																		
09																																		
10	WAS *	584	84	24	73	21	238	232	200	218	291	416	707	7	73	28	0.28	46	8	46	120	133	18%	114	27%	60%	6	50%	50%	3.79	-5.6	41	89	$18
11	WAS	573	72	21	66	17	236	241	283	222	305	414	718	9	71	30	0.34	44	16	40	132	130	14%	113	17%	74%	27	37%	41%	4.18	1.2	43	96	$14
12	WAS	594	82	17	56	20	247	234	281	234	302	402	704	7	68	34	0.24	47	19	34	123	109	13%	105	19%	77%	27	33%	52%	4.11	0.0	19	48	$16
1st Half		279	38	6	22	11	226	224	324	190	294	362	656	9	69	31	0.31	48	16	36	111	104	9%	99	22%	79%	13	31%	46%	3.54	-4.0	16	40	$11
2nd Half		315	44	11	34	9	267	243	247	275	308	438	746	6	68	36	0.19	46	22	32	133	114	16%	108	17%	75%	14	36%	57%	4.66	6.0	19	48	$21
13	**Proj**	**581**	**78**	**20**	**62**	**19**	**226**	**235**	**251**	**218**	**286**	**396**	**683**	**8**	**70**	**29**	**0.28**	**46**	**17**	**38**	**125**	**120**	**13%**	**108**	**21%**	**72%**				**3.69**	**-10.1**	**31**	**78**	**$14**

RAY MURPHY

Ethier,Andre

Age 31	Bats L	Pos RF	Health B	LIMA Plan	C+
Ht 6' 2"	Wt 205		PT/Exp A	Rand Var	-1
			Consist A	MM	3135

In between 2010 (finger) and 2011 (knee) injuries, had been flashing hot streaks that made us wonder if he had another step forward in him. After a healthy but stagnant 2012, the answer seems to be "apparently not." Regular 300-pt left/right OPS splits suggest he would net out as more valuable if he sat down vs. LHPs.

Yr	Tm	AB	R	HR	RBI	SB	BA	xBA	vL	vR	OB	Slg	OPS	bb%	ct%	h%	Eye	G	L	F	PX	xPX	hr/f	Spd	SBO	SB%	#Wk	DOM	DIS	RC/G	RAR	BPV	BPX	R$
08	LA	525	90	20	77	6	305	308	243	326	375	510	885	10	83	34	0.67	41	27	32	130	111	14%	101	6%	67%	27	56%	15%	6.95	26.0	87	171	$23
09	LA	596	92	31	106	6	272	296	194	302	350	508	859	11	81	29	0.62	38	20	42	148	132	15%	86	6%	60%	27	52%	22%	6.14	17.0	87	178	$22
10	LA	517	71	23	82	2	292	286	233	318	365	493	858	10	80	33	0.58	39	22	40	135	142	14%	88	2%	67%	25	56%	28%	6.46	18.8	66	143	$21
11	LA	487	67	11	62	0	292	265	220	321	367	421	788	11	79	35	0.56	44	25	31	97	80	9%	85	1%	0%	24	33%	42%	5.52	5.0	24	53	$16
12	LA	556	79	20	89	2	284	271	222	325	343	460	804	8	78	33	0.40	43	24	33	120	106	14%	85	3%	50%	26	54%	35%	5.57	6.6	41	103	$20
1st Half		275	36	10	55	1	291	279	241	325	350	491	841	8	76	35	0.37	41	25	34	144	119	14%	85	3%	50%	13	62%	31%	6.11	8.5	52	130	$23
2nd Half		281	43	10	34	1	278	264	202	326	337	431	767	8	80	32	0.44	46	23	31	98	95	14%	88	3%	50%	13	46%	38%	5.06	0.5	29	73	$18
13	Proj	508	73	19	75	2	297	273	228	333	362	474	835	9	79	35	0.48	42	24	34	118	106	14%	83	2%	52%				6.16	16.3	46	114	$19

Fielder,Prince

Age 29	Bats L	Pos 1B	Health A	LIMA Plan	B
Ht 5' 11"	Wt 275		PT/Exp A	Rand Var	-1
			Consist C	MM	4045

Doubled down on 2011's ct% gains, trading a little power for BA in the process, but net return was stable per R$. Even though 1H power suffered in the transition, the overall trend is more contact and more LDs. Hard to find fault with that, and as a result is a healthier skill set that can support... UP: 40-120-.320.

Yr	Tm	AB	R	HR	RBI	SB	BA	xBA	vL	vR	OB	Slg	OPS	bb%	ct%	h%	Eye	G	L	F	PX	xPX	hr/f	Spd	SBO	SB%	#Wk	DOM	DIS	RC/G	RAR	BPV	BPX	R$
08	MIL	588	86	34	102	3	276	276	239	295	366	507	873	13	77	30	0.63	41	19	40	146	142	18%	36	3%	60%	27	59%	26%	6.48	20.0	69	135	$21
09	MIL	591	103	46	141	2	299	302	292	303	409	602	1012	16	77	32	0.80	41	16	43	187	175	23%	37	2%	40%	27	74%	7%	8.85	58.2	105	214	$32
10	MIL	578	94	32	83	1	261	266	226	280	383	471	854	16	76	29	0.83	42	18	40	138	134	18%	22	0%	100%	27	52%	33%	6.23	15.8	61	133	$19
11	MIL	569	95	38	120	1	299	306	282	306	410	566	976	16	81	31	1.01	43	20	37	170	145	22%	39	1%	50%	27	74%	19%	8.40	48.7	107	238	$32
12	DET	581	83	30	108	1	313	304	289	328	401	528	929	13	86	33	1.01	41	25	33	126	128	18%	39	0%	100%	27	67%	11%	7.88	40.5	81	203	$30
1st Half		293	42	12	52	1	297	298	295	298	370	488	858	10	85	32	0.79	44	25	32	116	110	15%	50	1%	100%	13	54%	15%	6.58	9.8	73	183	$27
2nd Half		288	41	18	56	0	330	312	283	360	431	569	1000	15	86	34	1.24	39	26	35	136	147	21%	29	0%	0%	14	79%	7%	9.33	30.1	88	220	$32
13	Proj	570	87	33	107	1	301	292	275	315	401	534	935	14	82	32	0.94	42	22	36	139	138	19%	33	1%	68%				7.80	38.1	81	204	$29

Figgins,Chone

Age 35	Bats B	Pos LF	Health B	LIMA Plan	F
Ht 5' 8"	Wt 180		PT/Exp C	Rand Var	+4
			Consist C	MM	0301

Last winter, you could have looked at that 2011 collapse, and reasonably concluded that regression would drag his value upward, creating a profit opportunity. As it turns out, you would have been very wrong. Posting a BA lower than your LD% is just plain hard, and he's now done it two years running. He's done.

Yr	Tm	AB	R	HR	RBI	SB	BA	xBA	vL	vR	OB	Slg	OPS	bb%	ct%	h%	Eye	G	L	F	PX	xPX	hr/f	Spd	SBO	SB%	#Wk	DOM	DIS	RC/G	RAR	BPV	BPX	R$
08	LAA	453	72	1	22	34	276	240	272	277	363	318	681	12	82	33	0.78	46	24	30	33	47	1%	118	27%	72%	23	13%	39%	4.11	-5.8	15	29	$18
09	LAA	615	114	5	54	42	298	253	246	323	397	393	790	14	81	36	0.89	41	24	36	65	50	3%	126	24%	71%	27	33%	33%	5.61	18.7	48	98	$31
10	SEA	602	62	1	35	42	259	232	286	247	340	306	646	11	81	32	0.65	47	21	32	38	24	1%	120	28%	74%	27	15%	63%	3.64	-16.3	9	20	$19
11	SEA	288	24	1	15	11	188	238	152	204	243	243	486	7	85	22	0.50	50	18	32	42	31	1%	99	27%	65%	19	37%	42%	1.80	-25.7	20	44	-$3
12	SEA	166	18	2	11	4	181	207	183	179	265	271	536	10	71	24	0.40	40	23	37	64	54	5%	92	13%	80%	24	21%	63%	2.28	-12.1	-8	-20	-$2
1st Half		138	13	2	10	3	181	200	188	178	242	275	517	7	71	24	0.28	38	20	43	70	59	5%	80	11%	100%	14	21%	64%	2.16	-10.7	-15	-38	-$2
2nd Half		28	5	0	1	1	179	254	167	188	361	250	611	22	71	25	1.00	53	37	11	36	28	0%	103	17%	50%	10	20%	60%	2.67	-1.8	-4	-10	-$3
13	Proj	95	11	0	6	5	229	239	214	237	302	288	591	10	79	29	0.50	47	25	28	45	36	2%	83	23%	74%				2.92	-5.1	3	8	$2

Flaherty,Ryan

Age 26	Bats L	Pos 2B	Health A	LIMA Plan	F
Ht 6' 3"	Wt 210		PT/Exp F	Rand Var	-3
			Consist B	MM	3101

6-19-.216 in 153 AB at BAL. xBA hates this Rule 5er's "swing at everything and don't hit it often enough" approach. But average power and speed in an LH-hitting middle infielder is probably enough of a calling-card skill to keep him employed for a while, if not fanalytically relevant.

Yr	Tm	AB	R	HR	RBI	SB	BA	xBA	vL	vR	OB	Slg	OPS	bb%	ct%	h%	Eye	G	L	F	PX	xPX	hr/f	Spd	SBO	SB%	#Wk	DOM	DIS	RC/G	RAR	BPV	BPX	R$
08																																		
09																																		
10	aa	71	7	1	6	1	154	222			230	210	440	9	81	18	0.53				39			99	5%	100%				1.49		-6	0	-$3
11	a/a	475	48	13	57	3	224	244			275	365	640	7	75	27	0.28				104			83	10%	31%				3.10		18	0	$5
12	BAL *	191	19	8	21	1	224	208	250	213	254	380	633	4	72	27	0.14	43	13	44	96	107	13%	117	3%	100%	24	21%	67%	3.19	-5.6	-2	-5	$1
1st Half		85	6	1	5	1	188	154	333	177	207	224	430	2	69	26	0.08	50	12	38	21	79	5%	106	6%	100%	12	0%	92%	1.49	-7.5	-84	-210	-$5
2nd Half		106	13	7	16	0	253	245	167	258	290	505	795	5	74	28	0.21	34	14	52	151	139	19%	109	0%	0%	12	42%	42%	5.00	2.3	51	128	$5
13	Proj	233	24	11	27	1	226	224	231	226	264	411	674	5	74	26	0.19	40	13	46	117	115	13%	105	6%	48%				3.49	-5.5	20	49	$4

Flores,Jesus

Age 28	Bats R	Pos CA	Health A	LIMA Plan	F
Ht 6' 1"	Wt 210		PT/Exp F	Rand Var	+4
			Consist A	MM	2001

Another year removed from 2009 torn labrum, with skills in transition. The pre-injury power hasn't come back, but there's more contact... not that anything is happening afterwards, but contact is good. He's still young for a catcher, and these sample sizes are small. There may yet be a sneaky-serviceable 2nd CA here.

Yr	Tm	AB	R	HR	RBI	SB	BA	xBA	vL	vR	OB	Slg	OPS	bb%	ct%	h%	Eye	G	L	F	PX	xPX	hr/f	Spd	SBO	SB%	#Wk	DOM	DIS	RC/G	RAR	BPV	BPX	R$
08	WAS *	360	30	9	65	0	236	245	308	238	279	372	651	6	72	30	0.22	37	25	38	103	101	9%	68	1%	0%	20	25%	55%	3.42	-9.4	-4	-8	$2
09	WAS	93	13	4	15	0	301	232	276	313	375	505	880	11	72	38	0.42	28	18	54	128	138	11%	148	0%	0%	6	33%	33%	6.91	6.7	35	71	$2
10																																		
11	WAS *	295	17	5	24	0	196	247	200	212	218	306	524	3	69	27	0.09	37	31	32	99	52	5%	63	0%	0%	13	23%	69%	2.12	-20.1	-30	-67	-$4
12	WAS	277	22	6	26	1	213	228	189	225	248	329	577	4	79	25	0.22	43	18	39	78	72	7%	84	6%	33%	26	23%	58%	2.56	-14.8	3	8	-$1
1st Half		159	13	3	13	1	252	247	163	291	292	384	675	5	79	30	0.27	45	20	36	93	79	7%	93	9%	33%	12	25%	50%	3.63	-2.8	22	55	$1
2nd Half		118	9	3	13	0	161	198	220	130	189	254	443	3	78	18	0.15	40	16	43	57	62	8%	73	0%	0%	14	21%	64%	1.46	-10.7	-26	-65	-$3
13	Proj	167	14	4	19	0	247	229	234	252	282	376	658	5	75	31	0.20	38	22	40	90	78	8%	85	2%	31%				3.55	-3.3	-5	-12	$2

Florimon Jr.,Pedro

Age 26	Bats B	Pos SS	Health A	LIMA Plan	F
Ht 6' 2"	Wt 180		PT/Exp D	Rand Var	-2
			Consist C	MM	1201

1-10-.219 with 3 SB in 137 AB at MIN. Searching for a fanalytic skill? No sign of a third digit in the PX column. Average Spd might be something... no, wait, SB% says he should be given a red light. How about BA? Not with that ct%. Reputed to have a glove, that's going to have to be enough. Safe to disregard.

Yr	Tm	AB	R	HR	RBI	SB	BA	xBA	vL	vR	OB	Slg	OPS	bb%	ct%	h%	Eye	G	L	F	PX	xPX	hr/f	Spd	SBO	SB%	#Wk	DOM	DIS	RC/G	RAR	BPV	BPX	R$
08																																		
09	aa	22	0	0	1	0	89	120			127	89	216	4	58	15	0.10				0			100	0%	0%				0.32		-160	0	-$3
10	aa	120	12	1	9	3	159	196			213	202	415	6	72	21	0.24				36			99	18%	73%				1.33		-43	0	-$3
11	BAL *	462	44	7	51	12	234	310		125	298	347	645	8	71	31	0.31	50	50	0	93	2	0%	103	23%	47%				3.14	-11.0	2	4	$6
12	MIN *	561	54	4	37	14	219	223	255	200	266	295	561	6	70	30	0.22	58	20	22	62	32	4%	109	19%	57%	8	13%	50%	2.45	-25.7	-26	-65	$3
1st Half		311	28	3	15	10	216	197			264	290	554	6	69	30	0.21				57			120	23%	59%				2.37		-36	-90	$3
2nd Half		250	26	1	22	4	221	231	255	200	269	300	569	6	72	30	0.23	58	20	22	67	32	4%	104	13%	53%	8	13%	50%	2.55	-11.4	-18	-45	$2
13	Proj	163	16	1	14	4	215	225	250	196	269	290	558	7	71	30	0.25	58	20	22	63	29	4%	102	19%	55%				2.40	-8.3	-24	-59	$1

Flowers,Tyler

Age 27	Bats R	Pos CA	Health A	LIMA Plan	F
Ht 6' 4"	Wt 245		PT/Exp F	Rand Var	-2
			Consist C	MM	5101

Amid a lot of small-sample size noise, we can say two things for certain: he has pop in the bat, and he strikes out WAY too much. More AB may be coming his way, but struggles vR suggest that's a bad idea. If he ends up in a job share where bulk of his AB come vL, that's when he gets interesting. UP: 300 AB, 15 HR.

Yr	Tm	AB	R	HR	RBI	SB	BA	xBA	vL	vR	OB	Slg	OPS	bb%	ct%	h%	Eye	G	L	F	PX	xPX	hr/f	Spd	SBO	SB%	#Wk	DOM	DIS	RC/G	RAR	BPV	BPX	R$
08																																		
09	CHW *	369	62	15	49	3	270	243	250	125	377	469	846	15	65	38	0.49	50	13	38	160	89	0%	89	2%	100%	5	20%	80%	6.23	22.1	42	86	$11
10	CHW *	357	34	14	40	1	186	177	0	125	283	363	646	12	59	27	0.33	33	0	67	158	120	0%	94	3%	57%	5	0%	100%	3.20	-10.7	5	11	-$1
11	CHW *	332	41	19	41	2	223	210	135	247	320	432	752	13	58	32	0.34	32	16	51	179	180	13%	82	3%	61%	10	40%	50%	4.50	3.7	17	38	$6
12	CHW	136	19	7	13	2	213	225	269	179	277	412	689	8	59	30	0.21	53	18	29	165	87	30%	74	11%	67%	26	27%	69%	3.64	-2.0	4	10	$1
1st Half		54	8	2	2	2	167	208	286	91	224	315	539	7	54	26	0.16	55	24	21	137	118	33%	77	22%	100%	12	25%	75%	2.30	-3.4	-29	-73	-$3
2nd Half		82	11	5	11	0	244	233	258	235	311	476	787	9	62	33	0.26	52	14	34	181	69	29%	77	5%	0%	14	29%	64%	4.74	1.3	23	58	$3
13	Proj	219	29	12	29	2	231	222	235	229	312	441	753	10	59	33	0.29	45	17	38	172	126	24%	67	6%	68%				4.52	2.0	15	38	$5

RAY MURPHY

Forsythe,Logan

Age 26	Bats R	Pos 2B	Health	C	LIMA Plan	D
Ht 6' 1"	Wt 205		PT/Exp	D	Rand Var	-1
			Consist	B	MM	2403

6-28-.273 with 8 SB in 315 AB at SD. Made gains in two areas—ct% and SB%—that have the potential to boost him into fanalytic relevance. xPX also hints at some power growth, well-aligned with shortening PETCO fences. Serious struggles vs. RHP (career .595 OPS) temper our optimism, but still... UP: 15 HR, 15 SB.

Yr	Tm	AB	R	HR	RBI	SB	BA	xBA	vL	vR	OB	Slg	OPS	bb%	ct%	h%	Eye	G	L	F	PX	xPX	hr/f	Spd	SBO	SB%	#Wk	DOM	DIS	RC/G	RAR	BPV	BPX	R$
08																																		
09	aa	244	30	2	25	4	236	206			331	312	643	12	69	33	0.46				57			114	5%	100%				3.55		-18	0	$1
10	aa	392	56	2	32	14	215	212			329	283	612	15	71	29	0.60				62			102	15%	72%				3.06		-4	0	$3
11	SD *	328	36	4	32	8	226	217	217	212	297	326	623	9	70	31	0.34	43	20	37	87	98	0%	87	16%	57%	15	33%	60%	3.06	-13.0	-4	-9	$3
12	SD *	373	53	7	32	10	262	249	384	222	328	381	709	9	79	32	0.47	36	29	35	77	107	7%	147	11%	83%	18	28%	33%	4.39	0.4	33	83	$9
1st Half		125	15	2	12	3	237	239	167	306	319	377	696	11	70	33	0.40	38	31	31	94	138	6%	174	11%	75%	4	25%	50%	4.02	-0.9	12	30	$0
2nd Half		248	38	5	20	7	274	257	432	198	333	383	716	8	83	31	0.52	36	28	36	69	99	7%	110	11%	88%	14	29%	29%	4.59	2.3	35	88	$14
13	Proj	314	41	7	28	8	243	235	280	226	321	367	688	10	74	31	0.45	39	25	36	86	108	8%	125	13%	73%				3.96	-2.8	21	52	$5

Fowler,Dexter

Age 27	Bats B	Pos CF	Health	B	LIMA Plan	C
Ht 6' 4"	Wt 190		PT/Exp	B	Rand Var	-5
			Consist	C	MM	4525

Do we believe in this breakout? PRO: hit equally well vL/vR; subtle power growth fully validated (and then some) by xPX. CON: ct% and xBA weak; has no idea how to turn Spd into SB; 2H h% unsustainable, massive home/road split (.984 OPS home/.720 road). Best use: home-only play in daily games.

Yr	Tm	AB	R	HR	RBI	SB	BA	xBA	vL	vR	OB	Slg	OPS	bb%	ct%	h%	Eye	G	L	F	PX	xPX	hr/f	Spd	SBO	SB%	#Wk	DOM	DIS	RC/G	RAR	BPV	BPX	R$
08	COL *	447	70	7	47	15	296	273	364	0	362	441	803	9	78	36	0.48	62	14	24	100	53	0%	135	18%	60%	5	0%	60%	5.51	10.4	51	100	$17
09	COL	433	73	4	34	27	266	247	321	240	364	406	770	13	73	35	0.58	42	21	37	104	83	4%	159	27%	73%	26	38%	38%	5.10	5.3	50	102	$15
10	COL *	545	87	7	44	14	266	261	260	260	346	422	768	11	76	34	0.50	45	22	33	107	95	6%	165	14%	63%	24	38%	29%	4.94	4.0	51	111	$15
11	COL *	578	92	6	49	13	251	250	254	270	338	406	743	12	73	34	0.48	43	21	35	119	102	4%	155	15%	56%	22	41%	27%	4.48	-3.5	50	111	$12
12	COL	454	72	13	53	12	300	249	315	293	391	474	864	13	72	39	0.53	39	27	34	115	125	12%	169	10%	71%	27	30%	48%	6.67	25.1	43	108	$20
1st Half		224	43	10	35	7	286	267	260	299	382	536	918	14	70	37	0.52	43	22	34	163	145	19%	171	11%	88%	13	46%	31%	7.42	16.7	79	198	$24
2nd Half		230	29	3	18	5	313	237	379	287	399	413	812	13	73	42	0.54	35	32	33	69	108	6%	146	10%	56%	14	14%	64%	5.91	7.2	3	8	$16
13	Proj	491	77	16	48	17	278	260	292	271	367	474	841	12	73	35	0.53	41	25	34	130	109	13%	160	16%	70%				6.03	17.9	61	154	$21

Francisco,Ben

Age 31	Bats R	Pos RF LF	Health	B	LIMA Plan	F
Ht 6' 1"	Wt 185		PT/Exp	F	Rand Var	+2
			Consist	B	MM	2211

4-15-.240 in 192 AB at TOR/HOU/TAM. Back in the late-aughts, there was some power/speed intrigue in this skill set, but it never materialized. Now there's just a corner OF with a free-swinging approach, average power and speed, who doesn't even merit a bad-side platoon role or a place on your draft list.

Yr	Tm	AB	R	HR	RBI	SB	BA	xBA	vL	vR	OB	Slg	OPS	bb%	ct%	h%	Eye	G	L	F	PX	xPX	hr/f	Spd	SBO	SB%	#Wk	DOM	DIS	RC/G	RAR	BPV	BPX	R$
08	CLE *	539	72	16	59	6	254	243	269	265	317	409	726	8	78	30	0.43	34	18	48	108	136	9%	120	7%	68%	23	35%	26%	4.40	-7.3	40	78	$10
09	2 TM	405	58	15	46	14	257	271	247	260	321	447	767	9	80	29	0.46	38	18	44	127	122	11%	93	22%	67%	27	52%	33%	4.76	-1.1	67	137	$12
10	PHI	179	24	6	28	8	268	265	284	253	321	441	763	7	80	30	0.40	38	17	45	123	136	9%	82	19%	100%	27	37%	37%	5.22	1.8	64	139	$7
11	PHI	250	24	6	34	4	244	235	245	243	332	364	696	12	83	27	0.79	40	17	43	79	105	7%	99	10%	50%	26	42%	38%	3.92	-7.0	38	84	$4
12	3 TM *	228	15	4	16	0	229	252	213	265	277	362	639	6	76	28	0.28	35	26	39	102	104	7%	92	2%	0%	22	32%	45%	3.25	-11.1	12	30	-$1
1st Half		78	6	0	1	0	208	261	286	143	256	290	547	6	86	24	0.46	39	25	36	69	107	0%	90	7%	0%	8	50%	25%	2.25	-6.8	24	60	-$6
2nd Half		150	9	4	15	0	240	247	182	286	288	400	688	6	71	31	0.23	34	26	40	121	103	9%	96	0%	0%	14	21%	57%	3.86	-5.1	5	13	$1
13	Proj	194	18	4	20	3	240	246	248	233	299	376	676	8	79	28	0.41	37	21	41	96	112	7%	89	9%	63%				3.72	-7.5	30	75	$3

Francisco,Juan

Age 26	Bats L	Pos 3B	Health	A	LIMA Plan	F
Ht 6' 2"	Wt 245		PT/Exp	D	Rand Var	+1
			Consist	A	MM	4013

Chipper's heir apparent? Above-average PX is something to build on, but it needs more contact to flourish. Unfair to judge him on part-time 2012 work: K'd in more than half his PH AB, made better contact (67%) in his starts. If that earns him a regular role, then maybe there's very speculative hope for... UP: 2011.

Yr	Tm	AB	R	HR	RBI	SB	BA	xBA	vL	vR	OB	Slg	OPS	bb%	ct%	h%	Eye	G	L	F	PX	xPX	hr/f	Spd	SBO	SB%	#Wk	DOM	DIS	RC/G	RAR	BPV	BPX	R$
08																																		
09	CIN *	550	73	27	87	5	284	317	333	444	314	497	811	4	76	33	0.18	57	29	14	138	66	50%	81	6%	70%	4	50%	50%	5.51	14.0	47	96	$20
10	CIN *	363	39	16	53	1	258	269	222	283	291	477	768	4	69	33	0.15	60	11	29	168	45	10%	94	3%	44%	10	20%	60%	4.72	1.1	42	91	$9
11	CIN *	393	44	15	52	1	261	278	143	278	282	454	736	3	75	32	0.11	45	25	30	142	125	14%	70	1%	100%	8	38%	25%	4.44	-1.9	38	84	$10
12	ATL	192	17	9	32	1	234	240	189	245	276	432	708	5	64	32	0.16	43	24	33	158	114	23%	50	6%	50%	25	36%	56%	3.90	-4.0	2	5	$2
1st Half		111	10	5	17	1	225	246	269	212	246	414	660	3	67	29	0.08	44	24	32	144	105	21%	59	12%	50%	13	23%	69%	3.23	-4.6	2	5	$2
2nd Half		81	7	4	15	0	247	229	0	286	315	457	771	9	59	36	0.24	43	23	34	181	127	25%	55	0%	0%	12	50%	42%	4.87	0.7	4	10	$2
13	Proj	266	27	10	42	1	252	247	150	273	290	436	726	5	68	33	0.17	46	22	32	141	110	18%	56	3%	59%				4.27	-2.4	11	27	$7

Francoeur,Jeff

Age 29	Bats R	Pos RF	Health	A	LIMA Plan	D
Ht 6' 4"	Wt 210		PT/Exp	A	Rand Var	+2
			Consist	D	MM	3213

Following 2011, KC chose to deal Melky Cabrera and extend this guy for two years. That's an "oops," even if they knew about Melky's chemistry problems. Gave back all of 2011's gains, plus forgot how to hit LHPs (his only consistent skill). May have some platoon utility, but should never get 500+ AB again.

Yr	Tm	AB	R	HR	RBI	SB	BA	xBA	vL	vR	OB	Slg	OPS	bb%	ct%	h%	Eye	G	L	F	PX	xPX	hr/f	Spd	SBO	SB%	#Wk	DOM	DIS	RC/G	RAR	BPV	BPX	R$
08	ATL	599	70	11	71	0	239	256	210	251	285	359	644	6	81	28	0.35	45	21	34	82	71	7%	91	1%	0%	27	26%	44%	3.40	-26.0	22	43	$4
09	2 NL	593	72	15	76	6	280	266	344	256	307	423	730	4	84	31	0.25	38	21	41	89	106	7%	109	7%	60%	26	46%	27%	4.52	-5.7	44	90	$16
10	2 TM	454	52	13	65	8	249	238	300	231	295	383	679	6	82	28	0.37	41	14	45	86	107	8%	108	10%	73%	27	37%	37%	3.83	-13.9	37	80	$10
11	KC	601	77	20	87	22	285	276	302	279	326	476	802	6	80	33	0.30	40	20	40	137	113	10%	101	23%	69%	26	62%	23%	5.36	8.7	74	164	$27
12	KC	561	58	16	49	4	235	252	225	239	279	378	657	6	79	27	0.29	45	21	34	93	106	11%	95	9%	36%	27	30%	41%	3.35	-25.8	21	53	$7
1st Half		292	28	7	24	1	257	257	253	258	289	390	679	4	82	29	0.24	46	21	33	86	96	9%	92	6%	25%	13	23%	38%	3.70	-11.3	22	55	$8
2nd Half		269	30	9	25	3	212	247	200	217	269	364	633	7	76	25	0.32	44	21	35	102	118	13%	98	13%	43%	14	36%	43%	3.00	-17.0	22	55	$6
13	Proj	363	41	11	41	6	249	254	255	247	293	404	696	6	80	29	0.30	43	20	38	101	108	10%	93	13%	57%				3.88	-12.2	37	92	$9

Frandsen,Kevin

Age 31	Bats R	Pos 3B	Health	B	LIMA Plan	F
Ht 6' 0"	Wt 185		PT/Exp	D	Rand Var	-1
			Consist	B	MM	1121

2-14-.338 in 195 AB at PHI. Turned heads with a late-season hot streak, but that was driven by a fluky 37% h%. When you put the ball in play nine times out of 10, you at least create the opportunity for good things to happen. Then again, this many GBs from a non-speedster isn't a winning value proposition.

Yr	Tm	AB	R	HR	RBI	SB	BA	xBA	vL	vR	OB	Slg	OPS	bb%	ct%	h%	Eye	G	L	F	PX	xPX	hr/f	Spd	SBO	SB%	#Wk	DOM	DIS	RC/G	RAR	BPV	BPX	R$
08	SF	1	0	0	0	0	0	0		0	0	0	0	0	100	0	0.00	100	0	0	0	5	0%	108	0%	0%	1	0%	0%	0.00	-0.1	2	4	-$2
09	SF *	477	47	8	37	2	223	252	154	135	251	315	566	4	91	23	0.39	55	14	32	53	120	0%	105	7%	28%	9	22%	44%	2.48	-31.3	30	61	-$1
10	LAA *	359	45	2	24	4	221	266	226	262	255	294	549	4	90	24	0.43	56	15	28	55	51	0%	106	8%	78%	16	44%	19%	2.47	-23.5	39	85	$0
11	a/a	288	23	4	28	7	234	244			256	320	576	3	86	26	0.20				57			92	20%	58%				2.59		21	0	$2
12	PHI *	586	52	3	39	1	272	287	400	308	295	361	656	3	90	30	0.34	54	24	22	62	48	5%	98	6%	20%	10	40%	30%	3.56	-17.7	32	80	$8
1st Half		297	23	0	19	1	231	251			254	303	557	3	90	26	0.29				57			82	12%	23%				2.35		24	60	$2
2nd Half		289	29	3	19	0	313	294	400	308	337	420	758	4	91	34	0.39	54	24	22	67	48	5%	114	1%	0%	10	40%	30%	5.19	4.7	42	105	$14
13	Proj	135	13	1	10	1	255	259	269	248	281	332	613	4	89	28	0.33	55	18	27	54	78	2%	97	8%	46%				3.08	-6.0	29	72	$2

Frazier,Todd

Age 27	Bats R	Pos 3B 1B	Health	A	LIMA Plan	B
Ht 6' 3"	Wt 215		PT/Exp	C	Rand Var	-2
			Consist	B	MM	4325

19-67-.273 in 422 AB at CIN. Muddled through 1H, then leapt forward when Votto injury got him in the lineup every day. This wasn't some h% or hr/f anomaly, either: ct% jumped in 2H, xPX moved in lockstep with PX. He should be a lineup fixture now, so with 500 AB and just a touch more growth... UP: 30 HR.

Yr	Tm	AB	R	HR	RBI	SB	BA	xBA	vL	vR	OB	Slg	OPS	bb%	ct%	h%	Eye	G	L	F	PX	xPX	hr/f	Spd	SBO	SB%	#Wk	DOM	DIS	RC/G	RAR	BPV	BPX	R$
08																																		
09	a/a	514	57	15	64	8	268	289			323	446	768	7	83	30	0.46				118			81	14%	46%				4.74		62	0	$13
10	aaa	480	54	14	50	11	224	245			277	383	660	7	69	29	0.24				125			100	16%	70%				3.44		24	0	$7
11	CIN *	427	51	18	48	13	221	255	360	195	275	396	671	7	71	27	0.25	48	21	31	130	138	23%	89	20%	74%	12	42%	50%	3.53	-15.8	31	69	$8
12	CIN *	461	58	20	72	5	265	258	298	262	321	480	801	8	75	32	0.32	33	22	45	143	127	13%	120	7%	72%	25	52%	28%	5.32	7.8	59	148	$15
1st Half		193	18	8	27	3	245	252	304	241	305	479	783	8	70	31	0.28	24	27	50	168	108	13%	116	11%	76%	11	55%	27%	4.91	1.5	60	150	$7
2nd Half		268	40	12	45	2	280	261	295	274	332	481	814	7	78	32	0.36	38	20	42	127	136	13%	112	4%	67%	14	50%	29%	5.62	7.4	55	138	$20
13	Proj	520	63	25	70	7	260	264	305	242	313	477	790	7	74	31	0.30	38	22	40	147	130	16%	108	8%	76%				5.12	8.3	56	140	$17

RAY MURPHY

Freeman,Freddie

Age 23	Bats L	Pos 1B	Health	A	LIMA Plan	B
Ht 6' 5"	Wt 225		PT/Exp	B	Rand Var	+1
			Consist	A	MM	4135

Early-season hand, vision issues zapped 1H power. At age 23, that 2H is what should draw you in. Odds of further growth supported by enticing PX and shedding of extreme GB tilt. xBA suggests he'll split '11 and '12 BA, especially with return of '10-'11 h%. Eye growth gives hope for even more. For now, UP: .290-30-110

Yr	Tm	AB	R	HR	RBI	SB	BA	xBA	vL	vR	OB	Slg	OPS	bb%	ct%	h%	Eye	G	L	F	PX	xPX	hr/f	Spd	SBO	SB%	#Wk	DOM	DIS	RC/G	RAR	BPV	BPX	R$
08																																		
09	aa	149	14	2	23	0	238	251			291	326	617	7	86	27	0.54				60			80	0%	0%				3.17		17	0	$0
10	ATL *	485	64	16	74	5	285	272	667	95	335	457	792	7	79	33	0.36	44	19	38	122	120	17%	91	6%	70%	5	20%	40%	5.42	0.0	52	113	$17
11	ATL	571	67	21	76	4	282	260	247	299	343	448	791	8	75	34	0.37	42	23	35	122	138	14%	73	5%	50%	27	33%	44%	5.35	-1.2	29	64	$20
12	ATL	540	91	23	94	2	259	271	237	276	338	456	793	11	76	30	0.50	37	26	37	132	137	15%	81	1%	100%	27	44%	33%	5.32	-1.6	55	138	$18
1st Half		248	41	9	44	0	262	277	202	299	312	444	756	7	74	32	0.28	35	33	33	129	137	15%	88	0%	0%	13	38%	46%	4.78	-4.1	33	83	$15
2nd Half		292	50	14	50	2	257	267	261	253	358	466	824	14	78	29	0.71	39	20	40	135	137	15%	80	2%	100%	14	50%	21%	5.77	3.5	69	173	$21
13	Proj	**570**	**82**	**25**	**97**	**3**	**267**	**273**	**241**	**283**	**336**	**462**	**798**	**9**	**77**	**31**	**0.46**	**39**	**25**	**36**	**129**	**137**	**15%**	**75**	**3%**	**69%**				**5.38**	**0.3**	**52**	**129**	**$18**

Freese,David

Age 30	Bats R	Pos 3B	Health	D	LIMA Plan	C
Ht 6' 2"	Wt 220		PT/Exp	C	Rand Var	-3
			Consist	A	MM	3125

'11 October hero stayed healthy enough for first 500-AB season...at age 30. Problem is, friendly hr/f drove HR spike more than anything. Hits too many GB to be a reliable power source. And xBA says he's no .290 lock. 2H calf, wrist, ankle woes remind us that chronically injured players don't get healthy in their 30s.

Yr	Tm	AB	R	HR	RBI	SB	BA	xBA	vL	vR	OB	Slg	OPS	bb%	ct%	h%	Eye	G	L	F	PX	xPX	hr/f	Spd	SBO	SB%	#Wk	DOM	DIS	RC/G	RAR	BPV	BPX	R$
08	aaa	464	62	18	68	4	253	253			297	430	728	6	73	31	0.23				124			89	6%	61%				4.31		27	0	$10
09	STL *	247	31	8	38	1	258	228	176	500	313	422	736	7	72	33	0.29	44	12	44	121	145	9%	77	1%	100%	4	25%	50%	4.57	-0.2	14	29	$4
10	STL	240	28	4	36	1	296	248	357	271	352	404	757	8	75	38	0.36	49	22	29	83	102	8%	100	3%	50%	13	15%	54%	5.10	3.3	2	4	$7
11	STL	333	41	10	55	1	297	273	347	283	345	441	786	7	77	36	0.32	52	25	23	102	121	17%	73	1%	100%	20	25%	55%	5.54	8.5	23	51	$12
12	STL	501	70	20	79	3	293	265	320	285	366	467	833	10	76	35	0.47	52	22	26	116	119	20%	89	4%	50%	27	33%	30%	6.06	20.3	33	83	$20
1st Half		268	35	13	48	1	280	264	300	275	330	481	811	7	74	34	0.28	46	22	32	135	139	21%	82	4%	33%	13	38%	31%	5.47	6.8	33	83	$22
2nd Half		233	35	7	31	2	309	266	333	298	404	451	854	14	78	37	0.73	58	21	20	96	97	19%	94	3%	67%	14	29%	29%	6.68	13.3	32	80	$18
13	Proj	**413**	**55**	**14**	**64**	**2**	**281**	**264**	**318**	**268**	**347**	**437**	**783**	**9**	**76**	**34**	**0.42**	**52**	**23**	**25**	**106**	**115**	**18%**	**81**	**3%**	**60%**				**5.33**	**8.7**	**25**	**63**	**$15**

Furcal,Rafael

Age 35	Bats B	Pos SS	Health	F	LIMA Plan	C+
Ht 5' 8"	Wt 190		PT/Exp	C	Rand Var	0
			Consist	D	MM	1225

Torn elbow ligament puts 2013 at risk, but even when healthy, this was far from the Furcal of old. All that's left is great plate control. Marginal wheels and slap hitter profile won't bring back BA. And 20 SB are a distant memory as he enters mid-30s with fading green light. Even if he avoids surgery, an end-gamer at best.

Yr	Tm	AB	R	HR	RBI	SB	BA	xBA	vL	vR	OB	Slg	OPS	bb%	ct%	h%	Eye	G	L	F	PX	xPX	hr/f	Spd	SBO	SB%	#Wk	DOM	DIS	RC/G	RAR	BPV	BPX	R$
08	LA	143	34	5	16	8	357	321	365	352	436	573	1009	12	88	38	1.18	49	19	32	131	93	13%	124	21%	73%	7	86%	14%	9.68	20.7	124	243	$10
09	LA	613	92	9	47	12	269	274	296	261	335	375	711	9	85	30	0.69	53	19	28	66	75	6%	118	10%	67%	26	31%	31%	4.34	4.1	45	92	$14
10	LA	383	66	8	43	22	300	287	277	310	366	460	826	9	84	34	0.67	47	20	33	102	77	8%	121	22%	85%	21	57%	33%	6.30	23.3	85	185	$20
11	2 NL	333	44	8	28	9	231	276	235	230	291	348	639	8	88	24	0.72	54	18	28	75	65	10%	74	17%	64%	18	67%	28%	3.27	-8.5	55	122	$5
12	STL	477	69	5	49	12	264	261	284	255	326	346	672	8	88	29	0.77	54	19	27	51	46	4%	101	11%	75%	22	32%	32%	3.93	-2.4	42	105	$12
1st Half		300	52	5	31	9	280	265	300	271	347	377	724	9	88	31	0.86	57	17	26	59	47	7%	95	12%	75%	13	38%	15%	4.65	5.5	49	123	$20
2nd Half		177	17	0	18	3	237	252	262	223	289	294	583	7	88	27	0.62	48	22	29	37	44	0%	101	9%	75%	9	22%	56%	2.86	-6.1	25	63	$0
13	Proj	**417**	**59**	**6**	**41**	**9**	**261**	**268**	**273**	**256**	**323**	**368**	**691**	**8**	**87**	**29**	**0.72**	**52**	**20**	**29**	**66**	**59**	**6%**	**98**	**11%**	**66%**				**4.05**	**0.5**	**51**	**127**	**$11**

Galvis,Freddy

Age 23	Bats B	Pos 2B	Health	D	LIMA Plan	F
Ht 5' 10"	Wt 170		PT/Exp	C	Rand Var	+3
			Consist	B	MM	1211

Former all-glove, no-bat prospect endured fractured back, PED suspension on way to miserable year. Previous Spd flashes are useless with sub-.300 OBP, and that's a mark that won't move given chronically dismal bb%. You wantBA or SB upside out of young middle infielders. There's none of that here.

Yr	Tm	AB	R	HR	RBI	SB	BA	xBA	vL	vR	OB	Slg	OPS	bb%	ct%	h%	Eye	G	L	F	PX	xPX	hr/f	Spd	SBO	SB%	#Wk	DOM	DIS	RC/G	RAR	BPV	BPX	R$
08																																		
09	aa	61	5	1	4	0	186	229			207	230	438	3	88	20	0.23				21			102	9%	0%				1.35		-8	0	-$3
10	aa	501	44	4	36	11	206	227			240	268	508	4	81	25	0.24				44			111	15%	72%				2.06		0	0	-$1
11	a/a	543	63	7	35	19	250	245			283	347	630	4	82	29	0.26				70			107	26%	57%				3.10		29	0	$11
12	PHI	190	14	3	24	0	226	265	267	208	254	363	617	4	85	25	0.24	41	21	38	95	116	5%	76	0%	0%	10	30%	50%	3.04	-7.5	35	88	-$1
1st Half		190	14	3	24	0	226	265	267	208	254	363	617	4	85	25	0.24	41	21	38	95	116	5%	76	0%	0%	10	30%	50%	3.04	-7.0	35	88	-$1
2nd Half																																		
13	Proj	**235**	**21**	**3**	**21**	**4**	**233**	**245**	**274**	**213**	**265**	**340**	**605**	**4**	**83**	**27**	**0.25**	**41**	**21**	**38**	**72**	**104**	**5%**	**88**	**13%**	**65%**				**2.93**	**-9.5**	**23**	**58**	**$3**

Gamel,Mat

Age 27	Bats L	Pos 1B	Health	F	LIMA Plan	D
Ht 6' 0"	Wt 223		PT/Exp	D	Rand Var	0
			Consist	B	MM	3213

Torn ACL in May prevented first extended everyday MLB look. Still owns that '08-'10 PX, but without loft, his HR ceiling is limited (and note the three-year PX free-fall). Eroding bb% will be exploited in MLB and will keep him a BA liability. With health, there's modest post-hype profit here, but only in your end-game.

Yr	Tm	AB	R	HR	RBI	SB	BA	xBA	vL	vR	OB	Slg	OPS	bb%	ct%	h%	Eye	G	L	F	PX	xPX	hr/f	Spd	SBO	SB%	#Wk	DOM	DIS	RC/G	RAR	BPV	BPX	R$
08	MIL *	531	77	16	77	5	285	387		500	343	454	797	8	73	36	0.33	0	100	0	121	255	0%	91	9%	41%	2	50%	50%	5.28	-2.1	33	65	$17
09	MIL *	401	43	14	57	2	239	215	304	229	321	405	726	11	60	36	0.30	23	27	51	142	138	13%	83	2%	100%	16	25%	69%	4.39	-12.4	-5	-10	$5
10	MIL *	354	45	11	54	2	261	274	500	154	324	419	743	9	73	33	0.34	43	29	29	124	31	0%	65	4%	65%	4	0%	75%	4.66	-7.8	23	50	$8
11	MIL *	519	60	20	65	1	240	277	0	150	284	401	684	6	79	27	0.29	41	27	32	110	92	0%	51	1%	100%	2	0%	50%	3.83	-24.7	31	69	$9
12	MIL	69	10	1	6	3	246	240	286	236	288	348	635	5	78	30	0.27	36	29	35	64	120	5%	92	18%	100%	5	20%	60%	3.62	-3.6	16	40	$0
1st Half		69	10	1	6	3	246	240	286	236	288	348	635	5	78	30	0.27	36	29	35	64	120	5%	92	18%	100%	5	20%	60%	3.62	-3.6	16	40	$0
2nd Half																																		
13	Proj	**292**	**38**	**9**	**37**	**5**	**251**	**243**	**295**	**240**	**305**	**406**	**711**	**7**	**74**	**31**	**0.30**	**31**	**28**	**41**	**108**	**127**	**10%**	**70**	**8%**	**88%**				**4.27**	**-9.4**	**26**	**64**	**$8**

Garcia,Avisail

Age 22	Bats R	Pos RF	Health	A	LIMA Plan	F
Ht 6' 4"	Wt 240		PT/Exp	F	Rand Var	0
			Consist	F	MM	1301

0-3-.319 in 47 AB at DET. Miggy look-a-like went from High-A in April to starting RF w/DET in Sept. While physical tools entice and speed surprises, tiny bb%, big holes in swing say he's not ready to put them to use yet. Needs more seasoning in high-minors to consolidate his 2012 gains. Save him for keeper leagues.

Yr	Tm	AB	R	HR	RBI	SB	BA	xBA	vL	vR	OB	Slg	OPS	bb%	ct%	h%	Eye	G	L	F	PX	xPX	hr/f	Spd	SBO	SB%	#Wk	DOM	DIS	RC/G	RAR	BPV	BPX	R$
08																																		
09																																		
10																																		
11																																		
12	DET *	262	33	5	21	7	295	291	333	294	317	404	721	3	81	35	0.17	62	27	11	67	63	0%	125	20%	54%	6	0%	100%	4.31	-4.1	18	45	$8
1st Half																																		
2nd Half		262	33	5	21	7	295	291	333	294	317	404	721	3	81	35	0.17	62	27	11	67	63	0%	125	20%	54%	6	0%	100%	4.31	-5.2	18	45	$8
13	Proj	**238**	**27**	**4**	**17**	**6**	**265**	**239**	**276**	**244**	**284**	**357**	**642**	**3**	**83**	**31**	**0.16**	**42**	**22**	**36**	**56**	**57**	**5%**	**124**	**19%**	**54%**				**3.30**	**-12.0**	**14**	**36**	**$6**

Gardner,Brett

Age 29	Bats L	Pos LF	Health	F	LIMA Plan	D+
Ht 5' 10"	Wt 183		PT/Exp	C	Rand Var	-3
			Consist	B	MM	1515

Elbow injury torpedoed season before it could get going. When healthy, he may be a one-trick pony, but he's an elite one. Mediocre xBA history makes '11 BA more likely than '10, so invest only in wheels. If elbow is sound, he's one of the lower-risk 40 SB locks that you'll find.

Yr	Tm	AB	R	HR	RBI	SB	BA	xBA	vL	vR	OB	Slg	OPS	bb%	ct%	h%	Eye	G	L	F	PX	xPX	hr/f	Spd	SBO	SB%	#Wk	DOM	DIS	RC/G	RAR	BPV	BPX	R$
08	NYY *	468	75	3	43	44	251	220	125	252	344	343	687	12	75	33	0.56	48	17	35	62	77	0%	164	35%	79%	12	25%	67%	4.20	-5.2	25	49	$20
09	NYY	248	48	3	23	26	270	255	291	264	339	379	718	9	84	31	0.65	49	18	33	59	43	4%	172	40%	84%	21	33%	48%	4.77	1.4	58	118	$13
10	NYY	477	97	5	47	47	277	256	252	286	379	379	759	14	79	34	0.78	53	19	28	72	34	5%	151	31%	84%	27	44%	19%	5.41	11.7	52	113	$28
11	NYY	510	87	7	36	49	259	260	233	265	337	369	705	11	82	30	0.65	52	19	28	72	48	6%	161	39%	79%	27	48%	30%	4.40	-2.5	57	127	$24
12	NYY	31	7	0	3	2	323	266	857	167	417	387	804	14	77	42	0.71	38	38	25	60	51	0%	93	31%	50%	5	40%	60%	5.24	0.6	14	35	$0
1st Half		28	5	0	3	2	321	274	857	143	424	393	817	15	75	43	0.71	33	43	24	69	60	0%	92	17%	100%	3	33%	67%	6.89	1.7	10	25	$0
2nd Half		3	2	0	0	0	333	226		333	333	333	667	0	100	33	0.00	67	0	33	0	-11	0%	96	200%	0%	2	50%	50%	-2.13	-1.1	99	248	-$1
13	Proj	**435**	**80**	**3**	**38**	**43**	**265**	**253**	**246**	**265**	**347**	**359**	**706**	**11**	**81**	**32**	**0.66**	**46**	**26**	**28**	**58**	**50**	**3%**	**156**	**37%**	**82%**				**4.57**	**-1.1**	**45**	**114**	**$24**

STEPHEN NICKRAND

Gentry,Craig

Age 29	Bats R	Pos CF	Health	A	LIMA Plan	F
Ht 6' 2"	Wt 190		PT/Exp	F	Rand Var	-5
			Consist	B	MM	1513

Not all players regress as perfectly as he did in the second half. His 100-point BA-xBA 1H differential returned to normal, leaving season-long BA 50 points too high. Double-digit steals have some value, but's that all he offers.

Yr	Tm	AB	R	HR	RBI	SB	BA	xBA	vL	vR	OB	Slg	OPS	bb%	ct%	h%	Eye	G	L	F	PX	xPX	hr/f	Spd	SBO	SB%	#Wk	DOM	DIS	RC/G	RAR	BPV	BPX	R$
08	a/a	360	36	3	25	12	221	219			260	289	549	5	76	28	0.22				55			87	26%	56%				2.28		-15	0	$1
09	TEX *	529	79	6	41	37	255	245	250	77	306	354	660	7	85	29	0.48	33	25	42	59	57	0%	167	31%	84%	5	20%	40%	3.88	-15.4	49	100	$18
10	TEX *	292	34	3	27	9	249	183	174	300	300	323	623	7	77	31	0.32	43	9	48	48	103	0%	179	19%	60%	7	14%	57%	3.16	-14.9	-4	-9	$5
11	TEX *	243	38	2	19	21	232	248	265	277	281	303	585	6	80	28	0.35	50	23	27	52	62	4%	150	37%	94%	21	33%	52%	3.20	-12.1	26	58	$7
12	TEX	240	31	1	26	13	304	245	343	277	343	392	734	6	83	36	0.34	47	20	33	61	57	2%	132	28%	65%	27	30%	41%	4.67	-1.2	29	73	$10
1st Half		122	15	1	18	9	352	251	375	328	402	451	852	8	84	42	0.50	38	27	35	62	59	3%	143	27%	75%	13	38%	46%	7.06	7.4	38	95	$14
2nd Half		118	16	0	8	4	254	239	286	241	279	331	609	3	82	31	0.19	56	14	30	60	56	0%	112	31%	50%	14	21%	36%	2.81	-7.1	20	50	$5
13	Proj	264	35	1	24	15	250	242	266	239	293	329	622	6	81	30	0.32	49	21	30	55	59	2%	135	31%	73%				3.26	-12.1	21	53	$6

Getz,Chris

Age 29	Bats L	Pos 2B	Health	D	LIMA Plan	D
Ht 5' 11"	Wt 185		PT/Exp	D	Rand Var	+1
			Consist	A	MM	0423

0-17-9-.275 in 189 AB at KC. Injuries kept him on the DL much of the first half, but his skill deficiencies hurt him more. Though he does possess strong ct% and good Spd—making him capable of 20 SB—he's unlikely to get the playing time he needs to make that happen.

Yr	Tm	AB	R	HR	RBI	SB	BA	xBA	vL	vR	OB	Slg	OPS	bb%	ct%	h%	Eye	G	L	F	PX	xPX	hr/f	Spd	SBO	SB%	#Wk	DOM	DIS	RC/G	RAR	BPV	BPX	R$
08	CHW*	411	52	10	44	11	264	373	500	200	321	393	714	8	85	29	0.55	50	50	0	82	5	0%	88	15%	66%	5	0%	100%	4.27	1.2	46	90	$10
09	CHW	375	49	2	31	25	261	259	246	265	316	347	663	7	86	30	0.56	47	19	33	57	46	2%	114	26%	93%	24	33%	38%	4.09	-0.8	47	96	$12
10	KC	224	23	0	18	15	237	247	304	219	296	277	573	8	88	27	0.68	52	18	30	35	29	0%	102	27%	88%	23	35%	30%	2.98	-8.0	25	54	$4
11	KC	380	50	0	26	21	255	239	286	245	310	287	597	7	88	29	0.67	54	18	28	20	16	0%	144	24%	75%	26	23%	42%	3.10	-12.0	22	49	$9
12	KC *	232	26	0	22	10	264	284	229	291	304	347	651	5	91	29	0.62	43	29	28	53	50	0%	119	21%	76%	16	50%	31%	3.67	-3.3	55	138	$4
1st Half		123	15	0	13	6	300	296	200	313	336	399	735	5	91	33	0.58	36	36	29	61	64	0%	135	20%	86%	10	50%	40%	5.04	2.7	63	158	$6
2nd Half		89	10	0	9	3	258	277	250	262	298	337	635	5	91	28	0.63	51	22	27	53	34	0%	92	23%	60%	6	50%	17%	3.28	-2.6	50	125	$2
13	Proj	262	31	0	24	13	263	264	263	263	309	330	639	6	89	29	0.62	48	23	29	45	36	0%	112	23%	76%				3.57	-5.4	43	107	$8

Giavotella,Johnny

Age 25	Bats R	Pos 2B	Health	A	LIMA Plan	D+
Ht 5' 8"	Wt 185		PT/Exp	B	Rand Var	+1
			Consist	A	MM	1223

1-15-.238 in 181 AB at KC. Yeah, he puts up decent minor league numbers. So what? It's the minors. He doesn't get on base enough for his modest Spd to be a factor. It would take a breakout season for him to even be rosterable in most leagues. Nothing to see here; move along.

Yr	Tm	AB	R	HR	RBI	SB	BA	xBA	vL	vR	OB	Slg	OPS	bb%	ct%	h%	Eye	G	L	F	PX	xPX	hr/f	Spd	SBO	SB%	#Wk	DOM	DIS	RC/G	RAR	BPV	BPX	R$
08																																		
09																																		
10	aa	522	68	6	48	10	284	268			340	396	736	8	86	32	0.61				78			109	12%	55%				4.62		52	0	$15
11	KC *	631	68	8	72	11	277	262	262	243	314	393	708	5	85	32	0.36	43	21	36	82	66	4%	105	12%	59%	9	33%	33%	4.23	1.1	46	102	$17
12	KC *	543	67	7	64	8	257	259	203	259	308	351	659	7	85	29	0.49	47	23	30	61	50	2%	95	6%	87%	14	7%	50%	3.76	-6.4	33	83	$11
1st Half		252	32	3	25	2	243	286	176	257	310	328	638	9	88	27	0.78	42	32	26	55	50	0%	90	3%	100%	6	0%	67%	3.47	-5.9	36	90	$7
2nd Half		291	35	4	39	6	270	244	229	260	306	371	677	5	83	31	0.30	51	17	33	67	51	3%	97	9%	83%	8	13%	38%	4.01	-2.1	25	63	$16
13	Proj	394	47	3	45	7	269	256	245	281	315	360	675	6	85	31	0.45	45	22	32	62	57	3%	98	9%	68%				3.92	-3.8	32	81	$10

Goldschmidt,Paul

Age 25	Bats R	Pos 1B	Health	A	LIMA Plan	B
Ht 6' 3"	Wt 245		PT/Exp	D	Rand Var	0
			Consist	A	MM	4225

Solid first full season. Lots of positives, including improving his ct% without sacrificing power. However, despite solid SB%, his sub-par Spd makes the SB increase looks shaky. That ct% is barely adequate right now, but trends are good, and there's still plenty of room for growth. UP: 30 HR.

Yr	Tm	AB	R	HR	RBI	SB	BA	xBA	vL	vR	OB	Slg	OPS	bb%	ct%	h%	Eye	G	L	F	PX	xPX	hr/f	Spd	SBO	SB%	#Wk	DOM	DIS	RC/G	RAR	BPV	BPX	R$
08																																		
09																																		
10																																		
11	ARI *	522	87	30	92	10	260	270	162	277	354	498	852	13	70	32	0.48	42	21	37	174	155	21%	84	9%	74%	9	56%	44%	6.04	9.3	76	169	$23
12	ARI	514	82	20	82	18	286	274	343	257	361	490	851	10	75	35	0.46	40	24	36	149	160	14%	71	15%	86%	27	48%	26%	6.41	14.3	70	175	$25
1st Half		225	34	11	35	6	293	286	386	239	367	542	909	10	73	36	0.43	43	20	36	182	153	18%	75	12%	86%	13	54%	46%	7.24	11.8	87	218	$21
2nd Half		289	48	9	47	12	280	267	303	270	356	450	806	11	76	34	0.49	38	26	36	124	165	11%	68	17%	86%	14	43%	7%	5.80	3.6	54	135	$28
13	Proj	558	91	25	93	12	276	269	314	258	358	489	847	11	73	34	0.47	41	23	36	152	158	17%	75	10%	79%				6.18	13.1	67	167	$25

Gomes,Jonny

Age 32	Bats R	Pos DH LF	Health	A	LIMA Plan	D
Ht 6' 1"	Wt 225		PT/Exp	C	Rand Var	-5
			Consist	C	MM	4203

PRO: Power, speed still intact; still hits LHP very well.
CON: Drastic decline in ct% and inability to hit RHP make him a one-trick pony.
Huge BA downside may kill playing time. Way too much risk for his expected production level.

Yr	Tm	AB	R	HR	RBI	SB	BA	xBA	vL	vR	OB	Slg	OPS	bb%	ct%	h%	Eye	G	L	F	PX	xPX	hr/f	Spd	SBO	SB%	#Wk	DOM	DIS	RC/G	RAR	BPV	BPX	R$
08	TAM *	261	37	9	31	8	188	203	182	182	256	356	612	8	67	24	0.28	34	10	56	129	156	13%	88	21%	78%	23	43%	52%	2.87	-14.1	25	49	$0
09	CIN *	412	52	28	71	6	256	270	307	244	314	521	834	8	68	31	0.27	34	20	46	188	156	22%	66	9%	73%	20	60%	25%	5.55	9.9	61	124	$13
10	CIN	511	77	18	86	5	266	239	285	257	318	431	749	7	76	32	0.32	29	21	50	113	125	9%	109	6%	63%	27	41%	41%	4.70	1.9	37	80	$17
11	2 NL	311	41	14	43	7	209	219	311	167	315	389	704	13	66	27	0.46	34	18	48	138	136	14%	87	12%	70%	27	26%	56%	3.92	-6.3	28	62	$5
12	OAK	279	46	18	47	3	262	225	299	209	362	491	853	14	63	35	0.42	31	19	50	171	159	20%	95	4%	75%	28	43%	43%	6.13	12.7	32	80	$10
1st Half		138	23	8	21	2	239	219	250	227	352	457	808	15	62	32	0.46	31	17	52	168	149	18%	81	7%	67%	14	29%	50%	5.33	2.8	31	78	$8
2nd Half		141	23	10	26	1	284	232	337	184	373	525	897	12	63	38	0.38	31	20	48	174	168	23%	96	2%	100%	14	57%	36%	7.01	9.4	30	75	$13
13	Proj	278	42	16	44	4	244	226	294	199	333	455	788	12	66	31	0.40	32	19	50	153	149	17%	90	7%	73%				5.09	1.6	32	81	$10

Gomes,Yan

Age 25	Bats R	Pos 1B	Health	A	LIMA Plan	F
Ht 6' 2"	Wt 215		PT/Exp	F	Rand Var	-1
			Consist	C	MM	4201

4-13-.204 in 98 AB at TOR. His decent power is overwhelmed by poor contact, patience, and speed. If you're reading this, you've already spent too much time considering him. There are plenty of better ways to kill your BA. (see teammate Arencibia, J.P.)

Yr	Tm	AB	R	HR	RBI	SB	BA	xBA	vL	vR	OB	Slg	OPS	bb%	ct%	h%	Eye	G	L	F	PX	xPX	hr/f	Spd	SBO	SB%	#Wk	DOM	DIS	RC/G	RAR	BPV	BPX	R$
08																																		
09																																		
10																																		
11	a/a	290	24	10	36	0	206	233			252	366	618	6	68	27	0.19				130			77	0%	0%				2.96		0	0	$0
12	TOR *	403	38	13	51	3	252	236	217	192	291	424	715	5	70	33	0.19	48	15	37	133	127	16%	66	3%	100%	15	27%	67%	4.24	-3.5	17	43	$8
1st Half		243	26	9	31	1	275	241	188	227	307	467	773	4	71	35	0.16	44	15	41	149	201	27%	62	1%	100%	5	40%	60%	5.05	3.3	24	60	$12
2nd Half		160	12	5	20	2	217	220	233	167	268	361	629	7	69	28	0.23	50	15	35	108	76	7%	83	6%	100%	10	20%	70%	3.21	-6.8	-3	-8	$1
13	Proj	165	14	7	21	1	228	234	253	205	273	414	686	6	69	29	0.20	48	15	37	139	126	15%	77	3%	100%				3.75	-8.0	15	38	$2

Gomez,Carlos

Age 27	Bats R	Pos CF	Health	C	LIMA Plan	C+
Ht 6' 4"	Wt 210		PT/Exp	D	Rand Var	-2
			Consist	B	MM	3505

It looks like a major breakout season for a post-hype prospect. What changed? More playing time and a modest improvement in contact are the only leaps. But his 2012 is very repeatable, and his defense plays even if his hitting slides. Expect some BA regression, but 15 HR and 30 SB look pretty safe.

Yr	Tm	AB	R	HR	RBI	SB	BA	xBA	vL	vR	OB	Slg	OPS	bb%	ct%	h%	Eye	G	L	F	PX	xPX	hr/f	Spd	SBO	SB%	#Wk	DOM	DIS	RC/G	RAR	BPV	BPX	R$
08	MIN	577	79	7	59	33	258	221	270	254	289	360	650	4	75	33	0.18	43	17	39	72	80	5%	166	32%	75%	27	33%	48%	3.56	-19.4	15	29	$19
09	MIN	315	51	3	28	14	229	241	204	242	279	337	615	7	77	29	0.31	45	19	35	74	56	4%	147	30%	67%	27	41%	41%	2.99	-16.5	30	61	$5
10	MIL *	319	43	5	25	19	246	224	196	273	292	347	639	6	74	32	0.25	48	16	36	72	48	7%	143	29%	82%	24	29%	50%	3.54	-10.9	10	22	$9
11	MIL	231	37	8	24	16	225	235	278	191	272	403	675	6	72	28	0.23	44	12	44	127	122	11%	145	40%	89%	22	50%	32%	3.79	-6.3	55	122	$7
12	MIL	415	72	19	51	37	260	250	261	260	294	463	757	5	76	30	0.20	40	17	43	128	124	14%	128	50%	86%	25	44%	36%	4.85	2.0	70	175	$24
1st Half		140	21	4	15	8	243	246	265	222	284	429	712	5	79	28	0.28	33	20	47	117	142	8%	137	41%	73%	11	55%	27%	3.97	-3.4	70	175	$3
2nd Half		275	51	15	36	29	269	253	259	274	300	480	780	4	75	31	0.17	44	15	41	134	115	18%	110	54%	91%	14	36%	43%	5.35	4.6	64	160	$34
13	Proj	511	82	18	55	38	247	240	255	242	286	419	705	5	75	30	0.22	43	17	41	113	107	11%	136	42%	84%				4.18	-9.2	53	133	$24

MATT CEDERHOLM

Gomez,Mauro

Age 28	Bats R	Pos 1B	PT/Exp	B	Rand Var	0
Ht 6' 2"	Wt 230		Consist	B	MM	3203
			Health	A	LIMA Plan	D

2-17-.275 in 102 AB at BOS. Injuries created opportunity for MLB debut at age 27. Has some pop, but BA gains largely due to slowly rising h%. Doesn't take walks, makes poor contact, and provides below average defense at 1B. In short, if he's logging significant ABs for a team in Aug/Sept, it's been a bad year.

Yr	Tm	AB	R	HR	RBI	SB	BA	xBA	vL	vR	OB	Slg	OPS	bb%	ct%	h%	Eye	G	L	F	PX	xPX	hr/f	Spd	SBO	SB%	#Wk	DOM	DIS	RC/G	RAR	BPV	BPX	R$
08																																		
09																																		
10	aa	495	51	12	61	1	230	244			281	378	659	7	70	30	0.24				124			86	3%	24%				3.45		9	0	$4
11	aaa	506	58	18	69	5	249	238			291	416	707	6	68	33	0.18				135			77	6%	65%				4.07		13	0	$12
12	BOS *	489	63	19	73	1	266	265	229	315	313	471	784	6	73	33	0.26	38	23	39	149	89	7%	91	1%	100%	11	36%	55%	5.13	-2.2	45	113	$14
1st Half		271	35	12	40	0	257	271	0	0	299	485	784	6	71	32	0.21	100	0	0	172	-11	0%	65	0%	0%	1	0%	100%	4.98	-3.0	47	118	$16
2nd Half		218	28	7	33	1	276	257	234	321	330	453	784	7	76	34	0.33	37	24	39	122	91	7%	104	1%	100%	10	40%	50%	5.30	-0.4	39	98	$12
13	**Proj**	**328**	**39**	**6**	**46**	**2**	**256**	**233**	**214**	**293**	**302**	**391**	**694**	**6**	**71**	**34**	**0.23**	**37**	**24**	**39**	**108**	**82**	**7%**	**95**	**3%**	**72%**				**4.05**	**-12.6**	**6**	**15**	**$5**

Gonzalez,Adrian

Age 31	Bats L	Pos 1B	PT/Exp	A	Rand Var	0
Ht 6' 2"	Wt 225		Consist	F	MM	4145
			Health	A	LIMA Plan	B

History said not to pay for '11 BA, but bb% collapse is a mystery. Fluky 1H hr/f sapped power; 2H regression yielded more familiar results. Track record makes approach/power rebound likely, but 31 y/o sluggers rarely age gracefully. 2nd half resurgence says to bet on some bounceback.

Yr	Tm	AB	R	HR	RBI	SB	BA	xBA	vL	vR	OB	Slg	OPS	bb%	ct%	h%	Eye	G	L	F	PX	xPX	hr/f	Spd	SBO	SB%	#Wk	DOM	DIS	RC/G	RAR	BPV	BPX	R$
08	SD	616	103	36	119	0	279	280	213	320	357	510	866	11	77	31	0.52	43	20	37	147	153	21%	62	0%	0%	27	44%	30%	6.43	17.4	59	116	$24
09	SD	552	90	40	99	1	277	305	234	305	405	551	956	18	80	28	1.09	39	21	40	160	165	22%	61	1%	50%	27	63%	15%	7.84	37.8	99	202	$22
10	SD	591	87	31	101	0	298	286	337	278	393	511	904	14	81	33	0.82	39	21	39	138	151	16%	56	0%	0%	27	59%	19%	7.30	30.4	68	148	$26
11	BOS	630	108	27	117	1	338	296	321	347	408	548	955	11	81	38	0.62	47	21	32	142	128	16%	73	0%	100%	27	59%	22%	8.61	52.1	79	176	$39
12	2 TM	629	75	18	108	2	299	279	322	286	343	463	805	6	83	34	0.38	40	24	36	111	134	10%	55	1%	100%	27	48%	37%	5.79	6.2	48	120	$24
1st Half		307	38	6	43	0	274	261	291	263	324	410	735	7	80	33	0.37	42	23	35	102	123	7%	63	0%	0%	13	46%	46%	4.67	-6.0	25	63	$17
2nd Half		322	37	12	65	2	323	294	354	306	361	512	873	6	85	35	0.40	39	25	36	119	144	12%	53	2%	100%	14	50%	29%	7.01	14.1	64	160	$31
13	**Proj**	**603**	**85**	**26**	**108**	**1**	**292**	**285**	**299**	**288**	**358**	**493**	**851**	**9**	**82**	**32**	**0.56**	**42**	**23**	**36**	**129**	**138**	**15%**	**58**	**1%**	**96%**				**6.37**	**17.0**	**65**	**164**	**$26**

Gonzalez,Carlos

Age 27	Bats L	Pos LF	PT/Exp	A	Rand Var	-1
Ht 6' 1"	Wt 220		Consist	B	MM	4335
			Health	A	LIMA Plan	D+

Road games (.234/.301/.405) and injuries (knee, hamstring) continue to haunt him. 2H leg injuries wiped out potent power/speed combo, but are there bigger issues? GB/FB, xPX, and Spd are all trending in the wrong direction. We'll chalk up the 2H power outage to injuries for now, but 20 SB days may be numbered.

Yr	Tm	AB	R	HR	RBI	SB	BA	xBA	vL	vR	OB	Slg	OPS	bb%	ct%	h%	Eye	G	L	F	PX	xPX	hr/f	Spd	SBO	SB%	#Wk	DOM	DIS	RC/G	RAR	BPV	BPX	R$
08	OAK *	475	48	7	47	5	241	240	188	263	279	354	633	5	75	31	0.21	49	18	33	89	90	6%	73	7%	69%	17	29%	53%	3.30	-20.2	5	10	$3
09	COL *	470	82	20	69	20	290	287	276	286	349	526	875	8	78	34	0.41	38	23	39	143	113	17%	125	23%	73%	18	50%	33%	6.45	23.0	88	180	$23
10	COL	587	111	34	117	26	336	302	320	345	378	598	976	6	77	39	0.30	43	21	37	171	140	20%	102	21%	76%	26	54%	31%	8.55	59.6	102	222	$46
11	COL	481	92	26	92	20	295	291	272	307	359	526	885	9	78	33	0.46	48	18	34	153	123	21%	94	19%	80%	24	58%	17%	6.84	28.5	92	204	$30
12	COL	518	89	22	85	20	303	285	266	325	371	510	881	10	78	35	0.49	49	22	29	134	116	19%	86	16%	80%	26	42%	27%	6.94	31.8	77	193	$30
1st Half		288	59	17	58	10	337	305	306	356	394	604	998	9	78	38	0.44	46	23	31	165	138	25%	93	13%	91%	13	54%	15%	9.31	35.1	106	265	$42
2nd Half		230	30	5	27	10	261	257	214	288	344	391	735	11	77	32	0.55	52	21	27	93	87	10%	77	20%	71%	13	31%	38%	4.59	-0.4	35	88	$14
13	**Proj**	**510**	**87**	**23**	**94**	**19**	**296**	**281**	**266**	**313**	**360**	**510**	**870**	**9**	**78**	**34**	**0.44**	**48**	**20**	**32**	**137**	**116**	**18%**	**86**	**17%**	**77%**				**6.60**	**27.9**	**77**	**192**	**$30**

Gonzalez,Marwin

Age 24	Bats B	Pos SS	PT/Exp	D	Rand Var	+1
Ht 6' 1"	Wt 195		Consist	A	MM	1121
			Health	B	LIMA Plan	F

2-12-.234 with 3 SB in 205 AB at HOU. Slick fielder's debut came amidst lost season in Houston. Solid ct% is greatest asset at the plate, but lack of patience and little power limit his impact. Below average Spd/SB production adds very little value. Great glove helps in MLB and sim games; not so much in Roto.

Yr	Tm	AB	R	HR	RBI	SB	BA	xBA	vL	vR	OB	Slg	OPS	bb%	ct%	h%	Eye	G	L	F	PX	xPX	hr/f	Spd	SBO	SB%	#Wk	DOM	DIS	RC/G	RAR	BPV	BPX	R$
08																																		
09																																		
10	aa	305	18	3	31	4	220	245			251	298	549	4	86	25	0.29				51			103	14%	51%				2.34		14	0	$0
11	a/a	413	37	3	27	5	246	255			286	335	621	5	87	28	0.43				67			89	9%	59%				3.18		35	0	$3
12	HOU *	244	22	3	19	3	241	262	113	276	285	341	626	6	85	27	0.40	54	20	27	74	67	4%	82	11%	50%	20	15%	35%	3.15	-7.0	27	68	$1
1st Half		69	11	1	3	0	261	244	278	255	292	348	639	4	86	29	0.30	51	18	31	58	71	6%	102	0%	0%	10	10%	30%	3.50	-1.0	14	35	-$3
2nd Half		168	11	2	16	3	238	271	29	287	289	349	638	7	84	27	0.46	55	20	25	83	65	4%	78	16%	50%	10	20%	40%	3.20	-4.2	33	83	$2
13	**Proj**	**132**	**12**	**1**	**10**	**2**	**242**	**259**	**144**	**276**	**283**	**335**	**618**	**5**	**86**	**27**	**0.40**	**54**	**19**	**27**	**66**	**67**	**4%**	**89**	**9%**	**54%**				**3.10**	**-3.6**	**25**	**61**	**$1**

Gordon,Alex

Age 29	Bats L	Pos LF	PT/Exp	A	Rand Var	-2
Ht 6' 1"	Wt 220		Consist	D	MM	4125
			Health	B	LIMA Plan	C+

Saw a drop-off from breakout '11, but solid patience and hard contact make a valuable OBP threat. HR and SB went missing in 1H, but peripherals held or improved in 2H leading to rebound. There is risk (h% regression could threaten BA) but versatile skills are a solid investment.

Yr	Tm	AB	R	HR	RBI	SB	BA	xBA	vL	vR	OB	Slg	OPS	bb%	ct%	h%	Eye	G	L	F	PX	xPX	hr/f	Spd	SBO	SB%	#Wk	DOM	DIS	RC/G	RAR	BPV	BPX	R$
08	KC	493	72	16	59	9	260	249	234	273	347	432	779	12	76	31	0.55	31	21	48	125	121	9%	78	8%	82%	24	46%	33%	5.20	9.1	53	104	$12
09	KC *	261	44	9	38	5	254	238	163	261	342	410	752	12	75	31	0.53	44	14	42	106	133	12%	93	6%	100%	13	31%	46%	4.91	2.6	38	78	$6
10	KC *	502	76	17	51	6	239	250	200	220	332	405	736	12	71	30	0.48	38	23	39	125	134	11%	76	9%	45%	15	27%	47%	4.31	-3.9	34	74	$10
11	KC	611	101	23	87	17	303	276	278	314	372	502	874	10	77	36	0.48	40	22	38	144	117	13%	79	14%	68%	26	58%	27%	6.69	36.1	77	171	$32
12	KC	642	93	14	72	10	294	272	248	320	366	455	821	10	78	36	0.52	42	25	33	116	103	8%	79	8%	67%	27	59%	26%	5.95	24.9	55	138	$24
1st Half		300	46	5	24	3	277	268	242	294	364	420	784	12	79	33	0.66	43	24	32	105	110	6%	82	6%	50%	13	54%	38%	5.25	5.2	50	125	$17
2nd Half		342	47	9	48	7	310	275	252	346	369	485	854	9	77	38	0.41	41	26	33	125	96	10%	80	9%	78%	14	64%	14%	6.62	18.4	56	140	$30
13	**Proj**	**626**	**95**	**20**	**86**	**9**	**278**	**266**	**241**	**296**	**354**	**457**	**811**	**11**	**77**	**34**	**0.50**	**40**	**23**	**36**	**127**	**113**	**11%**	**75**	**8%**	**60%**				**5.60**	**17.1**	**56**	**141**	**$23**

Gordon,Dee

Age 25	Bats L	Pos SS	PT/Exp	C	Rand Var	+2
Ht 5' 11"	Wt 160		Consist	C	MM	0513
			Health	C	LIMA Plan	F

1-17-.228 with 32 SB in 303 AB at LA. Began 2012 as starting SS, but a thumb injury wiped out half his season. Not that skills were so great before the injury, mind you. Has elite speed, and you can't ignore 32 SB, but empty bat and an uncertain role reduce him to a risky speculation for '13. Still... UP: 50+ SB.

Yr	Tm	AB	R	HR	RBI	SB	BA	xBA	vL	vR	OB	Slg	OPS	bb%	ct%	h%	Eye	G	L	F	PX	xPX	hr/f	Spd	SBO	SB%	#Wk	DOM	DIS	RC/G	RAR	BPV	BPX	R$
08																																		
09																																		
10	aa	555	65	1	29	40	236	226			274	291	565	5	82	29	0.28				38			141	45%	64%				2.47		11	0	$14
11	LA *	512	64	0	25	42	277	266	275	316	301	329	630	3	85	32	0.23	56	23	21	38	14	0%	159	39%	78%	11	45%	27%	3.56	-8.1	24	53	$20
12	LA *	333	40	1	18	33	225	246	172	255	272	276	548	6	80	28	0.32	59	21	21	36	20	2%	140	53%	75%	18	17%	56%	2.51	-16.8	7	18	$9
1st Half		289	34	1	16	25	225	244	172	253	270	277	547	6	79	28	0.30	60	20	19	37	12	3%	134	46%	76%	13	15%	62%	2.52	-13.6	0	0	$11
2nd Half		44	6	0	2	8	229	231		286	281	273	554	7	90	26	0.70	38	23	38	27	142	0%	135	97%	72%	5	20%	40%	2.43	-2.3	44	110	-$3
13	**Proj**	**266**	**32**	**1**	**14**	**21**	**242**	**252**	**193**	**267**	**279**	**297**	**577**	**5**	**82**	**29**	**0.28**	**58**	**21**	**20**	**37**	**13**	**2%**	**143**	**44%**	**72%**				**2.75**	**-10.4**	**9**	**24**	**$9**

Gose,Anthony

Age 22	Bats L	Pos RF CF	PT/Exp	D	Rand Var	0
Ht 6' 1"	Wt 190		Consist	B	MM	1503
			Health	A	LIMA Plan	D+

1-11-.223 with 15 SB in 166 AB at TOR. Speedy prospect earned late run with TOR, but forgot his bat. Elite speed and willingness to take a walk offers huge SB upside, but poor contact skills are holding him back. He offers a bit of cheap speed for now, with potential for more. But ct% says not to hold your breath for it.

Yr	Tm	AB	R	HR	RBI	SB	BA	xBA	vL	vR	OB	Slg	OPS	bb%	ct%	h%	Eye	G	L	F	PX	xPX	hr/f	Spd	SBO	SB%	#Wk	DOM	DIS	RC/G	RAR	BPV	BPX	R$
08																																		
09																																		
10																																		
11	aa	509	74	15	50	59	239	225			309	389	698	9	67	33	0.31				115			123	57%	79%				4.09		31	0	$25
12	TOR *	586	86	5	41	39	240	239	290	207	301	345	646	8	70	33	0.29	60	19	21	79	51	5%	159	37%	70%	11	18%	73%	3.40	-26.3	10	25	$18
1st Half		336	50	2	25	20	253	218			311	360	671	8	72	34	0.30	44	20	36	78			143	30%	75%				3.82		15	38	$21
2nd Half		250	35	2	16	18	223	232	290	207	288	326	613	8	68	32	0.28	60	19	21	79	51	5%	149	46%	66%	11	18%	73%	2.89	-15.1	2	5	$13
13	**Proj**	**384**	**55**	**2**	**31**	**33**	**237**	**228**	**288**	**260**	**302**	**323**	**625**	**9**	**69**	**34**	**0.30**	**60**	**19**	**21**	**68**	**31**	**3%**	**148**	**44%**	**73%**				**3.24**	**-21.1**	**-2**	**-6**	**$14**

DAN BECKER

Grandal,Yasmani

Grandal,Yasmani		Health	A	LIMA Plan	D
Age 24	Bats B Pos CA	PT/Exp	F	Rand Var	-2
Ht 6' 2"	Wt 210	Consist	C	MM	3013

8-36-.297 in 192 AB at SD. He looked the part in first MLB audition, but post-season suspension for elevated testosterone level sours the outlook. Modest PX and GB profile already limited his power ceiling, now 50-game suspension chops his value. No choice but to forget what we have seen and treat him as a blank slate.

Yr	Tm	AB	R	HR	RBI	SB	BA	xBA	vL	vR	OB	Slg	OPS	bb%	ct%	h%	Eye	G	L	F	PX	xPX	hr/f	Spd	SBO	SB%	#Wk	DOM	DIS	RC/G	RAR	BPV	BPX	R$
08																																		
09																																		
10																																		
11	a/a	168	16	3	20	0	267	242			319	409	728	7	72	35	0.28				124			75	3%	0%				4.41		12	0	$2
12	SD *	386	56	12	60	0	278	247	308	293	373	429	802	13	78	33	0.70	53	17	30	102	87	17%	101	0%	0%	15	40%	33%	5.66	14.9	34	85	$12
1st Half		199	30	6	27	0	264	167	500	333	352	421	773	12	78	31	0.61	20	0	80	112	438	50%	77	0%	0%	2	50%	0%	5.13	5.3	36	90	$10
2nd Half		187	26	6	33	0	294	246	300	292	394	439	833	14	79	35	0.79	54	17	29	90	75	14%	112	0%	0%	13	38%	38%	6.25	10.5	31	78	$13
13	Proj	**312**	**39**	**7**	**45**	**0**	**243**	**243**	**248**	**242**	**325**	**380**	**705**	**11**	**76**	**30**	**0.50**	**54**	**17**	**29**	**101**	**68**	**11%**	**101**	**1%**	**0%**				**4.12**	**-0.9**	**20**	**50**	**$4**

Granderson,Curtis

Granderson,Curtis		Health	A	LIMA Plan	B
Age 32	Bats L Pos CF	PT/Exp	A	Rand Var	0
Ht 6' 1"	Wt 185	Consist	C	MM	5315

Another 40 HR, but he's at a crossroads now. Consistent ct% erosion has put him in hacker territory. And with '11 h% looking like the outlier, even a .250 BA won't come easy. Power is elite, but friendly hr/f and home park fueled this HR output. 20 SB threshold a product of green light more than skill. Don't overpay.

Yr	Tm	AB	R	HR	RBI	SB	BA	xBA	vL	vR	OB	Slg	OPS	bb%	ct%	h%	Eye	G	L	F	PX	xPX	hr/f	Spd	SBO	SB%	#Wk	DOM	DIS	RC/G	RAR	BPV	BPX	R$
08	DET	553	112	22	66	12	280	273	259	288	362	494	856	11	80	32	0.64	40	19	41	127	123	12%	174	10%	75%	24	75%	13%	6.31	22.9	88	173	$22
09	DET	631	91	30	71	20	249	254	183	275	326	453	779	10	78	28	0.51	29	21	49	122	133	13%	120	15%	77%	27	56%	22%	5.01	2.7	68	139	$19
10	NYY	466	76	24	67	12	247	258	234	253	324	468	792	10	75	28	0.46	33	20	47	142	150	14%	121	12%	86%	24	50%	38%	5.19	4.6	76	165	$16
11	NYY	583	136	41	119	25	262	272	272	258	356	552	909	13	71	30	0.50	34	18	48	198	161	21%	124	22%	71%	27	67%	7%	6.64	30.7	117	260	$36
12	NYY	596	102	43	106	10	232	251	218	239	317	492	809	11	67	27	0.38	33	23	44	175	132	24%	100	9%	77%	27	48%	30%	5.17	5.6	65	163	$22
1st Half		302	54	23	46	6	245	267	265	235	343	510	853	13	70	27	0.49	36	25	40	172	125	28%	93	10%	67%	13	54%	15%	5.80	9.3	69	173	$25
2nd Half		294	48	20	60	4	218	237	178	244	290	473	763	9	65	26	0.29	30	21	49	179	140	21%	106	6%	100%	14	43%	43%	4.54	-2.1	56	140	$19
13	Proj	**573**	**106**	**38**	**101**	**11**	**243**	**254**	**228**	**251**	**327**	**502**	**829**	**11**	**70**	**28**	**0.42**	**33**	**21**	**46**	**168**	**143**	**20%**	**113**	**11%**	**72%**				**5.48**	**12.1**	**77**	**193**	**$24**

Greene,Tyler

Greene,Tyler		Health	A	LIMA Plan	F
Age 29	Bats R Pos 2B SS	PT/Exp	D	Rand Var	0
Ht 6' 2"	Wt 190	Consist	B	MM	3501

Fun fact: One of a handful of middle infielders with a 120+ PX and SX. Problem is, horrible plate control won't let him shed part-time label. And all of his damage came against LHers (.500 Slg), with a .198/.246/.337 line against righties. Sexy Spd won't matter with sub-.300 OBP. At best, an end-game MI in deep leagues.

Yr	Tm	AB	R	HR	RBI	SB	BA	xBA	vL	vR	OB	Slg	OPS	bb%	ct%	h%	Eye	G	L	F	PX	xPX	hr/f	Spd	SBO	SB%	#Wk	DOM	DIS	RC/G	RAR	BPV	BPX	R$
08	a/a	485	59	11	36	15	209	218			247	326	573	5	69	28	0.16				87			112	23%	68%				2.53		-7	0	$2
09	STL *	448	62	12	39	27	236	224	188	237	288	365	653	7	70	31	0.25	44	18	38	87	23	7%	146	28%	88%	11	18%	82%	3.69	-8.8	10	20	$13
10	STL *	442	58	7	32	10	217	216	208	232	274	329	603	7	70	29	0.26	41	19	41	88	55	6%	152	16%	61%	14	21%	64%	2.85	-20.6	1	2	$3
11	STL *	358	57	9	39	23	230	225	209	213	304	366	670	10	65	33	0.30	50	19	31	118	87	5%	129	28%	90%	16	38%	38%	3.92	-4.5	14	31	$11
12	2 NL	305	34	11	30	12	230	240	280	198	275	400	675	6	69	30	0.20	44	22	34	125	111	15%	121	26%	75%	26	31%	62%	3.60	-6.9	22	55	$6
1st Half		154	16	4	16	8	227	240	260	198	279	383	662	7	69	30	0.23	46	22	32	115	112	12%	132	31%	80%	12	33%	67%	3.56	-3.3	24	60	$6
2nd Half		151	18	7	14	4	232	241	311	198	270	417	688	5	68	29	0.17	42	22	36	135	110	18%	97	21%	67%	14	29%	57%	3.63	-2.9	14	35	$7
13	Proj	**228**	**29**	**6**	**22**	**10**	**227**	**223**	**255**	**211**	**281**	**362**	**643**	**7**	**68**	**31**	**0.23**	**45**	**20**	**35**	**104**	**88**	**11%**	**118**	**24%**	**78%**				**3.38**	**-6.2**	**6**	**15**	**$6**

Gutierrez,Franklin

Gutierrez,Franklin		Health	F	LIMA Plan	D
Age 30	Bats R Pos CF	PT/Exp	C	Rand Var	+1
Ht 6' 2"	Wt 190	Consist	C	MM	2303

Torn pectoral sidelined him early. Health grade confirms we can't count on him. RAR says it's been three years since he's added value anyway. OPS v. RH since '09 tells why: .681, .653, .528, .397. The speed he owns needs 500 AB and .300 OBP to materialize, and given other issues, that ain't happening.

Yr	Tm	AB	R	HR	RBI	SB	BA	xBA	vL	vR	OB	Slg	OPS	bb%	ct%	h%	Eye	G	L	F	PX	xPX	hr/f	Spd	SBO	SB%	#Wk	DOM	DIS	RC/G	RAR	BPV	BPX	R$
08	CLE	399	54	8	41	9	248	244	252	246	296	383	679	6	78	30	0.31	42	17	41	98	108	6%	112	13%	75%	27	33%	37%	3.84	-12.0	37	73	$7
09	SEA	565	85	18	70	16	283	255	335	262	337	425	762	8	78	33	0.38	45	19	36	91	114	11%	109	13%	76%	27	37%	33%	5.09	3.7	32	65	$21
10	SEA	568	61	12	64	25	245	228	248	244	306	363	669	8	76	30	0.36	42	16	42	86	108	7%	121	19%	89%	27	26%	41%	3.90	-16.1	24	52	$15
11	SEA *	362	30	1	22	13	220	220	224	224	260	273	533	5	82	27	0.30	48	17	36	44	76	1%	111	18%	87%	17	12%	65%	2.42	-27.1	4	9	$1
12	SEA *	212	25	5	22	3	237	251	400	153	285	384	669	6	77	29	0.29	43	21	36	105	125	9%	98	12%	57%	9	44%	33%	3.56	-8.3	31	78	$2
1st Half		83	8	2	10	0	212	198	458	48	253	334	587	5	77	25	0.24	51	8	41	86	178	13%	90	0%	0%	3	33%	33%	2.74	-5.2	-1	-3	-$2
2nd Half		129	17	3	12	3	254	268	366	188	306	417	723	7	77	31	0.32	39	27	34	117	102	7%	103	19%	56%	6	50%	33%	4.15	-2.4	45	113	$5
13	Proj	**328**	**36**	**7**	**31**	**8**	**239**	**236**	**358**	**181**	**286**	**360**	**646**	**6**	**78**	**29**	**0.31**	**45**	**18**	**37**	**85**	**113**	**7%**	**102**	**14%**	**77%**				**3.46**	**-13.0**	**22**	**54**	**$6**

Guzman,Jesus

Guzman,Jesus		Health	A	LIMA Plan	D
Age 29	Bats R Pos LF	PT/Exp	C	Rand Var	0
Ht 6' 1"	Wt 215	Consist	A	MM	4123

Lefty masher lived up to that billing (.942 OPS in 122 AB vs. LH). Has big holes and no power against righties, so full time duty is not in the cards yet. 2H bb%, PX, FB all suggest he could be a late bloomer. With adjustment vs. RH and opportunity... UP: .280-20-80

Yr	Tm	AB	R	HR	RBI	SB	BA	xBA	vL	vR	OB	Slg	OPS	bb%	ct%	h%	Eye	G	L	F	PX	xPX	hr/f	Spd	SBO	SB%	#Wk	DOM	DIS	RC/G	RAR	BPV	BPX	R$
08	a/a	400	46	11	64	4	288	257			334	429	763	6	81	33	0.35				92			84	8%	44%				4.94		29	0	$12
09	SF *	472	51	10	49	0	266	288	231	286	302	396	698	5	79	32	0.25	76	18	6	85	10	0%	110	2%	0%	7	0%	86%	4.06	-9.0	14	29	$7
10	aaa	445	45	12	49	4	260	262			300	397	697	5	82	29	0.32				93			87	9%	46%				3.95		29	0	$9
11	SD *	491	55	9	76	11	270	264	333	299	328	411	739	8	79	32	0.42	42	22	36	108	97	7%	83	15%	61%	16	69%	19%	4.56	-2.4	48	107	$15
12	SD	287	32	9	48	3	247	246	303	206	316	418	735	9	75	30	0.41	42	18	40	120	102	10%	82	8%	50%	27	48%	48%	4.35	-3.2	38	95	$6
1st Half		176	16	2	26	3	233	233	284	202	289	352	642	7	74	30	0.31	44	19	37	96	71	4%	79	13%	60%	13	46%	46%	3.30	-7.2	13	33	$5
2nd Half		111	16	7	22	0	270	266	327	214	357	523	880	12	77	29	0.58	39	16	45	155	150	18%	89	3%	0%	14	50%	50%	6.30	5.3	73	183	$8
13	Proj	**257**	**30**	**10**	**40**	**3**	**262**	**259**	**294**	**237**	**323**	**446**	**769**	**8**	**78**	**30**	**0.41**	**41**	**19**	**39**	**122**	**109**	**12%**	**82**	**9%**	**50%**				**4.82**	**1.3**	**49**	**122**	**$8**

Gwynn,Tony

Gwynn,Tony		Health	A	LIMA Plan	F
Age 30	Bats L Pos CF LF	PT/Exp	D	Rand Var	0
Ht 5' 11"	Wt 193	Consist	C	MM	0401

0-17-.232 w/13 SB in 259 AB at LA. Slap hitter needs some sense slapped into him. Concurrent bb%, ct% slides make even a .300 OBP out of reach. Without it, his wheels are useless. It all came crashing down in 2H collapse. He no longer belongs on your radar, let alone your roster.

Yr	Tm	AB	R	HR	RBI	SB	BA	xBA	vL	vR	OB	Slg	OPS	bb%	ct%	h%	Eye	G	L	F	PX	xPX	hr/f	Spd	SBO	SB%	#Wk	DOM	DIS	RC/G	RAR	BPV	BPX	R$
08	MIL *	414	38	1	19	17	218	231	1000	150	264	259	523	6	82	26	0.35	40	26	34	28	34	0%	132	24%	68%	9	22%	44%	2.20	-32.3	-2	-4	$1
09	SD *	545	84	3	28	22	264	257	215	290	340	336	676	10	83	31	0.69	46	24	30	46	47	2%	149	17%	73%	21	24%	38%	3.96	-11.6	30	61	$13
10	SD	289	30	3	20	17	204	240	325	185	303	287	590	12	83	24	0.82	46	19	35	54	38	4%	113	25%	81%	23	26%	48%	2.93	-16.1	37	80	$3
11	LA	312	37	2	22	22	256	260	200	273	307	353	660	7	80	31	0.38	51	23	25	65	45	3%	131	34%	79%	26	35%	38%	3.79	-8.3	35	78	$9
12	LA *	327	36	0	21	15	232	228	209	243	277	292	569	6	79	29	0.30	53	19	28	43	43	0%	123	28%	67%	19	16%	68%	2.62	-20.9	3	8	$4
1st Half		205	23	0	17	10	259	244	229	274	300	332	631	6	81	32	0.31	53	21	27	48	27	0%	124	30%	63%	13	23%	62%	3.23	-9.6	15	38	$8
2nd Half		122	13	0	4	5	188	186	125	132	239	226	465	6	76	25	0.28	54	10	36	33	110	0%	103	24%	79%	6	0%	83%	1.77	-11.8	-23	-58	-$2
13	Proj	**97**	**11**	**0**	**6**	**5**	**227**	**228**	**213**	**232**	**284**	**295**	**579**	**7**	**80**	**28**	**0.40**	**51**	**18**	**31**	**47**	**60**	**2%**	**106**	**27%**	**76%**				**2.81**	**-5.9**	**9**	**24**	**$2**

Hafner,Travis

Hafner,Travis		Health	D	LIMA Plan	D
Age 36	Bats L Pos DH	PT/Exp	C	Rand Var	+4
Ht 6' 3"	Wt 240	Consist	A	MM	3013

Knee, back were his maladies this go-around. By now, we know that 400 AB is his upside and 300 AB is our baseline. Part-time DHs with sub-elite power DO grow on trees, so his downside is even worse. Even with modest h% rebound, xBA says days of .280 BA are likely gone. Speculate elsewhere.

Yr	Tm	AB	R	HR	RBI	SB	BA	xBA	vL	vR	OB	Slg	OPS	bb%	ct%	h%	Eye	G	L	F	PX	xPX	hr/f	Spd	SBO	SB%	#Wk	DOM	DIS	RC/G	RAR	BPV	BPX	R$
08	CLE *	220	24	5	27	1	203	245	220	189	297	328	625	12	73	26	0.49	42	25	33	96	108	10%	45	4%	50%	13	15%	69%	3.08	-12.4	5	10	-$2
09	CLE *	377	50	17	55	0	271	278	210	292	352	462	814	11	81	29	0.67	39	21	40	120	121	15%	70	0%	0%	22	45%	27%	5.69	8.6	52	106	$9
10	CLE	396	46	13	50	2	278	264	273	279	360	449	810	11	76	34	0.54	43	19	38	129	106	11%	60	3%	67%	25	40%	44%	5.70	9.1	44	96	$11
11	CLE	325	41	13	57	0	280	253	233	302	352	449	801	10	76	33	0.46	43	21	36	119	121	14%	52	0%	0%	22	41%	41%	5.60	6.5	27	60	$11
12	CLE	219	23	12	34	0	228	254	197	241	327	438	765	13	79	24	0.68	43	17	39	122	123	17%	73	0%	0%	17	59%	29%	4.73	-0.9	51	128	$3
1st Half		132	14	6	23	0	242	264	150	283	367	439	806	16	81	26	1.04	45	18	36	118	118	15%	66	0%	0%	8	63%	13%	5.43	2.1	64	160	$4
2nd Half		87	9	6	11	0	207	239	286	182	258	437	695	6	75	20	0.27	40	15	45	128	131	21%	85	0%	0%	9	56%	44%	3.62	-3.4	31	78	$1
13	Proj	**251**	**28**	**11**	**37**	**0**	**246**	**247**	**232**	**251**	**324**	**427**	**751**	**10**	**77**	**28**	**0.50**	**42**	**19**	**39**	**113**	**121**	**15%**	**62**	**1%**	**62%**				**4.67**	**-1.6**	**33**	**83**	**$6**

STEPHEN NICKRAND

Hairston,Jerry

Age 37	Bats R	Pos 3B 2B	Health	D	LIMA Plan	D
Ht 5' 10"	Wt 195		PT/Exp	C	Rand Var	0
			Consist	B	MM	1123

There was a time when he'd qualify all over the place and give you a decent shot at 20 SB. That was five years ago. This version controls plate better than ever, but Spd is gone, and it isn't coming back at age 37. Neither is double-digit HR. An empty .270 BA is all you can hope for now. Pass.

Yr Tm	AB	R	HR	RBI	SB	BA	xBA	vL	vR	OB	Slg	OPS	bb%	ct%	h%	Eye	G	L	F	PX	xPX	hr/f	Spd	SBO	SB%	#Wk	DOM	DIS	RC/G	RAR	BPV	BPX	R$
08 CIN *	340	55	9	49	16	320	291	345	316	367	497	864	7	86	35	0.53	32	28	41	113	74	7%	104	21%	79%	20	50%	25%	6.83	20.5	87	171	$19
09 2 TM	383	62	10	39	7	251	272	242	255	308	394	703	8	86	27	0.59	34	23	43	90	74	7%	89	12%	64%	27	41%	41%	4.05	-6.2	61	124	$8
10 SD	430	53	10	50	9	244	241	244	244	295	353	648	7	87	26	0.57	40	16	44	65	71	6%	100	14%	60%	22	41%	32%	3.41	-15.5	43	93	$8
11 2 NL	337	43	5	31	3	270	256	228	288	335	383	718	9	86	30	0.72	39	20	41	80	62	4%	82	5%	60%	25	40%	32%	4.43	-1.7	48	107	$7
12 LA	238	19	4	26	1	273	269	293	260	337	387	724	9	89	29	0.85	36	25	39	72	82	5%	76	4%	33%	18	44%	39%	4.44	-1.0	43	108	$3
1st Half	155	12	2	18	1	297	266	333	274	366	400	766	10	90	32	1.13	40	23	37	64	69	4%	83	4%	50%	12	42%	33%	5.23	2.8	48	120	$5
2nd Half	83	7	2	8	0	229	275	219	235	281	361	642	7	86	25	0.50	30	28	42	86	108	7%	68	6%	0%	6	50%	50%	3.17	-3.6	35	88	-$1
13 Proj	257	28	5	27	3	261	260	256	263	320	381	701	8	87	28	0.68	36	23	41	77	80	5%	76	7%	51%				4.10	-3.7	44	110	$4

Hairston,Scott

Age 33	Bats R	Pos LF RF	Health	C	LIMA Plan	C
Ht 6' 0"	Wt 205		PT/Exp	D	Rand Var	0
			Consist	B	MM	4213

First 20 HR MLB season at age 32. Power is for real, but elite version of it comes only vs. LH (.550 Slg). Getting out of Citi Field might help (.528 Slg on road). xBA suggests he's no longer a BA drag, but bb%, Eye temper that enthusiasm. Given health and splits, keep viewing him as a part-timer with premium pop.

Yr Tm	AB	R	HR	RBI	SB	BA	xBA	vL	vR	OB	Slg	OPS	bb%	ct%	h%	Eye	G	L	F	PX	xPX	hr/f	Spd	SBO	SB%	#Wk	DOM	DIS	RC/G	RAR	BPV	BPX	R$
08 SD	326	42	17	31	3	248	256	280	224	308	479	786	8	74	28	0.33	37	14	48	152	133	14%	131	6%	75%	22	45%	41%	4.99	2.5	62	122	$6
09 2 TM	430	50	17	64	11	265	256	318	243	305	456	761	5	81	29	0.30	34	15	51	121	101	10%	92	15%	79%	23	48%	17%	4.83	1.2	61	124	$13
10 SD	295	34	10	36	6	210	218	233	198	285	346	631	10	77	24	0.45	34	15	51	92	81	9%	88	10%	86%	25	20%	40%	3.24	-13.6	22	48	$3
11 NYM	132	20	7	24	1	235	251	247	216	294	470	763	8	74	26	0.32	32	13	55	165	131	13%	96	8%	50%	22	45%	45%	4.48	-0.9	72	160	$2
12 NYM	377	52	20	57	8	263	273	286	239	298	504	802	5	78	29	0.23	33	21	46	155	117	15%	83	14%	80%	27	59%	22%	5.19	5.0	80	200	$14
1st Half	161	26	10	31	4	255	279	300	197	298	522	820	6	76	27	0.26	32	21	47	173	115	17%	69	17%	80%	13	69%	15%	5.31	3.1	89	223	$14
2nd Half	216	26	10	26	4	269	269	273	265	298	491	789	4	79	30	0.20	33	21	46	141	119	13%	95	12%	80%	14	50%	29%	5.09	2.7	67	168	$14
13 Proj	360	49	18	54	6	253	254	274	232	301	474	775	6	77	28	0.30	33	18	50	143	115	13%	87	11%	76%				4.84	2.0	65	162	$13

Hamilton,Josh

Age 32	Bats L	Pos CF LF	Health	B	LIMA Plan	B
Ht 6' 4"	Wt 240		PT/Exp	A	Rand Var	-1
			Consist	D	MM	5235

MVP-caliber Apr + May hid huge ct% tailspin, maddening inconsistency by month. Still hasn't posted 500 AB in back-to-back seasons, so view health grade with more skepticism. xBA trend another warning sign, especially as he opens up swing to hacker levels. This likely was his peak. DN: 400 AB, .270 BA, 20 HR

Yr Tm	AB	R	HR	RBI	SB	BA	xBA	vL	vR	OB	Slg	OPS	bb%	ct%	h%	Eye	G	L	F	PX	xPX	hr/f	Spd	SBO	SB%	#Wk	DOM	DIS	RC/G	RAR	BPV	BPX	R$
08 TEX	624	98	32	130	9	304	297	288	313	369	530	900	9	80	34	0.51	46	22	33	140	103	19%	80	5%	90%	27	63%	22%	7.24	40.6	82	161	$32
09 TEX *	368	46	10	55	9	259	250	327	239	310	412	723	7	76	32	0.31	36	22	42	105	116	9%	81	14%	76%	18	28%	39%	4.39	-4.9	36	73	$9
10 TEX	518	95	32	100	8	359	326	271	401	408	633	1041	8	82	39	0.45	42	22	36	176	135	21%	88	6%	89%	24	75%	4%	10.35	71.6	113	246	$39
11 TEX	487	80	25	94	8	298	297	260	314	350	536	886	7	81	33	0.42	41	21	38	154	126	16%	91	7%	89%	22	64%	14%	6.86	27.0	97	216	$26
12 TEX	562	103	43	128	7	285	282	291	282	354	577	930	10	71	33	0.37	38	21	41	196	166	26%	71	8%	64%	27	52%	30%	7.15	36.5	86	215	$33
1st Half	276	51	25	73	6	319	305	316	320	388	652	1040	10	73	36	0.42	41	21	38	214	166	32%	77	12%	67%	13	54%	31%	9.25	33.5	109	273	$42
2nd Half	286	52	18	55	1	252	260	260	249	321	503	824	9	69	30	0.33	34	21	45	177	167	20%	66	3%	50%	14	50%	29%	5.44	5.6	59	148	$23
13 Proj	493	86	31	101	7	282	284	266	289	343	543	886	9	76	32	0.38	39	21	39	169	146	21%	76	7%	75%				6.57	25.2	85	213	$26

Hanigan,Ryan

Age 32	Bats R	Pos CA	Health	B	LIMA Plan	D
Ht 6' 0"	Wt 210		PT/Exp	D	Rand Var	-2
			Consist	A	MM	0215

On surface, still a #2 catcher worth owning, given consistent history of .270-ish BA. xBA tells a different story. As PX and FB dip, he just doesn't have the pop to sustain it, even with fantastic plate control. He'll hurt you less than most, but with zero power and a BA at risk, there's not much value in his consistency.

Yr Tm	AB	R	HR	RBI	SB	BA	xBA	vL	vR	OB	Slg	OPS	bb%	ct%	h%	Eye	G	L	F	PX	xPX	hr/f	Spd	SBO	SB%	#Wk	DOM	DIS	RC/G	RAR	BPV	BPX	R$
08 CIN *	357	36	5	34	1	263	250	237	298	318	345	663	7	84	30	0.49	51	21	28	55	49	10%	97	1%	100%	8	38%	50%	3.81	-4.9	6	12	$4
09 CIN	251	22	3	11	0	263	264	291	255	358	331	688	13	88	29	1.19	48	24	27	40	62	5%	90	0%	0%	26	23%	46%	4.09	-1.3	19	39	$1
10 CIN *	249	29	5	41	0	278	271	291	304	369	392	761	13	88	30	1.24	48	21	31	75	79	9%	75	0%	0%	21	57%	19%	5.11	5.8	47	102	$6
11 CIN	266	27	6	31	0	267	249	275	265	352	357	709	12	88	29	1.09	48	22	30	54	69	9%	71	0%	0%	25	28%	48%	4.37	0.6	25	56	$4
12 CIN	317	25	2	24	0	274	241	329	259	363	338	700	12	88	31	1.19	53	21	26	45	48	3%	70	0%	0%	27	22%	37%	4.30	0.1	19	48	$3
1st Half	154	12	1	8	0	286	230	345	272	360	351	711	10	88	32	0.95	54	19	27	47	41	3%	79	0%	0%	13	23%	46%	4.51	1.3	15	38	$2
2nd Half	163	13	1	16	0	264	254	317	246	365	325	690	14	89	29	1.44	52	24	24	44	55	3%	65	0%	0%	14	21%	29%	4.11	-0.5	24	60	$4
13 Proj	400	37	4	40	0	258	247	289	250	347	331	678	12	88	28	1.14	51	22	28	48	59	5%	66	0%	100%				3.95	-3.1	22	54	$6

Hannahan,Jack

Age 33	Bats L	Pos 3B	Health	A	LIMA Plan	F
Ht 6' 2"	Wt 210		PT/Exp	D	Rand Var	-1
			Consist	C	MM	2001

Keeps getting trotted out due to glove and "intangibles." Those days may finally come to an end after this 2H collapse. With no hope for BA, power, or speed, he's now interesting only for his pseudo-palindromic last name, a full eight characters long, but made up of just three unique letters. THAT'S intangible value!

Yr Tm	AB	R	HR	RBI	SB	BA	xBA	vL	vR	OB	Slg	OPS	bb%	ct%	h%	Eye	G	L	F	PX	xPX	hr/f	Spd	SBO	SB%	#Wk	DOM	DIS	RC/G	RAR	BPV	BPX	R$
08 OAK	436	48	9	47	2	218	224	204	223	305	342	647	11	70	29	0.42	37	21	42	102	112	7%	66	2%	100%	26	27%	58%	3.43	-14.9	0	0	-$1
09 2 AL *	348	32	5	26	1	202	216	191	225	274	314	589	9	70	27	0.33	40	18	42	90	96	5%	95	4%	31%	24	33%	58%	2.69	-20.4	-9	-18	-$4
10 aaa	334	33	6	31	2	190	221			268	296	564	10	70	25	0.35				87			88	3%	100%				2.53		-11	0	-$3
11 CLE	320	38	8	40	2	250	241	296	226	330	388	717	11	75	31	0.48	52	16	32	101	85	10%	91	3%	67%	26	38%	50%	4.33	-2.0	25	56	$5
12 CLE	287	23	4	29	0	244	232	167	270	309	341	650	9	78	30	0.43	40	23	38	74	99	5%	62	3%	0%	25	16%	56%	3.45	-9.3	-3	-8	$1
1st Half	133	9	3	18	0	248	222	174	287	324	361	685	10	79	29	0.54	41	19	40	77	89	7%	61	5%	0%	11	18%	55%	3.73	-3.4	4	10	$2
2nd Half	154	14	1	11	0	240	240	154	258	295	325	620	7	77	31	0.34	39	26	35	71	108	2%	74	0%	0%	14	14%	57%	3.22	-6.3	-11	-28	$1
13 Proj	191	18	3	20	1	234	227	209	243	304	344	648	9	75	30	0.41	42	21	37	83	97	6%	74	3%	41%				3.44	-6.6	0	0	$2

Hardy,J.J.

Age 30	Bats R	Pos SS	Health	B	LIMA Plan	C+
Ht 6' 1"	Wt 190		PT/Exp	B	Rand Var	+1
			Consist	C	MM	2115

Counting stats propped up by huge AB total; '11 power looks like the clear outlier. With mediocre PX and a return to GB ways, 20 HR will come only with 600 AB, and injury history says not to count on that. xBA says BA rebounds some, but you buy him for power, not BA. 15-20 HR should be your baseline.

Yr Tm	AB	R	HR	RBI	SB	BA	xBA	vL	vR	OB	Slg	OPS	bb%	ct%	h%	Eye	G	L	F	PX	xPX	hr/f	Spd	SBO	SB%	#Wk	DOM	DIS	RC/G	RAR	BPV	BPX	R$
08 MIL	569	78	24	74	2	283	277	304	276	343	478	821	8	83	31	0.53	48	15	36	119	111	14%	129	2%	67%	27	41%	19%	5.81	30.5	65	127	$18
09 MIL *	485	58	14	56	0	225	232	169	245	292	356	648	9	80	25	0.47	46	14	40	81	124	8%	112	1%	0%	25	36%	40%	3.39	-10.5	18	37	$3
10 MIN	340	44	6	38	1	268	264	210	294	323	394	717	8	84	30	0.52	49	17	34	85	89	6%	121	2%	50%	23	48%	30%	4.40	4.8	44	96	$7
11 BAL	527	76	30	80	0	269	274	268	270	310	491	801	6	83	28	0.34	40	16	43	139	130	16%	77	0%	0%	23	52%	17%	5.32	21.3	63	140	$19
12 BAL	663	85	22	68	0	238	249	277	225	280	389	669	5	84	25	0.36	43	17	40	91	109	10%	97	0%	0%	27	33%	33%	3.64	-5.2	35	88	$10
1st Half	322	38	12	32	0	236	263	312	212	270	407	677	4	85	24	0.31	41	19	40	100	116	11%	103	0%	0%	13	15%	23%	3.67	-3.3	46	115	$9
2nd Half	341	47	10	36	0	240	235	247	238	288	372	661	6	83	26	0.40	45	15	39	83	102	9%	90	0%	0%	14	50%	43%	3.61	-4.1	24	60	$11
13 Proj	559	75	20	66	0	252	253	257	251	297	414	711	6	83	27	0.38	44	16	40	99	111	11%	94	1%	49%				4.18	2.9	42	106	$13

Harper,Bryce

Age 20	Bats L	Pos CF RF	Health	A	LIMA Plan	B
Ht 6' 3"	Wt 215		PT/Exp	F	Rand Var	0
			Consist	C	MM	4435

22-59-.270 in 533 AB at WAS. Phenom overshadowed by Trout, but a near 20-20 season at age 19 is amazing. Flashed elite ceiling in May (134 PX, 149 Spd, 91 BPV) and Sept (198 PX, 145 Spd, 130 BPV). 2H confirms that he's got 30-30 upside as he moves along growth curve. Unlike Trout, there's profit here.

Yr Tm	AB	R	HR	RBI	SB	BA	xBA	vL	vR	OB	Slg	OPS	bb%	ct%	h%	Eye	G	L	F	PX	xPX	hr/f	Spd	SBO	SB%	#Wk	DOM	DIS	RC/G	RAR	BPV	BPX	R$
08																																	
09																																	
10																																	
11 aa	129	12	3	10	6	245	251			311	372	684	9	80	29	0.48				91			95	24%	75%				3.91		40	0	$1
12 WAS *	607	105	23	62	19	265	272	240	286	334	459	793	9	78	31	0.47	45	23	33	122	107	16%	137	16%	73%	24	54%	8%	5.26	10.2	70	175	$23
1st Half	291	43	9	25	9	264	264	250	287	335	442	777	10	78	31	0.49	44	21	35	114	116	14%	127	16%	69%	10	60%	0%	5.03	2.2	61	153	$18
2nd Half	314	62	14	37	10	268	278	234	285	335	478	813	9	77	31	0.45	45	23	32	129	100	18%	136	16%	77%	14	50%	14%	5.56	7.2	75	188	$28
13 Proj	585	84	26	75	22	276	281	245	292	342	488	830	9	79	31	0.47	45	23	33	131	106	17%	117	19%	74%				5.81	17.6	76	189	$27

STEPHEN NICKRAND

Harrison,Josh

Age 25	Bats R	Pos 2B SS	Health	B	LIMA Plan	F
Ht 5' 8"	Wt 190		PT/Exp	C	Rand Var	+2
			Consist	A	MM	1411

Look at that Spd! Then look at everything else—it says "won't ever get to use it." But if we dig a little deeper, we see nuggets of hope: decent ct%, above-average xPX, and good LD%. Do these portend an uptick in production? Don't get crazy, now. He's more worth watching than worth buying.

Yr	Tm	AB	R	HR	RBI	SB	BA	xBA	vL	vR	OB	Slg	OPS	bb%	ct%	h%	Eye	G	L	F	PX	xPX	hr/f	Spd	SBO	SB%	#Wk	DOM	DIS	RC/G	RAR	BPV	BPX	R$
08																																		
09																																		
10	aa	520	59	3	59	15	268	265			302	352	654	5	89	29	0.46				61			94	18%	66%				3.61		47	0	$13
11	PIT *	421	48	5	34	14	269	257	226	293	293	381	674	3	87	30	0.26	45	17	38	78	88	2%	111	22%	67%	16	13%	50%	3.78	-10.1	52	116	$11
12	PIT	249	34	3	16	7	233	241	198	252	263	345	608	4	85	26	0.27	37	22	41	66	111	3%	152	20%	70%	27	26%	44%	2.96	-12.4	46	115	$2
1st Half		114	16	2	9	5	228	257	226	230	261	395	655	4	83	26	0.26	29	26	45	103	110	5%	126	42%	63%	13	46%	38%	3.15	-5.1	72	180	$3
2nd Half		135	18	1	7	2	237	226	152	265	264	304	568	4	87	27	0.28	43	19	38	35	113	2%	150	6%	100%	14	7%	50%	2.75	-7.4	19	48	$2
13	Proj	**168**	**21**	**2**	**13**	**5**	**251**	**244**	**208**	**272**	**279**	**350**	**630**	**4**	**87**	**28**	**0.30**	**40**	**20**	**40**	**63**	**102**	**3%**	**118**	**19%**	**69%**				**3.27**	**-5.0**	**42**	**104**	**$2**

Hart,Corey

Age 31	Bats R	Pos 1B RF	Health	B	LIMA Plan	B
Ht 6' 6"	Wt 237		PT/Exp	A	Rand Var	0
			Consist	A	MM	4235

A safe source of power, but there are a couple of warning signs elsewhere. The bigger concern is his slow decline in ct%. His 5-year high in DIS% indicates a growing inconsistency. Both could eventually erode his overall game. Reliability score now says "safe," but be careful.

Yr	Tm	AB	R	HR	RBI	SB	BA	xBA	vL	vR	OB	Slg	OPS	bb%	ct%	h%	Eye	G	L	F	PX	xPX	hr/f	Spd	SBO	SB%	#Wk	DOM	DIS	RC/G	RAR	BPV	BPX	R$
08	MIL	612	76	20	91	23	268	279	281	263	299	459	758	4	82	30	0.25	40	19	40	124	127	10%	104	25%	77%	27	63%	22%	4.74	-12.2	75	147	$22
09	MIL	419	64	12	48	11	260	252	248	264	329	418	747	9	78	31	0.47	41	17	42	105	118	9%	122	15%	65%	21	38%	29%	4.62	-10.0	48	98	$11
10	MIL	558	91	31	102	7	283	279	318	271	337	525	862	7	75	33	0.32	38	18	44	166	160	17%	109	10%	54%	27	59%	26%	6.09	10.5	76	165	$26
11	MIL	492	80	26	63	7	285	283	333	272	352	510	862	9	77	32	0.45	45	21	35	150	156	20%	113	10%	54%	23	57%	13%	6.18	10.6	75	167	$22
12	MIL	562	91	30	83	5	270	267	290	265	323	507	831	7	73	32	0.29	40	19	41	161	162	18%	98	4%	100%	27	56%	30%	5.79	5.8	67	168	$22
1st Half		287	45	15	36	2	251	259	273	244	302	502	804	7	69	31	0.24	39	16	45	182	181	17%	95	4%	100%	13	54%	23%	5.20	-1.4	69	173	$19
2nd Half		275	46	15	47	3	291	276	308	286	346	513	858	8	77	33	0.37	41	22	36	140	144	20%	96	4%	100%	14	57%	36%	6.45	8.3	61	153	$25
13	Proj	**548**	**88**	**29**	**82**	**7**	**277**	**270**	**304**	**269**	**335**	**507**	**842**	**8**	**75**	**32**	**0.35**	**41**	**20**	**39**	**151**	**155**	**18%**	**99**	**8%**	**69%**				**5.93**	**8.9**	**68**	**169**	**$24**

Headley,Chase

Age 29	Bats B	Pos 3B	Health	B	LIMA Plan	C
Ht 6' 2"	Wt 200		PT/Exp	A	Rand Var	-3
			Consist	C	MM	4225

REGRESSION ALERT! Yes, this was a significant power spike, without sacrificing plate discipline. And yes, he did show power potential in the minors. However, more than 1 out of every 4 flyballs went yard in the 2nd half, an unsustainable rate. Do not pay for more than 20 HR in 2013.

Yr	Tm	AB	R	HR	RBI	SB	BA	xBA	vL	vR	OB	Slg	OPS	bb%	ct%	h%	Eye	G	L	F	PX	xPX	hr/f	Spd	SBO	SB%	#Wk	DOM	DIS	RC/G	RAR	BPV	BPX	R$
08	SD *	590	70	18	67	4	256	245	276	265	317	418	735	8	69	34	0.28	38	25	37	127	133	11%	89	3%	80%	16	31%	56%	4.54	-1.0	17	33	$10
09	SD	543	62	12	64	10	262	240	244	270	337	392	729	10	76	33	0.47	45	17	38	94	111	8%	92	8%	83%	27	30%	37%	4.62	0.1	24	49	$12
10	SD	610	77	11	58	17	264	240	217	285	326	375	701	8	77	33	0.40	46	18	36	82	85	6%	109	13%	77%	27	30%	33%	4.26	-6.1	24	52	$16
11	SD	381	43	4	44	13	289	249	352	264	374	399	773	12	76	37	0.57	46	22	32	95	101	4%	81	12%	87%	21	29%	29%	5.49	9.5	31	69	$13
12	SD	604	95	31	115	17	286	268	265	296	375	498	874	12	74	34	0.55	48	19	32	141	134	21%	87	12%	74%	27	41%	41%	6.64	34.8	62	155	$32
1st Half		284	37	8	38	10	271	249	277	268	371	415	786	14	73	35	0.59	50	21	29	108	104	13%	81	14%	71%	13	31%	62%	5.35	6.4	29	73	$20
2nd Half		320	58	23	77	7	300	285	253	319	380	572	951	11	75	34	0.51	47	18	35	170	161	27%	96	9%	78%	14	50%	21%	7.88	29.3	87	218	$42
13	Proj	**590**	**82**	**22**	**86**	**16**	**282**	**257**	**275**	**285**	**363**	**457**	**820**	**11**	**75**	**34**	**0.50**	**47**	**20**	**33**	**121**	**119**	**15%**	**87**	**11%**	**79%**				**5.91**	**22.3**	**47**	**117**	**$26**

Hechavarria,Adeiny

Age 24	Bats R	Pos 3B	Health	A	LIMA Plan	D
Ht 5' 11"	Wt 180		PT/Exp	C	Rand Var	-4
			Consist	B	MM	1305

2-15-.254 in 126 AB at TOR. Had a hitting breakout of sorts at AAA-Las Vegas, but who doesn't hit well in the PCL? His peripherals, though, are not kind. xBA says his BA was a mirage. Sub-.300 OBP limits SB opps. Power is nonexistent. Could claim an IF slot, but his stat line won't be pretty.

Yr	Tm	AB	R	HR	RBI	SB	BA	xBA	vL	vR	OB	Slg	OPS	bb%	ct%	h%	Eye	G	L	F	PX	xPX	hr/f	Spd	SBO	SB%	#Wk	DOM	DIS	RC/G	RAR	BPV	BPX	R$
08																																		
09																																		
10	aa	253	28	2	26	5	239	238			266	314	580	4	82	28	0.21				54			99	14%	58%				2.71		7	0	$2
11	a/a	572	53	6	41	14	229	239			259	327	586	4	81	27	0.21				70			111	26%	46%				2.51		19	0	$5
12	TOR *	569	64	6	58	6	261	236	234	266	298	356	654	5	77	33	0.23	48	21	31	69	98	7%	121	5%	71%	10	10%	50%	3.65	-4.1	2	5	$10
1st Half		325	39	3	37	5	263	229			299	360	660	5	77	33	0.23	44	20	36	72			113	9%	68%				3.69		7	18	$14
2nd Half		244	24	3	21	1	259	230	234	266	296	351	648	5	76	33	0.22	48	21	31	64	98	7%	119	1%	100%	10	10%	50%	3.60	-2.9	-13	-33	$5
13	Proj	**435**	**45**	**4**	**39**	**7**	**246**	**239**	**227**	**258**	**279**	**337**	**617**	**4**	**79**	**30**	**0.22**	**48**	**21**	**31**	**64**	**59**	**4%**	**126**	**13%**	**54%**				**3.06**	**-19.8**	**5**	**12**	**$7**

Heisey,Chris

Age 28	Bats R	Pos LF CF	Health	A	LIMA Plan	D+
Ht 6' 0"	Wt 220		PT/Exp	D	Rand Var	-2
			Consist	C	MM	4413

With the exception of August 2011, has gotten at-bats in every week over the past two years, but has seen even 25 AB in a single week only once. It is tough to gain footing with such sporadic usage and some players need that regular playing time. Looking at his 2009 line, he might be one of them.

Yr	Tm	AB	R	HR	RBI	SB	BA	xBA	vL	vR	OB	Slg	OPS	bb%	ct%	h%	Eye	G	L	F	PX	xPX	hr/f	Spd	SBO	SB%	#Wk	DOM	DIS	RC/G	RAR	BPV	BPX	R$
08	aa	79	8	2	7	4	273	260			294	421	715	3	78	33	0.13				105			99	23%	100%				4.60		37	0	$1
09	a/a	516	73	20	62	17	278	288			329	465	794	7	83	30	0.44				116			92	16%	83%				5.46		72	0	$19
10	CIN *	280	37	11	30	2	239	234	169	321	292	410	702	7	70	30	0.25	35	19	45	127	135	13%	99	7%	55%	23	39%	43%	3.93	-6.6	18	39	$4
11	CIN	279	44	18	50	6	254	249	197	271	302	487	789	6	72	29	0.24	32	19	49	157	129	19%	102	11%	86%	24	50%	33%	5.08	2.8	57	127	$11
12	CIN	347	44	7	31	6	265	234	274	262	301	401	702	5	77	33	0.22	37	22	41	90	71	7%	130	11%	67%	27	41%	44%	4.12	-6.0	25	63	$8
1st Half		199	19	2	15	2	261	227	225	270	290	362	652	4	78	33	0.18	39	21	40	72	53	3%	114	11%	40%	13	38%	46%	3.42	-7.2	3	8	$5
2nd Half		148	25	5	16	4	270	243	318	250	316	453	769	6	75	33	0.27	35	23	42	115	96	11%	129	11%	100%	14	43%	43%	5.17	2.2	47	118	$11
13	Proj	**395**	**57**	**16**	**48**	**8**	**261**	**241**	**238**	**269**	**305**	**447**	**752**	**6**	**75**	**31**	**0.25**	**35**	**21**	**45**	**121**	**105**	**12%**	**116**	**11%**	**78%**				**4.69**	**0.5**	**43**	**108**	**$14**

Helton,Todd

Age 39	Bats L	Pos 1B	Health	F	LIMA Plan	F
Ht 6' 2"	Wt 220		PT/Exp	C	Rand Var	+5
			Consist	D	MM	2111

His season ended in August with a torn hip labrum. That shouldn't be an issue going forward— if only it was the last injury he'll suffer. Terrific skills are pretty much still intact, but at 39 with his health history, his value - even as an end-gamer - is questionable.

Yr	Tm	AB	R	HR	RBI	SB	BA	xBA	vL	vR	OB	Slg	OPS	bb%	ct%	h%	Eye	G	L	F	PX	xPX	hr/f	Spd	SBO	SB%	#Wk	DOM	DIS	RC/G	RAR	BPV	BPX	R$
08	COL	299	39	7	29	0	264	261	246	270	389	388	777	17	83	30	1.22	38	23	38	82	111	7%	63	0%	0%	16	31%	25%	5.23	-1.6	41	80	$4
09	COL	544	79	15	86	0	325	299	311	332	420	489	909	14	87	36	1.22	40	25	36	102	97	9%	84	0%	0%	26	62%	15%	7.72	33.0	71	145	$22
10	COL	398	48	8	37	0	256	237	272	248	363	367	730	14	77	31	0.74	34	23	43	81	119	6%	78	0%	0%	23	17%	57%	4.57	-9.9	14	30	$5
11	COL	421	59	14	69	0	302	288	292	307	388	466	853	12	83	34	0.83	35	27	38	112	128	10%	64	1%	0%	25	52%	20%	6.53	12.7	56	124	$17
12	COL	240	31	7	37	1	238	277	184	268	344	400	744	14	82	26	0.89	41	25	34	108	126	10%	61	3%	50%	18	50%	39%	4.56	-6.2	58	145	$3
1st Half		211	29	7	34	1	246	285	200	275	343	417	760	13	83	27	0.89	39	26	35	108	133	11%	64	2%	100%	13	54%	31%	4.87	-3.1	66	165	$5
2nd Half		29	2	0	3	0	172	214	0	227	351	276	627	22	69	25	0.89	57	14	29	108	60	0%	67	10%	0%	5	40%	60%	2.65	-2.7	15	38	-$11
13	Proj	**181**	**24**	**3**	**25**	**0**	**274**	**255**	**222**	**297**	**374**	**394**	**768**	**14**	**82**	**32**	**0.90**	**43**	**22**	**35**	**83**	**105**	**7%**	**66**	**1%**	**65%**				**5.17**	**-1.0**	**37**	**93**	**$5**

Hernandez,Gorkys

Age 25	Bats R	Pos CF	Health	A	LIMA Plan	F
Ht 6' 0"	Wt 190		PT/Exp	C	Rand Var	+3
			Consist	A	MM	1401

3-13-7-.192 in 156 AB at PIT/MIA. Yet another player on the Esix Snead List, but even worse. Yes, he has solid speed skill. Yes, his SB potential is derailed by a sub-.300 OBP. But worse - his sub-70% SB success rate is pitiful, so there is no reason to ever give him a green light even if he did reach base.

Yr	Tm	AB	R	HR	RBI	SB	BA	xBA	vL	vR	OB	Slg	OPS	bb%	ct%	h%	Eye	G	L	F	PX	xPX	hr/f	Spd	SBO	SB%	#Wk	DOM	DIS	RC/G	RAR	BPV	BPX	R$
08																																		
09	aa	556	65	2	42	17	258	220			297	323	621	5	76	34	0.23				52			104	23%	49%				3.00		-14	0	$10
10	aa	368	36	2	21	14	237	205			287	293	580	7	73	32	0.26				44			126	17%	80%				2.88		-23	0	$4
11	aaa	424	37	1	30	16	244	228			288	331	619	6	77	32	0.27				69			110	26%	61%				3.05		12	0	$6
12	2 NL *	393	53	5	33	18	212	225	159	215	284	299	583	9	72	28	0.36	58	18	24	62	72	12%	141	27%	64%	17	12%	53%	2.64	-31.3	-3	-8	$5
1st Half		226	33	2	22	11	241	232	0	333	317	318	635	10	72	33	0.41	50	25	25	62	82	0%	111	26%	61%	3	0%	33%	3.22	-12.5	-6	-15	$9
2nd Half		167	20	3	11	7	173	223	169	207	238	275	513	8	71	22	0.30	59	17	24	62	71	13%	167	28%	68%	14	14%	57%	1.98	-16.8	-6	-15	$0
13	Proj	**162**	**18**	**3**	**12**	**7**	**222**	**238**	**197**	**240**	**280**	**335**	**615**	**7**	**74**	**28**	**0.30**	**59**	**17**	**24**	**76**	**64**	**10%**	**130**	**26%**	**65%**				**2.96**	**-9.2**	**7**	**18**	**$3**

MATT CEDERHOLM

Hernandez,Ramon

Age	37	Bats	R	Pos CA	Health	D	LIMA Plan	F
Ht	6' 0"	Wt	220		PT/Exp	D	Rand Var	+5
					Consist	C	MM	2021

Missed six weeks with tendinitis in his hand, then popped his hamstring in September, leading to off-season surgery. Yes, his xBA says the awful BA was mostly bad luck, but ct%, bb%, and PX all point to an overall decline. Rand Var is optimistic, but 2012 with better BA is about the best you can hope for.

Yr	Tm	AB	R	HR	RBI	SB	BA	xBA	vL	vR	OB	Slg	OPS	bb%	ct%	h%	Eye	G	L	F	PX	xPX	hr/f	Spd	SBO	SB%	#Wk	DOM	DIS	RC/G	RAR	BPV	BPX	R$
08	BAL	463	49	15	65	0	257	272	283	245	305	406	711	6	87	27	0.52	47	20	33	89	116	11%	63	0%	0%	27	44%	26%	4.25	-0.4	42	82	$7
09	CIN	287	25	5	37	1	258	266	288	246	334	362	697	10	88	28	0.97	49	19	32	64	92	6%	68	1%	100%	17	35%	35%	4.19	-0.8	40	82	$3
10	CIN	313	30	7	48	0	297	269	303	295	357	428	785	8	84	33	0.59	52	20	29	89	81	9%	84	0%	0%	26	42%	50%	5.54	10.8	35	76	$9
11	CIN	298	28	12	36	0	282	265	323	271	333	446	780	7	86	29	0.56	52	19	29	101	99	16%	61	0%	0%	27	33%	33%	5.28	8.3	45	100	$8
12	COL	184	16	5	28	0	217	264	152	239	242	353	595	3	83	24	0.19	53	21	26	89	106	13%	54	3%	0%	18	22%	50%	2.71	-8.9	19	48	$0
1st Half		93	8	4	15	0	215	275	143	246	255	398	653	5	87	21	0.42	52	17	30	107	114	16%	44	6%	0%	8	25%	38%	3.12	-3.2	54	135	$0
2nd Half		91	8	1	13	0	220	254	167	233	228	308	536	1	78	27	0.05	54	25	21	69	96	7%	72	0%	0%	10	20%	60%	2.30	-5.3	-19	-48	-$1
13	**Proj**	**232**	**21**	**6**	**33**	**0**	**250**	**260**	**230**	**256**	**289**	**381**	**669**	**5**	**84**	**28**	**0.34**	**52**	**21**	**27**	**84**	**99**	**11%**	**60**	**1%**	**7%**				**3.70**	**-3.5**	**22**	**55**	**$2**

Herrera,Elian

Age	28	Bats	B	Pos LF 3B	Health	A	LIMA Plan	F
Ht	5' 10"	Wt	188		PT/Exp	C	Rand Var	0
					Consist	B	MM	1311

1-17-4-.251 in 187 AB at LA. When you hit ~60% ground balls, you'd better have some serious speed to leg them out. He doesn't. Nor does he have power, patience, or great contact ability, and at 28, they're not likely to develop. Only his mom would find these skills rosterable, but she already has a LF/3Bman.

Yr	Tm	AB	R	HR	RBI	SB	BA	xBA	vL	vR	OB	Slg	OPS	bb%	ct%	h%	Eye	G	L	F	PX	xPX	hr/f	Spd	SBO	SB%	#Wk	DOM	DIS	RC/G	RAR	BPV	BPX	R$
08																																		
09																																		
10	a/a	347	33	1	29	20	193	199			265	241	506	9	72	26	0.35				39			114	37%	61%				1.90		-26	0	$2
11	aa	378	47	2	24	22	218	194			290	286	576	9	67	32	0.31				61			115	34%	62%				2.56		-24	0	$5
12	LA *	460	55	3	40	10	250	256	265	244	299	345	645	7	76	32	0.30	56	23	20	73	34	4%	113	19%	49%	14	14%	57%	3.27	-18.6	9	23	$7
1st Half		268	32	1	23	9	256	258	271	236	310	352	662	7	76	33	0.33	54	24	21	76	37	0%	107	22%	61%	7	14%	43%	3.57	-8.1	16	40	$11
2nd Half		192	23	2	17	1	241	253	222	267	285	336	621	6	76	31	0.25	64	20	16	68	19	25%	112	14%	19%	7	14%	71%	2.87	-10.1	-2	-5	$3
13	**Proj**	**129**	**15**	**2**	**10**	**5**	**236**	**246**	**231**	**238**	**295**	**338**	**633**	**8**	**72**	**31**	**0.30**	**60**	**22**	**18**	**75**	**26**	**10%**	**108**	**26%**	**55%**				**3.08**	**-6.3**	**-1**	**-3**	**$3**

Herrera,Jonathan

Age	28	Bats	B	Pos SS	Health	C	LIMA Plan	F
Ht	5' 9"	Wt	180		PT/Exp	D	Rand Var	0
					Consist	A	MM	0211

3-12-4-.262 in 225 AB at COL. It's always interesting to see these guys with poor skill, questionable health and not a lot of experience, but boy are they CONSISTENT. He's like a restaurant where the food is terrible, the portions are small, the prices are high, the wallpaper is peeling... but the service is great.

Yr	Tm	AB	R	HR	RBI	SB	BA	xBA	vL	vR	OB	Slg	OPS	bb%	ct%	h%	Eye	G	L	F	PX	xPX	hr/f	Spd	SBO	SB%	#Wk	DOM	DIS	RC/G	RAR	BPV	BPX	R$
08	COL *	287	31	2	23	11	251	265	200	244	291	305	596	5	85	29	0.37	56	23	21	35	52	0%	108	18%	76%	7	14%	43%	3.06	-11.0	10	20	$4
09	aaa	381	41	1	22	11	225	236			284	283	567	8	85	26	0.57				35			131	16%	64%				2.59		19	0	$1
10	COL *	444	52	2	31	4	245	233	292	280	308	298	606	8	85	29	0.59	50	18	32	36	26	2%	123	7%	40%	17	18%	53%	2.98	-18.2	6	13	$3
11	COL	281	28	3	14	4	242	246	250	239	311	299	610	9	86	27	0.70	49	23	28	35	48	5%	115	9%	50%	23	13%	52%	3.02	-11.3	10	22	$1
12	COL *	254	31	4	13	4	248	260	231	272	293	339	632	6	84	28	0.40	52	22	26	59	39	6%	107	8%	80%	23	22%	35%	3.39	-7.1	23	58	$1
1st Half		95	18	3	6	2	242	283	136	274	273	389	662	4	86	25	0.31	43	25	32	90	57	12%	91	11%	100%	10	30%	20%	3.68	-1.6	58	145	$1
2nd Half		130	11	0	6	2	277	232	300	270	338	323	661	8	80	35	0.46	59	20	22	35	26	0%	112	7%	67%	13	15%	46%	3.83	-1.6	-13	-33	$1
13	**Proj**	**130**	**15**	**1**	**7**	**2**	**253**	**246**	**252**	**253**	**308**	**318**	**626**	**7**	**84**	**29**	**0.49**	**52**	**22**	**27**	**43**	**40**	**4%**	**104**	**9%**	**65%**				**3.30**	**-2.7**	**10**	**26**	**$2**

Heyward,Jason

Age	23	Bats	L	Pos RF	Health	A	LIMA Plan	B
Ht	6' 5"	Wt	240		PT/Exp	A	Rand Var	0
					Consist	D	MM	4325

Looks like a breakout, but more like a baby step in the right direction. Stagnant, sub-par ct% will cap BA, and average speed / SB% say he's reached SB ceiling, too. But that's not the good part—those growing flyball and power skills suggest a budding slugger in the making. UP: 40 HR

Yr	Tm	AB	R	HR	RBI	SB	BA	xBA	vL	vR	OB	Slg	OPS	bb%	ct%	h%	Eye	G	L	F	PX	xPX	hr/f	Spd	SBO	SB%	#Wk	DOM	DIS	RC/G	RAR	BPV	BPX	R$
08																																		
09	a/a	173	32	6	29	5	338	312			433	560	993	14	87	36	1.27				127			114	10%	84%				9.42		116	0	$9
10	ATL	520	83	18	72	11	277	278	249	291	385	456	840	15	75	34	0.71	55	18	27	126	100	17%	109	9%	65%	25	60%	36%	6.08	13.9	64	139	$20
11	ATL	396	50	14	42	9	227	251	192	240	315	389	704	11	77	26	0.55	54	13	33	112	106	14%	87	10%	82%	24	42%	42%	4.09	-12.7	48	107	$7
12	ATL	587	93	27	82	21	269	261	224	300	335	479	814	9	74	32	0.38	44	19	37	138	132	17%	105	19%	72%	27	56%	22%	5.51	6.1	63	158	$26
1st Half		261	42	12	38	10	272	268	228	300	340	502	842	9	75	32	0.41	39	21	40	152	129	15%	110	20%	77%	13	62%	23%	5.95	7.1	80	200	$24
2nd Half		326	51	15	44	11	267	255	221	300	331	460	791	9	74	32	0.36	48	18	34	127	135	19%	98	18%	69%	14	50%	21%	5.16	1.5	47	118	$28
13	**Proj**	**573**	**88**	**28**	**94**	**17**	**266**	**269**	**228**	**287**	**347**	**485**	**832**	**11**	**76**	**31**	**0.52**	**47**	**17**	**36**	**140**	**118**	**18%**	**94**	**14%**	**74%**				**5.80**	**13.3**	**74**	**185**	**$26**

Hill,Aaron

Age	31	Bats	R	Pos 2B	Health	B	LIMA Plan	B+
Ht	5' 11"	Wt	205		PT/Exp	A	Rand Var	-4
					Consist	D	MM	4235

At first glance, it looks like skills are all over the place. But really, 2011 looks like the outlier, with power outage fueled by injuries. Throw that out and factor in consistent Eye and FB rate, and suddenly his overall trends look more consistent, and gives us more confidence he will follow up well.

Yr	Tm	AB	R	HR	RBI	SB	BA	xBA	vL	vR	OB	Slg	OPS	bb%	ct%	h%	Eye	G	L	F	PX	xPX	hr/f	Spd	SBO	SB%	#Wk	DOM	DIS	RC/G	RAR	BPV	BPX	R$
08	TOR	205	19	2	20	4	263	234	286	258	317	361	678	7	85	30	0.52	35	17	47	73	93	2%	90	11%	67%	9	33%	44%	3.91	-2.6	31	61	$2
09	TOR	682	103	36	108	6	286	294	298	282	327	499	826	6	86	29	0.43	39	20	41	122	120	15%	81	5%	75%	27	48%	11%	5.81	28.0	73	149	$27
10	TOR	528	70	26	68	2	205	245	125	228	262	394	656	7	84	20	0.48	35	11	54	115	132	11%	73	4%	50%	25	56%	24%	3.26	-17.9	60	130	$5
11	2 TM	520	61	8	61	21	246	250	241	248	294	356	649	6	86	27	0.49	37	21	42	75	85	4%	89	22%	75%	25	36%	28%	3.53	-12.7	53	118	$13
12	ARI	609	93	26	85	14	302	286	271	316	357	522	879	8	86	32	0.60	34	21	45	132	145	11%	107	12%	74%	27	59%	11%	6.75	40.5	98	245	$30
1st Half		279	35	11	38	7	301	270	350	281	359	516	875	8	84	33	0.56	30	22	48	127	147	10%	130	12%	78%	13	46%	8%	6.74	19.1	89	223	$25
2nd Half		330	58	15	47	7	303	300	213	347	356	527	883	8	88	31	0.66	38	20	42	136	143	13%	84	12%	70%	14	71%	14%	6.76	22.8	102	255	$34
13	**Proj**	**584**	**81**	**25**	**77**	**14**	**288**	**276**	**259**	**298**	**340**	**493**	**832**	**7**	**86**	**30**	**0.55**	**36**	**19**	**45**	**122**	**124**	**11%**	**92**	**13%**	**73%**				**5.93**	**27.6**	**84**	**211**	**$27**

Hinske,Eric

Age	35	Bats	L	Pos 1B	Health	A	LIMA Plan	F
Ht	6' 2"	Wt	235		PT/Exp	F	Rand Var	+2
					Consist	C	MM	3001

Imagine for a moment that Eric Hinske is your life-long idol; you're the kind of fan who would buy scalped tickets on Eric Hinske bobblehead day. You'd go a buck for him at the end of the auction, right? No? Really, Hinske's #1 fan? Not even you?

Yr	Tm	AB	R	HR	RBI	SB	BA	xBA	vL	vR	OB	Slg	OPS	bb%	ct%	h%	Eye	G	L	F	PX	xPX	hr/f	Spd	SBO	SB%	#Wk	DOM	DIS	RC/G	RAR	BPV	BPX	R$
08	TAM	381	59	20	60	10	247	273	143	262	329	465	794	11	77	27	0.53	39	20	41	141	110	17%	61	13%	77%	27	52%	33%	5.17	0.3	71	139	$11
09	2 TM	190	31	8	25	1	242	251	244	242	336	432	768	12	73	29	0.52	37	18	45	135	114	13%	92	2%	100%	27	41%	52%	4.92	-1.2	41	84	$3
10	ATL	281	38	11	51	0	256	263	381	246	334	456	790	11	73	31	0.44	33	20	47	151	129	11%	48	0%	0%	27	44%	41%	5.22	0.6	49	107	$7
11	ATL	236	24	10	28	0	233	234	114	252	309	403	712	10	70	29	0.37	45	19	35	127	129	17%	42	2%	0%	27	33%	59%	4.06	-7.6	9	20	$2
12	ATL	132	9	2	13	0	197	203	118	209	274	311	585	10	69	27	0.34	47	15	37	91	101	6%	55	0%	0%	27	30%	56%	2.70	-10.1	-17	-43	-$3
1st Half		96	6	1	10	0	208	203	71	232	276	292	568	9	72	28	0.33	51	17	32	60	94	5%	66	0%	0%	13	15%	69%	2.59	-7.2	-32	-80	-$3
2nd Half		36	3	1	3	0	167	209	333	152	268	361	629	12	61	24	0.36	36	9	55	189	125	8%	57	0%	0%	14	43%	43%	2.96	-2.4	27	68	-$3
13	**Proj**	**126**	**14**	**3**	**17**	**0**	**234**	**219**	**207**	**238**	**313**	**377**	**690**	**10**	**72**	**30**	**0.42**	**41**	**16**	**43**	**104**	**119**	**9%**	**54**	**2%**	**68%**				**3.92**	**-5.4**	**12**	**29**	**$2**

Holliday,Matt

Age	33	Bats	R	Pos LF	Health	A	LIMA Plan	B
Ht	6' 4"	Wt	235		PT/Exp	A	Rand Var	-2
					Consist	A	MM	4135

Strong year-to-year consistency. Slipping ct% is worth noting, though, as is a series of minor health issues the last couple of seasons. He played through those this year, but as he moves deeper into his 30s, nagging injuries can nag a bit harder. If his health holds up, though, count on him to produce. Again.

Yr	Tm	AB	R	HR	RBI	SB	BA	xBA	vL	vR	OB	Slg	OPS	bb%	ct%	h%	Eye	G	L	F	PX	xPX	hr/f	Spd	SBO	SB%	#Wk	DOM	DIS	RC/G	RAR	BPV	BPX	R$
08	COL	539	107	25	88	28	321	300	293	329	403	538	941	12	81	36	0.71	46	22	33	140	102	17%	112	16%	93%	24	58%	21%	8.46	53.8	97	190	$37
09	2 TM	581	94	24	109	14	313	286	289	322	389	515	904	11	83	35	0.71	44	17	39	125	120	13%	97	11%	67%	27	52%	22%	7.29	40.7	81	165	$30
10	STL	596	95	28	103	9	312	298	344	301	383	532	915	10	84	33	0.74	42	17	41	142	133	14%	77	8%	64%	27	67%	7%	7.44	44.1	94	204	$32
11	STL	446	83	22	75	2	296	298	256	306	379	525	904	12	79	33	0.65	46	21	34	160	128	18%	73	2%	67%	25	60%	20%	7.18	30.3	86	191	$22
12	STL	599	95	27	102	4	295	270	316	288	374	497	871	11	78	34	0.57	46	19	35	132	145	16%	90	4%	50%	27	44%	30%	6.61	31.4	60	150	$27
1st Half		290	51	12	48	3	307	274	342	295	389	500	889	12	80	35	0.67	45	20	35	124	139	15%	103	5%	60%	13	38%	23%	7.06	19.1	66	165	$29
2nd Half		309	44	15	54	1	285	265	293	282	359	495	855	10	76	33	0.49	47	18	35	139	152	18%	74	3%	33%	14	50%	36%	6.21	13.6	52	130	$26
13	**Proj**	**560**	**93**	**26**	**96**	**3**	**299**	**279**	**304**	**298**	**377**	**512**	**889**	**11**	**79**	**34**	**0.61**	**45**	**19**	**36**	**139**	**136**	**17%**	**80**	**3%**	**54%**				**6.95**	**35.7**	**69**	**173**	**$27**

MATT CEDERHOLM

Hosmer,Eric

Age	23	Bats	L	Pos	1B	Health	A	LIMA Plan	B
Ht	6' 4"	Wt	230			PT/Exp	C	Rand Var	+4
						Consist	C	MM	2235

CON: Power outage that got worse in 2H; declining GB% didn't help. Spd didn't support SBs. Ended year with small rotator cuff tear. PRO: Contact and patience held up from rookie year. xBA more optimistic. Should be healthy come March. He's only 23. Draft price will be depressed. Near-guaranteed built-in profit here.

Yr	Tm	AB	R	HR	RBI	SB	BA	xBA	vL	vR	OB	Slg	OPS	bb%	ct%	h%	Eye	G	L	F	PX	xPX	hr/f	Spd	SBO	SB%	#Wk	DOM	DIS	RC/G	RAR	BPV	BPX	R$
08																																		
09																																		
10	aa	195	30	9	27	2	282	314			321	514	835	5	85	29	0.40				142			111	8%	68%				5.79		100	0	$7
11	KC *	621	82	21	89	13	309	279	237	315	359	471	830	7	84	34	0.49	50	19	32	104	106	13%	80	10%	73%	22	45%	32%	6.18	15.2	62	138	$30
12	KC	535	65	14	60	16	232	262	220	238	305	359	663	9	82	26	0.59	54	18	28	80	95	11%	78	12%	94%	26	46%	31%	3.76	-24.6	45	113	$11
1st Half		275	29	9	36	7	225	285	202	236	290	378	668	8	87	23	0.71	55	18	27	90	98	14%	73	13%	88%	13	62%	15%	3.68	-14.1	65	163	$11
2nd Half		260	36	5	24	9	238	236	235	241	320	338	658	11	77	29	0.52	52	19	29	68	90	8%	88	12%	100%	13	31%	46%	3.83	-11.9	16	40	$11
13	**Proj**	**559**	**74**	**18**	**70**	**12**	**267**	**271**	**237**	**282**	**328**	**421**	**749**	**8**	**83**	**30**	**0.52**	**52**	**19**	**30**	**95**	**98**	**13%**	**82**	**9%**	**83%**				**4.84**	**-8.4**	**54**	**135**	**$17**

Howard,Ryan

Age	33	Bats	L	Pos	1B	Health	D	LIMA Plan	C+
Ht	6' 4"	Wt	242			PT/Exp	B	Rand Var	+2
						Consist	C	MM	4115

Missed half the season recovering from a torn Achilles tendon. While power held up on his return, bb% and ct% stayed on the DL. With an abysmal BA vs. LHP, he'd be in danger of becoming a platoon player—if it weren't for the $105M left on his contract. As is, he might not get pitches to hit. DN: .200 BA, 20 HR.

Yr	Tm	AB	R	HR	RBI	SB	BA	xBA	vL	vR	OB	Slg	OPS	bb%	ct%	h%	Eye	G	L	F	PX	xPX	hr/f	Spd	SBO	SB%	#Wk	DOM	DIS	RC/G	RAR	BPV	BPX	R$
08	PHI	610	105	48	146	1	251	281	224	268	339	543	881	12	67	29	0.41	41	22	36	201	194	32%	64	1%	50%	27	48%	33%	6.22	14.3	76	149	$23
09	PHI	616	105	45	141	8	279	291	207	320	357	571	929	11	70	33	0.40	36	23	41	199	202	25%	69	6%	89%	26	54%	15%	7.27	32.1	91	186	$30
10	PHI	550	87	31	108	1	276	273	264	283	346	505	852	10	71	33	0.38	40	23	37	157	153	21%	98	1%	50%	26	38%	38%	6.14	11.1	55	120	$23
11	PHI	557	81	33	116	1	253	264	224	266	342	488	830	12	69	31	0.44	40	21	39	175	175	22%	46	1%	100%	27	41%	44%	5.71	4.6	56	124	$21
12	PHI	260	28	14	56	0	219	237	173	247	288	423	711	9	62	29	0.25	43	26	31	159	143	27%	47	0%	0%	13	31%	54%	3.98	-11.5	0	0	$4
1st Half																																		
2nd Half		260	28	14	56	0	219	237	173	247	288	423	711	9	62	29	0.25	43	26	31	159	143	27%	47	0%	0%	13	31%	54%	3.98	-11.0	-1	-3	$4
13	**Proj**	**502**	**62**	**25**	**87**	**1**	**243**	**252**	**207**	**262**	**320**	**447**	**767**	**10**	**67**	**31**	**0.35**	**44**	**24**	**32**	**148**	**166**	**23%**	**60**	**1%**	**77%**				**4.82**	**-8.1**	**27**	**68**	**$14**

Hudson,Orlando

Age	35	Bats	B	Pos	2B 3B	Health	C	LIMA Plan	F
Ht	6' 0"	Wt	190			PT/Exp	C	Rand Var	+5
						Consist	B	MM	2421

The Baseball Forecaster research department spent six weeks trying to find a fantasy league where "Veteran Leadership" was a scoring category. We found one: an 8-team, 24x24 league of sabermetric ranchers in Ulm, MT. Free-falling BPV tells you all you need to know about his outlook in all the traditional categories.

Yr	Tm	AB	R	HR	RBI	SB	BA	xBA	vL	vR	OB	Slg	OPS	bb%	ct%	h%	Eye	G	L	F	PX	xPX	hr/f	Spd	SBO	SB%	#Wk	DOM	DIS	RC/G	RAR	BPV	BPX	R$
08	ARI	407	54	8	41	4	305	291	269	321	367	450	817	9	85	34	0.65	48	23	29	97	91	8%	98	4%	80%	19	47%	26%	6.06	21.1	61	120	$13
09	LA	551	74	9	62	8	283	284	293	280	356	417	773	10	82	33	0.63	56	19	26	90	75	8%	101	5%	89%	27	37%	30%	5.34	18.2	54	110	$15
10	MIN	497	80	6	37	10	268	263	261	272	335	372	707	9	82	31	0.57	49	21	31	72	90	5%	120	9%	77%	24	42%	38%	4.36	2.7	43	93	$12
11	SD	398	54	7	43	19	246	248	226	256	329	352	681	11	79	30	0.58	58	15	27	73	85	8%	110	18%	86%	23	30%	35%	4.08	-1.0	34	76	$11
12	2 TM	260	21	3	28	6	204	233	221	198	261	312	572	7	80	24	0.39	47	20	33	56	63	4%	157	15%	67%	25	16%	56%	2.56	-13.2	16	40	-$1
1st Half		216	18	2	22	4	199	229	237	185	258	306	563	7	81	24	0.43	43	20	37	55	63	3%	149	15%	57%	13	15%	46%	2.42	-12.7	18	45	$0
2nd Half		44	3	1	6	2	227	251	167	280	277	341	618	6	75	28	0.27	69	19	13	60	59	25%	117	18%	100%	12	17%	67%	3.34	-1.2	-7	-18	-$3
13	**Proj**	**159**	**20**	**4**	**16**	**4**	**230**	**266**	**207**	**242**	**299**	**373**	**672**	**9**	**80**	**27**	**0.49**	**56**	**19**	**25**	**89**	**73**	**12%**	**117**	**12%**	**75%**				**3.70**	**-2.7**	**44**	**109**	**$3**

Huff,Aubrey

Age	36	Bats	L	Pos	1B	Health	D	LIMA Plan	D+
Ht	6' 4"	Wt	225			PT/Exp	C	Rand Var	+5
						Consist	F	MM	2023

Opened the year in a battle for PT and never found a groove in the sporadic ABs. Lost 3 weeks with anxiety disorder. Then, hurt his knee during Matt Cain's no-hitter celebration, which capped a lost season. There are still glimmers of skill here, but odds are against a 36 year-old getting the opportunity to find them again.

Yr	Tm	AB	R	HR	RBI	SB	BA	xBA	vL	vR	OB	Slg	OPS	bb%	ct%	h%	Eye	G	L	F	PX	xPX	hr/f	Spd	SBO	SB%	#Wk	DOM	DIS	RC/G	RAR	BPV	BPX	R$
08	BAL	598	96	32	108	4	304	306	270	321	361	552	913	8	85	31	0.60	41	17	42	151	137	15%	79	3%	100%	27	67%	19%	7.35	31.3	102	200	$28
09	2 AL	536	59	15	85	0	241	254	232	245	307	384	691	9	84	26	0.59	48	15	36	91	103	9%	61	4%	0%	27	37%	37%	3.77	-26.8	36	73	$7
10	SF	569	100	26	86	7	290	300	296	287	380	506	887	13	84	31	0.91	45	18	37	135	120	14%	94	4%	100%	27	63%	11%	7.01	25.0	103	224	$25
11	SF	521	45	12	59	5	246	244	270	237	308	370	679	8	83	28	0.52	46	16	38	86	94	7%	73	6%	63%	27	33%	41%	3.82	-24.9	34	76	$8
12	SF	78	7	1	7	0	192	226	111	203	330	282	612	17	85	22	1.33	36	19	45	63	123	3%	69	0%	0%	16	31%	56%	2.94	-6.1	29	73	-$3
1st Half		58	7	1	5	0	155	229	111	163	300	259	559	17	86	16	1.50	35	18	47	69	97	4%	67	0%	0%	9	44%	44%	2.34	-5.8	44	110	-$3
2nd Half		20	0	0	2	0	300	224		300	417	350	767	17	80	38	1.00	38	25	38	45	207	0%	82	0%	0%	7	14%	71%	5.31	0.0	-11	-28	-$2
13	**Proj**	**308**	**40**	**10**	**39**	**1**	**251**	**256**	**257**	**249**	**341**	**409**	**751**	**12**	**84**	**27**	**0.88**	**42**	**17**	**41**	**99**	**107**	**9%**	**68**	**2%**	**46%**				**4.72**	**-5.8**	**58**	**145**	**$7**

Hundley,Nick

Age	29	Bats	R	Pos	CA	Health	F	LIMA Plan	D
Ht	6' 1"	Wt	205			PT/Exp	D	Rand Var	+5
						Consist	F	MM	2003

3-22-.157 in 204 AB at SD. Finally succumbed to torn meniscus with knee surgery in August. Knee may have been an issue all year, but regardless, underlying power indicators—hard-hit balls, FB%, and xPX—all remain solid. Low ct% means BA will remain mediocre, but past power skills and regression point to a rebound.

Yr	Tm	AB	R	HR	RBI	SB	BA	xBA	vL	vR	OB	Slg	OPS	bb%	ct%	h%	Eye	G	L	F	PX	xPX	hr/f	Spd	SBO	SB%	#Wk	DOM	DIS	RC/G	RAR	BPV	BPX	R$
08	SD *	422	44	13	51	0	204	222	224	243	245	338	583	5	75	24	0.21	39	17	44	91	108	8%	98	0%	0%	14	7%	50%	2.65	-21.5	-3	-6	-$2
09	SD	256	23	8	30	5	238	236	159	267	313	406	720	10	70	31	0.37	31	22	47	123	127	9%	99	9%	83%	20	30%	55%	4.30	0.1	26	53	$3
10	SD	273	33	8	43	0	249	259	274	242	312	418	730	8	76	30	0.38	41	19	40	124	116	10%	98	8%	0%	26	27%	50%	4.09	-1.6	37	80	$4
11	SD *	315	36	10	32	1	272	249	286	289	329	449	779	8	71	35	0.30	41	21	38	132	107	12%	136	2%	50%	19	37%	47%	5.14	7.6	35	78	$7
12	SD *	246	16	3	26	0	153	193	98	197	209	234	442	7	72	20	0.26	39	18	43	59	100	5%	94	10%	0%	14	14%	79%	1.33	-24.6	-32	-80	-$7
1st Half		193	14	3	22	0	166	203	108	202	222	259	481	7	74	21	0.28	38	19	43	67	104	5%	89	9%	0%	13	15%	77%	1.61	-16.7	-20	-50	-$6
2nd Half		53	2	0	4	0	104	161	0	0	160	141	300	6	66	16	0.19	80	0	20	27	-11	0%	97	17%	0%	1	0%	100%	0.53	-7.0	-76	-190	-$9
13	**Proj**	**325**	**27**	**8**	**35**	**1**	**241**	**219**	**197**	**259**	**295**	**381**	**676**	**7**	**71**	**32**	**0.27**	**39**	**20**	**42**	**98**	**111**	**8%**	**112**	**6%**	**12%**				**3.58**	**-6.2**	**-3**	**-8**	**$4**

Hunter,Torii

Age	37	Bats	R	Pos	RF	Health	A	LIMA Plan	C+
Ht	6' 2"	Wt	225			PT/Exp	A	Rand Var	-5
						Consist	B	MM	2115

Across the board declines in all skills show his advance down the aging curve. Outsized BA and hr/f hide the risks, while BPV, xBA and h% are huge red flags. At 37, there's a real chance he falls off a skills cliff, taking his production with him. You've been warned.

Yr	Tm	AB	R	HR	RBI	SB	BA	xBA	vL	vR	OB	Slg	OPS	bb%	ct%	h%	Eye	G	L	F	PX	xPX	hr/f	Spd	SBO	SB%	#Wk	DOM	DIS	RC/G	RAR	BPV	BPX	R$
08	LAA	551	85	21	78	19	278	282	304	268	338	466	804	8	80	31	0.46	46	19	35	124	124	14%	97	17%	79%	27	48%	15%	5.58	11.3	71	139	$23
09	LAA	451	74	22	90	18	299	284	336	287	365	508	873	9	80	34	0.51	47	16	36	130	134	17%	79	17%	82%	22	55%	27%	6.80	24.4	73	149	$25
10	LAA	573	76	23	90	9	281	283	257	292	350	464	814	10	82	31	0.58	48	18	34	123	102	15%	71	13%	43%	27	44%	26%	5.40	8.9	60	130	$22
11	LAA	580	80	23	82	5	262	264	287	252	333	429	763	10	78	30	0.50	46	21	33	111	136	15%	84	7%	42%	27	30%	33%	4.76	-1.6	42	93	$18
12	LAA	534	81	16	92	9	313	257	340	303	358	451	810	7	75	39	0.29	52	23	25	96	88	16%	77	6%	90%	25	36%	56%	6.08	17.6	18	45	$26
1st Half		217	35	10	32	3	281	252	319	264	342	442	784	8	74	34	0.35	53	21	26	102	94	25%	79	5%	100%	11	27%	55%	5.46	2.8	15	38	$18
2nd Half		317	46	6	60	6	334	259	360	326	370	457	828	5	76	43	0.24	51	24	25	91	83	10%	74	7%	86%	14	43%	57%	6.55	12.8	15	38	$32
13	**Proj**	**516**	**75**	**15**	**84**	**7**	**274**	**255**	**290**	**267**	**331**	**413**	**743**	**8**	**77**	**33**	**0.38**	**49**	**21**	**30**	**94**	**106**	**13%**	**75**	**7%**	**68%**				**4.75**	**-3.8**	**25**	**64**	**$19**

Iannetta,Chris

Age	30	Bats	R	Pos	CA	Health	C	LIMA Plan	D
Ht	6' 0"	Wt	230			PT/Exp	D	Rand Var	-2
						Consist	B	MM	3003

9-26-.240 in 221 AB at LAA. Broken wrist in May cost him twelve weeks and some 2H power, which obscures his 1H reversal of a declining PX trend. With power as his only asset, any decline is a value killer. But given his pre-injury PX, a rebound is a decent bet. UP: A nostalgic return to 2008

Yr	Tm	AB	R	HR	RBI	SB	BA	xBA	vL	vR	OB	Slg	OPS	bb%	ct%	h%	Eye	G	L	F	PX	xPX	hr/f	Spd	SBO	SB%	#Wk	DOM	DIS	RC/G	RAR	BPV	BPX	R$
08	COL	333	50	18	65	0	264	275	275	261	370	505	875	14	72	31	0.61	38	21	41	167	158	18%	78	0%	0%	27	56%	33%	6.47	22.4	68	133	$10
09	COL	289	41	16	52	0	228	256	296	202	328	460	789	13	74	25	0.57	32	16	52	150	152	14%	82	1%	0%	24	54%	42%	4.93	6.9	59	120	$5
10	COL *	251	30	12	39	1	217	251	222	184	314	418	732	12	76	24	0.60	41	13	45	134	126	14%	69	2%	100%	22	32%	36%	4.30	0.1	54	117	$3
11	COL	345	51	14	55	6	238	245	241	237	366	414	781	17	74	28	0.79	35	20	44	126	104	12%	67	8%	67%	27	48%	37%	5.04	9.3	55	122	$9
12	LAA *	243	29	9	27	1	235	228	208	249	321	385	706	11	72	29	0.44	44	20	36	100	115	16%	79	6%	25%	16	25%	56%	3.94	-1.3	6	15	$3
1st Half		66	10	3	9	0	197	255	50	261	303	394	697	13	73	22	0.56	42	21	38	139	134	17%	56	6%	0%	6	33%	50%	3.55	-1.4	44	110	-$3
2nd Half		177	19	6	18	1	250	219	321	244	328	382	710	10	71	32	0.41	45	20	35	85	107	15%	94	5%	33%	10	20%	60%	4.10	-0.6	-8	-20	$5
13	**Proj**	**365**	**48**	**15**	**51**	**2**	**244**	**237**	**226**	**250**	**343**	**415**	**758**	**13**	**73**	**29**	**0.56**	**40**	**19**	**41**	**116**	**119**	**14%**	**67**	**5%**	**43%**				**4.68**	**5.1**	**29**	**72**	**$9**

MATT CEDERHOLM

Ibanez,Raul

Age	41	Bats	L	Pos	LF DH	Health	A	LIMA Plan	D+
Ht	6' 2"	Wt	220			PT/Exp	B	Rand Var	+5
						Consist	B	MM	4233

Reduced role as RHP killer injected life into fading career. As helpless in the field as he is vs LHP, but power stroke fits well in parks with a short RF porch. Expect a modest BA bounceback courtesy of h% regression, but value hinges on HR production. Owners with room for a platoon player could do worse.

Yr Tm	AB	R	HR	RBI	SB	BA	xBA	vL	vR	OB	Slg	OPS	bb%	ct%	h%	Eye	G	L	F	PX	xPX	hr/f	Spd	SBO	SB%	#Wk	DOM	DIS	RC/G	RAR	BPV	BPX	R$
08 SEA	635	85	23	110	2	293	276	305	288	358	479	836	9	83	32	0.58	41	19	40	119	134	11%	77	3%	33%	27	44%	37%	6.04	20.5	62	122	$23
09 PHI	500	93	34	93	4	272	297	285	267	345	552	897	10	76	29	0.47	43	15	42	177	179	21%	83	3%	100%	25	56%	20%	6.73	26.3	97	198	$21
10 PHI	561	75	16	83	4	275	273	268	277	353	444	797	11	81	32	0.63	45	18	37	116	121	9%	87	4%	57%	27	56%	30%	5.44	8.8	63	137	$17
11 PHI	535	65	20	84	2	245	270	211	256	289	419	707	6	80	27	0.31	46	19	35	119	117	13%	60	2%	100%	27	48%	37%	4.10	-12.4	48	107	$12
12 NYY	384	50	19	62	3	240	278	197	248	303	453	756	8	83	24	0.52	41	19	39	126	112	15%	75	3%	100%	27	52%	19%	4.65	-2.7	73	183	$9
1st Half	206	23	11	35	2	233	284	179	242	291	451	743	8	87	22	0.63	39	19	42	122	113	14%	62	5%	100%	13	54%	8%	4.43	-2.9	82	205	$10
2nd Half	178	27	8	27	1	247	271	212	255	316	455	771	9	78	28	0.45	44	20	36	131	110	16%	89	2%	100%	14	50%	29%	4.91	0.1	61	153	$9
13 Proj	385	52	18	61	2	251	275	231	257	314	458	771	8	81	27	0.47	44	19	37	128	119	15%	73	3%	85%				4.90	2.9	66	165	$10

Iglesias,Jose

Age	23	Bats	R	Pos	SS	Health	A	LIMA Plan	F
Ht	5' 11"	Wt	185			PT/Exp	D	Rand Var	+1
						Consist	B	MM	1301

1-2-.118 with 1 SB in 68 AB at BOS. Improving patience and contact skills hardly distract from the fact that batting average gains have been non-existent. Runs enough to generate double digit stolen bases, but awful OBP limits the upside. Unless your league counts defensive highlights, better to steer clear.

Yr Tm	AB	R	HR	RBI	SB	BA	xBA	vL	vR	OB	Slg	OPS	bb%	ct%	h%	Eye	G	L	F	PX	xPX	hr/f	Spd	SBO	SB%	#Wk	DOM	DIS	RC/G	RAR	BPV	BPX	R$
08																																	
09																																	
10 aa	221	22	0	10	4	267	226			287	335	622	3	77	35	0.12				58			120	11%	64%				3.28		-8	0	$2
11 BOS *	363	33	1	27	10	228	285	1000	200	264	262	526	5	83	27	0.28	75	25	0	28	2	0%	86	16%	71%	4	0%	75%	2.29	-18.0	-11	-24	$2
12 BOS *	421	44	2	22	11	233	233	172	77	278	277	556	6	85	27	0.41	59	16	25	32	23	8%	103	13%	78%	7	0%	43%	2.61	-16.6	5	13	$3
1st Half	181	20	1	12	7	242	224			282	283	565	5	87	27	0.43				25			117	16%	87%				2.81		11	28	$4
2nd Half	240	25	1	10	4	225	227	172	77	275	273	548	6	83	27	0.40	59	16	25	37	23	8%	96	11%	67%	7	0%	43%	2.46	-11.4	-5	-13	$2
13 Proj	167	17	2	10	4	236	240	264	216	273	315	588	5	83	27	0.30	59	16	25	51	21	7%	101	14%	74%				2.88	-5.7	7	18	$2

Infante,Omar

Age	31	Bats	R	Pos	2B	Health	C	LIMA Plan	B
Ht	6' 0"	Wt	197			PT/Exp	A	Rand Var	0
						Consist	B	MM	1425

Not as much of a surprise for those with longer memories. Had 16 HR, 13 SB in his first full season - 2004. That was not repeated; can 2012 be? Power skills stable so HR will be driven by FB and hr/f. Speed skills also stable so SB will be all about the opps (SB). 550 AB could well produce a comparable follow-up.

Yr Tm	AB	R	HR	RBI	SB	BA	xBA	vL	vR	OB	Slg	OPS	bb%	ct%	h%	Eye	G	L	F	PX	xPX	hr/f	Spd	SBO	SB%	#Wk	DOM	DIS	RC/G	RAR	BPV	BPX	R$
08 ATL	317	45	3	40	0	293	288	325	273	339	416	756	6	86	33	0.50	33	30	37	86	87	3%	119	1%	0%	20	50%	20%	5.03	7.6	49	96	$7
09 ATL	203	24	2	27	2	305	259	323	298	365	389	754	9	86	35	0.68	32	27	41	55	77	3%	109	3%	100%	16	38%	38%	5.29	6.2	27	55	$5
10 ATL	471	65	8	47	7	321	255	276	342	360	416	776	6	87	36	0.47	47	19	34	59	65	6%	144	8%	54%	27	33%	41%	5.44	16.2	32	70	$20
11 FLA	579	55	7	49	4	276	263	273	277	316	382	698	6	88	30	0.51	42	22	36	66	64	4%	140	4%	67%	26	23%	19%	4.23	1.1	45	100	$12
12 2 TM	554	69	12	53	17	274	267	317	257	301	419	720	4	88	29	0.32	41	20	39	86	97	6%	125	16%	85%	27	52%	22%	4.49	5.1	69	173	$18
1st Half	263	35	7	27	8	289	272	280	293	313	460	773	3	87	31	0.26	38	19	43	108	130	7%	104	16%	89%	13	62%	23%	5.25	7.3	75	188	$20
2nd Half	291	34	5	26	9	261	263	354	226	290	381	672	4	90	28	0.40	43	21	36	66	69	5%	143	16%	82%	14	43%	21%	3.87	-3.3	60	150	$16
13 Proj	566	67	10	55	14	283	260	304	275	318	406	723	5	88	31	0.42	40	21	38	73	81	5%	127	12%	81%				4.62	5.8	56	141	$19

Inge,Brandon

Age	36	Bats	R	Pos	3B	Health	D	LIMA Plan	F
Ht	5' 11"	Wt	190			PT/Exp	C	Rand Var	+1
						Consist	C	MM	3001

12-54-.218 in 303 AB at DET/OAK. Shoulder surgery ended his season in Sept. Athletic gifts have long since faded, leaving so-so power as lone fantasy relevant skill. Age and abysmal ct% mean his days as a starter are over. He's expected to be ready for spring training, but there's no rehabbing his fantasy value.

Yr Tm	AB	R	HR	RBI	SB	BA	xBA	vL	vR	OB	Slg	OPS	bb%	ct%	h%	Eye	G	L	F	PX	xPX	hr/f	Spd	SBO	SB%	#Wk	DOM	DIS	RC/G	RAR	BPV	BPX	R$
08 DET	347	41	11	51	4	205	230	232	196	292	369	661	11	73	25	0.46	37	17	46	113	120	9%	113	8%	57%	26	27%	38%	3.39	-12.6	34	67	$0
09 DET	562	71	27	84	2	230	224	243	225	297	406	703	9	70	28	0.32	41	15	44	117	111	15%	109	5%	29%	27	26%	63%	3.85	-11.9	5	10	$9
10 DET	514	47	13	70	4	247	233	254	245	319	397	716	10	74	31	0.40	38	17	45	110	116	7%	106	5%	57%	26	35%	54%	4.23	-4.9	27	59	$9
11 DET *	377	42	8	37	1	205	203	245	170	274	314	588	9	71	27	0.32	34	20	46	83	84	3%	98	2%	50%	22	23%	59%	2.74	-21.3	-12	-27	-$1
12 2 AL *	339	37	13	60	0	218	235	209	223	280	384	664	8	69	27	0.28	40	22	37	123	114	15%	51	1%	0%	17	29%	53%	3.46	-11.3	1	3	$1
1st Half	168	16	7	36	0	208	242	206	210	281	381	662	9	71	25	0.35	41	23	36	122	132	16%	49	0%	0%	10	30%	50%	3.45	-5.9	8	20	$2
2nd Half	135	17	5	18	0	230	226	212	241	268	385	653	5	68	30	0.16	40	22	39	116	91	14%	70	4%	0%	7	29%	57%	3.29	-5.3	-10	-25	$0
13 Proj	226	25	7	32	1	220	221	229	216	282	363	645	8	71	28	0.29	38	20	42	103	104	11%	75	3%	36%				3.29	-8.9	-2	-4	$3

Ishikawa,Travis

Age	29	Bats	L	Pos	1B	Health	A	LIMA Plan	F
Ht	6' 3"	Wt	224			PT/Exp	F	Rand Var	-1
						Consist	F	MM	3111

Former prospect turned bench bat missed time with an oblique strain. He has some pop when he runs into one, but weak Eye and poor contact rate make this an infrequent occurrence. Late-game pinch-hitting AB just aren't enough to merit a roster spot in most leagues.

Yr Tm	AB	R	HR	RBI	SB	BA	xBA	vL	vR	OB	Slg	OPS	bb%	ct%	h%	Eye	G	L	F	PX	xPX	hr/f	Spd	SBO	SB%	#Wk	DOM	DIS	RC/G	RAR	BPV	BPX	R$
08 SF *	500	64	19	86	9	258	287	0	280	320	460	780	8	76	30	0.38	56	18	26	141	119	17%	88	13%	60%	8	38%	50%	4.91	-7.6	61	120	$14
09 SF	326	49	9	39	2	261	229	278	259	323	387	710	8	73	33	0.34	45	18	37	84	108	10%	122	4%	50%	26	15%	54%	4.23	-11.3	1	2	$6
10 SF	158	18	3	22	0	266	278	111	286	322	392	714	8	82	31	0.45	42	25	32	95	114	7%	68	0%	0%	26	38%	46%	4.38	-4.7	28	61	$2
11 aaa	175	12	2	10	2	180	190			250	267	517	9	60	29	0.23				95			79	8%	58%				2.04		-49	0	-$4
12 MIL	152	19	4	30	0	257	252	286	250	315	428	743	8	72	33	0.31	36	24	40	131	130	9%	84	0%	0%	23	30%	52%	4.62	-3.5	28	70	$2
1st Half	71	8	4	15	0	239	255	250	237	299	479	778	8	69	29	0.27	40	19	42	177	134	20%	72	0%	0%	9	44%	56%	4.80	-1.2	40	100	$2
2nd Half	81	11	0	15	0	272	247	313	262	330	383	712	8	75	36	0.35	33	28	38	95	126	0%	94	0%	0%	14	21%	50%	4.42	-2.2	18	45	$2
13 Proj	129	14	3	19	1	241	242	212	246	302	389	691	8	71	32	0.31	41	23	36	116	121	9%	80	3%	64%				3.93	-5.5	14	35	$2

Izturis,Cesar

Age	33	Bats	B	Pos	SS	Health	F	LIMA Plan	F
Ht	5' 9"	Wt	180			PT/Exp	F	Rand Var	+3
						Consist	C	MM	1331

Utility, thy name is Cesar, an extreme contact hitter with far less patience and power than Caesar. There was a time when he brought some baserunning ability, but Spd faded along with SB upside. Can still pick it so he's likely to earn a bench role somewhere, but his bat makes him well cast as a defensive replacement.

Yr Tm	AB	R	HR	RBI	SB	BA	xBA	vL	vR	OB	Slg	OPS	bb%	ct%	h%	Eye	G	L	F	PX	xPX	hr/f	Spd	SBO	SB%	#Wk	DOM	DIS	RC/G	RAR	BPV	BPX	R$
08 STL	414	50	1	24	24	263	263	304	237	312	309	621	7	94	28	1.12	47	22	31	28	24	1%	123	24%	80%	25	32%	16%	3.45	-8.0	48	94	$11
09 BAL	387	34	2	30	12	256	269	290	238	289	328	617	4	90	28	0.47	49	20	30	44	23	2%	114	16%	75%	22	50%	36%	3.26	-9.7	39	80	$6
10 BAL	473	42	1	28	11	230	235	205	240	269	268	538	5	89	26	0.47	46	19	35	28	26	1%	94	13%	69%	27	19%	48%	2.38	-24.9	15	33	$2
11 BAL *	55	6	0	3	0	196	200	333	143	244	211	454	6	71	28	0.21	50	25	25	16	48	0%	88	9%	0%	8	0%	88%	1.44	-4.7	-72	-160	-$3
12 2 NL	166	13	2	11	1	241	286	188	263	254	343	598	2	92	25	0.23	55	21	24	59	28	6%	102	6%	50%	17	24%	35%	2.87	-6.1	44	110	-$1
1st Half	103	3	1	7	1	204	243	118	246	226	252	479	3	92	21	0.38	57	19	24	29	20	5%	72	10%	50%	10	0%	40%	1.77	-7.3	7	18	-$3
2nd Half	63	10	1	4	0	302	330	357	286	302	492	794	0	92	32	0.00	51	25	25	109	41	7%	120	0%	0%	7	57%	29%	5.42	2.4	87	218	$2
13 Proj	102	10	1	7	2	254	275	248	256	277	349	626	3	91	27	0.37	50	21	29	57	29	4%	102	12%	71%				3.28	-2.2	47	117	$2

Izturis,Maicer

Age	32	Bats	B	Pos	3B 2B SS	Health	C	LIMA Plan	F
Ht	5' 8"	Wt	170			PT/Exp	D	Rand Var	0
						Consist	B	MM	1321

After 2011's career high in AB, super-utility man fell back into a reduced role. Value hinges on OB, but even then, has to at least TRY to drive the ball, or BA is simply too poor. Green light helped SB, but questionable Spd jeopardizes future production. Position flexibility is nice, but he's still just a part-time singles hitter.

Yr Tm	AB	R	HR	RBI	SB	BA	xBA	vL	vR	OB	Slg	OPS	bb%	ct%	h%	Eye	G	L	F	PX	xPX	hr/f	Spd	SBO	SB%	#Wk	DOM	DIS	RC/G	RAR	BPV	BPX	R$
08 LAA	290	44	3	37	11	269	284	258	272	329	362	691	8	91	29	0.96	49	23	29	59	60	4%	108	15%	85%	19	47%	26%	4.27	-2.2	63	124	$8
09 LAA	387	74	8	65	13	300	278	380	288	358	434	792	8	89	32	0.85	43	19	38	81	77	6%	108	15%	72%	26	58%	19%	5.60	11.3	77	157	$18
10 LAA	212	27	3	27	7	250	261	280	241	318	363	681	9	87	27	0.78	42	18	40	78	86	4%	99	18%	70%	15	53%	33%	3.88	-4.2	59	128	$4
11 LAA	449	51	5	38	9	276	267	295	265	326	388	713	7	86	31	0.51	39	23	38	87	71	3%	78	13%	60%	27	37%	37%	4.32	-2.9	47	104	$11
12 LAA	289	35	2	20	17	256	252	231	265	315	315	630	8	87	29	0.66	47	23	30	42	39	3%	92	22%	89%	26	15%	42%	3.64	-7.6	28	70	$7
1st Half	148	16	0	7	10	230	240	262	217	309	270	579	10	86	27	0.81	47	22	31	34	44	0%	90	22%	100%	13	15%	38%	3.15	-6.4	21	53	$5
2nd Half	141	19	2	13	7	284	264	194	314	322	362	684	5	88	31	0.47	48	24	28	49	34	6%	93	22%	78%	13	15%	46%	4.19	-1.6	30	75	$10
13 Proj	194	25	2	18	8	266	258	259	269	320	354	674	7	87	30	0.61	44	22	34	61	57	4%	88	19%	80%				4.01	-3.3	40	100	$6

DAN BECKER

Jackson,Austin

Age 26	Bats R	Pos CF	Health	A	LIMA Plan	C
Ht 6' 1"	Wt 185		PT/Exp	A	Rand Var	-4
			Consist	D	MM	3515

This mini-breakout was fueled by improved plate control and blossoming power. Growing bb%, sexy Spd suggest there's plenty more SB potential with a friendlier green light. And with steady PX growth and decreasing GB, there's 20 HR pop here. BA still a risk due to low ct%, but that's nitpicking. UP: 20 HR, 30 SB

Yr Tm	AB	R	HR	RBI	SB	BA	xBA	vL	vR	OB	Slg	OPS	bb%	ct%	h%	Eye	G	L	F	PX	xPX	hr/f	Spd	SBO	SB%	#Wk	DOM	DIS	RC/G	RAR	BPV	BPX	R$
08 aa	520	72	9	66	18	275	249			342	404	747	9	77	34	0.44				94			97	16%	74%				4.85		36	0	$17
09 aaa	504	64	4	62	23	283	225			336	375	711	7	74	38	0.30				67			114	18%	84%				4.61		5	0	$18
10 DET	618	103	4	41	27	293	249	226	317	343	400	743	7	72	40	0.28	48	24	27	86	94	3%	198	18%	82%	27	26%	48%	5.03	3.0	22	48	$25
11 DET	591	90	10	45	22	249	218	257	245	314	374	688	9	69	34	0.31	47	17	36	94	96	7%	197	17%	81%	27	22%	52%	4.05	-14.1	17	38	$15
12 DET	543	103	16	66	12	300	260	289	305	377	479	856	11	75	37	0.50	42	24	34	118	117	11%	172	12%	57%	25	40%	32%	6.33	22.4	57	143	$25
1st Half	218	45	8	34	7	326	264	258	355	407	537	944	12	74	41	0.54	40	20	39	147	136	13%	141	12%	78%	11	55%	27%	8.26	20.3	79	198	$26
2nd Half	325	58	8	32	5	283	259	312	272	356	440	796	10	76	35	0.47	43	26	31	99	105	11%	186	12%	42%	14	29%	36%	5.22	4.2	39	98	$24
13 Proj	**570**	**98**	**15**	**58**	**18**	**284**	**247**	**272**	**289**	**352**	**449**	**801**	**9**	**73**	**36**	**0.39**	**44**	**21**	**35**	**112**	**106**	**11%**	**172**	**15%**	**71%**				**5.55**	**12.6**	**45**	**112**	**$23**

Jackson,Brett

Age 24	Bats L	Pos CF	Health	A	LIMA Plan	D
Ht 6' 2"	Wt 210		PT/Exp	C	Rand Var	-1
			Consist	A	MM	4403

4-9-.175 in 120 AB at CHC. Premium OF prospect flashed intriguing power + speed combo in minors. But that won't matter if he whiffs in nearly half of his AB, as he did in MLB debut. Showed better discipline in the minors, so there's hope, and he's got time. You'll need a bench for him in '12, but he's a keeper league gem.

Yr Tm	AB	R	HR	RBI	SB	BA	xBA	vL	vR	OB	Slg	OPS	bb%	ct%	h%	Eye	G	L	F	PX	xPX	hr/f	Spd	SBO	SB%	#Wk	DOM	DIS	RC/G	RAR	BPV	BPX	R$
08																																	
09																																	
10 aa	228	35	5	21	13	247	240			314	398	712	9	70	33	0.33				114			132	31%	75%				4.21		37	0	$7
11 a/a	431	57	14	39	14	229	222			310	387	697	10	64	33	0.32				130			108	20%	64%				3.84		15	0	$9
12 CHC *	527	61	15	43	19	209	200	167	176	285	379	664	10	55	35	0.24	30	31	39	153	165	17%	128	24%	69%	9	22%	78%	3.41	-21.3	2	5	$7
1st Half	301	36	9	24	11	222	208			279	403	683	7	56	36	0.18				156			131	26%	72%				3.62		6	15	$10
2nd Half	226	25	6	19	8	191	192	167	176	292	348	640	12	53	33	0.30	30	31	39	147	165	17%	114	21%	65%	9	22%	78%	3.12	-12.1	-9	-23	$2
13 Proj	**378**	**48**	**10**	**33**	**12**	**219**	**213**	**208**	**221**	**297**	**374**	**671**	**10**	**60**	**34**	**0.28**	**40**	**26**	**34**	**129**	**149**	**13%**	**119**	**20%**	**68%**				**3.55**	**-14.4**	**3**	**8**	**$7**

Janish,Paul

Age 30	Bats R	Pos SS	Health	A	LIMA Plan	F
Ht 6' 2"	Wt 200		PT/Exp	D	Rand Var	+5
			Consist	C	MM	1101

0-9-.186 in 167 AB at ATL. Fun fact: Had 3rd-lowest OPS of NL batters with at least 150 AB. Sure, that h% might normalize a bit, but he'll still be a BA drag. Marginal speed is totally worthless with chronic sub-.300 OBP. One positive note: his surname is close to Danish, a delectable treat that sounds really good right now.

Yr Tm	AB	R	HR	RBI	SB	BA	xBA	vL	vR	OB	Slg	OPS	bb%	ct%	h%	Eye	G	L	F	PX	xPX	hr/f	Spd	SBO	SB%	#Wk	DOM	DIS	RC/G	RAR	BPV	BPX	R$
08 CIN *	398	39	7	38	2	206	227	323	102	257	310	566	6	74	26	0.26	35	23	42	78	93	4%	92	2%	100%	11	27%	64%	2.57	-19.0	-9	-18	-$3
09 CIN	256	36	1	16	2	211	247	230	203	284	305	588	9	84	25	0.65	37	19	44	75	67	1%	99	3%	100%	27	33%	26%	2.83	-10.0	39	80	-$2
10 CIN	200	23	5	25	1	260	242	308	237	333	385	718	10	85	28	0.73	30	19	51	83	67	6%	93	7%	25%	27	33%	44%	4.19	0.5	39	85	$3
11 CIN *	379	33	1	25	4	212	234	210	215	256	264	520	6	86	24	0.44	43	21	37	41	54	0%	102	7%	65%	25	20%	44%	2.18	-22.7	12	27	-$3
12 ATL *	336	36	3	16	1	182	236	194	181	250	263	514	8	81	22	0.48	38	25	37	58	86	0%	95	3%	44%	10	10%	50%	2.03	-22.4	9	23	-$5
1st Half	131	16	3	6	0	203	252			264	350	614	8	78	24	0.37				105			104	0%	0%				2.96		29	73	-$4
2nd Half	205	21	0	10	1	169	223	194	181	242	208	450	9	83	20	0.56	38	25	37	30	86	0%	93	5%	44%	10	10%	50%	1.52	-16.7	-3	-8	-$6
13 Proj	**129**	**14**	**1**	**9**	**1**	**213**	**226**	**251**	**196**	**276**	**288**	**563**	**8**	**83**	**25**	**0.50**	**36**	**21**	**42**	**55**	**73**	**2%**	**94**	**4%**	**52%**				**2.54**	**-5.9**	**11**	**28**	**$0**

Jaso,John

Age 29	Bats L	Pos DH CA	Health	B	LIMA Plan	C+
Ht 6' 2"	Wt 205		PT/Exp	D	Rand Var	-1
			Consist	F	MM	2233

Where did this come from? Friendly h% deserves credit for the BA boost, and xBA says it was no fluke. GB profile, hr/f regression temper HR enthusiasm. With excellent plate control, BA won't be a liability again even if he gives back some power. .927 OPS vs. RH puts him on good side of platoon. A premium caddy.

Yr Tm	AB	R	HR	RBI	SB	BA	xBA	vL	vR	OB	Slg	OPS	bb%	ct%	h%	Eye	G	L	F	PX	xPX	hr/f	Spd	SBO	SB%	#Wk	DOM	DIS	RC/G	RAR	BPV	BPX	R$
08 TAM *	402	52	9	52	2	229	267	500	125	324	348	672	12	86	25	0.99	38	25	38	73	5	0%	94	2%	57%	4	0%	50%	3.71	-5.1	45	88	$2
09 aaa	331	34	4	24	1	225	239			302	307	609	10	82	26	0.63				53			103	1%	100%				3.07		11	0	-$1
10 TAM	339	57	5	44	4	263	266	191	274	372	378	749	15	88	28	1.51	46	17	37	75	81	5%	103	3%	100%	25	60%	12%	4.94	7.8	74	161	$8
11 TAM	246	26	5	27	1	224	256	161	233	295	354	649	9	85	24	0.69	43	18	39	90	89	6%	73	5%	33%	22	36%	36%	3.33	-6.0	50	111	$0
12 SEA	294	41	10	50	5	276	294	119	302	391	456	847	16	83	30	1.10	46	25	28	115	86	14%	85	5%	100%	26	62%	23%	6.41	18.9	82	205	$10
1st Half	117	16	3	20	0	274	301	59	310	375	453	828	14	83	31	0.95	46	26	27	121	85	11%	85	0%	0%	12	67%	25%	5.96	5.8	74	185	$4
2nd Half	177	25	7	30	5	277	289	160	296	402	458	859	17	82	30	1.19	46	25	29	110	88	16%	88	7%	100%	14	57%	21%	6.71	12.5	78	195	$14
13 Proj	**303**	**40**	**8**	**43**	**4**	**272**	**275**	**153**	**291**	**371**	**428**	**799**	**14**	**84**	**30**	**1.00**	**45**	**21**	**33**	**98**	**87**	**10%**	**82**	**4%**	**84%**				**5.60**	**6.2**	**66**	**166**	**$10**

Jay,Jon

Age 28	Bats L	Pos CF	Health	B	LIMA Plan	C
Ht 5' 11"	Wt 200		PT/Exp	C	Rand Var	-3
			Consist	A	MM	1335

PRO: Consistent xBA, bb% provide OB floor on which he can run; a nice end-game speed pick even as a part-timer. CON: He's not really a .300 hitter, and as GB rate continues to rise, chances of ever again reaching double digit HR are gone. Overall, he can be a valuable asset if you don't expect a '12 repeat.

Yr Tm	AB	R	HR	RBI	SB	BA	xBA	vL	vR	OB	Slg	OPS	bb%	ct%	h%	Eye	G	L	F	PX	xPX	hr/f	Spd	SBO	SB%	#Wk	DOM	DIS	RC/G	RAR	BPV	BPX	R$
08 a/a	430	51	9	45	8	271	259			326	387	713	8	86	30	0.57				71			103	14%	46%				4.14		41	0	$10
09 aaa	505	57	7	43	16	243	253			281	331	612	5	86	27	0.37				56			95	21%	64%				3.02		28	0	$8
10 STL *	452	68	7	49	11	284	275	308	297	337	407	743	7	83	33	0.47	49	19	32	91	76	5%	103	12%	73%	21	24%	43%	4.85	2.1	52	113	$15
11 STL	455	56	10	37	6	297	278	287	299	337	424	762	6	82	34	0.35	54	23	23	88	69	11%	96	10%	46%	27	44%	33%	4.94	3.3	33	73	$15
12 STL	443	70	4	40	19	305	278	281	314	354	400	754	7	84	36	0.48	59	22	19	64	53	6%	117	19%	73%	23	30%	22%	5.15	5.7	40	100	$19
1st Half	134	25	2	10	6	321	272	269	333	359	403	762	6	87	36	0.44	56	22	21	47	51	8%	126	16%	86%	9	22%	22%	5.59	2.9	33	83	$9
2nd Half	309	45	2	30	13	298	281	284	304	352	398	750	8	83	35	0.49	60	22	18	72	54	4%	109	20%	68%	14	36%	21%	4.98	1.8	41	103	$24
13 Proj	**457**	**67**	**7**	**41**	**14**	**285**	**276**	**268**	**290**	**333**	**394**	**727**	**7**	**84**	**33**	**0.45**	**56**	**22**	**23**	**72**	**62**	**8%**	**106**	**16%**	**68%**				**4.59**	**-2.4**	**41**	**101**	**$17**

Jennings,Desmond

Age 26	Bats R	Pos LF CF	Health	A	LIMA Plan	C+
Ht 6' 2"	Wt 200		PT/Exp	B	Rand Var	0
			Consist	B	MM	2515

On surface, a nice follow-up to his MLB debut. But power and patience both regressed. Steadily eroding Eye, marginal PX, and lack of uppercut in swing cap his BA and HR ceilings for now. Elite speed will net him 30 SB in his sleep, but odds are against an age-26 breakout.

Yr Tm	AB	R	HR	RBI	SB	BA	xBA	vL	vR	OB	Slg	OPS	bb%	ct%	h%	Eye	G	L	F	PX	xPX	hr/f	Spd	SBO	SB%	#Wk	DOM	DIS	RC/G	RAR	BPV	BPX	R$
08																																	
09 a/a	497	81	9	54	46	291	278			365	443	808	10	85	33	0.78				92			125	34%	86%				6.09		86	0	$29
10 TAM *	420	68	2	30	30	236	229	273	100	300	335	636	8	80	29	0.47	47	12	41	72	142	0%	159	35%	82%	6	33%	50%	3.51	-13.5	50	109	$12
11 TAM *	585	96	19	55	33	242	248	256	260	318	404	722	10	74	30	0.43	47	18	35	113	100	16%	152	26%	82%	11	82%	18%	4.42	-2.5	52	116	$21
12 TAM	505	85	13	47	31	246	236	246	245	309	388	697	8	76	30	0.38	42	20	38	92	99	9%	157	25%	94%	24	50%	29%	4.32	-3.6	46	115	$19
1st Half	207	27	5	21	12	242	226	226	247	302	372	674	8	77	29	0.38	38	21	41	81	99	8%	157	24%	92%	10	40%	40%	4.02	-3.9	33	83	$11
2nd Half	298	58	8	26	19	248	244	260	244	313	399	712	9	76	30	0.39	44	20	36	99	100	10%	144	26%	95%	14	57%	21%	4.55	-0.9	52	130	$24
13 Proj	**541**	**90**	**15**	**50**	**30**	**248**	**245**	**259**	**244**	**317**	**401**	**718**	**9**	**77**	**30**	**0.44**	**44**	**19**	**37**	**98**	**100**	**10%**	**153**	**24%**	**88%**				**4.50**	**-2.5**	**53**	**133**	**$21**

Jeter,Derek

Age 39	Bats R	Pos SS DH	Health	B	LIMA Plan	C+
Ht 6' 3"	Wt 195		PT/Exp	A	Rand Var	-3
			Consist	B	MM	1235

A typically remarkable season, right? Not so fast. Solid ct% is all he's got left—bb% in freefall, Spd average w/green light barely flickering, and HR were product of hr/f, not skill. Post-season ankle fracture another reason to temper expectations. An empty .300 BA is his new upside. DN: .260 BA, 5 HR, 5 SB

Yr Tm	AB	R	HR	RBI	SB	BA	xBA	vL	vR	OB	Slg	OPS	bb%	ct%	h%	Eye	G	L	F	PX	xPX	hr/f	Spd	SBO	SB%	#Wk	DOM	DIS	RC/G	RAR	BPV	BPX	R$
08 NYY	596	88	11	69	11	300	275	302	300	356	408	764	8	86	34	0.61	58	18	24	67	86	9%	133	8%	69%	26	35%	27%	5.25	22.2	42	82	$22
09 NYY	634	107	18	66	30	334	295	395	311	402	465	868	10	86	37	0.80	57	20	23	78	86	15%	106	15%	86%	27	44%	26%	7.35	57.6	58	118	$37
10 NYY	663	111	10	67	18	270	282	321	246	333	370	703	9	84	31	0.59	65	16	18	68	57	10%	121	12%	78%	27	26%	26%	4.34	8.2	43	93	$21
11 NYY	546	84	6	61	16	297	279	349	277	351	388	740	8	85	34	0.57	62	19	19	63	63	7%	132	13%	73%	25	40%	28%	4.93	15.5	42	93	$22
12 NYY	683	99	15	58	9	316	290	364	294	359	429	788	6	87	35	0.50	62	22	16	71	44	16%	102	6%	69%	27	22%	33%	5.69	33.0	38	95	$28
1st Half	323	41	7	25	6	300	290	382	269	349	406	754	7	87	33	0.56	66	22	13	65	41	20%	106	8%	75%	13	23%	46%	5.15	10.2	33	83	$24
2nd Half	360	58	8	33	3	331	288	352	319	367	450	817	6	87	36	0.45	60	22	19	76	47	14%	95	4%	60%	14	21%	21%	6.22	21.1	39	98	$32
13 Proj	**519**	**79**	**8**	**50**	**6**	**277**	**278**	**318**	**259**	**330**	**372**	**702**	**7**	**86**	**31**	**0.56**	**62**	**20**	**18**	**63**	**55**	**10%**	**109**	**6%**	**67%**				**4.30**	**4.3**	**34**	**85**	**$15**

STEPHEN NICKRAND

Johnson,Chris

Age 28 Bats R Pos 3B	Health A	LIMA Plan D	
Ht 6' 3" Wt 220	PT/Exp C	Rand Var -4	
	Consist D	MM 3215	

Chronic hacker took step forward on surface due to BA gains. But that jump was entirely h% driven. The holes in his swing haven't gone anywhere; xBA confirms he's a .250 hitter. You'll buy him for power, and that 2H PX is enticing. Lack of uppercut in swing caps his HR ceiling, so don't go crazy. Use 20 HR as his upside.

Yr	Tm	AB	R	HR	RBI	SB	BA	xBA	vL	vR	OB	Slg	OPS	bb%	ct%	h%	Eye	G	L	F	PX	xPX	hr/f	Spd	SBO	SB%	#Wk	DOM	DIS	RC/G	RAR	BPV	BPX	R$
08	a/a	435	40	10	50	4	255	243			286	383	668	4	76	31	0.18				91			80	4%	100%				3.79		8	0	$6
09	HOU *	406	40	11	35	2	239	237	0	133	271	383	654	4	72	30	0.16	81	0	19	99	-5	0%	112	3%	59%	4	0%	100%	3.45	-14.0	2	4	$3
10	HOU *	490	58	17	75	3	296	274	286	316	326	472	798	4	76	36	0.18	41	24	35	127	117	13%	83	3%	100%	18	39%	50%	5.61	13.5	36	78	$18
11	HOU *	459	44	10	52	3	245	247	260	248	280	380	660	5	72	32	0.18	46	23	31	107	110	8%	91	6%	45%	23	22%	57%	3.50	-15.1	5	11	$6
12	2 NL	488	48	15	76	5	281	254	245	295	324	451	775	6	73	36	0.23	39	26	35	120	112	12%	102	5%	83%	27	30%	52%	5.19	8.0	27	68	$16
1st Half		268	31	6	34	4	280	242	196	302	318	414	732	5	72	37	0.20	42	25	33	99	103	9%	104	6%	100%	13	31%	46%	4.76	1.3	9	23	$16
2nd Half		220	17	9	42	1	282	270	277	285	331	495	826	7	74	35	0.28	36	26	38	146	122	15%	95	4%	50%	14	29%	57%	5.73	7.2	46	115	$15
13	Proj	464	45	13	67	4	260	252	247	265	299	417	716	5	73	33	0.21	42	25	34	113	113	11%	92	5%	71%				4.28	-4.1	19	48	$10

Johnson,Elliot

Age 29 Bats B Pos SS	Health A	LIMA Plan F	
Ht 6' 1" Wt 190	PT/Exp D	Rand Var -2	
	Consist C	MM 2401	

Utility type got regular duty from May-July and showed why he's no full-timer. Growing Spd and friendly SBO: should we hope for a SB breakout? Sorry—chronically low ct%, long history of sub-.300 OBP make that very unlikely. Dismal xBA shows this is about his BA upside. Chase steals elsewhere.

Yr	Tm	AB	R	HR	RBI	SB	BA	xBA	vL	vR	OB	Slg	OPS	bb%	ct%	h%	Eye	G	L	F	PX	xPX	hr/f	Spd	SBO	SB%	#Wk	DOM	DIS	RC/G	RAR	BPV	BPX	R$
08	TAM *	406	38	7	39	12	222	235	167	143	269	350	619	6	69	30	0.21	42	25	33	101	47	0%	104	20%	73%	4	0%	100%	3.07	-10.5	6	12	$2
09	aaa	233	25	9	29	6	226	242			269	380	649	6	72	28	0.21				102			93	16%	71%				3.32		8	0	$3
10	aaa	427	53	8	42	22	263	237			308	384	692	6	74	34	0.25				90			115	27%	76%				4.07		20	0	$14
11	TAM	160	20	4	17	6	194	216	213	176	259	338	596	8	67	26	0.26	48	13	39	114	116	10%	120	41%	46%	25	16%	64%	2.35	-8.2	16	36	$0
12	TAM	297	32	6	33	18	242	226	175	275	299	350	649	7	72	32	0.29	47	22	31	76	81	10%	122	31%	75%	26	15%	58%	3.53	-3.4	0	0	$8
1st Half		180	22	4	20	13	272	245	156	336	338	394	733	9	74	35	0.38	52	23	26	81	75	13%	129	31%	76%	13	15%	46%	4.70	3.6	17	43	$13
2nd Half		117	10	2	13	5	197	198	212	190	236	282	518	5	68	27	0.16	40	21	39	68	89	7%	101	30%	71%	13	15%	69%	2.08	-7.2	-37	-93	$1
13	Proj	163	18	4	18	8	224	219	208	233	277	349	626	7	70	30	0.24	46	18	36	91	96	10%	114	31%	66%				3.04	-5.0	2	5	$4

Johnson,Kelly

Age 31 Bats L Pos 2B	Health A	LIMA Plan C	
Ht 6' 1" Wt 200	PT/Exp A	Rand Var 0	
	Consist C	MM 3305	

Another year removed from his '10 breakout, another season of regression. This one was steep, and with both power and speed in freefall, it's time to temper our expectations. When you open up swing AND lose power, that's a recipe for trouble. BA trend vs. LH another reason to heed... DN: .220-10-50, bench

Yr	Tm	AB	R	HR	RBI	SB	BA	xBA	vL	vR	OB	Slg	OPS	bb%	ct%	h%	Eye	G	L	F	PX	xPX	hr/f	Spd	SBO	SB%	#Wk	DOM	DIS	RC/G	RAR	BPV	BPX	R$
08	ATL	547	86	12	69	11	287	271	333	270	349	446	795	9	79	34	0.46	39	25	36	110	111	8%	99	11%	65%	27	44%	22%	5.46	20.0	58	114	$19
09	ATL *	355	54	10	41	8	229	266	325	188	298	402	700	9	82	25	0.55	39	18	43	108	102	8%	97	12%	80%	25	44%	40%	3.98	-3.9	73	149	$5
10	ARI	585	93	26	71	13	284	277	310	272	369	496	865	12	75	34	0.53	41	21	38	149	139	16%	109	11%	65%	26	58%	23%	6.38	36.8	73	159	$25
11	2 TM	545	75	21	58	16	222	245	224	221	299	413	712	10	70	28	0.37	39	20	40	141	156	14%	108	17%	73%	27	44%	44%	4.01	-2.6	53	118	$12
12	TOR	507	61	16	55	14	225	226	201	234	309	365	674	11	69	30	0.39	45	21	34	102	113	14%	87	12%	88%	27	30%	52%	3.80	-5.6	9	23	$9
1st Half		277	37	9	34	7	245	227	224	254	334	383	717	12	68	33	0.42	46	24	30	95	113	16%	108	9%	88%	13	23%	54%	4.42	1.3	3	8	$14
2nd Half		230	24	7	21	7	200	223	175	210	278	343	622	10	70	25	0.36	45	17	38	109	112	12%	69	15%	88%	14	36%	50%	3.13	-8.2	9	23	$4
13	Proj	470	62	15	51	13	233	237	234	233	314	393	707	11	71	29	0.41	43	20	37	114	127	12%	91	13%	78%				4.13	-1.9	32	79	$11

Johnson,Reed

Age 36 Bats R Pos LF CF RF	Health C	LIMA Plan F	
Ht 5' 10" Wt 180	PT/Exp F	Rand Var -3	
	Consist D	MM 2223	

Reserve OF always seems to luck into more AB than he deserves. On surface, BA suggests he can add value to your squad. But he's no .300 hitter, as dismal Eye predicts and xBA reveals. His legs could have value, but he never gets a green light, and that likely won't change in his mid-30s.

Yr	Tm	AB	R	HR	RBI	SB	BA	xBA	vL	vR	OB	Slg	OPS	bb%	ct%	h%	Eye	G	L	F	PX	xPX	hr/f	Spd	SBO	SB%	#Wk	DOM	DIS	RC/G	RAR	BPV	BPX	R$
08	CHC	333	52	6	50	5	303	259	333	280	341	420	761	5	80	37	0.28	41	24	35	86	84	7%	95	12%	45%	26	35%	46%	4.95	-1.7	20	39	$12
09	CHC	165	23	4	22	2	255	280	324	206	309	412	721	7	84	28	0.48	50	17	33	98	91	9%	112	8%	67%	18	39%	39%	4.31	-4.0	59	120	$2
10	LA	202	24	2	15	2	262	234	301	222	280	366	647	2	75	34	0.10	43	19	37	82	75	4%	148	9%	50%	24	29%	63%	3.43	-10.1	3	7	$2
11	CHC	246	33	5	28	2	309	263	305	312	323	467	790	2	74	40	0.08	43	21	35	132	89	8%	107	6%	67%	25	36%	48%	5.52	2.5	32	71	$8
12	2 NL	269	30	3	20	2	290	263	311	263	323	398	720	5	77	37	0.21	57	24	19	77	58	8%	125	6%	50%	27	30%	41%	4.51	-4.8	6	15	$5
1st Half		131	16	2	11	1	290	266	279	300	331	427	758	6	74	38	0.24	54	27	19	93	58	11%	134	6%	50%	13	38%	38%	4.97	-0.1	13	33	$6
2nd Half		138	14	1	9	1	290	253	333	208	315	370	684	3	80	35	0.19	59	21	20	63	59	5%	98	6%	50%	14	21%	43%	4.09	-3.6	-6	-15	$5
13	Proj	270	33	4	24	2	278	256	300	255	304	401	705	4	77	35	0.16	50	22	28	91	72	7%	114	7%	54%				4.22	-3.3	14	34	$7

Jones,Adam

Age 27 Bats R Pos CF	Health A	LIMA Plan C+	
Ht 6' 3" Wt 225	PT/Exp A	Rand Var 0	
	Consist A	MM 4335	

Age 26 breakout...and then some. $30 guys don't grow on trees, and he's still young enough for more growth. But while R$ trend gives hope for that, continued lack of patience, all those groundballs are reasons to temper enthusiasm. Use 2nd half times 2 as your baseline. In other words, 2011 more likely than 2012.

Yr	Tm	AB	R	HR	RBI	SB	BA	xBA	vL	vR	OB	Slg	OPS	bb%	ct%	h%	Eye	G	L	F	PX	xPX	hr/f	Spd	SBO	SB%	#Wk	DOM	DIS	RC/G	RAR	BPV	BPX	R$
08	BAL	477	61	9	57	10	270	244	256	275	304	400	704	5	77	33	0.21	47	18	35	86	92	7%	151	11%	77%	23	22%	52%	4.25	-8.2	27	53	$12
09	BAL	473	83	19	70	10	277	287	246	295	328	457	785	7	80	31	0.39	55	17	28	110	104	18%	107	11%	71%	22	36%	36%	5.23	5.0	59	120	$18
10	BAL	581	76	19	69	7	284	260	259	293	311	442	754	4	80	33	0.19	46	17	37	103	99	11%	127	10%	50%	27	26%	33%	4.71	-2.4	37	80	$20
11	BAL	567	68	25	83	12	280	273	242	295	315	466	781	5	80	31	0.26	49	18	33	120	106	17%	97	12%	75%	27	44%	26%	5.17	5.0	53	118	$23
12	BAL	648	103	32	82	16	287	290	292	285	323	505	827	5	81	31	0.27	46	21	33	136	108	19%	102	16%	70%	27	56%	26%	5.70	15.5	74	185	$30
1st Half		307	51	19	41	10	300	302	304	298	334	554	888	5	82	31	0.30	49	18	33	149	116	22%	110	21%	67%	13	69%	15%	6.49	14.8	93	233	$35
2nd Half		341	52	13	41	6	276	281	280	274	312	460	772	5	79	32	0.25	43	25	32	123	101	15%	92	11%	75%	14	43%	36%	5.03	2.5	54	135	$26
13	Proj	599	86	27	78	13	283	278	268	288	318	483	800	5	80	31	0.26	47	20	33	125	105	17%	101	13%	69%				5.36	9.9	60	150	$26

Jones,Andruw

Age 36 Bats R Pos LF RF	Health B	LIMA Plan F	
Ht 6' 1" Wt 225	PT/Exp D	Rand Var +3	
	Consist C	MM 4101	

Former lefty masher couldn't even produce in a platoon. While power skills remain strong, you need daily transactions to get any value from him. It's pretty sad when a 30% h% is needed just to approach a .250 BA. Such is the case here, and that mark in '11 is clearly the outlier. His career is at a crossroads.

Yr	Tm	AB	R	HR	RBI	SB	BA	xBA	vL	vR	OB	Slg	OPS	bb%	ct%	h%	Eye	G	L	F	PX	xPX	hr/f	Spd	SBO	SB%	#Wk	DOM	DIS	RC/G	RAR	BPV	BPX	R$
08	LA *	240	25	5	20	1	168	192	178	147	257	277	534	11	65	23	0.35	48	13	39	85	102	6%	81	4%	54%	15	13%	73%	2.15	-20.2	-26	-51	-$6
09	TEX	281	43	17	43	5	214	269	218	210	322	459	781	14	74	22	0.63	34	16	50	163	146	16%	72	9%	83%	25	48%	44%	4.83	2.2	77	157	$5
10	CHW	278	41	19	48	9	230	272	256	219	337	486	823	14	74	24	0.62	44	11	44	170	143	21%	79	14%	82%	26	50%	38%	5.47	7.7	87	189	$9
11	NYY	190	27	13	33	0	247	246	286	172	347	495	842	13	67	30	0.47	45	15	41	183	120	25%	61	0%	0%	26	50%	46%	5.82	7.0	50	111	$5
12	NYY	233	27	14	34	0	197	222	202	185	284	408	691	11	70	22	0.39	36	15	48	141	128	18%	59	0%	0%	27	37%	48%	3.67	-6.5	19	48	$1
1st Half		106	12	7	16	0	226	229	222	235	317	462	779	12	65	27	0.38	36	17	47	170	167	21%	69	0%	0%	13	38%	46%	4.83	0.6	25	63	$2
2nd Half		127	15	7	18	0	173	216	188	129	255	362	618	10	73	17	0.41	37	14	49	118	99	15%	57	0%	0%	14	36%	50%	2.85	-7.4	16	40	$1
13	Proj	154	20	9	24	1	213	234	228	189	307	434	741	12	70	24	0.45	40	14	46	149	127	19%	62	3%	80%				4.32	-1.6	37	93	$3

Jones,Chipper

Age 41 Bats B Pos 3B	Health	LIMA Plan	
Ht 6' 4" Wt 210	PT/Exp	Rand Var	
	Consist	MM	

Ends career with .303 BA, 468 HR, 1,623 RBI over parts of 19 seasons with ATL. Records include most HR in NL by a switch-hitter in a season (45), most HR in NL over a career by a switch-hitter (468), most consecutive games with an extra-base hit (14), most consecutive 20-HR seasons to start career (14).

Yr	Tm	AB	R	HR	RBI	SB	BA	xBA	vL	vR	OB	Slg	OPS	bb%	ct%	h%	Eye	G	L	F	PX	xPX	hr/f	Spd	SBO	SB%	#Wk	DOM	DIS	RC/G	RAR	BPV	BPX	R$
08	ATL	439	82	22	75	4	364	309	394	349	473	574	1047	17	86	39	1.48	43	24	33	122	114	17%	103	2%	100%	26	54%	12%	10.98	69.7	97	190	$30
09	ATL	488	80	18	71	4	264	275	289	252	390	430	821	17	82	29	1.13	45	20	35	101	121	13%	90	3%	80%	27	63%	37%	5.84	17.4	65	133	$13
10	ATL	317	47	10	46	5	265	271	245	275	384	426	809	16	85	28	1.30	38	18	44	107	116	8%	84	4%	100%	19	63%	16%	5.78	10.7	79	172	$9
11	ATL	455	56	18	70	2	275	280	268	278	348	470	818	10	82	30	0.64	49	16	35	133	117	14%	77	3%	50%	25	52%	16%	5.68	13.9	72	160	$15
12	ATL	387	58	14	62	1	287	284	298	278	378	455	833	13	87	30	1.12	46	22	32	102	130	13%	79	1%	100%	24	50%	29%	6.17	16.9	68	170	$14
1st Half		151	22	6	28	0	291	269	286	295	374	450	825	12	88	30	1.11	51	19	31	90	114	15%	84	0%	0%	10	50%	30%	6.07	6.2	57	143	$10
2nd Half		236	36	8	34	1	284	290	304	264	381	458	839	14	86	30	1.12	43	23	34	110	141	12%	79	1%	100%	14	50%	29%	6.24	11.0	73	183	$16
13	Proj																																	

STEPHEN NICKRAND

Jones,Garrett

Age 32	Bats L	Pos 1B RF	Health	A	LIMA Plan	C+
Ht 6' 4"	Wt 230		PT/Exp	B	Rand Var	0
			Consist	B	MM	4225

PRO: PX and xBA support power totals and BA; high reliability.
CON: Simply cannot hit LHP, which puts a ceiling on PT; that and age limit upside.
At 32, this is more likely a peak than a new level of performance. Expect regression.

Yr	Tm	AB	R	HR	RBI	SB	BA	xBA	vL	vR	OB	Slg	OPS	bb%	ct%	h%	Eye	G	L	F	PX	xPX	hr/f	Spd	SBO	SB%	#Wk	DOM	DIS	RC/G	RAR	BPV	BPX	R$
08	aaa	530	62	17	70	7	225	255			274	379	653	6	77	26	0.29				105			87	8%	73%				3.41		32	0	$5
09	PIT *	591	78	30	81	21	273	277	208	333	333	488	821	8	78	31	0.40	40	18	41	139	146	21%	82	19%	75%	15	53%	20%	5.63	3.5	67	137	$24
10	PIT	592	64	21	86	7	247	261	220	262	309	414	722	8	79	28	0.43	44	17	39	115	116	11%	71	7%	70%	27	41%	33%	4.29	-19.9	45	98	$13
11	PIT	423	51	16	58	6	243	258	147	262	321	433	753	10	75	29	0.46	36	20	45	141	140	11%	63	9%	67%	27	52%	37%	4.62	-10.1	57	127	$10
12	PIT	475	68	27	86	2	274	277	189	289	321	516	837	6	78	30	0.32	40	18	42	152	155	17%	88	2%	100%	27	44%	22%	5.84	5.5	72	180	$19
1st Half		182	23	10	30	2	258	268	0	275	289	489	778	4	75	29	0.18	43	18	39	150	141	19%	86	6%	100%	13	38%	31%	4.93	-2.3	54	135	$9
2nd Half		293	45	17	56	0	283	282	222	300	340	532	872	8	80	30	0.43	38	19	43	153	162	16%	88	0%	0%	14	50%	14%	6.43	8.8	77	193	$25
13	Proj	**485**	**63**	**24**	**77**	**5**	**259**	**267**	**188**	**278**	**316**	**478**	**794**	**8**	**78**	**29**	**0.37**	**40**	**18**	**42**	**142**	**144**	**15%**	**76**	**6%**	**75%**				**5.19**	**-2.4**	**64**	**159**	**$15**

Joyce,Matt

Age 28	Bats L	Pos RF LF	Health	C	LIMA Plan	C+
Ht 6' 2"	Wt 205		PT/Exp	C	Rand Var	+1
			Consist	C	MM	4115

Missed a month in June/July with an oblique injury, and that likely explains his 2H power outage. That's really the only difference in skills from his 2011 mini-breakout—bb%, ct%, and Spd all held up. With his low BA vs. LHP, there's little playing time upside, but expect a power rebound nonetheless.

Yr	Tm	AB	R	HR	RBI	SB	BA	xBA	vL	vR	OB	Slg	OPS	bb%	ct%	h%	Eye	G	L	F	PX	xPX	hr/f	Spd	SBO	SB%	#Wk	DOM	DIS	RC/G	RAR	BPV	BPX	R$
08	DET *	445	70	22	66	2	246	255	227	255	323	481	804	10	70	30	0.38	35	17	47	166	135	14%	117	7%	31%	18	44%	50%	5.03	2.2	62	122	$9
09	TAM *	449	63	16	61	13	232	237	250	179	320	415	735	11	73	28	0.47	38	12	50	132	197	23%	91	16%	68%	3	67%	33%	4.34	-7.1	50	102	$10
10	TAM *	308	43	12	49	3	240	259	80	262	358	448	806	16	74	29	0.70	33	18	49	151	179	13%	87	9%	33%	16	63%	31%	5.08	2.1	71	154	$7
11	TAM	462	69	19	75	13	277	269	217	292	346	478	825	10	77	32	0.46	36	21	42	144	128	12%	84	11%	93%	27	59%	30%	5.98	14.7	76	169	$20
12	TAM	399	55	17	59	4	241	244	209	250	333	429	761	12	74	28	0.54	38	19	43	124	117	13%	90	6%	57%	24	46%	29%	4.71	-1.8	47	118	$9
1st Half		201	36	11	34	2	279	261	259	287	375	512	887	13	76	32	0.65	39	18	43	143	136	17%	112	3%	100%	12	58%	8%	6.87	10.6	77	193	$16
2nd Half		198	19	6	25	2	202	226	121	218	288	343	632	11	73	25	0.44	36	20	43	103	97	10%	69	10%	40%	12	33%	50%	3.01	-12.6	9	23	$2
13	Proj	**433**	**60**	**18**	**65**	**7**	**245**	**249**	**183**	**260**	**334**	**441**	**774**	**12**	**75**	**29**	**0.52**	**36**	**20**	**44**	**133**	**129**	**13%**	**84**	**9%**	**62%**				**4.88**	**-1.6**	**54**	**135**	**$13**

Kalish,Ryan

Age 25	Bats L	Pos CF	Health	A	LIMA Plan	F
Ht 6' 0"	Wt 215		PT/Exp	F	Rand Var	0
			Consist	F	MM	1303

0-5-.229 in 96 AB at BOS. Missed two months recovering from off-season shoulder and neck surgery, and wasn't really right all season, so there's still some hope for his future. But contact, power, and speed skills are middling across the board, and there's little here that portends much of a rebound in 2013.

Yr	Tm	AB	R	HR	RBI	SB	BA	xBA	vL	vR	OB	Slg	OPS	bb%	ct%	h%	Eye	G	L	F	PX	xPX	hr/f	Spd	SBO	SB%	#Wk	DOM	DIS	RC/G	RAR	BPV	BPX	R$
08																																		
09	aa	391	54	11	48	12	265	261			326	419	745	8	77	32	0.40				103			101	15%	79%				4.76		44	0	$11
10	BOS *	456	71	14	61	30	265	275	233	258	331	433	763	9	79	31	0.48	46	18	36	118	116	9%	100	28%	87%	11	45%	45%	5.17	4.1	71	154	$22
11	aaa	86	7	0	7	3	199	224			256	272	527	7	75	27	0.30				73			83	38%	51%				1.96		-1	0	-$2
12	BOS *	216	27	3	16	9	233	219	333	210	297	319	616	8	72	31	0.33	57	16	26	68	106	0%	82	22%	67%	10	0%	90%	3.09	-11.7	-13	-33	$3
1st Half		85	15	3	12	3	278	268	250	226	360	438	798	11	71	36	0.45	63	22	15	114	81	0%	80	13%	100%	2	0%	100%	5.86	2.1	26	65	$6
2nd Half		131	12	0	4	5	205	183	429	200	255	243	498	6	73	28	0.24	54	12	34	38	123	0%	88	31%	55%	8	0%	88%	1.84	-13.5	-42	-105	$1
13	Proj	**289**	**40**	**5**	**30**	**13**	**251**	**232**	**302**	**239**	**314**	**356**	**670**	**8**	**75**	**32**	**0.37**	**51**	**17**	**32**	**79**	**110**	**7%**	**84**	**22%**	**78%**				**3.85**	**-8.0**	**15**	**37**	**$9**

Kawasaki,Munenori

Age 32	Bats L	Pos SS	Health	A	LIMA Plan	F
Ht 5' 10"	Wt 165		PT/Exp	C	Rand Var	+5
			Consist	C	MM	0431

Couldn't find playing time in SEA (which is a statement unto itself), and didn't do anything with the few ABs he did find. Was already on the far end of the bell curve when he crossed over (note BPV trend), but then took a short path to oblivion. Speed is his only fantasy-relevant skill and that can't function in a vacuum.

Yr	Tm	AB	R	HR	RBI	SB	BA	xBA	vL	vR	OB	Slg	OPS	bb%	ct%	h%	Eye	G	L	F	PX	xPX	hr/f	Spd	SBO	SB%	#Wk	DOM	DIS	RC/G	RAR	BPV	BPX	R$
08	for *	424	54	1	33	17	299	258			320	385	704	3	91	33	0.34				49	5	0%	143	24%	63%				4.25	-7.6	52	0	$15
09	for *	540	71	2	33	40	242	256			291	349	640	7	84	28	0.44				66	-5	0%	144	46%	68%				3.24	-27.7	53	0	$15
10	for *	602	72	2	52	27	294	252			333	376	709	5	86	34	0.43				56	-5	0%	121	22%	69%				4.41	-8.1	40	0	$23
11	for *	603	69	1	36	28	249	239			283	319	603	5	87	29	0.36				45	2	0%	141	26%	72%				3.04	-33.6	37	0	$12
12	SEA	104	13	0	7	2	192	224	105	212	250	202	452	7	83	23	0.44	61	19	20	8	30	0%	102	15%	50%	25	4%	64%	1.52	-8.0	-23	-58	-$2
1st Half		59	8	0	6	1	186	203	0	208	262	203	465	9	83	22	0.60	52	16	32	15	40	0%	94	19%	33%	13	8%	46%	1.48	-5.0	-13	-33	-$3
2nd Half		45	5	0	1	1	200	251	154	219	234	200	434	4	82	24	0.25	71	23	6	0	17	0%	109	9%	100%	12	0%	83%	1.58	-3.4	-38	-95	-$2
13	Proj	**98**	**12**	**0**	**8**	**4**	**245**	**272**	**157**	**269**	**292**	**308**	**600**	**6**	**86**	**29**	**0.47**	**64**	**20**	**16**	**41**	**26**	**1%**	**118**	**25%**	**61%**				**2.88**	**-3.4**	**25**	**61**	**$2**

Kearns,Austin

Age 33	Bats R	Pos LF	Health	C	LIMA Plan	F
Ht 6' 3"	Wt 240		PT/Exp	D	Rand Var	-2
			Consist	F	MM	2001

It's rare that a player is lucky to hit 4 HR, but here he is, with 4 of his 18 fly balls leaving the park. Pick a number—70% ct%, -2 BPV, 58% Dis%—they all add up to a whole lot of nothing to offer. Always fun to mention that he was once considered the better CIN prospect next to Adam Dunn.

Yr	Tm	AB	R	HR	RBI	SB	BA	xBA	vL	vR	OB	Slg	OPS	bb%	ct%	h%	Eye	G	L	F	PX	xPX	hr/f	Spd	SBO	SB%	#Wk	DOM	DIS	RC/G	RAR	BPV	BPX	R$
08	WAS	313	40	7	32	2	217	242	153	241	296	316	612	10	80	25	0.56	47	21	32	65	98	9%	69	5%	50%	16	31%	50%	3.00	-16.7	9	18	-$1
09	WAS	174	20	3	17	1	195	217	122	224	320	305	625	16	71	26	0.63	46	18	37	77	101	7%	103	4%	50%	18	17%	67%	3.06	-9.2	1	2	-$2
10	2 AL	403	55	10	49	4	263	246	252	270	339	395	733	10	71	35	0.40	44	23	33	104	104	11%	72	4%	80%	26	19%	50%	4.64	-1.0	12	26	$10
11	CLE	150	18	2	7	0	200	215	235	171	286	287	572	11	68	28	0.38	51	22	27	71	105	7%	112	10%	0%	20	30%	65%	2.32	-11.6	-27	-60	-$3
12	MIA	147	21	4	16	2	245	252	196	340	343	367	711	13	70	32	0.50	54	28	17	91	52	22%	59	6%	67%	26	38%	58%	4.23	-2.1	-2	-5	$1
1st Half		68	9	3	9	1	279	289	217	409	319	471	790	6	69	36	0.19	55	34	11	142	95	60%	53	6%	100%	12	58%	42%	5.41	1.5	18	45	$2
2nd Half		79	12	1	7	1	215	215	176	286	361	278	639	19	71	29	0.78	54	23	23	48	16	8%	72	6%	50%	14	21%	71%	3.20	-3.6	-24	-60	$1
13	Proj	**184**	**25**	**5**	**17**	**2**	**231**	**238**	**206**	**258**	**326**	**348**	**674**	**12**	**70**	**30**	**0.48**	**51**	**25**	**24**	**87**	**76**	**15%**	**74**	**7%**	**44%**				**3.64**	**-5.7**	**-5**	**-14**	**$3**

Kelly,Don

Age 33	Bats L	Pos RF	Health	A	LIMA Plan	F
Ht 6' 4"	Wt 190		PT/Exp	F	Rand Var	+3
			Consist	B	MM	0300

1-7-.186 in 113 AB at DET. His contact and power disappeared, and with no injury to explain it, age seems like an adequate scapegoat. Still... regression works both ways and his numbers will likely rebound some by mere chance... unless gravity is the stronger force now, in which case he's probably done.

Yr	Tm	AB	R	HR	RBI	SB	BA	xBA	vL	vR	OB	Slg	OPS	bb%	ct%	h%	Eye	G	L	F	PX	xPX	hr/f	Spd	SBO	SB%	#Wk	DOM	DIS	RC/G	RAR	BPV	BPX	R$
08	aaa	436	36	5	32	1	212	257			245	309	554	4	88	23	0.36				61			106	3%	48%				2.42		31	0	-$5
09	DET *	428	52	5	34	22	269	270	125	271	327	377	704	8	83	31	0.51	46	24	30	68	49	0%	125	22%	81%	11	27%	45%	4.39	-2.1	44	90	$13
10	DET	238	30	9	27	3	244	233	217	247	268	374	642	3	82	26	0.19	32	19	49	76	91	9%	103	6%	100%	27	30%	56%	3.45	-7.8	20	43	$4
11	DET	257	35	7	28	2	245	248	190	250	284	381	665	5	88	26	0.44	29	23	48	79	72	7%	131	5%	67%	27	41%	37%	3.63	-7.1	55	122	$4
12	DET *	186	20	2	15	5	183	192	83	198	270	240	510	11	77	23	0.52	40	18	42	38	44	3%	117	12%	79%	24	17%	67%	2.08	-14.9	-10	-25	-$2
1st Half		86	10	1	7	1	186	187	143	190	293	244	537	13	84	21	0.93	37	15	48	28	42	3%	132	4%	100%	13	23%	62%	2.30	-6.5	11	28	-$3
2nd Half		100	10	1	8	4	181	228	0	227	249	237	486	8	71	25	0.32	53	26	21	48	55	0%	96	22%	75%	11	9%	73%	1.88	-9.1	-35	-88	-$1
13	Proj	**65**	**8**	**1**	**6**	**1**	**213**	**222**	**112**	**224**	**271**	**286**	**557**	**7**	**81**	**25**	**0.42**	**40**	**22**	**38**	**47**	**61**	**4%**	**107**	**10%**	**82%**				**2.56**	**-4.9**	**5**	**12**	**$1**

Kemp,Matt

Age 28	Bats R	Pos CF	Health	B	LIMA Plan	D+
Ht 6' 4"	Wt 225		PT/Exp	A	Rand Var	-3
			Consist	F	MM	4335

A monster start was derailed by a hamstring injury, costing him two months and 2H power and speed. That all comes back; note, however, that xBA history puts .300 BA at risk. Off-season shoulder surgery may delay his 2013 start, tempering expectations for a full rebound.

Yr	Tm	AB	R	HR	RBI	SB	BA	xBA	vL	vR	OB	Slg	OPS	bb%	ct%	h%	Eye	G	L	F	PX	xPX	hr/f	Spd	SBO	SB%	#Wk	DOM	DIS	RC/G	RAR	BPV	BPX	R$
08	LA	606	93	18	76	35	290	267	369	260	340	459	799	7	75	36	0.30	45	23	32	119	122	12%	134	29%	76%	27	44%	33%	5.56	15.1	50	98	$31
09	LA	606	97	26	101	34	297	268	362	278	353	490	843	8	77	35	0.37	40	21	38	119	124	14%	138	24%	81%	27	48%	22%	6.31	27.7	63	129	$35
10	LA	602	82	28	89	19	249	257	295	233	310	450	760	8	72	30	0.31	41	20	39	139	146	16%	115	24%	56%	27	48%	33%	4.41	-5.0	49	107	$21
11	LA	602	115	39	126	40	324	284	341	319	398	586	984	11	74	39	0.47	36	23	41	181	164	21%	116	26%	78%	27	70%	19%	8.73	66.2	100	222	$51
12	LA	403	74	23	69	9	303	277	363	276	366	538	904	9	74	36	0.39	43	22	35	155	158	22%	92	11%	69%	21	43%	33%	7.08	26.7	70	175	$23
1st Half		121	30	12	28	2	355	326	486	298	451	719	1170	15	75	39	0.70	44	24	32	222	195	40%	111	11%	40%	8	75%	13%	11.91	22.7	135	338	$19
2nd Half		282	44	11	41	7	280	255	310	267	326	461	787	6	74	34	0.26	43	21	36	125	142	14%	80	11%	88%	13	23%	46%	5.39	4.9	40	100	$24
13	Proj	**538**	**97**	**32**	**96**	**20**	**297**	**275**	**352**	**277**	**364**	**539**	**903**	**9**	**74**	**35**	**0.40**	**41**	**22**	**37**	**158**	**157**	**21%**	**102**	**19%**	**70%**				**6.94**	**32.9**	**76**	**190**	**$34**

MATT CEDERHOLM

Kendrick,Howie

Age	29	Bats	R	Pos	2B	Health	A	LIMA Plan	C+
Ht	5' 10"	Wt	205			PT/Exp	A	Rand Var	-2
						Consist	B	MM	2335

At this point, can we all finally give up on the dream of him ever challenging for a batting title? Is there anyone out there who is still harboring a man-crush? Get over it!! Soft ct%, PX fall-back came with a huge GB shift, and xBA shows further BA vulnerability. Must. Resist. Going. One. Dollar. More.

Yr	Tm	AB	R	HR	RBI	SB	BA	xBA	vL	vR	OB	Slg	OPS	bb%	ct%	h%	Eye	G	L	F	PX	xPX	hr/f	Spd	SBO	SB%	#Wk	DOM	DIS	RC/G	RAR	BPV	BPX	R$
08	LAA	340	43	3	37	11	306	280	300	308	330	421	750	3	83	36	0.21	54	20	26	86	85	4%	90	18%	73%	19	32%	53%	5.04	8.2	41	80	$13
09	LAA *	452	69	11	69	14	290	284	313	278	327	439	767	5	81	34	0.29	54	19	27	97	86	12%	103	18%	68%	25	48%	20%	5.04	11.2	49	100	$18
10	LAA	616	67	10	75	14	279	285	264	286	311	407	718	4	85	32	0.30	53	19	28	90	93	7%	90	12%	78%	27	33%	37%	4.48	5.5	51	111	$19
11	LAA	537	86	18	63	14	285	284	295	280	326	464	790	6	78	34	0.28	52	22	27	123	127	17%	110	15%	70%	26	42%	23%	5.30	17.3	60	133	$23
12	LAA	550	57	8	67	14	287	265	309	278	323	400	723	5	79	35	0.25	59	21	21	81	87	9%	92	14%	70%	27	30%	44%	4.56	6.1	20	50	$18
1st Half		267	27	4	29	4	273	248	287	267	312	378	690	5	79	33	0.26	59	18	23	72	94	8%	102	13%	44%	13	31%	54%	3.89	-2.9	7	18	$14
2nd Half		283	30	4	38	10	300	280	333	288	333	420	754	5	80	37	0.24	58	23	19	90	81	10%	82	15%	91%	14	29%	36%	5.26	7.8	30	75	$22
13	Proj	**565**	**69**	**11**	**69**	**15**	**282**	**273**	**295**	**277**	**318**	**417**	**736**	**5**	**80**	**34**	**0.26**	**56**	**21**	**24**	**93**	**97**	**10%**	**91**	**15%**	**73%**				**4.68**	**6.8**	**37**	**93**	**$19**

Kennedy,Adam

Age	37	Bats	L	Pos	3B	Health	B	LIMA Plan	F
Ht	6' 1"	Wt	195			PT/Exp	D	Rand Var	-3
						Consist	B	MM	1211

Well-traveled and bi-coastal, if nothing else. Even if he consolidated all of his best skills: his 2012 bb%, 2010 ct%, etc. he'd still be replacement level at best. And he'd still be 37-years old.

Yr	Tm	AB	R	HR	RBI	SB	BA	xBA	vL	vR	OB	Slg	OPS	bb%	ct%	h%	Eye	G	L	F	PX	xPX	hr/f	Spd	SBO	SB%	#Wk	DOM	DIS	RC/G	RAR	BPV	BPX	R$
08	STL	339	42	2	36	7	280	271	270	283	322	372	694	6	87	32	0.49	43	25	32	60	56	2%	107	9%	88%	27	30%	48%	4.32	-2.7	45	88	$8
09	OAK *	611	73	13	70	21	280	269	241	307	337	400	737	8	83	32	0.52	41	24	36	79	90	7%	87	16%	75%	23	35%	35%	4.76	2.6	40	82	$20
10	WAS	342	43	3	31	14	249	253	316	240	322	327	649	10	87	28	0.84	43	20	37	56	64	3%	105	16%	88%	27	37%	26%	3.73	-8.8	45	98	$7
11	SEA	380	36	7	38	8	234	253	191	243	276	355	631	5	82	27	0.33	37	23	41	88	55	5%	67	13%	80%	26	31%	38%	3.29	-15.1	37	82	$4
12	LA	168	22	2	16	1	262	238	233	268	351	357	708	12	80	32	0.70	42	22	36	67	75	4%	104	4%	50%	21	24%	52%	4.27	-1.6	20	50	$1
1st Half		106	14	0	9	0	217	213	304	193	325	274	599	14	78	28	0.74	45	20	35	43	56	0%	113	0%	0%	13	15%	69%	2.90	-5.5	-4	-10	$0
2nd Half		62	8	2	7	1	339	281	0	382	397	500	897	9	84	38	0.60	37	26	37	104	104	10%	83	10%	50%	8	38%	25%	7.32	4.5	51	128	$4
13	Proj	**127**	**15**	**2**	**13**	**2**	**269**	**251**	**204**	**281**	**335**	**379**	**714**	**9**	**83**	**31**	**0.58**	**40**	**23**	**37**	**75**	**73**	**5%**	**88**	**9%**	**71%**				**4.40**	**-0.7**	**33**	**83**	**$4**

Keppinger,Jeff

Age	33	Bats	R	Pos	3B 2B 1B	Health	D	LIMA Plan	D
Ht	6' 0"	Wt	185			PT/Exp	C	Rand Var	-5
						Consist	D	MM	1133

9-40-.325 in 385 AB at TAM. Missed a month with a broken toe, but the real story is that he was able to again accumulate almost 400 AB with only one acceptable skill. Okay, it IS a really good skill—phenomenal ct% does provide a safe BA floor. But xBA says take the under on .300 BA. Another 400 AB? Pushing it.

Yr	Tm	AB	R	HR	RBI	SB	BA	xBA	vL	vR	OB	Slg	OPS	bb%	ct%	h%	Eye	G	L	F	PX	xPX	hr/f	Spd	SBO	SB%	#Wk	DOM	DIS	RC/G	RAR	BPV	BPX	R$
08	CIN *	481	47	4	44	3	273	288	360	225	317	358	675	6	95	28	1.25	51	21	28	55	52	2%	96	3%	75%	21	43%	5%	3.99	-4.9	56	110	$7
09	HOU	305	35	7	29	0	256	282	314	227	316	387	703	8	89	27	0.82	53	18	29	74	75	9%	113	2%	0%	26	35%	31%	4.08	-0.7	51	104	$3
10	HOU	514	62	6	59	4	288	292	304	282	352	393	745	9	93	30	1.42	51	20	30	72	79	4%	86	3%	80%	26	54%	12%	4.97	11.5	68	148	$14
11	2 NL *	423	43	7	37	0	273	287	290	273	296	369	665	3	94	28	0.55	47	24	29	62	61	6%	69	1%	0%	19	47%	21%	3.79	-6.7	43	96	$7
12	TAM *	406	49	9	41	1	319	283	376	302	361	429	790	6	92	33	0.80	49	23	27	63	57	9%	97	1%	100%	23	48%	35%	5.82	17.9	45	113	$15
1st Half		132	16	3	14	0	315	280	417	270	362	419	781	7	93	32	1.13	48	24	28	59	57	10%	86	0%	0%	9	67%	33%	5.64	4.9	44	110	$6
2nd Half		274	33	6	27	1	321	283	348	312	361	434	795	6	91	34	0.68	50	23	27	65	56	9%	101	1%	100%	14	36%	36%	5.91	12.1	45	113	$19
13	Proj	**329**	**38**	**6**	**33**	**1**	**288**	**283**	**337**	**268**	**332**	**397**	**728**	**6**	**93**	**30**	**0.87**	**49**	**22**	**28**	**64**	**62**	**7%**	**85**	**1%**	**66%**				**4.70**	**1.1**	**50**	**125**	**$9**

Kinsler,Ian

Age	31	Bats	R	Pos	2B	Health	B	LIMA Plan	B+
Ht	6' 0"	Wt	200			PT/Exp	A	Rand Var	+1
						Consist	B	MM	3325

If you were disappointed with his performance, just imagine his counting stats without the huge AB total. Small signs of decline across the board. Even at just-past peak, recent skills suggest that the declines are reversible, but factor in that there's only downside possible in his AB totals.

Yr	Tm	AB	R	HR	RBI	SB	BA	xBA	vL	vR	OB	Slg	OPS	bb%	ct%	h%	Eye	G	L	F	PX	xPX	hr/f	Spd	SBO	SB%	#Wk	DOM	DIS	RC/G	RAR	BPV	BPX	R$
08	TEX	518	102	18	71	26	319	292	281	332	373	517	890	8	87	34	0.67	32	24	43	123	128	9%	117	19%	93%	21	57%	5%	7.49	46.2	107	210	$33
09	TEX	566	101	31	86	31	253	276	310	230	323	488	811	9	86	24	0.77	30	16	54	132	133	12%	107	27%	86%	26	73%	8%	5.50	22.4	114	233	$26
10	TEX	391	73	9	45	15	286	257	376	258	376	412	788	13	85	32	0.98	40	18	42	83	90	7%	105	14%	75%	20	55%	25%	5.54	15.3	65	141	$17
11	TEX	620	121	32	77	30	255	286	263	252	348	477	826	13	89	24	1.25	35	18	47	130	125	12%	103	19%	88%	27	81%	7%	5.86	30.9	124	276	$30
12	TEX	655	105	19	72	21	256	268	350	226	319	423	742	8	86	27	0.67	38	20	42	103	88	8%	100	19%	70%	27	52%	19%	4.54	7.3	81	203	$22
1st Half		333	60	9	40	15	276	287	341	252	331	450	781	8	86	30	0.59	37	26	38	110	89	8%	98	24%	75%	13	62%	15%	5.19	9.0	90	225	$29
2nd Half		322	45	10	32	6	236	247	362	202	307	394	701	9	86	25	0.75	38	14	47	95	88	8%	99	13%	60%	14	43%	21%	3.93	-3.2	68	170	$14
13	Proj	**597**	**104**	**21**	**70**	**23**	**261**	**267**	**326**	**240**	**337**	**439**	**775**	**10**	**87**	**27**	**0.86**	**37**	**19**	**44**	**106**	**102**	**9%**	**99**	**18%**	**78%**				**5.11**	**14.8**	**89**	**222**	**$25**

Kipnis,Jason

Age	26	Bats	L	Pos	2B	Health	A	LIMA Plan	C+
Ht	5' 11"	Wt	185			PT/Exp	B	Rand Var	+1
						Consist	A	MM	3425

PRO: Increases in bb% and ct% show growth as a hitter; more green lights led to 30+ SB.
CON: 2H plummet is concerning; couldn't hit LHP; Spd doesn't support SB if 2H SB% repeats.
Keep SB and BA expectations realistic, but there is solid power upside here. UP: 25 HR.

Yr	Tm	AB	R	HR	RBI	SB	BA	xBA	vL	vR	OB	Slg	OPS	bb%	ct%	h%	Eye	G	L	F	PX	xPX	hr/f	Spd	SBO	SB%	#Wk	DOM	DIS	RC/G	RAR	BPV	BPX	R$
08																																		
09																																		
10	aa	315	49	7	33	5	270	261			323	417	741	7	78	33	0.36				104			115	8%	83%				4.75		47	0	$8
11	CLE *	479	74	16	61	14	248	262	263	276	312	424	736	8	76	30	0.38	45	21	34	121	126	21%	104	13%	93%	8	50%	38%	4.61	6.2	61	136	$15
12	CLE	591	86	14	76	31	257	259	215	280	333	379	712	10	82	29	0.61	47	23	30	76	91	10%	102	21%	82%	27	33%	30%	4.44	4.7	46	115	$23
1st Half		305	47	11	46	19	275	262	227	303	332	426	759	8	82	30	0.48	44	23	33	84	103	13%	122	22%	95%	13	46%	23%	5.31	9.2	54	135	$31
2nd Half		286	39	3	30	12	238	255	202	257	333	329	662	13	81	29	0.75	51	23	27	66	77	5%	88	20%	67%	14	21%	36%	3.61	-5.7	31	78	$14
13	Proj	**570**	**85**	**19**	**69**	**21**	**254**	**266**	**212**	**275**	**325**	**417**	**742**	**10**	**79**	**29**	**0.50**	**47**	**22**	**31**	**103**	**103**	**13%**	**104**	**17%**	**82%**				**4.70**	**7.4**	**56**	**139**	**$21**

Konerko,Paul

Age	37	Bats	R	Pos	1B DH	Health	A	LIMA Plan	B
Ht	6' 2"	Wt	220			PT/Exp	A	Rand Var	-1
						Consist	B	MM	3035

PX drop hints at age-related decline, but bone chip in wrist likely explains much of 2H power outage. The bigger story here is the steady decline in FB%, which even with health makes a full HR rebound unlikely. And now at age 37, is the wrist a sign that the breakdown is coming?

Yr	Tm	AB	R	HR	RBI	SB	BA	xBA	vL	vR	OB	Slg	OPS	bb%	ct%	h%	Eye	G	L	F	PX	xPX	hr/f	Spd	SBO	SB%	#Wk	DOM	DIS	RC/G	RAR	BPV	BPX	R$
08	CHW	438	59	22	62	2	240	280	236	241	338	438	776	13	82	25	0.81	41	22	38	119	116	16%	68	2%	100%	24	58%	25%	5.00	-3.7	66	129	$8
09	CHW	546	75	28	88	1	277	281	338	253	346	489	835	10	84	29	0.65	36	19	46	125	140	13%	59	1%	100%	26	58%	23%	5.98	10.6	70	143	$17
10	CHW	548	89	39	111	0	312	301	339	304	392	584	976	12	80	33	0.65	35	20	45	170	164	20%	72	1%	0%	27	56%	26%	8.43	46.5	90	196	$31
11	CHW	543	69	31	105	1	300	289	292	303	387	517	905	12	84	31	0.87	37	22	41	133	136	16%	46	1%	50%	27	56%	26%	7.26	29.5	74	164	$27
12	CHW	533	66	26	75	0	298	274	271	307	365	486	851	10	84	31	0.67	41	22	37	108	96	16%	68	0%	0%	27	56%	22%	6.45	17.0	50	125	$21
1st Half		259	38	14	40	0	336	298	271	355	407	556	963	11	84	36	0.76	37	25	38	131	114	17%	63	0%	0%	13	77%	15%	8.69	22.4	71	178	$27
2nd Half		274	28	12	35	0	263	251	271	260	324	420	744	8	85	27	0.60	45	20	35	87	80	15%	74	0%	0%	14	36%	29%	4.71	-5.2	31	78	$15
13	Proj	**501**	**65**	**24**	**82**	**0**	**284**	**272**	**278**	**286**	**359**	**474**	**834**	**11**	**83**	**30**	**0.71**	**40**	**22**	**38**	**112**	**118**	**15%**	**61**	**0%**	**52%**				**6.06**	**9.8**	**54**	**135**	**$20**

Kotchman,Casey

Age	30	Bats	L	Pos	1B	Health	A	LIMA Plan	D+
Ht	6' 3"	Wt	220			PT/Exp	B	Rand Var	+4
						Consist	F	MM	1125

That .306 BA in 2011 suddenly made him rosterable in the end game, but xBA told the true story. From a skills perspective, it wasn't a near-80 point BA drop; it was a gentler decline. Still, it shows the volatility of his only redeeming offensive skill. His defense makes him valuable in the real game and sim, but not roto.

Yr	Tm	AB	R	HR	RBI	SB	BA	xBA	vL	vR	OB	Slg	OPS	bb%	ct%	h%	Eye	G	L	F	PX	xPX	hr/f	Spd	SBO	SB%	#Wk	DOM	DIS	RC/G	RAR	BPV	BPX	R$
08	2 TM	525	65	14	74	2	272	289	303	261	319	410	729	6	93	27	0.92	53	18	30	80	86	10%	76	2%	67%	26	58%	12%	4.57	-10.8	64	125	$12
09	2 TM	385	37	7	48	1	268	276	250	275	335	382	717	9	89	29	0.93	51	19	29	73	79	7%	63	1%	100%	26	42%	23%	4.47	-9.0	45	92	$6
10	SEA	414	37	9	51	0	217	264	179	231	278	336	614	8	86	23	0.61	55	17	27	77	72	9%	64	0%	0%	26	31%	50%	3.05	-28.4	33	72	$1
11	TAM	500	44	10	48	2	306	267	289	313	367	422	789	9	87	34	0.73	56	18	26	76	74	9%	86	2%	50%	26	38%	31%	5.63	4.6	40	89	$16
12	CLE	463	46	12	55	3	229	253	221	231	270	333	603	5	89	23	0.53	56	16	29	58	51	10%	63	3%	100%	27	30%	44%	3.00	-31.9	33	83	$5
1st Half		237	26	6	27	3	224	256	215	227	267	333	600	6	86	24	0.44	58	16	27	65	51	11%	67	6%	100%	13	31%	46%	2.98	-17.1	30	75	$5
2nd Half		226	20	6	28	0	235	237	229	236	273	332	605	5	92	23	0.71	54	16	30	50	51	10%	69	0%	0%	14	29%	43%	3.02	-15.9	28	70	$4
13	Proj	**424**	**40**	**10**	**49**	**2**	**251**	**257**	**241**	**255**	**302**	**361**	**664**	**7**	**89**	**26**	**0.65**	**55**	**17**	**28**	**65**	**63**	**9%**	**68**	**2%**	**78%**				**3.72**	**-20.4**	**35**	**87**	**$8**

MATT CEDERHOLM

Kotsay,Mark

Age 37	Bats L	Pos LF	Health	C	LIMA Plan F
Ht 6' 0"	Wt 210		PT/Exp	D	Rand Var 0
			Consist	B	MM 1021

BPV decline tells what you need to know about this part/old-timer. Has the power of a slap hitter and the speed of a lumbering 1B, which is a bad combo. His contact rate remains excellent, but all the balls in play don't go very far (sub-.380 Slg from '09 on). Some team might give him another shot; you shouldn't.

Yr	Tm	AB	R	HR	RBI	SB	BA	xBA	vL	vR	OB	Slg	OPS	bb%	ct%	h%	Eye	G	L	F	PX	xPX	hr/f	Spd	SBO	SB%	#Wk	DOM	DIS	RC/G	RAR	BPV	BPX	R$
08	2 TM	402	45	6	49	2	276	279	250	288	329	403	732	7	89	30	0.71	42	22	36	80	95	5%	88	6%	33%	23	39%	35%	4.52	-7.2	56	110	$8
09	2 AL *	220	18	4	27	4	276	267	219	290	322	376	698	6	90	29	0.68	47	19	34	62	85	7%	69	9%	66%	18	39%	28%	4.21	-5.9	38	78	$4
10	CHW	327	30	8	31	1	239	262	0	258	306	376	683	9	89	25	0.89	44	16	40	85	101	7%	70	5%	25%	27	48%	37%	3.73	-14.0	58	126	$2
11	MIL	233	18	3	31	3	270	267	462	259	331	373	704	8	88	30	0.78	47	20	33	71	76	4%	61	4%	100%	27	37%	44%	4.40	-4.9	47	104	$4
12	SD	143	9	2	14	0	259	257	250	260	312	357	668	7	90	28	0.79	42	22	36	64	99	4%	62	5%	0%	22	32%	36%	3.60	-6.5	33	83	$0
1st Half		67	4	1	6	0	313	254	429	300	387	403	790	11	91	33	1.33	46	21	33	56	116	5%	85	8%	0%	8	25%	38%	5.16	0.3	37	93	$0
2nd Half		76	5	1	8	0	211	261	0	225	241	316	556	4	89	22	0.38	38	22	40	72	84	4%	47	0%	0%	14	36%	36%	2.45	-6.0	30	75	-$1
13	**Proj**	**130**	**10**	**2**	**14**	**1**	**257**	**260**	**235**	**259**	**313**	**365**	**677**	**7**	**89**	**27**	**0.77**	**43**	**20**	**36**	**69**	**92**	**5%**	**62**	**5%**	**37%**				**3.80**	**-3.2**	**41**	**103**	**$0**

Kottaras,George

Age 30	Bats L	Pos CA	Health	A	LIMA Plan D
Ht 6' 0"	Wt 200		PT/Exp	F	Rand Var +3
			Consist	A	MM 4011

Fluky 1H walk rate and unsustainable 2H hr/f aside, the power and patience are legit. Hit rate rebound will boost BA, and PX history says PT bump would mean 15+ HR. But contact rate, poor defense and platoon issues make it unlikely. Proved he can produce as a #2; backing into more PT could be very profitable.

Yr	Tm	AB	R	HR	RBI	SB	BA	xBA	vL	vR	OB	Slg	OPS	bb%	ct%	h%	Eye	G	L	F	PX	xPX	hr/f	Spd	SBO	SB%	#Wk	DOM	DIS	RC/G	RAR	BPV	BPX	R$
08	BOS *	400	50	15	51	0	215	194	500	0	302	381	683	11	69	27	0.40	67	0	33	123	5	0%	79	0%	0%	3	33%	67%	3.74	-4.9	7	14	$1
09	BOS *	117	16	1	10	0	247	257	111	267	339	395	734	12	73	33	0.52	30	23	48	134	129	3%	80	0%	0%	22	36%	50%	4.53	1.3	36	73	-$1
10	MIL	212	24	9	26	2	203	258	200	204	310	396	706	13	79	21	0.75	43	12	45	129	120	12%	84	4%	100%	27	52%	37%	3.98	-0.9	69	150	$1
11	MIL *	213	27	8	30	0	257	253	174	273	322	439	760	9	70	33	0.32	51	19	30	140	126	19%	84	4%	0%	20	40%	50%	4.63	2.1	29	64	$4
12	2 TM	171	20	9	31	0	211	246	231	207	351	415	766	18	72	24	0.77	45	19	36	134	120	20%	72	0%	0%	27	37%	48%	4.71	3.0	43	108	$1
1st Half		74	9	3	11	0	230	230	125	242	436	405	841	27	72	28	1.29	38	19	42	126	166	14%	72	0%	0%	13	46%	46%	5.85	3.6	45	113	-$1
2nd Half		97	11	6	20	0	196	257	278	177	271	423	694	9	72	20	0.37	50	19	31	139	85	27%	84	0%	0%	14	29%	50%	3.63	-1.8	36	90	$3
13	**Proj**	**212**	**25**	**10**	**33**	**0**	**232**	**250**	**211**	**237**	**336**	**435**	**771**	**13**	**72**	**27**	**0.57**	**45**	**18**	**37**	**137**	**121**	**18%**	**72**	**1%**	**38%**				**4.82**	**3.9**	**43**	**108**	**$5**

Kratz,Erik

Age 33	Bats R	Pos CA	Health	A	LIMA Plan F
Ht 6' 4"	Wt 255		PT/Exp	F	Rand Var 0
			Consist	B	MM 4011

9-26-.248 in 141 ABs at PHI. What is it about veteran catchers in Philly? Made the most of his opportunity, but at age 33 there's no guarantee he gets another. He's got some power, but HR outburst in limited ABs was driven by inflated hr/f. Weak Eye caps BA potential, so if he isn't going yard then he's not even worth a look.

Yr	Tm	AB	R	HR	RBI	SB	BA	xBA	vL	vR	OB	Slg	OPS	bb%	ct%	h%	Eye	G	L	F	PX	xPX	hr/f	Spd	SBO	SB%	#Wk	DOM	DIS	RC/G	RAR	BPV	BPX	R$
08	a/a	247	26	13	32	2	197	261			247	414	661	6	69	23	0.22				156			85	6%	100%				3.28		38	0	$0
09	aaa	319	33	8	32	5	216	253			267	366	633	6	73	27	0.25				117			77	9%	100%				3.26		21	0	$1
10	PIT *	264	22	6	28	1	194	211	143	111	258	327	585	8	71	25	0.30	28	16	56	109	65	0%	65	6%	20%	3	0%	67%	2.55	-14.6	3	7	-$2
11	PHI *	364	40	11	38	1	226	307	0	1000	280	362	642	7	74	28	0.29	0	60	40	100	102	0%	61	2%	100%	1	100%	0%	3.36	-10.1	6	13	$3
12	PHI *	265	27	15	48	0	231	263	256	245	281	465	746	6	77	24	0.31	42	17	41	153	134	20%	42	0%	0%	16	31%	44%	4.33	0.3	51	128	$5
1st Half		131	15	8	25	0	215	224	250	333	257	461	717	5	78	21	0.26	50	0	50	156	363	####	48	0%	0%	5	40%	60%	3.84	-1.5	56	140	$4
2nd Half		134	12	7	23	0	246	257	256	242	303	470	774	8	77	27	0.35	42	18	41	149	125	16%	46	0%	0%	11	27%	36%	4.83	2.4	46	115	$5
13	**Proj**	**163**	**16**	**7**	**23**	**0**	**223**	**247**	**232**	**219**	**277**	**408**	**685**	**7**	**75**	**26**	**0.30**	**42**	**18**	**41**	**128**	**113**	**14%**	**50**	**2%**	**59%**				**3.69**	**-2.6**	**29**	**72**	**$2**

Kubel,Jason

Age 31	Bats L	Pos LF	Health	B	LIMA Plan B
Ht 6' 0"	Wt 220		PT/Exp	B	Rand Var 0
			Consist	B	MM 4025

PRO: PX/xPX support power production; patience remains solid; LD% grew for second straight year. CON: Unsustainable hr/f fed 2H HR binge; big swings sent declining ct% rate down; struggles against LHP continue to cost him ABs. Has skills to repeat power output, but big flies come at a price. There are safer buys.

Yr	Tm	AB	R	HR	RBI	SB	BA	xBA	vL	vR	OB	Slg	OPS	bb%	ct%	h%	Eye	G	L	F	PX	xPX	hr/f	Spd	SBO	SB%	#Wk	DOM	DIS	RC/G	RAR	BPV	BPX	R$
08	MIN	463	74	20	78	0	272	270	232	283	339	471	810	9	80	30	0.52	40	20	41	121	138	13%	88	1%	0%	27	48%	41%	5.55	10.8	60	118	$14
09	MIN	514	73	28	103	1	300	292	243	323	368	539	907	10	79	33	0.53	39	20	42	151	139	16%	55	1%	50%	27	59%	22%	7.19	34.8	74	151	$22
10	MIN	518	68	21	92	0	249	256	225	260	322	427	749	10	78	28	0.48	38	19	43	117	128	12%	62	1%	0%	27	37%	41%	4.63	-1.4	40	87	$13
11	MIN	366	37	12	58	1	273	250	254	283	332	434	766	8	77	33	0.37	35	21	43	117	144	10%	53	2%	50%	19	32%	47%	5.02	3.0	29	64	$10
12	ARI	506	75	30	90	1	253	265	234	264	329	506	835	10	70	30	0.38	33	23	44	176	179	19%	66	2%	50%	27	48%	30%	5.64	13.5	63	158	$17
1st Half		262	36	11	50	1	294	267	289	297	369	508	876	11	73	36	0.44	30	28	43	151	171	13%	71	3%	50%	13	46%	23%	6.69	14.9	56	140	$20
2nd Half		244	39	19	40	0	209	264	181	227	285	504	789	10	67	22	0.32	38	18	45	205	188	26%	68	0%	0%	14	50%	36%	4.63	-0.1	72	180	$14
13	**Proj**	**519**	**70**	**28**	**89**	**1**	**260**	**262**	**235**	**272**	**331**	**490**	**821**	**10**	**73**	**30**	**0.40**	**36**	**21**	**43**	**154**	**160**	**17%**	**59**	**1%**	**44%**				**5.55**	**13.6**	**55**	**136**	**$18**

LaHair,Bryan

Age 30	Bats L	Pos 1B RF	Health	A	LIMA Plan F
Ht 6' 5"	Wt 240		PT/Exp	C	Rand Var -4
			Consist	B	MM 4101

All-Star selection exposes flaws of half season sample, as 1H hit rate and hr/f warned of harsh 2H correction. Takes walks (note OBP trend) and crushes mistakes (strong PX), but serious problems vs LHP and contact issues make him a BA liability. Age and uncertain PT means he's risky even as a deep league matchups play.

Yr	Tm	AB	R	HR	RBI	SB	BA	xBA	vL	vR	OB	Slg	OPS	bb%	ct%	h%	Eye	G	L	F	PX	xPX	hr/f	Spd	SBO	SB%	#Wk	DOM	DIS	RC/G	RAR	BPV	BPX	R$
08	SEA *	452	41	11	46	1	218	216	91	281	288	347	635	9	67	30	0.30	43	20	38	107	94	8%	86	3%	23%	11	9%	82%	3.20	-27.1	-18	-35	-$2
09	aaa	457	49	17	58	0	223	235			274	389	662	6	67	29	0.21				123			81	7%	0%				3.27		-6	0	$3
10	aaa	422	44	17	51	2	238	254			291	411	703	7	72	29	0.27				130			79	3%	60%				3.98		20	0	$6
11	CHC *	515	60	24	67	1	244	254	250	298	303	450	753	8	68	31	0.26	40	21	38	163	180	13%	64	1%	100%	4	50%	50%	4.61	-8.2	34	76	$12
12	CHC	340	42	16	40	4	259	236	63	291	335	450	785	10	64	36	0.31	39	25	36	151	137	21%	71	6%	67%	27	33%	48%	5.14	0.0	12	30	$9
1st Half		211	30	13	28	1	284	259	79	329	366	526	892	11	65	38	0.36	41	25	35	183	148	27%	78	3%	50%	13	46%	31%	6.76	10.5	40	100	$15
2nd Half		129	12	3	12	3	217	199	0	235	284	326	609	9	61	33	0.24	35	27	38	94	118	10%	67	13%	75%	14	21%	64%	3.02	-7.9	-44	-110	$0
13	**Proj**	**192**	**21**	**7**	**22**	**2**	**241**	**227**	**165**	**252**	**307**	**397**	**704**	**9**	**66**	**33**	**0.28**	**39**	**23**	**37**	**124**	**142**	**14%**	**70**	**6%**	**67%**				**4.06**	**-7.4**	**-3**	**-8**	**$4**

Laird,Gerald

Age 33	Bats R	Pos CA	Health	B	LIMA Plan F
Ht 6' 1"	Wt 225		PT/Exp	F	Rand Var -4
			Consist	B	MM 1101

Hard to believe he posted 400+ ABs as recently as 2009; back-up duty suits these skills. This resurgence was mostly fraudulent—success vs RHP, contact rate and LD% are all prime targets for regression. No power or speed, so without the empty BA there's nothing left to covet. Note BPV and Rand Var, then steer clear.

Yr	Tm	AB	R	HR	RBI	SB	BA	xBA	vL	vR	OB	Slg	OPS	bb%	ct%	h%	Eye	G	L	F	PX	xPX	hr/f	Spd	SBO	SB%	#Wk	DOM	DIS	RC/G	RAR	BPV	BPX	R$
08	TEX	344	54	6	41	2	276	255	245	288	322	398	720	6	82	32	0.37	38	22	41	89	89	5%	68	7%	33%	22	32%	18%	4.32	1.8	30	59	$7
09	DET	413	49	4	33	5	225	229	248	218	294	320	613	9	84	26	0.59	41	14	44	66	67	3%	89	5%	100%	27	22%	41%	3.15	-12.3	35	71	$1
10	DET	270	22	5	25	3	207	218	183	224	257	304	561	6	79	25	0.32	43	15	42	70	106	6%	67	7%	75%	25	20%	48%	2.51	-13.6	1	2	-$1
11	STL	95	11	1	12	1	232	229	286	222	298	358	656	9	80	28	0.47	38	14	49	98	76	3%	82	9%	50%	20	40%	40%	3.43	-1.9	44	98	-$1
12	DET	174	24	2	11	0	282	256	204	382	335	374	709	7	88	31	0.67	40	23	37	59	80	4%	92	0%	0%	25	44%	48%	4.44	1.5	32	80	$2
1st Half		92	13	2	5	0	293	257	178	404	343	402	746	7	89	31	0.70	33	24	44	66	95	6%	74	0%	0%	12	42%	42%	4.99	2.0	35	88	$3
2nd Half		82	11	0	6	0	268	259	226	345	326	341	667	8	87	31	0.64	49	23	29	51	64	0%	96	0%	0%	13	46%	54%	3.88	-0.8	26	65	$1
13	**Proj**	**194**	**24**	**2**	**17**	**1**	**243**	**237**	**228**	**253**	**301**	**341**	**642**	**8**	**84**	**28**	**0.51**	**41**	**19**	**40**	**68**	**81**	**3%**	**83**	**4%**	**58%**				**3.43**	**-4.5**	**28**	**70**	**$2**

LaPorta,Matt

Age 28	Bats R	Pos 1B	Health	A	LIMA Plan F
Ht 6' 2"	Wt 215		PT/Exp	C	Rand Var 0
			Consist	B	MM 2003

1-5-.241 in 58 ABs at CLE. Safe to call former top prospect a bust? Deteriorating ct% and unremarkable power continue to yield ugly results. Formerly solid Eye has fallen off dramatically leading to negative OBP trend. Poor track record vs LHP makes even platoon ABs a bad idea.

Yr	Tm	AB	R	HR	RBI	SB	BA	xBA	vL	vR	OB	Slg	OPS	bb%	ct%	h%	Eye	G	L	F	PX	xPX	hr/f	Spd	SBO	SB%	#Wk	DOM	DIS	RC/G	RAR	BPV	BPX	R$
08	aa	362	53	18	64	2	254	281			335	476	812	11	77	28	0.52				146			85	3%	61%				5.42		65	0	$9
09	CLE *	519	79	20	68	3	256	269	211	266	317	438	755	8	80	29	0.45	40	18	42	118	108	11%	77	5%	45%	12	58%	25%	4.66	-9.6	52	106	$12
10	CLE *	445	46	15	53	0	233	226	216	223	317	383	700	11	79	26	0.59	42	13	45	99	112	9%	81	1%	0%	24	33%	50%	3.99	-17.3	27	59	$5
11	CLE	352	34	11	53	1	247	239	207	260	293	412	705	6	75	30	0.26	34	18	49	124	147	8%	74	1%	100%	25	40%	32%	4.11	-12.2	29	64	$6
12	CLE *	433	42	14	49	0	213	202	286	174	267	353	620	7	73	26	0.28	54	10	37	97	62	7%	106	4%	0%	8	13%	75%	2.94	-31.7	-5	-13	$2
1st Half		231	30	11	28	0	239	243	125	333	303	420	723	8	70	29	0.31	44	22	33	125	-11	0%	87	4%	0%	1	0%	100%	4.08	-9.0	9	23	$8
2nd Half		202	12	3	21	0	184	186	333	150	225	277	503	5	76	23	0.23	56	6	38	68	82	8%	106	3%	0%	7	14%	71%	1.89	-22.6	-17	-43	-$5
13	**Proj**	**260**	**26**	**8**	**33**	**0**	**244**	**216**	**328**	**210**	**299**	**388**	**687**	**7**	**75**	**30**	**0.32**	**44**	**13**	**43**	**100**	**109**	**9%**	**80**	**2%**	**24%**				**3.85**	**-11.7**	**9**	**23**	**$4**

DAN BECKER

LaRoche,Adam

Age	33	Bats	L	Pos	1B	Health	D	LIMA Plan	C+
Ht	6' 3"	Wt	210			PT/Exp	B	Rand Var	-1
						Consist	F	MM	4115

Rebounded from shoulder surgery in fine fashion as power bounced back to pre-injury levels. A legit .270 hitter, and lack of LH/RH splits, history of consistency make him undervalued. Errants gusts of wind propped HR rate more than any true PX gains, but he's back to being a steady 25 HR, 100 RBI producer again.

Yr Tm	AB	R	HR	RBI	SB	BA	xBA	vL	vR	OB	Slg	OPS	bb%	ct%	h%	Eye	G	L	F	PX	xPX	hr/f	Spd	SBO	SB%	#Wk	DOM	DIS	RC/G	RAR	BPV	BPX	R$
08 PIT	492	66	25	85	1	270	274	241	282	342	500	842	10	75	31	0.44	37	20	43	154	133	16%	72	2%	50%	26	46%	35%	5.95	7.3	63	124	$15
09 3 TM	555	78	25	83	2	277	271	243	293	357	488	846	11	74	33	0.49	35	22	43	145	157	14%	74	3%	50%	27	52%	41%	6.10	10.6	53	108	$17
10 ARI	560	75	25	100	0	261	253	264	259	319	468	787	8	69	33	0.28	38	18	44	160	172	15%	73	1%	0%	26	38%	46%	5.11	-5.1	36	78	$17
11 WAS	151	15	3	15	1	172	211	98	200	290	258	548	14	75	21	0.68	43	19	38	62	119	7%	69	2%	100%	8	13%	63%	2.34	-15.1	-5	-11	-$3
12 WAS	571	76	33	100	1	271	274	268	273	348	510	858	11	76	31	0.49	34	22	44	157	164	17%	68	1%	50%	27	48%	26%	6.18	12.2	63	158	$22
1st Half	255	32	15	49	1	251	274	250	251	344	506	850	12	71	30	0.49	32	25	44	181	173	19%	65	3%	50%	13	54%	15%	5.85	3.7	70	175	$17
2nd Half	316	44	18	51	0	288	271	281	291	352	513	864	9	80	31	0.48	35	20	44	139	158	16%	74	0%	0%	14	43%	36%	6.46	9.7	56	140	$25
13 Proj	**561**	**70**	**27**	**97**	**2**	**268**	**254**	**246**	**277**	**347**	**466**	**814**	**11**	**75**	**31**	**0.49**	**37**	**21**	**43**	**133**	**152**	**15%**	**62**	**1%**	**67%**				**5.62**	**4.3**	**42**	**106**	**$18**

Lavarnway,Ryan

Age	25	Bats	R	Pos	CA	Health	A	LIMA Plan	D
Ht	6' 4"	Wt	225			PT/Exp	D	Rand Var	0
						Consist	C	MM	3103

2-12-.157 in 153 AB at BOS. Top backstop prospect exploded onto radar with '11 breakout. This version showed gains behind plate, big losses at it. Still owns elite power skills, and at age 25, he's got time to tap into them again. There's post-hype profit here as a second catcher in deep leagues.

Yr Tm	AB	R	HR	RBI	SB	BA	xBA	vL	vR	OB	Slg	OPS	bb%	ct%	h%	Eye	G	L	F	PX	xPX	hr/f	Spd	SBO	SB%	#Wk	DOM	DIS	RC/G	RAR	BPV	BPX	R$
08																																	
09																																	
10 aa	158	18	6	28	0	253	245			333	417	750	11	71	32	0.41				128			83	0%	0%				4.74		16	0	$3
11 BOS *	474	62	25	79	1	254	237	294	182	321	467	788	9	73	30	0.36	31	14	55	153	113	13%	86	2%	40%	6	33%	67%	5.09	13.2	42	93	$15
12 BOS *	472	53	8	47	1	231	212	180	146	295	347	642	8	77	29	0.38	43	13	44	89	120	4%	61	1%	100%	10	0%	60%	3.41	-10.3	8	20	$3
1st Half	233	34	5	28	0	288	252			362	431	793	10	79	34	0.55				104			77	0%	0%				5.59		32	80	$11
2nd Half	239	19	3	18	1	176	194	180	146	227	266	493	6	74	23	0.25	43	13	44	73	120	4%	63	2%	100%	10	0%	60%	1.88	-18.0	-19	-48	-$4
13 Proj	**320**	**37**	**10**	**42**	**1**	**247**	**219**	**283**	**229**	**311**	**398**	**710**	**9**	**74**	**30**	**0.36**	**43**	**13**	**44**	**110**	**108**	**10%**	**57**	**1%**	**73%**				**4.20**	**-0.2**	**14**	**34**	**$7**

Lawrie,Brett

Age	23	Bats	R	Pos	3B	Health	B	LIMA Plan	C+
Ht	6' 0"	Wt	215			PT/Exp	B	Rand Var	0
						Consist	F	MM	3425

Elite prospect was a mixed bag in first full MLB campaign. PRO: Steadily increasing ct%; one year removed from enticing power + speed combo; consistent Eye gains. CON: High GB limits short-term HR outlook; .697 OPS vs. RH; deep 2H slide. Remains a gem in keeper leagues, but don't expect a breakout just yet.

Yr Tm	AB	R	HR	RBI	SB	BA	xBA	vL	vR	OB	Slg	OPS	bb%	ct%	h%	Eye	G	L	F	PX	xPX	hr/f	Spd	SBO	SB%	#Wk	DOM	DIS	RC/G	RAR	BPV	BPX	R$
08																																	
09 aa	52	5	0	0	0	254	183			254	286	540	0	71	36	0.00				16			132	17%	0%				1.99		-69	0	-$2
10 aa	554	73	7	51	24	263	255			312	407	719	7	76	33	0.30				103			134	29%	64%				4.16		46	0	$17
11 TOR *	442	67	21	64	15	297	282	295	292	345	546	891	7	79	33	0.35	38	17	45	162	147	17%	128	18%	82%	8	63%	38%	6.86	28.4	103	229	$23
12 TOR	494	73	11	48	13	273	265	319	256	319	405	724	6	83	31	0.38	50	20	30	85	78	9%	105	16%	62%	23	39%	39%	4.37	-2.5	43	108	$16
1st Half	297	48	8	33	11	293	276	344	271	331	438	769	5	85	32	0.39	50	20	30	88	89	11%	107	24%	58%	13	46%	31%	4.87	2.4	57	143	$24
2nd Half	197	25	3	15	2	244	248	267	237	300	355	656	8	79	30	0.38	51	20	29	80	59	7%	97	4%	100%	10	30%	50%	3.66	-5.4	20	50	$3
13 Proj	**555**	**79**	**17**	**61**	**16**	**275**	**265**	**308**	**263**	**324**	**451**	**775**	**7**	**80**	**32**	**0.36**	**46**	**19**	**36**	**113**	**102**	**11%**	**116**	**16%**	**71%**				**5.06**	**7.7**	**62**	**155**	**$21**

Lee,Carlos

Age	37	Bats	R	Pos	1B	Health	B	LIMA Plan	C+
Ht	6' 2"	Wt	270			PT/Exp	A	Rand Var	0
						Consist	C	MM	2025

Once feared power hitter has turned into singles hitter in mammoth body. Excellent control of plate would give him value back when he was a 20 SB threat... 10 years ago. Dwindling FB, distant pop make power rebound unlikely. Heed HR trend. Without power to hit ball hard, days of .300 BA are officially gone too.

Yr Tm	AB	R	HR	RBI	SB	BA	xBA	vL	vR	OB	Slg	OPS	bb%	ct%	h%	Eye	G	L	F	PX	xPX	hr/f	Spd	SBO	SB%	#Wk	DOM	DIS	RC/G	RAR	BPV	BPX	R$
08 HOU	436	61	28	100	4	314	314	330	309	368	569	937	8	89	30	0.76	35	21	44	143	152	16%	39	4%	80%	19	74%	5%	7.78	27.6	101	198	$24
09 HOU	610	65	26	102	5	300	296	325	293	344	489	833	6	92	29	0.80	36	20	44	104	120	11%	53	5%	63%	27	63%	7%	6.05	10.5	78	159	$23
10 HOU	605	67	24	89	3	246	271	274	238	290	417	706	6	90	24	0.63	39	16	46	99	125	10%	48	5%	50%	27	59%	22%	4.02	-25.3	68	148	$13
11 HOU	585	66	18	94	4	275	282	348	253	342	446	788	9	90	28	0.98	35	21	44	106	111	8%	55	4%	57%	27	63%	7%	5.30	-2.1	82	182	$19
12 2 NL	550	53	9	77	3	264	264	206	284	334	365	699	10	91	28	1.18	41	22	37	63	79	5%	37	2%	100%	25	48%	20%	4.26	-18.5	51	128	$11
1st Half	242	22	5	29	0	285	286	143	328	337	405	742	7	93	29	1.12	40	25	35	70	88	6%	46	0%	0%	11	55%	9%	4.87	-3.3	53	133	$10
2nd Half	308	31	4	48	3	247	248	247	247	331	334	666	11	90	26	1.22	42	20	39	58	72	4%	32	3%	100%	14	43%	29%	3.81	-14.1	44	110	$13
13 Proj	**448**	**47**	**12**	**68**	**3**	**268**	**268**	**262**	**269**	**330**	**406**	**736**	**9**	**90**	**27**	**0.98**	**39**	**21**	**41**	**82**	**99**	**7%**	**41**	**3%**	**72%**				**4.65**	**-9.1**	**62**	**155**	**$13**

LeMahieu,DJ

Age	24	Bats	R	Pos	2B	Health	A	LIMA Plan	F
Ht	6' 4"	Wt	205			PT/Exp	D	Rand Var	-1
						Consist	B	MM	1421

2-22-.297 in in 229 AB at COL. 2Bmen with speed skills and a .300 BA don't grow on trees, so this one will get some attention in many leagues. But inflated h% drove BA, and xBA paints a less rosy picture. 2H Spd would be worth tucking away for a SB flier late in your draft—alas, he'll probably be gone by then.

Yr Tm	AB	R	HR	RBI	SB	BA	xBA	vL	vR	OB	Slg	OPS	bb%	ct%	h%	Eye	G	L	F	PX	xPX	hr/f	Spd	SBO	SB%	#Wk	DOM	DIS	RC/G	RAR	BPV	BPX	R$
08																																	
09																																	
10																																	
11 CHC *	474	40	4	38	6	266	260	292	222	294	341	635	4	86	30	0.27	65	17	19	54	38	0%	111	13%	40%	9	11%	67%	3.24	-15.4	14	31	$7
12 COL *	484	46	3	41	9	280	261	233	320	318	370	688	5	85	33	0.37	56	19	25	61	72	4%	139	14%	50%	17	29%	35%	3.94	-5.7	27	68	$11
1st Half	245	17	1	18	8	253	257	214	200	285	314	598	4	86	29	0.32	45	26	29	43	21	0%	106	23%	59%	5	0%	60%	2.89	-10.2	14	35	$8
2nd Half	239	30	2	23	1	307	269	239	340	351	427	778	6	83	36	0.41	58	18	24	80	82	5%	147	5%	16%	12	42%	25%	5.24	6.5	37	93	$14
13 Proj	**200**	**19**	**1**	**17**	**6**	**276**	**262**	**329**	**256**	**310**	**356**	**665**	**5**	**85**	**32**	**0.32**	**58**	**19**	**23**	**55**	**49**	**2%**	**126**	**18%**	**62%**				**3.74**	**-3.0**	**24**	**60**	**$6**

Liddi,Alex

Age	24	Bats	R	Pos	3B	Health	A	LIMA Plan	F
Ht	6' 4"	Wt	230			PT/Exp	B	Rand Var	0
						Consist	A	MM	4203

3-10-.224 in 116 AB at SEA. Young slugger has 30 HR upside when bat meets ball consistently. Problem is, those times have been few and far between. Closer fences could help if he stays with SEA (.271 Slg at home, .412 Slg on road). If you can bear his .200ish BA, he's got power worth speculating on.

Yr Tm	AB	R	HR	RBI	SB	BA	xBA	vL	vR	OB	Slg	OPS	bb%	ct%	h%	Eye	G	L	F	PX	xPX	hr/f	Spd	SBO	SB%	#Wk	DOM	DIS	RC/G	RAR	BPV	BPX	R$
08																																	
09																																	
10 aa	502	61	11	72	4	244	237			299	395	694	7	67	34	0.24				128			103	10%	33%				3.76		12	0	$9
11 SEA *	599	82	21	71	4	199	209	429	115	252	354	606	7	63	28	0.19	39	17	43	132	175	30%	87	5%	78%	4	75%	25%	2.84	-32.1	-1	-2	$4
12 SEA *	412	35	10	31	8	218	208	197	255	265	348	612	6	66	30	0.19	38	21	41	103	114	11%	111	19%	51%	12	25%	75%	2.81	-22.4	-16	-40	$2
1st Half	162	11	4	14	2	227	196	212	250	294	362	656	9	60	35	0.24	36	21	43	115	120	12%	107	13%	34%	9	22%	78%	3.26	-6.7	-29	-73	-$1
2nd Half	250	24	6	17	7	212	242	111	333	245	338	583	4	69	28	0.14	60	20	20	96	39	0%	99	25%	59%	3	33%	67%	2.53	-16.2	-8	-20	$5
13 Proj	**262**	**28**	**9**	**26**	**4**	**234**	**216**	**215**	**254**	**283**	**395**	**678**	**6**	**65**	**33**	**0.19**	**36**	**21**	**43**	**126**	**108**	**12%**	**111**	**13%**	**53%**				**3.58**	**-8.0**	**-2**	**-6**	**$5**

Lillibridge,Brent

Age	29	Bats	R	Pos	1B SS LF	Health	A	LIMA Plan	F
Ht	5' 11"	Wt	185			PT/Exp	F	Rand Var	0
						Consist	F	MM	1501

Utilityman extraordinare drew some bidders in due to '11 power outburst. To no one's surprise, that was a hr/f-driven fluke. With poor bb% and ct% in freefall, we can't even bank on a BA much over .200. Owns nice speed skills and is young enough to use them, but ineptitude with bat won't give him chances to do so.

Yr Tm	AB	R	HR	RBI	SB	BA	xBA	vL	vR	OB	Slg	OPS	bb%	ct%	h%	Eye	G	L	F	PX	xPX	hr/f	Spd	SBO	SB%	#Wk	DOM	DIS	RC/G	RAR	BPV	BPX	R$
08 ATL *	435	46	4	39	21	192	202	171	222	244	300	544	6	71	26	0.23	45	11	44	83	119	4%	130	36%	73%	13	31%	54%	2.29	-34.3	8	16	$0
09 CHW *	341	37	3	23	20	200	213	214	134	282	269	552	10	72	27	0.41	47	19	34	50	46	0%	129	26%	83%	16	13%	69%	2.57	-21.6	-8	-16	$2
10 CHW*	283	37	5	27	19	219	214	303	185	261	330	591	5	67	31	0.17	36	25	39	90	88	9%	122	42%	74%	19	21%	58%	2.77	-16.0	-3	-7	$6
11 CHW	186	38	13	29	10	258	239	287	228	320	505	826	8	67	32	0.27	32	17	50	176	179	21%	132	35%	63%	24	54%	33%	5.12	3.1	65	144	$9
12 3 AL	190	25	3	10	13	195	190	184	204	239	274	512	5	63	29	0.15	43	23	34	68	65	7%	97	38%	87%	27	15%	74%	2.23	-14.1	-45	-113	$1
1st Half	66	10	0	2	7	167	156	71	237	214	182	396	6	61	28	0.15	51	17	32	18	62	0%	104	64%	78%	13	15%	62%	1.32	-7.5	-86	-215	-$2
2nd Half	124	15	3	8	6	210	209	237	185	252	323	574	5	64	30	0.16	40	26	35	94	66	11%	87	24%	100%	14	14%	86%	2.84	-7.0	-28	-70	$3
13 Proj	**229**	**34**	**5**	**20**	**15**	**213**	**194**	**215**	**212**	**264**	**313**	**577**	**6**	**65**	**31**	**0.20**	**40**	**21**	**39**	**79**	**98**	**8%**	**108**	**37%**	**77%**				**2.71**	**-19.2**	**-23**	**-57**	**$6**

STEPHEN NICKRAND

Lind,Adam

Age 29	Bats L	Pos 1B DH	Health	B	LIMA Plan	C
Ht 6' 2"	Wt 210		PT/Exp	B	Rand Var	-2
			Consist	B	MM	3115

11-45-.255 in 321 AB at TOR. Sent to the minors for a while, and his GM called him out late in the year. Not good. But he battled back problems, and that's a sure-fire way to kill power. xPX shows it, and also that he's been better when healthy. Forget about '09, but a rebound to '11 HR levels nets a profit here.

Yr	Tm	AB	R	HR	RBI	SB	BA	xBA	vL	vR	OB	Slg	OPS	bb%	ct%	h%	Eye	G	L	F	PX	xPX	hr/f	Spd	SBO	SB%	#Wk	DOM	DIS	RC/G	RAR	BPV	BPX	R$
08	TOR *	515	68	15	83	3	288	279	253	294	330	458	788	6	80	34	0.32	51	19	30	112	116	11%	104	3%	71%	18	39%	39%	5.40	1.5	51	100	$16
09	TOR	587	93	35	114	1	305	311	275	317	367	562	930	9	81	33	0.53	43	20	37	161	141	20%	62	1%	50%	26	65%	15%	7.54	36.1	85	173	$27
10	TOR	569	57	23	72	0	237	258	117	275	285	425	710	6	75	28	0.26	41	19	40	133	135	13%	68	0%	0%	27	33%	37%	4.05	-21.0	31	67	$8
11	TOR	499	56	26	87	1	251	263	243	253	296	439	735	6	79	27	0.30	40	22	38	119	135	17%	64	2%	50%	24	42%	42%	4.39	-13.2	32	71	$14
12	TOR *	457	45	17	65	1	273	250	202	276	332	445	777	8	78	32	0.40	48	17	35	111	101	12%	87	1%	100%	18	39%	33%	5.19	-1.3	32	80	$11
1st Half		257	26	10	33	1	245	243	156	210	312	418	730	9	76	28	0.41	47	17	36	117	90	13%	66	1%	100%	8	38%	38%	4.42	-7.1	26	65	$11
2nd Half		189	17	6	30	0	296	253	228	326	342	455	797	6	81	34	0.37	49	17	34	96	108	11%	108	0%	0%	10	40%	30%	5.63	1.4	31	78	$10
13	**Proj**	**489**	**51**	**20**	**75**	**1**	**266**	**255**	**216**	**284**	**316**	**443**	**759**	**7**	**79**	**30**	**0.34**	**44**	**19**	**37**	**113**	**117**	**14%**	**81**	**1%**	**71%**				**4.85**	**-7.1**	**34**	**85**	**$12**

Lobaton,Jose

Age 28	Bats B	Pos CA	Health	C	LIMA Plan	F
Ht 6' 0"	Wt 195		PT/Exp	F	Rand Var	0
			Consist	B	MM	1001

2-20-.222 in 167 AB at TAM. For some hitters, you really have to look hard for a positive. But not here! What, not seeing it? Look at those walk and strikeout rates. He clearly made opposing pitchers throw lots of pitches before walking to first, or walking to the dugout bat in hand. He's a professional tire-outerer.

Yr	Tm	AB	R	HR	RBI	SB	BA	xBA	vL	vR	OB	Slg	OPS	bb%	ct%	h%	Eye	G	L	F	PX	xPX	hr/f	Spd	SBO	SB%	#Wk	DOM	DIS	RC/G	RAR	BPV	BPX	R$
08	aa	294	29	7	37	1	214	224			292	340	632	10	69	29	0.36				102			76	3%	42%				3.18		-9	0	-$1
09	SD *	234	23	5	16	0	213	215		176	277	324	601	8	71	28	0.31	50	17	33	85	-5	0%	102	0%	0%	2	0%	100%	2.91	-8.8	-21	-43	-$2
10	a/a	265	22	5	27	1	214	221			279	309	588	8	74	27	0.35				72			85	1%	100%				2.81		-18	0	-$1
11	TAM *	218	20	6	23	0	216	237	150	71	314	344	658	12	68	29	0.44	46	27	27	102	21	0%	73	0%	0%	7	14%	71%	3.52	-4.1	-11	-24	-$1
12	TAM *	195	17	2	21	0	201	200	310	174	296	291	587	12	71	27	0.47	48	16	36	78	100	5%	71	2%	0%	21	19%	71%	2.69	-8.8	-19	-48	-$3
1st Half		92	9	0	5	0	177	199	333	135	279	248	527	12	71	25	0.49	60	13	28	72	63	0%	75	4%	0%	7	29%	71%	2.04	-6.5	-22	-55	-$6
2nd Half		103	8	2	16	0	223	203	290	194	310	330	640	11	72	29	0.45	41	18	41	83	123	6%	80	0%	0%	14	14%	71%	3.36	-2.7	-18	-45	$0
13	**Proj**	**218**	**19**	**2**	**24**	**0**	**209**	**196**	**303**	**161**	**296**	**292**	**588**	**11**	**71**	**29**	**0.42**	**48**	**16**	**36**	**71**	**99**	**4%**	**74**	**1%**	**24%**				**2.76**	**-9.9**	**-27**	**-68**	**$0**

Lombardozzi,Steve

Age 24	Bats B	Pos 2B LF	Health	A	LIMA Plan	D
Ht 6' 0"	Wt 195		PT/Exp	D	Rand Var	-1
			Consist	B	MM	1423

Latent SB threat, but so far minor league bb% hasn't surfaced. That's the skill to watch for the potential SB spike. Trivia: his dad, Steve Sr., finished a six-year career with a .654 OPS. Junior's is now up to .655. Every good parent wants their child to have it better than they did, so Pop must be pretty proud right now.

Yr	Tm	AB	R	HR	RBI	SB	BA	xBA	vL	vR	OB	Slg	OPS	bb%	ct%	h%	Eye	G	L	F	PX	xPX	hr/f	Spd	SBO	SB%	#Wk	DOM	DIS	RC/G	RAR	BPV	BPX	R$
08																																		
09																																		
10	aa	105	17	4	10	3	276	294			341	477	818	9	85	29	0.65				118			125	20%	62%				5.47		89	0	$3
11	WAS *	587	73	7	43	24	273	244	0	200	310	371	681	5	85	31	0.35	44	19	37	64	29	0%	121	22%	73%	4	25%	75%	3.99	-6.0	41	91	$18
12	WAS	384	40	3	27	5	273	252	231	287	308	354	662	5	88	30	0.41	47	20	33	52	46	3%	114	8%	63%	27	26%	48%	3.77	-6.3	30	75	$7
1st Half		167	17	1	8	0	257	255	111	286	303	335	639	6	89	28	0.61	47	21	32	57	39	2%	85	2%	0%	13	23%	38%	3.40	-4.2	27	68	$1
2nd Half		217	23	2	19	5	286	247	281	288	311	369	680	4	87	32	0.29	47	20	33	48	52	3%	138	12%	71%	14	29%	57%	4.06	-1.2	27	68	$11
13	**Proj**	**331**	**40**	**4**	**25**	**8**	**274**	**255**	**235**	**286**	**314**	**370**	**684**	**5**	**86**	**31**	**0.43**	**47**	**20**	**33**	**60**	**47**	**4%**	**124**	**14%**	**68%**				**4.01**	**-2.4**	**39**	**97**	**$9**

Loney,James

Age 29	Bats L	Pos 1B	Health	A	LIMA Plan	C
Ht 6' 3"	Wt 220		PT/Exp	A	Rand Var	+3
			Consist	C	MM	1035

And it keeps getting better for the perennial underachiever. Was this one due to a hidden injury? Long-lasting whiplash from sketchy Nov car accident? Whatever the reason, even a full rebound is likely sub-replacement. Once had a high ceilng; only hope is that a full year in his new environs will spark something.

Yr	Tm	AB	R	HR	RBI	SB	BA	xBA	vL	vR	OB	Slg	OPS	bb%	ct%	h%	Eye	G	L	F	PX	xPX	hr/f	Spd	SBO	SB%	#Wk	DOM	DIS	RC/G	RAR	BPV	BPX	R$
08	LA	595	66	13	90	7	289	280	249	305	339	434	773	7	86	32	0.53	44	22	34	91	83	7%	92	7%	64%	27	52%	26%	5.20	-1.3	57	112	$18
09	LA	576	73	13	90	7	281	276	274	283	359	399	758	11	88	30	1.03	43	22	35	70	65	7%	75	5%	70%	27	44%	26%	5.07	-3.5	54	110	$17
10	LA	588	67	10	88	10	267	284	222	286	327	395	721	8	84	30	0.55	43	25	32	92	79	6%	71	10%	67%	27	41%	33%	4.43	-14.6	51	111	$16
11	LA	531	56	12	65	4	288	272	213	312	340	416	757	7	87	31	0.63	41	22	37	85	79	7%	81	3%	100%	27	48%	33%	5.12	-2.4	51	113	$16
12	2 TM	434	37	6	41	0	249	266	217	257	294	336	631	6	88	27	0.55	46	25	29	58	65	5%	56	3%	0%	27	22%	41%	3.26	-26.1	19	48	$4
1st Half		220	18	2	21	0	236	247	246	233	303	323	626	9	88	26	0.78	44	20	35	62	75	3%	59	5%	0%	13	23%	38%	3.08	-15.3	26	65	$2
2nd Half		214	19	4	20	0	262	286	161	279	285	350	636	3	89	28	0.29	47	29	23	53	55	9%	63	0%	0%	14	21%	43%	3.45	-11.8	12	30	$5
13	**Proj**	**490**	**48**	**11**	**57**	**3**	**283**	**273**	**231**	**298**	**330**	**403**	**733**	**7**	**87**	**31**	**0.56**	**43**	**24**	**33**	**76**	**71**	**8%**	**64**	**4%**	**55%**				**4.67**	**-9.5**	**37**	**93**	**$14**

Longoria,Evan

Age 27	Bats R	Pos 3B DH	Health	F	LIMA Plan	B
Ht 6' 2"	Wt 210		PT/Exp	B	Rand Var	-2
			Consist	B	MM	4135

17-55-.289 in 273 AB at TAM. Struggled a bit immediately after returning from hammy, but rebounded well late. So that 40-HR potential is still there... except for that little thing called Health. The injuries keep coming, and will keep rate stats in jeopardy. Otherwise, the skills remain superb, and he's at peak age now.

Yr	Tm	AB	R	HR	RBI	SB	BA	xBA	vL	vR	OB	Slg	OPS	bb%	ct%	h%	Eye	G	L	F	PX	xPX	hr/f	Spd	SBO	SB%	#Wk	DOM	DIS	RC/G	RAR	BPV	BPX	R$
08	TAM *	473	69	27	86	7	267	276	242	284	336	512	849	9	73	31	0.39	39	20	42	169	158	19%	91	6%	100%	22	45%	45%	6.09	20.9	75	147	$17
09	TAM	584	100	33	113	9	281	289	289	277	360	526	885	11	76	32	0.51	39	19	42	164	148	18%	74	6%	100%	27	48%	22%	6.81	37.3	83	169	$26
10	TAM	574	96	22	104	15	294	283	324	281	373	507	880	11	78	34	0.58	37	20	43	150	142	11%	117	12%	75%	25	68%	8%	6.80	36.2	91	198	$29
11	TAM	483	78	31	99	3	244	286	258	240	352	495	847	14	81	24	0.86	37	18	45	158	137	18%	79	4%	60%	23	65%	17%	5.82	18.3	96	213	$18
12	TAM *	303	39	17	57	2	276	264	318	280	357	491	848	11	76	31	0.53	38	22	40	137	147	20%	77	6%	40%	14	50%	21%	5.99	12.6	48	120	$11
1st Half		82	15	4	19	2	329	288	423	286	433	561	994	15	79	38	0.88	42	20	38	156	158	16%	88	16%	40%	5	60%	20%	8.33	8.5	90	225	$5
2nd Half		216	24	13	38	0	259	257	250	278	331	472	803	10	75	29	0.43	36	23	41	132	142	21%	74	0%	0%	9	44%	22%	5.37	5.0	31	78	$13
13	**Proj**	**510**	**77**	**31**	**100**	**6**	**276**	**278**	**302**	**267**	**365**	**520**	**884**	**12**	**78**	**30**	**0.63**	**38**	**20**	**42**	**155**	**145**	**18%**	**81**	**7%**	**55%**				**6.52**	**28.4**	**78**	**196**	**$24**

Lopez,Jose

Age 29	Bats R	Pos 3B	Health	A	LIMA Plan	D
Ht 6' 0"	Wt 205		PT/Exp	C	Rand Var	-2
			Consist	A	MM	2111

4-28-.246 in 236 AB at CLE/CHW. Continues to ply trade based on that 25-HR season, but that was four years ago, and as much as he tried by opening up his swing, it's not coming back. Each year that passes will put his dwindling PT even more at risk. There's nothing here to offer going forward.

Yr	Tm	AB	R	HR	RBI	SB	BA	xBA	vL	vR	OB	Slg	OPS	bb%	ct%	h%	Eye	G	L	F	PX	xPX	hr/f	Spd	SBO	SB%	#Wk	DOM	DIS	RC/G	RAR	BPV	BPX	R$
08	SEA	644	80	17	89	6	297	286	299	296	325	443	767	4	90	31	0.40	44	20	36	90	90	8%	88	6%	67%	27	48%	15%	5.17	11.0	60	118	$22
09	SEA	613	69	25	96	3	272	294	286	266	300	463	763	4	89	27	0.35	41	19	41	113	102	11%	58	5%	50%	27	56%	15%	4.79	4.2	68	139	$17
10	SEA	593	49	10	58	3	239	256	277	226	268	339	607	4	89	26	0.35	43	18	38	66	80	5%	67	4%	60%	27	30%	30%	3.02	-27.1	31	67	$5
11	2 NL *	356	38	13	40	3	246	273	203	223	268	409	677	3	88	25	0.25	44	17	38	101	115	10%	76	5%	100%	19	47%	42%	3.75	-9.0	58	129	$6
12	2 AL *	308	24	5	39	0	260	249	277	225	294	377	672	5	82	30	0.28	45	21	34	85	99	6%	72	1%	0%	22	23%	55%	3.77	-6.9	15	38	$4
1st Half		167	11	4	29	0	281	265	265	253	309	427	736	4	85	31	0.28	44	22	34	98	87	10%	66	0%	0%	10	30%	30%	4.68	0.5	31	78	$7
2nd Half		141	13	1	10	0	236	227	289	170	277	319	597	5	79	29	0.28	46	19	35	69	117	0%	85	3%	0%	12	17%	75%	2.86	-7.4	-5	-13	$0
13	**Proj**	**202**	**18**	**4**	**23**	**1**	**252**	**251**	**288**	**232**	**282**	**370**	**652**	**4**	**85**	**28**	**0.28**	**44**	**19**	**37**	**80**	**103**	**6%**	**72**	**3%**	**53%**				**3.52**	**-6.3**	**25**	**63**	**$3**

Lowrie,Jed

Age 29	Bats B	Pos SS	Health	F	LIMA Plan	C+
Ht 6' 0"	Wt 180		PT/Exp	D	Rand Var	0
			Consist	F	MM	3215

Alas, another promising season derailed by still more injuries, and he shows no signs of bringing up that "F" he earned in Health. Clearly owns the tools for a massive power breakout (see FB%, xPX), but betting on enough AB to see it realized is mining for fool's gold. But for a minute, imagine 500 AB... 30 HR? *drool*

Yr	Tm	AB	R	HR	RBI	SB	BA	xBA	vL	vR	OB	Slg	OPS	bb%	ct%	h%	Eye	G	L	F	PX	xPX	hr/f	Spd	SBO	SB%	#Wk	DOM	DIS	RC/G	RAR	BPV	BPX	R$
08	BOS *	458	62	6	71	2	254	251	338	222	340	397	737	11	75	33	0.52	32	25	43	115	131	2%	98	1%	100%	17	29%	47%	4.64	7.1	43	84	$7
09	BOS *	141	14	4	20	0	171	191	211	122	260	311	571	11	76	19	0.50	24	10	66	95	155	6%	86	0%	0%	10	20%	60%	2.49	-7.3	9	18	-$3
10	BOS	171	31	9	24	1	287	292	338	250	378	526	904	13	85	29	1.00	29	16	54	153	166	11%	87	4%	50%	12	58%	25%	6.99	13.9	106	230	$6
11	BOS	309	40	6	36	1	252	226	330	210	304	382	686	7	81	30	0.38	33	18	49	87	120	5%	124	3%	50%	20	35%	45%	3.92	-1.6	34	76	$5
12	HOU	340	43	16	42	2	244	253	184	265	329	438	767	11	81	26	0.66	29	19	51	121	162	11%	91	2%	100%	18	33%	33%	4.90	8.0	58	145	$7
1st Half		253	35	14	33	2	261	264	194	283	346	486	832	12	80	28	0.66	27	20	53	140	180	13%	95	3%	100%	12	42%	33%	5.86	13.6	72	180	$12
2nd Half		87	8	2	9	0	195	217	160	210	278	299	577	10	83	21	0.67	36	18	47	65	112	6%	91	0%	0%	6	17%	33%	2.64	-3.8	12	30	-$8
13	**Proj**	**440**	**56**	**18**	**54**	**2**	**265**	**246**	**289**	**254**	**340**	**445**	**785**	**10**	**81**	**29**	**0.61**	**32**	**18**	**50**	**112**	**139**	**10%**	**94**	**2%**	**67%**				**5.23**	**15.6**	**53**	**132**	**$13**

ROD TRUESDELL

Lucroy,Jonathan

Age	27	Bats	R	Pos CA	Health	C	LIMA Plan C+
Ht	6' 0"	Wt	185		PT/Exp	C	Rand Var -5
					Consist	D	MM 3335

Only freakishly broken hand and two months lost to it stood between this and a full breakout. As it is, some remarkable growth—but is it repeatable? Eye gains the main driver, and past skills suggest it was a progression, not aberration. Likely to give some back in the short haul, but he's moving into top CA tier.

Yr	Tm	AB	R	HR	RBI	SB	BA	xBA	vL	vR	OB	Slg	OPS	bb%	ct%	h%	Eye	G	L	F	PX	xPX	hr/f	Spd	SBO	SB%	#Wk	DOM	DIS	RC/G	RAR	BPV	BPX	R$
08																																		
09	aa	419	50	8	54	1	236	264			341	367	707	14	82	27	0.86				92			85	2%	42%				4.14		43	0	$3
10	MIL *	399	36	6	38	4	256	237	284	241	298	336	634	6	84	29	0.36	44	19	38	56	79	5%	88	6%	67%	20	20%	55%	3.41	-10.2	8	17	$5
11	MIL	430	45	12	59	2	265	248	291	259	312	391	702	6	77	32	0.29	42	24	34	87	83	11%	91	3%	67%	25	32%	48%	4.21	-0.9	7	16	$10
12	MIL	316	46	12	58	4	320	284	400	292	364	513	877	7	86	34	0.50	41	21	37	112	129	12%	121	6%	80%	20	45%	25%	7.00	22.9	77	193	$16
1st Half		139	17	5	30	2	345	304	459	304	377	583	959	5	84	38	0.32	40	25	36	140	145	12%	125	6%	100%	9	44%	22%	8.67	15.9	89	223	$15
2nd Half		177	29	7	28	2	299	265	349	284	354	458	812	8	88	31	0.68	43	18	39	90	118	11%	100	6%	67%	11	45%	27%	5.84	8.0	57	143	$16
13	Proj	422	53	16	64	4	287	271	343	270	338	460	798	7	83	32	0.46	42	22	36	104	105	12%	105	5%	74%				5.55	15.8	55	137	$15

Ludwick,Ryan

Age	34	Bats	R	Pos LF	Health	B	LIMA Plan C
Ht	6' 3"	Wt	215		PT/Exp	B	Rand Var 0
					Consist	D	MM 4025

One man's shipwreck is another's fortune. Took advantage of teammates' injuries to find PT and resurrect his career. The ironic part is, there was no real skills change at all—just look at xPX. Leaving PETCO didn't make him a big-time slugger again. So expect HR to regress; use 20 as your baseline, and hope for gravy.

Yr	Tm	AB	R	HR	RBI	SB	BA	xBA	vL	vR	OB	Slg	OPS	bb%	ct%	h%	Eye	G	L	F	PX	xPX	hr/f	Spd	SBO	SB%	#Wk	DOM	DIS	RC/G	RAR	BPV	BPX	R$
08	STL	538	104	37	113	4	299	294	266	316	372	591	963	10	73	35	0.42	27	26	47	200	177	20%	95	6%	50%	27	67%	22%	7.82	46.2	98	192	$29
09	STL	486	63	22	97	4	265	251	269	264	323	447	769	8	78	30	0.39	33	19	48	112	126	12%	83	5%	67%	26	35%	50%	4.96	3.3	38	78	$15
10	2 NL	490	63	17	69	0	251	255	194	275	318	418	736	9	75	30	0.40	32	23	45	120	126	10%	111	3%	0%	24	38%	46%	4.37	-5.1	29	63	$10
11	2 NL	490	56	13	75	1	237	222	264	228	309	363	672	9	75	29	0.41	34	19	47	95	124	7%	69	2%	50%	26	23%	54%	3.73	-14.7	6	13	$8
12	CIN	422	53	26	80	0	275	288	263	280	341	531	871	9	77	30	0.43	33	24	43	166	127	18%	64	1%	0%	27	56%	30%	6.30	18.8	69	173	$16
1st Half		186	19	11	33	0	226	256	246	217	301	473	774	10	74	24	0.42	35	16	49	169	134	16%	58	0%	0%	13	46%	31%	4.69	0.2	56	140	$8
2nd Half		236	34	15	47	0	314	307	279	326	372	576	948	9	79	34	0.45	31	30	39	163	122	21%	75	2%	0%	14	64%	29%	7.83	20.4	79	198	$23
13	Proj	476	61	21	83	1	264	259	253	268	333	458	791	9	76	31	0.43	35	23	43	130	128	13%	72	2%	27%				5.21	7.7	41	101	$16

Machado,Manny

Age	20	Bats	R	Pos 3B	Health	A	LIMA Plan B
Ht	6' 3"	Wt	185		PT/Exp	F	Rand Var 0
					Consist	F	MM 3415

7-26-.252 in 191 AB at BAL. More than held his own, with memorable HRs, solid Spd, and even reasonable contact. Exciting! But (is there always a but?) you can count the 20/21-year-old breakout superstars in MLB history on, what, two hands? So for 2013, don't go crazy. In keeper leagues? By all means, go nuts.

Yr	Tm	AB	R	HR	RBI	SB	BA	xBA	vL	vR	OB	Slg	OPS	bb%	ct%	h%	Eye	G	L	F	PX	xPX	hr/f	Spd	SBO	SB%	#Wk	DOM	DIS	RC/G	RAR	BPV	BPX	R$
08																																		
09																																		
10																																		
11																																		
12	BAL *	593	73	17	74	13	253	250	280	255	308	415	723	7	81	29	0.43	46	14	40	102	100	12%	128	12%	75%	9	33%	56%	4.35	-3.4	56	140	$16
1st Half		289	29	5	33	7	245	253			309	375	684	8	81	29	0.47				91			102	16%	64%				3.81		39	98	$12
2nd Half		304	44	11	42	5	260	261	280	255	308	452	760	6	82	28	0.39	46	14	40	112	100	12%	147	8%	100%	9	33%	56%	4.91	2.9	69	173	$20
13	Proj	555	70	18	71	11	251	254	268	244	302	426	728	7	81	28	0.39	43	16	39	109	90	11%	129	11%	78%				4.38	-3.4	62	154	$16

Maldonado,Martin

Age	26	Bats	R	Pos CA	Health	A	LIMA Plan F
Ht	6' 1"	Wt	224		PT/Exp	D	Rand Var 0
					Consist	A	MM 3001

8-30-.266 in 233 AB at MIL. Shows league-average pop, and often that's about all you can ask for from a second catcher. Good thing you're not greedy, because that's all he has to offer. BA has no upside; even his pedestrian 2H .267 was h%-inflated. So $3 is what you got, and $3 is about what you'll get. And 1 SB.

Yr	Tm	AB	R	HR	RBI	SB	BA	xBA	vL	vR	OB	Slg	OPS	bb%	ct%	h%	Eye	G	L	F	PX	xPX	hr/f	Spd	SBO	SB%	#Wk	DOM	DIS	RC/G	RAR	BPV	BPX	R$
08	aa	98	3	2	6	0	169	176			197	236	433	3	72	22	0.12				47			91	0%	0%				1.43		-63	0	-$4
09	aaa																																	
10	a/a	277	21	7	28	1	214	225			261	337	598	6	70	28	0.22				97			82	7%	18%				2.69		-18	0	-$1
11	MIL *	343	33	8	42	1	236	225	0		288	353	641	7	73	30	0.27	44	20	36	91	2	0%	65	3%	55%	3	0%	100%	3.36	-9.5	-9	-20	$3
12	MIL *	354	30	11	40	1	232	230	250	271	281	368	648	6	72	29	0.24	43	23	34	97	78	14%	70	5%	23%	19	32%	58%	3.29	-10.7	-13	-33	$3
1st Half		204	17	8	26	0	207	221	292	254	258	358	616	6	70	25	0.23	36	22	42	105	67	19%	55	6%	0%	5	60%	40%	2.80	-9.1	-16	-40	$3
2nd Half		150	13	3	14	1	267	239	219	280	313	380	693	6	74	34	0.26	48	23	29	86	85	10%	86	5%	50%	14	21%	64%	4.05	-0.7	-11	-28	$3
13	Proj	230	19	8	24	1	230	234	232	229	275	371	646	6	72	29	0.23	43	23	34	100	78	13%	76	4%	34%				3.29	-6.5	-10	-25	$3

Markakis,Nick

Age	29	Bats	L	Pos RF	Health	B	LIMA Plan B
Ht	6' 1"	Wt	190		PT/Exp	A	Rand Var 0
					Consist	B	MM 3245

When he did this at 24, we were ready to coronate the next star. Things haven't worked out that way, but only time lost from two broken bones (hamate, thumb) prevented his best year since. He's so consistent, even this small uptick feels like a new, shinier level. Welcome back, '08 Nick, we've been expecting you.

Yr	Tm	AB	R	HR	RBI	SB	BA	xBA	vL	vR	OB	Slg	OPS	bb%	ct%	h%	Eye	G	L	F	PX	xPX	hr/f	Spd	SBO	SB%	#Wk	DOM	DIS	RC/G	RAR	BPV	BPX	R$
08	BAL	595	106	20	87	10	306	290	297	310	405	491	896	14	81	35	0.88	46	21	33	127	102	13%	95	8%	59%	27	59%	15%	7.13	37.4	76	149	$27
09	BAL	642	94	18	101	6	293	272	262	314	350	453	803	8	85	32	0.57	43	17	41	103	118	8%	106	4%	75%	27	52%	19%	5.71	15.1	62	127	$22
10	BAL	629	79	12	60	7	297	274	361	269	370	436	806	10	85	33	0.78	46	18	36	97	82	6%	123	5%	78%	27	44%	19%	5.86	17.5	63	137	$21
11	BAL	641	72	15	73	12	284	275	261	294	347	406	753	9	88	30	0.83	43	23	34	78	96	8%	86	8%	80%	27	48%	26%	5.04	3.3	57	127	$21
12	BAL	420	59	13	54	1	298	303	313	291	361	471	833	9	88	31	0.82	42	27	31	105	111	11%	97	2%	50%	18	61%	11%	6.15	14.9	74	185	$15
1st Half		199	25	8	26	1	256	293	231	265	330	452	783	10	81	28	0.59	47	24	29	125	114	17%	82	4%	50%	9	33%	22%	5.05	0.3	65	163	$11
2nd Half		221	34	5	28	0	335	314	368	317	390	489	879	8	94	34	1.43	38	29	33	90	109	7%	110	0%	0%	9	89%	0%	7.31	13.3	81	203	$18
13	Proj	603	81	20	89	5	297	294	308	292	362	471	834	9	88	31	0.82	43	24	34	105	103	11%	92	4%	72%				6.18	19.6	76	191	$25

Marson,Lou

Age	27	Bats	R	Pos CA	Health	A	LIMA Plan F
Ht	6' 1"	Wt	200		PT/Exp	D	Rand Var +1
					Consist	A	MM 1301

You know that Einstein quote about insanity? Doing the same thing over and over, expecting different results? Maybe Marson's managers qualify as insane for playing him. Few have been more consistent, yet so stunningly poor, at batting. (Turns out Einstein didn't actually say that... so Acta's off the hook.)

Yr	Tm	AB	R	HR	RBI	SB	BA	xBA	vL	vR	OB	Slg	OPS	bb%	ct%	h%	Eye	G	L	F	PX	xPX	hr/f	Spd	SBO	SB%	#Wk	DOM	DIS	RC/G	RAR	BPV	BPX	R$
08	PHI *	326	44	5	37	2	280	165	500	500	376	376	752	13	75	36	0.63	50	0	50	74	379	####	97	5%	41%	1	100%	0%	4.87	5.5	1	2	$7
09	2 TM *	375	43	1	31	3	245	241	111	269	323	322	644	10	77	32	0.49	46	22	32	66	111	0%	96	4%	74%	7	29%	43%	3.51	-6.9	0	0	$2
10	CLE *	386	43	6	32	12	186	250	286	161	266	288	554	10	79	22	0.52	56	15	29	78	68	5%	95	15%	92%	19	32%	42%	2.51	-20.1	28	61	-$1
11	CLE	243	26	1	19	4	230	229	297	191	300	296	596	9	72	32	0.35	54	24	23	55	61	3%	114	9%	67%	25	28%	64%	2.92	-8.9	-20	-44	$0
12	CLE	195	27	0	13	4	226	243	221	229	346	287	633	16	77	29	0.82	61	20	19	48	58	0%	122	9%	67%	26	35%	58%	3.28	-5.1	10	25	$0
1st Half		81	15	0	5	2	284	269	250	306	389	395	785	15	78	37	0.78	54	25	21	80	108	0%	126	7%	100%	12	42%	50%	5.67	3.3	42	105	$1
2nd Half		114	12	0	8	2	184	212	204	167	316	211	527	16	77	24	0.85	65	17	18	25	23	0%	94	10%	50%	14	29%	64%	2.03	-8.1	-22	-55	-$1
13	Proj	183	23	0	14	4	224	235	226	222	323	289	612	13	76	29	0.61	57	21	23	52	65	1%	108	9%	70%				3.08	-6.4	0	-1	$1

Marte,Starling

Age	24	Bats	R	Pos LF	Health	A	LIMA Plan C
Ht	6' 0"	Wt	180		PT/Exp	D	Rand Var 0
					Consist	B	MM 3525

5-17-.257, 12 SB in 167 AB at PIT. For want of a batting Eye. He's got everything else to become a star—some power, plus wheels. A really cool name. But .300 OB, mid-70s ct% guys don't become stars. Contact's the key, and he's shown better. Even a return to '11 MLE could make him the real deal.

Yr	Tm	AB	R	HR	RBI	SB	BA	xBA	vL	vR	OB	Slg	OPS	bb%	ct%	h%	Eye	G	L	F	PX	xPX	hr/f	Spd	SBO	SB%	#Wk	DOM	DIS	RC/G	RAR	BPV	BPX	R$
08																																		
09																																		
10																																		
11	aa	536	74	9	40	19	297	260			319	436	755	3	80	36	0.16				100			112	26%	59%				4.71		46	0	$21
12	PIT *	555	71	14	68	29	256	263	318	236	295	431	726	5	74	32	0.21	57	18	25	112	83	18%	179	40%	61%	9	33%	56%	3.98	-12.0	39	98	$20
1st Half		296	41	6	39	13	254	246			292	415	707	5	76	32	0.22				104			152	42%	50%				3.52		40	100	$21
2nd Half		259	30	8	29	16	259	260	318	236	298	450	748	5	71	33	0.19	57	18	25	121	83	18%	184	37%	76%	9	33%	56%	4.55	-1.8	37	93	$20
13	Proj	469	61	12	48	22	251	257	310	230	283	423	706	4	74	32	0.17	52	18	30	114	75	12%	163	38%	62%				3.77	-12.6	41	103	$16

ROD TRUESDELL

Martin,Leonys

Martin,Leonys						Health	A	LIMA Plan	C
Age	25	Bats	L	Pos	CF	PT/Exp	F	Rand Var	0
Ht	6' 2"	Wt	190			Consist	D	MM	3253

0-6-.174 in 46 AB at TEX. Intriguing growth year for former Cuban refugee, especially in the power dept. Didn't bring BA to short stints in majors, but showed a little pop there too (7 of 8 hits were for extra bases). In short, lots to like, but opportunity is the key for '13: UP: 400+ AB DN: rides AAA shuttle

Yr	Tm	AB	R	HR	RBI	SB	BA	xBA	vL	vR	OB	Slg	OPS	bb%	ct%	h%	Eye	G	L	F	PX	xPX	hr/f	Spd	SBO	SB%	#Wk	DOM	DIS	RC/G	RAR	BPV	BPX	R$
08																																		
09																																		
10																																		
11	TEX *	295	38	3	29	13	262	314	0	375	306	364	669	6	88	29	0.52	57	29	14	68	37	0%	115	33%	54%	4	25%	50%	3.45	-12.6	53	118	$8
12	TEX *	277	40	10	36	10	290	295	125	184	340	496	837	7	80	33	0.38	47	24	29	135	55	0%	97	30%	49%	12	33%	42%	5.38	4.3	78	195	$12
1st Half		153	16	4	20	7	289	326	143	278	347	476	823	8	81	34	0.47	60	30	10	121	76	0%	101	37%	46%	3	67%	0%	5.00	1.0	72	180	$12
2nd Half		124	23	6	15	3	292	254	0	100	332	522	853	6	79	33	0.29	29	14	57	152	25	0%	101	20%	57%	9	22%	56%	5.90	4.0	84	210	$12
13	**Proj**	**295**	**42**	**8**	**34**	**11**	**278**	**303**	**165**	**322**	**325**	**445**	**770**	**6**	**83**	**31**	**0.41**	**45**	**25**	**40**	**107**	**68**	**8%**	**96**	**29%**	**53%**				**4.61**	**-1.5**	**66**	**165**	**$10**

Martin,Russell

Martin,Russell						Health	B	LIMA Plan	C
Age	30	Bats	R	Pos	CA	PT/Exp	C	Rand Var	+4
Ht	5' 10"	Wt	231			Consist	A	MM	3025

As he's increasingly swung from the heels, the HR have returned with a vengeance—at the expense of everything else, save bb%. But h% looks unlucky, and 50-point BA/xBA gap shows the pop should be offsetting the whiffs. A h% regression gives .265 upside, which with 15-20 HR is darned attractive.

Yr	Tm	AB	R	HR	RBI	SB	BA	xBA	vL	vR	OB	Slg	OPS	bb%	ct%	h%	Eye	G	L	F	PX	xPX	hr/f	Spd	SBO	SB%	#Wk	DOM	DIS	RC/G	RAR	BPV	BPX	R$
08	LA	553	87	13	69	18	280	268	253	291	381	396	777	14	85	31	1.08	51	19	30	74	89	9%	63	12%	75%	27	48%	22%	5.37	19.5	53	104	$20
09	LA	505	63	7	53	11	250	254	275	243	340	329	668	12	84	28	0.86	49	21	31	53	81	5%	72	10%	65%	26	27%	38%	3.75	-5.8	25	51	$8
10	LA	331	45	5	26	6	248	253	235	252	343	332	675	13	82	29	0.79	51	21	28	61	69	6%	65	7%	75%	18	39%	44%	3.89	-2.4	22	48	$5
11	NYY	417	57	18	65	8	237	268	211	248	319	408	727	11	81	25	0.62	47	19	33	110	110	16%	47	9%	80%	27	37%	30%	4.37	2.9	55	122	$11
12	NYY	422	50	21	53	6	211	264	226	205	299	403	702	11	77	22	0.56	48	19	33	121	107	20%	37	7%	86%	27	37%	33%	3.93	-2.7	49	123	$6
1st Half		190	21	8	21	1	189	260	295	158	294	368	662	13	76	20	0.62	49	20	31	120	98	18%	44	2%	100%	13	38%	31%	3.43	-4.7	40	100	$0
2nd Half		232	29	13	32	5	228	266	188	250	304	431	735	10	78	24	0.50	47	19	34	122	114	21%	38	11%	83%	14	36%	36%	4.36	1.0	51	128	$11
13	**Proj**	**403**	**52**	**16**	**51**	**7**	**239**	**260**	**234**	**242**	**327**	**400**	**727**	**11**	**80**	**26**	**0.64**	**48**	**20**	**32**	**101**	**100**	**16%**	**43**	**8%**	**80%**				**4.41**	**2.3**	**43**	**107**	**$10**

Martinez,Fernando

Martinez,Fernando						Health	A	LIMA Plan	D
Age	24	Bats	L	Pos	LF	PT/Exp	D	Rand Var	-5
Ht	6' 1"	Wt	205			Consist	B	MM	4005

6-14-.237 in 118 AB at HOU. Perhaps saved fading prospect status with a decent year at Triple-A, but did little in a late look in majors. Suffers from the first of the Three True Handicaps: has power, but can't make contact. Should get another, longer look, but with that plate approach, he's likely going to struggle.

Yr	Tm	AB	R	HR	RBI	SB	BA	xBA	vL	vR	OB	Slg	OPS	bb%	ct%	h%	Eye	G	L	F	PX	xPX	hr/f	Spd	SBO	SB%	#Wk	DOM	DIS	RC/G	RAR	BPV	BPX	R$
08	aa	352	42	7	38	5	267	248			315	396	711	6	78	33	0.31				89			104	8%	71%				4.32		25	0	$7
09	NYM *	267	34	9	35	4	244	280	158	181	285	439	723	5	81	27	0.30	52	10	38	129	63	3%	83	10%	79%	6	33%	50%	4.21	-7.4	69	141	$4
10	NYM *	275	30	9	27	1	212	231		167	251	356	607	5	72	26	0.18	50	14	36	110	66	0%	82	4%	43%	3	0%	67%	2.85	-19.5	1	2	$0
11	NYM *	245	26	7	26	0	211	166	250	222	256	344	601	6	70	27	0.20	47	0	53	104	151	13%	78	0%	0%	4	25%	50%	2.85	-17.3	-13	-29	$0
12	HOU *	459	48	15	55	1	250	222	77	257	284	415	699	5	70	32	0.16	56	9	34	122	112	21%	86	4%	16%	11	36%	27%	3.89	-17.1	5	13	$8
1st Half		226	23	6	29	0	261	214	0	77	290	400	690	4	72	34	0.14	83	0	17	106	114	0%	83	2%	0%	2	0%	50%	3.90	-7.3	-6	-15	$8
2nd Half		233	25	9	26	1	241	233	91	283	279	430	709	5	69	31	0.18	54	10	35	137	112	21%	92	6%	23%	9	44%	22%	3.87	-8.0	18	45	$8
13	**Proj**	**432**	**47**	**16**	**49**	**1**	**235**	**229**	**139**	**250**	**273**	**407**	**681**	**5**	**71**	**29**	**0.19**	**53**	**10**	**36**	**124**	**92**	**14%**	**81**	**4%**	**42%**				**3.65**	**-13.1**	**14**	**36**	**$7**

Martinez,J.D.

Martinez,J.D.						Health	A	LIMA Plan	D
Age	25	Bats	R	Pos	LF	PT/Exp	D	Rand Var	+2
Ht	6' 3"	Wt	205			Consist	C	MM	2015

11-55-.241 in 395 AB at HOU. Where do the Astros dig up all these mediocre Martinezes? Followed up encouraging '11 growth with a thud, losing all the power gains. HOU hopes a season of winter ball will help clear up swing issues, and 2011 is not that long ago. Keep him on your radar, but off your roster.

Yr	Tm	AB	R	HR	RBI	SB	BA	xBA	vL	vR	OB	Slg	OPS	bb%	ct%	h%	Eye	G	L	F	PX	xPX	hr/f	Spd	SBO	SB%	#Wk	DOM	DIS	RC/G	RAR	BPV	BPX	R$
08																																		
09																																		
10	aa	189	21	3	22	2	279	229			324	375	700	6	75	36	0.27				74			99	7%	44%				4.15		-5	0	$4
11	HOU *	525	64	16	85	1	279	275	360	247	332	435	768	7	78	33	0.37	37	28	36	115	124	10%	78	1%	41%	10	40%	40%	5.09	5.3	33	73	$17
12	HOU *	485	38	11	58	0	230	224	255	235	292	349	640	8	76	28	0.37	52	17	32	80	79	12%	97	3%	0%	22	23%	50%	3.27	-21.5	-2	-5	$3
1st Half		251	24	10	46	0	235	227	275	220	319	394	714	11	74	28	0.48	51	16	34	103	86	16%	90	1%	0%	13	31%	31%	4.13	-3.9	12	30	$10
2nd Half		234	14	1	12	0	224	226	216	262	260	299	559	5	78	28	0.22	54	18	28	57	68	3%	108	4%	0%	9	11%	78%	2.44	-15.9	-16	-40	-$5
13	**Proj**	**454**	**44**	**12**	**57**	**1**	**253**	**244**	**278**	**244**	**307**	**391**	**698**	**7**	**77**	**31**	**0.34**	**46**	**20**	**33**	**94**	**95**	**10%**	**90**	**3%**	**29%**				**4.02**	**-8.5**	**13**	**34**	**$9**

Martinez,Victor

Martinez,Victor						Health	F	LIMA Plan	C+
Age	34	Bats	B	Pos	DH	PT/Exp	C	Rand Var	-3
Ht	6' 2"	Wt	210			Consist	A	MM	2235

Instead of ACL reconstruction, doctors opted for a procedure to "promote healing" in the ligament to try and get him back in 2012. He couldn't return, and now second-guessers will be out in force if the knee isn't fully healed by spring. He was thriving at DH before the injuries, so offseason health reports are critical.

Yr	Tm	AB	R	HR	RBI	SB	BA	xBA	vL	vR	OB	Slg	OPS	bb%	ct%	h%	Eye	G	L	F	PX	xPX	hr/f	Spd	SBO	SB%	#Wk	DOM	DIS	RC/G	RAR	BPV	BPX	R$
08	CLE *	292	32	3	37	0	275	262	339	260	339	367	706	9	86	31	0.70	45	22	33	67	67	3%	73	0%	0%	16	31%	13%	4.38	-4.1	26	51	$4
09	2 AL	588	88	23	108	1	303	294	273	316	382	480	861	11	87	32	1.01	43	21	35	103	108	13%	72	1%	100%	27	67%	19%	6.71	29.2	70	143	$23
10	BOS	493	64	20	79	1	302	291	400	257	355	493	847	8	89	31	0.77	41	17	42	116	112	11%	80	1%	100%	23	57%	26%	6.40	20.4	81	176	$20
11	DET	540	76	12	103	1	330	298	311	337	382	470	853	8	91	35	0.90	43	24	33	95	94	7%	67	1%	100%	26	42%	19%	6.85	27.9	68	151	$27
12																																		
1st Half																																		
2nd Half																																		
13	**Proj**	**477**	**65**	**14**	**82**	**1**	**296**	**281**	**308**	**291**	**360**	**449**	**809**	**9**	**89**	**31**	**0.88**	**43**	**21**	**36**	**95**	**98**	**9%**	**66**	**1%**	**100%**				**5.86**	**12.8**	**63**	**157**	**$19**

Mastroianni,Darin

Mastroianni,Darin						Health	A	LIMA Plan	F
Age	27	Bats	R	Pos	RF LF	PT/Exp	C	Rand Var	-2
Ht	5' 11"	Wt	190			Consist	C	MM	1511

3-17-.252, 21 SB in 163 AB at MIN. Attempted 24 steals in majors, and only reached 1st or 2nd base 55 times! Imagine what he'd do if he, oh I don't know, put the ball in play a little, maybe? As it is, he's nearly Sneadian. Still, as vs-LHP platooner, he might not be too bad—and you know he'll be off and running.

Yr	Tm	AB	R	HR	RBI	SB	BA	xBA	vL	vR	OB	Slg	OPS	bb%	ct%	h%	Eye	G	L	F	PX	xPX	hr/f	Spd	SBO	SB%	#Wk	DOM	DIS	RC/G	RAR	BPV	BPX	R$
08																																		
09	aa	247	36	1	23	35	251	228			347	320	667	13	79	32	0.69				50			112	52%	80%				4.08		26	0	$13
10	aa	525	72	3	33	33	248	229			320	328	648	10	78	31	0.48				59			133	29%	74%				3.58		21	0	$15
11	TOR *	490	60	2	24	22	214	88		0	274	298	571	8	80	26	0.42	0	0	100	61	2	0%	151	30%	65%	1	0%	100%	2.55	-35.9	28	62	$4
12	MIN *	276	34	3	25	32	245	232	288	227	308	324	631	8	73	33	0.33	46	29	25	52	59	10%	164	46%	85%	21	33%	57%	3.69	-9.7	-1	-3	$12
1st Half		169	19	1	16	16	229	243	235	205	287	298	585	8	75	30	0.33	49	29	22	45	44	11%	136	40%	87%	8	38%	50%	3.10	-9.9	0	0	$11
2nd Half		107	15	2	9	16	271	223	306	241	339	364	703	9	69	38	0.33	44	29	27	63	68	10%	150	54%	84%	13	31%	62%	4.72	-0.9	-9	-23	$13
13	**Proj**	**191**	**25**	**4**	**14**	**19**	**243**	**254**	**257**	**233**	**311**	**359**	**670**	**9**	**75**	**30**	**0.40**	**46**	**29**	**25**	**75**	**58**	**10%**	**158**	**44%**	**80%**				**3.90**	**-6.5**	**25**	**63**	**$9**

Mather,Joe

Mather,Joe						Health	A	LIMA Plan	F
Age	30	Bats	R	Pos	CF LF	PT/Exp	D	Rand Var	+1
Ht	6' 4"	Wt	215			Consist	A	MM	1201

Good news: He's making more contact. Bad news: It didn't help his BA. Good news: Scouting reports said he has enough offensive skills to become a starter. Bad news: That report was in 2007. Good news: He got a career-high 225 AB. Bad news: He got a career-high 225 AB.

Yr	Tm	AB	R	HR	RBI	SB	BA	xBA	vL	vR	OB	Slg	OPS	bb%	ct%	h%	Eye	G	L	F	PX	xPX	hr/f	Spd	SBO	SB%	#Wk	DOM	DIS	RC/G	RAR	BPV	BPX	R$
08	STL *	344	53	20	48	6	243	273	219	261	314	475	789	9	78	26	0.48	30	22	48	145	115	16%	95	11%	72%	12	50%	42%	4.97	3.7	76	149	$9
09	a/a	194	14	3	18	5	146	231			188	237	425	5	77	18	0.22				62			96	32%	58%				1.25		0	0	-$5
10	STL *	395	42	6	32	5	206	219	219	214	255	307	562	6	74	26	0.25	40	19	42	78	73	0%	117	13%	44%	11	36%	55%	2.37	-28.0	-2	-4	-$1
11	ATL *	346	26	5	25	2	214	205	250	196	252	309	561	5	74	27	0.20	35	18	47	78	60	4%	85	7%	50%	8	25%	63%	2.47	-23.0	-14	-31	-$2
12	CHC	225	18	5	19	5	209	235	202	216	255	324	580	6	80	24	0.30	42	19	39	80	66	7%	77	16%	71%	27	22%	48%	2.65	-13.7	14	35	$0
1st Half		123	9	4	12	2	244	253	273	221	301	398	699	8	80	28	0.40	43	20	37	103	78	11%	81	10%	67%	13	23%	46%	3.99	-2.2	29	73	$1
2nd Half		102	9	1	7	3	167	210	136	209	198	235	433	4	79	20	0.19	40	18	41	51	53	3%	80	25%	75%	14	21%	50%	1.44	-10.6	-7	-18	-$2
13	**Proj**	**132**	**12**	**3**	**11**	**2**	**218**	**221**	**198**	**238**	**262**	**326**	**588**	**6**	**77**	**26**	**0.26**	**38**	**19**	**43**	**77**	**69**	**6%**	**85**	**13%**	**65%**				**2.73**	**-8.4**	**3**	**8**	**$1**

ROD TRUESDELL

Mathis,Jeff

Age 30 Bats R Pos CA	Health	B	LIMA Plan	F
Ht 6' 0" Wt 200	PT/Exp	F	Rand Var	-1
	Consist	B	MM	3201

Threw patience to the wind and swung for the fences, and mostly it worked. Well, "worked" in this context means having any positive value whatsoever. Some perspective: when his very best, peak season earned but a single dollar's value, that tells you all you need to know about how much to bid next year.

Yr	Tm	AB	R	HR	RBI	SB	BA	xBA	vL	vR	OB	Slg	OPS	bb%	ct%	h%	Eye	G	L	F	PX	xPX	hr/f	Spd	SBO	SB%	#Wk	DOM	DIS	RC/G	RAR	BPV	BPX	R$
08	LAA	283	35	9	42	2	194	182	224	184	272	318	590	10	68	25	0.33	36	11	53	89	92	9%	91	6%	50%	26	27%	73%	2.68	-13.1	-18	-35	-$1
09	LAA	237	26	5	28	2	211	196	228	203	278	308	586	8	69	28	0.30	37	17	46	73	77	7%	96	8%	40%	27	22%	67%	2.65	-11.0	-30	-61	-$1
10	LAA *	238	23	4	21	3	193	184	204	192	221	280	500	3	70	26	0.12	39	13	48	66	72	4%	122	7%	100%	19	5%	74%	2.00	-16.0	-28	-61	-$2
11	LAA	247	18	3	22	1	174	196	180	170	221	259	480	6	70	24	0.20	39	18	43	76	81	4%	77	7%	33%	27	22%	59%	1.71	-19.5	-34	-76	-$5
12	TOR	211	25	8	27	1	218	229	219	218	250	393	643	4	68	28	0.13	36	20	44	136	118	13%	75	3%	100%	26	42%	50%	3.23	-5.8	6	15	$1
1st Half		64	13	4	7	1	234	243	278	217	290	484	774	7	63	31	0.21	39	16	45	199	179	24%	93	8%	100%	12	50%	50%	4.76	1.0	51	128	$0
2nd Half		147	12	4	20	0	211	224	196	218	232	354	586	3	70	27	0.09	35	21	44	112	95	9%	69	0%	0%	14	36%	50%	2.65	-7.1	-16	-40	$2
13	Proj	199	22	6	22	1	203	211	209	200	244	346	590	5	68	26	0.17	38	18	45	111	104	10%	82	6%	69%				2.69	-9.5	-8	-20	-$1

Mauer,Joe

Age 30 Bats L Pos CA DH 1B	Health	C	LIMA Plan	C+
Ht 6' 6" Wt 231	PT/Exp	B	Rand Var	-3
	Consist	F	MM	1145

Most everything bounced all the way back; xPX shows that even the power returned in 2H. Note though that it came at the expense of contact rate—as xBA reveals, that's putting his gaudy BA numbers at risk. Still, are a few more HR at the expense of a few BA points a reasonable trade-off? Your call.

Yr	Tm	AB	R	HR	RBI	SB	BA	xBA	vL	vR	OB	Slg	OPS	bb%	ct%	h%	Eye	G	L	F	PX	xPX	hr/f	Spd	SBO	SB%	#Wk	DOM	DIS	RC/G	RAR	BPV	BPX	R$
08	MIN	536	98	9	85	1	328	295	361	312	419	451	871	14	91	35	1.68	49	23	28	76	103	6%	93	1%	50%	27	63%	19%	7.16	42.7	73	143	$24
09	MIN	523	94	28	96	4	365	325	345	377	446	587	1033	13	88	38	1.21	48	23	30	124	118	20%	79	2%	80%	24	71%	13%	10.51	83.2	97	198	$35
10	MIN	510	88	9	75	1	327	310	272	365	403	469	872	11	90	35	1.23	47	24	29	98	126	7%	84	3%	20%	27	63%	19%	6.98	38.7	74	161	$23
11	MIN	296	38	3	30	0	287	270	234	319	357	368	725	10	87	32	0.84	55	23	22	60	75	5%	89	0%	0%	17	29%	47%	4.70	4.6	27	60	$6
12	MIN	545	81	10	85	8	319	286	287	336	416	446	862	14	84	37	1.02	53	25	22	83	113	10%	91	5%	67%	27	52%	22%	6.89	40.4	56	140	$25
1st Half		252	37	4	36	3	325	291	366	309	416	448	864	13	85	37	1.05	59	22	19	84	88	10%	82	4%	75%	13	62%	15%	7.05	19.0	57	143	$22
2nd Half		293	44	6	49	5	314	280	239	364	416	444	859	15	83	36	1.00	47	27	26	82	134	10%	101	7%	63%	14	43%	29%	6.75	20.3	52	130	$28
13	Proj	520	78	9	75	4	305	286	266	328	392	427	819	13	86	34	1.03	52	24	24	79	107	9%	87	4%	61%				6.09	26.8	54	135	$22

Maxwell,Justin

Age 29 Bats R Pos CF LF RF	Health	B	LIMA Plan	D+
Ht 6' 5" Wt 235	PT/Exp	D	Rand Var	0
	Consist	C	MM	4405

Power/speed combo held up well in majors, but he has SO many holes in his swing. Horrific ct% keeps BA right where it is, he doesn't hit righties, and xPX, hr/f say he won't keep all of the power gains. Now 29, this is probably about as good as it gets. UP: 500 AB nets 20/20/.240. DN: Drops into wrong side of a platoon.

Yr	Tm	AB	R	HR	RBI	SB	BA	xBA	vL	vR	OB	Slg	OPS	bb%	ct%	h%	Eye	G	L	F	PX	xPX	hr/f	Spd	SBO	SB%	#Wk	DOM	DIS	RC/G	RAR	BPV	BPX	R$
08	aa	146	26	5	21	10	197	260			307	367	674	14	79	22	0.74				103			123	36%	68%				3.44		71	0	$2
09	WAS *	473	67	14	42	34	214	201	242	250	295	351	646	10	61	32	0.29	48	14	38	106	120	19%	159	36%	76%	10	30%	70%	3.39	-19.4	-3	-6	$12
10	WAS *	334	42	8	28	17	209	195	155	130	315	338	653	13	61	32	0.39	35	16	49	125	110	10%	95	29%	65%	18	28%	56%	3.31	-14.7	-3	-7	$5
11	aaa	177	28	14	27	8	222	240			302	507	810	10	51	33	0.24				268			89	28%	78%				4.98		76	0	$6
12	HOU	315	46	18	53	9	229	239	272	208	300	460	760	9	64	30	0.28	44	16	39	171	134	23%	115	19%	69%	25	52%	40%	4.46	-2.1	47	118	$10
1st Half		121	22	8	24	1	231	229	224	236	316	471	787	11	59	32	0.30	44	17	39	193	161	29%	84	10%	33%	12	58%	42%	4.66	-0.4	31	78	$6
2nd Half		194	24	10	29	8	227	243	315	193	289	454	743	8	67	28	0.27	45	16	39	158	119	20%	125	25%	80%	13	46%	38%	4.33	-2.6	51	128	$12
13	Proj	408	60	19	60	16	234	214	276	209	313	428	742	10	61	33	0.30	41	16	43	154	124	18%	110	22%	71%				4.39	-4.8	23	59	$15

Mayberry,John

Age 29 Bats R Pos LF CF 1B	Health	A	LIMA Plan	D
Ht 6' 6" Wt 225	PT/Exp	C	Rand Var	+2
	Consist	C	MM	4213

One good month followed by a really bad one in first real shot at full-time play. Fly rate collapsed, which bears watching, since HR pop is about all he contributes now. Assuming FB ways return, let's focus on the big picture: at 29, this is what he is. He'll hit lefties, strike out a lot, and smack 15 HR or so.

Yr	Tm	AB	R	HR	RBI	SB	BA	xBA	vL	vR	OB	Slg	OPS	bb%	ct%	h%	Eye	G	L	F	PX	xPX	hr/f	Spd	SBO	SB%	#Wk	DOM	DIS	RC/G	RAR	BPV	BPX	R$
08	a/a	519	47	15	52	7	224	263			259	398	658	5	76	27	0.20				120			101	12%	68%				3.35		42	0	$2
09	PHI *	373	43	15	42	5	219	224	243	150	275	402	676	7	64	30	0.21	35	18	47	143	164	25%	109	10%	67%	12	33%	50%	3.56	-12.9	11	22	$4
10	PHI *	507	63	14	57	16	226	194	500	167	270	353	623	6	73	28	0.23	50	0	50	94	182	50%	110	19%	78%	5	40%	60%	3.16	-23.7	11	24	$9
11	PHI *	380	49	18	60	9	256	273	306	250	310	466	775	7	78	28	0.36	42	18	40	144	109	17%	75	15%	76%	23	52%	22%	4.91	2.5	69	153	$13
12	PHI	441	53	14	46	1	245	248	271	229	299	395	694	7	75	30	0.31	52	20	28	106	74	15%	86	1%	100%	27	30%	56%	4.00	-9.0	13	33	$7
1st Half		195	20	6	23	1	226	243	259	200	260	379	639	4	71	29	0.16	51	20	29	118	73	15%	87	3%	100%	13	31%	69%	3.27	-8.9	2	5	$3
2nd Half		246	33	8	23	0	260	250	284	248	328	407	735	9	78	30	0.46	52	20	28	98	74	15%	88	0%	0%	14	29%	43%	4.60	-1.2	19	48	$10
13	Proj	392	48	16	46	5	243	254	292	211	294	423	717	7	75	29	0.29	46	19	35	123	100	15%	85	8%	76%				4.18	-5.5	35	88	$10

Maybin,Cameron

Age 26 Bats R Pos CF	Health	A	LIMA Plan	C
Ht 6' 3" Wt 210	PT/Exp	B	Rand Var	+2
	Consist	B	MM	2515

Ran a little less, and slightly less effectively, and dropped 19 points of BA. That's all it took to lose 35% of his SB. Any glimmers of hope? That 2nd half. Contact and BA were little more than a correction from the poor 1st half, but a .283 BA over 247 AB is still something. Will it carry over into '13? At 26, it's possible.

Yr	Tm	AB	R	HR	RBI	SB	BA	xBA	vL	vR	OB	Slg	OPS	bb%	ct%	h%	Eye	G	L	F	PX	xPX	hr/f	Spd	SBO	SB%	#Wk	DOM	DIS	RC/G	RAR	BPV	BPX	R$
08	FLA *	422	70	10	43	22	276	247	375	542	361	427	788	12	65	40	0.38	50	29	21	113	89	0%	211	22%	75%	3	33%	33%	5.41	8.9	18	35	$17
09	FLA *	474	65	6	44	7	275	259	254	248	342	412	754	9	75	35	0.41	55	17	28	97	80	12%	144	9%	59%	12	50%	50%	4.84	2.0	32	65	$10
10	FLA *	421	62	11	45	13	252	230	222	239	308	379	687	8	71	33	0.28	53	14	33	90	100	13%	162	14%	80%	16	25%	56%	4.02	-8.3	12	26	$11
11	SD	516	82	9	40	40	264	251	296	251	321	393	715	8	76	33	0.35	55	16	29	93	93	8%	166	35%	83%	25	44%	40%	4.54	-2.2	44	98	$22
12	SD	507	67	8	45	26	243	242	240	244	303	349	652	8	78	30	0.40	55	16	28	71	88	7%	130	25%	79%	27	33%	37%	3.62	-16.3	26	65	$14
1st Half		260	37	3	23	16	204	228	165	221	279	292	571	9	77	25	0.45	58	14	28	55	73	5%	149	28%	84%	13	31%	38%	2.76	-16.6	19	48	$12
2nd Half		247	30	5	22	10	283	256	324	267	330	409	738	6	80	34	0.34	53	18	29	87	104	9%	110	21%	71%	14	36%	36%	4.72	-0.4	31	78	$16
13	Proj	517	73	10	46	30	267	243	279	262	323	391	715	8	76	33	0.35	55	16	29	84	92	9%	138	26%	81%				4.49	-4.3	29	73	$21

McCann,Brian

Age 29 Bats L Pos CA	Health	A	LIMA Plan	D+
Ht 6' 3" Wt 230	PT/Exp	B	Rand Var	+4
	Consist	B	MM	3113

It's pretty clear in hindsight that the rather badly-torn labrum in his shoulder caused this collapse. Now, after surgery, he's not expected to be ready when the season starts, so he'll be doing well to grab 400 AB again. Once healed, though, expect a healthy McCann to return to solid 2010-11 skills and production.

Yr	Tm	AB	R	HR	RBI	SB	BA	xBA	vL	vR	OB	Slg	OPS	bb%	ct%	h%	Eye	G	L	F	PX	xPX	hr/f	Spd	SBO	SB%	#Wk	DOM	DIS	RC/G	RAR	BPV	BPX	R$
08	ATL	509	68	23	87	5	301	304	299	301	371	523	894	10	87	31	0.89	37	20	43	136	129	12%	62	3%	100%	27	67%	19%	7.14	39.8	101	198	$22
09	ATL	488	63	21	94	4	281	291	225	308	346	486	832	9	83	30	0.59	38	21	41	128	137	13%	55	4%	80%	26	58%	19%	5.97	23.2	73	149	$17
10	ATL	479	63	21	77	5	269	268	263	272	367	453	820	13	80	30	0.76	37	20	43	122	144	13%	62	4%	71%	27	52%	33%	5.79	20.7	59	128	$16
11	ATL	466	51	24	71	3	270	252	265	273	350	466	816	11	81	29	0.64	38	16	47	123	162	14%	59	4%	60%	25	48%	32%	5.64	18.1	55	122	$16
12	ATL	439	44	20	67	3	230	252	236	227	300	399	699	9	83	24	0.58	40	19	41	98	131	13%	51	3%	100%	27	41%	44%	4.00	-3.7	42	105	$8
1st Half		234	23	9	35	1	226	253	247	215	296	385	680	9	85	23	0.68	40	18	42	93	138	11%	62	2%	100%	13	38%	38%	3.77	-3.1	46	115	$7
2nd Half		205	21	11	32	2	234	249	222	241	305	415	720	9	80	24	0.50	39	20	40	103	124	17%	52	4%	100%	14	43%	50%	4.27	0.3	32	80	$9
13	Proj	377	42	17	59	3	253	252	247	255	329	426	755	10	82	27	0.62	39	19	43	105	140	13%	53	3%	81%				4.79	6.4	45	112	$11

McCutchen,Andrew

Age 26 Bats R Pos CF	Health	A	LIMA Plan	D+
Ht 5' 10" Wt 185	PT/Exp	A	Rand Var	-5
	Consist	C	MM	4435

Exciting breakout, but not without caveats. H% spike not fully supported by skills, meaning his BA should regression. Lingering knee pain likely cut into SBO and SB%, and needs monitoring. His peak may still be 1-2 years away, but growth often comes in fits and starts, even at this level. Expect some regression in'13.

Yr	Tm	AB	R	HR	RBI	SB	BA	xBA	vL	vR	OB	Slg	OPS	bb%	ct%	h%	Eye	G	L	F	PX	xPX	hr/f	Spd	SBO	SB%	#Wk	DOM	DIS	RC/G	RAR	BPV	BPX	R$
08	aaa	512	63	7	42	29	263	248			335	363	699	10	82	31	0.61				69			100	32%	58%				3.87		35	0	$16
09	PIT *	634	108	15	71	30	283	273	310	279	352	457	810	10	83	32	0.62	42	19	39	104	114	9%	178	21%	81%	19	63%	16%	5.79	19.9	82	167	$27
10	PIT	570	94	16	56	33	286	279	324	273	364	449	813	11	84	32	0.79	43	19	38	106	115	9%	148	24%	77%	27	63%	22%	5.84	18.8	85	185	$28
11	PIT	572	87	23	89	23	259	266	277	253	359	456	815	13	78	30	0.71	38	20	42	135	142	12%	109	19%	70%	27	56%	19%	5.52	14.2	82	182	$24
12	PIT	593	107	31	96	20	327	281	392	309	398	553	951	11	78	38	0.53	44	22	34	140	147	19%	135	16%	63%	27	52%	26%	7.99	53.3	78	195	$40
1st Half		280	47	15	51	14	346	290	451	311	402	593	995	8	78	40	0.43	42	23	35	152	147	19%	126	20%	78%	13	46%	23%	9.21	32.5	91	228	$43
2nd Half		313	60	16	45	6	310	270	322	307	395	518	913	12	77	36	0.62	46	21	34	128	147	20%	134	13%	43%	14	57%	29%	7.01	19.6	63	158	$37
13	Proj	591	100	29	84	23	297	279	336	286	376	515	891	11	79	33	0.61	43	21	36	135	138	17%	128	19%	66%				6.78	33.5	82	204	$34

ROD TRUESDELL

McDonald,John			Health	C	LIMA Plan	F
Age 38	Bats R	Pos SS	PT/Exp	F	Rand Var	-1
Ht 5' 9"	Wt 181		Consist	C	MM	1011

He's 38. He's earned more than a dollar in only one season since there was a Bush in the White House. He hits for a poor average, has little speed, and shows only fleeting, unreliable glimpses of power. And yet, in deep leagues, when your SS goes down, you always see his name in the pool and think, "just this once."

Yr	Tm	AB	R	HR	RBI	SB	BA	xBA	vL	vR	OB	Slg	OPS	bb%	ct%	h%	Eye	G	L	F	PX	xPX	hr/f	Spd	SBO	SB%	#Wk	DOM	DIS	RC/G	RAR	BPV	BPX	R$
08	TOR	186	21	1	18	3	210	220	250	184	250	269	519	5	87	24	0.40	42	15	43	44	76	1%	79	10%	75%	23	22%	57%	2.18	-11.1	16	31	-$2
09	TOR	151	18	4	13	0	258	245	260	257	263	384	647	1	88	27	0.06	32	17	50	75	76	6%	93	7%	0%	27	15%	56%	3.24	-3.8	30	61	$1
10	TOR	152	27	6	23	2	250	278	250	250	278	454	732	4	83	27	0.23	34	20	45	128	96	10%	114	11%	67%	23	43%	43%	4.23	0.5	83	180	$3
11	2 TM	227	21	2	22	2	229	239	241	225	268	308	576	5	88	25	0.44	38	20	42	55	39	2%	98	12%	33%	25	28%	40%	2.54	-10.9	27	60	$0
12	ARI	197	16	6	22	0	249	241	318	214	292	386	678	6	83	27	0.36	41	19	40	86	91	9%	68	2%	0%	24	38%	50%	3.73	-2.1	21	53	$1
1st Half		86	9	4	12	0	267	297	321	241	308	488	796	5	87	27	0.45	38	21	41	135	112	13%	58	6%	0%	13	62%	23%	4.97	2.4	78	195	$2
2nd Half		111	7	2	10	0	234	193	316	192	280	306	586	6	80	28	0.32	43	17	40	45	74	6%	86	0%	0%	11	9%	82%	2.85	-3.9	-26	-65	$0
13	**Proj**	**166**	**17**	**4**	**18**	**1**	**242**	**244**	**286**	**222**	**279**	**368**	**647**	**5**	**85**	**26**	**0.34**	**39**	**19**	**42**	**79**	**76**	**7%**	**83**	**6%**	**37%**				**3.34**	**-3.3**	**29**	**72**	**$1**

McGehee,Casey			Health	A	LIMA Plan	F
Age 30	Bats R	Pos 1B 3B	PT/Exp	B	Rand Var	+4
Ht 6' 1"	Wt 220		Consist	C	MM	2011

In retrospect, it's often so easy to see the peak. It's a bit more unusual to see it look this much like the Matterhorn. As he still owns those '09 and '10 skills, it wouldn't be too surprising to see a secondary, Appalachian-sized peak over the next year or three. But it's chasing shadows to try and predict it.

Yr	Tm	AB	R	HR	RBI	SB	BA	xBA	vL	vR	OB	Slg	OPS	bb%	ct%	h%	Eye	G	L	F	PX	xPX	hr/f	Spd	SBO	SB%	#Wk	DOM	DIS	RC/G	RAR	BPV	BPX	R$
08	CHC *	521	46	9	67	0	236	210	125	188	273	336	609	5	77	29	0.22	59	12	29	75	123	0%	71	3%	0%	4	0%	75%	2.96	-26.0	-12	-24	$2
09	MIL	355	58	16	66	0	301	282	303	301	362	499	861	9	81	33	0.51	38	22	40	122	138	14%	87	2%	0%	27	37%	44%	6.45	18.6	54	110	$14
10	MIL	610	70	23	104	1	285	276	316	274	339	464	803	8	83	31	0.49	47	17	36	117	106	13%	71	1%	50%	27	41%	19%	5.59	17.8	54	117	$21
11	MIL	546	46	13	67	0	223	237	169	239	283	346	629	8	81	25	0.43	50	16	34	84	97	9%	78	2%	0%	27	37%	48%	3.13	-23.6	17	38	$3
12	2 TM	318	36	9	41	1	217	240	231	209	282	358	641	8	78	25	0.41	51	16	33	95	104	11%	67	3%	50%	25	28%	56%	3.27	-12.5	23	58	$2
1st Half		179	18	5	22	1	235	244	259	223	315	374	689	11	79	27	0.55	50	17	33	91	104	11%	84	4%	50%	13	38%	54%	3.87	-3.8	27	68	$3
2nd Half		139	18	4	19	0	194	233	203	188	238	338	576	5	77	22	0.25	53	13	34	101	104	11%	52	0%	0%	12	17%	58%	2.55	-8.9	15	38	$0
13	**Proj**	**194**	**21**	**6**	**27**	**0**	**231**	**243**	**227**	**232**	**288**	**376**	**664**	**7**	**80**	**26**	**0.39**	**49**	**16**	**35**	**97**	**106**	**11%**	**67**	**2%**	**29%**				**3.54**	**-10.7**	**25**	**63**	**$3**

McKenry,Michael			Health	A	LIMA Plan	F
Age 28	Bats R	Pos CA	PT/Exp	D	Rand Var	-2
Ht 5' 10"	Wt 215		Consist	C	MM	4003

PRO: Wow, 12 part-time HR and a skills-supported 151 PX from a catcher! CON: Regressed when exposed to more PT in Aug/Sept; a terrible BA drag with shrinking ct%. VERDICT: David Ross redux? Maybe, but our multi-year regression model says to temper those power comparisons for now.

Yr	Tm	AB	R	HR	RBI	SB	BA	xBA	vL	vR	OB	Slg	OPS	bb%	ct%	h%	Eye	G	L	F	PX	xPX	hr/f	Spd	SBO	SB%	#Wk	DOM	DIS	RC/G	RAR	BPV	BPX	R$
08																																		
09	aa	358	41	10	40	2	256	269			335	414	748	11	80	30	0.58				107			85	4%	42%				4.66		41	0	$5
10	COL *	355	26	7	29	1	210	195		0	252	326	577	5	75	26	0.22	67	0	33	90	-5	0%	75	3%	34%	4	25%	50%	2.61	-18.5	-5	-11	-$2
11	PIT *	275	25	4	20	1	229	220	167	239	292	337	629	8	72	30	0.32	39	20	41	93	86	4%	77	3%	44%	15	20%	60%	3.22	-8.9	-8	-18	$0
12	PIT	240	25	12	39	0	233	222	241	231	316	442	758	11	70	28	0.40	35	14	51	151	147	14%	57	0%	0%	27	44%	52%	4.64	2.5	26	65	$4
1st Half		87	9	5	12	0	241	210	250	239	327	471	798	11	67	30	0.38	42	8	50	171	122	17%	78	0%	0%	13	46%	54%	5.17	2.5	31	78	$0
2nd Half		153	16	7	27	0	229	229	237	226	310	425	735	11	71	27	0.41	32	16	52	141	161	12%	49	0%	0%	14	43%	50%	4.35	0.6	25	63	$6
13	**Proj**	**285**	**28**	**11**	**35**	**1**	**232**	**225**	**214**	**237**	**304**	**403**	**707**	**9**	**72**	**29**	**0.37**	**37**	**16**	**47**	**125**	**121**	**11%**	**65**	**2%**	**50%**				**4.04**	**-1.5**	**18**	**44**	**$4**

McLouth,Nate			Health	D	LIMA Plan	D+
Age 31	Bats L	Pos LF	PT/Exp	D	Rand Var	+2
Ht 5' 11"	Wt 180		Consist	A	MM	2315

7-20-.241 in 266 AB at ATL/BAL. Sometimes you've gotta hit rock bottom. After a fully earned release from ATL, flashes of the old power/speed combo resurfaced with BAL. Can't hit lefties, health remains a risk, and two months is hardly a definitive sample. But he owns the skills, and in a platoon... UP .270, 20/20.

Yr	Tm	AB	R	HR	RBI	SB	BA	xBA	vL	vR	OB	Slg	OPS	bb%	ct%	h%	Eye	G	L	F	PX	xPX	hr/f	Spd	SBO	SB%	#Wk	DOM	DIS	RC/G	RAR	BPV	BPX	R$
08	PIT	597	113	26	94	23	276	285	261	282	347	497	845	10	84	29	0.70	35	19	47	138	133	11%	97	17%	88%	27	67%	11%	6.22	28.2	109	214	$28
09	2 NL	507	86	20	70	19	256	262	230	269	344	436	780	12	80	28	0.69	40	17	43	112	100	11%	87	17%	76%	25	56%	12%	5.15	8.6	69	141	$18
10	ATL *	370	43	10	37	12	187	226	135	205	277	309	586	11	77	21	0.55	40	16	44	83	120	8%	90	15%	86%	18	33%	44%	2.77	-23.1	28	61	$1
11	ATL	267	35	4	16	4	228	237	179	251	338	333	671	14	81	27	0.85	47	17	36	74	82	5%	112	7%	67%	15	33%	33%	3.70	-7.0	36	80	$1
12	2 TM *	446	61	15	45	16	224	250	197	255	290	378	668	8	79	25	0.44	43	20	37	97	116	9%	96	16%	94%	18	28%	39%	3.75	-11.0	48	120	$10
1st Half		135	10	2	10	2	156	225	0	157	219	225	444	8	74	20	0.31	38	28	33	53	66	0%	69	9%	100%	8	0%	75%	1.55	-13.9	-27	-68	-$13
2nd Half		311	51	14	35	14	254	267	217	289	320	445	765	9	81	27	0.52	44	18	38	114	128	11%	108	18%	93%	10	50%	10%	5.06	3.8	74	185	$19
13	**Proj**	**407**	**54**	**11**	**38**	**12**	**231**	**241**	**174**	**252**	**313**	**364**	**677**	**11**	**79**	**27**	**0.57**	**42**	**20**	**38**	**86**	**102**	**9%**	**93**	**12%**	**87%**				**3.87**	**-9.7**	**39**	**98**	**$9**

Mesoraco,Devin			Health	A	LIMA Plan	D
Age 25	Bats R	Pos CA	PT/Exp	D	Rand Var	+3
Ht 6' 1"	Wt 225		Consist	C	MM	3013

Safe to say no one predicted his biggest headline would be bumping an umpire. Of course, that's the way things can go for rookie catchers. Still has the power skills history that made many expect a more positive first impression, but a history of problems hitting RHP suggests his development will take some time.

Yr	Tm	AB	R	HR	RBI	SB	BA	xBA	vL	vR	OB	Slg	OPS	bb%	ct%	h%	Eye	G	L	F	PX	xPX	hr/f	Spd	SBO	SB%	#Wk	DOM	DIS	RC/G	RAR	BPV	BPX	R$
08																																		
09																																		
10	a/a	239	37	14	35	1	255	293			310	501	811	7	76	28	0.34				161			109	4%	42%				5.23		75	0	$7
11	CIN *	486	50	15	60	1	244	245	250	167	304	409	713	8	78	28	0.40	40	15	45	121	83	11%	73	2%	40%	5	40%	20%	4.16	-1.8	41	91	$8
12	CIN	165	17	5	14	1	212	238	308	183	286	352	637	9	80	24	0.52	45	17	38	92	80	10%	65	5%	50%	22	32%	41%	3.19	-5.5	26	65	-$1
1st Half		105	12	4	9	1	200	238	290	162	288	362	650	11	77	22	0.54	44	16	40	107	106	13%	62	8%	50%	13	31%	38%	3.23	-3.3	31	78	$0
2nd Half		60	5	1	5	0	233	233	375	212	281	333	615	6	85	26	0.44	47	18	35	67	38	6%	80	0%	0%	9	33%	44%	3.12	-2.0	14	35	-$2
13	**Proj**	**290**	**31**	**10**	**31**	**1**	**244**	**246**	**332**	**222**	**304**	**406**	**709**	**8**	**80**	**27**	**0.43**	**44**	**16**	**40**	**107**	**73**	**11%**	**68**	**3%**	**50%**				**4.11**	**-0.9**	**36**	**89**	**$5**

Middlebrooks,Will			Health	B	LIMA Plan	D+
Age 24	Bats R	Pos 3B	PT/Exp	F	Rand Var	-1
Ht 6' 4"	Wt 225		Consist	D	MM	4215

15-54-.288 in 267 AB at BOS. Broken wrist prematurely ended what was shaping up to be a productive indoctrination to the bigs. Clearly, there are some holes: mainly, that poor Eye all but assures a BA drop. That said, beefy power skills held up well with BOS, and HR-hitting 3B are valuable commodities.

Yr	Tm	AB	R	HR	RBI	SB	BA	xBA	vL	vR	OB	Slg	OPS	bb%	ct%	h%	Eye	G	L	F	PX	xPX	hr/f	Spd	SBO	SB%	#Wk	DOM	DIS	RC/G	RAR	BPV	BPX	R$
08																																		
09																																		
10																																		
11	a/a	427	45	15	68	7	258	248			288	425	713	4	71	33	0.15				131			72	9%	86%				4.24		23	0	$12
12	BOS *	360	49	22	76	6	292	276	300	282	327	529	856	5	75	34	0.21	44	22	35	152	119	21%	72	10%	75%	15	40%	33%	6.19	16.6	55	138	$18
1st Half		261	40	17	59	4	304	285	304	304	338	561	899	5	76	34	0.22	43	20	36	163	128	21%	72	11%	68%	9	33%	22%	6.82	16.2	70	175	$26
2nd Half		99	9	5	17	2	263	250	294	246	298	444	743	5	72	32	0.18	44	24	32	119	101	22%	81	9%	100%	6	50%	50%	4.70	0.3	6	15	-$2
13	**Proj**	**534**	**60**	**23**	**88**	**9**	**271**	**253**	**288**	**262**	**304**	**452**	**756**	**5**	**73**	**33**	**0.18**	**44**	**22**	**34**	**125**	**112**	**18%**	**75**	**9%**	**86%**				**4.85**	**4.1**	**24**	**61**	**$21**

Molina,Jose			Health	B	LIMA Plan	F
Age 38	Bats R	Pos CA	PT/Exp	F	Rand Var	+1
Ht 6' 2"	Wt 250		Consist	C	MM	2111

Don't say we didn't warn you. Why, in this very space a mere one year ago, it was stated quite clearly that the one-and-only positive-RAR, over-$1 season in his long and sibling-overshadowed career was, without a shadow of a doubt, NOT repeatable in any way. We said that. But with fewer hyphens.

Yr	Tm	AB	R	HR	RBI	SB	BA	xBA	vL	vR	OB	Slg	OPS	bb%	ct%	h%	Eye	G	L	F	PX	xPX	hr/f	Spd	SBO	SB%	#Wk	DOM	DIS	RC/G	RAR	BPV	BPX	R$
08	NYY	268	32	3	18	0	216	245	188	230	250	313	563	4	81	26	0.23	48	19	33	75	76	4%	55	0%	0%	27	30%	48%	2.55	-13.0	6	12	-$3
09	NYY	138	15	1	11	0	217	206	220	216	289	268	558	9	80	27	0.50	39	19	42	37	69	2%	73	0%	0%	19	32%	63%	2.53	-6.7	-21	-43	-$2
10	TOR	167	13	6	12	1	246	249	174	273	284	377	661	5	78	28	0.25	43	22	35	83	123	13%	65	3%	100%	26	23%	58%	3.65	-2.3	1	2	$1
11	TOR	171	19	3	15	2	281	249	276	283	339	415	754	8	74	36	0.34	43	22	35	109	90	7%	72	6%	67%	26	31%	58%	4.94	3.9	24	53	$3
12	TAM	251	27	8	32	3	223	239	170	235	280	355	635	7	76	26	0.33	52	18	29	87	83	14%	46	7%	75%	27	19%	67%	3.26	-6.6	7	18	$2
1st Half		123	12	4	13	0	195	223	130	210	256	333	589	8	75	23	0.32	57	15	28	94	76	15%	53	0%	0%	13	23%	62%	2.70	-5.9	-2	-5	-$1
2nd Half		128	15	4	19	3	250	243	208	260	304	375	679	7	77	29	0.34	48	21	31	80	91	13%	47	12%	75%	14	14%	71%	3.88	-1.3	8	20	$6
13	**Proj**	**195**	**21**	**5**	**21**	**2**	**243**	**241**	**213**	**253**	**297**	**372**	**669**	**7**	**77**	**29**	**0.33**	**47**	**20**	**32**	**88**	**91**	**11%**	**55**	**6%**	**74%**				**3.71**	**-2.9**	**9**	**22**	**$4**

ROD TRUESDELL

Molina,Yadier

Age 30 Bats R Pos CA
Ht 5' 11" Wt 225

Health	A	LIMA Plan	B
PT/Exp	B	Rand Var	-3
Consist	D	MM	2145

Shattered previous high for total bases in ascent to top-tier C. While line drive, hr/f rates may regress, now pairing excellent ct% with punch. Can't count on double-digit SB again, but opportunistic baserunner has earned an amber light. With no significant 1H/2H or LH/RH splits, his bat now warrants an aggressive bid.

Yr	Tm	AB	R	HR	RBI	SB	BA	xBA	vL	vR	OB	Slg	OPS	bb%	ct%	h%	Eye	G	L	F	PX	xPX	hr/f	Spd	SBO	SB%	#Wk	DOM	DIS	RC/G	RAR	BPV	BPX	R$
08	STL	444	37	7	56	0	304	262	323	296	351	392	743	7	93	31	1.10	46	21	33	53	72	5%	63	1%	0%	26	35%	19%	4.95	8.0	36	71	$12
09	STL	481	45	6	54	9	293	278	248	307	360	383	742	9	92	31	1.28	51	19	30	56	70	5%	61	7%	75%	27	44%	33%	4.97	9.2	51	104	$13
10	STL	465	34	6	62	8	262	269	217	281	323	342	665	8	89	28	0.82	51	21	28	54	85	5%	54	9%	67%	25	32%	44%	3.79	-6.7	32	70	$9
11	STL	475	55	14	65	4	305	291	284	311	350	465	816	6	91	31	0.75	45	20	35	101	101	9%	57	7%	44%	27	56%	22%	5.79	19.7	74	164	$19
12	STL	505	65	22	76	12	315	300	342	307	371	501	872	8	89	32	0.82	40	25	35	107	112	14%	62	10%	80%	27	67%	7%	6.93	36.2	80	200	$26
1st Half		257	33	12	44	7	311	311	388	293	359	510	868	7	89	31	0.70	43	25	32	113	92	16%	56	11%	88%	13	69%	8%	6.86	18.5	84	210	$29
2nd Half		248	32	10	32	5	319	289	306	323	383	492	875	9	89	33	0.93	37	25	38	100	133	12%	73	9%	71%	14	64%	7%	6.99	18.6	72	180	$24
13	**Proj**	**516**	**58**	**18**	**72**	**9**	**303**	**289**	**296**	**306**	**358**	**463**	**820**	**8**	**90**	**31**	**0.83**	**43**	**22**	**34**	**93**	**103**	**11%**	**57**	**8%**	**69%**				**5.99**	**25.4**	**68**	**169**	**$21**

Montero,Jesus

Age 23 Bats R Pos DH CA
Ht 6' 3" Wt 235

Health	A	LIMA Plan	C
PT/Exp	B	Rand Var	0
Consist	B	MM	3035

Disappointing year in light of hype machine. Minor-league power and 2011's hr/f raised expectations but he didn't get airborne enough. Walk rate and Eye show more work is needed, but 2H gains in ct% and BA vs. RHP confirm his still enormous upside. Patience.

Yr	Tm	AB	R	HR	RBI	SB	BA	xBA	vL	vR	OB	Slg	OPS	bb%	ct%	h%	Eye	G	L	F	PX	xPX	hr/f	Spd	SBO	SB%	#Wk	DOM	DIS	RC/G	RAR	BPV	BPX	R$
08																																		
09	aa	167	19	10	33	0	318	302			373	557	930	8	87	32	0.68				134			76	0%	0%				7.76		76	0	$7
10	aaa	453	58	21	66	0	275	291			336	495	831	8	79	31	0.43				149			90	0%	0%				5.85		66	0	$14
11	NYY *	481	55	22	70	0	281	273	500	216	336	469	804	8	75	33	0.33	39	27	34	130	155	27%	75	0%	0%	5	60%	40%	5.58	9.4	27	60	$16
12	SEA	515	46	15	62	0	260	253	322	228	300	386	686	5	81	30	0.29	43	25	33	80	92	11%	61	2%	0%	28	25%	54%	3.92	-14.5	4	10	$10
1st Half		265	24	8	28	0	253	246	359	209	290	389	679	5	75	31	0.22	43	24	33	94	87	12%	75	3%	0%	14	29%	57%	3.72	-9.2	-5	-13	$9
2nd Half		250	22	7	34	0	268	264	293	252	309	384	693	6	86	29	0.44	42	25	33	68	96	10%	56	0%	0%	14	21%	50%	4.14	-5.4	18	45	$10
13	**Proj**	**490**	**51**	**22**	**68**	**0**	**274**	**278**	**389**	**211**	**323**	**459**	**782**	**7**	**80**	**30**	**0.37**	**41**	**26**	**33**	**114**	**117**	**17%**	**64**	**1%**	**0%**				**5.18**	**4.0**	**34**	**84**	**$16**

Montero,Miguel

Age 29 Bats L Pos CA
Ht 5' 11" Wt 213

Health	B	LIMA Plan	C
PT/Exp	B	Rand Var	-5
Consist	A	MM	3015

2012 results mirrored previous years despite continued disparities in hit tool. Fluctuations in BA vs LHP, BA/xBA gap and ct% drop are disconcerting for veteran hitter. Lots of grounders and plateau in flyball rate limit the possibility of a power spike. Inconsistent BPIs raise his risk factor. Feeling lucky?

Yr	Tm	AB	R	HR	RBI	SB	BA	xBA	vL	vR	OB	Slg	OPS	bb%	ct%	h%	Eye	G	L	F	PX	xPX	hr/f	Spd	SBO	SB%	#Wk	DOM	DIS	RC/G	RAR	BPV	BPX	R$
08	ARI *	216	26	6	21	0	251	262	286	250	321	422	743	9	76	31	0.42	36	22	41	127	136	9%	79	0%	0%	24	38%	58%	4.62	2.1	39	76	$1
09	ARI	425	61	16	59	1	294	281	329	286	352	478	830	8	82	33	0.49	44	20	36	119	126	13%	74	3%	33%	27	48%	26%	5.98	20.0	51	104	$14
10	ARI	297	36	9	43	0	266	257	213	286	331	438	769	9	76	32	0.41	38	19	43	126	134	9%	76	1%	0%	18	28%	39%	4.97	5.8	41	89	$7
11	ARI	493	65	18	86	1	282	281	195	308	344	469	813	9	80	32	0.48	42	22	36	131	136	13%	53	2%	50%	27	48%	33%	5.70	19.6	59	131	$18
12	ARI	486	65	15	88	0	286	239	259	299	379	438	818	13	73	36	0.56	43	21	36	108	121	12%	91	0%	0%	27	33%	52%	5.94	22.4	20	50	$17
1st Half		226	32	8	43	0	279	232	188	318	366	434	799	12	71	36	0.48	47	19	34	108	125	15%	88	0%	0%	13	23%	54%	5.61	8.9	11	28	$16
2nd Half		260	33	7	45	0	292	246	312	281	391	442	833	14	75	37	0.65	39	23	38	108	118	9%	91	0%	0%	14	43%	50%	6.23	14.5	26	65	$17
13	**Proj**	**480**	**63**	**14**	**80**	**0**	**271**	**250**	**237**	**284**	**351**	**429**	**780**	**11**	**76**	**33**	**0.52**	**41**	**21**	**37**	**112**	**128**	**10%**	**74**	**1%**	**33%**				**5.24**	**14.1**	**31**	**78**	**$15**

Moore,Scott

Age 29 Bats L Pos 3B
Ht 6' 2" Wt 195

Health	A	LIMA Plan	F
PT/Exp	D	Rand Var	-1
Consist	B	MM	4111

9-26-.259 in 201 AB at HOU. PRO: Doubled his career plate appearances; strong FB, PX and hr/f speak to power. CON: Lots of Ks will cap BA; at 29, this might have been his peak season. Sock and strong defense have likely earned him a bench role, but has little upside.

Yr	Tm	AB	R	HR	RBI	SB	BA	xBA	vL	vR	OB	Slg	OPS	bb%	ct%	h%	Eye	G	L	F	PX	xPX	hr/f	Spd	SBO	SB%	#Wk	DOM	DIS	RC/G	RAR	BPV	BPX	R$
08	BAL *	295	33	7	35	2	210	130		125	257	351	608	6	74	26	0.24	0	0	100	104	155	20%	98	4%	100%	2	50%	50%	2.94	-15.1	17	33	-$1
09	aaa	123	16	7	18	1	225	284			264	433	698	5	80	23	0.27				126			84	4%	100%				3.80		49	0	$1
10	BAL *	311	33	12	43	4	226	244	0	222	279	376	655	7	76	26	0.31	46	18	37	98	76	12%	89	11%	55%	10	20%	70%	3.35	-12.0	17	37	$4
11	aaa	363	34	5	30	2	216	215			272	311	583	7	72	29	0.28				74			97	4%	57%				2.73		-15	0	-$1
12	HOU *	446	51	15	58	2	244	250	182	263	301	416	718	8	72	31	0.29	29	27	45	129	133	14%	79	7%	26%	15	27%	53%	4.05	-7.4	21	53	$8
1st Half		252	28	6	32	2	237	350	0	500	295	396	691	8	71	31	0.28	33	67	0	127	72	0%	90	11%	31%	1	0%	100%	3.67	-7.0	20	50	$8
2nd Half		194	23	9	26	0	253	255	200	255	310	443	753	8	73	30	0.31	28	26	46	131	134	14%	78	2%	0%	14	29%	50%	4.58	0.0	23	58	$8
13	**Proj**	**162**	**18**	**7**	**19**	**1**	**233**	**245**	**116**	**239**	**289**	**410**	**699**	**7**	**73**	**28**	**0.30**	**35**	**22**	**42**	**122**	**111**	**13%**	**85**	**6%**	**43%**				**3.84**	**-3.6**	**24**	**60**	**$3**

Moore,Tyler

Age 26 Bats R Pos LF
Ht 6' 2" Wt 215

Health	A	LIMA Plan	F
PT/Exp	D	Rand Var	0
Consist	D	MM	4311

10-29-.263 in 156 AB at WAS. MLEs speak to thunder and problems with contact and patience. 4-11-.425 June made 2012's 2nd half fade inevitable as AB dwindled and plate discipline eroded. Still, overall line as fill-in was impressive, and the power is enticing. If he can elevate to a platoon role, a nice endgame pick.

Yr	Tm	AB	R	HR	RBI	SB	BA	xBA	vL	vR	OB	Slg	OPS	bb%	ct%	h%	Eye	G	L	F	PX	xPX	hr/f	Spd	SBO	SB%	#Wk	DOM	DIS	RC/G	RAR	BPV	BPX	R$
08																																		
09																																		
10																																		
11	aa	519	56	25	72	2	237	265			269	453	722	4	71	29	0.15				162			82	2%	100%				4.09		43	0	$11
12	WAS *	257	32	17	49	4	263	273	247	286	323	522	845	8	71	31	0.30	40	22	38	178	148	24%	77	6%	100%	22	41%	50%	5.92	3.6	63	158	$10
1st Half		159	22	11	31	4	293	281	297	409	358	561	919	9	71	35	0.35	37	26	37	178	146	25%	91	9%	100%	8	38%	63%	7.40	9.0	72	180	$15
2nd Half		97	10	6	18	0	216	257	214	220	262	464	726	6	69	25	0.20	42	19	39	178	149	23%	68	0%	0%	14	43%	43%	3.96	-4.2	37	93	$1
13	**Proj**	**197**	**22**	**9**	**33**	**2**	**244**	**252**	**233**	**260**	**290**	**446**	**736**	**6**	**70**	**30**	**0.22**	**40**	**22**	**38**	**145**	**148**	**17%**	**78**	**4%**	**100%**				**4.41**	**-1.4**	**31**	**78**	**$5**

Morales,Kendrys

Age 30 Bats B Pos DH 1B
Ht 6' 1" Wt 225

Health	F	LIMA Plan	C
PT/Exp	F	Rand Var	0
Consist	B	MM	4035

Shed 1H rust to earn 500 plate appearances for the first time in 3 years. Be aware of 2H hr/f, groundball tendency and shadow of health issues, but he gained traction and strength as season progressed. As ct% and Eye inch back to pre-injury levels, a return to 2009 heights may be just around the corner.

Yr	Tm	AB	R	HR	RBI	SB	BA	xBA	vL	vR	OB	Slg	OPS	bb%	ct%	h%	Eye	G	L	F	PX	xPX	hr/f	Spd	SBO	SB%	#Wk	DOM	DIS	RC/G	RAR	BPV	BPX	R$
08	LAA *	378	39	13	52	1	270	243	214	213	301	419	720	4	85	29	0.29	41	15	44	92	70	13%	66	6%	13%	7	29%	43%	4.18	-7.7	31	61	$8
09	LAA	566	86	34	108	3	306	300	296	309	358	569	927	8	79	33	0.39	42	17	41	166	159	18%	75	7%	30%	27	59%	19%	7.15	35.4	83	169	$27
10	LAA	193	29	11	39	0	290	289	208	339	332	487	819	6	84	30	0.39	48	21	31	113	110	22%	60	2%	0%	8	50%	0%	5.68	4.3	50	109	$8
11																																		
12	LAA	484	61	22	73	0	273	267	229	280	317	467	783	6	76	32	0.27	51	20	28	129	109	21%	60	1%	0%	27	37%	44%	5.14	3.4	32	80	$15
1st Half		217	25	8	28	0	281	240	270	283	322	429	750	6	75	34	0.24	49	21	29	98	98	17%	66	0%	0%	13	23%	54%	4.89	0.0	-3	-8	$11
2nd Half		267	36	14	45	0	266	288	182	278	312	498	810	6	77	30	0.30	53	20	28	152	117	25%	61	2%	0%	14	50%	36%	5.32	3.3	58	145	$19
13	**Proj**	**526**	**71**	**27**	**89**	**1**	**281**	**273**	**233**	**295**	**325**	**491**	**815**	**6**	**79**	**31**	**0.31**	**48**	**19**	**33**	**130**	**113**	**20%**	**56**	**3%**	**16%**				**5.52**	**9.5**	**45**	**114**	**$21**

Morel,Brent

Age 26 Bats R Pos 3B
Ht 6' 2" Wt 220

Health	C	LIMA Plan	F
PT/Exp	C	Rand Var	+5
Consist	D	MM	1201

0-5-.177 in 113 AB at CHW. The mirage of Sept 2011 (30% hr/f) quickly evaporated to the 2012 reality of TWO XBH. Last seen in mid-May; gave way to sore back and then hit below .200 in Triple-A. MLEs indicate a (soft) BA proficiency, so injury may have plagued him all year. Best left for someone else to speculate on.

Yr	Tm	AB	R	HR	RBI	SB	BA	xBA	vL	vR	OB	Slg	OPS	bb%	ct%	h%	Eye	G	L	F	PX	xPX	hr/f	Spd	SBO	SB%	#Wk	DOM	DIS	RC/G	RAR	BPV	BPX	R$
08																																		
09																																		
10	CHW*	555	61	12	58	8	280	250	375	184	314	424	738	5	79	34	0.23	49	12	39	105	117	16%	109	11%	60%	5	40%	40%	4.59	0.6	37	80	$15
11	CHW	413	44	10	41	5	245	266	240	246	283	366	648	5	86	26	0.39	49	19	32	78	93	9%	83	10%	56%	27	26%	33%	3.39	-14.2	39	87	$6
12	CHW*	237	24	1	13	4	174	196	200	170	221	209	430	6	70	25	0.20	47	23	30	32	60	0%	79	10%	80%	7	0%	100%	1.46	-23.8	-58	-145	-$4
1st Half		143	18	0	5	4	189	184	200	170	237	209	446	6	67	28	0.19	47	23	30	22	60	0%	91	15%	80%	7	0%	100%	1.61	-13.6	-73	-183	-$4
2nd Half		94	6	1	8	0	150	195			198	209	407	6	74	19	0.22	44	20	36	45			78	0%	0%				1.24		-49	-123	-$6
13	**Proj**	**132**	**13**	**2**	**11**	**2**	**210**	**224**	**221**	**194**	**253**	**294**	**547**	**5**	**77**	**26**	**0.26**	**49**	**19**	**33**	**61**	**62**	**6%**	**82**	**9%**	**65%**				**2.38**	**-9.1**	**-10**	**-25**	**$0**

ROB CARROLL

Moreland,Mitch

Moreland,Mitch		Health	B	LIMA Plan	C
Age 27	Bats L Pos 1B	PT/Exp	C	Rand Var	-1
Ht 6' 2"	Wt 230	Consist	B	MM	4025

Power returned after offseason wrist surgery, until June hamstring injury shelved him for 6 weeks. Roared back with h%-fueled August, but brutal .205/.247/.274 Sept hurt 2H numbers. Just 41 AB vs. LHP, but .457 Slg says he's not hopeless. R$ history, xPX say he'll repeat. With health, more PT... UP: 25 HR, 80 RBI.

Yr	Tm	AB	R	HR	RBI	SB	BA	xBA	vL	vR	OB	Slg	OPS	bb%	ct%	h%	Eye	G	L	F	PX	xPX	hr/f	Spd	SBO	SB%	#Wk	DOM	DIS	RC/G	RAR	BPV	BPX	R$
08																																		
09	aa	301	40	7	46	1	291	273			331	436	767	6	84	33	0.38				90			99	2%	41%				5.12		45	0	$8
10	TEX *	498	57	18	72	4	249	273	200	264	329	425	754	11	78	28	0.55	40	23	38	121	152	21%	59	5%	67%	11	36%	36%	4.72	-8.3	52	113	$11
11	TEX	464	60	16	51	2	259	250	234	266	316	414	730	8	80	29	0.42	42	18	40	104	105	11%	75	3%	50%	27	41%	41%	4.44	-11.4	38	84	$11
12	TEX	327	41	15	50	1	275	262	239	281	323	468	791	7	78	31	0.32	42	20	38	125	128	15%	70	3%	50%	22	36%	32%	5.26	-0.1	39	98	$10
1st Half		158	25	10	25	0	272	281	167	291	324	513	836	7	80	28	0.39	45	19	37	145	119	21%	69	0%	0%	12	50%	17%	5.81	2.0	63	158	$12
2nd Half		169	16	5	25	1	278	244	318	272	322	426	748	6	76	34	0.28	40	21	39	105	136	10%	77	5%	50%	10	20%	50%	4.76	-2.9	13	33	$9
13	Proj	422	52	20	64	2	269	266	239	275	322	467	789	7	79	30	0.38	41	20	39	126	124	15%	70	3%	54%				5.19	-2.0	48	120	$12

Morgan,Nyjer

Morgan,Nyjer		Health	C	LIMA Plan	F
Age 32	Bats L Pos CF RF	PT/Exp	C	Rand Var	0
Ht 5' 10"	Wt 184	Consist	F	MM	1513

A ct% dip, another h% regression, and a .523 OPS with 0 RBI start through the end of May buried him. Spd is intact, but SBO hasn't recovered—and neither his bb% nor SB% have helped. Void of power, his BA will likely determine his playing time. And the past five years of volatility just emphasize his unpredictability.

Yr	Tm	AB	R	HR	RBI	SB	BA	xBA	vL	vR	OB	Slg	OPS	bb%	ct%	h%	Eye	G	L	F	PX	xPX	hr/f	Spd	SBO	SB%	#Wk	DOM	DIS	RC/G	RAR	BPV	BPX	R$
08	PIT *	482	66	1	32	42	261	261	240	304	295	327	621	5	82	32	0.26	50	25	26	52	76	0%	130	47%	74%	14	21%	50%	3.29	-20.3	22	43	$19
09	2 NL	469	73	3	39	42	307	264	175	344	361	388	750	8	84	36	0.54	54	19	26	49	41	3%	143	37%	71%	21	29%	29%	5.02	4.4	38	78	$27
10	WAS	509	60	0	24	34	253	256	200	273	308	314	622	7	83	31	0.45	53	22	25	43	53	0%	155	35%	67%	26	27%	46%	3.18	-23.4	23	50	$14
11	MIL	378	61	4	37	13	304	268	209	316	338	421	758	5	81	37	0.27	45	26	29	81	80	5%	125	16%	76%	24	33%	42%	5.20	5.3	45	100	$16
12	MIL	289	44	3	16	12	239	230	263	237	288	308	596	6	78	30	0.32	52	21	27	42	58	5%	135	22%	71%	27	19%	67%	2.95	-15.3	2	5	$5
1st Half		180	29	2	4	7	239	232	200	241	286	294	581	6	80	29	0.33	49	23	29	38	60	5%	112	20%	70%	13	23%	62%	2.80	-10.8	-5	-13	$6
2nd Half		109	15	1	12	5	239	228	333	230	291	330	621	7	75	31	0.30	59	17	24	51	53	5%	141	24%	71%	14	14%	71%	3.18	-5.3	-1	-3	$4
13	Proj	263	38	2	20	13	262	244	230	266	308	347	655	6	80	32	0.33	52	21	27	54	62	4%	131	25%	71%				3.64	-8.9	18	46	$9

Morneau,Justin

Morneau,Justin		Health	F	LIMA Plan	B
Age 32	Bats L Pos 1B DH	PT/Exp	C	Rand Var	0
Ht 6' 4"	Wt 222	Consist	F	MM	3225

Healthy enough to stay on the field for first full season in 3 years. Flashed power of old in April and May, but not afterward—physical repercussions from wrist surgery were reportedly a factor. 2H aided by inflated h%, but bb% and FB% say he's not vintage. Should repeat, maybe more with health and conditioning.

Yr	Tm	AB	R	HR	RBI	SB	BA	xBA	vL	vR	OB	Slg	OPS	bb%	ct%	h%	Eye	G	L	F	PX	xPX	hr/f	Spd	SBO	SB%	#Wk	DOM	DIS	RC/G	RAR	BPV	BPX	R$
08	MIN	623	97	23	129	0	300	294	284	310	376	499	875	11	86	32	0.89	43	19	38	123	109	11%	81	1%	0%	27	56%	15%	6.80	25.9	82	161	$26
09	MIN	508	85	30	100	0	274	289	277	272	364	516	880	12	83	28	0.84	41	16	43	143	141	16%	68	0%	0%	23	61%	13%	6.59	18.8	85	173	$19
10	MIN	296	53	18	56	0	345	312	325	358	439	618	1058	14	79	39	0.81	33	22	45	185	187	17%	93	0%	0%	14	71%	7%	10.57	40.1	107	233	$19
11	MIN *	294	25	5	36	0	233	238	144	270	281	345	626	6	84	26	0.42	35	18	46	84	97	4%	63	0%	0%	15	33%	47%	3.23	-18.1	24	53	$1
12	MIN	505	63	19	77	1	267	263	232	290	332	440	772	9	80	30	0.48	41	22	37	110	115	13%	77	1%	100%	26	27%	35%	5.09	-2.7	42	105	$14
1st Half		222	24	10	34	1	239	270	96	309	305	441	746	9	78	26	0.44	39	22	39	131	126	14%	78	2%	100%	12	25%	33%	4.53	-5.5	53	133	$10
2nd Half		283	39	9	43	0	290	257	312	272	354	438	792	9	81	33	0.52	43	22	35	94	106	11%	78	0%	0%	14	29%	36%	5.56	1.6	31	78	$18
13	Proj	539	69	21	84	0	273	267	237	295	341	459	800	9	81	30	0.55	39	21	41	119	122	12%	71	0%	92%				5.50	2.1	53	132	$18

Morrison,Logan

Morrison,Logan		Health	C	LIMA Plan	C+
Age 25	Bats L Pos LF 1B	PT/Exp	C	Rand Var	+3
Ht 6' 3"	Wt 240	Consist	B	MM	3125

He was never right following Dec. knee surgery. Struggled physically from spring training on, until his season ended in July—another knee surgery in Sept. PX/xPX and hr/f declined, but physical issues make his power and chronically underachieving BA tough reads. If healthy, could be overlooked on draft day.

Yr	Tm	AB	R	HR	RBI	SB	BA	xBA	vL	vR	OB	Slg	OPS	bb%	ct%	h%	Eye	G	L	F	PX	xPX	hr/f	Spd	SBO	SB%	#Wk	DOM	DIS	RC/G	RAR	BPV	BPX	R$
08																																		
09	aa	278	42	7	42	8	260	271			389	411	800	17	81	30	1.11				100			93	12%	65%				5.42		68	0	$7
10	FLA *	482	69	6	51	1	273	277	342	257	375	425	800	14	81	33	0.84	48	20	32	108	100	3%	105	3%	18%	11	45%	36%	5.47	0.5	63	137	$10
11	FLA *	486	56	24	75	2	241	281	241	249	318	457	776	10	79	26	0.53	47	18	35	143	129	18%	74	3%	67%	24	63%	25%	4.88	-7.9	71	158	$12
12	MIA	296	30	11	36	1	230	252	213	236	303	399	701	9	80	25	0.53	41	18	41	107	117	11%	59	1%	100%	17	35%	41%	4.01	-12.6	42	105	$3
1st Half		227	25	8	27	0	233	250	221	239	310	401	710	10	81	25	0.60	42	17	40	105	126	11%	64	0%	0%	13	38%	31%	4.13	-8.4	42	105	$5
2nd Half		69	5	3	9	1	217	251	167	228	280	391	671	8	77	24	0.38	36	23	42	112	88	14%	67	7%	100%	4	25%	75%	3.64	-3.6	24	60	-$4
13	Proj	500	55	19	66	4	263	263	265	262	343	447	790	11	79	30	0.58	43	19	37	118	112	13%	67	4%	75%				5.30	9.4	55	137	$15

Morse,Michael

Morse,Michael		Health	F	LIMA Plan	C
Age 31	Bats R Pos LF RF	PT/Exp	C	Rand Var	-2
Ht 6' 5"	Wt 245	Consist	C	MM	4025

Season was delayed until June due to strained lat. Battled thumb, hand and wrist issues from mid-Aug on. GB% spike can likely be traced to injuries, bb% dip and poor pitch selection, but h% and hr/f repeats are tributes to some legit raw power. Durability is now a concern, but he'll be a force once more if healthy.

Yr	Tm	AB	R	HR	RBI	SB	BA	xBA	vL	vR	OB	Slg	OPS	bb%	ct%	h%	Eye	G	L	F	PX	xPX	hr/f	Spd	SBO	SB%	#Wk	DOM	DIS	RC/G	RAR	BPV	BPX	R$
08	SEA	9	0	0	0	0	222	174	250	200	300	333	633	10	56	40	0.25	60	20	20	145	5	0%	88	0%	0%	3	33%	67%	3.28	-0.3	-41	-80	-$2
09	WAS *	477	50	15	77	2	267	255	250	250	310	425	736	6	78	32	0.28	61	11	28	104	127	30%	89	2%	56%	8	38%	38%	4.56	-2.2	25	51	$11
10	WAS *	317	45	17	47	0	276	269	295	287	335	495	829	8	76	32	0.36	46	16	38	144	141	19%	112	1%	0%	22	45%	41%	5.75	9.3	52	113	$10
11	WAS	522	73	31	95	2	303	287	297	304	348	550	897	6	76	35	0.29	44	20	37	173	154	21%	56	4%	40%	27	52%	30%	6.85	30.5	67	149	$27
12	WAS	406	53	18	62	0	291	263	290	291	318	470	788	4	76	34	0.16	55	20	25	116	111	23%	81	1%	0%	19	37%	32%	5.31	6.6	19	48	$15
1st Half		107	16	3	13	0	299	259	314	292	318	439	757	3	77	37	0.12	56	21	23	99	90	16%	83	0%	0%	5	20%	40%	5.08	1.3	5	13	$0
2nd Half		299	37	15	49	0	288	265	278	291	317	482	799	4	76	33	0.18	55	20	25	122	119	26%	82	1%	0%	14	43%	29%	5.39	6.2	24	60	$20
13	Proj	531	71	27	84	1	290	268	289	290	327	496	823	5	76	34	0.23	52	19	30	134	126	22%	76	2%	31%				5.75	16.3	37	93	$22

Moss,Brandon

Moss,Brandon		Health	A	LIMA Plan	D
Age 29	Bats L Pos 1B	PT/Exp	C	Rand Var	-4
Ht 6' 0"	Wt 210	Consist	C	MM	4013

21-52-.291 in 265 AB at OAK. PX/xPX history says power shouldn't be a complete surprise. But until we see confirmation, the double-digit GB% plunge and BA vs. LHPs look like outliers. As does a 36% h% with OAK. Handedness will help him be productive again if he can keep his BA above water. But that's the big question.

Yr	Tm	AB	R	HR	RBI	SB	BA	xBA	vL	vR	OB	Slg	OPS	bb%	ct%	h%	Eye	G	L	F	PX	xPX	hr/f	Spd	SBO	SB%	#Wk	DOM	DIS	RC/G	RAR	BPV	BPX	R$
08	2 TM *	399	42	14	57	3	249	253	267	239	307	440	747	8	69	33	0.27	44	20	36	140	129	13%	95	5%	56%	18	33%	50%	4.52	-9.0	34	67	$6
09	PIT	385	47	7	41	1	236	251	232	237	298	364	662	8	78	29	0.40	44	20	36	86	88	6%	84	6%	17%	27	41%	44%	3.43	-21.7	22	45	$2
10	PIT *	526	53	15	69	8	208	245	0	160	250	347	598	5	73	26	0.21	55	15	30	106	145	0%	83	18%	49%	5	20%	80%	2.64	-46.5	11	24	$4
11	PHI *	442	49	17	60	3	219	196	0	0	293	399	693	9	64	30	0.29	50	0	50	154	2	0%	66	10%	29%	2	0%	50%	3.58	-25.4	13	29	$6
12	OAK *	461	68	30	73	4	255	259	293	290	314	507	822	8	69	30	0.28	33	21	46	179	176	26%	66	4%	78%	18	56%	33%	5.45	2.1	56	140	$16
1st Half		263	31	16	33	3	211	233	176	240	269	437	706	7	70	23	0.27	29	17	55	153	232	30%	68	5%	100%	4	50%	50%	3.84	-12.3	40	100	$12
2nd Half		198	37	14	40	1	313	277	341	306	373	601	974	9	67	40	0.29	34	23	43	214	159	24%	68	4%	50%	14	57%	29%	8.20	15.3	73	183	$21
13	Proj	257	34	13	39	2	246	247	264	242	307	461	768	8	68	31	0.28	38	20	42	158	144	18%	65	8%	48%				4.64	-5.5	37	93	$8

Moustakas,Mike

Moustakas,Mike		Health	A	LIMA Plan	C+
Age 24	Bats L Pos 3B	PT/Exp	B	Rand Var	0
Ht 6' 0"	Wt 215	Consist	C	MM	3115

Signs of growth faded in 2H, completely collapsing after he sustained a bruised knee in late July. 2H hr/f plunge may be partly injury-related, but xPX says power isn't all that. Combination of stagnant patience and deteriorating ct% aren't BA-friendly. Still young enough to improve, for which there's plenty of room.

Yr	Tm	AB	R	HR	RBI	SB	BA	xBA	vL	vR	OB	Slg	OPS	bb%	ct%	h%	Eye	G	L	F	PX	xPX	hr/f	Spd	SBO	SB%	#Wk	DOM	DIS	RC/G	RAR	BPV	BPX	R$
08																																		
09																																		
10	a/a	484	72	25	95	2	286	316			322	520	842	5	85	29	0.36				149			77	3%	58%				5.94		87	0	$21
11	KC *	561	54	11	62	3	256	249	191	289	301	380	681	6	82	29	0.36	38	20	41	88	83	4%	75	3%	71%	17	24%	47%	3.92	-10.3	31	69	$10
12	KC	563	69	20	73	5	242	236	254	236	291	412	703	6	78	28	0.31	34	16	50	115	109	9%	65	6%	71%	27	41%	41%	4.01	-9.0	40	100	$12
1st Half		269	37	13	38	2	264	250	211	285	322	472	794	8	79	29	0.41	35	14	51	135	115	12%	60	5%	67%	13	62%	15%	5.23	5.1	57	143	$17
2nd Half		294	32	7	35	3	221	224	290	189	261	357	618	5	77	26	0.24	32	19	49	97	102	6%	75	7%	75%	14	21%	64%	3.05	-13.8	20	50	$7
13	Proj	573	67	21	76	4	252	251	233	259	296	428	724	6	81	28	0.32	36	18	46	115	98	10%	67	5%	72%				4.30	-4.7	46	116	$14

JOCK THOMPSON

Murphy,Daniel

Age 28	Bats L	Pos 2B	Health	D	LIMA Plan	C+
Ht 6' 2"	Wt 205		PT/Exp	C	Rand Var	-1
			Consist	D	MM	2245

Decent rebound from torn MCL that put premature end to 2011. Power remains subpar amid ct% dip and stagnant plate patience. But he reprised the LD stroke and even upped his SB count via unexpected SB%. His xBA history says to expect more BA-heavy numbers, but shaky defense threatens his playing time.

Yr	Tm	AB	R	HR	RBI	SB	BA	xBA	vL	vR	OB	Slg	OPS	bb%	ct%	h%	Eye	G	L	F	PX	xPX	hr/f	Spd	SBO	SB%	#Wk	DOM	DIS	RC/G	RAR	BPV	BPX	R$
08	NYM *	492	72	13	72	12	282	310	400	306	350	439	789	9	84	32	0.64	41	33	25	102	86	8%	103	14%	60%	10	50%	50%	5.28	13.2	66	129	$18
09	NYM	508	60	12	63	4	266	280	223	275	317	427	744	7	86	29	0.55	40	19	41	103	96	7%	83	5%	67%	27	48%	30%	4.67	4.7	68	139	$10
10	aaa	34	3	1	6	1	238	294			254	370	624	2	93	24	0.30				87			93	13%	100%				3.24		64	0	-$1
11	NYM	391	49	6	49	5	320	289	299	326	359	448	807	6	89	35	0.57	47	22	31	88	95	6%	91	9%	50%	20	40%	25%	5.80	15.4	63	140	$16
12	NYM	571	62	6	65	10	291	285	283	294	333	403	736	6	86	33	0.44	51	24	25	79	55	5%	86	8%	83%	27	41%	37%	4.86	8.2	46	115	$17
1st Half		289	30	3	38	5	280	288	248	298	325	391	716	6	88	31	0.53	53	23	24	78	62	5%	73	8%	83%	13	46%	31%	4.54	2.3	50	125	$17
2nd Half		282	32	3	27	5	301	280	326	291	341	415	756	6	84	35	0.37	48	26	26	80	48	5%	102	8%	83%	14	36%	43%	5.21	7.4	39	98	$18
13	Proj	**491**	**58**	**8**	**59**	**8**	**295**	**286**	**286**	**297**	**340**	**427**	**766**	**6**	**86**	**33**	**0.50**	**47**	**24**	**29**	**88**	**74**	**7%**	**88**	**8%**	**69%**				**5.19**	**12.7**	**55**	**137**	**$16**

Murphy,David

Age 31	Bats L	Pos LF	Health	A	LIMA Plan	C+
Ht 6' 4"	Wt 205		PT/Exp	B	Rand Var	-3
			Consist	D	MM	3335

Weird route to a fine season. Followed up power-and-patience-driven 1H with successful ct%-fueled 2H. Zero HR—for second straight year—and anomalous 44% h% vs. LHP. Just one 2H HR in Arlington summer, in spite of season-long FB rebound. History says he'll be profitable again; consistency warns against betting on how.

Yr	Tm	AB	R	HR	RBI	SB	BA	xBA	vL	vR	OB	Slg	OPS	bb%	ct%	h%	Eye	G	L	F	PX	xPX	hr/f	Spd	SBO	SB%	#Wk	DOM	DIS	RC/G	RAR	BPV	BPX	R$
08	TEX	415	64	15	74	7	275	278	258	282	325	465	790	7	83	30	0.44	42	18	40	120	105	11%	108	9%	78%	19	68%	21%	5.31	8.8	75	147	$14
09	TEX	432	61	17	57	9	269	255	235	279	343	447	790	10	75	32	0.46	38	19	43	120	97	12%	98	11%	69%	27	44%	41%	5.28	8.9	43	88	$13
10	TEX	419	54	12	65	14	291	277	272	298	360	449	809	10	83	33	0.63	44	19	36	106	95	9%	99	13%	88%	26	58%	27%	5.94	16.0	68	148	$18
11	TEX	404	46	11	46	11	275	264	215	296	330	401	731	8	85	30	0.54	54	17	29	78	82	11%	113	15%	65%	27	41%	44%	4.53	-0.4	45	100	$13
12	TEX	457	65	15	61	10	304	279	347	296	378	479	857	11	84	34	0.73	43	21	35	110	109	11%	102	10%	67%	27	48%	22%	6.52	24.7	72	180	$20
1st Half		191	28	9	32	6	288	274	321	282	379	497	876	13	79	33	0.68	44	20	37	134	131	16%	97	11%	86%	13	38%	15%	6.85	11.8	74	185	$19
2nd Half		266	37	6	29	4	316	283	362	306	377	466	843	9	88	34	0.79	43	22	35	95	96	7%	105	10%	50%	14	57%	29%	6.28	11.9	69	173	$21
13	Proj	**443**	**59**	**14**	**59**	**11**	**292**	**270**	**280**	**295**	**359**	**452**	**811**	**9**	**84**	**32**	**0.64**	**46**	**20**	**35**	**100**	**100**	**11%**	**101**	**12%**	**70%**				**5.77**	**14.0**	**61**	**153**	**$20**

Murphy,Donnie

Age 30	Bats R	Pos 3B	Health	D	LIMA Plan	F
Ht 5' 10"	Wt 190		PT/Exp	F	Rand Var	+2
			Consist	F	MM	3201

3-12-.216 in 116 AB at FLA. Still flashing a little pop whenever he gets a chance, but age and BA/xBA history keep him locked into utility infielder / bench role. Sub-par patience, contact, running game... what am I missing? Oh, and sub-par chance of being profitable to any meaningful degree, regardless of format.

Yr	Tm	AB	R	HR	RBI	SB	BA	xBA	vL	vR	OB	Slg	OPS	bb%	ct%	h%	Eye	G	L	F	PX	xPX	hr/f	Spd	SBO	SB%	#Wk	DOM	DIS	RC/G	RAR	BPV	BPX	R$
08	OAK *	244	28	11	33	3	204	232	196	175	255	391	646	6	63	27	0.19	38	23	39	147	122	12%	106	9%	73%	14	14%	71%	3.18	-10.9	10	20	$0
09	aaa																																	
10	FLA *	250	30	11	40	0	234	281	500	250	273	439	711	5	71	29	0.18	32	32	36	154	214	33%	101	0%	0%	9	67%	33%	3.98	-4.6	35	76	$4
11	FLA *	115	12	2	10	0	160	209	160	197	200	276	476	5	77	19	0.23	39	13	49	84	109	6%	95	0%	0%	9	22%	56%	1.68	-11.0	11	24	-$4
12	MIA *	222	28	11	29	2	220	242	128	275	282	436	718	8	68	27	0.27	40	18	41	154	104	9%	99	6%	63%	17	24%	65%	3.98	-4.2	37	93	$3
1st Half		91	13	6	11	1	163	240	118	143	237	390	628	9	70	16	0.33	44	13	44	152	153	14%	72	7%	100%	9	22%	67%	2.87	-5.1	42	105	-$1
2nd Half		131	15	5	18	1	260	240	133	366	314	468	782	7	66	35	0.23	38	22	40	154	74	5%	113	6%	41%	8	25%	63%	4.92	1.3	30	75	$5
13	Proj	**131**	**16**	**3**	**16**	**1**	**205**	**215**	**159**	**230**	**257**	**347**	**604**	**7**	**70**	**27**	**0.23**	**39**	**17**	**44**	**105**	**109**	**8%**	**92**	**4%**	**68%**				**2.85**	**-7.1**	**5**	**12**	**$1**

Myers,Wil

Age 22	Bats R	Pos RF	Health	A	LIMA Plan	D+
Ht 6' 3"	Wt 205		PT/Exp	D	Rand Var	-1
			Consist	F	MM	3203

Highly-touted KC rookie with both BA and power upside blasted 37 HR between AA and AAA at a reasonable age. Should get a shot at substantial playing time sooner than later in 2013. Could turn a small profit, but ct% warns against expecting too much too soon. It may be a year early to be buying in big on this one.

Yr	Tm	AB	R	HR	RBI	SB	BA	xBA	vL	vR	OB	Slg	OPS	bb%	ct%	h%	Eye	G	L	F	PX	xPX	hr/f	Spd	SBO	SB%	#Wk	DOM	DIS	RC/G	RAR	BPV	BPX	R$
08																																		
09																																		
10																																		
11	aa	354	37	5	37	7	225	233			301	334	636	10	74	29	0.43				90			83	10%	76%				3.33		14	0	$3
12	a/a	522	75	25	83	5	279	256			338	492	830	8	72	35	0.31				143			100	6%	58%				5.79		46	0	$21
1st Half		298	51	18	52	4	289	278			352	552	904	9	71	35	0.34				178			115	6%	78%				6.96		80	200	$30
2nd Half		224	24	7	31	1	266	227			319	412	731	7	72	34	0.28				96			115	5%	26%				4.39		-1	-3	$9
13	Proj	**384**	**47**	**10**	**51**	**5**	**256**	**216**			**321**	**402**	**722**	**9**	**73**	**33**	**0.35**	**37**	**16**	**47**	**103**		**8%**	**104**	**7%**	**67%**				**4.38**	**-7.1**	**18**	**46**	**$10**

Nady,Xavier

Age 34	Bats R	Pos LF	Health	F	LIMA Plan	F
Ht 6' 2"	Wt 215		PT/Exp	F	Rand Var	+5
			Consist	B	MM	2200

4-13-.184 in 152 AB at WAS/SF. Never recovered from 2009 elbow injury, struggled again after fractured hand prematurely ended 2011. 2010 GB% is now a baseline; depressed 2011 h% just added to his issues. September power flash suggests bench player upside at best, but health and now age aren't on his side.

Yr	Tm	AB	R	HR	RBI	SB	BA	xBA	vL	vR	OB	Slg	OPS	bb%	ct%	h%	Eye	G	L	F	PX	xPX	hr/f	Spd	SBO	SB%	#Wk	DOM	DIS	RC/G	RAR	BPV	BPX	R$
08	2 TM	555	76	25	97	2	305	298	262	317	350	510	860	7	81	34	0.38	41	25	34	131	122	16%	69	2%	67%	26	58%	15%	6.52	16.6	61	120	$23
09	NYY	28	4	0	2	0	286	299	333	273	310	429	739	3	79	36	0.17	41	27	32	130	63	0%	79	0%	0%	2	50%	0%	4.75	-0.4	41	84	-$1
10	CHC	317	33	6	33	0	256	223	242	265	293	353	647	5	73	33	0.20	47	20	33	76	93	8%	70	0%	0%	27	19%	63%	3.55	-17.3	-25	-54	$4
11	ARI	206	26	4	35	2	248	231	248	248	282	359	642	5	78	30	0.22	47	16	37	86	116	7%	79	4%	100%	20	35%	40%	3.49	-11.7	10	22	$3
12	2 NL *	241	20	7	24	1	187	238	213	156	240	326	566	7	74	22	0.27	51	19	30	96	95	12%	73	2%	100%	16	25%	50%	2.47	-22.6	3	8	-$2
1st Half		102	6	3	6	1	157	236	176	137	211	275	486	6	76	17	0.29	53	21	27	76	78	14%	63	6%	100%	11	18%	64%	1.79	-12.1	-9	-23	-$6
2nd Half		139	14	4	18	0	208	229	292	192	262	364	626	7	72	26	0.25	49	16	35	110	130	8%	89	0%	0%	5	40%	20%	3.07	-9.9	6	15	$0
13	Proj	**66**	**7**	**2**	**8**	**0**	**225**	**231**	**239**	**213**	**270**	**349**	**619**	**6**	**75**	**28**	**0.25**	**48**	**18**	**34**	**88**	**110**	**10%**	**76**	**2%**	**96%**				**3.12**	**-3.1**	**0**	**0**	**$1**

Nakajima,Hiroyuki

Age 30	Bats R	Pos SS	Health	A	LIMA Plan	D+
Ht 5' 11"	Wt 183		PT/Exp	C	Rand Var	-2
			Consist	B	MM	2323

Reportedly didn't want MLB utility/bench job, signed a one-year contract in Japan after spurning NYY offer last winter. Soft MLB MI market suggests he may have better luck this off-season. MLEs suggest mostly-BA plate skills, with a touch of declining speed. The name Tsuyoshi Nishioka should inspire caution, if not fear.

Yr	Tm	AB	R	HR	RBI	SB	BA	xBA	vL	vR	OB	Slg	OPS	bb%	ct%	h%	Eye	G	L	F	PX	xPX	hr/f	Spd	SBO	SB%	#Wk	DOM	DIS	RC/G	RAR	BPV	BPX	R$
08	for *	486	73	13	79	23	309	265			366	452	818	8	81	36	0.49				98			76	19%	80%				6.16	17.0	50	0	$27
09	for *	560	98	13	90	18	288	265			357	430	787	10	81	34	0.56				92			98	18%	57%				5.21	5.2	52	0	$23
10	for *	503	78	12	91	14	293	275			347	448	795	8	82	34	0.46				106			98	14%	71%				5.53	9.1	63	0	$23
11	for *	566	80	10	98	19	277	251			319	380	699	6	84	31	0.40				71			77	14%	89%				4.41	-7.7	41	0	$23
12	for *	497	67	8	72	6	291	255			344	402	745	7	86	33	0.57				74			77	9%	49%				4.78	-1.5	39	0	$16
1st Half																																		
2nd Half																																		
13	Proj	**387**	**61**	**9**	**65**	**13**	**276**	**258**			**333**	**412**	**745**	**8**	**82**	**32**	**0.49**	**45**	**20**	**35**	**89**		**8%**	**96**	**17%**	**72%**				**4.78**	**8.6**	**50**	**125**	**$17**

Napoli,Mike

Age 31	Bats R	Pos CA 1B	Health	C	LIMA Plan	C+
Ht 6' 0"	Wt 215		PT/Exp	C	Rand Var	+1
			Consist	F	MM	5123

Prodigious power at a scarce position is a given. The wildcards are h%, ct% and the resulting BA that are all fluctuating wildly from season to season. Second consecutive year of DL time (strained quad) suggests that durability is becoming an issue. Pay for the HR; still a worthy investment, particularly if he remains in Texas.

Yr	Tm	AB	R	HR	RBI	SB	BA	xBA	vL	vR	OB	Slg	OPS	bb%	ct%	h%	Eye	G	L	F	PX	xPX	hr/f	Spd	SBO	SB%	#Wk	DOM	DIS	RC/G	RAR	BPV	BPX	R$
08	LAA	227	39	20	49	7	273	272	286	270	370	586	956	13	69	31	0.50	31	17	52	208	152	24%	109	15%	70%	22	59%	23%	7.45	21.8	97	190	$12
09	LAA	382	60	20	56	3	272	265	330	253	341	492	833	9	73	32	0.39	38	19	43	149	138	17%	98	6%	50%	27	44%	30%	5.75	17.7	51	104	$12
10	LAA	453	60	26	68	4	238	264	305	208	303	468	771	8	70	28	0.31	38	20	42	168	148	19%	55	6%	67%	26	54%	31%	4.71	7.7	51	111	$12
11	TEX	369	72	30	75	4	320	312	319	320	412	631	1044	14	77	35	0.68	39	20	41	207	187	25%	71	5%	67%	24	63%	25%	9.66	54.8	119	264	$26
12	TEX	352	53	24	56	1	227	239	179	250	333	469	802	14	64	28	0.45	40	19	41	169	157	26%	98	1%	100%	23	39%	48%	5.17	11.0	41	103	$9
1st Half		223	36	12	30	0	238	231	162	275	325	444	769	12	64	31	0.36	39	23	39	146	157	21%	111	0%	0%	13	23%	62%	4.83	4.1	18	45	$11
2nd Half		129	17	12	26	1	209	248	211	209	346	512	858	17	65	21	0.60	42	13	45	206	155	32%	67	3%	100%	10	60%	30%	5.76	6.2	69	173	$6
13	Proj	**364**	**57**	**27**	**65**	**3**	**253**	**261**	**250**	**255**	**353**	**522**	**875**	**13**	**69**	**29**	**0.50**	**39**	**18**	**43**	**182**	**161**	**25%**	**74**	**4%**	**73%**				**6.27**	**22.0**	**69**	**172**	**$15**

JOCK THOMPSON

Nava,Daniel

Age 30	Bats B	Pos LF	Health	B	LIMA Plan	F
Ht 5' 10"	Wt 200		PT/Exp	C	Rand Var	0
			Consist	B	MM	2103

6-33-.243 in 267 AB at BOS. Turned a 36% h% in May/June into signficant fill-in PT. Then he injured his wrist, h% balanced itself out, and his 2H was horrific. Welcome to the temporal existence and pendulum swings of a 30-year-old quad-A player. Catch the right half, and he's a valuable injury fill-in. Otherwise ...

Yr	Tm	AB	R	HR	RBI	SB	BA	xBA	vL	vR	OB	Slg	OPS	bb%	ct%	h%	Eye	G	L	F	PX	xPX	hr/f	Spd	SBO	SB%	#Wk	DOM	DIS	RC/G	RAR	BPV	BPX	R$
08																																		
09	aa	118	19	3	18	0	328	302			422	505	927	14	89	35	1.42				112			92	0%	0%				8.08		88	0	$4
10	BOS *	445	53	8	62	4	245	226	207	250	307	374	681	8	73	32	0.33	39	16	45	106	102	2%	76	7%	54%	16	25%	63%	3.80	-10.2	16	35	$7
11	aaa	441	52	7	36	7	226	238			307	339	646	10	76	28	0.49				89			89	9%	67%				3.41		22	0	$4
12	BOS *	366	53	9	46	4	248	258	185	269	336	399	735	12	78	30	0.60	38	23	38	111	104	8%	64	5%	75%	17	41%	41%	4.55	-0.1	46	115	$7
1st Half		234	40	5	39	4	286	267	200	343	377	449	826	13	80	34	0.72	37	23	40	120	118	7%	74	7%	75%	8	63%	25%	6.05	9.2	66	165	$15
2nd Half		128	12	3	7	0	180	230	171	184	255	297	552	9	73	22	0.38	40	23	36	86	87	9%	65	0%	0%	9	22%	56%	2.36	-9.4	-10	-25	-$7
13	Proj	282	35	5	30	2	238	235	191	254	318	360	678	11	77	29	0.51	39	20	41	92	101	6%	66	5%	68%				3.82	-7.1	24	61	$2

Nelson,Chris

Age 27	Bats R	Pos 3B 2B	Health	D	LIMA Plan	D
Ht 5' 11"	Wt 205		PT/Exp	D	Rand Var	-5
			Consist	C	MM	3223

9-53-.301 in 345 AB at COL. Mgr Jim Tracy kept him out of the last two games of the season to preserve his 38% h%—er, I mean, his .301 BA. Given that his hr/f also looks a bit suspect, a production repeat is a long-shot. Perhaps if he got more AB and rediscovered his contact, but Reliability underscores the risk.

Yr	Tm	AB	R	HR	RBI	SB	BA	xBA	vL	vR	OB	Slg	OPS	bb%	ct%	h%	Eye	G	L	F	PX	xPX	hr/f	Spd	SBO	SB%	#Wk	DOM	DIS	RC/G	RAR	BPV	BPX	R$
08	aa	283	27	2	30	4	207	227			269	299	568	8	75	27	0.34				74			93	9%	79%				2.61		0	0	-$3
09	aa	107	17	3	13	4	260	271			320	437	757	8	80	30	0.42				106			118	23%	64%				4.61		60	0	$2
10	COL *	344	43	8	33	5	259	267	444	188	296	383	679	5	82	30	0.29	52	19	29	81	42	0%	102	11%	60%	8	13%	38%	3.80	-8.1	31	67	$7
11	COL *	469	46	10	48	4	249	264	245	252	273	386	658	3	81	29	0.17	47	21	32	95	101	9%	101	10%	49%	13	46%	38%	3.44	-16.2	31	69	$7
12	COL *	396	52	9	58	3	293	266	307	299	340	441	781	7	75	37	0.29	50	25	25	106	105	14%	109	4%	54%	24	38%	38%	5.32	7.8	24	60	$12
1st Half		186	23	5	26	2	263	262	362	233	320	419	739	8	74	33	0.33	53	22	25	110	105	17%	97	5%	61%	12	33%	33%	4.59	0.1	27	68	$9
2nd Half		195	27	4	30	1	323	269	259	348	362	467	829	6	75	41	0.25	48	28	25	103	104	11%	115	2%	100%	12	42%	42%	6.41	9.5	22	55	$14
13	Proj	297	36	7	37	3	274	267	276	274	316	423	739	6	78	33	0.27	49	24	28	101	103	12%	109	7%	62%				4.62	0.4	30	75	$9

Nickeas,Mike

Age 30	Bats R	Pos CA	Health	A	LIMA Plan	F
Ht 6' 0"	Wt 215		PT/Exp	F	Rand Var	-2
			Consist	C	MM	1000

1-13-.174 in 109 AB at NYM. His .364/.405/.500 line in 66 AB in Triple-A in 2012 (pick one): a) was abnormal; b) should be considered his career peak; c) shows that ANYONE can get hot in a small sample. (Okay, pick all three.) While a 1.000 OPS is impressive, a 1000 Mayberry score is not.

Yr	Tm	AB	R	HR	RBI	SB	BA	xBA	vL	vR	OB	Slg	OPS	bb%	ct%	h%	Eye	G	L	F	PX	xPX	hr/f	Spd	SBO	SB%	#Wk	DOM	DIS	RC/G	RAR	BPV	BPX	R$
08	a/a	214	14	2	16	0	175	207			234	247	481	7	73	23	0.29				58			82	3%	0%				1.74		-36	0	-$7
09	a/a	61	2	0	6	0	136	181			232	149	381	11	76	18	0.52				13			91	0%	0%				1.02		-58	0	-$4
10	NYM *	303	19	3	22	1	210	216	0	286	289	282	571	10	78	26	0.50	40	20	40	57	-5	0%	76	2%	35%	4	0%	75%	2.60	-15.8	-15	-33	-$3
11	NYM *	221	15	2	17	0	161	195	115	259	214	226	440	6	80	19	0.34	36	17	48	49	55	5%	68	2%	0%	10	20%	70%	1.43	-20.8	-16	-36	-$6
12	NYM *	175	15	2	17	0	207	207	217	122	258	277	535	6	78	26	0.31	43	19	38	54	54	3%	61	0%	0%	18	17%	61%	2.29	-10.8	-22	-55	-$2
1st Half		85	7	1	12	0	188	215	250	133	250	259	509	8	79	23	0.39	42	21	37	51	56	4%	67	0%	0%	12	25%	42%	2.03	-5.9	-19	-48	-$3
2nd Half		90	8	1	5	0	224	170	150	0	266	294	559	5	77	28	0.25	50	7	43	56	42	0%	65	0%	0%	6	0%	100%	2.56	-4.5	-26	-65	-$2
13	Proj	65	5	1	5	0	194	209	203	186	250	275	525	7	78	24	0.33	39	19	41	59	56	4%	72	1%	19%				2.15	-4.3	-18	-45	-$1

Nieuwenhuis,Kirk

Age 25	Bats L	Pos CF LF RF	Health	A	LIMA Plan	F
Ht 6' 3"	Wt 215		PT/Exp	C	Rand Var	-1
			Consist	B	MM	2201

An obscene 45% hit rate led to .325/.379/.475 April; writers and analysts brushed up on spelling skills. It was irrelevant by early August, when foot injury ended his season after pitchers had found and exploited the ample holes in his swing. Versatile in OF, but ct%, fluky hr/f, poor SB% point to future backup.

Yr	Tm	AB	R	HR	RBI	SB	BA	xBA	vL	vR	OB	Slg	OPS	bb%	ct%	h%	Eye	G	L	F	PX	xPX	hr/f	Spd	SBO	SB%	#Wk	DOM	DIS	RC/G	RAR	BPV	BPX	R$
08																																		
09	aa	32	7	1	2	1	371	267			428	592	1021	9	67	54	0.30				170			117	18%	42%				9.25		60	0	$0
10	a/a	514	65	12	55	9	228	248			271	379	650	6	71	30	0.20				124			96	18%	54%				3.23		23	0	$7
11	aaa	188	26	5	11	4	236	231			324	396	721	12	64	34	0.36				143			108	13%	63%				4.20		25	0	$1
12	NYM	282	40	7	28	4	252	222	180	271	313	376	689	8	65	36	0.26	51	22	27	99	90	14%	92	11%	50%	17	18%	76%	3.85	-7.0	-18	-45	$5
1st Half		244	39	7	25	4	275	236	182	302	335	414	749	8	67	38	0.28	51	23	26	107	95	16%	96	10%	57%	13	23%	69%	4.73	-0.3	-1	-3	$8
2nd Half		38	1	0	3	0	105	132	167	94	171	132	302	7	53	20	0.17	53	16	32	36	41	0%	86	17%	0%	4	0%	100%	0.53	-5.8	-135	-338	-$14
13	Proj	226	32	3	21	4	232	214	234	232	293	339	632	8	65	35	0.24	52	19	29	97	63	7%	86	13%	58%				3.20	-10.9	-17	-43	$3

Nix,Jayson

Age 30	Bats R	Pos 3B	Health	A	LIMA Plan	F
Ht 5' 11"	Wt 195		PT/Exp	D	Rand Var	-3
			Consist	C	MM	3201

4-18-.243 in 177 AB at NYY. About the only plus tool here is his power—and that's only barely. Poor patience, abysmal contact rate, inconsistent speed skills, and a baffling lack of line drives (the AL average in 2012 was 21%) all point in one direction. He is a healthy below-average player, though.

Yr	Tm	AB	R	HR	RBI	SB	BA	xBA	vL	vR	OB	Slg	OPS	bb%	ct%	h%	Eye	G	L	F	PX	xPX	hr/f	Spd	SBO	SB%	#Wk	DOM	DIS	RC/G	RAR	BPV	BPX	R$
08	COL *	320	41	11	33	8	222	255	0	179	275	398	673	7	72	27	0.26	49	18	33	127	31	0%	102	22%	56%	6	0%	83%	3.39	-12.1	34	67	$3
09	CHW*	285	40	12	39	11	236	236	256	194	315	403	718	10	78	26	0.52	39	13	48	106	118	13%	91	17%	84%	23	39%	39%	4.33	-1.8	44	90	$7
10	2 AL	331	32	14	34	1	224	231	233	220	268	396	664	6	74	26	0.23	36	15	49	122	104	12%	92	5%	33%	26	31%	50%	3.39	-11.6	15	33	$3
11	TOR *	299	31	9	32	6	181	196	273	149	231	328	559	6	69	23	0.21	36	9	55	114	115	8%	93	13%	85%	11	27%	64%	2.39	-20.8	14	31	-$1
12	NYY *	207	28	4	21	6	233	216	255	228	289	369	658	7	69	32	0.25	46	12	42	117	107	8%	75	20%	67%	22	36%	55%	3.46	-6.8	10	25	$3
1st Half		82	10	2	9	2	211	194	259	200	266	358	625	7	67	29	0.22	42	6	53	126	224	11%	84	19%	67%	9	33%	67%	3.02	-4.0	4	10	-$1
2nd Half		125	18	2	12	4	248	226	254	241	304	376	680	7	70	34	0.27	48	15	37	111	59	6%	73	21%	67%	13	38%	46%	3.78	-3.0	12	30	$5
13	Proj	163	20	4	17	4	224	212	236	214	276	371	647	7	70	29	0.24	41	12	47	115	114	8%	80	16%	69%				3.32	-6.4	13	33	$3

Nix,Laynce

Age 32	Bats L	Pos LF	Health	D	LIMA Plan	F
Ht 6' 1"	Wt 220		PT/Exp	F	Rand Var	-2
			Consist	B	MM	4011

First borns always have it better—in this case bigger physique for more raw power potential and the timing to parlay a career-high AB total in 2011 into a guaranteed two-year contract. But calf injury sidelined him from early May to late July, and that ct% trend looks ominous. Call him an unhealthy average player.

Yr	Tm	AB	R	HR	RBI	SB	BA	xBA	vL	vR	OB	Slg	OPS	bb%	ct%	h%	Eye	G	L	F	PX	xPX	hr/f	Spd	SBO	SB%	#Wk	DOM	DIS	RC/G	RAR	BPV	BPX	R$
08	MIL *	388	43	15	40	3	217	195	0	91	267	390	657	7	70	27	0.23	22	11	67	123	5	0%	96	9%	48%	3	0%	67%	3.28	-17.4	14	27	$1
09	CIN	309	42	15	46	0	239	282	156	249	290	476	766	7	74	28	0.27	38	20	43	167	107	15%	65	2%	0%	26	46%	35%	4.56	-1.5	59	120	$5
10	CIN	165	16	4	18	0	291	265	313	289	350	455	805	8	76	36	0.38	40	22	37	119	133	9%	96	2%	0%	24	29%	58%	5.58	3.9	38	83	$3
11	WAS	324	38	16	44	2	250	255	111	263	300	451	750	7	75	29	0.28	38	20	43	138	136	15%	77	6%	50%	27	44%	44%	4.50	-2.1	41	91	$8
12	PHI	114	13	3	16	0	246	232	222	248	317	412	730	10	63	36	0.29	39	24	38	153	110	11%	53	0%	0%	17	24%	59%	4.42	-0.9	3	8	$0
1st Half		46	7	2	11	0	326	308	1000	311	392	587	979	10	76	39	0.45	41	24	35	196	136	17%	49	0%	0%	6	33%	33%	8.71	4.9	90	225	$2
2nd Half		68	6	1	5	0	191	181	125	200	267	294	561	9	54	33	0.23	37	24	39	112	87	7%	74	0%	0%	11	18%	73%	2.47	-4.7	-65	-163	-$1
13	Proj	128	15	4	17	0	252	241	201	256	313	427	740	8	69	33	0.29	38	22	40	138	118	12%	65	2%	38%				4.51	-0.5	19	46	$3

Norris,Derek

Age 24	Bats R	Pos CA	Health	A	LIMA Plan	F
Ht 6' 0"	Wt 210		PT/Exp	F	Rand Var	+1
			Consist	B	MM	3303

7-34-.201 in 209 AB at OAK. Well, there's a switch: Traded to OAK, power-and-patience hitter ditches the latter, makes his mark with the former. Still too much swing-and-miss (68% MLB ct%) to recommend for BA, and difficult to know where his hr/f will settle. But should provide moderate value at CA over short-term.

Yr	Tm	AB	R	HR	RBI	SB	BA	xBA	vL	vR	OB	Slg	OPS	bb%	ct%	h%	Eye	G	L	F	PX	xPX	hr/f	Spd	SBO	SB%	#Wk	DOM	DIS	RC/G	RAR	BPV	BPX	R$
08																																		
09																																		
10																																		
11	aa	334	62	17	38	11	190	240			314	392	706	15	63	24	0.49				164			98	17%	71%				3.85		49	0	$6
12	OAK *	427	47	13	61	9	212	235	209	195	274	361	635	8	73	26	0.32	40	22	39	103	93	13%	94	12%	80%	16	25%	63%	3.23	-12.0	22	55	$5
1st Half		232	29	7	31	4	237	259	273	417	285	395	680	6	78	27	0.31	33	28	39	103	100	29%	93	9%	76%	2	50%	50%	3.77	-3.1	38	95	$8
2nd Half		186	16	5	29	5	183	214	200	171	262	317	579	10	67	24	0.33	40	21	39	103	92	10%	91	15%	83%	14	21%	64%	2.65	-9.4	-1	-3	$1
13	Proj	280	38	7	37	8	200	217	219	187	289	331	620	11	69	27	0.40	40	21	39	101	83	9%	97	14%	78%				3.08	-10.1	9	22	$4

BRENT HERSHEY

Nunez,Eduardo

Age 26	Bats R	Pos SS	Health	A	LIMA Plan	D+
Ht 6' 0"	Wt 155		PT/Exp	D	Rand Var	+1
			Consist	B	MM	1513

1-11-.292 with 11 SB in 89 AB at NYY. Early-season defensive lapses resulted in demotion, and his sub-par effort at the plate in the minors (.228 BA; 0.24 Eye in 180 AB) suppressed his season value. But his MLB BPI were fine (6/87/0.50 bb%/ct%/Eye), and his SB pace spiked. Should be an undervalued end-gamer.

Yr	Tm	AB	R	HR	RBI	SB	BA	xBA	vL	vR	OB	Slg	OPS	bb%	ct%	h%	Eye	G	L	F	PX	xPX	hr/f	Spd	SBO	SB%	#Wk	DOM	DIS	RC/G	RAR	BPV	BPX	R$
08																																		
09	aa	497	68	10	54	19	310	266			340	420	760	4	86	34	0.33				70			89	18%	71%				5.18		40	0	$22
10	NYY *	514	59	5	50	25	265	247	269	292	307	348	655	6	87	30	0.46	65	6	29	57	52	7%	138	22%	82%	7	43%	0%	3.80	-11.2	40	87	$16
11	NYY	309	38	5	30	22	265	274	277	259	314	385	699	7	88	29	0.59	45	21	34	80	70	5%	130	35%	79%	26	46%	15%	4.25	-2.7	68	151	$11
12	NYY *	252	28	3	23	23	229	216	360	200	263	299	562	4	83	27	0.26	44	16	39	46	90	3%	140	50%	81%	12	33%	42%	2.73	-14.1	17	43	$6
1st Half		51	7	0	5	6	294	221	323	238	357	373	730	9	88	33	0.83	40	16	44	48	89	0%	144	41%	86%	6	33%	50%	5.21	0.9	54	135	-$2
2nd Half		188	20	3	18	16	214	230	421	158	240	287	527	3	82	25	0.19	50	18	32	48	92	9%	125	50%	83%	6	33%	33%	2.36	-13.2	9	23	$8
13	**Proj**	**330**	**40**	**6**	**32**	**26**	**260**	**249**	**309**	**215**	**301**	**365**	**667**	**6**	**86**	**29**	**0.42**	**49**	**17**	**35**	**66**	**78**	**6%**	**136**	**37%**	**82%**				**3.93**	**-0.8**	**47**	**117**	**$13**

Olivo,Miguel

Age 34	Bats R	Pos CA	Health	B	LIMA Plan	F
Ht 6' 0"	Wt 230		PT/Exp	C	Rand Var	+3
			Consist	C	MM	3103

Used to be his big and consistent power would overshadow the poor approach and Eye ratios. But now that's fleeting, his xBA is spinning, age is ascending and AB are declining. When you have almost as many CS (6) as you do BB (7) over the course of the season, it's time to move on.

Yr	Tm	AB	R	HR	RBI	SB	BA	xBA	vL	vR	OB	Slg	OPS	bb%	ct%	h%	Eye	G	L	F	PX	xPX	hr/f	Spd	SBO	SB%	#Wk	DOM	DIS	RC/G	RAR	BPV	BPX	R$
08	KC	306	29	12	41	7	255	251	262	251	272	444	716	2	73	31	0.09	38	17	44	139	114	12%	69	14%	100%	25	36%	52%	4.25	1.0	33	65	$7
09	KC	390	51	23	65	5	249	256	265	238	284	490	773	5	68	31	0.15	45	14	40	163	116	22%	96	10%	71%	26	38%	38%	4.67	6.1	45	92	$11
10	COL	394	55	14	58	7	269	243	295	259	316	449	765	6	70	35	0.23	42	18	40	129	104	12%	134	11%	64%	26	35%	46%	4.84	8.0	35	76	$13
11	SEA	477	54	19	62	6	224	222	236	220	256	388	643	4	71	28	0.14	41	15	45	120	122	12%	71	13%	55%	27	33%	56%	3.14	-14.6	10	22	$8
12	SEA	315	27	12	29	3	222	233	221	223	239	381	620	2	73	27	0.08	41	20	40	110	97	13%	72	18%	33%	26	31%	58%	2.73	-13.8	0	0	$2
1st Half		150	16	6	16	1	213	244	240	200	229	373	602	2	77	24	0.09	39	21	41	103	66	13%	65	17%	25%	12	33%	58%	2.49	-8.2	14	35	$2
2nd Half		165	11	6	13	2	230	223	211	253	249	388	636	2	69	30	0.08	42	19	39	117	128	14%	77	18%	40%	14	29%	57%	2.95	-6.5	-13	-33	$3
13	**Proj**	**271**	**28**	**11**	**31**	**3**	**233**	**230**	**235**	**232**	**259**	**402**	**661**	**3**	**71**	**29**	**0.12**	**41**	**18**	**41**	**118**	**109**	**13%**	**78**	**15%**	**48%**				**3.28**	**-7.7**	**9**	**22**	**$5**

Olt,Mike

Age 24	Bats R	Pos 1B	Health	A	LIMA Plan	D
Ht 6' 2"	Wt 210		PT/Exp	F	Rand Var	0
			Consist	F	MM	4303

0-5-.152 in 33 AB at TEX. Surprise callup from AA in August; missed most of September with foot injury. Boasts classic 3B power and knows how to take a walk, but strikeouts will cap his BA for now. Reputation as an excellent defender should hasten his rise to the majors, though could see additional Triple-A seasoning.

Yr	Tm	AB	R	HR	RBI	SB	BA	xBA	vL	vR	OB	Slg	OPS	bb%	ct%	h%	Eye	G	L	F	PX	xPX	hr/f	Spd	SBO	SB%	#Wk	DOM	DIS	RC/G	RAR	BPV	BPX	R$
08																																		
09																																		
10																																		
11																																		
12	TEX *	387	52	25	69	4	253	255	176	125	343	492	835	12	69	30	0.43	45	18	36	166	125	0%	102	5%	80%	8	0%	75%	5.77	5.5	50	125	$14
1st Half		267	37	19	47	3	277	268			363	540	903	12	69	33	0.44				181			84	4%	100%				6.99		65	163	$21
2nd Half		120	15	6	22	1	201	228	176	125	299	386	685	12	68	24	0.43	45	18	36	129	125	0%	102	6%	50%	8	0%	75%	3.59	-6.7	13	33	-$2
13	**Proj**	**308**	**40**	**13**	**56**	**3**	**231**	**221**	**269**	**190**	**323**	**403**	**726**	**12**	**68**	**29**	**0.43**	**40**	**17**	**42**	**124**	**113**	**15%**	**116**	**5%**	**66%**				**4.29**	**-10.0**	**15**	**37**	**$8**

Ortiz,David

Age 37	Bats L	Pos DH	Health	D	LIMA Plan	C+
Ht 6' 4"	Wt 250		PT/Exp	B	Rand Var	-1
			Consist	C	MM	4045

Nagging Achilles injury destroyed his 2H; a nagging manager couldn't stop him in the 1H. Was on pace for a ridiculous season on par with his 2004-07 glory days. Alas, at his age the body just doesn't hold up like it used to. Incredibly, 2008-10 is beginning to look like the outliers. High risk, though.

Yr	Tm	AB	R	HR	RBI	SB	BA	xBA	vL	vR	OB	Slg	OPS	bb%	ct%	h%	Eye	G	L	F	PX	xPX	hr/f	Spd	SBO	SB%	#Wk	DOM	DIS	RC/G	RAR	BPV	BPX	R$
08	BOS	416	74	23	89	1	264	292	221	279	370	507	878	14	82	27	0.95	37	19	45	151	147	15%	56	1%	100%	21	67%	24%	6.53	19.7	97	190	$14
09	BOS	541	77	28	99	0	238	262	212	250	330	462	792	12	75	27	0.55	32	17	50	149	153	13%	53	1%	0%	27	44%	37%	5.03	2.3	56	114	$12
10	BOS	518	86	32	102	0	270	279	222	297	370	529	899	14	72	32	0.57	38	17	45	188	168	19%	56	1%	0%	27	63%	22%	6.79	28.2	79	172	$21
11	BOS	525	84	29	96	1	309	311	329	298	398	554	952	13	84	32	0.94	41	21	37	158	167	17%	57	1%	50%	27	56%	22%	8.10	45.8	104	231	$28
12	BOS	324	65	23	60	0	318	318	320	317	418	611	1030	15	84	32	1.10	37	21	42	175	150	20%	54	1%	0%	17	71%	12%	9.46	39.8	118	295	$19
1st Half		282	57	21	53	0	305	322	321	295	395	613	1009	13	85	30	1.02	38	19	43	182	142	20%	54	1%	0%	13	77%	8%	8.78	30.0	126	315	$23
2nd Half		42	8	2	7	0	405	310	313	462	554	595	1149	25	76	50	1.40	30	39	30	124	208	20%	64	0%	0%	4	50%	25%	14.12	9.0	61	153	-$10
13	**Proj**	**447**	**80**	**23**	**82**	**0**	**292**	**290**	**266**	**306**	**397**	**515**	**911**	**15**	**80**	**32**	**0.85**	**36**	**25**	**39**	**143**	**173**	**17%**	**53**	**1%**	**26%**				**7.31**	**30.1**	**76**	**190**	**$21**

Overbay,Lyle

Age 36	Bats L	Pos 1B	Health	A	LIMA Plan	F
Ht 6' 2"	Wt 235		PT/Exp	C	Rand Var	0
			Consist	B	MM	3111

2-10-.259 in 116 AB at ARI/ATL. Maybe his 1H h% gave him hope. Or his ability to recognize pitches—that's one skill that hadn't deteriorated. Regardless, he kept plugging away, even though his AB and contributions were minimal. But being DFA'd in July to make way for Chris Johnson? That could be the final straw.

Yr	Tm	AB	R	HR	RBI	SB	BA	xBA	vL	vR	OB	Slg	OPS	bb%	ct%	h%	Eye	G	L	F	PX	xPX	hr/f	Spd	SBO	SB%	#Wk	DOM	DIS	RC/G	RAR	BPV	BPX	R$
08	TOR	544	74	15	69	1	270	265	215	291	358	419	777	12	79	32	0.64	44	23	33	102	111	10%	73	2%	33%	27	44%	33%	5.18	-3.9	36	71	$12
09	TOR	423	57	16	64	0	265	280	190	282	374	466	840	15	78	31	0.78	42	20	37	139	123	13%	49	0%	0%	27	52%	41%	6.05	7.5	62	127	$10
10	TOR	534	75	20	67	1	243	264	222	250	328	433	760	11	75	29	0.51	45	16	39	138	129	13%	64	1%	100%	27	37%	30%	4.79	-10.0	54	117	$10
11	2 NL	394	43	9	47	2	234	243	241	231	307	360	668	10	78	28	0.48	46	19	35	94	120	8%	63	3%	67%	26	38%	50%	3.67	-20.8	23	51	$4
12	2 NL *	138	14	2	12	0	249	265	214	265	332	382	713	11	70	35	0.41	43	33	24	118	157	10%	58	0%	0%	20	25%	60%	4.30	-4.5	3	8	$0
1st Half		78	11	2	10	0	333	316	250	343	416	526	941	12	77	41	0.61	43	34	23	150	169	14%	59	0%	0%	12	33%	42%	8.36	6.1	61	153	$3
2nd Half		60	3	0	2	0	140	191	167	94	219	194	413	9	60	23	0.25	45	27	27	65	125	0%	63	0%	0%	8	13%	88%	1.26	-8.3	-83	-208	-$5
13	**Proj**	**125**	**13**	**2**	**12**	**0**	**228**	**242**	**219**	**231**	**310**	**354**	**663**	**11**	**72**	**30**	**0.42**	**45**	**24**	**31**	**102**	**132**	**8%**	**60**	**1%**	**67%**				**3.61**	**-6.6**	**3**	**8**	**$1**

Pacheco,Jordan

Age 27	Bats R	Pos 3B 1B	Health	A	LIMA Plan	C
Ht 6' 1"	Wt 200		PT/Exp	D	Rand Var	-5
			Consist	F	MM	2245

5-54-.309 in 475 AB at COL. Catcher-turned-corner guy turned in surprise season, though he lacks the power associated with the positions. He did smack line drives all over the place, but one would best be skeptical of his 35% hit rate. Still, xBA likes that he makes tons of contact. Usable, but not much upside.

Yr	Tm	AB	R	HR	RBI	SB	BA	xBA	vL	vR	OB	Slg	OPS	bb%	ct%	h%	Eye	G	L	F	PX	xPX	hr/f	Spd	SBO	SB%	#Wk	DOM	DIS	RC/G	RAR	BPV	BPX	R$
08																																		
09																																		
10	aa	78	8	1	15	1	303	271			341	397	738	5	92	32	0.71				65			87	8%	41%				4.72		46	0	$2
11	COL *	447	33	4	39	1	225	277	385	241	255	297	552	4	86	25	0.28	53	27	20	51	49	13%	90	4%	29%	4	25%	50%	2.43	-29.7	8	18	$0
12	COL *	542	57	7	60	8	315	283	351	294	344	431	775	4	88	35	0.36	42	26	31	77	83	4%	88	6%	79%	23	35%	22%	5.53	13.5	47	118	$20
1st Half		245	25	3	22	5	318	273	333	289	344	426	771	4	88	35	0.34	41	26	33	66	92	2%	111	7%	100%	9	33%	22%	5.62	6.8	44	110	$18
2nd Half		297	32	4	38	3	313	290	365	296	344	434	778	5	87	35	0.37	43	27	30	86	77	5%	75	6%	60%	14	36%	21%	5.46	7.1	43	108	$22
13	**Proj**	**436**	**40**	**9**	**44**	**4**	**280**	**288**	**356**	**250**	**310**	**410**	**720**	**4**	**87**	**30**	**0.34**	**44**	**27**	**29**	**82**	**70**	**9%**	**88**	**6%**	**70%**				**4.48**	**-1.3**	**42**	**106**	**$12**

Pagan,Angel

Age 31	Bats B	Pos CF	Health	D	LIMA Plan	B
Ht 6' 2"	Wt 200		PT/Exp	A	Rand Var	-1
			Consist	C	MM	2525

2011 now looks like the outlier, as Spd, 2H SBO, h% and thus BA all recovered in 2012. Even with 600 AB, he couldn't crack the double-digit HR barrier, but hits line drives at an impressive pace that sets a nice BA floor. Add in the SB and runs, and he should continue to return twentysomething value with full health.

Yr	Tm	AB	R	HR	RBI	SB	BA	xBA	vL	vR	OB	Slg	OPS	bb%	ct%	h%	Eye	G	L	F	PX	xPX	hr/f	Spd	SBO	SB%	#Wk	DOM	DIS	RC/G	RAR	BPV	BPX	R$
08	NYM	91	12	0	13	4	275	245	250	294	353	374	727	11	80	34	0.61	36	23	41	80	63	0%	106	14%	100%	7	43%	57%	4.94	0.6	43	84	$1
09	NYM	343	54	6	32	14	306	283	280	316	353	487	840	7	84	35	0.45	41	21	38	108	102	6%	144	23%	67%	18	56%	17%	6.08	13.3	79	161	$14
10	NYM	579	80	11	69	37	290	251	261	300	340	425	765	7	83	33	0.45	36	20	44	89	99	5%	133	28%	80%	27	41%	33%	5.27	9.5	62	135	$29
11	NYM	478	68	7	56	32	262	256	262	261	324	372	696	8	87	29	0.71	35	24	41	74	93	4%	108	29%	82%	22	41%	18%	4.30	-5.4	66	147	$19
12	SF	605	95	8	56	29	288	270	271	296	340	440	780	7	84	33	0.49	42	23	35	95	96	4%	145	22%	81%	27	59%	19%	5.40	12.3	74	185	$26
1st Half		294	38	5	30	14	293	263	253	312	342	415	757	7	85	33	0.50	46	22	33	74	99	6%	123	19%	88%	13	54%	23%	5.28	4.2	54	135	$25
2nd Half		311	57	3	26	15	283	276	287	281	338	463	801	8	83	33	0.49	39	23	38	115	94	3%	152	27%	75%	14	64%	14%	5.51	6.5	88	220	$26
13	**Proj**	**548**	**83**	**8**	**57**	**30**	**281**	**260**	**269**	**287**	**338**	**422**	**760**	**8**	**84**	**32**	**0.54**	**39**	**22**	**39**	**90**	**94**	**4%**	**131**	**25%**	**81%**				**5.13**	**5.6**	**72**	**180**	**$25**

BRENT HERSHEY

Paredes,Jimmy

Age 24	Bats B	Pos RF	Health	A	LIMA Plan	D
Ht 6' 3"	Wt 200		PT/Exp	D	Rand Var	-2
			Consist	A	MM	1403

0-3-.189 in 74 AB at HOU. Free swinger couldn't escape Triple-A until late Aug; MLEs expose lousy approach. Can run but won't take a walk, and abysmal OBP and SB% curtail baserunning returns. Having some juice in his bat adds intrigue, but until he proves more than a work-in-progress, those SB will come at a steep cost.

Yr	Tm	AB	R	HR	RBI	SB	BA	xBA	vL	vR	OB	Slg	OPS	bb%	ct%	h%	Eye	G	L	F	PX	xPX	hr/f	Spd	SBO	SB%	#Wk	DOM	DIS	RC/G	RAR	BPV	BPX	R$
08																																		
09																																		
10																																		
11	HOU *	553	64	9	47	25	246	251	216	305	271	362	634	3	74	32	0.14	54	21	25	89	96	7%	124	37%	59%	9	11%	78%	3.02	-36.1	13	29	$14
12	HOU *	581	67	9	42	26	250	223	63	224	275	357	633	3	76	32	0.14	47	16	36	75	98	0%	125	31%	67%	6	0%	100%	3.21	-34.0	9	23	$15
1st Half		305	39	4	24	17	256	221			275	352	627	3	75	33	0.10				67			119	37%	67%				3.15		1	3	$18
2nd Half		276	29	5	18	9	243	229	63	224	276	363	639	4	76	30	0.19	47	16	36	83	98	0%	122	23%	67%	6	0%	100%	3.27	-14.5	14	35	$10
13	Proj	**371**	**43**	**2**	**28**	**16**	**247**	**222**	**135**	**278**	**274**	**330**	**604**	**4**	**75**	**32**	**0.15**	**50**	**18**	**32**	**63**	**97**	**3%**	**122**	**31%**	**63%**				**2.88**	**-24.1**	**-3**	**-9**	**$7**

Parmelee,Chris

Age 25	Bats L	Pos 1B	Health	A	LIMA Plan	C
Ht 6' 1"	Wt 228		PT/Exp	C	Rand Var	-2
			Consist	C	MM	4025

5-20-.229 in 192 AB in MIN. Plate discipline (0.25 MLB Eye) didn't follow him from Triple-A to bigs, and neither did success. A 73% ct% shows more major-league AB are needed to flesh out power upside. Developing patience and emerging pop fuel modest hope for 2013 growth.

Yr	Tm	AB	R	HR	RBI	SB	BA	xBA	vL	vR	OB	Slg	OPS	bb%	ct%	h%	Eye	G	L	F	PX	xPX	hr/f	Spd	SBO	SB%	#Wk	DOM	DIS	RC/G	RAR	BPV	BPX	R$
08																																		
09																																		
10	aa	411	39	4	34	2	246	249			304	340	644	8	82	29	0.47				72			96	4%	51%				3.44		21	0	$3
11	MIN *	606	64	12	75	0	259	239	316	368	328	386	714	9	81	30	0.53	38	19	43	90	132	15%	92	1%	0%	4	75%	0%	4.32	-17.0	27	60	$11
12	MIN *	420	56	18	61	1	267	249	245	223	354	468	821	12	74	32	0.51	38	18	44	139	106	8%	68	2%	43%	20	20%	55%	5.71	5.1	48	120	$12
1st Half		148	19	4	14	1	236	227	300	163	324	390	714	12	76	28	0.55	30	19	51	107	83	3%	81	5%	43%	11	9%	64%	4.12	-5.6	36	90	$0
2nd Half		272	37	14	47	0	284	262	212	305	370	510	880	12	72	35	0.49	46	18	36	157	130	17%	66	0%	0%	9	33%	44%	6.72	10.4	53	133	$19
13	Proj	**408**	**48**	**17**	**52**	**1**	**260**	**255**	**254**	**262**	**337**	**454**	**791**	**10**	**77**	**30**	**0.51**	**39**	**19**	**42**	**127**	**119**	**12%**	**74**	**2%**	**44%**				**5.22**	**-1.6**	**50**	**125**	**$11**

Parra,Gerardo

Age 26	Bats L	Pos CF LF	Health	A	LIMA Plan	D+
Ht 5' 11"	Wt 200		PT/Exp	C	Rand Var	0
			Consist	C	MM	2323

Back-to-back run of niceties in mostly platoon role. Sneaky speed lands double-digit steals, BA and OBP won't kill you. While the slight uptick in xPX may be offset by groundball tendencies, there's really nothing wrong here. For the price you'll pay, enjoy the little bit of this and the little bit of that.

Yr	Tm	AB	R	HR	RBI	SB	BA	xBA	vL	vR	OB	Slg	OPS	bb%	ct%	h%	Eye	G	L	F	PX	xPX	hr/f	Spd	SBO	SB%	#Wk	DOM	DIS	RC/G	RAR	BPV	BPX	R$
08	aa	265	30	4	28	15	274	276			325	422	747	7	87	30	0.59				87			131	35%	61%				4.42		74	0	$9
09	ARI *	563	79	8	70	11	301	264	220	310	351	417	768	7	82	36	0.43	53	18	29	72	97	5%	117	13%	49%	22	32%	45%	5.05	5.0	34	69	$19
10	ARI *	400	36	4	35	3	270	263	283	257	311	384	695	6	80	33	0.30	51	20	29	83	92	4%	102	4%	72%	26	31%	54%	4.16	-6.4	26	57	$6
11	ARI	445	55	8	46	15	292	272	277	296	355	427	781	9	82	34	0.52	50	22	28	88	84	8%	125	12%	94%	27	41%	33%	5.64	11.3	57	127	$17
12	ARI	385	58	7	36	15	273	267	256	278	330	392	722	8	80	33	0.43	53	22	24	83	101	9%	96	22%	63%	27	26%	37%	4.34	-4.4	36	90	$13
1st Half		198	37	6	23	10	268	284	195	287	341	429	770	10	81	31	0.58	52	23	25	102	103	15%	103	25%	71%	13	46%	23%	5.00	2.0	65	163	$18
2nd Half		187	21	1	13	5	278	247	311	268	318	353	671	6	79	35	0.28	55	21	24	62	98	3%	87	20%	50%	14	7%	50%	3.67	-5.4	-1	-3	$8
13	Proj	**388**	**50**	**7**	**37**	**12**	**279**	**268**	**268**	**282**	**334**	**411**	**745**	**8**	**81**	**33**	**0.42**	**52**	**21**	**26**	**87**	**95**	**9%**	**104**	**17%**	**67%**				**4.73**	**-0.5**	**42**	**104**	**$14**

Parrino,Andy

Age 27	Bats B	Pos SS	Health	A	LIMA Plan	F
Ht 6' 0"	Wt 180		PT/Exp	D	Rand Var	-2
			Consist	A	MM	1201

1-6-.207 in 116 AB at SD. Career minor leaguer rode best campaign to SD for second trial, but was again overmatched. Proved he can take a walk, but contact rate, Eye, and overall batting skills lag. It's always good copy when a 26th rounder reaches The Show, but it doesn't mean he needs to play.

Yr	Tm	AB	R	HR	RBI	SB	BA	xBA	vL	vR	OB	Slg	OPS	bb%	ct%	h%	Eye	G	L	F	PX	xPX	hr/f	Spd	SBO	SB%	#Wk	DOM	DIS	RC/G	RAR	BPV	BPX	R$
08																																		
09																																		
10	aa	410	57	8	40	3	200	222			300	328	628	12	66	28	0.41				110			109	5%	58%				3.10		4	0	$0
11	SD *	349	37	7	39	4	223	240	143	189	292	333	625	9	71	30	0.33	50	25	25	88	28	0%	99	8%	62%	6	17%	83%	3.15	-10.2	-6	-13	$2
12	SD *	351	37	2	27	4	229	220	214	203	297	316	613	9	71	32	0.34	37	26	38	77	71	3%	103	8%	62%	15	20%	73%	3.07	-11.0	-8	-20	$1
1st Half		131	13	1	6	1	201	232	152	186	277	299	576	10	72	27	0.37	37	27	35	83	73	5%	102	3%	100%	10	20%	70%	2.68	-5.4	-5	-13	-$5
2nd Half		220	24	1	20	3	246	199	444	267	309	327	636	8	71	34	0.32	35	20	45	73	64	0%	106	10%	56%	5	20%	80%	3.33	-4.5	-14	-35	$4
13	Proj	**95**	**11**	**1**	**9**	**1**	**222**	**223**	**193**	**238**	**295**	**315**	**610**	**9**	**70**	**31**	**0.35**	**37**	**27**	**35**	**78**	**66**	**4%**	**98**	**7%**	**58%**				**2.99**	**-3.0**	**-15**	**-38**	**$1**

Pastornicky,Tyler

Age 23	Bats R	Pos SS	Health	A	LIMA Plan	F
Ht 5' 11"	Wt 190		PT/Exp	D	Rand Var	+3
			Consist	B	MM	1431

2-13-.243 in 169 AB at ATL. After 2011's good-not-great minor-league season, he was rushed to the majors at 22. But flaws in plate discipline, lack of power and shoddy defense bid him adios; mustered only 24 MLB AB in 2H. Wheels may develop, but xPX is not a misprint: he had four total extra-base hits after April.

Yr	Tm	AB	R	HR	RBI	SB	BA	xBA	vL	vR	OB	Slg	OPS	bb%	ct%	h%	Eye	G	L	F	PX	xPX	hr/f	Spd	SBO	SB%	#Wk	DOM	DIS	RC/G	RAR	BPV	BPX	R$
08																																		
09																																		
10	aa	134	18	2	12	9	231	244			301	326	627	9	82	27	0.55				62			123	31%	81%				3.38		38	0	$3
11	a/a	459	52	6	36	22	281	248			319	362	681	5	89	31	0.51				50			114	26%	64%				3.91		40	0	$16
12	ATL *	322	32	3	28	4	236	269	196	265	278	331	608	5	83	28	0.33	64	18	17	69	36	8%	100	11%	56%	22	27%	50%	2.98	-10.9	22	55	$2
1st Half		267	23	1	23	4	234	263	205	264	263	310	573	4	83	28	0.23	63	19	18	59	37	5%	97	14%	56%	9	22%	56%	2.62	-11.3	9	23	$3
2nd Half		55	9	2	6	0	248	291	176	286	343	433	775	13	82	27	0.82	74	11	16	115	28	33%	104	0%	0%	13	31%	46%	5.03	1.7	72	180	-$2
13	Proj	**193**	**24**	**1**	**18**	**6**	**256**	**273**	**211**	**272**	**315**	**341**	**656**	**8**	**84**	**30**	**0.55**	**63**	**19**	**18**	**56**	**33**	**4%**	**125**	**15%**	**69%**				**3.64**	**-2.1**	**33**	**83**	**$5**

Pearce,Steve

Age 30	Bats R	Pos LF	Health	F	LIMA Plan	F
Ht 5' 11"	Wt 210		PT/Exp	F	Rand Var	-1
			Consist	F	MM	2101

3-26-.239 in 159 AB at BAL, HOU, and NYY. Finally fleeing PIT org did little to further his cause. Had moments with each new employer but not enough to sustain interest. Throughout catch-and-release, he maintained patience and good power, and hr/f trend might translate to another major-league gig or two. Or three.

Yr	Tm	AB	R	HR	RBI	SB	BA	xBA	vL	vR	OB	Slg	OPS	bb%	ct%	h%	Eye	G	L	F	PX	xPX	hr/f	Spd	SBO	SB%	#Wk	DOM	DIS	RC/G	RAR	BPV	BPX	R$
08	PIT *	495	43	13	63	11	225	241	321	222	268	368	637	6	79	26	0.28	38	17	45	101	101	10%	75	16%	70%	12	33%	50%	3.21	-33.7	31	61	$4
09	PIT *	438	48	14	58	3	229	258	268	174	303	397	700	10	78	26	0.49	38	19	43	114	136	8%	60	11%	29%	15	53%	33%	3.71	-23.3	41	84	$4
10	PIT *	158	22	2	16	5	264	266	294	250	360	418	777	13	76	34	0.63	44	20	36	121	85	0%	109	16%	67%	4	25%	75%	5.11	-1.4	64	139	$3
11	PIT *	124	12	3	14	0	203	197	213	191	246	304	550	5	75	25	0.22	43	15	43	73	98	3%	71	0%	0%	14	21%	71%	2.39	-11.7	-22	-49	-$2
12	3 TM *	351	42	13	47	3	247	240	240	238	326	420	746	10	77	29	0.50	38	17	45	117	128	7%	71	7%	49%	15	33%	53%	4.52	-8.0	40	100	$7
1st Half		246	33	11	32	2	255	233	273	235	329	454	783	10	78	29	0.49	34	11	55	132	136	8%	62	5%	63%	4	50%	50%	5.06	-2.2	52	130	$12
2nd Half		103	9	2	15	1	233	220	226	240	325	350	674	12	74	30	0.52	40	21	40	81	123	6%	91	10%	33%	11	27%	55%	3.54	-5.8	6	15	-$3
13	Proj	**127**	**14**	**3**	**16**	**1**	**234**	**220**	**228**	**239**	**308**	**362**	**670**	**10**	**75**	**29**	**0.43**	**39**	**17**	**45**	**92**	**119**	**7%**	**78**	**8%**	**52%**				**3.62**	**-4.0**	**16**	**40**	**$2**

Pedroia,Dustin

Age 29	Bats R	Pos 2B	Health	C	LIMA Plan	D+
Ht 5' 8"	Wt 165		PT/Exp	A	Rand Var	0
			Consist	B	MM	3345

Did his game lose altitude during the 2012 BOS free fall? Weathered 5-year lows or near lows in BA, Slg, bb%, Eye. But couldn't play through May thumb injury and didn't hit with authority until after AS Break. Rode torrid 2H to post typical final line, then had pinkie surgery. When healthy, still among the very best 2B plays.

Yr	Tm	AB	R	HR	RBI	SB	BA	xBA	vL	vR	OB	Slg	OPS	bb%	ct%	h%	Eye	G	L	F	PX	xPX	hr/f	Spd	SBO	SB%	#Wk	DOM	DIS	RC/G	RAR	BPV	BPX	R$
08	BOS	653	118	17	83	20	326	306	313	331	374	493	867	7	92	34	0.96	43	21	36	104	98	8%	115	11%	95%	28	68%	7%	7.18	52.0	101	198	$36
09	BOS	626	115	15	72	20	296	295	277	302	370	447	817	11	93	30	1.64	39	20	41	93	92	6%	110	14%	71%	27	78%	4%	5.93	30.9	98	200	$26
10	BOS	302	53	12	41	9	288	310	236	304	366	493	859	11	87	30	0.97	39	22	39	131	97	11%	98	11%	90%	13	62%	15%	6.59	20.5	109	237	$14
11	BOS	635	102	21	91	26	307	288	358	287	390	474	864	12	87	33	1.01	48	19	33	106	115	11%	116	15%	76%	27	63%	22%	6.80	46.1	87	193	$36
12	BOS	563	81	15	65	20	290	288	305	283	345	449	795	8	89	30	0.80	46	20	35	98	108	9%	101	17%	77%	26	62%	15%	5.56	22.2	85	213	$24
1st Half		293	40	5	31	4	263	265	247	270	321	392	713	8	86	29	0.63	43	20	37	85	111	5%	105	9%	57%	13	46%	31%	4.25	-0.1	57	143	$17
2nd Half		270	41	10	34	16	319	313	373	297	372	511	883	8	93	32	1.15	48	20	32	111	106	12%	96	24%	84%	13	77%	0%	7.24	21.9	109	273	$32
13	Proj	**583**	**92**	**20**	**74**	**22**	**299**	**295**	**316**	**293**	**366**	**480**	**846**	**10**	**89**	**31**	**0.96**	**45**	**20**	**35**	**109**	**107**	**11%**	**101**	**16%**	**80%**				**6.42**	**35.2**	**95**	**237**	**$31**

ROB CARROLL

Pena,Brayan

Age	31	Bats	B	Pos	CA	Health	A	LIMA Plan	F
Ht	5' 9"	Wt	230			PT/Exp	F	Rand Var	+4
						Consist	A	MM	1021

Can man live on high ct% alone? If he dons the tools of ignorance and switch-hits, the answer is yes. But sometimes, it can be a hollow life—with no power or speed and a ton of ground balls, not much happens when he makes contact. xBA hints at some BA upside, but that's not enough to make him draft-worthy.

Yr	Tm	AB	R	HR	RBI	SB	BA	xBA	vL	vR	OB	Slg	OPS	bb%	ct%	h%	Eye	G	L	F	PX	xPX	hr/f	Spd	SBO	SB%	#Wk	DOM	DIS	RC/G	RAR	BPV	BPX	R$
08	ATL *	248	27	4	23	5	258	373	333	273	315	381	696	8	91	27	0.95	33	50	17	79	68	0%	63	14%	59%	5	20%	0%	4.00	-1.0	67	131	$3
09	KC *	253	26	9	32	2	269	310	258	282	311	442	753	6	89	27	0.54	51	22	28	101	61	15%	46	5%	57%	22	50%	27%	4.73	4.3	64	131	$5
10	KC	158	11	1	19	2	253	233	204	275	306	335	641	7	83	30	0.44	45	16	39	67	93	2%	49	5%	100%	24	21%	58%	3.58	-2.5	14	30	$1
11	KC	222	17	3	24	0	248	262	250	247	286	338	624	5	89	27	0.50	44	23	33	62	60	5%	36	0%	0%	25	32%	44%	3.28	-5.5	24	53	$1
12	KC	212	16	2	25	0	236	271	265	222	267	321	588	4	89	26	0.38	48	25	27	56	92	4%	43	2%	0%	27	30%	52%	2.79	-8.5	22	55	$0
1st Half		127	7	1	13	0	260	302	225	276	288	346	634	4	90	28	0.38	52	30	18	62	87	5%	32	3%	0%	13	38%	54%	3.31	-3.4	24	60	$0
2nd Half		85	9	1	12	0	200	225	321	140	236	282	518	4	87	22	0.36	43	17	40	46	99	3%	71	0%	0%	14	21%	50%	2.12	-5.6	18	45	-$1
13	**Proj**	**199**	**17**	**3**	**24**	**1**	**253**	**259**	**277**	**242**	**291**	**351**	**641**	**5**	**88**	**28**	**0.43**	**46**	**21**	**33**	**63**	**82**	**5%**	**44**	**2%**	**56%**				**3.46**	**-4.4**	**28**	**69**	**$1**

Pena,Carlos

Age	35	Bats	L	Pos	1B	Health	B	LIMA Plan	D
Ht	6' 2"	Wt	225			PT/Exp	A	Rand Var	0
						Consist	D	MM	4005

When a third of your ABs end in a whiff, you need prodigous power to balance the low BA. That used to be the case, but now his power is on the wane. He's never hit LHP (career .206/.308/.416), and has gotten worse in recent years. When a one-dimensional player loses that one dimension, he disappears.

Yr	Tm	AB	R	HR	RBI	SB	BA	xBA	vL	vR	OB	Slg	OPS	bb%	ct%	h%	Eye	G	L	F	PX	xPX	hr/f	Spd	SBO	SB%	#Wk	DOM	DIS	RC/G	RAR	BPV	BPX	R$
08	TAM	490	76	31	102	1	247	247	190	280	370	494	864	16	66	31	0.58	32	18	50	180	176	19%	73	1%	50%	24	54%	29%	6.16	12.6	58	114	$14
09	TAM	471	91	39	100	3	227	270	211	236	348	537	885	16	65	25	0.53	29	17	54	221	203	24%	61	5%	50%	23	61%	26%	6.06	11.0	93	190	$15
10	TAM	484	64	28	84	5	196	242	179	204	319	407	726	15	67	22	0.55	45	14	41	155	149	21%	52	4%	83%	25	40%	32%	4.14	-17.5	42	91	$7
11	CHC	493	72	28	80	2	225	248	133	255	357	462	819	17	67	27	0.63	37	15	47	181	201	18%	61	3%	50%	27	48%	41%	5.38	1.3	68	151	$12
12	TAM	497	72	19	61	2	197	207	176	206	317	354	671	15	63	27	0.48	37	20	43	120	128	14%	87	3%	40%	27	26%	63%	3.50	-28.1	0	0	$3
1st Half		275	45	11	33	1	200	205	170	219	327	356	684	16	64	27	0.53	39	18	43	119	127	14%	77	2%	50%	13	23%	62%	3.69	-14.5	0	0	$6
2nd Half		222	27	8	28	1	194	207	191	194	304	351	655	14	62	27	0.42	35	23	42	120	129	14%	94	5%	33%	14	29%	64%	3.27	-14.8	-5	-13	$0
13	**Proj**	**384**	**55**	**15**	**57**	**2**	**208**	**213**	**172**	**222**	**331**	**378**	**709**	**16**	**65**	**27**	**0.53**	**37**	**18**	**44**	**129**	**156**	**14%**	**72**	**3%**	**49%**				**3.97**	**-16.7**	**14**	**36**	**$5**

Pence,Hunter

Age	30	Bats	R	Pos	RF	Health	A	LIMA Plan	C+
Ht	6' 4"	Wt	220			PT/Exp	A	Rand Var	+1
						Consist	F	MM	3325

On the surface, his consistent HR totals are encouraging. But something happened in San Francisco that sent his 2nd half into a tailspin. hr/f, h% should bounce back, but if 2H ct% and GB% remain, the future is cloudier. Power production is tied to a 600-AB seasons, so pray that the health grade holds up.

Yr	Tm	AB	R	HR	RBI	SB	BA	xBA	vL	vR	OB	Slg	OPS	bb%	ct%	h%	Eye	G	L	F	PX	xPX	hr/f	Spd	SBO	SB%	#Wk	DOM	DIS	RC/G	RAR	BPV	BPX	R$
08	HOU	595	78	25	83	11	269	273	250	275	315	466	781	6	79	30	0.32	52	14	34	126	110	15%	120	15%	52%	27	52%	26%	4.85	-5.1	58	114	$19
09	HOU	585	76	25	72	14	282	280	294	279	347	472	819	9	81	31	0.53	53	15	33	112	100	16%	128	15%	56%	27	44%	15%	5.53	6.5	62	127	$21
10	HOU	614	93	25	91	18	282	284	292	279	327	461	788	6	83	31	0.39	53	15	32	112	96	15%	116	17%	67%	27	56%	30%	5.19	0.8	67	146	$27
11	2 NL	606	84	22	97	8	314	282	317	313	372	502	873	8	80	37	0.45	51	18	31	129	115	15%	124	6%	80%	27	56%	22%	6.93	29.3	68	151	$31
12	2 NL	617	87	24	104	5	253	254	235	259	315	425	740	8	76	29	0.39	51	17	32	110	96	16%	111	4%	71%	27	41%	48%	4.55	-10.8	38	95	$18
1st Half		315	56	16	47	4	286	282	250	296	350	498	848	9	80	31	0.50	53	17	31	128	111	21%	118	7%	67%	13	62%	31%	6.15	10.2	71	178	$27
2nd Half		302	31	8	57	1	219	224	222	217	278	348	626	8	73	27	0.30	49	18	33	89	79	11%	100	1%	100%	14	21%	64%	3.17	-16.9	-2	-5	$9
13	**Proj**	**612**	**84**	**23**	**99**	**8**	**279**	**265**	**271**	**282**	**337**	**455**	**792**	**8**	**80**	**32**	**0.43**	**51**	**17**	**32**	**110**	**100**	**15%**	**110**	**7%**	**69%**				**5.37**	**6.4**	**51**	**128**	**$25**

Pennington,Cliff

Age	29	Bats	B	Pos	SS 2B	Health	A	LIMA Plan	D
Ht	5' 10"	Wt	193			PT/Exp	B	Rand Var	+3
						Consist	B	MM	1303

Big drop in BA partly due to h%, but consistent xBA says to split the difference. Slowly eroding ct%; low PX and hr/f mean nothing exciting happens when he makes contact. Spd is average, but in 2012 low h% = low BA = low OBA = fewer SB opportunities. Good for a handful of SBs, but that's about it.

Yr	Tm	AB	R	HR	RBI	SB	BA	xBA	vL	vR	OB	Slg	OPS	bb%	ct%	h%	Eye	G	L	F	PX	xPX	hr/f	Spd	SBO	SB%	#Wk	DOM	DIS	RC/G	RAR	BPV	BPX	R$
08	OAK *	539	80	1	34	27	233	206	289	213	334	288	622	13	82	28	0.85	36	19	46	40	42	0%	133	19%	77%	8	25%	50%	3.31	-14.2	24	47	$9
09	OAK *	568	63	6	51	27	239	241	200	307	304	340	644	9	81	29	0.49	42	18	39	70	67	6%	104	25%	74%	11	36%	36%	3.46	-12.2	35	71	$11
10	OAK	508	64	6	46	29	250	242	258	247	317	368	685	9	81	30	0.52	36	21	43	81	70	3%	114	25%	85%	27	44%	44%	4.13	-0.5	54	117	$15
11	OAK	515	57	8	58	14	264	243	270	262	320	369	689	8	80	32	0.40	36	25	40	78	76	5%	80	16%	61%	26	31%	54%	3.94	-3.4	24	53	$14
12	OAK	418	50	6	28	15	215	233	168	232	276	311	587	8	78	26	0.39	41	23	37	67	63	5%	98	21%	71%	26	23%	54%	2.77	-18.2	17	43	$4
1st Half		257	29	3	16	11	206	232	156	228	266	300	566	8	79	25	0.40	41	22	38	68	57	4%	95	23%	85%	14	29%	50%	2.66	-12.9	22	55	$5
2nd Half		161	21	3	12	4	230	234	200	237	291	329	621	8	77	28	0.38	40	25	35	66	71	7%	99	19%	50%	12	17%	58%	2.95	-6.6	7	18	$3
13	**Proj**	**385**	**47**	**6**	**32**	**14**	**237**	**234**	**227**	**241**	**301**	**340**	**641**	**8**	**79**	**29**	**0.44**	**38**	**23**	**39**	**70**	**68**	**5%**	**95**	**20%**	**69%**				**3.37**	**-7.6**	**24**	**59**	**$8**

Peralta,Jhonny

Age	31	Bats	R	Pos	SS	Health	A	LIMA Plan	C+
Ht	6' 2"	Wt	215			PT/Exp	A	Rand Var	+2
						Consist	D	MM	3015

2011 BA was aided by h%, but then the pendulum swung back in 2012; xBA shows the truth. Power production was suppressed by 1H FB% and hr/f; those returned in 2H. Regression to the mean will bump up his performance; he's a solid, if unspectacular, player at a scarce position.

Yr	Tm	AB	R	HR	RBI	SB	BA	xBA	vL	vR	OB	Slg	OPS	bb%	ct%	h%	Eye	G	L	F	PX	xPX	hr/f	Spd	SBO	SB%	#Wk	DOM	DIS	RC/G	RAR	BPV	BPX	R$
08	CLE	605	104	23	89	3	276	281	247	285	329	473	802	7	79	32	0.38	44	20	36	131	127	13%	101	3%	75%	27	56%	30%	5.48	27.0	65	127	$19
09	CLE	582	57	11	83	0	254	245	235	261	314	375	689	8	77	31	0.38	50	19	31	88	78	8%	74	1%	0%	27	26%	56%	3.97	1.0	4	8	$8
10	2 AL	551	60	15	81	1	249	260	241	251	315	392	707	9	81	28	0.51	34	22	43	98	99	8%	90	1%	100%	26	35%	35%	4.20	4.6	38	83	$10
11	DET	525	68	21	86	0	299	262	240	323	349	478	827	7	82	33	0.42	36	20	44	114	116	11%	88	1%	0%	27	44%	37%	5.97	29.9	48	107	$22
12	DET	531	58	13	63	1	239	257	214	249	303	384	688	8	80	28	0.47	41	22	37	98	124	8%	76	2%	33%	27	41%	33%	3.85	-0.8	34	85	$7
1st Half		246	25	4	24	1	260	275	215	276	331	390	721	10	81	31	0.57	39	29	32	90	104	6%	78	3%	50%	13	46%	31%	4.40	2.8	36	90	$5
2nd Half		285	33	9	39	0	221	241	213	224	279	379	658	7	79	25	0.39	43	15	41	105	142	10%	76	2%	0%	14	36%	36%	3.41	-5.3	32	80	$8
13	**Proj**	**548**	**64**	**16**	**76**	**1**	**257**	**254**	**227**	**269**	**316**	**410**	**726**	**8**	**81**	**29**	**0.44**	**40**	**21**	**40**	**101**	**118**	**9%**	**78**	**2%**	**30%**				**4.40**	**6.2**	**35**	**89**	**$13**

Perez,Salvador

Age	23	Bats	R	Pos	CA	Health	C	LIMA Plan	C+
Ht	6' 3"	Wt	245			PT/Exp	F	Rand Var	0
						Consist	C	MM	2055

11-39-.301 in 289 AB at KC. Made a splash with strong 2011 debut; picked up where he left off after return in June from knee surgery. Defense got him to the majors; high ct% and LD will keep him there. hr/f growth, xPX says there's power upside in this bat. With more experience and regular playing time, UP: 25 HR.

Yr	Tm	AB	R	HR	RBI	SB	BA	xBA	vL	vR	OB	Slg	OPS	bb%	ct%	h%	Eye	G	L	F	PX	xPX	hr/f	Spd	SBO	SB%	#Wk	DOM	DIS	RC/G	RAR	BPV	BPX	R$
08																																		
09																																		
10																																		
11	KC *	482	50	10	61	0	280	296	484	291	307	401	708	4	88	30	0.33	42	29	29	79	86	8%	87	1%	0%	8	50%	38%	4.31	2.4	37	82	$12
12	KC *	339	46	11	44	0	301	291	358	279	328	451	779	4	90	31	0.42	44	24	32	87	116	13%	71	0%	0%	16	63%	25%	5.39	11.6	50	125	$12
1st Half		74	10	2	10	0	311	276	333	333	325	444	769	2	91	32	0.23	57	17	26	78	152	33%	72	0%	0%	2	100%	0%	5.34	2.2	44	110	-$2
2nd Half		265	36	9	34	0	298	294	360	274	329	453	781	4	90	30	0.46	43	25	32	90	113	12%	73	0%	0%	14	57%	29%	5.40	8.7	53	133	$15
13	**Proj**	**439**	**54**	**16**	**57**	**0**	**294**	**303**	**355**	**271**	**318**	**459**	**778**	**3**	**90**	**30**	**0.34**	**42**	**27**	**31**	**95**	**102**	**13%**	**75**	**0%**	**0%**				**5.26**	**12.7**	**54**	**135**	**$16**

Petersen,Bryan

Age	27	Bats	L	Pos	LF CF	Health	A	LIMA Plan	F
Ht	6' 0"	Wt	190			PT/Exp	C	Rand Var	0
						Consist	F	MM	1201

0-17-.195 with 8 SBs in 241 AB at MIA. Rode the AAA shuttle all year and wasn't productive in either place. Low PX, high GB% indicate the 2011 power was a fluke. Awful SB% says he's doing more damage than good when he runs. He's got "part-time player" written all over him. No, wait. That's just a bad tattoo of a fish.

Yr	Tm	AB	R	HR	RBI	SB	BA	xBA	vL	vR	OB	Slg	OPS	bb%	ct%	h%	Eye	G	L	F	PX	xPX	hr/f	Spd	SBO	SB%	#Wk	DOM	DIS	RC/G	RAR	BPV	BPX	R$
08	aa	37	4	1	8	1	321	249			394	438	831	11	81	38	0.63				80			90	22%	28%				5.29		26	0	$0
09	aa	431	56	6	43	11	275	247			344	378	722	10	82	32	0.59				62			127	18%	46%				4.19		30	0	$11
10	FLA *	346	35	3	21	4	203	161	0	87	260	273	533	7	76	26	0.32	50	0	50	53	36	0%	105	10%	44%	7	0%	71%	2.17	-27.6	-16	-35	-$3
11	FLA *	452	49	9	27	11	272	259	294	255	346	407	753	10	78	33	0.52	38	25	37	102	77	4%	110	14%	61%	16	31%	50%	4.78	1.2	42	93	$11
12	MIA *	484	62	2	38	14	230	222	137	211	289	293	582	8	77	29	0.37	48	21	31	45	68	0%	109	19%	57%	16	13%	63%	2.68	-30.2	-3	-8	$6
1st Half		220	30	1	17	5	240	224	222	209	303	291	594	8	76	31	0.37	61	18	21	37	41	0%	128	16%	45%	5	0%	60%	2.74	-13.8	-21	-53	$5
2nd Half		264	32	1	21	9	221	227	119	211	277	294	572	7	79	28	0.37	45	21	34	52	74	0%	95	21%	67%	11	18%	64%	2.62	-17.7	9	23	$6
13	**Proj**	**225**	**27**	**1**	**16**	**6**	**240**	**228**	**227**	**244**	**303**	**309**	**611**	**8**	**78**	**30**	**0.41**	**46**	**22**	**32**	**52**	**67**	**1%**	**104**	**16%**	**55%**				**2.99**	**-11.4**	**1**	**2**	**$3**

DAVE ADLER

Phillips,Brandon

Age 32	Bats R	Pos 2B	Health	A	LIMA Plan	C+
Ht 6' 0"	Wt 200		PT/Exp	A	Rand Var	0
			Consist	B	MM	2235

Stats mirror consistent (but average) power metrics; PX, FB% and hr/f have barely changed. The days of 25 SBs? Not so much—Spd and SBO in decline. Hard to quibble with the eerily repeatable production over the past three years, but tons of ABs also a constant. At 32, that won't last forever.

Yr	Tm	AB	R	HR	RBI	SB	BA	xBA	vL	vR	OB	Slg	OPS	bb%	ct%	h%	Eye	G	L	F	PX	xPX	hr/f	Spd	SBO	SB%	#Wk	DOM	DIS	RC/G	RAR	BPV	BPX	R$
08	CIN	559	80	21	78	23	261	279	296	247	309	442	751	7	83	28	0.42	50	16	34	106	103	13%	129	25%	70%	24	50%	21%	4.58	3.8	71	139	$20
09	CIN	584	78	20	98	25	276	291	301	267	326	447	773	7	87	29	0.59	50	17	33	98	103	12%	103	23%	74%	27	59%	19%	5.06	12.1	77	157	$25
10	CIN	626	100	18	59	16	275	283	291	268	324	430	754	7	87	29	0.55	51	15	33	96	97	10%	121	17%	57%	27	56%	7%	4.66	5.7	72	157	$22
11	CIN	610	94	18	82	14	300	282	316	295	347	457	804	7	86	33	0.52	45	20	35	104	112	10%	88	14%	61%	27	67%	15%	5.59	21.2	70	156	$28
12	CIN	580	86	18	77	15	281	277	269	286	314	429	743	5	86	30	0.35	47	21	32	90	79	11%	85	12%	88%	27	41%	22%	4.87	8.5	58	145	$23
1st Half		271	42	10	46	4	288	280	215	318	328	446	774	6	87	30	0.47	47	21	33	90	87	13%	87	6%	100%	13	38%	31%	5.33	8.1	61	153	$24
2nd Half		309	44	8	31	11	275	275	321	259	302	414	716	4	85	30	0.27	47	21	32	90	72	9%	88	19%	85%	14	43%	14%	4.48	1.9	52	130	$22
13	Proj	594	89	16	75	16	283	273	289	281	325	428	752	6	86	31	0.44	48	19	33	89	92	10%	89	15%	73%				4.89	10.7	60	150	$23

Pierre,Juan

Age 35	Bats L	Pos LF	Health	A	LIMA Plan	C
Ht 5' 11"	Wt 175		PT/Exp	A	Rand Var	-2
			Consist	B	MM	0533

You have to appreciate someone who understands his limitations. He hits hardly any fly balls, which is fine, since he has no power. Consistently high ct% sets a nice BA foundation. He's getting up in years and sliding into a platoon role, so while his wheels are still fine, expect 30 SB rather than 60.

Yr	Tm	AB	R	HR	RBI	SB	BA	xBA	vL	vR	OB	Slg	OPS	bb%	ct%	h%	Eye	G	L	F	PX	xPX	hr/f	Spd	SBO	SB%	#Wk	DOM	DIS	RC/G	RAR	BPV	BPX	R$
08	LA	375	44	1	28	40	283	287	346	257	322	328	650	6	94	30	0.92	53	25	22	28	25	1%	127	45%	77%	25	32%	24%	3.84	-9.7	47	92	$19
09	LA	380	57	0	31	30	308	302	320	304	354	392	746	7	93	33	1.00	51	24	24	49	45	0%	152	35%	71%	27	44%	22%	4.98	2.7	73	149	$19
10	CHW	651	96	1	47	68	275	277	297	268	322	316	638	6	93	30	0.96	59	19	23	28	21	1%	131	43%	79%	27	30%	4%	3.75	-18.7	50	109	$34
11	CHW	639	80	2	50	27	279	270	329	264	324	327	651	6	94	30	1.05	53	21	26	31	34	1%	128	22%	61%	27	41%	30%	3.57	-21.6	45	100	$20
12	PHI	394	59	1	25	37	307	291	190	329	345	371	716	6	93	33	0.85	56	24	20	35	23	1%	164	35%	84%	27	26%	19%	4.98	2.7	60	150	$22
1st Half		220	28	1	16	19	314	286	175	344	349	377	726	5	95	33	1.00	54	23	23	34	23	2%	143	31%	86%	13	23%	15%	5.20	3.3	59	148	$23
2nd Half		174	31	0	9	18	299	297	217	311	341	362	703	6	91	33	0.73	58	25	16	36	23	0%	159	40%	82%	14	29%	21%	4.71	0.3	57	143	$20
13	Proj	362	53	1	25	30	293	283	273	298	335	349	684	6	93	31	0.90	56	23	22	33	27	1%	145	34%	78%				4.31	-3.5	54	134	$19

Pierzynski,A.J.

Age 36	Bats L	Pos CA	Health	A	LIMA Plan	C
Ht 6' 3"	Wt 235		PT/Exp	B	Rand Var	0
			Consist	B	MM	2025

Nice little surprise for a player who had been trending into irrelevance; okay, how did he do it? Yes, catchers often see power peaks in their later years—but, seriously now. A career year at 36? Power barrage came at the expense of ct%, but BA wasn't impacted. Can he repeat? Whatever you think, I'll take the under.

Yr	Tm	AB	R	HR	RBI	SB	BA	xBA	vL	vR	OB	Slg	OPS	bb%	ct%	h%	Eye	G	L	F	PX	xPX	hr/f	Spd	SBO	SB%	#Wk	DOM	DIS	RC/G	RAR	BPV	BPX	R$
08	CHW	534	66	13	60	1	281	264	286	279	306	416	721	3	87	30	0.27	44	18	38	86	105	7%	65	1%	100%	27	48%	33%	4.52	5.7	40	78	$12
09	CHW	504	57	13	49	1	300	277	277	307	331	425	756	5	90	31	0.46	47	20	33	72	81	9%	71	1%	50%	26	42%	35%	5.09	13.2	39	80	$14
10	CHW	474	43	9	56	3	270	268	250	276	292	388	681	3	92	28	0.38	49	16	36	77	80	6%	52	7%	43%	27	33%	22%	3.84	-4.0	49	107	$10
11	CHW	464	38	8	48	0	287	285	305	283	320	405	726	5	93	30	0.70	51	21	29	78	72	6%	58	0%	0%	25	44%	24%	4.64	6.5	53	118	$10
12	CHW	479	68	27	77	0	278	289	248	287	318	501	819	6	84	28	0.36	42	22	36	125	104	19%	79	0%	0%	27	48%	22%	5.62	20.0	65	163	$18
1st Half		242	36	14	45	0	285	300	268	290	332	517	849	7	88	28	0.57	48	20	32	121	81	20%	88	0%	0%	13	46%	15%	6.12	12.9	81	203	$21
2nd Half		237	32	13	32	0	270	279	228	283	302	485	788	4	80	29	0.23	35	25	40	129	130	17%	68	0%	0%	14	50%	29%	5.13	6.2	46	115	$15
13	Proj	467	54	12	62	0	279	267	261	284	313	414	726	5	87	30	0.38	45	21	34	81	95	8%	64	1%	5%				4.55	4.4	38	96	$14

Pill,Brett

Age 28	Bats L	Pos 1B	Health	A	LIMA Plan	F
Ht 6' 4"	Wt 225		PT/Exp	C	Rand Var	+2
			Consist	A	MM	3121

4-11-.210 in 105 AB at SF. While he showed good pop at AAA, it hasn't really translated to the majors. Lefties give him trouble (.214/.270/.359 in 103 AB), and doesn't take many walks. At this age, he's officially graduated from prospect to suspect.

Yr	Tm	AB	R	HR	RBI	SB	BA	xBA	vL	vR	OB	Slg	OPS	bb%	ct%	h%	Eye	G	L	F	PX	xPX	hr/f	Spd	SBO	SB%	#Wk	DOM	DIS	RC/G	RAR	BPV	BPX	R$
08																																		
09	aa	527	59	15	90	5	266	280			305	419	724	5	85	29	0.37				98			74	7%	59%				4.36		49	0	$13
10	aaa	520	43	11	57	5	220	263			250	336	585	4	85	24	0.26				79			78	7%	66%				2.71		29	0	$3
11	SF *	586	56	16	73	4	237	289	250	364	258	383	641	3	87	25	0.22	42	26	33	93	118	14%	80	12%	30%	4	50%	0%	3.09	-41.8	48	107	$9
12	SF *	351	32	10	39	1	210	228	200	233	240	349	590	4	81	23	0.21	48	12	41	90	73	11%	80	2%	100%	15	27%	47%	2.72	-29.3	21	53	$0
1st Half		163	13	4	18	1	219	229	200	263	249	350	598	4	82	24	0.22	54	10	37	83	76	13%	90	3%	100%	10	30%	70%	2.86	-12.5	21	53	$0
2nd Half		188	19	6	21	0	203	228	200	182	233	349	583	4	81	22	0.20	30	17	52	95	65	8%	71	0%	0%	5	20%	0%	2.61	-16.2	17	43	$1
13	Proj	101	9	4	12	1	234	265	216	272	263	412	675	4	84	24	0.24	41	19	40	108	89	12%	82	6%	52%				3.54	-5.6	46	115	$2

Plouffe,Trevor

Age 27	Bats R	Pos 3B	Health	A	LIMA Plan	C+
Ht 6' 2"	Wt 203		PT/Exp	C	Rand Var	+2
			Consist	C	MM	4115

All signs pointed to a power breakout in 2012; with playing time, he obliged. Contact is trending in the right direction, so there's some upside—xBA shows the possibilities. High PX and rising FB% means the power is legit. With continued growth in plate approach, he'll approach the upper echelon at 3B. UP: .260, 30 HR.

Yr	Tm	AB	R	HR	RBI	SB	BA	xBA	vL	vR	OB	Slg	OPS	bb%	ct%	h%	Eye	G	L	F	PX	xPX	hr/f	Spd	SBO	SB%	#Wk	DOM	DIS	RC/G	RAR	BPV	BPX	R$
08	a/a	477	55	7	50	4	236	254			272	367	639	5	79	29	0.24				93			103	8%	56%				3.26		31	0	$3
09	aaa	430	44	8	50	3	233	259			279	359	638	6	82	27	0.36				80			102	10%	27%				3.12		29	0	$3
10	MIN *	443	46	11	42	4	201	230	200	139	237	339	576	4	75	24	0.19	50	11	39	100	173	18%	103	13%	39%	11	18%	73%	2.43	-29.8	14	30	$0
11	MIN *	478	72	18	56	5	248	256	308	212	307	433	741	8	76	29	0.35	43	17	40	132	128	10%	118	9%	56%	17	41%	35%	4.41	-1.9	53	118	$12
12	MIN	422	56	24	55	1	235	262	242	232	296	455	751	8	78	25	0.40	38	18	44	136	114	17%	86	4%	25%	24	54%	33%	4.36	-2.3	53	133	$9
1st Half		196	33	16	29	0	245	279	291	227	324	541	865	11	76	24	0.49	38	16	47	184	136	23%	83	4%	0%	13	54%	31%	5.68	6.5	84	210	$13
2nd Half		226	23	8	26	1	226	248	203	236	271	381	651	6	80	25	0.31	38	21	41	96	97	11%	93	4%	50%	11	55%	36%	3.34	-8.5	27	68	$5
13	Proj	520	67	23	62	3	251	252	275	242	305	441	746	7	77	28	0.34	40	18	42	122	119	13%	99	6%	41%				4.45	-2.1	43	106	$14

Podsednik,Scott

Age 37	Bats L	Pos LF CF	Health	B	LIMA Plan	F
Ht 6' 0"	Wt 185		PT/Exp	D	Rand Var	-1
			Consist	C	MM	1401

1-12-.302 with 8 SB in 199 AB at BOS. Ex-burner spent 2011 with a wiffle bat in the minors, then went even more sub-Mendoza early in 2012. But then he came to New England. Batted .281 in Pawtucket and over .300 in Fenway. Skills are down but might still be a useful set of legs off the bench.

Yr	Tm	AB	R	HR	RBI	SB	BA	xBA	vL	vR	OB	Slg	OPS	bb%	ct%	h%	Eye	G	L	F	PX	xPX	hr/f	Spd	SBO	SB%	#Wk	DOM	DIS	RC/G	RAR	BPV	BPX	R$
08	COL	162	22	1	15	12	253	269	167	264	320	333	654	9	83	30	0.57	51	24	24	58	66	3%	108	34%	75%	24	29%	54%	3.68	-4.3	33	65	$4
09	CHW*	579	80	7	50	31	297	273	320	297	345	402	747	7	86	34	0.53	53	18	30	67	56	5%	135	25%	70%	24	38%	33%	4.91	5.7	51	104	$24
10	2 TM	539	63	6	51	35	297	252	289	300	345	382	728	7	85	34	0.48	50	19	31	52	57	4%	157	29%	70%	23	26%	35%	4.66	1.4	33	72	$26
11	aaa	112	11	0	4	4	195	221			257	288	545	8	72	27	0.30				79			108	16%	100%				2.49		10	0	-$2
12	BOS *	364	36	2	23	15	254	224	395	280	288	298	587	5	82	31	0.26	49	20	31	33	66	2%	115	22%	73%	14	7%	64%	2.94	-17.7	-7	-18	$7
1st Half		176	22	2	14	12	251	262	375	389	293	310	603	6	84	29	0.38	55	25	21	37	83	9%	112	29%	84%	5	20%	20%	3.27	-7.3	15	38	$10
2nd Half		188	14	0	9	3	257	198	400	224	283	288	571	4	80	32	0.18	47	17	36	28	58	0%	105	14%	50%	9	0%	89%	2.64	-11.3	-35	-88	$3
13	Proj	131	14	1	8	6	248	238	275	240	294	329	623	4	80	30	0.33	51	20	29	55	63	4%	115	23%	74%				3.28	-5.4	10	25	$3

Polanco,Placido

Age 37	Bats R	Pos 3B	Health	D	LIMA Plan	D
Ht 5' 10"	Wt 189		PT/Exp	B	Rand Var	+1
			Consist	B	MM	0223

Another year with back issues that kept him out most of the 2nd half. Makes great ct%, but not much happens when he puts the ball into play—except lots and lots of GB outs. Continued BA erosion, age and health grade makes him safely irrelevant.

Yr	Tm	AB	R	HR	RBI	SB	BA	xBA	vL	vR	OB	Slg	OPS	bb%	ct%	h%	Eye	G	L	F	PX	xPX	hr/f	Spd	SBO	SB%	#Wk	DOM	DIS	RC/G	RAR	BPV	BPX	R$
08	DET	580	90	8	58	7	307	279	321	301	346	417	764	6	93	32	0.81	47	19	35	69	46	4%	113	5%	88%	26	54%	19%	5.36	11.9	67	131	$20
09	DET	618	82	10	72	7	285	279	266	292	324	396	721	6	93	30	0.78	43	20	37	66	50	5%	105	5%	78%	27	59%	26%	4.59	-0.3	63	129	$16
10	PHI	554	76	6	52	5	298	272	280	305	336	386	722	5	92	32	0.68	45	20	35	59	39	3%	106	3%	100%	25	36%	20%	4.78	2.5	52	113	$17
11	PHI	469	46	5	50	3	277	265	336	257	337	339	676	8	91	30	0.95	42	26	32	41	44	4%	73	2%	100%	23	17%	39%	4.07	-7.1	28	62	$10
12	PHI	303	28	2	19	0	257	262	226	271	299	327	626	6	92	28	0.72	56	21	24	48	22	3%	81	0%	0%	20	30%	35%	3.36	-11.0	26	65	$1
1st Half		245	25	2	18	0	278	276	244	293	317	359	676	5	91	30	0.61	53	23	23	57	24	4%	80	0%	0%	13	38%	23%	4.01	-3.9	29	73	$4
2nd Half		58	3	0	1	0	172	196	133	186	226	190	415	6	97	18	2.00	65	11	25	13	15	0%	83	0%	0%	7	14%	57%	1.32	-6.1	17	43	-$9
13	Proj	328	31	2	23	1	251	255	245	253	297	311	608	6	93	26	0.91	52	19	29	39	31	3%	83	2%	94%				3.17	-13.6	31	77	$3

DAVE ADLER

Posey,Buster

Age	26	Bats	R	Pos CA 1B	Health	D	LIMA Plan	C+
Ht	6' 1"	Wt	220		PT/Exp	C	Rand Var	-5
					Consist	F	MM	3135

Impressive comeback by a rising star—but step back and take a deep breath. The 2H h% and PX are unrepeatable, and he won't always dominate LHP like that. He hits tons of GBs, and xPX suggests regression. But 1H production is a reasonable benchmark; double it, and he's still a top-flight catcher.

Yr Tm	AB	R	HR	RBI	SB	BA	xBA	vL	vR	OB	Slg	OPS	bb%	ct%	h%	Eye	G	L	F	PX	xPX	hr/f	Spd	SBO	SB%	#Wk	DOM	DIS	RC/G	RAR	BPV	BPX	R$
08																																	
09 SF *	148	16	3	16	0	264	236	0	167	319	395	714	8	80	31	0.41	62	8	31	85	53	0%	103	3%	0%	4	0%	75%	4.22	-0.2	21	43	$1
10 SF *	578	81	22	90	1	305	291	309	304	360	493	853	8	85	33	0.57	49	18	33	119	121	15%	89	2%	19%	20	55%	25%	6.38	33.2	66	143	$24
11 SF	162	17	4	21	3	284	243	205	314	356	389	744	10	81	33	0.60	53	18	29	69	84	10%	78	5%	100%	9	22%	44%	5.05	3.5	18	40	$4
12 SF	530	78	24	103	1	336	301	433	292	412	549	961	12	82	38	0.72	47	25	29	137	104	19%	75	1%	50%	27	59%	19%	8.65	60.3	74	185	$30
1st Half	250	31	10	40	1	296	272	370	266	367	472	839	10	82	33	0.61	50	20	30	111	109	16%	70	1%	100%	13	54%	31%	6.30	14.4	47	118	$21
2nd Half	280	47	14	63	0	371	325	484	317	452	618	1070	13	82	42	0.82	43	29	28	159	100	21%	81	1%	0%	14	64%	7%	11.18	48.4	94	235	$38
13 Proj	**502**	**67**	**20**	**83**	**2**	**304**	**283**	**333**	**292**	**376**	**489**	**865**	**10**	**82**	**34**	**0.64**	**49**	**22**	**30**	**117**	**99**	**16%**	**76**	**2%**	**59%**				**6.69**	**34.1**	**58**	**144**	**$21**

Prado,Martin

Age	29	Bats	R	Pos LF 3B	Health	B	LIMA Plan	B
Ht	6' 1"	Wt	190		PT/Exp	A	Rand Var	-1
					Consist	F	MM	2335

Fine rebound from injury-plagued 2011. As always, solid ct% virtually assured a lofty BA. SB boost was a perfect storm of SBO and SB%; history casts doubt on a repeat. Hit plenty of line drives, but low hr/f tempered HR totals. BA is the main attraction here; in his prime years, so expect more of the same.

Yr Tm	AB	R	HR	RBI	SB	BA	xBA	vL	vR	OB	Slg	OPS	bb%	ct%	h%	Eye	G	L	F	PX	xPX	hr/f	Spd	SBO	SB%	#Wk	DOM	DIS	RC/G	RAR	BPV	BPX	R$
08 ATL	228	36	2	33	3	320	286	283	349	378	461	838	8	87	36	0.72	42	23	35	93	111	3%	130	6%	75%	20	45%	25%	6.51	10.9	75	147	$8
09 ATL	450	64	11	49	1	307	289	301	309	358	464	822	7	87	33	0.61	44	20	37	105	108	8%	91	3%	25%	27	48%	19%	5.97	15.3	59	120	$14
10 ATL	599	100	15	66	5	307	295	275	320	351	459	810	6	86	34	0.47	48	21	31	102	91	9%	119	5%	63%	24	46%	25%	5.86	18.5	65	141	$24
11 ATL *	577	69	13	59	4	255	259	245	265	299	374	673	6	90	27	0.62	51	15	35	75	71	8%	114	8%	33%	23	48%	17%	3.63	-18.8	51	113	$11
12 ATL	617	81	10	70	17	301	291	323	290	361	438	799	9	89	33	0.84	48	23	29	86	76	6%	119	11%	81%	27	52%	15%	5.82	18.6	76	190	$25
1st Half	291	45	5	31	9	323	294	376	295	388	467	856	10	89	35	0.97	51	21	29	91	83	7%	130	10%	90%	13	69%	15%	6.99	18.2	83	208	$28
2nd Half	326	36	5	39	8	282	290	276	286	337	411	748	8	89	31	0.73	46	25	30	82	70	6%	104	12%	73%	14	36%	14%	4.89	2.3	66	165	$22
13 Proj	**614**	**82**	**13**	**69**	**11**	**299**	**284**	**299**	**298**	**352**	**442**	**794**	**8**	**88**	**32**	**0.71**	**48**	**21**	**31**	**89**	**80**	**8%**	**112**	**8%**	**72%**				**5.63**	**16.6**	**70**	**174**	**$25**

Presley,Alex

Age	27	Bats	L	Pos LF	Health	B	LIMA Plan	D
Ht	5' 10"	Wt	185		PT/Exp	C	Rand Var	+1
					Consist	B	MM	2433

10-25-.237 with 9 SB in 346 AB at PIT. Won the LF job with a hot March, but lost it with a cold April that relegated him to the AAA shuttle all season. PRO: Good speed; some pop in the bat. CON: Low bb% in the majors; SB% might warrant a red light going forward. More bus rides await.

Yr Tm	AB	R	HR	RBI	SB	BA	xBA	vL	vR	OB	Slg	OPS	bb%	ct%	h%	Eye	G	L	F	PX	xPX	hr/f	Spd	SBO	SB%	#Wk	DOM	DIS	RC/G	RAR	BPV	BPX	R$
08																																	
09																																	
10 PIT *	541	67	9	64	11	272	261	500	238	312	401	712	5	83	31	0.34	64	7	29	83	13	0%	126	16%	51%	4	25%	75%	4.12	-16.2	45	98	$15
11 PIT *	557	70	10	50	25	285	275	231	327	325	419	744	6	82	33	0.33	50	23	27	89	89	8%	131	26%	67%	10	50%	10%	4.66	-7.9	51	113	$22
12 PIT *	499	65	14	42	14	243	271	262	232	294	398	693	7	80	28	0.36	60	17	23	92	85	16%	139	20%	61%	22	45%	50%	3.77	-20.9	46	115	$11
1st Half	268	38	10	24	11	235	282	268	228	286	407	693	7	81	26	0.37	59	17	24	103	80	16%	114	26%	74%	11	45%	45%	3.82	-9.7	59	148	$15
2nd Half	231	27	4	18	3	253	257	250	236	304	388	693	7	78	31	0.34	61	17	22	78	92	17%	153	15%	38%	11	45%	55%	3.70	-9.1	22	55	$6
13 Proj	**262**	**33**	**7**	**24**	**8**	**263**	**276**	**263**	**263**	**309**	**421**	**730**	**6**	**81**	**30**	**0.35**	**56**	**20**	**25**	**94**	**88**	**13%**	**128**	**21%**	**60%**				**4.28**	**-2.9**	**50**	**125**	**$8**

Profar,Jurickson

Age	20	Bats	B	Pos 2B	Health	A	LIMA Plan	D
Ht	6' 0"	Wt	165		PT/Exp	F	Rand Var	-1
					Consist	F	MM	3421

1-2-.176 in 17 AB at TEX. NEWS FLASH: He's good. Great plate patience, makes contact, has power and speed, a solid defender. But don't go overboard in redraft leagues. We expect there to be some rampant Trout-inflation this spring. He's not going to hit 30 HRs and steal 45 bases. Not yet, anyway.

Yr Tm	AB	R	HR	RBI	SB	BA	xBA	vL	vR	OB	Slg	OPS	bb%	ct%	h%	Eye	G	L	F	PX	xPX	hr/f	Spd	SBO	SB%	#Wk	DOM	DIS	RC/G	RAR	BPV	BPX	R$
08																																	
09																																	
10																																	
11																																	
12 TEX *	497	67	15	55	14	276	256	0	231	350	448	798	10	84	31	0.69	54	8	38	105	123	20%	124	12%	77%	4	25%	75%	5.52	23.0	75	188	$18
1st Half	295	42	8	31	8	290	278			361	471	832	10	84	32	0.71				109			135	12%	71%				6.04		82	205	$22
2nd Half	202	24	7	24	6	254	243	0	231	333	415	748	11	82	28	0.68	54	8	38	99	123	20%	105	12%	85%	4	25%	75%	4.81	4.8	58	145	$11
13 Proj	**188**	**24**	**6**	**21**	**5**	**268**	**259**			**346**	**447**	**793**	**11**	**83**	**29**	**0.71**	**45**	**14**	**41**	**108**		**10%**	**118**	**12%**	**80%**				**5.42**	**6.3**	**73**	**183**	**$7**

Pujols,Albert

Age	33	Bats	R	Pos 1B DH	Health	A	LIMA Plan	C
Ht	6' 3"	Wt	230		PT/Exp	A	Rand Var	+2
					Consist	C	MM	4155

Two slow starts in a row. Was homerless with a .190 BA on May 8, then hit in 9 of his next 10 games and never looked back, batting .309 the rest of the way. PX, hr/f recovered, but most BPIs declined for a 3rd straight year. There may be some rebound in '13, but the days of $40+ value are in the past.

Yr Tm	AB	R	HR	RBI	SB	BA	xBA	vL	vR	OB	Slg	OPS	bb%	ct%	h%	Eye	G	L	F	PX	xPX	hr/f	Spd	SBO	SB%	#Wk	DOM	DIS	RC/G	RAR	BPV	BPX	R$
08 STL	524	100	37	116	7	357	347	411	333	463	653	1116	17	90	35	1.93	40	22	37	168	143	21%	62	5%	70%	26	92%	0%	11.90	88.1	144	282	$40
09 STL	568	124	47	135	16	327	343	338	324	441	658	1099	17	89	30	1.80	39	16	46	182	155	20%	75	10%	80%	27	81%	7%	11.00	86.4	161	329	$43
10 STL	587	115	42	118	14	312	323	306	314	414	596	1011	15	87	30	1.36	38	17	44	167	146	18%	65	9%	78%	27	81%	7%	9.14	61.6	137	298	$40
11 STL	579	105	37	99	9	299	311	295	300	366	541	906	10	90	28	1.05	45	17	38	137	140	18%	75	6%	90%	26	77%	4%	7.25	31.3	114	253	$33
12 LAA	607	85	30	105	8	285	303	290	283	341	516	857	8	87	29	0.68	41	19	40	140	126	14%	54	6%	89%	27	70%	7%	6.32	17.6	100	250	$27
1st Half	301	39	12	47	4	269	288	273	268	331	458	790	9	88	27	0.78	42	20	38	114	116	12%	57	5%	100%	13	54%	8%	5.38	0.2	80	200	$22
2nd Half	306	46	18	58	4	301	316	313	297	352	572	923	7	87	30	0.60	40	18	42	164	137	16%	55	7%	80%	14	86%	7%	7.32	16.6	113	283	$32
13 Proj	**566**	**94**	**33**	**104**	**9**	**291**	**308**	**297**	**289**	**363**	**542**	**905**	**10**	**88**	**28**	**0.96**	**41**	**18**	**40**	**145**	**136**	**17%**	**60**	**7%**	**84%**				**7.11**	**27.6**	**112**	**281**	**$30**

Punto,Nick

Age	35	Bats	B	Pos 3B 2B	Health	F	LIMA Plan	F
Ht	5' 9"	Wt	190		PT/Exp	F	Rand Var	0
					Consist	C	MM	1311

Utility infielder, or futility infielder? Yes, he plays all over the diamond, but that's all he has to offer. Used to make decent contact, but that dropped steeply. Great xBA in 2011, but that was an outlier. No power—15 HR in 10 years. And nothing in the metrics that presages a regression. That's sad.

Yr Tm	AB	R	HR	RBI	SB	BA	xBA	vL	vR	OB	Slg	OPS	bb%	ct%	h%	Eye	G	L	F	PX	xPX	hr/f	Spd	SBO	SB%	#Wk	DOM	DIS	RC/G	RAR	BPV	BPX	R$
08 MIN	338	43	2	28	15	284	253	302	272	346	382	728	9	83	34	0.56	45	21	35	68	54	2%	112	20%	71%	22	36%	41%	4.65	5.3	42	82	$11
09 MIN	359	56	1	38	16	228	234	236	225	340	284	625	15	81	28	0.87	48	19	33	44	31	1%	86	15%	84%	26	31%	46%	3.36	-8.1	20	41	$6
10 MIN	252	24	1	20	6	238	225	253	231	314	302	616	10	80	29	0.56	52	15	33	51	20	2%	86	11%	75%	21	19%	52%	3.20	-6.8	7	15	$2
11 STL *	172	24	1	21	2	260	294	273	281	364	375	738	14	85	30	1.07	46	31	23	75	41	4%	110	4%	61%	14	57%	36%	4.65	2.7	59	131	$2
12 2 TM	160	20	1	10	6	219	222	280	207	324	281	606	14	74	29	0.60	46	24	30	54	78	3%	84	12%	100%	27	19%	56%	3.20	-4.4	-8	-20	$0
1st Half	76	10	1	7	4	197	220	91	215	322	276	599	16	70	27	0.61	41	28	31	65	86	6%	78	16%	100%	13	31%	54%	3.13	-2.1	-13	-33	$0
2nd Half	84	10	0	3	2	238	222	429	200	326	286	612	12	77	31	0.58	51	21	29	44	72	0%	86	7%	100%	14	7%	57%	3.26	-1.9	-12	-30	$0
13 Proj	**122**	**15**	**1**	**10**	**3**	**238**	**242**	**280**	**224**	**336**	**316**	**652**	**13**	**79**	**30**	**0.70**	**47**	**24**	**29**	**59**	**56**	**3%**	**90**	**10%**	**88%**				**3.67**	**-3.3**	**17**	**41**	**$2**

Quentin,Carlos

Age	30	Bats	R	Pos LF	Health	D	LIMA Plan	B
Ht	6' 2"	Wt	235		PT/Exp	C	Rand Var	+1
					Consist	A	MM	4035

A trade to a pitcher's park didn't slow him; another injury did. Missed first two months after knee surgery, which also acted up in Sept. When he was on the field, his power profile was unchanged, though his plate approach did improve. Unfortunately, that health grade makes regular AB a risky proposition.

Yr Tm	AB	R	HR	RBI	SB	BA	xBA	vL	vR	OB	Slg	OPS	bb%	ct%	h%	Eye	G	L	F	PX	xPX	hr/f	Spd	SBO	SB%	#Wk	DOM	DIS	RC/G	RAR	BPV	BPX	R$
08 CHW	480	96	36	100	7	288	304	246	303	374	571	944	12	83	28	0.83	41	15	43	163	141	21%	83	7%	70%	23	87%	0%	7.56	38.3	114	224	$26
09 CHW *	388	55	22	63	3	245	277	213	245	308	457	765	8	86	23	0.65	37	16	47	118	143	15%	53	3%	100%	20	50%	25%	4.79	0.7	74	151	$10
10 CHW	453	73	26	87	2	243	277	211	253	318	479	797	10	82	24	0.60	37	14	49	147	125	14%	79	4%	50%	26	54%	4%	5.06	4.5	87	189	$14
11 CHW	421	53	24	77	1	254	273	297	241	310	499	809	7	80	27	0.40	32	14	54	165	143	13%	67	2%	50%	22	55%	23%	5.24	6.4	79	176	$14
12 SD	284	44	16	46	0	261	290	329	233	344	504	847	11	86	26	0.88	35	18	47	146	165	14%	47	1%	0%	19	68%	21%	5.89	9.6	93	233	$9
1st Half	90	15	7	16	0	311	315	323	305	404	622	1026	13	84	30	1.00	32	20	49	183	196	19%	59	0%	0%	5	80%	20%	9.30	11.3	119	298	$6
2nd Half	194	29	9	30	0	237	278	333	203	315	448	763	10	86	23	0.81	36	18	46	129	152	12%	48	2%	0%	14	64%	21%	4.62	-0.2	81	203	$10
13 Proj	**410**	**62**	**22**	**72**	**1**	**260**	**275**	**296**	**246**	**334**	**494**	**828**	**10**	**83**	**26**	**0.67**	**35**	**16**	**49**	**143**	**154**	**13%**	**54**	**2%**	**43%**				**5.63**	**11.7**	**82**	**204**	**$15**

DAVE ADLER

Quintanilla,Omar

Age 31	Bats L	Pos 2B SS	Health	A	LIMA Plan	F
Ht 5' 9"	Wt 185		PT/Exp	F	Rand Var	0
			Consist	B	MM	1001

4-16-.243 in 169 AB at BAL and NYM. There's not much going on here: sub-average power, sub-average speed and sub-average contact. One thing he does do well is hit the ball on the ground. Basically, he just provides in-game infield practice.

Yr	Tm	AB	R	HR	RBI	SB	BA	xBA	vL	vR	OB	Slg	OPS	bb%	ct%	h%	Eye	G	L	F	PX	xPX	hr/f	Spd	SBO	SB%	#Wk	DOM	DIS	RC/G	RAR	BPV	BPX	R$
08	COL *	283	39	3	20	2	243	257	209	246	303	343	646	8	79	30	0.42	52	20	28	80	81	4%	95	3%	100%	21	33%	62%	3.54	-6.7	18	35	$1
09	COL	58	7	0	2	0	172	153	83	196	273	207	480	12	53	32	0.30	39	23	39	46	59	0%	96	0%	0%	24	13%	79%	1.74	-4.5	-110	-224	-$3
10	aaa	119	8	1	8	1	187	219			225	259	484	5	75	24	0.19				60			98	9%	30%				1.74		-21	0	-$3
11	TEX *	230	29	3	16	2	205	222	0	91	248	309	558	5	78	25	0.26	58	8	33	69	126	0%	126	6%	57%	6	17%	67%	2.43	-12.5	15	33	-$2
12	2 TM *	325	37	8	34	1	221	242	261	236	277	350	627	7	76	27	0.33	56	17	27	90	88	12%	85	8%	12%	18	22%	56%	2.97	-13.9	9	23	$1
1st Half		225	25	5	22	1	217	255	133	296	273	351	623	7	77	26	0.34	60	17	23	93	74	8%	87	10%	15%	5	40%	40%	2.87	-9.8	19	48	$3
2nd Half		100	12	3	12	0	230	222	323	188	287	350	637	7	74	28	0.31	53	17	29	80	99	14%	80	4%	0%	13	15%	62%	3.18	-3.3	-12	-30	-$1
13	Proj	98	11	1	9	0	216	231	200	221	266	315	581	6	76	27	0.29	49	20	31	70	77	6%	91	6%	36%				2.63	-5.0	-1	-3	-$2

Quintero,Humberto

Age 33	Bats R	Pos CA	Health	B	LIMA Plan	F
Ht 5' 9"	Wt 215		PT/Exp	F	Rand Var	+2
			Consist	A	MM	1001

1-19-.232 in 138 AB at MIL. Rarely walks, makes mediocre contact, and doesn't contribute in the power or speed categories. The general rule of thumb for backup catchers is "do no harm." Unfortunately, all those negative numbers in the final four columns equal a world of harm.

Yr	Tm	AB	R	HR	RBI	SB	BA	xBA	vL	vR	OB	Slg	OPS	bb%	ct%	h%	Eye	G	L	F	PX	xPX	hr/f	Spd	SBO	SB%	#Wk	DOM	DIS	RC/G	RAR	BPV	BPX	R$
08	HOU *	298	25	4	25	0	208	223	273	215	232	289	521	3	82	24	0.17	59	12	29	53	82	5%	95	4%	0%	16	6%	81%	2.06	-20.8	-6	-12	-$4
09	HOU	157	11	4	14	0	236	226	273	226	268	376	644	4	74	29	0.17	57	10	32	99	88	11%	67	0%	0%	25	24%	48%	3.36	-4.3	-3	-6	-$1
10	HOU	265	13	4	20	0	234	212	165	263	256	317	573	3	78	29	0.14	47	19	34	62	50	6%	55	0%	0%	27	19%	70%	2.71	-12.5	-28	-61	-$1
11	HOU	262	22	2	25	1	240	231	268	233	257	317	574	2	80	29	0.11	52	18	30	60	78	3%	61	2%	100%	22	14%	64%	2.76	-11.9	-8	-18	$0
12	KC *	248	14	2	30	0	214	223	152	257	233	309	542	2	76	27	0.10	47	18	35	83	95	3%	45	3%	0%	12	17%	58%	2.28	-15.3	-15	-38	-$2
1st Half		138	7	1	19	0	232	238	152	257	254	341	594	3	80	28	0.14	47	18	35	90	95	3%	45	4%	0%	12	17%	58%	2.76	-6.1	5	13	-$1
2nd Half		110	7	1	11	0	191	206			206	270	476	2	71	26	0.07				72			52	0%	0%				1.75		-43	-108	-$3
13	Proj	102	7	1	10	0	221	219	189	231	241	317	558	3	77	28	0.11	51	17	33	74	78	5%	52	2%	33%				2.48	-5.4	-17	-43	$0

Raburn,Ryan

Age 32	Bats R	Pos 2B LF RF	Health	B	LIMA Plan	F
Ht 6' 0"	Wt 185		PT/Exp	D	Rand Var	+5
			Consist	D	MM	3201

1-12-.171 in 205 AB at DET. BA was hurt by low h%; poor plate approach didn't help. xBA shows that his hitting ability has been regressing for years. Hit more HR in March (six) than he did all season. Problem wasn't just PX drop, but miniscule hr/f. xPX hints at a power rebound, but first he'll need an opportunity.

Yr	Tm	AB	R	HR	RBI	SB	BA	xBA	vL	vR	OB	Slg	OPS	bb%	ct%	h%	Eye	G	L	F	PX	xPX	hr/f	Spd	SBO	SB%	#Wk	DOM	DIS	RC/G	RAR	BPV	BPX	R$
08	DET	182	26	4	20	3	236	228	238	235	298	368	666	8	73	30	0.33	47	14	39	98	111	8%	116	9%	75%	26	31%	46%	3.66	-4.9	17	33	$1
09	DET *	308	53	20	52	7	279	269	278	302	346	531	877	9	75	31	0.42	38	15	48	155	143	17%	119	14%	56%	25	48%	32%	6.21	14.6	74	151	$13
10	DET *	398	58	15	63	3	285	265	295	273	333	478	811	7	76	34	0.30	39	18	44	142	128	12%	106	6%	45%	27	41%	41%	5.52	10.8	51	111	$14
11	DET	387	53	14	49	1	256	238	274	245	294	432	726	5	71	33	0.18	35	21	45	135	142	11%	118	2%	50%	27	41%	44%	4.31	-2.8	23	51	$9
12	DET *	265	20	4	20	2	176	202	165	175	224	277	500	6	73	23	0.23	43	14	43	83	138	2%	81	6%	63%	19	21%	42%	1.90	-22.9	-13	-33	-$5
1st Half		182	12	2	10	1	174	183	190	172	218	251	469	5	72	23	0.20	41	14	45	66	139	2%	89	6%	50%	12	17%	50%	1.66	-17.8	-35	-88	-$6
2nd Half		83	8	2	10	1	180	241	121	190	236	334	570	7	76	21	0.30	50	14	36	117	136	0%	74	6%	100%	7	29%	29%	2.48	-5.8	27	68	-$2
13	Proj	164	19	5	19	1	234	233	227	239	282	391	673	6	73	29	0.25	42	16	42	117	136	9%	88	6%	68%				3.64	-3.1	20	50	$3

Ramirez,Alexei

Age 31	Bats R	Pos SS	Health	A	LIMA Plan	C
Ht 6' 2"	Wt 180		PT/Exp	A	Rand Var	0
			Consist	B	MM	1325

Aggressive approach at the plate—fewer walks—didn't result in more production. Increased aggressiveness on the basepaths, though, led to more SBs. 2H xBA, PX, hr/f all rebounded after slow start, so should return to usual levels. Consistent $15-20 value plus good health make him a good target at a scarce position.

Yr	Tm	AB	R	HR	RBI	SB	BA	xBA	vL	vR	OB	Slg	OPS	bb%	ct%	h%	Eye	G	L	F	PX	xPX	hr/f	Spd	SBO	SB%	#Wk	DOM	DIS	RC/G	RAR	BPV	BPX	R$
08	CHW	480	65	21	77	13	290	284	312	281	315	475	790	4	87	30	0.30	47	17	37	105	104	14%	121	20%	59%	27	44%	19%	5.09	16.2	69	135	$21
09	CHW	542	71	15	68	14	277	251	370	248	337	389	726	8	88	29	0.74	46	16	38	62	71	8%	110	11%	74%	27	44%	33%	4.61	10.9	43	88	$17
10	CHW	585	83	18	70	13	282	281	278	283	314	431	744	4	86	30	0.33	48	19	33	93	82	11%	122	15%	62%	27	44%	26%	4.64	12.3	57	124	$22
11	CHW	614	81	15	70	7	269	266	268	269	325	399	724	8	86	29	0.61	45	19	35	85	77	8%	108	7%	58%	27	37%	26%	4.43	9.3	51	113	$17
12	CHW	593	59	9	73	20	265	254	290	258	284	364	648	3	87	29	0.21	46	20	34	61	69	5%	123	20%	74%	27	30%	44%	3.56	-6.0	35	88	$17
1st Half		293	28	2	37	9	249	242	286	239	269	317	587	3	85	29	0.18	49	20	31	45	75	3%	120	16%	82%	13	15%	54%	2.95	-9.2	15	38	$13
2nd Half		300	31	7	36	11	280	267	294	276	299	410	709	3	89	30	0.24	44	20	36	76	62	7%	122	23%	69%	14	43%	36%	4.21	1.7	52	130	$21
13	Proj	601	71	13	73	16	272	261	288	267	306	393	699	5	87	29	0.38	46	19	35	74	74	7%	114	15%	69%				4.13	2.1	46	116	$20

Ramirez,Aramis

Age 35	Bats R	Pos 3B	Health	B	LIMA Plan	B+
Ht 6' 1"	Wt 205		PT/Exp	A	Rand Var	0
			Consist	C	MM	4235

PX rose to lofty level; xPX fully buys in. However, 2nd half fueled this surge, making it the 4th straight year he's gone nuts after the Break. But he's 35 now; odds are it's going to get tougher to turn around these slow starts. If you're still in the bidding when it hits $25, you're spending away any possible profit.

Yr	Tm	AB	R	HR	RBI	SB	BA	xBA	vL	vR	OB	Slg	OPS	bb%	ct%	h%	Eye	G	L	F	PX	xPX	hr/f	Spd	SBO	SB%	#Wk	DOM	DIS	RC/G	RAR	BPV	BPX	R$
08	CHC	554	97	27	111	2	289	289	239	305	373	518	891	12	83	31	0.79	31	20	48	146	133	12%	83	2%	50%	27	56%	22%	6.85	34.8	91	178	$23
09	CHC	306	46	15	65	2	317	285	350	312	374	516	891	8	86	33	0.65	35	21	44	112	105	13%	88	3%	67%	18	50%	28%	7.17	21.1	70	143	$15
10	CHC	465	61	25	83	0	241	255	259	235	293	452	744	7	81	25	0.38	27	16	57	132	147	12%	66	0%	0%	26	54%	31%	4.44	-2.3	55	120	$11
11	CHC	565	80	26	93	1	306	297	305	307	355	510	865	7	88	31	0.62	34	23	43	125	129	12%	90	1%	50%	27	59%	15%	6.62	31.0	79	176	$27
12	MIL	570	92	27	105	9	300	299	338	288	350	540	891	7	86	31	0.54	39	19	42	148	164	13%	87	8%	82%	27	67%	7%	6.90	36.1	106	265	$29
1st Half		267	44	9	45	2	262	287	258	263	330	464	794	9	85	28	0.68	40	20	41	130	147	10%	75	5%	67%	13	62%	0%	5.26	5.3	90	225	$19
2nd Half		303	48	18	60	7	333	311	403	310	369	607	976	5	86	34	0.40	38	18	44	165	179	16%	96	11%	88%	14	71%	14%	8.63	32.2	116	290	$38
13	Proj	585	89	25	98	5	292	284	314	285	342	500	842	7	85	31	0.52	36	21	43	128	149	12%	85	5%	79%				6.16	25.7	83	208	$27

Ramirez,Hanley

Age 29	Bats R	Pos 3B SS	Health	B	LIMA Plan	C+
Ht 6' 2"	Wt 229		PT/Exp	B	Rand Var	+1
			Consist	D	MM	3225

Made his debut in Tinseltown, but the reviews were decidedly mixed. PRO: Fully healthy; switched to SS; PX and hr/f returned to 2010 levels. CON: Erosion in bb%, ct% continued; ran less. This flick gets two stars; not the blockbusters of 2008-2010, but better than 2011's "Ishtar."

Yr	Tm	AB	R	HR	RBI	SB	BA	xBA	vL	vR	OB	Slg	OPS	bb%	ct%	h%	Eye	G	L	F	PX	xPX	hr/f	Spd	SBO	SB%	#Wk	DOM	DIS	RC/G	RAR	BPV	BPX	R$
08	FLA	589	125	33	67	35	301	292	258	313	395	540	935	14	79	33	0.75	46	17	37	149	122	19%	136	24%	74%	26	65%	15%	7.65	58.9	103	202	$38
09	FLA	576	101	24	106	27	342	287	316	352	405	543	948	10	82	38	0.60	39	20	42	128	105	12%	105	18%	77%	26	58%	27%	8.48	66.3	82	167	$40
10	FLA	543	92	21	76	32	300	285	286	305	374	475	849	11	83	33	0.69	51	16	33	112	108	14%	112	24%	76%	26	54%	38%	6.44	35.7	78	170	$33
11	FLA	338	55	10	45	20	243	255	315	223	330	379	709	12	80	27	0.67	51	16	33	94	96	11%	76	30%	67%	18	33%	22%	4.05	-0.6	51	113	$12
12	2 NL	604	79	24	92	21	257	262	263	254	318	437	755	8	78	29	0.41	47	18	34	115	115	15%	87	18%	75%	27	44%	37%	4.73	11.1	55	138	$23
1st Half		297	40	11	41	10	259	263	266	257	329	441	770	9	80	29	0.53	42	19	40	116	129	12%	85	18%	71%	13	46%	31%	4.93	8.1	65	163	$22
2nd Half		307	39	13	51	11	254	262	260	251	306	433	739	7	76	30	0.31	53	18	29	114	101	19%	87	19%	79%	14	43%	43%	4.54	4.8	42	105	$24
13	Proj	570	86	21	84	21	266	261	279	261	336	433	768	10	79	30	0.51	49	17	34	106	108	14%	86	18%	73%				4.99	6.9	54	135	$25

Ramos,Wilson

Age 25	Bats R	Pos CA	Health	F	LIMA Plan	D
Ht 6' 0"	Wt 250		PT/Exp	D	Rand Var	-3
			Consist	C	MM	3013

Talk about a rough year: kidnapped from the Venezuelan Winter League; then tore a knee ligament in May. Showed his power in 2011; just don't expect 2012's small-sample hr/f to hold up. Step one is getting back on the field; all signs point to him being ready for spring training.

Yr	Tm	AB	R	HR	RBI	SB	BA	xBA	vL	vR	OB	Slg	OPS	bb%	ct%	h%	Eye	G	L	F	PX	xPX	hr/f	Spd	SBO	SB%	#Wk	DOM	DIS	RC/G	RAR	BPV	BPX	R$
08																																		
09	aa	205	28	3	26	0	294	277			312	419	731	2	88	32	0.21				85			82	0%	0%				4.73		37	0	$4
10	2 TM *	436	38	8	37	1	241	226	563	206	265	349	614	3	82	28	0.18	43	13	43	77	118	3%	64	3%	28%	8	25%	50%	3.04	-16.3	11	24	$3
11	WAS	389	48	15	52	0	267	257	276	265	333	445	777	9	80	30	0.50	50	15	36	120	119	13%	58	2%	0%	27	52%	33%	5.04	8.4	48	107	$10
12	WAS	83	11	3	10	0	265	224	300	260	358	398	755	13	77	31	0.63	66	14	20	82	96	23%	53	0%	0%	6	17%	50%	4.94	1.5	8	20	$0
1st Half		83	11	3	10	0	265	224	300	260	358	398	755	13	77	31	0.63	66	14	20	82	96	23%	53	0%	0%	6	17%	50%	4.94	1.7	8	20	$0
2nd Half																																		
13	Proj	390	45	14	44	0	261	245	291	255	314	423	737	7	81	29	0.41	53	14	33	102	111	14%	47	1%	23%				4.54	3.7	32	80	$10

DAVE ADLER

Ransom,Cody

Age 37	Bats R	Pos SS 3B	Health	A	LIMA Plan	F
Ht 6' 2"	Wt 203		PT/Exp	D	Rand Var	-5
			Consist	A	MM	4101

11-42-.220 in 246 AB at ARI and MIL. It's all about the power. Hasn't seen this level of hr/f in four years. Contact rate dropped to absurd level. It's rare when someone who strikes out so much gets this many ABs; at 37, it won't happen again. Short term goal: to hit .225. We all need goals.

Yr Tm	AB	R	HR	RBI	SB	BA	xBA	vL	vR	OB	Slg	OPS	bb%	ct%	h%	Eye	G	L	F	PX	xPX	hr/f	Spd	SBO	SB%	#Wk	DOM	DIS	RC/G	RAR	BPV	BPX	R$
08 NYY *	466	61	21	61	7	212	228	214	345	279	404	683	8	66	27	0.27	39	16	45	144	142	29%	101	14%	52%	8	50%	50%	3.49	-16.3	23	45	$4
09 NYY *	175	30	3	23	2	191	227	158	220	285	338	623	12	70	26	0.44	38	15	47	121	80	0%	107	5%	100%	9	44%	56%	3.10	-8.3	37	76	-$1
10 PHI *	436	49	16	51	5	205	199	194	182	260	361	621	7	66	27	0.22	42	6	52	124	51	13%	92	8%	65%	6	33%	50%	2.97	-22.4	2	4	$3
11 ARI *	405	46	15	50	6	215	231	125	176	268	391	659	7	67	28	0.22	42	17	42	143	85	10%	78	13%	60%	6	33%	67%	3.31	-16.3	22	49	$5
12 2 NL *	280	32	12	47	0	218	201	264	195	301	403	704	11	55	35	0.26	40	19	42	174	156	20%	82	2%	0%	23	30%	57%	3.90	-6.0	-12	-30	$3
1st Half	172	20	8	33	0	210	194	209	211	293	395	687	10	53	34	0.25	39	19	42	173	157	23%	72	2%	0%	10	40%	60%	3.64	-5.1	-20	-50	$5
2nd Half	108	12	4	14	0	231	211	318	172	314	417	731	11	57	36	0.28	40	18	42	175	155	16%	93	0%	0%	13	23%	54%	4.34	-0.8	-1	-3	$0
13 Proj	96	11	3	13	1	216	204	230	206	286	370	657	9	61	32	0.26	39	17	44	135	126	11%	88	5%	56%				3.40	-1.8	-9	-22	-$1

Rasmus,Colby

Age 26	Bats L	Pos CF	Health	A	LIMA Plan	C+
Ht 6' 2"	Wt 200		PT/Exp	A	Rand Var	+2
			Consist	C	MM	3205

Still struggling to live up to the prospect label from years ago. Combination of low h% and ct% eliminates BA upside, as does the fact that he still gets ABs vs LHP. 1H showed a servicable BA when he made contact, but he started hacking again in 2H. If he continues to see lefties and swing freely... DN: 15 HR.

Yr Tm	AB	R	HR	RBI	SB	BA	xBA	vL	vR	OB	Slg	OPS	bb%	ct%	h%	Eye	G	L	F	PX	xPX	hr/f	Spd	SBO	SB%	#Wk	DOM	DIS	RC/G	RAR	BPV	BPX	R$
08 aaa	331	44	8	28	12	219	236			300	331	631	10	77	26	0.50				77			92	17%	78%				3.29		18	0	$3
09 STL	474	72	16	52	3	251	250	160	277	304	407	711	7	80	28	0.38	35	20	46	98	114	9%	99	3%	75%	27	30%	48%	4.21	-9.0	38	78	$9
10 STL	464	85	23	66	12	276	251	270	278	362	498	860	12	68	36	0.43	32	19	49	170	130	15%	113	15%	60%	27	44%	37%	6.12	16.9	65	141	$21
11 2 TM	471	75	14	53	5	225	233	215	229	299	391	690	10	75	27	0.43	36	16	48	117	139	8%	114	6%	71%	25	40%	52%	3.84	-14.6	51	113	$7
12 TOR	565	75	23	75	4	223	237	182	238	283	400	683	8	74	26	0.32	38	20	42	115	123	13%	103	6%	57%	27	33%	41%	3.66	-20.8	29	73	$10
1st Half	292	40	14	46	4	257	273	241	263	309	476	785	7	79	28	0.35	40	20	40	137	131	15%	100	8%	80%	13	54%	15%	5.05	2.3	70	175	$18
2nd Half	273	35	9	29	0	187	200	120	212	255	319	574	8	68	24	0.29	35	20	45	88	114	11%	111	3%	0%	14	14%	64%	2.46	-20.3	-17	-43	$1
13 Proj	510	75	20	63	6	242	232	204	256	309	417	726	9	73	29	0.36	36	19	45	117	126	12%	104	7%	62%				4.28	-7.7	34	84	$13

Reddick,Josh

Age 26	Bats L	Pos RF	Health	A	LIMA Plan	B
Ht 6' 2"	Wt 180		PT/Exp	B	Rand Var	0
			Consist	B	MM	4315

In retrospect, we might have seen this breakout coming with additional ABs; the trends were there, but hindsight is always 20/20. Still, 2nd half PX, hr/f are more realistic going forward. Falling ct%, low h% mean there's no BA upside; his value is completely rooted in HR.

Yr Tm	AB	R	HR	RBI	SB	BA	xBA	vL	vR	OB	Slg	OPS	bb%	ct%	h%	Eye	G	L	F	PX	xPX	hr/f	Spd	SBO	SB%	#Wk	DOM	DIS	RC/G	RAR	BPV	BPX	R$
08 aa	117	18	4	20	2	200	262			261	377	639	8	78	22	0.38				109			112	15%	69%				3.10		54	0	-$1
09 BOS *	386	49	13	36	5	234	243	200	167	296	422	719	8	76	28	0.37	31	17	52	126	161	9%	128	13%	42%	9	22%	56%	3.93	-10.9	50	102	$4
10 BOS *	513	53	15	57	4	241	259	400	175	271	408	680	4	82	27	0.23	45	13	43	113	69	5%	101	13%	36%	9	44%	44%	3.50	-21.1	49	107	$8
11 BOS *	445	71	18	57	4	249	268	275	280	319	449	767	9	79	28	0.49	31	23	46	135	121	7%	115	7%	58%	16	56%	31%	4.77	-1.0	73	162	$12
12 OAK	611	85	32	85	11	242	249	237	245	305	463	768	8	75	27	0.36	29	21	50	141	131	14%	119	9%	92%	28	54%	25%	4.82	-0.7	65	163	$19
1st Half	288	49	18	39	8	260	263	269	256	339	517	856	11	74	29	0.46	31	23	47	160	143	18%	139	11%	100%	14	64%	21%	6.22	10.1	87	218	$25
2nd Half	323	36	14	46	3	226	239	214	234	273	415	688	6	76	25	0.27	28	20	52	125	121	11%	99	6%	75%	14	43%	29%	3.73	-12.6	39	98	$14
13 Proj	581	80	25	77	8	250	249	206	270	308	448	756	8	77	28	0.37	32	20	48	127	122	11%	115	8%	68%				4.65	-6.2	57	144	$17

Reimold,Nolan

Age 29	Bats R	Pos LF	Health	F	LIMA Plan	C
Ht 6' 4"	Wt 205		PT/Exp	D	Rand Var	-3
			Consist	F	MM	4323

Blistered the ball in April; missed the rest of the year with a herniated disk in neck. Only had two walks before injury, but exhibited fine plate patience in the past. Has previously shown power, but high GB% and xPX temper expectations going forward. Can't draw any conclusions until he's on the field.

Yr Tm	AB	R	HR	RBI	SB	BA	xBA	vL	vR	OB	Slg	OPS	bb%	ct%	h%	Eye	G	L	F	PX	xPX	hr/f	Spd	SBO	SB%	#Wk	DOM	DIS	RC/G	RAR	BPV	BPX	R$
08 aa	507	70	22	67	6	251	280			317	441	758	9	82	27	0.54				116			90	7%	62%				4.68		63	0	$11
09 BAL *	467	67	23	68	13	297	279	271	284	379	515	894	12	78	34	0.59	48	14	37	139	98	14%	112	11%	80%	19	53%	26%	7.10	32.9	74	151	$21
10 BAL *	453	47	11	41	7	206	218	265	164	285	312	598	10	78	24	0.51	49	12	39	72	65	8%	83	8%	73%	11	27%	55%	2.87	-24.1	11	24	$1
11 BAL *	406	51	18	61	8	228	238	225	258	298	410	708	9	73	27	0.37	45	14	41	124	107	15%	128	12%	72%	20	55%	30%	4.01	-6.9	42	93	$9
12 BAL	67	10	5	10	1	313	333	313	314	333	627	960	3	79	33	0.14	43	26	30	201	92	31%	98	8%	100%	5	40%	20%	7.86	5.9	100	250	$2
1st Half	67	10	5	10	1	313	334	313	314	333	627	960	3	79	33	0.14	43	26	30	201	92	31%	98	8%	100%	5	40%	20%	7.86	5.8	100	250	$2
2nd Half																																	
13 Proj	323	42	14	43	6	261	262	302	243	319	454	773	8	78	30	0.38	46	17	37	126	86	15%	100	9%	81%				5.01	3.4	52	131	$11

Revere,Ben

Age 25	Bats L	Pos RF CF	Health	A	LIMA Plan	C
Ht 5' 9"	Wt 172		PT/Exp	C	Rand Var	-2
			Consist	A	MM	0535

0-32-.294 with 40 SB in 511 AB at MIN. Slap hitter who put few balls in the air; only 19 of 150 hits were XBH. Huge GB% takes advantage of blazing speed to get on base (although more walks would be nice). xBA fortells a dip in BA, but SBs are money in the bank.

Yr Tm	AB	R	HR	RBI	SB	BA	xBA	vL	vR	OB	Slg	OPS	bb%	ct%	h%	Eye	G	L	F	PX	xPX	hr/f	Spd	SBO	SB%	#Wk	DOM	DIS	RC/G	RAR	BPV	BPX	R$
08																																	
09																																	
10 MIN *	389	35	1	20	28	267	262	154	200	316	314	631	7	88	30	0.58	68	14	18	31	40	0%	135	37%	65%	5	0%	80%	3.27	-18.6	24	52	$12
11 MIN *	582	68	1	37	40	267	291	265	268	304	311	615	5	91	29	0.58	69	20	12	27	18	0%	146	31%	78%	22	36%	32%	3.38	-25.3	38	84	$20
12 MIN *	605	78	0	37	45	294	278	314	284	330	337	667	5	90	33	0.53	67	19	15	26	23	0%	150	30%	80%	24	29%	38%	4.15	-12.1	33	83	$27
1st Half	272	29	0	16	20	312	299	413	288	337	352	689	4	93	33	0.55	67	23	11	25	28	0%	125	30%	76%	10	30%	30%	4.43	-4.3	35	88	$24
2nd Half	333	49	0	21	25	279	264	276	281	324	324	648	6	87	32	0.52	67	16	17	27	21	0%	158	29%	83%	14	29%	43%	3.93	-10.4	29	73	$30
13 Proj	596	71	0	36	43	280	281	288	276	319	322	641	5	90	31	0.55	68	19	13	26	22	0%	146	31%	77%				3.72	-22.3	32	80	$25

Reyes,Jose

Age 30	Bats B	Pos SS	Health	C	LIMA Plan	C
Ht 6' 1"	Wt 195		PT/Exp	A	Rand Var	+1
			Consist	F	MM	2535

At face value, a disappointment compared to 2011, but skills were virtually unchanged. BA drop seems the most damning, but that red herring was driven by high h% in 2011; xBA was identical both years. Double-digit HRs now in question due to eroding FB%, but continued high SB are assured due to consistent SBO.

Yr Tm	AB	R	HR	RBI	SB	BA	xBA	vL	vR	OB	Slg	OPS	bb%	ct%	h%	Eye	G	L	F	PX	xPX	hr/f	Spd	SBO	SB%	#Wk	DOM	DIS	RC/G	RAR	BPV	BPX	R$
08 NYM	688	113	16	68	56	297	299	280	303	358	475	833	9	88	32	0.80	44	23	33	101	81	8%	165	36%	79%	27	70%	4%	6.18	40.6	101	198	$41
09 NYM	147	18	2	15	11	279	259	400	248	358	395	752	11	87	31	0.95	41	19	40	70	76	4%	144	27%	85%	7	43%	14%	5.22	4.7	67	137	$5
10 NYM	563	83	11	54	30	282	274	309	274	320	428	748	5	89	30	0.49	43	18	40	88	67	6%	132	29%	75%	25	52%	20%	4.81	11.3	83	180	$24
11 NYM	537	101	7	44	39	337	290	325	341	386	493	880	7	92	36	1.05	42	21	37	91	88	4%	176	27%	85%	23	70%	9%	7.53	48.7	109	242	$36
12 MIA	642	86	11	57	40	287	291	277	291	350	433	783	9	91	30	1.13	46	22	32	84	83	6%	123	27%	78%	27	70%	4%	5.46	24.8	94	235	$29
1st Half	306	37	2	19	18	271	287	237	286	348	386	734	11	90	30	1.13	48	24	28	70	82	3%	117	23%	82%	13	62%	8%	4.83	7.3	77	193	$21
2nd Half	336	49	9	38	22	301	296	316	295	353	476	829	7	93	30	1.13	44	20	36	97	83	8%	125	31%	76%	14	79%	0%	6.04	19.3	108	270	$37
13 Proj	580	88	10	53	38	300	284	300	300	355	451	806	8	91	32	0.95	44	21	35	86	81	5%	139	28%	80%				5.89	30.6	96	239	$32

Reynolds,Mark

Age 29	Bats R	Pos 1B	Health	A	LIMA Plan	C+
Ht 6' 2"	Wt 220		PT/Exp	A	Rand Var	+2
			Consist	B	MM	5105

Early season oblique injury slowed his 1st half, and he didn't click into gear until Aug. But he hit 15 HRs and batted .250 over the last two months. Decreasing FB% tempers expectations for more runs at 40+ HRs but power output in the 30s is money in the bank, if he's healthy. Along with a BA that toes the Mendoza Line.

Yr Tm	AB	R	HR	RBI	SB	BA	xBA	vL	vR	OB	Slg	OPS	bb%	ct%	h%	Eye	G	L	F	PX	xPX	hr/f	Spd	SBO	SB%	#Wk	DOM	DIS	RC/G	RAR	BPV	BPX	R$
08 ARI	539	87	28	97	11	239	233	279	226	320	458	778	11	62	33	0.31	36	19	45	173	149	18%	106	10%	85%	27	30%	52%	4.96	-5.2	43	84	$15
09 ARI	578	98	44	102	24	260	257	235	266	346	543	889	12	61	34	0.34	35	17	47	217	169	26%	92	22%	73%	27	63%	26%	6.34	17.9	73	149	$29
10 ARI	499	79	32	85	7	198	218	218	191	313	433	746	14	58	26	0.39	32	13	55	196	149	20%	85	8%	64%	26	42%	38%	4.24	-16.5	43	93	$10
11 BAL	534	84	37	86	6	221	248	208	225	317	483	800	12	63	27	0.38	39	13	48	209	171	23%	67	8%	60%	27	59%	22%	4.92	-5.9	67	149	$16
12 BAL	457	65	23	69	1	221	236	227	219	328	429	757	14	65	28	0.46	37	20	42	161	138	18%	65	3%	25%	25	28%	56%	4.50	-11.0	28	70	$8
1st Half	177	24	6	22	1	209	221	267	189	327	379	705	15	62	30	0.46	34	23	43	148	131	13%	68	4%	50%	11	18%	64%	3.94	-7.9	11	28	-$1
2nd Half	280	41	17	47	0	229	245	203	238	329	461	790	13	67	27	0.46	39	19	42	168	143	22%	67	3%	0%	14	36%	50%	4.87	-4.2	39	98	$14
13 Proj	547	82	32	87	5	231	232	235	230	333	459	792	13	63	30	0.41	37	17	46	176	150	20%	67	6%	56%				4.98	-6.3	40	100	$16

DAVE ADLER

Rhymes,Will

Age	30	Bats	L	Pos 2B	Health	A	LIMA Plan	F
Ht	5' 9"	Wt	155		PT/Exp	C	Rand Var	+5
					Consist	B	MM	0311

1-8-.228 in 123 AB in TAM. Passed out after getting hit in the wrist with a pitch on May 16. No break, but a .195 MLB BA for the balance of the season implies that it bothered him. Not that it matters given his history of zero power and bad SB technique. But he does have end-game speed, unless your category is net steals.

Yr	Tm	AB	R	HR	RBI	SB	BA	xBA	vL	vR	OB	Slg	OPS	bb%	ct%	h%	Eye	G	L	F	PX	xPX	hr/f	Spd	SBO	SB%	#Wk	DOM	DIS	RC/G	RAR	BPV	BPX	R$
08	a/a	541	61	2	47	13	263	239			307	334	640	6	85	30	0.43				45			126	13%	65%				3.47		24	0	$9
09	aaa	404	39	3	34	16	228	244			280	311	591	7	84	27	0.44				52			120	26%	64%				2.76		28	0	$4
10	DET *	555	73	2	45	16	269	278	351	292	318	364	682	7	90	30	0.69	44	23	33	62	35	2%	143	17%	64%	11	73%	27%	3.93	-3.9	61	133	$13
11	DET *	490	56	2	20	11	248	265	143	244	311	310	621	8	86	28	0.67	47	26	26	43	67	0%	141	14%	52%	11	18%	55%	3.11	-15.6	25	56	$6
12	TAM *	295	24	4	23	2	210	251	0	272	266	290	556	7	86	23	0.54	39	27	34	45	39	3%	116	11%	29%	14	21%	57%	2.29	-17.5	17	43	-$2
1st Half		191	15	1	12	2	200	240	0	275	246	249	494	6	86	23	0.42	42	25	33	31	31	0%	106	11%	34%	9	11%	78%	1.82	-15.0	2	5	-$3
2nd Half		104	9	3	11	1	228	269	0	261	302	365	667	10	87	24	0.79	27	32	41	70	68	11%	127	11%	22%	5	40%	20%	3.31	-3.1	46	115	$0
13	**Proj**	**129**	**13**	**0**	**10**	**4**	**236**	**250**	**165**	**250**	**296**	**298**	**594**	**8**	**87**	**27**	**0.64**	**44**	**25**	**31**	**39**	**42**	**1%**	**119**	**20%**	**61%**				**2.84**	**-5.6**	**25**	**64**	**$0**

Rios,Alex

Age	32	Bats	R	Pos RF	Health	A	LIMA Plan	B
Ht	6' 5"	Wt	215		PT/Exp	A	Rand Var	-4
					Consist	F	MM	3435

When skills consolidate for a five-category player, it looks like this. A h% bump produced the .300 BA, but other metrics supportive: PX and FB%, Spd skills, equal vR/vL splits. But he's 32, not 26, and with declining Eye and that BA/xBA gap, a repeat is unlikely. The ghost of 2011 should always temper your enthusiasm.

Yr	Tm	AB	R	HR	RBI	SB	BA	xBA	vL	vR	OB	Slg	OPS	bb%	ct%	h%	Eye	G	L	F	PX	xPX	hr/f	Spd	SBO	SB%	#Wk	DOM	DIS	RC/G	RAR	BPV	BPX	R$
08	TOR	635	91	15	79	32	291	277	289	292	337	461	799	6	82	33	0.39	41	21	38	113	131	7%	119	25%	80%	27	41%	26%	5.63	13.8	76	149	$30
09	2 AL	582	63	17	71	24	247	256	261	242	292	395	688	6	82	28	0.35	43	16	41	94	103	9%	91	22%	83%	27	44%	37%	3.98	-15.2	47	96	$16
10	CHW	567	89	21	88	34	284	277	259	292	329	457	786	6	84	31	0.41	45	17	38	109	107	12%	111	33%	71%	26	54%	19%	5.16	4.9	73	159	$31
11	CHW	537	64	13	44	11	227	255	287	204	264	348	612	5	87	24	0.40	42	18	39	76	76	7%	100	15%	65%	27	37%	33%	2.96	-31.2	50	111	$7
12	CHW	605	93	25	91	23	304	288	293	308	333	516	849	4	85	33	0.28	40	22	38	125	111	13%	118	21%	79%	27	56%	22%	6.27	23.6	90	225	$34
1st Half		291	43	10	41	13	306	284	266	317	336	491	827	4	85	33	0.30	41	24	35	106	83	11%	131	22%	81%	13	54%	31%	6.08	8.7	77	193	$32
2nd Half		314	50	15	50	10	303	293	313	299	330	538	868	4	84	32	0.27	39	20	41	142	138	14%	103	19%	77%	14	57%	14%	6.44	12.5	96	240	$35
13	**Proj**	**567**	**81**	**19**	**75**	**21**	**278**	**272**	**286**	**276**	**313**	**452**	**765**	**5**	**85**	**30**	**0.33**	**41**	**20**	**39**	**105**	**105**	**10%**	**106**	**22%**	**75%**				**4.94**	**-1.1**	**72**	**180**	**$25**

Rivera,Juan

Age	34	Bats	R	Pos 1B LF	Health	F	LIMA Plan	F
Ht	6' 2"	Wt	220		PT/Exp	C	Rand Var	+2
					Consist	A	MM	2021

Hamstring injury cost him nearly a month; still put up some useful part-time power stats. But PX/xPX are droppping in tandem, and a sub-30% hit rate means he's unlikely to ever best his decidely mediocre xBA. Tons of contact, but doesn't run well. Health grade says high-risk, BPI says low-reward.

Yr	Tm	AB	R	HR	RBI	SB	BA	xBA	vL	vR	OB	Slg	OPS	bb%	ct%	h%	Eye	G	L	F	PX	xPX	hr/f	Spd	SBO	SB%	#Wk	DOM	DIS	RC/G	RAR	BPV	BPX	R$
08	LAA	256	31	12	45	1	246	262	233	253	290	438	728	6	87	24	0.48	37	14	48	111	100	11%	67	4%	50%	25	32%	44%	4.24	-3.6	63	124	$4
09	LAA	529	72	25	88	0	287	287	333	271	333	478	811	6	89	28	0.63	44	18	38	104	111	14%	82	1%	0%	26	58%	12%	5.65	13.6	64	131	$18
10	LAA	416	53	15	52	2	252	266	264	246	307	409	716	7	86	26	0.57	46	16	39	97	98	11%	71	4%	50%	26	50%	35%	4.22	-6.1	52	113	$9
11	2 TM	466	46	11	74	5	258	260	289	247	320	382	702	8	84	29	0.57	43	21	35	84	88	8%	76	6%	63%	27	33%	44%	4.15	-7.8	38	84	$11
12	LA	312	30	9	47	1	244	256	260	232	285	375	660	5	89	25	0.51	49	17	34	78	68	9%	59	6%	25%	24	46%	21%	3.46	-11.8	40	100	$4
1st Half		153	14	3	24	0	261	231	257	265	307	353	660	6	92	27	0.83	52	14	34	52	51	6%	70	5%	0%	10	50%	20%	3.53	-5.1	32	80	$4
2nd Half		159	16	6	23	1	226	278	263	206	263	396	660	5	86	23	0.35	46	20	33	104	87	13%	55	7%	50%	14	43%	21%	3.37	-6.2	50	125	$5
13	**Proj**	**164**	**17**	**5**	**25**	**1**	**249**	**259**	**267**	**239**	**298**	**391**	**689**	**7**	**87**	**26**	**0.53**	**46**	**18**	**36**	**85**	**84**	**10%**	**66**	**5%**	**44%**				**3.86**	**-7.3**	**42**	**104**	**$4**

Rizzo,Anthony

Age	23	Bats	L	Pos 1B	Health	A	LIMA Plan	C+
Ht	6' 3"	Wt	220		PT/Exp	C	Rand Var	-1
					Consist	D	MM	3125

15-48-.285 in 337 AB at CHC. Now THAT's more like it. Vastly improved ct% had a ripple affect on other numbers. Inflated hr/f may overestimate short-term power outlook, and lefties still give him fits, but nice line-drive foundation could sustain him for now. Plenty more to come, but it may not materialize immediately.

Yr	Tm	AB	R	HR	RBI	SB	BA	xBA	vL	vR	OB	Slg	OPS	bb%	ct%	h%	Eye	G	L	F	PX	xPX	hr/f	Spd	SBO	SB%	#Wk	DOM	DIS	RC/G	RAR	BPV	BPX	R$
08																																		
09																																		
10	aa	414	49	14	60	5	242	270			299	422	722	8	75	29	0.32				138			80	7%	83%				4.27		45	0	$8
11	SD *	484	49	16	72	6	222	228	172	131	294	396	690	9	68	29	0.32	43	13	44	146	126	3%	62	14%	44%	11	18%	73%	3.61	-27.4	27	60	$7
12	CHC *	594	80	33	94	4	291	292	208	318	341	513	853	7	80	32	0.37	45	24	30	136	119	18%	85	6%	51%	15	53%	33%	6.15	12.0	59	148	$26
1st Half		272	37	19	49	1	298	271	286	250	342	579	922	6	77	33	0.30	25	17	58	178	238	14%	85	6%	40%	1	100%	0%	6.99	12.4	83	208	$28
2nd Half		322	43	14	45	3	286	280	202	320	339	457	796	7	82	31	0.44	46	25	29	103	113	18%	84	5%	60%	14	50%	36%	5.45	0.8	40	100	$25
13	**Proj**	**582**	**70**	**20**	**88**	**6**	**259**	**259**	**206**	**280**	**316**	**432**	**747**	**8**	**77**	**31**	**0.35**	**45**	**20**	**35**	**119**	**118**	**13%**	**79**	**8%**	**51%**				**4.56**	**-13.7**	**38**	**94**	**$17**

Roberts,Brian

Age	35	Bats	B	Pos 2B	Health	F	LIMA Plan	F
Ht	5' 9"	Wt	175		PT/Exp	F	Rand Var	+5
					Consist	D	MM	1301

0-5-.182 in 66 AB at BAL. A sad tale of injuries wrecking the career a very productive fanalytic player. Eased his way back from 2011's concussion, but then groin and ultimately hip labrum surgery in Aug ended his season. Said to be ready by spring; but age, rust, Reliability point to spending resources elsewhere.

Yr	Tm	AB	R	HR	RBI	SB	BA	xBA	vL	vR	OB	Slg	OPS	bb%	ct%	h%	Eye	G	L	F	PX	xPX	hr/f	Spd	SBO	SB%	#Wk	DOM	DIS	RC/G	RAR	BPV	BPX	R$
08	BAL	611	107	9	57	40	296	281	313	289	380	450	830	12	83	35	0.79	40	24	36	107	94	5%	116	26%	80%	27	59%	15%	6.28	36.5	87	171	$32
09	BAL	632	110	16	79	30	283	279	294	278	358	451	809	10	82	32	0.66	36	22	42	117	106	7%	94	21%	81%	27	63%	19%	5.82	29.8	78	159	$28
10	BAL	230	28	4	15	12	278	248	288	275	352	391	743	10	83	32	0.65	34	22	45	83	112	5%	96	19%	86%	12	50%	33%	5.04	5.7	45	98	$8
11	BAL	163	18	3	19	6	221	240	188	235	274	331	606	7	87	24	0.57	29	23	49	71	121	4%	91	19%	86%	8	50%	25%	3.07	-5.4	52	116	$1
12	BAL *	103	6	1	8	1	185	202	250	167	252	246	498	8	80	22	0.45	45	16	39	47	25	0%	78	8%	50%	4	0%	100%	1.89	-7.5	-12	-30	-$3
1st Half		99	6	1	8	1	193	207	250	180	261	256	518	9	80	23	0.47	45	17	38	48	27	0%	79	8%	50%	3	0%	100%	2.06	-7.0	-11	-28	-$3
2nd Half		4	0	0	0	0	0	0		0	0	0	0	0	75	0	0.00	33	0	67	0	-11	0%	84	0%	0%	1	0%	100%	0.00	-0.7	-98	-245	-$4
13	**Proj**	**159**	**18**	**2**	**15**	**4**	**262**	**237**	**272**	**259**	**331**	**363**	**695**	**9**	**83**	**31**	**0.60**	**37**	**21**	**42**	**72**	**86**	**4%**	**85**	**10%**	**88%**				**4.26**	**0.0**	**31**	**78**	**$4**

Roberts,Ryan

Age	32	Bats	R	Pos 3B 2B	Health	A	LIMA Plan	D+
Ht	5' 11"	Wt	185		PT/Exp	B	Rand Var	0
					Consist	D	MM	2203

Regression in just about every area—perfectly expected given his age and the out-of-nowhere career year of 2011. Still useful as roster piece (positional flexiblity, xPX holding steady), but doesn't deserve to be running this much, and plate approach is not pretty. Not worth elevating beyond your end-game list.

Yr	Tm	AB	R	HR	RBI	SB	BA	xBA	vL	vR	OB	Slg	OPS	bb%	ct%	h%	Eye	G	L	F	PX	xPX	hr/f	Spd	SBO	SB%	#Wk	DOM	DIS	RC/G	RAR	BPV	BPX	R$
08	TEX *	454	49	7	45	10	240	247	0		310	367	677	9	78	29	0.47	44	20	36	85	5	0%	140	12%	73%	1	0%	100%	3.82	-9.9	36	71	$5
09	ARI *	347	47	8	31	11	274	249	325	250	355	407	761	11	82	32	0.70	38	19	43	85	118	6%	113	13%	79%	24	29%	50%	5.11	5.0	51	104	$10
10	ARI *	413	42	8	39	9	192	205	143	292	252	315	567	7	73	24	0.30	39	10	51	96	142	8%	84	21%	53%	11	36%	45%	2.36	-30.0	12	26	-$1
11	ARI	482	86	19	65	18	249	266	278	238	339	427	767	12	80	28	0.67	35	24	41	119	119	12%	94	19%	67%	27	59%	22%	4.79	3.5	71	158	$18
12	2 TM	439	51	12	52	10	235	229	231	238	299	360	658	8	79	27	0.43	38	19	43	83	122	8%	75	14%	63%	27	30%	41%	3.49	-14.2	21	53	$8
1st Half		220	21	6	32	4	236	235	250	229	285	359	644	6	82	26	0.38	37	19	43	78	140	8%	71	13%	57%	13	31%	38%	3.30	-8.6	22	55	$8
2nd Half		219	30	6	20	6	233	223	211	246	311	361	672	10	76	28	0.47	40	18	43	89	103	8%	85	15%	67%	14	29%	43%	3.67	-6.1	18	45	$9
13	**Proj**	**349**	**46**	**11**	**40**	**9**	**248**	**235**	**261**	**241**	**318**	**393**	**711**	**9**	**78**	**29**	**0.47**	**38**	**19**	**44**	**96**	**122**	**9%**	**85**	**16%**	**64%**				**4.12**	**-4.8**	**34**	**86**	**$10**

Robinson,Shane

Age	28	Bats	R	Pos CF	Health	A	LIMA Plan	F
Ht	5' 9"	Wt	160		PT/Exp	F	Rand Var	-5
					Consist	B	MM	1501

3-16-.253 in 166 AB at STL. In the second half, he was wedded to Lance Berkman's health—was promoted when Berkman went down, was demoted when Big Puma was activated. His lackluster hit tool, anemic power and underutilized speed (terrible OBP) assures that this was a short-term relationship.

Yr	Tm	AB	R	HR	RBI	SB	BA	xBA	vL	vR	OB	Slg	OPS	bb%	ct%	h%	Eye	G	L	F	PX	xPX	hr/f	Spd	SBO	SB%	#Wk	DOM	DIS	RC/G	RAR	BPV	BPX	R$
08	a/a	385	43	4	32	11	259	244			290	347	637	4	83	30	0.26				61			105	22%	55%				3.24		22	0	$7
09	STL *	370	37	3	32	13	203	288	143	278	246	286	533	5	87	23	0.43	67	17	17	54	26	0%	110	23%	79%	3	0%	33%	2.30	-27.9	37	76	$0
10	aaa	86	6	1	9	2	216	243			257	305	562	5	82	25	0.30				65			91	31%	35%				2.13		8	0	-$1
11	STL *	205	27	4	19	6	237	262	0	0	292	347	639	7	89	25	0.69	80	0	20	67	2	0%	121	16%	69%	5	20%	40%	3.34	-8.3	56	124	$3
12	STL *	236	30	3	18	4	246	226	256	250	304	341	644	8	78	30	0.39	57	12	31	68	45	7%	140	7%	100%	25	36%	52%	3.60	-7.5	14	35	$2
1st Half		119	13	2	10	1	244	221	226	258	291	336	627	6	79	29	0.32	59	13	28	65	44	7%	127	3%	100%	13	23%	62%	3.35	-5.0	-3	-8	$1
2nd Half		113	16	1	8	3	236	213	310	222	307	326	633	9	78	29	0.47	51	10	38	68	46	7%	113	11%	100%	12	50%	42%	3.50	-4.3	18	45	$3
13	**Proj**	**130**	**16**	**3**	**11**	**3**	**237**	**239**	**273**	**199**	**290**	**355**	**644**	**7**	**83**	**27**	**0.44**	**54**	**11**	**34**	**76**	**45**	**7%**	**132**	**13%**	**78%**				**3.45**	**-5.2**	**37**	**92**	**$2**

BRENT HERSHEY

Robinson,Trayvon

Age	25	Bats	B	Pos	LF	Health	A	LIMA Plan	F
Ht	5' 10"	Wt	200			PT/Exp	C	Rand Var	+4
						Consist	B	MM	2201

3-12-.221 in 145 AB at SEA. Called up when Ichiro was traded, but again failed to adjust in his second MLB go-around. Made better contact (70%, as opposed to 57% in 2011), but h% killed BA, impressive PX disappeared, and Spd/SB% showed that SB level is flimsy at best. Still needs time, but doesn't have much.

Yr	Tm	AB	R	HR	RBI	SB	BA	xBA	vL	vR	OB	Slg	OPS	bb%	ct%	h%	Eye	G	L	F	PX	xPX	hr/f	Spd	SBO	SB%	#Wk	DOM	DIS	RC/G	RAR	BPV	BPX	R$
08																																		
09	aa	57	7	2	9	3	221	217			319	373	692	13	64	31	0.40				102			122	33%	61%				3.62		3	0	$0
10	aa	434	59	7	42	28	249	213			329	352	681	11	67	36	0.35				88			109	35%	62%				3.68		-4	0	$15
11	SEA *	520	56	17	58	7	216	215	158	229	270	363	633	7	58	34	0.18	41	29	30	131	136	8%	78	12%	48%	9	44%	44%	3.04	-24.8	-22	-49	$6
12	SEA *	485	50	9	40	19	211	242	192	237	268	311	579	7	69	29	0.25	50	30	20	77	68	15%	90	25%	68%	11	18%	64%	2.63	-29.6	-13	-33	$5
1st Half		277	28	5	24	10	202	216			250	305	555	6	71	27	0.22				79			85	28%	62%				2.32		-8	-20	$5
2nd Half		208	22	4	16	9	222	231	192	237	291	320	611	9	67	31	0.29	50	30	20	73	68	15%	97	22%	76%	11	18%	64%	3.09	-10.1	-26	-65	$5
13	Proj	**206**	**23**	**4**	**19**	**7**	**219**	**224**	**184**	**237**	**281**	**325**	**606**	**8**	**65**	**32**	**0.24**	**46**	**29**	**24**	**85**	**95**	**12%**	**89**	**22%**	**64%**				**2.89**	**-11.4**	**-26**	**-66**	**$1**

Rodriguez,Alex

Age	37	Bats	R	Pos	3B DH	Health	D	LIMA Plan	C
Ht	6' 3"	Wt	225			PT/Exp	B	Rand Var	-2
						Consist	A	MM	3215

Often lost in all the surrounding drama is his eroding skill set over the past four seasons. Power leads the way, due largely to a nastly G/L/F flip, and xBA says this is now a .250 hitter. At 37, his 2012 SB spike won't hold. He's likely to rebound some and benefits from the 3B wasteland, but low $20s value is his peak.

Yr	Tm	AB	R	HR	RBI	SB	BA	xBA	vL	vR	OB	Slg	OPS	bb%	ct%	h%	Eye	G	L	F	PX	xPX	hr/f	Spd	SBO	SB%	#Wk	DOM	DIS	RC/G	RAR	BPV	BPX	R$
08	NYY	510	104	35	103	18	302	296	263	316	381	573	953	11	77	33	0.56	42	18	40	174	148	22%	89	14%	86%	25	60%	24%	8.06	49.4	101	198	$33
09	NYY	444	78	30	100	14	286	290	277	289	395	532	927	15	78	31	0.82	42	20	38	145	138	23%	72	10%	88%	23	57%	26%	7.62	38.4	87	178	$25
10	NYY	522	74	30	125	4	270	287	217	290	344	506	850	10	81	28	0.60	46	14	40	148	139	17%	75	5%	57%	25	60%	28%	5.99	21.7	84	183	$23
11	NYY	373	67	16	62	4	276	261	277	276	357	461	818	11	79	31	0.59	49	14	37	127	116	15%	78	4%	80%	21	52%	43%	5.82	13.4	61	136	$15
12	NYY	463	74	18	57	13	272	250	308	256	344	430	774	10	75	33	0.44	45	22	32	103	118	16%	91	10%	93%	22	41%	32%	5.33	10.3	33	83	$18
1st Half		279	43	13	35	6	265	252	271	263	345	437	782	11	75	31	0.49	46	21	33	110	110	19%	71	7%	100%	13	38%	23%	5.38	6.4	33	83	$21
2nd Half		184	31	5	22	7	283	247	361	244	343	418	762	8	75	35	0.37	44	24	32	93	130	11%	110	15%	88%	9	44%	44%	5.24	3.5	26	65	$13
13	Proj	**440**	**73**	**16**	**70**	**10**	**265**	**249**	**283**	**258**	**341**	**426**	**767**	**10**	**76**	**32**	**0.47**	**46**	**19**	**35**	**108**	**125**	**14%**	**84**	**9%**	**86%**				**5.11**	**6.8**	**40**	**101**	**$18**

Rodriguez,Sean

Age	28	Bats	R	Pos	3B SS 2B	Health	A	LIMA Plan	F
Ht	6' 0"	Wt	200			PT/Exp	C	Rand Var	+3
						Consist	B	MM	2301

Missed most of Sept due to broken hand suffered in post-game meeting with a locker at Triple-A. If he connected with his on-field swings as successfully, he'd 1) quite possibly not been demoted, and 2) actually be able to help you. Once-promising power has declined and SB dried up. And this should be his prime.

Yr	Tm	AB	R	HR	RBI	SB	BA	xBA	vL	vR	OB	Slg	OPS	bb%	ct%	h%	Eye	G	L	F	PX	xPX	hr/f	Spd	SBO	SB%	#Wk	DOM	DIS	RC/G	RAR	BPV	BPX	R$
08	LAA *	415	67	17	47	6	237	243	178	213	296	429	724	8	75	28	0.33	41	12	47	132	93	6%	104	9%	73%	15	13%	73%	4.22	3.8	50	98	$7
09	LAA *	410	77	26	86	8	257	261	91	286	336	518	854	11	64	33	0.33	63	0	37	186	74	29%	146	9%	77%	6	17%	50%	5.96	24.7	69	141	$17
10	TAM	343	53	9	40	13	251	239	292	229	294	397	690	6	72	32	0.22	42	19	39	112	120	10%	102	21%	81%	27	37%	48%	4.01	1.0	29	63	$10
11	TAM	373	45	8	36	11	223	235	273	192	294	357	651	9	77	27	0.44	41	17	41	98	91	7%	109	20%	61%	27	41%	30%	3.31	-6.9	37	82	$5
12	TAM	301	36	6	32	5	213	220	228	205	277	326	603	8	75	26	0.36	47	15	38	82	76	7%	97	7%	100%	25	16%	56%	3.01	-8.3	11	28	$1
1st Half		224	25	5	22	3	214	222	239	203	261	330	591	6	78	25	0.29	47	14	39	77	75	7%	102	6%	100%	13	23%	46%	2.86	-8.0	14	35	$3
2nd Half		77	11	1	10	2	208	212	200	213	322	312	634	14	66	30	0.50	47	20	33	96	82	6%	87	9%	100%	12	8%	67%	3.38	-1.5	-7	-18	-$2
13	Proj	**222**	**30**	**5**	**26**	**6**	**232**	**224**	**249**	**223**	**305**	**363**	**668**	**9**	**72**	**30**	**0.38**	**44**	**17**	**39**	**98**	**90**	**8%**	**94**	**12%**	**80%**				**3.71**	**-5.8**	**18**	**44**	**$5**

Rolen,Scott

Age	38	Bats	R	Pos	3B	Health	F	LIMA Plan	D+
Ht	6' 4"	Wt	245			PT/Exp	C	Rand Var	0
						Consist	D	MM	3123

Sore shoulder and balky back again torpedoed his season, enough that there was retirement talk in October. If he comes back, his body (age, Health grade) and bat (career low ct%) will prevent him from providing much value. If he hangs them up, remember the Gold Gloves instead of the past two seasons.

Yr	Tm	AB	R	HR	RBI	SB	BA	xBA	vL	vR	OB	Slg	OPS	bb%	ct%	h%	Eye	G	L	F	PX	xPX	hr/f	Spd	SBO	SB%	#Wk	DOM	DIS	RC/G	RAR	BPV	BPX	R$
08	TOR	408	58	11	50	5	262	269	250	266	337	431	768	10	83	29	0.65	36	21	44	113	108	7%	81	5%	100%	22	45%	23%	5.10	5.8	72	141	$9
09	2 TM	475	76	11	67	5	305	284	374	283	365	455	820	9	87	33	0.73	37	23	41	97	117	6%	86	6%	56%	25	56%	20%	5.97	17.9	66	135	$18
10	CIN	471	66	20	83	1	285	289	260	295	353	497	850	10	83	31	0.61	37	19	44	139	129	12%	77	2%	33%	26	54%	23%	6.16	20.6	80	174	$18
11	CIN	252	31	5	36	1	242	275	246	241	271	397	668	4	86	27	0.28	38	21	41	108	96	6%	90	2%	100%	15	53%	20%	3.64	-7.2	63	140	$3
12	CIN	294	26	8	39	2	245	252	234	249	315	398	713	9	79	29	0.48	41	20	38	103	105	9%	81	4%	67%	22	50%	36%	4.21	-3.4	36	90	$4
1st Half		125	9	3	16	1	184	230	176	187	239	312	551	7	76	22	0.30	43	19	39	93	95	8%	51	5%	100%	8	38%	50%	2.36	-8.9	5	13	-$2
2nd Half		169	17	5	23	1	290	265	279	294	368	462	830	11	81	33	0.66	40	22	38	109	111	9%	101	4%	50%	14	57%	29%	6.01	6.8	54	135	$8
13	Proj	**322**	**36**	**10**	**46**	**2**	**255**	**266**	**250**	**257**	**315**	**428**	**743**	**8**	**82**	**29**	**0.48**	**39**	**20**	**40**	**113**	**107**	**9%**	**80**	**4%**	**67%**				**4.60**	**0.1**	**55**	**138**	**$8**

Rollins,Jimmy

Age	34	Bats	B	Pos	SS	Health	C	LIMA Plan	B+
Ht	5' 8"	Wt	180			PT/Exp	A	Rand Var	0
						Consist	A	MM	2325

Drew fans' ire by repeatedly not running out groundballs, but got his body back in shape, scored 100 runs, and led the team in HR. Though he again topped 30 SB with below-average speed, his ct% was his lowest since 2003 and BA will keep him from being a five-category player. Should have another year at this level.

Yr	Tm	AB	R	HR	RBI	SB	BA	xBA	vL	vR	OB	Slg	OPS	bb%	ct%	h%	Eye	G	L	F	PX	xPX	hr/f	Spd	SBO	SB%	#Wk	DOM	DIS	RC/G	RAR	BPV	BPX	R$
08	PHI	556	76	11	59	47	277	308	288	272	345	437	782	9	90	29	1.05	45	24	31	96	92	7%	100	32%	94%	24	67%	4%	5.76	26.2	105	206	$28
09	PHI	672	100	21	77	31	250	290	230	257	296	423	719	6	90	25	0.63	40	19	41	101	95	8%	94	27%	79%	26	58%	12%	4.27	3.3	94	192	$22
10	PHI	350	48	8	41	17	243	276	297	218	321	374	695	10	91	25	1.25	46	17	37	78	82	7%	91	18%	94%	17	59%	12%	4.28	1.8	86	187	$10
11	PHI	567	87	16	63	30	268	263	240	278	336	399	735	9	90	28	0.98	39	20	41	78	94	8%	95	22%	79%	26	58%	19%	4.72	10.2	76	169	$24
12	PHI	632	102	23	68	30	250	266	218	265	317	427	744	9	85	26	0.65	39	19	42	106	95	10%	91	22%	86%	27	67%	19%	4.73	11.6	83	208	$24
1st Half		320	45	8	27	14	263	262	240	272	318	409	727	8	85	29	0.53	42	20	38	91	82	8%	98	21%	82%	13	46%	38%	4.58	5.3	65	163	$21
2nd Half		312	57	15	41	16	237	270	198	257	316	446	762	10	85	24	0.77	36	18	45	121	108	13%	82	23%	89%	14	86%	0%	4.87	8.1	99	248	$27
13	Proj	**604**	**94**	**19**	**68**	**31**	**253**	**266**	**237**	**261**	**322**	**413**	**736**	**9**	**87**	**26**	**0.81**	**40**	**19**	**41**	**93**	**94**	**9%**	**89**	**22%**	**86%**				**4.69**	**12.2**	**83**	**208**	**$25**

Rosario,Wilin

Age	24	Bats	R	Pos	CA	Health	A	LIMA Plan	C
Ht	5' 11"	Wt	215			PT/Exp	C	Rand Var	0
						Consist	F	MM	4115

Incredible power display in less than 400 AB, though season-long hr/f played a large part. That's likely not sustainable (2011's figure was in 16 MLB AB) though previous MLEs, xPX indicate that this is not your average backstop. Patience needs work, but 2H Eye shows some growth. With a full-time gig ... UP: 35 HR

Yr	Tm	AB	R	HR	RBI	SB	BA	xBA	vL	vR	OB	Slg	OPS	bb%	ct%	h%	Eye	G	L	F	PX	xPX	hr/f	Spd	SBO	SB%	#Wk	DOM	DIS	RC/G	RAR	BPV	BPX	R$
08																																		
09																																		
10	aa	270	34	17	42	1	275	297			316	520	837	6	79	29	0.29				155			92	1%	100%				5.81		68	0	$9
11	COL *	459	43	20	42	1	225	251	286	175	250	406	656	3	75	26	0.14	40	20	40	121	137	21%	100	4%	24%	4	25%	25%	3.27	-14.2	24	53	$5
12	COL	396	67	28	71	4	270	278	348	239	314	530	844	6	75	29	0.25	46	17	37	165	142	25%	72	11%	44%	27	59%	22%	5.55	14.6	64	160	$18
1st Half		175	28	13	35	3	246	284	273	233	275	526	800	4	72	27	0.14	46	18	36	188	162	28%	58	22%	50%	13	62%	23%	4.57	1.9	71	178	$14
2nd Half		221	39	15	36	1	290	273	421	244	343	534	877	8	77	31	0.36	46	17	37	149	127	23%	89	5%	33%	14	57%	21%	6.36	13.4	60	150	$20
13	Proj	**431**	**59**	**20**	**62**	**3**	**256**	**252**	**333**	**226**	**294**	**443**	**738**	**5**	**76**	**29**	**0.23**	**44**	**18**	**38**	**121**	**140**	**16%**	**84**	**6%**	**44%**				**4.35**	**1.7**	**32**	**81**	**$13**

Ross,Cody

Age	32	Bats	R	Pos	RF LF	Health	B	LIMA Plan	C+
Ht	5' 10"	Wt	195			PT/Exp	B	Rand Var	-1
						Consist	B	MM	4115

Nice free-agent find who won more 2H AB with hr/f-aided 1H performance. xPX is skeptical of extent of the power outburst; and at his age, declining ct% is never a good thing. But hits enough LD and FB to do some damage and BA is of the doesn't help/doesn't hurt variety. Worked himself into another full-time shot.

Yr	Tm	AB	R	HR	RBI	SB	BA	xBA	vL	vR	OB	Slg	OPS	bb%	ct%	h%	Eye	G	L	F	PX	xPX	hr/f	Spd	SBO	SB%	#Wk	DOM	DIS	RC/G	RAR	BPV	BPX	R$
08	FLA	461	59	22	73	6	260	271	285	249	310	488	798	7	75	30	0.28	36	21	43	153	136	15%	95	7%	86%	27	48%	22%	5.24	5.1	67	131	$13
09	FLA	559	73	24	90	5	270	266	284	266	312	469	781	6	78	31	0.28	33	19	48	131	128	11%	75	6%	71%	25	52%	32%	5.08	3.6	52	106	$17
10	2 NL	525	71	14	65	9	269	261	287	263	317	413	730	7	77	33	0.31	46	21	34	103	94	10%	99	8%	82%	27	26%	44%	4.59	-4.0	35	76	$15
11	SF	405	54	14	52	5	240	241	234	241	322	405	727	11	76	28	0.51	34	18	48	122	120	9%	75	7%	71%	22	41%	41%	4.35	-6.1	44	98	$8
12	BOS	476	70	22	81	2	267	262	295	256	326	481	807	8	73	32	0.33	36	22	42	153	118	15%	74	4%	40%	23	48%	39%	5.34	6.7	48	120	$16
1st Half		177	34	12	39	1	282	289	302	274	349	576	925	9	72	33	0.37	37	21	42	203	167	22%	83	5%	50%	9	78%	11%	7.02	10.1	96	240	$17
2nd Half		299	36	10	42	1	258	248	291	245	313	425	737	7	73	32	0.30	35	23	42	124	90	11%	67	4%	33%	14	29%	57%	4.45	-4.9	20	50	$16
13	Proj	**514**	**73**	**19**	**79**	**5**	**260**	**251**	**280**	**254**	**321**	**444**	**765**	**8**	**75**	**31**	**0.35**	**37**	**21**	**43**	**130**	**118**	**12%**	**75**	**6%**	**63%**				**4.86**	**-2.2**	**41**	**103**	**$16**

BRENT HERSHEY

Ross,David

Age	36	Bats	R	Pos	CA	Health	A	LIMA Plan	F
Ht	6' 2"	Wt	205			PT/Exp	F	Rand Var	-2
						Consist	B	MM	4001

Displayed his power—and then some—again in limited PT as backup CA. His 2H HR were found money in deep-league #2 CA slots. All you had to do was coordinate his injury-dependent AB and streaks with your roster-fill needs. History says he won't hurt, but good luck timing his brief/limited moments of upside.

Yr	Tm	AB	R	HR	RBI	SB	BA	xBA	vL	vR	OB	Slg	OPS	bb%	ct%	h%	Eye	G	L	F	PX	xPX	hr/f	Spd	SBO	SB%	#Wk	DOM	DIS	RC/G	RAR	BPV	BPX	R$
08	2 TM *	200	24	4	17	0	208	230	206	241	326	334	659	15	69	28	0.56	38	25	37	100	135	8%	89	2%	0%	20	25%	60%	3.43	-5.2	0	0	-$2
09	ATL	128	18	7	20	0	273	267	250	284	376	508	884	14	70	34	0.54	30	22	49	171	106	16%	81	0%	0%	22	41%	36%	6.70	8.8	51	104	$3
10	ATL	121	15	2	28	0	289	281	308	256	390	479	869	14	77	36	0.71	38	21	41	150	125	5%	93	3%	0%	26	35%	50%	6.51	7.6	79	172	$3
11	ATL	152	14	6	23	0	263	236	240	275	333	428	761	10	66	36	0.31	28	26	45	132	154	14%	76	2%	0%	24	38%	58%	4.80	2.3	-2	-4	$2
12	ATL	176	18	9	23	1	256	233	241	268	325	449	774	9	66	34	0.30	34	23	43	142	152	18%	73	2%	100%	25	40%	56%	5.03	3.8	6	15	$3
1st Half		68	7	3	7	0	279	265	357	225	355	456	811	11	66	38	0.35	23	36	41	132	125	17%	77	0%	0%	11	45%	55%	5.73	2.9	-3	-8	$0
2nd Half		108	11	6	16	1	241	221	176	298	305	444	750	8	66	31	0.27	41	15	44	147	168	19%	75	4%	100%	14	36%	57%	4.61	1.3	9	23	$5
13	Proj	**157**	**17**	**7**	**23**	**0**	**261**	**239**	**254**	**267**	**339**	**449**	**789**	**11**	**68**	**34**	**0.37**	**33**	**24**	**43**	**140**	**145**	**15%**	**77**	**2%**	**47%**				**5.22**	**4.6**	**19**	**47**	**$3**

Ruggiano,Justin

Age	31	Bats	R	Pos	CF LF	Health	A	LIMA Plan	C
Ht	6' 2"	Wt	205			PT/Exp	D	Rand Var	-4
						Consist	C	MM	4315

13-36-.313 with 14 SB in 288 AB at MIA. PX/xPX history says HR shouldn't shock us, but this is still a notable surge. Even with ct% and bb% upticks, 40% h% with MIA will regress and take BA down with it. SB%, age, and Spd aren't optimistic about his running game. Risk is greater than the reward; pay for HR only.

Yr	Tm	AB	R	HR	RBI	SB	BA	xBA	vL	vR	OB	Slg	OPS	bb%	ct%	h%	Eye	G	L	F	PX	xPX	hr/f	Spd	SBO	SB%	#Wk	DOM	DIS	RC/G	RAR	BPV	BPX	R$
08	TAM *	333	46	10	46	17	247	238	174	233	292	413	705	6	64	35	0.18	41	27	33	135	122	13%	102	29%	83%	15	27%	53%	4.15	-5.3	18	35	$10
09	aaa	471	56	11	57	18	208	212			270	334	603	8	62	31	0.22				108			82	22%	79%				2.93		-15	0	$6
10	aaa	457	55	10	50	17	223	216			271	343	614	6	64	32	0.18				108			84	25%	69%				2.98		-15	0	$8
11	TAM *	273	31	9	37	9	238	233	217	271	285	392	677	6	70	31	0.22	53	13	35	119	108	14%	95	22%	73%	15	13%	60%	3.69	-8.2	19	42	$6
12	MIA *	405	50	16	53	17	290	261	330	305	353	497	850	9	71	37	0.34	41	21	38	156	165	17%	100	27%	59%	17	53%	29%	5.84	13.6	56	140	$19
1st Half		168	20	5	26	5	282	289	438	316	353	502	855	10	75	35	0.44	38	26	36	165	209	13%	81	29%	41%	5	100%	0%	5.49	3.6	82	205	$12
2nd Half		237	30	11	27	12	295	243	271	303	353	494	846	8	68	39	0.28	42	19	39	148	154	17%	101	26%	71%	12	33%	42%	6.11	9.0	32	80	$24
13	Proj	**421**	**51**	**15**	**54**	**16**	**253**	**245**	**306**	**223**	**310**	**436**	**746**	**8**	**69**	**33**	**0.26**	**45**	**19**	**36**	**140**	**144**	**15%**	**98**	**26%**	**63%**				**4.38**	**-5.1**	**33**	**83**	**$15**

Ruiz,Carlos

Age	34	Bats	R	Pos	CA	Health	C	LIMA Plan	B
Ht	5' 10"	Wt	206			PT/Exp	C	Rand Var	-3
						Consist	F	MM	3145

2011 Forecaster said: "Mid-30s power spike not in the cards," perhaps in response to 2010 Forecaster note: "Plate control is rock solid, and he still has... UP: 15 HRs." It's all in the timing. And the patience. Plantar fasciitis and DL stint interrupted 2H, raising durability questions. If healthy, could follow up well.

Yr	Tm	AB	R	HR	RBI	SB	BA	xBA	vL	vR	OB	Slg	OPS	bb%	ct%	h%	Eye	G	L	F	PX	xPX	hr/f	Spd	SBO	SB%	#Wk	DOM	DIS	RC/G	RAR	BPV	BPX	R$
08	PHI	320	47	4	31	1	219	252	212	220	313	300	613	12	88	24	1.16	54	17	29	54	72	5%	70	3%	33%	26	35%	31%	3.01	-12.6	36	71	-$1
09	PHI	322	32	9	43	3	255	290	293	242	350	425	775	13	88	27	1.21	42	19	39	108	96	8%	66	5%	60%	24	58%	21%	5.03	7.0	80	163	$5
10	PHI	371	43	8	53	0	302	279	327	291	392	447	839	13	85	34	1.02	45	20	35	102	87	7%	78	1%	0%	25	56%	32%	6.34	20.9	60	130	$12
11	PHI	410	49	6	40	1	283	258	265	288	358	383	741	10	88	31	1.00	42	21	37	70	95	4%	65	1%	100%	26	50%	27%	4.89	7.0	43	96	$9
12	PHI	372	56	16	68	4	325	313	320	327	374	540	914	7	87	34	0.58	43	24	33	135	131	15%	52	4%	100%	22	73%	14%	7.72	33.8	89	223	$20
1st Half		229	38	11	43	3	358	324	365	355	400	585	985	7	87	38	0.53	45	26	29	139	117	19%	60	4%	100%	13	69%	15%	9.41	30.0	92	230	$28
2nd Half		143	18	5	25	1	273	293	250	282	333	469	802	8	86	29	0.65	41	21	38	128	154	11%	46	3%	100%	9	78%	11%	5.52	5.3	78	195	$7
13	Proj	**411**	**54**	**14**	**61**	**2**	**293**	**289**	**291**	**294**	**361**	**468**	**829**	**10**	**87**	**31**	**0.81**	**43**	**22**	**35**	**111**	**115**	**11%**	**55**	**2%**	**85%**				**6.12**	**21.7**	**71**	**178**	**$16**

Rutledge,Josh

Age	24	Bats	R	Pos	SS	Health	A	LIMA Plan	C+
Ht	6' 1"	Wt	190			PT/Exp	F	Rand Var	0
						Consist	F	MM	4535

8-37-.274 with 7 SB in 277 AB at COL. Jumped from AA, exploded at SS after Tulo injury until Aug quad issues and Sept slump slowed him down. Needs more patience, but history says he'll hit for BA, steal some bases, and has enough pop to be dangerous. Playing time up in the air; but buy skills, not roles.

Yr	Tm	AB	R	HR	RBI	SB	BA	xBA	vL	vR	OB	Slg	OPS	bb%	ct%	h%	Eye	G	L	F	PX	xPX	hr/f	Spd	SBO	SB%	#Wk	DOM	DIS	RC/G	RAR	BPV	BPX	R$
08																																		
09																																		
10																																		
11																																		
12	COL *	633	86	21	67	19	289	289	247	286	312	487	800	3	80	33	0.17	49	20	31	130	112	12%	125	18%	82%	13	54%	31%	5.47	24.3	74	185	$26
1st Half		317	42	10	26	11	295	281			319	480	798	3	83	33	0.21				119			116	23%	72%				5.41		70	175	$26
2nd Half		316	44	11	40	8	284	287	247	286	306	495	801	3	78	34	0.14	49	20	31	141	112	12%	125	13%	100%	13	54%	31%	5.54	13.6	72	180	$27
13	Proj	**441**	**60**	**13**	**48**	**13**	**281**	**279**	**253**	**293**	**303**	**469**	**772**	**3**	**79**	**33**	**0.15**	**48**	**20**	**32**	**127**	**101**	**11%**	**125**	**17%**	**85%**				**5.09**	**13.5**	**65**	**161**	**$18**

Ryan,Brendan

Age	31	Bats	R	Pos	SS	Health	A	LIMA Plan	D
Ht	6' 2"	Wt	195			PT/Exp	B	Rand Var	+3
						Consist	B	MM	1403

That rare Mendoza-line infielder for whom a confluence of terrific defense and organizational weakness assures him regular playing time. Zero power and declining contact aren't likely to be offset by a patience uptick and moderate running game. The big debate: When will his string of 400 AB seasons end? Now.

Yr	Tm	AB	R	HR	RBI	SB	BA	xBA	vL	vR	OB	Slg	OPS	bb%	ct%	h%	Eye	G	L	F	PX	xPX	hr/f	Spd	SBO	SB%	#Wk	DOM	DIS	RC/G	RAR	BPV	BPX	R$
08	STL *	296	43	3	19	8	233	249	261	229	280	312	592	6	81	28	0.34	52	19	28	61	37	0%	114	15%	81%	21	29%	48%	2.96	-10.3	15	29	$2
09	STL	390	55	3	37	14	292	273	265	306	333	400	733	6	86	34	0.43	51	19	30	67	45	3%	153	19%	67%	25	52%	36%	4.67	8.4	49	100	$13
10	STL	439	50	2	36	11	223	247	224	223	278	294	571	7	86	25	0.55	47	18	35	51	43	2%	128	14%	73%	27	33%	37%	2.69	-16.5	33	72	$3
11	SEA	436	51	3	39	13	248	232	255	245	302	326	628	7	80	30	0.39	45	20	35	59	60	2%	127	14%	81%	23	26%	52%	3.40	-6.5	17	38	$8
12	SEA	407	42	3	31	11	194	215	234	169	273	278	550	10	76	25	0.45	41	20	39	64	60	2%	116	16%	69%	28	29%	54%	2.39	-19.8	6	15	-$1
1st Half		205	27	2	19	5	176	213	195	164	278	268	546	12	75	23	0.56	44	18	38	68	69	3%	117	15%	63%	14	43%	57%	2.27	-11.7	13	33	-$1
2nd Half		202	15	1	12	6	213	217	272	174	267	287	554	7	77	27	0.33	39	22	40	59	50	2%	108	17%	75%	14	14%	50%	2.51	-9.5	-3	-8	-$1
13	Proj	**387**	**42**	**2**	**31**	**11**	**221**	**225**	**245**	**208**	**283**	**299**	**582**	**8**	**79**	**27**	**0.42**	**44**	**20**	**37**	**58**	**54**	**2%**	**117**	**15%**	**73%**				**2.78**	**-14.7**	**13**	**33**	**$4**

Saltalamacchia,Jarrod

Age	28	Bats	B	Pos	CA	Health	A	LIMA Plan	D+
Ht	6' 4"	Wt	235			PT/Exp	C	Rand Var	0
						Consist	A	MM	4015

More HR, less BA, but ultimately the same skill set. Year-long hr/f spike in synch with 2H gains from last season bode well for his power. Mid-season attempt at patience chilled his 2H numbers and value to H2Hers. Remains profitable at a scarce position, but poor ct% and struggles vs. LHPs have him platoon-bound.

Yr	Tm	AB	R	HR	RBI	SB	BA	xBA	vL	vR	OB	Slg	OPS	bb%	ct%	h%	Eye	G	L	F	PX	xPX	hr/f	Spd	SBO	SB%	#Wk	DOM	DIS	RC/G	RAR	BPV	BPX	R$
08	TEX *	253	35	5	36	0	254	219	160	311	348	378	726	13	64	38	0.40	31	27	42	110	125	6%	76	3%	0%	19	21%	58%	4.36	1.7	-12	-24	$3
09	TEX	283	34	9	34	0	233	222	229	235	289	371	660	7	66	32	0.23	36	23	41	107	99	12%	92	3%	0%	20	20%	65%	3.45	-5.8	-24	-49	$2
10	2 AL *	298	34	9	32	1	217	216	143	200	285	381	666	9	72	27	0.35	42	5	53	127	8	0%	88	1%	100%	6	67%	33%	3.55	-5.3	29	63	$1
11	BOS	358	52	16	56	1	235	245	209	247	283	450	732	6	67	30	0.20	32	21	47	172	145	14%	79	2%	100%	27	41%	33%	4.25	1.2	46	102	$8
12	BOS	405	55	25	59	0	222	242	170	230	289	454	743	9	66	27	0.27	31	23	47	168	160	20%	73	1%	0%	27	41%	33%	4.26	1.4	29	73	$8
1st Half		205	31	15	37	0	254	281	206	263	301	537	838	6	71	28	0.24	27	24	49	194	191	21%	61	0%	0%	13	54%	8%	5.53	7.9	64	160	$14
2nd Half		200	24	10	22	0	190	203	105	199	277	370	647	11	60	25	0.30	36	21	44	135	123	19%	97	2%	0%	14	29%	57%	3.15	-6.8	-13	-33	$2
13	Proj	**417**	**55**	**23**	**62**	**1**	**231**	**248**	**198**	**240**	**295**	**454**	**749**	**8**	**69**	**28**	**0.29**	**32**	**23**	**45**	**158**	**139**	**18%**	**76**	**2%**	**35%**				**4.40**	**2.3**	**36**	**90**	**$10**

Sanchez,Gaby

Age	29	Bats	R	Pos	1B	Health	A	LIMA Plan	D
Ht	6' 1"	Wt	230			PT/Exp	B	Rand Var	+3
						Consist	C	MM	3113

7-30-.217 in 299 AB at MIA/PIT. Fresh ct% plunge and continuation of 2011 2H PX outage produced a miserable 1H—and a mid-May demotion. 2H hr/f offers glimmer of hope, highlighted by 3 MLB HR in Sept, but we need to see more. That stagnant long-term power trend has put his offense and career in jeopardy.

Yr	Tm	AB	R	HR	RBI	SB	BA	xBA	vL	vR	OB	Slg	OPS	bb%	ct%	h%	Eye	G	L	F	PX	xPX	hr/f	Spd	SBO	SB%	#Wk	DOM	DIS	RC/G	RAR	BPV	BPX	R$
08	FLA *	486	55	13	74	13	271	276	0	429	347	435	782	11	82	31	0.65	50	17	33	114	172	0%	66	17%	59%	2	50%	0%	5.06	-5.2	63	124	$15
09	FLA *	339	42	13	44	4	238	252	333	200	306	385	691	9	83	25	0.57	44	17	39	84	134	29%	62	4%	100%	8	25%	38%	4.00	-14.4	36	73	$5
10	FLA	572	72	19	85	5	273	265	324	256	339	448	786	9	82	30	0.56	37	17	46	117	144	9%	90	3%	100%	27	48%	15%	5.37	-0.9	67	146	$18
11	FLA	572	72	19	78	3	266	261	295	257	350	427	776	11	83	29	0.76	36	20	45	109	103	9%	53	2%	75%	27	52%	26%	5.18	-4.0	57	127	$16
12	2 NL *	415	44	10	42	2	220	227	240	207	291	345	635	9	79	25	0.48	41	17	42	85	111	7%	67	5%	48%	21	33%	43%	3.22	-28.2	18	45	$2
1st Half		233	16	4	23	2	205	199	231	179	275	301	576	9	79	24	0.46	40	13	47	69	106	3%	60	8%	40%	10	10%	60%	2.55	-20.7	0	0	$0
2nd Half		182	28	6	20	1	241	261	250	250	310	401	712	9	80	27	0.50	43	21	36	106	117	14%	79	2%	100%	11	55%	27%	4.20	-6.3	40	100	$6
13	Proj	**316**	**39**	**10**	**39**	**3**	**246**	**249**	**276**	**236**	**320**	**401**	**720**	**10**	**81**	**28**	**0.57**	**39**	**19**	**43**	**101**	**114**	**9%**	**65**	**4%**	**67%**				**4.31**	**-9.9**	**43**	**108**	**$7**

JOCK THOMPSON

Sanchez,Hector

Sanchez,Hector			Health	A	LIMA Plan	F
Age 23	Bats B	Pos CA	PT/Exp	F	Rand Var	-3
Ht 5' 11"	Wt 225		Consist	D	MM	2011

Free-swinger traded contact for more power, still came up short on HRs. But he cut his GB%, and wrung the best out of what he had via an inflated h%. Age, xPX history and small sample PX/bb% spikes in 2H hint at some upside. But poor pitch selection, inexperience and lack of opportunity leave him unrosterable for now.

Yr	Tm	AB	R	HR	RBI	SB	BA	xBA	vL	vR	OB	Slg	OPS	bb%	ct%	h%	Eye	G	L	F	PX	xPX	hr/f	Spd	SBO	SB%	#Wk	DOM	DIS	RC/G	RAR	BPV	BPX	R$
08																																		
09																																		
10																																		
11	SF *	184	10	1	18	0	221	197	91	350	266	283	550	6	83	26	0.37	52	12	36	53	161	0%	54	3%	0%	7	29%	71%	2.40	-10.6	-5	-11	-$2
12	SF	218	22	3	34	0	280	237	304	266	296	390	686	2	76	36	0.10	44	22	34	88	101	5%	58	0%	0%	25	32%	56%	4.09	-1.2	-9	-23	$4
1st Half		110	11	2	21	0	264	225	260	267	270	364	634	1	77	33	0.04	43	20	36	72	99	6%	56	0%	0%	12	17%	58%	3.40	-2.6	-21	-53	$4
2nd Half		108	11	1	13	0	296	250	379	266	321	417	738	4	75	39	0.15	44	23	32	105	103	4%	70	0%	0%	13	46%	54%	4.85	1.9	1	3	$4
13	Proj	**168**	**14**	**2**	**22**	**0**	**259**	**242**	**289**	**243**	**288**	**363**	**651**	**4**	**79**	**32**	**0.20**	**44**	**22**	**34**	**81**	**101**	**5%**	**62**	**1%**	**0%**				**3.56**	**-3.2**	**-3**	**-7**	**$1**

Sandoval,Pablo

Sandoval,Pablo			Health	D	LIMA Plan	C+
Age 26	Bats B	Pos 3B	PT/Exp	B	Rand Var	0
Ht 5' 11"	Wt 240		Consist	F	MM	3035

Injuries (broken hamate bone, hamstring) and off-field issues fueled near-repeat of 2010. Apart from power outage, basic plate skills remain intact, but conditioning remains an ongoing issue. High-risk, high-reward; is house arrest with Jenny Craig an option? Minus some poundage... UP: .310-25-90.

Yr	Tm	AB	R	HR	RBI	SB	BA	xBA	vL	vR	OB	Slg	OPS	bb%	ct%	h%	Eye	G	L	F	PX	xPX	hr/f	Spd	SBO	SB%	#Wk	DOM	DIS	RC/G	RAR	BPV	BPX	R$
08	SF *	320	50	9	57	0	330	314	237	383	353	497	850	3	89	35	0.32	45	26	29	103	72	8%	93	1%	0%	8	50%	38%	6.59	16.7	62	122	$15
09	SF	572	79	25	90	5	330	310	379	314	386	556	942	8	85	35	0.63	45	19	36	136	115	14%	79	6%	50%	27	63%	19%	7.97	51.2	91	186	$28
10	SF	563	61	13	63	3	268	267	227	282	325	409	733	8	86	29	0.58	44	17	38	93	106	7%	59	3%	60%	27	44%	22%	4.58	-0.3	53	115	$12
11	SF	426	55	23	70	2	315	301	281	324	362	552	914	7	85	33	0.51	42	19	39	145	125	16%	66	5%	33%	21	57%	19%	7.19	30.0	89	198	$22
12	SF	396	59	12	63	1	283	274	299	275	346	447	793	9	85	31	0.64	43	20	37	103	117	10%	59	2%	50%	21	52%	29%	5.45	9.4	61	153	$13
1st Half		166	26	6	25	0	307	291	375	286	365	482	847	8	85	33	0.60	36	27	37	110	142	11%	60	0%	0%	9	44%	33%	6.47	8.5	56	140	$12
2nd Half		230	33	6	38	1	265	265	264	266	332	422	754	9	85	29	0.68	48	16	36	98	100	8%	62	3%	50%	12	58%	25%	4.80	1.5	62	155	$14
13	Proj	**549**	**76**	**19**	**85**	**2**	**293**	**278**	**288**	**295**	**348**	**471**	**819**	**8**	**85**	**32**	**0.58**	**43**	**20**	**37**	**109**	**115**	**11%**	**60**	**3%**	**44%**				**5.82**	**19.0**	**64**	**161**	**$22**

Santana,Carlos

Santana,Carlos			Health	A	LIMA Plan	B+
Age 27	Bats B	Pos CA DH 1B	PT/Exp	B	Rand Var	+1
Ht 5' 11"	Wt 200		Consist	B	MM	4125

Wrestled with power and ct% issues in 1H—perhaps a hidden/nagging injury—before real deal showed up. Though BA/xBA trend appears stagnant; 2H ct%, Eye and xBA gains show real promise in upping his entire offensive game. Legitimate skills, experience, age... and with a complete power rebound: UP: .275-30-100.

Yr	Tm	AB	R	HR	RBI	SB	BA	xBA	vL	vR	OB	Slg	OPS	bb%	ct%	h%	Eye	G	L	F	PX	xPX	hr/f	Spd	SBO	SB%	#Wk	DOM	DIS	RC/G	RAR	BPV	BPX	R$
08	aa																																	
09	aa	429	82	19	87	2	265	284			384	472	856	16	78	30	0.88				135			84	3%	45%				6.20		73	0	$14
10	CLE *	346	52	15	60	7	263	280	146	314	389	469	858	17	79	30	0.96	35	21	44	144	147	11%	65	6%	100%	9	67%	33%	6.48	23.3	89	193	$12
11	CLE	552	84	27	79	5	239	268	318	201	353	457	809	15	76	27	0.73	45	15	40	153	137	16%	65	5%	63%	27	59%	26%	5.35	20.0	78	173	$15
12	CLE	507	72	18	76	3	252	256	272	243	366	420	786	15	80	28	0.90	43	19	38	108	104	12%	82	5%	38%	26	46%	31%	5.10	14.5	54	135	$13
1st Half		223	30	5	29	2	220	229	200	229	343	336	680	16	74	28	0.72	45	21	35	86	89	8%	70	4%	67%	12	25%	42%	3.77	-3.1	13	33	$5
2nd Half		284	42	13	47	1	278	278	323	254	384	486	870	15	85	29	1.14	42	18	40	122	115	13%	93	5%	20%	14	64%	21%	6.29	17.0	84	210	$20
13	Proj	**532**	**80**	**23**	**84**	**5**	**263**	**264**	**299**	**245**	**378**	**460**	**838**	**16**	**79**	**29**	**0.87**	**42**	**18**	**39**	**128**	**122**	**14%**	**72**	**5%**	**55%**				**5.93**	**26.6**	**69**	**172**	**$19**

Santiago,Ramon

Santiago,Ramon			Health	A	LIMA Plan	F
Age 33	Bats B	Pos 2B SS	PT/Exp	D	Rand Var	+4
Ht 5' 11"	Wt 175		Consist	C	MM	1201

R$ history notes dip from unproductive consistency to something worse. Rand Var projects a rebound near previous insignificance. AB are always dependent on productivity and health of his teammates. Zero power, no running game, empty/mediocre contact as he enters his mid-30s. Just telling you how we really feel.

Yr	Tm	AB	R	HR	RBI	SB	BA	xBA	vL	vR	OB	Slg	OPS	bb%	ct%	h%	Eye	G	L	F	PX	xPX	hr/f	Spd	SBO	SB%	#Wk	DOM	DIS	RC/G	RAR	BPV	BPX	R$
08	DET *	152	32	4	20	1	261	279	320	273	360	416	775	13	83	29	0.92	44	23	33	95	66	12%	132	2%	100%	21	48%	43%	5.20	4.6	69	135	$3
09	DET	262	29	7	35	1	267	235	270	267	312	385	697	6	78	32	0.30	46	18	36	71	98	10%	116	4%	33%	27	19%	56%	4.07	-0.7	2	4	$4
10	DET	320	38	3	22	2	263	241	313	249	326	325	651	9	83	31	0.54	49	21	30	43	30	4%	123	4%	50%	26	15%	62%	3.60	-5.2	0	0	$4
11	DET	258	29	5	30	0	260	262	320	245	305	384	689	6	85	29	0.45	43	21	35	79	55	7%	109	0%	0%	26	31%	46%	4.04	-0.9	37	82	$3
12	DET	228	19	2	17	1	206	224	140	228	270	272	542	8	83	24	0.51	52	17	31	44	53	4%	101	2%	100%	24	17%	63%	2.38	-12.6	1	3	-$3
1st Half		147	14	2	17	1	224	240	133	248	283	306	589	8	84	25	0.52	51	19	30	49	60	6%	99	3%	100%	13	23%	54%	2.88	-6.2	14	35	$0
2nd Half		81	5	0	0	0	173	180	148	185	247	210	457	9	80	22	0.50	56	13	32	33	40	0%	103	0%	0%	11	9%	73%	1.60	-7.0	-27	-68	-$7
13	Proj	**129**	**13**	**2**	**10**	**0**	**228**	**232**	**212**	**232**	**290**	**310**	**600**	**8**	**83**	**26**	**0.51**	**50**	**18**	**32**	**54**	**50**	**4%**	**104**	**2%**	**68%**				**2.97**	**-5.1**	**9**	**22**	**$1**

Saunders,Michael

Saunders,Michael			Health	A	LIMA Plan	C
Age 26	Bats L	Pos CF LF	PT/Exp	C	Rand Var	-1
Ht 6' 4"	Wt 215		Consist	C	MM	4405

Minor league career always pointed to raw power/speed skills; improved contact, BA vs. LHP finally made them MLB-playable. But sub-par ct%, marginal BA—particularly against RHPs—could put his playing time at risk. PX/xPX and SB% are encouraging, but BA/xBA track record says let someone else pay for a repeat.

Yr	Tm	AB	R	HR	RBI	SB	BA	xBA	vL	vR	OB	Slg	OPS	bb%	ct%	h%	Eye	G	L	F	PX	xPX	hr/f	Spd	SBO	SB%	#Wk	DOM	DIS	RC/G	RAR	BPV	BPX	R$
08	a/a	343	45	8	35	10	240	229			303	384	687	8	67	33	0.28				115			103	23%	53%				3.63		11	0	$5
09	SEA *	370	56	9	28	8	249	229	200	239	297	386	683	6	74	31	0.26	48	13	39	90	52	0%	135	14%	66%	12	17%	67%	3.80	-8.4	19	39	$6
10	SEA *	369	33	10	37	9	201	208	202	215	284	325	609	10	72	25	0.41	36	16	48	89	81	11%	94	13%	75%	22	32%	55%	2.96	-18.7	6	13	$1
11	SEA *	397	47	6	31	12	187	167	143	152	266	273	540	10	63	28	0.29	36	15	50	76	78	4%	102	18%	68%	14	14%	79%	2.27	-29.6	-34	-76	-$1
12	SEA	507	71	19	57	21	247	259	261	239	305	432	737	8	74	30	0.33	45	20	35	130	136	15%	102	22%	84%	28	29%	36%	4.54	-0.3	54	135	$17
1st Half		260	35	8	24	12	258	259	276	250	320	427	747	8	74	32	0.35	45	22	33	124	110	13%	101	23%	80%	14	36%	36%	4.74	0.7	44	110	$17
2nd Half		247	36	11	33	9	235	259	250	224	289	437	727	7	74	27	0.30	45	18	36	135	164	17%	103	20%	90%	14	21%	36%	4.33	-2.4	58	145	$17
13	Proj	**449**	**67**	**20**	**51**	**15**	**234**	**239**	**242**	**230**	**299**	**426**	**725**	**8**	**71**	**29**	**0.31**	**42**	**17**	**41**	**134**	**108**	**15%**	**104**	**19%**	**77%**				**4.23**	**-7.5**	**43**	**107**	**$14**

Schafer,Jordan

Schafer,Jordan			Health	B	LIMA Plan	F
Age 26	Bats L	Pos CF	PT/Exp	D	Rand Var	-3
Ht 6' 1"	Wt 190		Consist	C	MM	1501

Showed wheels again in extended playing time before season was torpedoed by assorted injuries and more behavioral issues. Ct% and bb% still gyrating in opposing directions, leaving BA/xBA history—and future—as troubling as ever. With power gone and sub-par defense, his speed isn't a sufficient silver lining.

Yr	Tm	AB	R	HR	RBI	SB	BA	xBA	vL	vR	OB	Slg	OPS	bb%	ct%	h%	Eye	G	L	F	PX	xPX	hr/f	Spd	SBO	SB%	#Wk	DOM	DIS	RC/G	RAR	BPV	BPX	R$
08	aa	297	38	8	42	10	245	237			337	414	752	12	67	34	0.42				128			112	18%	65%				4.58		33	0	$7
09	ATL *	202	23	4	10	4	203	193	212	200	302	296	599	12	63	30	0.39	44	18	39	80	77	5%	107	11%	68%	9	22%	78%	2.86	-11.6	-36	-73	-$1
10	a/a	252	18	1	10	8	166	200			220	209	429	6	73	22	0.26				37			108	35%	44%				1.20		-37	0	-$5
11	2 NL *	486	64	3	30	28	238	236	216	251	295	305	600	7	77	30	0.36	44	26	30	53	84	3%	120	28%	76%	16	19%	56%	3.06	-24.1	8	18	$11
12	HOU	313	40	4	23	27	211	196	100	232	292	294	586	10	66	31	0.34	44	21	35	66	76	6%	120	42%	75%	23	4%	74%	2.84	-18.5	-20	-50	$7
1st Half		232	31	3	18	18	237	201	116	265	311	323	635	10	67	34	0.32	45	21	35	71	70	6%	122	36%	75%	13	8%	69%	3.41	-9.8	-19	-48	$11
2nd Half		81	9	1	5	9	136	184	0	149	239	210	449	12	64	20	0.38	43	22	35	52	91	6%	107	63%	75%	10	0%	80%	1.58	-9.1	-29	-73	-$3
13	Proj	**190**	**22**	**2**	**12**	**13**	**195**	**205**	**153**	**205**	**273**	**274**	**547**	**10**	**69**	**27**	**0.35**	**44**	**22**	**34**	**59**	**82**	**5%**	**111**	**39%**	**71%**				**2.37**	**-14.9**	**-15**	**-39**	**$3**

Schierholtz,Nate

Schierholtz,Nate			Health	B	LIMA Plan	D
Age 29	Bats L	Pos RF	PT/Exp	D	Rand Var	0
Ht 6' 2"	Wt 217		Consist	B	MM	2223

Only his patience is trending upward, with no positive impact on his other metrics. Ongoing deterioration vs. LHP and an .826 OPS vs. RHP solidify his upside as a platoon player. As an underpowered corner OF with no standout skills, consistency may be his most valuable asset.

Yr	Tm	AB	R	HR	RBI	SB	BA	xBA	vL	vR	OB	Slg	OPS	bb%	ct%	h%	Eye	G	L	F	PX	xPX	hr/f	Spd	SBO	SB%	#Wk	DOM	DIS	RC/G	RAR	BPV	BPX	R$
08	SF *	425	56	12	57	6	280	322	333	315	309	476	785	4	85	31	0.27	46	30	24	118	76	6%	102	12%	59%	5	60%	20%	5.06	-1.0	78	153	$12
09	SF	285	33	5	29	3	267	264	370	242	306	400	706	5	80	32	0.28	45	21	35	94	101	6%	97	6%	75%	25	28%	52%	4.25	-7.3	32	65	$4
10	SF	227	34	3	17	4	242	260	294	227	304	366	669	8	83	28	0.53	44	18	37	85	85	4%	117	16%	44%	27	30%	48%	3.48	-11.5	53	115	$2
11	SF	335	42	9	41	7	278	269	234	288	320	430	750	6	82	32	0.34	40	22	38	108	114	9%	73	13%	64%	22	41%	23%	4.74	-3.9	50	111	$10
12	2 NL	241	20	6	21	3	257	253	175	287	322	407	729	9	81	30	0.50	46	20	34	87	67	9%	114	8%	60%	26	23%	50%	4.41	-5.1	39	98	$3
1st Half		125	10	3	12	2	248	244	103	292	314	400	714	9	80	29	0.48	47	19	34	81	60	9%	130	12%	50%	13	15%	54%	4.06	-3.5	30	75	$3
2nd Half		116	10	3	9	1	267	260	235	280	331	414	745	9	82	30	0.52	45	21	34	93	75	9%	88	3%	100%	13	31%	46%	4.82	-0.6	40	100	$4
13	Proj	**259**	**28**	**6**	**25**	**4**	**263**	**259**	**224**	**275**	**319**	**407**	**726**	**8**	**82**	**30**	**0.45**	**44**	**21**	**35**	**91**	**85**	**8%**	**96**	**10%**	**59%**				**4.39**	**-4.7**	**44**	**111**	**$6**

JOCK THOMPSON

Schumaker,Skip

Age	33	Bats	L	Pos 2B	Health	C	LIMA Plan	D
Ht	5' 10"	Wt	195		PT/Exp	C	Rand Var	0
					Consist	A	MM	1123

1-28-.276 in 272 AB at STL. Began season on DL with oblique injury, missed more time with hamstring and wrist issues. Value has always been dependent on ct% that is no longer elite. Even if healthy, ongoing futility vs LHP screams platoon role at best. Minus power or running game, his full-time days are over.

Yr	Tm	AB	R	HR	RBI	SB	BA	xBA	vL	vR	OB	Slg	OPS	bb%	ct%	h%	Eye	G	L	F	PX	xPX	hr/f	Spd	SBO	SB%	#Wk	DOM	DIS	RC/G	RAR	BPV	BPX	R$
08	STL	540	87	8	46	8	302	296	168	340	358	406	763	8	89	33	0.78	58	22	20	62	59	8%	111	6%	80%	27	30%	26%	5.33	14.5	55	108	$18
09	STL	532	85	4	35	2	303	294	220	322	365	393	758	9	87	34	0.75	61	22	17	65	40	5%	105	2%	50%	27	37%	19%	5.19	12.3	37	76	$13
10	STL	476	66	5	42	5	265	279	211	275	326	338	664	8	87	30	0.67	59	22	20	51	58	6%	86	6%	63%	27	33%	33%	3.78	-7.7	28	61	$9
11	STL	367	34	2	38	0	283	257	250	287	332	351	684	7	86	32	0.54	52	23	25	54	51	2%	63	2%	0%	22	27%	45%	4.06	-2.9	11	24	$6
12	STL *	293	40	1	28	2	271	262	158	295	338	361	699	9	82	33	0.55	54	23	23	64	52	2%	109	3%	62%	23	26%	48%	4.25	-0.8	25	63	$5
1st Half		124	19	0	13	1	277	272	250	297	354	386	740	11	82	34	0.67	47	26	28	81	64	0%	95	4%	39%	9	22%	44%	4.70	1.6	46	115	$3
2nd Half		169	21	1	15	1	266	253	115	294	326	343	669	8	81	32	0.47	59	21	20	51	45	4%	111	2%	100%	14	29%	50%	3.93	-1.6	8	20	$5
13	Proj	321	41	2	30	2	275	265	187	290	336	359	695	8	84	32	0.58	55	23	23	58	53	3%	92	3%	58%				4.21	-0.5	24	60	$5

Scott,Luke

Age	35	Bats	L	Pos DH	Health	F	LIMA Plan	C+
Ht	6' 0"	Wt	205		PT/Exp	C	Rand Var	+3
					Consist	D	MM	4125

Fast April start fizzled due to repeated interruptions by back problems; later said he returned too fast from 2011 labrum surgery. But 1H BA issues look like a h% blip, power is intact, and he gets a bb% mulligan for pressing with a bad offense. If healthy, he's still a streaky, low-BA platoon hitter who is good for 20 HR.

Yr	Tm	AB	R	HR	RBI	SB	BA	xBA	vL	vR	OB	Slg	OPS	bb%	ct%	h%	Eye	G	L	F	PX	xPX	hr/f	Spd	SBO	SB%	#Wk	DOM	DIS	RC/G	RAR	BPV	BPX	R$
08	BAL	475	67	23	65	2	257	269	215	269	331	472	803	10	79	28	0.52	39	17	44	139	112	14%	79	3%	50%	27	67%	30%	5.30	5.7	64	125	$11
09	BAL	449	61	25	77	0	258	272	260	257	339	488	827	11	77	28	0.53	40	17	43	147	138	17%	68	0%	0%	26	46%	42%	5.69	10.4	58	118	$12
10	BAL	447	70	27	72	2	284	295	240	297	368	535	902	12	78	31	0.60	40	19	41	166	147	19%	68	2%	100%	25	64%	16%	7.03	26.9	87	189	$19
11	BAL	209	24	9	22	1	220	244	167	231	300	402	702	10	74	25	0.44	43	16	41	131	134	14%	58	4%	50%	16	31%	38%	3.89	-6.3	35	78	$1
12	TAM	314	35	14	55	5	229	261	149	260	278	439	717	6	75	26	0.26	42	17	40	147	132	15%	47	9%	100%	21	48%	38%	4.12	-7.2	55	138	$7
1st Half		188	18	9	36	3	207	255	155	239	255	399	654	6	78	22	0.29	46	17	38	122	113	16%	46	9%	100%	11	55%	36%	3.35	-9.0	38	95	$7
2nd Half		126	17	5	19	2	262	265	125	282	311	500	811	7	70	34	0.24	36	19	45	187	166	13%	61	9%	100%	10	40%	40%	5.47	2.1	72	180	$5
13	Proj	416	52	19	62	4	243	261	176	262	309	458	767	9	75	28	0.37	41	17	42	149	140	15%	52	5%	88%				4.80	-1.1	58	146	$12

Scutaro,Marco

Age	37	Bats	R	Pos 2B SS	Health	B	LIMA Plan	B
Ht	5' 10"	Wt	185		PT/Exp	A	Rand Var	-2
					Consist	B	MM	1235

Repeated solid ct% and h% combination, turned them into career year with stratospheric LD% and 600+ AB. Without HR and SB, all of the aforementioned and continued durability are the keys to his value. His new aggressive approach comes with bb% cost, but it obviously works for him. Advancing age is his biggest risk.

Yr	Tm	AB	R	HR	RBI	SB	BA	xBA	vL	vR	OB	Slg	OPS	bb%	ct%	h%	Eye	G	L	F	PX	xPX	hr/f	Spd	SBO	SB%	#Wk	DOM	DIS	RC/G	RAR	BPV	BPX	R$
08	TOR	517	76	7	60	7	267	261	268	267	340	356	696	10	87	29	0.88	43	23	35	58	89	4%	104	5%	78%	27	26%	30%	4.23	-1.7	41	80	$11
09	TOR	574	100	12	60	14	282	262	269	287	380	409	789	14	87	31	1.20	37	19	44	82	92	6%	100	9%	74%	25	48%	12%	5.52	19.1	68	139	$19
10	BOS	632	92	11	56	5	275	258	282	273	331	388	719	8	89	30	0.75	41	17	42	77	69	5%	99	5%	56%	26	35%	19%	4.45	1.8	52	113	$16
11	BOS	395	59	7	54	4	299	279	303	297	360	423	783	9	91	32	1.06	46	19	35	83	74	6%	92	5%	67%	23	52%	13%	5.50	12.6	70	156	$14
12	2 NL	620	87	7	74	9	306	281	301	309	348	405	753	6	92	32	0.82	41	26	33	61	93	4%	116	7%	69%	27	48%	15%	5.15	13.6	58	145	$23
1st Half		292	41	4	24	6	284	277	282	285	332	390	723	7	91	30	0.78	42	25	33	63	95	5%	129	10%	75%	13	38%	0%	4.62	3.0	60	150	$19
2nd Half		328	46	3	50	3	326	286	315	332	363	418	781	5	93	34	0.86	41	26	33	60	92	3%	101	5%	60%	14	57%	29%	5.67	12.3	54	135	$28
13	Proj	551	80	8	66	7	289	272	288	290	342	396	738	7	91	31	0.88	42	22	35	68	85	4%	101	6%	67%				4.82	8.6	59	148	$19

Seager,Kyle

Age	25	Bats	L	Pos 3B	Health	A	LIMA Plan	C+
Ht	5' 10"	Wt	195		PT/Exp	C	Rand Var	0
					Consist	A	MM	2125

2011 PX/xPX combo hinted at potential HR spike, 1H FB surge touched it off. Even with 2H PX fade, hr/f says enough of the gains are real. But speed metrics say SBs won't last as he ages, and average plate skills leave him with limited ceiling. Should be profitable again, but how long can he hold starting job over the long haul?

Yr	Tm	AB	R	HR	RBI	SB	BA	xBA	vL	vR	OB	Slg	OPS	bb%	ct%	h%	Eye	G	L	F	PX	xPX	hr/f	Spd	SBO	SB%	#Wk	DOM	DIS	RC/G	RAR	BPV	BPX	R$
08																																		
09																																		
10																																		
11	SEA *	554	62	8	51	11	264	261	229	265	313	383	697	7	82	31	0.40	30	28	42	91	118	5%	83	14%	57%	12	33%	58%	4.01	-8.7	41	91	$12
12	SEA	594	62	20	86	13	259	259	237	272	313	423	735	7	81	29	0.42	36	22	42	106	115	10%	70	13%	72%	28	36%	25%	4.51	-0.6	48	120	$18
1st Half		274	34	10	46	7	252	259	220	266	310	442	751	8	80	28	0.41	33	20	47	128	124	10%	67	15%	78%	14	50%	29%	4.66	0.7	64	160	$19
2nd Half		320	28	10	40	6	266	260	248	278	315	406	721	7	83	29	0.43	38	24	39	88	108	10%	75	11%	67%	14	21%	21%	4.37	-1.9	33	83	$17
13	Proj	553	59	15	68	12	261	259	239	273	314	409	723	7	82	30	0.42	34	24	42	99	116	8%	74	13%	66%				4.35	-3.8	45	112	$16

Segura,Jean

Age	23	Bats	R	Pos SS	Health	A	LIMA Plan	D+
Ht	5' 10"	Wt	165		PT/Exp	F	Rand Var	0
					Consist	F	MM	1505

0-14-.258, 7 SB in 151 AB at LAA/MIL. Pedigreed prospect flashed solid 85% ct% and elite wheels in MLB debut. Dogged by leg injuries (ankle, hamstring) in minors, making 137 SB, 79% SB% in 1570 AB even more impressive. Should be profitable quickly, regardless of power and patience shortcomings.

Yr	Tm	AB	R	HR	RBI	SB	BA	xBA	vL	vR	OB	Slg	OPS	bb%	ct%	h%	Eye	G	L	F	PX	xPX	hr/f	Spd	SBO	SB%	#Wk	DOM	DIS	RC/G	RAR	BPV	BPX	R$
08																																		
09																																		
10																																		
11																																		
12	2 TM *	555	66	6	50	38	273	262	81	316	317	361	678	6	83	32	0.39	66	15	19	53	57	0%	168	33%	71%	10	30%	60%	3.92	-3.0	29	73	$22
1st Half		308	34	6	30	23	261	237			292	370	662	4	81	30	0.23	44	20	36	65			137	46%	66%				3.43		25	63	$25
2nd Half		247	32	0	21	15	288	262	81	316	347	351	698	8	87	33	0.67	66	15	19	39	57	0%	169	22%	82%	10	30%	60%	4.52	3.6	35	88	$18
13	Proj	491	60	4	44	33	276	234	237	288	323	361	683	6	84	32	0.44	51	15	34	51	34	3%	170	31%	74%				4.09	1.1	34	85	$21

Shoppach,Kelly

Age	33	Bats	R	Pos CA	Health	B	LIMA Plan	F
Ht	6' 0"	Wt	220		PT/Exp	F	Rand Var	-4
					Consist	C	MM	4301

Productive 1H in small sample was fueled by crazy h%, fell back to earth with more AB following trade to NYM. But the profile remains the same: Contact-and-BA challenged backup C with terrific power, and BA/AB history that says the positive will usually be cancelled out by the negative. Rosterable only in non-BA/OBA leagues.

Yr	Tm	AB	R	HR	RBI	SB	BA	xBA	vL	vR	OB	Slg	OPS	bb%	ct%	h%	Eye	G	L	F	PX	xPX	hr/f	Spd	SBO	SB%	#Wk	DOM	DIS	RC/G	RAR	BPV	BPX	R$
08	CLE	352	67	21	55	0	261	256	304	246	330	517	847	9	62	36	0.27	38	19	43	211	159	22%	69	0%	0%	27	37%	48%	5.89	16.3	51	100	$10
09	CLE	271	33	12	40	0	214	236	304	191	299	399	698	11	64	29	0.34	41	22	37	145	123	18%	66	0%	0%	26	35%	54%	3.87	-3.4	2	4	$1
10	TAM	158	17	5	17	0	196	180	261	114	287	342	628	11	55	32	0.28	44	11	44	145	173	13%	82	0%	0%	20	15%	75%	3.11	-5.8	-31	-67	-$1
11	TAM	221	23	11	22	0	176	185	241	115	242	339	581	8	64	21	0.24	37	12	51	119	153	15%	89	0%	0%	26	27%	62%	2.54	-12.4	-22	-49	-$2
12	2 TM	219	23	8	27	1	233	217	239	226	285	425	710	7	59	35	0.18	35	21	44	167	142	14%	104	2%	100%	27	33%	52%	4.05	-1.5	10	25	$2
1st Half		87	13	4	12	1	276	263	255	300	330	540	870	7	61	41	0.21	42	19	38	232	94	20%	96	6%	100%	13	54%	38%	6.35	5.3	76	190	$4
2nd Half		132	10	4	15	0	205	189	227	182	255	348	604	6	58	32	0.16	30	22	48	122	174	11%	96	0%	0%	14	14%	64%	2.85	-5.6	-40	-100	$1
13	Proj	226	25	9	27	1	214	208	246	183	276	396	672	8	60	31	0.22	37	17	46	151	149	15%	90	1%	100%				3.55	-4.6	-2	-6	$2

Sierra,Moises

Age	24	Bats	R	Pos RF	Health	A	LIMA Plan	F
Ht	6' 0"	Wt	225		PT/Exp	D	Rand Var	+2
					Consist	A	MM	2103

6-15-.224 in 147 AB at TOR. His recent minor league numbers—36 HR in last 876 AB—suggest that his power is on the uptick. MLB small sample and xPX add confirmation. But lofty GB%, struggles vs RHP and otherwise mediocre plate skills say it probably won't be enough. Still, he's young enough to keep an eye on.

Yr	Tm	AB	R	HR	RBI	SB	BA	xBA	vL	vR	OB	Slg	OPS	bb%	ct%	h%	Eye	G	L	F	PX	xPX	hr/f	Spd	SBO	SB%	#Wk	DOM	DIS	RC/G	RAR	BPV	BPX	R$
08																																		
09	aa	34	1	1	6	0	342	218			361	461	822	3	73	44	0.11				80			90	10%	0%				5.64		-31	0	$0
10																																		
11	aa	495	67	16	55	13	252	251			297	396	693	6	79	29	0.30				95			99	24%	46%				3.60		33	0	$14
12	TOR *	524	56	18	57	6	234	228	286	187	281	375	656	6	72	29	0.23	53	17	30	96	134	19%	54	11%	45%	10	20%	50%	3.35	-24.1	-4	-10	$9
1st Half		289	35	9	32	4	251	232			298	390	688	6	74	31	0.25	44	20	36	96			66	14%	41%				3.68		2	5	$12
2nd Half		235	21	9	25	2	214	222	286	187	260	357	617	6	70	26	0.21	53	17	30	96	134	19%	65	6%	59%	10	20%	50%	2.97	-14.8	-13	-33	$4
13	Proj	263	30	8	29	4	239	231	279	199	284	366	651	6	75	29	0.25	48	19	33	85	80	12%	69	15%	47%				3.27	-13.9	2	6	$5

JOCK THOMPSON

Simmons,Andrelton

Age 23	Bats R	Pos SS	Health	C	LIMA Plan	D+
Ht 6' 2"	Wt 170		PT/Exp	F	Rand Var	0
			Consist	F	MM	1525

3-19-.289 in 166 AB at ATL. Terrific defender whose MLB debut gave preview of his offensive MO. Solid contact, less-than-elite patience, gap power, and excellent speed that has yet to translate into a productive running game. Doesn't look overmatched; his glove will keep him in the lineup while he learns on the job.

Yr	Tm	AB	R	HR	RBI	SB	BA	xBA	vL	vR	OB	Slg	OPS	bb%	ct%	h%	Eye	G	L	F	PX	xPX	hr/f	Spd	SBO	SB%	#Wk	DOM	DIS	RC/G	RAR	BPV	BPX	R$
08																																		
09																																		
10																																		
11																																		
12	ATL *	340	42	5	37	9	276	270	305	280	333	393	726	8	87	30	0.66	56	17	27	71	45	8%	133	12%	81%	11	45%	45%	4.67	5.4	54	135	$9
1st Half		261	34	5	32	8	287	273	333	333	343	424	767	8	87	31	0.67	49	19	33	83	67	12%	128	14%	79%	5	60%	20%	5.24	9.1	65	163	$14
2nd Half		76	7	0	5	1	237	241	261	226	301	289	591	8	86	28	0.64	64	15	21	33	19	0%	138	5%	100%	6	33%	67%	2.99	-2.3	11	28	-$7
13	**Proj**	**515**	**55**	**5**	**46**	**10**	**257**	**260**	**275**	**248**	**316**	**350**	**666**	**8**	**86**	**29**	**0.63**	**58**	**16**	**25**	**57**	**38**	**5%**	**147**	**8%**	**87%**				**3.87**	**-2.1**	**40**	**101**	**$9**

Sizemore,Grady

Age 30	Bats L	Pos CF	Health	F	LIMA Plan	D
Ht 6' 2"	Wt 200		PT/Exp	F	Rand Var	+1
			Consist	C	MM	4003

Missed entire season after March back surgery, which just adds to the injuries dimming his outlook. Once you display a skill you own it, but the last time he showed elite skills was 2008. The combination of a bad back, balky knees and two years on the shelf say that return to productivity won't come quickly, if it comes at all.

Yr	Tm	AB	R	HR	RBI	SB	BA	xBA	vL	vR	OB	Slg	OPS	bb%	ct%	h%	Eye	G	L	F	PX	xPX	hr/f	Spd	SBO	SB%	#Wk	DOM	DIS	RC/G	RAR	BPV	BPX	R$
08	CLE	634	101	33	90	38	268	277	224	286	366	502	868	13	79	29	0.75	35	19	46	147	139	14%	98	23%	88%	27	70%	22%	6.62	32.4	103	202	$32
09	CLE	436	73	18	64	13	248	255	216	262	339	445	784	12	79	28	0.65	36	16	48	119	128	11%	106	17%	62%	19	63%	26%	4.92	0.8	73	149	$13
10	CLE	128	15	0	13	4	211	207	122	266	263	289	552	7	73	29	0.26	39	19	42	65	116	0%	108	21%	67%	7	14%	57%	2.41	-9.8	-2	-4	-$1
11	CLE *	296	35	11	36	0	229	248	183	239	280	424	703	7	69	29	0.23	40	18	42	160	137	13%	78	4%	0%	16	31%	38%	3.80	-9.5	34	76	$3
12																																		
1st Half																																		
2nd Half																																		
13	**Proj**	**253**	**36**	**8**	**33**	**1**	**238**	**240**	**187**	**261**	**311**	**415**	**726**	**10**	**75**	**29**	**0.42**	**38**	**18**	**45**	**122**	**130**	**10%**	**90**	**6%**	**13%**				**4.10**	**-5.2**	**40**	**100**	**$5**

Sizemore,Scott

Age 28	Bats R	Pos 3B	Health	F	LIMA Plan	D
Ht 6' 0"	Wt 185		PT/Exp	D	Rand Var	+1
			Consist	B	MM	3303

Missed entire season after sustaining torn ACL in Feb. Had 3B job until injury, thanks largely to power and patience surge in 2011. But struggles vs. RHP, ct% plunge, and BA/xBA combo over 2010-2011 leave us with questions. Opportunity would offer profit potential at scarce position, making him an interesting March watch.

Yr	Tm	AB	R	HR	RBI	SB	BA	xBA	vL	vR	OB	Slg	OPS	bb%	ct%	h%	Eye	G	L	F	PX	xPX	hr/f	Spd	SBO	SB%	#Wk	DOM	DIS	RC/G	RAR	BPV	BPX	R$
08																																		
09	a/a	520	73	15	55	17	277	276			343	446	789	9	80	32	0.50				112			102	15%	79%				5.43		64	0	$18
10	DET *	442	57	10	42	2	244	237	224	223	304	376	680	8	71	32	0.30	38	22	40	107	87	7%	95	4%	40%	12	33%	50%	3.79	-9.9	5	11	$6
11	2 AL *	474	69	13	68	8	254	239	294	221	350	405	754	13	70	34	0.49	44	20	36	122	119	12%	105	9%	60%	21	38%	48%	4.74	2.7	29	64	$13
12																																		
1st Half																																		
2nd Half																																		
13	**Proj**	**315**	**44**	**8**	**37**	**6**	**252**	**238**	**292**	**232**	**327**	**408**	**735**	**10**	**71**	**33**	**0.39**	**41**	**21**	**38**	**119**	**106**	**10%**	**105**	**11%**	**70%**				**4.51**	**-0.6**	**30**	**74**	**$9**

Smith,Seth

Age 30	Bats L	Pos LF DH	Health	A	LIMA Plan	D+
Ht 6' 3"	Wt 210		PT/Exp	C	Rand Var	+1
			Consist	C	MM	4223

Move from extreme LHB park to polar opposite altered his plate approach, as shown by bb% hike and ct% plunge. PX/xPX and HR metrics remain solid; he may even improve in second AL season. But upside looks capped by platoon profile. Career home numbers of note: .299/.370/.567 in Coors; .244/.348/.411 in OAK.

Yr	Tm	AB	R	HR	RBI	SB	BA	xBA	vL	vR	OB	Slg	OPS	bb%	ct%	h%	Eye	G	L	F	PX	xPX	hr/f	Spd	SBO	SB%	#Wk	DOM	DIS	RC/G	RAR	BPV	BPX	R$
08	COL *	356	47	11	48	8	259	266	0	289	339	414	753	11	79	30	0.57	45	21	34	104	108	14%	108	8%	100%	17	41%	47%	4.97	2.5	49	96	$9
09	COL	335	61	15	55	4	293	282	259	300	378	510	888	12	80	33	0.69	39	19	42	134	112	13%	111	5%	80%	27	70%	30%	6.97	22.4	85	173	$13
10	COL	358	55	17	52	2	246	275	154	261	313	469	782	9	81	26	0.52	36	16	48	139	132	12%	105	4%	67%	27	56%	37%	4.94	3.9	85	185	$9
11	COL	476	67	15	59	10	284	276	217	299	347	483	830	9	80	33	0.49	38	22	40	133	127	10%	117	10%	83%	27	59%	26%	6.00	19.3	86	191	$18
12	OAK	383	55	14	52	2	240	258	157	259	328	420	748	12	74	29	0.51	41	23	36	126	130	14%	78	4%	50%	26	42%	35%	4.56	0.0	43	108	$8
1st Half		202	30	8	27	2	252	258	242	254	360	436	796	14	76	29	0.71	42	21	37	122	126	14%	87	5%	67%	14	36%	29%	5.32	4.0	53	133	$10
2nd Half		181	25	6	25	0	227	259	81	264	289	403	693	8	72	28	0.32	40	25	34	130	134	13%	73	3%	0%	12	50%	42%	3.75	-5.0	32	80	$5
13	**Proj**	**347**	**50**	**13**	**47**	**3**	**245**	**264**	**161**	**264**	**320**	**438**	**757**	**10**	**77**	**28**	**0.48**	**40**	**22**	**39**	**128**	**128**	**12%**	**91**	**6%**	**70%**				**4.70**	**0.5**	**61**	**151**	**$9**

Smoak,Justin

Age 26	Bats B	Pos 1B	Health	A	LIMA Plan	D+
Ht 6' 4"	Wt 230		PT/Exp	B	Rand Var	+2
			Consist	B	MM	3205

19-51-.217 in 483 AB at SEA. Almost lost in another disappointing season was a terrific Sept (5 HR, .338 BA, 11% bb%, 87% ct%) that will tempt owners again in 2013... just like his .301 BA in Sept 2011 tempted owners last March. But while xPX history holds out hope, repeated failures have shortened his leash.

Yr	Tm	AB	R	HR	RBI	SB	BA	xBA	vL	vR	OB	Slg	OPS	bb%	ct%	h%	Eye	G	L	F	PX	xPX	hr/f	Spd	SBO	SB%	#Wk	DOM	DIS	RC/G	RAR	BPV	BPX	R$
08																																		
09	a/a	380	45	9	43	0	259	239			362	380	742	14	77	32	0.69				85			81	0%	0%				4.73		11	0	$5
10	2 AL *	531	64	19	70	1	222	251	215	220	318	376	694	12	74	26	0.54	38	23	39	112	140	13%	50	1%	100%	19	26%	47%	3.93	-21.9	22	48	$6
11	SEA	427	38	15	55	0	234	222	252	227	322	396	717	11	75	28	0.52	44	14	43	119	129	11%	64	0%	0%	25	36%	40%	4.24	-13.4	25	56	$5
12	SEA *	549	56	19	54	2	213	225	235	208	291	353	644	10	76	25	0.46	40	18	42	91	116	12%	66	1%	100%	26	31%	58%	3.34	-32.9	11	28	$3
1st Half		277	25	11	32	1	202	204	200	203	268	332	600	8	77	22	0.40	41	14	44	75	107	12%	64	1%	100%	14	21%	64%	2.86	-21.6	-3	-8	$3
2nd Half		272	31	8	22	1	225	245	271	215	313	374	687	11	75	27	0.51	37	23	40	107	129	13%	80	1%	100%	12	42%	50%	3.87	-12.3	23	58	$3
13	**Proj**	**530**	**55**	**20**	**59**	**1**	**245**	**234**	**263**	**235**	**328**	**404**	**731**	**11**	**76**	**29**	**0.51**	**40**	**18**	**42**	**107**	**126**	**12%**	**65**	**1%**	**100%**				**4.48**	**-13.8**	**22**	**55**	**$10**

Snider,Travis

Age 25	Bats L	Pos RF	Health	B	LIMA Plan	D+
Ht 6' 0"	Wt 235		PT/Exp	D	Rand Var	-1
			Consist	C	MM	3115

4-17-.250 in 164 AB at TOR/PIT. PRO: MLEs point to mild power rebound; bb% recovery; progress vs. LHP. CON: Most of 2012 power numbers from extreme AAA environment didn't translate to MLB; GB% is spiking; power potential has dimmed. He still has time for an MLB career, but his upside has faded.

Yr	Tm	AB	R	HR	RBI	SB	BA	xBA	vL	vR	OB	Slg	OPS	bb%	ct%	h%	Eye	G	L	F	PX	xPX	hr/f	Spd	SBO	SB%	#Wk	DOM	DIS	RC/G	RAR	BPV	BPX	R$
08	TOR *	499	74	20	87	2	268	268	286	305	339	451	791	10	66	37	0.32	37	35	29	146	144	13%	57	2%	63%	6	17%	33%	5.31	8.3	17	33	$14
09	TOR *	416	58	20	60	3	266	251	225	244	345	482	827	11	68	34	0.38	44	15	41	159	125	14%	73	6%	37%	15	33%	40%	5.58	10.3	41	84	$11
10	TOR *	379	47	18	45	8	256	279	254	255	298	463	760	6	73	31	0.22	41	24	35	152	129	18%	72	16%	67%	16	38%	31%	4.61	-1.3	47	102	$11
11	TOR *	435	52	6	56	16	247	239	116	257	290	367	658	6	75	32	0.24	47	17	37	102	97	6%	66	22%	80%	10	30%	50%	3.65	-13.9	28	62	$11
12	2 TM *	373	56	13	56	3	266	258	364	221	337	435	772	10	74	33	0.41	56	19	26	119	74	13%	73	8%	42%	12	17%	58%	4.90	1.8	29	73	$11
1st Half		155	22	6	28	1	273	267			339	458	797	9	78	32	0.46	44	20	36	127			57	15%	22%				4.86		49	123	$9
2nd Half		218	35	8	27	2	261	245	364	221	335	419	755	10	70	34	0.38	56	19	26	113	74	13%	86	3%	100%	12	17%	58%	4.91	1.7	17	43	$13
13	**Proj**	**418**	**58**	**10**	**58**	**7**	**260**	**244**	**284**	**253**	**320**	**401**	**721**	**8**	**73**	**33**	**0.33**	**48**	**20**	**32**	**107**	**79**	**11%**	**68**	**11%**	**61%**				**4.32**	**-8.5**	**20**	**49**	**$13**

Snyder,Chris

Age 32	Bats R	Pos CA	Health	F	LIMA Plan	F
Ht 6' 4"	Wt 240		PT/Exp	F	Rand Var	+4
			Consist	D	MM	2001

Recovered from 2011 back surgery and stayed injury-free. Retained customary patience, but the good news ends there. Rising GB% and back issues are sapping his power upside, while ct% and BA skills remain unplayable. The 2H hr/f, PX upticks provide glimmer of hope with more off-season rest, but that's all we see.

Yr	Tm	AB	R	HR	RBI	SB	BA	xBA	vL	vR	OB	Slg	OPS	bb%	ct%	h%	Eye	G	L	F	PX	xPX	hr/f	Spd	SBO	SB%	#Wk	DOM	DIS	RC/G	RAR	BPV	BPX	R$
08	ARI	334	47	16	64	0	237	252	250	231	346	452	798	14	70	29	0.55	38	18	44	159	118	16%	64	0%	0%	24	42%	33%	5.23	9.4	48	94	$5
09	ARI	165	20	6	22	0	200	221	161	220	330	352	681	16	72	24	0.68	37	17	46	106	124	11%	79	0%	0%	15	33%	60%	3.70	-3.0	11	22	-$1
10	2 NL	319	34	15	48	0	207	215	192	212	318	376	694	14	71	24	0.55	42	15	43	118	118	15%	67	0%	0%	25	24%	48%	3.85	-4.3	10	22	$2
11	PIT	96	13	3	17	0	271	247	310	254	381	396	776	15	76	33	0.74	43	25	32	86	90	13%	80	3%	0%	9	33%	44%	5.07	2.2	13	29	$1
12	HOU	221	23	7	24	0	176	207	169	181	283	308	591	13	68	22	0.47	48	18	34	97	78	13%	52	0%	0%	26	27%	62%	2.70	-11.2	-14	-35	-$3
1st Half		114	10	3	17	0	184	199	158	197	273	298	572	11	68	24	0.39	47	18	35	86	78	11%	57	0%	0%	13	23%	69%	2.55	-6.1	-29	-73	-$3
2nd Half		107	13	4	7	0	168	215	179	162	294	318	611	15	68	20	0.56	48	18	34	109	78	16%	63	0%	0%	13	31%	54%	2.86	-4.7	-1	-3	-$3
13	**Proj**	**180**	**21**	**6**	**24**	**0**	**219**	**219**	**221**	**218**	**329**	**360**	**689**	**14**	**71**	**27**	**0.56**	**45**	**19**	**36**	**99**	**91**	**14%**	**58**	**1%**	**0%**				**3.83**	**-2.1**	**0**	**0**	**$2**

JOCK THOMPSON

Sogard,Eric

Sogard,Eric				Health	B	LIMA Plan	F
Age	27	Bats L	Pos SS	PT/Exp	D	Rand Var	+2
Ht	5' 10"	Wt	190	Consist	A	MM	1211

2-7-.167 in 103 AB with OAK. Bench player offering a little infield versatility, a lot of nothing else. Without any power or real speed, it's nearly impossible to leverage mediocre plate skills into a sum greater than the parts. The best news about this season is that he's still just 27 and another step closer to an MLB pension.

Yr Tm	AB	R	HR	RBI	SB	BA	xBA	vL	vR	OB	Slg	OPS	bb%	ct%	h%	Eye	G	L	F	PX	xPX	hr/f	Spd	SBO	SB%	#Wk	DOM	DIS	RC/G	RAR	BPV	BPX	R$
08																																	
09 aa	458	63	4	41	8	243	255			314	324	638	9	87	27	0.82				53			103	11%	54%				3.31		39	0	$5
10 OAK *	521	55	3	44	9	243	362	1000	200	312	320	632	9	84	28	0.64	50	50	0	55	78	0%	117	14%	45%	3	33%	33%	3.15	-16.1	26	57	$6
11 OAK *	385	44	5	29	9	229	230	0	237	287	318	605	8	86	26	0.58	37	19	44	60	71	8%	94	13%	71%	12	42%	50%	3.01	-13.6	35	78	$3
12 OAK *	259	28	5	22	9	224	255	200	159	282	329	611	7	85	25	0.55	39	26	35	60	61	7%	97	20%	72%	14	21%	36%	3.02	-9.1	38	95	$3
1st Half	154	19	3	15	6	204	256	188	132	277	296	573	9	86	22	0.71	34	30	36	52	88	11%	92	18%	82%	10	10%	40%	2.71	-7.5	39	98	$3
2nd Half	105	9	2	6	4	253	254	250	207	288	378	666	5	84	28	0.32	48	19	33	73	7	0%	103	25%	60%	4	50%	25%	3.50	-2.4	34	85	$2
13 Proj	97	11	2	7	3	235	247	163	250	293	344	636	8	85	26	0.56	40	21	38	65	53	6%	93	17%	67%				3.29	-2.1	36	91	$0

Solano,Donovan

Solano,Donovan				Health	A	LIMA Plan	D
Age	25	Bats R	Pos 2B	PT/Exp	D	Rand Var	-5
Ht	5' 9"	Wt	190	Consist	B	MM	1413

2-28-.295 with 10 SB in 285 AB at MIA. Productive rookie season driven by inflated h%, crazy LD%, and perfect SB%. Prior history offers no precedent for this—.281 BA and 5 SB are his high watermarks. Zero power and nothing suggesting table-setting plate skills. Both his success and opportunity look short-lived.

Yr Tm	AB	R	HR	RBI	SB	BA	xBA	vL	vR	OB	Slg	OPS	bb%	ct%	h%	Eye	G	L	F	PX	xPX	hr/f	Spd	SBO	SB%	#Wk	DOM	DIS	RC/G	RAR	BPV	BPX	R$
08 aa	106	9	1	9	2	235	220			263	297	560	4	78	29	0.17				50			89	11%	60%				2.54		-21	0	-$1
09 a/a	415	39	1	24	3	223	224			267	262	529	6	83	27	0.35				30			98	3%	100%				2.33		-10	0	-$2
10 aaa	330	29	3	19	1	210	242			228	268	496	2	88	23	0.20				39			103	4%	55%				1.95		9	0	-$3
11 a/a	330	18	2	22	1	209	241			244	296	539	4	82	25	0.26				72			77	2%	100%				2.34		8	0	-$4
12 MIA *	426	39	2	38	10	270	248	291	297	316	340	656	6	79	34	0.32	45	28	27	51	72	3%	121	8%	100%	20	20%	60%	3.90	-5.4	3	8	$8
1st Half	174	11	0	15	4	246	276	350	385	290	305	595	6	78	31	0.29	32	43	25	50	87	0%	95	9%	100%	6	50%	50%	3.12	-5.9	-11	-28	$2
2nd Half	252	28	2	23	6	286	247	277	290	333	365	698	7	79	35	0.35	47	26	27	52	70	4%	133	8%	100%	14	7%	64%	4.50	1.7	6	15	$13
13 Proj	398	33	2	31	6	242	241	239	243	281	315	596	5	81	29	0.29	46	23	31	54	77	2%	110	6%	94%				3.04	-14.5	5	13	$4

Soriano,Alfonso

Soriano,Alfonso				Health	B	LIMA Plan	B
Age	37	Bats R	Pos LF	PT/Exp	B	Rand Var	-1
Ht	6' 1"	Wt	195	Consist	B	MM	4225

Looked finished after April, with no HR, 25 PX and .237 BA. Put up a season-best .290/.347/.591 line in May and never looked back. Power still intact, while slowly ebbing contact remains barely adequate. R$ driven by health and first 500+ AB season in the last five. At his age, pay for another 20+ HR, but not a full repeat.

Yr Tm	AB	R	HR	RBI	SB	BA	xBA	vL	vR	OB	Slg	OPS	bb%	ct%	h%	Eye	G	L	F	PX	xPX	hr/f	Spd	SBO	SB%	#Wk	DOM	DIS	RC/G	RAR	BPV	BPX	R$
08 CHC	453	76	29	75	19	280	280	351	252	343	532	875	9	77	31	0.42	29	23	48	161	129	17%	67	19%	86%	21	62%	19%	6.56	23.6	86	169	$24
09 CHC	477	64	20	55	9	241	247	184	256	300	423	723	8	75	28	0.34	33	19	48	121	108	11%	90	10%	82%	22	41%	36%	4.29	-6.2	41	84	$10
10 CHC	496	67	24	79	5	258	269	295	243	320	496	816	8	75	30	0.37	29	16	54	171	159	12%	98	6%	83%	27	63%	19%	5.47	10.6	82	178	$16
11 CHC	475	50	26	88	2	244	263	271	235	285	469	754	5	76	27	0.24	29	20	51	154	148	14%	68	3%	67%	26	38%	35%	4.49	-3.3	55	122	$13
12 CHC	561	68	32	108	6	262	262	260	263	316	499	815	7	73	31	0.29	36	20	44	161	153	18%	78	6%	75%	27	44%	30%	5.43	11.3	56	140	$21
1st Half	267	30	15	46	1	273	261	221	291	322	494	816	7	76	31	0.29	42	19	40	144	132	19%	71	3%	50%	13	38%	38%	5.52	6.6	42	105	$19
2nd Half	294	38	17	62	5	252	259	302	238	310	503	814	8	70	30	0.28	30	22	48	178	173	17%	84	10%	83%	14	50%	21%	5.34	6.0	68	170	$24
13 Proj	520	64	27	85	5	256	256	274	250	310	480	790	7	74	30	0.30	32	20	48	152	151	15%	78	6%	75%				5.08	6.6	55	137	$18

Soto,Geovany

Soto,Geovany				Health	D	LIMA Plan	D
Age	30	Bats R	Pos CA	PT/Exp	C	Rand Var	+5
Ht	6' 1"	Wt	220	Consist	D	MM	3113

More injuries (knee, groin, back) finally dragged down power along with BA metrics. xPX says the HR should return with better health. But with more than 340 AB just once in four years, he's now flyer material. BA will rebound some with h%. He looks old, but with health, opportunity... UP: .260 BA, 20+ HR.

Yr Tm	AB	R	HR	RBI	SB	BA	xBA	vL	vR	OB	Slg	OPS	bb%	ct%	h%	Eye	G	L	F	PX	xPX	hr/f	Spd	SBO	SB%	#Wk	DOM	DIS	RC/G	RAR	BPV	BPX	R$
08 CHC	494	66	23	86	0	285	274	312	276	365	504	869	11	76	34	0.51	38	21	41	150	146	15%	79	1%	0%	26	50%	19%	6.52	33.0	57	112	$17
09 CHC	331	27	11	47	1	218	250	205	221	320	381	701	13	77	25	0.65	41	18	41	110	147	10%	58	1%	100%	24	33%	54%	3.99	-1.4	35	71	$1
10 CHC	322	47	17	53	0	280	281	367	235	393	497	893	16	74	33	0.75	36	24	40	153	179	18%	71	1%	0%	22	55%	36%	6.89	25.1	59	128	$11
11 CHC	421	46	17	54	0	228	241	296	207	303	411	714	10	71	28	0.36	41	19	40	143	125	14%	64	0%	0%	25	32%	44%	4.11	-0.3	24	53	$6
12 2 TM	324	45	11	39	1	198	237	239	182	266	343	608	8	77	22	0.39	40	21	40	94	139	11%	80	1%	100%	23	22%	30%	2.91	-12.5	21	53	$1
1st Half	122	16	5	9	0	172	245	143	181	257	336	593	10	80	17	0.56	45	18	37	95	138	14%	93	0%	0%	9	22%	11%	2.66	-6.1	36	90	-$5
2nd Half	202	29	6	30	1	213	232	283	183	271	347	617	7	75	26	0.31	36	23	41	93	139	10%	75	2%	100%	14	21%	43%	3.06	-7.2	8	20	$4
13 Proj	346	45	14	46	1	237	244	294	216	314	407	721	10	75	28	0.45	39	21	40	115	142	13%	70	1%	74%				4.27	0.6	27	68	$7

Span,Denard

Span,Denard				Health	D	LIMA Plan	B
Age	29	Bats L	Pos CF	PT/Exp	B	Rand Var	0
Ht	6' 0"	Wt	212	Consist	B	MM	1435

Overcame effects of 2011 concussion to post productive season, in spite of August shoulder injury that limited AB down the stretch. Continues to live off near-elite ct% and legs, though post-injury running game was a tick off. Offers consistency marred only by durability questions. Expect more of the same.

Yr Tm	AB	R	HR	RBI	SB	BA	xBA	vL	vR	OB	Slg	OPS	bb%	ct%	h%	Eye	G	L	F	PX	xPX	hr/f	Spd	SBO	SB%	#Wk	DOM	DIS	RC/G	RAR	BPV	BPX	R$
08 MIN *	507	97	8	58	30	294	289	283	299	379	426	805	12	80	35	0.68	54	26	20	88	66	11%	119	26%	65%	17	65%	29%	5.57	10.4	59	116	$26
09 MIN	578	97	8	68	23	311	266	330	303	386	415	801	11	85	36	0.79	53	19	28	58	39	6%	151	15%	70%	26	42%	31%	5.85	15.8	47	96	$27
10 MIN	629	85	3	58	26	264	271	279	256	328	348	676	9	88	30	0.81	54	18	28	53	48	2%	123	16%	87%	27	44%	33%	4.10	-13.7	57	124	$18
11 MIN *	322	40	2	17	8	253	267	240	273	311	339	650	8	87	29	0.64	53	21	26	55	55	3%	123	10%	89%	15	27%	33%	3.70	-10.9	46	102	$4
12 MIN	516	71	4	41	17	283	290	301	275	343	395	738	8	88	32	0.76	54	21	24	78	48	4%	103	16%	74%	26	50%	23%	4.81	-0.7	65	163	$16
1st Half	284	38	3	20	8	275	291	275	275	344	391	735	10	88	30	0.86	57	20	22	79	43	5%	101	13%	73%	13	38%	23%	4.71	-0.5	64	160	$16
2nd Half	232	33	1	21	9	293	288	329	276	341	401	742	7	88	33	0.63	51	23	27	77	54	2%	100	19%	75%	13	62%	23%	4.93	1.0	64	160	$16
13 Proj	545	76	4	43	19	276	279	287	271	337	380	717	8	87	31	0.73	53	21	26	68	51	4%	109	15%	77%				4.54	-3.7	59	147	$18

Stanton,Giancarlo

Stanton,Giancarlo				Health	B	LIMA Plan	B+
Age	23	Bats R	Pos RF	PT/Exp	B	Rand Var	-2
Ht	6' 5"	Wt	245	Consist	B	MM	5135

Scary power. Soaring hr/f is driving performance gains, trumping sub-par ct%. HR every 9 AB in 2H says overaggressiveness and bb% dip aren't issues for now. This after missing most of spring training, finishing April with one HR, losing July to knee surgery, and battling oblique issues in Sept. With health... UP: 50+ HR.

Yr Tm	AB	R	HR	RBI	SB	BA	xBA	vL	vR	OB	Slg	OPS	bb%	ct%	h%	Eye	G	L	F	PX	xPX	hr/f	Spd	SBO	SB%	#Wk	DOM	DIS	RC/G	RAR	BPV	BPX	R$
08																																	
09 aa	299	45	14	48	1	222	244			292	428	720	9	63	30	0.27				157			94	3%	47%				4.05		23	0	$4
10 FLA *	551	80	39	103	6	269	280	218	271	355	551	906	12	67	33	0.40	43	16	41	214	138	23%	100	5%	75%	18	39%	44%	6.79	26.1	86	187	$24
11 FLA	516	79	34	87	5	262	276	293	253	350	537	887	12	68	32	0.42	45	16	38	205	172	25%	98	7%	50%	27	56%	26%	6.31	17.5	87	193	$21
12 MIA	449	75	37	86	6	290	288	302	285	356	608	964	9	68	35	0.32	36	22	42	226	163	29%	73	7%	75%	23	61%	22%	7.72	32.3	95	238	$25
1st Half	276	44	18	49	5	283	283	351	256	357	547	904	10	72	33	0.42	37	24	39	183	137	23%	62	8%	83%	13	54%	23%	6.97	15.4	76	190	$28
2nd Half	173	31	19	37	1	301	299	205	328	353	705	1058	7	62	38	0.21	34	19	47	305	211	37%	93	6%	50%	10	70%	20%	8.90	18.7	129	323	$21
13 Proj	569	91	44	106	6	274	275	270	276	345	578	923	10	66	34	0.32	40	19	41	220	172	28%	85	6%	63%				6.91	31.1	85	214	$29

Stewart,Chris

Stewart,Chris				Health	A	LIMA Plan	F
Age	31	Bats R	Pos CA	PT/Exp	F	Rand Var	-3
Ht	6' 4"	Wt	210	Consist	B	MM	1301

Another journeyman working for an MLB paycheck, and there's nothing wrong with it. But you don't want him trying to earn it on your fantasy team. Put it this way: That MLB career-high OPS only ensured that he didn't hurt you at your deep-league #2 catching spot (per R$). And a repeat is even money at best.

Yr Tm	AB	R	HR	RBI	SB	BA	xBA	vL	vR	OB	Slg	OPS	bb%	ct%	h%	Eye	G	L	F	PX	xPX	hr/f	Spd	SBO	SB%	#Wk	DOM	DIS	RC/G	RAR	BPV	BPX	R$
08 NYY *	275	26	2	20	2	237	173	0		295	315	610	8	83	28	0.50	50	0	50	61	5	0%	91	4%	58%	1	0%	100%	3.07	-8.7	13	25	-$1
09 aaa	232	28	1	15	1	238	234			305	289	594	9	85	28	0.65				38			91	3%	42%				2.91		4	0	-$1
10 SD *	266	21	4	26	1	180	240			242	275	516	7	81	21	0.43	44	20	36	65	-5	0%	112	1%	100%	2	0%	100%	2.08	-18.8	10	22	-$4
11 SF *	257	25	3	16	2	185	215	295	169	250	266	515	8	85	21	0.57	35	16	49	59	64	5%	94	5%	57%	19	32%	37%	2.05	-18.4	20	44	-$4
12 NYY	141	15	1	13	2	241	224	214	259	291	319	611	7	85	28	0.48	34	19	47	59	43	2%	88	6%	100%	26	27%	54%	3.20	-3.8	21	53	$0
1st Half	72	7	0	9	0	264	228	258	268	274	306	580	1	83	32	0.08	33	26	41	36	36	0%	94	0%	0%	12	17%	67%	2.90	-2.7	-23	-58	-$1
2nd Half	69	8	1	4	2	217	226	160	250	308	333	641	12	87	24	1.00	34	13	52	81	50	3%	86	11%	100%	14	36%	43%	3.50	-1.5	57	143	$0
13 Proj	97	10	1	8	1	215	220	214	216	276	304	580	8	85	24	0.54	34	17	48	63	52	3%	89	6%	90%				2.77	-4.3	21	54	$0

JOCK THOMPSON

Stewart,Ian

Age 28 Bats L Pos 3B
Ht 6' 3" Wt 215

Health	F	LIMA Plan	D
PT/Exp	D	Rand Var	+3
Consist	C	MM	4103

Season ended with surgery to correct wrist problem dating back to 2011, so can't determine trade impact. The plusses include bb%, ct% rebounds, but BA remains sub-Mendoza. If GB% spike and and PX/xPX crash are injury-related, his power potential remains intriguing. If healthy, speculate... UP: 20+ HR, .250 BA.

Yr	Tm	AB	R	HR	RBI	SB	BA	xBA	vL	vR	OB	Slg	OPS	bb%	ct%	h%	Eye	G	L	F	PX	xPX	hr/f	Spd	SBO	SB%	#Wk	DOM	DIS	RC/G	RAR	BPV	BPX	R$
08	COL *	523	75	24	78	6	250	254	370	231	318	469	787	9	69	32	0.32	31	25	44	159	163	13%	110	7%	63%	17	35%	53%	5.00	6.1	53	104	$13
09	COL	425	74	25	70	7	228	249	178	244	318	464	782	12	68	27	0.41	40	14	46	164	149	19%	84	10%	64%	27	48%	48%	4.78	2.2	58	118	$11
10	COL	386	54	18	61	5	256	250	231	264	334	443	777	10	72	31	0.41	37	22	41	129	124	16%	98	6%	71%	24	38%	54%	5.05	5.0	35	76	$12
11	COL *	293	28	8	26	3	184	199	91	170	248	321	568	8	67	24	0.26	39	12	49	111	117	0%	78	10%	64%	12	8%	58%	2.45	-20.3	0	0	-$2
12	CHC	179	16	5	17	0	201	231	179	207	285	335	620	11	74	24	0.46	56	16	27	86	90	14%	106	7%	0%	11	36%	55%	2.83	-10.1	6	15	-$2
1st Half		179	16	5	17	0	201	231	179	207	285	335	620	11	74	24	0.46	56	16	27	86	90	14%	106	7%	0%	11	36%	55%	2.83	-10.0	6	15	-$2
2nd Half																																		
13	Proj	**315**	**38**	**13**	**39**	**3**	**230**	**234**	**209**	**236**	**308**	**414**	**722**	**10**	**71**	**28**	**0.38**	**43**	**17**	**40**	**125**	**120**	**15%**	**92**	**7%**	**48%**				**4.10**	**-4.6**	**27**	**67**	**$4**

Stubbs,Drew

Age 28 Bats R Pos CF
Ht 6' 4" Wt 205

Health	A	LIMA Plan	C
PT/Exp	A	Rand Var	+1
Consist	C	MM	3505

Poor ct% always forecast risk, but increased struggles vRHP made 2012 painful. Running game still near-elite, but power upside is fading as GB% rises and bb% stagnates. BA should rebound some, but playing time will continue to dwindle if he can't find a way to steal 1B. DIS frequency makes him lethal to H2Hers.

Yr	Tm	AB	R	HR	RBI	SB	BA	xBA	vL	vR	OB	Slg	OPS	bb%	ct%	h%	Eye	G	L	F	PX	xPX	hr/f	Spd	SBO	SB%	#Wk	DOM	DIS	RC/G	RAR	BPV	BPX	R$
08	a/a	167	20	2	15	5	265	230			319	376	695	7	72	36	0.28				91			101	13%	80%				4.21		7	0	$2
09	CIN *	591	73	11	49	47	244	227	286	261	311	354	665	9	71	33	0.33	42	21	37	83	139	17%	143	38%	78%	8	13%	38%	3.79	-16.1	8	16	$21
10	CIN	514	91	22	77	30	255	237	240	262	327	444	770	10	67	34	0.33	44	16	40	138	139	16%	170	26%	83%	27	56%	30%	5.07	5.8	47	102	$24
11	CIN	604	92	15	44	40	243	216	319	226	315	364	679	9	66	34	0.31	47	20	33	98	115	11%	162	29%	80%	27	30%	56%	3.96	-13.2	2	4	$21
12	CIN	493	75	14	40	30	213	206	283	186	275	333	607	8	66	29	0.25	51	15	34	87	85	13%	140	31%	81%	25	24%	60%	3.05	-25.3	-6	-15	$12
1st Half		221	38	8	19	16	231	235	259	221	306	376	682	10	71	29	0.37	54	17	30	102	94	18%	117	34%	80%	11	36%	45%	3.90	-6.0	19	48	$15
2nd Half		272	37	6	21	14	199	181	300	156	248	298	546	6	63	29	0.18	49	13	37	74	76	10%	149	29%	82%	14	14%	71%	2.44	-20.3	-33	-83	$10
13	Proj	**513**	**78**	**16**	**46**	**31**	**230**	**215**	**279**	**213**	**295**	**370**	**665**	**8**	**67**	**31**	**0.28**	**48**	**17**	**35**	**102**	**105**	**13%**	**143**	**30%**	**81%**				**3.70**	**-17.0**	**8**	**19**	**$18**

Sutton,Drew

Age 30 Bats B Pos LF
Ht 6' 3" Wt 200

Health	A	LIMA Plan	F
PT/Exp	F	Rand Var	+3
Consist	D	MM	3101

1-13-.254 in 122 AB at PIT and TAM. Journeyman with a brief window of regular playing time thanks to injuries and demotions—and who again was unable to turn his brief power and speed flashes into anything lasting. Age, inconsistency and mediocre plate skills work against him. Don't wait up for his next opportunity.

Yr	Tm	AB	R	HR	RBI	SB	BA	xBA	vL	vR	OB	Slg	OPS	bb%	ct%	h%	Eye	G	L	F	PX	xPX	hr/f	Spd	SBO	SB%	#Wk	DOM	DIS	RC/G	RAR	BPV	BPX	R$
08	aa	524	73	15	49	14	264	262			333	425	758	9	77	32	0.45				112			101	16%	63%				4.75		48	0	$14
09	CIN *	238	36	5	26	1	219	235	167	217	305	374	679	11	71	28	0.43	37	19	44	116	198	5%	106	9%	15%	15	40%	33%	3.47	-6.5	27	55	$0
10	2 TM *	398	36	5	37	6	219	218	429	219	300	313	613	10	68	31	0.37	58	15	27	84	148	29%	96	9%	63%	5	40%	60%	3.03	-16.2	-18	-39	$1
11	BOS *	220	29	4	27	0	266	237	214	350	323	409	732	8	73	35	0.31	34	20	46	123	99	0%	87	5%	0%	10	20%	60%	4.39	0.2	25	56	$4
12	2 TM *	280	28	1	25	2	219	232	275	244	279	322	600	8	72	30	0.30	35	28	38	90	82	3%	117	12%	32%	11	27%	55%	2.74	-14.0	0	0	-$1
1st Half		198	19	0	20	1	235	253	250	297	300	321	621	8	76	31	0.39	29	36	36	74	36	0%	117	11%	28%	6	33%	50%	2.99	-7.7	3	8	$1
2nd Half		82	8	1	5	1	180	213	313	200	226	324	550	6	62	28	0.15	42	18	39	135	133	7%	107	16%	42%	5	20%	60%	2.16	-5.6	2	5	-$4
13	Proj	**97**	**11**	**1**	**9**	**1**	**226**	**220**	**212**	**231**	**287**	**340**	**628**	**8**	**70**	**32**	**0.29**	**36**	**22**	**42**	**100**	**111**	**3%**	**98**	**10%**	**39%**				**3.08**	**-4.7**	**0**	**1**	**$1**

Suzuki,Ichiro

Age 39 Bats L Pos RF LF
Ht 5' 11" Wt 170

Health	A	LIMA Plan	C
PT/Exp	A	Rand Var	+2
Consist	C	MM	1535

NYY trade seemed to rejuvenate him, as .322/.340/.454, 5 HR, 14 SB after July 22 suggest. Arrested 2011 decline with LD% spike and 2H surge fueled by SBO, h%. Elite contact is intact, speed is still playable, bb% still trending the wrong way without consequence. A FA who is no longer vintage, but aging remarkably well.

Yr	Tm	AB	R	HR	RBI	SB	BA	xBA	vL	vR	OB	Slg	OPS	bb%	ct%	h%	Eye	G	L	F	PX	xPX	hr/f	Spd	SBO	SB%	#Wk	DOM	DIS	RC/G	RAR	BPV	BPX	R$
08	SEA	686	103	6	42	43	310	283	288	320	358	386	745	7	91	34	0.78	57	20	23	44	50	4%	174	20%	91%	27	30%	22%	5.44	16.3	55	108	$35
09	SEA	639	88	11	46	26	352	288	339	359	383	465	848	5	89	38	0.45	56	18	26	68	48	7%	157	17%	74%	26	38%	31%	6.94	39.2	53	108	$35
10	SEA	680	74	6	43	42	315	271	309	318	357	394	751	6	87	35	0.52	57	17	25	55	44	4%	135	23%	82%	27	26%	37%	5.39	15.3	40	87	$34
11	SEA	677	80	5	47	40	272	275	281	268	311	335	647	5	90	30	0.57	60	19	21	42	29	4%	126	24%	85%	27	30%	30%	3.83	-14.4	41	91	$23
12	2 AL	629	77	9	55	29	283	292	284	283	307	390	697	3	90	30	0.36	51	25	24	63	40	7%	127	23%	81%	28	43%	25%	4.31	-4.6	58	145	$24
1st Half		325	39	4	26	11	274	289	250	288	304	372	676	4	91	29	0.50	47	26	27	58	36	5%	118	16%	85%	14	43%	21%	4.06	-5.5	56	140	$20
2nd Half		304	38	5	29	18	293	296	321	277	311	408	719	3	89	32	0.24	55	23	22	69	44	8%	127	31%	78%	14	43%	29%	4.58	-0.6	57	143	$27
13	Proj	**568**	**69**	**7**	**44**	**26**	**282**	**282**	**286**	**280**	**315**	**374**	**689**	**5**	**90**	**31**	**0.46**	**55**	**21**	**23**	**56**	**39**	**6%**	**128**	**20%**	**82%**				**4.27**	**-12.0**	**50**	**125**	**$22**

Suzuki,Kurt

Age 29 Bats R Pos CA
Ht 5' 11" Wt 195

Health	A	LIMA Plan	D
PT/Exp	B	Rand Var	0
Consist	A	MM	1113

Full-year numbers show BA wallowing in three-year trough, with continued ct% deterioration and GB relapse dragging power down. But 2H shows across-the-board turnaround, both skills and bottom line. Post-June hr/f, xPX hint at power upside. With 2H contact level and 500 AB... UP: 20 HR, .260 BA, and a #2 CA sleeper.

Yr	Tm	AB	R	HR	RBI	SB	BA	xBA	vL	vR	OB	Slg	OPS	bb%	ct%	h%	Eye	G	L	F	PX	xPX	hr/f	Spd	SBO	SB%	#Wk	DOM	DIS	RC/G	RAR	BPV	BPX	R$
08	OAK	530	54	7	42	2	279	248	246	291	334	370	704	8	87	31	0.64	45	19	36	60	71	4%	108	3%	40%	28	29%	39%	4.30	0.1	25	49	$9
09	OAK	570	74	15	88	8	274	290	250	283	308	421	729	5	90	28	0.47	44	19	36	90	100	8%	79	8%	80%	27	63%	22%	4.56	4.4	66	135	$16
10	OAK	495	55	13	71	3	242	259	213	253	290	366	655	6	90	25	0.67	42	17	41	72	87	7%	85	4%	60%	24	42%	25%	3.53	-11.1	52	113	$8
11	OAK	460	54	14	44	2	237	262	233	239	295	385	680	8	86	25	0.59	36	20	44	97	80	8%	77	4%	50%	27	56%	19%	3.75	-7.4	52	116	$6
12	2 TM	408	36	6	43	2	235	223	242	233	271	328	599	5	82	27	0.27	41	17	42	66	102	4%	79	2%	100%	28	14%	54%	2.99	-15.8	6	15	$3
1st Half		226	16	0	16	1	208	200	224	202	238	257	495	4	80	26	0.20	40	17	43	44	88	0%	84	2%	100%	14	0%	71%	1.99	-15.6	-22	-55	-$3
2nd Half		182	20	6	27	1	269	250	270	269	311	418	728	6	85	29	0.39	42	18	41	91	118	10%	77	2%	100%	14	29%	36%	4.56	1.8	36	90	$9
13	Proj	**329**	**34**	**8**	**38**	**2**	**246**	**243**	**239**	**248**	**291**	**366**	**658**	**6**	**85**	**27**	**0.44**	**40**	**18**	**42**	**77**	**95**	**7%**	**76**	**3%**	**72%**				**3.60**	**-6.0**	**30**	**76**	**$6**

Sweeney,Ryan

Age 28 Bats L Pos RF
Ht 6' 4" Wt 225

Health	F	LIMA Plan	D
PT/Exp	D	Rand Var	0
Consist	A	MM	1111

Re-ignited BA skills and LD% early on with aggressive plate approach. Began June hitting .321 before assorted injuries (fractured toe, hamstring) intervened. Fractured knuckle from a door punch ended his season in July. With zero power, offers singles vs. RHP only. And a reckless style that shelves him too often.

Yr	Tm	AB	R	HR	RBI	SB	BA	xBA	vL	vR	OB	Slg	OPS	bb%	ct%	h%	Eye	G	L	F	PX	xPX	hr/f	Spd	SBO	SB%	#Wk	DOM	DIS	RC/G	RAR	BPV	BPX	R$
08	OAK *	418	57	6	49	9	292	255	216	307	354	394	749	9	83	34	0.56	45	21	34	70	85	5%	92	8%	90%	26	27%	42%	5.14	3.2	36	71	$13
09	OAK	484	68	6	53	6	293	284	268	301	347	407	754	8	86	33	0.60	45	24	31	76	84	5%	93	8%	55%	25	32%	40%	4.97	1.5	47	96	$14
10	OAK	303	41	1	36	1	294	274	246	307	346	383	728	7	86	34	0.59	52	20	28	68	36	1%	96	2%	50%	15	47%	20%	4.73	-1.0	37	80	$7
11	OAK	264	34	1	25	1	265	241	159	286	347	341	688	11	82	32	0.69	48	21	31	55	65	1%	116	2%	50%	25	28%	56%	4.07	-6.0	19	42	$3
12	BOS	204	22	0	16	0	260	264	100	277	301	373	673	6	79	33	0.28	47	24	29	94	60	0%	82	0%	0%	15	40%	33%	3.86	-5.8	22	55	$1
1st Half		171	19	0	13	0	292	271	111	314	328	404	731	5	77	38	0.23	49	27	24	98	58	0%	79	0%	0%	10	40%	40%	4.77	-1.1	14	35	$2
2nd Half		33	3	0	3	0	91	221	0	97	167	212	379	8	88	10	0.75	38	10	52	75	66	0%	98	0%	0%	5	40%	20%	0.99	-4.7	60	150	-$7
13	Proj	**226**	**29**	**1**	**23**	**1**	**287**	**243**	**211**	**299**	**341**	**380**	**722**	**8**	**82**	**35**	**0.47**	**45**	**19**	**36**	**72**	**62**	**1%**	**84**	**3%**	**62%**				**4.62**	**-2.5**	**26**	**65**	**$6**

Swisher,Nick

Age 32 Bats B Pos RF 1B
Ht 5' 11" Wt 200

Health	A	LIMA Plan	C+
PT/Exp	A	Rand Var	-1
Consist	A	MM	4025

The S stands for "same old." Same old GLF, same old 1H and 2H surface stats. Pretty much the same or near-same old everything, with mild bb% and ct% dips neutralized by h% uptick. Even his volatile vL, vR history is consistent. Gravity will win out eventually, but there's nothing here that leads us to bet against 2013.

Yr	Tm	AB	R	HR	RBI	SB	BA	xBA	vL	vR	OB	Slg	OPS	bb%	ct%	h%	Eye	G	L	F	PX	xPX	hr/f	Spd	SBO	SB%	#Wk	DOM	DIS	RC/G	RAR	BPV	BPX	R$
08	CHW	497	86	24	69	3	219	247	197	227	330	410	740	14	73	25	0.61	35	21	44	128	123	15%	78	4%	50%	27	33%	48%	4.35	-7.6	43	84	$6
09	NYY	498	84	29	82	0	249	276	244	251	371	498	869	16	75	28	0.77	38	16	46	167	146	17%	67	0%	0%	27	56%	26%	6.28	20.8	78	159	$13
10	NYY	566	91	29	89	1	288	272	294	286	354	511	865	9	75	34	0.42	36	20	45	153	163	15%	81	2%	33%	27	59%	22%	6.40	24.4	62	135	$23
11	NYY	526	81	23	85	2	260	264	327	232	374	449	822	15	76	30	0.76	39	22	39	133	133	14%	63	2%	50%	27	44%	26%	5.73	13.3	55	122	$17
12	NYY	537	75	24	93	2	272	261	270	273	363	473	836	13	74	33	0.55	39	22	39	142	127	15%	71	3%	40%	27	44%	37%	5.92	16.3	46	115	$19
1st Half		252	34	12	46	1	270	278	247	279	336	492	828	9	76	31	0.42	35	24	42	154	149	15%	67	3%	50%	13	54%	23%	5.70	5.1	59	148	$18
2nd Half		285	41	12	47	1	274	246	286	266	386	456	842	15	72	34	0.64	42	21	37	131	107	16%	77	3%	33%	14	36%	50%	6.05	8.6	33	83	$20
13	Proj	**517**	**78**	**24**	**85**	**2**	**268**	**259**	**284**	**260**	**363**	**468**	**831**	**13**	**74**	**32**	**0.59**	**38**	**21**	**40**	**138**	**133**	**15%**	**69**	**3%**	**42%**				**5.84**	**12.5**	**49**	**121**	**$19**

JOCK THOMPSON

Tabata,Jose

Age	24	Bats	R	Pos	RF LF	Health	B	LIMA Plan	D	
Ht	5' 11"	Wt	215			PT/Exp	C	Rand Var	+2	
						Consist	B	MM	1333	

3-16-.243 and 8 SB in 333 at PIT. Elite running game flashed in 2010 still hasn't returned, but injuries weren't the reason in 2012. SB% trend is discouraging; SBO plunge in 2H is telling. Without SBs, GB-fueled plate profile looks mediocre. Age may offer him more opportunities, but needs to show something soon.

Yr	Tm	AB	R	HR	RBI	SB	BA	xBA	vL	vR	OB	Slg	OPS	bb%	ct%	h%	Eye	G	L	F	PX	xPX	hr/f	Spd	SBO	SB%	#Wk	DOM	DIS	RC/G	RAR	BPV	BPX	R$
08	aa	379	51	5	44	16	262	242			315	351	667	7	83	31	0.45				60			97	17%	89%				3.99		29	0	$10
09	a/a	362	44	4	30	9	273	267			319	373	692	6	88	30	0.56				67			96	19%	52%				3.91		45	0	$8
10	PIT *	629	94	6	50	38	290	277	247	315	338	389	727	7	85	33	0.49	59	16	25	69	82	5%	137	28%	74%	18	39%	28%	4.69	-0.7	50	109	$28
11	PIT *	367	58	4	23	16	269	270	297	258	347	371	718	11	82	32	0.67	61	17	22	79	89	7%	101	22%	63%	18	39%	50%	4.32	-4.3	45	100	$11
12	PIT *	491	60	3	28	12	250	267	241	244	303	339	642	7	84	29	0.47	62	18	20	64	52	6%	98	21%	46%	21	29%	43%	3.18	-23.1	29	73	$7
1st Half		247	32	3	11	8	231	270	213	237	280	344	624	6	83	27	0.40	63	16	22	75	51	7%	117	29%	50%	13	23%	38%	2.88	-13.8	40	100	$7
2nd Half		244	28	0	17	4	270	277	333	265	326	333	659	8	85	32	0.55	60	24	16	53	53	0%	77	15%	40%	8	38%	50%	3.49	-8.4	17	43	$8
13	**Proj**	**322**	**44**	**3**	**22**	**16**	**265**	**273**	**278**	**261**	**323**	**360**	**683**	**8**	**84**	**31**	**0.54**	**61**	**19**	**20**	**68**	**70**	**5%**	**95**	**27%**	**67%**				**3.91**	**-10.6**	**39**	**97**	**$9**

Taveras,Oscar

Age	21	Bats	L	Pos	RF	Health	A	LIMA Plan	D+	
Ht	6' 2"	Wt	180			PT/Exp	F	Rand Var	0	
						Consist	F	MM	3331	

Prodigious STL prospect who has been compared skills-wise to Vlad Guerrero. Leapfrogged High-A ball after impressive spring, then led AA Texas League in batting, finished 2nd in Slg while posting near-elite ct% and decent patience. MLEs suggest that he can be productive at the MLB level sooner rather than later.

Yr	Tm	AB	R	HR	RBI	SB	BA	xBA	vL	vR	OB	Slg	OPS	bb%	ct%	h%	Eye	G	L	F	PX	xPX	hr/f	Spd	SBO	SB%	#Wk	DOM	DIS	RC/G	RAR	BPV	BPX	R$
08																																		
09																																		
10																																		
11																																		
12	aa	477	67	17	76	8	287	294			336	484	820	7	87	30	0.59				118			90	8%	88%				5.87		91	0	$19
1st Half		286	36	12	46	5	291	295			338	506	844	7	85	31	0.46				132			102	7%	100%				6.26		87	218	$24
2nd Half		191	32	5	30	3	281	293			334	450	784	7	92	29	0.94				98			111	9%	75%				5.32		92	230	$13
13	**Proj**	**228**	**34**	**8**	**36**	**4**	**286**	**284**			**336**	**481**	**817**	**7**	**89**	**29**	**0.67**	**48**	**13**	**39**	**115**		**10%**	**107**	**8%**	**84%**				**5.79**	**5.1**	**93**	**232**	**$10**

Teixeira,Mark

Age	33	Bats	B	Pos	1B	Health	A	LIMA Plan	B	
Ht	6' 3"	Wt	215			PT/Exp	A	Rand Var	+3	
						Consist	A	MM	4135	

Played early with breathing issues found later to be vocal chord nerve damage. Slowed by nagging injuries (wrist, calf) in 2H that benched him for most of Sept. Eye deterioration, zero speed help keep BA buried, while GB spike gnawed at power. With health, HR will rebound. Not what he was, but better than this.

Yr	Tm	AB	R	HR	RBI	SB	BA	xBA	vL	vR	OB	Slg	OPS	bb%	ct%	h%	Eye	G	L	F	PX	xPX	hr/f	Spd	SBO	SB%	#Wk	DOM	DIS	RC/G	RAR	BPV	BPX	R$
08	2 TM	574	102	33	121	2	308	309	303	311	408	552	961	14	84	32	1.04	43	21	36	149	135	19%	82	1%	100%	27	70%	11%	8.34	47.5	99	194	$30
09	NYY	609	103	39	122	2	292	308	305	287	375	565	940	12	81	30	0.71	36	20	44	165	156	18%	74	1%	100%	27	63%	15%	7.66	40.1	103	210	$28
10	NYY	601	113	33	108	0	256	281	278	247	356	481	837	13	80	27	0.76	36	19	45	147	147	15%	66	1%	0%	27	67%	22%	5.83	9.5	76	165	$21
11	NYY	589	90	39	111	4	248	281	302	223	334	494	828	11	81	24	0.69	35	18	47	151	133	17%	62	3%	80%	27	59%	26%	5.60	5.3	88	196	$23
12	NYY	451	66	24	84	2	251	281	269	239	331	475	805	11	82	26	0.65	41	19	39	137	120	16%	63	3%	67%	24	58%	25%	5.32	0.4	76	190	$14
1st Half		275	41	13	44	1	244	279	232	250	318	451	769	10	84	25	0.68	44	18	38	127	108	14%	70	3%	50%	13	54%	23%	4.78	-4.7	73	183	$16
2nd Half		176	25	11	40	1	261	282	316	220	350	511	861	12	78	28	0.62	36	22	41	154	141	19%	59	2%	100%	11	64%	27%	6.22	4.4	77	193	$12
13	**Proj**	**587**	**92**	**31**	**104**	**3**	**258**	**273**	**290**	**240**	**345**	**477**	**822**	**12**	**81**	**27**	**0.69**	**40**	**19**	**42**	**135**	**134**	**16%**	**62**	**2%**	**76%**				**5.65**	**4.9**	**74**	**184**	**$21**

Tejada,Ruben

Age	23	Bats	R	Pos	SS	Health	B	LIMA Plan	D+	
Ht	5' 11"	Wt	185			PT/Exp	C	Rand Var	-4	
						Consist	B	MM	0215	

Underpowered SS with decent contact and LD swing hit for BA in his first full season. But promising 2011 flashes of patience and a running game are no longer visible. Age says there's plenty of time for improvement, but xBA, Eye and h% regression say his BA will head south. Just empty contact for now.

Yr	Tm	AB	R	HR	RBI	SB	BA	xBA	vL	vR	OB	Slg	OPS	bb%	ct%	h%	Eye	G	L	F	PX	xPX	hr/f	Spd	SBO	SB%	#Wk	DOM	DIS	RC/G	RAR	BPV	BPX	R$
08																																		
09	aa	488	49	4	38	16	265	254			307	348	655	6	86	30	0.45				55			99	15%	83%				3.78		34	0	$10
10	NYM *	434	47	2	27	3	228	239	296	185	283	290	572	7	82	27	0.42	41	23	36	52	71	2%	87	7%	34%	19	37%	47%	2.59	-20.2	1	2	$0
11	NYM *	535	52	2	53	8	252	255	266	289	316	316	632	9	85	29	0.61	45	26	30	47	39	0%	109	7%	72%	18	39%	61%	3.41	-11.0	19	42	$7
12	NYM	464	53	1	25	4	289	264	320	273	328	351	679	5	84	34	0.37	40	30	30	51	55	1%	112	6%	50%	21	14%	52%	4.03	-0.9	6	15	$9
1st Half		136	19	0	11	1	309	257	377	265	352	397	749	6	79	39	0.32	35	29	36	80	82	0%	110	5%	50%	7	29%	43%	5.05	3.9	12	30	$5
2nd Half		328	34	1	14	3	280	268	290	276	318	332	650	5	86	32	0.40	42	30	28	40	45	1%	110	6%	50%	14	7%	57%	3.65	-3.4	4	10	$11
13	**Proj**	**524**	**57**	**1**	**37**	**6**	**270**	**254**	**287**	**262**	**317**	**331**	**648**	**6**	**84**	**32**	**0.43**	**41**	**27**	**31**	**49**	**54**	**1%**	**104**	**7%**	**61%**				**3.61**	**-6.1**	**10**	**26**	**$10**

Thames,Eric

Age	26	Bats	L	Pos	LF RF	Health	A	LIMA Plan	D	
Ht	6' 0"	Wt	205			PT/Exp	B	Rand Var	-1	
						Consist	B	MM	4213	

9-25-.232 in 271 AB at TOR/SEA. Both 1H GB spike and 2H hr/f look anomalous. Power potential remains, but poor contact and impatience aren't helping. Good speed shows no signs of turning into a running game. Still young enough to have productive years as a LH power bat, but only if he recaptures that 2011 ct%.

Yr	Tm	AB	R	HR	RBI	SB	BA	xBA	vL	vR	OB	Slg	OPS	bb%	ct%	h%	Eye	G	L	F	PX	xPX	hr/f	Spd	SBO	SB%	#Wk	DOM	DIS	RC/G	RAR	BPV	BPX	R$
08																																		
09																																		
10	aa	496	69	20	76	7	244	256			296	431	727	7	71	30	0.26				133			109	11%	53%				4.15		37	0	$13
11	TOR *	572	81	16	64	5	268	272	209	279	312	459	771	6	76	33	0.26	40	23	37	142	122	12%	93	7%	59%	18	44%	22%	4.91	0.8	61	136	$16
12	2 AL *	468	47	13	46	2	246	233	212	237	294	404	698	6	70	32	0.23	44	19	37	116	115	13%	117	4%	43%	19	26%	63%	3.95	-12.6	11	28	$6
1st Half		253	27	4	21	1	243	229	286	233	296	359	655	7	73	31	0.29	53	17	30	86	96	9%	110	3%	39%	9	11%	78%	3.52	-11.2	-3	-8	$5
2nd Half		215	20	9	25	1	249	234	125	242	291	459	749	5	67	33	0.17	30	22	47	154	143	17%	114	5%	45%	10	40%	50%	4.43	-3.6	26	65	$8
13	**Proj**	**362**	**43**	**14**	**41**	**3**	**254**	**252**	**207**	**266**	**299**	**457**	**756**	**6**	**72**	**32**	**0.23**	**40**	**20**	**40**	**143**	**123**	**14%**	**104**	**6%**	**56%**				**4.58**	**-0.7**	**41**	**104**	**$9**

Theriot,Ryan

Age	33	Bats	R	Pos	2B	Health	A	LIMA Plan	D	
Ht	5' 11"	Wt	185			PT/Exp	B	Rand Var	0	
						Consist	A	MM	0321	

Still owns near-elite contact and decent speed. But neither are quite as good as they once were, making his issues more glaring. Zero power caps his BA. Even with SB uptick, mediocre SB% will limit his SBO on most teams. Sub-par patience and now poor defense at 2B will likely help cement his new bench role.

Yr	Tm	AB	R	HR	RBI	SB	BA	xBA	vL	vR	OB	Slg	OPS	bb%	ct%	h%	Eye	G	L	F	PX	xPX	hr/f	Spd	SBO	SB%	#Wk	DOM	DIS	RC/G	RAR	BPV	BPX	R$
08	CHC	580	85	1	38	22	307	281	305	308	384	359	743	11	90	34	1.26	57	23	20	34	51	1%	139	15%	63%	27	26%	22%	4.93	9.4	40	78	$22
09	CHC	602	81	7	54	21	284	258	306	279	340	369	709	8	85	33	0.55	50	20	30	52	59	5%	136	16%	68%	27	30%	41%	4.38	0.6	30	61	$19
10	2 NL	586	72	2	29	20	270	253	286	264	317	312	630	7	87	31	0.55	54	20	26	30	35	2%	140	16%	69%	27	19%	44%	3.43	-15.7	18	39	$14
11	STL	442	46	1	47	4	271	267	310	256	316	342	658	6	91	30	0.71	51	21	29	54	39	1%	84	8%	40%	27	26%	30%	3.62	-9.3	37	82	$8
12	SF	352	45	0	28	13	270	267	272	269	316	321	638	6	87	31	0.51	52	25	23	40	56	0%	110	18%	72%	26	27%	31%	3.55	-8.2	22	55	$8
1st Half		188	18	0	16	8	266	269	219	296	299	309	608	5	88	30	0.41	55	25	20	30	40	0%	106	21%	73%	12	33%	50%	3.21	-5.8	17	43	$8
2nd Half		164	27	0	12	5	274	265	346	241	335	335	671	8	85	32	0.60	49	26	26	52	74	0%	111	14%	71%	14	21%	14%	3.94	-1.5	25	63	$9
13	**Proj**	**228**	**29**	**0**	**18**	**7**	**273**	**263**	**295**	**264**	**323**	**331**	**654**	**7**	**88**	**31**	**0.59**	**52**	**23**	**25**	**43**	**51**	**1%**	**102**	**15%**	**66%**				**3.69**	**-3.8**	**26**	**65**	**$6**

Thole,Josh

Age	26	Bats	L	Pos	CA	Health	A	LIMA Plan	D	
Ht	6' 1"	Wt	215			PT/Exp	D	Rand Var	+1	
						Consist	B	MM	1013	

Marginal platoon-BA-only profile of #2 fantasy catcher collapsed. Miniscule bb%, ct%, h% dips, coupled with significant LD-to-GB shift crushed any value he may have offered. Likely to rebound some as the offending numbers retrace. But without any hope for power, why bother? You have better options.

Yr	Tm	AB	R	HR	RBI	SB	BA	xBA	vL	vR	OB	Slg	OPS	bb%	ct%	h%	Eye	G	L	F	PX	xPX	hr/f	Spd	SBO	SB%	#Wk	DOM	DIS	RC/G	RAR	BPV	BPX	R$
08																																		
09	NYM *	437	40	1	46	7	291	323	200	349	347	373	720	8	90	32	0.82	46	34	20	58	85	0%	81	9%	62%	6	50%	17%	4.58	3.5	45	92	$10
10	NYM *	367	32	4	29	1	251	273	143	299	325	359	685	10	85	28	0.74	44	23	33	78	73	5%	105	1%	100%	16	31%	31%	4.00	-3.0	41	89	$2
11	NYM	340	22	3	40	0	268	257	167	280	341	344	685	10	86	30	0.81	49	25	26	58	55	4%	47	2%	0%	27	33%	41%	3.99	-2.8	16	36	$4
12	NYM	321	24	1	21	0	234	228	211	241	293	290	583	8	84	27	0.54	58	19	24	45	58	2%	77	0%	0%	25	16%	60%	2.83	-14.0	-2	-5	-$1
1st Half		163	13	1	10	0	264	216	233	275	322	319	641	8	87	30	0.64	61	15	24	40	64	3%	93	0%	0%	11	18%	55%	3.56	-3.1	1	3	$0
2nd Half		158	11	0	11	0	203	240	182	208	263	259	523	8	82	25	0.46	55	22	23	50	50	0%	66	0%	0%	14	14%	64%	2.18	-10.0	-8	-20	-$3
13	**Proj**	**351**	**26**	**2**	**30**	**1**	**247**	**255**	**184**	**261**	**313**	**318**	**631**	**9**	**85**	**29**	**0.65**	**52**	**23**	**25**	**53**	**61**	**2%**	**69**	**2%**	**43%**				**3.35**	**-9.0**	**12**	**31**	**$3**

JOCK THOMPSON

Thome,Jim

Age 42	Bats L	Pos DH	Health	F	LIMA Plan	F
Ht 6' 4"	Wt 250		PT/Exp	D	Rand Var	-4
			Consist	F	MM	4101

PRO: Can still do some damage to RHPs. CON: DH-only, GB% spiked, ct% continues to deteriorate, zero durability. May have another opportunity, but both his role and level of production will likely be limited. Can't rule out one more 2011 repeat, but if this is the end, he leaves with 612 HR.

Yr	Tm	AB	R	HR	RBI	SB	BA	xBA	vL	vR	OB	Slg	OPS	bb%	ct%	h%	Eye	G	L	F	PX	xPX	hr/f	Spd	SBO	SB%	#Wk	DOM	DIS	RC/G	RAR	BPV	BPX	R$
08	CHW	503	93	34	90	1	245	271	233	249	360	503	863	15	71	28	0.62	40	18	42	178	160	23%	43	1%	100%	27	63%	11%	6.13	18.5	71	139	$14
09	2 TM	362	55	23	77	0	249	252	209	262	369	481	850	16	66	31	0.56	44	20	36	165	149	26%	48	0%	0%	27	33%	56%	6.02	12.0	36	73	$10
10	MIN	276	48	25	59	0	283	316	241	302	411	627	1038	18	70	31	0.73	41	21	38	239	195	34%	63	0%	0%	27	59%	37%	9.15	33.1	124	270	$14
11	2 AL	277	32	15	50	0	256	244	253	257	362	477	839	14	67	33	0.50	45	18	37	174	179	22%	45	0%	0%	22	45%	32%	5.92	8.3	40	89	$8
12	2 TM	163	17	8	25	0	252	230	179	267	341	442	782	12	63	35	0.36	55	24	22	149	128	36%	56	0%	0%	15	33%	60%	5.12	1.1	-1	-3	$2
1st Half		62	9	5	15	0	242	260	200	262	329	516	845	11	66	28	0.38	56	20	24	189	117	50%	56	0%	0%	8	38%	63%	5.70	1.5	46	115	$3
2nd Half		101	8	3	10	0	257	214	125	269	348	396	744	12	60	40	0.35	54	26	20	121	136	25%	63	0%	0%	7	29%	57%	4.73	-0.5	-33	-83	$2
13	Proj	181	23	9	32	0	257	240	219	268	358	456	814	14	65	34	0.46	49	21	30	151	154	25%	54	0%	100%				5.60	3.8	18	46	$4

Torrealba,Yorvit

Age 34	Bats R	Pos CA	Health	A	LIMA Plan	F
Ht 5' 11"	Wt 200		PT/Exp	D	Rand Var	+2
			Consist	B	MM	1011

Drop in line drives, h% led to BA collapse and his release from Rangers. Has little power to speak of, as he's never reached double digit home runs, and hasn't homered off a LH in two years. xBA confirms BA collapse, and that removes him from the ranks of serviceable #2 catchers.

Yr	Tm	AB	R	HR	RBI	SB	BA	xBA	vL	vR	OB	Slg	OPS	bb%	ct%	h%	Eye	G	L	F	PX	xPX	hr/f	Spd	SBO	SB%	#Wk	DOM	DIS	RC/G	RAR	BPV	BPX	R$
08	COL	236	19	6	31	0	246	255	279	234	282	394	676	5	81	28	0.27	50	17	33	104	96	9%	71	9%	0%	22	41%	41%	3.47	-5.8	27	53	$1
09	COL	213	27	2	31	1	291	259	220	318	355	380	735	9	80	36	0.50	50	23	28	65	92	4%	103	3%	50%	22	27%	50%	4.79	3.0	12	24	$4
10	SD	325	31	7	37	7	271	258	227	287	338	378	716	9	79	32	0.49	55	20	25	77	75	11%	74	12%	58%	27	19%	44%	4.33	0.4	15	33	$8
11	TEX	396	40	7	37	0	273	281	256	280	308	399	707	5	84	31	0.31	48	25	27	92	81	8%	75	2%	0%	27	44%	37%	4.21	-0.8	30	67	$7
12	3 TM	194	19	4	14	1	227	231	203	243	289	330	619	8	79	27	0.43	51	18	31	70	67	8%	77	4%	50%	23	30%	52%	3.10	-6.9	3	8	-$1
1st Half		125	14	2	11	1	224	243	211	235	292	328	620	9	79	27	0.46	48	21	32	77	85	6%	75	3%	100%	13	31%	46%	3.19	-3.9	12	30	$0
2nd Half		69	5	2	3	0	232	203	182	255	284	333	617	7	80	26	0.36	58	13	29	59	34	13%	83	6%	0%	10	30%	60%	2.94	-2.7	-12	-30	-$2
13	Proj	162	15	3	14	1	250	244	218	266	304	361	665	7	81	29	0.40	52	19	29	75	68	9%	76	5%	36%				3.61	-2.9	10	26	$2

Torres,Andres

Age 35	Bats B	Pos CF	Health	D	LIMA Plan	D
Ht 5' 10"	Wt 195		PT/Exp	C	Rand Var	+3
			Consist	C	MM	1403

PRO: Above-average speed, career-best bb%, got on base vs LH at .382 clip. CON: SBO collapsed in 2H, .214 BA vs RH past 2 years, power he displayed in 2009-10 not coming back. As a BA drag with little power, needs to run to have value, but age and SB% trend not on his side.

Yr	Tm	AB	R	HR	RBI	SB	BA	xBA	vL	vR	OB	Slg	OPS	bb%	ct%	h%	Eye	G	L	F	PX	xPX	hr/f	Spd	SBO	SB%	#Wk	DOM	DIS	RC/G	RAR	BPV	BPX	R$
08	aaa	409	56	7	31	18	230	222			288	365	653	8	66	33	0.24				107			124	25%	77%				3.50		13	0	$6
09	SF *	195	34	7	24	7	261	228	338	210	319	486	805	8	65	37	0.24	34	16	49	152	165	13%	148	17%	87%	20	35%	40%	5.43	4.2	44	90	$6
10	SF	507	84	16	63	26	268	280	226	283	341	479	820	10	75	33	0.44	39	22	39	157	117	11%	99	26%	79%	26	50%	27%	5.70	15.0	91	198	$22
11	SF *	403	56	6	25	20	217	216	170	229	296	336	632	10	72	29	0.40	40	16	44	100	83	4%	105	26%	77%	21	38%	48%	3.27	-17.8	27	60	$6
12	NYM	374	47	3	35	13	230	247	286	194	324	337	661	12	76	30	0.58	48	25	28	74	65	4%	123	16%	72%	24	29%	46%	3.62	-12.2	27	68	$5
1st Half		158	25	1	20	9	209	244	298	158	332	297	629	16	78	26	0.83	54	20	26	63	58	3%	104	23%	75%	10	40%	30%	3.27	-7.6	34	85	$6
2nd Half		216	22	2	15	4	245	249	278	222	318	366	684	10	75	32	0.42	43	28	29	83	71	4%	125	10%	67%	14	21%	57%	3.89	-5.8	17	43	$5
13	Proj	343	47	2	31	12	234	226	266	219	318	336	654	11	74	31	0.47	43	21	36	78	88	2%	111	17%	73%				3.56	-12.7	20	51	$7

Trout,Mike

Age 21	Bats R	Pos CF LF	Health	A	LIMA Plan	D+
Ht 6' 1"	Wt 210		PT/Exp	D	Rand Var	-4
			Consist	F	MM	4525

30-83-.326 with 49 SB in 559 AB with LAA. Exploded onto the scene following late-April callup, with across the board production that topped even the loftiest expectations. Power/speed combo at his age is unheard of. BA will regress as h% normalizes, though, so paying full price for a repeat is likely a losing proposition.

Yr	Tm	AB	R	HR	RBI	SB	BA	xBA	vL	vR	OB	Slg	OPS	bb%	ct%	h%	Eye	G	L	F	PX	xPX	hr/f	Spd	SBO	SB%	#Wk	DOM	DIS	RC/G	RAR	BPV	BPX	R$
08																																		
09																																		
10																																		
11	LAA *	476	93	15	50	33	282	253	245	203	349	460	808	9	77	34	0.44	39	21	40	119	105	14%	159	32%	76%	11	55%	36%	5.63	10.7	72	160	$26
12	LAA *	636	144	31	92	53	328	276	267	346	398	554	953	11	75	40	0.47	44	23	33	143	113	22%	152	28%	90%	24	58%	13%	8.75	66.1	90	225	$54
1st Half		309	63	9	41	26	338	269	323	341	394	516	910	9	78	41	0.41	44	24	32	116	94	14%	140	30%	86%	10	50%	20%	8.12	27.3	71	178	$48
2nd Half		327	81	22	51	27	318	284	222	350	402	590	992	12	73	38	0.52	45	21	34	171	127	27%	152	26%	93%	14	64%	7%	9.35	40.3	107	268	$59
13	Proj	597	104	25	78	41	286	265	291	285	359	494	853	10	76	34	0.46	42	22	36	132	110	15%	147	28%	86%				6.53	29.7	77	193	$37

Trumbo,Mark

Age 27	Bats R	Pos LF RF DH	Health	A	LIMA Plan	C+
Ht 6' 4"	Wt 225		PT/Exp	B	Rand Var	-4
			Consist	B	MM	4115

Couldn't handle third base, but forced way into lineup with early season power display. 2H PX, ct% crashes may or may not have had anything to do with back spasms he suffered in July. Power is now well-established, but so is poor OBP. Pay for the power, but forget the 1H BA ever happened.

Yr	Tm	AB	R	HR	RBI	SB	BA	xBA	vL	vR	OB	Slg	OPS	bb%	ct%	h%	Eye	G	L	F	PX	xPX	hr/f	Spd	SBO	SB%	#Wk	DOM	DIS	RC/G	RAR	BPV	BPX	R$
08	aa	123	11	5	21	1	254	259			287	434	721	4	75	30	0.18				123			89	12%	28%				3.94		27	0	$1
09	aa	533	48	13	78	5	272	266			314	419	733	6	80	32	0.30				100			80	7%	62%				4.55		32	0	$12
10	LAA *	547	71	24	84	2	237	275	0	100	287	421	709	7	72	29	0.25	43	29	29	130	31	0%	99	6%	30%	5	0%	100%	3.91	-10.9	25	54	$11
11	LAA	539	65	29	87	9	254	276	264	249	287	477	764	4	78	28	0.21	46	16	38	150	135	18%	76	13%	69%	27	56%	22%	4.61	0.6	65	144	$19
12	LAA	544	66	32	95	4	268	248	266	269	314	491	805	6	72	32	0.24	45	16	39	144	132	21%	90	7%	44%	27	52%	44%	5.20	9.9	36	90	$21
1st Half		259	37	19	53	4	313	298	310	314	360	614	974	7	76	35	0.31	46	16	38	187	147	25%	95	10%	67%	13	77%	15%	8.05	24.0	97	243	$30
2nd Half		285	29	13	42	0	228	198	216	232	272	379	650	6	68	29	0.18	43	16	41	100	117	16%	75	5%	0%	14	29%	71%	3.23	-12.4	-30	-75	$12
13	Proj	528	62	28	87	5	256	249	259	255	299	464	764	6	74	30	0.23	45	16	39	136	132	18%	83	8%	49%				4.62	-0.4	36	89	$18

Tulowitzki,Troy

Age 28	Bats R	Pos SS	Health	F	LIMA Plan	A
Ht 6' 3"	Wt 215		PT/Exp	C	Rand Var	+2
			Consist	C	MM	4245

8-27-.287 in 181 AB at COL. Groin injury cost him final four months of season. Prior to that, plate discipline as strong as ever, but power was slow-starting. Still among the elite SS, and shortened season could make him undervalued. But with just two 500+ AB seasons, Health grade shows why he's a risky early-round pick.

Yr	Tm	AB	R	HR	RBI	SB	BA	xBA	vL	vR	OB	Slg	OPS	bb%	ct%	h%	Eye	G	L	F	PX	xPX	hr/f	Spd	SBO	SB%	#Wk	DOM	DIS	RC/G	RAR	BPV	BPX	R$
08	COL *	405	53	9	49	2	266	271	330	242	333	407	740	9	86	29	0.70	42	20	37	91	104	7%	99	7%	22%	19	37%	26%	4.45	4.0	52	102	$7
09	COL	543	101	32	92	20	297	293	269	307	380	552	932	12	79	32	0.65	42	18	40	149	134	18%	143	18%	65%	26	62%	23%	7.31	49.2	101	206	$30
10	COL	470	89	27	95	11	315	309	342	302	378	568	946	9	83	33	0.62	45	15	40	158	142	17%	107	10%	85%	21	52%	5%	8.05	50.0	114	248	$30
11	COL	537	81	30	105	9	302	307	349	284	371	544	915	10	85	31	0.75	42	20	39	150	126	17%	83	8%	75%	26	73%	19%	7.33	47.7	106	236	$30
12	COL *	208	35	10	31	2	286	287	173	333	347	499	846	9	88	29	0.76	46	17	37	117	98	13%	117	7%	50%	9	56%	11%	6.01	11.2	88	220	$7
1st Half		181	33	8	27	2	287	287	173	333	355	486	841	10	90	29	1.00	46	17	37	107	98	13%	123	8%	50%	9	56%	11%	5.98	10.1	91	228	$9
2nd Half		25	1	1	3	0	230	249			250	474	724	2	72	26	0.09				170			84	0%	0%				3.92		28	70	-$9
13	Proj	504	87	28	87	9	296	296	281	303	367	539	906	10	85	30	0.75	44	17	39	139	121	17%	106	10%	65%				7.02	42.4	103	257	$28

Turner,Justin

Age 28	Bats R	Pos 2B	Health	A	LIMA Plan	D
Ht 6' 0"	Wt 210		PT/Exp	D	Rand Var	0
			Consist	A	MM	1131

Versatility may help him keep part-time role, and ct% gives him solid BA floor. Unfortunately, doesn't draw walks and lacks above-average power or speed. A long shot to find regular at-bats, or to be of any fanalytic use if he does.

Yr	Tm	AB	R	HR	RBI	SB	BA	xBA	vL	vR	OB	Slg	OPS	bb%	ct%	h%	Eye	G	L	F	PX	xPX	hr/f	Spd	SBO	SB%	#Wk	DOM	DIS	RC/G	RAR	BPV	BPX	R$
08	aa	280	34	7	31	1	249	241			311	370	681	8	78	30	0.40				82			90	4%	57%				3.87		12	0	$3
09	BAL *	405	48	2	40	8	266	327	429	0	321	342	663	7	89	29	0.74	67	27	7	56	28	0%	80	11%	63%	5	40%	40%	3.74	-7.1	39	80	$7
10	2 TM *	413	49	8	30	5	243	269	0	91	286	366	652	6	84	27	0.38	57	14	29	86	84	0%	85	9%	57%	4	50%	50%	3.45	-11.1	41	89	$5
11	NYM *	475	53	4	52	7	257	276	234	270	315	355	671	8	86	29	0.61	49	23	28	75	60	4%	81	7%	78%	24	38%	42%	3.86	-6.7	45	100	$8
12	NYM	171	20	2	19	1	269	283	241	295	306	392	697	5	86	30	0.38	47	24	29	86	68	5%	86	5%	50%	25	36%	28%	4.10	-1.1	45	113	$2
1st Half		85	11	0	12	1	271	273	213	342	311	341	652	6	85	32	0.38	44	29	27	60	61	0%	70	5%	100%	11	36%	36%	3.78	-1.2	18	45	$2
2nd Half		86	9	2	7	0	267	295	278	260	300	442	742	4	87	29	0.36	49	20	31	111	75	9%	100	6%	0%	14	36%	21%	4.37	0.3	70	175	$2
13	Proj	230	26	3	23	2	261	276	237	278	305	374	679	6	86	30	0.44	48	23	29	79	66	5%	86	7%	57%				3.87	-2.6	40	101	$5

MATT GELFAND

Uggla,Dan

Age	33	Bats	R	Pos	2B	Health	A	LIMA Plan	C+
Ht	5' 11"	Wt	205			PT/Exp	A	Rand Var	0
						Consist	C	MM	4105

When people talk about "old player skills," they're usually thinking about the big, hulking 1B/DH-types -- the Mo Vaughns and Richie Sexsons. But big power, low BA, good bb% - and rapid decline - is not necessarily limited to those types. Looks like a classic case study here. If so, don't expect much of a rebound.

Yr	Tm	AB	R	HR	RBI	SB	BA	xBA	vL	vR	OB	Slg	OPS	bb%	ct%	h%	Eye	G	L	F	PX	xPX	hr/f	Spd	SBO	SB%	#Wk	DOM	DIS	RC/G	RAR	BPV	BPX	R$
08	FLA	531	97	32	92	5	260	260	191	283	354	514	868	13	68	32	0.45	36	16	48	190	150	18%	98	7%	50%	26	50%	35%	6.10	27.3	71	139	$18
09	FLA	564	84	31	90	2	243	255	208	253	349	459	808	14	73	28	0.61	37	17	46	142	135	16%	79	2%	67%	27	41%	37%	5.39	17.4	52	106	$13
10	FLA	589	100	33	105	4	287	269	306	281	370	508	878	12	75	33	0.52	40	18	43	152	146	17%	84	3%	80%	27	48%	26%	6.73	39.3	63	137	$27
11	ATL	600	88	36	82	1	233	252	201	245	305	453	758	9	74	25	0.40	41	15	43	147	127	19%	94	3%	25%	27	48%	26%	4.51	2.9	48	107	$16
12	ATL	523	86	19	78	4	220	222	220	220	339	384	723	15	68	29	0.56	34	20	46	127	119	11%	73	4%	57%	27	33%	44%	4.21	-2.2	22	55	$10
1st Half		268	51	11	43	0	235	223	267	220	357	414	772	16	66	31	0.57	36	19	46	139	126	13%	76	2%	0%	13	31%	46%	4.80	4.4	23	58	$13
2nd Half		255	35	8	35	4	204	219	171	220	319	353	672	14	69	26	0.55	31	21	47	114	111	10%	70	7%	80%	14	36%	43%	3.64	-5.0	18	45	$6
13	**Proj**	**519**	**82**	**21**	**78**	**4**	**235**	**228**	**218**	**241**	**333**	**407**	**740**	**13**	**71**	**29**	**0.51**	**36**	**18**	**45**	**124**	**126**	**13%**	**77**	**4%**	**59%**				**4.47**	**3.3**	**26**	**66**	**$11**

Upton,B.J.

Age	28	Bats	R	Pos	CF	Health	A	LIMA Plan	C+
Ht	6' 3"	Wt	185			PT/Exp	A	Rand Var	0
						Consist	A	MM	4515

Spent first two weeks of season on DL with back injury, power remained MIA for entire 1H. Found his stroke in 2H, peaking with a 12 HR, 248 PX Sept. Consistent ct%, xBA indicate you can take .240ish BA to the bank. Speed is a given, but 2H power and looming escape from TAM has us thinking... UP: 40/40.

Yr	Tm	AB	R	HR	RBI	SB	BA	xBA	vL	vR	OB	Slg	OPS	bb%	ct%	h%	Eye	G	L	F	PX	xPX	hr/f	Spd	SBO	SB%	#Wk	DOM	DIS	RC/G	RAR	BPV	BPX	R$
08	TAM	531	85	9	67	44	273	253	271	275	385	401	786	15	75	35	0.72	51	19	31	100	93	7%	116	31%	73%	27	33%	33%	5.41	8.7	46	90	$27
09	TAM	560	79	11	55	42	241	233	190	262	311	373	684	9	73	31	0.38	44	15	40	99	113	7%	138	39%	75%	26	31%	50%	3.89	-16.6	31	63	$20
10	TAM	536	89	18	62	42	237	247	278	218	322	424	745	11	69	31	0.41	40	17	44	149	119	11%	129	38%	82%	27	41%	33%	4.68	-2.8	66	143	$23
11	TAM	560	82	23	81	36	243	244	238	245	328	429	757	11	71	30	0.44	41	18	41	136	134	14%	127	31%	75%	27	33%	30%	4.70	-2.7	56	124	$24
12	TAM	573	79	28	78	31	246	246	238	249	301	454	755	7	71	30	0.27	40	19	41	145	105	17%	119	29%	84%	25	40%	36%	4.70	-2.7	51	128	$24
1st Half		243	27	5	25	14	243	221	179	273	303	362	665	8	71	32	0.30	43	20	37	91	66	8%	125	27%	82%	11	18%	55%	3.81	-7.1	7	18	$11
2nd Half		330	52	23	53	17	248	265	301	233	299	521	821	7	70	28	0.24	38	17	44	184	134	22%	111	31%	85%	14	57%	21%	5.36	5.8	82	205	$34
13	**Proj**	**590**	**86**	**30**	**89**	**32**	**245**	**252**	**246**	**245**	**316**	**464**	**780**	**9**	**71**	**30**	**0.36**	**41**	**18**	**41**	**153**	**115**	**18%**	**116**	**28%**	**81%**				**5.01**	**4.1**	**63**	**157**	**$27**

Upton,Justin

Age	25	Bats	R	Pos	RF	Health	A	LIMA Plan	B
Ht	6' 2"	Wt	205			PT/Exp	A	Rand Var	-1
						Consist	C	MM	4425

Maintained ct% gains but suffered major power outage. He hinted that April thumb injury may have been a factor. Finished strong with 6 HR, 137 PX in Sept. That doesn't erase April-August, but given age and previous track record, could bounce back in a big way. Buy at a discount if you can... UP: 2011, or more.

Yr	Tm	AB	R	HR	RBI	SB	BA	xBA	vL	vR	OB	Slg	OPS	bb%	ct%	h%	Eye	G	L	F	PX	xPX	hr/f	Spd	SBO	SB%	#Wk	DOM	DIS	RC/G	RAR	BPV	BPX	R$
08	ARI *	417	61	17	49	2	250	239	253	249	342	459	801	12	64	35	0.40	37	21	42	159	130	15%	150	5%	37%	21	43%	38%	5.18	0.3	39	76	$7
09	ARI	526	84	26	86	20	300	282	377	277	367	532	899	9	74	36	0.40	45	19	36	152	122	19%	134	17%	80%	25	60%	28%	7.12	28.8	78	159	$28
10	ARI	495	73	17	69	18	273	243	276	272	356	442	798	11	69	36	0.42	41	19	39	131	134	12%	119	17%	69%	25	36%	40%	5.42	3.9	38	83	$20
11	ARI	592	105	31	88	21	289	280	268	295	353	529	882	9	79	32	0.47	37	18	45	160	142	15%	118	19%	70%	27	63%	15%	6.53	23.3	99	220	$33
12	ARI	554	107	17	67	18	280	250	275	282	353	430	783	10	78	33	0.52	44	21	36	96	107	11%	120	15%	69%	27	37%	33%	5.29	2.2	47	118	$24
1st Half		256	48	7	34	10	277	235	286	274	358	398	756	11	74	35	0.48	43	23	34	85	106	11%	95	20%	59%	13	31%	38%	4.76	-1.9	13	33	$23
2nd Half		298	59	10	33	8	282	264	265	288	350	456	806	9	82	32	0.57	44	19	37	105	107	11%	132	10%	89%	14	43%	29%	5.77	6.5	72	180	$26
13	**Proj**	**567**	**101**	**26**	**75**	**18**	**284**	**259**	**280**	**286**	**356**	**491**	**847**	**10**	**76**	**33**	**0.47**	**40**	**19**	**41**	**134**	**122**	**15%**	**118**	**16%**	**70%**				**6.11**	**17.9**	**69**	**171**	**$29**

Uribe,Juan

Age	34	Bats	R	Pos	3B	Health	D	LIMA Plan	F
Ht	6' 0"	Wt	240			PT/Exp	D	Rand Var	+4
						Consist	C	MM	2001

Followed up awful 2011 campaign with nearly identical BPIs. Miserable .601 OPS vs RH past two years, and that's the good news (.439 vs LH). Chances of finding 2009-10 power stroke or consistent at-bats appear slim at this point.

Yr	Tm	AB	R	HR	RBI	SB	BA	xBA	vL	vR	OB	Slg	OPS	bb%	ct%	h%	Eye	G	L	F	PX	xPX	hr/f	Spd	SBO	SB%	#Wk	DOM	DIS	RC/G	RAR	BPV	BPX	R$
08	CHW	324	38	7	40	1	247	249	254	245	295	386	681	6	80	29	0.34	34	20	45	98	89	6%	77	6%	25%	24	29%	46%	3.71	-8.6	31	61	$3
09	SF	398	50	16	55	3	289	282	255	299	331	495	826	6	79	33	0.30	39	21	40	131	117	13%	93	4%	75%	27	41%	37%	5.86	13.9	62	127	$13
10	SF	521	64	24	85	1	248	264	231	252	307	440	747	8	82	26	0.49	40	15	44	119	115	12%	68	2%	33%	27	56%	33%	4.51	-1.4	57	124	$13
11	LA	270	21	4	28	2	204	216	159	219	251	293	543	6	78	25	0.28	42	17	41	69	76	5%	37	4%	100%	15	13%	60%	2.38	-18.7	-5	-11	-$2
12	LA	162	15	2	17	0	191	218	143	222	251	284	535	7	77	24	0.35	48	17	35	72	81	5%	44	3%	0%	20	15%	70%	2.18	-12.5	-5	-13	-$3
1st Half		122	9	1	12	0	205	218	146	243	236	287	523	4	77	26	0.18	46	18	35	67	80	3%	48	5%	0%	10	10%	70%	2.08	-9.6	-18	-45	-$3
2nd Half		40	6	1	5	0	150	221	133	160	292	275	567	17	78	17	0.89	53	13	34	87	82	9%	48	0%	0%	10	20%	70%	2.41	-2.9	26	65	-$3
13	**Proj**	**99**	**10**	**2**	**12**	**0**	**232**	**232**	**186**	**253**	**277**	**359**	**636**	**6**	**79**	**27**	**0.30**	**45**	**16**	**39**	**88**	**87**	**7%**	**51**	**4%**	**42%**				**3.25**	**-4.0**	**15**	**37**	**$1**

Utley,Chase

Age	34	Bats	L	Pos	2B	Health	F	LIMA Plan	B+
Ht	6' 1"	Wt	200			PT/Exp	C	Rand Var	+2
						Consist	B	MM	3335

Missed half the season due to knee issues, returned with skills nearly identical to 2010-11. Struggles vs LH last two years not as bad as it seems, as 22% h% a major factor. League average power and speed still has value, particularly given 95% SB% past four years. But AB trend, health suggest having a solid backup.

Yr	Tm	AB	R	HR	RBI	SB	BA	xBA	vL	vR	OB	Slg	OPS	bb%	ct%	h%	Eye	G	L	F	PX	xPX	hr/f	Spd	SBO	SB%	#Wk	DOM	DIS	RC/G	RAR	BPV	BPX	R$
08	PHI	607	113	33	104	14	292	299	277	301	359	535	895	10	83	31	0.62	33	24	42	148	151	15%	88	10%	88%	26	65%	15%	6.99	44.8	106	208	$30
09	PHI	571	112	31	93	23	282	273	288	279	378	508	886	13	81	30	0.80	34	18	48	134	152	14%	112	12%	100%	26	65%	15%	7.11	44.4	98	200	$30
10	PHI	425	75	16	65	13	275	279	294	266	369	445	814	13	85	29	1.00	41	20	39	104	127	11%	99	11%	87%	21	48%	14%	5.89	18.7	83	180	$18
11	PHI	398	54	11	44	14	259	258	187	285	325	425	750	9	88	27	0.83	41	13	46	100	132	7%	114	13%	100%	19	58%	16%	4.96	7.1	93	207	$12
12	PHI	301	48	11	45	11	256	278	215	283	349	429	777	13	86	27	1.00	42	21	36	102	110	12%	85	13%	92%	15	53%	13%	5.29	8.3	85	213	$11
1st Half		13	2	1	1	0	385	188	500	333	429	615	1044	7	69	50	0.25	67	0	33	140	238	33%	96	0%	0%	1	0%	0%	10.93	2.1	10	25	-$17
2nd Half		288	46	10	44	11	250	280	205	281	345	420	766	13	86	26	1.08	42	22	36	100	105	11%	82	14%	92%	14	57%	14%	5.11	7.3	87	218	$12
13	**Proj**	**432**	**72**	**17**	**64**	**15**	**267**	**271**	**243**	**280**	**354**	**451**	**806**	**12**	**85**	**28**	**0.91**	**39**	**19**	**41**	**109**	**128**	**11%**	**93**	**12%**	**93%**				**5.74**	**18.4**	**88**	**221**	**$19**

Valbuena,Luis

Age	27	Bats	L	Pos	3B	Health	A	LIMA Plan	F
Ht	5' 10"	Wt	195			PT/Exp	C	Rand Var	+1
						Consist	A	MM	2001

4-28-.219 in 265 AB at CHC. Strikes out a lot for a player with merely average power. Has shown flashes of something better (see 1H PX), but nothing in his skill set suggests he merits a full-time role. And with a .618 career OPS vs RH, he's not an ideal candidate for the larger half of a platoon anyway.

Yr	Tm	AB	R	HR	RBI	SB	BA	xBA	vL	vR	OB	Slg	OPS	bb%	ct%	h%	Eye	G	L	F	PX	xPX	hr/f	Spd	SBO	SB%	#Wk	DOM	DIS	RC/G	RAR	BPV	BPX	R$
08	SEA *	501	70	8	47	14	257	225	429	214	325	357	682	9	81	30	0.54	39	17	44	69	109	0%	118	16%	60%	5	20%	60%	3.84	-7.5	26	51	$11
09	CLE *	446	64	12	41	4	255	269	205	255	315	420	735	8	78	30	0.40	41	22	37	111	92	10%	104	10%	40%	23	48%	30%	4.30	-0.5	45	92	$8
10	CLE *	371	39	6	39	2	209	234	318	169	290	312	602	10	77	26	0.49	47	18	35	79	67	3%	62	5%	55%	23	17%	65%	2.89	-16.8	9	20	$0
11	CLE *	463	51	13	56	5	244	205	250	194	296	368	664	7	73	31	0.28	42	12	45	93	100	7%	88	8%	60%	9	22%	67%	3.61	-10.1	0	0	$8
12	CHC *	476	52	10	49	1	229	243	196	225	309	363	672	10	76	28	0.48	43	21	35	102	82	5%	69	3%	17%	17	24%	41%	3.61	-10.6	16	40	$3
1st Half		261	30	9	31	1	237	237	190	241	298	409	706	8	74	29	0.33	47	14	40	125	105	18%	67	3%	36%	3	67%	0%	4.00	-2.1	28	70	$8
2nd Half		215	22	1	18	0	219	238	200	222	323	307	630	13	78	28	0.69	43	23	34	77	76	2%	74	3%	0%	14	14%	50%	3.11	-7.6	9	23	-$2
13	**Proj**	**158**	**18**	**3**	**16**	**1**	**231**	**232**	**305**	**217**	**305**	**346**	**652**	**10**	**76**	**29**	**0.44**	**45**	**19**	**36**	**87**	**81**	**6%**	**71**	**5%**	**43%**				**3.42**	**-5.6**	**10**	**25**	**$2**

Valdespin,Jordany

Age	25	Bats	L	Pos	LF	Health	A	LIMA Plan	D+
Ht	6' 0"	Wt	190			PT/Exp	D	Rand Var	0
						Consist	B	MM	2303

8-26-.241 with 10 SB in 191 AB at NYM. Was decent source of power and speed in part-time role. But low bb% provides little hope for even a .300 OBP, and SB success rate in minors was less than stellar. Youth provides hope for more growth, but short-term prospects not so promising.

Yr	Tm	AB	R	HR	RBI	SB	BA	xBA	vL	vR	OB	Slg	OPS	bb%	ct%	h%	Eye	G	L	F	PX	xPX	hr/f	Spd	SBO	SB%	#Wk	DOM	DIS	RC/G	RAR	BPV	BPX	R$
08																																		
09																																		
10	aa	112	6	0	6	3	188	223			198	247	445	1	77	25	0.05				57			92	32%	55%				1.42		-23	0	-$3
11	a/a	511	52	13	45	28	229	249			256	358	614	3	79	27	0.17				90			89	51%	57%				2.63		30	0	$12
12	NYM *	342	45	12	43	18	232	244	226	244	269	376	645	5	80	26	0.25	49	15	35	87	64	17%	93	41%	58%	21	33%	57%	3.00	-18.6	34	85	$10
1st Half		185	26	5	24	6	214	210	235	217	239	348	587	3	83	23	0.19	43	6	51	80	68	8%	107	44%	42%	8	50%	38%	2.21	-14.7	42	105	$8
2nd Half		157	19	7	19	12	254	254	214	254	304	409	713	7	76	30	0.29	53	20	27	96	62	25%	81	40%	72%	13	23%	69%	4.11	-2.6	22	55	$13
13	**Proj**	**336**	**36**	**10**	**34**	**18**	**243**	**236**	**278**	**237**	**274**	**379**	**652**	**4**	**78**	**28**	**0.20**	**49**	**15**	**37**	**88**	**64**	**10%**	**85**	**40%**	**61%**				**3.18**	**-15.3**	**24**	**61**	**$11**

BRIAN RUDD

Valdez,Wilson

Age 35	Bats R	Pos SS 2B	Health	A	LIMA Plan	F
Ht 5' 11"	Wt 170		PT/Exp	D	Rand Var	+4
			Consist	C	MM	0221

GB% uptick further solidifies notoriety as a powerless worm-killer off the bench. Spd and ct% plunges helped kill h% luck and BA. Likely to rebound some, but to what end? Mediocre ct% at 35 offers near-zero upside for utility off the bench. A '11 relief Win in an 18-inning game may be his most memorable recent effort.

Yr	Tm	AB	R	HR	RBI	SB	BA	xBA	vL	vR	OB	Slg	OPS	bb%	ct%	h%	Eye	G	L	F	PX	xPX	hr/f	Spd	SBO	SB%	#Wk	DOM	DIS	RC/G	RAR	BPV	BPX	R$
08	for *	78	8	1	8	1	239	213	0	0	297	275	572	8	83	28	0.49				23	5	0%	90	4%	100%				2.80	-4.8	-17	0	-$1
09	NYM *	321	35	0	17	6	213	259	115	317	262	247	509	6	85	25	0.44	64	19	17	24	41	0%	130	11%	61%	12	25%	42%	2.06	-20.5	1	2	-$2
10	PHI *	355	39	4	38	9	265	285	242	265	310	361	671	6	87	30	0.50	60	19	21	63	48	7%	119	12%	77%	26	38%	46%	3.89	-2.1	41	89	$8
11	PHI	273	39	1	30	3	249	293	250	249	296	341	636	6	85	29	0.44	63	23	14	65	56	3%	122	9%	50%	26	31%	54%	3.31	-6.4	39	87	$3
12	CIN	194	15	0	15	3	206	238	308	169	238	227	464	4	81	25	0.22	68	20	13	18	37	0%	86	9%	75%	26	0%	73%	1.75	-14.3	-31	-78	-$2
1st Half		76	6	0	9	0	237	238	368	193	247	276	523	1	82	29	0.07	72	19	9	35	37	0%	86	0%	0%	13	0%	77%	2.28	-3.9	-32	-80	-$3
2nd Half		118	9	0	6	3	186	230	273	153	232	195	427	6	81	23	0.32	65	20	15	8	37	0%	94	14%	75%	13	0%	69%	1.45	-9.7	-35	-88	-$2
13	Proj	166	17	0	15	3	226	259	258	214	266	276	542	5	83	27	0.32	65	20	15	36	44	2%	101	10%	67%				2.41	-8.2	0	0	-$1

Valencia,Danny

Age 28	Bats R	Pos 3B	Health	A	LIMA Plan	F
Ht 6' 2"	Wt 220		PT/Exp	B	Rand Var	+3
			Consist	C	MM	2011

3-21-.188 in 154 AB at MIN and BOS. Underpowered, slow, defensively-mediocre 3B without basic plate skills to recommend. Proficiency as lefty-killer vanished, and needs to return for him to extend his MLB career. The xPX hints that a friendlier venue might help some. But that OPS makes his 2011 look like a career year.

Yr	Tm	AB	R	HR	RBI	SB	BA	xBA	vL	vR	OB	Slg	OPS	bb%	ct%	h%	Eye	G	L	F	PX	xPX	hr/f	Spd	SBO	SB%	#Wk	DOM	DIS	RC/G	RAR	BPV	BPX	R$
08	aa	266	32	7	26	2	249	239			286	405	691	5	69	33	0.17				120			98	5%	58%				3.89		8	0	$2
09	a/a	487	65	11	58	0	247	272			292	399	691	6	82	28	0.35				102			93	4%	0%				3.78		40	0	$6
10	MIN *	484	46	7	57	3	285	253	374	280	327	397	723	6	82	33	0.36	43	19	38	84	89	7%	74	3%	100%	19	53%	37%	4.67	1.6	29	63	$12
11	MIN	564	63	15	72	2	246	252	309	224	296	383	679	7	82	28	0.39	46	18	36	93	85	9%	86	6%	25%	27	26%	33%	3.68	-14.6	32	71	$10
12	2 AL *	471	39	9	55	1	209	229	226	168	236	325	561	3	79	25	0.16	43	18	39	82	114	6%	70	8%	11%	13	23%	69%	2.31	-33.1	3	8	$0
1st Half		277	25	5	30	1	203	236	231	176	229	329	558	3	80	24	0.17	50	14	36	86	104	4%	83	10%	18%	6	17%	67%	2.26	-20.4	16	40	$0
2nd Half		194	14	3	25	0	218	227	222	148	245	320	565	3	77	27	0.15	31	24	45	75	131	11%	59	7%	0%	7	29%	71%	2.39	-13.2	-16	-40	-$1
13	Proj	134	13	3	16	0	234	241	312	200	270	370	639	5	79	27	0.23	42	19	39	92	103	8%	78	6%	25%				3.20	-5.6	18	44	$2

Venable,Will

Age 30	Bats L	Pos RF CF	Health	A	LIMA Plan	C+
Ht 6' 2"	Wt 200		PT/Exp	C	Rand Var	0
			Consist	B	MM	3515

Achieved BA respectability with modest across-the-board bumps in plate skills. Running game was slow out of the gate, but 2H rebound confirmed value. GB% and PETCO capped 2H power—one HR at home—and again hurt BA (.239/.286 home/road). But this platooner is still getting consistent mileage out of limited skills.

Yr	Tm	AB	R	HR	RBI	SB	BA	xBA	vL	vR	OB	Slg	OPS	bb%	ct%	h%	Eye	G	L	F	PX	xPX	hr/f	Spd	SBO	SB%	#Wk	DOM	DIS	RC/G	RAR	BPV	BPX	R$
08	SD *	552	64	11	50	6	230	217	324	237	286	347	633	7	72	30	0.28	49	13	37	85	98	6%	123	8%	55%	6	33%	33%	3.21	-32.6	0	0	$3
09	SD *	493	63	20	61	7	233	240	225	266	291	415	706	8	70	29	0.27	44	16	40	126	119	15%	108	7%	87%	18	28%	44%	4.05	-16.2	28	57	$8
10	SD	392	60	13	51	29	245	218	154	259	323	408	731	10	67	33	0.35	39	17	44	116	109	11%	158	33%	81%	25	36%	48%	4.54	-7.1	32	70	$17
11	SD *	428	56	10	50	28	237	241	174	256	293	385	678	7	74	30	0.31	43	21	36	101	100	9%	143	30%	90%	26	35%	42%	3.99	-14.9	43	96	$14
12	SD	417	62	9	45	24	264	270	231	270	330	429	759	9	77	32	0.44	48	22	29	111	97	10%	127	28%	80%	27	52%	30%	4.96	-2.3	64	160	$16
1st Half		228	28	6	21	8	259	281	233	265	316	434	750	8	77	31	0.37	47	26	27	121	98	13%	99	26%	57%	13	62%	15%	4.39	-4.2	56	140	$14
2nd Half		189	34	3	24	16	270	256	227	275	346	423	769	10	78	33	0.52	49	18	32	99	97	6%	151	29%	100%	14	43%	43%	5.68	3.6	64	160	$19
13	Proj	415	61	12	48	25	252	252	225	256	317	427	744	9	75	31	0.38	45	20	35	115	101	12%	135	28%	86%				4.76	-3.0	56	140	$18

Viciedo,Dayan

Age 24	Bats R	Pos LF	Health	A	LIMA Plan	C+
Ht 5' 11"	Wt 240		PT/Exp	C	Rand Var	0
			Consist	B	MM	3025

Growth-age free-swinger showed raw power with hr/f spike. GB% retrace helped profitability in first full season. Upside is limited by drifting ct%, mediocre bb% and poor pitch selection. Power isn't a Cell product, but unless he can hike his BA and/or build on LD/FB growth, he may continue to cause heartburn for H2Hers.

Yr	Tm	AB	R	HR	RBI	SB	BA	xBA	vL	vR	OB	Slg	OPS	bb%	ct%	h%	Eye	G	L	F	PX	xPX	hr/f	Spd	SBO	SB%	#Wk	DOM	DIS	RC/G	RAR	BPV	BPX	R$
08	for *	177	40	6	37	2	274	267			356	422	778	11	86	29	0.88				82	5	0%	113	5%	62%				5.21	1.6	64	0	$6
09	aa	504	65	12	70	5	267	248			297	377	675	4	81	31	0.22				70			79	5%	68%				3.88		10	0	$12
10	CHW*	447	50	23	50	2	264	265	340	278	282	467	749	2	75	30	0.10	42	19	39	138	124	16%	66	3%	62%	13	38%	46%	4.53	-0.5	30	65	$12
11	CHW*	554	61	20	72	3	271	251	406	186	332	433	765	8	79	31	0.43	58	13	29	112	62	4%	57	2%	71%	5	20%	80%	5.02	7.1	36	80	$16
12	CHW	505	64	25	78	0	255	261	350	225	295	444	738	5	76	29	0.23	47	22	31	118	97	20%	58	2%	0%	27	41%	52%	4.39	-2.5	23	58	$14
1st Half		243	31	14	37	0	255	252	321	237	287	449	736	4	76	28	0.19	46	21	33	116	96	23%	66	0%	0%	13	38%	54%	4.41	-1.7	14	35	$14
2nd Half		262	33	11	41	0	256	269	371	214	301	439	740	6	77	29	0.28	47	23	30	119	98	18%	53	3%	0%	14	43%	50%	4.38	-2.1	30	75	$14
13	Proj	560	70	27	81	2	262	260	419	204	305	451	756	6	77	29	0.27	49	18	33	119	89	19%	55	3%	46%				4.70	0.8	33	83	$18

Victorino,Shane

Age 32	Bats B	Pos CF LF	Health	B	LIMA Plan	B+
Ht 5' 9"	Wt 190		PT/Exp	A	Rand Var	+1
			Consist	D	MM	2525

Stable h%, ct% suggest that season-long power collapse may have also factored into BA plunge. HR all but vanished in 2H, likely impacted by nagging injuries (hand, back, wrist, elbow). But return of healthy wheels and SBO restored running game. Power should rebound, but his legs are the best bet for ongoing value.

Yr	Tm	AB	R	HR	RBI	SB	BA	xBA	vL	vR	OB	Slg	OPS	bb%	ct%	h%	Eye	G	L	F	PX	xPX	hr/f	Spd	SBO	SB%	#Wk	DOM	DIS	RC/G	RAR	BPV	BPX	R$
08	PHI	570	102	14	58	36	293	282	282	298	345	447	792	7	88	31	0.65	45	19	36	91	92	8%	147	29%	77%	24	54%	21%	5.53	13.0	87	171	$30
09	PHI	620	102	10	62	25	292	296	314	283	354	445	800	9	89	32	0.85	45	22	33	90	59	5%	130	18%	76%	27	70%	22%	5.66	16.4	90	184	$25
10	PHI	587	84	18	69	34	259	281	321	235	320	429	750	8	87	27	0.67	45	17	38	100	86	9%	119	26%	85%	26	62%	19%	4.87	2.4	90	196	$24
11	PHI	519	95	17	61	19	279	286	308	271	348	491	840	10	88	29	0.87	42	16	42	121	91	9%	141	16%	86%	25	72%	12%	6.16	21.2	115	256	$23
12	2 NL	595	72	11	55	39	255	260	323	230	316	383	700	8	87	28	0.66	46	18	36	78	72	6%	120	28%	87%	27	52%	30%	4.35	-6.6	68	170	$22
1st Half		307	32	8	36	19	254	251	329	231	320	388	708	9	88	27	0.79	45	15	40	78	68	8%	103	25%	90%	13	38%	31%	4.49	-1.4	65	163	$23
2nd Half		288	40	3	19	20	257	268	319	228	312	378	690	7	85	29	0.55	48	21	32	77	76	4%	129	33%	83%	14	64%	29%	4.20	-3.9	66	165	$20
13	Proj	577	85	13	58	32	266	269	316	247	327	421	748	8	87	29	0.70	45	18	37	90	80	7%	127	25%	85%				4.92	2.5	83	208	$25

Vitters,Josh

Age 23	Bats R	Pos 3B	Health	A	LIMA Plan	D
Ht 6' 2"	Wt 200		PT/Exp	C	Rand Var	-1
			Consist	B	MM	2103

2-5-.121 in 99 AB at CHC. Former #3 overall draft pick turned disappointment, had a "career season" in the PCL's favorable offensive environment. But the MLEs don't suggest any real improvement, nor does his small sample with CHC. Has plenty of time, but avg power with sub-par plate skills are never a good mix.

Yr	Tm	AB	R	HR	RBI	SB	BA	xBA	vL	vR	OB	Slg	OPS	bb%	ct%	h%	Eye	G	L	F	PX	xPX	hr/f	Spd	SBO	SB%	#Wk	DOM	DIS	RC/G	RAR	BPV	BPX	R$
08																																		
09																																		
10	aa	206	21	6	19	1	199	255			235	332	567	4	79	23	0.22				95			89	4%	100%				2.51		19	0	-$1
11	aa	449	42	11	60	3	249	267			276	382	657	4	87	27	0.28				87			78	15%	21%				3.19		41	0	$8
12	CHC *	514	47	15	55	6	236	237	111	130	278	387	665	5	77	28	0.25	52	12	36	105	63	8%	82	9%	66%	9	11%	78%	3.54	-16.6	24	60	$7
1st Half		286	29	10	32	1	254	264			290	421	711	5	82	28	0.28				106			88	5%	25%				4.03		36	90	$11
2nd Half		228	17	5	24	6	213	217	111	130	263	345	607	6	70	28	0.22	52	12	36	103	63	8%	83	15%	83%	9	11%	78%	2.98	-11.4	1	3	$3
13	Proj	333	30	7	38	4	233	232	213	249	269	359	628	5	80	27	0.24	52	12	36	87	57	7%	83	11%	51%				3.09	-15.2	19	47	$4

Vizquel,Omar

Age 46	Bats B	Pos 2B	Health		LIMA Plan	
Ht 5' 9"	Wt 180		PT/Exp		Rand Var	
			Consist		MM	

11-time Gold Glove-winning defensive wizard also parlayed career 90% ct%, good wheels and longevity into HOF consideration. Gained reputation with his glove, but also a decent offensive player at his peak—as noted by career .272 BA and 404 SBs. But per the recent seasons, no one beats the reaper. Retiring at 45.

Yr	Tm	AB	R	HR	RBI	SB	BA	xBA	vL	vR	OB	Slg	OPS	bb%	ct%	h%	Eye	G	L	F	PX	xPX	hr/f	Spd	SBO	SB%	#Wk	DOM	DIS	RC/G	RAR	BPV	BPX	R$
08	SF	266	24	0	23	5	222	239	121	250	286	267	553	8	89	25	0.83	42	21	37	34	33	0%	74	13%	56%	22	27%	50%	2.43	-17.5	24	47	-$1
09	TEX	177	17	1	14	4	266	236	485	215	316	345	660	7	85	31	0.48	34	22	43	51	46	2%	109	8%	100%	25	36%	52%	3.91	-3.1	25	51	$2
10	CHW	344	36	2	30	11	276	247	207	290	341	331	673	9	87	31	0.76	46	21	33	39	36	2%	103	16%	61%	26	19%	46%	3.86	-6.8	21	46	$9
11	CHW	167	18	0	8	1	251	248	200	259	290	305	595	5	89	28	0.50	39	24	37	41	30	0%	94	7%	33%	22	32%	45%	2.88	-8.2	23	51	-$1
12	TOR	153	13	0	7	3	235	269	217	243	269	281	550	4	89	26	0.41	34	34	32	32	15	0%	94	14%	60%	25	16%	56%	2.45	-9.7	16	40	-$1
1st Half		62	5	0	2	1	226	262	235	222	262	226	487	5	92	25	0.60	41	31	28	0	3	0%	81	6%	100%	12	0%	67%	2.02	-4.8	-6	-15	-$3
2nd Half		91	8	0	5	2	242	273	207	258	274	319	592	4	87	28	0.33	30	35	35	55	23	0%	96	20%	50%	13	31%	46%	2.73	-5.1	29	73	$0
13	Proj																																	

JOCK THOMPSON

Votto,Joey			Health	B	LIMA Plan	C
Age 29	Bats L	Pos 1B	PT/Exp	A	Rand Var	-3
Ht 6' 3"	Wt 225		Consist	D	MM	5155

Tore meniscus to begin 2H, finally diagnosed/operated on in mid-July, shelving him until September. Forget his 2H, elite offensive performer was either consolidating or improving on 2010-2011 gains prior to his injury. 1H BA and PX in particular jump off this page. With health, we'll say it again... UP: .330 BA, 40+ HR.

Yr	Tm	AB	R	HR	RBI	SB	BA	xBA	vL	vR	OB	Slg	OPS	bb%	ct%	h%	Eye	G	L	F	PX	xPX	hr/f	Spd	SBO	SB%	#Wk	DOM	DIS	RC/G	RAR	BPV	BPX	R$
08	CIN	526	69	24	84	7	297	300	292	299	368	506	873	10	81	33	0.58	44	25	31	132	125	18%	85	8%	58%	27	41%	22%	6.59	17.0	71	139	$22
09	CIN	469	82	25	84	4	322	299	329	319	410	567	977	13	77	37	0.66	39	22	39	163	153	17%	71	3%	80%	24	54%	25%	8.75	41.5	87	178	$24
10	CIN	547	106	37	113	16	324	313	283	347	420	600	1020	14	77	36	0.73	45	20	35	183	150	25%	84	11%	76%	27	81%	11%	9.44	59.0	113	246	$40
11	CIN	599	101	29	103	8	309	299	333	299	416	531	947	16	78	35	0.85	39	28	33	152	145	18%	75	6%	57%	27	67%	15%	7.98	42.0	90	200	$33
12	CIN	374	59	14	56	5	337	311	288	359	470	567	1037	20	77	41	1.11	38	30	32	171	161	15%	68	5%	63%	21	71%	10%	10.12	46.1	101	253	$20
1st Half		266	50	14	47	4	350	328	306	370	469	632	1101	18	77	41	0.98	36	31	33	203	177	20%	71	7%	57%	13	85%	8%	11.35	41.3	124	310	$30
2nd Half		108	9	0	9	1	306	269	242	333	472	407	879	24	78	39	1.42	43	29	29	95	123	0%	68	2%	100%	8	50%	13%	7.15	5.3	44	110	-$3
13	Proj	**545**	**91**	**29**	**93**	**8**	**318**	**307**	**290**	**331**	**441**	**573**	**1014**	**18**	**78**	**36**	**0.99**	**39**	**27**	**34**	**172**	**145**	**20%**	**67**	**5%**	**69%**				**9.37**	**59.1**	**105**	**263**	**$31**

Walker,Neil			Health	A	LIMA Plan	C+
Age 27	Bats B	Pos 2B	PT/Exp	A	Rand Var	-3
Ht 6' 3"	Wt 210		Consist	B	MM	3125

On his way to career season until dislocated finger knocked him out the lineup in mid-August—and back woes torpedoed the rest. Always hinted at more power, but not to degree shown in 2H, when hr/f spike came out of nowhere. Solid MI run-producer; at his age, a clean March health report will keep us intrigued.

Yr	Tm	AB	R	HR	RBI	SB	BA	xBA	vL	vR	OB	Slg	OPS	bb%	ct%	h%	Eye	G	L	F	PX	xPX	hr/f	Spd	SBO	SB%	#Wk	DOM	DIS	RC/G	RAR	BPV	BPX	R$
08	aaa	505	57	12	66	8	219	253			253	360	612	4	79	25	0.21				93			104	16%	56%				2.84		32	0	$3
09	PIT *	392	36	11	56	5	230	249	143	207	275	396	671	6	81	26	0.32	32	16	52	113	125	0%	98	10%	69%	6	17%	67%	3.58	-9.1	48	98	$4
10	PIT *	594	75	16	85	9	288	275	295	296	341	460	801	7	80	34	0.40	36	22	41	122	125	9%	103	9%	69%	20	40%	20%	5.56	20.3	62	135	$22
11	PIT	596	76	12	83	9	273	262	269	275	334	408	742	8	81	32	0.48	44	21	35	96	120	7%	90	9%	60%	27	41%	33%	4.68	5.6	46	102	$18
12	PIT	472	62	14	69	7	280	259	246	291	345	426	771	9	78	33	0.45	42	24	34	101	115	11%	80	9%	58%	25	20%	32%	5.08	9.8	30	75	$16
1st Half		279	33	4	34	7	269	243	270	268	336	366	701	9	77	34	0.43	43	25	32	74	91	6%	77	10%	88%	13	8%	46%	4.37	0.9	8	20	$16
2nd Half		193	29	10	35	0	295	282	205	322	358	513	871	9	80	33	0.49	42	22	36	138	148	18%	88	7%	0%	12	33%	17%	6.12	10.2	58	145	$16
13	Proj	**514**	**67**	**15**	**76**	**6**	**276**	**262**	**251**	**285**	**336**	**431**	**767**	**8**	**80**	**32**	**0.44**	**42**	**23**	**36**	**105**	**123**	**10%**	**85**	**9%**	**52%**				**4.94**	**10.1**	**41**	**102**	**$18**

Wallace,Brett			Health	A	LIMA Plan	C
Age 26	Bats L	Pos 1B	PT/Exp	C	Rand Var	-2
Ht 6' 2"	Wt 260		Consist	B	MM	3005

9-24-.253 in 229 AB at HOU. One-time "natural hitter" prospect with .307 career BA in minors—and projected to hit for MLB average. Now selling out for power and flirting with success there, but it may not help if he can't reverse a steep ct% plunge and maintain patience. Age helps give him modest profit potential.

Yr	Tm	AB	R	HR	RBI	SB	BA	xBA	vL	vR	OB	Slg	OPS	bb%	ct%	h%	Eye	G	L	F	PX	xPX	hr/f	Spd	SBO	SB%	#Wk	DOM	DIS	RC/G	RAR	BPV	BPX	R$
08	aa	49	11	2	9	0	326	310			348	555	903	3	84	35	0.21				147			91	0%	0%				7.30		81	0	$1
09	a/a	532	57	14	47	1	246	237			293	368	661	6	76	30	0.28				84			84	2%	25%				3.58		-5	0	$5
10	HOU *	529	52	13	49	1	228	218	240	218	262	356	618	4	71	30	0.16	39	17	44	98	122	5%	78	2%	33%	11	18%	73%	3.05	-38.1	-10	-22	$3
11	HOU *	440	48	6	46	2	268	237	211	269	338	376	714	10	72	36	0.37	52	21	27	98	91	8%	53	2%	63%	23	30%	57%	4.40	-12.9	-1	-2	$8
12	HOU *	539	58	20	60	0	242	232	273	247	288	396	684	6	66	33	0.19	38	27	35	117	138	16%	53	1%	0%	12	17%	33%	3.79	-26.3	-16	-40	$8
1st Half		265	29	11	31	0	235	244	286	345	271	407	678	5	64	32	0.14	32	32	36	137	125	25%	62	2%	0%	2	50%	0%	3.59	-14.1	-13	-33	$9
2nd Half		274	29	9	28	0	248	228	271	228	304	385	689	7	68	33	0.25	39	26	35	98	140	15%	59	0%	0%	10	10%	40%	3.97	-11.3	-21	-53	$8
13	Proj	**587**	**62**	**19**	**60**	**1**	**256**	**236**	**242**	**259**	**306**	**405**	**711**	**7**	**69**	**34**	**0.24**	**42**	**24**	**34**	**111**	**117**	**14%**	**54**	**1%**	**45%**				**4.22**	**-19.6**	**-6**	**-14**	**$12**

Weeks,Jemile			Health	A	LIMA Plan	D+
Age 26	Bats B	Pos 2B	PT/Exp	C	Rand Var	+1
Ht 5' 9"	Wt 160		Consist	D	MM	1505

2-20-.221, 16 SB in 444 AB at OAK. The h% reversal suggests he's regularly getting his bat knocked out of his hands. Distressed power makes average plate skills that much more glaring, even with bb% uptick. Checkered running game history shortchanges terrific speed. Sub-par defense doesn't help.

Yr	Tm	AB	R	HR	RBI	SB	BA	xBA	vL	vR	OB	Slg	OPS	bb%	ct%	h%	Eye	G	L	F	PX	xPX	hr/f	Spd	SBO	SB%	#Wk	DOM	DIS	RC/G	RAR	BPV	BPX	R$
08																																		
09	aa	105	7	1	9	3	197	243			250	277	527	7	83	22	0.42				54			87	13%	100%				2.32		10	0	-$2
10	aa	273	34	2	26	9	232	258			289	341	630	7	85	27	0.52				70			132	23%	56%				3.07		51	0	$3
11	OAK *	590	71	4	51	29	290	253	287	310	337	400	736	7	83	34	0.41	40	23	37	76	66	2%	149	27%	65%	17	47%	18%	4.60	7.4	48	107	$23
12	OAK *	489	57	2	27	17	225	242	232	215	302	307	610	10	84	27	0.68	49	19	32	53	49	2%	151	16%	77%	26	38%	31%	3.11	-15.9	37	93	$5
1st Half		284	31	2	11	11	222	255	232	216	307	317	624	11	85	25	0.83	47	22	31	58	59	3%	151	20%	69%	14	43%	21%	3.16	-9.8	47	118	$5
2nd Half		205	26	0	16	6	230	221	231	213	296	294	590	9	82	28	0.51	54	14	33	44	32	0%	139	10%	100%	12	33%	42%	3.03	-7.6	18	45	$4
13	Proj	**514**	**59**	**2**	**39**	**19**	**240**	**239**	**239**	**241**	**303**	**323**	**627**	**8**	**83**	**29**	**0.54**	**47**	**19**	**34**	**55**	**52**	**1%**	**142**	**19%**	**72%**				**3.29**	**-15.2**	**33**	**82**	**$10**

Weeks,Rickie			Health	D	LIMA Plan	C
Age 30	Bats R	Pos 2B	PT/Exp	A	Rand Var	+2
Ht 5' 10"	Wt 213		Consist	B	MM	4315

Beat the odds by staying healthy, but couldn't arrest whiff-itis in time to help H2Hers avoid nightmarish 1H. Increased aggressiveness, h% rebound and ct% return fueled huge 2H. Uptick in 2H SBO bodes well for future SB totals. Bottom-line skills remain strong despite early slump. Health remains biggest concern.

Yr	Tm	AB	R	HR	RBI	SB	BA	xBA	vL	vR	OB	Slg	OPS	bb%	ct%	h%	Eye	G	L	F	PX	xPX	hr/f	Spd	SBO	SB%	#Wk	DOM	DIS	RC/G	RAR	BPV	BPX	R$
08	MIL	475	89	14	46	19	234	247	250	227	327	398	725	12	76	28	0.57	46	15	39	108	93	10%	155	18%	79%	24	46%	25%	4.38	0.5	61	120	$11
09	MIL	147	28	9	24	2	272	267	276	271	327	517	844	8	73	31	0.31	38	19	44	151	138	19%	153	11%	50%	7	43%	29%	5.67	5.7	67	137	$5
10	MIL	651	112	29	83	11	269	259	329	251	345	464	809	10	72	33	0.41	49	15	36	140	115	17%	112	8%	73%	27	33%	33%	5.56	22.8	53	115	$24
11	MIL	453	77	20	49	9	269	270	261	271	342	468	810	10	76	31	0.47	48	17	35	138	109	16%	99	9%	82%	22	59%	32%	5.61	16.5	68	151	$17
12	MIL	588	85	21	63	16	230	236	248	224	316	400	715	11	71	29	0.44	45	17	38	120	114	13%	111	12%	84%	27	37%	41%	4.24	-1.8	38	95	$14
1st Half		268	27	6	22	6	183	200	230	169	294	306	600	14	65	26	0.45	47	15	38	98	101	9%	105	8%	100%	13	15%	62%	2.92	-11.5	-4	-10	-$1
2nd Half		320	58	15	41	10	269	266	264	270	335	478	813	9	77	31	0.43	44	18	38	136	123	16%	107	16%	77%	14	57%	21%	5.57	12.2	69	173	$26
13	Proj	**564**	**91**	**23**	**64**	**13**	**261**	**248**	**277**	**256**	**339**	**446**	**785**	**11**	**73**	**32**	**0.44**	**46**	**17**	**37**	**126**	**113**	**15%**	**108**	**10%**	**79%**				**5.23**	**15.9**	**49**	**122**	**$20**

Wells,Casper			Health	A	LIMA Plan	D
Age 28	Bats R	Pos LF RF	PT/Exp	D	Rand Var	+2
Ht 6' 2"	Wt 220		Consist	C	MM	4303

10-36-.228 in 285 AB at SEA. More AB, a touch more contact, fewer HR, and no change vs. RHP. PX/xPX combo hints at less power upside than previously. Still not taking advantage of solid speed, with SBO trending badly. Career .838 OPS vs. LHP point to his likely career path.

Yr	Tm	AB	R	HR	RBI	SB	BA	xBA	vL	vR	OB	Slg	OPS	bb%	ct%	h%	Eye	G	L	F	PX	xPX	hr/f	Spd	SBO	SB%	#Wk	DOM	DIS	RC/G	RAR	BPV	BPX	R$
08	aa	270	44	13	39	6	249	276			305	484	789	8	73	30	0.30				157			119	17%	63%				4.86		74	0	$7
09	aa	311	40	12	32	6	226	236			301	415	716	10	63	32	0.29				147			110	21%	40%				3.71		21	0	$4
10	DET *	480	56	20	51	5	219	253	265	386	266	417	682	6	70	27	0.21	42	19	39	145	157	14%	151	18%	33%	9	56%	22%	3.29	-19.2	36	78	$6
11	2 AL *	242	33	12	32	3	247	241	260	218	305	468	773	8	67	32	0.25	42	13	45	170	135	17%	111	9%	60%	23	35%	57%	4.72	1.1	47	104	$6
12	SEA *	356	53	11	45	4	217	222	267	195	295	382	677	10	71	27	0.38	40	15	45	116	109	11%	132	7%	77%	25	32%	44%	3.68	-9.7	33	83	$4
1st Half		136	21	3	18	2	227	220	239	293	325	374	699	13	67	32	0.45	46	14	41	127	99	8%	100	8%	56%	11	45%	45%	3.93	-3.0	23	58	$0
2nd Half		220	32	9	27	3	211	223	282	159	275	388	663	8	73	25	0.33	37	16	47	110	113	12%	150	6%	100%	14	21%	43%	3.50	-7.8	36	90	$7
13	Proj	**320**	**45**	**13**	**40**	**4**	**242**	**233**	**263**	**225**	**308**	**440**	**748**	**9**	**70**	**31**	**0.31**	**41**	**15**	**44**	**139**	**125**	**13%**	**127**	**10%**	**61%**				**4.47**	**-1.7**	**41**	**102**	**$8**

Wells,Vernon			Health	D	LIMA Plan	D
Age 34	Bats R	Pos LF	PT/Exp	B	Rand Var	+2
Ht 6' 1"	Wt 230		Consist	C	MM	3223

11-29-.230 in 243 AB at LAA. On pace for repeat of 2011 stinker in mid-May. Torn thumb-ligament DL'd him thru July, keeping bad year from becoming worse. Most of his skills remain near career norms, but his h% and BA have fallen off a cliff. Without an early-season reversal of this, his PT will follow suit in 2013.

Yr	Tm	AB	R	HR	RBI	SB	BA	xBA	vL	vR	OB	Slg	OPS	bb%	ct%	h%	Eye	G	L	F	PX	xPX	hr/f	Spd	SBO	SB%	#Wk	DOM	DIS	RC/G	RAR	BPV	BPX	R$
08	TOR	427	63	20	78	4	300	296	333	290	344	496	841	6	89	30	0.63	47	17	36	111	104	14%	76	5%	67%	20	65%	10%	6.17	18.9	80	157	$18
09	TOR	630	84	15	66	17	260	260	206	278	313	400	713	7	86	28	0.56	43	15	42	87	90	6%	92	13%	81%	27	48%	19%	4.35	-4.0	62	127	$16
10	TOR	590	79	31	88	6	273	307	195	291	330	515	845	8	86	27	0.60	42	16	42	150	126	15%	76	8%	60%	26	62%	4%	5.85	21.8	103	224	$22
11	LAA	505	60	25	66	9	218	250	284	187	248	412	660	4	83	22	0.23	40	12	48	114	107	12%	106	15%	69%	24	54%	38%	3.27	-20.3	63	140	$10
12	LAA *	269	37	12	31	5	229	253	227	232	272	400	673	6	84	23	0.37	42	16	42	99	110	13%	66	10%	83%	19	47%	42%	3.63	-7.6	52	130	$5
1st Half		135	18	6	12	2	244	276	222	253	282	422	704	5	87	24	0.41	42	19	38	101	112	13%	71	7%	100%	8	50%	38%	4.09	-2.2	61	153	$4
2nd Half		134	19	6	19	3	214	227	231	203	263	379	642	6	81	22	0.35	42	11	47	97	108	12%	65	14%	73%	11	45%	45%	3.21	-6.0	38	95	$6
13	Proj	**297**	**40**	**14**	**39**	**5**	**237**	**255**	**248**	**233**	**280**	**423**	**703**	**6**	**84**	**24**	**0.37**	**42**	**14**	**44**	**108**	**110**	**12%**	**74**	**11%**	**75%**				**3.94**	**-6.4**	**60**	**150**	**$8**

JOCK THOMPSON

Werth,Jayson

Age 34	Bats R	Pos RF	Health	D	LIMA Plan	B
Ht 6' 5"	Wt 225		PT/Exp	B	Rand Var	-3
			Consist	F	MM	4415

5-31-.300 in 300 AB at WAS. No surprise to see power loss after DL stint, since wrists take time to heal. While a power rebound is likely, as long as FB% continues to decline, he won't approach 2008-10 levels. Even with big ct% boost, xBA says to expect BA regression. Having trouble living up to the big contract.

Yr	Tm	AB	R	HR	RBI	SB	BA	xBA	vL	vR	OB	Slg	OPS	bb%	ct%	h%	Eye	G	L	F	PX	xPX	hr/f	Spd	SBO	SB%	#Wk	DOM	DIS	RC/G	RAR	BPV	BPX	R$
08	PHI	418	73	24	67	20	273	263	303	255	360	498	858	12	72	33	0.48	39	23	38	148	125	21%	124	16%	95%	26	50%	31%	6.55	16.8	69	135	$21
09	PHI	571	98	36	99	20	268	267	302	256	369	506	875	14	73	31	0.58	36	20	44	155	143	19%	90	13%	87%	27	44%	44%	6.62	24.2	73	149	$27
10	PHI	554	106	27	85	13	296	278	287	300	387	532	919	13	73	36	0.56	37	18	45	176	163	14%	110	9%	81%	27	63%	22%	7.49	36.1	92	200	$29
11	WAS	561	69	20	58	19	232	233	184	244	321	389	710	12	71	29	0.46	43	17	40	118	132	12%	89	14%	86%	27	41%	33%	4.25	-15.2	33	73	$13
12	WAS *	321	45	5	34	8	292	249	395	268	381	428	809	13	80	35	0.73	42	19	39	96	88	5%	119	9%	80%	16	56%	13%	5.92	7.0	54	135	$11
1st Half		98	10	3	12	3	276	238	400	244	366	439	805	13	79	32	0.67	43	14	43	105	70	9%	102	9%	100%	6	50%	33%	5.87	2.4	51	128	$3
2nd Half		223	35	2	22	5	300	254	393	281	387	423	811	13	81	36	0.76	42	21	37	92	96	3%	119	9%	71%	10	60%	0%	5.94	5.8	54	135	$14
13	Proj	**520**	**75**	**19**	**62**	**15**	**275**	**254**	**318**	**260**	**366**	**461**	**828**	**13**	**76**	**33**	**0.61**	**41**	**18**	**41**	**127**	**114**	**12%**	**106**	**11%**	**85%**				**6.03**	**15.2**	**64**	**160**	**$19**

Wheeler,Ryan

Age 24	Bats L	Pos 3B	Health	A	LIMA Plan	D
Ht 6' 3"	Wt 237		PT/Exp	D	Rand Var	-2
			Consist	A	MM	2123

1-10-.239 in 109 AB at ARI. Called up in July to solve 3B problem; got a week before a trade ended that experiment. Decent plate approach in majors, so BA will come eventually; crushed it to the tune of .351 in hitter-happy PCL. Middling power and platoon role (15 AB vs LHP) limit upside.

Yr	Tm	AB	R	HR	RBI	SB	BA	xBA	vL	vR	OB	Slg	OPS	bb%	ct%	h%	Eye	G	L	F	PX	xPX	hr/f	Spd	SBO	SB%	#Wk	DOM	DIS	RC/G	RAR	BPV	BPX	R$
08																																		
09																																		
10	aa	67	7	3	9	0	241	249			286	404	690	6	75	28	0.25				114			94	0%	0%				3.88		11	0	$0
11	aa	480	49	12	64	2	258	247			303	397	700	6	76	32	0.28				104			80	5%	39%				4.03		19	0	$10
12	ARI *	471	45	10	65	3	276	267	67	266	312	423	735	5	79	33	0.24	49	23	28	101	111	4%	88	4%	71%	12	33%	58%	4.63	0.3	29	73	$12
1st Half		302	27	8	47	1	300	249			329	453	782	4	77	37	0.19				105			80	2%	100%				5.45		21	53	$18
2nd Half		169	18	3	18	2	235	274	67	266	283	368	651	6	82	27	0.38	49	23	28	93	111	4%	88	8%	58%	12	33%	58%	3.41	-6.0	39	98	$1
13	Proj	**264**	**27**	**6**	**34**	**2**	**261**	**262**	**73**	**291**	**302**	**404**	**706**	**6**	**79**	**31**	**0.27**	**48**	**22**	**30**	**100**	**100**	**10%**	**87**	**5%**	**59%**				**4.16**	**-3.3**	**27**	**68**	**$6**

Wieters,Matt

Age 27	Bats B	Pos CA	Health	A	LIMA Plan	B
Ht 6' 5"	Wt 240		PT/Exp	B	Rand Var	+1
			Consist	B	MM	4125

2010-2011 growth combined with a hot April (6 HR) made it seem like breakout was imminent; instead, it was more of the same. It's a fine level; despite struggles vs RHP, xBA hints at BA upside, and reliable power virtually assures 20-25 HR. Entering prime years... UP: 30 HR, .280.

Yr	Tm	AB	R	HR	RBI	SB	BA	xBA	vL	vR	OB	Slg	OPS	bb%	ct%	h%	Eye	G	L	F	PX	xPX	hr/f	Spd	SBO	SB%	#Wk	DOM	DIS	RC/G	RAR	BPV	BPX	R$
08	aa	208	35	11	44	1	345	309			432	587	1019	13	85	36	1.05				140			92	1%	100%				9.90		101	0	$12
09	BAL *	495	57	14	70	0	289	241	248	313	348	431	780	8	76	35	0.39	42	19	40	95	101	8%	81	0%	0%	20	25%	60%	5.39	17.2	12	24	$13
10	BAL	446	37	11	55	0	249	231	210	263	320	377	697	10	79	29	0.50	46	15	38	90	108	8%	70	1%	0%	25	32%	48%	4.06	-0.9	16	35	$6
11	BAL	500	72	22	68	1	262	273	339	237	327	450	777	9	83	28	0.57	43	18	39	122	130	14%	66	1%	100%	27	37%	22%	5.09	13.8	63	140	$15
12	BAL	526	67	23	83	3	249	265	323	224	326	435	761	10	79	28	0.54	44	20	35	119	113	16%	58	2%	100%	27	48%	33%	4.85	11.0	50	125	$14
1st Half		257	33	11	38	1	249	264	403	195	323	440	762	10	81	27	0.56	44	18	38	119	109	14%	68	2%	100%	13	62%	23%	4.84	4.8	55	138	$13
2nd Half		269	34	12	45	2	249	266	242	251	329	431	760	11	77	28	0.52	44	23	33	119	117	17%	55	3%	100%	14	36%	43%	4.86	5.1	40	100	$15
13	Proj	**536**	**73**	**26**	**90**	**2**	**268**	**270**	**310**	**254**	**342**	**470**	**812**	**10**	**80**	**29**	**0.55**	**44**	**19**	**37**	**126**	**116**	**16%**	**59**	**1%**	**92%**				**5.61**	**21.5**	**58**	**145**	**$20**

Wigginton,Ty

Age 35	Bats R	Pos 1B 3B	Health	A	LIMA Plan	D
Ht 6' 0"	Wt 230		PT/Exp	B	Rand Var	0
			Consist	A	MM	2113

Never seems to have a job on Opening Day but always finds a way to 400 AB. It started the same this year, but numbers couldn't support continued PT. Contact dropped for third straight year; even with bb% bump, BA isn't coming back. Power dipped as well; high GB% isn't helping.

Yr	Tm	AB	R	HR	RBI	SB	BA	xBA	vL	vR	OB	Slg	OPS	bb%	ct%	h%	Eye	G	L	F	PX	xPX	hr/f	Spd	SBO	SB%	#Wk	DOM	DIS	RC/G	RAR	BPV	BPX	R$
08	HOU	386	50	23	58	4	285	290	340	265	340	526	866	8	82	30	0.46	45	16	39	145	129	19%	75	10%	40%	23	52%	22%	6.04	15.8	77	151	$15
09	BAL	410	44	11	41	1	273	255	252	285	312	400	712	5	86	30	0.40	43	18	39	77	76	8%	62	3%	33%	26	42%	31%	4.30	-3.6	29	59	$7
10	BAL	581	63	22	76	0	248	253	237	252	307	415	722	8	80	28	0.43	47	16	37	111	116	13%	70	1%	0%	27	37%	44%	4.29	-5.4	35	76	$11
11	COL	401	52	15	47	8	242	266	259	235	308	416	724	9	79	27	0.45	46	18	36	118	117	13%	82	9%	89%	26	50%	27%	4.37	-2.7	58	129	$9
12	PHI	315	40	11	43	1	235	227	234	236	315	375	690	11	74	28	0.46	46	18	36	93	97	13%	65	1%	100%	27	19%	48%	3.96	-6.1	7	18	$5
1st Half		218	30	8	33	1	248	224	224	258	320	394	714	10	74	30	0.41	46	16	38	98	103	13%	62	2%	100%	13	15%	31%	4.30	-1.8	10	25	$9
2nd Half		97	10	3	10	0	206	236	246	150	306	330	636	13	74	25	0.56	45	24	31	83	83	13%	71	0%	0%	14	21%	64%	3.25	-4.0	-4	-10	-$4
13	Proj	**347**	**41**	**12**	**43**	**2**	**246**	**244**	**256**	**239**	**320**	**397**	**718**	**10**	**77**	**28**	**0.48**	**46**	**19**	**35**	**99**	**102**	**13%**	**69**	**3%**	**77%**				**4.31**	**-10.8**	**25**	**63**	**$8**

Willingham,Josh

Age 34	Bats R	Pos LF DH	Health	C	LIMA Plan	B
Ht 6' 2"	Wt 228		PT/Exp	B	Rand Var	0
			Consist	C	MM	5125

A bit of a surprise, since MIN is harsher on RH HR than OAK. Also hit fewer FB than in 2011, but made up for it with better hr/f. On the plus side, xBA fortells a better BA; on the down side, xPX says the power will retreat a bit. But a late-career power spike at 34 is rarely repeatable.

Yr	Tm	AB	R	HR	RBI	SB	BA	xBA	vL	vR	OB	Slg	OPS	bb%	ct%	h%	Eye	G	L	F	PX	xPX	hr/f	Spd	SBO	SB%	#Wk	DOM	DIS	RC/G	RAR	BPV	BPX	R$
08	FLA *	377	58	15	55	3	248	266	242	258	336	454	790	12	76	29	0.56	39	19	42	136	122	13%	117	5%	60%	20	45%	40%	5.11	4.3	68	133	$8
09	WAS	427	70	24	61	4	260	285	300	251	352	496	849	13	76	29	0.59	36	22	42	157	148	17%	79	6%	57%	27	52%	37%	5.93	17.0	71	145	$13
10	WAS	370	54	16	56	8	268	256	277	264	380	459	839	15	77	31	0.79	31	20	49	129	149	11%	87	6%	100%	20	45%	35%	6.23	17.7	71	154	$13
11	OAK	488	69	29	98	4	246	251	208	264	324	477	801	10	69	29	0.37	35	17	48	173	161	17%	66	4%	80%	25	52%	32%	5.23	9.5	54	120	$17
12	MIN	519	85	35	110	3	260	272	231	273	355	524	879	13	73	29	0.54	38	19	43	176	136	21%	66	3%	60%	26	58%	19%	6.35	26.9	76	190	$22
1st Half		265	42	16	52	2	268	279	265	269	360	532	892	13	72	31	0.51	39	20	41	185	131	21%	66	4%	67%	13	62%	15%	6.62	15.1	81	203	$22
2nd Half		254	43	19	58	1	252	264	205	277	349	516	865	13	74	27	0.57	37	18	45	167	141	22%	65	3%	50%	13	54%	23%	6.07	10.7	68	170	$22
13	Proj	**490**	**76**	**30**	**96**	**4**	**256**	**260**	**229**	**268**	**350**	**496**	**846**	**13**	**73**	**29**	**0.53**	**36**	**19**	**45**	**161**	**145**	**18%**	**70**	**4%**	**74%**				**5.94**	**18.4**	**66**	**166**	**$20**

Wise,DeWayne

Age 35	Bats L	Pos LF CF	Health	B	LIMA Plan	D
Ht 6' 0"	Wt 200		PT/Exp	F	Rand Var	-1
			Consist	C	MM	3401

8-30-.259 with 19 SB in 224 AB at NYY and CHW. High SBO; baby, he was born to run. Unfortunately, low bb% and struggles vs LHP limited his opportunities. PX and hr/f boost led to more HRs; xPX sheds doubt on whether that will be repeated. Future remains as a platooner and late-inning defensive replacement.

Yr	Tm	AB	R	HR	RBI	SB	BA	xBA	vL	vR	OB	Slg	OPS	bb%	ct%	h%	Eye	G	L	F	PX	xPX	hr/f	Spd	SBO	SB%	#Wk	DOM	DIS	RC/G	RAR	BPV	BPX	R$
08	CHW*	320	49	14	35	20	251	262	143	261	305	449	754	7	77	29	0.34	35	23	42	125	127	15%	114	40%	69%	17	29%	41%	4.43	-1.3	68	133	$12
09	CHW*	169	19	2	13	4	232	242	400	205	249	372	620	2	81	28	0.12	36	17	47	92	112	4%	122	33%	44%	20	35%	45%	2.70	-9.8	43	88	$0
10	TOR *	249	33	6	24	5	230	256	231	253	260	393	653	4	75	29	0.16	41	22	37	112	74	10%	135	18%	68%	18	22%	61%	3.31	-10.7	40	87	$3
11	2 TM *	241	27	4	18	11	226	207	150	215	247	342	589	3	71	30	0.10	41	16	44	88	122	7%	116	38%	64%	16	19%	69%	2.61	-15.9	4	9	$3
12	2 AL *	331	46	12	40	21	249	247	188	288	290	419	709	6	75	30	0.23	40	22	39	115	74	12%	91	36%	84%	21	24%	43%	4.23	-3.2	46	115	$13
1st Half		116	20	6	13	8	270	260	143	294	316	497	813	6	73	33	0.25	37	20	43	156	89	15%	96	30%	100%	9	22%	44%	5.89	4.1	74	185	$9
2nd Half		215	26	6	27	14	237	238	193	286	276	377	654	5	76	29	0.22	40	22	38	93	70	11%	87	38%	77%	12	25%	42%	3.48	-7.7	28	70	$15
13	Proj	**201**	**26**	**6**	**21**	**10**	**239**	**238**	**162**	**262**	**273**	**401**	**674**	**4**	**74**	**29**	**0.18**	**39**	**20**	**41**	**110**	**92**	**10%**	**102**	**35%**	**76%**				**3.62**	**-6.3**	**38**	**96**	**$7**

Wright,David

Age 30	Bats R	Pos 3B	Health	B	LIMA Plan	C+
Ht 6' 0"	Wt 210		PT/Exp	A	Rand Var	-2
			Consist	C	MM	4225

Positively scorching in the 1H; looked like his younger self with high bb%, ct%, h%. But couldn't sustain those in 2H, most disappointingly ct%. On the bright side, FB% came back in 2H, and xPX buys the 2H power gains. Net: 25 HR more likely than a .300 repeat.

Yr	Tm	AB	R	HR	RBI	SB	BA	xBA	vL	vR	OB	Slg	OPS	bb%	ct%	h%	Eye	G	L	F	PX	xPX	hr/f	Spd	SBO	SB%	#Wk	DOM	DIS	RC/G	RAR	BPV	BPX	R$
08	NYM	626	115	33	124	15	302	300	382	275	393	534	927	13	81	33	0.80	36	26	38	145	125	17%	85	10%	75%	27	56%	7%	7.62	52.2	96	188	$35
09	NYM	535	88	10	72	27	307	258	416	277	391	447	838	12	74	40	0.53	38	26	36	108	113	7%	104	19%	75%	25	40%	36%	6.41	26.8	41	84	$27
10	NYM	587	87	29	103	19	283	267	339	267	358	503	861	11	73	35	0.43	38	19	43	158	147	16%	83	18%	63%	27	56%	30%	6.16	26.2	67	146	$29
11	NYM	389	60	14	61	13	254	252	256	254	342	427	769	12	75	31	0.54	42	18	40	126	142	12%	69	13%	87%	19	42%	21%	5.11	5.7	56	124	$14
12	NYM	581	91	21	93	15	306	278	320	300	391	492	883	12	81	35	0.72	42	22	35	123	134	13%	84	13%	60%	27	56%	22%	6.83	36.0	71	178	$30
1st Half		273	52	9	50	8	355	309	363	352	452	564	1016	15	85	39	1.17	45	23	32	136	123	12%	91	14%	53%	13	85%	8%	9.49	35.2	106	265	$37
2nd Half		308	39	12	43	7	263	251	286	252	334	429	763	10	77	31	0.46	40	21	39	110	144	13%	73	11%	70%	14	29%	36%	4.90	2.9	36	90	$24
13	Proj	**587**	**91**	**22**	**94**	**17**	**286**	**263**	**314**	**277**	**371**	**471**	**841**	**12**	**77**	**34**	**0.59**	**41**	**21**	**38**	**125**	**137**	**13%**	**77**	**14%**	**69%**				**6.13**	**25.9**	**62**	**154**	**$29**

DAVE ADLER

Youkilis,Kevin

Youkilis,Kevin	Health C	LIMA Plan	C+
Age 34 Bats R Pos 3B 1B	PT/Exp B	Rand Var	+3
Ht 6' 1" Wt 220	Consist F	MM	4225

Injuries slowed him again; this time, it was back woes. The question is, for a player with such fundamentally sound core skill, will good health be enough to elevate him back to solid productivity? H%, ct% rebounds will help. 2H showed exciting glimmers of the past. There might another big year left IF he can stay healthy.

Yr Tm	AB	R	HR	RBI	SB	BA	xBA	vL	vR	OB	Slg	OPS	bb%	ct%	h%	Eye	G	L	F	PX	xPX	hr/f	Spd	SBO	SB%	#Wk	DOM	DIS	RC/G	RAR	BPV	BPX	R$
08 BOS	538	91	29	115	3	312	299	288	318	383	569	952	10	80	35	0.57	34	22	44	165	142	15%	91	5%	38%	28	64%	29%	7.85	48.5	94	184	$28
09 BOS	491	99	27	94	7	305	282	309	304	400	548	948	14	75	36	0.62	35	21	44	164	161	16%	80	6%	78%	26	65%	31%	8.04	46.9	83	169	$26
10 BOS	362	77	19	62	4	307	297	404	275	402	564	966	14	81	33	0.87	37	16	47	164	166	14%	121	4%	80%	18	67%	11%	8.35	37.5	119	259	$20
11 BOS	431	68	17	80	3	258	275	311	234	359	459	818	14	77	30	0.68	42	20	38	146	136	13%	81	2%	100%	24	58%	25%	5.71	14.5	76	169	$14
12 2 AL	438	72	19	60	0	235	247	275	220	315	409	724	10	75	27	0.47	43	21	36	110	119	16%	87	0%	0%	24	38%	33%	4.29	-3.3	30	75	$9
1st Half	168	26	4	17	0	232	240	244	228	291	363	654	8	74	29	0.33	50	20	30	92	106	11%	83	0%	0%	10	30%	40%	3.51	-5.4	9	23	$0
2nd Half	270	46	15	43	0	237	253	293	215	329	437	766	12	76	26	0.57	39	21	40	121	127	18%	86	0%	0%	14	43%	29%	4.81	1.8	41	103	$15
13 Proj	**458**	**79**	**20**	**73**	**2**	**281**	**264**	**330**	**262**	**373**	**479**	**852**	**13**	**78**	**32**	**0.67**	**41**	**20**	**39**	**127**	**133**	**14%**	**85**	**2%**	**80%**				**6.34**	**22.7**	**63**	**158**	**$17**

Young Jr.,Eric

Young Jr.,Eric	Health D	LIMA Plan	D+
Age 28 Bats B Pos CF	PT/Exp D	Rand Var	-5
Ht 5' 10" Wt 180	Consist D	MM	1513

Started seeing regular PT time in 2H until intercostal strain ended his season. Not surprisingly, h% was main driver of ridiculous 2H BA. Still, there is a monster SB machine lurking here, waiting for an opportunity and a green light. But at 28, the window for those opps could be closing soon.

Yr Tm	AB	R	HR	RBI	SB	BA	xBA	vL	vR	OB	Slg	OPS	bb%	ct%	h%	Eye	G	L	F	PX	xPX	hr/f	Spd	SBO	SB%	#Wk	DOM	DIS	RC/G	RAR	BPV	BPX	R$
08 aa	403	53	2	23	33	255	237			327	340	666	10	80	31	0.53				63			118	42%	65%				3.56		28	0	$14
09 COL *	529	86	6	30	42	257	277	304	206	311	361	672	7	82	31	0.42	59	20	22	64	68	11%	170	44%	68%	7	43%	57%	3.65	-17.5	43	88	$20
10 COL *	308	41	1	14	24	230	223	238	248	293	279	572	8	78	29	0.40	54	17	29	39	55	0%	142	34%	80%	11	36%	45%	2.85	-17.8	0	0	$7
11 COL *	421	64	1	24	35	264	262	234	256	335	355	691	10	81	32	0.56	58	19	23	64	69	0%	152	32%	87%	17	29%	41%	4.43	-3.5	46	102	$16
12 COL	174	36	4	15	14	316	257	383	291	364	448	812	7	82	37	0.42	49	19	32	81	73	9%	141	29%	88%	20	20%	55%	6.37	7.8	55	138	$10
1st Half	74	18	0	3	10	243	215	300	222	317	284	601	10	80	31	0.53	45	23	32	24	83	0%	140	46%	91%	12	17%	75%	3.61	-2.3	16	40	$6
2nd Half	100	18	4	12	4	370	288	444	342	400	570	970	5	84	41	0.31	51	17	33	120	67	15%	122	16%	80%	8	25%	25%	9.21	11.4	76	190	$13
13 Proj	**322**	**56**	**4**	**23**	**26**	**286**	**252**	**335**	**265**	**343**	**390**	**733**	**8**	**81**	**34**	**0.46**	**53**	**19**	**29**	**67**	**69**	**6%**	**145**	**31%**	**84%**				**4.97**	**1.8**	**43**	**106**	**$17**

Young,Chris

Young,Chris	Health B	LIMA Plan	C+
Age 29 Bats R Pos CF	PT/Exp A	Rand Var	+3
Ht 6' 2" Wt 192	Consist A	MM	4215

Roared out of the gate with 5 HR in first 12 games until injured shoulder shelved him for a month. PRO: Plenty of fly balls and consistent PX will result in the usual HRs. CON: Struggles vs RHP nothing new, and now impacting PT; lower OBA and loss of Spd impacted SBs. Power should rebound; speed questionable.

Yr Tm	AB	R	HR	RBI	SB	BA	xBA	vL	vR	OB	Slg	OPS	bb%	ct%	h%	Eye	G	L	F	PX	xPX	hr/f	Spd	SBO	SB%	#Wk	DOM	DIS	RC/G	RAR	BPV	BPX	R$
08 ARI	625	85	22	85	14	248	255	285	236	316	443	759	9	74	30	0.38	38	19	43	138	115	11%	121	13%	74%	27	52%	22%	4.72	0.5	60	118	$15
09 ARI *	487	65	17	48	12	223	229	262	196	314	414	728	12	70	28	0.44	26	18	56	141	141	9%	118	16%	66%	26	31%	38%	4.17	-7.7	49	100	$7
10 ARI	584	94	27	91	28	257	250	264	255	340	452	792	11	75	30	0.51	34	17	50	137	135	12%	91	21%	80%	26	54%	19%	5.33	11.0	64	139	$26
11 ARI	567	89	20	71	22	236	247	285	222	331	420	751	12	75	28	0.58	32	20	49	135	137	10%	118	20%	71%	27	56%	33%	4.57	-1.9	69	153	$18
12 ARI	325	36	14	41	8	231	259	267	210	307	434	741	10	76	26	0.46	31	22	47	143	136	12%	72	15%	73%	24	42%	38%	4.38	-2.9	58	145	$7
1st Half	154	17	7	18	2	214	241	320	163	301	416	716	11	74	24	0.48	32	17	51	141	125	12%	85	11%	50%	10	40%	30%	3.90	-4.2	46	115	$3
2nd Half	171	19	7	23	6	246	274	229	257	314	450	764	9	77	28	0.44	30	27	44	144	146	12%	67	18%	86%	14	43%	43%	4.86	0.4	65	163	$10
13 Proj	**437**	**58**	**18**	**57**	**12**	**238**	**251**	**267**	**225**	**319**	**434**	**753**	**11**	**75**	**28**	**0.49**	**32**	**21**	**48**	**137**	**136**	**11%**	**86**	**16%**	**71%**				**4.59**	**-2.5**	**59**	**148**	**$13**

Young,Delmon

Young,Delmon	Health B	LIMA Plan	C+
Age 27 Bats R Pos DH LF	PT/Exp B	Rand Var	0
Ht 6' 3" Wt 240	Consist B	MM	2025

Never a patient hitter; now a declining ct% has sent OBA and Eye into a tailspin. In two short years, he's given back almost all the plate approach gains that led to his 2010 breakout (see xBA bell curve). Age, LD% trend, 2H hr/f and post-post hype status remain intriguing, but underlying skills are soft.

Yr Tm	AB	R	HR	RBI	SB	BA	xBA	vL	vR	OB	Slg	OPS	bb%	ct%	h%	Eye	G	L	F	PX	xPX	hr/f	Spd	SBO	SB%	#Wk	DOM	DIS	RC/G	RAR	BPV	BPX	R$
08 MIN	575	80	10	69	14	290	262	300	286	331	405	736	6	82	34	0.33	55	17	28	76	80	8%	103	12%	74%	27	30%	48%	4.80	-1.4	33	65	$20
09 MIN	395	50	12	60	2	284	246	310	271	305	425	730	3	77	34	0.13	50	16	34	92	94	11%	97	7%	29%	25	28%	56%	4.38	-5.7	8	16	$11
10 MIN	570	77	21	112	5	298	291	312	292	331	493	824	5	86	32	0.35	45	15	40	129	119	11%	62	7%	56%	27	67%	7%	5.81	14.6	76	165	$25
11 2 AL *	504	58	13	68	1	267	251	301	256	300	397	696	5	82	30	0.26	47	18	35	88	88	9%	80	1%	100%	23	22%	39%	4.14	-10.7	25	56	$12
12 DET	574	54	18	74	0	267	255	308	247	291	411	702	3	80	30	0.18	43	22	35	93	107	11%	56	2%	0%	27	26%	48%	4.10	-13.1	12	30	$13
1st Half	269	22	6	29	0	268	244	317	246	289	387	675	3	80	32	0.15	44	22	34	82	111	8%	58	2%	0%	13	15%	62%	3.82	-8.3	-1	-3	$9
2nd Half	305	32	12	45	0	266	265	300	249	293	433	726	4	81	29	0.21	42	23	35	102	103	13%	61	1%	0%	14	36%	36%	4.34	-4.8	27	68	$17
13 Proj	**571**	**63**	**19**	**81**	**2**	**273**	**259**	**305**	**259**	**303**	**428**	**730**	**4**	**82**	**31**	**0.23**	**45**	**20**	**35**	**99**	**102**	**11%**	**64**	**3%**	**46%**				**4.48**	**-6.7**	**29**	**73**	**$17**

Young,Michael

Young,Michael	Health A	LIMA Plan	C+
Age 36 Bats R Pos DH 1B 3B	PT/Exp A	Rand Var	+2
Ht 6' 1" Wt 200	Consist F	MM	1235

Great ct%, and still plenty of line drives—so there's room for BA recovery. Power, though, is another story—too many GBs, and rapidly decreasing PX and hr/f. He's turned into a one-trick pony. While that might play well if he still qualified at MI, it's not what you're looking for from a corner infielder.

Yr Tm	AB	R	HR	RBI	SB	BA	xBA	vL	vR	OB	Slg	OPS	bb%	ct%	h%	Eye	G	L	F	PX	xPX	hr/f	Spd	SBO	SB%	#Wk	DOM	DIS	RC/G	RAR	BPV	BPX	R$
08 TEX	645	102	12	82	10	284	271	305	276	340	402	742	8	83	33	0.50	47	23	31	80	102	7%	95	5%	100%	27	37%	41%	4.96	1.3	44	86	$20
09 TEX	541	76	22	68	8	322	302	297	331	376	518	893	8	83	35	0.52	45	22	33	121	140	15%	98	7%	73%	24	50%	25%	7.27	34.5	71	145	$25
10 TEX	656	99	21	91	4	284	276	322	270	334	444	778	7	82	32	0.43	47	18	34	105	104	11%	91	3%	67%	27	37%	30%	5.25	6.7	53	115	$23
11 TEX	631	88	11	106	6	338	301	361	330	383	474	857	7	88	37	0.60	47	26	27	91	112	7%	110	4%	75%	27	52%	19%	6.98	34.5	66	147	$33
12 TEX	611	79	8	67	2	277	277	333	257	314	370	684	5	89	30	0.47	53	23	24	59	68	6%	105	2%	50%	27	30%	30%	4.05	-14.5	33	83	$14
1st Half	308	37	3	31	2	273	271	356	239	309	357	666	5	87	31	0.40	53	23	24	55	56	5%	112	4%	67%	13	23%	31%	3.85	-9.2	26	65	$13
2nd Half	303	42	5	36	0	281	282	303	274	319	383	702	5	90	30	0.57	54	22	24	63	79	8%	93	1%	0%	14	36%	29%	4.26	-5.4	38	95	$16
13 Proj	**559**	**77**	**9**	**73**	**3**	**296**	**278**	**332**	**284**	**339**	**408**	**747**	**6**	**87**	**33**	**0.50**	**50**	**23**	**27**	**72**	**91**	**7%**	**99**	**3%**	**66%**				**4.98**	**1.4**	**42**	**106**	**$20**

Zimmerman,Ryan

Zimmerman,Ryan	Health C	LIMA Plan	B
Age 28 Bats R Pos 3B	PT/Exp A	Rand Var	0
Ht 6' 3" Wt 230	Consist B	MM	4235

Shoulder injury slowed him in 1H, so we'll give him a mulligan. Solid plate approach, xBA history show there's little BA risk. FB% drop in 2011 led to power outage; while it continued in 2012, inflated 2nd half hr/f boosted HRs. If FB% doesn't rebound, HR upside will be limited. Pay for a repeat, with room for more.

Yr Tm	AB	R	HR	RBI	SB	BA	xBA	vL	vR	OB	Slg	OPS	bb%	ct%	h%	Eye	G	L	F	PX	xPX	hr/f	Spd	SBO	SB%	#Wk	DOM	DIS	RC/G	RAR	BPV	BPX	R$
08 WAS	428	51	14	51	1	283	274	333	259	331	442	773	7	83	31	0.44	46	20	34	101	110	12%	95	2%	50%	19	37%	26%	5.16	6.7	43	84	$11
09 WAS	610	110	33	106	2	292	289	270	298	367	525	891	11	80	32	0.61	40	19	42	142	131	16%	98	1%	100%	27	52%	22%	6.95	39.6	81	165	$26
10 WAS	525	85	25	85	4	307	280	331	300	387	510	898	12	81	34	0.70	41	18	41	133	139	14%	80	3%	80%	25	52%	28%	7.28	38.2	73	159	$26
11 WAS	395	52	12	49	3	289	261	338	279	356	443	799	9	82	33	0.56	50	16	34	104	114	11%	102	3%	75%	18	39%	28%	5.64	11.4	51	113	$13
12 WAS	578	93	25	95	5	282	274	307	273	346	478	824	9	80	32	0.49	48	18	33	126	144	16%	80	4%	71%	25	48%	28%	5.85	20.3	60	150	$24
1st Half	252	34	5	31	3	234	242	222	238	296	345	641	8	81	27	0.47	53	16	32	77	116	8%	82	6%	75%	11	18%	55%	3.40	-9.0	25	63	$8
2nd Half	326	59	20	64	2	319	299	367	301	385	580	965	10	79	35	0.51	44	21	35	166	165	22%	79	3%	67%	14	71%	7%	8.31	32.6	89	223	$36
13 Proj	**582**	**89**	**27**	**104**	**4**	**289**	**276**	**319**	**280**	**357**	**494**	**851**	**10**	**81**	**32**	**0.55**	**47**	**18**	**35**	**129**	**134**	**16%**	**80**	**4%**	**73%**				**6.31**	**28.3**	**66**	**165**	**$27**

Zobrist,Ben

Zobrist,Ben	Health A	LIMA Plan	B+
Age 32 Bats B Pos RF 2B SS	PT/Exp A	Rand Var	+1
Ht 6' 3" Wt 210	Consist B	MM	4235

BA, power repeated from 2011; 2010 now looks like the outlier. High bb% and an acceptable ct% make a decent BA likely. However, advancing age and eroding SB% puts his thefts at risk. The consistent BA and HR are gold in H2H (DOM%/DIS%), particularly factoring in the positional flexibility.

Yr Tm	AB	R	HR	RBI	SB	BA	xBA	vL	vR	OB	Slg	OPS	bb%	ct%	h%	Eye	G	L	F	PX	xPX	hr/f	Spd	SBO	SB%	#Wk	DOM	DIS	RC/G	RAR	BPV	BPX	R$
08 TAM *	269	43	15	40	6	265	269	269	242	353	490	843	12	79	29	0.64	44	13	42	137	126	17%	107	9%	83%	17	71%	18%	6.04	16.6	79	155	$9
09 TAM	501	91	27	91	17	297	295	319	287	405	543	948	15	79	33	0.88	42	20	39	148	132	18%	120	13%	74%	27	59%	26%	7.92	56.3	105	214	$27
10 TAM	541	77	10	75	24	238	246	247	235	349	353	702	15	80	28	0.86	44	18	38	82	93	6%	94	15%	89%	27	33%	37%	4.32	6.7	50	109	$15
11 TAM	588	99	20	91	19	269	284	303	253	353	469	823	12	78	31	0.60	45	20	35	144	120	12%	90	15%	76%	27	67%	22%	5.77	31.8	90	200	$25
12 TAM	560	88	20	74	14	270	285	308	253	377	471	849	15	82	30	0.94	43	22	35	128	114	13%	102	13%	61%	27	63%	19%	6.03	34.7	92	230	$21
1st Half	262	44	10	32	7	252	283	258	249	374	458	832	16	82	27	1.09	41	22	37	126	118	13%	104	15%	54%	13	62%	23%	5.54	12.2	96	240	$18
2nd Half	298	44	10	42	7	285	288	368	257	381	483	864	13	81	32	0.82	45	22	33	130	111	12%	99	11%	70%	14	64%	14%	6.49	21.0	85	213	$24
13 Proj	**575**	**91**	**21**	**82**	**15**	**267**	**279**	**301**	**252**	**366**	**467**	**834**	**14**	**80**	**30**	**0.79**	**44**	**20**	**36**	**129**	**114**	**13%**	**96**	**12%**	**69%**				**5.87**	**14.6**	**85**	**214**	**$23**

DAVE ADLER

The following section contains player boxes for every pitcher who had significant playing time in 2012 and/or is expected to get fantasy roster-worthy innings in 2013. In most cases, high-end prospects who have yet to make their major league debuts will not appear here; you can find scouting reports for them in the Prospects section.

Snapshot Section

The top band of each player box contains the following information:

Age as of Opening Day 2013.

Throws right (R) or left (L).

Role: Starters (SP) are those projected to face 18+ batters per game; the rest are relievers (RP).

Ht/Wt: Each batter's height and weight.

Type evaluates the extent to which a pitcher allows the ball to be put into play and his ground ball or fly ball tendency. CON (contact) represents pitchers who allow the ball to be put into play a great deal. PWR (power) represents those with high strikeout and/or walk totals who keep the ball out of play. GB are those who have a ground ball rate more than 50%; xGB are those who have a GB rate more than 55%. FB are those who have a fly ball rate more than 40%; xFB are those who have a FB rate more than 45%.

Reliability Grades analyze each pitcher's forecast risk, on an A-F scale. High grades go to those who have accumulated few disabled list days (Health), have a history of substantial and regular major league playing time (PT/Exp) and have displayed consistent performance over the past three years, using xERA (Consist).

LIMA Plan Grade evaluates how well that pitcher would be a good fit for a team using the LIMA Plan draft strategy. Best grades go to pitchers who have excellent base skills and had a 2012 dollar value less than $20. Lowest grades will go to poor skills and values more than $20.

Random Variance Score (Rand Var) measures the impact random variance had on the pitcher's 2012 stats and the probability that his 2013 performance will exceed or fall short of 2012. The variables tracked are those prone to regression—H%, S%, hr/f and xERA. Players are rated on a scale of –5 to +5 with positive scores indicating rebounds and negative scores indicating corrections. Note that this score is computer-generated and the projections will override it on occasion.

Mayberry Method (MM) acknowledges the imprecision of the forecasting process by projecting player performance in broad strokes. The four digits of MM each represent a fantasy-relevant skill—ERA, strikeout rate, saves potential and playing time (IP)—and are all on a scale of 0 to 5.

Commentaries for each pitcher provide a brief analysis of BPIs and the potential impact on performance in 2013. MLB statistics are listed first for those who played only a portion of 2012 at the major league level. Note that these commentaries generally look at performance related issues only. Role and playing time expectations may impact these analyses, so you will have to adjust accordingly. Upside (UP) and downside (DN) statistical potential appears for some players; these are less grounded in hard data and more speculative of skills potential.

Player Stat Section

The past five years' statistics represent the total accumulated in the majors as well as in Triple-A, Double-A ball and various foreign leagues during each year. All non-major league stats have been converted to a major league equivalent (MLE) performance level. Minor league levels below Double-A are not included.

Nearly all baseball publications separate a player's statistical experiences in the major leagues from the minor leagues and outside leagues. While this may be appropriate for official record-keeping purposes, it is not an easy-to-analyze snapshot of a player's complete performance for a given year.

Bill James has proven that minor league statistics (converted to MLEs), at Double-A level or above, provide as accurate a record of a player's performance as Major league statistics. Other researchers have also devised conversion factors for foreign leagues. Since these are adequate barometers, we include them in the pool of historical data for each year.

Team designations: An asterisk (*) appearing with a team name means that Triple-A and/or Double-A numbers are included in that year's stat line. Any stints of less than 10 IP are not included (to screen out most rehab appearances). A designation of "a/a" means the stats were accumulated at both AA and AAA levels that year. "for" represents a foreign or independent league. The designation "2TM" appears whenever a player was on more than one major league team, crossing leagues, in a season. "2AL" and "2NL" represent more than one team in the same league. Players who were cut during the season and finished 2012 as a free agent are designated as FAA (Free agent, AL) and FAN (Free agent, NL).

Stats: Descriptions of all the categories appear in the Encyclopedia.

- The leading decimal point has been suppressed on some categories to conserve space.
- Data for platoons (vL, vR), balls-in-play (G/L/F) and consistency (Wk#, DOM, DIS) are for major league performance only.
- Formulas that use BIP data, like xERA and BPV, are used for years in which G/L/F data is available. Where feasible, older versions of these formulas are used otherwise.

Earned run average is presented alongside skills-based xERA. WHIP and Opposition Batting Average—which essentially measure the same thing—appear next, and then OBA versus left-handed and right-handed batters. Batters faced per game (BF/G) provide a quick view of a pitcher's role—starters will generally have levels over 20.

Basic pitching skills are measured with Control, or walk rate (Ctl), Dominance, or strikeout rate (Dom), and Command, or strikeout-to-walk rate (Cmd).

Once the ball leaves the bat, it will either be a (G)round ball, (L)ine drive or (F)ly ball. Home runs per 9 innings (hr/9) measures a pitcher's ability to keep the ball in the park. The ratio of home runs to fly balls (hr/f) is the sanity check; levels far from 10% are prone to regression.

Other random variance indicators include hit rate (H%)—often referred to as batting average on balls-in-play (BABIP)—which tends to regress to 30%. Normal strand rates (S%) fall within the tolerances of 65% to 80%.

In looking at consistency for starting pitchers, we track games started (GS), average pitch counts (APC) for all outings (for starters and relievers), the percentage of DOMinating starts (PQS 4 or 5) and DISaster starts (PQS 0 or 1). The larger the variance between DOM and DIS, the greater the consistency.

For relievers, we look at their saves success rate (Sv%) and Leverage Index (LI). A Doug Dennis study showed little correlation between saves success and future opportunity. However, you can increase your odds by prospecting for pitchers who have *both* a high saves percentage (80% or better) *and* high skills. Relievers with LI levels over 1.0 are being used more often by managers to win ballgames.

The final section includes several overall performance measures: runs above replacement (RAR), Base performance value (BPV), Base performance index (BPX, which is BPV indexed to each year's league average) and the Rotisserie value (R$).

2013 Projections

Forecasts are computed from a player's trends over the past five years. Adjustments were made for leading indicators and variances between skill and statistical output. After reviewing the leading indicators, you might opt to make further adjustments.

Although each year's numbers include all playing time at the Double-A level or above, the 2013 forecast only represents potential playing time at the major league level, and again is highly preliminary.

Note that the projected Rotisserie values in this book will not necessarily align with each player's historical actuals. Since we currently have no idea who is going to close games for the Tigers, or whether Dylan Bundy is going to break camp with Baltimore, it is impossible to create a finite pool of playing time, something which is required for valuation. So the projections are roughly based on a 12-team AL/NL league, and include an inflated number of innings, league-wide. This serves to flatten the spread of values and depress individual player dollar projections. In truth, a $25 player in this book might actually be worth $21, or $28. This level of precision is irrelevant in a process that is driven by market forces anyway. So, don't obsess over it.

Be aware of other sources that publish perfectly calibrated Rotisserie values over the winter. They are likely making arbitrary decisions as to where free agents are going to sign and who is going to land jobs in the spring. We do not make those leaps of faith here.

Bottom line… It is far too early to be making definitive projections for 2013, especially on playing time. Focus on the skill levels and trends, then consult BaseballHQ.com for playing time revisions as players change teams and roles become more defined. A free projections update will be available online in March.

Do-it-yourself analysis

Here are some data points you can look at in doing your own player analysis:

- Variance between vLH and vRH opposition batting avg
- Variance in 2012 hr/f rate from 10%
- Variance in 2012 hit rate (H%) from 30%
- Variance in 2012 strand rate (S%) to tolerances (65% - 75%)
- Variance between ERA and xERA each year
- Growth or decline in Base Performance Value (BPV)
- Spikes in innings pitched
- Trends in average pitch counts (APC)
- Trends in DOM/DIS splits
- Trends in saves success rate (Sv%)

Abad,Fernando

Abad,Fernando	Health	D	LIMA Plan	C
Age: 27 Th: L Role RP	PT/Exp	D	Rand Var	+1
Ht: 6' 2" Wt: 215 Type	Consist	C	MM	2300

0-6, 5.09 ERA in 46 IP at HOU. From the That Didn't Work So Well Dept.: As a RP to start the season, logged 24 IP, 0-0 W-L, 3.80 ERA, 3.7 Cmd. As late-season SP, hurled 22 IP, 0-6, 6.45 ERA, 1.2 Cmd. With 1H Cmd and GB%, can't completely write him off, but OBA history says he's not fooling anyone.

Yr Tm	W	L	Sv	IP	K	ERA	xERA	WHIP	OBA	vL	vR	BF/G	Ctl	Dom	Cmd	G	L	F	hr/9	hr/f	H%	S%	GS	APC	DOM%	DIS%	Sv%	LI	RAR	BPV	BPX	R$
08																																
09																																
10 HOU *	4	4	0	65	47	2.84	4.77	1.38	294	179	214	6.7	1.8	6.5	3.6	32	8	59	1.1	9%	34%	84%	0	14			0	1.29	9.9	78	126	$2
11 HOU *	3	7	0	50	40	6.13	6.24	1.60	316	273	381	3.8	2.7	7.3	2.7	35	20	45	1.7	16%	36%	65%	0	15			0	0.93	-13.4	41	62	-$7
12 HOU *	2	6	2	74	60	4.68	5.67	1.62	310	277	331	6.5	3.2	7.4	2.3	43	21	36	1.1	12%	36%	73%	6	22	0%	83%	50	0.67	-6.0	53	69	-$7
1st Half	1	0	2	25	23	1.78	3.86	1.18	243	200	259	3.6	2.5	8.3	3.4	52	16	32	1.4	29%	28%	96%	0	11			67	0.72	7.0	84	109	$3
2nd Half	1	6	0	48	37	6.20	6.57	1.85	341	343	352	10.3	3.5	6.9	2.0	39	24	37	0.9	5%	40%	66%	6	37	0%	83%	0	0.60	-13.0	41	53	-$13
13 Proj	2	4	0	44	35	4.79	4.27	1.56	308	271	330	5.1	2.8	7.2	2.6	44	20	35	1.3	13%	36%	73%	0						-4.2	77	100	-$4

Accardo,Jeremy

Accardo,Jeremy	Health	A	LIMA Plan	F
Age: 31 Th: R Role RP	PT/Exp	D	Rand Var	0
Ht: 6' 1" Wt: 200 Type	Consist	B	MM	0100

0-0, 4.82 ERA in 37 IP at CLE/OAK. The combined numbers say he improved, but his MLB line disagrees. He's not registered a 2.0+ Cmd since 2007; 2012's BPV (46) his first non-negative mark since 2008. There's little use for a reliever that gives up bushels of BB and LD—and can't get RHBs out.

Yr Tm	W	L	Sv	IP	K	ERA	xERA	WHIP	OBA	vL	vR	BF/G	Ctl	Dom	Cmd	G	L	F	hr/9	hr/f	H%	S%	GS	APC	DOM%	DIS%	Sv%	LI	RAR	BPV	BPX	R$
08 TOR	0	3	4	12	5	6.57	5.31	1.54	300	300	300	3.5	2.9	3.6	1.3	46	15	39	0.7	6%	32%	56%	0	13			67	1.38	-3.4	11	20	-$3
09 TOR *	2	1	14	55	40	3.08	4.63	1.59	285	143	386	4.5	4.2	6.5	1.6	46	13	41	0.5	7%	34%	81%	0	17			88	0.87	8.4	55	103	$5
10 TOR *	3	3	24	51	23	3.96	5.28	1.71	326	462	353	4.9	3.1	4.1	1.3	44	33	22	0.2	0%	36%	75%	0	27			86	0.95	0.7	37	60	$6
11 BAL *	4	4	2	71	42	4.46	4.68	1.52	279	257	329	5.4	3.9	5.4	1.4	37	22	41	0.8	10%	31%	72%	0	22			29	0.77	-4.5	36	55	-$3
12 2AL *	1	2	6	61	44	3.96	4.20	1.50	274	217	358	5.6	3.9	6.5	1.6	46	23	31	0.4	8%	33%	73%	0	23			86	0.18	0.4	60	78	-$2
1st Half	0	2	4	37	33	3.64	3.34	1.37	251	143	340	5.3	3.8	8.1	2.1	50	21	29	0.2	6%	32%	72%	0	20			100	0.23	1.7	90	117	-$1
2nd Half	1	0	2	25	11	4.44	5.43	1.69	305	281	382	6.2	4.1	4.0	1.0	42	25	33	0.7	10%	33%	74%	0	27			67	0.10	-1.3	17	22	-$5
13 Proj	1	1	0	36	22	4.31	5.08	1.59	291	235	338	5.4	3.9	5.4	1.4	42	23	35	0.5	5%	33%	73%	0						-1.3	13	17	-$4

Aceves,Alfredo

Aceves,Alfredo	Health	D	LIMA Plan	B
Age: 31 Th: R Role RP	PT/Exp	C	Rand Var	+4
Ht: 6' 3" Wt: 220 Type FB	Consist	B	MM	2311

More effective at stranding his manager than stranding runners. ERA was inflated, and showed in the 1H he still has his 2009 skills. But repeated implosions on the mound and explosions in the clubhouse probably nixed future Sv opps. Should bounce back; might even surprise if given chance to start.

Yr Tm	W	L	Sv	IP	K	ERA	xERA	WHIP	OBA	vL	vR	BF/G	Ctl	Dom	Cmd	G	L	F	hr/9	hr/f	H%	S%	GS	APC	DOM%	DIS%	Sv%	LI	RAR	BPV	BPX	R$
08 NYY *	5	5	0	124	77	3.72	4.27	1.28	268	238	213	22.1	2.3	5.6	2.5	42	17	41	1.2	11%	29%	76%	4	77	50%	25%	0	0.74	9.3	51	96	$6
09 NYY *	12	1	1	108	83	4.01	3.30	1.07	235	212	228	8.9	1.9	6.9	3.7	35	17	48	1.2	9%	26%	67%	1	29	0%	100%	50	1.20	4.2	92	172	$12
10 NYY	3	0	1	12	2	3.00	5.36	1.17	208	235	194	5.3	3.0	1.5	0.5	50	20	30	0.8	7%	22%	77%	0	19			100	0.81	1.6	-26	-42	-$1
11 BOS	10	2	2	114	80	2.61	4.22	1.11	204	190	216	8.6	3.3	6.3	1.9	40	15	45	0.6	5%	24%	79%	4	32	25%	25%	40	0.97	18.8	42	63	$14
12 BOS	2	10	25	84	75	5.36	4.20	1.32	254	269	239	5.2	3.3	8.0	2.4	37	22	41	1.2	11%	30%	61%	0	21			76	1.28	-13.9	70	91	$5
1st Half	0	5	18	40	40	4.28	3.51	1.15	228	256	194	4.5	2.9	9.0	3.1	43	23	34	0.7	8%	29%	63%	0	18			86	1.42	-1.3	104	135	$13
2nd Half	2	5	7	44	35	6.34	4.83	1.48	277	280	273	6.1	3.7	7.2	1.9	32	22	46	1.6	13%	30%	60%	0	24			58	1.12	-12.6	40	52	-$2
13 Proj	5	6	8	87	69	4.38	4.24	1.24	242	247	238	6.7	3.0	7.1	2.4	38	19	43	1.1	10%	28%	67%	0						-3.9	62	81	$5

Acosta,Manny

Acosta,Manny	Health	A	LIMA Plan	D+
Age: 32 Th: R Role RP	PT/Exp	D	Rand Var	+3
Ht: 6' 4" Wt: 215 Type Pwr	Consist	A	MM	2300

1-3, 6.46 ERA in 47 IP at NYM. Designated for assignment in late May, he righted himself at Triple-A and was much improved in the 2H. Or was he? BPI didn't move that much, but good fortune went to the extreme (see 2H hr/f and H%). As long as his Cmd holds, he'll have a seat on the quad-A shuttle.

Yr Tm	W	L	Sv	IP	K	ERA	xERA	WHIP	OBA	vL	vR	BF/G	Ctl	Dom	Cmd	G	L	F	hr/9	hr/f	H%	S%	GS	APC	DOM%	DIS%	Sv%	LI	RAR	BPV	BPX	R$
08 ATL	3	5	3	53	31	3.57	4.63	1.40	247	280	218	4.9	4.4	5.3	1.2	53	19	28	1.2	16%	26%	79%	0	18			60	1.00	5.0	7	12	$1
09 ATL *	2	4	2	65	51	3.99	5.40	1.64	283	297	302	5.3	4.8	7.2	1.5	44	19	37	1.2	9%	33%	80%	0	19			100	0.55	2.6	36	68	-$2
10 NYM *	5	5	6	76	69	3.50	3.57	1.30	230	163	245	4.5	4.1	8.2	2.0	42	18	41	1.0	10%	28%	76%	0	16			55	0.90	5.4	71	116	$6
11 NYM *	5	1	8	67	65	3.04	4.20	1.47	258	247	286	4.5	4.4	8.7	2.0	37	24	39	0.8	11%	32%	82%	0	17			67	1.05	7.5	73	110	$4
12 NYM *	1	4	1	75	64	5.04	4.37	1.41	267	253	264	5.1	3.5	7.6	2.2	39	26	35	1.0	15%	32%	65%	0	18			33	0.71	-9.6	64	84	-$6
1st Half	1	2	0	37	35	7.69	6.74	1.80	330	362	360	6.0	3.7	8.6	2.3	35	30	35	1.5	23%	40%	58%	0	23			0	0.78	-16.6	46	60	-$16
2nd Half	0	2	1	39	29	2.53	2.07	1.05	195	94	179	4.4	3.3	6.7	2.0	44	22	34	0.5	5%	23%	77%	0	14			50	0.66	7.1	84	109	$4
13 Proj	2	2	0	51	44	4.15	4.27	1.38	252	239	262	4.8	3.9	7.8	2.0	41	23	36	0.9	9%	30%	72%	0						-0.8	54	70	-$2

Adams,Mike

Adams,Mike	Health	C	LIMA Plan	A+
Age: 34 Th: R Role RP	PT/Exp	C	Rand Var	-1
Ht: 6' 5" Wt: 195 Type Pwr	Consist	B	MM	3400

A relief horse for years, but concerns mushroomed in 2012: big Dom dip; Ctl on the rise; thoroughly mediocre 2H. Then he was diagnosed with mild thoratic outlet syndrome in Sept, which could result in surgery and delay his 2013. At 34, he could recover—but no one will blame you if you dismount.

Yr Tm	W	L	Sv	IP	K	ERA	xERA	WHIP	OBA	vL	vR	BF/G	Ctl	Dom	Cmd	G	L	F	hr/9	hr/f	H%	S%	GS	APC	DOM%	DIS%	Sv%	LI	RAR	BPV	BPX	R$
08 SD	2	3	0	65	74	2.48	3.13	1.04	209	228	190	4.8	2.6	10.2	3.9	42	18	40	1.0	11%	28%	82%	0	19			0	0.92	14.9	133	249	$7
09 SD	0	0	0	37	45	0.73	2.53	0.59	111	130	88	3.7	1.9	10.9	5.6	51	7	42	0.2	3%	18%	90%	0	15			0	1.13	16.4	173	325	$7
10 SD	4	1	0	67	73	1.76	3.25	1.07	196	185	206	3.8	3.1	9.9	3.2	41	20	39	0.3	3%	29%	84%	0	15			0	1.33	19.1	113	182	$9
11 2TM	5	4	2	74	74	1.47	2.88	0.79	169	189	143	3.7	1.7	9.0	5.3	45	14	41	0.6	7%	23%	87%	0	14			40	1.20	22.5	140	210	$15
12 TEX	5	3	1	52	45	3.27	3.97	1.39	269	290	248	3.7	2.9	7.7	2.6	47	21	32	0.7	8%	34%	78%	0	14			50	1.32	4.8	85	111	$0
1st Half	1	2	1	27	23	2.96	3.76	1.32	266	281	244	3.6	2.3	7.6	3.3	48	23	30	0.3	4%	34%	77%	0	13			50	1.30	3.6	100	130	$0
2nd Half	4	1	0	25	22	3.60	4.21	1.48	273	302	250	3.9	3.6	7.9	2.2	46	19	35	1.1	12%	33%	79%	0	15			0	1.35	1.3	69	90	$1
13 Proj	5	2	1	55	50	3.44	3.68	1.24	250	266	233	3.8	2.7	8.2	3.1	45	18	37	0.6	7%	31%	73%	0						3.9	99	129	$3

Adcock,Nathan

Adcock,Nathan	Health	A	LIMA Plan	D
Age: 25 Th: R Role RP	PT/Exp	D	Rand Var	+2
Ht: 6' 4" Wt: 225 Type Con GB	Consist	B	MM	1100

0-3, 2.34 ERA in 35 IP at KC. The things second-division clubs can do: Pick a high-A arm in the Rule 5 draft, baby his 2011 innings, give him the high-minors time he desparately needs in 2012, reap the rewards in 2013. Or not. Do these look like MLB skills? Sigh ... the things second-division clubs do.

Yr Tm	W	L	Sv	IP	K	ERA	xERA	WHIP	OBA	vL	vR	BF/G	Ctl	Dom	Cmd	G	L	F	hr/9	hr/f	H%	S%	GS	APC	DOM%	DIS%	Sv%	LI	RAR	BPV	BPX	R$
08																																
09																																
10																																
11 KC	1	1	1	60	36	4.62	4.31	1.48	272	260	281	11.0	3.9	5.4	1.4	56	19	26	0.7	10%	30%	69%	3	40	33%	33%	100	0.53	-5.1	26	39	-$4
12 KC *	8	9	0	134	70	5.04	4.89	1.54	304	237	319	18.9	2.8	4.7	1.7	50	17	33	0.6	11%	34%	66%	2	43	50%	50%	0	0.89	-16.9	40	53	-$11
1st Half	4	5	0	68	33	4.07	3.96	1.39	264	277	333	16.7	3.4	4.4	1.3	48	17	34	0.6	10%	29%	71%	2	45	50%	50%	0	0.98	-0.5	37	48	-$4
2nd Half	4	4	0	66	37	6.02	5.79	1.70	340	83	278	21.4	2.2	5.0	2.2	55	18	27	0.5	17%	38%	63%	0	38			0	0.63	-16.4	49	64	-$18
13 Proj	2	2	0	44	24	4.97	4.72	1.53	294	271	314	14.7	3.2	5.0	1.6	51	18	31	0.7	7%	33%	67%	6						-5.1	33	43	-$5

Affeldt,Jeremy

Affeldt,Jeremy	Health	B	LIMA Plan	A
Age: 34 Th: L Role RP	PT/Exp	C	Rand Var	-3
Ht: 6' 4" Wt: 230 Type Pwr xGB	Consist	A	MM	4410

Home, freak home? In 2011, he sliced a finger separating frozen hamburgers; in 2012, it was a sprained knee picking up his child. But a favorable H%/S% (2011) and hr/f (2012) have provided counterbalance and a sub-3.00 ERA. xERA, GB%, Dom all strong. But DN: Another domestic disaster.

Yr Tm	W	L	Sv	IP	K	ERA	xERA	WHIP	OBA	vL	vR	BF/G	Ctl	Dom	Cmd	G	L	F	hr/9	hr/f	H%	S%	GS	APC	DOM%	DIS%	Sv%	LI	RAR	BPV	BPX	R$
08 CIN	1	1	0	78	80	3.33	3.26	1.31	260	269	255	4.5	2.9	9.2	3.2	54	18	28	1.0	15%	33%	79%	0	18			0	0.65	9.6	120	225	$3
09 SF	2	2	0	62	55	1.73	3.29	1.17	197	211	187	3.4	4.5	7.9	1.8	65	17	18	0.4	10%	24%	87%	0	13			0	1.44	19.9	65	122	$6
10 SF	4	3	4	50	44	4.14	3.93	1.60	290	290	290	4.3	4.3	7.9	1.8	56	19	26	0.7	11%	35%	75%	0	15			57	1.17	-0.4	60	97	$0
11 SF	3	2	3	62	54	2.63	3.24	1.15	207	144	248	3.9	3.5	7.9	2.3	62	16	22	0.7	14%	26%	80%	0	15			50	1.18	10.0	87	131	$5
12 SF	1	2	3	63	57	2.70	3.37	1.26	241	236	244	4.0	3.3	8.1	2.5	60	20	20	0.1	3%	32%	77%	0	15			75	1.22	10.3	96	125	$3
1st Half	0	1	1	29	25	2.48	3.39	1.21	239	227	246	4.4	2.8	7.8	2.8	58	22	20	0.3	6%	31%	79%	0	16			50	1.10	5.5	100	130	$1
2nd Half	1	1	2	34	32	2.88	3.35	1.31	242	242	242	3.7	3.7	8.4	2.3	62	19	19	0.0	0%	32%	76%	0	14			100	1.30	4.8	92	120	$5
13 Proj	2	2	3	58	52	3.05	3.43	1.29	240	224	252	3.8	3.6	8.1	2.3	60	19	21	0.4	8%	31%	76%	0						6.9	88	114	$3

BRENT HERSHEY

Albers,Matt		Health	B	LIMA Plan	B
Age: 30	Th: R Role RP	PT/Exp	C	Rand Var	-5
Ht: 6' 0"	Wt: 225 Type Pwr GB	Consist	A	MM	2300

Pay attention: Might be the only time you'll see 20% hr/f and a 2.39 ERA in the same stat line. Chalk it up to the power of a fortunate H%/S% (with a close 2nd to GB profile). Regardless, his 1H/2H splits showcase the quest for a Ctl/Dom Happy Zone. ERA will regress, but could still be useful.

Yr	Tm	W	L	Sv	IP	K	ERA	xERA	WHIP	OBA	vL	vR	BF/G	Ctl	Dom	Cmd	G	L	F	hr/9	hr/f	H%	S%	GS	APC	DOM%	DIS%	Sv%	LI	RAR	BPV	BPX	R$
08	BAL	3	3	0	49	26	3.49	4.75	1.33	240	163	312	7.4	4.0	4.8	1.2	53	12	34	0.7	8%	26%	75%	3	28	33%	33%	0	1.11	5.0	8	15	$0
09	BAL	3	6	0	67	49	5.51	4.86	1.73	303	342	273	5.5	4.8	6.6	1.4	48	20	31	0.4	4%	35%	66%	0	21			0	1.01	-9.8	14	26	-$7
10	BAL	5	3	0	76	49	4.52	4.32	1.48	269	297	250	5.3	4.0	5.8	1.4	56	15	29	0.7	9%	30%	70%	0	21			0	0.82	-4.1	30	48	-$2
11	BOS	4	4	0	65	68	4.73	3.76	1.44	251	263	243	5.2	4.3	9.5	2.2	46	18	35	1.0	11%	32%	69%	0	21			0	0.83	-6.3	78	117	-$3
12	2 TM	3	1	0	60	44	2.39	3.76	1.13	215	207	220	3.8	3.3	6.6	2.0	55	19	26	1.3	20%	23%	88%	0	14			0	1.02	12.1	63	82	$4
1st Half		2	0	0	30	19	2.67	3.88	1.09	221	231	216	4.4	2.4	5.6	2.4	54	18	28	1.5	19%	23%	86%	0	16			0	0.97	5.0	69	90	$4
2nd Half		1	1	0	30	25	2.10	3.64	1.17	208	186	224	3.4	4.2	7.5	1.8	57	19	23	1.2	22%	22%	90%	0	13			0	1.06	7.1	57	74	$5
13	**Proj**	**2**	**2**	**0**	**44**	**35**	**3.47**	**4.01**	**1.30**	**236**	**237**	**236**	**4.4**	**3.9**	**7.2**	**1.9**	**53**	**18**	**29**	**1.1**	**14%**	**27%**	**77%**	**0**						**2.9**	**56**	**73**	**$0**

Alburquerque,Al		Health	F	LIMA Plan	C
Age: 27	Th: R Role RP	PT/Exp	D	Rand Var	-5
Ht: 6' 0"	Wt: 195 Type Pwr xGB	Consist	C	MM	4500

Returned in Sept from elbow surgery and looked like his 2011 self: Tons of Ks, too many walks, bushels of GBs. It's an acceptable reliever profile, especially when you reduce your opponents to Mario Mendoza. With an adjustment to reduce the free passes (and opportunity) ... UP: 25 saves.

Yr	Tm	W	L	Sv	IP	K	ERA	xERA	WHIP	OBA	vL	vR	BF/G	Ctl	Dom	Cmd	G	L	F	hr/9	hr/f	H%	S%	GS	APC	DOM%	DIS%	Sv%	LI	RAR	BPV	BPX	R$
08																																	
09	aa	1	3	0	26	25	5.02	3.92	1.57	273			5.0	4.6	8.4	1.8				0.0		36%	65%							-2.3	89	167	-$4
10	aa	2	4	3	34	25	6.69	4.90	1.72	289			6.2	5.2	6.5	1.3				0.4		35%	58%							-11.1	52	84	-$5
11	DET	6	1	0	43	67	1.87	2.65	1.15	142	176	113	4.4	6.0	13.9	2.3	57	14	30	0.0	0%	28%	82%	0	19			0	1.08	11.1	123	185	$6
12	DET	0	0	0	13	18	0.68	2.80	1.05	133	136	130	6.6	5.4	12.2	2.3	63	11	26	0.0	0%	23%	93%	0	29			0	1.55	5.5	114	149	-$1
1st Half																																	
2nd Half		0	0	0	13	18	0.68	2.80	1.05	133	136	130	6.6	5.4	12.2	2.3	63	11	26	0.0	0%	23%	93%	0	29			0	1.55	5.5	114	148	-$1
13	**Proj**	**5**	**3**	**0**	**44**	**53**	**3.85**	**3.56**	**1.38**	**209**	**260**	**166**	**4.9**	**5.7**	**11.0**	**1.9**	**57**	**14**	**30**	**0.1**	**2%**	**31%**	**70%**	**0**						**0.9**	**78**	**101**	**$0**

Alvarez,Henderson		Health	A	LIMA Plan	D+
Age: 23	Th: R Role SP	PT/Exp	C	Rand Var	+3
Ht: 6' 1"	Wt: 210 Type Con xGB	Consist	B	MM	2003

Numbers looked completely different than his 10-start sample in 2011. Lack of strikeouts and opponents ability to square balls up doomed his season. Still has a nice xGB foundation, Dom was closer to respectable in 2H, and hr/f was not kind—but it's a long road even with youth on his side.

Yr	Tm	W	L	Sv	IP	K	ERA	xERA	WHIP	OBA	vL	vR	BF/G	Ctl	Dom	Cmd	G	L	F	hr/9	hr/f	H%	S%	GS	APC	DOM%	DIS%	Sv%	LI	RAR	BPV	BPX	R$
08																																	
09																																	
10																																	
11	TOR *	9	7	0	152	99	3.51	3.84	1.20	268	252	274	24.4	1.5	5.9	4.0	53	20	26	1.0	15%	30%	74%	10	98	50%	0%			8.1	91	137	$9
12	TOR	9	14	0	187	79	4.85	4.57	1.44	290	312	265	26.0	2.6	3.8	1.5	57	19	24	1.4	18%	29%	70%	31	92	32%	19%			-19.3	33	43	-$9
1st Half		5	6	0	102	32	4.15	4.53	1.34	287	308	263	26.9	1.9	2.8	1.5	58	17	25	1.5	19%	28%	75%	16	94	31%	13%			-1.6	37	48	-$3
2nd Half		4	8	0	85	47	5.70	4.61	1.56	294	316	267	25.1	3.5	5.0	1.4	55	21	24	1.3	17%	31%	65%	15	91	33%	27%			-17.7	29	38	-$17
13	**Proj**	**9**	**11**	**0**	**174**	**93**	**4.43**	**4.17**	**1.36**	**282**	**291**	**271**	**25.1**	**2.3**	**4.8**	**2.1**	**55**	**20**	**25**	**1.2**	**16%**	**30%**	**71%**	**29**						**-8.9**	**58**	**76**	**$1**

Anderson,Brett		Health	F	LIMA Plan	B+
Age: 25	Th: L Role SP	PT/Exp	C	Rand Var	-1
Ht: 6' 4"	Wt: 235 Type xGB	Consist	A	MM	4203

4-2, 2.57 ERA in 35 IP at OAK. Picked right up where he left off before 2011's Tommy John surgery: Flashed the Ctl, Cmd and xGB that produce BPVs near triple digits. Oh, and another injury that wiped out the season's final two weeks. Stellar results when he gets the ball. WHEN. Rich Harden, anyone?

Yr	Tm	W	L	Sv	IP	K	ERA	xERA	WHIP	OBA	vL	vR	BF/G	Ctl	Dom	Cmd	G	L	F	hr/9	hr/f	H%	S%	GS	APC	DOM%	DIS%	Sv%	LI	RAR	BPV	BPX	R$
08	aa	2	1	0	31	32	2.57	3.05	1.14	239			20.5	2.3	9.4	4.1				0.7		31%	81%							6.7	128	240	$1
09	OAK	11	11	0	175	150	4.06	3.62	1.28	265	313	247	24.5	2.3	7.7	3.3	51	15	34	1.0	11%	32%	71%	30	94	50%	20%			5.8	105	197	$11
10	OAK	7	6	0	112	75	2.80	3.57	1.19	257	299	243	24.7	1.8	6.0	3.4	55	17	28	0.5	6%	30%	77%	19	95	58%	11%			17.7	94	151	$9
11	OAK	3	6	0	83	61	4.00	3.55	1.33	270	303	252	27.4	2.7	6.6	2.4	57	18	25	0.9	13%	31%	72%	13	104	54%	31%			-0.6	81	121	-$1
12	OAK *	5	3	0	58	40	3.30	3.50	1.20	261	219	227	21.3	1.8	6.2	3.4	60	24	17	0.7	6%	30%	74%	6	88	83%	17%			5.1	91	119	$2
1st Half																																	
2nd Half		5	3	0	58	40	3.30	3.48	1.20	261	219	227	21.3	1.8	6.2	3.4	60	24	17	0.7	6%	30%	74%	6	88	83%	17%			5.2	91	118	$2
13	**Proj**	**9**	**8**	**0**	**145**	**109**	**3.34**	**3.51**	**1.23**	**261**	**291**	**250**	**23.1**	**2.1**	**6.8**	**3.2**	**56**	**19**	**25**	**0.7**	**10%**	**31%**	**75%**	**25**						**12.1**	**99**	**128**	**$11**

Archer,Chris		Health	A	LIMA Plan	B
Age: 24	Th: R Role SP	PT/Exp	D	Rand Var	+2
Ht: 6' 3"	Wt: 200 Type Pwr GB	Consist	D	MM	2401

1-3, 4.60 ERA in 29 IP at TAM. Hard thrower with swing-and-miss stuff finally reined in his Ctl; overall BPV marks the progress. Surface stats misleading, and didn't wilt upon his MLB promotion: 11.0 Dom, 3.29 xERA, 113 BPV in small sample. Might not happen right away, but UP: another young TAM SP stud.

Yr	Tm	W	L	Sv	IP	K	ERA	xERA	WHIP	OBA	vL	vR	BF/G	Ctl	Dom	Cmd	G	L	F	hr/9	hr/f	H%	S%	GS	APC	DOM%	DIS%	Sv%	LI	RAR	BPV	BPX	R$
08																																	
09																																	
10	aa	8	2	0	70	57	2.02	2.69	1.29	211			22.1	4.8	7.4	1.5				0.3		27%	85%							17.7	81	130	$7
11	a/a	9	7	0	147	112	4.36	4.74	1.63	277			24.3	4.9	6.9	1.4				0.6		33%	73%							-7.7	51	76	-$6
12	TAM *	8	12	0	157	154	4.26	3.28	1.33	234	300	164	21.1	4.2	8.8	2.1	44	18	38	0.5	11%	30%	67%	4	82	75%	0%	0	0.99	-4.7	89	116	$3
1st Half		4	10	0	88	90	5.28	3.72	1.45	247	238	136	23.6	4.7	9.2	2.0	34	24	41	0.5	8%	33%	62%	2	88	100%	0%			-13.8	86	112	-$3
2nd Half		4	2	0	69	63	2.94	2.67	1.18	216	368	178	18.4	3.6	8.3	2.3	50	14	36	0.5	13%	27%	76%	2	79	50%	0%	0	1.05	9.1	94	122	$10
13	**Proj**	**8**	**6**	**0**	**116**	**104**	**3.79**	**4.14**	**1.37**	**244**	**384**	**185**	**21.7**	**4.1**	**8.1**	**2.0**	**50**	**14**	**36**	**0.5**	**5%**	**31%**	**72%**	**22**						**3.3**	**63**	**82**	**$4**

Arredondo,Jose		Health	B	LIMA Plan	C+
Age: 29	Th: R Role RP	PT/Exp	D	Rand Var	-3
Ht: 6' 0"	Wt: 175 Type Pwr	Consist	B	MM	2400

The effect of 1st half H%/S% gift still felt in season-ending ERA despite the reality of 2nd half ERA/xERA regression. Truth is, skills metrics didn't move that much after June. Logs loads of Ks, but all the free passes mean he can't be trusted with the lead in the 9th. Which is all we really care about.

Yr	Tm	W	L	Sv	IP	K	ERA	xERA	WHIP	OBA	vL	vR	BF/G	Ctl	Dom	Cmd	G	L	F	hr/9	hr/f	H%	S%	GS	APC	DOM%	DIS%	Sv%	LI	RAR	BPV	BPX	R$
08	LAA *	11	3	10	78	67	1.76	2.17	1.04	200	148	236	4.5	3.0	7.8	2.6	51	17	31	0.6	6%	25%	86%	0	18			59	1.23	24.6	100	187	$18
09	LAA *	3	4	1	66	66	4.90	4.34	1.50	251	238	295	4.6	5.0	9.0	1.8	44	18	38	1.0	12%	32%	69%	0	18			50	0.95	-4.7	68	127	-$2
10																																	
11	CIN *	6	5	0	69	65	3.09	3.25	1.34	220	238	218	4.4	4.9	8.5	1.7	42	19	39	0.7	9%	28%	79%	0	18			0	0.85	7.2	79	118	$3
12	CIN	6	2	1	61	62	2.95	4.16	1.38	225	165	277	4.0	5.0	9.1	1.8	45	20	34	1.0	13%	28%	83%	0	17			50	0.83	8.0	52	68	$2
1st Half		4	1	1	33	37	1.89	3.88	1.17	164	89	233	4.0	5.4	10.0	1.9	45	19	36	0.8	11%	22%	89%	0	16			50	0.82	8.7	57	74	$9
2nd Half		2	1	0	28	25	4.23	4.52	1.63	293	255	322	3.9	4.6	8.1	1.8	46	21	33	1.3	14%	34%	78%	0	17			0	0.84	-0.7	47	61	-$5
13	**Proj**	**5**	**3**	**0**	**58**	**56**	**3.66**	**4.22**	**1.40**	**234**	**200**	**263**	**4.2**	**4.9**	**8.7**	**1.8**	**45**	**19**	**36**	**0.9**	**11%**	**29%**	**77%**	**0**						**2.6**	**48**	**62**	**$1**

Arrieta,Jake		Health	B	LIMA Plan	D
Age: 27	Th: R Role SP	PT/Exp	C	Rand Var	+5
Ht: 6' 4"	Wt: 225 Type Pwr	Consist	A	MM	1301

3-9, 6.20 ERA in 109 IP at BAL. How much longer to wait? Cmd headed in right direction but got killed by H%, S%, hr/f again. With a career 5.33 ERA, many have moved on, but rising PQS DOM and 1H BPV indicate he might be close. Speculative profit potential, and dirt cheap at that. UP: Sub-4.00 ERA

Yr	Tm	W	L	Sv	IP	K	ERA	xERA	WHIP	OBA	vL	vR	BF/G	Ctl	Dom	Cmd	G	L	F	hr/9	hr/f	H%	S%	GS	APC	DOM%	DIS%	Sv%	LI	RAR	BPV	BPX	R$
08																																	
09	a/a	11	11	0	151	120	5.02	5.48	1.60	299			23.8	3.6	7.2	2.0				1.2		35%	71%							-13.0	45	85	-$3
10	BAL *	12	8	0	173	104	3.67	3.87	1.41	250	315	213	24.5	4.3	5.4	1.3	42	19	39	0.7	7%	28%	75%	18	95	17%	33%			8.8	44	71	$5
11	BAL	10	8	0	119	93	5.05	4.45	1.46	253	253	252	23.8	4.4	7.0	1.6	46	16	39	1.6	15%	28%	70%	22	95	32%	23%			-16.3	30	45	-$4
12	BAL *	8	13	0	171	151	6.08	4.68	1.45	274	291	249	21.5	3.5	8.0	2.3	44	24	32	1.1	15%	33%	58%	18	82	44%	50%	0	0.79	-43.4	64	83	-$14
1st Half		3	9	0	98	86	5.81	3.90	1.38	276	288	260	24.9	2.6	7.9	3.1	43	24	32	1.2	13%	33%	59%	17	98	47%	47%			-21.5	94	122	-$13
2nd Half		5	4	0	73	65	6.44	4.63	1.55	267	320	194	18.8	4.7	8.0	1.7	48	20	33	0.9	23%	32%	58%	1	41	0%	100%	0	0.84	-21.8	58	76	-$17
13	**Proj**	**8**	**8**	**0**	**116**	**94**	**4.94**	**4.46**	**1.48**	**267**	**297**	**237**	**22.0**	**4.0**	**7.3**	**1.8**	**45**	**19**	**36**	**1.1**	**11%**	**31%**	**69%**	**23**						**-13.2**	**45**	**59**	**-$3**

BRENT HERSHEY

Arroyo,Bronson

Age: 36 Th: R Role SP	Health A	LIMA Plan C	
Ht: 6' 4" Wt: 195 Type Con	PT/Exp A	Rand Var 0	
	Consist A	MM 2105	

Now here's an outlier: After disastrous 2011, the 35-year-old came to camp in "best shape of my life"—and had his best skills season since 2004. Improved Cmd and OBA were key. At his age, a full repeat is unlikely, though he's proven his knack to log innings and outpitch his xERA.

Yr Tm	W	L	Sv	IP	K	ERA	xERA	WHIP	OBA	vL	vR	BF/G	Ctl	Dom	Cmd	G	L	F	hr/9	hr/f	H%	S%	GS	APC	DOM%	DIS%	Sv%	LI	RAR	BPV	BPX	R$
08 CIN	15	11	0	200	163	4.77	4.18	1.44	281	314	254	25.6	3.1	7.3	2.4	41	23	36	1.3	13%	32%	70%	34	101	50%	18%			-11.0	68	128	$4
09 CIN	15	13	0	220	127	3.84	4.41	1.27	256	278	236	28.0	2.7	5.2	2.0	45	19	37	1.3	12%	27%	75%	33	103	45%	18%			13.1	45	84	$15
10 CIN	17	10	0	216	121	3.88	4.27	1.15	234	285	185	26.7	2.5	5.0	2.1	43	16	40	1.2	11%	25%	71%	33	99	52%	21%			5.3	45	73	$15
11 CIN	9	12	0	199	108	5.07	4.51	1.37	286	317	258	26.7	2.0	4.9	2.4	39	19	43	2.1	16%	29%	71%	32	97	38%	22%			-27.6	50	75	-$6
12 CIN	12	10	0	202	129	3.74	4.14	1.21	267	287	245	26.1	1.6	5.7	3.7	41	21	37	1.2	11%	29%	73%	32	92	50%	9%			6.8	80	105	$11
1st Half	3	5	0	94	64	4.13	4.21	1.25	278	320	224	26.2	1.4	6.1	4.3	37	21	41	1.4	12%	30%	73%	15	95	40%	13%			-1.3	87	113	$4
2nd Half	9	5	0	108	65	3.41	4.09	1.17	258	254	262	26.0	1.7	5.4	3.3	45	21	34	0.9	9%	29%	74%	17	91	59%	6%			8.2	75	98	$18
13 Proj	**12**	**10**	**0**	**198**	**120**	**4.13**	**4.31**	**1.25**	**268**	**294**	**242**	**25.7**	**2.0**	**5.5**	**2.8**	**41**	**20**	**39**	**1.4**	**12%**	**28%**	**72%**	**31**						**-2.7**	**65**	**84**	**$9**

Atchison,Scott

Age: 37 Th: R Role RP	Health C	LIMA Plan B+	
Ht: 6' 2" Wt: 200 Type	PT/Exp D	Rand Var -5	
	Consist A	MM 3200	

Bailed out beleaguered BOS bullpen in 1H, but then came the dreaded "forearm tightness"-to-torn UCL story. Chose rehab over TJS—understandable given his age and one-last-shot mentality—and returned in Sept. Excellent skills, but health risk precludes giving him one last shot on YOUR roster.

Yr Tm	W	L	Sv	IP	K	ERA	xERA	WHIP	OBA	vL	vR	BF/G	Ctl	Dom	Cmd	G	L	F	hr/9	hr/f	H%	S%	GS	APC	DOM%	DIS%	Sv%	LI	RAR	BPV	BPX	R$
08 for	7	6	0	104	81	4.62	4.72	1.38	276			10.4	2.8	7.0	2.5				1.3		31%	70%							-3.8	56	104	$2
09 for	5	3	0	90	77	2.11	2.02	0.99	202			4.6	2.5	7.7	3.1				0.5		25%	81%							24.5	111	207	$13
10 BOS	2	3	0	60	41	4.50	4.21	1.28	252	290	220	5.9	2.9	6.2	2.2	48	11	41	1.4	12%	28%	69%	1	23	0%	100%	0	0.95	-3.1	60	97	-$1
11 BOS *	7	2	6	92	69	3.81	3.95	1.28	281	289	273	7.1	1.6	6.8	4.1	46	26	28	0.7	0%	33%	71%	0	28			60	0.38	1.5	107	160	$5
12 BOS	2	1	0	51	36	1.58	3.41	0.99	223	188	252	4.8	1.6	6.3	4.0	55	17	28	0.4	5%	27%	86%	0	17			0	0.79	15.4	104	136	$6
1st Half	2	1	0	41	30	1.54	3.50	1.00	216	197	232	4.8	2.0	6.6	3.3	53	17	30	0.2	3%	27%	85%	0	17			0	0.88	12.5	97	126	$8
2nd Half	0	0	0	10	6	1.74	3.07	0.97	250	158	333	4.4	0.0	5.2	0.0	62	18	21	0.9	14%	28%	89%	0	17			0	0.46	2.9	134	174	-$3
13 Proj	**2**	**1**	**0**	**38**	**28**	**3.60**	**3.78**	**1.17**	**244**	**255**	**235**	**5.7**	**2.3**	**6.7**	**2.9**	**49**	**17**	**34**	**1.0**	**11%**	**28%**	**72%**	**0**						**2.0**	**86**	**112**	**$0**

Aumont,Phillippe

Age: 24 Th: R Role RP	Health A	LIMA Plan D+	
Ht: 6' 7" Wt: 260 Type Pwr xGB	PT/Exp F	Rand Var -1	
	Consist D	MM 3510	

0-0, 3.68 ERA with 2 Sv in 15 IP at PHI. In Tall Pitcher University, "Repeating Your Delivery" is class 101. Ctl history says he's not yet passed the exam—frustrating since two big-league out pitches await (Dom, OBA). If he graduates, the upside is significant, but it's a field littered with drop-outs.

Yr Tm	W	L	Sv	IP	K	ERA	xERA	WHIP	OBA	vL	vR	BF/G	Ctl	Dom	Cmd	G	L	F	hr/9	hr/f	H%	S%	GS	APC	DOM%	DIS%	Sv%	LI	RAR	BPV	BPX	R$
08																																
09 aa	1	4	4	18	22	6.09	6.09	1.96	321			5.6	5.7	11.4	2.0				0.5		45%	67%							-3.9	86	160	-$4
10 aa	1	6	0	50	33	7.93	5.77	1.89	295			21.3	6.4	5.9	0.9				0.7		34%	56%							-23.6	30	48	-$12
11 a/a	2	5	7	54	68	3.10	3.34	1.37	245			5.2	4.1	11.4	2.8				0.4		36%	77%							5.6	122	184	$4
12 PHI *	3	2	17	59	64	5.05	4.00	1.61	233	167	195	4.4	6.8	9.8	1.4	74	3	23	0.5	0%	32%	68%	0	14			81	1.10	-7.6	81	106	$0
1st Half	2	1	9	23	28	5.98	5.00	1.81	246	0	0	4.9	8.1	10.9	1.4				0.9	0%	34%	67%	0	0					-5.6	72	94	$0
2nd Half	1	1	8	36	36	4.45	3.31	1.48	224	167	195	4.1	6.0	9.1	1.5	74	3	23	0.3	0%	30%	68%	0	14			80	1.10	-1.9	88	115	$1
13 Proj	**2**	**4**	**5**	**58**	**63**	**4.77**	**3.93**	**1.57**	**246**			**5.4**	**5.8**	**9.8**	**1.7**	**58**	**15**	**27**	**0.6**	**9%**	**33%**	**69%**	**0**						**-5.4**	**55**	**72**	**-$2**

Avilan,Luis

Age: 23 Th: L Role RP	Health A	LIMA Plan B	
Ht: 6' 2" Wt: 220 Type Pwr GB	PT/Exp D	Rand Var -2	
	Consist C	MM 2200	

1-0, 2.00 ERA in 36 IP at ATL. Mainly a starter at Double-A in the 1H, he pitched exclusively out of the bullpen upon his July promotion; 2H BPI confirmed his comfort level. Improving Dom and Cmd, xGB profile and the ability to retire both LHers and RHers point to a middle reliever with value.

Yr Tm	W	L	Sv	IP	K	ERA	xERA	WHIP	OBA	vL	vR	BF/G	Ctl	Dom	Cmd	G	L	F	hr/9	hr/f	H%	S%	GS	APC	DOM%	DIS%	Sv%	LI	RAR	BPV	BPX	R$
08																																
09																																
10																																
11 aa	4	8	1	105	68	4.82	4.62	1.46	288			12.5	2.9	5.9	2.0				0.8		33%	67%							-11.4	51	77	-$5
12 ATL *	4	6	1	97	81	3.26	3.55	1.31	237	180	231	8.5	3.9	7.5	1.9	47	20	33	0.8	3%	28%	78%	0	18			100	0.91	9.1	69	90	$4
1st Half	2	6	1	56	44	4.35	4.81	1.51	265	0	0	16.3	4.4	7.0	1.6				1.2	0%	30%	75%	0	0					-2.3	40	52	-$1
2nd Half	2	0	0	41	37	1.76	1.78	1.03	196	180	231	4.9	3.1	8.2	2.6	47	20	33	0.2	3%	26%	83%	0	18			0	0.91	11.4	114	148	$11
13 Proj	**2**	**3**	**0**	**58**	**45**	**3.61**	**4.19**	**1.32**	**252**	**215**	**275**	**8.7**	**3.4**	**6.9**	**2.1**	**47**	**19**	**34**	**0.7**	**7%**	**30%**	**74%**	**0**						**2.9**	**59**	**77**	**$0**

Axelrod,Dylan

Age: 27 Th: R Role RP	Health A	LIMA Plan D+	
Ht: 6' 0" Wt: 195 Type Pwr	PT/Exp D	Rand Var 0	
	Consist D	MM 1200	

2-2, 5.47 ERA in 51 IP at CHW. Three stints in AAA, three in majors. Seven GS in MLB, seven relief appearances. Is it a surprise that his numbers got worse in 2012? Cmd, xERA, PQS, BPV from 2011 all preach patience—but at 27, it's high time to give him a consistent home and role to see what you have.

Yr Tm	W	L	Sv	IP	K	ERA	xERA	WHIP	OBA	vL	vR	BF/G	Ctl	Dom	Cmd	G	L	F	hr/9	hr/f	H%	S%	GS	APC	DOM%	DIS%	Sv%	LI	RAR	BPV	BPX	R$
08																																
09																																
10																																
11 CHW *	10	3	0	169	128	3.54	3.58	1.35	270	256	259	23.5	2.7	6.8	2.5	41	22	37	0.3	5%	33%	72%	3	79	67%	33%	0	0.62	8.3	86	129	$6
12 CHW *	9	7	0	148	114	4.71	5.15	1.52	283	277	273	21.4	3.7	7.0	1.9	45	19	36	1.2	13%	32%	72%	7	68	14%	43%	0	0.73	-12.6	42	55	-$7
1st Half	5	5	0	88	66	4.70	5.07	1.47	287	194	311	23.6	3.0	6.8	2.3	46	13	40	1.3	11%	33%	71%	3	74	0%	33%	0	0.61	-7.4	48	62	-$5
2nd Half	4	2	0	60	48	4.72	5.20	1.60	276	328	246	19.0	4.8	7.2	1.5	44	22	34	1.2	15%	32%	73%	4	64	25%	50%	0	0.80	-5.2	38	49	-$10
13 Proj	**3**	**1**	**0**	**44**	**33**	**4.23**	**4.43**	**1.46**	**276**	**277**	**275**	**6.5**	**3.5**	**6.9**	**2.0**	**45**	**19**	**36**	**0.8**	**8%**	**32%**	**72%**	**0**						**-1.1**	**53**	**69**	**-$2**

Axford,John

Age: 30 Th: R Role RP	Health A	LIMA Plan B+	
Ht: 6' 5" Wt: 195 Type Pwr	PT/Exp A	Rand Var +5	
	Consist A	MM 4531	

Here's the risk with stud relievers who have periodic Ctl issues: Double-digit Dom usually covers wildness woes. But when hr/f or S% go haywire, any baserunners become toxic. High ERA + blown saves = panicked chaos. In this case, Dom/Cmd is fine and GB% still strong, so bet on a return.

Yr Tm	W	L	Sv	IP	K	ERA	xERA	WHIP	OBA	vL	vR	BF/G	Ctl	Dom	Cmd	G	L	F	hr/9	hr/f	H%	S%	GS	APC	DOM%	DIS%	Sv%	LI	RAR	BPV	BPX	R$
08																																
09 MIL *	5	0	2	48	47	4.22	3.72	1.48	231	67	308	6.3	5.6	8.8	1.6	33	22	44	0.6	0%	30%	72%	0	20			67	0.19	0.6	75	141	$1
10 MIL	8	2	24	58	76	2.48	2.90	1.19	204	225	183	4.8	4.2	11.8	2.8	48	19	33	0.2	2%	32%	78%	0	20			89	1.37	11.4	125	203	$17
11 MIL	2	2	46	74	86	1.95	3.02	1.14	212	188	233	4.1	3.1	10.5	3.4	50	15	35	0.5	6%	31%	85%	0	17			96	1.15	18.1	135	202	$26
12 MIL	5	8	35	69	93	4.67	3.47	1.44	229	225	234	4.1	5.1	12.1	2.4	46	24	30	1.3	19%	33%	71%	0	19			80	1.22	-5.6	105	136	$12
1st Half	1	5	13	29	41	5.22	3.59	1.53	231	238	222	4.4	5.5	12.6	2.3	45	26	29	1.2	18%	36%	68%	0	20			76	1.36	-4.3	100	130	$5
2nd Half	4	3	22	40	52	4.28	3.38	1.38	228	213	243	4.0	4.7	11.7	2.5	47	22	30	1.4	20%	32%	73%	0	18			81	1.13	-1.3	108	141	$17
13 Proj	**5**	**5**	**40**	**73**	**91**	**3.62**	**3.30**	**1.33**	**228**	**220**	**235**	**4.2**	**4.5**	**11.3**	**2.5**	**48**	**20**	**32**	**0.9**	**12%**	**32%**	**75%**	**0**						**3.6**	**108**	**141**	**$20**

Ayala,Luis

Age: 35 Th: R Role RP	Health B	LIMA Plan B	
Ht: 6' 2" Wt: 175 Type Con	PT/Exp D	Rand Var -4	
	Consist D	MM 2101	

Second year of sub-3.00 ERA in well-used relief role, but xERA again scoffs. At least in 2012, though, a big improvement in Ctl (rather than extreme S% luck) propelled the results. The question is whether you believe in a 35-year-old journeyman with a BDD Reliability rating. Rand Var advises against.

Yr Tm	W	L	Sv	IP	K	ERA	xERA	WHIP	OBA	vL	vR	BF/G	Ctl	Dom	Cmd	G	L	F	hr/9	hr/f	H%	S%	GS	APC	DOM%	DIS%	Sv%	LI	RAR	BPV	BPX	R$
08 2 NL	2	10	9	76	50	5.71	4.41	1.45	287	285	288	4.1	2.9	5.9	2.1	46	22	32	1.1	11%	32%	61%	0	16			60	1.17	-12.9	54	101	-$1
09 2 TM	1	5	0	40	28	5.63	4.73	1.60	318	396	279	4.7	3.2	6.3	2.0	37	19	43	1.1	9%	35%	66%	0	18			0	0.89	-6.4	43	81	-$6
10 aaa	2	10	4	48	21	7.60	7.05	1.94	354			6.3	3.5	4.0	1.1				0.9		38%	59%							-20.7	5	8	-$10
11 NYY	2	2	0	56	39	2.09	3.83	1.27	256	250	263	4.5	3.2	6.3	2.0	50	20	30	0.8	10%	28%	88%	0	17			0	0.83	12.8	54	81	$3
12 BAL	5	5	1	75	51	2.64	3.97	1.27	272	284	262	4.8	1.7	6.1	3.6	49	19	32	0.8	9%	32%	83%	0	18			33	1.08	12.7	92	120	$4
1st Half	2	1	1	37	23	1.96	4.33	1.15	236	239	237	4.9	2.0	5.6	2.9	45	17	38	0.7	7%	28%	87%	0	19			33	1.04	9.3	72	94	$6
2nd Half	3	4	0	38	28	3.29	3.63	1.38	303	328	284	4.8	1.4	6.6	4.7	52	22	25	0.9	13%	35%	80%	0	17			0	1.12	3.5	111	145	$3
13 Proj	**4**	**7**	**0**	**73**	**47**	**3.60**	**4.28**	**1.41**	**287**	**299**	**277**	**4.8**	**2.5**	**5.9**	**2.4**	**47**	**20**	**33**	**0.9**	**9%**	**32%**	**77%**	**0**						**3.7**	**65**	**84**	**$0**

BRENT HERSHEY

Badenhop,Burke

Age: 30	Th: R	Role RP	Health	B	LIMA Plan	B+
Ht: 6' 5"	Wt: 220	Type GB	PT/Exp	D	Rand Var	-1
			Consist	A	MM	3200

Slow but steady improvement since being moved to the bullpen three years ago. Having a consistent GB profile is always an asset; vastly improved Ctl was the big step forward in 2012. But 2H Dom drop and ERA due to rise temper our enthusiasm. Shouldn't hurt you, but doesn't look like late-inning material.

Yr	Tm	W	L	Sv	IP	K	ERA	xERA	WHIP	OBA	vL	vR	BF/G	Ctl	Dom	Cmd	G	L	F	hr/9	hr/f	H%	S%	GS	APC	DOM%	DIS%	Sv%	LI	RAR	BPV	BPX	R$
08	FLA	2	3	0	47	35	6.08	4.39	1.61	289	298	281	16.8	4.0	6.7	1.7	54	20	26	1.3	18%	33%	64%	8	62	25%	38%	0	0.71	-10.3	44	83	-$6
09	FLA	7	4	0	72	57	3.75	3.70	1.32	260	250	269	8.7	3.0	7.1	2.4	54	20	26	0.6	9%	31%	72%	2	34	50%	50%	0	1.06	5.1	79	148	$3
10	FLA *	2	6	1	84	54	3.87	3.57	1.31	256	238	252	5.3	3.1	5.9	1.9	57	14	29	0.5	8%	30%	70%	0	20			33	0.88	2.2	63	101	$1
11	FLA	2	3	1	64	51	4.10	3.54	1.40	265	264	266	5.5	3.4	7.2	2.1	58	21	21	0.1	2%	33%	68%	0	20			100	1.03	-1.2	74	112	-$2
12	TAM	3	2	0	62	42	3.03	3.76	1.20	259	300	239	4.0	1.7	6.1	3.5	53	23	25	0.9	12%	30%	78%	0	14			0	0.78	7.6	93	122	$2
1st Half		1	2	0	33	27	3.78	3.80	1.41	282	250	295	4.2	2.4	7.3	3.0	53	23	24	1.4	19%	33%	79%	0	15			0	0.86	1.0	97	126	-$2
2nd Half		2	0	0	29	15	2.17	3.68	0.97	232	350	162	3.7	0.9	4.7	5.0	53	22	25	0.3	4%	26%	78%	0	12			0	0.68	6.6	89	116	$6
13	**Proj**	**2**	**2**	**0**	**51**	**35**	**3.51**	**3.75**	**1.26**	**261**	**288**	**245**	**4.6**	**2.4**	**6.2**	**2.6**	**55**	**20**	**25**	**0.6**	**8%**	**30%**	**73%**	**0**						**3.2**	**79**	**103**	**$0**

Bailey,Andrew

Age: 29	Th: R	Role RP	Health	F	LIMA Plan	C
Ht: 6' 3"	Wt: 240	Type Pwr FB	PT/Exp	C	Rand Var	+5
			Consist	B	MM	2430

Earned a "D" Health grade in last year's book before thumb surgery sidelined him for almost the entire season. Was predictably erratic upon return, though still flashed solid, though not overwhelming, Dom. Assuming Ctl snaps back, expect his save total to be inversely proportional to his DL days.

Yr	Tm	W	L	Sv	IP	K	ERA	xERA	WHIP	OBA	vL	vR	BF/G	Ctl	Dom	Cmd	G	L	F	hr/9	hr/f	H%	S%	GS	APC	DOM%	DIS%	Sv%	LI	RAR	BPV	BPX	R$
08	aa	5	9	0	111	89	4.52	4.29	1.45	256			12.5	4.3	7.2	1.7				1.0		30%	71%							-2.7	53	100	$0
09	OAK	6	3	26	83	91	1.84	3.18	0.88	167	146	185	4.8	2.6	9.8	3.8	42	13	45	0.5	6%	23%	82%	0	19			87	1.05	25.6	127	238	$27
10	OAK	1	3	25	49	42	1.47	3.55	0.96	199	195	202	4.0	2.4	7.7	3.2	39	16	45	0.6	5%	24%	89%	0	16			89	1.44	15.8	91	148	$16
11	OAK	0	4	24	42	41	3.24	3.57	1.10	218	227	206	4.0	2.6	8.9	3.4	37	17	46	0.6	6%	29%	72%	0	17			92	1.27	3.6	104	157	$10
12	BOS	1	1	6	15	14	7.04	5.29	1.89	318	364	273	3.9	4.7	8.2	1.8	33	23	44	1.2	9%	39%	63%	0	16			67	1.20	-5.7	32	42	-$5
1st Half																																	
2nd Half		1	1	6	15	14	7.04	5.29	1.89	318	364	273	3.9	4.7	8.2	1.8	33	23	44	1.2	9%	39%	63%	0	16			67	1.20	-5.7	32	42	-$5
13	**Proj**	**2**	**4**	**28**	**58**	**54**	**3.86**	**4.11**	**1.30**	**249**	**265**	**233**	**4.3**	**3.3**	**8.4**	**2.5**	**37**	**18**	**45**	**0.8**	**7%**	**31%**	**72%**	**0**						**1.1**	**75**	**98**	**$11**

Bailey,Homer

Age: 27	Th: R	Role SP	Health	D	LIMA Plan	B
Ht: 6' 3"	Wt: 225	Type	PT/Exp	B	Rand Var	0
			Consist	A	MM	3305

Breakthough season was really just a breakthrough 2H, as his pre-July numbers were in lockstep with his history. Then, BOOM: Ctl dipped under 2.0, Dom rose over 8.0, nearly half of BIP ended up on the ground. Luck factors stable, so it may continue. But Health, regression provide counterbalance.

Yr	Tm	W	L	Sv	IP	K	ERA	xERA	WHIP	OBA	vL	vR	BF/G	Ctl	Dom	Cmd	G	L	F	hr/9	hr/f	H%	S%	GS	APC	DOM%	DIS%	Sv%	LI	RAR	BPV	BPX	R$
08	CIN *	4	13	0	148	102	6.40	6.33	1.76	319	305	423	25.0	3.9	6.2	1.6	43	25	31	1.3	19%	36%	65%	8	85	13%	50%			-37.9	23	44	-$16
09	CIN *	16	10	0	203	157	4.09	4.82	1.48	277	283	248	25.7	3.6	7.0	1.9	43	21	37	1.1	9%	32%	76%	20	101	30%	20%			5.8	48	90	$8
10	CIN *	6	3	0	128	113	4.22	3.89	1.34	259	238	272	23.2	3.2	7.9	2.5	42	21	37	0.8	9%	32%	69%	19	102	58%	21%			-2.2	80	129	$3
11	CIN *	11	8	0	162	124	4.26	4.38	1.32	277	274	256	24.0	2.2	6.9	3.2	39	22	38	1.1	12%	32%	71%	22	96	45%	18%			-6.3	76	114	$3
12	CIN	13	10	0	208	168	3.68	3.90	1.24	256	245	265	26.5	2.3	7.3	3.2	45	20	35	1.1	12%	30%	75%	33	101	52%	24%			8.6	93	121	$12
1st Half		5	6	0	90	61	4.42	4.54	1.37	271	262	279	25.9	2.7	6.1	2.3	41	21	38	1.4	13%	30%	72%	15	98	40%	33%			-4.4	56	73	$0
2nd Half		8	4	0	118	107	3.12	3.44	1.14	244	231	255	26.9	1.9	8.1	4.3	48	19	33	0.9	11%	30%	76%	18	104	61%	17%			13.1	121	158	$22
13	**Proj**	**12**	**9**	**0**	**203**	**163**	**3.91**	**3.97**	**1.31**	**268**	**258**	**275**	**24.8**	**2.5**	**7.2**	**2.9**	**43**	**21**	**36**	**1.1**	**11%**	**31%**	**73%**	**34**						**2.6**	**84**	**109**	**$10**

Baker,Scott

Age: 31	Th: R	Role SP	Health	F	LIMA Plan	A
Ht: 6' 4"	Wt: 215	Type xFB	PT/Exp	B	Rand Var	0
			Consist	A	MM	3301

Though he took a step forward in 2011 and had slowly overcome early-career HR woes, he has always been one of those frustrating big-skills, little results players. Tommy John surgery in April 2012 only encourages the choice to let someone burden the frustration for 2013. Call back in 2014.

Yr	Tm	W	L	Sv	IP	K	ERA	xERA	WHIP	OBA	vL	vR	BF/G	Ctl	Dom	Cmd	G	L	F	hr/9	hr/f	H%	S%	GS	APC	DOM%	DIS%	Sv%	LI	RAR	BPV	BPX	R$
08	MIN	11	4	0	172	141	3.45	4.01	1.18	247	263	230	25.1	2.2	7.4	3.4	33	21	46	1.0	9%	29%	75%	28	96	50%	14%			18.6	84	158	$16
09	MIN	15	9	0	200	162	4.37	4.09	1.19	247	217	275	25.1	2.2	7.3	3.4	33	19	47	1.3	10%	29%	67%	33	99	58%	15%			-1.1	84	157	$15
10	MIN	12	9	0	170	148	4.49	3.89	1.34	277	277	277	25.0	2.3	7.8	3.4	36	21	43	1.2	10%	33%	70%	29	92	48%	28%			-8.7	93	151	$4
11	MIN	8	6	0	135	123	3.14	3.59	1.17	248	267	215	23.8	2.1	8.2	3.8	34	21	45	1.0	9%	30%	78%	21	93	48%	10%	0	0.72	13.3	102	154	$11
12																																	
1st Half																																	
2nd Half																																	
13	**Proj**	**5**	**3**	**0**	**73**	**62**	**4.13**	**3.97**	**1.21**	**256**	**255**	**257**	**24.1**	**2.2**	**7.7**	**3.5**	**34**	**21**	**45**	**1.1**	**9%**	**30%**	**69%**	**12**						**-1.0**	**91**	**119**	**$2**

Balfour,Grant

Age: 35	Th: R	Role RP	Health	B	LIMA Plan	C+
Ht: 6' 2"	Wt: 200	Type Pwr FB	PT/Exp	C	Rand Var	-5
			Consist	A	MM	3530

Second half success sets him up as a favorite for Svs going into 2013. But wagonload of caveats caution hitching to him long-term: very favorable H%, hr/f% in 2012; dubious LD+FB history; prone to Ctl lapses; how long can 35-yr-old run on emotion? Elite Dom covers much for now, but take this one year-by-year.

Yr	Tm	W	L	Sv	IP	K	ERA	xERA	WHIP	OBA	vL	vR	BF/G	Ctl	Dom	Cmd	G	L	F	hr/9	hr/f	H%	S%	GS	APC	DOM%	DIS%	Sv%	LI	RAR	BPV	BPX	R$
08	TAM *	7	2	12	82	111	1.24	0.82	0.86	130	120	159	4.6	3.9	12.2	3.1	29	19	52	0.5	5%	20%	89%	0	20			92	1.54	31.1	153	288	$23
09	TAM	5	4	4	67	69	4.81	4.14	1.37	235	240	232	4.0	4.4	9.2	2.1	36	21	43	0.8	8%	30%	65%	0	17			44	1.26	-4.1	61	114	$2
10	TAM	2	1	0	55	56	2.28	3.63	1.08	216	267	174	3.9	2.8	9.1	3.3	31	20	50	0.5	4%	29%	81%	0	17			0	1.25	12.3	98	159	$5
11	OAK	5	2	2	62	59	2.47	3.50	1.03	199	191	207	3.9	2.9	8.6	3.0	38	17	45	1.2	11%	24%	84%	0	16			29	1.18	11.3	92	138	$8
12	OAK	3	2	24	75	72	2.53	3.68	0.92	160	157	163	3.9	3.4	8.7	2.6	36	24	41	0.5	5%	21%	74%	0	17			92	1.33	13.7	79	103	$19
1st Half		1	2	7	39	30	3.49	4.42	1.11	187	194	177	4.1	4.2	7.0	1.7	36	24	40	0.7	7%	22%	70%	0	18			78	1.29	2.5	27	35	$11
2nd Half		2	0	17	36	42	1.50	2.97	0.72	130	113	148	3.6	2.5	10.5	4.2	35	23	41	0.3	3%	20%	80%	0	16			100	1.37	11.2	135	176	$28
13	**Proj**	**4**	**2**	**33**	**65**	**66**	**2.96**	**3.61**	**1.05**	**199**	**198**	**199**	**3.9**	**3.1**	**9.1**	**2.9**	**35**	**21**	**44**	**0.6**	**6%**	**26%**	**74%**	**0**						**8.5**	**92**	**120**	**$19**

Bard,Daniel

Age: 28	Th: R	Role RP	Health	A	LIMA Plan	F
Ht: 6' 4"	Wt: 215	Type Pwr	PT/Exp	C	Rand Var	+5
			Consist	D	MM	1310

5-6, 6.22 ERA in 59 IP at BOS. S% and hr/f contributed, but most of this was his own doing. Since Sept. 1, 2011, his combined (MLB/minors) Cmd is 1.0—81 BB, 81 K in 102 IP. Role is irrelevant; no pitcher can succeed with that many walks. Perhaps an off-season will help clear his head. Or not.

Yr	Tm	W	L	Sv	IP	K	ERA	xERA	WHIP	OBA	vL	vR	BF/G	Ctl	Dom	Cmd	G	L	F	hr/9	hr/f	H%	S%	GS	APC	DOM%	DIS%	Sv%	LI	RAR	BPV	BPX	R$
08	aa	4	1	7	50	53	2.47	2.66	1.24	200			6.5	4.8	9.5	2.0				0.6		27%	82%							11.4	97	182	$7
09	BOS *	3	2	7	65	86	3.20	3.09	1.18	210	263	200	4.4	3.8	11.9	3.1	45	19	36	1.1	12%	30%	78%	0	17			64	0.81	9.0	117	219	$8
10	BOS	1	2	3	75	76	1.93	3.33	1.00	176	141	215	4.0	3.6	9.2	2.5	47	15	38	0.7	9%	22%	86%	0	16			30	1.72	19.8	92	149	$10
11	BOS	2	9	1	73	74	3.33	2.99	0.96	179	211	136	4.1	3.0	9.1	3.1	53	16	31	0.6	9%	24%	66%	0	16			17	1.53	5.5	115	173	$6
12	BOS *	8	8	0	91	63	7.65	6.10	1.94	282	260	286	9.1	7.5	6.2	0.8	44	22	34	1.1	14%	31%	60%	10	61	20%	20%	0	0.66	-41.0	19	25	-$23
1st Half		5	6	0	66	45	6.13	5.04	1.70	263	237	287	15.0	6.3	6.1	1.0	47	20	33	1.0	11%	29%	64%	10	86	20%	20%	0	0.97	-17.3	30	39	-$20
2nd Half		3	2	0	25	18	11.69	8.77	2.58	329	556	273	4.8	10.8	6.4	0.6	12	35	53	1.5	33%	36%	53%	0	17			0	0.08	-23.7	-6	-8	-$32
13	**Proj**	**4**	**5**	**5**	**58**	**51**	**5.31**	**4.66**	**1.55**	**251**	**242**	**261**	**5.1**	**5.4**	**7.9**	**1.5**	**48**	**18**	**35**	**1.0**	**11%**	**30%**	**66%**	**0**						**-9.2**	**21**	**27**	**-$2**

Bass,Anthony

Age: 25	Th: R	Role RP	Health	C	LIMA Plan	D+
Ht: 6' 2"	Wt: 190	Type Pwr	PT/Exp	D	Rand Var	+2
			Consist	C	MM	2201

Super-skilled April (104 BPV) turned south quickly. Right shoulder inflammation kept him out two-plus months; both Ctl and Dom suffered upon his return. Cmd, GB history, PQS scores show some potential but it's still just mid-rotation upside. Assure a clean bill of health before taking the plunge.

Yr	Tm	W	L	Sv	IP	K	ERA	xERA	WHIP	OBA	vL	vR	BF/G	Ctl	Dom	Cmd	G	L	F	hr/9	hr/f	H%	S%	GS	APC	DOM%	DIS%	Sv%	LI	RAR	BPV	BPX	R$
08																																	
09																																	
10																																	
11	SD *	9	4	0	123	81	2.55	3.04	1.20	237	243	230	12.1	2.9	5.9	2.0	46	23	31	0.5	6%	27%	80%	3	27	0%	0%	0	0.67	21.1	69	104	$11
12	SD	2	8	1	97	80	4.73	4.10	1.32	243	251	234	17.1	3.6	7.4	2.1	48	20	32	0.9	11%	29%	65%	15	64	47%	27%	100	1.13	-8.6	62	81	-$3
1st Half		2	7	0	84	72	4.70	3.99	1.34	251	252	250	22.3	3.5	7.7	2.2	48	21	31	0.9	11%	30%	66%	14	83	50%	21%	0	0.83	-7.1	69	90	-$3
2nd Half		0	1	1	13	8	4.97	4.90	1.18	188	250	143	6.8	4.3	5.7	1.3	49	13	38	1.4	13%	20%	62%	1	24	0%	100%	100	1.72	-1.5	14	18	-$7
13	**Proj**	**4**	**6**	**0**	**102**	**79**	**4.02**	**4.06**	**1.31**	**252**	**256**	**249**	**16.7**	**3.3**	**7.0**	**2.1**	**47**	**22**	**31**	**0.8**	**10%**	**30%**	**71%**	**17**						**0.0**	**62**	**81**	**$2**

BRENT HERSHEY

Bastardo,Antonio

Age: 27	Th: L	Role RP	Health A	LIMA Plan B	
			PT/Exp D	Rand Var +4	
Ht: 5' 11"	Wt: 197	Type Pwr xFB	Consist A	MM 4500	

Concerns about a dip in velocity started in camp and followed him all season long. But BPI say that 1H's shoddy Ctl, 2H blasts of unlucky hr/f and H%—not Dom—were the main problem. xFB profile lessens his wiggle room. ERA should rebound some, but walks and balls in the air remain his nemeses.

Yr Tm	W	L	Sv	IP	K	ERA	xERA	WHIP	OBA	vL	vR	BF/G	Ctl	Dom	Cmd	G	L	F	hr/9	hr/f	H%	S%	GS	APC	DOM%	DIS%	Sv%	LI	RAR	BPV	BPX	R$
08 aa	1	5	0	67	53	4.14	5.07	1.44	246			20.4	4.7	7.1	1.5				1.9		26%	80%							1.5	22	42	-$2
09 PHI *	5	5	3	73	63	3.70	3.27	1.17	243	303	258	15.3	2.4	7.8	3.3	23	25	52	0.8	10%	29%	70%	5	74	40%	40%	100	0.70	5.5	98	183	$6
10 PHI *	3	1	3	36	48	3.59	3.31	1.37	250	200	300	3.4	3.9	11.9	3.1	32	15	53	0.2	4%	38%	72%	0	14			75	0.60	2.2	134	217	$2
11 PHI	6	1	8	58	70	2.64	3.46	0.93	144	145	143	3.5	4.0	10.9	2.7	25	16	59	0.9	8%	19%	77%	0	15			80	1.47	9.3	90	135	$11
12 PHI	2	5	1	52	81	4.33	3.26	1.27	207	169	236	3.4	4.5	14.0	3.1	28	22	50	1.2	13%	33%	69%	0	15			20	1.37	-2.0	137	178	$0
1st Half	2	2	0	26	36	3.46	3.80	1.35	217	225	211	3.7	4.8	12.5	2.6	27	22	52	1.0	10%	33%	78%	0	15			0	1.55	1.8	98	128	$0
2nd Half	0	3	1	26	45	5.19	2.76	1.19	198	116	264	3.2	4.2	15.6	3.8	29	23	48	1.4	16%	35%	59%	0	14			33	1.20	-3.8	175	228	-$1
13 Proj	**3**	**4**	**0**	**58**	**80**	**3.83**	**3.39**	**1.19**	**207**	**176**	**228**	**3.6**	**4.1**	**12.4**	**3.0**	**27**	**20**	**53**	**1.0**	**10%**	**30%**	**71%**	**0**						**1.3**	**117**	**152**	**$3**

Bauer,Trevor

Age: 22	Th: R	Role SP	Health A	LIMA Plan B+	
			PT/Exp D	Rand Var 0	
Ht: 6' 1"	Wt: 185	Type Pwr	Consist F	MM 4501	

1-2, 6.06 ERA in 16 IP at ARI. Though he struggled in first MLB exposure, MLEs show his upside. Most concerns center on his Ctl, as his non-traditional delivery is easily sidetracked and free passes result. But he's got strikeout ability and a GB tilt. Big return someday, but expect growing pains for now.

Yr Tm	W	L	Sv	IP	K	ERA	xERA	WHIP	OBA	vL	vR	BF/G	Ctl	Dom	Cmd	G	L	F	hr/9	hr/f	H%	S%	GS	APC	DOM%	DIS%	Sv%	LI	RAR	BPV	BPX	R$
08																																
09																																
10																																
11 aa	1	1	0	17	23	8.11	5.80	1.70	311			18.9	3.9	12.4	3.2				1.1		44%	51%							-8.6	101	152	-$6
12 ARI *	13	4	0	147	153	2.93	3.43	1.33	235	281	172	23.4	4.2	9.4	2.2	45	25	30	0.7	15%	31%	80%	4	81	25%	75%			19.7	91	119	$12
1st Half	11	1	0	97	103	2.42	3.26	1.35	236	333	400	23.8	4.3	9.6	2.2	42	8	50	0.5	0%	32%	83%	1	74	0%	100%			19.1	99	129	$23
2nd Half	2	3	0	50	49	3.91	3.71	1.30	234	261	125	22.7	3.9	9.0	2.3	47	31	22	1.1	29%	29%	73%	3	83	33%	67%			0.6	78	102	-$8
13 Proj	**10**	**4**	**0**	**102**	**103**	**2.91**	**3.32**	**1.27**	**225**			**22.9**	**4.1**	**9.2**	**2.2**	**43**	**19**	**38**	**0.8**		**29%**	**80%**	**18**						**13.8**	**87**	**113**	**$10**

Beachy,Brandon

Age: 26	Th: R	Role RP	Health F	LIMA Plan B+	
			PT/Exp C	Rand Var -5	
Ht: 6' 3"	Wt: 215	Type Pwr FB	Consist A	MM 4501	

Made-for-TV movie hit roadblock, as TJS will sideline him for start of 2013. Base skills regressed, but a fortunate H% led to improved results. At 26, he should return to pre-injury levels by 2014, giving him keeper league value. Nothing an undrafted college kid churning out three-digit BPVs can't handle.

Yr Tm	W	L	Sv	IP	K	ERA	xERA	WHIP	OBA	vL	vR	BF/G	Ctl	Dom	Cmd	G	L	F	hr/9	hr/f	H%	S%	GS	APC	DOM%	DIS%	Sv%	LI	RAR	BPV	BPX	R$
08																																
09																																
10 ATL *	5	3	2	134	140	2.19	2.94	1.19	247	273	259	14.2	2.4	9.4	3.9	36	29	36	0.4	0%	33%	82%	3	93	33%	33%			31.3	133	216	$15
11 ATL	7	3	0	142	169	3.68	3.27	1.21	236	236	237	23.6	2.9	10.7	3.7	34	21	45	1.0	10%	32%	73%	25	97	60%	12%			4.5	126	190	$9
12 ATL	5	5	0	81	68	2.00	3.94	0.96	171	148	189	24.5	3.2	7.6	2.3	41	18	41	0.7	7%	21%	83%	13	102	69%	8%			20.1	68	89	$12
1st Half	5	5	0	81	68	2.00	3.93	0.96	171	148	189	24.5	3.2	7.6	2.3	41	18	41	0.7	7%	21%	83%	13	102	69%	8%			20.2	68	89	$12
2nd Half																																
13 Proj	**4**	**4**	**0**	**73**	**73**	**2.88**	**3.57**	**1.12**	**221**	**204**	**234**	**18.4**	**2.8**	**9.1**	**3.2**	**38**	**19**	**43**	**0.6**	**6%**	**29%**	**76%**	**13**						**10.2**	**104**	**134**	**$6**

Beavan,Blake

Age: 24	Th: R	Role SP	Health A	LIMA Plan B	
			PT/Exp C	Rand Var 0	
Ht: 6' 7"	Wt: 240	Type Con FB	Consist A	MM 1003	

11-11, 4.43 ERA in 152 IP at SEA. Our crack stats dept. reports that he's one of only 2 AL P in 2012 — 125 IP min — whose height in inches (79) actually exceeded his MLB strikeouts (67). His LD tendency, OBA and BPV all cancel out playable Cmd. What's that? Oh, you don't want Derek Lowe, either.

Yr Tm	W	L	Sv	IP	K	ERA	xERA	WHIP	OBA	vL	vR	BF/G	Ctl	Dom	Cmd	G	L	F	hr/9	hr/f	H%	S%	GS	APC	DOM%	DIS%	Sv%	LI	RAR	BPV	BPX	R$
08																																
09 aa	4	4	0	90	30	4.72	5.22	1.54	331			26.1	1.3	3.0	2.4				0.5		35%	68%							-4.4	43	81	-$5
10 a/a	14	8	0	168	92	3.96	3.61	1.19	276			25.0	1.0	4.9	4.7				0.6		31%	67%							2.4	110	178	$10
11 SEA *	10	9	0	190	100	3.96	4.40	1.31	288	314	236	25.3	1.5	4.7	3.1	38	23	39	0.9	10%	31%	72%	15	99	33%	13%			-0.3	63	95	$4
12 SEA *	15	11	0	190	80	4.05	4.44	1.26	280	304	258	24.3	1.5	3.8	2.5	37	22	42	1.2	10%	29%	72%	26	89	23%	31%			-0.9	38	49	$6
1st Half	5	6	0	80	37	5.14	5.57	1.45	306	323	271	22.9	1.9	4.2	2.2	35	22	43	1.5	12%	31%	69%	12	83	17%	42%			-11.1	20	26	-$8
2nd Half	10	5	0	110	43	3.26	3.57	1.13	259	290	247	25.6	1.3	3.5	2.7	38	21	41	1.0	9%	27%	75%	14	93	29%	21%			10.3	53	69	$16
13 Proj	**12**	**9**	**0**	**174**	**79**	**4.22**	**4.69**	**1.31**	**290**	**319**	**258**	**25.0**	**1.4**	**4.1**	**2.8**	**37**	**22**	**41**	**1.0**	**8%**	**31%**	**70%**	**29**						**-4.3**	**50**	**65**	**$4**

Beckett,Josh

Age: 33	Th: R	Role SP	Health C	LIMA Plan C+	
			PT/Exp A	Rand Var 0	
Ht: 6' 5"	Wt: 225	Type Pwr	Consist B	MM 3303	

Paltry win total siphoned his roto value again. But this time, the ERA/xERA gap, BPV and 2H slide are more ominous. Dogged by shoulder and back injuries for much of the year, he did recover nicely after the trade (2.93 ERA, 2.7 Cmd in 43 IP). Skills support a mild rebound, but don't pay for much more.

Yr Tm	W	L	Sv	IP	K	ERA	xERA	WHIP	OBA	vL	vR	BF/G	Ctl	Dom	Cmd	G	L	F	hr/9	hr/f	H%	S%	GS	APC	DOM%	DIS%	Sv%	LI	RAR	BPV	BPX	R$
08 BOS	12	10	0	174	172	4.03	3.31	1.19	256	260	252	26.9	1.8	8.9	5.1	41	25	34	0.9	11%	33%	68%	27	100	70%	11%			6.4	131	247	$15
09 BOS	17	6	0	212	199	3.86	3.41	1.19	244	258	226	27.6	2.3	8.4	3.6	47	21	32	1.1	13%	30%	71%	32	105	78%	6%			12.2	114	213	$21
10 BOS	6	6	0	128	116	5.78	3.94	1.54	292	310	267	27.5	3.2	8.2	2.6	46	19	35	1.4	14%	35%	65%	21	103	43%	19%			-26.8	86	138	-$7
11 BOS	13	7	0	193	175	2.89	3.43	1.03	211	186	245	25.6	2.4	8.2	3.4	40	18	42	1.0	10%	25%	77%	30	100	70%	7%			25.0	99	149	$24
12 2 TM	7	14	0	170	132	4.65	4.23	1.33	264	280	245	26.1	2.7	7.0	2.5	43	21	37	1.1	11%	31%	67%	28	94	50%	18%			-13.3	72	94	-$2
1st Half	4	7	0	84	60	4.06	4.05	1.15	242	257	221	26.5	2.1	6.4	3.0	42	22	36	1.0	10%	28%	67%	13	95	69%	15%			-0.4	78	102	$6
2nd Half	3	7	0	86	72	5.23	4.41	1.50	284	305	263	25.7	3.3	7.5	2.3	43	20	37	1.3	12%	33%	68%	15	93	33%	20%			-12.9	66	86	-$9
13 Proj	**9**	**11**	**0**	**174**	**148**	**4.36**	**3.92**	**1.29**	**259**	**264**	**252**	**25.3**	**2.7**	**7.7**	**2.8**	**43**	**20**	**38**	**1.1**	**11%**	**30%**	**69%**	**28**						**-7.5**	**85**	**111**	**$6**

Bedard,Erik

Age: 34	Th: L	Role SP	Health F	LIMA Plan C	
			PT/Exp C	Rand Var +1	
Ht: 6' 1"	Wt: 200	Type Pwr	Consist B	MM 3400	

Used to be you could count on him for excellent numbers in between the DL stints. But with his first 5.00+ ERA season, that's no longer the case, and he was released in Aug. He'll land somewhere with strikeout stuff like this, but Ctl, OBA, LD% all trending the wrong way. Only for the well-prepared realist.

Yr Tm	W	L	Sv	IP	K	ERA	xERA	WHIP	OBA	vL	vR	BF/G	Ctl	Dom	Cmd	G	L	F	hr/9	hr/f	H%	S%	GS	APC	DOM%	DIS%	Sv%	LI	RAR	BPV	BPX	R$
08 SEA	6	4	0	81	72	3.67	4.33	1.32	231	253	224	23.1	4.1	8.0	1.9	40	17	43	1.0	9%	28%	76%	15	91	40%	27%			6.6	51	96	$4
09 SEA	5	3	0	83	90	2.82	3.60	1.19	212	214	211	23.2	3.7	9.8	2.6	42	17	40	0.9	9%	28%	80%	15	97	40%	27%			15.4	96	180	$8
10																																
11 2 AL	5	9	0	129	125	3.62	3.65	1.28	241	245	239	22.5	3.3	8.7	2.6	42	20	38	1.0	10%	30%	75%	24	93	54%	25%			5.2	86	130	$5
12 FAN	7	14	0	126	118	5.01	4.21	1.47	263	218	272	23.2	4.0	8.5	2.1	43	23	33	1.0	11%	33%	67%	24	89	38%	33%			-15.5	65	85	-$6
1st Half	4	8	0	78	72	4.27	4.25	1.44	260	226	269	22.7	3.9	8.3	2.1	40	25	35	0.7	8%	33%	71%	15	88	47%	20%			-2.4	61	79	-$2
2nd Half	3	6	0	48	46	6.23	4.14	1.53	267	200	277	24.1	4.2	8.7	2.1	49	21	30	1.5	19%	33%	62%	9	91	22%	56%			-13.0	71	92	-$13
13 Proj	**3**	**5**	**0**	**58**	**56**	**4.42**	**3.96**	**1.38**	**253**	**232**	**258**	**22.4**	**3.8**	**8.7**	**2.3**	**43**	**21**	**36**	**1.1**	**12%**	**31%**	**70%**	**11**						**-2.9**	**75**	**97**	**-$1**

Belisario,Ronald

Age: 30	Th: R	Role RP	Health A	LIMA Plan B	
			PT/Exp D	Rand Var -2	
Ht: 6' 3"	Wt: 243	Type Pwr xGB	Consist B	MM 4311	

New training regimen? Visa and drug abuse issues kept him in Venezuela for all of 2011. Returned in May 2012 with career-best skills. Got some H% help, but experienced big gains in GB, Dom (especially 2H), and against RHB. Notched 8 wins, even. We don't recommend this plan for everyone, though.

Yr Tm	W	L	Sv	IP	K	ERA	xERA	WHIP	OBA	vL	vR	BF/G	Ctl	Dom	Cmd	G	L	F	hr/9	hr/f	H%	S%	GS	APC	DOM%	DIS%	Sv%	LI	RAR	BPV	BPX	R$
08 aa	4	4	9	57	27	6.43	6.44	1.86	331			7.0	4.2	4.3	1.0				0.9		36%	65%							-14.8	9	18	-$5
09 LA	4	3	0	71	64	2.04	3.56	1.15	201	270	157	4.3	3.7	8.2	2.2	56	16	28	0.5	8%	26%	84%	0	16			0	1.03	19.9	81	152	$8
10 LA	3	1	2	55	38	5.04	3.62	1.28	250	257	246	3.9	3.1	6.2	2.0	61	17	22	1.0	16%	28%	62%	0	15			50	1.08	-6.6	67	108	-$1
11																																
12 LA	8	1	1	71	69	2.54	2.98	1.07	187	250	142	4.2	3.7	8.7	2.4	64	21	15	0.4	11%	25%	77%	0	16			20	1.12	13.0	100	131	$9
1st Half	3	0	0	24	16	1.11	3.85	0.95	138	114	156	3.9	4.4	5.9	1.3	59	23	17	0.4	9%	16%	91%	0	15			0	0.73	8.7	24	31	$6
2nd Half	5	1	1	47	53	3.28	2.57	1.14	209	319	136	4.4	3.3	10.2	3.1	67	19	13	0.4	13%	30%	71%	0	16			25	1.34	4.2	141	184	$11
13 Proj	**6**	**2**	**5**	**73**	**60**	**3.79**	**3.48**	**1.24**	**228**	**271**	**201**	**4.2**	**3.6**	**7.4**	**2.1**	**62**	**19**	**19**	**0.6**	**12%**	**28%**	**70%**	**0**						**2.0**	**76**	**99**	**$5**

BRENT HERSHEY

Belisle,Matt

Age: 33 Th: R Role RP	Health A	LIMA Plan A+	
Ht: 6' 4" Wt: 225 Type	PT/Exp C	Rand Var +1	
	Consist A	MM 3311	

Third straight season of closer-worthy BPV and a trusted (LI) arm when the game is close. For the most part, his 2H results can be ignored; H%/S% accounted for the bloated ERA. Improved GB% the past two seasons lessens the risk of implosion. Not a young pup, but durable and with opportunity ... UP: 20 Sv.

Yr Tm	W	L	Sv	IP	K	ERA	xERA	WHIP	OBA	vL	vR	BF/G	Ctl	Dom	Cmd	G	L	F	hr/9	hr/f	H%	S%	GS	APC	DOM%	DIS%	Sv%	LI	RAR	BPV	BPX	R$
08 CIN *	7	5	4	77	37	6.02	5.95	1.70	341	296	419	10.5	2.2	4.3	2.0	51	26	23	0.6	14%	37%	63%	6	86	0%	50%			-16.1	35	66	-$5
09 COL *	4	2	9	89	55	4.45	4.82	1.44	300	241	313	6.7	2.1	5.5	2.6	40	21	40	0.9	15%	34%	70%	0	22			100	0.56	-1.4	57	107	$2
10 COL	7	5	1	92	91	2.93	2.94	1.09	246	232	253	4.8	1.6	8.9	5.7	46	20	33	0.7	9%	31%	75%	0	19			50	1.03	13.0	142	230	$10
11 COL	10	4	0	72	58	3.25	3.28	1.26	276	250	291	4.1	1.8	7.3	4.1	53	19	28	0.6	8%	33%	76%	0	16			0	1.20	6.1	114	172	$5
12 COL	3	8	3	80	69	3.71	3.58	1.36	282	313	259	4.4	2.0	7.8	3.8	51	24	26	0.6	8%	35%	73%	0	16			30	1.42	3.0	114	149	$0
1st Half	3	2	0	42	34	1.93	3.25	1.17	252	250	252	4.6	1.5	7.3	4.9	60	20	21	0.2	4%	33%	83%	0	16			0	1.36	10.8	128	167	$7
2nd Half	0	6	3	38	35	5.68	3.94	1.58	314	371	267	4.1	2.6	8.3	3.2	41	28	31	0.9	11%	38%	64%	0	16			43	1.48	-7.8	98	128	-$7
13 Proj	**5**	**6**	**5**	**73**	**61**	**3.86**	**3.60**	**1.34**	**285**	**295**	**278**	**4.4**	**2.0**	**7.6**	**3.8**	**48**	**22**	**29**	**0.7**	**8%**	**35%**	**72%**	**0**						**1.4**	**110**	**142**	**$3**

Bell,Heath

Age: 35 Th: R Role RP	Health A	LIMA Plan B+	
Ht: 6' 0" Wt: 260 Type Pwr	PT/Exp A	Rand Var +3	
	Consist B	MM 3321	

His age and three-season BPV trend are a volatile mix for a closer—and sure enough, he didn't last the season. By the end, his Dom recovery was a good sign and his 2H (including the return of GB) will be enough to tempt some into a late-draft bidding war. ERA will be better, but Svs may tough to come by.

Yr Tm	W	L	Sv	IP	K	ERA	xERA	WHIP	OBA	vL	vR	BF/G	Ctl	Dom	Cmd	G	L	F	hr/9	hr/f	H%	S%	GS	APC	DOM%	DIS%	Sv%	LI	RAR	BPV	BPX	R$
08 SD	6	6	0	78	71	3.58	3.72	1.21	229	207	254	4.4	3.2	8.2	2.5	46	19	35	0.6	7%	29%	71%	0	18			0	1.37	7.2	84	158	$6
09 SD	6	4	42	70	79	2.71	3.07	1.12	213	275	138	4.1	3.1	10.2	3.3	48	18	35	0.4	5%	30%	76%	0	18			88	1.40	13.8	126	236	$26
10 SD	6	1	47	70	86	1.93	3.09	1.20	221	200	241	4.3	3.6	11.1	3.1	44	18	38	0.1	2%	33%	83%	0	18			94	1.42	18.6	124	200	$28
11 SD	3	4	43	63	51	2.44	3.74	1.15	223	283	164	4.0	3.0	7.3	2.4	43	21	35	0.6	6%	27%	81%	0	17			90	1.45	11.6	71	107	$22
12 MIA	4	5	19	64	59	5.09	4.18	1.55	282	239	317	3.9	4.1	8.3	2.0	47	23	30	0.7	9%	35%	67%	0	16			70	1.09	-8.4	64	84	$1
1st Half	2	3	16	29	28	6.14	4.90	1.77	297	241	350	4.1	5.2	8.6	1.6	40	25	35	0.6	6%	38%	64%	0	17			80	1.17	-7.7	32	42	$3
2nd Half	2	2	3	34	31	4.19	3.59	1.37	269	235	291	3.7	3.1	8.1	2.6	53	22	25	0.8	12%	33%	70%	0	15			43	1.01	-0.8	92	120	$0
13 Proj	**5**	**5**	**10**	**73**	**64**	**3.70**	**3.97**	**1.35**	**252**	**244**	**258**	**3.9**	**3.6**	**7.9**	**2.2**	**46**	**21**	**33**	**0.6**	**7%**	**31%**	**73%**	**0**						**2.8**	**70**	**91**	**$6**

Below,Duane

Age: 27 Th: L Role RP	Health A	LIMA Plan D	
Ht: 6' 4" Wt: 218 Type Con	PT/Exp D	Rand Var 0	
	Consist C	MM 0000	

2-1, 3.88 ERA in 46 IP at DET. PRO: Actual MLB BPI, mostly in relief, show at least a shred of utility: 4.08 xERA, 1.6 Ctl, 5.6 Dom, 3.6 Cmd, 75 BPV. CON: MLB skills still soft; don't let him start (12 ER in 17 IP in Triple-A); age does him no favors. If he can't get lefties out, there's no reason to roster him.

Yr Tm	W	L	Sv	IP	K	ERA	xERA	WHIP	OBA	vL	vR	BF/G	Ctl	Dom	Cmd	G	L	F	hr/9	hr/f	H%	S%	GS	APC	DOM%	DIS%	Sv%	LI	RAR	BPV	BPX	R$
08																																
09																																
10 aa	7	12	0	126	81	5.97	5.84	1.58	313			19.8	2.6	5.8	2.2				1.4		34%	64%							-29.5	33	53	-$10
11 DET *	9	6	0	144	77	4.21	4.48	1.40	272	255	250	19.0	3.1	4.8	1.5	51	15	34	1.0	6%	29%	72%	2	35	0%	50%	0	0.79	-4.8	31	47	-$1
12 DET *	3	3	0	64	34	5.07	5.74	1.57	306	304	260	9.0	2.9	4.8	1.6	38	27	35	1.3	12%	32%	71%	1	26	0%	100%	0	0.72	-8.2	17	22	-$8
1st Half	2	1	0	33	22	2.70	3.53	0.93	231	263	200	6.0	1.1	5.9	5.5	40	26	34	0.5	6%	26%	72%	0	21			0	0.84	5.4	95	124	$2
2nd Half	1	2	0	30	12	7.66	9.59	2.27	379	409	361	15.5	5.0	3.6	0.7	36	28	36	2.2	21%	38%	70%	1	41	0%	100%	0	0.30	-13.6	-51	-66	-$20
13 Proj	**3**	**3**	**0**	**58**	**31**	**4.44**	**5.00**	**1.51**	**296**	**338**	**257**	**12.9**	**2.9**	**4.8**	**1.7**	**40**	**26**	**34**	**1.4**	**12%**	**31%**	**75%**	**6**						**-3.1**	**26**	**33**	**-$4**

Benoit,Joaquin

Age: 35 Th: R Role RP	Health D	LIMA Plan A+	
Ht: 6' 3" Wt: 220 Type Pwr xFB	PT/Exp C	Rand Var +2	
	Consist A	MM 4511	

Can't help but wonder if hr/f going all willy-nilly cost him a legit shot as closer in post-Valverde era. Still could happen, as skills are worthy and have a track record. But HRs come from FBs—which he serves up aplenty—and are hazardous to your save-opps health. A rock-solid setup guy with upside.

Yr Tm	W	L	Sv	IP	K	ERA	xERA	WHIP	OBA	vL	vR	BF/G	Ctl	Dom	Cmd	G	L	F	hr/9	hr/f	H%	S%	GS	APC	DOM%	DIS%	Sv%	LI	RAR	BPV	BPX	R$
08 TEX	3	2	1	45	43	5.00	5.75	1.67	233	184	282	4.8	7.0	8.6	1.2	27	17	56	1.2	8%	29%	72%	0	19			25	0.98	-3.8	-29	-55	-$3
09																																
10 TAM	1	2	1	60	75	1.34	2.51	0.68	147	144	150	3.4	1.6	11.2	6.8	39	12	49	0.9	9%	20%	91%	0	15			25	1.11	20.4	174	282	$12
11 DET	4	3	2	61	63	2.95	3.23	1.05	218	248	184	3.7	2.5	9.3	3.7	39	18	43	0.7	7%	28%	75%	0	15			29	1.26	7.5	117	175	$6
12 DET	5	3	2	71	84	3.68	3.33	1.14	228	237	217	3.9	2.8	10.6	3.8	36	20	44	1.8	18%	28%	78%	0	17			33	1.05	3.0	130	170	$5
1st Half	1	1	1	36	46	2.25	3.36	1.22	229	262	200	4.2	3.5	11.5	3.3	35	23	42	0.8	8%	33%	85%	0	18			50	1.19	7.8	125	163	$6
2nd Half	4	2	1	35	38	5.14	3.30	1.06	227	218	240	3.7	2.1	9.8	4.8	37	18	46	2.8	27%	23%	65%	0	16			25	0.92	-4.9	135	176	$4
13 Proj	**5**	**3**	**5**	**73**	**81**	**3.43**	**3.40**	**1.09**	**215**	**221**	**208**	**3.8**	**2.9**	**10.1**	**3.5**	**36**	**18**	**46**	**1.4**	**14%**	**26%**	**76%**	**0**						**5.2**	**118**	**153**	**$8**

Betancourt,Rafael

Age: 38 Th: R Role RP	Health B	LIMA Plan B	
Ht: 6' 2" Wt: 220 Type Pwr xFB	PT/Exp C	Rand Var -3	
	Consist B	MM 3430	

Finally got the chance that his BPIs had been screaming for (90+ BPV eight of the past nine seasons). But cautions abound: 1) age-related BPV decline; 2) xFB profile is at the whim of hr/f; 3) favorable MLB contract, so attractive (setup) target for contenders. Don't draft as a sole saves source.

Yr Tm	W	L	Sv	IP	K	ERA	xERA	WHIP	OBA	vL	vR	BF/G	Ctl	Dom	Cmd	G	L	F	hr/9	hr/f	H%	S%	GS	APC	DOM%	DIS%	Sv%	LI	RAR	BPV	BPX	R$
08 CLE	3	4	4	71	64	5.07	4.45	1.42	276	252	295	4.5	3.2	8.1	2.6	29	21	50	1.4	10%	32%	68%	0	18			50	1.15	-6.5	67	127	$0
09 2 TM	4	3	2	56	61	2.73	3.77	1.11	209	265	169	3.7	3.2	9.8	3.1	30	16	54	0.6	5%	28%	78%	0	15			33	1.37	11.0	98	183	$6
10 COL	5	1	1	62	89	3.61	2.61	0.96	220	279	187	3.4	1.2	12.9	11.1	26	22	52	1.3	12%	33%	69%	0	13			20	1.26	3.6	204	330	$7
11 COL	2	0	8	62	73	2.89	2.83	0.87	203	220	189	3.5	1.2	10.5	9.1	31	18	51	1.0	9%	28%	72%	0	14			67	1.08	8.1	168	252	$10
12 COL	1	4	31	58	57	2.81	3.66	1.13	241	304	186	3.9	1.9	8.9	4.8	36	18	46	0.9	8%	31%	80%	0	15			82	1.22	8.6	124	161	$15
1st Half	1	3	12	29	30	3.14	3.67	1.08	222	298	164	4.0	2.2	9.4	4.3	33	18	49	0.9	8%	29%	75%	0	17			75	1.15	3.1	122	159	$14
2nd Half	0	1	19	29	27	2.48	3.66	1.17	259	309	211	3.8	1.6	8.4	5.4	38	19	43	0.9	8%	32%	84%	0	14			86	1.29	5.5	125	163	$17
13 Proj	**2**	**2**	**30**	**58**	**56**	**3.34**	**3.65**	**1.09**	**235**	**282**	**198**	**3.6**	**2.0**	**8.6**	**4.3**	**33**	**19**	**48**	**1.2**	**10%**	**28%**	**75%**	**0**						**4.9**	**112**	**145**	**$15**

Billingsley,Chad

Age: 28 Th: R Role SP	Health B	LIMA Plan B	
Ht: 6' 1" Wt: 240 Type Pwr	PT/Exp A	Rand Var -1	
	Consist A	MM 3301	

Sparkled in 2H as we await that full-fledged breakout season. But elbow woes that shut him down in August cast a dark shadow; the progression of "inflammation" to "platelet-rich plasma injections" to "possible Tommy John surgery" is not one that usually ends well. Even if he breaks camp, a huge risk.

Yr Tm	W	L	Sv	IP	K	ERA	xERA	WHIP	OBA	vL	vR	BF/G	Ctl	Dom	Cmd	G	L	F	hr/9	hr/f	H%	S%	GS	APC	DOM%	DIS%	Sv%	LI	RAR	BPV	BPX	R$
08 LA	16	10	0	201	201	3.14	3.61	1.34	248	274	225	24.5	3.6	9.0	2.5	49	20	31	0.6	8%	32%	78%	32	95	56%	6%	0	0.77	29.3	92	173	$19
09 LA	12	11	0	196	179	4.03	3.93	1.32	244	257	229	24.9	3.9	8.2	2.1	45	18	36	0.8	9%	29%	71%	32	98	63%	9%	0	0.77	7.0	64	120	$12
10 LA	12	11	0	192	171	3.57	3.65	1.28	244	252	236	26.4	3.2	8.0	2.5	50	18	32	0.4	4%	31%	71%	31	101	48%	10%			12.1	85	138	$12
11 LA	11	11	0	188	152	4.21	4.20	1.45	264	282	248	25.9	4.0	7.3	1.8	45	21	34	0.7	7%	32%	71%	32	101	41%	19%			-6.3	45	68	$0
12 LA	10	9	0	150	128	3.55	3.87	1.29	257	260	255	25.4	2.7	7.7	2.8	45	21	33	0.7	7%	32%	74%	25	95	72%	16%			8.6	88	115	$8
1st Half	4	7	0	93	87	4.18	3.99	1.44	274	264	287	25.3	3.3	8.4	2.6	44	21	35	0.9	10%	34%	73%	16	95	63%	19%			-1.8	85	111	$4
2nd Half	6	2	0	57	41	2.53	3.69	1.05	229	252	206	25.4	1.7	6.5	3.7	47	22	31	0.3	4%	28%	76%	9	95	89%	11%			10.5	95	124	$13
13 Proj	**5**	**4**	**0**	**73**	**61**	**3.79**	**3.90**	**1.29**	**252**	**264**	**240**	**24.8**	**3.0**	**7.5**	**2.5**	**47**	**21**	**33**	**0.7**	**8%**	**31%**	**72%**	**12**						**2.0**	**77**	**101**	**$2**

Blackburn,Nick

Age: 31 Th: R Role SP	Health B	LIMA Plan D	
Ht: 6' 4" Wt: 238 Type Con	PT/Exp C	Rand Var +3	
	Consist D	MM 0001	

4-9, 7.39 ERA in 99 IP at MIN. Consider: A Twilight Zone season... The Dom column looks like Cmd. A GB pitcher struggles with gopheritis. A 7.39 ERA pitcher gets NINETEEN starts. But take heart—his Aug 20 demotion sewed up 2012's "Most Inconsequential MLB Roster Move, Current SP" award.

Yr Tm	W	L	Sv	IP	K	ERA	xERA	WHIP	OBA	vL	vR	BF/G	Ctl	Dom	Cmd	G	L	F	hr/9	hr/f	H%	S%	GS	APC	DOM%	DIS%	Sv%	LI	RAR	BPV	BPX	R$
08 MIN	11	11	0	193	96	4.05	4.44	1.36	292	295	289	24.9	1.8	4.5	2.5	45	21	34	1.1	10%	31%	73%	33	87	39%	33%			6.5	54	102	$7
09 MIN	11	11	0	206	98	4.03	4.56	1.37	290	300	277	26.7	1.8	4.3	2.4	46	18	36	1.1	9%	31%	74%	33	94	30%	27%			7.5	53	99	$7
10 MIN *	11	12	0	183	77	5.14	5.25	1.45	297	285	318	24.3	2.3	3.8	1.7	51	17	32	1.3	14%	30%	67%	26	85	23%	31%	0	0.78	-23.9	14	22	-$5
11 MIN	7	10	0	148	76	4.49	4.54	1.60	305	295	316	25.8	3.3	4.6	1.4	54	21	26	1.2	14%	32%	75%	26	93	23%	31%			-10.0	27	40	-$8
12 MIN *	7	10	0	135	50	6.44	7.14	1.75	344	376	311	23.8	2.4	3.3	1.4	45	19	36	1.7	17%	34%	66%	19	86	5%	42%			-40.5	-16	-20	-$25
1st Half	4	5	0	65	30	8.02	7.00	1.77	328	370	296	21.4	3.6	4.2	1.2	50	15	35	1.8	17%	33%	56%	12	83	0%	42%			-32.2	-14	-18	-$29
2nd Half	3	5	0	70	20	4.97	7.19	1.72	357	385	333	26.5	1.4	2.5	1.8	39	24	37	1.6	17%	35%	76%	7	91	14%	43%			-8.2	-11	-14	-$21
13 Proj	**4**	**5**	**0**	**77**	**32**	**5.40**	**5.10**	**1.63**	**324**	**334**	**314**	**24.6**	**2.5**	**3.8**	**1.5**	**47**	**20**	**33**	**1.4**	**13%**	**33%**	**70%**	**14**						**-13.0**	**26**	**33**	**-$8**

BRENT HERSHEY

Blackley,Travis

Age: 30	Th: L	Role RP	Health	A	LIMA Plan	D
Ht: 6' 3"	Wt: 205	Type	PT/Exp	D	Rand Var	-1
			Consist	D	MM	1201

6-4, 4.10 ERA in 108 IP at SF and OAK. Melbourne Aces refugee had mid-season run of PQS3+ starts before Ctl, Cmd lagged and gopheritis struck in 2H. Pitched true to GB profile, but nothing in recent past—any league or continent—says ERA, WHIP, OBA, are close to being repeatable. Watch from afar.

Yr	Tm	W	L	Sv	IP	K	ERA	xERA	WHIP	OBA	vL	vR	BF/G	Ctl	Dom	Cmd	G	L	F	hr/9	hr/f	H%	S%	GS	APC	DOM%	DIS%	Sv%	LI	RAR	BPV	BPX	R$
08	aaa	5	10	0	123	70	7.59	7.11	1.90	328			20.8	4.7	5.1	1.1				1.6		35%	61%							-49.6	-4	-7	-$21
09	aaa	4	7	3	111	76	5.59	6.24	1.76	332			13.4	3.2	6.2	1.9				1.0		38%	69%							-17.4	37	70	-$9
10	aaa	2	1	0	42	30	3.71	4.91	1.70	265			10.0	6.2	6.4	1.0				0.8		31%	80%							1.9	39	63	-$3
11																																	
12	2 TM *	9	4	1	131	85	3.44	3.05	1.13	235	241	244	16.2	2.4	5.8	2.4	48	18	35	0.8	9%	26%	72%	15	59	47%	33%	100	0.65	9.2	72	93	$10
1st Half		4	2	1	70	42	2.60	2.03	1.00	220	229	238	15.6	1.8	5.4	3.0	46	21	33	0.2	2%	26%	73%	6	53	50%	33%	100	0.50	12.2	99	129	$16
2nd Half		5	2	0	61	43	4.40	4.16	1.29	251	250	248	16.8	3.1	6.3	2.0	49	15	36	1.3	13%	27%	70%	9	65	44%	33%	0	0.77	-2.9	46	60	$3
13	**Proj**	**5**	**3**	**0**	**87**	**58**	**4.35**	**4.67**	**1.47**	**270**	**269**	**271**	**13.9**	**3.8**	**6.0**	**1.6**	**48**	**17**	**35**	**1.0**	**10%**	**30%**	**72%**	**10**						**-3.5**	**32**	**41**	**-$2**

Blanton,Joe

Age: 32	Th: R	Role SP	Health	F	LIMA Plan	A+
Ht: 6' 3"	Wt: 235	Type	PT/Exp	B	Rand Var	+3
			Consist	A	MM	3305

Rebound from injury-ravaged 2011 didn't clear up the mystery of the perpetual disconnect between skill and results. Do you trust the bests/near bests for Ctl, Dom, and Cmd? Or are you held back by the repeated ERA/xERA gaps, hr/f and S% issues? There is a sub-3.50 ERA lurking, but it's tough to bet on.

Yr	Tm	W	L	Sv	IP	K	ERA	xERA	WHIP	OBA	vL	vR	BF/G	Ctl	Dom	Cmd	G	L	F	hr/9	hr/f	H%	S%	GS	APC	DOM%	DIS%	Sv%	LI	RAR	BPV	BPX	R$
08	2 TM	9	12	0	198	111	4.69	4.70	1.40	271	256	286	25.9	3.0	5.1	1.7	44	20	35	1.0	9%	30%	68%	33	98	33%	18%			-8.9	32	60	$1
09	PHI	12	8	0	195	163	4.05	4.04	1.32	262	252	271	27.0	2.7	7.5	2.8	41	20	39	1.4	13%	30%	74%	31	105	55%	16%			6.4	81	151	$11
10	PHI	9	6	0	176	134	4.82	4.06	1.42	291	266	314	26.4	2.2	6.9	3.1	42	19	39	1.4	12%	33%	70%	28	95	50%	14%	0	0.74	-16.0	84	136	-$1
11	PHI	1	2	0	41	35	5.01	3.38	1.48	319	299	333	16.4	2.0	7.6	3.9	55	17	28	1.1	14%	37%	68%	8	53	25%	50%	0	0.66	-5.4	117	176	-$4
12	2 NL	10	13	0	191	166	4.71	3.60	1.26	273	293	254	26.0	1.6	7.8	4.9	45	23	32	1.4	15%	32%	67%	30	94	63%	10%	0	0.83	-16.4	121	157	$2
1st Half		7	6	0	98	82	4.87	3.68	1.24	275	292	254	26.2	1.2	7.5	6.3	44	22	34	1.7	17%	32%	66%	15	92	60%	13%	0	0.90	-10.3	125	163	$5
2nd Half		3	7	0	93	84	4.55	3.53	1.28	272	294	254	25.8	2.0	8.1	4.0	45	25	30	1.1	13%	33%	67%	15	97	67%	7%			-6.1	115	150	-$1
13	**Proj**	**11**	**11**	**0**	**196**	**163**	**4.52**	**3.68**	**1.32**	**282**	**281**	**282**	**22.0**	**2.0**	**7.5**	**3.8**	**47**	**21**	**32**	**1.2**	**14%**	**33%**	**69%**	**37**						**-12.1**	**107**	**139**	**$5**

Blevins,Jerry

Age: 29	Th: L	Role RP	Health	A	LIMA Plan	B
Ht: 6' 6"	Wt: 175	Type Pwr FB	PT/Exp	D	Rand Var	-5
			Consist	D	MM	2300

Neither lefties or righties hit him much and a nifty WHIP speaks to overall effectiveness. Strand rate made for showy ERA, but troubles stemmed from Dom drop and 2H BB. If he were used in more crucial spots, it might have been a Year of Living Dangerously. But until he corrals his walk rate, he won't.

Yr	Tm	W	L	Sv	IP	K	ERA	xERA	WHIP	OBA	vL	vR	BF/G	Ctl	Dom	Cmd	G	L	F	hr/9	hr/f	H%	S%	GS	APC	DOM%	DIS%	Sv%	LI	RAR	BPV	BPX	R$
08	OAK *	3	5	10	70	63	3.08	3.36	1.22	253	193	256	4.4	2.4	8.1	3.3	43	18	38	0.6	5%	32%	76%	0	17			83	1.06	10.7	105	197	$8
09	OAK *	5	3	2	86	71	4.58	4.33	1.40	283	250	218	5.6	2.6	7.5	2.9	32	17	52	0.7	6%	34%	68%	0	19			33	0.36	-2.8	82	153	$1
10	OAK	2	1	1	49	46	3.70	4.10	1.48	274	231	311	3.5	3.3	8.5	2.6	38	23	39	1.3	12%	34%	80%	0	13			50	1.19	2.3	79	128	-$1
11	OAK *	2	0	0	58	53	4.13	3.50	1.28	245	256	220	4.5	3.3	8.2	2.5	38	18	44	0.7	6%	30%	69%	0	17			0	0.62	-1.3	86	129	-$1
12	OAK	5	1	1	65	54	2.48	4.07	1.07	201	182	219	4.1	3.4	7.4	2.2	38	18	44	1.0	9%	23%	83%	0	16			100	0.92	12.4	57	74	$7
1st Half		1	0	0	32	27	2.51	3.80	1.08	216	226	207	4.6	3.1	7.5	2.5	43	20	37	1.1	13%	24%	84%	0	18			0	0.59	6.0	73	95	$4
2nd Half		4	1	1	33	27	2.45	4.33	1.06	186	140	232	3.8	3.8	7.4	1.9	34	15	51	0.8	7%	21%	81%	0	15			100	1.17	6.4	42	55	$10
13	**Proj**	**4**	**2**	**0**	**58**	**50**	**3.69**	**4.07**	**1.21**	**229**	**195**	**259**	**4.0**	**3.3**	**7.8**	**2.4**	**38**	**20**	**42**	**0.9**	**9%**	**27%**	**72%**	**0**						**2.3**	**67**	**88**	**$2**

Boggs,Mitchell

Age: 29	Th: R	Role RP	Health	A	LIMA Plan	B
Ht: 6' 4"	Wt: 215	Type GB	PT/Exp	C	Rand Var	-5
			Consist	A	MM	3210

Completed his 3rd straight season of improved BPIs across the board to move into top tier of setup men. Watch out - studies warn us that year #4 ends in give-backs more often than not. Unswerving groundball resume will prevent him from slipping too far, but regression can be a powerful force.

Yr	Tm	W	L	Sv	IP	K	ERA	xERA	WHIP	OBA	vL	vR	BF/G	Ctl	Dom	Cmd	G	L	F	hr/9	hr/f	H%	S%	GS	APC	DOM%	DIS%	Sv%	LI	RAR	BPV	BPX	R$
08	STL *	12	5	0	159	78	4.64	4.36	1.44	266	321	283	23.4	3.8	4.4	1.2	52	19	29	0.9	14%	28%	69%	6	72	17%	33%	0	0.58	-6.2	27	50	$2
09	STL *	8	7	0	134	92	5.14	5.92	1.81	319	410	234	20.7	4.4	6.2	1.4	53	18	29	0.7	6%	37%	72%	9	64	11%	33%	0	0.77	-13.6	36	67	-$10
10	STL	2	3	0	67	52	3.61	3.88	1.29	243	253	238	4.7	3.6	7.0	1.9	53	16	31	0.7	8%	29%	73%	0	18			0	0.72	3.9	59	95	$1
11	STL	2	3	4	61	48	3.56	3.73	1.37	266	247	276	5.1	3.1	7.1	2.3	51	21	28	0.6	8%	32%	75%	0	19			50	0.62	2.9	73	110	$1
12	STL	4	1	0	73	58	2.21	3.55	1.05	211	241	191	3.8	2.6	7.1	2.8	53	19	28	0.6	9%	26%	82%	0	14			0	1.21	16.3	90	117	$8
1st Half		1	1	0	34	27	2.12	3.49	1.06	220	313	160	4.1	2.4	7.1	3.0	53	20	27	0.5	8%	27%	82%	0	15			0	1.04	8.0	95	124	$5
2nd Half		3	0	0	39	31	2.29	3.61	1.04	204	183	220	3.6	2.7	7.1	2.6	53	18	29	0.7	9%	25%	82%	0	13			0	1.34	8.4	84	109	$11
13	**Proj**	**3**	**2**	**5**	**58**	**45**	**3.50**	**3.86**	**1.27**	**250**	**266**	**239**	**4.5**	**3.0**	**6.9**	**2.3**	**52**	**19**	**29**	**0.6**	**8%**	**30%**	**74%**	**0**						**3.7**	**73**	**95**	**$3**

Bowden,Michael

Age: 26	Th: R	Role RP	Health	A	LIMA Plan	D
Ht: 6' 3"	Wt: 215	Type Pwr xFB	PT/Exp	D	Rand Var	-2
			Consist	B	MM	1300

0-0, 2.95 ERA in 40 IP at BOS and CHC. It's like we've hearing about him as a starter-closer forever but still has fewer than 100 career IP over 5 years. Other than unrelenting BB rate, numbers seem randomly generated. Good trick, having no decisions in 40 IP with that degree of volatility.

Yr	Tm	W	L	Sv	IP	K	ERA	xERA	WHIP	OBA	vL	vR	BF/G	Ctl	Dom	Cmd	G	L	F	hr/9	hr/f	H%	S%	GS	APC	DOM%	DIS%	Sv%	LI	RAR	BPV	BPX	R$
08	BOS *	10	7	0	149	112	3.25	2.98	1.12	245	222	417	21.8	1.8	6.7	3.7	17	22	61	0.6	0%	29%	72%	1	89	0%	0%			19.8	106	198	$16
09	BOS *	5	7	0	142	84	5.51	5.26	1.57	289	395	258	19.5	3.8	5.3	1.4	42	14	44	1.2	12%	31%	66%	1	38	0%	100%	0	0.45	-20.8	24	45	-$8
10	BOS *	6	5	1	121	76	4.72	4.43	1.36	262	379	273	11.2	3.2	5.6	1.8	29	18	53	1.2	8%	28%	68%	0	19			33	1.20	-9.6	36	59	-$1
11	BOS *	3	3	16	73	66	3.88	4.50	1.43	264	258	229	5.6	3.8	8.2	2.2	29	18	53	1.1	9%	32%	77%	0	27			94	0.22	0.6	63	95	$5
12	2 TM *	3	2	2	72	60	3.10	3.14	1.24	211	212	233	5.3	4.4	7.4	1.7	39	15	46	0.9	10%	25%	78%	0	20			40	0.46	8.1	66	87	$4
1st Half		1	0	0	24	21	4.79	4.74	1.50	267	261	370	4.9	4.3	7.8	1.8	38	20	43	1.1	18%	32%	71%	0	18			0	0.39	-2.2	52	68	-$8
2nd Half		2	2	2	49	39	2.29	2.33	1.11	180	172	175	5.6	4.4	7.3	1.7	40	13	47	0.8	6%	21%	84%	0	22			50	0.49	10.4	74	96	$9
13	**Proj**	**2**	**1**	**0**	**44**	**35**	**3.77**	**4.65**	**1.32**	**240**	**238**	**241**	**6.4**	**3.9**	**7.3**	**1.9**	**40**	**13**	**47**	**1.0**	**7%**	**28%**	**75%**	**0**						**1.3**	**44**	**57**	**-$1**

Brach,Brad

Age: 27	Th: R	Role RP	Health	A	LIMA Plan	A+
Ht: 6' 6"	Wt: 210	Type Pwr FB	PT/Exp	D	Rand Var	0
			Consist	C	MM	4500

Four possible closer seeds planted in 2H: 1) Terrific strikeout rate 2) Halved walks over more IP 3) sliced ERA, pitched to xERA 4) Dual lefty-righty dominance. Still a small sample size, but more gains in Ctl, ground ball rate could inspire fierce bidding in 2014.

Yr	Tm	W	L	Sv	IP	K	ERA	xERA	WHIP	OBA	vL	vR	BF/G	Ctl	Dom	Cmd	G	L	F	hr/9	hr/f	H%	S%	GS	APC	DOM%	DIS%	Sv%	LI	RAR	BPV	BPX	R$
08																																	
09																																	
10																																	
11	SD *	3	7	34	79	91	2.78	2.59	1.11	238	333	286	4.1	2.1	10.4	5.0	26	53	21	0.3	0%	34%	75%	0	17			92	1.06	11.3	165	248	$20
12	SD	2	4	0	67	75	3.78	3.96	1.25	207	239	188	4.2	4.5	10.1	2.3	35	20	45	1.5	15%	26%	76%	0	17			0	1.17	1.9	75	98	$1
1st Half		0	1	0	28	31	4.23	4.91	1.59	225	233	218	4.5	7.2	10.1	1.4	33	24	43	1.6	17%	27%	79%	0	19			0	1.19	-0.7	-1	-1	-$7
2nd Half		2	3	0	39	44	3.46	3.40	1.00	196	245	170	4.0	2.5	10.2	4.0	37	18	46	1.4	13%	25%	73%	0	16			0	1.15	2.7	129	168	$6
13	**Proj**	**2**	**5**	**0**	**65**	**74**	**3.37**	**3.58**	**1.19**	**221**	**256**	**200**	**4.1**	**3.5**	**10.2**	**2.9**	**35**	**20**	**45**	**1.0**	**10%**	**29%**	**76%**	**0**						**5.2**	**103**	**134**	**$3**

Breslow,Craig

Age: 32	Th: L	Role RP	Health	A	LIMA Plan	B+
Ht: 6' 0"	Wt: 190	Type Pwr	PT/Exp	C	Rand Var	-3
			Consist	B	MM	3400

Well-traveled ex-LOOGY renewed emphasis on cut fastball and saw jump in strikeout rate plus improved Cmd. But true accomplishment is annually outpitching his xERA. A Yale biophysics major can do that, apparently. Value is capped by iffy control and non-closer role, but a nice complementary piece.

Yr	Tm	W	L	Sv	IP	K	ERA	xERA	WHIP	OBA	vL	vR	BF/G	Ctl	Dom	Cmd	G	L	F	hr/9	hr/f	H%	S%	GS	APC	DOM%	DIS%	Sv%	LI	RAR	BPV	BPX	R$
08	2 AL	0	2	1	47	39	1.91	4.05	1.13	202	183	221	3.9	3.6	7.5	2.1	42	17	42	0.2	2%	26%	83%	0	14			50	0.85	14.0	56	105	$4
09	2 AL	8	7	0	70	55	3.36	4.35	1.11	197	204	191	3.6	3.7	7.1	1.9	32	20	48	1.0	9%	22%	74%	0	14			0	1.07	8.3	37	69	$7
10	OAK	4	4	5	75	71	3.01	4.07	1.10	194	181	201	4.1	3.5	8.6	2.4	30	15	56	1.1	8%	24%	78%	0	16			71	1.03	9.8	68	109	$8
11	OAK	0	2	0	59	44	3.79	4.41	1.52	296	352	261	3.9	3.2	6.7	2.1	38	20	41	0.6	5%	35%	76%	0	15			0	0.78	1.1	50	75	-$4
12	2 TM	3	0	0	63	61	2.70	3.67	1.17	225	222	228	4.1	3.1	8.7	2.8	45	19	36	0.7	8%	29%	80%	0	17			0	0.83	10.3	95	123	$4
1st Half		2	0	0	35	32	3.09	3.91	1.23	246	271	227	4.6	2.6	8.2	3.2	39	21	41	1.3	12%	30%	82%	0	19			0	0.84	4.0	95	124	$3
2nd Half		1	0	0	28	29	2.22	3.33	1.09	196	163	229	3.7	3.8	9.2	2.4	54	17	29	0.0	0%	27%	77%	0	15			0	0.82	6.3	95	124	$5
13	**Proj**	**2**	**1**	**0**	**58**	**52**	**3.41**	**3.99**	**1.26**	**240**	**244**	**238**	**3.9**	**3.3**	**8.1**	**2.4**	**42**	**18**	**40**	**0.6**	**6%**	**30%**	**74%**	**0**						**4.3**	**75**	**97**	**$1**

ROB CARROLL

Britton,Zach

Age: 25	Th: L Role SP	Health	C	LIMA Plan	D
Ht: 6' 3"	Wt: 195 Type xGB	PT/Exp	D	Rand Var	+2
		Consist	A	MM	2203

5-3, 5.07 ERA in 60 IP at BAL. Remnant of '11 shoulder injury shelved him until July, then pitched brilliantly or dreadfully (see DOM%/DIS%). Sinkerballer induces tons of GBs, strikes out some, walks too many. But has he ever been pain free? Health will define his value, but.. UP: 3.50 ERA

Yr	Tm	W	L	Sv	IP	K	ERA	xERA	WHIP	OBA	vL	vR	BF/G	Ctl	Dom	Cmd	G	L	F	hr/9	hr/f	H%	S%	GS	APC	DOM%	DIS%	Sv%	LI	RAR	BPV	BPX	R$
08																																	
09																																	
10	a/a	10	7	0	153	103	3.28	3.91	1.37	271			23.8	2.9	6.0	2.1				0.5		32%	77%							15.1	65	105	$7
11	BAL *	11	14	0	171	112	4.70	4.44	1.45	274	260	281	22.8	3.4	5.9	1.7	53	19	28	0.8	9%	31%	68%	28	90	36%	21%			-16.0	46	70	-$3
12	BAL *	10	5	0	124	91	5.26	4.68	1.51	273	235	273	23.3	4.1	6.6	1.6	61	16	23	0.9	14%	32%	66%	11	89	45%	45%	0	0.73	-18.9	47	61	-$8
1st Half		3	1	0	39	20	5.52	5.06	1.59	305	0	0	24.4	3.2	4.6	1.5				0.6	0%	34%	64%	0	0					-7.2	34	44	-$13
2nd Half		7	4	0	85	71	5.13	4.46	1.48	258	235	273	22.8	4.5	7.5	1.7	61	16	23	1.0	14%	30%	67%	11	89	45%	45%	0	0.73	-11.7	53	69	-$6
13	Proj	**9**	**7**	**0**	**131**	**89**	**4.43**	**4.24**	**1.48**	**275**	**252**	**286**	**23.3**	**3.7**	**6.2**	**1.7**	**58**	**17**	**25**	**0.8**	**11%**	**31%**	**71%**	**24**						**-6.6**	**48**	**62**	**-$1**

Brothers,Rex

Age: 25	Th: L Role RP	Health	A	LIMA Plan	A+
Ht: 6' 0"	Wt: 210 Type Pwr	PT/Exp	D	Rand Var	+2
		Consist	A	MM	4520

He lets 'em rip, one 95-mph heater after another, inducing swings and misses aplenty. But oh, that strike zone is so elusive, and RHB have had their successes. Dom, emerging ground ball profile are enticing, and just one fewer BB per week could translate to....UP: 25 saves

Yr	Tm	W	L	Sv	IP	K	ERA	xERA	WHIP	OBA	vL	vR	BF/G	Ctl	Dom	Cmd	G	L	F	hr/9	hr/f	H%	S%	GS	APC	DOM%	DIS%	Sv%	LI	RAR	BPV	BPX	R$
08																																	
09																																	
10	aa	2	1	4	23	21	5.15	3.96	1.53	206			4.2	7.2	8.4	1.2				1.1		25%	68%							-3.0	57	92	-$1
11	COL *	4	4	1	69	94	2.74	3.69	1.38	242	193	232	4.0	4.3	12.3	2.9	46	16	37	0.8	12%	36%	83%	0	15			20	1.01	10.2	118	177	$4
12	COL	8	2	0	68	83	3.86	3.59	1.48	251	206	282	3.9	4.9	11.0	2.2	47	23	30	0.7	10%	35%	75%	0	15			0	1.09	1.3	91	118	$0
1st Half		3	2	0	29	42	3.41	3.05	1.52	261	200	303	3.6	4.7	13.0	2.8	51	23	27	0.3	5%	41%	77%	0	15			0	1.12	2.2	138	180	$0
2nd Half		5	0	0	39	41	4.19	4.03	1.45	243	211	265	4.3	5.1	9.5	1.9	44	23	32	0.9	13%	31%	73%	0	16			0	1.07	-0.8	56	73	$0
13	Proj	**6**	**3**	**10**	**65**	**84**	**3.42**	**3.42**	**1.44**	**246**	**208**	**270**	**3.9**	**4.7**	**11.5**	**2.5**	**47**	**20**	**33**	**0.7**	**10%**	**35%**	**78%**	**0**						**4.8**	**106**	**137**	**$7**

Broxton,Jonathan

Age: 29	Th: R Role RP	Health	D	LIMA Plan	B+
Ht: 6' 4"	Wt: 300 Type Pwr GB	PT/Exp	C	Rand Var	-4
		Consist	D	MM	4420

Were reports of his demise premature? YES: Ctl south of 3.0 for first time in 5 yrs; career-low ERA; dramatic increase in GB%. NO: Dom didn't recover; S% artificially lowered ERA; increasingly ineffective from Jun-Aug. Will need more distance from that Sept '11 elbow surgery before we know for sure.

Yr	Tm	W	L	Sv	IP	K	ERA	xERA	WHIP	OBA	vL	vR	BF/G	Ctl	Dom	Cmd	G	L	F	hr/9	hr/f	H%	S%	GS	APC	DOM%	DIS%	Sv%	LI	RAR	BPV	BPX	R$
08	LA	3	5	14	69	88	3.13	2.98	1.17	217	270	181	4.1	3.5	11.5	3.3	45	23	32	0.3	4%	33%	72%	0	17			64	1.29	10.2	135	252	$12
09	LA	7	2	36	76	114	2.61	2.20	0.96	165	138	190	4.1	3.4	13.5	3.9	56	16	28	0.5	9%	29%	74%	0	17			86	1.32	16.1	184	345	$28
10	LA	5	6	22	62	73	4.04	3.35	1.48	270	243	292	4.2	4.0	10.5	2.6	47	21	32	0.6	8%	37%	73%	0	17			76	1.31	0.3	106	171	$9
11	LA	1	2	7	13	10	5.68	5.30	1.89	283	238	313	4.4	6.4	7.1	1.1	42	33	26	1.4	18%	34%	73%	0	18			88	1.04	-2.7	-25	-37	-$2
12	2 TM	4	5	27	58	45	2.48	3.58	1.26	260	219	294	4.0	2.6	7.0	2.6	54	22	24	0.3	5%	31%	80%	0	16			82	1.33	11.0	86	113	$14
1st Half		1	1	20	31	23	2.05	3.96	1.34	257	218	293	4.3	3.5	6.8	1.9	54	21	25	0.3	5%	31%	85%	0	16			87	1.37	7.4	58	76	$18
2nd Half		3	4	7	27	22	2.96	3.19	1.17	265	220	295	3.6	1.6	7.2	4.4	54	23	24	0.3	5%	32%	74%	0	15			70	1.29	3.6	118	154	$10
13	Proj	**5**	**5**	**10**	**58**	**55**	**3.01**	**3.44**	**1.25**	**243**	**215**	**266**	**4.0**	**3.1**	**8.6**	**2.8**	**51**	**21**	**27**	**0.4**	**6%**	**32%**	**76%**	**0**						**7.2**	**100**	**130**	**$7**

Buchholz,Clay

Age: 28	Th: R Role SP	Health	F	LIMA Plan	B
Ht: 6' 3"	Wt: 190 Type	PT/Exp	A	Rand Var	+1
		Consist	A	MM	2205

Slow start was likely residue from his truncated 2011 (back), but BPIs show his skill levels are intact. Maintained Dom, tightened control, and check out that 2H DOM%/DIS%. Throw out his first and last games of 2012, and ERA drops to 3.98. And he set a new career-high in IP. A return to profit potential.

Yr	Tm	W	L	Sv	IP	K	ERA	xERA	WHIP	OBA	vL	vR	BF/G	Ctl	Dom	Cmd	G	L	F	hr/9	hr/f	H%	S%	GS	APC	DOM%	DIS%	Sv%	LI	RAR	BPV	BPX	R$
08	BOS *	7	11	0	135	121	5.10	4.74	1.52	276	293	305	21.6	4.0	8.1	2.0	48	21	31	0.9	15%	34%	67%	15	86	20%	40%	0	0.76	-12.9	62	117	-$2
09	BOS *	14	6	0	191	138	4.06	4.11	1.34	254	284	228	24.1	3.4	6.5	1.9	54	18	29	1.1	16%	29%	73%	16	95	38%	25%			6.2	51	95	$11
10	BOS	17	7	0	174	120	2.33	3.96	1.20	226	230	221	25.4	3.5	6.2	1.8	51	18	32	0.5	6%	26%	82%	28	100	43%	21%			37.4	47	76	$21
11	BOS	6	3	0	83	60	3.48	4.15	1.29	241	241	242	25.2	3.4	6.5	1.9	51	11	39	1.1	10%	28%	77%	14	97	43%	21%			4.7	55	83	$3
12	BOS	11	8	0	189	129	4.56	4.27	1.33	263	266	260	27.7	3.0	6.1	2.0	48	20	33	1.2	13%	29%	69%	29	100	52%	21%			-12.8	54	71	$0
1st Half		8	2	0	86	58	5.53	4.55	1.54	295	332	241	27.2	3.5	6.0	1.7	49	19	32	1.6	17%	31%	68%	14	100	36%	36%			-16.1	40	52	-$7
2nd Half		3	6	0	103	71	3.76	4.06	1.15	235	193	273	28.1	2.6	6.2	2.4	46	20	33	0.9	10%	26%	69%	15	100	67%	7%			3.3	65	85	$6
13	Proj	**12**	**11**	**0**	**210**	**149**	**3.91**	**4.22**	**1.30**	**250**	**250**	**249**	**25.5**	**3.2**	**6.4**	**2.0**	**49**	**17**	**34**	**1.0**	**11%**	**28%**	**73%**	**34**						**2.8**	**54**	**71**	**$10**

Buehrle,Mark

Age: 34	Th: L Role SP	Health	A	LIMA Plan	C
Ht: 6' 2"	Wt: 245 Type Con	PT/Exp	A	Rand Var	0
		Consist	A	MM	2105

So predictable, was considering a blind copy & paste from this space last year. (He does it, why can't we?) OK, he gave up a few more HR and his ground ball rate is in slow fade, but Dom and Cmd were his best in years. With twelve straight 200-IP seasons, look for number 13. But that'll be his win total, too.

Yr	Tm	W	L	Sv	IP	K	ERA	xERA	WHIP	OBA	vL	vR	BF/G	Ctl	Dom	Cmd	G	L	F	hr/9	hr/f	H%	S%	GS	APC	DOM%	DIS%	Sv%	LI	RAR	BPV	BPX	R$
08	CHW	15	12	0	219	140	3.79	4.02	1.34	281	293	277	27.0	2.1	5.8	2.7	50	19	32	0.9	10%	31%	74%	34	100	53%	15%			14.5	74	139	$13
09	CHW	13	10	0	213	105	3.84	4.32	1.25	275	298	267	26.5	1.9	4.4	2.3	45	19	36	1.1	11%	28%	73%	33	97	33%	18%			12.7	51	96	$13
10	CHW	13	13	0	210	99	4.28	4.55	1.40	295	275	303	27.2	2.1	4.2	2.0	46	16	38	0.7	6%	32%	70%	33	100	33%	15%			-5.2	44	71	$2
11	CHW	13	9	0	205	109	3.59	4.20	1.30	277	251	288	27.7	2.0	4.8	2.4	45	20	35	0.9	9%	30%	75%	31	101	45%	10%			8.8	56	84	$8
12	MIA	13	13	0	202	125	3.74	4.16	1.17	258	217	271	26.7	1.8	5.6	3.1	41	22	36	1.2	11%	28%	73%	31	99	55%	13%			7.0	71	93	$13
1st Half		7	8	0	106	58	3.48	4.17	1.15	265	224	278	26.8	1.4	4.9	3.6	43	20	37	1.1	10%	28%	74%	16	99	50%	6%			7.0	73	95	$16
2nd Half		6	5	0	96	67	4.02	4.15	1.19	251	207	263	26.7	2.2	6.3	2.8	40	25	35	1.2	13%	28%	71%	15	98	60%	20%			0.0	70	91	$9
13	Proj	**13**	**11**	**0**	**200**	**115**	**4.00**	**4.29**	**1.25**	**268**	**242**	**278**	**26.5**	**2.0**	**5.2**	**2.7**	**43**	**21**	**36**	**1.0**	**10%**	**29%**	**71%**	**31**						**0.3**	**62**	**81**	**$9**

Bumgarner,Madison

Age: 23	Th: L Role SP	Health	A	LIMA Plan	C+
Ht: 6' 5"	Wt: 235 Type	PT/Exp	A	Rand Var	0
		Consist	B	MM	4305

Another profile that has developed its own rhythm. It's full of high notes—Dom and Cmd settling in, pitching to xERA, fine DOM%/DIS%. Only September was decidedly off key, when velocity and control abandoned him on the way to career-high IP. He's a young virtuoso. Bid accordingly.

Yr	Tm	W	L	Sv	IP	K	ERA	xERA	WHIP	OBA	vL	vR	BF/G	Ctl	Dom	Cmd	G	L	F	hr/9	hr/f	H%	S%	GS	APC	DOM%	DIS%	Sv%	LI	RAR	BPV	BPX	R$
08																																	
09	SF *	9	1	0	117	70	2.38	2.91	1.13	232	83	304	19.2	2.5	5.4	2.2	58	15	27	0.7	29%	26%	82%	1	39	0%	0%	0	0.38	28.0	67	125	$15
10	SF *	14	7	0	194	137	3.12	4.12	1.33	279	243	283	25.1	2.1	6.4	3.0	45	17	38	0.7	8%	32%	79%	18	96	50%	22%			23.0	78	126	$13
11	SF	13	13	0	205	191	3.21	3.25	1.21	260	243	264	25.6	2.0	8.4	4.2	46	21	33	0.5	6%	33%	74%	33	97	70%	15%			18.5	121	181	$17
12	SF	16	11	0	208	191	3.37	3.43	1.11	234	208	241	26.5	2.1	8.3	3.9	48	19	33	1.0	12%	29%	74%	32	102	66%	13%			16.6	117	153	$23
1st Half		10	4	0	111	92	2.85	3.47	1.06	229	158	250	27.9	1.8	7.5	4.2	50	17	33	0.8	10%	28%	77%	16	104	63%	6%			16.0	114	148	$32
2nd Half		6	7	0	98	99	3.96	3.39	1.18	240	274	231	25.2	2.5	9.1	3.7	45	21	34	1.2	14%	30%	71%	16	100	69%	19%			0.7	120	156	$12
13	Proj	**14**	**10**	**0**	**203**	**177**	**3.27**	**3.55**	**1.18**	**250**	**234**	**254**	**24.4**	**2.2**	**7.8**	**3.6**	**46**	**19**	**34**	**0.8**	**9%**	**30%**	**75%**	**33**						**18.8**	**107**	**138**	**$20**

Bundy,Dylan

Age: 20	Th: R Role RP	Health	A	LIMA Plan	C+
Ht: 6' 1"	Wt: 195 Type Pwr xFB	PT/Exp	F	Rand Var	-3
		Consist	F	MM	1201

0-0, 0.00 ERA in 2 IP at BAL. Began year with 13 hitless IP in Low-A, ended it by getting Colby Rasmus to hit into a DP in Camden Yards. Has three plus pitches, mechanics, command, control. Precious few prospects earn a 10C rating in these pages. It may not happen this year, but get your wallets out now.

Yr	Tm	W	L	Sv	IP	K	ERA	xERA	WHIP	OBA	vL	vR	BF/G	Ctl	Dom	Cmd	G	L	F	hr/9	hr/f	H%	S%	GS	APC	DOM%	DIS%	Sv%	LI	RAR	BPV	BPX	R$
08																																	
09																																	
10																																	
11																																	
12	BAL *	2	0	0	18	11	3.31	3.43	1.34	238	500	0	15.3	4.1	5.6	1.3	20	0	80	0.5	0%	27%	76%	0	15			0	0.40	1.6	53	69	-$3
1st Half																																	
2nd Half		2	0	0	18	11	3.31	3.41	1.34	238	500	0	15.3	4.1	5.6	1.3	20	0	80	0.5	0%	27%	76%	0	15			0	0.40	1.6	53	69	-$3
13	Proj	**6**	**3**	**0**	**73**	**55**	**3.78**	**4.72**	**1.34**	**254**			**13.9**	**3.5**	**6.8**	**2.0**	**36**	**13**	**51**	**0.8**	**6%**	**30%**	**74%**	**8**						**2.1**	**43**	**56**	**$2**

ROB CARROLL

Burnett,A.J.

Age: 36 | Th: R | Role SP | Ht: 6' 4" | Wt: 230 | Type Pwr GB

Health A | PT/Exp A | Consist A | LIMA Plan C+ | Rand Var +1 | MM 3305

BPV says it was, in fact, recovery from a 3-year case of EdWhitsonitis. Friendlier home park helped some, but home/road splits were minor. Credit rebound to righting FB/GB rates (40% fewer HR allowed than last year), still-solid Dom and shaving a walk per game. At 36, expect some regression.

Yr	Tm	W	L	Sv	IP	K	ERA	xERA	WHIP	OBA	vL	vR	BF/G	Ctl	Dom	Cmd	G	L	F	hr/9	hr/f	H%	S%	GS	APC	DOM%	DIS%	Sv%	LI	RAR	BPV	BPX	R$
08	TOR	18	10	0	221	231	4.07	3.56	1.34	249	262	231	27.3	3.5	9.4	2.7	49	20	32	0.8	10%	33%	71%	34	104	59%	12%	0	0.81	7.0	102	191	$16
09	NYY	13	9	0	207	195	4.04	4.15	1.40	247	217	282	27.2	4.2	8.5	2.0	43	18	39	1.1	11%	30%	74%	33	105	58%	12%			7.1	60	112	$11
10	NYY	10	15	0	187	145	5.26	4.31	1.51	285	286	285	25.1	3.8	7.0	1.9	45	18	37	1.2	12%	32%	67%	33	94	45%	33%			-27.1	47	77	-$6
11	NYY	11	11	0	190	173	5.15	3.86	1.43	260	256	264	25.4	3.9	8.2	2.1	49	18	32	1.5	17%	30%	68%	32	98	47%	16%	0	0.76	-28.4	68	103	-$5
12	PIT	16	10	0	202	180	3.51	3.42	1.24	246	248	245	27.5	2.8	8.0	2.9	57	19	24	0.8	13%	30%	74%	31	98	55%	6%			12.5	105	137	$16
1st Half		9	2	0	82	69	3.31	3.60	1.24	235	231	239	26.4	3.2	7.6	2.4	57	20	23	0.8	13%	29%	76%	13	96	62%	8%			7.2	86	112	$17
2nd Half		7	8	0	121	111	3.65	3.31	1.24	254	261	248	28.2	2.5	8.3	3.4	57	18	26	0.8	13%	32%	73%	18	99	50%	6%			5.4	117	152	$15
13	Proj	13	11	0	189	167	3.95	3.74	1.34	257	256	258	25.6	3.3	8.0	2.4	52	19	29	1.0	14%	31%	74%	31						1.5	85	110	$9

Burnett,Alex

Age: 25 | Th: R | Role RP | Ht: 6' 0" | Wt: 221 | Type

Health A | PT/Exp D | Consist B | LIMA Plan D | Rand Var -2 | MM 1100

One of the first things we're told growing up: "If you can't think of anything nice to say, don't say anything at all." Has 93-mph fastball (but only half the number of Ks than IP). Had a 0.00 ERA in June (and 7.50 in Jul-Aug). Gave up only one HR in 2H (but check that 2H Ctl and WHIP). Mom, we're trying...

Yr	Tm	W	L	Sv	IP	K	ERA	xERA	WHIP	OBA	vL	vR	BF/G	Ctl	Dom	Cmd	G	L	F	hr/9	hr/f	H%	S%	GS	APC	DOM%	DIS%	Sv%	LI	RAR	BPV	BPX	R$
08																																	
09	aa	1	2	9	55	45	2.85	2.37	1.12	216			5.4	3.1	7.4	2.4				0.4		27%	74%							10.0	96	180	$7
10	MIN *	2	4	2	67	52	5.51	5.39	1.66	298	351	258	5.5	4.1	6.9	1.7	47	19	34	0.9	12%	35%	67%	0	20			40	0.76	-11.8	44	72	-$6
11	MIN	2	5	0	51	33	5.51	4.45	1.40	263	263	264	3.4	3.7	5.9	1.6	46	18	36	0.7	7%	30%	60%	0	13			0	1.13	-9.8	29	43	-$5
12	MIN	4	4	0	72	36	3.52	4.73	1.35	257	215	279	4.6	3.3	4.5	1.4	52	18	30	0.5	6%	29%	74%	0	17			0	0.97	4.4	23	30	-$1
1st Half		2	0	0	39	16	1.83	4.40	0.99	207	170	230	4.8	2.3	3.7	1.6	49	17	34	0.7	7%	22%	86%	0	18			0	0.62	10.6	31	40	$6
2nd Half		2	4	0	32	20	5.57	5.10	1.79	309	275	323	4.4	4.5	5.6	1.3	55	20	25	0.3	3%	37%	67%	0	16			0	1.29	-6.2	13	17	-$9
13	Proj	3	4	0	58	36	4.53	4.63	1.45	270	258	276	4.2	3.7	5.6	1.5	50	18	32	0.6	6%	31%	68%	0						-3.7	30	40	-$3

Burnett,Sean

Age: 30 | Th: L | Role RP | Ht: 6' 1" | Wt: 180 | Type Pwr xGB

Health A | PT/Exp C | Consist C | LIMA Plan A+ | Rand Var -1 | MM 4311

Former 1st-rounder was again solid in middle relief, managing to tiptoe high H% and S% for excellent ERA. Skills have always been a bit inconsistent and RHB can give him fits, but Dom, Cmd soared and Ctl plunged—all lifetime bests. This may not be the career he envisioned, but he's become pretty good at it.

Yr	Tm	W	L	Sv	IP	K	ERA	xERA	WHIP	OBA	vL	vR	BF/G	Ctl	Dom	Cmd	G	L	F	hr/9	hr/f	H%	S%	GS	APC	DOM%	DIS%	Sv%	LI	RAR	BPV	BPX	R$
08	PIT *	2	2	3	74	53	3.96	4.30	1.49	246	171	328	4.6	5.1	6.5	1.3	48	19	33	1.0	13%	28%	76%	0	17			75	0.88	3.3	42	78	$0
09	2 NL	2	3	1	58	43	3.12	4.13	1.11	181	186	176	3.3	4.4	6.7	1.5	49	21	30	0.9	13%	20%	76%	0	14			33	0.87	8.5	30	56	$4
10	WAS	1	7	3	63	62	2.14	3.09	1.14	220	273	182	3.6	2.9	8.9	3.1	54	21	24	0.4	7%	30%	83%	0	15			75	1.25	15.0	114	185	$6
11	WAS	5	5	4	57	33	3.81	4.20	1.32	254	200	297	3.5	3.3	5.2	1.6	53	17	30	1.0	11%	27%	74%	0	14			36	1.37	0.9	35	53	$2
12	WAS	1	2	2	57	57	2.38	2.98	1.24	262	211	298	3.4	1.9	9.1	4.8	57	20	23	0.6	11%	34%	83%	0	14			40	1.02	11.4	146	191	$3
1st Half		1	1	2	29	28	1.57	3.02	0.94	198	170	222	3.2	2.2	8.8	4.0	54	13	33	0.6	8%	25%	88%	0	13			67	1.00	8.7	131	171	$7
2nd Half		0	1	0	28	29	3.21	2.94	1.54	317	256	351	3.6	1.6	9.3	5.8	60	26	14	0.6	15%	42%	80%	0	14			0	1.04	2.8	162	211	-$1
13	Proj	3	4	3	73	63	2.91	3.44	1.28	259	220	286	3.4	2.7	7.9	3.0	55	20	25	0.7	11%	32%	80%	0						9.9	103	133	$4

Burton,Jared

Age: 32 | Th: R | Role RP | Ht: 6' 6" | Wt: 225 | Type Pwr

Health D | PT/Exp D | Consist F | LIMA Plan C+ | Rand Var -5 | MM 3310

Made a case for more save opps. Boasted career-best ctl and cmd, and stinginess with baserunners, GB profile and handedness (BA vR) speak to BPV. Caveats: Did benefit from abnormally low H% and missed most of 2011 with shoulder surgery. Worth an extra buck if he's in the endgame mix.

Yr	Tm	W	L	Sv	IP	K	ERA	xERA	WHIP	OBA	vL	vR	BF/G	Ctl	Dom	Cmd	G	L	F	hr/9	hr/f	H%	S%	GS	APC	DOM%	DIS%	Sv%	LI	RAR	BPV	BPX	R$
08	CIN	5	1	0	59	58	3.22	3.86	1.38	249	247	250	4.8	3.8	8.9	2.3	51	14	36	0.9	10%	32%	80%	0	18			0	0.79	8.0	86	161	$3
09	CIN	1	0	0	59	45	4.40	4.58	1.42	261	222	289	5.0	3.5	6.8	2.0	43	15	42	0.8	6%	31%	70%	0	20			0	0.76	-0.6	50	93	-$2
10	CIN *	3	2	4	41	27	3.19	4.09	1.35	243	0	0	4.7	4.0	5.8	1.4	44	11	44	1.2	0%	26%	82%	0	11			67	0.47	4.5	37	60	$2
11	CIN	0	0	0	5	3	3.86	5.95	1.93	316	500	231	3.8	5.8	5.8	1.0	38	19	44	1.9	14%	33%	88%	0	16			0	0.46	0.0	-36	-54	-$4
12	MIN	3	2	5	62	55	2.18	3.39	0.92	186	235	154	3.8	2.3	8.0	3.4	49	17	35	0.7	9%	23%	81%	0	15			56	1.13	14.1	108	141	$10
1st Half		1	0	2	32	29	2.81	3.30	0.91	198	286	149	3.8	1.7	8.2	4.8	47	16	38	1.1	12%	24%	76%	0	14			67	1.05	4.8	126	164	$8
2nd Half		2	2	3	30	26	1.50	3.49	0.93	171	186	161	3.8	3.0	7.8	2.6	51	18	32	0.3	4%	22%	85%	0	15			50	1.22	9.3	88	115	$12
13	Proj	4	2	5	65	53	2.81	3.88	1.14	220	226	217	4.1	3.1	7.4	2.4	47	16	37	0.8	9%	26%	79%	0						9.7	73	95	$7

Cahill,Trevor

Age: 25 | Th: R | Role SP | Ht: 6' 4" | Wt: 222 | Type Pwr xGB

Health A | PT/Exp A | Consist A | LIMA Plan B | Rand Var 0 | MM 3205

Made some nice strides with Dom hike for third straight year and best-yet Cmd. Still had to win 4 of last 5 decisions to finish above .500. Adept at bailing himself out of trouble by inducing the 3rd-most GB in MLB, minimizing impact of borderline S%. It all makes him a bit enigmatic, but still.... UP: 2010.

Yr	Tm	W	L	Sv	IP	K	ERA	xERA	WHIP	OBA	vL	vR	BF/G	Ctl	Dom	Cmd	G	L	F	hr/9	hr/f	H%	S%	GS	APC	DOM%	DIS%	Sv%	LI	RAR	BPV	BPX	R$
08	aa	6	1	0	37	28	2.15	2.10	1.11	189			20.8	4.1	6.9	1.7				0.4		23%	82%							9.9	81	153	$4
09	OAK	10	13	0	179	90	4.63	4.90	1.44	270	286	252	24.2	3.6	4.5	1.3	48	18	34	1.4	13%	28%	72%	32	94	22%	34%			-6.9	10	18	$1
10	OAK	18	8	0	197	118	2.97	3.79	1.11	220	237	198	26.1	2.9	5.4	1.9	56	15	29	0.9	11%	24%	77%	30	101	47%	10%			26.8	53	86	$22
11	OAK	12	14	0	208	147	4.16	3.93	1.43	269	264	274	26.5	3.6	6.4	1.8	56	19	25	0.8	12%	31%	72%	34	100	47%	26%			-5.6	53	79	$1
12	ARI	13	12	0	200	156	3.78	3.65	1.29	250	253	246	26.2	3.3	7.0	2.1	61	16	23	0.7	12%	29%	72%	32	99	59%	19%			5.8	75	98	$9
1st Half		6	6	0	96	70	3.67	3.75	1.28	244	251	232	26.3	3.6	6.6	1.8	61	17	22	0.6	10%	28%	72%	15	100	53%	20%			4.1	61	79	$10
2nd Half		7	6	0	104	86	3.88	3.57	1.30	255	255	255	26.2	3.1	7.4	2.4	61	15	24	0.9	14%	30%	72%	17	98	65%	18%			1.7	89	116	$9
13	Proj	15	12	0	203	157	3.50	3.77	1.31	252	255	247	25.4	3.2	7.0	2.2	58	17	26	0.8	12%	30%	75%	33						12.8	74	96	$13

Cain,Matt

Age: 28 | Th: R | Role SP | Ht: 6' 3" | Wt: 230 | Type FB

Health A | PT/Exp A | Consist A | LIMA Plan D+ | Rand Var -3 | MM 3305

0% DIS in 32 starts. Top ten in IP again. Career-low walks, career high Ks. This is the profile of an ace in his prime. He did have a slight Dom drop in the 2H but still went 6-0 after Aug 6. Studies do warn of H% regressions when outpitching xERA every year, but if this isn't THAT year...UP: 20 Wins, Cy Young.

Yr	Tm	W	L	Sv	IP	K	ERA	xERA	WHIP	OBA	vL	vR	BF/G	Ctl	Dom	Cmd	G	L	F	hr/9	hr/f	H%	S%	GS	APC	DOM%	DIS%	Sv%	LI	RAR	BPV	BPX	R$
08	SF	8	14	0	218	186	3.76	4.42	1.36	251	268	235	27.4	3.8	7.7	2.0	33	23	44	0.8	7%	30%	74%	34	106	56%	9%			15.1	48	90	$11
09	SF	14	8	0	218	171	2.89	4.09	1.18	232	233	231	26.8	3.0	7.1	2.3	39	19	42	0.9	8%	27%	80%	33	102	61%	9%			38.3	63	117	$26
10	SF	13	11	0	223	177	3.14	3.90	1.08	221	225	217	27.2	2.5	7.1	2.9	36	17	47	0.9	7%	26%	75%	33	106	67%	6%			25.8	76	123	$23
11	SF	12	11	0	222	179	2.88	3.70	1.08	217	185	250	27.5	2.6	7.3	2.8	42	19	39	0.4	4%	27%	73%	33	106	73%	3%			29.0	82	123	$24
12	SF	16	5	0	219	193	2.79	3.67	1.04	222	257	191	27.4	2.1	7.9	3.8	37	21	42	0.9	8%	27%	77%	32	105	63%	0%			33.1	101	132	$32
1st Half		9	3	0	114	114	2.53	3.40	0.95	207	255	165	27.9	1.8	9.0	5.0	34	21	45	0.8	8%	27%	78%	16	108	81%	0%			20.8	125	163	$41
2nd Half		7	2	0	106	79	3.07	4.00	1.14	238	258	219	26.8	2.4	6.7	2.8	41	21	38	0.9	9%	27%	77%	16	101	44%	0%			12.4	75	98	$21
13	Proj	17	7	0	203	168	3.04	3.83	1.09	226	234	218	26.4	2.4	7.4	3.1	38	20	42	0.7	7%	27%	75%	30						24.5	85	110	$25

Camp,Shawn

Age: 37 | Th: R | Role RP | Ht: 6' 0" | Wt: 205 | Type Con GB

Health A | PT/Exp C | Consist A | LIMA Plan B | Rand Var -1 | MM 2100

Very erratic year-to-year, with in-season unpredictability even more pronounced. Throwing the stats onto a scatter diagram, you can discern trends: Dom down, GB% down, xERA up—or is that down? Too confusing. Moving into his late 30s, don't expect anything different...which is to say everything.

Yr	Tm	W	L	Sv	IP	K	ERA	xERA	WHIP	OBA	vL	vR	BF/G	Ctl	Dom	Cmd	G	L	F	hr/9	hr/f	H%	S%	GS	APC	DOM%	DIS%	Sv%	LI	RAR	BPV	BPX	R$
08	TOR	3	1	0	39	31	4.12	3.63	1.30	263	356	204	4.2	2.5	7.1	2.8	54	19	27	0.5	6%	32%	67%	0	15			0	1.20	1.0	92	172	$0
09	TOR	2	6	1	80	58	3.50	3.86	1.28	245	260	230	5.6	3.3	6.6	2.0	55	17	28	0.8	11%	28%	75%	0	20			100	0.91	8.1	62	117	$3
10	TOR	4	3	2	72	46	2.99	3.80	1.23	259	299	234	4.3	2.2	5.7	2.6	52	17	31	1.0	11%	29%	80%	0	15			50	1.21	9.7	73	117	$5
11	TOR	6	3	1	66	32	4.21	4.36	1.52	303	347	263	4.4	3.0	4.3	1.5	54	21	26	0.4	5%	33%	71%	0	15			25	0.92	-2.2	30	44	-$2
12	CHC	3	6	2	78	54	3.59	4.16	1.29	261	263	259	4.1	2.4	6.3	2.6	47	19	33	0.8	8%	30%	74%	0	15			33	0.84	4.0	72	94	$1
1st Half		2	4	1	42	33	3.02	3.86	1.15	238	206	261	4.4	2.2	7.1	3.3	45	21	34	0.6	7%	29%	76%	0	16			33	0.89	5.1	93	121	$5
2nd Half		1	2	1	36	21	4.45	4.53	1.44	287	348	258	3.8	2.8	5.3	1.9	50	17	33	1.0	10%	31%	73%	0	14			33	0.78	-1.0	48	62	-$3
13	Proj	3	3	0	58	36	4.07	4.24	1.36	274	307	252	4.1	2.6	5.6	2.1	51	19	31	0.9	10%	31%	72%	0						-0.4	59	76	-$1

ROB CARROLL

Capps,Carter

Age: 22	Th: R	Role RP	Health	A	LIMA Plan	A+
Ht: 6' 5"	Wt : 220	Type Pwr	PT/Exp	F	Rand Var	-3
			Consist	F	MM	4500

0-0, 3.96 ERA in 25 IP at SEA. Converted starter saved 19 games in Double-A (72 K in 50 IP, 1.26 ERA) by pounding 94-97mph fastballs. Wasn't overmatched in first MLB trial (28 K in 25 IP with .260 OBA), but command predictably lagged. Closer-in-waiting could be worth a few holds from the get-go.

Yr Tm	W	L	Sv	IP	K	ERA	xERA	WHIP	OBA	vL	vR	BF/G	Ctl	Dom	Cmd	G	L	F	hr/9	hr/f	H%	S%	GS	APC	DOM%	DIS%	Sv%	LI	RAR	BPV	BPX	R$
08																																
09																																
10																																
11																																
12 SEA *	2	3	19	76	96	2.18	2.69	1.19	240	318	212	5.4	2.7	11.3	4.2	41	28	32	0.2	0%	36%	81%	0	26			90	0.50	17.3	158	205	$15
1st Half	2	2	12	38	53	1.45	2.48	1.09	224	0	0	5.3	2.5	12.5	5.1				0.5	0%	35%	90%	0	0					12.0	177	230	$22
2nd Half	0	1	7	38	43	3.09	3.24	1.35	265	318	212	5.5	3.0	10.2	3.4	41	28	32	0.0	0%	38%	75%	0	26			88	0.50	4.4	134	174	$8
13 Proj	1	2	0	65	75	3.23	3.39	1.26	246	301	200	5.5	3.1	10.4	3.4	39	26	36	0.7	8%	33%	77%	0						6.4	121	158	$2

Capps,Matt

Age: 29	Th: R	Role RP	Health	D	LIMA Plan	B+
Ht: 6' 2"	Wt : 260	Type Con	PT/Exp	B	Rand Var	-1
			Consist	A	MM	2110

Second year in a row he was replaced as closer by mid-season, this time due to inflamed shoulder. Until then, he had regained some Dom and topped Cmd/Ctl from '11, but GB stayed down, hr/f stayed up. Even if skills prove intact through injury, he won't find himself in position to lose the closer role thrice.

Yr Tm	W	L	Sv	IP	K	ERA	xERA	WHIP	OBA	vL	vR	BF/G	Ctl	Dom	Cmd	G	L	F	hr/9	hr/f	H%	S%	GS	APC	DOM%	DIS%	Sv%	LI	RAR	BPV	BPX	R$
08 PIT	2	3	21	54	39	3.02	3.72	0.97	234	222	245	4.3	0.8	6.5	7.8	31	23	46	0.8	7%	27%	72%	0	15			81	1.30	8.6	104	195	$13
09 PIT	4	8	27	54	46	5.80	4.41	1.66	324	342	306	4.4	2.8	7.6	2.7	41	19	41	1.7	14%	37%	69%	0	16			84	1.04	-9.9	80	150	$6
10 2 TM	5	3	42	73	59	2.47	3.53	1.26	265	248	280	4.1	2.1	7.3	3.5	50	19	31	0.7	9%	32%	84%	0	14			88	1.31	14.5	102	166	$23
11 MIN	4	7	15	66	34	4.25	4.28	1.20	262	264	260	4.0	1.8	4.7	2.6	42	17	41	1.4	11%	27%	70%	0	13			63	1.34	-2.5	56	84	$6
12 MIN	1	4	14	29	18	3.68	4.14	1.09	241	175	305	4.0	1.2	5.5	4.5	42	19	39	1.5	13%	26%	74%	0	15			93	1.09	1.2	86	113	$4
1st Half	1	4	14	26	16	3.42	4.19	1.06	233	157	308	4.0	1.4	5.5	4.0	41	18	40	1.4	11%	26%	75%	0	15			93	1.21	1.9	81	105	$5
2nd Half	0	0	0	3	2	6.00	3.72	1.33	308	333	286	4.3	0.0	6.0	0.0	45	27	27	3.0	33%	32%	67%	0	15			0	0.02	-0.7	131	171	-$9
13 Proj	3	6	8	58	37	3.97	4.16	1.22	266	241	289	4.0	1.8	5.7	3.2	42	19	39	1.2	11%	29%	72%	0						0.3	75	97	$3

Capuano,Chris

Age: 34	Th: L	Role SP	Health	A	LIMA Plan	B
Ht: 6' 3"	Wt : 215	Type	PT/Exp	A	Rand Var	0
			Consist	A	MM	3305

A Tale of Two Halves? Not so much. While Dom/Ctl did regress, fortuitous strand, hit rates tilted ERA to his favor through June. Other BPIs (xERA, G/L/F, hr/f) shows he stayed steady throughout, even hiked Cmd. It was a good luck/bad luck season as much as anything. Talk down that 2H and grab him low.

Yr Tm	W	L	Sv	IP	K	ERA	xERA	WHIP	OBA	vL	vR	BF/G	Ctl	Dom	Cmd	G	L	F	hr/9	hr/f	H%	S%	GS	APC	DOM%	DIS%	Sv%	LI	RAR	BPV	BPX	R$
08																																
09																																
10 MIL *	5	5	0	91	66	3.48	3.92	1.29	263	224	272	13.3	2.5	6.5	2.6	43	17	40	0.9	11%	30%	76%	9	44	44%	33%	0	0.65	6.7	70	112	$4
11 NYM	11	12	0	186	168	4.55	3.76	1.35	270	224	283	24.3	2.6	8.1	3.2	43	17	40	1.3	12%	32%	70%	31	90	45%	6%	0	0.82	-13.9	98	147	$1
12 LA	12	12	0	198	162	3.72	3.97	1.22	254	231	260	24.8	2.5	7.4	3.0	40	21	39	1.1	11%	29%	74%	33	90	55%	18%			7.2	84	110	$12
1st Half	9	3	0	100	89	2.69	3.76	1.10	219	214	221	25.1	2.8	8.0	2.9	41	20	39	1.0	10%	26%	81%	16	95	69%	19%			16.4	88	115	$28
2nd Half	3	9	0	98	73	4.78	4.20	1.35	286	244	298	24.4	2.1	6.7	3.2	40	21	39	1.3	12%	32%	68%	17	85	41%	18%			-9.2	82	107	-$4
13 Proj	11	12	0	189	156	3.89	3.99	1.29	264	229	275	21.4	2.5	7.4	3.0	42	19	40	1.2	11%	31%	74%	36						2.9	87	112	$9

Carpenter,Chris

Age: 38	Th: R	Role SP	Health	F	LIMA Plan	C+
Ht: 6' 6"	Wt : 230	Type	PT/Exp	A	Rand Var	0
			Consist	A	MM	3203

Can't ignore the numbers as they pile up. From 2007-2012, had 703 IP and 580 DL days. In same period, led majors in starts twice and was 4th in IP twice. Skills are intact well into 30s and his come- backs always impress, but it's never a good thing when the pitcher has more stitches than the baseball.

Yr Tm	W	L	Sv	IP	K	ERA	xERA	WHIP	OBA	vL	vR	BF/G	Ctl	Dom	Cmd	G	L	F	hr/9	hr/f	H%	S%	GS	APC	DOM%	DIS%	Sv%	LI	RAR	BPV	BPX	R$
08 STL	0	1	0	15	7	1.76	4.22	1.30	286	158	351	15.8	2.3	4.1	1.8	51	24	24	0.0	0%	31%	85%	3	52	0%	67%	0	0.63	4.8	40	74	-$2
09 STL	17	4	0	193	144	2.24	3.24	1.01	226	239	214	26.8	1.8	6.7	3.8	55	17	28	0.3	5%	27%	78%	28	95	71%	4%			49.4	106	199	$33
10 STL	16	9	0	235	179	3.22	3.59	1.18	244	239	248	27.7	2.4	6.9	2.8	51	17	32	0.8	9%	29%	75%	35	101	57%	6%			25.0	87	141	$21
11 STL	11	9	0	237	191	3.45	3.50	1.26	264	259	268	29.3	2.1	7.2	3.5	47	24	29	0.6	8%	32%	73%	34	106	68%	6%			14.4	99	149	$14
12 STL	0	2	0	17	12	3.71	4.11	1.12	242	385	150	24.0	1.6	6.4	4.0	39	20	41	1.1	9%	28%	71%	3	86	67%	0%			0.6	88	115	-$3
1st Half																																
2nd Half	0	2	0	17	12	3.71	4.10	1.12	242	385	150	24.0	1.6	6.4	4.0	39	20	41	1.1	9%	28%	71%	3	86	67%	0%			0.7	88	115	-$3
13 Proj	7	9	0	145	109	3.76	3.78	1.22	261	303	229	26.0	2.0	6.8	3.4	47	19	34	0.8	8%	31%	71%	23						4.6	93	120	$8

Carpenter,David

Age: 25	Th: R	Role RP	Health	A	LIMA Plan	D
Ht: 6' 3"	Wt : 180	Type GB	PT/Exp	F	Rand Var	0
			Consist	F	MM	1100

1-2, 4.76 ERA in 40 IP at LAA. Unheralded rookie didn't flash minor-league Dom (10.2) in brief trial but didn't wilt until the very end. Toss out his trio of Aug clunkers (3 HR against) and the ERA drops to 3.55. But this same logic can be applied to just about any RP. At this point, he's just a guy.

Yr Tm	W	L	Sv	IP	K	ERA	xERA	WHIP	OBA	vL	vR	BF/G	Ctl	Dom	Cmd	G	L	F	hr/9	hr/f	H%	S%	GS	APC	DOM%	DIS%	Sv%	LI	RAR	BPV	BPX	R$
08																																
09																																
10																																
11 aa	1	0	5	19	13	0.00	1.75	1.02	211			3.8	2.4	6.4	2.6				0.0		26%	100%							9.1	106	160	$3
12 LAA *	1	2	1	59	39	4.06	3.90	1.29	239	308	253	5.7	3.7	6.0	1.6	46	22	33	1.2	15%	26%	72%	0	23			100	1.16	-0.3	42	55	-$2
1st Half	1	1	0	31	25	3.77	3.35	1.29	243	306	236	5.5	3.5	7.1	2.1	46	23	30	0.6	8%	29%	71%	0	21			0	1.23	0.9	75	98	-$2
2nd Half	0	1	1	28	15	4.38	4.47	1.30	235	313	281	5.8	3.9	4.7	1.2	44	19	37	1.8	25%	22%	74%	0	28			100	0.95	-1.3	7	9	-$3
13 Proj	0	1	0	29	19	4.18	4.52	1.30	240	273	211	5.7	3.7	5.8	1.6	46	23	30	1.4	15%	25%	73%	0						-0.6	29	37	-$3

Carrasco,Carlos

Age: 26	Th: R	Role SP	Health	F	LIMA Plan	B+
Ht: 6' 3"	Wt : 210	Type GB	PT/Exp	C	Rand Var	0
			Consist	A	MM	2201

Missed all of 2012 recovering from Sept 2011 TJS surgery. Before injury, was building nicely on 2010 surprise season, tightening Cmd and bolstering GB profile. Not a soft tosser (despite modest Dom), and good news is that he's touching the mid-90s during rehab. Expect a consolidation year.

Yr Tm	W	L	Sv	IP	K	ERA	xERA	WHIP	OBA	vL	vR	BF/G	Ctl	Dom	Cmd	G	L	F	hr/9	hr/f	H%	S%	GS	APC	DOM%	DIS%	Sv%	LI	RAR	BPV	BPX	R$
08 a/a	9	9	0	151	137	4.29	4.49	1.43	273			24.7	3.3	8.1	2.5				1.0		33%	72%							0.6	71	134	$4
09 CLE *	11	14	0	179	141	5.79	4.97	1.46	290	367	431	24.8	2.8	7.1	2.5	48	27	25	1.1	27%	34%	61%	5	80	0%	80%			-32.5	58	109	-$4
10 CLE *	12	8	0	195	151	3.87	4.04	1.31	264	193	356	25.2	2.7	6.9	2.6	57	14	29	0.9	16%	31%	73%	7	97	57%	0%			5.0	70	114	$9
11 CLE	8	9	0	125	85	4.62	4.08	1.36	270	318	216	25.5	2.9	6.1	2.1	49	17	34	1.1	11%	30%	68%	21	94	52%	24%			-10.4	59	89	-$1
12																																
1st Half																																
2nd Half																																
13 Proj	7	8	0	116	89	4.05	4.01	1.40	276	274	278	24.9	2.9	6.9	2.4	52	16	32	1.1	12%	32%	74%	20						-0.4	77	100	$2

Cashner,Andrew

Age: 26	Th: R	Role RP	Health	F	LIMA Plan	A
Ht: 6' 6"	Wt : 200	Type Pwr GB	PT/Exp	D	Rand Var	+3
			Consist	A	MM	4301

3-4, 4.27 ERA in 46 IP at SD. Transitioned from RP to SP then lost 60 days to lat strain (after rotator cuff injury washed out 2011). Health poses questions, skills not so much. Throws gas; had 23/3 K/BB in 19 IP as starter, 10.0 Cmd overall. Induces grounders. If body parts cooperate, a breakout candidate.

Yr Tm	W	L	Sv	IP	K	ERA	xERA	WHIP	OBA	vL	vR	BF/G	Ctl	Dom	Cmd	G	L	F	hr/9	hr/f	H%	S%	GS	APC	DOM%	DIS%	Sv%	LI	RAR	BPV	BPX	R$
08																																
09 aa	3	4	0	58	35	4.55	3.28	1.43	249			20.7	4.5	5.4	1.2				0.0		30%	65%							-1.6	62	117	-$2
10 CHC *	8	7	0	111	98	3.54	3.48	1.29	240	300	246	7.2	3.6	8.0	2.2	48	19	33	0.7	16%	29%	74%	0	18			0	0.90	7.4	79	127	$6
11 CHC	0	0	0	11	8	1.69	3.31	0.66	86	83	87	5.6	3.4	6.8	2.0	59	7	33	0.8	11%	8%	83%	1	21	0%	0%	0	0.56	3.0	67	101	-$1
12 SD *	5	5	0	70	77	3.64	3.21	1.23	239	197	281	7.2	3.1	10.0	3.2	53	23	24	0.6	17%	32%	71%	5	24	40%	60%	0	1.25	3.3	115	150	$3
1st Half	5	3	0	49	61	3.18	3.00	1.23	217	164	261	6.2	4.1	11.3	2.8	52	28	20	0.7	25%	31%	76%	2	21	50%	50%	0	1.33	5.1	115	150	$7
2nd Half	0	2	0	21	16	4.82	3.77	1.25	290	286	333	12.0	0.9	6.8	7.7	56	10	33	0.4	8%	35%	59%	3	43	33%	67%	0	0.66	-2.1	187	243	-$9
13 Proj	6	9	0	116	102	3.98	3.58	1.29	253	229	270	8.9	3.0	7.9	2.6	50	25	25	0.5	8%	32%	69%	0						0.6	90	116	$4

ROB CARROLL

Casilla,Santiago

Age: 32 | Th: R | Role: RP | Ht: 6' 0" | Wt: 220 | Type: Pwr GB

Health	C	LIMA Plan	C+
PT/Exp	C	Rand Var	-2
Consist	A	MM	3310

Answered the "opportunity knock" when SF needed a closer in April. High GB%, domination of RH hitters, and improved Ctl served him well. High H%, hr/f in June/July cost him the job. With Dom eroding, he's going to need to hold Ctl gains to maintain the requisite Cmd to maybe get the gig back.

Yr	Tm	W	L	Sv	IP	K	ERA	xERA	WHIP	OBA	vL	vR	BF/G	Ctl	Dom	Cmd	G	L	F	hr/9	hr/f	H%	S%	GS	APC	DOM%	DIS%	Sv%	LI	RAR	BPV	BPX	R$
08	OAK	2	1	2	50	43	3.93	4.37	1.59	299	308	291	4.5	3.6	7.7	2.2	43	20	36	0.9	9%	36%	77%	0	17			67	0.90	2.4	63	118	-$1
09	OAK	1	2	0	48	35	5.96	4.96	1.78	303	354	257	5.1	4.7	6.5	1.4	50	20	30	1.1	12%	35%	68%	0	19			0	0.80	-9.8	20	37	-$8
10	SF	7	2	2	55	56	1.95	3.33	1.19	208	203	211	4.3	4.2	9.1	2.2	51	21	29	0.3	5%	28%	84%	0	17			67	1.22	14.5	79	127	$7
11	SF	2	2	6	52	45	1.74	3.65	1.12	183	234	155	4.3	4.4	7.8	1.8	52	20	29	0.2	3%	24%	84%	0	17			86	0.95	14.0	54	80	$7
12	SF	7	6	25	63	55	2.84	3.80	1.22	224	265	197	3.7	3.1	7.8	2.5	55	15	30	1.1	14%	28%	83%	0	14			81	1.37	9.2	89	116	$15
1st Half		1	3	21	30	28	2.70	3.61	1.20	217	212	221	3.9	3.0	8.4	2.8	60	11	29	1.5	19%	27%	87%	0	15			91	1.38	4.9	108	141	$19
2nd Half		6	3	4	33	27	2.97	3.96	1.23	232	326	177	3.6	3.2	7.3	2.3	51	19	30	0.8	10%	28%	79%	0	13			50	1.36	4.3	72	94	$11
13	Proj	**5**	**4**	**5**	**58**	**51**	**2.65**	**3.75**	**1.24**	**226**	**271**	**199**	**3.8**	**3.7**	**7.9**	**2.1**	**52**	**18**	**30**	**0.7**	**10%**	**28%**	**82%**	**0**						**9.8**	**72**	**94**	**$6**

Cecil,Brett

Age: 26 | Th: L | Role: RP | Ht: 6' 1" | Wt: 215 | Type: FB

Health	A	LIMA Plan	D+
PT/Exp	B	Rand Var	+2
Consist	A	MM	1201

2-4, 5.72 ERA in 61 IP at TOR. Strikingly similar year to 2011; same issues had him shuttling between AAA and majors. Maintained decent Cmd; was occasionally dominant. But still couldn't solve RHers; lots of FBs were trouble, and hr/f did him in. Still lots to work on here.

Yr	Tm	W	L	Sv	IP	K	ERA	xERA	WHIP	OBA	vL	vR	BF/G	Ctl	Dom	Cmd	G	L	F	hr/9	hr/f	H%	S%	GS	APC	DOM%	DIS%	Sv%	LI	RAR	BPV	BPX	R$
08	a/a	8	5	0	108	107	3.65	3.68	1.36	261			18.9	3.3	8.9	2.7				0.5		34%	73%							9.0	99	185	$6
09	TOR *	8	9	0	142	98	5.54	5.58	1.61	301	295	314	23.4	3.5	6.2	1.7	43	20	38	1.2	15%	34%	67%	17	89	35%	41%	0	0.71	-21.4	32	61	-$8
10	TOR	15	7	0	173	117	4.22	4.20	1.33	264	224	275	25.9	2.8	6.1	2.2	44	18	38	0.9	9%	30%	70%	28	97	50%	18%			-3.0	56	90	$6
11	TOR *	12	13	0	202	139	4.80	4.94	1.37	273	186	282	26.5	2.8	6.2	2.2	38	18	43	1.6	13%	29%	70%	20	96	50%	10%			-21.5	36	54	-$2
12	TOR *	6	8	0	144	105	4.46	4.75	1.46	289	214	319	17.1	2.8	6.6	2.4	37	22	41	0.9	14%	33%	71%	9	49	44%	22%	0	0.72	-7.8	59	77	-$5
1st Half		5	3	0	66	45	4.61	5.59	1.60	315	167	328	22.3	2.8	6.2	2.2	24	27	49	1.0	21%	36%	73%	3	89	0%	0%			-4.8	46	60	-$6
2nd Half		1	5	0	78	60	4.33	4.00	1.33	266	220	315	14.1	2.8	6.9	2.5	41	20	39	0.8	12%	31%	69%	6	42	67%	33%	0	0.71	-3.0	71	92	-$4
13	Proj	**5**	**5**	**0**	**87**	**63**	**4.54**	**4.52**	**1.41**	**279**	**215**	**300**	**19.9**	**2.9**	**6.5**	**2.3**	**38**	**20**	**42**	**1.2**	**10%**	**32%**	**71%**	**18**						**-5.6**	**56**	**73**	**-$2**

Cedeno,Xavier

Age: 26 | Th: L | Role: RP | Ht: 6' 1" | Wt: 205 | Type: Pwr xFB

Health	A	LIMA Plan	D+
PT/Exp	D	Rand Var	0
Consist	B	MM	1300

0-1, 3.77 ERA in 31 IP at HOU. Keeps the ball on the ground. Sometimes. Can blow people away with solid Dom. Sometimes. Would be good if he could do those things more times, and also at the same time. Until that time, he'll work towards buying more time, but at 26, he's running out of time.

Yr	Tm	W	L	Sv	IP	K	ERA	xERA	WHIP	OBA	vL	vR	BF/G	Ctl	Dom	Cmd	G	L	F	hr/9	hr/f	H%	S%	GS	APC	DOM%	DIS%	Sv%	LI	RAR	BPV	BPX	R$
08	aa	7	7	0	103	42	4.58	5.93	1.68	323			24.3	3.0	3.7	1.2				1.0		34%	75%							-3.2	9	17	-$5
09	aa	3	2	0	47	20	6.39	5.96	1.67	296			7.5	4.4	3.8	0.9				1.5		30%	64%							-12.0	-8	-15	-$7
10																																	
11	HOU *	7	9	0	139	113	4.94	4.44	1.45	277	500	714	15.7	3.3	7.3	2.2	27	45	27	0.8	67%	33%	66%	0	12			0	1.04	-17.2	66	99	-$5
12	HOU *	2	1	2	59	56	3.07	3.79	1.39	264	213	298	3.7	3.5	8.6	2.5	50	15	35	0.5	10%	34%	78%	0	13			29	1.05	6.8	93	121	$0
1st Half		2	0	2	31	23	1.17	2.83	1.24	233	357	190	4.3	3.4	6.8	2.0	71	7	21	0.3	17%	29%	92%	0	12			50	0.94	10.8	82	107	$6
2nd Half		0	1	0	28	33	5.14	4.80	1.57	294	170	361	3.3	3.5	10.6	3.0	39	20	41	0.6	9%	40%	67%	0	13			0	1.09	-3.9	104	135	-$6
13	Proj	**2**	**2**	**0**	**44**	**35**	**4.42**	**4.64**	**1.50**	**282**	**190**	**402**	**5.7**	**3.6**	**7.3**	**2.1**	**39**	**20**	**41**	**0.8**	**6%**	**34%**	**71%**	**0**						**-2.2**	**53**	**68**	**-$3**

Chacin,Jhoulys

Age: 25 | Th: R | Role: SP | Ht: 6' 3" | Wt: 225 | Type: Pwr

Health	D	LIMA Plan	D
PT/Exp	C	Rand Var	0
Consist	C	MM	1203

3-5, 4.43 ERA in 69 IP at COL. Terrible in first five starts; that turned into a demotion, which turned into three months on the DL with shoulder inflammation. ERA bounced back in 2H, but Dom plunge and xERA show that skills still weren't solid. Without return to high Dom and GB% days, too dangerous to roster.

Yr	Tm	W	L	Sv	IP	K	ERA	xERA	WHIP	OBA	vL	vR	BF/G	Ctl	Dom	Cmd	G	L	F	hr/9	hr/f	H%	S%	GS	APC	DOM%	DIS%	Sv%	LI	RAR	BPV	BPX	R$
08																																	
09	COL *	9	9	0	129	93	3.86	3.90	1.34	242	263	59	17.3	4.0	6.5	1.6	48	9	43	1.0	10%	27%	74%	1	23	0%	100%	0	0.29	7.3	49	91	$6
10	COL *	12	13	0	173	166	2.92	3.05	1.26	226	266	201	20.2	4.0	8.6	2.2	47	22	32	0.6	9%	29%	78%	21	82	57%	10%	0	0.70	24.8	90	146	$16
11	COL	11	14	0	194	150	3.62	3.90	1.31	231	232	230	26.7	4.0	7.0	1.7	56	15	28	0.9	12%	27%	75%	31	101	52%	16%			7.7	50	76	$8
12	COL *	4	7	0	92	54	4.59	5.25	1.55	284	293	282	22.3	3.9	5.3	1.4	39	24	37	1.2	12%	31%	74%	14	83	29%	50%			-6.5	22	29	-$8
1st Half		0	3	0	25	22	7.30	5.19	1.86	304	385	220	23.8	5.5	8.0	1.5	41	23	37	2.6	24%	34%	67%	5	93	20%	60%			-10.0	15	20	-$19
2nd Half		4	4	0	67	32	3.60	4.35	1.43	275	242	321	21.9	3.3	4.3	1.3	38	25	38	0.8	5%	30%	77%	9	77	33%	44%			3.5	31	40	-$3
13	Proj	**8**	**12**	**0**	**152**	**111**	**4.27**	**4.57**	**1.45**	**262**	**274**	**251**	**22.1**	**4.1**	**6.6**	**1.6**	**46**	**21**	**33**	**1.2**	**13%**	**29%**	**74%**	**29**						**-4.8**	**33**	**43**	**$0**

Chamberlain,Joba

Age: 27 | Th: R | Role: RP | Ht: 6' 2" | Wt: 250 | Type: Pwr

Health	F	LIMA Plan	B
PT/Exp	D	Rand Var	+5
Consist	B	MM	4500

Dr. HQ, what's the typical recovery time for TJS rehab coupled with a trampoline mishap? Velocity consistent with 2010/11; Cmd excellent upon return. But ERA was hurt by high LD%, H%, and hr/f; xERA portends improvement. No more RP/SP questions; should thrive as long as health cooperates.

Yr	Tm	W	L	Sv	IP	K	ERA	xERA	WHIP	OBA	vL	vR	BF/G	Ctl	Dom	Cmd	G	L	F	hr/9	hr/f	H%	S%	GS	APC	DOM%	DIS%	Sv%	LI	RAR	BPV	BPX	R$
08	NYY	4	3	0	100	118	2.60	3.15	1.26	233	247	219	9.9	3.5	10.6	3.0	52	14	34	0.4	6%	33%	80%	12	41	58%	33%	0	1.07	21.3	126	237	$10
09	NYY	9	6	0	157	133	4.75	4.48	1.54	274	266	282	22.2	4.3	7.6	1.8	43	21	36	1.2	12%	32%	72%	31	85	39%	52%	0	0.75	-8.3	41	76	-$1
10	NYY	3	4	3	72	77	4.40	3.36	1.30	253	246	258	4.2	2.8	9.7	3.5	46	17	37	0.8	8%	34%	67%	0	16			43	1.02	-2.8	123	200	$2
11	NYY	2	0	0	29	24	2.83	2.88	1.05	228	250	208	4.1	2.2	7.5	3.4	60	16	25	0.9	16%	26%	78%	0	16			0	1.08	3.9	114	172	$1
12	NYY	1	0	0	21	22	4.35	3.65	1.55	302	226	345	4.3	2.6	9.6	3.7	45	23	31	1.3	15%	39%	76%	0	16			0	1.12	-0.9	125	163	-$5
1st Half																																	
2nd Half		1	0	0	21	22	4.35	3.65	1.55	302	226	345	4.3	2.6	9.6	3.7	45	23	31	1.3	15%	39%	76%	0	16			0	1.12	-0.9	125	163	-$5
13	Proj	**3**	**2**	**0**	**58**	**58**	**3.77**	**3.55**	**1.33**	**267**	**244**	**286**	**4.5**	**2.8**	**9.1**	**3.3**	**46**	**20**	**34**	**1.0**	**12%**	**33%**	**75%**	**0**						**1.8**	**112**	**145**	**$0**

Chapman,Aroldis

Age: 25 | Th: L | Role: RP | Ht: 6' 4" | Wt: 200 | Type: Pwr

Health	B	LIMA Plan	C
PT/Exp	C	Rand Var	-4
Consist	B	MM	5530

First two closer candidates fell by the wayside; he seized the role. Drop in velocity—though he still averaged 98 mph—seemed to help, as Ctl plummeted and Dom rose. S% and xERA say he won't repeat the sub-2.00 ERA, but that's a quibble. Even with the drop in GB%, he's dominant.

Yr	Tm	W	L	Sv	IP	K	ERA	xERA	WHIP	OBA	vL	vR	BF/G	Ctl	Dom	Cmd	G	L	F	hr/9	hr/f	H%	S%	GS	APC	DOM%	DIS%	Sv%	LI	RAR	BPV	BPX	R$
08	for	6	7	0	74	75	4.83	3.41	1.42	220			19.6	5.6	9.1	1.6				0.6		29%	65%							-4.7	82	153	$0
09	for	11	4	0	118	123	5.02	4.74	1.64	260			23.9	5.9	9.4	1.6				0.9		33%	70%							-10.2	67	125	-$2
10	CIN *	11	8	8	109	129	3.84	3.56	1.39	235	154	212	8.5	4.7	10.7	2.3	73	12	15	0.7	0%	33%	73%	0	15			80	1.68	3.2	100	162	$9
11	CIN	4	1	1	50	71	3.60	3.25	1.30	147	77	180	3.8	7.4	12.8	1.7	53	16	31	0.4	7%	24%	71%	0	16			33	1.13	2.1	62	93	$2
12	CIN	5	5	38	72	122	1.51	2.13	0.81	141	108	155	4.1	2.9	15.3	5.3	37	20	43	0.5	7%	28%	85%	0	18			88	1.42	22.2	213	278	$32
1st Half		4	4	9	36	64	1.98	2.15	0.77	127	136	122	4.4	3.0	15.9	5.3	35	17	48	0.7	10%	25%	80%	0	20			69	1.45	9.1	218	284	$29
2nd Half		1	1	29	35	58	1.02	2.10	0.85	156	67	185	3.8	2.8	14.8	5.3	40	22	38	0.3	4%	30%	90%	0	16			97	1.40	13.1	208	271	$36
13	Proj	**5**	**3**	**40**	**65**	**97**	**2.27**	**2.59**	**1.02**	**173**	**109**	**200**	**4.5**	**3.9**	**13.3**	**3.4**	**44**	**19**	**38**	**0.5**	**8%**	**29%**	**80%**	**0**						**14.1**	**157**	**204**	**$26**

Chatwood,Tyler

Age: 23 | Th: R | Role: SP | Ht: 6' 0" | Wt: 185 | Type: GB

Health	A	LIMA Plan	F
PT/Exp	D	Rand Var	+4
Consist	B	MM	0101

5-6, 5.43 ERA in 65 IP at COL. PRO: Kept the ball on the ground; H% should revert; hr/f caused some of his struggles; small improvement to Cmd. CON: Cmd needed a lot more than a small improvement; hammered by lefties. Still young, but at this point there's not enough upside to warrant attention.

Yr	Tm	W	L	Sv	IP	K	ERA	xERA	WHIP	OBA	vL	vR	BF/G	Ctl	Dom	Cmd	G	L	F	hr/9	hr/f	H%	S%	GS	APC	DOM%	DIS%	Sv%	LI	RAR	BPV	BPX	R$
08																																	
09																																	
10	a/a	5	6	0	74	34	4.11	4.36	1.47	289			24.4	2.9	4.1	1.4				0.5		32%	71%							-0.3	38	62	-$2
11	LAA *	7	13	0	158	84	4.73	5.42	1.69	295	321	281	23.0	4.6	4.8	1.0	47	22	31	0.9	10%	32%	73%	25	90	20%	44%	0	0.77	-15.4	20	30	-$12
12	COL *	6	9	1	126	83	5.65	5.71	1.70	304	311	268	17.8	4.2	5.9	1.4	56	21	23	1.0	19%	34%	68%	12	61	8%	58%	100	0.62	-25.4	29	38	-$17
1st Half		1	2	1	46	32	6.32	6.97	1.97	353	348	412	15.8	3.8	6.2	1.6	55	24	21	0.8	29%	40%	67%	0	33			100	0.23	-13.1	31	40	-$26
2nd Half		5	7	0	80	52	4.75	4.52	1.47	260	303	245	19.0	4.3	5.8	1.4	57	21	23	1.1	17%	29%	70%	12	71	8%	58%	0	0.75	-7.2	34	44	-$11
13	Proj	**5**	**7**	**0**	**94**	**56**	**4.79**	**4.86**	**1.65**	**297**	**322**	**268**	**20.0**	**4.1**	**5.3**	**1.3**	**53**	**21**	**26**	**0.9**	**11%**	**33%**	**72%**	**21**						**-9.0**	**16**	**20**	**-$7**

DAVE ADLER

Chen,Bruce

Age: 36 Th: L Role SP	Health D	LIMA Plan D+	
Ht: 6' 2" Wt: 201 Type xFB	PT/Exp B	Rand Var +1	
	Consist A	MM 1203	

Soft-tosser improved Cmd quite a bit, but it didn't help his bottom line. xERA identical to 2011; small swings in LD%, H%, S%, hr/f contributed to ERA boost. For the future, split the difference. Advanced age, tons of fly balls, and struggles against lefties are all reasons to let someone else take him.

Yr	Tm	W	L	Sv	IP	K	ERA	xERA	WHIP	OBA	vL	vR	BF/G	Ctl	Dom	Cmd	G	L	F	hr/9	hr/f	H%	S%	GS	APC	DOM%	DIS%	Sv%	LI	RAR	BPV	BPX	R$
08																																	
09	KC *	5	8	0	144	93	5.37	4.84	1.42	272	292	305	19.8	3.3	5.8	1.8	31	17	51	1.4	12%	29%	65%	9	64	22%	33%	0	0.46	-18.7	31	59	-$4
10	KC *	12	8	1	161	112	3.85	3.96	1.34	252	259	253	18.6	3.5	6.3	1.8	34	18	48	1.0	8%	28%	74%	23	73	35%	26%	100	0.87	4.5	51	83	$7
11	KC	12	8	0	155	97	3.77	4.51	1.30	258	259	258	26.2	2.9	5.6	1.9	35	20	45	1.0	8%	28%	74%	25	101	56%	36%			3.2	36	54	$6
12	KC	11	14	0	192	140	5.07	4.51	1.37	281	314	271	24.3	2.2	6.6	3.0	33	22	45	1.5	12%	31%	67%	34	94	44%	21%			-25.0	70	91	-$5
1st Half		7	6	0	89	64	4.53	4.37	1.25	266	268	265	23.6	1.9	6.4	3.4	32	24	44	1.0	8%	31%	66%	16	90	50%	19%			-5.7	74	96	$4
2nd Half		4	8	0	102	76	5.54	4.64	1.47	295	349	275	24.9	2.5	6.7	2.7	33	21	45	2.0	15%	32%	69%	18	97	39%	22%			-19.2	65	85	-$13
13	Proj	**10**	**10**	**0**	**164**	**113**	**4.63**	**4.65**	**1.36**	**273**	**290**	**267**	**22.7**	**2.7**	**6.2**	**2.3**	**33**	**21**	**46**	**1.3**	**10%**	**30%**	**70%**	**30**						**-12.3**	**50**	**66**	**$1**

Chen,Wei-Yin

Age: 27 Th: L Role SP	Health A	LIMA Plan B	
Ht: 6' 0" Wt: 195 Type FB	PT/Exp A	Rand Var 0	
	Consist C	MM 2205	

Workhorse didn't miss a beat in his transition from Japan to the US. Improved Cmd in 2H; ERA rose due to high hr/f. Pedestrian Dom may keep him from being a #1 starter, but PQS-DOM/DIS ratings make him a reliable rotation option.

Yr	Tm	W	L	Sv	IP	K	ERA	xERA	WHIP	OBA	vL	vR	BF/G	Ctl	Dom	Cmd	G	L	F	hr/9	hr/f	H%	S%	GS	APC	DOM%	DIS%	Sv%	LI	RAR	BPV	BPX	R$
08	for	7	6	0	114	102	3.63	3.85	1.31	252			12.1	3.2	8.0	2.5				0.9		31%	75%							9.8	77	145	$7
09	for	8	4	0	164	139	1.91	2.60	1.04	208			26.4	2.7	7.6	2.8				0.9		24%	88%							48.8	90	169	$26
10	for	13	10	0	188	145	3.57	4.46	1.27	251			26.5	2.9	6.9	2.4				1.7		27%	81%							11.9	47	75	$12
11	for	8	10	0	165	89	3.32	3.18	1.13	241			26.1	2.1	4.9	2.3				0.8		26%	73%							12.7	60	90	$11
12	BAL	12	11	0	193	154	4.02	4.29	1.26	250	232	257	25.6	2.7	7.2	2.7	37	21	42	1.4	12%	29%	73%	32	98	56%	16%			-0.1	73	95	$8
1st Half		7	4	0	92	64	3.73	4.58	1.32	257	270	252	26.1	2.9	6.3	2.1	38	20	41	1.1	9%	29%	75%	15	99	47%	7%			3.2	50	65	$9
2nd Half		5	7	0	101	90	4.28	4.04	1.21	244	194	262	25.1	2.4	8.0	3.3	36	21	43	1.6	14%	28%	71%	17	97	65%	24%			-3.2	93	121	$7
13	Proj	**11**	**11**	**0**	**189**	**140**	**3.92**	**4.28**	**1.27**	**259**	**234**	**268**	**24.3**	**2.6**	**6.7**	**2.6**	**37**	**21**	**42**	**1.2**	**11%**	**29%**	**74%**	**32**						**2.3**	**66**	**86**	**$9**

Choate,Randy

Age: 37 Th: L Role RP	Health B	LIMA Plan C	
Ht: 6' 1" Wt: 203 Type Pwr xGB	PT/Exp D	Rand Var -1	
	Consist B	MM 4400	

Take a looky at this LOOGY. While he dominates lefties, righties hit him hard, so he sees very few batters. Most of them put the ball on the ground; he gave up only one HR in 2012. Great Dom, but Ctl occasionally gets him into trouble. Basically, he's the 21st-century Jesse Orosco.

Yr	Tm	W	L	Sv	IP	K	ERA	xERA	WHIP	OBA	vL	vR	BF/G	Ctl	Dom	Cmd	G	L	F	hr/9	hr/f	H%	S%	GS	APC	DOM%	DIS%	Sv%	LI	RAR	BPV	BPX	R$
08	aaa	0	4	2	36	23	6.99	7.13	2.02	333			7.0	5.6	5.7	1.0				1.2		37%	66%							-12.0	9	16	-$8
09	TAM *	4	0	5	56	39	4.11	3.36	1.28	240	141	321	2.8	3.5	6.3	1.8	65	10	25	0.6	16%	28%	68%	0	10			83	0.94	1.4	64	119	$3
10	TAM	4	3	0	45	40	4.23	3.29	1.30	252	202	410	2.2	3.4	8.1	2.4	60	15	24	0.6	10%	31%	67%	0	8			0	1.19	-0.8	91	147	$0
11	FLA	1	1	0	25	31	1.82	2.68	1.05	149	145	167	1.9	4.7	11.3	2.4	63	18	20	1.1	27%	21%	91%	0	8			0	1.44	6.4	117	175	$1
12	2 NL	0	0	1	39	38	3.03	3.37	1.22	206	158	325	2.1	4.2	8.8	2.1	62	19	18	0.2	5%	28%	74%	0	8			100	1.26	4.7	86	112	-$1
1st Half		0	0	1	22	19	2.49	3.46	1.02	169	135	240	2.5	3.7	7.9	2.1	61	17	22	0.0	0%	24%	73%	0	10			100	1.49	4.1	80	104	$1
2nd Half		0	0	0	17	19	3.71	3.24	1.47	250	184	467	1.8	4.8	10.1	2.1	64	23	14	0.5	17%	34%	75%	0	7			0	1.07	0.7	94	122	-$2
13	Proj	**1**	**1**	**0**	**44**	**39**	**3.55**	**3.56**	**1.36**	**243**	**187**	**389**	**2.2**	**4.1**	**8.1**	**2.0**	**62**	**17**	**21**	**0.5**	**10%**	**31%**	**74%**	**0**						**2.5**	**75**	**98**	**-$1**

Cishek,Steve

Age: 27 Th: R Role RP	Health A	LIMA Plan A	
Ht: 6' 6" Wt: 215 Type Pwr GB	PT/Exp D	Rand Var -3	
	Consist B	MM 4531	

1H ERA looked great, but that was despite all the walks he allowed (thank you strand rate!). But when he was put into the closer's role, he responded with much better Cmd and BA vs LH. With high GB%, Dom, and domination of righties, he'll do well if he keeps getting save opportunities.

Yr	Tm	W	L	Sv	IP	K	ERA	xERA	WHIP	OBA	vL	vR	BF/G	Ctl	Dom	Cmd	G	L	F	hr/9	hr/f	H%	S%	GS	APC	DOM%	DIS%	Sv%	LI	RAR	BPV	BPX	R$
08																																	
09																																	
10	FLA *	3	1	2	36	33	4.76	3.33	1.37	267	0	111	6.0	3.0	8.4	2.8	45	9	45	0.0	0%	35%	61%	0	21			67	0.14	-3.0	110	177	-$1
11	FLA *	3	2	3	78	70	2.57	2.66	1.23	228	225	218	5.2	3.6	8.2	2.3	57	17	26	0.2	3%	30%	78%	0	20			100	0.86	13.2	100	150	$6
12	MIA	5	2	15	64	68	2.69	3.58	1.30	230	279	185	4.0	4.1	9.6	2.3	52	16	31	0.4	6%	31%	80%	0	16			79	1.20	10.4	92	120	$10
1st Half		4	1	1	32	30	2.53	4.26	1.44	237	327	167	4.3	5.1	8.4	1.7	53	14	33	0.8	10%	29%	86%	0	17			25	1.29	5.9	46	60	$7
2nd Half		1	1	14	32	38	2.84	2.96	1.17	222	237	207	3.8	3.1	10.8	3.5	52	19	29	0.0	0%	34%	73%	0	16			93	1.12	4.6	140	182	$13
13	Proj	**4**	**2**	**35**	**73**	**73**	**3.09**	**3.47**	**1.28**	**236**	**267**	**211**	**4.5**	**3.7**	**9.0**	**2.5**	**54**	**17**	**29**	**0.5**	**7%**	**31%**	**76%**	**0**						**8.3**	**95**	**124**	**$18**

Clippard,Tyler

Age: 28 Th: R Role RP	Health A	LIMA Plan B	
Ht: 6' 3" Wt: 200 Type Pwr xFB	PT/Exp B	Rand Var -1	
	Consist B	MM 3521	

H%, S% swings have affected him the past two years. 2H ERA was awful, but skills were actually better than in the 1H. 2011 ERA was unsustainable for the same reason. High Dom looks good on a closer, but history of high Ctl, extreme FB tendencies, and opportunity make the chances of a Saves repeat risky.

Yr	Tm	W	L	Sv	IP	K	ERA	xERA	WHIP	OBA	vL	vR	BF/G	Ctl	Dom	Cmd	G	L	F	hr/9	hr/f	H%	S%	GS	APC	DOM%	DIS%	Sv%	LI	RAR	BPV	BPX	R$
08	WAS *	7	14	0	153	111	5.86	5.03	1.57	276	333	261	23.2	4.4	6.5	1.5	21	15	64	1.1	10%	31%	63%	2	95	0%	100%			-29.1	36	68	-$8
09	WAS *	8	3	1	99	101	2.10	2.45	1.09	177	122	234	6.0	4.3	9.1	2.1	30	13	57	1.0	11%	21%	88%	0	24			50	0.71	27.2	88	165	$16
10	WAS	11	8	1	91	112	3.07	3.64	1.21	212	242	188	4.8	4.1	11.1	2.7	28	17	56	0.8	7%	30%	77%	0	20			9	1.23	11.4	96	155	$10
11	WAS	3	0	0	88	104	1.83	3.15	0.84	162	169	156	4.6	2.6	10.6	4.0	20	20	60	1.1	9%	20%	89%	0	19			0	1.49	23.0	117	176	$15
12	WAS	2	6	32	73	84	3.72	3.97	1.16	204	170	239	4.1	3.6	10.4	2.9	30	14	57	0.9	7%	28%	70%	0	17			86	1.25	2.7	98	128	$16
1st Half		1	2	13	33	39	1.89	3.76	0.93	140	121	161	3.9	4.1	10.5	2.6	34	8	58	0.0	0%	23%	77%	0	17			93	1.48	8.7	92	120	$20
2nd Half		1	4	19	39	45	5.26	4.15	1.35	252	208	295	4.4	3.2	10.3	3.2	27	17	56	1.6	11%	33%	65%	0	18			83	1.04	-6.0	103	134	$12
13	Proj	**3**	**4**	**13**	**73**	**83**	**3.27**	**3.76**	**1.11**	**205**	**186**	**224**	**4.5**	**3.5**	**10.3**	**3.0**	**27**	**16**	**57**	**1.0**	**8%**	**27%**	**75%**	**0**						**6.7**	**96**	**125**	**$11**

Cloyd,Tyler

Age: 26 Th: R Role SP	Health A	LIMA Plan B	
Ht: 6' 3" Wt: 210 Type Con xFB	PT/Exp D	Rand Var 0	
	Consist A	MM 1201	

2-2, 4.91 ERA in 33 IP at PHI. Soft-tosser with excellent Ctl was lights-out at AAA, with a 12-1 record and 2.35 ERA. Has a history of high Cmd, though Dom has dropped as he's moved up the organizational ladder. Durable frame casts him as a mid-rotation innings-eating type.

Yr	Tm	W	L	Sv	IP	K	ERA	xERA	WHIP	OBA	vL	vR	BF/G	Ctl	Dom	Cmd	G	L	F	hr/9	hr/f	H%	S%	GS	APC	DOM%	DIS%	Sv%	LI	RAR	BPV	BPX	R$
08																																	
09																																	
10																																	
11	aa	6	3	0	107	83	3.17	3.64	1.21	275			23.9	1.3	7.0	5.6				0.6		33%	75%							10.2	140	211	$6
12	PHI *	17	3	0	200	123	3.22	3.74	1.18	248	314	224	25.0	2.3	5.5	2.4	32	19	49	1.2	17%	27%	78%	6	88	50%	33%			19.7	55	72	$19
1st Half		11	1	0	102	60	2.59	3.15	1.15	250	0	0	25.2	1.9	5.3	2.8				0.6	0%	28%	80%	0	0					17.9	77	100	$28
2nd Half		6	2	0	98	63	3.86	4.31	1.22	247	314	224	24.8	2.7	5.7	2.1	32	19	49	1.7	17%	25%	77%	6	88	50%	33%			1.9	34	44	$8
13	Proj	**6**	**3**	**0**	**102**	**70**	**3.71**	**4.46**	**1.20**	**259**	**313**	**223**	**24.5**	**1.9**	**6.1**	**3.2**	**32**	**19**	**49**	**1.0**	**7%**	**29%**	**72%**	**17**						**3.9**	**70**	**90**	**$5**

Cobb,Alex

Age: 25 Th: R Role SP	Health B	LIMA Plan B+	
Ht: 6' 2" Wt: 195 Type Pwr xGB	PT/Exp D	Rand Var +1	
	Consist B	MM 4303	

11-9, 4.03 ERA in 136 IP at TAM. GBer acquitted himself well in extended trial. 1H/2H splits were due to shift in H%, S%; skills were similar. Plenty of DOMinant starts mixed in with a few DISasters—not surprising for a young pitcher. Keep an eye on the workload increase, but growth is likely.

Yr	Tm	W	L	Sv	IP	K	ERA	xERA	WHIP	OBA	vL	vR	BF/G	Ctl	Dom	Cmd	G	L	F	hr/9	hr/f	H%	S%	GS	APC	DOM%	DIS%	Sv%	LI	RAR	BPV	BPX	R$
08																																	
09																																	
10	aa	7	5	0	120	111	3.14	4.33	1.44	288			22.1	2.7	8.3	3.1				0.6		36%	79%							13.8	96	155	$5
11	TAM *	8	3	0	120	96	2.69	3.50	1.29	258	259	224	23.5	2.7	7.2	2.6	54	20	26	0.5	7%	31%	80%	9	94	22%	22%			18.6	86	129	$9
12	TAM *	12	13	0	178	142	4.21	3.85	1.35	265	256	252	23.9	2.9	7.2	2.5	59	20	21	0.6	13%	32%	69%	23	94	48%	26%			-4.4	78	102	$3
1st Half		4	8	0	87	69	4.78	4.13	1.45	281	257	257	24.8	3.1	7.2	2.3	62	17	21	0.4	10%	34%	65%	7	104	43%	0%			-8.2	78	102	-$4
2nd Half		8	5	0	91	73	3.67	3.53	1.25	250	255	250	23.0	2.8	7.2	2.6	57	22	21	0.8	14%	30%	72%	16	90	50%	38%			3.8	80	104	$10
13	Proj	**11**	**8**	**0**	**160**	**131**	**3.92**	**3.57**	**1.33**	**265**	**272**	**255**	**23.4**	**2.8**	**7.4**	**2.6**	**57**	**20**	**23**	**0.6**	**9%**	**32%**	**71%**	**28**						**1.9**	**92**	**119**	**$7**

DAVE ADLER

Coke,Phil

Age: 30	Th: L	Role RP	Health A	LIMA Plan C	
			PT/Exp C	Rand Var +3	
Ht: 6' 1"	Wt: 210	Type Pwr	Consist A	MM 2410	

Bullpen definitely suits him better than the rotation; more ground balls and Ks with limited exposure. H% and 2H hr/f indicate that there's some ERA upside. But if you think the playoff saves set him up for a bigger role, take a closer look—struggles vs righties will limit his opportunities.

Yr	Tm	W	L	Sv	IP	K	ERA	xERA	WHIP	OBA	vL	vR	BF/G	Ctl	Dom	Cmd	G	L	F	hr/9	hr/f	H%	S%	GS	APC	DOM%	DIS%	Sv%	LI	RAR	BPV	BPX	R$
08	NYY *	12	6	0	150	123	3.67	4.38	1.47	285	207	95	13.1	3.1	7.4	2.4	50	17	33	0.6	0%	35%	75%	0	17			0	0.84	12.2	75	141	$7
09	NYY	4	3	2	60	49	4.50	3.99	1.07	209	195	227	3.3	3.0	7.4	2.5	35	20	45	1.5	14%	22%	63%	0	13			29	1.42	-1.3	64	120	$3
10	DET	7	5	2	65	53	3.76	4.31	1.44	275	273	276	3.8	3.6	7.4	2.0	35	21	43	0.3	2%	33%	73%	1	14	0%	100%	50	1.12	2.6	48	78	$2
11	DET	3	9	1	109	69	4.47	4.46	1.45	279	215	314	9.9	3.3	5.7	1.7	43	22	35	0.4	4%	32%	68%	14	35	36%	43%	50	1.05	-7.1	34	52	-$4
12	DET	2	3	1	54	51	4.00	3.93	1.65	324	263	396	3.7	3.0	8.5	2.8	49	21	30	0.8	10%	39%	77%	0	14			33	1.25	0.1	99	129	-$5
1st Half		1	3	1	32	30	3.62	3.84	1.55	318	303	333	4.1	2.5	8.4	3.3	46	22	31	0.3	3%	40%	76%	0	15			50	1.25	1.6	107	139	-$4
2nd Half		1	0	0	22	21	4.57	4.07	1.80	333	212	500	3.2	3.7	8.7	2.3	52	19	29	1.7	20%	39%	80%	0	13			0	1.26	-1.5	86	112	-$7
13	Proj	3	3	3	58	52	4.03	4.08	1.47	281	225	335	4.3	3.3	8.0	2.4	44	21	35	1.0	10%	34%	75%	0						-0.1	78	101	-$1

Cole,Gerrit

Age: 22	Th: R	Role SP	Health A	LIMA Plan D+	
			PT/Exp F	Rand Var +1	
Ht: 6' 4"	Wt: 220	Type Pwr	Consist F	MM 2300	

Hard-throwing youngster made it through three levels. In AA, kept the ball on the ground and whiffed many (9.2 Dom). In keeper leagues, he's a no-brainer, as his future looks bright. Redraft leagues, think twice; while he'll likely be up with PIT in the 2H. Initial ups and downs wouldn't be surprising.

Yr	Tm	W	L	Sv	IP	K	ERA	xERA	WHIP	OBA	vL	vR	BF/G	Ctl	Dom	Cmd	G	L	F	hr/9	hr/f	H%	S%	GS	APC	DOM%	DIS%	Sv%	LI	RAR	BPV	BPX	R$
08																																	
09																																	
10																																	
11																																	
12	a/a	4	6	0	65	54	3.73	3.85	1.42	273			21.2	3.2	7.5	2.3				0.3		34%	72%							2.3	86	112	-$2
1st Half		1	1	0	6	6	9.07	6.98	1.90	403			14.2	0.0	9.7	0.0				0.0		52%	47%							-3.7	0	0	-$14
2nd Half		3	5	0	59	48	3.17	3.50	1.37	257			22.5	3.6	7.3	2.0				0.3		32%	76%							6.1	81	105	$0
13	Proj	3	5	0	58	50	4.30	4.38	1.53	274			21.2	4.2	7.7	1.9	48	16	36	1.0	10%	33%	74%	12						-2.0	53	69	-$3

Coleman,Louis

Age: 27	Th: R	Role RP	Health A	LIMA Plan C+	
			PT/Exp D	Rand Var 0	
Ht: 6' 4"	Wt: 205	Type Pwr xFB	Consist B	MM 2500	

0-0, 3.71 ERA in 51 IP at KC. You fell in love with that Dom, particularly in the 2H. You broke up over that combo of inflated FB% & hr/f. But he dominates righties, and you know it hurts so good to be dominated. If only he had better control. But who needs control when you're getting off on the power?

Yr	Tm	W	L	Sv	IP	K	ERA	xERA	WHIP	OBA	vL	vR	BF/G	Ctl	Dom	Cmd	G	L	F	hr/9	hr/f	H%	S%	GS	APC	DOM%	DIS%	Sv%	LI	RAR	BPV	BPX	R$
08																																	
09																																	
10	a/a	7	3	7	92	82	2.44	2.35	1.02	212			8.4	2.4	8.0	3.4				0.6		26%	79%							18.6	113	182	$15
11	KC	1	4	1	60	64	2.87	3.83	1.17	207	257	180	5.1	3.9	9.7	2.5	30	13	57	1.4	11%	25%	84%	0	21			50	1.43	7.9	76	114	$3
12	KC *	0	2	3	71	85	3.68	3.76	1.27	219	235	210	5.5	4.3	10.8	2.5	20	23	58	1.4	14%	28%	77%	0	23			100	0.53	2.9	87	113	$1
1st Half		0	2	3	42	43	4.30	3.83	1.32	224	242	220	6.2	4.5	9.3	2.0	18	22	60	1.3	14%	27%	72%	0	25			100	0.37	-1.4	70	91	$0
2nd Half		0	0	0	29	42	2.79	3.61	1.21	212	229	203	4.7	4.0	13.0	3.2	22	23	55	1.6	15%	30%	87%	0	21			0	0.64	4.4	112	146	$3
13	Proj	1	2	0	51	58	4.14	4.09	1.31	234	266	216	5.6	4.0	10.3	2.6	24	19	57	1.3	10%	30%	73%	0						-0.7	80	104	-$1

Collins,Tim

Age: 23	Th: L	Role RP	Health A	LIMA Plan A	
			PT/Exp D	Rand Var 0	
Ht: 5' 7"	Wt: 165	Type Pwr FB	Consist F	MM 3500	

Lefty complement to Coleman—power pitcher with tons of Ks, too many walks, and a bunch of fly balls. But the Cmd growth is encouraging; success against righties means he can be more than a specialist. Closer at AA/AAA, but being a southpaw works against him.

Yr	Tm	W	L	Sv	IP	K	ERA	xERA	WHIP	OBA	vL	vR	BF/G	Ctl	Dom	Cmd	G	L	F	hr/9	hr/f	H%	S%	GS	APC	DOM%	DIS%	Sv%	LI	RAR	BPV	BPX	R$
08																																	
09																																	
10	a/a	3	1	15	71	90	2.17	1.63	0.95	176			4.8	3.1	11.4	3.6				0.6		26%	80%							16.8	148	240	$16
11	KC	4	4	0	67	60	3.63	4.83	1.49	216	210	221	4.3	6.4	8.1	1.3	41	17	42	0.7	7%	27%	77%	0	18			0	1.20	2.6	-10	-15	-$1
12	KC	5	4	0	70	93	3.36	3.40	1.28	216	239	196	4.1	4.4	12.0	2.7	41	16	43	1.0	12%	31%	78%	0	17			0	1.09	5.6	117	152	$3
1st Half		4	2	0	38	52	3.35	3.22	1.14	190	226	167	4.6	4.1	12.4	3.1	40	14	45	0.7	8%	30%	73%	0	19			0	1.04	3.1	132	172	$7
2nd Half		1	2	0	32	41	3.38	3.64	1.44	246	250	241	3.7	4.8	11.5	2.4	41	19	40	1.4	17%	33%	83%	0	16			0	1.14	2.5	98	128	-$1
13	Proj	4	3	0	65	76	3.82	3.81	1.32	222	232	213	4.1	4.7	10.5	2.2	41	17	42	1.0	11%	29%	74%	0						1.6	80	104	$2

Collmenter,Josh

Age: 27	Th: R	Role RP	Health A	LIMA Plan A	
			PT/Exp C	Rand Var 0	
Ht: 6' 2"	Wt: 235	Type xFB	Consist A	MM 2301	

42% S% and 25% hr/f in April (9.82 ERA) cost his rotation slot, but skills were solid all year; excelled as starter in 2H. Dom remained high over both halves, but fly balls started sailing in 2H. Command isn't an issue, but he needs to reduce the fly balls to maintain a rotation spot.

Yr	Tm	W	L	Sv	IP	K	ERA	xERA	WHIP	OBA	vL	vR	BF/G	Ctl	Dom	Cmd	G	L	F	hr/9	hr/f	H%	S%	GS	APC	DOM%	DIS%	Sv%	LI	RAR	BPV	BPX	R$
08																																	
09																																	
10	a/a	12	6	0	137	91	4.01	4.15	1.38	269			26.2	3.1	6.0	1.9				0.8		31%	72%							1.1	55	88	$4
11	ARI	10	10	0	154	100	3.38	4.02	1.07	237	250	225	20.0	1.6	5.8	3.6	33	20	47	1.0	8%	26%	72%	24	79	58%	21%	0	0.71	10.7	72	108	$13
12	ARI	5	3	0	90	80	3.69	3.92	1.26	264	313	215	13.4	2.2	8.0	3.6	37	19	43	1.3	12%	31%	76%	11	54	36%	27%	0	0.66	3.7	99	130	$2
1st Half		0	2	0	45	41	4.80	3.82	1.40	288	348	224	12.8	2.4	8.2	3.4	43	21	36	1.6	17%	33%	71%	5	50	0%	60%	0	0.53	-4.3	104	135	-$6
2nd Half		5	1	0	45	39	2.58	4.01	1.13	240	274	207	14.1	2.0	7.7	3.9	31	18	51	1.0	8%	29%	83%	6	58	67%	0%	0	0.82	8.0	95	124	$11
13	Proj	9	6	0	127	100	3.94	4.07	1.20	255	288	221	16.3	2.1	7.1	3.4	35	19	46	1.3	11%	29%	72%	20						1.1	84	109	$7

Colon,Bartolo

Age: 40	Th: R	Role SP	Health B	LIMA Plan C	
			PT/Exp B	Rand Var -1	
Ht: 5' 11"	Wt: 265	Type Con	Consist A	MM 1101	

You really have to admire and respect a guy who shows solid growth and posts career-best pinpoint control at such an advanced age. Oh... wait.

Yr	Tm	W	L	Sv	IP	K	ERA	xERA	WHIP	OBA	vL	vR	BF/G	Ctl	Dom	Cmd	G	L	F	hr/9	hr/f	H%	S%	GS	APC	DOM%	DIS%	Sv%	LI	RAR	BPV	BPX	R$
08	BOS *	7	3	0	71	42	3.67	4.22	1.31	275	309	253	18.3	2.2	5.3	2.4	40	21	39	0.9	10%	30%	75%	7	83	43%	14%			5.7	55	103	$3
09	CHW	3	6	0	62	38	4.19	4.75	1.44	280	288	273	23.0	3.0	5.5	1.8	44	16	40	1.9	16%	29%	79%	12	83	25%	25%			1.0	39	73	-$2
10																																	
11	NYY	8	10	0	164	135	4.00	3.69	1.29	267	297	238	23.9	2.2	7.4	3.4	44	20	36	1.2	11%	31%	73%	26	88	50%	27%	0	0.77	-1.1	96	144	$5
12	OAK	10	9	0	152	91	3.43	4.18	1.21	266	274	257	26.5	1.4	5.4	4.0	46	18	36	1.0	9%	30%	75%	24	89	50%	25%			11.1	84	110	$9
1st Half		6	7	0	90	55	4.22	4.28	1.30	283	276	291	25.3	1.6	5.5	3.4	45	18	37	1.2	11%	31%	71%	15	86	33%	33%			-2.2	79	103	$7
2nd Half		4	2	0	63	36	2.30	4.04	1.07	242	271	204	28.6	1.0	5.2	5.1	47	18	35	0.7	7%	28%	82%	9	94	78%	11%			13.3	91	118	$13
13	Proj	4	6	0	87	52	4.25	4.67	1.42	282	301	261	24.7	2.9	5.3	1.9	45	18	37	1.3	12%	30%	75%	15						-2.5	41	54	-$2

Cook,Aaron

Age: 34	Th: R	Role SP	Health F	LIMA Plan F	
			PT/Exp C	Rand Var +2	
Ht: 6' 3"	Wt: 215	Type Con xGB	Consist B	MM 0001	

4-11, 5.65 ERA in 94 IP at BOS. Those are not typos-Dom really was that low, and PQS DOM/DIS split was that bad. Contact pitcher keeps the ball on the ground, but when S% is low (64% in majors), bad things will happen. If you're considering him, slap yourself. Seriously. Why are you still reading this?

Yr	Tm	W	L	Sv	IP	K	ERA	xERA	WHIP	OBA	vL	vR	BF/G	Ctl	Dom	Cmd	G	L	F	hr/9	hr/f	H%	S%	GS	APC	DOM%	DIS%	Sv%	LI	RAR	BPV	BPX	R$
08	COL	16	9	0	211	96	3.96	4.14	1.34	287	297	276	27.7	2.0	4.1	2.0	56	20	24	0.6	8%	31%	70%	32	96	25%	6%			9.5	52	98	$10
09	COL	11	6	0	158	78	4.16	4.29	1.41	284	282	285	25.0	2.7	4.4	1.7	57	19	25	1.1	14%	30%	73%	27	89	22%	26%			3.2	43	80	$4
10	COL	6	8	0	128	62	5.08	4.61	1.56	290	337	258	24.9	3.7	4.4	1.2	58	17	25	0.8	10%	31%	68%	23	86	26%	35%			-15.7	16	25	-$7
11	COL *	4	11	0	126	60	6.14	5.56	1.63	314	349	303	24.3	3.0	4.3	1.4	55	22	23	0.9	11%	34%	62%	17	82	6%	35%	0	0.73	-34.1	21	32	-$16
12	BOS *	7	11	0	131	32	5.11	5.41	1.51	306	340	261	23.7	2.4	2.2	0.9	59	18	23	1.1	18%	30%	68%	18	75	6%	44%			-17.7	-8	-11	-$12
1st Half		5	1	0	54	14	3.92	4.27	1.44	290	326	95	25.6	2.6	2.3	0.9	57	15	28	0.4	6%	30%	72%	3	69	33%	67%			0.6	17	22	-$2
2nd Half		2	10	0	77	18	5.94	6.15	1.56	317	343	284	22.6	2.3	2.1	0.9	59	19	22	1.6	21%	30%	65%	15	76	0%	40%			-18.3	-26	-34	-$18
13	Proj	4	7	0	85	31	5.29	4.82	1.53	303	340	263	24.1	2.7	3.3	1.2	57	19	24	1.0	12%	31%	66%	15						-13.2	20	26	-$7

DAVE ADLER

Cook,Ryan

Age: 26	Th: R	Role RP	Health	A	LIMA Plan B
Ht: 6' 2"	Wt: 215	Type Pwr	PT/Exp	D	Rand Var -5
			Consist	C	MM 4421

PRO: Huge Dom held up all season; developing GB tilt; massive 2H skills gains. CON: H%-S%-hr/f coincided to drive near-2.00 ERA; limited track record. Got a taste of the ninth and has hard fastball/ slider profile of many successful closers. If 2nd half Ctl is for real ... UP: 35 Sv

Yr	Tm	W	L	Sv	IP	K	ERA	xERA	WHIP	OBA	vL	vR	BF/G	Ctl	Dom	Cmd	G	L	F	hr/9	hr/f	H%	S%	GS	APC	DOM%	DIS%	Sv%	LI	RAR	BPV	BPX	R$
08																																	
09																																	
10	a/a	1	1	0	24	14	5.15	4.04	1.43	250			25.1	4.4	5.4	1.2				0.8		28%	64%							-3.1	39	63	-$3
11	ARI *	1	6	19	69	58	2.75	2.51	1.20	219	313	353	4.6	3.6	7.6	2.1	46	19	35	0.2	0%	28%	76%	0	14			79	0.44	10.1	93	140	$11
12	OAK	6	2	14	73	80	2.09	3.24	0.94	166	171	162	4.1	3.3	9.8	3.0	47	16	38	0.5	6%	23%	80%	0	16			67	1.40	17.4	112	146	$18
1st Half		2	2	6	34	37	1.59	3.89	0.97	109	75	140	4.0	5.6	9.8	1.8	45	11	44	0.0	0%	17%	82%	0	16			67	1.45	10.2	49	64	$16
2nd Half		4	0	8	39	43	2.52	2.76	0.92	210	250	177	4.1	1.4	9.8	7.2	48	19	33	0.9	12%	28%	78%	0	16			67	1.36	7.3	166	216	$19
13	Proj	**4**	**4**	**23**	**73**	**72**	**2.38**	**3.45**	**1.04**	**192**	**203**	**183**	**4.2**	**3.3**	**8.9**	**2.7**	**47**	**16**	**37**	**0.4**	**5%**	**25%**	**78%**	**0**						**14.6**	**96**	**124**	**$18**

Corbin,Patrick

Age: 23	Th: L	Role SP	Health	A	LIMA Plan A+
Ht: 6' 2"	Wt: 187	Type	PT/Exp	D	Rand Var +1
			Consist	A	MM 3303

6-8, 4.54 ERA in 107 IP at ARI. Survived both the organizational yo-yo and ups and downs in MLB performance (DOM%/DIS%). But good signs underneath: Ctl, Dom, GB% improving in concert; MLB xERA (3.72) and BPV (97) confirm his readiness. Underrated, with profit potential.

Yr	Tm	W	L	Sv	IP	K	ERA	xERA	WHIP	OBA	vL	vR	BF/G	Ctl	Dom	Cmd	G	L	F	hr/9	hr/f	H%	S%	GS	APC	DOM%	DIS%	Sv%	LI	RAR	BPV	BPX	R$
08																																	
09																																	
10																																	
11	aa	9	8	0	160	121	4.65	4.63	1.40	293			26.0	2.1	6.8	3.3				0.9		34%	68%							-14.1	80	120	-$2
12	ARI *	11	10	1	186	153	3.91	4.27	1.34	279	325	269	22.1	2.2	7.4	3.3	46	23	31	0.9	13%	33%	73%	17	73	47%	35%	100	0.77	2.3	87	113	$6
1st Half		7	5	0	95	70	3.68	4.20	1.39	280	357	245	24.9	2.6	6.6	2.5	50	24	27	0.7	11%	33%	75%	5	84	20%	40%	0	0.72	3.9	72	94	$7
2nd Half		4	5	1	92	83	4.16	4.28	1.29	277	308	279	19.8	1.8	8.2	4.4	44	23	33	1.1	14%	34%	71%	12	68	58%	33%	100	0.79	-1.6	110	143	$4
13	Proj	**7**	**7**	**0**	**131**	**105**	**4.23**	**3.79**	**1.36**	**285**	**339**	**271**	**23.3**	**2.1**	**7.2**	**3.4**	**46**	**23**	**30**	**0.9**	**10%**	**34%**	**70%**	**23**						**-3.5**	**96**	**125**	**$2**

Corpas,Manuel

Age: 30	Th: R	Role RP	Health	A	LIMA Plan D+
Ht: 6' 3"	Wt: 210	Type	PT/Exp	D	Rand Var 0
			Consist	B	MM 1100

0-2, 5.01 ERA in 47 IP at CHC. Showed considerable rust after missing 2011 with Tommy John surgery. Without an adequate strikeout pitch, his effectiveness is severely limited. Still only 30, there's time for late life—though his skills weren't exactly thriving before the operation either. Let rest.

Yr	Tm	W	L	Sv	IP	K	ERA	xERA	WHIP	OBA	vL	vR	BF/G	Ctl	Dom	Cmd	G	L	F	hr/9	hr/f	H%	S%	GS	APC	DOM%	DIS%	Sv%	LI	RAR	BPV	BPX	R$
08	COL	3	4	4	80	50	4.52	4.21	1.46	296	285	308	4.6	2.6	5.6	2.2	50	23	28	0.8	10%	33%	70%	0	16			31	0.94	-1.9	60	112	$0
09	COL	1	3	1	34	24	5.88	3.89	1.51	326	400	267	4.2	1.9	6.4	3.4	49	22	30	0.8	9%	37%	60%	0	15			33	0.78	-6.5	92	172	-$5
10	COL	3	5	10	62	47	4.62	4.31	1.41	269	326	239	4.9	3.2	6.8	2.1	43	19	39	1.0	9%	31%	69%	0	18			71	1.05	-4.2	57	93	$2
11																																	
12	CHC *	0	4	0	80	42	5.09	4.98	1.43	281	328	248	5.1	2.9	4.7	1.6	44	19	37	1.3	12%	29%	67%	0	15			0	0.84	-10.6	21	27	-$8
1st Half		0	2	0	45	22	4.31	4.42	1.36	265	100	214	6.2	3.1	4.4	1.4	43	13	43	1.2	8%	28%	72%	0	14			0	1.13	-1.6	23	30	-$7
2nd Half		0	2	0	36	20	6.06	5.62	1.51	299	375	258	4.2	2.8	5.0	1.8	44	20	35	1.5	14%	31%	63%	0	15			0	0.75	-9.0	18	23	-$10
13	Proj	**1**	**4**	**0**	**58**	**36**	**4.84**	**4.48**	**1.45**	**288**	**343**	**251**	**4.6**	**2.8**	**5.6**	**2.0**	**46**	**21**	**33**	**1.1**	**12%**	**32%**	**69%**	**0**						**-5.9**	**51**	**66**	**-$4**

Correia,Kevin

Age: 32	Th: R	Role SP	Health	B	LIMA Plan C+
Ht: 6' 3"	Wt: 200	Type Con	PT/Exp	A	Rand Var 0
			Consist	A	MM 1103

The latest episode of "As Pittsburgh Turns": journeyman SP with a Dom barely higher than his xERA moans about being replaced with his team 15 games over .500 in July for the first time in eons. Good karma is ruined, chaos ensues, team limps to a 21-40 finish. And the SP escapes into free agency.

Yr	Tm	W	L	Sv	IP	K	ERA	xERA	WHIP	OBA	vL	vR	BF/G	Ctl	Dom	Cmd	G	L	F	hr/9	hr/f	H%	S%	GS	APC	DOM%	DIS%	Sv%	LI	RAR	BPV	BPX	R$
08	SF	3	8	0	110	66	6.05	5.30	1.71	310	307	312	20.6	3.8	5.4	1.4	38	25	37	1.2	10%	34%	66%	19	76	37%	32%	0	0.67	-23.5	9	18	-$11
09	SD	12	11	0	198	142	3.91	4.16	1.30	259	247	269	25.2	2.9	6.5	2.2	45	19	36	0.8	8%	30%	71%	33	96	52%	15%			10.1	61	113	$12
10	SD	10	10	0	145	115	5.40	4.16	1.49	271	248	290	22.9	4.0	7.1	1.8	49	21	30	1.2	15%	31%	66%	26	90	35%	19%	0	0.75	-23.6	48	78	-$5
11	PIT	12	11	0	154	77	4.79	4.45	1.39	287	277	294	24.4	2.3	4.5	2.0	45	18	36	1.4	13%	30%	69%	26	87	27%	27%	0	0.73	-16.1	42	64	-$3
12	PIT	12	11	0	171	89	4.21	4.43	1.30	267	248	284	22.8	2.4	4.7	1.9	51	20	29	1.1	12%	28%	70%	28	80	36%	18%	0	0.76	-4.1	48	63	$3
1st Half		4	6	0	85	34	4.32	4.77	1.30	263	234	289	24.1	2.6	3.6	1.4	53	17	31	1.5	16%	26%	72%	15	87	27%	20%			-3.2	24	31	-$1
2nd Half		8	5	0	86	55	4.10	4.11	1.30	272	263	279	21.5	2.2	5.8	2.6	50	23	28	0.6	8%	31%	69%	13	74	46%	15%	0	0.75	-0.8	72	94	$6
13	Proj	**12**	**12**	**0**	**174**	**101**	**4.60**	**4.42**	**1.37**	**275**	**260**	**288**	**22.4**	**2.7**	**5.2**	**1.9**	**48**	**20**	**32**	**1.1**	**12%**	**30%**	**69%**	**33**						**-12.5**	**48**	**62**	**$1**

Crain,Jesse

Age: 31	Th: R	Role RP	Health	C	LIMA Plan A
Ht: 6' 1"	Wt: 215	Type Pwr xFB	PT/Exp	C	Rand Var -5
			Consist	A	MM 3510

Entered the spring with a shot at the closer's job, but missed time with oblique (early May) and shoulder (July) injuries. Still, most skills were stellar all season, led by a jump in strikeout rate. H%/S% say the ERA won't be quite as good, and 2H Ctl a mild concern. But a solid LIMA choice with some saves upside.

Yr	Tm	W	L	Sv	IP	K	ERA	xERA	WHIP	OBA	vL	vR	BF/G	Ctl	Dom	Cmd	G	L	F	hr/9	hr/f	H%	S%	GS	APC	DOM%	DIS%	Sv%	LI	RAR	BPV	BPX	R$
08	MIN	5	4	0	63	50	3.59	4.40	1.37	257	250	261	4.1	3.4	7.2	2.1	41	17	42	0.9	7%	31%	76%	0	16			0	1.29	5.7	55	104	$2
09	MIN *	8	4	1	69	60	4.39	3.66	1.45	249	297	220	4.4	4.6	7.8	1.7	43	16	41	0.4	5%	31%	68%	0	16			100	0.76	-0.6	75	141	$2
10	MIN	1	1	1	68	62	3.04	3.87	1.18	215	196	228	3.9	3.6	8.2	2.3	39	17	44	0.7	6%	27%	76%	0	15			25	1.10	8.7	68	110	$4
11	CHW	8	3	1	65	70	2.62	3.83	1.24	215	184	233	4.0	4.3	9.6	2.3	33	18	49	1.0	9%	27%	84%	0	17			14	1.71	10.7	69	104	$7
12	CHW	2	3	0	48	60	2.44	3.46	1.08	171	232	129	3.8	4.3	11.3	2.6	37	19	44	0.9	11%	24%	83%	0	17			0	1.28	9.3	101	132	$4
1st Half		2	1	0	23	28	2.38	3.29	1.10	191	294	120	3.9	3.6	11.1	3.1	42	20	38	0.8	10%	28%	83%	0	16			0	1.02	4.6	123	160	$4
2nd Half		0	2	0	25	32	2.49	3.62	1.07	151	171	137	3.7	5.0	11.4	2.3	32	19	49	1.1	12%	20%	83%	0	17			0	1.51	4.8	80	104	$4
13	Proj	**3**	**3**	**3**	**58**	**65**	**3.04**	**3.81**	**1.22**	**210**	**231**	**197**	**3.9**	**4.2**	**10.0**	**2.4**	**36**	**18**	**45**	**0.9**	**9%**	**28%**	**79%**	**0**						**7.0**	**81**	**105**	**$4**

Crow,Aaron

Age: 26	Th: R	Role RP	Health	A	LIMA Plan A
Ht: 6' 3"	Wt: 190	Type Pwr GB	PT/Exp	D	Rand Var 0
			Consist	C	MM 3410

Fine-tuning his Ctl fueled another excellent season, further highlighting his attributes: a strikeout per inning, heavy ground-ball tilt, very good OBA. ERA snapped back as hr/f, S% corrected, but overall skills sharpened and improved in 2H. If he stays in pen, he's as a sure thing as you'll find.

Yr	Tm	W	L	Sv	IP	K	ERA	xERA	WHIP	OBA	vL	vR	BF/G	Ctl	Dom	Cmd	G	L	F	hr/9	hr/f	H%	S%	GS	APC	DOM%	DIS%	Sv%	LI	RAR	BPV	BPX	R$
08																																	
09																																	
10	aa	7	7	0	119	72	6.33	5.56	1.70	302			24.5	4.3	5.4	1.3				0.9		34%	62%							-33.1	27	43	-$13
11	KC	4	4	0	62	65	2.76	3.49	1.39	237	311	175	4.7	4.5	9.4	2.1	52	21	27	1.2	18%	30%	86%	0	18			0	1.30	9.1	78	118	$2
12	KC	3	1	2	65	65	3.48	3.25	1.18	231	188	255	3.6	3.1	9.0	3.0	53	19	28	0.6	8%	30%	71%	0	13			25	1.09	4.3	111	145	$3
1st Half		1	1	1	34	32	2.65	3.42	1.18	228	106	303	3.7	3.2	8.5	2.7	51	22	27	0.3	4%	30%	77%	0	14			33	1.22	5.7	95	124	$4
2nd Half		2	0	1	31	33	4.40	3.06	1.17	234	289	205	3.4	2.9	9.7	3.3	56	15	29	0.9	13%	30%	64%	0	12			20	0.95	-1.5	129	168	$2
13	Proj	**4**	**2**	**3**	**65**	**63**	**3.77**	**3.60**	**1.33**	**245**	**268**	**229**	**4.5**	**3.7**	**8.7**	**2.3**	**53**	**19**	**28**	**0.9**	**12%**	**31%**	**74%**	**0**						**2.0**	**87**	**113**	**$2**

Cruz,Juan

Age: 34	Th: R	Role RP	Health	B	LIMA Plan D
Ht: 6' 2"	Wt: 170	Type Pwr xFB	PT/Exp	D	Rand Var -4
			Consist	A	MM 1400

Won a bullpen spot in camp, then oupitched his xERA by almost two full runs before he missed most of the second half with elbow issues and his subsequent release. Always had nice Dom, but also can't find the plate (4.8 career Ctl). xERA string, RAR, BPV all agree: Move on.

Yr	Tm	W	L	Sv	IP	K	ERA	xERA	WHIP	OBA	vL	vR	BF/G	Ctl	Dom	Cmd	G	L	F	hr/9	hr/f	H%	S%	GS	APC	DOM%	DIS%	Sv%	LI	RAR	BPV	BPX	R$
08	ARI	4	0	0	52	71	2.61	3.71	1.26	192	159	221	3.8	5.4	12.4	2.3	27	16	57	0.9	8%	28%	83%	0	17			0	0.75	10.9	82	153	$5
09	KC	3	4	2	50	38	5.72	5.37	1.49	246	244	247	4.8	5.2	6.8	1.3	24	22	54	1.1	8%	28%	62%	0	21			33	0.98	-8.7	-16	-29	-$3
10	KC	0	0	0	5	7	3.38	4.66	2.44	391	333	429	5.6	6.8	11.8	1.8	31	38	31	0.0	0%	53%	85%	0	22			0	1.39	0.5	39	64	-$4
11	TAM	5	0	0	49	46	3.88	4.26	1.32	211	171	238	3.6	5.2	8.5	1.6	35	18	46	0.9	9%	25%	73%	0	16			0	0.94	0.4	26	40	$0
12	PIT	1	1	3	36	33	2.78	4.56	1.63	289	254	316	3.8	4.8	8.3	1.7	37	30	32	0.8	9%	35%	85%	0	16			75	1.05	5.5	35	46	-$2
1st Half		1	1	3	26	28	2.73	4.15	1.67	304	289	316	3.7	4.4	9.6	2.2	39	28	33	1.0	12%	38%	88%	0	15			100	1.15	4.2	69	90	-$1
2nd Half		0	0	0	9	5	2.89	5.83	1.50	242	143	316	3.9	5.8	4.8	0.8	33	37	30	0.0	0%	27%	79%	0	16			0	0.76	1.3	-58	-76	-$5
13	Proj	**2**	**1**	**0**	**29**	**28**	**4.30**	**4.67**	**1.47**	**246**	**229**	**260**	**4.0**	**5.0**	**8.8**	**1.8**	**31**	**22**	**47**	**1.0**	**9%**	**31%**	**73%**	**0**						**-1.0**	**33**	**43**	**-$3**

BRENT HERSHEY

Cruz,Rhiner

Age: 26 Th: R Role RP	Health	A	LIMA Plan	F
Ht: 6' 2" Wt: 205 Type Pwr	PT/Exp	D	Rand Var	+4
	Consist	D	MM	1200

Well-travelled 26-year-old was Rule 5 pick last winter. Spent most of season showing mid/high-90s velocity and little else. Serious Ctl problems suggests more minor league seasoning. But that Sept. flash from nowhere—11/0 K/BB, 1.08/2.53 ERA/xERA combo in 8 IP—says to heed the Rand Var.

Yr Tm	W	L	Sv	IP	K	ERA	xERA	WHIP	OBA	vL	vR	BF/G	Ctl	Dom	Cmd	G	L	F	hr/9	hr/f	H%	S%	GS	APC	DOM%	DIS%	Sv%	LI	RAR	BPV	BPX	R$
08																																
09																																
10																																
11 aa	3	2	7	59	40	4.08	3.24	1.38	217			6.8	5.4	6.2	1.1				0.5		25%	70%							-1.0	56	84	$1
12 HOU	1	1	0	55	46	6.05	4.94	1.71	297	315	285	4.9	4.7	7.5	1.6	39	25	36	1.3	13%	34%	66%	0	19			0	0.33	-13.8	24	32	-$11
1st Half	1	0	0	25	20	6.75	5.05	1.70	301	348	263	5.1	4.3	7.1	1.7	40	20	39	1.8	15%	34%	63%	0	20			0	0.57	-8.5	31	40	-$12
2nd Half	0	1	0	30	26	5.46	4.86	1.72	293	279	301	4.7	5.2	7.9	1.5	38	29	33	0.9	10%	35%	69%	0	18			0	0.13	-5.3	19	25	-$10
13 Proj	**1**	**2**	**0**	**58**	**45**	**4.48**	**4.75**	**1.47**	**256**	**268**	**248**	**5.3**	**4.6**	**7.0**	**1.5**	**39**	**25**	**36**	**1.0**	**10%**	**30%**	**72%**	**0**						**-3.3**	**20**	**26**	**-$4**

Cueto,Johnny

Age: 27 Th: R Role SP	Health	B	LIMA Plan	C
Ht: 5' 10" Wt: 215 Type	PT/Exp	A	Rand Var	-2
	Consist	A	MM	3205

Avoided DL, nagging injuries to notch first 200+ IP campaign, as season-long Ctl gains and 2H Dom spike fueled career year. Held much of GB advance from 2011, while making one-time gopheritis problems seem like long ago. Entering a prime age; there's little to criticize about this performance.

Yr Tm	W	L	Sv	IP	K	ERA	xERA	WHIP	OBA	vL	vR	BF/G	Ctl	Dom	Cmd	G	L	F	hr/9	hr/f	H%	S%	GS	APC	DOM%	DIS%	Sv%	LI	RAR	BPV	BPX	R$
08 CIN	9	14	0	174	158	4.81	4.22	1.41	264	249	275	24.8	3.5	8.2	2.3	39	21	41	1.5	14%	31%	71%	31	98	45%	23%			-10.4	69	130	$3
09 CIN	11	11	0	171	132	4.41	4.31	1.36	262	250	274	24.7	3.2	6.9	2.2	42	18	41	1.3	11%	30%	71%	30	97	47%	17%			-1.9	58	109	$6
10 CIN	12	7	0	186	138	3.64	4.03	1.28	257	234	276	25.2	2.7	6.7	2.5	42	19	39	0.9	9%	30%	74%	31	101	58%	13%			10.2	67	109	$11
11 CIN	9	5	0	156	104	2.31	3.66	1.09	220	209	229	26.3	2.7	6.0	2.2	54	16	30	0.5	6%	26%	80%	24	100	54%	13%			31.5	67	100	$18
12 CIN	19	9	0	217	170	2.78	3.60	1.17	252	279	220	26.9	2.0	7.1	3.5	49	22	29	0.6	8%	30%	78%	33	105	58%	12%			33.1	99	129	$26
1st Half	9	4	0	108	79	2.26	3.64	1.14	246	294	182	27.2	2.1	6.6	3.2	49	21	29	0.4	5%	29%	81%	16	107	75%	13%			23.4	90	117	$31
2nd Half	10	5	0	109	91	3.29	3.55	1.20	257	263	250	26.6	2.0	7.5	3.8	49	22	30	0.8	10%	31%	75%	17	102	41%	12%			9.8	108	141	$21
13 Proj	**16**	**9**	**0**	**210**	**159**	**3.02**	**3.79**	**1.19**	**246**	**252**	**240**	**25.5**	**2.4**	**6.8**	**2.8**	**48**	**20**	**32**	**0.7**	**8%**	**29%**	**77%**	**33**						**25.8**	**83**	**108**	**$22**

Danks,John

Age: 28 Th: L Role SP	Health	F	LIMA Plan	C
Ht: 6' 1" Wt: 215 Type	PT/Exp	A	Rand Var	+2
	Consist	B	MM	2205

Season never got lift-off, as final start was May 19. BPIs took a dive en masse, fueled by shoulder issues that ended in arthroscopic surgery in August. Early reports say damage was minor and he's good to go in March. But given diminished velocity and expected rust, best to err on the side of caution.

Yr Tm	W	L	Sv	IP	K	ERA	xERA	WHIP	OBA	vL	vR	BF/G	Ctl	Dom	Cmd	G	L	F	hr/9	hr/f	H%	S%	GS	APC	DOM%	DIS%	Sv%	LI	RAR	BPV	BPX	R$
08 CHW	12	9	0	195	159	3.32	3.84	1.23	246	264	240	24.4	2.6	7.3	2.8	43	22	35	0.7	7%	30%	75%	33	95	55%	21%			24.1	82	154	$18
09 CHW	13	11	0	200	149	3.77	4.27	1.28	245	244	246	26.2	3.3	6.7	2.0	44	15	41	1.3	11%	27%	76%	32	100	50%	13%			13.5	54	101	$14
10 CHW	15	11	0	213	162	3.72	3.94	1.22	237	273	221	27.4	3.0	6.8	2.3	45	16	39	0.8	7%	28%	71%	32	106	63%	9%			9.5	66	107	$15
11 CHW	8	12	0	170	135	4.33	3.83	1.34	274	270	275	27.0	2.4	7.1	2.9	44	20	36	1.0	10%	32%	70%	27	102	59%	19%			-8.2	85	127	$1
12 CHW	3	4	0	54	30	5.70	5.21	1.49	273	307	248	26.4	3.9	5.0	1.3	41	22	37	1.2	11%	29%	63%	9	93	33%	33%			-11.2	5	7	-$8
1st Half	3	4	0	54	30	5.70	5.22	1.49	273	307	248	26.4	3.9	5.0	1.3	41	22	37	1.2	11%	29%	63%	9	93	33%	33%			-11.2	6	8	-$8
2nd Half																																
13 Proj	**13**	**10**	**0**	**189**	**144**	**3.93**	**4.18**	**1.31**	**259**	**283**	**247**	**25.7**	**2.9**	**6.9**	**2.4**	**43**	**19**	**38**	**1.0**	**10%**	**30%**	**73%**	**30**						**2.1**	**67**	**87**	**$9**

Darvish,Yu

Age: 26 Th: R Role SP	Health	A	LIMA Plan	B+
Ht: 6' 5" Wt: 215 Type Pwr	PT/Exp	A	Rand Var	0
	Consist	C	MM	4505

Nice debut from the long-hyped import. Harnessing Ctl is a work in progress, but scary-good Dom held firm all season. Scuffled in July-Aug Texas heat (5.49 ERA), but DOM/DIS says he was just fine. Sept finish (2.21 ERA/xERA, 5.6 Cmd) points to upside. With better Ctl and S% luck... UP: sub-3.00 ERA

Yr Tm	W	L	Sv	IP	K	ERA	xERA	WHIP	OBA	vL	vR	BF/G	Ctl	Dom	Cmd	G	L	F	hr/9	hr/f	H%	S%	GS	APC	DOM%	DIS%	Sv%	LI	RAR	BPV	BPX	R$
08 for	16	4	0	200	197	2.35	2.38	1.00	206			30.6	2.5	8.9	3.6				0.8		26%	81%							48.8	118	222	$34
09 for	15	5	0	182	158	2.15	2.22	1.00	198			30.2	2.8	7.8	2.8				0.7		24%	83%							48.8	100	187	$33
10 for	12	8	0	202	211	2.21	2.56	1.13	229			30.7	2.6	9.4	3.6				0.4		31%	81%							46.5	130	211	$27
11 for	18	6	0	232	262	1.78	1.65	0.91	204			30.9	1.7	10.2	5.9				0.3		29%	82%							61.8	189	283	$46
12 TEX	16	9	0	191	221	3.90	3.51	1.28	220	231	207	28.1	4.2	10.4	2.5	46	22	32	0.7	9%	31%	70%	29	109	72%	3%			2.6	98	128	$13
1st Half	10	4	0	96	106	3.57	3.76	1.38	228	253	187	27.9	4.7	10.0	2.1	48	22	30	0.8	11%	31%	76%	15	108	60%	7%			5.2	78	102	$16
2nd Half	6	5	0	96	115	4.23	3.28	1.18	212	202	222	28.4	3.7	10.8	2.9	44	22	33	0.6	8%	31%	64%	14	110	86%	0%			-2.6	118	154	$9
13 Proj	**15**	**8**	**0**	**203**	**226**	**3.43**	**3.38**	**1.23**	**222**	**229**	**213**	**29.5**	**3.8**	**10.0**	**2.6**	**46**	**22**	**32**	**0.7**	**9%**	**30%**	**73%**	**28**						**14.6**	**102**	**132**	**$20**

Davis,Wade

Age: 27 Th: R Role RP	Health	A	LIMA Plan	A
Ht: 6' 5" Wt: 225 Type Pwr FB	PT/Exp	A	Rand Var	-3
	Consist	B	MM	4501

New calling as a reliever? Struggling SP with declining Dom adds a couple of MPH to FB and slider out of the pen and voila! The kicker is that his velocity, Dom and overall skill kept improving as season progressed. Obviously this performance needs confirmation. But 2H BPV suggests a closer-in-waiting.

Yr Tm	W	L	Sv	IP	K	ERA	xERA	WHIP	OBA	vL	vR	BF/G	Ctl	Dom	Cmd	G	L	F	hr/9	hr/f	H%	S%	GS	APC	DOM%	DIS%	Sv%	LI	RAR	BPV	BPX	R$
08 a/a	13	8	0	161	116	4.03	4.10	1.42	263			24.3	3.7	6.5	1.7				0.7		31%	73%							5.8	57	106	$7
09 TAM *	12	10	0	195	153	4.20	4.17	1.40	265	238	250	24.2	3.5	7.1	2.0	39	25	36	0.8	6%	31%	71%	6	100	33%	17%			3.0	63	118	$7
10 TAM	12	10	0	168	113	4.07	4.56	1.35	255	260	250	24.9	3.3	6.1	1.8	39	17	44	1.3	10%	28%	74%	29	96	31%	17%			0.2	36	59	$5
11 TAM	11	10	0	184	105	4.45	4.73	1.38	267	289	246	27.4	3.1	5.1	1.7	36	21	43	1.1	9%	29%	70%	29	102	38%	21%			-11.5	23	35	-$1
12 TAM	3	0	0	70	87	2.43	3.31	1.09	189	161	211	5.3	3.7	11.1	3.0	39	22	40	0.6	8%	28%	81%	0	23			0	0.85	13.7	117	153	$7
1st Half	1	0	0	37	37	2.92	4.14	1.24	214	167	250	6.0	3.9	9.0	2.3	35	24	41	1.0	10%	28%	81%	0	25			0	1.12	5.0	70	91	$3
2nd Half	2	0	0	33	50	1.89	2.46	0.93	158	154	161	4.5	3.5	13.5	3.8	44	17	38	0.3	4%	28%	80%	0	21			0	0.60	8.7	171	223	$12
13 Proj	**5**	**2**	**0**	**87**	**94**	**3.29**	**3.60**	**1.22**	**228**	**227**	**229**	**8.5**	**3.5**	**9.8**	**2.8**	**39**	**20**	**40**	**0.9**	**10%**	**30%**	**76%**	**0**						**7.8**	**99**	**129**	**$6**

de la Rosa,Jorge

Age: 32 Th: L Role SP	Health	F	LIMA Plan	C
Ht: 6' 1" Wt: 220 Type Pwr	PT/Exp	C	Rand Var	+5
	Consist	C	MM	3401

Slowed by forearm tightness, fluid build-up in return from June 2011 TJS. Mid-season target pushed back till September, and he didn't look sharp on his return. Historical Dom, GB rates point to upside; Ctl, age, durability questions suggest caution. A return to full health offers real profit potential.

Yr Tm	W	L	Sv	IP	K	ERA	xERA	WHIP	OBA	vL	vR	BF/G	Ctl	Dom	Cmd	G	L	F	hr/9	hr/f	H%	S%	GS	APC	DOM%	DIS%	Sv%	LI	RAR	BPV	BPX	R$
08 COL *	13	8	0	152	145	4.51	4.15	1.45	260	289	253	20.3	4.1	8.6	2.1	46	20	34	0.8	10%	33%	70%	23	81	43%	30%	0	0.69	-3.4	75	141	$5
09 COL	16	9	0	185	193	4.38	3.74	1.38	249	204	262	24.2	4.0	9.4	2.3	45	21	34	1.0	12%	32%	70%	32	92	50%	19%	0	0.75	-1.3	83	155	$11
10 COL	8	7	0	122	113	4.22	3.60	1.32	235	206	244	25.6	4.1	8.4	2.1	52	19	29	1.1	16%	28%	71%	20	101	60%	10%			-2.1	71	114	$4
11 COL	5	2	0	59	52	3.51	3.74	1.19	222	111	244	24.5	3.4	7.9	2.4	43	20	38	0.6	7%	28%	71%	10	96	70%	20%			3.2	73	110	$3
12 COL	0	2	0	11	6	9.28	5.80	1.78	340	125	381	17.7	1.7	5.1	3.0	34	14	52	4.2	22%	33%	57%	3	68	0%	100%			-6.9	58	75	-$8
1st Half																																
2nd Half	0	2	0	11	6	9.28	5.80	1.78	340	125	381	17.7	1.7	5.1	3.0	34	14	52	4.2	22%	33%	57%	3	68	0%	100%			-6.9	58	76	-$8
13 Proj	**7**	**7**	**0**	**116**	**111**	**4.10**	**3.87**	**1.32**	**240**	**197**	**251**	**23.3**	**3.9**	**8.6**	**2.2**	**46**	**20**	**34**	**0.9**	**10%**	**30%**	**71%**	**21**						**-1.2**	**75**	**97**	**$4**

De La Rosa,Rubby

Age: 24 Th: R Role SP	Health	B	LIMA Plan	C
Ht: 5' 11" Wt: 205 Type Pwr GB	PT/Exp	F	Rand Var	+5
	Consist	F	MM	3401

August 2011 TJS victim returned to LA for an inning. Mega-trade forced him back to minors for waiver protection as a player to be named later. Reported return of mid-90s velocity and GB-generating repertoire point to big future. 2011 MLEs and 3.71 ERA in 61 IP at LA say future may start now.

Yr Tm	W	L	Sv	IP	K	ERA	xERA	WHIP	OBA	vL	vR	BF/G	Ctl	Dom	Cmd	G	L	F	hr/9	hr/f	H%	S%	GS	APC	DOM%	DIS%	Sv%	LI	RAR	BPV	BPX	R$
08																																
09																																
10 aa	3	1	0	51	35	1.39	2.15	1.11	213			25.1	3.2	6.1	1.9				0.2		26%	88%							16.9	85	138	$5
11 LA *	6	7	0	101	105	3.30	3.28	1.32	231	235	255	19.8	4.3	9.4	2.2	48	22	30	0.6	13%	30%	76%	10	79	50%	20%	0	0.85	8.0	93	140	$5
12 BOS	0	0	0	1	0	27.00	29.98	3.00	0	0	0	4.0	27.0	0.0	0.0	0	0	100	0.0	0%	0%	0%	0	20			0	0.14	-1.9	-751	-980	-$5
1st Half																																
2nd Half	0	0	0	1	0	27.00	29.99	3.00	0	0	0	4.0	27.0	0.0	0.0	0	0	100	0.0	0%	0%	0%	0	20			0	0.14	-1.9	-751	-978	-$5
13 Proj	**4**	**4**	**0**	**73**	**65**	**3.79**	**3.93**	**1.31**	**238**	**229**	**248**	**22.0**	**3.8**	**8.1**	**2.1**	**48**	**22**	**30**	**0.7**	**8%**	**30%**	**72%**	**14**						**2.0**	**68**	**88**	**$2**

JOCK THOMPSON

Deduno,Samuel

Age: 29 Th: R Role RP	Health A	LIMA Plan F	
Ht: 6' 3" Wt: 190 Type Pwr xGB	PT/Exp D	Rand Var +3	
	Consist A	MM 1203	

6-5, 4.44 ERA in 79 IP at MIN. Keeps infielders busy with GB%, which he ran up to 60%+ in Aug/Sept at MIN. But poor Ctl also keeps them standing around for too long between contact. Dom is enough that only walks prevent him from being really interesting. But age, history say an improvement isn't likely.

Yr Tm	W	L	Sv	IP	K	ERA	xERA	WHIP	OBA	vL	vR	BF/G	Ctl	Dom	Cmd	G	L	F	hr/9	hr/f	H%	S%	GS	APC	DOM%	DIS%	Sv%	LI	RAR	BPV	BPX	R$
08																																
09 a/a	12	5	0	139	98	3.51	3.39	1.45	237			23.7	5.2	6.4	1.2				0.2		29%	75%							13.9	64	120	$7
10 COL *	3	1	0	33	24	3.29	3.78	1.35	218	200	333	13.9	5.0	6.5	1.3	38	25	38	1.2	33%	24%	81%	0	13			0	0.37	3.2	42	68	$0
11 SD *	4	6	0	108	72	3.32	3.79	1.53	261	333	375	11.2	4.8	6.0	1.2	70	20	10	0.1	0%	31%	77%	0	35			0	0.16	8.3	61	92	-$1
12 MIN *	7	7	0	121	91	3.96	4.18	1.52	235	256	221	21.9	5.9	6.8	1.2	58	21	20	0.9	21%	27%	76%	15	89	27%	47%			0.9	45	59	-$3
1st Half	1	1	0	35	30	3.65	3.83	1.55	229	0	0	19.1	6.4	7.8	1.2				0.6	0%	28%	77%	0	0					1.6	64	83	-$7
2nd Half	6	6	0	86	61	4.08	4.29	1.51	238	256	221	23.3	5.7	6.3	1.1	58	21	20	1.0	21%	27%	76%	15	89	27%	47%			-0.7	38	49	-$1
13 Proj	10	8	0	174	127	4.23	4.63	1.58	256	272	235	16.8	5.5	6.6	1.2	58	21	20	0.6	10%	30%	73%	31						-4.6	7	9	-$2

Delabar,Steve

Age: 29 Th: R Role RP	Health A	LIMA Plan A+	
Ht: 6' 5" Wt: 220 Type Pwr FB	PT/Exp D	Rand Var +3	
	Consist B	MM 4500	

4-3, 3.82 ERA in 66 IP at SEA/TOR. Rookie with electric stuff shows serious skills growth. Career once stalled by injuries and wildness. But health, Ctl gains and ungodly Dom spike change his outlook. Ks are legit, Ctl remains volatile, and needs to stabilize fluky HR metrics. But BPV says to keep him radar'd.

Yr Tm	W	L	Sv	IP	K	ERA	xERA	WHIP	OBA	vL	vR	BF/G	Ctl	Dom	Cmd	G	L	F	hr/9	hr/f	H%	S%	GS	APC	DOM%	DIS%	Sv%	LI	RAR	BPV	BPX	R$
08																																
09																																
10																																
11 SEA *	3	5	12	51	45	1.86	3.62	1.59	234	125	267	5.7	6.5	8.0	1.2	31	25	44	0.2	14%	30%	88%	0	18			80	1.06	13.0	77	116	$6
12 2 AL	4	3	0	66	92	3.82	2.97	1.09	193	171	211	4.5	3.5	12.5	3.5	43	16	42	1.6	20%	27%	73%	0	19			0	0.90	1.6	151	197	$4
1st Half	1	1	0	26	34	4.78	2.92	0.99	188	98	255	4.2	2.7	11.6	4.3	44	15	41	2.4	28%	21%	63%	0	17			0	0.72	-2.5	158	206	-$1
2nd Half	3	2	0	40	58	3.18	3.00	1.16	197	219	179	4.7	4.1	13.2	3.2	42	16	42	1.1	14%	30%	78%	0	20			0	1.04	4.1	146	190	$7
13 Proj	3	4	0	58	69	3.48	3.54	1.24	213	189	233	4.7	4.3	10.7	2.5	43	16	42	1.1	12%	28%	76%	0						3.8	98	127	$3

Delgado,Randall

Age: 23 Th: R Role SP	Health A	LIMA Plan D+	
Ht: 6' 3" Wt: 200 Type Pwr	PT/Exp D	Rand Var 0	
	Consist B	MM 2301	

4-9, 4.37 ERA in 93 IP at ATL. Good prospect with growing pains. Dom is there, ability to induce GBs took step forward, notwithstanding the 2H drop-off. Ctl and Cmd still need work, and H%/S% swings a factor. Has time, but volatility points to some more short-term bumpiness.

Yr Tm	W	L	Sv	IP	K	ERA	xERA	WHIP	OBA	vL	vR	BF/G	Ctl	Dom	Cmd	G	L	F	hr/9	hr/f	H%	S%	GS	APC	DOM%	DIS%	Sv%	LI	RAR	BPV	BPX	R$
08																																
09																																
10 aa	3	5	0	44	38	5.32	3.28	1.33	241			22.7	3.9	7.9	2.0				0.4		30%	58%							-6.7	83	135	-$2
11 ATL *	8	8	0	174	139	3.98	4.33	1.40	263	196	237	23.0	3.6	7.2	2.0	38	20	42	1.0	11%	31%	74%	7	89	29%	14%			-0.9	58	87	$2
12 ATL *	8	12	0	137	121	4.37	4.44	1.47	266	263	250	22.6	4.1	8.0	2.0	50	22	28	0.9	11%	32%	72%	17	90	35%	29%	0	0.80	-6.1	64	83	-$3
1st Half	4	8	0	80	64	4.52	4.28	1.44	254	257	252	23.2	4.4	7.2	1.6	52	22	26	0.8	11%	30%	69%	15	94	27%	33%			-4.9	41	53	-$3
2nd Half	4	4	0	57	57	4.17	4.90	1.51	283	296	238	22.6	3.6	9.0	2.5	39	22	39	1.1	7%	35%	75%	2	69	100%	0%	0	0.88	-1.1	73	95	-$4
13 Proj	4	5	0	73	63	4.25	4.09	1.39	256	250	261	22.5	3.8	7.8	2.1	47	21	32	0.9	11%	31%	71%	14						-2.1	63	81	-$1

Dempster,Ryan

Age: 36 Th: R Role SP	Health B	LIMA Plan B	
Ht: 6' 2" Wt: 215 Type Pwr	PT/Exp A	Rand Var 0	
	Consist A	MM 3405	

Terrific start supercharged by fortunate H% and S%. Slowed by mid-season lat injury and 3-week DL stint. 2H wasn't nearly as lucky, even though Cmd and xERA barely budged. Still a consistent, low-upside workhorse, though age, injury and recent ERA/WHIP swings are becoming red flags.

Yr Tm	W	L	Sv	IP	K	ERA	xERA	WHIP	OBA	vL	vR	BF/G	Ctl	Dom	Cmd	G	L	F	hr/9	hr/f	H%	S%	GS	APC	DOM%	DIS%	Sv%	LI	RAR	BPV	BPX	R$
08 CHC	17	6	0	207	187	2.96	3.66	1.21	227	243	213	25.9	3.3	8.1	2.5	48	20	32	0.6	8%	29%	77%	33	101	64%	3%			34.7	83	156	$25
09 CHC	11	9	0	200	172	3.65	3.79	1.31	260	281	241	27.2	2.9	7.7	2.6	47	18	34	1.0	11%	31%	75%	31	102	65%	6%			16.7	85	160	$14
10 CHC	15	12	0	215	208	3.85	3.69	1.32	244	234	252	27.0	3.6	8.7	2.4	47	16	37	1.0	11%	30%	74%	34	106	62%	15%			6.2	84	137	$12
11 CHC	10	14	0	202	191	4.80	3.82	1.45	271	303	245	25.9	3.6	8.5	2.3	44	21	35	1.0	11%	33%	69%	34	103	62%	18%			-21.5	76	115	-$4
12 2 TM	12	8	0	173	153	3.38	3.81	1.20	237	218	257	25.6	2.7	8.0	2.9	43	21	36	1.0	11%	29%	76%	28	98	68%	21%			13.5	91	119	$14
1st Half	3	3	0	81	66	2.11	3.78	1.02	204	197	210	27.1	2.4	7.3	3.0	41	24	35	0.7	8%	25%	83%	12	102	75%	17%			19.0	85	111	$20
2nd Half	9	5	0	92	87	4.50	3.85	1.35	265	232	311	24.5	2.9	8.5	2.9	45	19	36	1.3	13%	32%	70%	16	95	63%	25%			-5.5	97	126	$9
13 Proj	13	10	0	196	179	3.93	3.82	1.29	251	247	255	25.2	3.1	8.2	2.6	45	20	36	1.0	11%	30%	73%	32						2.2	87	112	$11

Detwiler,Ross

Age: 27 Th: L Role SP	Health C	LIMA Plan D+	
Ht: 6' 5" Wt: 190 Type	PT/Exp C	Rand Var -1	
	Consist B	MM 1103	

An example of the sum being greater than the parts. Turned good control, GB% spike and fortunate H% into career year and a small profit for his owners. Ctl and Dom history are stable, but don't show enough upside to get excited about. DOM/DIS is another indicator of his low ceiling. Unlikely to repeat.

Yr Tm	W	L	Sv	IP	K	ERA	xERA	WHIP	OBA	vL	vR	BF/G	Ctl	Dom	Cmd	G	L	F	hr/9	hr/f	H%	S%	GS	APC	DOM%	DIS%	Sv%	LI	RAR	BPV	BPX	R$
08																																
09 WAS *	5	11	0	152	100	4.51	5.06	1.66	305	288	289	22.0	3.8	5.9	1.6	43	25	32	0.5	4%	35%	72%	14	84	36%	29%	0	0.73	-3.6	49	91	-$6
10 WAS *	4	5	0	67	44	3.60	5.40	1.61	311	381	268	18.6	3.0	5.9	2.0	43	20	37	0.8	14%	35%	80%	5	62	0%	60%	0	0.53	4.0	44	72	-$2
11 WAS *	10	11	0	153	91	4.45	4.71	1.50	293	167	281	21.4	3.0	5.3	1.8	43	24	33	0.7	11%	33%	71%	10	65	50%	10%	0	0.90	-9.6	45	68	-$4
12 WAS	10	8	0	164	105	3.40	4.24	1.22	241	170	263	20.8	2.8	5.8	2.0	51	16	33	0.8	9%	27%	75%	27	77	33%	22%	0	0.83	12.6	56	73	$10
1st Half	4	3	0	74	50	3.30	4.25	1.18	232	113	274	18.1	2.9	6.1	2.1	49	13	37	0.9	9%	26%	75%	11	67	36%	18%	0	0.91	6.5	58	76	$10
2nd Half	6	5	0	91	55	3.47	4.24	1.26	249	224	256	23.7	2.8	5.5	2.0	52	19	29	0.8	9%	28%	75%	16	88	31%	25%			6.1	53	69	$11
13 Proj	10	11	0	174	110	4.01	4.45	1.40	274	206	293	20.5	3.0	5.7	1.9	47	20	32	0.7	8%	31%	72%	36						0.1	46	60	$3

DeVries,Cole

Age: 28 Th: R Role RP	Health A	LIMA Plan D+	
Ht: 6' 2" Wt: 180 Type Con FB	PT/Exp D	Rand Var 0	
	Consist C	MM 1103	

5-5, 4.11 ERA in 88 IP at MIN. Surprisingly good Ctl kept him competitive in MIN; even 6.0 Dom was better than minor league stats. But minus a GB pitch, his average stuff/velocity permits too much solid contact. A 2.1 hr/9 and .513 Slg allowed in the AL's most HR-repressive home venue is a tell. Avoid.

Yr Tm	W	L	Sv	IP	K	ERA	xERA	WHIP	OBA	vL	vR	BF/G	Ctl	Dom	Cmd	G	L	F	hr/9	hr/f	H%	S%	GS	APC	DOM%	DIS%	Sv%	LI	RAR	BPV	BPX	R$
08																																
09 aa	7	14	0	138	75	6.32	6.55	1.77	336			24.3	3.1	4.9	1.6				1.2		36%	65%							-33.9	15	28	-$16
10 a/a	1	8	1	92	68	6.63	6.51	1.84	332			8.9	4.0	6.7	1.7				1.0		38%	64%							-28.8	33	54	-$14
11 a/a	4	2	9	90	59	3.97	4.58	1.45	296			8.5	2.4	5.9	2.5				0.7		34%	73%							-0.4	64	96	$1
12 MIN *	8	10	0	158	96	4.92	4.96	1.35	292	236	266	22.7	1.7	5.5	3.3	31	24	45	1.3	12%	31%	67%	16	87	44%	19%	0	0.77	-17.6	58	76	-$5
1st Half	5	6	0	91	53	5.36	5.38	1.46	309	158	302	24.3	1.8	5.3	2.9	35	25	40	1.2	19%	33%	65%	4	91	25%	0%			-15.0	49	64	-$8
2nd Half	3	4	0	67	43	4.32	4.34	1.20	268	260	255	20.6	1.5	5.8	3.9	30	24	47	1.5	10%	29%	70%	12	85	50%	25%	0	0.76	-2.5	74	96	-$1
13 Proj	6	8	0	131	83	4.98	4.78	1.47	301	266	331	13.6	2.3	5.8	2.5	32	24	44	1.1	9%	33%	68%	15						-15.6	51	66	-$5

Diamond,Scott

Age: 26 Th: L Role SP	Health A	LIMA Plan B	
Ht: 6' 3" Wt: 220 Type Con GB	PT/Exp C	Rand Var 0	
	Consist D	MM 2103	

12-9, 3.54 ERA in 173 IP at MIN. Unremarkable journeyman turned improved Ctl, GB spike into a serviceable season. Mind-boggling DOM/DIS accompanied weak Dom. Reversal of S% fortune caught up to him in 2H. But this is called wringing the most out of what you have. Don't bet on a repeat.

Yr Tm	W	L	Sv	IP	K	ERA	xERA	WHIP	OBA	vL	vR	BF/G	Ctl	Dom	Cmd	G	L	F	hr/9	hr/f	H%	S%	GS	APC	DOM%	DIS%	Sv%	LI	RAR	BPV	BPX	R$
08																																
09 aa	5	10	0	131	96	4.67	5.96	1.86	333			26.6	4.1	6.6	1.6				0.4		39%	74%							-5.6	50	93	-$10
10 a/a	8	7	0	159	103	4.17	4.73	1.57	302			25.8	3.2	5.9	1.8				0.4		35%	72%							-1.8	57	92	-$3
11 MIN *	5	19	0	162	91	6.28	6.28	1.79	341	323	315	24.9	3.0	5.1	1.7	46	21	33	0.8	6%	38%	64%	7	91	14%	29%			-46.6	30	45	-$25
12 MIN *	16	10	0	208	110	3.52	4.08	1.28	280	291	268	25.8	1.7	4.8	2.9	53	21	26	0.8	11%	31%	75%	27	93	52%	11%			12.6	64	84	$11
1st Half	11	4	0	107	61	2.89	4.15	1.30	285	324	255	25.8	1.6	5.2	3.3	59	21	20	0.8	16%	32%	81%	11	95	64%	9%			14.8	75	98	$21
2nd Half	5	6	0	101	49	4.19	3.97	1.27	275	272	278	25.8	1.8	4.4	2.5	50	21	29	0.8	9%	30%	68%	16	92	44%	13%			-2.1	54	70	$0
13 Proj	9	12	0	174	99	4.03	4.36	1.42	289	299	286	25.1	2.5	5.1	2.1	51	21	28	0.7	8%	32%	72%	29						-0.3	54	70	$2

JOCK THOMPSON

Dickey,R.A.

Age: 38	Th: R Role SP	Health	A	LIMA Plan	D+
Ht: 6' 2"	Wt: 216 Type	PT/Exp	A	Rand Var	-1
		Consist	B	MM	3305

Just your garden variety 37-year-old knuckleball pitcher. Um, not quite. Stunning Dom spike driven by the Fastest Knuckler in the East, while he solidified elite Ctl. Post-season abdomen surgery a concern, but capable of a worthy encore as health allows.

Yr Tm	W	L	Sv	IP	K	ERA	xERA	WHIP	OBA	vL	vR	BF/G	Ctl	Dom	Cmd	G	L	F	hr/9	hr/f	H%	S%	GS	APC	DOM%	DIS%	Sv%	LI	RAR	BPV	BPX	R$
08 SEA *	7	13	0	162	81	4.84	5.23	1.57	299	259	309	18.2	3.3	4.5	1.4	46	17	36	0.9	11%	32%	70%	14	60	14%	36%	0	0.55	-10.3	23	42	-$5
09 MIN *	3	2	0	98	55	5.51	5.71	1.70	314	246	326	11.0	3.7	5.1	1.4	47	18	35	0.9	11%	35%	68%	1	32	0%	0%	0	0.70	-14.3	26	49	-$9
10 NYM *	15	11	0	235	131	2.79	3.44	1.21	260	226	269	27.0	1.9	5.0	2.6	55	17	28	0.6	8%	29%	79%	26	97	50%	4%	0	0.78	37.2	69	112	$21
11 NYM	8	13	0	209	134	3.28	3.89	1.23	256	263	251	26.5	2.3	5.8	2.5	51	16	33	0.8	8%	29%	76%	32	95	47%	9%	0	0.79	17.1	70	105	$12
12 NYM	20	6	0	234	230	2.73	3.21	1.05	226	237	218	27.3	2.1	8.9	4.3	46	20	34	0.9	11%	28%	79%	33	99	70%	3%	0	0.76	36.9	127	166	$36
1st Half	12	1	0	113	116	2.15	2.80	0.88	190	212	172	26.8	2.0	9.2	4.6	53	18	29	0.7	11%	25%	80%	16	99	69%	6%			26.0	143	186	$50
2nd Half	8	5	0	121	114	3.28	3.60	1.21	258	259	257	27.7	2.2	8.5	3.9	41	21	38	1.1	12%	31%	78%	17	99	71%	0%	0	0.75	10.9	113	147	$23
13 Proj	**14**	**10**	**0**	**214**	**168**	**3.21**	**3.72**	**1.19**	**250**	**248**	**251**	**24.0**	**2.3**	**7.1**	**3.1**	**48**	**18**	**33**	**0.9**	**10%**	**29%**	**76%**	**34**						**21.2**	**92**	**120**	**$20**

Diekman,Jake

Age: 26	Th: L Role RP	Health	A	LIMA Plan	D
Ht: 6' 4"	Wt: 200 Type Pwr GB	PT/Exp	F	Rand Var	0
		Consist	A	MM	2500

1-1, 3.95 ERA in 27 IP at PHI. Rookie with interesting-but-volatile dominance and GB skills. Ability to avoid HR ball neutralizes his chronic Ctl issues, allowing him to be marginally effective. Needs to harness wavering Cmd for regular high-leverage innings, but this doesn't appear to be happening soon.

Yr Tm	W	L	Sv	IP	K	ERA	xERA	WHIP	OBA	vL	vR	BF/G	Ctl	Dom	Cmd	G	L	F	hr/9	hr/f	H%	S%	GS	APC	DOM%	DIS%	Sv%	LI	RAR	BPV	BPX	R$
08																																
09																																
10																																
11 aa	0	1	3	65	70	3.47	3.47	1.49	225			5.3	6.0	9.6	1.6				0.4		31%	77%							3.8	88	132	-$1
12 PHI *	2	2	7	54	65	3.12	3.55	1.53	242	200	258	4.1	5.7	10.9	1.9	52	25	23	0.2	6%	35%	78%	0	17			70	1.18	5.9	107	140	$1
1st Half	2	0	5	30	41	2.18	3.01	1.37	248	200	233	4.2	3.9	12.2	3.1	47	27	27	0.0	0%	39%	82%	0	16			83	1.24	6.9	143	186	$6
2nd Half	0	2	2	24	24	4.33	4.19	1.75	235	200	281	4.0	7.9	9.2	1.2	56	23	21	0.4	13%	31%	74%	0	17			50	1.10	-0.9	77	100	-$6
13 Proj	**1**	**2**	**0**	**44**	**49**	**3.78**	**4.17**	**1.54**	**232**	**213**	**248**	**4.5**	**6.2**	**10.1**	**1.6**	**47**	**27**	**27**	**0.3**	**4%**	**33%**	**74%**	**0**						**1.3**	**39**	**51**	**-$3**

Dillard,Tim

Age: 29	Th: R Role RP	Health	A	LIMA Plan	D
Ht: 6' 4"	Wt: 219 Type xGB	PT/Exp	D	Rand Var	+2
		Consist	F	MM	1200

0-2, 4.38 ERA in 37 IP at MIL. His new side-armed delivery emphasizes sinker, but consistency remains elusive. Dom and GB% look pitchable, if he can ever harness Ctl. 2H gopheritis occurred in PCL, 0.7 HR/9 at MIL says it's mostly a fluke. Still, mid-80s velocity and .816 OPS say he's too hittable to roster.

Yr Tm	W	L	Sv	IP	K	ERA	xERA	WHIP	OBA	vL	vR	BF/G	Ctl	Dom	Cmd	G	L	F	hr/9	hr/f	H%	S%	GS	APC	DOM%	DIS%	Sv%	LI	RAR	BPV	BPX	R$
08 MIL *	6	1	2	78	51	2.69	4.67	1.53	274	269	313	6.8	4.2	6.0	1.4	44	26	30	0.9	13%	31%	86%	0	19			50	0.62	15.6	40	76	$4
09 MIL *	11	8	0	152	54	5.64	5.77	1.72	318	500	364	26.5	3.7	3.2	0.9	59	24	18	0.8	33%	33%	67%	0	43			0	0.72	-24.6	5	10	-$12
10 aaa	5	7	1	109	66	4.85	4.02	1.38	274			11.2	2.8	5.5	1.9				0.6		31%	64%							-10.4	57	92	-$2
11 MIL *	5	3	1	66	50	4.03	3.48	1.20	250	300	206	6.5	2.4	6.8	2.9	54	17	29	0.8	13%	29%	68%	0	19			25	0.56	-0.7	81	122	$2
12 MIL *	1	3	0	56	42	6.80	7.64	2.00	357	340	281	5.3	3.9	6.7	1.7	54	19	27	1.3	9%	41%	67%	0	18			0	0.38	-19.3	20	26	-$17
1st Half	0	2	0	37	28	4.42	4.22	1.58	301	346	277	4.9	3.4	6.9	2.0	53	19	27	0.7	9%	35%	73%	0	18			0	0.39	-1.8	62	81	-$13
2nd Half	1	1	0	20	14	11.23	12.40	2.78	443	0	500	6.1	4.8	6.4	1.3	100	0	0	2.4	0%	48%	61%	0	8			0	0.06	-17.5	-40	-52	-$25
13 Proj	**2**	**2**	**0**	**36**	**25**	**4.74**	**4.44**	**1.55**	**289**	**332**	**265**	**6.2**	**3.6**	**6.3**	**1.7**	**53**	**19**	**27**	**1.0**	**11%**	**33%**	**71%**	**0**						**-3.2**	**46**	**60**	**-$4**

Dolis,Rafael

Age: 25	Th: R Role RP	Health	A	LIMA Plan	F
Ht: 6' 4"	Wt: 215 Type Pwr GB	PT/Exp	D	Rand Var	+2
		Consist	F	MM	1200

2-4, 6.39 ERA and 4 saves in 55 IP at CHC. Ctl was never a strength, particularly when Dom is only a tick or two better. GB% wasn't enough to hold onto closer opportunity inherited by default. Things didn't improve in 2H pursuit of dominance, as he coughed up HRs in bunches. Needs to put things together.

Yr Tm	W	L	Sv	IP	K	ERA	xERA	WHIP	OBA	vL	vR	BF/G	Ctl	Dom	Cmd	G	L	F	hr/9	hr/f	H%	S%	GS	APC	DOM%	DIS%	Sv%	LI	RAR	BPV	BPX	R$
08																																
09																																
10 aa	5	4	0	55	38	4.57	5.57	1.76	315			21.1	4.2	6.3	1.5				0.5		37%	74%							-3.4	45	72	-$4
11 CHC *	8	5	17	74	42	3.51	3.34	1.39	244	0	0	6.0	4.3	5.1	1.2	100	0	0	0.3	0%	28%	73%	0	20			89	0.57	4.0	54	81	$8
12 CHC *	2	5	7	54	37	5.27	5.19	1.64	280	141	388	4.9	4.8	6.2	1.3	45	31	23	1.0	18%	32%	69%	0	19			70	1.06	-8.4	32	42	-$6
1st Half	2	5	7	39	22	5.02	4.12	1.49	251	93	380	4.8	4.9	5.1	1.0	49	30	20	0.7	12%	28%	66%	0	18			70	1.30	-4.8	35	46	-$4
2nd Half	0	0	0	16	15	5.74	7.59	1.97	340	238	400	5.4	4.6	8.9	1.9	37	34	29	1.7	27%	41%	75%	0	23			0	0.49	-3.3	29	38	-$11
13 Proj	**2**	**2**	**0**	**29**	**20**	**4.67**	**4.67**	**1.65**	**289**	**109**	**443**	**6.1**	**4.5**	**6.3**	**1.4**	**49**	**30**	**20**	**0.8**	**12%**	**33%**	**73%**	**0**						**-2.3**	**19**	**25**	**-$4**

Doolittle,Sean

Age: 26	Th: L Role RP	Health	A	LIMA Plan	A+
Ht: 6' 3"	Wt: 190 Type Pwr xFB	PT/Exp	F	Rand Var	0
		Consist	F	MM	4510

Former no-hit 1B with outstanding arm suddenly looks like a potential closer. Ability vs RHB mitigates the bias against him being a LHer. Monster Dom, elite Ctl are revelations given his 72 IP of pro experience. Okay, that's one data point. Let's see it again.

Yr Tm	W	L	Sv	IP	K	ERA	xERA	WHIP	OBA	vL	vR	BF/G	Ctl	Dom	Cmd	G	L	F	hr/9	hr/f	H%	S%	GS	APC	DOM%	DIS%	Sv%	LI	RAR	BPV	BPX	R$
08																																
09																																
10																																
11																																
12 OAK	2	1	1	47	60	3.04	3.13	1.08	227	286	195	4.3	2.1	11.4	5.5	35	15	50	0.6	5%	33%	73%	0	18			50	1.38	5.7	162	211	$3
1st Half	1	0	0	10	18	3.48	1.99	1.35	300	545	207	5.5	1.7	15.7	9.0	38	33	29	0.0	0%	52%	71%	0	25			0	1.26	0.7	251	327	-$5
2nd Half	1	1	1	37	42	2.92	3.46	1.00	206	231	190	4.1	2.2	10.2	4.7	34	11	55	0.7	6%	29%	74%	0	16			100	1.40	5.0	137	178	$5
13 Proj	**2**	**2**	**3**	**58**	**72**	**3.52**	**3.33**	**1.10**	**228**	**255**	**211**	**3.7**	**2.4**	**11.2**	**4.7**	**34**	**11**	**55**	**1.0**	**7%**	**32%**	**71%**	**0**						**3.5**	**150**	**194**	**$4**

Dotel,Octavio

Age: 39	Th: R Role RP	Health	B	LIMA Plan	A+
Ht: 6' 0"	Wt: 230 Type Pwr xFB	PT/Exp	C	Rand Var	0
		Consist	A	MM	4500

Another age-defying performance fueled by unexpected Cmd surge and squashing the long-ball. Added some craft by way of 1H GB spike, then compensated with exquisite Ctl during 2H Dom plunge. Has lost little off of power FB/slider combo. Still shreds RH batters, so he remains a reliable LIMA pick.

Yr Tm	W	L	Sv	IP	K	ERA	xERA	WHIP	OBA	vL	vR	BF/G	Ctl	Dom	Cmd	G	L	F	hr/9	hr/f	H%	S%	GS	APC	DOM%	DIS%	Sv%	LI	RAR	BPV	BPX	R$
08 CHW	4	4	1	67	92	3.76	3.26	1.21	208	240	194	4.0	3.9	12.4	3.2	38	16	46	1.6	17%	29%	77%	0	16			20	1.22	4.6	133	250	$5
09 CHW	3	3	0	62	75	3.32	4.13	1.44	239	268	226	4.3	5.2	10.8	2.1	30	19	51	1.0	9%	32%	81%	0	18			0	0.99	7.7	63	117	$2
10 3 NL	3	4	22	64	75	4.08	4.00	1.31	218	301	166	4.1	4.5	10.5	2.3	32	14	54	1.3	10%	29%	73%	0	17			79	1.08	0.0	78	127	$10
11 2 TM	5	4	3	54	62	3.50	3.32	0.98	185	236	154	3.4	2.8	10.3	3.6	30	20	50	1.0	9%	25%	68%	0	13			100	1.25	2.9	118	177	$6
12 DET	5	3	1	58	62	3.57	3.27	1.07	230	288	197	4.1	1.9	9.6	5.2	40	19	41	0.5	5%	32%	66%	0	16			25	0.90	3.2	141	184	$4
1st Half	1	2	1	24	37	4.07	2.50	1.11	217	233	210	4.0	2.6	13.7	5.3	48	13	39	0.7	10%	36%	64%	0	17			33	0.87	-0.2	203	264	$1
2nd Half	4	1	0	34	25	3.21	3.83	1.04	240	320	187	4.2	1.3	6.7	5.0	36	23	42	0.3	2%	29%	68%	0	16			0	0.93	3.4	98	128	$6
13 Proj	**5**	**3**	**0**	**58**	**65**	**3.62**	**3.40**	**1.11**	**222**	**281**	**187**	**3.7**	**2.8**	**10.1**	**3.7**	**36**	**18**	**46**	**0.8**	**8%**	**30%**	**69%**	**0**						**2.9**	**121**	**157**	**$4**

Doubront,Felix

Age: 25	Th: L Role RP	Health	A	LIMA Plan	D+
Ht: 6' 2"	Wt: 165 Type Pwr	PT/Exp	C	Rand Var	+3
		Consist	C	MM	2403

Maintained impressive Dom and xERA growth for entire year after stepping into rotation following BOS injuries. But real Ctl gains remain elusive, and gopheritis has killed him for two straight seasons. Abysmal .894 OPS with RISP. And .815 OPS at Fenway (.732 on the road) says there's work to be done.

Yr Tm	W	L	Sv	IP	K	ERA	xERA	WHIP	OBA	vL	vR	BF/G	Ctl	Dom	Cmd	G	L	F	hr/9	hr/f	H%	S%	GS	APC	DOM%	DIS%	Sv%	LI	RAR	BPV	BPX	R$
08																																
09 aa	8	6	0	121	85	4.35	4.94	1.61	292			20.6	4.0	6.3	1.6				0.7		34%	73%							-0.4	47	89	-$2
10 BOS *	10	5	2	105	83	3.58	4.09	1.48	276	189	317	15.6	3.7	7.1	1.9	47	10	42	0.3	9%	34%	75%	3	35	0%	67%	67	0.97	6.5	72	117	$4
11 BOS *	3	5	1	86	63	5.22	5.03	1.50	280	412	238	12.3	3.6	6.7	1.8	44	28	28	1.3	11%	32%	68%	0	16			100	0.33	-13.5	40	60	-$6
12 BOS	11	10	0	161	167	4.86	3.93	1.45	259	259	259	24.4	4.0	9.3	2.4	44	23	33	1.3	16%	32%	70%	29	99	45%	24%			-16.8	83	108	-$3
1st Half	8	4	0	85	87	4.54	3.78	1.39	266	260	269	24.8	3.1	9.2	3.0	41	24	34	1.4	15%	33%	72%	15	98	47%	13%			-5.5	102	133	$4
2nd Half	3	6	0	76	80	5.23	4.12	1.51	251	257	249	24.1	5.0	9.5	1.9	46	22	31	1.3	17%	31%	68%	14	100	43%	36%			-11.4	61	79	-$12
13 Proj	**10**	**10**	**0**	**174**	**156**	**4.50**	**4.19**	**1.49**	**271**	**272**	**271**	**17.9**	**4.0**	**8.0**	**2.0**	**44**	**23**	**33**	**1.1**	**13%**	**32%**	**72%**	**33**						**-10.4**	**61**	**79**	**$0**

JOCK THOMPSON

Downs,Scott

Age: 37	Th: L	Role RP	Health	C	LIMA Plan B+
			PT/Exp	C	Rand Var -1
Ht: 6' 2"	Wt: 215	Type xGB	Consist	A	MM 3200

Outstanding 1H gave way to nagging injuries. August shoulder strain shelved him for 3 weeks and cut into his velocity. Arrested Dom slide, but struggled with 2H Ctl as RHBs began to torch him. Still a GB machine who eats LHBs for breakfast, but age and velocity drop are concerning for 2013.

Yr	Tm	W	L	Sv	IP	K	ERA	xERA	WHIP	OBA	vL	vR	BF/G	Ctl	Dom	Cmd	G	L	F	hr/9	hr/f	H%	S%	GS	APC	DOM%	DIS%	Sv%	LI	RAR	BPV	BPX	R$
08	TOR	0	3	5	71	57	1.78	3.37	1.15	213	194	226	4.4	3.4	7.3	2.1	66	12	22	0.4	7%	26%	86%	0	17			56	1.32	22.1	82	154	$9
09	TOR	1	3	9	47	43	3.09	3.30	1.26	251	263	246	4.2	2.5	8.3	3.3	56	21	24	0.8	12%	32%	78%	0	15			69	1.35	7.1	116	216	$5
10	TOR	5	5	0	61	48	2.64	3.14	0.99	211	152	243	3.6	2.1	7.0	3.4	58	13	29	0.4	6%	26%	74%	0	14			0	1.37	10.9	107	174	$7
11	LAA	6	3	1	54	35	1.34	3.42	1.01	199	179	214	3.6	2.5	5.9	2.3	63	15	22	0.5	8%	24%	90%	0	13			25	1.77	17.2	79	118	$8
12	LAA	1	1	9	46	32	3.15	3.94	1.31	246	190	297	3.4	3.4	6.3	1.9	60	18	22	0.6	10%	29%	77%	0	12			75	1.26	4.9	61	80	$2
1st Half		1	0	6	26	18	0.35	3.19	1.04	219	200	235	3.6	2.1	6.2	3.0	67	16	16	0.0	0%	28%	96%	0	14			75	1.50	11.8	101	131	$9
2nd Half		0	1	3	20	14	6.86	5.01	1.68	279	179	375	3.3	5.0	6.4	1.3	52	20	28	1.4	17%	31%	60%	0	11			75	1.01	-6.9	10	13	-$7
13	Proj	**2**	**2**	**0**	**44**	**31**	**3.72**	**3.80**	**1.30**	**252**	**199**	**294**	**3.5**	**3.2**	**6.5**	**2.0**	**60**	**17**	**24**	**0.7**	**10%**	**29%**	**72%**	**0**						**1.6**	**69**	**89**	**-$1**

Drabek,Kyle

Age: 25	Th: R	Role SP	Health	D	LIMA Plan F
			PT/Exp	C	Rand Var 0
Ht: 6' 1"	Wt: 230	Type Pwr GB	Consist	F	MM 1100

Showed breakthrough signs in 5 April starts, but 2.40 ERA was mostly the product of 24% h% and 88% S%. Season fell apart as Ctl and hr/9 soared again, in spite of GB% reclamation. June TJS will keep him out until mid-2013. Has time and stuff—and serious Cmd issues. Longshot for 2013 profitability.

Yr	Tm	W	L	Sv	IP	K	ERA	xERA	WHIP	OBA	vL	vR	BF/G	Ctl	Dom	Cmd	G	L	F	hr/9	hr/f	H%	S%	GS	APC	DOM%	DIS%	Sv%	LI	RAR	BPV	BPX	R$
08																																	
09	aa	8	2	0	96	66	4.42	4.57	1.41	279			27.2	2.9	6.2	2.2				1.0		32%	71%							-1.2	52	97	$1
10	TOR *	14	12	0	179	127	3.32	3.33	1.26	235	292	308	24.3	3.5	6.4	1.8	62	12	26	0.7	15%	27%	75%	3	87	33%	0%			16.8	63	102	$13
11	TOR *	9	9	0	154	89	6.43	6.54	1.89	315	304	269	21.9	5.3	5.2	1.0	45	24	31	1.2	13%	34%	67%	14	82	14%	50%	0	0.68	-47.1	7	11	-$25
12	TOR	4	7	0	71	47	4.67	5.18	1.60	250	199	307	24.4	5.9	5.9	1.0	54	18	28	1.3	16%	27%	74%	13	100	23%	38%			-5.7	-21	-28	-$7
1st Half		4	7	0	71	47	4.67	5.19	1.60	250	199	307	24.4	5.9	5.9	1.0	54	18	28	1.3	16%	27%	74%	13	100	23%	38%			-5.7	-21	-27	-$7
2nd Half																																	
13	Proj	**3**	**3**	**0**	**44**	**29**	**4.51**	**4.76**	**1.51**	**263**	**241**	**290**	**24.1**	**4.5**	**6.0**	**1.3**	**50**	**20**	**29**	**1.0**	**12%**	**29%**	**72%**	**8**						**-2.6**	**14**	**18**	**-$3**

Duensing,Brian

Age: 30	Th: L	Role RP	Health	A	LIMA Plan D+
			PT/Exp	B	Rand Var +2
Ht: 6' 0"	Wt: 205	Type Con	Consist	A	MM 2100

Marginal Dom says he's obviously not a world-beater. But solid Ctl, and recent xERA/GB histories say he shouldn't be this bad. H% says he's too hittable too often, and RHBs have crushed him for two years. Role splits—6.92 ERA, 52 IP as SP; 3.47 ERA, 57 IP out of the pen—likely point to his future.

Yr	Tm	W	L	Sv	IP	K	ERA	xERA	WHIP	OBA	vL	vR	BF/G	Ctl	Dom	Cmd	G	L	F	hr/9	hr/f	H%	S%	GS	APC	DOM%	DIS%	Sv%	LI	RAR	BPV	BPX	R$
08	aaa	5	12	0	144	66	5.34	5.28	1.51	308			24.0	2.3	4.1	1.8				1.0		33%	65%							-18.1	26	49	-$7
09	MIN *	9	8	0	159	88	4.79	4.70	1.52	299	244	269	18.7	2.9	5.0	1.7	45	15	40	0.5	7%	34%	68%	9	55	33%	33%	0	0.76	-9.3	46	86	-$3
10	MIN	10	3	0	131	78	2.62	3.90	1.20	247	162	282	10.1	2.4	5.4	2.2	53	16	31	0.8	9%	28%	82%	13	36	54%	8%	0	0.82	23.6	63	101	$12
11	MIN	9	14	0	162	115	5.23	4.25	1.52	299	217	330	22.2	2.9	6.4	2.2	43	21	36	1.2	11%	34%	67%	28	83	50%	32%	0	0.71	-25.7	58	87	-$9
12	MIN	4	12	0	109	69	5.12	4.35	1.40	288	250	310	8.6	2.2	5.7	2.6	47	20	33	0.8	8%	33%	64%	11	31	27%	45%	0	1.00	-14.8	67	88	-$7
1st Half		1	4	0	42	24	4.10	4.60	1.22	253	183	296	5.3	2.4	5.2	2.2	38	19	43	0.6	5%	28%	67%	2	20	0%	100%	0	0.93	-0.4	45	59	-$4
2nd Half		3	8	0	67	45	5.75	4.19	1.51	307	288	318	13.1	2.1	6.0	2.8	53	20	27	0.9	11%	35%	62%	9	46	33%	33%	0	1.08	-14.4	81	105	-$9
13	Proj	**3**	**5**	**0**	**58**	**37**	**4.29**	**4.34**	**1.38**	**281**	**230**	**306**	**5.7**	**2.5**	**5.7**	**2.3**	**47**	**19**	**34**	**0.9**	**9%**	**31%**	**70%**	**0**						**-1.9**	**61**	**79**	**-$2**

Duffy,Danny

Age: 24	Th: L	Role SP	Health	F	LIMA Plan D+
			PT/Exp	D	Rand Var -2
Ht: 6' 3"	Wt: 200	Type Pwr FB	Consist	B	MM 2401

Stop us if you've heard this before: Youngster flashes good stuff in April, ends season with TJS in June, won't be ready until mid-year. Ctl eruption likely an injury symptom, as his minors history is better than this. Needs to develop a GB pitch but Dom and overall stuff keep us interested. Check back in June.

Yr	Tm	W	L	Sv	IP	K	ERA	xERA	WHIP	OBA	vL	vR	BF/G	Ctl	Dom	Cmd	G	L	F	hr/9	hr/f	H%	S%	GS	APC	DOM%	DIS%	Sv%	LI	RAR	BPV	BPX	R$
08																																	
09																																	
10	aa	5	2	0	40	34	3.17	3.59	1.24	268			23.0	1.9	7.7	4.1				0.6		33%	76%							4.5	116	187	$2
11	KC *	7	9	0	147	126	5.09	4.90	1.49	277	266	295	22.7	3.7	7.7	2.1	38	22	40	1.2	11%	33%	68%	20	98	20%	25%			-20.8	54	81	-$7
12	KC	2	2	0	28	28	3.90	4.80	1.59	252	192	273	20.2	5.9	9.1	1.6	35	21	44	0.7	6%	32%	76%	6	88	17%	50%			0.4	19	25	-$4
1st Half		2	2	0	28	28	3.90	4.81	1.59	252	192	273	20.2	5.9	9.1	1.6	35	21	44	0.7	6%	32%	76%	6	88	17%	50%			0.4	19	25	-$4
2nd Half																																	
13	Proj	**6**	**4**	**0**	**73**	**66**	**4.15**	**4.34**	**1.42**	**264**	**221**	**279**	**21.9**	**3.7**	**8.2**	**2.2**	**36**	**22**	**43**	**0.8**	**7%**	**33%**	**72%**	**14**						**-1.2**	**61**	**80**	**$0**

Dunn,Mike

Age: 28	Th: L	Role RP	Health	A	LIMA Plan D
			PT/Exp	D	Rand Var +2
Ht: 6' 0"	Wt: 220	Type Pwr FB	Consist	C	MM 1500

Improving control line is now a memory. Reversed hr/9, but FBs turned into LDs and exploding H%. Even LHBs jumped on him, as only an anomalous S% saved him from even bigger 2H disaster. Terrific Dom keeps him watchable. Should rebound, but he's unrosterable without more consistency. And Ctl.

Yr	Tm	W	L	Sv	IP	K	ERA	xERA	WHIP	OBA	vL	vR	BF/G	Ctl	Dom	Cmd	G	L	F	hr/9	hr/f	H%	S%	GS	APC	DOM%	DIS%	Sv%	LI	RAR	BPV	BPX	R$
08																																	
09	NYY *	4	3	2	77	87	4.82	4.89	1.74	259	0	273	8.4	6.8	10.1	1.5	40	30	30	0.8	33%	35%	73%	0	20			50	0.05	-4.7	71	133	-$3
10	ATL *	4	0	7	66	80	1.88	3.09	1.43	217	211	212	4.5	5.9	10.9	1.8	34	18	48	0.3	5%	32%	87%	0	15			78	1.04	18.0	107	173	$8
11	FLA	5	6	0	63	68	3.43	3.83	1.30	224	198	244	3.7	4.4	9.7	2.2	39	16	46	1.3	12%	28%	79%	0	16			0	1.20	4.0	72	109	$2
12	MIA *	1	4	1	62	66	5.15	5.15	1.77	294	293	272	3.9	5.4	9.6	1.8	34	28	38	0.4	6%	39%	70%	0	15			14	1.11	-8.6	78	102	-$10
1st Half		1	1	0	34	40	5.96	4.50	1.70	293	250	250	5.1	4.8	10.6	2.2	30	33	37	0.0	0%	42%	61%	0	18			0	0.86	-8.1	107	139	-$10
2nd Half		0	3	1	28	26	4.18	5.86	1.86	295	317	286	3.1	6.1	8.4	1.4	35	26	39	1.0	9%	36%	80%	0	14			20	1.22	-0.6	46	60	-$9
13	Proj	**2**	**4**	**0**	**58**	**63**	**4.05**	**4.53**	**1.61**	**262**	**262**	**263**	**4.0**	**5.5**	**9.7**	**1.8**	**35**	**23**	**41**	**0.7**	**7%**	**35%**	**76%**	**0**						**-0.2**	**41**	**53**	**-$3**

Durbin,Chad

Age: 35	Th: R	Role RP	Health	B	LIMA Plan B
			PT/Exp	C	Rand Var -4
Ht: 6' 2"	Wt: 220	Type Pwr	Consist	A	MM 2300

Older, craftier, luckier. Lofty S% and depressed H% helped minimize 1H Ctl and hr/9 issues. Figured out how to induce more 2H GBs without sacrificing any good fortune in the process. Mediocre Cmd, xERA are trading within narrow ranges. Age, limited upside say avoid betting on his next ERA move.

Yr	Tm	W	L	Sv	IP	K	ERA	xERA	WHIP	OBA	vL	vR	BF/G	Ctl	Dom	Cmd	G	L	F	hr/9	hr/f	H%	S%	GS	APC	DOM%	DIS%	Sv%	LI	RAR	BPV	BPX	R$
08	PHI	5	4	1	88	63	2.87	4.20	1.32	254	311	214	5.1	3.6	6.5	1.8	46	21	34	0.5	6%	29%	79%	0	20			14	1.33	15.7	43	81	$6
09	PHI	2	2	2	70	62	4.39	4.97	1.48	220	223	218	5.3	6.1	8.0	1.3	39	18	42	1.0	10%	26%	73%	0	22			67	0.87	-0.6	-3	-5	-$1
10	PHI	4	1	0	69	63	3.80	3.85	1.31	246	324	195	4.6	3.5	8.3	2.3	42	17	41	0.9	9%	30%	73%	0	19			0	0.80	2.4	73	118	$2
11	CLE	2	2	0	68	59	5.53	4.40	1.64	306	289	319	5.7	3.4	7.8	2.3	40	20	40	1.6	13%	36%	70%	0	22			0	0.69	-13.4	65	98	-$8
12	ATL	4	1	1	61	49	3.10	4.37	1.31	231	274	206	3.4	4.1	7.2	1.8	48	16	36	1.3	14%	26%	83%	0	13			33	1.01	6.9	45	58	$2
1st Half		3	1	0	31	26	4.06	4.68	1.42	241	256	233	3.4	4.6	7.5	1.6	44	15	42	1.7	16%	26%	79%	0	14			0	1.03	-0.2	32	42	$0
2nd Half		1	0	1	30	23	2.10	4.05	1.20	220	293	176	3.3	3.6	6.9	1.9	52	17	31	0.9	11%	25%	88%	0	12			33	0.99	7.1	57	74	$3
13	Proj	**3**	**1**	**0**	**58**	**48**	**4.07**	**4.32**	**1.39**	**254**	**287**	**232**	**4.0**	**3.9**	**7.5**	**1.9**	**45**	**17**	**38**	**1.2**	**12%**	**29%**	**75%**	**0**						**-0.4**	**53**	**69**	**-$1**

Elbert,Scott

Age: 27	Th: L	Role RP	Health	C	LIMA Plan C
			PT/Exp	D	Rand Var -5
Ht: 6' 2"	Wt: 225	Type Pwr FB	Consist	B	MM 2400

GB plunge, hr/f regression fueled hr/9 hike. But he continued to parlay inflated S% into surprisingly good ERA until July shoulder soreness shelved him for 3 weeks. Season ended in Aug. with minor elbow surgery. Solid Dom, but handedness, otherwise unspectacular skills and now health set a limited ceiling.

Yr	Tm	W	L	Sv	IP	K	ERA	xERA	WHIP	OBA	vL	vR	BF/G	Ctl	Dom	Cmd	G	L	F	hr/9	hr/f	H%	S%	GS	APC	DOM%	DIS%	Sv%	LI	RAR	BPV	BPX	R$
08	LA *	4	2	0	47	49	3.92	2.81	1.20	202	417	286	5.4	4.4	9.3	2.1	44	17	39	0.8	29%	26%	69%	0	13			0	0.74	2.4	91	171	$2
09	LA *	6	4	0	116	129	4.46	4.53	1.49	275	222	282	12.8	3.8	10.0	2.7	44	17	39	0.9	19%	36%	71%	0	17			0	0.69	-1.9	90	169	$1
10	LA *	1	1	0	44	37	4.29	4.90	1.74	270	1000	0	20.1	6.3	7.6	1.2	0	33	67	0.6	0%	33%	76%	0	24			0	0.15	-1.2	54	88	-$5
11	LA	0	1	2	33	34	2.43	3.59	1.23	220	191	255	3.0	3.8	9.2	2.4	43	19	38	0.3	3%	30%	80%	0	12			100	0.86	6.2	84	127	$1
12	LA	1	1	0	33	29	2.20	4.10	1.22	231	271	170	3.1	3.6	8.0	2.2	34	24	41	0.8	8%	28%	86%	0	13			0	1.03	7.3	59	77	$0
1st Half		0	1	0	25	26	2.88	3.97	1.32	250	302	179	3.2	3.6	9.4	2.6	31	25	45	1.1	10%	31%	83%	0	13			0	0.99	3.5	80	104	-$1
2nd Half		1	0	0	8	3	0.00	4.54	0.91	160	176	125	2.8	3.5	3.5	1.0	45	23	32	0.0	0%	18%	100%	0	12			0	1.15	3.8	-8	-10	$1
13	Proj	**1**	**1**	**0**	**44**	**43**	**3.90**	**4.02**	**1.31**	**239**	**260**	**212**	**4.8**	**3.8**	**9.0**	**2.4**	**36**	**22**	**42**	**0.9**	**9%**	**30%**	**73%**	**0**						**0.6**	**73**	**95**	**-$1**

JOCK THOMPSON

Eovaldi,Nathan

Age: 23	Th: R	Role SP	Health	A	LIMA Plan	B
Ht: 6' 2"	Wt: 215	Type	PT/Exp	D	Rand Var	0
			Consist	D	MM	2203

4-13, 4.30 ERA in 119 IP at LA and MIA. Rookie with good stuff and just 168 IP above A+ ball learning on the job. Struggled with Dom and Ctl but made strides in keeping the ball on the ground. Sept. finish—3.72/3.32 ERA/xERA, 3.4 Cmd, 51% GB% in 29 IP—points to seeds of something good here.

Yr Tm	W	L	Sv	IP	K	ERA	xERA	WHIP	OBA	vL	vR	BF/G	Ctl	Dom	Cmd	G	L	F	hr/9	hr/f	H%	S%	GS	APC	DOM%	DIS%	Sv%	LI	RAR	BPV	BPX	R$
08																																
09																																
10																																
11 LA *	7	7	0	138	109	2.84	2.53	1.21	214	275	197	18.5	3.9	7.1	1.8	41	26	34	0.3	6%	27%	76%	6	60	33%	17%	0	0.63	18.7	84	127	$11
12 2 NL *	6	15	0	154	104	4.11	4.39	1.46	276	318	236	21.3	3.5	6.1	1.8	46	23	31	0.7	8%	32%	73%	22	94	32%	36%			-1.9	52	68	-$4
1st Half	2	7	0	76	47	4.09	3.92	1.37	267	344	197	19.9	3.1	5.6	1.8	47	22	30	0.6	7%	30%	70%	7	96	43%	29%			-0.7	55	72	-$4
2nd Half	4	8	0	78	57	4.14	4.80	1.54	285	304	256	22.8	3.8	6.5	1.7	44	24	32	0.8	9%	33%	75%	15	93	27%	40%			-1.2	49	64	-$4
13 Proj	**7**	**10**	**0**	**145**	**108**	**3.92**	**4.23**	**1.33**	**254**	**295**	**208**	**24.1**	**3.4**	**6.7**	**2.0**	**44**	**24**	**32**	**0.7**	**8%**	**30%**	**71%**	**25**						**1.8**	**52**	**68**	**$5**

Eppley,Cody

Age: 27	Th: R	Role RP	Health	A	LIMA Plan	D+
Ht: 6' 5"	Wt: 205	Type Pwr xGB	PT/Exp	D	Rand Var	0
			Consist	C	MM	3200

GBer rookie supreme struggled in PCL and rocky MLB debut in 2011 before getting settled. The depressed 1H H% helped. Needs to polish his Ctl and ability to put away LHBs. But his overall minor league numbers—2.75 ERA, 0.4 hr/9, 2.7 Ctl in 229 IP—say a valuable bullpen career is likely ahead.

Yr Tm	W	L	Sv	IP	K	ERA	xERA	WHIP	OBA	vL	vR	BF/G	Ctl	Dom	Cmd	G	L	F	hr/9	hr/f	H%	S%	GS	APC	DOM%	DIS%	Sv%	LI	RAR	BPV	BPX	R$
08																																
09																																
10 a/a	3	2	10	51	46	3.63	4.38	1.51	270			6.0	4.2	8.1	1.9				0.7		34%	77%							2.8	70	113	$3
11 TEX *	5	3	10	64	48	4.91	5.18	1.70	278	385	261	5.5	5.5	6.7	1.2	52	24	24	0.9	43%	32%	72%	0	18			83	1.51	-7.7	38	57	-$2
12 NYY	1	2	0	46	32	3.33	3.86	1.37	266	352	227	3.3	3.3	6.3	1.9	60	21	19	0.6	11%	31%	77%	0	13			0	0.84	3.9	61	79	-$2
1st Half	0	0	0	19	10	3.38	4.22	1.34	254	292	233	3.2	3.9	4.8	1.3	63	16	21	0.5	8%	27%	75%	0	12			0	0.83	1.5	24	31	-$5
2nd Half	1	2	0	27	22	3.29	3.63	1.39	274	400	224	3.4	3.0	7.2	2.4	58	24	18	0.7	13%	33%	78%	0	13			0	0.85	2.4	87	113	$0
13 Proj	**2**	**2**	**0**	**44**	**32**	**3.72**	**3.93**	**1.44**	**265**	**351**	**226**	**4.1**	**3.8**	**6.7**	**1.7**	**60**	**21**	**19**	**0.5**	**10%**	**32%**	**74%**	**0**						**1.6**	**55**	**72**	**-$2**

Estrada,Marco

Age: 29	Th: R	Role SP	Health	B	LIMA Plan	A
Ht: 5' 11"	Wt: 200	Type Pwr FB	PT/Exp	C	Rand Var	0
			Consist	A	MM	3403

FB pitcher with fine base skills overcomes ordinary stuff to record nice bottom line. Season-long Cmd move was huge, but 2H hr/9, hr/f and GB% swings were decisive. Terrific follow-up to '11 rotation shot, but how sustainable are the 2H gains? He's legit, but too-high DIS% tempers expectations.

Yr Tm	W	L	Sv	IP	K	ERA	xERA	WHIP	OBA	vL	vR	BF/G	Ctl	Dom	Cmd	G	L	F	hr/9	hr/f	H%	S%	GS	APC	DOM%	DIS%	Sv%	LI	RAR	BPV	BPX	R$
08 WAS *	9	6	0	152	104	4.29	5.06	1.59	296	348	273	18.7	3.6	6.1	1.7	48	20	33	0.8	27%	34%	74%	0	22			0	0.79	0.7	45	85	-$1
09 WAS *	9	6	0	144	85	5.01	4.93	1.49	301	300	167	20.0	2.5	5.3	2.1	37	5	58	0.8	9%	33%	67%	1	38	0%	100%	0	0.50	-12.2	46	87	-$3
10 MIL *	1	2	0	51	40	5.00	3.73	1.31	255	429	172	15.2	3.1	7.0	2.2	29	14	57	0.7	15%	30%	62%	1	34	0%	100%	0	0.60	-5.8	71	115	-$3
11 MIL	4	8	0	93	88	4.08	3.58	1.21	243	204	276	8.9	2.8	8.5	3.0	40	18	43	1.1	10%	29%	69%	7	36	86%	0%	0	0.66	-1.6	96	144	$2
12 MIL	5	7	0	138	143	3.64	3.54	1.14	247	247	246	19.4	1.9	9.3	4.9	34	20	45	1.2	10%	31%	73%	23	77	48%	26%	0	0.71	6.3	129	168	$9
1st Half	0	3	0	42	46	4.50	3.57	1.12	238	284	204	14.2	1.9	9.9	5.1	27	21	51	2.1	17%	28%	70%	7	56	43%	29%	0	0.64	-2.5	131	171	-$5
2nd Half	5	4	0	96	97	3.27	3.51	1.15	251	233	267	23.1	1.9	9.1	4.9	37	20	43	0.7	7%	32%	74%	16	93	50%	25%	0	0.76	8.9	128	167	$16
13 Proj	**6**	**9**	**0**	**160**	**150**	**4.05**	**3.82**	**1.22**	**253**	**241**	**262**	**24.6**	**2.4**	**8.5**	**3.5**	**36**	**19**	**45**	**1.1**	**10%**	**31%**	**70%**	**26**						**-0.6**	**100**	**130**	**$7**

Familia,Jeurys

Age: 23	Th: R	Role RP	Health	A	LIMA Plan	D+
Ht: 6' 4"	Wt: 230	Type Pwr	PT/Exp	D	Rand Var	0
			Consist	B	MM	2310

0-0, 5.84 ERA in 12 IP at NYM. Control-challenged rookie with swing-and-miss FB/slider combo. Improved 2H Ctl, but 9 BB with Mets says he has work to do. Dom, GB% and age point to upside. Has spent his entire career as a starter, but now reportedly moving to the pen. Wait for dust to settle.

Yr Tm	W	L	Sv	IP	K	ERA	xERA	WHIP	OBA	vL	vR	BF/G	Ctl	Dom	Cmd	G	L	F	hr/9	hr/f	H%	S%	GS	APC	DOM%	DIS%	Sv%	LI	RAR	BPV	BPX	R$
08																																
09																																
10																																
11 aa	4	4	0	88	80	3.33	3.84	1.31	256			21.3	3.1	8.3	2.7				0.9		31%	77%							6.6	84	127	$3
12 NYM *	9	9	0	149	115	4.90	4.53	1.59	280	316	167	18.3	4.5	6.9	1.5	48	18	33	0.4	0%	34%	68%	1	26	0%	100%	0	0.13	-16.3	60	78	-$10
1st Half	5	4	0	72	53	4.86	4.96	1.74	285	0	0	20.4	5.5	6.7	1.2				0.5	0%	34%	71%	0	0					-7.4	50	65	-$11
2nd Half	4	5	0	78	62	4.94	4.09	1.46	275	316	167	16.6	3.5	7.2	2.0	48	18	33	0.4	0%	34%	65%	1	26	0%	100%	0	0.13	-8.8	72	94	-$9
13 Proj	**3**	**3**	**3**	**58**	**48**	**4.28**	**4.19**	**1.47**	**270**			**7.6**	**3.9**	**7.5**	**1.9**	**50**	**19**	**31**	**0.8**	**9%**	**32%**	**72%**	**0**						**-1.9**	**58**	**75**	**-$1**

Farnsworth,Kyle

Age: 37	Th: R	Role RP	Health	D	LIMA Plan	C+
Ht: 6' 4"	Wt: 230	Type Pwr	PT/Exp	C	Rand Var	-1
			Consist	B	MM	3410

Elbow strain kept him out of action until the 2H and ended his short reign as closer. Returned minus a few ticks off his FB and missing recent Ctl gains, but with Dom and GB mojo intact. Off-season rest should help him rebound somewhat. But age and health keep future at risk, likely preclude more Svs.

Yr Tm	W	L	Sv	IP	K	ERA	xERA	WHIP	OBA	vL	vR	BF/G	Ctl	Dom	Cmd	G	L	F	hr/9	hr/f	H%	S%	GS	APC	DOM%	DIS%	Sv%	LI	RAR	BPV	BPX	R$
08 2 AL	2	3	1	60	61	4.48	4.04	1.52	299	275	318	4.3	3.3	9.1	2.8	35	19	46	2.2	19%	34%	81%	0	17			25	1.01	-1.1	88	165	-$2
09 KC	1	5	0	37	42	4.58	3.59	1.53	287	277	294	4.1	3.4	10.1	3.0	46	21	34	0.7	8%	39%	70%	0	16			0	0.70	-1.2	115	215	-$3
10 2 TM	3	2	0	65	61	3.34	3.46	1.14	230	264	202	4.5	2.6	8.5	3.2	41	22	36	0.6	6%	30%	71%	0	18			0	0.81	5.9	100	162	$4
11 TAM	5	1	25	58	51	2.18	3.13	0.99	211	194	225	3.7	1.9	8.0	4.3	51	16	33	0.8	9%	26%	83%	0	14			81	1.09	12.5	122	183	$17
12 TAM	1	6	0	27	25	4.00	4.19	1.33	216	225	210	3.5	4.7	8.3	1.8	55	13	32	0.3	4%	29%	69%	0	13			0	1.01	0.0	57	74	-$3
1st Half	0	0	0	1	2	0.00	4.06	2.00	250	0	333	5.0	9.0	18.0	2.0	0	50	50	0.0	0%	55%	100%	0	17			0	0.65	0.5	59	77	-$9
2nd Half	1	6	0	26	23	4.15	4.19	1.31	214	231	203	3.5	4.5	8.0	1.8	57	12	32	0.3	4%	28%	67%	0	13			0	1.02	-0.4	56	73	-$3
13 Proj	**3**	**6**	**3**	**58**	**55**	**3.65**	**3.67**	**1.26**	**242**	**248**	**237**	**3.7**	**3.2**	**8.5**	**2.6**	**48**	**17**	**35**	**0.7**	**8%**	**30%**	**72%**	**0**						**2.6**	**92**	**120**	**$2**

Feldman,Scott

Age: 30	Th: R	Role RP	Health	D	LIMA Plan	D+
Ht: 6' 6"	Wt: 230	Type	PT/Exp	C	Rand Var	+4
			Consist	A	MM	2101

Pressed into rotation due to injuries, responded with excellent 2H Cmd and hr/9, good overall BPV. But H%/S% undid him, as he went 6 IP in fewer than 40% of games. Arlington isn't a factor; road woes were worse. .802 OPS with baserunners is chronic (.808 career mark). DOM/DIS history says avoid.

Yr Tm	W	L	Sv	IP	K	ERA	xERA	WHIP	OBA	vL	vR	BF/G	Ctl	Dom	Cmd	G	L	F	hr/9	hr/f	H%	S%	GS	APC	DOM%	DIS%	Sv%	LI	RAR	BPV	BPX	R$
08 TEX	6	8	0	151	74	5.29	4.92	1.43	280	291	269	23.3	3.3	4.4	1.3	44	19	37	1.3	12%	28%	66%	25	89	24%	20%	0	0.75	-18.1	11	21	-$4
09 TEX	17	8	0	190	113	4.08	4.34	1.28	250	226	277	23.3	3.1	5.4	1.7	47	21	33	0.9	9%	27%	70%	31	94	35%	13%	0	0.76	5.6	38	72	$13
10 TEX	7	11	0	141	75	5.48	4.85	1.60	313	302	323	22.1	2.9	4.8	1.7	43	20	37	1.1	10%	34%	67%	22	83	27%	36%	0	0.73	-24.4	30	48	-$10
11 TEX *	5	2	0	82	45	4.76	4.63	1.39	283	155	276	16.4	2.4	5.0	2.0	62	13	25	1.1	13%	31%	68%	2	46	50%	0%	0	0.39	-8.2	40	60	-$3
12 TEX	6	11	0	124	96	5.09	4.12	1.38	279	276	283	18.5	2.3	7.0	3.0	42	26	32	1.0	11%	33%	64%	21	73	38%	33%	0	0.71	-16.5	83	108	-$6
1st Half	2	6	0	47	35	6.13	4.77	1.53	288	268	314	15.4	2.9	6.7	2.3	37	26	37	1.5	13%	33%	63%	9	62	22%	56%	0	0.54	-12.2	58	76	-$14
2nd Half	4	5	0	77	61	4.46	3.72	1.29	273	282	264	21.4	2.0	7.2	3.6	46	26	28	0.7	9%	33%	66%	12	83	50%	17%	0	0.86	-4.2	99	129	-$1
13 Proj	**6**	**7**	**0**	**107**	**71**	**4.79**	**4.26**	**1.42**	**287**	**268**	**307**	**18.3**	**2.5**	**5.9**	**2.3**	**48**	**21**	**31**	**1.1**	**12%**	**32%**	**68%**	**21**						**-10.2**	**64**	**83**	**-$3**

Feliz,Neftali

Age: 25	Th: R	Role RP	Health	F	LIMA Plan	C+
Ht: 6' 3"	Wt: 215	Type Pwr xFB	PT/Exp	B	Rand Var	-5
			Consist	B	MM	1300

Move to rotation didn't work as planned. Ulnar collateral ligament sprain that shelved him late May turned into TJS in August. Prior to this, his Ctl woes continued while his hr/f and hr/9 spiked. Only a depressed H% kept his ERA attractive. Aug/Sept return is a best-case scenario, perhaps out of the pen.

Yr Tm	W	L	Sv	IP	K	ERA	xERA	WHIP	OBA	vL	vR	BF/G	Ctl	Dom	Cmd	G	L	F	hr/9	hr/f	H%	S%	GS	APC	DOM%	DIS%	Sv%	LI	RAR	BPV	BPX	R$
08 aa	4	3	0	45	42	3.28	2.72	1.28	222			18.6	4.3	8.4	2.0				0.2		29%	73%							5.8	96	179	$2
09 TEX *	5	6	2	108	104	3.72	2.89	1.23	235	155	85	9.7	3.2	8.7	2.7	38	5	57	0.4	5%	31%	69%	0	25			67	1.50	8.1	105	197	$8
10 TEX	4	3	40	69	71	2.73	3.24	0.88	176	127	220	3.8	2.3	9.2	3.9	37	15	48	0.6	6%	23%	71%	0	15			93	1.27	11.6	118	191	$25
11 TEX	2	3	32	62	54	2.74	4.14	1.16	194	189	200	3.9	4.3	7.8	1.8	37	16	46	0.6	5%	24%	78%	0	17			84	1.10	9.2	38	58	$16
12 TEX	3	1	0	43	37	3.16	4.58	1.20	187	173	203	21.9	4.9	7.8	1.6	37	15	48	1.1	9%	22%	78%	7	92	57%	14%	0	0.74	4.5	24	32	$1
1st Half	3	1	0	43	37	3.16	4.59	1.20	187	173	203	21.9	4.9	7.8	1.6	37	15	48	1.1	9%	22%	78%	7	92	57%	14%	0	0.74	4.5	25	33	$1
2nd Half																																
13 Proj	**1**	**1**	**0**	**22**	**18**	**3.91**	**4.57**	**1.26**	**219**	**199**	**241**	**6.8**	**4.2**	**7.5**	**1.8**	**37**	**14**	**49**	**1.1**	**9%**	**25%**	**73%**	**0**						**0.3**	**36**	**47**	**-$2**

JOCK THOMPSON

Fien,Casey

Health: A | LIMA Plan: B
Age: 29 Th: R Role: RP | PT/Exp: D | Rand Var: 0
Ht: 6' 2" Wt: 105 Type: xFB | Consist: F | MM: 1200

2-1, 2.06 ERA in 35 IP at MIN. Extreme FBer makes good on third MLB try. MIN performance was a product of unprecedented Cmd, hr9, and hr/f—and further fueled by S% and H% luck. Clearly he's adjusted something, but career numbers and volatility say a repeat isn't likely.

Yr Tm	W	L	Sv	IP	K	ERA	xERA	WHIP	OBA	vL	vR	BF/G	Ctl	Dom	Cmd	G	L	F	hr/9	hr/f	H%	S%	GS	APC	DOM%	DIS%	Sv%	LI	RAR	BPV	BPX	R$
08 a/a	5	3	13	61	46	3.48	4.24	1.29	266			4.8	2.4	6.9	2.8				1.2		30%	78%							6.3	67	126	$8
09 DET *	2	2	14	69	60	5.43	4.99	1.48	289	188	345	5.8	3.0	7.8	2.6	29	18	53	1.1	10%	34%	65%	0	23			74	0.47	-9.4	65	122	$2
10 DET *	3	3	8	65	33	3.70	4.98	1.32	282	400	333	5.8	1.9	4.6	2.4	36	18	45	1.6	40%	29%	80%	0	23			80	0.11	3.0	28	45	$3
11 aaa	2	2	3	24	19	5.60	7.87	1.72	328			5.3	3.1	6.9	2.2				2.9		34%	78%							-5.0	-9	-14	-$4
12 MIN *	4	6	9	81	63	4.36	3.81	1.27	252	173	211	4.9	2.8	7.0	2.5	25	25	51	1.0	6%	29%	67%	0	17			75	0.98	-3.5	69	90	$3
1st Half	2	5	9	43	26	6.54	5.53	1.59	300	0	0	6.1	3.5	5.4	1.6				1.2	0%	33%	59%	0	0					-13.4	24	31	-$4
2nd Half	2	1	0	38	37	1.89	1.81	0.89	189	173	211	3.8	2.1	8.8	4.1	25	25	51	0.7	6%	24%	84%	0	17			0	0.98	9.9	135	176	$10
13 Proj	**3**	**3**	**0**	**58**	**43**	**3.96**	**4.63**	**1.27**	**260**	**230**	**280**	**5.1**	**2.5**	**6.7**	**2.7**	**25**	**25**	**51**	**1.2**	**8%**	**29%**	**73%**	**0**						**0.4**	**55**	**72**	**$0**

Fiers,Mike

Health: A | LIMA Plan: B
Age: 28 Th: R Role: RP | PT/Exp: D | Rand Var: 0
Ht: 6' 3" Wt: 195 Type: Pwr | Consist: C | MM: 3403

9-10, 3.74 ERA in 128 IP at MIL. PRO: MIL stats exceeded AAA; Dom/Cmd history; terrific change-up and LHB-neutralizing deception. CON: Sub-par velocity; Aug-Sept beating—6.12 ERA, 1.6 hr/9, but call fatigue a factor (career-high IP). MLB work needs confirmation, but UP: 14 W, 3.60 ERA.

Yr Tm	W	L	Sv	IP	K	ERA	xERA	WHIP	OBA	vL	vR	BF/G	Ctl	Dom	Cmd	G	L	F	hr/9	hr/f	H%	S%	GS	APC	DOM%	DIS%	Sv%	LI	RAR	BPV	BPX	R$
08																																
09																																
10 aa	1	1	1	32	30	4.27	3.87	1.28	258			13.0	2.7	8.6	3.3				0.9		32%	68%							-0.7	95	154	-$1
11 MIL *	13	3	5	128	110	2.08	2.70	1.08	213	500	200	13.9	2.8	7.7	2.7	40	40	20	0.9	0%	25%	86%	0	21			83	0.07	29.5	91	137	$21
12 MIL *	10	13	0	183	174	4.36	4.13	1.33	266	265	242	23.0	2.8	8.6	3.1	33	28	39	1.0	9%	33%	69%	22	94	59%	18%	0	0.74	-7.7	90	117	$3
1st Half	4	5	0	94	80	4.33	4.00	1.31	264	286	177	22.9	2.7	7.7	2.8	32	25	43	0.9	4%	32%	69%	6	87	83%	0%	0	0.68	-3.7	80	104	$3
2nd Half	6	8	0	88	94	4.38	4.22	1.35	268	257	272	23.0	2.9	9.6	3.4	33	29	37	1.0	11%	34%	70%	16	96	50%	25%			-4.0	99	129	$4
13 Proj	**12**	**9**	**0**	**174**	**162**	**3.96**	**3.85**	**1.23**	**247**	**264**	**230**	**17.2**	**2.8**	**8.4**	**3.0**	**33**	**28**	**40**	**0.9**	**9%**	**30%**	**70%**	**29**						**1.1**	**87**	**113**	**$11**

Fister,Doug

Health: C | LIMA Plan: B+
Age: 29 Th: R Role: SP | PT/Exp: A | Rand Var: 0
Ht: 6' 9" Wt: 200 Type: | Consist: A | MM: 3205

Strained rib cage limited him to one April start and shelved him for 2+ weeks in June. But injuries and short-lived 1H hr/f spike were the only blips on a stellar season. Dom repeats big step forward, Ctl remains stable as postive GB trend continues. Strong 2H finish says that with health... UP: 15 wins.

Yr Tm	W	L	Sv	IP	K	ERA	xERA	WHIP	OBA	vL	vR	BF/G	Ctl	Dom	Cmd	G	L	F	hr/9	hr/f	H%	S%	GS	APC	DOM%	DIS%	Sv%	LI	RAR	BPV	BPX	R$
08 aa	6	14	0	134	91	6.19	5.58	1.65	317			19.4	3.1	6.1	2.0				0.8		36%	62%							-30.9	45	85	-$11
09 SEA *	10	8	0	173	108	4.30	5.20	1.43	310	237	298	21.0	1.4	5.6	3.9	41	20	39	1.1	14%	34%	73%	10	87	50%	20%	0	0.70	0.4	75	140	$3
10 SEA	6	14	0	171	93	4.11	4.11	1.28	277	274	279	25.7	1.7	4.9	2.9	47	18	35	0.7	6%	31%	68%	28	96	39%	18%			-0.6	68	109	$4
11 2 AL	11	13	0	216	146	2.83	3.53	1.06	237	239	235	27.3	1.5	6.1	3.9	48	20	32	0.5	5%	28%	74%	31	100	65%	3%	0	0.77	29.7	94	141	$23
12 DET	10	10	0	162	137	3.45	3.47	1.19	249	270	220	25.9	2.1	7.6	3.7	51	22	27	0.8	12%	31%	74%	26	97	50%	23%			11.2	111	144	$12
1st Half	1	5	0	51	42	3.91	3.57	1.34	278	288	264	24.1	2.0	7.5	3.8	50	25	24	1.2	18%	33%	75%	9	90	44%	22%			0.7	110	143	-$7
2nd Half	9	5	0	111	95	3.24	3.42	1.13	235	261	196	26.8	2.1	7.7	3.7	51	21	28	0.6	9%	29%	73%	17	100	53%	24%			10.6	111	145	$20
13 Proj	**13**	**10**	**0**	**189**	**139**	**3.60**	**3.70**	**1.22**	**263**	**271**	**254**	**24.5**	**1.9**	**6.6**	**3.5**	**49**	**21**	**30**	**0.8**	**9%**	**31%**	**72%**	**31**						**9.7**	**95**	**124**	**$14**

Floyd,Gavin

Health: B | LIMA Plan: B+
Age: 30 Th: R Role: SP | PT/Exp: A | Rand Var: +1
Ht: 6' 6" Wt: 235 Type: Pwr | Consist: A | MM: 2305

Elbow woes began in 2H. July-Aug DL stints that followed—career firsts—were responsible for his 2H Cmd woes. Only GB% spike, S% luck and hr/f regression helped him outpitch 2H xERA. Pre-injury BPIs say he still has skills; with luck and health... UP: 15 W, 3.75 ERA.

Yr Tm	W	L	Sv	IP	K	ERA	xERA	WHIP	OBA	vL	vR	BF/G	Ctl	Dom	Cmd	G	L	F	hr/9	hr/f	H%	S%	GS	APC	DOM%	DIS%	Sv%	LI	RAR	BPV	BPX	R$
08 CHW	17	8	0	206	145	3.84	4.41	1.26	241	259	226	26.6	3.1	6.3	2.1	41	19	40	1.3	12%	27%	75%	33	98	42%	12%			12.4	50	95	$16
09 CHW	11	11	0	193	163	4.06	3.75	1.23	244	232	256	26.6	2.8	7.6	2.8	44	22	33	1.0	11%	29%	69%	30	99	53%	13%			6.3	85	158	$14
10 CHW	10	13	0	187	151	4.08	3.75	1.37	274	259	292	25.7	2.8	7.3	2.6	50	18	32	0.7	8%	33%	71%	31	97	61%	10%			-0.1	83	135	$5
11 CHW	12	13	0	194	151	4.37	3.64	1.16	247	272	211	25.7	2.1	7.0	3.4	44	19	37	1.0	10%	29%	65%	30	97	57%	13%	0	0.83	-10.2	92	138	$8
12 CHW	12	11	0	168	144	4.29	4.06	1.36	259	291	226	25.0	3.4	7.7	2.3	47	18	35	1.2	13%	30%	72%	29	95	48%	24%			-5.6	73	95	$2
1st Half	6	7	0	90	85	4.80	3.72	1.26	257	295	213	25.6	2.4	8.5	3.5	44	17	39	1.5	15%	30%	66%	15	99	60%	20%			-8.7	110	143	$4
2nd Half	6	4	0	78	59	3.69	4.49	1.49	262	285	240	24.3	4.5	6.8	1.5	51	19	30	0.8	10%	30%	77%	14	91	36%	29%			3.1	30	39	$0
13 Proj	**13**	**12**	**0**	**189**	**152**	**3.93**	**4.02**	**1.32**	**257**	**276**	**236**	**24.7**	**3.1**	**7.3**	**2.4**	**47**	**19**	**35**	**1.0**	**11%**	**30%**	**73%**	**32**						**2.1**	**73**	**95**	**$9**

Francis,Jeff

Health: F | LIMA Plan: C
Age: 32 Th: L Role: SP | PT/Exp: B | Rand Var: +2
Ht: 6' 5" Wt: 220 Type: Con | Consist: B | MM: 2103

6-7, 5.58 ERA in 113 IP at COL. Still generates GBs at a nice clip, still with outstanding Ctl but it doesn't matter. 2009 shoulder surgery robbed him of already mediocre velocity and it hasn't returned. Even with Dom rebound, .851 OPS with runners on (.809 career) says he's heading in the wrong direction.

Yr Tm	W	L	Sv	IP	K	ERA	xERA	WHIP	OBA	vL	vR	BF/G	Ctl	Dom	Cmd	G	L	F	hr/9	hr/f	H%	S%	GS	APC	DOM%	DIS%	Sv%	LI	RAR	BPV	BPX	R$
08 COL	4	10	0	144	94	5.01	4.62	1.48	286	248	295	26.5	3.1	5.9	1.9	44	20	36	1.3	12%	31%	69%	24	99	46%	21%			-12.2	45	85	-$4
09																																
10 COL	4	6	0	104	67	5.00	3.94	1.36	293	309	290	22.1	2.0	5.8	2.9	47	21	32	0.9	10%	32%	64%	19	83	37%	26%	0	0.72	-11.9	75	122	-$3
11 KC	6	16	0	183	91	4.82	4.41	1.44	301	277	309	25.9	1.9	4.5	2.3	47	18	35	0.9	8%	33%	68%	31	95	42%	23%			-19.8	54	81	-$8
12 COL *	9	13	0	190	125	5.34	5.71	1.56	322	270	329	23.2	2.0	5.9	2.9	50	19	31	1.1	13%	36%	67%	24	77	25%	42%			-31.0	55	72	-$16
1st Half	4	7	0	102	61	5.11	5.74	1.64	330	211	346	26.7	2.3	5.4	2.4	49	15	36	0.8	3%	37%	69%	5	78	20%	40%			-13.7	47	61	-$18
2nd Half	5	6	0	88	64	5.60	5.61	1.47	312	284	324	20.0	1.7	6.5	3.8	51	20	29	1.4	16%	35%	65%	19	77	26%	42%			-17.3	68	89	-$14
13 Proj	**5**	**9**	**0**	**131**	**81**	**5.16**	**4.34**	**1.48**	**308**	**269**	**318**	**23.2**	**2.1**	**5.6**	**2.7**	**48**	**19**	**33**	**1.1**	**11%**	**34%**	**67%**	**24**						**-18.4**	**71**	**93**	**-$6**

Francisco,Frank

Health: D | LIMA Plan: A
Age: 33 Th: R Role: RP | PT/Exp: C | Rand Var: +4
Ht: 6' 2" Wt: 250 Type: Pwr FB | Consist: B | MM: 3521

When consistency isn't a good thing. Four consecutive seasons with DL time, three seasons of coughing up his closer role at least once. Dom is still solid, Ctl spike and increasing hittablity are injury (knee, oblique elbow) related, but ominous. He's rapidly working himself out of anyone's closer plans.

Yr Tm	W	L	Sv	IP	K	ERA	xERA	WHIP	OBA	vL	vR	BF/G	Ctl	Dom	Cmd	G	L	F	hr/9	hr/f	H%	S%	GS	APC	DOM%	DIS%	Sv%	LI	RAR	BPV	BPX	R$
08 TEX	3	5	5	63	83	3.13	3.41	1.15	200	193	207	4.6	3.7	11.8	3.2	33	19	48	1.0	9%	29%	77%	0	19			45	1.37	9.4	124	232	$7
09 TEX	2	3	25	49	57	3.83	3.52	1.11	214	238	186	4.0	2.7	10.4	3.8	29	21	50	1.1	9%	29%	69%	0	16			86	1.07	3.0	120	225	$13
10 TEX	6	4	2	53	60	3.76	3.33	1.27	247	205	275	3.9	3.1	10.3	3.3	39	20	40	0.9	9%	33%	73%	0	16			33	1.24	2.1	119	192	$3
11 TOR	1	4	17	51	53	3.55	3.61	1.32	246	292	177	4.0	3.2	9.4	2.9	39	23	38	1.2	13%	32%	78%	0	16			81	1.04	2.4	100	151	$6
12 NYM	1	3	23	42	47	5.53	4.43	1.61	269	273	264	4.1	4.5	10.0	2.2	33	28	39	1.1	10%	37%	67%	0	17			88	0.98	-7.9	70	92	$2
1st Half	1	3	18	29	31	4.97	4.54	1.59	265	270	259	4.4	4.3	9.6	2.2	34	26	40	0.9	8%	36%	70%	0	18			86	1.16	-3.4	68	89	$6
2nd Half	0	0	5	13	16	6.75	4.19	1.65	278	280	276	3.6	4.7	10.8	2.3	29	34	37	1.4	14%	38%	60%	0	15			100	0.65	-4.5	74	96	-$6
13 Proj	**4**	**6**	**18**	**73**	**81**	**4.03**	**3.84**	**1.38**	**253**	**261**	**244**	**4.0**	**3.9**	**10.1**	**2.6**	**36**	**23**	**42**	**1.0**	**10%**	**33%**	**74%**	**0**						**-0.1**	**91**	**118**	**$8**

Frasor,Jason

Health: B | LIMA Plan: C
Age: 35 Th: R Role: RP | PT/Exp: D | Rand Var: +3
Ht: 5' 9" Wt: 180 Type: Pwr | Consist: A | MM: 3500

When consistency isn't enough. Continued his solid Dom run, but also his mediocre Ctl. Never induced enough GBs to combine with his Ks; now HR metrics suggest hitters are tagging him more often. His last shot a closer role was in 2009. His age and middling skills say he won't get another one.

Yr Tm	W	L	Sv	IP	K	ERA	xERA	WHIP	OBA	vL	vR	BF/G	Ctl	Dom	Cmd	G	L	F	hr/9	hr/f	H%	S%	GS	APC	DOM%	DIS%	Sv%	LI	RAR	BPV	BPX	R$
08 TOR	1	2	0	47	42	4.18	4.91	1.44	208	266	174	4.2	6.1	8.0	1.3	38	24	38	0.8	8%	26%	72%	0	18			0	0.75	0.8	-5	-9	-$2
09 TOR	7	3	11	58	56	2.50	3.47	1.02	209	274	140	3.7	2.5	8.7	3.5	38	18	43	0.6	6%	27%	78%	0	16			79	1.26	13.0	106	198	$13
10 TOR	3	4	4	64	65	3.68	3.69	1.38	247	248	247	4.0	3.8	9.2	2.4	46	19	35	0.6	6%	33%	74%	0	16			50	1.00	3.2	86	140	$2
11 2 AL	3	3	0	60	57	3.60	4.03	1.40	257	279	238	4.1	3.9	8.6	2.2	37	23	40	1.1	10%	31%	78%	0	18			0	1.19	2.5	64	96	$0
12 TOR	1	1	0	44	53	4.12	3.79	1.47	256	273	245	3.8	4.5	10.9	2.4	38	23	38	1.2	14%	34%	76%	0	16			0	1.06	-0.6	90	118	-$4
1st Half	0	1	0	30	38	3.94	3.69	1.45	243	244	243	3.7	4.9	11.5	2.4	39	23	38	1.2	14%	33%	77%	0	16			0	1.14	0.3	94	122	-$4
2nd Half	1	0	0	14	15	4.50	4.02	1.50	283	320	250	4.2	3.9	9.6	2.5	37	24	39	1.3	13%	35%	74%	0	17			0	0.88	-0.8	84	109	-$4
13 Proj	**2**	**3**	**0**	**58**	**62**	**3.93**	**3.89**	**1.36**	**241**	**262**	**225**	**3.8**	**4.2**	**9.6**	**2.3**	**40**	**21**	**38**	**0.9**	**10%**	**31%**	**73%**	**0**						**0.7**	**78**	**101**	**$0**

JOCK THOMPSON

Friedrich,Christian

Age: 25 Th: L Role SP	Health C	LIMA Plan C	
Ht: 6' 4" Wt: 215 Type	PT/Exp D	Rand Var +5	
	Consist B	MM 2201	

5-8, 6.17 ERA in 84 IP at COL. On surface, a miserable MLB debut ended in August due to stress fracture in his back. But that 1H Dom, Cmd are reasons to take another look. He was victimized by an unfriendly hr/f and S% in addition to ugly 8.92 ERA at Coors. If healthy, a $1 bid could return $5 profit.

Yr	Tm	W	L	Sv	IP	K	ERA	xERA	WHIP	OBA	vL	vR	BF/G	Ctl	Dom	Cmd	G	L	F	hr/9	hr/f	H%	S%	GS	APC	DOM%	DIS%	Sv%	LI	RAR	BPV	BPX	R$
08																																	
09																																	
10	aa	3	6	0	87	62	6.65	6.66	1.79	328			22.4	3.7	6.4	1.7				1.4		37%	64%							-27.6	23	36	-$13
11	aa	6	10	0	133	80	6.08	6.67	1.69	327			24.1	2.9	5.4	1.8				1.7		35%	68%							-35.1	10	15	-$17
12	COL *	7	9	0	115	95	5.42	4.82	1.41	283	288	307	23.1	2.7	7.4	2.8	42	23	35	1.2	15%	33%	63%	16	87	38%	31%			-19.9	66	86	-$7
1st Half		6	6	0	90	78	4.79	4.73	1.39	288	340	306	23.8	2.3	7.7	3.4	37	27	36	1.1	15%	34%	68%	11	91	45%	18%			-8.6	82	107	-$4
2nd Half		1	3	0	24	17	7.77	5.01	1.48	267	174	309	20.9	4.1	6.3	1.5	55	13	32	1.5	17%	29%	47%	5	78	20%	60%			-11.3	27	35	-$19
13	Proj	4	8	0	87	66	4.95	4.19	1.47	292	236	309	22.2	2.8	6.8	2.5	48	19	33	1.1	12%	33%	68%	17						-10.1	74	96	-$4

Frieri,Ernesto

Age: 27 Th: R Role RP	Health A	LIMA Plan B	
Ht: 6' 2" Wt: 200 Type Pwr xFB	PT/Exp C	Rand Var -5	
	Consist D	MM 4530	

Got first extended MLB run as closer and made most of it. 94 mph fastball was +2 mph vs. 2011, a pitch he threw 86% of time to generate even more Ks...including crazy 17.8 Dom vs. LH. As a FB pitcher with shaky control, he needs a friendly home park to avoid riding on closer carousel. With it... UP: 45 SV

Yr	Tm	W	L	Sv	IP	K	ERA	xERA	WHIP	OBA	vL	vR	BF/G	Ctl	Dom	Cmd	G	L	F	hr/9	hr/f	H%	S%	GS	APC	DOM%	DIS%	Sv%	LI	RAR	BPV	BPX	R$
08	a/a	2	0	0	17	15	3.26	1.88	0.78	166			20.4	2.0	8.0	4.1				1.3		18%	66%							2.2	115	215	$0
09	SD *	10	9	0	142	106	3.68	3.80	1.38	252	0	0	20.6	3.9	6.7	1.7	0	25	75	0.7	0%	30%	74%	0	13			0	0.03	11.2	61	113	$8
10	SD *	4	2	17	69	83	1.58	1.33	0.99	145	176	156	3.9	4.6	10.7	2.4	25	13	62	0.5	5%	21%	87%	0	18			89	0.62	21.4	126	203	$18
11	SD	1	2	0	63	76	2.71	3.95	1.35	221	258	196	4.7	4.9	10.9	2.2	24	21	55	0.4	4%	32%	80%	0	19			0	0.60	9.5	66	100	$2
12	2 TM	5	2	23	66	98	2.32	3.10	0.98	152	95	200	4.0	4.1	13.4	3.3	26	21	53	1.2	13%	23%	86%	0	18			88	1.03	13.8	134	175	$19
1st Half		1	0	10	35	58	0.77	2.77	0.97	129	115	141	4.1	4.9	14.9	3.1	22	29	48	0.5	7%	24%	97%	0	19			100	0.97	14.0	137	178	$22
2nd Half		4	2	13	31	40	4.06	3.50	1.00	175	75	262	3.9	3.2	11.6	3.6	29	15	56	2.0	17%	22%	71%	0	17			81	1.09	-0.2	130	169	$17
13	Proj	4	2	33	58	74	2.96	3.59	1.12	187	163	204	4.3	4.2	11.5	2.7	25	20	55	1.0	9%	26%	78%	0						7.5	96	125	$18

Fuentes,Brian

Age: 37 Th: L Role RP	Health D	LIMA Plan D+	
Ht: 6' 4" Wt: 230 Type Pwr xFB	PT/Exp C	Rand Var +5	
	Consist A	MM 1300	

Personal issues mercifully ended season in August. Inflated H%, low S% drove up ERA, but horrible skill base says he was at best a 5.00 ERA pitcher anyway. Steadily eroding Cmd gives little hope for rebound. At age 37, his MLB days are numbered, and days of being a part-time closer are gone.

Yr	Tm	W	L	Sv	IP	K	ERA	xERA	WHIP	OBA	vL	vR	BF/G	Ctl	Dom	Cmd	G	L	F	hr/9	hr/f	H%	S%	GS	APC	DOM%	DIS%	Sv%	LI	RAR	BPV	BPX	R$
08	COL	1	5	30	63	82	2.73	3.15	1.10	205	184	211	3.8	3.2	11.8	3.7	33	22	46	0.4	5%	32%	76%	0	17			88	1.27	12.3	138	258	$18
09	LAA	1	5	48	55	46	3.93	4.60	1.40	254	239	261	3.7	3.9	7.5	1.9	36	17	47	1.0	8%	30%	75%	0	15			87	1.38	2.7	43	81	$19
10	2 AL	4	1	24	48	47	2.81	4.11	1.06	181	128	202	4.1	3.8	8.8	2.4	23	19	59	0.9	7%	23%	78%	0	17			86	1.27	7.5	58	94	$14
11	OAK	2	8	12	58	42	3.70	4.33	1.23	237	265	221	3.7	3.1	6.5	2.1	37	19	44	0.9	8%	27%	73%	0	15			80	1.18	1.7	48	73	$5
12	2 TM	2	2	5	30	24	7.20	5.10	1.70	293	250	313	4.4	4.5	7.2	1.6	38	25	38	1.8	17%	33%	60%	0	16			63	0.94	-11.8	24	31	-$7
1st Half		2	2	5	25	18	6.84	4.94	1.60	291	265	304	4.5	3.6	6.5	1.8	39	23	38	1.8	16%	32%	60%	0	16			63	0.97	-8.7	36	47	-$6
2nd Half		0	0	0	5	6	9.00	6.04	2.20	300	167	357	4.3	9.0	10.8	1.2	29	36	36	1.8	20%	38%	60%	0	16			0	0.82	-3.1	-42	-55	-$10
13	Proj	2	3	0	44	37	4.98	4.52	1.43	268	253	275	3.9	3.5	7.7	2.2	33	20	46	1.1	9%	32%	67%	0						-5.2	55	72	-$3

Fujikawa,Kyuji

Age: 32 Th: R Role RP	Health A	LIMA Plan B+	
Ht: 0' 0" Wt: 0 Type Pwr	PT/Exp B	Rand Var -4	
	Consist F	MM 4501	

Top Japanese closer owns consistent 10.0+ Dom and solid control, but thinking he'll step in as a MLB closer w/o adjustment period would be a mistake. And at age 32, he's not a growth stock. Worth a flyer if he lands with MLB club, but don't base your bid on a sub-2.00 ERA.

Yr	Tm	W	L	Sv	IP	K	ERA	xERA	WHIP	OBA	vL	vR	BF/G	Ctl	Dom	Cmd	G	L	F	hr/9	hr/f	H%	S%	GS	APC	DOM%	DIS%	Sv%	LI	RAR	BPV	BPX	R$
08	for	8	1	38	67	85	0.83	0.95	0.78	161			3.8	2.2	11.4	5.3				0.4		24%	94%							28.9	189	355	$32
09	for	5	3	25	57	82	1.56	2.01	0.93	176			4.4	2.9	12.8	4.4				1.0		26%	93%							19.5	158	295	$21
10	for	3	4	28	62	77	2.52	3.91	1.21	223			4.3	3.6	11.1	3.1				1.7		28%	91%							12.0	92	148	$17
11	for	3	3	41	51	76	1.53	1.17	0.84	157			3.3	2.8	13.4	4.7				0.6		26%	86%							15.1	185	278	$25
12	for	2	2	24	47	55	1.66	2.43	1.17	215			3.9	3.6	10.5	3.0				0.3		31%	87%							13.7	127	166	$14
1st Half																																	
2nd Half																																	
13	Proj	5	4	0	71	83	2.91	3.22	1.17	210			4.2	3.8	10.6	2.8				1.2		27%	82%	0						9.7	98	128	$7

Furbush,Charlie

Age: 27 Th: L Role RP	Health B	LIMA Plan A	
Ht: 6' 5" Wt: 215 Type Pwr	PT/Exp D	Rand Var -3	
	Consist D	MM 4400	

Marginal SP prospect became dynamite RP overnight. Sure, a low H% helped. Real credit goes to a newfound slider, a pitch he threw 35% of time. Mid-season triceps injury derailed him in 2H, but Dom, Cmd trends and lack of LH/RH splits warrant optimism. If arm is healthy, LIMA gem regardless of role.

Yr	Tm	W	L	Sv	IP	K	ERA	xERA	WHIP	OBA	vL	vR	BF/G	Ctl	Dom	Cmd	G	L	F	hr/9	hr/f	H%	S%	GS	APC	DOM%	DIS%	Sv%	LI	RAR	BPV	BPX	R$
08																																	
09																																	
10	a/a	4	4	0	82	60	6.11	6.21	1.59	312			25.9	2.8	6.5	2.3				1.7		34%	65%							-20.6	29	47	-$8
11	2 AL *	9	13	0	139	115	4.96	4.67	1.34	263	293	294	15.2	3.0	7.4	2.5	42	19	39	1.6	15%	29%	68%	12	53	25%	42%	0	0.88	-17.5	52	78	-$2
12	SEA	5	2	0	46	53	2.72	3.13	0.95	174	147	198	3.8	3.1	10.3	3.3	42	22	37	0.6	8%	24%	73%	0	16			0	1.16	7.4	121	158	$5
1st Half		4	1	0	35	45	1.82	2.34	0.69	135	148	123	4.4	2.1	11.7	5.6	47	23	30	0.5	9%	21%	77%	0	18			0	0.98	9.4	179	233	$10
2nd Half		1	1	0	12	8	5.40	5.98	1.71	286	143	429	2.8	6.2	6.2	1.0	30	18	52	0.8	6%	31%	68%	0	12			0	1.44	-2.0	-47	-61	-$10
13	Proj	5	3	0	65	62	3.37	3.52	1.22	247	236	254	5.5	2.6	8.6	3.3	45	22	34	1.3	15%	30%	78%	0						5.2	106	138	$4

Gallardo,Yovani

Age: 27 Th: R Role SP	Health B	LIMA Plan B+	
Ht: 6' 2" Wt: 210 Type Pwr	PT/Exp A	Rand Var +1	
	Consist A	MM 4505	

ERA and WHIP erosion after '11 breakout might signal that he has peaked, but that 2H reminds us that the ingredients for a sub-3.50 ERA are there. Only Gio Gonzalez had a higher GB rate among SP with a 9.0+ Dom, and trend gives some hope for more. With a little hr/f help... UP: 20 W, 220 K, 3.00 ERA

Yr	Tm	W	L	Sv	IP	K	ERA	xERA	WHIP	OBA	vL	vR	BF/G	Ctl	Dom	Cmd	G	L	F	hr/9	hr/f	H%	S%	GS	APC	DOM%	DIS%	Sv%	LI	RAR	BPV	BPX	R$
08	MIL *	0	1	0	40	36	3.36	4.76	1.43	281	324	204	24.1	3.0	8.2	2.8	40	12	48	1.1	10%	34%	81%	4	96	50%	25%			4.7	72	135	-$2
09	MIL	13	12	0	186	204	3.73	3.73	1.31	219	213	225	26.4	4.6	9.9	2.2	45	19	36	1.0	12%	29%	75%	30	107	63%	3%			13.5	78	146	$15
10	MIL	14	7	0	185	200	3.84	3.53	1.37	251	280	228	25.9	3.6	9.7	2.7	43	24	33	0.6	7%	34%	72%	31	103	81%	13%			5.4	98	158	$10
11	MIL	17	10	0	207	207	3.52	3.34	1.22	245	257	235	26.2	2.6	9.0	3.5	47	17	36	1.2	13%	31%	76%	33	105	61%	15%			10.9	118	177	$17
12	MIL	16	9	0	204	204	3.66	3.69	1.30	243	256	230	26.1	3.6	9.0	2.5	48	21	31	1.1	15%	30%	76%	33	105	64%	9%			8.9	92	119	$13
1st Half		6	6	0	96	95	4.14	3.99	1.40	255	274	236	25.8	4.0	8.9	2.3	45	20	35	1.1	13%	31%	74%	16	103	63%	13%			-1.4	77	100	$6
2nd Half		10	3	0	108	109	3.24	3.42	1.22	232	240	225	26.3	3.2	9.1	2.8	50	22	28	1.2	17%	29%	79%	17	107	65%	6%			10.4	103	134	$19
13	Proj	15	9	0	203	206	3.52	3.55	1.27	242	254	230	25.2	3.3	9.1	2.7	47	20	33	1.1	13%	30%	76%	33						12.4	99	128	$17

Garcia,Freddy

Age: 37 Th: R Role RP	Health A	LIMA Plan D+	
Ht: 6' 4" Wt: 255 Type	PT/Exp B	Rand Var +4	
	Consist A	MM 2201	

Mid-30s skill spike hidden due to inflated hr/f. Not that it matters when you're a washed up two-pitch pitcher, one of which is a 87-mph fastball. If you're desperate to take a flyer, consider: 2.4 Cmd as SP, 3.4 Cmd as RP. Don't chase that '11 ERA; it was a mirage. His upside is as a 4.00 ERA middle man.

Yr	Tm	W	L	Sv	IP	K	ERA	xERA	WHIP	OBA	vL	vR	BF/G	Ctl	Dom	Cmd	G	L	F	hr/9	hr/f	H%	S%	GS	APC	DOM%	DIS%	Sv%	LI	RAR	BPV	BPX	R$
08	DET	1	1	0	15	12	4.20	4.20	1.13	204	100	265	20.3	3.6	7.2	2.0	40	14	45	1.8	16%	21%	71%	3	69	33%	0%			0.2	50	95	-$2
09	CHW *	3	7	0	73	48	5.73	4.85	1.41	291	196	316	25.7	2.3	5.9	2.6	45	14	41	1.1	5%	32%	60%	9	92	67%	11%			-12.6	54	101	-$4
10	CHW	12	6	0	157	89	4.64	4.48	1.38	279	271	287	24.0	2.6	5.1	2.0	41	21	38	1.3	12%	29%	70%	28	88	39%	25%			-10.9	41	67	$1
11	NYY	12	8	0	147	96	3.62	4.39	1.34	268	284	255	24.1	2.8	5.9	2.1	36	22	41	1.0	8%	30%	76%	25	88	40%	20%	0	0.76	5.8	45	68	$6
12	NYY	7	6	0	107	89	5.20	4.15	1.37	270	282	256	15.4	2.9	7.5	2.5	40	25	35	1.5	16%	31%	66%	17	59	24%	35%	0	0.71	-15.7	73	95	-$5
1st Half		2	2	0	31	23	6.39	4.31	1.45	296	246	357	9.8	2.3	6.7	2.9	39	28	33	1.2	12%	34%	56%	4	39	0%	75%	0	0.60	-9.1	74	96	-$12
2nd Half		5	4	0	76	66	4.72	4.08	1.34	259	298	216	20.3	3.2	7.8	2.4	41	24	36	1.7	18%	29%	70%	13	77	31%	23%	0	0.80	-6.6	73	95	-$2
13	Proj	6	5	0	87	63	4.86	4.35	1.37	276	273	278	17.4	2.7	6.5	2.4	40	23	37	1.3	12%	31%	68%	16						-9.1	61	80	-$2

STEPHEN NICKRAND

Garcia,Jaime

Age: 26	Th: L	Role SP	Health	C	LIMA Plan	A
Ht: 6' 2"	Wt: 215	Type GB	PT/Exp	B	Rand Var	0
			Consist	A	MM	3303

7-7, 3.92 ERA in 122 IP at STL. Missed two months with shoulder impingement and a frayed labrum found in October. Showed strong skills and maintained Ctl gains, but high H% and health held him back. Little upside, but consistent; you can rely on him if healthy.

Yr Tm	W	L	Sv	IP	K	ERA	xERA	WHIP	OBA	vL	vR	BF/G	Ctl	Dom	Cmd	G	L	F	hr/9	hr/f	H%	S%	GS	APC	DOM%	DIS%	Sv%	LI	RAR	BPV	BPX	R$
08 STL *	8	7	0	122	92	4.18	4.00	1.39	262	250	227	17.7	3.5	6.8	1.9	61	20	20	0.7	40%	31%	71%	1	26	0%	0%	0	0.76	2.1	63	117	$3
09 aaa	2	0	0	21	18	4.49	4.87	1.34	245			21.8	3.8	7.8	2.1				2.0		26%	75%							-0.4	35	66	-$2
10 STL	13	8	0	163	132	2.70	3.69	1.32	243	211	251	24.8	3.5	7.3	2.1	56	19	26	0.5	7%	30%	81%	28	93	61%	11%			27.8	70	113	$14
11 STL	13	7	0	195	156	3.56	3.49	1.32	273	308	264	25.8	2.3	7.2	3.1	54	18	28	0.7	9%	33%	74%	32	93	47%	16%			9.2	99	149	$9
12 STL *	8	8	0	137	113	4.07	4.05	1.34	279	260	297	24.8	2.2	7.4	3.4	54	20	26	0.6	7%	34%	70%	20	88	55%	20%			-1.0	96	125	$2
1st Half	3	4	0	66	51	4.48	3.90	1.46	304	286	309	25.9	2.6	6.9	2.7	54	18	28	0.3	3%	36%	67%	11	87	45%	18%			-3.8	87	113	-$4
2nd Half	5	4	0	71	62	3.70	3.84	1.22	265	212	283	23.8	1.8	7.9	4.4	54	23	23	1.0	13%	32%	73%	9	89	67%	22%			2.8	112	146	$7
13 Proj	11	9	0	174	142	3.72	3.61	1.32	270	261	273	23.7	2.5	7.3	2.9	54	20	26	0.7	9%	33%	73%	30						6.4	96	125	$9

Garza,Matt

Age: 29	Th: R	Role SP	Health	C	LIMA Plan	A+
Ht: 6' 4"	Wt: 215	Type Pwr	PT/Exp	A	Rand Var	+2
			Consist	B	MM	3405

Stress reaction in his elbow ended another strong season, skills-wise, in August. He's expected to recover by spring. Inflated hr/f pushed up ERA, but aside from a slight dip in strikeout rate, this was a mirror of 2011 skills. A rebound is in the cards.

Yr Tm	W	L	Sv	IP	K	ERA	xERA	WHIP	OBA	vL	vR	BF/G	Ctl	Dom	Cmd	G	L	F	hr/9	hr/f	H%	S%	GS	APC	DOM%	DIS%	Sv%	LI	RAR	BPV	BPX	R$
08 TAM	11	9	0	185	128	3.70	4.32	1.24	245	244	245	25.7	2.9	6.2	2.2	42	18	40	0.9	8%	28%	73%	30	98	37%	23%			14.1	55	103	$13
09 TAM	8	12	0	203	189	3.95	4.02	1.26	233	196	271	26.9	3.5	8.4	2.4	40	18	43	1.1	10%	28%	72%	32	107	50%	6%			9.4	74	139	$13
10 TAM	15	10	1	205	150	3.91	4.23	1.25	248	241	255	25.9	2.8	6.6	2.4	36	19	45	1.2	10%	28%	73%	32	99	50%	16%	100	0.76	4.2	58	94	$12
11 CHC	10	10	0	198	197	3.32	3.38	1.26	245	247	243	27.1	2.9	9.0	3.1	46	21	33	0.6	8%	32%	75%	31	103	68%	10%			15.2	108	162	$13
12 CHC	5	7	0	104	96	3.91	3.54	1.18	236	247	224	23.6	2.8	8.3	3.0	47	19	33	1.3	16%	28%	72%	18	94	56%	22%			1.4	100	130	$4
1st Half	4	6	0	90	80	4.01	3.62	1.16	235	246	224	24.5	2.6	8.0	3.1	46	19	35	1.2	14%	28%	70%	15	98	60%	13%			0.0	98	128	$6
2nd Half	1	1	0	14	16	3.21	3.05	1.29	240	261	222	19.0	3.9	10.3	2.7	56	21	24	1.9	38%	28%	87%	3	78	33%	67%			1.4	115	150	-$8
13 Proj	11	11	0	203	189	3.68	3.66	1.24	246	242	251	25.1	2.9	8.4	2.9	45	19	35	1.1	12%	30%	74%	33						8.5	97	126	$14

Gaudin,Chad

Age: 30	Th: R	Role RP	Health	F	LIMA Plan	D
Ht: 5' 10"	Wt: 185	Type Pwr	PT/Exp	D	Rand Var	0
			Consist	D	MM	1300

The good news is that this middle reliever posted his best ERA in the past four years; the bad news is pretty much everything else. Strand rate was unfair, but that just brings him to marginally respectable at best. ED NOTE: Stephen asked me, "Do I get hazard pay for looking at numbers like this?"

Yr Tm	W	L	Sv	IP	K	ERA	xERA	WHIP	OBA	vL	vR	BF/G	Ctl	Dom	Cmd	G	L	F	hr/9	hr/f	H%	S%	GS	APC	DOM%	DIS%	Sv%	LI	RAR	BPV	BPX	R$
08 2 TM	9	5	0	90	71	4.40	4.15	1.32	265	273	258	7.6	2.7	7.1	2.6	39	21	40	1.1	10%	31%	69%	6	29	67%	17%	0	0.66	-0.8	72	135	$4
09 2 TM	6	10	0	147	139	4.64	4.34	1.51	258	296	224	21.4	4.6	8.5	1.8	44	20	36	0.9	9%	32%	70%	25	83	40%	28%	0	0.79	-5.8	49	93	$0
10 2 AL	1	4	0	65	53	5.65	4.44	1.50	285	283	287	7.0	3.4	7.3	2.1	39	15	46	2.2	17%	30%	70%	0	26			0	0.64	-12.6	55	90	-$6
11 TOR *	3	6	0	50	31	5.75	6.09	1.83	337	429	273	10.6	3.5	5.6	1.6	31	15	54	0.5	7%	38%	67%	0	20			0	0.94	-11.2	38	58	-$9
12 MIA	4	2	0	69	57	4.54	4.29	1.41	274	322	232	6.6	3.4	7.4	2.2	41	24	35	0.8	8%	32%	68%	0	25			0	0.78	-4.5	61	80	-$4
1st Half	1	1	0	39	31	4.89	4.24	1.40	277	270	284	8.7	3.0	7.2	2.4	41	24	36	0.7	7%	33%	65%	0	33			0	0.65	-4.2	67	87	-$6
2nd Half	3	1	0	31	26	4.11	4.37	1.43	270	404	176	5.0	3.8	7.6	2.0	41	25	34	0.9	10%	32%	73%	0	19			0	0.88	-0.3	53	69	-$1
13 Proj	2	2	0	29	23	4.95	4.59	1.54	289	330	252	7.2	3.5	7.0	2.0	41	21	38	1.0	9%	34%	69%	0						-3.3	49	64	-$4

Gee,Dillon

Age: 27	Th: R	Role SP	Health	C	LIMA Plan	A
Ht: 6' 1"	Wt: 205	Type Pwr	PT/Exp	B	Rand Var	+1
			Consist	B	MM	3303

A breakout season, skills-wise, was ended in July by blood clot in shoulder. Struggles vs. LHB are likely anomalous and inflated hr/f cost him ERA. DOM/DIS shows how good he was, with nary a bad start. With that Cmd and GB rate, here's where you buy skills and not stats. UP: sub-3.50 ERA

Yr Tm	W	L	Sv	IP	K	ERA	xERA	WHIP	OBA	vL	vR	BF/G	Ctl	Dom	Cmd	G	L	F	hr/9	hr/f	H%	S%	GS	APC	DOM%	DIS%	Sv%	LI	RAR	BPV	BPX	R$
08 aa	2	0	0	27	17	1.56	1.85	0.93	210			25.3	1.7	5.8	3.5				0.3		25%	85%							9.2	111	207	$2
09 aaa	1	3	0	48	37	5.51	5.24	1.52	296			23.3	3.1	7.0	2.3				1.2		34%	65%							-7.1	50	94	-$5
10 NYM *	15	10	0	194	155	4.74	4.62	1.39	282	170	239	24.8	2.5	7.2	2.8	47	10	43	1.1	5%	33%	68%	5	98	20%	0%			-15.9	69	112	$3
11 NYM	13	6	0	161	114	4.43	4.31	1.38	248	224	265	23.5	4.0	6.4	1.6	47	19	33	1.0	11%	28%	70%	27	87	41%	22%	0	0.77	-9.6	33	49	$1
12 NYM	6	7	0	110	97	4.10	3.55	1.25	256	287	219	27.2	2.4	8.0	3.3	50	20	30	1.0	13%	31%	70%	17	103	71%	0%			-1.2	107	140	$2
1st Half	5	6	0	96	89	4.42	3.48	1.29	259	293	220	27.2	2.5	8.4	3.3	51	20	28	1.1	15%	32%	68%	15	103	67%	0%			-4.8	112	146	$4
2nd Half	1	1	0	14	8	1.93	4.00	1.00	235	250	211	27.5	1.3	5.1	4.0	43	19	38	0.0	0%	28%	79%	2	100	100%	0%			3.6	79	103	-$7
13 Proj	10	9	0	160	135	3.97	3.83	1.25	247	245	250	23.7	2.9	7.6	2.6	49	16	35	1.1	12%	29%	72%	27						0.9	85	110	$9

Germano,Justin

Age: 30	Th: R	Role RP	Health	A	LIMA Plan	C
Ht: 6' 2"	Wt: 210	Type Con	PT/Exp	D	Rand Var	0
			Consist	B	MM	2100

2-10, 6.20 ERA in 70 IP at CHC. Sure, control is great and all that, but low strikeout rate and middling GB% mean too many baserunners nonetheless. He wasn't unlucky—just bad, with almost half of starts ending in disaster. And L/R splits say he's not useful as a spot reliever, either. Okay, we've said enough.

Yr Tm	W	L	Sv	IP	K	ERA	xERA	WHIP	OBA	vL	vR	BF/G	Ctl	Dom	Cmd	G	L	F	hr/9	hr/f	H%	S%	GS	APC	DOM%	DIS%	Sv%	LI	RAR	BPV	BPX	R$
08 SD *	2	12	0	142	73	5.69	5.63	1.56	315	268	330	21.4	2.3	4.6	2.0	49	18	33	1.1	15%	34%	65%	6	58	17%	33%	0	0.44	-23.9	27	51	-$10
09 for	5	4	0	76	40	5.44	5.43	1.46	315			23.2	1.5	4.7	3.2				1.2		34%	64%							-10.5	52	98	-$4
10 CLE *	5	6	1	108	69	3.68	3.95	1.21	260	213	200	9.3	1.9	5.8	3.0	40	17	42	1.2	14%	28%	74%	1	22	0%	100%	50	0.78	5.3	66	106	$5
11 FAA *	1	3	3	62	34	5.40	4.98	1.41	309	273	316	10.4	1.4	5.0	3.6	36	17	47	0.9	5%	34%	62%	0	23			100	0.35	-11.1	71	107	-$5
12 2 TM *	11	14	0	175	104	4.71	5.01	1.36	290	274	320	23.6	1.9	5.4	2.8	46	22	32	1.4	9%	31%	69%	12	82	17%	42%	0	0.79	-15.1	47	61	-$3
1st Half	9	4	0	105	52	3.73	4.86	1.25	280	0	0	25.1	1.3	4.5	3.3				1.7	0%	28%	79%	0	0					3.7	44	57	$9
2nd Half	2	10	0	70	52	6.20	5.16	1.54	304	274	320	21.7	2.7	6.7	2.5	46	22	32	0.9	9%	35%	59%	12	82	17%	42%	0	0.79	-18.8	59	77	-$20
13 Proj	2	3	0	44	26	5.06	4.31	1.39	296	268	315	15.1	1.9	5.5	2.9	46	19	35	1.1	11%	32%	66%	6						-5.6	71	93	-$4

Gomez,Jeanmar

Age: 25	Th: R	Role SP	Health	A	LIMA Plan	D
Ht: 6' 3"	Wt: 200	Type	PT/Exp	C	Rand Var	+4
			Consist	C	MM	1103

4-5, 5.96 ERA in 91 IP at CLE. Minor-league numbers hide the ugly major league Dom history (5.3, 4.8, 4.7). This isn't good enough even with a strong groundball rate, and he's crossed 50% in that department only once. xERA, command, and DOM/DIS are all telling you to stay away.

Yr Tm	W	L	Sv	IP	K	ERA	xERA	WHIP	OBA	vL	vR	BF/G	Ctl	Dom	Cmd	G	L	F	hr/9	hr/f	H%	S%	GS	APC	DOM%	DIS%	Sv%	LI	RAR	BPV	BPX	R$
08																																
09 aa	10	4	0	123	97	4.42	4.61	1.46	283			24.0	3.1	7.1	2.3				0.9		33%	71%							-1.6	63	117	$2
10 CLE *	12	13	0	174	101	5.17	5.36	1.56	300	268	360	24.6	3.2	5.3	1.6	47	20	33	1.1	10%	33%	68%	11	91	18%	36%			-23.4	29	46	-$7
11 CLE *	15	10	0	196	122	3.31	4.07	1.38	274	319	289	25.7	2.8	5.6	2.0	53	20	27	0.6	10%	31%	77%	10	87	20%	50%	0	0.83	15.3	56	85	$9
12 CLE *	11	13	0	160	92	5.51	4.89	1.43	284	258	285	22.0	2.8	5.2	1.8	48	19	33	1.2	15%	31%	63%	17	73	12%	53%	0	0.68	-29.5	32	42	-$10
1st Half	5	7	0	80	39	4.73	4.64	1.40	276	258	270	22.5	2.9	4.4	1.5	49	18	33	1.1	12%	29%	69%	13	83	15%	46%	0	0.74	-7.0	24	31	-$6
2nd Half	6	6	0	80	53	6.30	5.08	1.47	291	258	353	21.4	2.8	5.9	2.1	47	21	32	1.2	28%	32%	58%	4	49	0%	75%	0	0.54	-22.5	41	53	-$14
13 Proj	9	9	0	131	81	4.88	4.44	1.45	285	270	299	23.3	2.9	5.6	1.9	49	20	31	1.0	11%	31%	68%	24						-14.0	48	63	-$3

Gonzalez,Gio

Age: 27	Th: L	Role SP	Health	A	LIMA Plan	C
Ht: 6' 0"	Wt: 200	Type Pwr	PT/Exp	A	Rand Var	-1
			Consist	A	MM	3405

What appears to be a growth season, skills-wise, can mostly be attributed to NL move. Don't get us wrong—these are outstanding skills. But they don't portend further growth; if anything, expect a slight pull-back in ERA. Even then, he's still very reliable, and still among the elite.

Yr Tm	W	L	Sv	IP	K	ERA	xERA	WHIP	OBA	vL	vR	BF/G	Ctl	Dom	Cmd	G	L	F	hr/9	hr/f	H%	S%	GS	APC	DOM%	DIS%	Sv%	LI	RAR	BPV	BPX	R$
08 OAK *	9	11	0	157	138	5.16	4.36	1.45	248	194	260	20.3	4.7	7.9	1.7	42	18	40	1.1	23%	29%	66%	7	71	29%	57%	0	0.59	-16.2	54	101	$0
09 OAK *	10	8	0	160	167	4.63	4.75	1.57	262	340	271	21.9	5.1	9.4	1.9	46	18	36	1.1	14%	33%	73%	17	91	41%	29%	0	0.80	-6.0	66	123	$1
10 OAK	15	9	0	201	171	3.23	4.00	1.31	229	209	235	25.8	4.1	7.7	1.9	49	15	35	0.7	7%	28%	77%	33	102	58%	18%			21.0	54	87	$15
11 OAK	16	12	0	202	197	3.12	3.70	1.32	230	253	224	27.0	4.1	8.8	2.2	47	18	34	0.8	9%	30%	79%	32	106	56%	13%			20.5	74	111	$16
12 WAS	21	8	0	199	207	2.89	3.43	1.13	206	231	199	25.7	3.4	9.3	2.7	48	22	30	0.4	6%	28%	75%	32	100	78%	13%			27.7	102	132	$28
1st Half	10	3	0	91	108	2.78	3.16	1.08	192	197	190	24.7	3.5	10.7	3.1	46	23	31	0.3	4%	29%	74%	15	99	80%	13%			13.8	123	160	$32
2nd Half	11	5	0	109	99	2.98	3.67	1.17	217	259	206	26.5	3.4	8.2	2.4	50	21	29	0.5	7%	28%	75%	17	101	76%	12%			13.9	84	109	$25
13 Proj	18	10	0	203	199	3.20	3.69	1.25	227	243	222	24.7	3.8	8.8	2.3	48	20	33	0.7	10%	29%	77%	33						20.4	81	105	$21

MATT CEDERHOLM

Gonzalez,Michael

Age: 35	Th: L	Role RP	Health	C	LIMA Plan B
			PT/Exp	D	Rand Var -2
Ht: 6' 2"	Wt : 215	Type Pwr FB	Consist	A	MM 3500

Shook off the rust in 2H after knee surgery delayed signing. Excellent Dom forgives some sins, but walks remain a problem and he's due for a hr/f correction. Age and Health are major red flags as he's topped 53 innings just once in past five seasons. Note xERA trend—let someone else weather the fall.

Yr Tm	W	L	Sv	IP	K	ERA	xERA	WHIP	OBA	vL	vR	BF/G	Ctl	Dom	Cmd	G	L	F	hr/9	hr/f	H%	S%	GS	APC	DOM%	DIS%	Sv%	LI	RAR	BPV	BPX	R$
08 ATL	0	3	14	34	44	4.28	3.38	1.19	210	259	196	3.9	3.7	11.8	3.1	31	25	44	1.6	17%	28%	71%	0	17			88	0.92	0.2	120	225	$5
09 ATL	5	4	10	74	90	2.42	3.48	1.20	209	194	218	3.9	4.0	10.9	2.7	38	18	44	0.8	9%	29%	84%	0	16			59	1.18	17.4	104	195	$13
10 BAL	1	3	1	25	31	4.01	3.74	1.30	205	324	130	3.7	5.1	11.3	2.2	33	22	45	0.4	4%	31%	68%	0	14			33	1.71	0.2	77	124	-$1
11 2 AL	2	2	1	53	51	4.39	3.79	1.35	250	214	287	4.1	3.5	8.6	2.4	41	23	36	1.2	13%	31%	71%	0	17			50	0.88	-2.9	78	118	-$2
12 WAS	0	0	0	36	39	3.03	3.82	1.32	237	179	297	3.2	4.0	9.8	2.4	40	23	38	0.5	6%	32%	78%	0	13			0	0.90	4.3	86	112	-$2
1st Half	0	0	0	9	9	1.93	4.19	1.50	235	77	333	2.9	5.8	8.7	1.5	56	16	28	0.0	0%	32%	86%	0	11			0	1.05	2.4	34	44	-$6
2nd Half	0	0	0	26	30	3.42	3.68	1.25	237	204	279	3.4	3.4	10.3	3.0	34	25	41	0.7	7%	32%	74%	0	14			0	0.83	1.9	104	135	$0
13 Proj	**1**	**1**	**0**	**36**	**42**	**3.89**	**3.60**	**1.27**	**234**	**215**	**248**	**3.6**	**3.7**	**10.4**	**2.8**	**36**	**22**	**42**	**1.0**	**10%**	**31%**	**72%**	**0**						**0.6**	**101**	**132**	**-$1**

Gonzalez,Miguel

Age: 29	Th: R	Role SP	Health	A	LIMA Plan C+
			PT/Exp	D	Rand Var -1
Ht: 6' 1"	Wt : 170	Type xFB	Consist	F	MM 1203

9-4, 3.25 ERA in 105 IP at BAL. Late bloomer made MLB debut and thrived in pennant race, but 2H BPV confirms skills are just average. Correction in store for hit and strand rates, so results will suffer. Will be overvalued, especially by those suffering from acute recency bias.

Yr Tm	W	L	Sv	IP	K	ERA	xERA	WHIP	OBA	vL	vR	BF/G	Ctl	Dom	Cmd	G	L	F	hr/9	hr/f	H%	S%	GS	APC	DOM%	DIS%	Sv%	LI	RAR	BPV	BPX	R$
08																																
09																																
10																																
11 a/a	0	6	0	52	38	7.70	6.47	1.84	331			15.0	4.0	6.7	1.7				1.0		38%	57%							-23.9	34	51	-$13
12 BAL *	12	6	1	150	116	3.01	2.99	1.12	224	250	220	18.5	2.8	7.0	2.5	35	22	43	0.9	10%	26%	77%	15	94	47%	20%	100	0.69	18.6	78	102	$17
1st Half	3	2	1	52	46	2.44	1.64	0.96	197	250	200	12.3	2.4	8.0	3.4	19	19	62	0.3	0%	26%	74%	0	55			100	0.31	10.1	127	165	$13
2nd Half	9	4	0	98	70	3.31	3.68	1.21	237	250	222	24.7	3.0	6.4	2.1	36	23	41	1.2	11%	26%	78%	15	99	47%	20%	0	0.74	8.6	55	72	$19
13 Proj	**8**	**12**	**0**	**174**	**133**	**4.31**	**4.61**	**1.40**	**269**	**284**	**252**	**24.6**	**3.3**	**6.9**	**2.1**	**36**	**23**	**41**	**1.0**	**8%**	**31%**	**72%**	**30**						**-6.3**	**50**	**65**	**$2**

Gorzelanny,Tom

Age: 30	Th: L	Role RP	Health	B	LIMA Plan B
			PT/Exp	B	Rand Var -4
Ht: 6' 2"	Wt : 205	Type Pwr	Consist	A	MM 2301

Move to bullpen benefitted results, but not skills. Erratic control negates the strikeouts, and it took a fluky strand rate to prop up that second-half ERA. xERA and BPV both show the truth: skills are just ordinary, and an ERA spike is on the way.

Yr Tm	W	L	Sv	IP	K	ERA	xERA	WHIP	OBA	vL	vR	BF/G	Ctl	Dom	Cmd	G	L	F	hr/9	hr/f	H%	S%	GS	APC	DOM%	DIS%	Sv%	LI	RAR	BPV	BPX	R$
08 PIT *	9	10	0	140	92	5.67	5.49	1.63	281	261	299	22.3	4.8	5.9	1.2	40	16	44	1.4	13%	31%	68%	21	91	10%	43%			-23.2	20	37	-$7
09 2 NL *	11	6	0	134	110	4.09	3.98	1.39	266	244	252	15.2	3.3	7.4	2.2	41	21	38	0.6	12%	32%	71%	7	35	43%	29%	0	1.16	3.8	74	139	$6
10 CHC	7	9	1	136	119	4.09	4.43	1.50	260	286	251	20.8	4.5	7.9	1.8	41	19	40	0.7	7%	32%	74%	23	80	48%	17%	100	0.77	-0.2	39	63	$1
11 WAS	4	6	0	105	95	4.03	3.91	1.29	258	157	287	14.9	2.8	8.1	2.9	36	17	47	1.3	11%	30%	73%	15	57	40%	27%	0	0.88	-1.1	84	127	$2
12 WAS	4	2	1	72	62	2.88	4.20	1.32	242	237	245	6.8	3.8	7.8	2.1	43	21	36	0.9	9%	29%	82%	1	26	0%	100%	100	0.93	10.1	59	77	$3
1st Half	2	1	1	39	32	3.69	4.28	1.33	245	246	244	7.3	3.5	7.4	2.1	44	19	37	0.9	9%	30%	75%	0	28			100	1.00	1.6	61	79	$1
2nd Half	2	1	0	33	30	1.91	4.12	1.30	237	224	246	6.3	4.1	8.2	2.0	41	23	36	0.8	10%	28%	90%	1	23	0%	100%	0	0.86	8.6	56	73	$5
13 Proj	**4**	**3**	**0**	**73**	**63**	**3.42**	**4.26**	**1.35**	**251**	**227**	**262**	**7.2**	**3.7**	**7.8**	**2.1**	**40**	**20**	**40**	**1.0**	**9%**	**30%**	**78%**	**0**						**5.3**	**59**	**77**	**$2**

Gregerson,Luke

Age: 29	Th: R	Role RP	Health	B	LIMA Plan B+
			PT/Exp	C	Rand Var -3
Ht: 6' 3"	Wt : 200	Type Pwr	Consist	C	MM 4421

Resurgent skills led to excellent results for perpetual closer-in-waiting. In retrospect, 2011's performance dip is the clear outlier. Positive GB% trend and improvement vs lefties make him ideally suited for the end of games. If he gets the opportunities... UP: 35 Sv

Yr Tm	W	L	Sv	IP	K	ERA	xERA	WHIP	OBA	vL	vR	BF/G	Ctl	Dom	Cmd	G	L	F	hr/9	hr/f	H%	S%	GS	APC	DOM%	DIS%	Sv%	LI	RAR	BPV	BPX	R$
08 aa	7	6	10	75	63	3.80	3.48	1.27	248			5.4	3.1	7.5	2.4				0.7		30%	71%							4.9	81	152	$8
09 SD	2	4	1	75	93	3.24	3.17	1.24	221	285	161	4.4	3.7	11.2	3.0	46	21	33	0.4	5%	33%	73%	0	16			14	1.28	10.0	124	233	$5
10 SD	4	7	2	78	89	3.22	2.66	0.83	170	180	162	3.7	2.1	10.2	4.9	48	15	37	0.9	12%	23%	65%	0	14			29	1.34	8.3	154	250	$11
11 SD	3	3	0	56	34	2.75	4.21	1.37	266	329	225	4.0	3.1	5.5	1.8	49	22	29	0.3	4%	31%	80%	0	14			0	1.15	8.2	43	65	$1
12 SD	2	0	9	72	72	2.39	3.31	1.09	215	214	216	3.8	2.6	9.0	3.4	50	18	32	0.9	11%	28%	83%	0	14			69	1.19	14.4	120	156	$10
1st Half	1	0	0	34	37	3.67	3.41	1.28	244	286	218	3.9	3.4	9.7	2.8	48	22	31	1.3	19%	30%	77%	0	14			0	1.15	1.5	108	141	$2
2nd Half	1	0	9	37	35	1.21	3.22	0.91	188	143	213	3.8	1.9	8.4	4.4	52	15	33	0.5	6%	25%	91%	0	14			90	1.23	12.9	130	169	$18
13 Proj	**3**	**2**	**10**	**73**	**67**	**2.74**	**3.44**	**1.15**	**232**	**255**	**217**	**3.8**	**2.7**	**8.3**	**3.1**	**49**	**19**	**32**	**0.7**	**9%**	**29%**	**79%**	**0**						**11.4**	**105**	**136**	**$10**

Greinke,Zack

Age: 29	Th: R	Role SP	Health	A	LIMA Plan B
			PT/Exp	A	Rand Var 0
Ht: 6' 2"	Wt : 200	Type Pwr	Consist	B	MM 4405

BPIs as a whole are elite, as is PQS DOM/DIS history, regardless of which city or league he pitches in. Factor in positive GB% & FB% trends along with manageable innings-pitched totals, and you have one of the safer starting pitchers available. Go the extra dollar here.

Yr Tm	W	L	Sv	IP	K	ERA	xERA	WHIP	OBA	vL	vR	BF/G	Ctl	Dom	Cmd	G	L	F	hr/9	hr/f	H%	S%	GS	APC	DOM%	DIS%	Sv%	LI	RAR	BPV	BPX	R$
08 KC	13	10	0	202	183	3.47	3.77	1.28	257	287	232	26.6	2.5	8.1	3.3	43	19	38	0.9	9%	32%	76%	32	101	66%	13%			21.3	100	188	$17
09 KC	16	8	0	229	242	2.16	3.19	1.07	230	250	211	27.7	2.0	9.5	4.7	40	19	41	0.4	5%	31%	81%	33	105	88%	0%			61.2	135	253	$39
10 KC	10	14	0	220	181	4.17	3.64	1.25	260	280	235	27.8	2.3	7.4	3.3	46	18	36	0.7	8%	31%	67%	33	104	55%	9%			-2.5	97	156	$9
11 MIL	16	6	0	172	201	3.83	2.84	1.20	245	245	245	25.5	2.4	10.5	4.5	47	22	31	1.0	14%	33%	71%	28	101	71%	11%			2.4	151	227	$14
12 2 TM	15	5	0	212	200	3.48	3.36	1.20	249	249	249	25.5	2.3	8.5	3.7	49	22	29	0.8	10%	31%	73%	34	100	65%	12%			14.1	118	154	$18
1st Half	9	2	0	102	102	2.82	3.00	1.17	251	254	249	25.7	1.9	9.0	4.6	52	23	25	0.4	6%	33%	76%	16	101	75%	13%			15.0	140	182	$27
2nd Half	6	3	0	110	98	4.08	3.69	1.22	247	245	249	25.4	2.6	8.0	3.1	46	21	33	1.1	13%	29%	70%	18	98	56%	11%			-0.8	98	128	$10
13 Proj	**16**	**8**	**0**	**218**	**213**	**3.53**	**3.32**	**1.20**	**251**	**257**	**245**	**26.1**	**2.3**	**8.8**	**3.8**	**47**	**21**	**32**	**0.8**	**11%**	**32%**	**73%**	**34**						**13.1**	**121**	**158**	**$20**

Griffin,A.J.

Age: 25	Th: R	Role SP	Health	A	LIMA Plan B
			PT/Exp	D	Rand Var 0
Ht: 6' 5"	Wt : 230	Type FB	Consist	F	MM 2203

7-1, 3.06 ERA in 82 IP at OAK. Excelled in upper minors and carried it over to MLB. Control is best asset, but also misses bats reasonably and handles righties/lefties equally well. MLB experience is limited and PQS DIS% is a bit of a red flag, but if BPIs continue on current track... UP: 200 IP, 15 W.

Yr Tm	W	L	Sv	IP	K	ERA	xERA	WHIP	OBA	vL	vR	BF/G	Ctl	Dom	Cmd	G	L	F	hr/9	hr/f	H%	S%	GS	APC	DOM%	DIS%	Sv%	LI	RAR	BPV	BPX	R$
08																																
09																																
10																																
11 a/a	2	4	0	38	24	5.91	5.70	1.56	306			23.8	2.9	5.7	2.0				1.4		33%	64%							-9.2	29	43	-$6
12 OAK *	14	4	0	184	141	3.04	2.94	1.07	236	245	225	22.4	1.8	6.9	3.8	37	24	39	0.8	10%	28%	75%	15	95	53%	27%			22.1	106	138	$22
1st Half	6	3	0	107	79	2.70	2.14	0.94	218	91	158	23.6	1.4	6.7	4.7	52	21	27	0.5	11%	26%	73%	2	107	100%	0%			17.3	135	176	$29
2nd Half	8	1	0	78	62	3.51	3.99	1.24	259	270	235	21.0	2.3	7.2	3.1	35	24	41	1.1	10%	30%	76%	13	93	46%	31%			4.9	77	100	$12
13 Proj	**10**	**8**	**0**	**145**	**109**	**3.95**	**4.30**	**1.29**	**269**	**287**	**250**	**22.7**	**2.3**	**6.8**	**2.9**	**35**	**24**	**41**	**1.1**	**9%**	**31%**	**73%**	**26**						**1.2**	**73**	**95**	**$6**

Grilli,Jason

Age: 36	Th: R	Role RP	Health	A	LIMA Plan A+
			PT/Exp	D	Rand Var 0
Ht: 6' 5"	Wt : 225	Type Pwr FB	Consist	B	MM 4510

Raise your hand if you saw this coming... Thought so. He always racked up Ks, but this was another stratosphere. More importantly, BPIs held all year. Age and track record each suggest some regression, but he's done this for two straight years now. A LIMA gem—who'da thunk it?

Yr Tm	W	L	Sv	IP	K	ERA	xERA	WHIP	OBA	vL	vR	BF/G	Ctl	Dom	Cmd	G	L	F	hr/9	hr/f	H%	S%	GS	APC	DOM%	DIS%	Sv%	LI	RAR	BPV	BPX	R$
08 2 TM	3	3	1	75	69	3.00	4.21	1.40	240	237	242	5.4	4.6	8.3	1.8	42	23	34	0.2	3%	31%	78%	0	22			50	0.62	12.2	46	86	$3
09 2 TM	2	3	1	46	49	5.32	4.68	1.69	276	262	289	4.1	5.3	9.7	1.8	34	21	46	0.8	7%	37%	68%	0	17			100	0.85	-5.6	42	79	-$4
10																																
11 PIT *	6	2	4	65	69	2.63	3.55	1.35	243	238	179	4.9	4.0	9.5	2.4	45	22	33	0.6	7%	32%	83%	0	19			100	1.41	10.6	94	141	$6
12 PIT	1	6	2	59	90	2.91	2.88	1.14	207	168	241	3.8	3.4	13.8	4.1	31	24	45	1.1	12%	33%	80%	0	16			40	1.20	8.0	166	217	$5
1st Half	1	2	1	31	48	2.05	2.92	1.04	157	130	185	3.9	4.4	14.1	3.2	33	20	47	1.2	14%	25%	89%	0	16			50	1.19	7.4	146	190	$7
2nd Half	0	4	1	28	42	3.86	2.83	1.25	257	213	290	3.7	2.3	13.5	6.0	28	28	43	1.0	10%	40%	72%	0	15			33	1.22	0.6	189	246	$1
13 Proj	**2**	**4**	**5**	**58**	**74**	**3.32**	**3.39**	**1.31**	**240**	**224**	**252**	**4.1**	**3.8**	**11.5**	**3.0**	**36**	**23**	**41**	**0.8**	**9%**	**34%**	**77%**	**0**						**5.0**	**118**	**154**	**$4**

DAN BECKER

Guerra,Javy

Age: 27	Th: R	Role	RP	Health	C	LIMA Plan	C+
Ht: 6' 1"	Wt: 200	Type	Pwr	PT/Exp	D	Rand Var	-5
				Consist	F	MM	2300

Nifty ERA will reel in the bidders, but it was driven by friendly S% and hr/f. Spotty control, especially that 2H blow-up, confirms he's not closer material yet. 94-mph fastball gives hope, but without consistent >2.0 Cmd, it won't matter. Use xERA as your guide. DN: 5.00 ERA

Yr Tm	W	L	Sv	IP	K	ERA	xERA	WHIP	OBA	vL	vR	BF/G	Ctl	Dom	Cmd	G	L	F	hr/9	hr/f	H%	S%	GS	APC	DOM%	DIS%	Sv%	LI	RAR	BPV	BPX	R$
08																																
09 aa	3	1	0	28	25	5.07	6.07	1.88	320			5.8	5.0	7.9	1.6				0.7		39%	73%							-2.6	51	96	-$5
10 aa	2	0	5	27	22	2.46	4.40	1.72	257			4.4	6.7	7.5	1.1				0.3		32%	86%							5.4	62	101	$0
11 LA *	3	2	24	64	50	2.00	2.20	1.08	204	164	258	4.1	3.2	7.1	2.2	43	20	37	0.4	4%	25%	83%	0	17			92	1.07	15.2	90	135	$16
12 LA	2	3	8	45	37	2.60	4.40	1.49	265	314	229	4.4	4.6	7.4	1.6	48	22	30	0.2	3%	32%	82%	0	17			62	1.12	7.9	35	46	$2
1st Half	2	3	8	24	20	3.38	3.93	1.50	289	400	200	3.9	3.8	7.5	2.0	53	26	21	0.0	0%	35%	75%	0	15			73	1.32	1.9	65	85	$4
2nd Half	0	0	0	21	17	1.71	4.97	1.48	237	200	261	5.1	5.6	7.3	1.3	43	17	40	0.4	4%	29%	90%	0	20			0	0.83	6.0	2	3	-$1
13 Proj	2	2	0	51	41	3.83	4.31	1.33	234	231	236	4.3	4.2	7.3	1.7	45	21	34	0.3	4%	29%	70%	0						1.2	41	53	-$1

Guthrie,Jeremy

Age: 34	Th: R	Role	SP	Health	B	LIMA Plan	D
Ht: 6' 1"	Wt: 205	Type	Con	PT/Exp	A	Rand Var	+1
				Consist	A	MM	1105

On surface, the picture of consistent mediocrity. But trade back to AL served him well. With KC: 3.16 ERA, 1.13 WHIP, 2.9 Cmd. While he won't turn into a new pitcher at age 34, as that hr/f comes down, so too will his ERA. With 93-mph fastball, he's no soft-tosser either. He remains a good end-rotation stash.

Yr Tm	W	L	Sv	IP	K	ERA	xERA	WHIP	OBA	vL	vR	BF/G	Ctl	Dom	Cmd	G	L	F	hr/9	hr/f	H%	S%	GS	APC	DOM%	DIS%	Sv%	LI	RAR	BPV	BPX	R$
08 BAL	10	12	0	191	120	3.63	4.36	1.23	242	241	243	26.5	2.7	5.7	2.1	44	18	38	1.1	10%	27%	75%	30	102	50%	10%			16.2	50	94	$14
09 BAL	10	17	0	200	110	5.04	5.02	1.42	281	289	274	26.5	2.7	5.0	1.8	35	19	47	1.6	11%	29%	69%	33	102	27%	21%			-17.7	29	55	-$1
10 BAL	11	14	0	209	119	3.83	4.30	1.16	243	253	234	27.3	2.1	5.1	2.4	42	14	43	1.1	9%	26%	71%	32	104	56%	13%			6.5	54	87	$12
11 BAL	9	17	0	208	130	4.33	4.40	1.34	267	270	263	26.1	2.9	5.6	2.0	40	21	40	1.1	10%	29%	71%	32	98	38%	13%	0	0.73	-9.9	42	63	$1
12 2 TM	8	12	0	182	101	4.76	4.72	1.41	288	303	272	23.9	2.5	5.0	2.0	41	23	36	1.5	14%	30%	71%	29	89	34%	21%	0	0.74	-16.6	42	55	-$7
1st Half	3	7	0	71	36	6.56	5.42	1.72	327	348	301	22.3	3.3	4.5	1.4	41	23	35	2.1	18%	33%	67%	11	82	0%	27%	0	0.73	-22.4	12	16	-$26
2nd Half	5	5	0	110	65	3.59	4.30	1.21	261	268	254	25.2	2.0	5.3	2.7	41	23	37	1.1	10%	28%	74%	18	94	56%	17%			5.8	61	79	$5
13 Proj	9	13	0	189	109	4.24	4.63	1.35	274	284	263	24.4	2.6	5.2	2.0	41	21	39	1.3	12%	29%	73%	32						-5.2	43	56	$3

Halladay,Roy

Age: 36	Th: R	Role	SP	Health	C	LIMA Plan	A+
Ht: 6' 6"	Wt: 230	Type		PT/Exp	A	Rand Var	+2
				Consist	A	MM	4303

Shoulder strain nagged him most of season, resulting in first sub-200 IP year since '05. That shoulder carried 240 IP per season from '08-'11, so we can't assume return to good health. 2H hr/f spike, slight S% erosion drove up ERA, but age, health make him a risky ace. Use 3.50-4.00 ERA as a new baseline.

Yr Tm	W	L	Sv	IP	K	ERA	xERA	WHIP	OBA	vL	vR	BF/G	Ctl	Dom	Cmd	G	L	F	hr/9	hr/f	H%	S%	GS	APC	DOM%	DIS%	Sv%	LI	RAR	BPV	BPX	R$
08 TOR	20	11	0	246	206	2.78	3.11	1.05	237	243	230	29.0	1.4	7.5	5.3	54	19	27	0.7	9%	29%	76%	33	105	76%	0%	0	0.85	46.8	129	242	$36
09 TOR	17	10	0	239	208	2.79	3.15	1.13	256	240	278	30.1	1.3	7.8	5.9	50	20	29	0.8	11%	31%	79%	32	106	78%	6%			45.3	133	250	$32
10 PHI	21	10	0	251	219	2.44	2.94	1.04	245	259	231	30.1	1.1	7.9	7.3	51	19	30	0.9	11%	30%	81%	33	108	70%	3%			50.6	141	229	$37
11 PHI	19	6	0	234	220	2.35	2.89	1.04	239	273	206	29.2	1.3	8.5	6.3	51	19	31	0.4	5%	31%	78%	32	108	84%	3%			45.9	145	218	$35
12 PHI	11	8	0	156	132	4.49	3.65	1.22	261	273	246	25.8	2.1	7.6	3.7	45	23	32	1.0	12%	31%	65%	25	96	60%	12%			-9.2	104	135	$5
1st Half	4	5	0	72	56	3.98	3.62	1.15	252	237	277	26.8	1.7	7.0	4.0	47	22	31	0.7	9%	30%	66%	11	98	64%	9%			0.3	104	135	$6
2nd Half	7	3	0	84	76	4.93	3.68	1.29	269	315	228	25.1	2.4	8.1	3.5	42	24	33	1.3	15%	32%	65%	14	94	57%	14%			-9.4	103	134	$3
13 Proj	12	7	0	168	147	3.51	3.32	1.14	252	271	233	26.8	1.7	7.9	4.7	48	21	31	0.8	10%	31%	72%	25						10.5	122	159	$16

Hamels,Cole

Age: 29	Th: L	Role	SP	Health	A	LIMA Plan	C+
Ht: 6' 3"	Wt: 200	Type	Pwr	PT/Exp	A	Rand Var	0
				Consist	A	MM	4405

3 reasons why he's a true ace... 1) 4.0+ Cmd in back-to-back seasons; 2) Zero PQS-DIS starts; 3) 100+ BPV last five years. Threw over 110 pitches in only ten out of his 31 starts, and posted only one start with more than 120 pitches. If you want to spend $30 on a SP, this is the place. UP: Cy Young

Yr Tm	W	L	Sv	IP	K	ERA	xERA	WHIP	OBA	vL	vR	BF/G	Ctl	Dom	Cmd	G	L	F	hr/9	hr/f	H%	S%	GS	APC	DOM%	DIS%	Sv%	LI	RAR	BPV	BPX	R$
08 PHI	14	10	0	227	196	3.09	3.63	1.08	227	262	215	27.7	2.1	7.8	3.7	40	22	39	1.1	11%	27%	77%	33	104	70%	6%			34.7	101	190	$29
09 PHI	10	11	0	194	168	4.32	3.74	1.29	273	242	282	25.4	2.0	7.8	3.9	40	21	39	1.1	11%	32%	69%	32	97	53%	25%			0.0	105	196	$10
10 PHI	12	11	0	209	211	3.06	3.29	1.18	237	196	247	25.9	2.6	9.1	3.5	45	17	38	1.1	12%	30%	80%	33	102	61%	12%			26.2	116	187	$21
11 PHI	14	9	0	216	194	2.79	3.02	0.99	214	249	204	26.6	1.8	8.1	4.4	52	15	33	0.8	10%	27%	75%	31	98	77%	10%	0	0.76	30.7	126	189	$29
12 PHI	17	6	0	215	216	3.05	3.31	1.12	237	242	235	28.0	2.2	9.0	4.2	43	22	35	1.0	12%	30%	78%	31	107	77%	0%			25.6	125	163	$27
1st Half	10	4	0	111	111	3.08	3.32	1.10	232	232	231	27.8	2.3	9.0	4.0	43	21	36	1.0	12%	29%	76%	16	106	81%	0%			12.8	122	159	$32
2nd Half	7	2	0	104	105	3.02	3.31	1.15	242	252	239	28.2	2.1	9.1	4.4	43	22	35	1.0	12%	31%	79%	15	108	73%	0%			12.8	128	167	$21
13 Proj	18	7	0	218	210	2.88	3.30	1.11	236	243	233	26.5	2.1	8.7	4.1	46	19	35	1.0	11%	29%	79%	32						30.4	122	159	$29

Hammel,Jason

Age: 30	Th: R	Role	SP	Health	C	LIMA Plan	B
Ht: 6' 6"	Wt: 225	Type	Pwr	PT/Exp	A	Rand Var	0
				Consist	C	MM	3303

Newfound sinker, added velocity worked wonders, driving both Dom and GB north before knee injury derailed him in mid-season. First sub-4.00 ERA came w/full skill support, even if 26% H% vs. LH helped a bit. With good health... UP: 3.25 ERA, 200 K

Yr Tm	W	L	Sv	IP	K	ERA	xERA	WHIP	OBA	vL	vR	BF/G	Ctl	Dom	Cmd	G	L	F	hr/9	hr/f	H%	S%	GS	APC	DOM%	DIS%	Sv%	LI	RAR	BPV	BPX	R$
08 TAM	4	4	2	78	44	4.60	4.94	1.51	272	281	265	8.7	4.0	5.1	1.3	47	21	32	1.3	13%	29%	73%	5	33	40%	20%	100	0.67	-2.6	7	14	-$2
09 COL	10	8	0	177	133	4.33	3.92	1.39	290	289	290	22.7	2.1	6.8	3.2	46	23	31	0.9	10%	34%	70%	30	82	50%	23%	0	0.73	-0.2	88	165	$5
10 COL	10	9	0	178	141	4.81	3.81	1.40	287	282	291	25.7	2.4	7.1	3.0	47	20	33	0.9	10%	34%	67%	30	95	47%	20%			-16.1	89	144	$0
11 COL	7	13	1	170	94	4.76	4.67	1.43	270	268	271	23.1	3.6	5.0	1.4	44	21	35	1.1	11%	29%	69%	27	85	41%	26%	100	0.78	-17.1	14	22	-$5
12 BAL	8	6	0	118	113	3.43	3.51	1.24	234	203	266	24.7	3.2	8.6	2.7	53	19	28	0.7	10%	30%	74%	20	97	50%	15%			8.5	100	130	$7
1st Half	8	3	0	93	89	3.29	3.48	1.19	227	202	255	25.6	3.1	8.6	2.8	54	16	30	0.8	10%	29%	75%	15	101	60%	7%			8.3	103	134	$13
2nd Half	0	3	0	25	24	3.96	3.66	1.40	258	208	306	21.8	3.6	8.6	2.4	51	27	22	0.4	6%	34%	71%	5	83	20%	40%			0.2	87	113	-$14
13 Proj	10	10	0	174	150	3.74	3.87	1.37	263	240	284	21.0	3.3	7.7	2.4	49	22	29	0.8	10%	32%	74%	35						6.0	78	101	$7

Hanrahan,Joel

Age: 31	Th: R	Role	RP	Health	A	LIMA Plan	C+
Ht: 6' 4"	Wt: 250	Type	Pwr	PT/Exp	B	Rand Var	-5
				Consist	B	MM	3531

On surface, has settled in as an elite closer. Not so fast. The Dom he gained was more than offset by the Ctl he lost, especially in 2H. That '11 Ctl is the clear outlier now, as is his GB% from the same year. Without a GB tilt, his shaky control is playing with fire. You'll need a plan B if you draft him. DN: 20 SV

Yr Tm	W	L	Sv	IP	K	ERA	xERA	WHIP	OBA	vL	vR	BF/G	Ctl	Dom	Cmd	G	L	F	hr/9	hr/f	H%	S%	GS	APC	DOM%	DIS%	Sv%	LI	RAR	BPV	BPX	R$
08 WAS	6	3	9	84	93	3.95	3.82	1.36	233	228	237	5.3	4.5	9.9	2.2	43	22	36	1.0	11%	31%	74%	0	22			69	1.10	3.9	79	148	$7
09 2 NL	1	4	5	64	72	4.78	4.25	1.67	282	269	293	4.4	4.8	10.1	2.1	36	25	39	0.4	4%	39%	70%	0	18			50	0.96	-3.6	67	126	-$3
10 PIT	4	1	6	70	100	3.62	2.78	1.21	221	219	222	4.1	3.4	12.9	3.8	42	18	40	0.8	9%	35%	72%	0	16			60	0.84	4.0	162	262	$7
11 PIT	1	4	40	69	61	1.83	3.07	1.05	220	195	241	3.9	2.1	8.0	3.8	52	19	29	0.1	2%	29%	82%	0	15			91	1.27	17.8	117	176	$23
12 PIT	5	2	36	60	67	2.72	4.20	1.27	187	135	236	4.0	5.4	10.1	1.9	39	16	45	1.2	13%	24%	85%	0	16			90	1.17	9.6	52	68	$18
1st Half	3	0	20	30	35	2.10	3.77	1.07	164	150	182	3.9	4.5	10.5	2.3	36	13	51	1.2	12%	21%	89%	0	16			91	1.30	7.1	81	105	$25
2nd Half	2	2	16	30	32	3.34	4.69	1.48	209	114	273	4.2	6.4	9.7	1.5	41	19	40	1.2	13%	27%	83%	0	16			89	1.04	2.5	22	29	$12
13 Proj	4	3	33	73	80	3.48	3.70	1.25	216	175	248	3.9	4.3	10.0	2.3	43	18	39	0.8	9%	29%	75%	0						4.8	84	109	$17

Hanson,Tommy

Age: 26	Th: R	Role	SP	Health	C	LIMA Plan	C+
Ht: 6' 6"	Wt: 220	Type	Pwr	PT/Exp	A	Rand Var	+1
				Consist	B	MM	3403

Partially torn rotator cuff led to new delivery, which led to his worst MLB results. High 2H hit rate left his owners with an especially bad taste, which means profit potential heading into '13. Problem is, cranky shoulder will keep him a big health risk. ERA trend underscores downside. High-risk, high-reward.

Yr Tm	W	L	Sv	IP	K	ERA	xERA	WHIP	OBA	vL	vR	BF/G	Ctl	Dom	Cmd	G	L	F	hr/9	hr/f	H%	S%	GS	APC	DOM%	DIS%	Sv%	LI	RAR	BPV	BPX	R$
08 aa	8	4	0	98	100	3.55	3.17	1.22	222			22.0	3.8	9.2	2.4				0.9		28%	74%							9.4	91	171	$8
09 ATL *	14	7	0	194	194	2.52	2.67	1.11	216	256	192	23.8	3.0	9.0	3.0	40	18	42	0.7	7%	28%	81%	21	95	57%	10%			43.2	108	202	$29
10 ATL	10	11	0	203	173	3.33	3.73	1.17	239	226	251	24.9	2.5	7.7	3.1	42	17	42	0.6	6%	30%	73%	34	96	65%	12%			18.7	91	147	$16
11 ATL	11	7	0	130	142	3.60	3.38	1.17	219	244	198	24.5	3.2	9.8	3.1	39	20	40	1.2	13%	28%	74%	22	99	73%	14%			5.5	108	162	$11
12 ATL	13	10	0	175	161	4.48	4.25	1.45	271	295	245	24.5	3.7	8.3	2.3	40	21	39	1.4	14%	32%	74%	31	94	45%	16%			-10.1	69	89	-$1
1st Half	9	4	0	93	79	3.59	4.34	1.35	255	284	225	24.7	3.5	7.7	2.2	40	17	43	1.5	13%	29%	80%	16	97	50%	13%			4.8	62	81	$10
2nd Half	4	6	0	82	82	5.49	4.15	1.57	288	307	267	24.4	3.8	9.0	2.3	40	25	36	1.3	14%	35%	68%	15	91	40%	20%			-14.9	76	99	-$14
13 Proj	12	10	0	174	169	3.97	3.91	1.33	253	273	232	23.8	3.4	8.8	2.6	40	20	40	1.2	11%	31%	74%	30						1.1	85	110	$9

STEPHEN NICKRAND

Happ,J.A.

Age: 30	Th: L	Role SP	Health C	LIMA Plan C
Ht: 6' 6"	Wt: 195	Type Pwr FB	PT/Exp C	Rand Var +2
			Consist B	MM 2405

Three years of near-5.00 ERA, 1.40+ WHIP will keep the bidders away. But there's something interesting here. Concurrent Ctl, Dom improvement were kept hidden by H% jump. PQS-DOM%, xERA confirm that he's got skills worth speculating on. A $1 bid could yield $10 profit. UP: 3.75 ERA, 200 K

Yr Tm	W	L	Sv	IP	K	ERA	xERA	WHIP	OBA	vL	vR	BF/G	Ctl	Dom	Cmd	G	L	F	hr/9	hr/f	H%	S%	GS	APC	DOM%	DIS%	Sv%	LI	RAR	BPV	BPX	R$
08 PHI *	9	7	0	167	147	4.79	4.82	1.46	273	209	247	22.3	3.6	7.9	2.2	31	27	43	1.2	8%	32%	70%	4	68	75%	25%	0	0.64	-9.6	57	108	$1
09 PHI	12	4	0	166	119	2.93	4.30	1.23	244	216	253	19.6	3.0	6.5	2.1	38	19	43	1.1	10%	27%	82%	23	76	43%	17%	0	0.71	28.5	50	94	$17
10 2 NL *	7	5	0	122	94	4.68	5.12	1.61	273	179	244	22.5	5.0	6.9	1.4	39	18	43	1.1	7%	31%	74%	16	99	56%	19%			-9.0	37	60	-$5
11 HOU *	7	15	0	174	146	4.99	4.58	1.51	257	270	264	24.3	4.8	7.5	1.6	33	23	44	1.1	10%	30%	69%	28	106	29%	21%			-22.4	49	74	-$8
12 2 TM	10	11	0	145	144	4.79	3.97	1.40	264	259	267	22.4	3.5	9.0	2.6	44	17	39	1.2	12%	33%	68%	24	91	54%	17%	0	0.73	-13.8	89	116	-$2
1st Half	6	8	0	92	90	4.81	4.05	1.48	277	257	284	25.3	3.6	8.8	2.4	46	16	37	1.4	14%	34%	71%	16	103	63%	19%			-9.0	85	111	-$1
2nd Half	4	3	0	53	54	4.75	3.85	1.26	242	261	237	18.6	3.2	9.2	2.8	40	18	42	0.8	8%	31%	63%	8	74	38%	13%	0	0.68	-4.8	96	125	-$4
13 Proj	11	12	0	189	171	4.34	4.16	1.34	252	244	255	21.1	3.5	8.2	2.3	39	19	42	1.1	10%	30%	70%	37						-7.6	69	90	$6

Harang,Aaron

Age: 35	Th: R	Role SP	Health D	LIMA Plan C+
Ht: 6' 7"	Wt: 260	Type Pwr FB	PT/Exp A	Rand Var -2
			Consist B	MM 1203

Seems to really, really like the NL West, but he's playing with fire now. Cmd eroding for three years, low PQS-DOM%. These mid-3.00s ERAs were the result of low hr/f and slightly elevated S%. Gradual Ctl erosion gives him a razor thin margin for error. Use a 4.00 ERA as an optimistic baseline. DN: 5.00 ERA

Yr Tm	W	L	Sv	IP	K	ERA	xERA	WHIP	OBA	vL	vR	BF/G	Ctl	Dom	Cmd	G	L	F	hr/9	hr/f	H%	S%	GS	APC	DOM%	DIS%	Sv%	LI	RAR	BPV	BPX	R$
08 CIN	6	17	0	184	153	4.78	4.22	1.38	284	298	274	26.4	2.4	7.5	3.1	34	22	44	1.7	14%	32%	71%	29	102	55%	24%	0	0.83	-10.5	81	151	$2
09 CIN	6	14	0	162	142	4.21	4.04	1.41	287	285	289	27.0	2.4	7.9	3.3	35	24	41	1.3	12%	34%	75%	26	103	58%	19%			2.2	90	169	$3
10 CIN	6	7	0	112	82	5.32	4.57	1.59	305	283	323	22.9	3.1	6.6	2.2	37	22	41	1.3	10%	35%	69%	20	94	40%	45%	0	0.70	-17.1	51	83	-$7
11 SD	14	7	0	171	124	3.64	4.19	1.37	269	277	261	25.7	3.1	6.5	2.1	41	18	41	1.1	9%	30%	77%	28	98	46%	18%			6.4	54	81	$7
12 LA	10	10	0	180	131	3.61	4.94	1.40	246	260	233	25.4	4.3	6.6	1.5	39	20	41	0.7	6%	29%	76%	31	100	32%	23%			9.0	20	26	$4
1st Half	5	5	0	93	73	3.68	4.78	1.48	265	269	260	26.0	4.2	7.1	1.7	40	23	38	0.7	7%	32%	76%	16	102	31%	25%			3.9	32	42	$3
2nd Half	5	5	0	87	58	3.53	5.11	1.32	226	250	204	24.7	4.4	6.0	1.4	37	18	45	0.7	6%	26%	75%	15	98	33%	20%			5.2	6	8	$5
13 Proj	10	10	0	174	128	4.06	4.67	1.41	264	270	258	24.4	3.6	6.6	1.8	38	20	42	1.1	9%	30%	74%	30						-0.8	38	49	$4

Haren,Dan

Age: 32	Th: R	Role SP	Health A	LIMA Plan A+
Ht: 6' 5"	Wt: 215	Type	PT/Exp A	Rand Var +1
			Consist A	MM 3305

Huge ERA spike due in part to nagging back problem. While skills foundation remained strong, real culprit was velocity. Former 92-mph fastball plummeted to just 88 mph, putting elite Cmd at risk. With health, LIMA grade highlights the potential profit, but only if you view him as a $10-15 pitcher now.

Yr Tm	W	L	Sv	IP	K	ERA	xERA	WHIP	OBA	vL	vR	BF/G	Ctl	Dom	Cmd	G	L	F	hr/9	hr/f	H%	S%	GS	APC	DOM%	DIS%	Sv%	LI	RAR	BPV	BPX	R$
08 ARI	16	8	0	216	206	3.33	3.27	1.13	247	241	253	26.7	1.7	8.6	5.2	44	21	35	0.8	9%	31%	73%	33	101	82%	9%			26.4	132	247	$26
09 ARI	14	10	0	229	223	3.14	3.14	1.00	224	229	219	27.5	1.5	8.8	5.9	43	20	37	1.1	12%	28%	74%	33	105	79%	0%			33.4	138	259	$33
10 2 TM	12	12	0	235	216	3.91	3.63	1.27	267	258	274	28.4	2.1	8.3	4.0	40	19	41	1.2	11%	32%	74%	35	107	60%	6%			5.0	111	180	$13
11 LAA	16	10	0	238	192	3.17	3.36	1.02	235	226	248	27.2	1.2	7.3	5.8	43	20	38	0.8	8%	28%	71%	34	108	71%	9%	0	0.82	22.6	118	177	$27
12 LAA	12	13	0	177	142	4.33	4.03	1.29	275	234	320	24.9	1.9	7.2	3.7	40	21	40	1.4	13%	31%	72%	30	95	53%	17%			-6.9	96	125	$4
1st Half	6	7	0	99	85	4.53	4.03	1.37	289	241	340	26.7	2.1	7.7	3.7	40	21	40	1.4	12%	33%	71%	16	101	56%	13%			-6.3	100	130	$3
2nd Half	6	6	0	77	57	4.07	4.04	1.19	257	225	293	22.9	1.7	6.6	3.8	40	21	39	1.5	14%	28%	72%	14	88	50%	21%			-0.5	90	117	$5
13 Proj	13	11	0	189	151	3.88	3.79	1.19	260	236	287	25.0	1.8	7.2	4.0	41	20	39	1.2	11%	30%	72%	30						3.2	100	129	$13

Harrell,Lucas

Age: 28	Th: R	Role SP	Health A	LIMA Plan C
Ht: 6' 2"	Wt: 210	Type xGB	PT/Exp B	Rand Var 0
			Consist C	MM 2205

At first glance, a league average pitcher. A closer look shows he's electric with the bases empty (8.8 Dom, 2.7 Ctl, 59% GB) but horrible with runners on (3.4 Dom, 4.9 Ctl, 55% GB). Dom + GB growth give him skills foundation to take step forward if he can solve this bugaboo. UP: 3.50 ERA, 1.25 WHIP

Yr Tm	W	L	Sv	IP	K	ERA	xERA	WHIP	OBA	vL	vR	BF/G	Ctl	Dom	Cmd	G	L	F	hr/9	hr/f	H%	S%	GS	APC	DOM%	DIS%	Sv%	LI	RAR	BPV	BPX	R$
08 aa	3	3	0	55	29	4.83	5.42	1.66	311			22.2	3.5	4.7	1.4				0.7		34%	71%							-3.4	29	54	-$4
09 a/a	12	4	0	146	79	4.58	5.17	1.70	293			26.4	4.8	4.8	1.0				0.6		33%	73%							-4.7	28	52	-$4
10 CHW *	11	10	0	162	85	5.65	5.94	1.79	309	396	271	21.9	4.8	4.7	1.0	51	28	22	0.9	11%	34%	69%	3	60	0%	33%	0	0.43	-31.3	15	24	-$15
11 2 TM *	12	7	0	145	91	3.13	3.84	1.42	266	421	268	19.8	3.6	5.7	1.6	55	15	30	0.4	0%	31%	78%	2	40	50%	50%	0	0.71	14.6	57	86	$6
12 HOU	11	11	0	194	140	3.76	4.04	1.36	253	248	258	25.8	3.6	6.5	1.8	57	20	22	0.6	10%	30%	73%	32	100	41%	13%			6.0	54	71	$5
1st Half	7	6	0	98	56	4.33	4.35	1.33	255	242	265	26.2	3.2	5.2	1.6	56	20	24	0.7	11%	28%	68%	16	97	31%	19%			-3.8	40	52	$4
2nd Half	4	5	0	96	84	3.19	3.73	1.39	251	253	250	25.5	4.0	7.9	2.0	58	21	21	0.5	9%	31%	77%	16	102	50%	6%			9.8	69	90	$7
13 Proj	11	13	0	203	135	3.91	4.14	1.40	260	256	264	22.6	3.7	6.0	1.6	58	20	22	0.7	11%	30%	73%	38						2.7	45	58	$5

Harrison,Matt

Age: 27	Th: L	Role SP	Health C	LIMA Plan D
Ht: 6' 4"	Wt: 240	Type	PT/Exp A	Rand Var -1
			Consist B	MM 2105

Third year of ERA improvement, wins spike will get him drafted as a rotation anchor in some leagues. The prudent move is not to follow suit. While GB tilt, 2.0+ Cmd give him less risk than most, marginal Dom puts fate in the hands of defense. xERA confirms he's a 4.00 ERA pitcher. Use that as your guide.

Yr Tm	W	L	Sv	IP	K	ERA	xERA	WHIP	OBA	vL	vR	BF/G	Ctl	Dom	Cmd	G	L	F	hr/9	hr/f	H%	S%	GS	APC	DOM%	DIS%	Sv%	LI	RAR	BPV	BPX	R$
08 TEX *	15	6	0	168	89	4.74	5.22	1.55	298	310	297	24.4	3.2	4.8	1.5	40	24	36	1.0	11%	32%	71%	15	91	20%	40%			-8.7	26	48	$0
09 TEX	4	5	0	63	34	6.11	4.81	1.64	316	210	351	25.7	3.3	4.8	1.5	47	23	31	1.3	13%	33%	64%	11	97	27%	45%			-14.0	24	44	-$7
10 TEX	3	2	2	78	46	4.71	5.00	1.52	262	235	273	9.6	4.5	5.3	1.2	47	21	32	1.1	12%	29%	72%	6	38	33%	17%	67	0.89	-6.1	-1	-1	-$3
11 TEX	14	9	0	186	126	3.39	3.93	1.28	257	275	249	24.9	2.8	6.1	2.2	47	20	32	0.6	7%	30%	75%	30	97	43%	13%	0	0.75	12.6	60	91	$11
12 TEX	18	11	0	213	133	3.29	4.15	1.26	258	209	276	27.4	2.5	5.6	2.3	49	20	31	0.9	11%	29%	77%	32	101	50%	13%			19.1	61	79	$16
1st Half	11	3	0	105	65	3.16	3.96	1.24	263	173	294	26.9	2.1	5.6	2.6	52	19	29	0.6	7%	30%	76%	16	101	50%	13%			11.1	72	94	$22
2nd Half	7	8	0	108	68	3.42	4.34	1.28	254	243	257	27.9	2.8	5.7	2.0	46	21	33	1.3	13%	27%	79%	16	102	50%	13%			8.0	49	64	$10
13 Proj	15	10	0	210	131	3.75	4.38	1.34	264	239	273	20.3	3.0	5.6	1.9	47	21	32	0.9	10%	29%	75%	43						6.8	46	60	$10

Harvey,Matt

Age: 24	Th: R	Role SP	Health A	LIMA Plan B
Ht: 6' 4"	Wt: 225	Type Pwr FB	PT/Exp D	Rand Var 0
			Consist A	MM 3403

3-5, 2.73 ERA in 59 IP at NYM. High-ceiling SP prospect looked the part in debut—dominant in 7 of 10 MLB starts. 95-mph fastball & four-pitch mix enticing, as is 4.5 Cmd vs. LHB. But oddly, struggled vs. RHB (5.4 Ctl, 1.6 Cmd). Keeper gem, but just enough command issues to keep expecations humble.

Yr Tm	W	L	Sv	IP	K	ERA	xERA	WHIP	OBA	vL	vR	BF/G	Ctl	Dom	Cmd	G	L	F	hr/9	hr/f	H%	S%	GS	APC	DOM%	DIS%	Sv%	LI	RAR	BPV	BPX	R$
08																																
09																																
10																																
11 aa	5	3	0	60	54	4.33	3.57	1.32	260			20.6	2.9	8.1	2.7				0.5		33%	66%							-2.9	94	141	-$1
12 NYM *	10	10	0	169	162	3.39	3.28	1.26	233	212	185	23.0	3.7	8.6	2.3	38	24	37	0.7	10%	29%	75%	10	98	70%	0%			13.0	88	115	$11
1st Half	7	3	0	92	79	3.47	3.57	1.34	252	0	0	22.6	3.5	7.7	2.2				0.5	0%	31%	75%	0	0					6.2	80	104	$12
2nd Half	3	7	0	77	83	3.29	2.89	1.17	207	212	185	23.6	3.9	9.7	2.5	38	24	37	0.9	10%	27%	75%	10	98	70%	0%			6.9	97	126	$10
13 Proj	11	10	0	160	152	3.94	3.94	1.27	240	255	222	22.1	3.4	8.6	2.5	40	23	37	0.9	9%	30%	71%	30						1.5	80	103	$9

Hawkins,LaTroy

Age: 40	Th: R	Role RP	Health F	LIMA Plan D
Ht: 6' 5"	Wt: 220	Type Con xGB	PT/Exp D	Rand Var 0
			Consist A	MM 2000

Fractured finger cost him a month, but it's not like it really mattered anyway. Hasn't topped 50 IP for three seasons. Credit him for extending career by becoming GB pitcher. But age, lack of health, Dom slide outside of tiny sample size '11 blip all confirm his days of providing value are over.

Yr Tm	W	L	Sv	IP	K	ERA	xERA	WHIP	OBA	vL	vR	BF/G	Ctl	Dom	Cmd	G	L	F	hr/9	hr/f	H%	S%	GS	APC	DOM%	DIS%	Sv%	LI	RAR	BPV	BPX	R$
08 2 TM	3	1	1	62	48	3.92	4.01	1.21	235	293	189	4.4	3.2	7.0	2.2	46	18	37	0.4	5%	28%	67%	0	17			50	0.60	3.1	63	119	$2
09 HOU	1	4	11	63	45	2.13	3.81	1.20	253	203	303	4.0	2.3	6.4	2.8	45	24	31	1.0	12%	28%	88%	0	16			73	1.08	17.1	77	144	$9
10 MIL	0	3	0	16	18	8.44	3.48	1.69	323	269	359	4.1	3.4	10.1	3.0	47	21	32	1.1	13%	41%	48%	0	18			0	0.84	-8.6	116	188	-$5
11 MIL	3	1	0	48	28	2.42	3.60	1.24	260	207	300	3.9	1.9	5.2	2.8	62	16	22	0.2	3%	31%	80%	0	14			0	0.81	9.1	84	126	$2
12 LAA	2	3	1	42	23	3.64	4.30	1.38	280	214	351	3.7	2.8	4.9	1.8	57	17	26	1.1	14%	30%	77%	0	15			25	0.80	1.9	49	63	-$3
1st Half	1	1	1	15	7	1.17	4.41	1.37	263	156	400	3.6	3.5	4.1	1.2	60	22	18	0.0	0%	29%	90%	0	14			100	0.96	5.4	17	22	-$1
2nd Half	1	2	0	27	16	5.06	4.25	1.39	289	250	327	3.8	2.4	5.4	2.3	55	15	30	1.7	19%	29%	69%	0	15			0	0.70	-3.4	66	86	-$4
13 Proj	1	2	0	29	15	4.00	4.33	1.34	266	216	313	3.8	2.8	4.8	1.7	55	18	27	0.7	9%	29%	71%	0						0.1	42	55	-$2

STEPHEN NICKRAND

Hefner,Jeremy

Age: 27	Th: R	Role SP	Health	A
Ht: 6' 4"	Wt: 215	Type Con	PT/Exp	D
			Consist	A

LIMA Plan	D+
Rand Var	0
MM	1100

4-7, 5.09 ERA in 94 IP at NYM. Rough MLB debut will keep most bidders away, and MLE skill history doesn't inspire much hope. Low Dom hurler needs pinpoint control to survive. That's not something he showed prior to '12. A $1 bid in deep leagues could yield a few bucks profit but keep expectations low.

Yr	Tm	W	L	Sv	IP	K	ERA	xERA	WHIP	OBA	vL	vR	BF/G	Ctl	Dom	Cmd	G	L	F	hr/9	hr/f	H%	S%	GS	APC	DOM%	DIS%	Sv%	LI	RAR	BPV	BPX	R$
08																																	
09																																	
10	aa	11	8	0	168	100	3.37	3.96	1.37	272			25.1	2.9	5.4	1.9				0.5		31%	76%							14.8	56	90	$7
11	aaa	9	7	0	157	102	3.95	4.36	1.42	277			23.8	3.1	5.9	1.9				0.8		31%	74%							-0.1	51	77	$1
12	NYM *	9	9	0	155	91	4.26	4.08	1.28	282	302	272	17.7	1.6	5.2	3.3	44	20	37	0.7	8%	31%	67%	13	58	54%	23%	0	0.62	-4.8	77	100	$1
1st Half		4	5	0	74	36	3.78	3.39	1.14	263	300	263	18.4	1.2	4.4	3.8	46	21	33	0.7	6%	28%	68%	3	49	33%	33%	0	0.50	2.2	86	112	$5
2nd Half		5	4	0	81	54	4.71	4.67	1.42	299	302	276	17.2	2.0	6.0	3.0	43	19	38	0.8	8%	34%	67%	10	63	60%	20%	0	0.69	-7.0	72	94	-$2
13	Proj	**3**	**3**	**0**	**51**	**31**	**4.04**	**4.41**	**1.36**	**280**	**295**	**265**	**20.4**	**2.4**	**5.5**	**2.3**	**44**	**20**	**36**	**0.7**	**7%**	**32%**	**71%**	**10**						**-0.1**	**58**	**75**	**-$1**

Hellickson,Jeremy

Age: 26	Th: R	Role SP	Health	A
Ht: 6' 1"	Wt: 190	Type FB	PT/Exp	A
			Consist	B

LIMA Plan	C
Rand Var	-4
MM	2205

Former top prospect's xERA continues to suggest he's no 3.00 ERA pitcher. In truth, his Cmd reappears at home (7.3 Dom, 2.8 Ctl). Consistency is the next step. Lack of LH/RH splits, Ctl, Dom, GB gains from MLB debut keep him a growth stock even though he'll still likely be overvalued in '13.

Yr	Tm	W	L	Sv	IP	K	ERA	xERA	WHIP	OBA	vL	vR	BF/G	Ctl	Dom	Cmd	G	L	F	hr/9	hr/f	H%	S%	GS	APC	DOM%	DIS%	Sv%	LI	RAR	BPV	BPX	R$
08	aa	4	4	0	75	70	4.43	5.72	1.42	302			24.6	1.8	8.3	4.7				1.8		35%	76%							-1.0	89	166	$0
09	a/a	9	2	0	114	115	3.05	2.22	0.99	206			21.7	2.3	9.1	4.0				0.7		27%	71%							17.9	131	244	$16
10	TAM *	16	3	0	154	139	2.90	3.30	1.22	252	301	154	20.1	2.5	8.1	3.3	37	13	50	0.6	10%	32%	78%	4	59	100%	0%	0	0.86	22.4	105	170	$16
11	TAM	13	10	0	189	117	2.95	4.54	1.15	210	230	188	26.7	3.4	5.6	1.6	35	20	45	1.0	8%	23%	79%	29	102	45%	7%			23.1	21	31	$17
12	TAM	10	11	0	177	124	3.10	4.37	1.25	244	241	247	23.9	3.0	6.3	2.1	42	21	37	1.3	12%	27%	82%	31	97	42%	23%			19.9	52	68	$12
1st Half		4	4	0	81	53	3.44	4.85	1.36	254	241	270	24.9	3.4	5.9	1.7	39	19	42	1.6	13%	27%	82%	14	98	36%	36%			5.7	30	39	$5
2nd Half		6	7	0	96	71	2.81	3.97	1.17	235	240	227	23.1	2.6	6.7	2.5	44	22	33	1.0	12%	27%	81%	17	95	47%	12%			14.3	71	92	$18
13	Proj	**12**	**9**	**0**	**181**	**134**	**3.58**	**4.26**	**1.21**	**240**	**257**	**220**	**23.2**	**2.9**	**6.7**	**2.3**	**39**	**20**	**41**	**1.1**	**10%**	**27%**	**75%**	**31**						**9.8**	**58**	**76**	**$13**

Hendriks,Liam

Age: 24	Th: R	Role SP	Health	A
Ht: 6' 1"	Wt: 205	Type Con	PT/Exp	D
			Consist	B

LIMA Plan	B+
Rand Var	+1
MM	2103

1-8, 5.59 ERA in 85 IP at MIN. MLE stats hid miserable end to season with MIN. Inflated 36% H% vs. RH bats gives hope for regression, and he still owns that command artist profile from '11. But there's just not a lot of upside here. If you're a gambler, consider him a LIMA end-gamer in very deep leagues.

Yr	Tm	W	L	Sv	IP	K	ERA	xERA	WHIP	OBA	vL	vR	BF/G	Ctl	Dom	Cmd	G	L	F	hr/9	hr/f	H%	S%	GS	APC	DOM%	DIS%	Sv%	LI	RAR	BPV	BPX	R$
08																																	
09																																	
10																																	
11	MIN *	12	8	0	163	111	3.98	3.57	1.25	278	333	282	22.8	1.4	6.1	4.3	46	24	29	0.4	13%	33%	67%	4	94	0%	0%			-0.7	114	171	$7
12	MIN *	10	11	0	192	119	4.01	4.16	1.30	265	257	357	24.7	2.6	5.6	2.2	41	24	35	1.0	17%	29%	72%	16	91	19%	44%			0.1	50	65	$4
1st Half		5	5	0	81	57	4.29	4.59	1.29	272	224	422	23.7	2.2	6.4	2.9	40	27	33	1.4	24%	30%	72%	7	87	29%	43%			-2.7	57	74	$3
2nd Half		5	6	0	111	62	3.81	3.80	1.31	260	273	282	25.5	2.9	5.0	1.7	42	22	36	0.7	11%	29%	72%	9	95	11%	44%			2.9	47	61	$5
13	Proj	**8**	**9**	**0**	**149**	**96**	**4.23**	**4.22**	**1.28**	**270**	**228**	**316**	**23.9**	**2.1**	**5.8**	**2.7**	**41**	**24**	**35**	**1.0**	**9%**	**30%**	**69%**	**26**						**-3.9**	**66**	**86**	**$4**

Hensley,Clay

Age: 33	Th: R	Role RP	Health	D
Ht: 5' 11"	Wt: 190	Type Pwr	PT/Exp	C
			Consist	B

LIMA Plan	D
Rand Var	0
MM	1300

Lucked into a few save opps due to lack of alternatives, but with these skills, don't expect it to happen again. Skill spike from '10 is a clear outlier now. Velocity has dropped from 89 mph that season to 86 mph in '12. Soft-tossing relievers have short MLB shelf lives.

Yr	Tm	W	L	Sv	IP	K	ERA	xERA	WHIP	OBA	vL	vR	BF/G	Ctl	Dom	Cmd	G	L	F	hr/9	hr/f	H%	S%	GS	APC	DOM%	DIS%	Sv%	LI	RAR	BPV	BPX	R$
08	SD *	2	3	0	87	53	4.73	4.51	1.50	267	288	221	7.8	4.3	5.4	1.3	51	18	31	0.9	5%	30%	69%	1	19	0%	100%	0	0.58	-4.3	35	66	-$4
09	aaa	9	4	0	124	68	4.85	5.46	1.68	306			22.3	3.9	4.9	1.2				0.8		34%	72%							-8.1	26	48	-$5
10	FLA	3	4	7	75	77	2.16	3.20	1.11	200	216	184	4.5	3.5	9.2	2.7	53	15	32	0.4	5%	27%	81%	0	17			70	1.12	17.8	103	167	$11
11	FLA	6	7	0	68	46	5.19	4.57	1.36	238	171	305	8.0	4.0	6.1	1.5	46	15	39	1.2	11%	27%	64%	9	30	11%	33%	0	1.23	-10.4	26	40	-$3
12	SF	4	5	3	51	42	4.62	4.89	1.58	258	241	270	3.9	5.3	7.5	1.4	51	14	36	0.9	9%	31%	72%	0	15			75	1.17	-3.8	19	25	-$4
1st Half		3	3	2	29	25	3.41	4.72	1.52	232	132	286	4.0	5.9	7.8	1.3	57	11	32	0.3	4%	30%	77%	0	16			67	1.56	2.2	15	20	$0
2nd Half		1	2	1	22	17	6.23	5.09	1.66	291	333	244	3.8	4.6	7.1	1.5	44	17	39	1.7	14%	32%	66%	0	14			100	0.71	-5.9	25	33	-$9
13	Proj	**3**	**4**	**0**	**44**	**34**	**4.65**	**4.56**	**1.47**	**256**	**245**	**265**	**4.7**	**4.5**	**7.1**	**1.6**	**49**	**15**	**36**	**1.0**	**10%**	**30%**	**70%**	**0**						**-3.4**	**34**	**44**	**-$3**

Hernandez,David

Age: 28	Th: R	Role RP	Health	A
Ht: 6' 3"	Wt: 230	Type Pwr xFB	PT/Exp	C
			Consist	B

LIMA Plan	A
Rand Var	-2
MM	4510

Blossoming closer just biding time until opportunity comes. Concurrent Dom, Ctl improvement crested in 2H with filthy Cmd, suggesting he hasn't reached ceiling yet. Previous struggles vs. RHBs seem like distant memories now. If you're looking for an elite closer-in-waiting, start here. UP: 2.00 ERA, 40 SV

Yr	Tm	W	L	Sv	IP	K	ERA	xERA	WHIP	OBA	vL	vR	BF/G	Ctl	Dom	Cmd	G	L	F	hr/9	hr/f	H%	S%	GS	APC	DOM%	DIS%	Sv%	LI	RAR	BPV	BPX	R$
08	aa	10	4	0	141	135	3.46	4.12	1.46	251			22.3	4.6	8.6	1.9				0.8		31%	79%							15.1	71	133	$8
09	BAL *	7	12	0	163	134	5.21	5.57	1.49	276	280	297	21.9	3.7	7.4	2.0	29	18	53	1.9	15%	30%	71%	19	96	26%	42%	0	0.75	-17.8	29	54	-$3
10	BAL	8	8	2	79	72	4.31	4.69	1.44	242	198	271	8.5	4.8	8.2	1.7	28	21	51	1.0	8%	29%	72%	8	35	13%	25%	33	1.13	-2.3	24	39	$2
11	ARI	5	3	11	69	77	3.38	3.68	1.14	193	171	212	3.9	3.9	10.0	2.6	31	23	46	0.5	5%	28%	71%	0	16			79	1.17	4.9	84	126	$9
12	ARI	2	3	4	68	98	2.50	2.92	1.02	190	240	145	3.9	2.9	12.9	4.5	31	22	46	0.5	6%	32%	77%	0	15			40	1.04	12.7	163	213	$10
1st Half		1	1	2	33	50	2.73	3.03	1.09	183	278	106	3.9	3.8	13.6	3.6	30	21	49	0.5	6%	32%	76%	0	15			33	1.01	5.2	150	195	$8
2nd Half		1	2	2	35	48	2.29	2.83	0.96	197	209	185	3.8	2.0	12.2	6.0	33	23	45	0.5	5%	32%	78%	0	15			50	1.06	7.5	176	229	$11
13	Proj	**3**	**3**	**8**	**58**	**70**	**3.16**	**3.46**	**1.15**	**214**	**224**	**205**	**4.5**	**3.5**	**10.9**	**3.1**	**31**	**22**	**47**	**0.7**	**7%**	**30%**	**75%**	**0**						**6.2**	**111**	**145**	**$7**

Hernandez,Felix

Age: 27	Th: R	Role SP	Health	A
Ht: 6' 3"	Wt: 230	Type Pwr GB	PT/Exp	A
			Consist	A

LIMA Plan	C+
Rand Var	0
MM	4405

Still rock solid...and with some added Cmd to boot. While he's as close to a 3.00 ERA lock as they come, there is a warning sign looming. Fastball velocity has decreased in five straight seasons, going from 96 mph in '07 to 92 mph in '12. Given workload at young age, it's a tidbit worth tucking away.

Yr	Tm	W	L	Sv	IP	K	ERA	xERA	WHIP	OBA	vL	vR	BF/G	Ctl	Dom	Cmd	G	L	F	hr/9	hr/f	H%	S%	GS	APC	DOM%	DIS%	Sv%	LI	RAR	BPV	BPX	R$
08	SEA	9	11	0	201	175	3.45	3.81	1.39	261	275	242	27.6	3.6	7.8	2.2	52	18	29	0.8	10%	32%	77%	31	103	58%	13%			21.5	74	140	$12
09	SEA	19	5	0	239	217	2.49	3.35	1.14	227	228	226	28.7	2.7	8.2	3.1	53	17	30	0.6	8%	29%	80%	34	107	74%	9%			54.0	106	198	$36
10	SEA	13	12	0	250	232	2.27	3.11	1.06	212	213	212	29.4	2.5	8.4	3.3	54	16	30	0.6	8%	27%	81%	34	110	76%	6%			55.7	114	185	$35
11	SEA	14	14	0	234	222	3.47	3.22	1.22	248	252	243	29.2	2.6	8.6	3.3	50	19	31	0.7	10%	31%	73%	33	109	70%	6%			13.7	112	169	$17
12	SEA	13	9	0	232	223	3.06	3.21	1.14	241	248	231	28.5	2.2	8.7	4.0	49	22	29	0.5	8%	31%	74%	33	104	70%	9%			27.2	124	162	$25
1st Half		6	5	0	111	114	3.09	3.31	1.22	248	251	242	28.6	2.6	9.3	3.6	45	23	31	0.7	10%	32%	77%	16	104	69%	6%			12.6	120	156	$23
2nd Half		7	4	0	121	109	3.04	3.11	1.07	235	245	223	28.4	1.8	8.1	4.5	52	22	26	0.4	6%	30%	71%	17	103	71%	12%			14.6	128	167	$28
13	Proj	**13**	**10**	**0**	**232**	**218**	**3.23**	**3.27**	**1.15**	**240**	**246**	**232**	**28.1**	**2.4**	**8.5**	**3.5**	**51**	**20**	**29**	**0.6**	**8%**	**30%**	**73%**	**33**						**22.6**	**117**	**151**	**$24**

Hernandez,Livan

Age: 38	Th: R	Role RP	Health	A
Ht: 6' 2"	Wt: 245	Type Con	PT/Exp	A
			Consist	A

LIMA Plan	D+
Rand Var	+5
MM	1101

Junkballer posted best skills since '03. Figures his ERA and WHIP would tank when his skills were actually good. Even though hr/f and S% conspired against him and Cmd is on multi-year upswing, there's no upside investing in a 40-something with an 84 mph fastball.

Yr	Tm	W	L	Sv	IP	K	ERA	xERA	WHIP	OBA	vL	vR	BF/G	Ctl	Dom	Cmd	G	L	F	hr/9	hr/f	H%	S%	GS	APC	DOM%	DIS%	Sv%	LI	RAR	BPV	BPX	R$
08	2 TM	13	11	0	180	67	6.05	5.12	1.67	342	340	344	26.2	2.2	3.4	1.6	44	22	34	1.3	11%	34%	65%	31	90	29%	32%			-38.3	24	45	-$13
09	2 NL	9	12	0	184	102	5.44	4.92	1.56	308	287	330	26.0	3.3	5.0	1.5	41	22	37	0.9	8%	33%	66%	31	96	32%	26%			-25.3	20	38	-$8
10	WAS	10	12	0	212	114	3.66	4.60	1.32	270	295	248	27.2	2.7	4.8	1.8	39	21	40	0.7	6%	29%	73%	33	98	30%	9%			11.0	31	50	$8
11	WAS	8	13	0	175	99	4.47	4.34	1.40	291	297	286	25.9	2.4	5.1	2.2	42	22	36	0.8	8%	32%	69%	29	93	45%	28%			-11.3	48	72	-$3
12	2 NL	4	1	1	67	48	6.42	4.36	1.49	317	323	311	6.6	2.1	6.4	3.0	40	22	39	2.0	18%	33%	61%	0	25			50	0.64	-19.9	76	99	-$10
1st Half		1	1	1	33	23	5.13	4.51	1.53	328	333	324	7.0	2.2	6.2	2.9	39	22	39	1.6	14%	34%	71%	0	25			100	0.73	-4.6	70	91	-$9
2nd Half		3	0	0	34	25	7.68	4.22	1.44	306	315	295	6.3	2.1	6.6	3.1	41	21	38	2.4	22%	31%	50%	0	25			0	0.55	-15.3	81	105	-$10
13	Proj	**3**	**4**	**0**	**73**	**45**	**5.57**	**4.55**	**1.45**	**296**	**304**	**289**	**6.5**	**2.3**	**5.6**	**2.4**	**41**	**21**	**38**	**1.5**	**13%**	**32%**	**64%**	**0**						**-13.9**	**57**	**74**	**-$6**

STEPHEN NICKRAND

Hernandez,Roberto

Age: 29	Th: R	Role SP	Health	A	LIMA Plan D
Ht: 6' 4"	Wt : 230	Type xGB	PT/Exp	B	Rand Var +5
			Consist	B	MM 1101

Identity fraud is a red herring for former Fausto Carmona's real issue: his skills are M.I.A. Has never been able to crack a 2.0 Cmd, and without it, odds of another sub-4.00 ERA are remote. Given hard-to-repeat mechanics, he should be tried in the bullpen to see if he can assume identity of his namesake.

Yr	Tm	W	L	Sv	IP	K	ERA	xERA	WHIP	OBA	vL	vR	BF/G	Ctl	Dom	Cmd	G	L	F	hr/9	hr/f	H%	S%	GS	APC	DOM%	DIS%	Sv%	LI	RAR	BPV	BPX	R$
08	CLE	8	7	0	121	58	5.44	5.03	1.62	271	303	230	25.0	5.2	4.3	0.8	63	15	22	0.5	8%	30%	65%	22	92	18%	32%			-16.7	-22	-41	-$7
09	CLE *	7	15	0	165	105	5.80	5.64	1.65	296	331	245	24.6	4.2	5.7	1.4	55	18	27	1.2	14%	32%	66%	24	94	17%	25%			-30.2	22	41	-$12
10	CLE	13	14	0	210	124	3.77	4.09	1.31	258	269	244	26.7	3.1	5.3	1.7	56	14	31	0.7	8%	28%	72%	33	100	39%	15%			8.1	46	75	$9
11	CLE	7	15	0	189	109	5.25	4.14	1.40	276	296	252	26.0	2.9	5.2	1.8	55	19	27	1.0	13%	30%	64%	32	94	34%	22%			-30.4	49	74	-$9
12	CLE	0	3	0	14	2	7.53	5.30	1.40	304	364	217	20.7	1.9	1.3	0.7	51	18	31	2.5	24%	25%	50%	3	77	0%	67%			-6.2	1	1	-$7
1st Half																																	
2nd Half		0	3	0	14	2	7.53	5.30	1.40	304	364	217	20.7	1.9	1.3	0.7	51	18	31	2.5	24%	25%	50%	3	77	0%	67%			-6.2	1	1	-$7
13	**Proj**	**4**	**6**	**0**	**74**	**43**	**4.94**	**4.58**	**1.50**	**279**	**305**	**245**	**25.0**	**3.7**	**5.3**	**1.4**	**56**	**17**	**27**	**1.0**	**12%**	**31%**	**68%**	**13**						**-8.4**	**29**	**37**	**-$5**

Herrera,Kelvin

Age: 23	Th: R	Role RP	Health	A	LIMA Plan A
Ht: 5' 9"	Wt : 190	Type Pwr xGB	PT/Exp	D	Rand Var -3
			Consist	C	MM 5411

3 reasons to believe in future closer hype: 1) Top-notch command; 2) Pronounced groundball tilt; 3) 99 mph average fastball. Sure, friendly hr/f + S% kept his ERA below 3.00, but that's nitpicking when you've got his skill diversity. At minimum, a premium LIMA reliever. With opportunity... UP: 30 Sv

Yr	Tm	W	L	Sv	IP	K	ERA	xERA	WHIP	OBA	vL	vR	BF/G	Ctl	Dom	Cmd	G	L	F	hr/9	hr/f	H%	S%	GS	APC	DOM%	DIS%	Sv%	LI	RAR	BPV	BPX	R$
08																																	
09																																	
10																																	
11	KC *	5	1	13	55	49	2.38	2.09	0.91	197	500	200	5.3	2.0	7.9	4.0	29	14	57	0.9	25%	24%	79%	0	16			81	1.25	10.6	122	184	$12
12	KC	4	3	3	84	77	2.35	3.20	1.19	250	275	235	4.5	2.2	8.2	3.7	56	20	25	0.4	7%	32%	81%	0	17			75	1.20	17.3	121	158	$9
1st Half		0	1	0	40	37	2.90	2.97	1.04	233	263	215	4.5	1.6	8.3	5.3	58	16	27	0.9	13%	29%	76%	0	17			0	1.05	5.6	142	185	$4
2nd Half		4	2	3	44	40	1.84	3.41	1.32	265	286	252	4.5	2.9	8.2	2.9	54	24	23	0.0	0%	34%	84%	0	17			75	1.33	11.8	102	133	$13
13	**Proj**	**5**	**2**	**3**	**80**	**72**	**2.80**	**3.11**	**1.12**	**238**	**261**	**224**	**4.8**	**2.2**	**8.1**	**3.7**	**55**	**21**	**24**	**0.7**	**11%**	**30%**	**77%**	**0**						**11.9**	**121**	**157**	**$9**

Hochevar,Luke

Age: 29	Th: R	Role SP	Health	B	LIMA Plan D+
Ht: 6' 5"	Wt : 220	Type	PT/Exp	A	Rand Var +5
			Consist	A	MM 2205

The epitome of frustration. 1st-round pedigree, sexy skill flashes keep reeling us back in. Inability to pitch with runners on makes it a moot point. Consistent Dom, BPV gains say we can't write him off yet, especially since you'll be able to get him for nothing. But don't roster him without a comfy bench slot.

Yr	Tm	W	L	Sv	IP	K	ERA	xERA	WHIP	OBA	vL	vR	BF/G	Ctl	Dom	Cmd	G	L	F	hr/9	hr/f	H%	S%	GS	APC	DOM%	DIS%	Sv%	LI	RAR	BPV	BPX	R$
08	KC *	7	13	0	146	81	5.24	4.45	1.43	274	314	244	24.9	3.3	5.0	1.5	52	17	32	0.9	9%	30%	64%	22	94	36%	27%			-16.5	36	68	-$3
09	KC *	12	14	0	191	133	5.42	5.01	1.46	289	292	289	24.8	2.8	6.3	2.2	47	18	36	1.2	14%	32%	65%	25	94	36%	32%			-25.9	46	86	-$3
10	KC	6	6	0	103	76	4.81	4.17	1.43	272	288	255	25.0	3.2	6.6	2.1	46	21	33	0.8	8%	32%	67%	17	91	41%	18%	0	0.73	-9.2	56	91	-$2
11	KC	11	11	0	198	128	4.68	4.01	1.28	252	269	231	26.9	2.8	5.8	2.1	50	18	32	1.0	12%	28%	65%	31	101	45%	16%			-18.1	57	85	$1
12	KC	8	16	0	185	144	5.73	4.22	1.42	281	298	261	25.0	3.0	7.0	2.4	43	22	35	1.3	14%	32%	61%	32	94	44%	31%			-39.2	67	87	-$13
1st Half		5	8	0	93	68	5.23	4.15	1.41	286	289	282	24.8	2.8	6.6	2.3	45	22	33	0.9	10%	32%	63%	16	91	44%	38%			-13.9	66	86	-$8
2nd Half		3	8	0	92	76	6.24	4.29	1.43	276	308	243	25.3	3.1	7.4	2.4	41	22	37	1.8	17%	31%	60%	16	97	44%	25%			-25.3	69	90	-$17
13	**Proj**	**9**	**14**	**0**	**189**	**137**	**4.77**	**4.26**	**1.39**	**273**	**291**	**252**	**24.9**	**3.0**	**6.6**	**2.2**	**46**	**20**	**34**	**1.2**	**12%**	**31%**	**68%**	**32**						**-17.4**	**61**	**79**	**-$1**

Holland,Derek

Age: 26	Th: L	Role SP	Health	C	LIMA Plan B+
Ht: 6' 2"	Wt : 195	Type Pwr	PT/Exp	A	Rand Var +2
			Consist	A	MM 2305

Shoulder fatigue derailed any possibility for growth. Blame ERA spike on 17% hr/f vs. RH bats and unsupportive S%. BA trend vs. RH confirms he's otherwise making gains. Cmd growth, enticing DOM% trends lay seeds for breakout, if healthy. UP: 3.50 ERA, 1.20 WHIP

Yr	Tm	W	L	Sv	IP	K	ERA	xERA	WHIP	OBA	vL	vR	BF/G	Ctl	Dom	Cmd	G	L	F	hr/9	hr/f	H%	S%	GS	APC	DOM%	DIS%	Sv%	LI	RAR	BPV	BPX	R$
08	aa	3	0	0	26	25	0.79	0.79	0.82	174			23.7	2.0	8.8	4.4				0.0		24%	89%							11.3	164	308	$4
09	TEX	8	13	0	138	107	6.12	4.40	1.50	288	287	289	18.5	3.1	7.0	2.3	41	19	39	1.7	15%	32%	62%	21	68	19%	33%	0	0.95	-30.6	62	116	-$7
10	TEX *	9	6	0	120	95	3.12	3.78	1.30	250	130	277	19.8	3.2	7.2	2.2	42	15	43	0.9	8%	29%	79%	10	76	40%	50%	0	0.74	14.2	68	110	$8
11	TEX	16	5	0	198	162	3.95	3.81	1.35	262	235	272	26.3	3.0	7.4	2.4	46	20	34	1.0	11%	31%	74%	32	100	47%	22%			-0.3	74	112	$7
12	TEX	12	7	0	175	145	4.67	4.05	1.22	243	243	243	25.2	2.7	7.4	2.8	43	17	40	1.6	15%	27%	68%	27	95	63%	15%	0	0.81	-14.2	83	108	$4
1st Half		5	4	0	67	59	5.10	4.27	1.33	251	284	240	23.8	3.2	7.9	2.5	38	20	41	1.5	13%	29%	65%	11	91	64%	18%	0	0.72	-9.0	72	94	-$2
2nd Half		7	3	0	108	86	4.40	3.92	1.15	238	208	245	26.1	2.3	7.1	3.1	46	15	39	1.7	17%	26%	69%	16	98	63%	13%	0	0.88	-5.2	90	117	$9
13	**Proj**	**14**	**9**	**0**	**196**	**160**	**4.00**	**4.07**	**1.29**	**257**	**233**	**263**	**23.1**	**2.9**	**7.3**	**2.5**	**44**	**18**	**39**	**1.4**	**13%**	**29%**	**74%**	**35**						**0.4**	**76**	**98**	**$10**

Holland,Greg

Age: 27	Th: R	Role RP	Health	A	LIMA Plan B+
Ht: 5' 10"	Wt : 195	Type Pwr	PT/Exp	D	Rand Var 0
			Consist	D	MM 4530

Harnessed stuff in 2H and took hold of closer job. Steadily increasing Dom gives him nice margin for error when chronic wildness appears again. And it will. Likely H%, hr/f regression will cancel out, so his risk of ERA erosion is minimal. With consistency, a 40 save source without the Prada pricetag.

Yr	Tm	W	L	Sv	IP	K	ERA	xERA	WHIP	OBA	vL	vR	BF/G	Ctl	Dom	Cmd	G	L	F	hr/9	hr/f	H%	S%	GS	APC	DOM%	DIS%	Sv%	LI	RAR	BPV	BPX	R$
08																																	
09	a/a	4	3	10	54	39	4.75	5.51	1.73	309			7.1	4.2	6.5	1.6				0.7		36%	73%							-2.9	45	84	$0
10	KC *	3	4	3	75	70	5.03	3.85	1.42	246	278	310	6.3	4.5	8.3	1.8	35	24	42	0.7	13%	31%	64%	0	21			60	0.68	-8.8	73	119	-$1
11	KC *	7	1	6	82	95	1.96	1.77	1.01	184	181	171	5.3	3.3	10.4	3.1	45	16	39	0.4	6%	26%	82%	0	21			67	1.38	20.0	133	201	$15
12	KC	7	4	16	67	91	2.96	3.34	1.37	234	194	264	4.3	4.6	12.2	2.7	45	18	36	0.3	3%	36%	78%	0	17			80	1.41	8.8	120	156	$10
1st Half		2	2	0	26	39	4.10	3.50	1.78	282	237	308	4.3	6.2	13.3	2.2	50	23	27	0.3	6%	44%	76%	0	17			0	1.18	-0.3	102	133	-$5
2nd Half		5	2	16	41	52	2.21	3.22	1.11	200	171	227	4.3	3.5	11.5	3.3	42	15	43	0.2	2%	31%	80%	0	17			89	1.58	9.0	132	172	$20
13	**Proj**	**6**	**3**	**30**	**65**	**77**	**3.21**	**3.45**	**1.25**	**217**	**194**	**235**	**4.8**	**4.2**	**10.6**	**2.5**	**45**	**17**	**37**	**0.6**	**7%**	**31%**	**75%**	**0**						**6.5**	**101**	**131**	**$17**

Howell,J.P.

Age: 30	Th: L	Role RP	Health	F	LIMA Plan B
Ht: 6' 0"	Wt : 190	Type Pwr GB	PT/Exp	D	Rand Var -3
			Consist	A	MM 3400

Lefty cut ERA in half, but buyer beware. Lives on curve + change mix, a necessity given his 84-mph fastball. Fantastic 2H was produced by H%-S% good fortune, not inherent skill. Middling command, health grade make him a LIMA reliever option in very deep leagues only. Use 1H x 2 as baseline.

Yr	Tm	W	L	Sv	IP	K	ERA	xERA	WHIP	OBA	vL	vR	BF/G	Ctl	Dom	Cmd	G	L	F	hr/9	hr/f	H%	S%	GS	APC	DOM%	DIS%	Sv%	LI	RAR	BPV	BPX	R$
08	TAM	6	1	3	89	92	2.22	3.39	1.13	194	188	197	5.8	3.9	9.3	2.4	54	17	30	0.6	9%	26%	83%	0	23			60	1.18	23.2	93	174	$13
09	TAM	7	5	17	67	79	2.84	3.34	1.20	197	280	159	4.0	4.5	10.7	2.4	49	16	35	0.9	13%	27%	81%	0	16			68	1.56	12.2	99	185	$15
10																																	
11	TAM	2	3	1	31	26	6.16	4.28	1.57	259	222	302	3.0	5.3	7.6	1.4	53	19	29	1.5	19%	29%	63%	0	12			50	1.04	-8.4	26	39	-$5
12	TAM	1	0	0	50	42	3.04	3.86	1.21	223	200	244	3.7	3.9	7.5	1.9	49	20	31	1.3	17%	24%	81%	0	15			0	0.71	6.1	56	73	$0
1st Half		1	0	0	26	21	4.44	3.99	1.22	232	209	250	3.7	3.4	7.2	2.1	44	22	34	1.4	16%	25%	68%	0	15			0	0.76	-1.4	59	77	-$2
2nd Half		0	0	0	24	21	1.50	3.70	1.21	213	190	237	3.7	4.5	7.9	1.8	55	17	28	1.1	19%	23%	96%	0	15			0	0.66	7.5	53	69	$3
13	**Proj**	**2**	**2**	**0**	**51**	**46**	**3.70**	**3.98**	**1.35**	**233**	**221**	**244**	**3.6**	**4.4**	**8.2**	**1.9**	**51**	**18**	**30**	**1.2**	**16%**	**28%**	**77%**	**0**						**2.0**	**58**	**76**	**$0**

Hudson,Daniel

Age: 26	Th: R	Role SP	Health	F	LIMA Plan C+
Ht: 6' 3"	Wt : 225	Type Pwr FB	PT/Exp	B	Rand Var +5
			Consist	A	MM 2300

Hard to find an unluckier season than this one. First, H%, S%, hr/f trifecta got him, then Tommy John put him to bed. Strong Cmd gives him solid foundation to reclaim once healthy, but also keep in mind that TJ returnees often struggle out of the gate. Likely out until 2H '13 at earliest, so dog-ear for '14.

Yr	Tm	W	L	Sv	IP	K	ERA	xERA	WHIP	OBA	vL	vR	BF/G	Ctl	Dom	Cmd	G	L	F	hr/9	hr/f	H%	S%	GS	APC	DOM%	DIS%	Sv%	LI	RAR	BPV	BPX	R$
08																																	
09	CHW *	10	1	0	99	91	2.84	2.95	1.18	238	194	257	19.8	2.7	8.2	3.1	30	12	58	0.5	9%	30%	77%	2	53	50%	0%	0	0.29	18.1	105	197	$12
10	2 TM *	19	6	0	189	178	3.32	3.50	1.18	233	203	201	24.3	2.9	8.5	2.9	35	19	45	1.2	7%	28%	77%	14	103	79%	7%			17.6	86	139	$20
11	ARI	16	12	0	222	169	3.49	3.77	1.20	255	251	258	27.9	2.0	6.9	3.4	42	19	39	0.7	6%	30%	72%	33	104	67%	6%			12.5	89	133	$16
12	ARI	3	2	0	45	37	7.35	4.31	1.63	332	340	321	22.4	2.4	7.3	3.1	37	27	36	1.8	17%	37%	57%	9	89	22%	44%			-18.6	83	108	-$11
1st Half		3	2	0	45	37	7.35	4.32	1.63	332	340	321	22.4	2.4	7.3	3.1	37	27	36	1.8	17%	37%	57%	9	89	22%	44%			-18.6	83	108	-$11
2nd Half																																	
13	**Proj**	**6**	**2**	**0**	**66**	**57**	**4.49**	**4.01**	**1.32**	**269**	**277**	**261**	**23.4**	**2.5**	**7.8**	**3.1**	**38**	**22**	**41**	**1.2**	**11%**	**32%**	**69%**	**12**						**-3.9**	**87**	**113**	**$0**

STEPHEN NICKRAND

Hudson,Tim

Age: 37	Th: R	Role SP	Health	D	LIMA Plan	C+
Ht: 6' 1"	Wt: 175	Type Con xGB	PT/Exp	A	Rand Var	-1
			Consist	A	MM	3105

Value he provides on the surface is slowly eroding. 2H Dom drop the first warning sign; two straight years of fastball decline, to sub-90 mph, suggests he might not get it back. xERA warns that first 4.00+ ERA since '06 is on horizon. He's middle-rotation filler now, and at 37, it could all go quickly.

Yr	Tm	W	L	Sv	IP	K	ERA	xERA	WHIP	OBA	vL	vR	BF/G	Ctl	Dom	Cmd	G	L	F	hr/9	hr/f	H%	S%	GS	APC	DOM%	DIS%	Sv%	LI	RAR	BPV	BPX	R$
08	ATL	11	7	0	142	85	3.17	3.70	1.16	239	255	223	24.9	2.5	5.4	2.1	59	19	22	0.7	11%	27%	75%	22	87	45%	23%	0	0.74	20.2	66	123	$14
09	ATL *	3	1	0	61	38	3.94	5.23	1.58	320	329	271	24.4	2.3	5.6	2.5	62	18	20	0.6	15%	36%	75%	7	86	29%	29%			2.9	59	111	-$3
10	ATL	17	9	0	229	139	2.83	3.55	1.15	229	233	225	27.1	2.9	5.5	1.9	64	14	22	0.8	13%	25%	79%	34	98	50%	9%			35.1	62	100	$24
11	ATL	16	10	0	215	158	3.22	3.36	1.14	236	249	226	26.8	2.3	6.6	2.8	57	19	25	0.6	9%	28%	73%	33	97	55%	9%			19.1	91	136	$20
12	ATL	16	7	0	179	102	3.62	4.06	1.21	248	235	263	26.8	2.4	5.1	2.1	55	19	25	0.6	8%	28%	71%	28	94	39%	11%			8.7	60	78	$12
1st Half		6	3	0	73	51	3.58	3.69	1.19	241	243	239	27.5	2.6	6.3	2.4	56	23	21	0.4	7%	29%	69%	11	96	45%	0%			4.0	77	100	$10
2nd Half		10	4	0	106	51	3.65	4.33	1.22	253	231	282	26.2	2.3	4.3	1.9	55	17	28	0.8	9%	27%	72%	17	92	35%	18%			4.8	49	64	$14
13	Proj	**14**	**8**	**0**	**183**	**113**	**3.74**	**3.80**	**1.20**	**247**	**245**	**248**	**25.7**	**2.5**	**5.6**	**2.3**	**58**	**18**	**24**	**0.6**	**9%**	**28%**	**69%**	**29**						**6.2**	**69**	**90**	**$13**

Hughes,Jared

Age: 27	Th: R	Role RP	Health	A	LIMA Plan	B+
Ht: 6' 7"	Wt: 245	Type xGB	PT/Exp	D	Rand Var	-2
			Consist	B	MM	3110

Sinkerballer used friendly H% and S% to produce first sub-3.00 ERA, but don't dismiss his potential as an impact reliever. That 2H gets our attention. Next step is strikeout pitch vs. LH, as 3.6 Dom, 1.3 Cmd hides behind decent OBA. With lefty adjustment, repeat of 2H, and opportunity... UP: 30 Sv

Yr	Tm	W	L	Sv	IP	K	ERA	xERA	WHIP	OBA	vL	vR	BF/G	Ctl	Dom	Cmd	G	L	F	hr/9	hr/f	H%	S%	GS	APC	DOM%	DIS%	Sv%	LI	RAR	BPV	BPX	R$
08	aa	2	2	0	31	15	6.29	6.60	1.85	322			24.1	4.6	4.2	0.9				1.3		34%	67%							-7.5	-2	-4	-$6
09	aa	1	6	3	46	29	4.73	5.42	1.73	330			12.4	3.1	5.6	1.8				0.2		38%	71%							-2.3	54	101	-$4
10	aa	12	8	0	151	93	5.42	5.55	1.58	317			22.1	2.5	5.5	2.2				0.9		35%	66%							-25.0	43	69	-$7
11	PIT *	6	6	0	115	68	4.08	4.05	1.45	280	214	222	8.2	3.2	5.3	1.7	66	21	14	0.3	25%	32%	70%	0	16			0	0.72	-2.0	56	85	-$2
12	PIT	2	2	2	76	50	2.85	3.77	1.15	226	248	206	4.8	2.6	5.9	2.3	60	17	23	0.8	13%	26%	79%	0	18			50	0.96	10.8	74	97	$5
1st Half		2	0	1	39	20	2.31	4.26	1.18	221	242	203	5.2	3.2	4.6	1.4	59	18	23	0.7	10%	24%	84%	0	20			100	0.72	8.2	33	43	$6
2nd Half		0	2	1	37	30	3.44	3.28	1.12	231	254	211	4.4	2.0	7.4	3.8	60	17	23	1.0	16%	28%	73%	0	16			33	1.17	2.6	118	154	$4
13	Proj	**3**	**3**	**3**	**66**	**43**	**3.87**	**3.91**	**1.35**	**269**	**296**	**246**	**6.6**	**2.8**	**5.8**	**2.1**	**60**	**17**	**23**	**0.7**	**11%**	**31%**	**72%**	**0**						**1.2**	**66**	**86**	**$1**

Hughes,Phil

Age: 27	Th: R	Role SP	Health	C	LIMA Plan	B
Ht: 6' 5"	Wt: 240	Type xFB	PT/Exp	A	Rand Var	0
			Consist	B	MM	2303

Rebounded from '11 back woes with near duplication of '10, and a nice Cmd uptick to boot. 4.9 Cmd vs. RH bats confirms his dominance. With a 34% H% and 18% hr/f against them, he's got even more growth potential if those items regress and he stays on field. If planets align... UP: 3.50 ERA, 200 K

Yr	Tm	W	L	Sv	IP	K	ERA	xERA	WHIP	OBA	vL	vR	BF/G	Ctl	Dom	Cmd	G	L	F	hr/9	hr/f	H%	S%	GS	APC	DOM%	DIS%	Sv%	LI	RAR	BPV	BPX	R$
08	NYY *	1	4	0	63	50	7.03	5.67	1.70	318	333	299	20.3	3.4	7.1	2.1	34	27	39	0.8	7%	38%	57%	8	79	25%	75%			-21.0	54	102	-$9
09	NYY *	11	3	3	105	112	2.95	3.12	1.14	230	257	184	7.7	2.7	9.6	3.6	34	22	44	0.9	8%	30%	78%	7	29	43%	43%	50	1.14	17.9	114	213	$15
10	NYY	18	8	0	176	146	4.19	4.11	1.25	244	235	253	23.5	3.0	7.5	2.5	36	16	47	1.3	10%	28%	71%	29	97	55%	14%	0	0.89	-2.3	68	110	$11
11	NYY	5	5	0	75	47	5.79	4.87	1.49	283	312	234	19.6	3.3	5.7	1.7	32	23	45	1.1	8%	31%	62%	14	76	29%	43%	0	0.86	-17.0	24	36	-$7
12	NYY	16	13	0	191	165	4.23	4.22	1.26	259	211	308	25.5	2.2	7.8	3.6	32	20	48	1.6	12%	30%	73%	32	101	53%	22%			-5.2	91	119	$8
1st Half		8	6	0	86	81	4.48	4.12	1.30	265	202	349	24.7	2.2	8.4	3.9	33	17	50	2.0	15%	31%	74%	15	100	47%	27%			-5.0	104	135	$8
2nd Half		8	7	0	105	84	4.03	4.31	1.24	254	221	281	26.2	2.1	7.2	3.4	32	22	46	1.4	11%	30%	73%	17	101	59%	18%			-0.2	82	107	$8
13	Proj	**14**	**11**	**0**	**174**	**140**	**4.16**	**4.35**	**1.33**	**269**	**258**	**282**	**24.6**	**2.6**	**7.2**	**2.7**	**33**	**21**	**46**	**1.4**	**11%**	**31%**	**74%**	**29**						**-3.0**	**70**	**90**	**$7**

Hultzen,Danny

Age: 23	Th: L	Role SP	Health	A	LIMA Plan	D+
Ht: 6' 3"	Wt: 200	Type Pwr FB	PT/Exp	F	Rand Var	0
			Consist	F	MM	0401

Second pick in '11 draft couldn't find plate in Triple-A (43 BB in 48 IP). High Dom is nice building block, and with mid-90s raw stuff, it's no fluke. Just don't let him work out his kinks on your active roster if he's rushed to the majors. Elite keeper league stash.

Yr	Tm	W	L	Sv	IP	K	ERA	xERA	WHIP	OBA	vL	vR	BF/G	Ctl	Dom	Cmd	G	L	F	hr/9	hr/f	H%	S%	GS	APC	DOM%	DIS%	Sv%	LI	RAR	BPV	BPX	R$
08																																	
09																																	
10																																	
11																																	
12	a/a	9	7	0	124	121	3.33	2.90	1.37	214			20.8	5.4	8.8	1.6				0.3		29%	75%							10.5	91	118	$6
1st Half		8	4	0	82	78	1.91	1.75	1.10	178			21.5	4.4	8.5	1.9				0.2		24%	82%							21.4	105	137	$20
2nd Half		1	3	0	42	43	6.13	5.13	1.89	277			19.6	7.3	9.2	1.3				0.4		37%	65%							-10.9	69	90	-$22
13	Proj	**5**	**5**	**0**	**85**	**85**	**4.37**	**4.91**	**1.58**	**240**			**22.8**	**6.2**	**9.0**	**1.4**	**39**	**17**	**44**	**0.9**	**8%**	**30%**	**74%**	**16**						**-3.7**	**11**	**15**	**-$3**

Humber,Philip

Age: 30	Th: R	Role RP	Health	B	LIMA Plan	D
Ht: 6' 3"	Wt: 210	Type FB	PT/Exp	B	Rand Var	+5
			Consist	C	MM	1201

Imagine these stats without a perfect game mixed in. There was bad strand and HR luck, but there's no ignoring that 2H skill collapse—and more troubling, how much it looks like the rest of his career. Move to bullpen might provide a boost given 9.0 Dom in short outings, but look elsewhere for SP help.

Yr	Tm	W	L	Sv	IP	K	ERA	xERA	WHIP	OBA	vL	vR	BF/G	Ctl	Dom	Cmd	G	L	F	hr/9	hr/f	H%	S%	GS	APC	DOM%	DIS%	Sv%	LI	RAR	BPV	BPX	R$
08	MIN *	10	8	0	148	92	5.47	5.99	1.61	306	150	333	18.2	3.3	5.6	1.7	50	16	34	1.5	31%	33%	70%	0	37			0	0.21	-20.9	17	32	-$6
09	MIN *	7	9	0	129	77	7.18	7.07	1.90	341	385	429	19.6	4.0	5.4	1.3	48	26	26	1.3	13%	37%	63%	0	28			0	0.47	-45.3	9	16	-$21
10	KC *	7	7	0	140	74	5.38	5.61	1.51	318	275	244	21.0	1.8	4.8	2.6	46	17	37	1.2	4%	34%	66%	1	46	0%	0%	0	1.64	-22.4	40	65	-$7
11	CHW	9	9	0	163	116	3.75	3.80	1.18	243	268	203	24.1	2.3	6.4	2.8	47	17	36	0.8	8%	29%	70%	26	89	46%	12%	0	0.71	3.8	79	119	$9
12	CHW	5	5	0	102	85	6.44	4.84	1.54	276	302	243	17.8	3.9	7.5	1.9	35	22	43	2.0	17%	31%	63%	16	68	38%	38%	0	0.59	-30.5	43	56	-$14
1st Half		3	4	0	67	63	6.01	4.59	1.49	261	282	223	25.1	4.1	8.4	2.0	33	24	43	1.6	14%	31%	63%	12	95	33%	33%			-16.6	51	66	-$12
2nd Half		2	1	0	35	22	7.27	5.35	1.64	303	355	265	11.5	3.4	5.7	1.7	38	19	43	2.9	20%	30%	63%	4	45	50%	50%	0	0.43	-13.9	27	35	-$17
13	Proj	**5**	**4**	**0**	**87**	**61**	**5.04**	**4.66**	**1.49**	**290**	**319**	**254**	**16.9**	**3.0**	**6.3**	**2.1**	**40**	**19**	**40**	**1.7**	**14%**	**31%**	**71%**	**15**						**-11.0**	**49**	**63**	**-$4**

Hunter,Tommy

Age: 26	Th: R	Role RP	Health	C	LIMA Plan	D+
Ht: 6' 3"	Wt: 260	Type Con	PT/Exp	D	Rand Var	+2
			Consist	B	MM	1001

7-8, 5.45 ERA in 133 IP at BAL. Remains utterly hittable, but there's at least a small foundation on which to build: another solid Cmd year, gradually fewer FB allowed, and hr/f will regress. It does feel a little like the famous Jim Carrey line, though—"so you're tellin' me there's a chance." Yeah, he has a chance.

Yr	Tm	W	L	Sv	IP	K	ERA	xERA	WHIP	OBA	vL	vR	BF/G	Ctl	Dom	Cmd	G	L	F	hr/9	hr/f	H%	S%	GS	APC	DOM%	DIS%	Sv%	LI	RAR	BPV	BPX	R$
08	TEX *	8	6	0	116	58	5.00	5.29	1.46	302	393	414	26.2	2.2	4.5	2.0	31	23	46	1.2	18%	32%	68%	3	71	0%	67%			-9.7	27	51	-$2
09	TEX *	13	8	0	183	107	4.59	4.85	1.45	291	288	228	24.4	2.6	5.3	2.0	38	20	42	1.0	8%	32%	70%	19	91	37%	21%			-6.0	40	75	$2
10	TEX *	14	6	0	155	79	3.92	4.50	1.31	267	272	231	22.0	2.6	4.6	1.8	42	18	40	1.4	12%	27%	75%	22	83	18%	23%	0	0.77	3.0	26	42	$7
11	2 AL *	6	6	1	115	61	5.01	5.34	1.44	311	316	261	16.9	1.5	4.8	3.2	41	21	38	1.2	11%	33%	68%	11	65	18%	18%	50	0.95	-15.2	52	78	-$5
12	BAL *	10	9	1	163	93	5.22	5.55	1.37	292	294	311	18.0	1.8	5.1	2.8	45	20	35	1.9	20%	30%	68%	20	63	25%	25%	50	0.87	-24.1	28	36	-$6
1st Half		4	4	0	88	46	5.77	6.00	1.43	305	305	312	23.4	1.8	4.7	2.7	46	20	34	2.0	21%	31%	66%	13	83	31%	15%	0	0.77	-19.1	17	22	-$12
2nd Half		6	5	1	75	47	4.57	4.99	1.30	278	278	309	14.1	2.0	5.6	2.9	45	20	35	1.8	20%	29%	72%	7	47	14%	43%	50	0.96	-5.2	40	52	$0
13	Proj	**5**	**4**	**0**	**73**	**40**	**4.83**	**4.50**	**1.38**	**292**	**299**	**284**	**18.1**	**1.9**	**5.0**	**2.6**	**43**	**20**	**37**	**1.6**	**14%**	**30%**	**70%**	**14**						**-7.2**	**59**	**77**	**-$2**

Hutchison,Drew

Age: 22	Th: R	Role SP	Health	D	LIMA Plan	C+
Ht: 6' 2"	Wt: 195	Type Pwr	PT/Exp	F	Rand Var	+1
			Consist	F	MM	3300

5-3, 4.60 ERA in 58 IP at TOR. Quick ascent through minors derailed by mid-season elbow injury that led to Tommy John surgery. Flashed MLB 8.3 Dom, 4.1 Cmd w/bases empty, so the seeds of something good are there. Given age, he's got time to bounce back and find consistency. Revisit in 2014.

Yr	Tm	W	L	Sv	IP	K	ERA	xERA	WHIP	OBA	vL	vR	BF/G	Ctl	Dom	Cmd	G	L	F	hr/9	hr/f	H%	S%	GS	APC	DOM%	DIS%	Sv%	LI	RAR	BPV	BPX	R$
08																																	
09																																	
10																																	
11	aa	3	0	0	15	19	1.46	1.39	0.89	212			18.6	1.2	11.2	9.4				0.0		33%	82%							4.6	278	418	$1
12	TOR *	7	4	0	75	60	4.17	4.30	1.33	267	254	259	22.3	2.7	7.1	2.6	45	25	30	1.1	15%	31%	72%	11	90	36%	27%			-1.4	66	86	$0
1st Half		7	4	0	75	60	4.17	4.27	1.33	267	254	259	22.3	2.7	7.1	2.6	45	25	30	1.1	15%	31%	72%	11	90	36%	27%			-1.4	66	86	$0
2nd Half																																	
13	Proj	**3**	**2**	**0**	**29**	**25**	**4.60**	**3.99**	**1.46**	**285**	**282**	**288**	**20.9**	**3.0**	**7.9**	**2.6**	**45**	**25**	**30**	**1.2**	**13%**	**34%**	**71%**	**6**						**-2.1**	**83**	**108**	**-$3**

STEPHEN NICKRAND

Isringhausen,Jason

Age: 40	Th: R	Role RP	Health	A	LIMA Plan	D
Ht: 6' 3"	Wt: 235	Type Pwr	PT/Exp	D	Rand Var	0
			Consist	A	MM	1300

Breaking his name down: in German, "Is" means "is"; "ring" means "lead"; "haus" means "house", but is also used for "safe"; and "sen", of course, translates to "Not". So his name translates to "Lead is not safe." Okay, maybe not. But he's a 40-year old ex-closer whose last glory days were 6 years ago.

Yr Tm	W	L	Sv	IP	K	ERA	xERA	WHIP	OBA	vL	vR	BF/G	Ctl	Dom	Cmd	G	L	F	hr/9	hr/f	H%	S%	GS	APC	DOM%	DIS%	Sv%	LI	RAR	BPV	BPX	R$
08 STL	1	5	12	43	36	5.70	4.43	1.64	279	186	327	4.8	4.6	7.6	1.6	51	22	28	1.1	14%	34%	66%	0	18			63	0.95	-7.2	40	76	$0
09 TAM	0	1	0	8	6	2.25	5.38	1.38	200	167	222	4.1	5.6	6.8	1.2	29	25	46	0.0	0%	27%	82%	0	18			0	0.27	2.0	-23	-44	-$3
10																																
11 NYM	3	3	7	47	44	4.05	4.26	1.29	211	257	178	3.8	4.6	8.5	1.8	39	14	47	1.2	10%	26%	72%	0	15			64	1.31	-0.6	45	67	$2
12 LAA	3	2	0	46	31	4.14	4.73	1.38	251	241	260	4.0	3.7	6.1	1.6	45	21	35	1.4	14%	27%	75%	0	16			0	0.63	-0.7	32	42	-$3
1st Half	2	0	0	27	17	2.33	4.80	1.15	182	191	173	4.1	4.3	5.7	1.3	46	21	33	0.7	7%	21%	83%	0	15			0	0.49	5.6	9	12	$1
2nd Half	1	2	0	19	14	6.75	4.62	1.71	342	313	364	3.8	2.9	6.8	2.3	42	20	38	2.4	21%	35%	67%	0	16			0	0.80	-6.3	64	83	-$9
13 Proj	2	2	0	30	24	4.76	4.51	1.44	260	254	264	3.9	4.1	7.3	1.8	43	18	38	1.4	14%	29%	71%	0						-2.7	43	55	-$3

Iwakuma,Hisashi

Age: 32	Th: R	Role SP	Health	A	LIMA Plan	B+
Ht: 6' 3"	Wt: 190	Type GB	PT/Exp	A	Rand Var	0
			Consist	A	MM	3203

A nice-looking debut for the Japanese import, but the real story is his second half, when he was moved into the rotation. 2H ERA was driven by a S% that's not likely to repeat, but 90 BPV and DOM/DIS show how well he pitched. Not much upside to a 32-year-old, but another solid year is very likely.

Yr Tm	W	L	Sv	IP	K	ERA	xERA	WHIP	OBA	vL	vR	BF/G	Ctl	Dom	Cmd	G	L	F	hr/9	hr/f	H%	S%	GS	APC	DOM%	DIS%	Sv%	LI	RAR	BPV	BPX	R$
08 for	21	4	0	201	151	2.34	2.39	1.08	234			28.0	2.0	6.8	3.4				0.2		29%	78%							49.3	113	212	$32
09 for	13	6	0	169	115	4.03	5.09	1.45	287			30.1	2.8	6.1	2.1				1.3		32%	77%							6.0	40	74	$6
10 for	10	9	0	201	145	3.50	3.59	1.20	258			28.9	2.0	6.5	3.2				0.8		30%	73%							14.3	86	139	$13
11 for	6	7	0	119	85	3.03	3.35	1.16	254			27.9	1.8	6.4	3.5				0.8		29%	77%							13.5	95	142	$9
12 SEA	9	5	2	125	101	3.16	3.77	1.28	248	246	251	17.3	3.1	7.3	2.3	52	20	27	1.2	17%	28%	81%	16	64	44%	13%	100	0.59	13.2	77	101	$9
1st Half	1	1	2	30	23	4.75	4.15	1.42	252	213	300	9.1	4.5	6.8	1.5	56	18	25	1.8	27%	26%	73%	0	32			100	0.39	-2.7	37	48	-$11
2nd Half	8	4	0	95	78	2.65	3.66	1.23	247	258	239	24.5	2.7	7.4	2.8	51	21	28	1.0	14%	29%	84%	16	92	44%	13%			16.0	90	117	$15
13 Proj	11	8	0	174	132	3.55	3.79	1.31	264	252	275	24.6	2.7	6.8	2.5	53	20	27	1.0	13%	30%	76%	29						10.0	81	105	$10

Jackson,Edwin

Age: 29	Th: R	Role SP	Health	A	LIMA Plan	B+
Ht: 6' 3"	Wt: 210	Type Pwr	PT/Exp	A	Rand Var	0
			Consist	A	MM	3305

Mr. Reliable, with another solid season and sub-4.00 xERA. Or so it seems. In fact, his skills jumped across the board in 2H. It's a small sample, but could it herald a step up? Maybe, but a 25% 2H DIS% is in that mix, too, so let's not go overboard. Most likely, he's simply Mr. Reliable yet again.

Yr Tm	W	L	Sv	IP	K	ERA	xERA	WHIP	OBA	vL	vR	BF/G	Ctl	Dom	Cmd	G	L	F	hr/9	hr/f	H%	S%	GS	APC	DOM%	DIS%	Sv%	LI	RAR	BPV	BPX	R$
08 TAM	14	11	0	183	108	4.42	5.00	1.51	281	295	268	24.8	3.8	5.3	1.4	39	21	40	1.1	10%	30%	74%	31	96	29%	26%	0	0.79	-2.1	10	19	$2
09 DET	13	9	0	214	161	3.62	4.25	1.26	247	247	248	27.0	2.9	6.8	2.3	39	18	42	1.1	10%	28%	76%	33	105	52%	12%			18.6	59	111	$17
10 2 TM	10	12	0	209	181	4.47	3.79	1.39	265	271	258	28.2	3.4	7.8	2.3	49	19	32	0.9	11%	32%	69%	32	105	53%	9%			-10.1	77	124	$2
11 2 TM	12	9	0	200	148	3.79	3.97	1.44	290	304	276	26.9	2.8	6.7	2.4	44	25	31	0.7	8%	33%	75%	31	101	52%	10%	0	0.76	3.8	67	100	$3
12 WAS	10	11	0	190	168	4.03	3.79	1.22	243	249	236	25.5	2.8	8.0	2.9	47	17	36	1.1	12%	29%	70%	31	96	48%	16%			-0.4	94	123	$9
1st Half	4	4	0	96	73	3.57	4.04	1.13	227	240	215	26.1	2.6	6.9	2.6	44	19	38	0.9	9%	26%	71%	15	93	53%	7%			5.2	74	96	$12
2nd Half	6	7	0	94	95	4.50	3.54	1.31	258	256	259	24.9	2.9	9.1	3.2	51	15	34	1.2	14%	32%	69%	16	98	44%	25%			-5.6	115	150	$6
13 Proj	11	10	0	189	158	3.94	3.93	1.33	262	268	255	25.6	2.9	7.5	2.6	46	19	34	1.0	11%	31%	73%	31						1.8	81	105	$8

Jansen,Kenley

Age: 25	Th: R	Role RP	Health	B	LIMA Plan	C+
Ht: 6' 5"	Wt: 260	Type Pwr xFB	PT/Exp	C	Rand Var	-3
			Consist	B	MM	5530

Missed a month with irregular heartbeat, but off-season surgery should correct that. Took over as full-time closer in 2H and continued to flash exceptional skills. Continues to trade Dom for Ctl, for which his Cmd is quite pleased (and he had plenty of Dom to spare). Sv% is a concern, but these skills are elite.

Yr Tm	W	L	Sv	IP	K	ERA	xERA	WHIP	OBA	vL	vR	BF/G	Ctl	Dom	Cmd	G	L	F	hr/9	hr/f	H%	S%	GS	APC	DOM%	DIS%	Sv%	LI	RAR	BPV	BPX	R$
08																																
09																																
10 LA *	5	0	12	54	84	1.18	1.06	1.05	150	205	63	4.4	5.0	14.0	2.8	34	16	50	0.0	0%	28%	88%	0	19			100	0.83	19.3	168	272	$14
11 LA	2	1	5	54	96	2.85	2.39	1.04	159	163	156	4.3	4.4	16.1	3.7	27	24	49	0.5	7%	33%	74%	0	19			83	0.88	7.2	177	266	$7
12 LA	5	3	25	65	99	2.35	2.62	0.85	146	147	145	3.9	3.0	13.7	4.5	33	19	48	0.8	10%	24%	78%	0	16			78	1.31	13.3	175	229	$22
1st Half	4	2	12	34	54	2.36	2.56	0.84	143	133	153	4.0	3.1	14.2	4.5	35	15	50	1.0	12%	23%	80%	0	17			80	1.48	7.0	183	238	$25
2nd Half	1	1	13	31	45	2.35	2.68	0.85	150	161	137	3.8	2.9	13.2	4.5	31	23	47	0.6	7%	25%	75%	0	15			76	1.12	6.3	167	217	$18
13 Proj	4	2	35	65	95	2.90	2.97	1.10	194	198	191	4.1	3.8	13.1	3.5	30	21	49	0.7	8%	31%	76%	0						9.0	143	185	$21

Janssen,Casey

Age: 31	Th: R	Role RP	Health	D	LIMA Plan	B
Ht: 6' 3"	Wt: 225	Type Pwr	PT/Exp	C	Rand Var	-2
			Consist	A	MM	4430

Early injury history is behind him, and skills are now at the top of a three-year run. There are nothing but good things to say about his 2012. A regression will likely bring skills down a step, but even a repeat of 2011's skills is more than closer-worthy. Sv% shows he was more than capable. Step right up.

Yr Tm	W	L	Sv	IP	K	ERA	xERA	WHIP	OBA	vL	vR	BF/G	Ctl	Dom	Cmd	G	L	F	hr/9	hr/f	H%	S%	GS	APC	DOM%	DIS%	Sv%	LI	RAR	BPV	BPX	R$
08																																
09 TOR *	3	4	1	62	39	5.36	5.38	1.63	314	313	367	8.1	3.0	5.7	1.9	50	24	26	0.7	13%	36%	67%	5	34	0%	40%	100	0.67	-7.9	44	83	-$5
10 TOR	5	2	0	69	63	3.67	3.59	1.38	272	283	264	5.3	2.8	8.3	3.0	47	22	31	1.0	12%	34%	77%	0	21			0	0.48	3.5	99	161	$1
11 TOR	6	0	2	56	53	2.26	3.09	1.10	228	216	242	4.1	2.3	8.6	3.8	47	21	31	0.3	4%	30%	80%	0	16			50	0.85	11.5	118	178	$7
12 TOR	1	1	22	64	67	2.54	2.90	0.86	195	172	218	3.9	1.6	9.5	6.1	43	21	36	1.0	12%	25%	77%	0	15			88	1.03	11.5	149	195	$17
1st Half	1	1	9	31	31	2.64	2.83	0.91	207	206	208	4.0	1.5	9.1	6.2	50	20	30	1.2	17%	26%	79%	0	16			90	1.02	5.2	152	198	$14
2nd Half	0	0	13	33	36	2.45	2.96	0.82	183	132	226	3.8	1.6	9.8	6.0	35	23	43	0.8	9%	24%	75%	0	14			87	1.04	6.4	146	190	$19
13 Proj	3	1	38	58	56	2.92	3.24	1.07	230	211	249	4.3	2.1	8.7	4.2	44	22	34	0.8	10%	29%	76%	0						7.8	123	160	$20

Jepsen,Kevin

Age: 28	Th: R	Role RP	Health	A	LIMA Plan	B+
Ht: 6' 3"	Wt: 230	Type Pwr	PT/Exp	D	Rand Var	0
			Consist	F	MM	2310

3-2, 3.02 ERA in 45 IP at LAA. These are the kinds of skills that can turn a closer-in-waiting into a closer-no-longer-in-waiting. He was in the mix at year-end, but it was a very muddled mix. Beware, too, his inconsistency. But a skills repeat is a reasonable bet, and could pay off if he stands out from the pack.

Yr Tm	W	L	Sv	IP	K	ERA	xERA	WHIP	OBA	vL	vR	BF/G	Ctl	Dom	Cmd	G	L	F	hr/9	hr/f	H%	S%	GS	APC	DOM%	DIS%	Sv%	LI	RAR	BPV	BPX	R$
08 LAA *	3	5	13	63	53	2.38	3.17	1.35	227	235	267	5.4	4.7	7.5	1.6	48	24	28	0.4	0%	28%	83%	0	16			93	1.54	15.1	75	142	$9
09 LAA *	7	4	3	73	64	6.27	6.02	1.82	322	373	208	5.0	4.3	7.9	1.8	57	16	27	0.8	4%	39%	65%	0	17			43	1.09	-17.5	53	100	-$7
10 LAA	2	4	0	59	61	3.97	3.43	1.41	250	239	263	3.7	4.4	9.3	2.1	56	18	26	0.3	5%	33%	70%	0	15			0	1.22	0.8	82	133	-$1
11 LAA *	2	5	7	41	22	5.42	6.33	1.75	324	333	423	4.7	3.6	4.7	1.3	55	16	29	1.2	13%	35%	71%	0	14			64	1.32	-7.6	10	14	-$4
12 LAA *	5	4	4	70	65	3.13	2.79	1.15	232	286	205	3.8	2.7	8.3	3.1	35	23	42	0.5	6%	30%	73%	0	14			67	1.16	7.6	109	142	$6
1st Half	2	3	2	31	29	5.01	3.23	1.25	243	353	333	4.1	3.1	8.4	2.7	35	30	35	0.6	13%	31%	58%	0	13			50	1.21	-3.8	97	126	$0
2nd Half	3	1	2	39	36	1.63	2.40	1.06	222	267	189	3.7	2.3	8.3	3.6	35	21	43	0.5	5%	28%	87%	0	15			100	1.14	11.4	121	158	$12
13 Proj	4	5	5	65	55	3.87	4.01	1.38	263	310	216	4.1	3.4	7.6	2.2	49	18	33	0.8	9%	32%	74%	0						1.2	72	94	$2

Jimenez,Ubaldo

Age: 29	Th: R	Role SP	Health	A	LIMA Plan	D+
Ht: 6' 5"	Wt: 210	Type Pwr	PT/Exp	A	Rand Var	+1
			Consist	B	MM	2305

Nothing here—whatsoever—points to a rebound. However, he posted strong xERA and skills over two-and-a-half years in one of the best hitters' parks, and his first two months in the AL were in line with that. If you're going out on a limb, he's a good place to try your luck—but have a backup plan.

Yr Tm	W	L	Sv	IP	K	ERA	xERA	WHIP	OBA	vL	vR	BF/G	Ctl	Dom	Cmd	G	L	F	hr/9	hr/f	H%	S%	GS	APC	DOM%	DIS%	Sv%	LI	RAR	BPV	BPX	R$
08 COL	12	12	0	199	172	3.99	4.09	1.43	245	248	241	25.5	4.7	7.8	1.7	54	18	28	0.5	7%	31%	72%	34	99	53%	15%			8.3	46	87	$8
09 COL	15	12	0	218	198	3.47	3.57	1.23	229	251	206	27.7	3.5	8.2	2.3	53	20	28	0.5	8%	29%	72%	33	108	79%	12%			23.0	83	156	$22
10 COL	19	8	0	222	214	2.88	3.45	1.15	209	191	227	27.1	3.7	8.7	2.3	49	16	35	0.4	5%	27%	75%	33	109	82%	6%			32.7	83	134	$26
11 2 TM	10	13	0	188	180	4.68	3.74	1.40	254	239	269	25.7	3.7	8.6	2.3	47	20	33	0.9	9%	32%	67%	32	102	44%	22%			-17.2	79	119	-$1
12 CLE	9	17	0	177	143	5.40	5.03	1.61	273	273	272	26.0	4.8	7.3	1.5	38	23	38	1.3	12%	32%	69%	31	101	35%	19%			-30.2	16	21	-$16
1st Half	7	6	0	88	65	4.69	5.32	1.54	245	254	234	26.3	5.4	6.6	1.2	38	23	39	1.2	11%	28%	73%	15	104	40%	20%			-7.3	-10	-13	-$6
2nd Half	2	11	0	88	78	6.11	4.78	1.69	299	293	304	25.6	4.3	7.9	1.9	38	24	38	1.3	12%	35%	65%	16	97	31%	19%			-22.8	44	57	-$25
13 Proj	10	15	0	189	165	4.60	4.23	1.43	261	256	267	25.1	3.9	7.9	2.0	44	21	35	1.0	10%	31%	69%	32						-13.6	58	76	$1

MATT CEDERHOLM

Johnson,Jim

Age: 30	Th: R	Role RP	PT/Exp	B	Rand Var -3
Ht: 6' 6"	Wt: 240	Type Con xGB	Consist	A	MM 3130
			Health	A	LIMA Plan D+

The only real difference between '11 and '12 is save opps and what he did with them (94% Sv%). 2H H% normalized, as did ERA, but success continued. This is not a typical closer skill set, and just barely good enough. He showed he can handle the role, but expect a bumpy road.

Yr Tm	W	L	Sv	IP	K	ERA	xERA	WHIP	OBA	vL	vR	BF/G	Ctl	Dom	Cmd	G	L	F	hr/9	hr/f	H%	S%	GS	APC	DOM%	DIS%	Sv%	LI	RAR	BPV	BPX	R$
08 BAL	2	4	1	69	38	2.23	4.21	1.19	219	227	212	5.2	3.7	5.0	1.4	59	14	27	0.0	0%	26%	79%	0	19			100	1.05	17.7	28	52	$5
09 BAL	4	6	10	70	49	4.11	4.06	1.37	270	262	278	4.7	3.0	6.3	2.1	52	18	30	1.0	12%	30%	73%	0	18			63	1.00	1.8	64	119	$4
10 BAL	1	1	1	26	22	3.42	3.44	1.41	296	264	327	4.5	1.7	7.5	4.4	51	24	24	0.7	10%	36%	77%	0	16			17	1.53	2.1	118	191	-$1
11 BAL	6	5	9	91	58	2.67	3.35	1.11	238	220	258	5.3	2.1	5.7	2.8	61	15	24	0.5	8%	27%	77%	0	18			64	1.11	14.3	86	130	$12
12 BAL	2	1	51	69	41	2.49	3.45	1.02	220	225	214	3.8	2.0	5.4	2.7	62	16	21	0.4	7%	25%	76%	0	14			94	1.29	12.9	84	109	$27
1st Half	1	0	23	35	22	1.30	3.14	0.78	154	176	122	3.8	2.3	5.7	2.4	67	14	19	0.8	17%	17%	92%	0	14			96	1.27	11.6	85	111	$31
2nd Half	1	1	28	34	19	3.71	3.77	1.26	278	271	286	3.8	1.6	5.0	3.2	58	19	23	0.0	0%	32%	67%	0	14			93	1.30	1.3	84	109	$22
13 Proj	**2**	**2**	**38**	**58**	**36**	**3.50**	**3.67**	**1.14**	**239**	**234**	**244**	**4.3**	**2.3**	**5.5**	**2.4**	**60**	**16**	**24**	**0.4**	**7%**	**28%**	**69%**	**0**						**3.7**	**76**	**99**	**$17**

Johnson,Josh

Age: 29	Th: R	Role SP	PT/Exp	A	Rand Var 0
Ht: 6' 7"	Wt: 250	Type Pwr	Consist	A	MM 4403
			Health	F	LIMA Plan B+

Decline in Dom and normalized H% and S% are all it took for him to go from elite to mediocre, though lingering effects of a shoulder injury may explain lost velocity (down 2 mph from 2010). But 2H was actually worse than 1H. Betting on a return to old form may require a leap of faith.

Yr Tm	W	L	Sv	IP	K	ERA	xERA	WHIP	OBA	vL	vR	BF/G	Ctl	Dom	Cmd	G	L	F	hr/9	hr/f	H%	S%	GS	APC	DOM%	DIS%	Sv%	LI	RAR	BPV	BPX	R$
08 FLA *	8	2	0	106	89	3.69	4.13	1.38	280	288	259	26.3	2.6	7.6	3.0	48	21	31	0.6	9%	34%	74%	14	101	50%	0%			8.3	89	166	$5
09 FLA	15	5	0	209	191	3.23	3.38	1.16	237	242	231	25.9	2.5	8.2	3.3	50	18	32	0.6	8%	30%	73%	33	100	70%	15%			28.2	109	203	$25
10 FLA	11	6	0	184	186	2.30	3.12	1.11	229	223	235	26.6	2.4	9.1	3.9	46	21	34	0.3	4%	31%	80%	28	107	71%	4%			40.2	125	202	$24
11 FLA	3	1	0	60	56	1.64	3.19	0.98	185	209	156	26.0	3.0	8.4	2.8	51	15	34	0.3	4%	24%	84%	9	104	67%	0%			17.1	99	149	$8
12 MIA	8	14	0	191	165	3.81	3.81	1.28	252	263	238	25.7	3.1	7.8	2.5	46	24	30	0.7	8%	31%	71%	31	101	65%	13%			4.8	81	106	$7
1st Half	5	5	0	97	83	3.80	3.74	1.37	279	314	231	25.3	2.9	7.7	2.7	47	25	28	0.5	6%	34%	72%	16	99	63%	13%			2.5	86	112	$7
2nd Half	3	9	0	94	82	3.82	3.89	1.19	225	209	247	26.3	3.2	7.8	2.4	45	23	32	0.9	10%	27%	70%	15	104	67%	13%			2.3	76	99	$8
13 Proj	**8**	**8**	**0**	**167**	**151**	**3.44**	**3.59**	**1.20**	**237**	**246**	**226**	**25.6**	**2.9**	**8.1**	**2.8**	**47**	**20**	**32**	**0.5**	**7%**	**30%**	**72%**	**26**						**11.9**	**94**	**121**	**$13**

Johnson,Steve

Age: 25	Th: R	Role RP	PT/Exp	D	Rand Var 0
Ht: 6' 1"	Wt: 220	Type Pwr xFB	Consist	C	MM 0301
			Health	A	LIMA Plan D

4-0, 2.11 ERA in 38 IP at BAL. Too soon to tell if this was a true step up, or a happy confluence of H% and a one-time Cmd spike. MLB Dom well above anything he's done in the minors, and it's too small a sample to rely on. At 25, he's young enough for more growth, but the safe bet is on a regression in '13.

Yr Tm	W	L	Sv	IP	K	ERA	xERA	WHIP	OBA	vL	vR	BF/G	Ctl	Dom	Cmd	G	L	F	hr/9	hr/f	H%	S%	GS	APC	DOM%	DIS%	Sv%	LI	RAR	BPV	BPX	R$
08																																
09 aa	4	3	0	49	43	3.93	3.70	1.29	230			22.2	4.0	8.0	2.0				1.1		27%	73%							2.4	64	121	$1
10 aa	7	8	0	145	106	6.24	6.18	1.67	289			23.3	4.7	6.6	1.4				1.8		31%	67%							-38.7	11	17	-$14
11 a/a	7	8	0	146	99	5.40	5.33	1.60	292			23.9	3.9	6.1	1.6				1.1		33%	68%							-26.2	33	50	-$12
12 BAL *	8	8	0	130	114	3.48	3.36	1.23	227	169	179	16.9	3.6	7.9	2.2	24	25	52	1.0	9%	27%	75%	4	56	75%	0%	0	0.59	8.6	75	98	$8
1st Half	3	5	0	63	50	3.87	3.50	1.29	237	0	0	18.4	3.8	7.2	1.9				0.8	0%	28%	72%	0	0					1.1	67	87	$3
2nd Half	5	3	0	67	64	3.11	3.19	1.16	217	169	179	15.7	3.4	8.6	2.5	24	25	52	1.1	9%	26%	79%	4	56	75%	0%	0	0.59	7.5	83	108	$13
13 Proj	**5**	**5**	**0**	**87**	**71**	**4.06**	**5.04**	**1.44**	**264**	**256**	**271**	**19.9**	**3.9**	**7.3**	**1.9**	**24**	**25**	**52**	**1.2**	**8%**	**31%**	**75%**	**18**						**-0.5**	**28**	**37**	**$0**

Jones,Nate

Age: 27	Th: R	Role RP	PT/Exp	D	Rand Var -5
Ht: 6' 5"	Wt: 185	Type Pwr	Consist	B	MM 2400
			Health	A	LIMA Plan B

Nice surface numbers, but the skill set says "replacement level." He's able to miss some bats, and that's about it—Ctl is shaky and xERA uninspiring; platoon splits are troublesome. He's a bit too old to be a true prospect anymore so don't expect him to sustain 2012's ERA or see much more growth.

Yr Tm	W	L	Sv	IP	K	ERA	xERA	WHIP	OBA	vL	vR	BF/G	Ctl	Dom	Cmd	G	L	F	hr/9	hr/f	H%	S%	GS	APC	DOM%	DIS%	Sv%	LI	RAR	BPV	BPX	R$
08																																
09																																
10																																
11 aa	2	3	12	63	57	4.33	4.83	1.63	286			6.7	4.6	8.0	1.8				0.6		36%	74%							-3.0	65	98	$0
12 CHW	8	0	0	72	65	2.39	4.02	1.38	256	170	304	4.6	4.0	8.2	2.0	46	23	32	0.5	6%	31%	84%	0	18			0	1.19	14.4	62	81	$5
1st Half	3	0	0	36	36	2.97	3.93	1.35	254	150	338	5.0	3.7	8.9	2.4	38	25	37	0.7	8%	32%	80%	0	20			0	1.03	4.7	76	99	$3
2nd Half	5	0	0	35	29	1.78	4.11	1.42	258	206	277	4.3	4.3	7.4	1.7	53	20	27	0.3	4%	31%	88%	0	17			0	1.33	9.7	47	61	$6
13 Proj	**5**	**1**	**0**	**65**	**58**	**3.76**	**4.19**	**1.48**	**264**	**181**	**306**	**5.3**	**4.3**	**8.1**	**1.9**	**47**	**22**	**31**	**0.8**	**10%**	**32%**	**76%**	**0**						**2.1**	**55**	**71**	**$0**

Jurrjens,Jair

Age: 27	Th: R	Role SP	PT/Exp	B	Rand Var +3
Ht: 6' 1"	Wt: 200	Type Con	Consist	C	MM 0001
			Health	F	LIMA Plan D

3-4, 6.89 ERA in 48 IP at ATL. Ugly bad, with skills in freefall. There's literally not a single good thing to say about 2012. While only a year removed from marginal acceptability, history of 4.00+ xERA says there's not much to hope for even, if he does rebound.

Yr Tm	W	L	Sv	IP	K	ERA	xERA	WHIP	OBA	vL	vR	BF/G	Ctl	Dom	Cmd	G	L	F	hr/9	hr/f	H%	S%	GS	APC	DOM%	DIS%	Sv%	LI	RAR	BPV	BPX	R$
08 ATL	13	10	0	188	139	3.68	4.06	1.37	260	261	260	26.2	3.3	6.6	2.0	52	22	27	0.5	7%	31%	73%	31	99	52%	13%			15.0	59	111	$11
09 ATL	14	10	0	215	152	2.60	4.23	1.21	237	264	212	26.0	3.1	6.4	2.0	43	18	39	0.6	6%	27%	81%	34	97	53%	9%			45.8	51	95	$26
10 ATL	7	6	0	116	86	4.64	4.34	1.39	270	294	250	25.0	3.2	6.7	2.0	40	18	42	1.0	9%	31%	68%	20	91	40%	15%			-8.1	50	81	$0
11 ATL	13	6	0	152	90	2.96	4.18	1.22	249	270	233	27.3	2.6	5.3	2.0	42	21	37	0.8	8%	27%	79%	23	99	48%	13%			18.4	46	69	$12
12 ATL *	7	10	0	121	51	6.26	6.30	1.65	326	345	355	21.6	2.6	3.8	1.5	39	22	39	1.4	11%	34%	64%	10	75	20%	70%	0	0.69	-33.4	2	3	-$19
1st Half	4	6	0	87	37	6.08	6.28	1.69	326	351	302	24.5	3.0	3.8	1.3	36	21	43	1.3	11%	34%	66%	6	87	17%	83%			-22.1	1	1	-$21
2nd Half	3	4	0	34	14	6.74	6.24	1.54	326	339	467	16.3	1.6	3.8	2.4	42	24	34	1.6	11%	33%	58%	4	62	25%	50%	0	0.61	-11.3	13	17	-$14
13 Proj	**8**	**8**	**0**	**106**	**57**	**4.55**	**4.80**	**1.45**	**292**	**295**	**289**	**21.7**	**2.5**	**4.9**	**1.9**	**41**	**21**	**38**	**1.1**	**10%**	**31%**	**71%**	**21**						**-6.9**	**38**	**49**	**-$2**

Karstens,Jeff

Age: 30	Th: R	Role RP	PT/Exp	C	Rand Var 0
Ht: 6' 3"	Wt: 185	Type Con	Consist	C	MM 2103
			Health	C	LIMA Plan B

5-4, 3.97 ERA in 91 IP at PIT. BPV alone shows a nice upward skills trend, driven by rising Dom. But we can't ignore the litany of injuries that have kept him sidelined for parts of the past three seasons. At 30, health and skills aren't likely to improve. Profit potential exists, but it's low probability.

Yr Tm	W	L	Sv	IP	K	ERA	xERA	WHIP	OBA	vL	vR	BF/G	Ctl	Dom	Cmd	G	L	F	hr/9	hr/f	H%	S%	GS	APC	DOM%	DIS%	Sv%	LI	RAR	BPV	BPX	R$
08 PIT *	8	10	0	120	67	4.74	5.09	1.41	293	265	293	24.2	2.2	5.0	2.3	42	20	39	1.3	10%	31%	70%	9	92	22%	22%			-6.1	34	65	$0
09 PIT	4	6	0	108	52	5.42	5.38	1.48	279	263	294	12.1	3.8	4.3	1.2	39	16	46	1.0	7%	29%	64%	13	44	8%	38%	0	0.73	-14.6	-6	-12	-$6
10 PIT *	4	12	0	139	81	5.39	5.61	1.45	305	364	249	19.1	1.9	5.2	2.8	42	18	40	1.6	13%	32%	67%	19	69	32%	16%	0	0.66	-22.4	36	59	-$7
11 PIT	9	9	0	162	96	3.38	3.96	1.21	263	288	242	22.3	1.8	5.3	2.9	46	17	36	1.2	12%	28%	78%	26	79	46%	19%	0	0.81	11.2	70	106	$9
12 PIT *	6	6	0	114	79	4.06	3.49	1.17	262	243	265	19.0	1.5	6.2	4.0	37	26	37	0.7	8%	30%	66%	15	69	60%	13%	0	0.75	-0.6	103	134	$3
1st Half	2	4	0	48	29	4.82	4.07	1.35	293	217	385	19.9	1.6	5.5	3.4	37	27	37	0.4	3%	34%	62%	5	73	40%	20%			-4.7	88	115	-$6
2nd Half	4	2	0	67	50	3.51	3.05	1.05	239	255	223	18.4	1.5	6.8	4.5	37	26	37	0.9	10%	27%	70%	10	68	70%	10%	0	0.73	4.2	115	150	$10
13 Proj	**7**	**9**	**0**	**149**	**94**	**3.89**	**4.21**	**1.25**	**271**	**272**	**270**	**19.3**	**1.8**	**5.7**	**3.1**	**40**	**22**	**38**	**1.0**	**9%**	**30%**	**72%**	**29**						**2.3**	**72**	**93**	**$6**

Kelley,Shawn

Age: 29	Th: R	Role RP	PT/Exp	D	Rand Var -2
Ht: 6' 2"	Wt: 220	Type Pwr xFB	Consist	C	MM 2400
			Health	F	LIMA Plan A

2-4, 3.25 ERA in 44 IP at SEA. Shoulder and elbow woes have kept his closer-worthy skills on the DL for much of the past four years. Even without that, he wouldn't be able to hold the 9th inning—nothing sours a manager quicker than a game-ending HR, and his 50%+ FB% will lead to many of those.

Yr Tm	W	L	Sv	IP	K	ERA	xERA	WHIP	OBA	vL	vR	BF/G	Ctl	Dom	Cmd	G	L	F	hr/9	hr/f	H%	S%	GS	APC	DOM%	DIS%	Sv%	LI	RAR	BPV	BPX	R$
08 aa	3	1	9	43	39	2.40	2.85	1.23	226			6.0	3.7	8.2	2.2				0.4		29%	81%							10.1	92	173	$6
09 SEA	5	4	0	46	41	4.50	3.88	1.17	257	209	303	4.7	1.8	8.0	4.6	31	17	51	1.8	13%	29%	69%	0	18			0	1.32	-1.0	106	198	$1
10 SEA	3	1	0	25	26	3.96	4.55	1.52	265	261	269	5.1	4.3	9.4	2.2	23	16	61	1.8	12%	32%	82%	0	20			0	0.88	0.4	53	85	-$2
11 SEA *	1	1	0	30	25	0.92	2.69	1.08	217	278	77	4.7	2.7	7.3	2.7	38	6	56	0.8	0%	26%	99%	0	17			0	0.56	11.3	89	134	$2
12 SEA *	4	4	6	64	65	2.54	2.85	1.13	227	265	252	4.2	2.7	9.1	3.4	29	20	51	0.7	8%	29%	81%	0	16			67	1.00	11.7	114	149	$8
1st Half	3	2	4	37	40	2.69	3.15	1.18	239	370	234	4.7	2.7	9.7	3.6	22	25	53	0.7	8%	32%	80%	0	17			67	0.84	6.1	119	155	$10
2nd Half	1	2	2	27	25	2.33	2.41	1.05	211	136	273	3.6	2.7	8.3	3.1	37	14	49	0.7	7%	26%	81%	0	15			67	1.15	5.6	108	141	$5
13 Proj	**3**	**2**	**0**	**44**	**40**	**3.39**	**4.08**	**1.23**	**250**	**221**	**267**	**4.5**	**2.6**	**8.3**	**3.1**	**31**	**18**	**51**	**1.5**	**11%**	**29%**	**80%**	**0**						**3.3**	**87**	**113**	**$1**

MATT CEDERHOLM

Kelly,Casey

Age: 23	Th: R	Role SP	Health A	LIMA Plan C+	
			PT/Exp D	Rand Var +5	
Ht: 6' 3"	Wt: 195	Type xGB	Consist C	MM	3301

2-3, 6.21 ERA in 29 IP at SD. Elbow inflammation cost him most of 1H, and was shut down at end of season with arm fatigue. In between, posted strong skills at all levels, including 3.79 xERA at SD. Step up in Dom and strong GB% bode well for success, but watch his health closely.

Yr Tm	W	L	Sv	IP	K	ERA	xERA	WHIP	OBA	vL	vR	BF/G	Ctl	Dom	Cmd	G	L	F	hr/9	hr/f	H%	S%	GS	APC	DOM%	DIS%	Sv%	LI	RAR	BPV	BPX	R$
08																																
09																																
10 aa	3	5	0	95	69	5.78	5.84	1.69	322			20.4	3.1	6.6	2.1				0.9		37%	66%							-19.9	47	76	-$10
11 aa	11	6	0	142	95	3.72	3.88	1.38	277			22.1	2.7	6.0	2.2				0.4		32%	72%							3.9	71	106	$4
12 SD *	2	4	0	58	54	4.62	4.20	1.31	278	318	327	21.6	2.0	8.5	4.2	56	17	27	0.9	19%	34%	66%	6	84	33%	50%			-4.3	112	146	-$3
1st Half	0	0	0	12	12	2.03	2.29	1.00	261	0	0	22.9	0.0	9.3	0.0				0.0	0%	36%	77%	0	0					2.9	0	0	-$4
2nd Half	2	4	0	46	42	5.27	4.63	1.38	281	318	327	21.3	2.5	8.3	3.3	56	17	27	1.1	19%	34%	64%	6	84	33%	50%			-7.0	83	108	-$3
13 Proj	5	7	0	116	90	4.33	3.90	1.42	281	277	285	20.7	2.8	7.0	2.5	56	17	27	0.8	10%	33%	71%	24						-4.5	84	109	-$1

Kelly,Joe

Age: 25	Th: R	Role SP	Health A	LIMA Plan D+	
			PT/Exp D	Rand Var -1	
Ht: 6' 1"	Wt: 185	Type GB	Consist B	MM	2201

5-7, 3.53 ERA in 107 IP at STL. "Pedestrian" is the best way to describe these skills. His lack of DISaster starts looks encouraging but there is a big difference between disaster avoidance and dominance. Regardless, he doesn't know how to miss bats, and that severely limits his upside.

Yr Tm	W	L	Sv	IP	K	ERA	xERA	WHIP	OBA	vL	vR	BF/G	Ctl	Dom	Cmd	G	L	F	hr/9	hr/f	H%	S%	GS	APC	DOM%	DIS%	Sv%	LI	RAR	BPV	BPX	R$
08																																
09																																
10																																
11 aa	6	4	0	59	43	4.33	4.78	1.53	290			23.4	3.4	6.5	1.9				0.8		34%	72%							-2.9	54	81	-$2
12 STL *	7	12	0	179	112	3.34	4.15	1.40	277	318	236	21.0	2.9	5.6	2.0	52	21	27	0.6	11%	32%	77%	16	71	44%	6%	0	0.78	14.9	57	74	$4
1st Half	3	5	0	94	48	3.13	4.28	1.44	294	326	310	25.0	2.4	4.6	1.9	46	28	26	0.4	10%	33%	78%	4	85	0%	25%			10.3	53	69	$2
2nd Half	4	7	0	86	64	3.57	3.97	1.35	258	315	221	17.9	3.4	6.7	2.0	53	19	28	0.8	11%	30%	76%	12	68	58%	0%	0	0.77	4.7	61	79	$5
13 Proj	7	7	0	102	69	4.07	4.24	1.44	280	316	250	21.5	3.1	6.1	2.0	50	22	27	0.7	9%	32%	73%	20						-0.6	54	71	$0

Kendrick,Kyle

Age: 28	Th: R	Role RP	Health A	LIMA Plan C+	
			PT/Exp A	Rand Var 0	
Ht: 6' 3"	Wt: 210	Type Con	Consist A	MM	2103

Can a chewing out by a manager turn a player around? After an Aug. meeting, he was a new pitcher, with Dom, Cmd, and GB% at or near career highs. He even solved LHBs, an Achilles heel. Small sample and career 36% DIS% advise caution, but those 2H skills say "breakout." UP: sub-3.50 ERA

Yr Tm	W	L	Sv	IP	K	ERA	xERA	WHIP	OBA	vL	vR	BF/G	Ctl	Dom	Cmd	G	L	F	hr/9	hr/f	H%	S%	GS	APC	DOM%	DIS%	Sv%	LI	RAR	BPV	BPX	R$
08 PHI	11	9	0	156	68	5.49	5.19	1.61	304	334	271	23.3	3.3	3.9	1.2	44	27	29	1.3	14%	32%	68%	30	85	20%	43%	0	0.73	-22.4	4	7	-$8
09 PHI *	12	8	0	169	66	4.32	4.41	1.41	287	267	278	21.7	2.5	3.5	1.4	56	22	22	0.7	5%	30%	70%	2	44	50%	50%	0	0.72	0.0	28	52	$3
10 PHI	11	10	0	181	84	4.73	4.65	1.37	283	312	254	23.4	2.4	4.2	1.7	45	17	38	1.3	11%	29%	69%	31	86	32%	32%	0	0.74	-14.6	32	52	-$1
11 PHI	8	6	0	115	59	3.22	4.25	1.22	255	234	270	14.1	2.4	4.6	2.0	45	19	36	1.1	11%	27%	79%	15	51	47%	40%	0	0.87	10.2	43	64	$6
12 PHI	11	12	0	159	116	3.90	4.20	1.27	254	238	269	18.2	2.8	6.6	2.4	47	18	36	1.1	11%	29%	73%	25	68	52%	28%	0	1.06	2.3	68	89	$6
1st Half	2	8	0	74	52	5.35	4.77	1.55	298	301	294	19.4	3.5	6.3	1.8	42	19	38	1.2	11%	33%	68%	12	72	42%	33%	0	0.79	-12.2	39	51	-$12
2nd Half	9	4	0	85	64	2.64	3.72	1.03	215	178	248	17.2	2.1	6.8	3.2	50	16	33	1.1	12%	25%	81%	13	64	62%	23%	0	1.28	14.5	93	121	$22
13 Proj	12	11	0	174	105	3.87	4.36	1.28	261	256	266	17.3	2.6	5.4	2.1	46	19	35	1.1	11%	28%	74%	30						3.3	52	68	$8

Kennedy,Ian

Age: 28	Th: R	Role SP	Health A	LIMA Plan B+	
			PT/Exp A	Rand Var 0	
Ht: 6' 0"	Wt: 190	Type Pwr FB	Consist B	MM	3305

Look at his main skill set, from Ctl to hr/f. This was the same season as 2011. The only differences are luck regression and run support. FB tilt means he may often seem to underperform his stellar Cmd, but his reliability and strong skills give him value. Just don't expect a repeat of 2011; let xERA guide you.

Yr Tm	W	L	Sv	IP	K	ERA	xERA	WHIP	OBA	vL	vR	BF/G	Ctl	Dom	Cmd	G	L	F	hr/9	hr/f	H%	S%	GS	APC	DOM%	DIS%	Sv%	LI	RAR	BPV	BPX	R$
08 NYY *	5	7	0	109	87	4.96	4.38	1.45	270	236	397	20.2	3.6	7.2	2.0	41	12	48	0.8	8%	32%	66%	9	79	22%	56%	0	0.74	-8.5	60	113	-$1
09 NYY *	1	0	0	24	21	2.18	3.28	1.41	257	0	0	20.0	3.9	8.1	2.1	0	50	50	0.0	0%	34%	83%	0	28			0	1.86	6.3	96	179	-$1
10 ARI	9	10	0	194	168	3.80	3.98	1.20	228	218	238	25.3	3.2	7.8	2.4	37	19	44	1.2	11%	27%	73%	32	99	63%	13%			6.6	68	109	$12
11 ARI	21	4	0	222	198	2.88	3.48	1.09	227	237	218	27.3	2.2	8.0	3.6	39	22	40	0.8	8%	28%	77%	33	104	70%	6%			29.1	101	152	$28
12 ARI	15	12	0	208	187	4.02	4.02	1.30	266	265	267	27.2	2.4	8.1	3.4	37	21	42	1.2	11%	32%	73%	33	102	58%	9%			-0.1	96	126	$9
1st Half	6	7	0	101	90	4.20	3.98	1.32	277	294	257	27.4	2.0	8.0	4.1	37	22	41	1.1	9%	34%	71%	16	102	63%	13%			-2.3	107	139	$6
2nd Half	9	5	0	108	97	3.85	4.07	1.28	256	234	277	27.1	2.8	8.1	2.9	38	19	43	1.3	12%	30%	75%	17	103	53%	6%			2.3	87	113	$11
13 Proj	15	9	0	203	179	3.78	3.94	1.24	253	244	262	25.1	2.6	7.9	3.0	38	20	42	1.1	10%	30%	73%	33						5.9	88	114	$14

Kershaw,Clayton

Age: 25	Th: L	Role SP	Health A	LIMA Plan C	
			PT/Exp A	Rand Var -2	
Ht: 6' 3"	Wt: 220	Type Pwr	Consist A	MM	4505

With GB% trending up and elite Dom and Cmd, he's one of the best and most consistent (85 DOM%, 5% DIS%, past two seasons). Even with three 200-IP seasons, workload is not an issue, as pitch counts were well managed. If you're going to pay top dollar for a elite starter, you won't do much better.

Yr Tm	W	L	Sv	IP	K	ERA	xERA	WHIP	OBA	vL	vR	BF/G	Ctl	Dom	Cmd	G	L	F	hr/9	hr/f	H%	S%	GS	APC	DOM%	DIS%	Sv%	LI	RAR	BPV	BPX	R$
08 LA *	7	8	0	169	155	3.47	3.37	1.31	240	250	269	19.9	3.7	8.3	2.2	48	21	31	0.6	12%	30%	74%	21	85	43%	33%	0	0.82	17.8	85	160	$12
09 LA	8	8	0	171	185	2.79	3.84	1.23	200	173	208	22.6	4.8	9.7	2.0	39	19	42	0.4	4%	27%	77%	30	98	50%	23%	0	0.76	32.3	63	118	$19
10 LA	13	10	0	204	212	2.91	3.61	1.18	214	200	218	26.5	3.6	9.3	2.6	40	18	42	0.6	6%	29%	77%	32	106	81%	13%			29.5	90	145	$22
11 LA	21	5	0	233	248	2.28	2.94	0.98	207	178	213	27.6	2.1	9.6	4.6	43	18	39	0.6	7%	28%	79%	33	105	88%	3%			48.0	137	206	$40
12 LA	14	9	0	228	229	2.53	3.23	1.02	210	181	216	27.3	2.5	9.1	3.6	47	19	34	0.6	8%	27%	78%	33	105	82%	6%			41.7	121	157	$36
1st Half	5	4	0	108	103	2.74	3.40	1.04	221	209	223	26.9	2.2	8.6	3.8	44	20	36	0.9	11%	27%	78%	16	101	75%	13%			17.0	115	150	$30
2nd Half	9	5	0	119	126	2.34	3.07	1.01	200	159	210	27.6	2.7	9.5	3.5	50	18	32	0.4	5%	27%	77%	17	109	88%	0%			24.7	126	164	$42
13 Proj	15	8	0	223	229	2.57	3.27	1.06	211	185	217	25.8	2.7	9.3	3.4	45	19	36	0.6	7%	28%	78%	34						39.9	115	150	$33

Keuchel,Dallas

Age: 25	Th: L	Role SP	Health A	LIMA Plan D	
			PT/Exp D	Rand Var +2	
Ht: 6' 3"	Wt: 210	Type Con GB	Consist A	MM	1003

3-8, 5.27 ERA in 85 IP at HOU. The ultimate pitch-to-contact hurler. Strikeouts and walks are few, and along with ground ball tilt, his fate rests squarely in the gloves of his backing defense. League average H% has kept him from completely blowing up, but boy is this a ticking time bomb.

Yr Tm	W	L	Sv	IP	K	ERA	xERA	WHIP	OBA	vL	vR	BF/G	Ctl	Dom	Cmd	G	L	F	hr/9	hr/f	H%	S%	GS	APC	DOM%	DIS%	Sv%	LI	RAR	BPV	BPX	R$
08																																
09																																
10 aa	2	6	0	54	32	5.84	4.68	1.48	311			25.6	1.9	5.3	2.9				0.4		36%	58%							-11.7	73	118	-$5
11 a/a	10	7	0	164	79	4.22	4.10	1.31	279			25.0	2.0	4.3	2.2				0.8		30%	69%							-5.7	48	72	$2
12 HOU *	9	12	0	178	80	4.48	4.40	1.38	273	250	296	23.3	2.9	4.1	1.4	52	17	31	0.9	16%	29%	69%	16	87	19%	38%			-10.1	26	34	-$4
1st Half	6	4	0	100	47	3.54	3.64	1.25	267	316	151	25.6	2.0	4.2	2.1	52	17	31	0.6	10%	29%	72%	3	98	33%	0%			5.9	53	69	$7
2nd Half	3	8	0	77	33	5.69	5.33	1.55	281	226	335	21.1	4.0	3.9	1.0	52	17	30	1.4	18%	28%	66%	13	84	15%	46%			-16.0	1	1	-$17
13 Proj	7	10	0	145	70	4.77	4.60	1.40	282	280	282	23.8	2.6	4.3	1.7	52	17	31	0.9	9%	30%	67%	26						-13.5	37	49	-$3

Kimbrel,Craig

Age: 25	Th: R	Role RP	Health A	LIMA Plan C	
			PT/Exp B	Rand Var -5	
Ht: 5' 11"	Wt: 205	Type Pwr	Consist B	MM	5530

It is this 2012 performance, not Rodney's, that has effectively obliterated Dennis Eckersely's BPV bar. His 2nd half gave us a taste of 300+ for the first time. Odds are there will be some regression but he's still just 25, so any reasonable closer bid could well have some built-in profit.

Yr Tm	W	L	Sv	IP	K	ERA	xERA	WHIP	OBA	vL	vR	BF/G	Ctl	Dom	Cmd	G	L	F	hr/9	hr/f	H%	S%	GS	APC	DOM%	DIS%	Sv%	LI	RAR	BPV	BPX	R$
08																																
09																																
10 ATL *	7	2	24	76	113	1.48	1.85	1.19	158	176	79	4.4	6.0	13.3	2.2	28	22	50	0.4	0%	27%	89%	0	18			89	0.53	24.4	139	226	$21
11 ATL	4	3	46	77	127	2.10	2.23	1.04	178	157	196	3.9	3.7	14.8	4.0	45	15	40	0.4	5%	33%	81%	0	17			85	1.32	17.5	189	284	$29
12 ATL	3	1	42	63	116	1.01	1.44	0.65	126	116	136	3.7	2.0	16.7	8.3	49	19	32	0.4	10%	28%	89%	0	15			93	1.29	23.3	273	356	$34
1st Half	0	1	23	30	50	1.50	1.78	0.77	126	43	193	3.8	3.0	15.0	5.0	58	13	28	0.3	7%	26%	82%	0	16			96	1.29	9.3	225	293	$31
2nd Half	3	0	19	33	66	0.55	1.17	0.55	125	167	65	3.6	1.1	18.2	16.5	38	27	36	0.6	13%	31%	100%	0	14			90	1.30	14.0	313	407	$37
13 Proj	4	2	40	65	108	1.98	1.95	0.88	165	153	177	3.7	2.9	15.0	5.2	46	19	35	0.5	10%	30%	80%	0						16.4	216	280	$28

MATT CEDERHOLM

Kirkman,Michael

Age: 26	Th: L	Role RP	Health A	LIMA Plan D
Ht: 6' 4"	Wt: 195	Type Pwr FB	PT/Exp D	Rand Var +1
			Consist C	MM 1400

1-2, 3.82 ERA in 35 IP at TEX. Here is a trend you don't often see: a consistent decline in batters faced per game. He was a starter in 2009, but as he progressed through the system and displayed mediocre skill, his team exposed him to opposing batters less and less. There is a message in there.

Yr Tm	W	L	Sv	IP	K	ERA	xERA	WHIP	OBA	vL	vR	BF/G	Ctl	Dom	Cmd	G	L	F	hr/9	hr/f	H%	S%	GS	APC	DOM%	DIS%	Sv%	LI	RAR	BPV	BPX	R$
08																																
09 aa	5	7	0	97	54	5.17	5.08	1.58	285			23.6	4.1	5.0	1.2				1.0		31%	68%							-10.2	24	45	-$5
10 TEX *	13	3	0	147	122	3.48	4.09	1.51	255	214	107	16.8	4.9	7.4	1.5	49	10	41	0.6	0%	31%	78%	0	20			0	0.71	10.9	63	102	$5
11 TEX *	4	4	1	100	86	5.86	5.78	1.72	305	214	274	10.9	4.4	7.8	1.8	35	24	41	1.1	14%	36%	67%	0	33			50	0.60	-23.7	46	69	-$12
12 TEX *	6	3	0	83	75	5.33	4.83	1.56	255	216	160	8.5	5.4	8.1	1.5	37	21	42	1.2	13%	30%	68%	0	22			0	1.03	-13.6	47	61	-$7
1st Half	5	1	0	59	46	5.97	5.36	1.69	268	91	138	13.4	5.9	6.9	1.2	31	16	53	1.3	12%	30%	66%	0	39			0	0.18	-14.3	29	38	-$9
2nd Half	1	2	0	24	29	3.75	3.43	1.25	219	250	173	4.2	4.1	10.9	2.6	40	24	37	1.1	13%	29%	74%	0	19			0	1.21	0.8	98	128	-$4
13 Proj	3	2	0	51	46	4.81	4.58	1.53	263	319	221	8.4	4.7	8.2	1.8	40	24	37	1.0	10%	32%	70%	0						-5.0	40	51	-$3

Kluber,Corey

Age: 27	Th: R	Role SP	Health A	LIMA Plan D
Ht: 6' 4"	Wt: 215	Type Pwr	PT/Exp C	Rand Var +2
			Consist B	MM 1303

2-5, 5.14 ERA in 63 IP at CLE. When you see a pitcher with a consistently elevated hit rate, one place to look is his pct of hard/med/soft hit balls. His soft hit ball rate was a tiny 15% which is why so many of his batted balls fell for hits. Decent 2nd half in CLE but not a high ceiling here.

Yr Tm	W	L	Sv	IP	K	ERA	xERA	WHIP	OBA	vL	vR	BF/G	Ctl	Dom	Cmd	G	L	F	hr/9	hr/f	H%	S%	GS	APC	DOM%	DIS%	Sv%	LI	RAR	BPV	BPX	R$
08																																
09 aa	2	4	0	45	31	4.69	5.23	1.78	273			23.0	6.5	6.3	1.0				0.8		31%	74%							-2.0	34	64	-$5
10 a/a	9	9	0	160	137	3.84	4.51	1.52	294			24.0	3.1	7.7	2.5				0.4		36%	74%							4.8	82	132	$2
11 CLE *	7	11	0	155	121	6.46	5.45	1.64	294	400	0	23.1	4.2	7.0	1.7	27	47	27	1.1	0%	34%	61%	0	30			0	0.15	-48.0	41	61	-$19
12 CLE *	13	12	0	188	156	4.51	4.87	1.51	290	301	286	24.7	3.2	7.4	2.3	45	22	33	0.9	13%	35%	71%	12	90	33%	25%			-11.4	64	84	-$5
1st Half	7	7	0	91	78	4.48	5.13	1.63	301	0	0	25.4	3.7	7.7	2.1				0.7	0%	37%	73%	0	0					-5.2	64	83	-$5
2nd Half	6	5	0	97	78	4.53	4.58	1.41	280	301	286	24.1	2.8	7.2	2.6	45	22	33	1.0	13%	33%	70%	12	90	33%	25%			-6.1	66	86	-$5
13 Proj	8	10	0	145	117	4.90	4.63	1.56	289	296	281	23.9	3.7	7.2	1.9	40	24	36	1.2	10%	34%	71%	27						-15.7	48	62	-$5

Kontos,George

Age: 28	Th: R	Role RP	Health A	LIMA Plan A
Ht: 6' 3"	Wt: 225	Type Pwr xGB	PT/Exp D	Rand Var -2
			Consist D	MM 3310

2-1, 2.47 ERA in 44 IP at SF. The big difference between 2012 and previous seasons was improved control. That inched backward in 2H, but overall, Cmd is trending nicely, giving us hope that he will have value in deeper leagues. While some regression is likely, he profiles out to be a solid LIMA pick.

Yr Tm	W	L	Sv	IP	K	ERA	xERA	WHIP	OBA	vL	vR	BF/G	Ctl	Dom	Cmd	G	L	F	hr/9	hr/f	H%	S%	GS	APC	DOM%	DIS%	Sv%	LI	RAR	BPV	BPX	R$
08 aa	6	11	0	152	129	5.15	4.90	1.50	280			24.3	3.6	7.6	2.1				1.1		33%	67%							-15.4	56	105	-$3
09 a/a	4	5	0	71	52	4.49	5.22	1.60	284			24.3	4.4	6.6	1.5				1.1		32%	75%							-1.4	36	67	-$3
10 a/a	0	3	0	35	24	5.14	5.60	1.62	306			8.1	3.4	6.3	1.8				1.1		35%	70%							-4.6	37	60	-$5
11 NYY *	4	4	2	95	78	3.74	5.06	1.37	267	200	188	8.5	3.1	7.3	2.3	20	7	73	1.8	9%	29%	82%	0	13			67	0.37	2.4	40	60	$1
12 SF *	4	1	1	75	64	2.18	2.41	1.06	223	167	229	4.4	2.2	7.7	3.5	51	15	34	0.5	8%	28%	81%	0	15			50	0.62	17.0	115	150	$9
1st Half	2	0	1	40	29	1.86	2.60	1.11	246	200	364	5.2	1.7	6.6	3.8	48	17	35	0.2	0%	30%	83%	0	16			100	0.29	10.6	120	156	$9
2nd Half	2	1	0	35	35	2.55	2.16	0.99	194	159	195	3.6	2.8	8.9	3.2	52	15	33	0.8	9%	25%	78%	0	15			0	0.68	6.4	114	148	$9
13 Proj	2	2	3	58	48	3.33	3.84	1.26	251	218	267	5.9	2.9	7.5	2.6	52	15	33	1.0	10%	29%	77%	0						4.9	87	112	$2

Kuroda,Hiroki

Age: 38	Th: R	Role SP	Health B	LIMA Plan C+
Ht: 6' 1"	Wt: 190	Type	PT/Exp A	Rand Var 0
			Consist A	MM 3205

Continues to thumb his nose at the aging curve, flourishing despite move to the AL. Skills even took a step up in a tough ballpark, especially in second half. Of course, the percentage play is to heed the "Age 38" and expect some eventual drop-off, but he's gamely fighting it off for now.

Yr Tm	W	L	Sv	IP	K	ERA	xERA	WHIP	OBA	vL	vR	BF/G	Ctl	Dom	Cmd	G	L	F	hr/9	hr/f	H%	S%	GS	APC	DOM%	DIS%	Sv%	LI	RAR	BPV	BPX	R$
08 LA	9	10	0	183	116	3.73	3.95	1.22	253	260	246	25.0	2.1	5.7	2.8	51	20	29	0.6	8%	30%	70%	31	88	55%	19%			13.4	76	142	$12
09 LA	8	7	0	117	87	3.76	3.71	1.14	243	233	253	23.1	1.8	6.7	3.6	49	17	33	0.9	10%	29%	70%	20	86	55%	15%	0	0.77	8.2	97	182	$9
10 LA	11	13	0	196	159	3.39	3.48	1.16	243	245	241	26.1	2.2	7.3	3.3	51	17	32	0.7	8%	29%	72%	31	98	68%	13%			16.6	101	163	$16
11 LA	13	16	0	202	161	3.07	3.64	1.21	254	264	244	26.2	2.2	7.2	3.3	43	22	35	1.1	11%	30%	80%	32	100	56%	13%			21.6	91	137	$17
12 NYY	16	11	0	220	167	3.32	3.60	1.17	249	253	244	27.0	2.1	6.8	3.3	52	18	30	1.0	13%	28%	76%	33	101	61%	9%			18.9	97	126	$20
1st Half	8	7	0	102	80	3.17	3.87	1.22	245	272	208	26.3	2.7	7.0	2.6	49	19	32	1.1	12%	28%	79%	16	99	63%	19%			10.7	80	104	$20
2nd Half	8	4	0	117	87	3.45	3.37	1.12	253	236	275	27.6	1.5	6.7	4.4	55	17	27	1.0	14%	29%	73%	17	103	59%	0%			8.2	112	146	$21
13 Proj	13	12	0	203	156	3.63	3.66	1.20	256	259	252	25.9	2.1	6.9	3.3	50	19	31	1.0	11%	30%	73%	32						9.7	96	125	$16

Lackey,John

Age: 34	Th: R	Role SP	Health F	LIMA Plan B
Ht: 6' 6"	Wt: 245	Type	PT/Exp B	Rand Var 0
			Consist A	MM 2205

Missed 2012 recovering from TJS and should be ready by the start of the season. But he's a pariah in Boston now, and why not? Kept his ERA south of 4.00 for 5 years until he arrived at Fenway, and 2011 was a disaster. But there is a history of better, even if its ancient history at this point. Speculate.

Yr Tm	W	L	Sv	IP	K	ERA	xERA	WHIP	OBA	vL	vR	BF/G	Ctl	Dom	Cmd	G	L	F	hr/9	hr/f	H%	S%	GS	APC	DOM%	DIS%	Sv%	LI	RAR	BPV	BPX	R$
08 LAA	12	5	0	163	130	3.75	3.72	1.23	260	221	301	28.1	2.2	7.2	3.3	45	20	34	1.4	15%	29%	76%	24	101	58%	4%			11.6	92	173	$13
09 LAA	11	8	0	176	139	3.83	3.87	1.27	263	276	247	27.7	2.4	7.1	3.0	45	20	35	0.9	9%	31%	72%	27	102	59%	22%			10.7	86	161	$12
10 BOS	14	11	0	215	156	4.35	4.16	1.42	277	298	251	28.2	3.0	6.5	2.2	46	18	36	0.8	7%	32%	70%	33	109	55%	12%			-7.3	60	97	$3
11 BOS	12	12	0	160	108	6.41	4.61	1.62	308	343	265	26.5	3.2	6.1	1.9	40	22	37	1.1	10%	35%	61%	28	102	29%	32%			-48.7	42	64	-$17
12																																
1st Half																																
2nd Half																																
13 Proj	13	10	0	189	135	4.22	4.39	1.43	280	294	262	26.7	3.0	6.4	2.2	44	20	36	1.0	10%	32%	73%	30						-4.7	58	75	$3

Laffey,Aaron

Age: 28	Th: L	Role RP	Health B	LIMA Plan F
Ht: 6' 0"	Wt: 200	Type Con	PT/Exp D	Rand Var +1
			Consist A	MM 0003

4-6, 4.56 ERA in 101 IP at TOR. Five years of the same, dull, lifeless skills. But right-brained arms will keep getting chances. If you're considering adding him to your roster, just take your league entry fee and donate it to charity. Either way, you'll be out some cash, but you'll have much better karma.

Yr Tm	W	L	Sv	IP	K	ERA	xERA	WHIP	OBA	vL	vR	BF/G	Ctl	Dom	Cmd	G	L	F	hr/9	hr/f	H%	S%	GS	APC	DOM%	DIS%	Sv%	LI	RAR	BPV	BPX	R$
08 CLE *	11	9	0	155	84	4.94	5.09	1.56	304	244	292	25.2	3.0	4.8	1.6	51	19	30	0.7	10%	34%	68%	16	93	38%	19%			-11.8	36	67	-$3
09 CLE *	7	11	1	139	67	5.19	5.53	1.74	305	255	310	21.2	4.5	4.4	1.0	49	21	30	0.7	7%	33%	70%	19	80	11%	21%	100	0.79	-15.0	19	35	-$10
10 CLE *	2	4	0	84	38	4.34	4.68	1.68	289	308	270	9.4	4.8	4.1	0.9	49	21	30	0.2	2%	32%	72%	5	35	20%	60%	0	0.85	-2.7	33	54	-$6
11 2 AL	3	2	0	53	30	3.88	4.80	1.65	306	242	358	5.3	3.5	5.1	1.4	48	19	33	1.2	11%	33%	80%	0	19			0	1.15	0.4	21	32	-$4
12 TOR *	7	11	0	164	78	4.73	5.24	1.49	289	239	269	21.5	3.1	4.3	1.4	50	19	31	1.3	16%	30%	72%	16	71	25%	38%	0	0.68	-14.5	13	17	-$10
1st Half	3	5	0	79	36	4.39	5.29	1.55	306	214	158	21.5	2.7	4.1	1.5	53	11	36	1.0	13%	32%	74%	1	41	0%	0%	0	0.44	-3.7	21	27	-$10
2nd Half	4	6	0	86	42	5.04	5.14	1.45	274	243	287	21.5	3.5	4.4	1.3	49	20	31	1.6	17%	28%	70%	15	80	27%	40%	0	0.76	-10.8	6	8	-$10
13 Proj	6	8	0	135	67	4.64	5.05	1.57	295	275	305	10.7	3.6	4.5	1.3	50	18	32	1.1	10%	31%	73%	4						-10.3	13	16	-$6

Lannan,John

Age: 28	Th: L	Role SP	Health A	LIMA Plan F
Ht: 6' 4"	Wt: 235	Type Con GB	PT/Exp B	Rand Var -2
			Consist C	MM 1001

4-1, 4.13 ERA in 33 IP at WAS. Here's how to trade him: "Hey, look at that ground ball trend! Isn't that great? No, don't look at anything else. Just ground balls! He keeps the ball down. That's all that matters. 5.00+ ERA? 1.2 Cmd? No, no. It's all about the GROUND BALLS."

Yr Tm	W	L	Sv	IP	K	ERA	xERA	WHIP	OBA	vL	vR	BF/G	Ctl	Dom	Cmd	G	L	F	hr/9	hr/f	H%	S%	GS	APC	DOM%	DIS%	Sv%	LI	RAR	BPV	BPX	R$
08 WAS	9	15	0	182	117	3.91	4.24	1.34	252	259	250	25.1	3.6	5.8	1.6	54	19	27	1.1	15%	27%	75%	31	95	29%	19%			9.4	40	75	$8
09 WAS	9	13	0	206	89	3.88	4.65	1.35	266	290	259	26.5	3.0	3.9	1.3	52	18	30	1.0	11%	28%	74%	33	95	27%	18%			11.2	20	37	$7
10 WAS *	9	12	0	184	93	4.89	5.50	1.61	314	287	307	25.5	2.9	4.5	1.6	51	21	27	0.9	10%	34%	71%	25	94	32%	28%			-18.4	26	42	-$9
11 WAS	10	13	0	185	106	3.70	4.32	1.46	272	211	293	24.5	3.7	5.2	1.4	54	21	25	0.7	10%	30%	76%	33	89	30%	21%			5.4	25	38	$1
12 WAS *	13	12	0	181	80	5.34	5.90	1.69	320	281	267	27.3	3.3	4.0	1.2	57	22	22	1.0	0%	34%	69%	6	85	17%	33%			-29.6	12	15	-$20
1st Half	6	6	0	89	34	5.78	6.82	1.82	336	0	0	27.6	3.5	3.4	1.0				1.3	0%	34%	70%	0	0					-19.4	-11	-14	-$25
2nd Half	7	6	0	92	46	4.91	4.94	1.57	303	281	267	26.9	3.1	4.5	1.5	57	22	22	0.6	0%	33%	68%	6	85	17%	33%			-10.1	35	46	-$15
13 Proj	6	7	0	102	51	4.67	4.78	1.58	300	290	303	25.9	3.3	4.5	1.3	54	21	25	0.9	11%	32%	72%	17						-8.1	23	30	-$5

MATT CEDERHOLM

Latos,Mat

	Health	A	LIMA Plan	B	
Age: 25 Th: R Role SP	PT/Exp	A	Rand Var	0	
Ht: 6' 6" Wt: 235 Type Pwr	Consist	A	MM	3405	

Moved from the best pitcher's park to a hitter's park, with ERA and WHIP virtually unchanged. Not the big rebound you hoped for, but it still soldifies his resume. H% and S% kept ERA down a bit, but that's nit-picking. At 25, there's still room to grow, making for an appealing combination: safety with upside.

Yr	Tm	W	L	Sv	IP	K	ERA	xERA	WHIP	OBA	vL	vR	BF/G	Ctl	Dom	Cmd	G	L	F	hr/9	hr/f	H%	S%	GS	APC	DOM%	DIS%	Sv%	LI	RAR	BPV	BPX	R$
08																																	
09	SD *	9	6	0	98	81	3.32	2.61	1.10	217	271	200	20.2	2.9	7.5	2.6	36	19	45	0.6	11%	26%	71%	10	87	30%	50%			12.1	91	171	$11
10	SD	14	10	0	185	189	2.92	3.27	1.08	217	220	214	24.1	2.4	9.2	3.8	45	15	40	0.8	8%	29%	76%	31	96	65%	13%			26.3	123	199	$23
11	SD	9	14	0	194	185	3.47	3.56	1.18	233	258	204	25.8	2.9	8.6	3.0	43	16	41	0.7	7%	30%	72%	31	102	71%	3%			11.2	98	147	$14
12	CIN	14	4	0	209	185	3.48	3.74	1.16	230	252	208	26.0	2.8	8.0	2.9	46	18	36	1.1	12%	28%	74%	33	99	52%	12%			13.7	93	121	$19
1st Half		7	2	0	98	90	4.42	3.86	1.23	246	290	188	25.6	2.6	8.3	3.2	42	18	41	1.6	15%	29%	70%	16	98	31%	19%			-4.9	99	129	$11
2nd Half		7	2	0	112	95	2.66	3.64	1.10	216	207	223	26.4	2.9	7.7	2.6	49	19	32	0.6	8%	26%	78%	17	100	71%	6%			18.7	87	113	$25
13	Proj	13	8	0	203	186	3.32	3.65	1.14	229	248	209	24.3	2.8	8.2	3.0	44	17	39	0.9	9%	28%	74%	33						17.4	96	124	$21

Layne,Tom

	Health	A	LIMA Plan	D	
Age: 28 Th: L Role RP	PT/Exp	D	Rand Var	+2	
Ht: 6' 3" Wt: 185 Type Pwr GB	Consist	B	MM	1200	

2-0, 2 Sv, 3.24 ERA in 17 IP at SD. Poor command history tells you he's someone to avoid, despite the two saves. He did crush left-handed hitters in a very, very small sample, and that's really where his value lies. Lefty one-out guys have value in "real" baseball, but not in fantasy. He is no exception.

Yr	Tm	W	L	Sv	IP	K	ERA	xERA	WHIP	OBA	vL	vR	BF/G	Ctl	Dom	Cmd	G	L	F	hr/9	hr/f	H%	S%	GS	APC	DOM%	DIS%	Sv%	LI	RAR	BPV	BPX	R$
08																																	
09	aa	0	3	0	31	19	6.94	4.62	1.79	282			23.8	6.1	5.5	0.9				0.0		33%	57%							-10.0	50	94	-$8
10	aa	12	7	0	149	71	5.34	5.50	1.69	310			25.9	3.8	4.3	1.1				0.7		34%	68%							-23.3	21	33	-$10
11	a/a	12	7	0	139	54	6.13	6.08	1.76	321			18.2	3.9	3.5	0.9				1.0		33%	65%							-37.5	2	2	-$18
12	SD *	2	10	3	94	80	6.19	5.27	1.66	294	83	240	6.2	4.3	7.6	1.8	50	22	28	0.8	0%	35%	62%	0	11			50	1.26	-25.3	54	70	-$14
1st Half		0	8	0	64	41	7.93	6.89	1.93	330	0	0	15.3	4.9	5.8	1.2				1.2	0%	37%	59%	0	0					-31.1	12	16	-$26
2nd Half		2	2	3	30	39	2.44	1.72	1.07	203	83	240	2.4	3.1	11.6	3.7	50	22	28	0.0	0%	32%	75%	0	11			60	1.26	5.8	161	210	$10
13	Proj	3	4	0	58	43	4.88	4.47	1.52	276	156	449	6.7	4.0	6.7	1.7	50	22	28	0.6	7%	33%	67%	0						-6.2	40	52	-$4

League,Brandon

	Health	A	LIMA Plan	B	
Age: 30 Th: R Role RP	PT/Exp	B	Rand Var	-3	
Ht: 6' 2" Wt: 210 Type xGB	Consist	B	MM	3231	

PRO: Low FB% limits HR; strong past Cmd gives hope for rebound; signed big deal to remain at closer.
CON: 2012 skills not close to closer-worthy; hr/f will regress; ERA will correct; OBA v. LH a concern.
Which guy will you draft, '12 or '11? That's the question. Answer: Have a backup plan.

Yr	Tm	W	L	Sv	IP	K	ERA	xERA	WHIP	OBA	vL	vR	BF/G	Ctl	Dom	Cmd	G	L	F	hr/9	hr/f	H%	S%	GS	APC	DOM%	DIS%	Sv%	LI	RAR	BPV	BPX	R$
08	TOR *	3	5	3	67	50	3.88	4.41	1.48	279	263	200	5.7	3.5	6.7	1.9	67	19	14	0.6	14%	33%	74%	0	16			75	0.87	3.7	61	114	$1
09	TOR	3	6	0	75	76	4.58	3.03	1.25	257	270	245	4.7	2.5	9.2	3.6	56	18	26	1.0	15%	32%	65%	0	17			0	0.79	-2.4	131	244	$1
10	SEA	9	7	6	79	56	3.42	3.47	1.19	229	243	218	4.7	3.1	6.4	2.1	63	16	21	0.8	14%	26%	74%	0	16			50	1.37	6.4	73	118	$8
11	SEA	1	5	37	61	45	2.79	3.17	1.08	239	254	224	3.8	1.5	6.6	4.5	57	19	24	0.4	7%	29%	75%	0	14			88	1.20	8.7	114	172	$18
12	2 TM	2	6	15	72	54	3.13	4.14	1.36	246	292	208	4.1	4.1	6.8	1.6	50	27	23	0.1	2%	30%	75%	0	15			71	1.09	7.9	38	50	$6
1st Half		0	4	9	35	21	3.38	4.94	1.56	284	347	210	4.3	4.2	5.5	1.3	45	26	29	0.3	3%	33%	77%	0	15			60	1.17	2.7	9	12	$2
2nd Half		2	2	6	37	33	2.89	3.40	1.18	208	208	207	3.8	4.1	8.0	1.9	57	28	15	0.0	0%	27%	73%	0	15			100	1.01	5.2	67	87	$10
13	Proj	3	6	35	73	55	3.55	3.75	1.32	255	284	229	4.2	3.2	6.9	2.2	56	22	22	0.5	8%	31%	73%	0						4.2	71	93	$16

Leake,Mike

	Health	A	LIMA Plan	C	
Age: 25 Th: R Role SP	PT/Exp	A	Rand Var	+3	
Ht: 6' 0" Wt: 180 Type Con	Consist	A	MM	2105	

A relatively stable skill set, yes, but DIS% shows how erratic he was in 2012. Solid command and GB% say he has the stuff to be better, leaving consistency as the one skill that was lacking last year. He'll never be close to elite, but is a reliable back-end starter with a smidge of upside. Yes, we said "smidge."

Yr	Tm	W	L	Sv	IP	K	ERA	xERA	WHIP	OBA	vL	vR	BF/G	Ctl	Dom	Cmd	G	L	F	hr/9	hr/f	H%	S%	GS	APC	DOM%	DIS%	Sv%	LI	RAR	BPV	BPX	R$
08																																	
09																																	
10	CIN	8	4	0	138	91	4.23	4.26	1.50	292	292	291	25.2	3.2	5.9	1.9	50	18	32	1.2	13%	32%	76%	22	89	41%	14%	0	0.75	-2.6	48	78	-$1
11	CIN	12	9	0	168	118	3.86	3.64	1.17	250	262	240	23.9	2.0	6.3	3.1	48	21	32	1.2	14%	28%	72%	26	88	50%	12%	0	0.81	1.6	85	128	$10
12	CIN	8	9	0	179	116	4.58	4.01	1.35	287	297	275	25.2	2.1	5.8	2.8	49	25	27	1.3	17%	31%	70%	30	90	40%	27%			-12.4	76	100	-$3
1st Half		3	5	0	92	62	4.12	3.94	1.30	275	292	252	25.6	2.2	6.1	2.8	47	27	26	1.1	15%	30%	71%	15	92	47%	27%			-1.2	77	100	$0
2nd Half		5	4	0	87	54	5.05	4.09	1.41	300	302	297	24.9	2.0	5.6	2.8	51	22	27	1.5	19%	32%	69%	15	89	33%	27%			-11.1	76	99	-$6
13	Proj	11	9	0	189	125	4.33	4.01	1.32	275	284	266	24.2	2.2	6.0	2.7	49	22	29	1.3	15%	30%	71%	32						-7.2	75	97	$5

LeBlanc,Wade

	Health	A	LIMA Plan	B	
Age: 28 Th: L Role RP	PT/Exp	C	Rand Var	0	
Ht: 6' 2" Wt: 215 Type FB	Consist	B	MM	1201	

2-5, 3.67 ERA in 69 IP at MIA. This might have looked like more of a growth year had he stayed in SD. Still, skills are borderline; never had a sub-4.00 xERA in the bigs. Marginal Dom, high FB and high DIS% walk a tightrope above disaster. He won't kill your pitching staff, but you may have to visit it in the ICU.

Yr	Tm	W	L	Sv	IP	K	ERA	xERA	WHIP	OBA	vL	vR	BF/G	Ctl	Dom	Cmd	G	L	F	hr/9	hr/f	H%	S%	GS	APC	DOM%	DIS%	Sv%	LI	RAR	BPV	BPX	R$
08	SD *	12	12	0	160	135	5.53	4.79	1.40	275	318	333	21.8	3.0	7.6	2.5	41	22	37	1.3	26%	32%	63%	4	81	50%	50%	0	0.73	-23.9	59	110	$0
09	SD *	7	10	0	167	112	4.12	3.78	1.25	251	235	203	20.6	2.7	6.0	2.2	36	16	48	1.0	9%	28%	70%	9	86	22%	22%			4.2	56	106	$8
10	SD	8	12	0	146	110	4.25	4.42	1.42	279	308	269	24.0	3.1	6.8	2.2	35	19	46	1.5	12%	31%	76%	25	93	36%	20%	0	0.76	-3.1	50	81	$1
11	SD *	14	7	0	186	126	4.02	3.79	1.32	267	408	236	24.9	2.6	6.1	2.3	32	33	35	0.6	8%	31%	70%	14	95	43%	29%			-1.8	69	104	$6
12	MIA *	7	10	0	167	112	4.33	4.43	1.36	282	280	273	17.0	2.3	6.0	2.7	34	20	46	0.9	7%	32%	70%	9	43	22%	56%	0	0.58	-6.6	63	82	-$2
1st Half		5	5	0	99	69	4.79	4.64	1.39	291	0	0	26.0	2.1	6.3	3.0				1.0	0%	33%	67%	0	0					-9.5	69	90	-$2
2nd Half		2	5	0	69	43	3.67	4.08	1.31	268	280	273	11.3	2.5	5.6	2.3	34	20	46	0.9	7%	30%	75%	9	43	22%	56%	0	0.58	2.9	55	72	-$1
13	Proj	6	7	0	123	84	4.19	4.57	1.35	273	316	259	18.2	2.6	6.2	2.4	34	22	44	1.2	9%	30%	72%	23						-2.6	54	70	$2

Lecure,Sam

	Health	A	LIMA Plan	A+	
Age: 29 Th: R Role RP	PT/Exp	C	Rand Var	-1	
Ht: 6' 1" Wt: 210 Type Pwr	Consist	B	MM	3400	

A second straight season with a 100+ BPV—it seems relieving agrees with him, and his 2H stuff, in particular, was electric. Career splits agree: 1.6 Cmd, 6.8 Dom as a starter; 3.0 Cmd, 9.1 Dom as a reliever. This is the kind of guy who sneaks his way into a closer role later in his career. Just sayin'.

Yr	Tm	W	L	Sv	IP	K	ERA	xERA	WHIP	OBA	vL	vR	BF/G	Ctl	Dom	Cmd	G	L	F	hr/9	hr/f	H%	S%	GS	APC	DOM%	DIS%	Sv%	LI	RAR	BPV	BPX	R$
08	aa	9	7	0	155	107	4.15	4.67	1.49	280			24.8	3.5	6.2	1.8				0.9		32%	74%							3.3	47	88	$2
09	aaa	10	8	0	143	104	6.07	5.88	1.59	307			25.3	3.1	6.5	2.1				1.5		34%	64%							-30.8	32	60	-$8
10	CIN *	10	8	0	146	108	4.55	4.93	1.49	290	304	252	21.0	3.1	6.6	2.2	46	20	34	1.0	12%	33%	71%	6	57	17%	17%	0	0.68	-8.5	53	85	-$1
11	CIN	2	1	0	78	73	3.71	3.24	1.00	205	186	216	7.1	2.4	8.5	3.5	46	14	40	1.2	13%	24%	68%	4	28	50%	50%	0	0.83	2.2	111	166	$4
12	CIN	3	3	0	57	61	3.14	3.46	1.20	221	208	232	4.9	3.6	9.6	2.7	48	21	31	0.5	7%	30%	74%	0	20			0	1.09	6.2	101	132	$2
1st Half		2	2	0	30	28	3.94	3.72	1.35	248	224	275	5.9	3.9	8.5	2.2	49	25	26	0.9	14%	30%	73%	0	24			0	0.55	0.3	73	95	$0
2nd Half		1	1	0	28	33	2.28	3.22	1.05	192	184	197	4.2	3.3	10.7	3.3	46	16	37	0.0	0%	30%	76%	0	17			0	1.52	5.9	130	169	$5
13	Proj	3	3	0	65	63	3.32	3.62	1.21	234	226	239	5.2	3.2	8.7	2.7	46	18	36	0.7	9%	30%	75%	0						5.6	95	123	$3

Lee,Cliff

	Health	B	LIMA Plan	C+	
Age: 34 Th: L Role SP	PT/Exp	A	Rand Var	0	
Ht: 6' 3" Wt: 205 Type	Consist	A	MM	5405	

Forget the win total. Yes, FORGET IT. This was virtually the same season as 2011. PHI averaged 4.2 runs/game last year, yet scored less than that in 21 of his 30 starts. That's just horrible support. He may see some age-related decline, but odds are he'll still be close to elite starter status.

Yr	Tm	W	L	Sv	IP	K	ERA	xERA	WHIP	OBA	vL	vR	BF/G	Ctl	Dom	Cmd	G	L	F	hr/9	hr/f	H%	S%	GS	APC	DOM%	DIS%	Sv%	LI	RAR	BPV	BPX	R$
08	CLE	22	3	0	223	170	2.54	3.51	1.11	253	272	245	28.7	1.4	6.9	5.0	46	19	35	0.5	5%	31%	78%	31	106	68%	3%			49.2	110	207	$33
09	2 TM	14	13	0	232	181	3.22	3.78	1.24	272	241	283	28.5	1.7	7.0	4.2	41	22	36	0.7	7%	33%	76%	34	104	59%	9%			31.4	100	188	$22
10	2 AL	12	9	0	212	185	3.18	3.22	1.00	240	281	227	30.1	0.8	7.8	10.3	42	18	40	0.7	6%	30%	70%	28	106	64%	4%			23.6	141	227	$25
11	PHI	17	8	0	233	238	2.40	2.84	1.03	229	196	239	28.8	1.6	9.2	5.7	46	21	32	0.7	9%	30%	80%	32	106	81%	9%			44.3	146	219	$35
12	PHI	6	9	0	211	207	3.16	3.20	1.11	255	263	253	28.2	1.2	8.8	7.4	45	18	37	1.1	12%	32%	77%	30	103	80%	3%			22.3	150	195	$20
1st Half		0	5	0	89	89	4.13	3.21	1.21	264	269	263	27.5	1.9	9.0	4.7	47	19	35	0.9	11%	33%	68%	13	103	77%	8%			-1.3	134	174	$3
2nd Half		6	4	0	122	118	2.44	3.19	1.04	248	258	246	28.8	0.7	8.7	13.1	44	18	38	1.3	12%	31%	85%	17	104	82%	0%			23.6	161	210	$34
13	Proj	15	9	0	218	207	3.25	3.16	1.08	250	251	250	28.0	1.3	8.6	6.8	45	19	36	0.9	10%	31%	73%	30						20.5	143	186	$26

MATT CEDERHOLM

Lester,Jon

Age: 29	Th: L	Role SP	Health	A	LIMA Plan C
Ht: 6' 4"	Wt: 240	Type Pwr GB	PT/Exp	A	Rand Var +2
			Consist	A	MM 3305

Primed to bounce back or beyond salvation? PRO: xERA says correction of strand rate and hr/f will improve results, GB% remains an asset, still a workhorse. CON: Negative Dom trend driving BPV fade, 2H DIS% spike is a red flag. There is still plenty of skill here; expect a rebound.

Yr Tm	W	L	Sv	IP	K	ERA	xERA	WHIP	OBA	vL	vR	BF/G	Ctl	Dom	Cmd	G	L	F	hr/9	hr/f	H%	S%	GS	APC	DOM%	DIS%	Sv%	LI	RAR	BPV	BPX	R$
08 BOS	16	6	0	210	152	3.21	3.95	1.27	256	217	273	26.5	2.8	6.5	2.3	47	21	32	0.6	7%	30%	76%	33	100	58%	12%			28.9	66	123	$19
09 BOS	15	8	0	203	225	3.41	3.22	1.23	242	257	237	26.3	2.8	10.0	3.5	48	18	35	0.9	11%	32%	75%	32	106	69%	13%			22.9	129	241	$22
10 BOS	19	9	0	208	225	3.25	3.12	1.20	220	226	219	26.9	3.6	9.7	2.7	54	17	30	0.6	9%	30%	74%	32	105	69%	6%			21.4	110	178	$22
11 BOS	15	9	0	192	182	3.47	3.48	1.26	234	207	244	25.8	3.5	8.5	2.4	50	16	34	0.9	11%	29%	76%	31	103	61%	16%			11.1	87	130	$14
12 BOS	9	14	0	205	166	4.82	3.94	1.38	273	259	278	26.5	3.0	7.3	2.4	49	22	29	1.1	14%	32%	67%	33	104	52%	18%			-20.4	77	101	-$4
1st Half	5	5	0	101	79	4.53	3.83	1.34	276	277	276	26.9	2.4	7.0	2.9	49	23	28	0.9	11%	32%	67%	16	105	50%	13%			-6.4	88	115	$0
2nd Half	4	9	0	104	87	5.11	4.06	1.42	270	240	279	26.2	3.5	7.5	2.1	50	21	30	1.3	16%	31%	67%	17	103	53%	24%			-14.0	67	87	-$8
13 Proj	**13**	**12**	**0**	**210**	**179**	**3.91**	**3.84**	**1.32**	**253**	**238**	**258**	**25.9**	**3.2**	**7.7**	**2.4**	**50**	**19**	**31**	**1.0**	**12%**	**30%**	**73%**	**34**						**2.8**	**78**	**102**	**$11**

Lewis,Colby

Age: 33	Th: R	Role SP	Health	D	LIMA Plan B+
Ht: 6' 4"	Wt: 230	Type Pwr xFB	PT/Exp	A	Rand Var 0
			Consist	A	MM 3301

Underwent Tommy John surgery in July; expected to miss most of 1H. Injury interrupted excellent campaign as BPIs flourished across the board. Extreme FB% isn't ideal, but check PQS splits—he makes it work. Uncertain recovery time is primary risk. Strong skills make him a great stash as 2H upside play.

Yr Tm	W	L	Sv	IP	K	ERA	xERA	WHIP	OBA	vL	vR	BF/G	Ctl	Dom	Cmd	G	L	F	hr/9	hr/f	H%	S%	GS	APC	DOM%	DIS%	Sv%	LI	RAR	BPV	BPX	R$
08 for	15	8	0	178	174	3.33	3.28	1.10	244			26.8	1.7	8.8	5.2				1.0		30%	74%							21.9	137	258	$22
09 for	11	9	0	176	176	3.68	3.44	1.09	252			23.7	1.2	9.0	7.5				1.1		31%	70%							13.9	183	342	$19
10 TEX	12	13	0	201	196	3.72	3.75	1.19	227	239	216	26.4	2.9	8.8	3.0	38	17	45	0.9	8%	29%	72%	32	103	66%	3%			9.0	95	154	$15
11 TEX	14	10	0	200	169	4.40	4.01	1.21	244	274	204	26.2	2.5	7.6	3.0	34	17	49	1.6	12%	28%	70%	32	100	59%	19%			-11.4	81	121	$8
12 TEX	6	6	0	105	93	3.43	3.69	1.08	245	252	236	26.7	1.2	8.0	6.6	33	21	46	1.4	11%	29%	75%	16	102	69%	6%			7.6	122	159	$9
1st Half	6	6	0	100	90	3.51	3.64	1.08	248	257	237	27.1	1.1	8.1	7.5	33	21	46	1.4	11%	30%	74%	15	103	73%	7%			6.3	128	167	$10
2nd Half	0	0	0	5	3	1.80	4.93	1.00	177	167	200	21.0	3.6	5.4	1.5	29	21	50	1.8	14%	15%	100%	1	75	0%	0%			1.4	7	9	-$17
13 Proj	**6**	**5**	**0**	**94**	**83**	**3.75**	**3.94**	**1.19**	**247**	**263**	**228**	**25.7**	**2.4**	**7.9**	**3.3**	**35**	**18**	**46**	**1.2**	**10%**	**29%**	**73%**	**15**						**3.1**	**91**	**118**	**$5**

Lilly,Ted

Age: 37	Th: L	Role SP	Health	F	LIMA Plan B+
Ht: 6' 0"	Wt: 190	Type xFB	PT/Exp	A	Rand Var -5
			Consist	A	MM 2303

Landed on DL in May with shoulder issue that eventually required surgery. Dramatic skill erosion was first clue he wasn't right; consistent BPV history says he deserves a mulligan. Correction to hit rate and hr/f will yield numbers much closer to useful 2011 line. Even at 37, he'll be a bargain if healthy.

Yr Tm	W	L	Sv	IP	K	ERA	xERA	WHIP	OBA	vL	vR	BF/G	Ctl	Dom	Cmd	G	L	F	hr/9	hr/f	H%	S%	GS	APC	DOM%	DIS%	Sv%	LI	RAR	BPV	BPX	R$
08 CHC	17	9	0	205	184	4.09	4.04	1.23	239	307	219	25.3	2.8	8.1	2.9	34	22	44	1.4	12%	28%	72%	34	95	68%	21%			5.9	82	153	$17
09 CHC	12	9	0	177	151	3.10	3.83	1.06	230	219	233	26.1	1.8	7.7	4.2	32	17	51	1.1	9%	27%	76%	27	99	74%	4%			26.6	99	185	$23
10 2 NL	10	12	0	194	166	3.62	3.87	1.08	229	301	213	26.2	2.0	7.7	3.8	30	18	53	1.5	11%	26%	74%	30	97	63%	10%			10.8	92	148	$17
11 LA	12	14	0	193	158	3.97	3.92	1.16	238	210	246	24.2	2.4	7.4	3.1	34	20	47	1.3	11%	27%	71%	33	92	55%	21%			-0.7	81	121	$11
12 LA	5	1	0	49	31	3.14	4.61	1.13	203	209	201	25.3	3.5	5.7	1.6	41	21	38	0.6	5%	24%	73%	8	88	75%	13%			5.2	27	36	$2
1st Half	5	1	0	49	31	3.14	4.61	1.13	203	209	201	25.3	3.5	5.7	1.6	41	21	38	0.6	5%	24%	73%	8	88	75%	13%			5.2	28	36	$2
2nd Half																																
13 Proj	**10**	**8**	**0**	**145**	**114**	**3.70**	**4.19**	**1.19**	**242**	**260**	**237**	**24.8**	**2.6**	**7.1**	**2.7**	**35**	**19**	**46**	**1.3**	**11%**	**27%**	**74%**	**23**						**5.6**	**70**	**91**	**$10**

Lincecum,Tim

Age: 29	Th: R	Role SP	Health	A	LIMA Plan C+
Ht: 5' 11"	Wt: 175	Type Pwr	PT/Exp	A	Rand Var +3
			Consist	A	MM 3505

Try not to overreact to ugly 2012. I know, it's tough. Yes, control finally blew up, but damage was also due to fluky hr/f spike. Still... racks up Ks, S% & hr/f will regress. But it might not be enough if his velocity is still off. Looked superb in relief in play-offs... they could ride with that, you know.

Yr Tm	W	L	Sv	IP	K	ERA	xERA	WHIP	OBA	vL	vR	BF/G	Ctl	Dom	Cmd	G	L	F	hr/9	hr/f	H%	S%	GS	APC	DOM%	DIS%	Sv%	LI	RAR	BPV	BPX	R$
08 SF	18	5	0	227	265	2.62	3.18	1.17	221	221	221	27.3	3.3	10.5	3.2	44	21	35	0.4	6%	31%	78%	33	108	79%	6%	0	0.79	47.8	121	227	$33
09 SF	15	7	0	225	261	2.48	2.93	1.05	206	209	203	28.3	2.7	10.4	3.8	48	19	33	0.4	5%	30%	77%	32	107	81%	6%			51.3	140	263	$38
10 SF	15	10	0	206	224	3.43	3.24	1.28	244	255	231	27.3	3.2	9.8	3.0	49	19	32	0.8	10%	32%	74%	32	104	63%	19%			13.9	116	187	$16
11 SF	13	14	0	217	220	2.74	3.38	1.21	222	217	226	27.3	3.6	9.1	2.6	48	19	33	0.6	8%	29%	79%	33	109	73%	6%			32.3	94	141	$22
12 SF	10	15	0	186	190	5.18	4.00	1.47	257	232	282	25.0	4.4	9.2	2.1	46	24	30	1.1	15%	32%	66%	33	100	48%	24%			-26.7	72	94	-$8
1st Half	3	8	0	90	99	5.60	4.01	1.49	250	228	271	25.2	4.7	9.9	2.1	44	25	31	0.8	10%	34%	62%	16	101	38%	19%			-17.6	73	95	-$11
2nd Half	7	7	0	96	91	4.78	4.01	1.45	263	236	293	24.8	4.0	8.5	2.1	48	23	29	1.4	19%	31%	71%	17	99	59%	29%			-9.1	70	91	-$4
13 Proj	**12**	**11**	**0**	**181**	**188**	**3.87**	**3.64**	**1.34**	**244**	**232**	**257**	**25.3**	**3.8**	**9.3**	**2.4**	**47**	**22**	**32**	**0.7**	**10%**	**32%**	**72%**	**30**						**3.2**	**90**	**116**	**$10**

Lincoln,Brad

Age: 28	Th: R	Role RP	Health	A	LIMA Plan A+
Ht: 6' 0"	Wt: 210	Type Pwr	PT/Exp	C	Rand Var +1
			Consist	B	MM 3400

Failed starter found his calling in bullpen and handled move to AL East well. Elite dominance? Yep. Excellent control? Check. Even rediscovered the GB% lean he'd shown as a starter in 2H. Throw in a hr/f correction and you have a closer-in-waiting. All he needs is the opportunity.

Yr Tm	W	L	Sv	IP	K	ERA	xERA	WHIP	OBA	vL	vR	BF/G	Ctl	Dom	Cmd	G	L	F	hr/9	hr/f	H%	S%	GS	APC	DOM%	DIS%	Sv%	LI	RAR	BPV	BPX	R$
08																																
09 a/a	7	7	0	136	85	4.15	4.46	1.37	292			22.9	1.8	5.6	3.0				0.8		33%	71%							2.9	71	132	$3
10 PIT *	8	9	0	147	90	5.43	4.59	1.36	281	299	319	21.9	2.4	5.5	2.3	37	19	44	1.1	11%	31%	61%	9	78	11%	44%	0	0.64	-24.5	48	77	-$4
11 PIT *	9	11	0	159	99	5.01	4.54	1.44	299	349	236	21.9	2.1	5.6	2.7	52	23	26	0.6	10%	34%	64%	8	63	38%	25%	0	0.64	-20.9	67	101	-$6
12 2 TM	5	2	1	88	88	3.68	3.58	1.18	241	212	265	7.0	2.5	9.0	3.7	40	22	38	1.4	15%	29%	76%	5	25	40%	60%	50	0.84	3.6	114	148	$5
1st Half	4	2	0	48	49	3.21	3.61	1.15	233	235	232	9.8	2.5	9.3	3.8	34	24	41	1.3	13%	29%	79%	5	36	40%	60%	0	0.83	4.7	113	147	$8
2nd Half	1	0	1	40	39	4.24	3.53	1.21	250	182	302	5.2	2.5	8.7	3.5	46	18	35	1.6	18%	29%	71%	0	19			50	0.84	-1.1	115	150	$0
13 Proj	**3**	**2**	**0**	**58**	**52**	**3.93**	**3.67**	**1.30**	**270**	**271**	**268**	**7.0**	**2.3**	**8.0**	**3.5**	**44**	**21**	**34**	**1.1**	**12%**	**32%**	**73%**	**0**						**0.6**	**105**	**136**	**$0**

Lindblom,Josh

Age: 26	Th: R	Role RP	Health	A	LIMA Plan B+
Ht: 6' 4"	Wt: 239	Type Pwr FB	PT/Exp	D	Rand Var -2
			Consist	F	MM 2400

Change of scenery did nothing for skills, as negative control trend came to a head in 2H. Trouble with LH along with FB%/gopheritis combo increase the risk, and '11 now looks like a fortuitous confluence. Strikeout ability is there, but he's best-suited for lower leverage innings... and someone else's roster.

Yr Tm	W	L	Sv	IP	K	ERA	xERA	WHIP	OBA	vL	vR	BF/G	Ctl	Dom	Cmd	G	L	F	hr/9	hr/f	H%	S%	GS	APC	DOM%	DIS%	Sv%	LI	RAR	BPV	BPX	R$
08																																
09 a/a	6	5	1	96	74	4.15	3.54	1.24	262			11.5	2.2	6.9	3.2				0.6		31%	67%							2.0	91	170	$5
10 aaa	3	2	0	95	73	5.22	5.91	1.67	334			10.7	2.4	6.9	2.9				0.8		39%	69%							-13.4	66	107	-$8
11 LA *	2	3	17	72	73	2.42	2.10	1.06	208	370	153	4.6	2.9	9.1	3.2	28	19	53	0.3	0%	28%	77%	0	17			81	0.87	13.5	125	187	$14
12 2 NL	3	5	1	71	70	3.55	4.31	1.35	232	261	209	4.1	4.4	8.9	2.0	36	21	44	1.6	16%	27%	82%	0	17			25	1.10	4.1	54	70	$0
1st Half	2	2	0	37	32	3.13	4.02	1.13	214	213	214	4.2	3.4	7.7	2.3	40	14	45	1.7	16%	22%	83%	0	17			0	1.06	4.1	66	86	$3
2nd Half	1	3	1	34	38	4.01	4.61	1.60	250	315	205	4.1	5.6	10.2	1.8	31	27	42	1.6	15%	32%	81%	0	16			50	1.15	0.0	40	52	-$3
13 Proj	**2**	**3**	**0**	**58**	**55**	**3.62**	**4.16**	**1.34**	**250**	**289**	**220**	**4.9**	**3.6**	**8.6**	**2.4**	**35**	**22**	**43**	**1.1**	**10%**	**30%**	**77%**	**0**						**2.9**	**69**	**90**	**$0**

Lindstrom,Matt

Age: 33	Th: R	Role RP	Health	D	LIMA Plan B+
Ht: 6' 3"	Wt: 220	Type	PT/Exp	C	Rand Var -3
			Consist	A	MM 3300

Coincidence best results came the year he wasn't closing? BPV says middle relief suits him—solid control held while Dom went up considerably. GB% is best weapon and helps stifle HRs. There's temporary LIMA potential here, but note Health/Rand Var warning signs.

Yr Tm	W	L	Sv	IP	K	ERA	xERA	WHIP	OBA	vL	vR	BF/G	Ctl	Dom	Cmd	G	L	F	hr/9	hr/f	H%	S%	GS	APC	DOM%	DIS%	Sv%	LI	RAR	BPV	BPX	R$
08 FLA	3	3	5	57	43	3.14	4.31	1.45	270	324	214	3.7	4.1	6.8	1.7	46	23	30	0.2	2%	32%	77%	0	14			83	0.98	8.4	35	66	$3
09 FLA	2	1	15	47	39	5.89	4.72	1.65	281	278	284	4.1	4.6	7.4	1.6	45	20	35	1.0	9%	34%	64%	0	15			88	0.84	-9.2	33	62	$0
10 HOU	2	5	23	53	43	4.39	4.22	1.65	306	268	336	4.2	3.4	7.3	2.2	49	19	32	0.8	9%	37%	75%	0	16			79	0.97	-2.0	66	108	$5
11 COL	2	2	2	54	36	3.00	3.83	1.22	256	253	258	3.6	2.3	6.0	2.6	47	21	31	0.5	6%	30%	76%	0	13			40	1.23	6.3	70	105	$2
12 2 TM	1	0	0	47	40	2.68	3.64	1.26	250	284	226	4.3	2.7	7.7	2.9	51	22	27	0.4	5%	32%	79%	0	17			0	0.77	7.7	94	123	$0
1st Half	1	0	0	16	15	2.25	3.58	1.38	266	360	205	4.5	2.8	8.4	3.0	54	22	24	0.0	0%	36%	82%	0	17			0	1.07	3.5	108	141	-$2
2nd Half	0	0	0	31	25	2.90	3.66	1.19	241	245	239	4.3	2.6	7.3	2.8	49	22	29	0.6	8%	29%	77%	0	17			0	0.62	4.3	87	113	$1
13 Proj	**2**	**1**	**0**	**51**	**40**	**3.18**	**3.89**	**1.34**	**266**	**281**	**255**	**3.9**	**2.9**	**7.2**	**2.5**	**49**	**21**	**29**	**0.5**	**6%**	**32%**	**77%**	**0**						**5.2**	**79**	**102**	**$0**

DAN BECKER

Liriano,Francisco	Health	B	LIMA Plan	D+
Age: 29 Th: L Role SP	PT/Exp	A	Rand Var	+3
Ht: 6' 2" Wt: 215 Type Pwr	Consist	B	MM	2403

This highwire act has grown tiresome. Neither temporary move to bullpen nor change of scenery helped him find the plate. GB% continues to fade, and has topped 160 IP once in four seasons. Two straight years of atrocious DIS% make 2010 feel like a distant memory. Time to move on.

Yr Tm	W	L	Sv	IP	K	ERA	xERA	WHIP	OBA	vL	vR	BF/G	Ctl	Dom	Cmd	G	L	F	hr/9	hr/f	H%	S%	GS	APC	DOM%	DIS%	Sv%	LI	RAR	BPV	BPX	R$
08 MIN *	16	6	0	194	161	3.90	3.78	1.32	261	217	266	24.3	2.9	7.4	2.6	42	18	40	0.7	8%	32%	71%	14	91	50%	29%			10.0	81	152	$14
09 MIN	5	13	0	137	122	5.80	4.49	1.55	279	255	287	21.0	4.3	8.0	1.9	40	19	41	1.4	13%	32%	65%	24	80	38%	33%	0	0.73	-24.8	47	88	-$7
10 MIN	14	10	0	192	201	3.62	3.03	1.26	252	218	262	26.0	2.7	9.4	3.5	54	19	27	0.4	6%	34%	71%	31	97	65%	13%			11.0	128	208	$14
11 MIN	9	10	0	134	112	5.09	4.37	1.49	249	235	253	22.7	5.0	7.5	1.5	49	15	36	0.9	10%	29%	67%	24	88	46%	29%	0	0.75	-19.0	26	40	-$5
12 2 AL	6	12	0	157	167	5.34	4.15	1.47	244	221	251	20.4	5.0	9.6	1.9	44	21	35	1.1	13%	31%	65%	28	80	50%	32%	0	0.83	-25.7	60	78	-$9
1st Half	2	7	0	71	70	5.30	4.23	1.46	244	155	270	18.4	5.0	8.8	1.8	45	24	31	0.9	12%	30%	64%	12	72	50%	33%	0	0.87	-11.3	46	60	-$10
2nd Half	4	5	0	85	97	5.38	4.10	1.48	243	268	235	22.4	5.0	10.2	2.1	43	19	38	1.3	14%	32%	66%	16	88	50%	31%	0	0.79	-14.3	71	92	-$8
13 Proj	**9**	**11**	**0**	**160**	**158**	**4.97**	**4.08**	**1.44**	**249**	**230**	**256**	**21.4**	**4.5**	**8.9**	**2.0**	**46**	**19**	**35**	**1.0**	**11%**	**31%**	**67%**	**32**						**-18.8**	**62**	**81**	**-$1**

Loe,Kameron	Health	A	LIMA Plan	C+
Age: 31 Th: R Role RP	PT/Exp	C	Rand Var	+5
Ht: 6' 8" Wt: 245 Type xGB	Consist	C	MM	4210

Exhibit A of how a reliever's season can get wrecked by a combination of smaller sample size and bad luck. Disastrous 2H hit rate and hr/f sabotaged results, while underlying skills very similar to 2011. Control is plus; ground ball rate is strong; Dom surged in 2H. xERA says he's worth a bullpen flyer.

Yr Tm	W	L	Sv	IP	K	ERA	xERA	WHIP	OBA	vL	vR	BF/G	Ctl	Dom	Cmd	G	L	F	hr/9	hr/f	H%	S%	GS	APC	DOM%	DIS%	Sv%	LI	RAR	BPV	BPX	R$
08 TEX *	4	5	1	89	44	5.81	6.32	1.72	329	400	200	10.1	3.0	4.5	1.5	50	16	33	1.2	9%	35%	68%	0	36			33	0.94	-16.2	12	23	-$9
09 for	0	4	0	27	19	7.87	7.00	1.98	337			25.9	5.0	6.3	1.3				1.1		38%	60%							-11.8	19	36	-$9
10 MIL *	7	8	0	121	76	3.36	4.20	1.33	268	274	228	8.0	2.7	5.7	2.1	59	16	25	1.0	14%	30%	78%	0	17			0	1.25	10.8	50	81	$5
11 MIL	4	7	1	72	61	3.50	2.84	1.13	240	250	233	4.0	2.0	7.6	3.8	63	17	19	0.5	10%	30%	69%	0	15			13	1.09	3.9	124	187	$4
12 MIL	6	5	2	68	55	4.61	3.73	1.43	284	307	267	4.3	2.6	7.2	2.8	57	20	23	1.2	18%	33%	71%	0	15			29	1.04	-5.0	94	123	-$3
1st Half	4	2	0	35	24	3.34	3.81	1.20	248	291	218	4.6	2.3	6.2	2.7	52	23	25	1.0	15%	28%	76%	0	16			0	1.14	2.9	78	102	$3
2nd Half	2	3	2	33	31	5.94	3.62	1.68	317	322	313	4.1	3.0	8.4	2.8	63	16	21	1.4	22%	39%	67%	0	15			50	0.96	-7.9	111	145	-$8
13 Proj	**4**	**5**	**3**	**65**	**50**	**3.99**	**3.57**	**1.32**	**269**	**297**	**249**	**4.6**	**2.6**	**6.9**	**2.7**	**59**	**18**	**23**	**1.0**	**16%**	**31%**	**73%**	**0**						**0.2**	**93**	**121**	**$1**

Logan,Boone	Health	A	LIMA Plan	A
Age: 28 Th: L Role RP	PT/Exp	D	Rand Var	0
Ht: 6' 5" Wt: 215 Type Pwr	Consist	A	MM	3500

Growth of excellent Dom distracts from some disturbing 2H trends: Command plummeted as a result of control issues, ground ball lean has disappeared, hr/9 and FB% are on the rise, even K/9 tailed off. As lefty specialist, small IP totals mean one or two outings can ruin stats. There's risk along with those K's.

Yr Tm	W	L	Sv	IP	K	ERA	xERA	WHIP	OBA	vL	vR	BF/G	Ctl	Dom	Cmd	G	L	F	hr/9	hr/f	H%	S%	GS	APC	DOM%	DIS%	Sv%	LI	RAR	BPV	BPX	R$
08 CHW	2	3	0	42	42	5.95	4.00	1.68	317	291	351	3.6	3.0	8.9	3.0	43	23	34	1.5	15%	39%	67%	0	14			0	0.83	-8.5	101	190	-$5
09 ATL *	5	3	2	53	42	4.46	4.09	1.51	259	231	364	4.7	4.7	7.2	1.5	64	20	16	0.5	10%	31%	70%	0	14			67	0.77	-0.9	62	116	$0
10 NYY *	2	1	0	61	56	2.94	3.61	1.33	248	190	279	3.9	3.6	8.2	2.3	46	17	37	0.7	8%	31%	80%	0	13			0	1.04	8.6	83	134	$2
11 NYY	5	3	0	42	46	3.46	3.43	1.34	261	260	262	2.9	2.8	9.9	3.5	42	19	39	0.9	9%	35%	77%	0	11			0	1.23	2.5	123	185	$1
12 NYY	7	2	1	55	68	3.74	3.72	1.37	234	231	238	3.0	4.6	11.1	2.4	38	22	39	1.0	11%	32%	76%	0	12			25	1.30	1.9	92	120	$1
1st Half	2	0	1	28	37	2.54	3.16	1.20	221	203	250	3.0	3.5	11.8	3.4	41	22	38	0.6	8%	33%	81%	0	12			100	1.39	5.2	136	177	$4
2nd Half	5	2	0	27	31	5.00	4.38	1.56	248	263	227	3.0	5.7	10.3	1.8	36	23	41	1.3	14%	32%	71%	0	12			0	1.22	-3.3	47	61	-$1
13 Proj	**6**	**3**	**0**	**58**	**64**	**3.83**	**3.80**	**1.40**	**253**	**245**	**264**	**3.0**	**4.0**	**10.0**	**2.5**	**41**	**21**	**38**	**0.9**	**10%**	**33%**	**75%**	**0**						**1.3**	**89**	**116**	**$1**

Lohse,Kyle	Health	C	LIMA Plan	D
Age: 34 Th: R Role SP	PT/Exp	A	Rand Var	-2
Ht: 6' 2" Wt: 210 Type Con	Consist	C	MM	2105

Minor skills boost, but significantly outperformed xERA again. Ctl is legit, but not THIS good, and history says not to trust 2H Dom spike. Sterling W-L record will not repeat, and S% likely to regress. Sure, he's an effective MLB starter—note PQS splits—but let someone else pay this year's inflated price tag.

Yr Tm	W	L	Sv	IP	K	ERA	xERA	WHIP	OBA	vL	vR	BF/G	Ctl	Dom	Cmd	G	L	F	hr/9	hr/f	H%	S%	GS	APC	DOM%	DIS%	Sv%	LI	RAR	BPV	BPX	R$
08 STL	15	6	0	200	119	3.78	4.20	1.30	272	254	285	25.4	2.2	5.4	2.4	46	22	32	0.8	9%	30%	73%	33	96	52%	15%			13.4	61	114	$13
09 STL	6	10	0	118	77	4.74	4.43	1.37	269	251	285	22.3	2.8	5.9	2.1	45	20	36	1.2	12%	30%	68%	22	85	45%	41%	0	0.74	-6.1	55	102	$0
10 STL *	5	9	0	111	67	6.40	6.17	1.73	331	344	330	23.0	3.0	5.4	1.8	43	19	38	1.0	7%	37%	63%	18	90	22%	39%			-31.7	30	49	-$14
11 STL	14	8	0	188	111	3.39	4.07	1.17	249	249	248	25.8	2.0	5.3	2.6	41	22	37	0.8	7%	28%	73%	30	93	47%	10%			12.8	60	91	$14
12 STL	16	3	0	211	143	2.86	3.99	1.09	239	253	226	26.2	1.6	6.1	3.8	41	24	36	0.8	8%	28%	77%	33	95	67%	0%			30.1	85	111	$26
1st Half	7	2	0	102	58	2.82	4.13	1.09	245	265	220	25.8	1.5	5.1	3.4	42	23	35	0.8	8%	27%	77%	16	92	56%	0%			15.0	72	94	$24
2nd Half	9	1	0	109	85	2.89	3.87	1.09	233	238	230	26.5	1.7	7.0	4.0	39	25	36	0.8	8%	28%	77%	17	97	76%	0%			15.2	97	126	$28
13 Proj	**13**	**7**	**0**	**189**	**114**	**3.67**	**4.24**	**1.23**	**263**	**268**	**259**	**24.4**	**2.0**	**5.5**	**2.7**	**41**	**22**	**36**	**0.8**	**8%**	**29%**	**72%**	**31**						**8.1**	**63**	**82**	**$12**

Lopez,Javier	Health	A	LIMA Plan	B
Age: 35 Th: L Role RP	PT/Exp	D	Rand Var	-5
Ht: 6' 4" Wt: 220 Type Pwr xGB	Consist	A	MM	3210

Notched some saves as part of closing committee, but check the beating he took from RHs—he's still just a lefty specialist. Even with modest skills growth and the extreme GB rate that limits gopher balls, he's a pretty ordinary talent. Unless you get credit for funky release points, his impact will be minimal.

Yr Tm	W	L	Sv	IP	K	ERA	xERA	WHIP	OBA	vL	vR	BF/G	Ctl	Dom	Cmd	G	L	F	hr/9	hr/f	H%	S%	GS	APC	DOM%	DIS%	Sv%	LI	RAR	BPV	BPX	R$
08 BOS	2	0	0	59	38	2.43	4.09	1.35	245	182	311	3.5	4.1	5.8	1.4	60	19	22	0.6	10%	27%	84%	0	14			0	0.91	13.9	31	58	$2
09 BOS *	1	3	0	51	21	6.61	6.58	1.94	337	429	367	4.7	4.6	3.7	0.8	49	26	26	0.7	8%	36%	65%	0	18			0	0.53	-14.5	5	10	-$11
10 2 NL	4	2	0	58	38	2.34	3.59	1.21	238	162	306	3.1	3.1	5.9	1.9	62	16	23	0.3	5%	28%	81%	0	11			0	0.94	12.4	62	101	$4
11 SF	5	2	1	53	40	2.72	3.70	1.28	221	163	276	3.2	4.4	6.8	1.5	63	15	22	0.0	0%	28%	76%	0	12			33	1.52	8.0	44	66	$3
12 SF	3	0	7	36	28	2.50	3.80	1.42	270	191	417	2.2	3.5	7.0	2.0	60	19	21	0.3	4%	33%	82%	0	8			78	1.85	6.7	70	91	$2
1st Half	3	0	1	16	14	2.76	4.38	1.71	284	205	435	2.3	5.0	7.7	1.6	58	23	19	0.0	0%	37%	82%	0	8			33	2.58	2.5	41	53	$0
2nd Half	0	0	6	20	14	2.29	3.34	1.17	257	178	400	2.1	2.3	6.4	2.8	61	16	23	0.5	8%	29%	82%	0	8			100	1.16	4.2	92	120	$3
13 Proj	**4**	**1**	**2**	**51**	**37**	**3.08**	**3.91**	**1.36**	**252**	**181**	**346**	**2.6**	**3.7**	**6.5**	**1.8**	**61**	**17**	**22**	**0.4**	**7%**	**30%**	**78%**	**0**						**5.9**	**57**	**74**	**$2**

Lopez,Wilton	Health	B	LIMA Plan	B+
Age: 29 Th: R Role RP	PT/Exp	C	Rand Var	-3
Ht: 6' 0" Wt: 205 Type xGB	Consist	A	MM	5330

Continues to thrive in bullpen, and didn't miss a beat after mid-season transition to closer. Improving Dom doesn't fit the closer ideal just yet, but fantastic control, GB% tilt and improvement vs LHB more than compensate. Let others fight over high profile relievers. These are elite skills at a bargain price.

Yr Tm	W	L	Sv	IP	K	ERA	xERA	WHIP	OBA	vL	vR	BF/G	Ctl	Dom	Cmd	G	L	F	hr/9	hr/f	H%	S%	GS	APC	DOM%	DIS%	Sv%	LI	RAR	BPV	BPX	R$
08 a/a	0	2	0	39	21	5.38	4.38	1.45	295			6.0	2.4	4.9	2.0				0.4		33%	61%							-5.1	55	103	-$5
09 HOU *	4	7	0	130	65	5.93	5.90	1.61	339	377	400	15.5	1.5	4.5	3.1	58	17	25	0.9	21%	37%	63%	2	42	0%	100%	0	0.51	-25.7	53	99	-$11
10 HOU	5	2	1	67	50	2.96	3.00	1.06	261	284	245	3.9	0.7	6.7	10.0	56	16	28	0.5	7%	31%	73%	0	14			33	0.87	9.3	137	221	$6
11 HOU	2	6	0	71	56	2.79	3.38	1.27	264	330	225	4.1	2.3	7.1	3.1	56	17	27	0.8	10%	31%	81%	0	15			0	1.06	10.1	100	151	$3
12 HOU	6	3	10	66	54	2.17	2.95	1.04	250	231	261	4.1	1.1	7.3	6.8	55	24	21	0.5	10%	30%	82%	0	15			77	1.23	15.1	136	177	$12
1st Half	3	0	0	32	26	2.51	2.88	0.96	237	265	225	3.9	1.1	7.2	6.5	58	19	22	0.8	15%	27%	79%	0	13			0	1.25	6.0	137	178	$9
2nd Half	3	3	10	34	28	1.85	3.02	1.12	262	211	301	4.3	1.1	7.4	7.0	52	28	20	0.3	5%	33%	84%	0	16			83	1.21	9.1	135	176	$16
13 Proj	**4**	**3**	**33**	**58**	**47**	**2.77**	**3.19**	**1.16**	**262**	**276**	**253**	**4.2**	**1.4**	**7.2**	**5.1**	**55**	**20**	**24**	**0.6**	**9%**	**32%**	**78%**	**0**						**8.9**	**125**	**163**	**$17**

Lowe,Derek	Health	A	LIMA Plan	D
Age: 40 Th: R Role RP	PT/Exp	A	Rand Var	0
Ht: 6' 6" Wt: 230 Type Con xGB	Consist	B	MM	1100

Skills got tired of waiting for results to catch up and collapsed completely. Got pounded as a starter, then got pounded working out of the pen in 2H. LHs always beat him up, but now RHs own him as well. At his age and reduced ability, both value and performance have bottomed out. It was a good run.

Yr Tm	W	L	Sv	IP	K	ERA	xERA	WHIP	OBA	vL	vR	BF/G	Ctl	Dom	Cmd	G	L	F	hr/9	hr/f	H%	S%	GS	APC	DOM%	DIS%	Sv%	LI	RAR	BPV	BPX	R$
08 LA	14	11	0	211	147	3.24	3.37	1.13	246	251	240	25.0	1.9	6.3	3.3	60	17	23	0.6	9%	29%	72%	34	92	65%	9%			28.2	99	186	$23
09 ATL	15	10	0	195	111	4.67	4.30	1.52	301	300	303	25.1	2.9	5.1	1.8	56	18	26	0.7	9%	33%	70%	34	95	26%	24%			-8.4	48	89	$0
10 ATL	16	12	0	194	136	4.00	3.65	1.37	273	287	259	25.0	2.8	6.3	2.2	59	19	23	0.8	13%	31%	72%	33	96	39%	9%			2.0	74	120	$7
11 ATL	9	17	0	187	137	5.05	3.83	1.51	285	285	286	24.4	3.4	6.6	2.0	59	18	23	0.7	10%	34%	66%	34	95	47%	24%			-25.6	65	97	-$9
12 2 AL	9	11	1	143	55	5.11	4.88	1.62	311	345	285	16.8	3.2	3.5	1.1	59	20	21	0.6	9%	33%	68%	21	62	24%	24%	100	0.68	-19.3	13	16	-$14
1st Half	7	6	0	96	33	4.42	4.72	1.57	310	330	293	26.4	2.9	3.1	1.1	63	18	20	0.6	9%	32%	72%	16	99	25%	19%			-4.8	18	23	-$9
2nd Half	2	5	1	47	22	6.51	5.21	1.72	314	380	270	9.9	3.8	4.2	1.1	52	24	24	0.8	10%	34%	61%	5	35	20%	40%	100	0.65	-14.5	2	3	-$22
13 Proj	**3**	**5**	**0**	**58**	**33**	**5.10**	**4.43**	**1.55**	**296**	**319**	**276**	**16.7**	**3.2**	**5.1**	**1.6**	**58**	**20**	**22**	**0.7**	**10%**	**33%**	**67%**	**10**						**-7.7**	**39**	**51**	**-$5**

DAN BECKER

Lowe,Mark

Age: 30 Th: R Role RP	Health	F	LIMA Plan	C
Ht: 6' 3" Wt: 210 Type Pwr	PT/Exp	D	Rand Var	-3
	Consist	B	MM	2300

Was on way to career-best stats and skills before a strained abdominal muscle cost him six weeks. With 32 IP avg last three seasons, we can't bank on health anyway. Sub-4.00 ERA was result of friendly hit rate, and he's never shown that 1H Ctl over an extended period before. High risk for too little reward.

Yr	Tm	W	L	Sv	IP	K	ERA	xERA	WHIP	OBA	vL	vR	BF/G	Ctl	Dom	Cmd	G	L	F	hr/9	hr/f	H%	S%	GS	APC	DOM%	DIS%	Sv%	LI	RAR	BPV	BPX	R$
08	SEA	1	5	1	64	55	5.37	4.80	1.76	301	354	250	5.3	4.8	7.8	1.6	45	21	35	0.8	8%	37%	70%	0	21			20	0.93	-8.2	33	62	-$6
09	SEA	2	7	3	80	69	3.26	4.13	1.25	232	253	213	4.5	3.3	7.8	2.4	39	21	40	0.8	7%	29%	76%	0	17			23	1.39	10.5	69	128	$5
10	2 AL	1	3	0	13	12	5.40	4.75	1.80	333	440	241	4.4	4.1	8.1	2.0	24	27	49	1.4	10%	38%	73%	0	17			0	1.39	-2.2	38	62	-$4
11	TEX	2	3	1	45	42	3.80	3.78	1.44	263	256	268	3.8	3.8	8.4	2.2	49	19	32	1.2	14%	32%	78%	0	15			33	1.00	0.8	76	114	-$1
12	TEX	0	2	0	39	28	3.43	4.54	1.22	240	239	240	4.5	3.0	6.4	2.2	34	22	44	1.1	9%	27%	77%	0	18			0	0.30	2.8	47	61	-$2
1st Half		0	0	0	31	25	2.30	3.84	0.96	198	167	228	4.7	2.3	7.2	3.1	39	18	43	0.9	8%	23%	81%	0	18			0	0.19	6.6	84	109	$0
2nd Half		0	2	0	8	3	7.88	7.63	2.25	371	471	278	4.1	5.6	3.4	0.6	21	33	45	2.3	13%	36%	69%	0	17			0	0.58	-3.8	-92	-120	-$10
13	**Proj**	**1**	**2**	**0**	**44**	**37**	**3.81**	**4.09**	**1.30**	**248**	**255**	**243**	**4.4**	**3.3**	**7.7**	**2.3**	**42**	**20**	**39**	**0.9**	**9%**	**30%**	**73%**	**0**						**1.1**	**69**	**90**	**-$1**

Luebke,Cory

Age: 28 Th: L Role SP	Health	F	LIMA Plan	A
Ht: 6' 4" Wt: 205 Type	PT/Exp	C	Rand Var	-4
	Consist	B	MM	3301

Follow-up to 2011 breakout halted by Tommy John surgery in May. 9.0+ Dom, 2.5+ Cmd in each month of '11 confirms consistency, but Dom in other years, marginal 91 mph fastball are why we need to see a repeat before anointing him an anchor. Mine for injury profit, but keep '13 expectations in check.

Yr	Tm	W	L	Sv	IP	K	ERA	xERA	WHIP	OBA	vL	vR	BF/G	Ctl	Dom	Cmd	G	L	F	hr/9	hr/f	H%	S%	GS	APC	DOM%	DIS%	Sv%	LI	RAR	BPV	BPX	R$
08																																	
09	aa	3	2	0	41	28	3.85	3.71	1.35	261			19.1	3.2	6.1	1.9				0.5		30%	71%							2.4	64	120	-$1
10	SD *	11	2	0	132	93	3.08	2.83	1.11	228	333	222	22.5	2.5	6.4	2.6	50	14	36	0.7	17%	26%	74%	3	76	33%	33%	0	0.61	16.2	81	131	$13
11	SD	6	10	0	140	154	3.29	3.12	1.07	209	157	229	12.1	2.8	9.9	3.5	39	22	39	0.8	9%	28%	72%	17	51	71%	12%	0	0.91	11.3	119	179	$13
12	SD	3	1	0	31	23	2.61	4.00	1.16	233	259	226	26.0	2.3	6.7	2.9	48	19	33	0.3	3%	30%	77%	5	102	40%	20%			5.4	83	109	$0
1st Half		3	1	0	31	23	2.61	3.99	1.16	233	259	226	26.0	2.3	6.7	2.9	48	19	33	0.3	3%	30%	77%	5	102	40%	20%			5.4	83	108	$0
2nd Half																																	
13	**Proj**	**9**	**4**	**0**	**112**	**92**	**3.51**	**3.82**	**1.20**	**243**	**233**	**247**	**24.6**	**2.6**	**7.4**	**2.8**	**44**	**20**	**36**	**0.8**	**8%**	**29%**	**73%**	**18**						**7.0**	**84**	**109**	**$8**

Luetge,Lucas

Age: 26 Th: L Role RP	Health	A	LIMA Plan	D+
Ht: 6' 4" Wt: 205 Type Pwr	PT/Exp	D	Rand Var	0
	Consist	C	MM	2410

Lefty reliever rode LOOGY dominance on way to near-4.00 ERA in MLB debut. With 12/12 K/BB in 16 IP vs. RH batters, chances of role expansion are remote. 89 mph fastball, 4.4 Ctl vs. LH suggest lefty dominance might be short-lived too. There's no value here.

Yr	Tm	W	L	Sv	IP	K	ERA	xERA	WHIP	OBA	vL	vR	BF/G	Ctl	Dom	Cmd	G	L	F	hr/9	hr/f	H%	S%	GS	APC	DOM%	DIS%	Sv%	LI	RAR	BPV	BPX	R$
08																																	
09																																	
10	aa	3	2	0	44	41	3.85	5.71	1.69	316			8.6	3.5	8.5	2.4				0.9		39%	79%							1.2	68	110	-$3
11	aa	1	3	3	69	59	3.65	3.84	1.39	270			6.3	3.1	7.7	2.5				0.4		34%	73%							2.5	86	130	$0
12	SEA	2	2	2	41	38	3.98	4.37	1.50	248	193	318	2.8	5.3	8.4	1.6	47	24	29	0.7	9%	31%	74%	0	11			67	1.22	0.2	33	43	-$3
1st Half		1	0	0	20	19	1.77	3.96	1.28	200	154	258	2.8	5.3	8.4	1.6	54	18	28	0.0	0%	27%	85%	0	12			0	0.85	5.6	40	52	$0
2nd Half		1	2	2	20	19	6.20	4.76	1.72	291	227	371	2.9	5.3	8.4	1.6	41	29	30	1.3	16%	34%	66%	0	11			67	1.56	-5.5	27	35	-$6
13	**Proj**	**2**	**3**	**3**	**51**	**46**	**4.07**	**4.17**	**1.51**	**269**	**209**	**344**	**4.0**	**4.3**	**8.2**	**1.9**	**46**	**24**	**29**	**0.7**	**8%**	**33%**	**74%**	**0**						**-0.4**	**56**	**72**	**-$2**

Lyles,Jordan

Age: 22 Th: R Role SP	Health	A	LIMA Plan	A
Ht: 6' 4" Wt: 210 Type	PT/Exp	D	Rand Var	+1
	Consist	A	MM	2205

5-12, 5.09 ERA in 141 IP at HOU. On surface, a young SP in stagnation. But there's something good here. 2H Cmd + GB was hidden by hr/f spike, S% dip. Gained 2 mph on fastball, too. Must consolidate skill flashes (4.3 Cmd vs. RH, 3.5 Cmd w/bases empty) as next step. A growth stock. UP: 3.75 ERA

Yr	Tm	W	L	Sv	IP	K	ERA	xERA	WHIP	OBA	vL	vR	BF/G	Ctl	Dom	Cmd	G	L	F	hr/9	hr/f	H%	S%	GS	APC	DOM%	DIS%	Sv%	LI	RAR	BPV	BPX	R$
08																																	
09																																	
10	a/a	7	12	0	159	124	3.95	4.88	1.50	303			25.4	2.4	7.1	2.9				0.7		36%	75%							2.6	76	123	$0
11	HOU *	5	11	0	156	104	4.69	4.56	1.38	283	271	295	20.5	2.4	6.0	2.5	41	21	38	1.0	12%	32%	68%	15	79	40%	13%	0	0.80	-14.3	56	85	-$4
12	HOU *	10	12	0	182	128	4.68	4.56	1.37	280	300	263	23.8	2.4	6.3	2.6	54	17	29	1.1	15%	32%	68%	25	95	36%	32%			-15.0	60	78	-$3
1st Half		7	4	0	92	59	4.00	4.08	1.33	268	320	234	23.8	2.6	5.8	2.2	51	16	33	0.9	12%	30%	72%	9	94	33%	22%			0.2	56	73	$5
2nd Half		3	8	0	90	69	5.38	5.01	1.41	292	291	282	23.9	2.2	6.9	3.1	56	18	27	1.3	16%	33%	64%	16	95	38%	38%			-15.2	65	85	-$11
13	**Proj**	**8**	**13**	**0**	**189**	**135**	**4.22**	**4.02**	**1.36**	**281**	**290**	**275**	**22.6**	**2.3**	**6.5**	**2.8**	**49**	**19**	**33**	**1.0**	**11%**	**32%**	**72%**	**35**						**-4.7**	**81**	**106**	**$3**

Lynn,Lance

Age: 26 Th: R Role RP	Health	B	LIMA Plan	B
Ht: 6' 5" Wt: 250 Type Pwr	PT/Exp	C	Rand Var	0
	Consist	A	MM	3403

Transitioned from relief to rotation without a hitch. 6+ ERA, 1.91 WHIP in Aug. might leave bad taste, but don't follow suit. Rebounded with elite Sept. Dom and Cmd trends confirm that there's plenty more growth on the horizon. With consistency, addition of third pitch, spot in rotation... UP: 3.25 ERA, 200 K

Yr	Tm	W	L	Sv	IP	K	ERA	xERA	WHIP	OBA	vL	vR	BF/G	Ctl	Dom	Cmd	G	L	F	hr/9	hr/f	H%	S%	GS	APC	DOM%	DIS%	Sv%	LI	RAR	BPV	BPX	R$
08																																	
09	a/a	11	4	0	133	91	3.23	3.63	1.39	263			24.3	3.5	6.1	1.8				0.3		31%	76%							17.9	67	126	$9
10	aaa	13	10	0	164	118	4.75	4.39	1.40	271			23.9	3.2	6.5	2.0				1.0		31%	67%							-13.6	54	87	$1
11	STL *	8	4	1	110	93	3.67	3.51	1.32	262	229	187	15.1	2.9	7.6	2.6	57	11	32	0.4	12%	33%	71%	2	31	50%	0%	50	0.94	3.7	92	138	$4
12	STL	18	7	0	176	180	3.78	3.60	1.32	253	272	237	21.3	3.3	9.2	2.8	44	24	32	0.8	10%	32%	73%	29	86	59%	14%	0	0.83	5.0	99	130	$11
1st Half		10	4	0	97	98	3.62	3.52	1.25	239	259	217	25.3	3.2	9.1	2.9	47	22	32	0.8	11%	31%	73%	16	102	63%	13%			4.8	103	134	$18
2nd Half		8	3	0	79	82	3.99	3.70	1.41	271	292	257	17.9	3.4	9.3	2.7	40	27	33	0.8	10%	34%	73%	13	72	54%	15%	0	0.88	0.3	94	122	$2
13	**Proj**	**13**	**6**	**0**	**145**	**131**	**3.88**	**3.80**	**1.35**	**261**	**286**	**242**	**19.2**	**3.2**	**8.1**	**2.5**	**49**	**19**	**32**	**0.8**	**10%**	**32%**	**73%**	**29**						**2.4**	**87**	**112**	**$7**

Lyon,Brandon

Age: 33 Th: R Role RP	Health	F	LIMA Plan	B+
Ht: 6' 1" Wt: 195 Type Pwr FB	PT/Exp	C	Rand Var	-2
	Consist	D	MM	2300

First sub-4.00 xERA... EVER, and it came the year after he had a detached biceps tendon and a torn labrum. Credit increased use of cutter. Previous Dom, Cmd slides and unchanged 90-mph fastball make it likely this will be just a blip. Health grade, creaky shoulder make him a poor risk/reward proposition.

Yr	Tm	W	L	Sv	IP	K	ERA	xERA	WHIP	OBA	vL	vR	BF/G	Ctl	Dom	Cmd	G	L	F	hr/9	hr/f	H%	S%	GS	APC	DOM%	DIS%	Sv%	LI	RAR	BPV	BPX	R$
08	ARI	3	5	26	59	44	4.70	4.34	1.48	301	278	321	4.3	2.0	6.7	3.4	40	22	38	1.1	9%	36%	70%	0	16			84	1.04	-2.8	85	159	$8
09	DET	6	5	3	79	57	2.86	4.03	1.11	205	205	205	4.8	3.5	6.5	1.8	47	17	36	0.8	9%	23%	78%	0	18			50	0.96	14.2	47	87	$9
10	HOU	6	6	20	78	54	3.12	4.44	1.27	231	195	257	4.2	3.6	6.2	1.7	40	20	40	0.2	2%	28%	74%	0	16			91	1.22	9.3	34	54	$12
11	HOU	3	3	4	13	6	11.48	5.82	2.40	409	652	279	4.7	3.4	4.1	1.2	46	24	31	2.7	22%	42%	54%	0	19			50	1.26	-12.4	6	9	-$6
12	2 TM	4	2	1	61	63	3.10	3.82	1.25	240	213	253	3.9	3.0	9.3	3.2	38	18	44	0.7	7%	32%	77%	0	15			33	0.90	6.9	104	135	$3
1st Half		0	2	0	30	30	2.73	3.79	1.28	261	250	265	3.9	2.4	9.1	3.8	35	20	45	0.6	5%	34%	81%	0	15			0	0.73	4.7	111	145	-$1
2nd Half		4	0	1	31	33	3.45	3.84	1.21	220	186	240	3.8	3.4	9.5	2.8	40	17	43	0.9	8%	29%	74%	0	15			33	1.05	2.2	96	125	$6
13	**Proj**	**4**	**3**	**0**	**58**	**51**	**3.88**	**4.03**	**1.25**	**242**	**217**	**258**	**3.9**	**3.1**	**7.9**	**2.5**	**40**	**19**	**41**	**0.7**	**6%**	**30%**	**70%**	**0**						**1.0**	**75**	**97**	**$1**

Madson,Ryan

Age: 32 Th: R Role RP	Health	F	LIMA Plan	A
Ht: 6' 6" Wt: 200 Type Pwr	PT/Exp	C	Rand Var	0
	Consist	A	MM	4420

Budding elite closer sidelined by Tommy John surgery in April before season even began. RP skill sets don't get much better than his: high Dom, great Cmd, and groundball tilt. With mid-90s fastball and devastating changeup, he's got the raw stuff to match. Bid on the skills, hope for health, role.

Yr	Tm	W	L	Sv	IP	K	ERA	xERA	WHIP	OBA	vL	vR	BF/G	Ctl	Dom	Cmd	G	L	F	hr/9	hr/f	H%	S%	GS	APC	DOM%	DIS%	Sv%	LI	RAR	BPV	BPX	R$
08	PHI	4	2	1	83	67	3.05	3.61	1.23	254	268	243	4.5	2.5	7.3	2.9	51	19	30	0.7	8%	31%	77%	0	17			33	0.91	13.0	93	174	$6
09	PHI	5	5	10	77	78	3.26	3.30	1.23	251	257	245	4.1	2.6	9.1	3.5	46	22	32	0.8	10%	32%	76%	0	15			63	1.10	10.1	118	221	$10
10	PHI	6	2	5	53	64	2.55	2.74	1.04	212	217	208	3.9	2.2	10.9	4.9	50	13	37	0.7	8%	31%	78%	0	15			50	1.14	10.0	164	265	$9
11	PHI	4	2	32	61	62	2.37	3.06	1.15	243	198	278	4.0	2.4	9.2	3.9	49	18	34	0.3	4%	32%	79%	0	16			94	1.18	11.7	128	193	$18
12																																	
1st Half																																	
2nd Half																																	
13	**Proj**	**3**	**2**	**15**	**41**	**39**	**3.26**	**3.45**	**1.19**	**242**	**234**	**248**	**4.0**	**2.6**	**8.5**	**3.2**	**48**	**18**	**33**	**0.8**	**10%**	**30%**	**75%**	**0**						**3.8**	**109**	**141**	**$7**

STEPHEN NICKRAND

Maholm,Paul

Health			B	LIMA Plan	C+	
Age: 31	Th: L	Role SP	PT/Exp	A	Rand Var	0
Ht: 6' 2"	Wt: 220	Type GB	Consist	A	MM	2205

PRO: 2H Dom bump, excellent Ctl, well-established GB bias, got improved support from ATL late in season. CON: Cockiness from career high win total. (Only kidding.) VERDICT: Could continue to stay below 4.00, but don't pay for the 2H edition.

Yr	Tm	W	L	Sv	IP	K	ERA	xERA	WHIP	OBA	vL	vR	BF/G	Ctl	Dom	Cmd	G	L	F	hr/9	hr/f	H%	S%	GS	APC	DOM%	DIS%	Sv%	LI	RAR	BPV	BPX	R$
08	PIT	9	9	0	206	139	3.71	3.86	1.28	263	183	279	27.5	2.7	6.1	2.2	54	19	28	0.9	12%	29%	74%	31	98	52%	13%			15.7	67	126	$12
09	PIT	8	9	0	195	119	4.44	4.23	1.44	290	182	316	27.0	2.8	5.5	2.0	52	18	30	0.6	7%	32%	69%	31	98	29%	13%			-2.8	54	101	$1
10	PIT	9	15	0	185	102	5.10	4.55	1.56	303	231	316	26.3	3.0	5.0	1.6	51	19	30	0.7	8%	34%	67%	32	96	34%	31%			-23.3	37	60	-$9
11	PIT	6	14	0	162	97	3.66	4.03	1.29	262	265	261	26.4	2.8	5.4	1.9	50	22	28	0.6	8%	29%	72%	26	94	35%	23%			5.7	50	75	$4
12	2 NL	13	11	0	189	140	3.67	3.78	1.22	250	265	246	24.6	2.5	6.7	2.6	51	21	27	1.0	13%	29%	73%	31	93	65%	19%	0	0.77	8.1	81	105	$12
1st Half		5	6	0	84	55	4.84	4.24	1.34	268	308	255	24.2	2.8	5.9	2.1	53	16	32	1.2	13%	29%	66%	15	91	40%	27%			-8.5	62	81	-$1
2nd Half		8	5	0	105	85	2.73	3.43	1.13	236	226	239	24.9	2.3	7.3	3.1	50	26	24	0.8	13%	28%	79%	16	95	88%	13%	0	0.79	16.7	96	125	$22
13	Proj	**12**	**11**	**0**	**189**	**126**	**3.92**	**4.03**	**1.30**	**263**	**251**	**266**	**24.9**	**2.7**	**6.0**	**2.3**	**51**	**21**	**28**	**0.8**	**10%**	**30%**	**71%**	**31**						**2.2**	**65**	**85**	**$9**

Marcum,Shaun

Health			F	LIMA Plan	B+	
Age: 31	Th: R	Role SP	PT/Exp	A	Rand Var	0
Ht: 6' 0"	Wt: 195	Type Pwr FB	Consist	A	MM	2303

Elbow injury cost him two months, but his skills remain those of a solid starter. Miller Park has done him no favors--he was over a run per game better on the road in 2012, over two runs better in 2011. He's a FA and a FB pitcher. If he lands in a decent pitcher's park and the elbow is sound... UP: sub-3.50 ERA

Yr	Tm	W	L	Sv	IP	K	ERA	xERA	WHIP	OBA	vL	vR	BF/G	Ctl	Dom	Cmd	G	L	F	hr/9	hr/f	H%	S%	GS	APC	DOM%	DIS%	Sv%	LI	RAR	BPV	BPX	R$
08	TOR	9	7	0	151	123	3.39	4.00	1.16	222	244	200	25.2	3.0	7.3	2.5	43	17	40	1.2	12%	26%	77%	25	93	52%	24%			17.4	72	136	$14
09																																	
10	TOR	13	8	0	195	165	3.64	3.69	1.15	242	190	298	25.8	2.0	7.6	3.8	38	18	43	1.1	10%	29%	73%	31	98	61%	13%			10.6	99	161	$16
11	MIL	13	7	0	201	158	3.54	3.92	1.16	232	271	195	24.9	2.6	7.1	2.8	37	20	43	1.0	9%	27%	73%	33	96	61%	12%			9.9	74	111	$15
12	MIL	7	4	0	124	109	3.70	4.18	1.27	245	263	227	25.1	3.0	7.9	2.7	35	23	41	1.2	11%	29%	75%	21	99	57%	14%			4.8	75	98	$5
1st Half		5	3	0	82	77	3.39	3.91	1.17	227	228	225	26.3	2.8	8.4	3.0	37	22	42	1.1	10%	28%	76%	13	102	69%	0%			6.4	90	117	$11
2nd Half		2	1	0	42	32	4.32	4.74	1.46	279	333	230	23.1	3.2	6.9	2.1	33	26	41	1.3	11%	32%	75%	8	92	38%	38%			-1.6	48	62	-$8
13	Proj	**10**	**6**	**0**	**174**	**143**	**3.85**	**4.12**	**1.25**	**250**	**270**	**231**	**23.9**	**2.8**	**7.4**	**2.7**	**37**	**21**	**42**	**1.1**	**10%**	**29%**	**73%**	**30**						**3.6**	**73**	**95**	**$10**

Marmol,Carlos

Health			A	LIMA Plan	C+	
Age: 30	Th: R	Role RP	PT/Exp	A	Rand Var	-3
Ht: 6' 2"	Wt: 215	Type Pwr FB	Consist	B	MM	3520

Ever see a Weasel Ball? It's a plastic ball with a fur tail attached. When powered up, it flops around in sudden, random directions. He has a 95-mph fastball and an 85-mph Weasel Ball. It's hard to hit, and it's hard to throw for a strike. Pay no attention to his pre-season role: skills are not closer-worthy.

Yr	Tm	W	L	Sv	IP	K	ERA	xERA	WHIP	OBA	vL	vR	BF/G	Ctl	Dom	Cmd	G	L	F	hr/9	hr/f	H%	S%	GS	APC	DOM%	DIS%	Sv%	LI	RAR	BPV	BPX	R$
08	CHC	2	4	7	87	114	2.68	3.34	0.93	135	182	98	4.2	4.2	11.7	2.8	35	10	55	1.0	10%	18%	77%	0	18			78	1.23	17.7	110	207	$15
09	CHC	2	4	15	74	93	3.41	4.63	1.46	170	136	200	4.2	7.9	11.3	1.4	36	16	48	0.2	3%	26%	75%	0	19			79	1.25	8.4	4	8	$8
10	CHC	2	3	38	78	138	2.55	2.74	1.18	147	130	161	4.3	6.0	16.0	2.7	35	17	48	0.1	2%	32%	77%	0	18			88	1.45	14.7	138	224	$23
11	CHC	2	6	34	74	99	4.01	3.56	1.38	205	192	215	4.4	5.8	12.0	2.1	39	20	40	0.6	7%	31%	71%	0	19			77	1.40	-0.6	76	114	$13
12	CHC	3	3	20	55	72	3.42	4.37	1.54	200	221	177	4.0	7.3	11.7	1.6	41	20	40	0.7	8%	30%	79%	0	18			87	0.80	4.1	32	42	$7
1st Half		1	2	7	23	28	5.16	6.07	1.85	198	200	196	4.0	9.9	11.1	1.1	36	17	47	0.8	7%	29%	73%	0	19			78	0.84	-3.2	-54	-70	-$2
2nd Half		2	1	13	33	44	2.20	3.36	1.32	202	234	160	4.1	5.5	12.1	2.2	44	21	34	0.6	8%	30%	85%	0	18			93	0.77	7.3	92	120	$13
13	Proj	**3**	**4**	**23**	**65**	**86**	**3.80**	**3.99**	**1.41**	**193**	**200**	**185**	**4.0**	**6.6**	**11.9**	**1.8**	**39**	**19**	**42**	**0.6**	**7%**	**29%**	**73%**	**0**						**1.8**	**52**	**68**	**$10**

Marquis,Jason

Health			F	LIMA Plan	D+	
Age: 34	Th: R	Role SP	PT/Exp	C	Rand Var	+2
Ht: 6' 1"	Wt: 220	Type GB	Consist	B	MM	2101

8-11, 5.22 ERA in 127 IP at MIN, SD. Think the home park doesn't matter? In his games with SD, his four worst ER outings were @COL, @CIN, @ARI, and @ATL. Had a nice 7.6 Dom/2.8 Ctl for SD. Was hurt by unlucky hr/9 and... he's probably a great guy, but do not let him on your roster.

Yr	Tm	W	L	Sv	IP	K	ERA	xERA	WHIP	OBA	vL	vR	BF/G	Ctl	Dom	Cmd	G	L	F	hr/9	hr/f	H%	S%	GS	APC	DOM%	DIS%	Sv%	LI	RAR	BPV	BPX	R$
08	CHC	11	9	0	167	91	4.53	4.89	1.45	267	244	287	25.4	3.8	4.9	1.3	48	20	33	0.8	8%	29%	70%	28	92	25%	18%	0	0.77	-4.2	12	23	$2
09	COL	15	13	0	216	115	4.04	4.42	1.38	267	275	258	27.9	3.3	4.8	1.4	56	17	27	0.6	8%	29%	71%	33	98	36%	21%			7.5	30	57	$9
10	WAS	2	9	0	59	31	6.60	4.79	1.70	315	336	296	21.2	3.7	4.8	1.3	53	18	29	1.4	15%	33%	63%	13	79	23%	54%			-18.2	17	28	-$9
11	2 NL	8	6	0	132	76	4.43	4.17	1.49	294	306	284	25.5	2.9	5.2	1.8	55	20	25	0.8	10%	33%	71%	23	89	26%	26%			-8.0	47	71	-$4
12	2 TM *	10	11	0	149	103	4.77	5.12	1.42	285	302	278	25.2	2.7	6.3	2.3	53	21	27	1.5	21%	31%	71%	22	93	41%	18%			-13.8	41	54	-$4
1st Half		5	8	0	87	56	4.92	5.36	1.52	299	295	342	25.3	2.9	5.8	2.0	55	21	25	1.2	20%	33%	70%	12	91	42%	25%			-9.7	35	46	-$7
2nd Half		5	3	0	61	47	4.55	4.70	1.27	264	312	226	25.1	2.3	6.9	2.9	50	21	29	1.8	21%	28%	71%	10	95	40%	10%			-4.0	52	68	-$1
13	Proj	**7**	**8**	**0**	**116**	**74**	**4.88**	**4.28**	**1.46**	**286**	**303**	**272**	**24.2**	**2.9**	**5.7**	**2.0**	**53**	**20**	**27**	**1.2**	**15%**	**31%**	**69%**	**20**						**-12.3**	**55**	**71**	**-$3**

Marshall,Sean

Health			A	LIMA Plan	A	
Age: 30	Th: L	Role RP	PT/Exp	C	Rand Var	0
Ht: 6' 7"	Wt: 220	Type Pwr GB	Consist	A	MM	5510

Got an early opportunity to close and lost it, but his Dom and Ctl were personal bests and he is absolutely closer-worthy. The chink in the armor is that RHB did OK against him (.725 OPS), but he's still much more than a LOOGY. Nice LIMA option with saves upside. If the opps come... UP: 35 Sv.

Yr	Tm	W	L	Sv	IP	K	ERA	xERA	WHIP	OBA	vL	vR	BF/G	Ctl	Dom	Cmd	G	L	F	hr/9	hr/f	H%	S%	GS	APC	DOM%	DIS%	Sv%	LI	RAR	BPV	BPX	R$
08	CHC *	4	6	1	97	78	3.89	3.73	1.23	248	269	236	9.6	2.7	7.3	2.7	41	17	42	1.0	11%	29%	72%	7	31	57%	29%	50	0.70	5.1	74	139	$5
09	CHC	3	7	0	85	68	4.32	4.04	1.44	274	243	289	6.8	3.4	7.2	2.1	49	23	28	1.1	14%	32%	73%	9	26	33%	22%	0	1.23	0.0	65	122	-$1
10	CHC	7	5	1	75	90	2.65	2.70	1.11	210	196	218	3.8	3.0	10.8	3.6	52	23	25	0.4	7%	31%	76%	0	15			33	1.16	13.1	144	233	$9
11	CHC	6	6	5	76	79	2.26	2.67	1.10	234	206	249	3.9	2.0	9.4	4.6	58	18	25	0.1	2%	33%	78%	0	15			56	1.36	15.7	150	225	$11
12	CIN	5	5	9	61	74	2.51	2.69	1.16	232	173	273	3.5	2.4	10.9	4.6	56	20	24	0.4	8%	35%	79%	0	14			69	1.20	11.3	167	218	$9
1st Half		2	3	9	29	36	2.79	2.43	1.17	244	231	250	3.6	1.9	11.2	6.0	63	15	22	0.6	12%	36%	78%	0	14			90	0.93	4.4	192	250	$11
2nd Half		3	2	0	32	38	2.25	2.93	1.16	221	136	302	3.4	2.8	10.7	3.8	49	25	26	0.3	5%	33%	81%	0	13			0	1.44	7.0	144	187	$8
13	Proj	**5**	**4**	**5**	**58**	**65**	**2.61**	**2.81**	**1.16**	**238**	**192**	**267**	**3.7**	**2.5**	**10.1**	**4.1**	**54**	**20**	**25**	**0.4**	**7%**	**33%**	**78%**	**0**						**10.1**	**148**	**192**	**$7**

Marte,Victor

Health			A	LIMA Plan	D	
Age: 32	Th: R	Role RP	PT/Exp	D	Rand Var	+5
Ht: 6' 2"	Wt: 255	Type GB	Consist	D	MM	1200

Had a 3.55 ERA through June 25, then got bludgeoned repeatedly. Was sent down in July, returned in Sept. and still wasn't good. PRO: GB% and big jump in Dom has our attention; unlucky h% and hr/9 should regress. CON: Can be easily hit. VERDICT: Need to see him get hitters out before buying.

Yr	Tm	W	L	Sv	IP	K	ERA	xERA	WHIP	OBA	vL	vR	BF/G	Ctl	Dom	Cmd	G	L	F	hr/9	hr/f	H%	S%	GS	APC	DOM%	DIS%	Sv%	LI	RAR	BPV	BPX	R$
08																																	
09	KC *	3	5	8	76	44	3.92	4.25	1.58	269	167	357	7.1	4.9	5.2	1.1	49	15	36	0.4	14%	31%	74%	0	25			73	0.21	3.8	44	83	$1
10	KC *	7	1	3	68	39	6.51	6.51	1.77	317	292	338	6.7	4.1	5.2	1.3	44	21	34	1.5	24%	34%	65%	0	23			75	0.43	-20.5	5	8	-$7
11	aaa	2	4	31	62	38	1.67	3.44	1.27	245			4.6	3.2	5.5	1.7				0.7		27%	91%							17.5	54	82	$16
12	STL	3	2	0	40	36	4.91	4.09	1.61	305	318	297	3.9	3.1	8.0	2.6	47	24	29	1.3	16%	37%	73%	0	13			0	1.17	-4.4	85	111	-$6
1st Half		2	1	0	35	31	3.82	3.91	1.42	270	276	265	4.3	3.1	7.9	2.6	48	24	28	0.8	10%	34%	74%	0	14			0	1.19	0.9	85	111	-$5
2nd Half		1	1	0	5	5	12.60	5.29	3.00	500	625	444	2.4	3.6	9.0	2.5	45	23	32	5.4	43%	52%	67%	0	10			0	1.11	-5.3	88	115	-$13
13	Proj	**2**	**1**	**0**	**29**	**19**	**4.65**	**4.62**	**1.53**	**284**	**290**	**279**	**5.3**	**3.7**	**6.0**	**1.6**	**48**	**24**	**28**	**0.9**	**10%**	**32%**	**71%**	**0**						**-2.2**	**34**	**45**	**-$4**

Martinez,Cristhian

Health			A	LIMA Plan	A	
Age: 31	Th: R	Role RP	PT/Exp	D	Rand Var	+1
Ht: 6' 1"	Wt: 185	Type	Consist	B	MM	3301

Dom spike joined already stellar Ctl to produce a very interesting pitcher. His problem was a brutal reverse platoon split (.629 OPS vL, .856 OPS vR). The good news is his two previous seasons show he has ability to get righties out. There's talent here. Expect a repeat, but UP: 3.50 ERA.

Yr	Tm	W	L	Sv	IP	K	ERA	xERA	WHIP	OBA	vL	vR	BF/G	Ctl	Dom	Cmd	G	L	F	hr/9	hr/f	H%	S%	GS	APC	DOM%	DIS%	Sv%	LI	RAR	BPV	BPX	R$
08																																	
09	FLA *	10	4	0	130	69	4.46	4.69	1.45	295	163	352	17.4	2.4	4.8	2.0	56	13	31	0.8	8%	32%	70%	0	27			0	0.72	-2.3	43	81	$1
10	ATL *	5	1	0	79	60	4.31	3.96	1.27	277	326	228	7.9	1.7	6.9	4.0	59	16	26	0.7	14%	33%	67%	0	24			0	0.36	-2.3	102	166	$1
11	ATL *	3	4	0	100	72	3.49	3.28	1.12	243	222	177	7.9	1.9	6.5	3.4	48	19	33	0.9	11%	28%	72%	0	24			0	0.92	5.5	88	132	$5
12	ATL	5	4	1	74	65	3.91	3.74	1.34	277	241	311	5.8	2.3	7.9	3.4	46	22	32	0.7	8%	34%	72%	0	22			100	0.61	1.0	104	136	$0
1st Half		3	1	1	39	37	4.42	3.24	1.34	294	225	354	6.2	1.6	8.6	5.3	48	27	26	1.2	17%	36%	70%	0	22			100	0.61	-1.9	137	178	$0
2nd Half		2	3	0	35	28	3.34	4.31	1.34	257	257	258	5.4	3.1	7.2	2.3	44	18	38	0.3	2%	32%	74%	0	22			0	0.61	2.9	69	90	$0
13	Proj	**4**	**3**	**0**	**73**	**57**	**3.87**	**3.84**	**1.29**	**269**	**261**	**276**	**6.8**	**2.2**	**7.0**	**3.2**	**47**	**20**	**33**	**0.7**	**8%**	**32%**	**71%**	**0**						**1.3**	**91**	**118**	**$1**

JOSH PALEY

Masterson,Justin

Age: 28	Th: R	Role SP	Health	A	LIMA Plan	D+
Ht: 6' 6"	Wt: 250	Type Pwr xGB	PT/Exp	A	Rand Var	+2
			Consist	A	MM	3205

PRO: High GB% means the ball stays in the park, xERA says 2H collapse wasn't rooted in his skills. CON: 2011's Cmd spike left as quickly as it came, LH batters continue to mash him (.825 OPS). VERDICT: 2011 appears the outlier; likely can't get to sub-4.00 again without Cmd or vLHB gains.

Yr	Tm	W	L	Sv	IP	K	ERA	xERA	WHIP	OBA	vL	vR	BF/G	Ctl	Dom	Cmd	G	L	F	hr/9	hr/f	H%	S%	GS	APC	DOM%	DIS%	Sv%	LI	RAR	BPV	BPX	R$
08	BOS *	8	8	0	136	105	3.80	3.44	1.30	236	238	196	11.7	3.8	6.9	1.8	54	18	27	0.7	15%	28%	72%	9	38	56%	0%	0	0.97	8.7	66	123	$8
09	2 AL	4	10	0	129	119	4.52	3.92	1.45	265	323	203	13.5	4.2	8.3	2.0	54	15	31	0.8	10%	32%	70%	16	52	38%	25%	0	0.78	-3.2	68	128	$0
10	CLE	6	13	0	180	140	4.70	3.84	1.50	278	290	263	23.6	3.7	7.0	1.9	60	15	25	0.7	10%	33%	69%	29	91	41%	28%	0	0.85	-13.8	65	106	-$4
11	CLE	12	10	0	216	158	3.21	3.60	1.28	257	291	210	26.7	2.7	6.6	2.4	55	18	27	0.5	6%	31%	75%	33	102	55%	12%	0	0.75	19.6	78	118	$14
12	CLE	11	15	0	206	159	4.93	4.13	1.45	269	296	232	26.6	3.8	6.9	1.8	56	19	25	0.8	11%	31%	66%	34	101	47%	26%			-23.3	55	72	-$7
1st Half		4	7	0	103	79	4.09	4.02	1.33	245	279	210	27.6	3.7	6.9	1.8	55	20	25	0.6	9%	29%	69%	16	102	50%	13%			-1.0	55	72	$0
2nd Half		7	8	0	103	80	5.77	4.22	1.58	291	309	260	25.8	3.9	7.0	1.8	57	19	25	1.0	14%	34%	64%	18	100	44%	39%			-22.2	54	70	-$15
13	Proj	**10**	**13**	**0**	**203**	**156**	**4.47**	**4.00**	**1.42**	**267**	**294**	**230**	**22.9**	**3.6**	**6.9**	**2.0**	**56**	**18**	**26**	**0.7**	**10%**	**32%**	**69%**	**38**						**-11.4**	**63**	**82**	**$1**

Matsuzaka,Daisuke

Age: 32	Th: R	Role SP	Health	F	LIMA Plan	F
Ht: 6' 0"	Wt: 185	Type Pwr xFB	PT/Exp	D	Rand Var	+4
			Consist	C	MM	0201

1-7, 8.28 ERA in 45 IP at BOS. Never seemed fully recovered from 2011 Tommy John surgery or 2009 thigh injury prepping for the World Baseball Classic. His skills set was suspect even before that, including in 2008 despite the ERA and wins. Cmd history is the only column you need to look at here.

Yr	Tm	W	L	Sv	IP	K	ERA	xERA	WHIP	OBA	vL	vR	BF/G	Ctl	Dom	Cmd	G	L	F	hr/9	hr/f	H%	S%	GS	APC	DOM%	DIS%	Sv%	LI	RAR	BPV	BPX	R$
08	BOS	18	3	0	168	154	2.90	4.49	1.32	211	225	195	24.7	5.0	8.3	1.6	39	18	43	0.6	6%	27%	80%	29	100	48%	14%			29.5	30	55	$19
09	BOS *	4	8	0	77	68	6.15	7.12	1.90	326	340	304	21.5	4.8	7.9	1.6	34	23	43	1.7	12%	38%	71%	12	92	25%	33%			-17.4	22	41	-$10
10	BOS *	11	6	0	170	142	4.46	3.61	1.33	240	265	211	25.3	4.0	7.5	1.9	33	22	45	0.8	7%	29%	67%	25	105	48%	16%			-8.0	69	112	$4
11	BOS	3	3	0	37	26	5.30	5.55	1.47	224	259	172	20.9	5.5	6.3	1.1	32	13	56	1.0	6%	26%	65%	7	82	43%	57%	0	0.90	-6.3	-27	-40	-$4
12	BOS *	2	10	0	101	76	6.33	6.02	1.62	297	333	280	19.5	3.8	6.7	1.8	40	18	42	1.7	17%	33%	64%	11	77	27%	45%			-29.0	22	29	-$16
1st Half		0	4	0	55	40	4.99	4.35	1.29	258	171	279	20.5	2.7	6.5	2.4	41	22	37	1.4	9%	28%	65%	4	94	50%	0%			-6.6	49	64	-$10
2nd Half		2	6	0	46	36	7.92	7.94	2.01	339	455	280	18.6	5.0	7.0	1.4	38	15	47	2.0	23%	37%	63%	7	67	14%	71%			-22.3	-1	-1	-$24
13	Proj	**5**	**9**	**0**	**102**	**78**	**5.02**	**5.15**	**1.59**	**278**	**308**	**242**	**20.5**	**4.5**	**6.9**	**1.5**	**36**	**17**	**46**	**1.3**	**10%**	**31%**	**72%**	**22**						**-12.5**	**16**	**21**	**-$6**

Mattheus,Ryan

Age: 29	Th: R	Role RP	Health	B	LIMA Plan	C+
Ht: 6' 3"	Wt: 205	Type	PT/Exp	D	Rand Var	-3
			Consist	D	MM	2101

Let's repeat the mantra... Skills over surface numbers... Skills over surface numbers... Unsustainable 1H S% produced a shiny ERA, 2H was more in line with what to expect. GB% and Ctl are good, but Dom puts him at risk of a rapid fall. xERA warns that this is not a LIMA safe haven... DN: 4.00+ ERA

Yr	Tm	W	L	Sv	IP	K	ERA	xERA	WHIP	OBA	vL	vR	BF/G	Ctl	Dom	Cmd	G	L	F	hr/9	hr/f	H%	S%	GS	APC	DOM%	DIS%	Sv%	LI	RAR	BPV	BPX	R$
08	aa	2	5	17	58	43	3.87	4.44	1.48	264			4.3	4.2	6.7	1.6				0.9		30%	76%							3.2	48	90	$6
09	a/a	1	2	0	22	19	5.35	6.18	1.68	307			6.1	3.9	7.8	2.0				1.6		35%	72%							-2.7	35	65	-$4
10																																	
11	WAS *	4	3	6	57	33	2.43	2.32	1.14	205	170	279	3.9	3.7	5.2	1.4	49	17	34	0.4	3%	23%	79%	0	14			100	0.99	10.6	64	96	$7
12	WAS	5	3	0	66	41	2.85	3.97	1.15	241	241	240	4.0	2.6	5.6	2.2	50	21	29	1.1	14%	25%	81%	0	15			0	0.98	9.5	59	76	$4
1st Half		2	1	0	26	16	1.75	4.17	1.21	245	313	210	4.0	2.8	5.6	2.0	44	26	30	0.4	4%	28%	87%	0	16			0	1.00	7.2	47	61	$3
2nd Half		3	2	0	41	25	3.54	3.84	1.11	238	200	261	4.0	2.4	5.5	2.3	53	18	28	1.5	21%	23%	76%	0	15			0	0.97	2.4	65	85	$5
13	Proj	**5**	**4**	**0**	**73**	**45**	**3.70**	**4.33**	**1.29**	**248**	**222**	**266**	**4.1**	**3.2**	**5.6**	**1.8**	**49**	**20**	**31**	**0.8**	**9%**	**28%**	**73%**	**0**						**2.8**	**42**	**55**	**$2**

Matusz,Brian

Age: 26	Th: L	Role RP	Health	B	LIMA Plan	D+
Ht: 6' 4"	Wt: 200	Type FB	PT/Exp	C	Rand Var	+2
			Consist	F	MM	1200

6-10, 4.87 in 98 IP at BAL. Starting was disagreeing with him, then he was sent to AAA and returned as a LOOGY with these numbers: 13 IP, 2 ER, 3 BB, 19K. It's a smallish sample size, but the results are encouraging. Pitched last 3 mos with abdominal tear that was repaired in Oct. so there's possible upside.

Yr	Tm	W	L	Sv	IP	K	ERA	xERA	WHIP	OBA	vL	vR	BF/G	Ctl	Dom	Cmd	G	L	F	hr/9	hr/f	H%	S%	GS	APC	DOM%	DIS%	Sv%	LI	RAR	BPV	BPX	R$
08																																	
09	BAL *	12	2	0	91	76	3.48	3.93	1.29	263	200	315	23.4	2.6	7.5	2.9	31	21	48	0.9	9%	31%	76%	8	93	25%	13%			9.5	82	154	$8
10	BAL	10	12	0	176	143	4.30	4.29	1.34	255	218	266	23.8	3.2	7.3	2.3	36	19	45	1.0	8%	30%	70%	32	94	44%	25%			-4.9	59	95	$4
11	BAL *	3	12	0	110	72	7.02	6.81	1.73	319	327	387	22.8	3.6	5.9	1.6	28	22	50	1.9	20%	34%	62%	12	79	0%	75%			-41.8	4	6	-$19
12	BAL *	8	11	1	145	106	5.23	5.18	1.55	290	175	327	14.4	3.6	6.6	1.9	41	20	40	1.1	12%	33%	68%	16	50	19%	38%	50	1.34	-21.7	42	55	-$11
1st Half		5	9	0	81	60	5.24	5.06	1.67	299	175	339	24.9	3.9	6.7	1.7	40	20	39	1.3	11%	34%	72%	15	96	20%	33%			-12.2	33	43	-$12
2nd Half		3	2	1	64	46	5.21	4.18	1.39	269	176	222	9.3	3.1	6.5	2.1	43	15	43	0.8	18%	31%	62%	1	14	0%	100%	50	1.80	-9.4	59	77	-$9
13	Proj	**3**	**4**	**0**	**58**	**44**	**4.57**	**4.63**	**1.48**	**288**	**217**	**321**	**16.1**	**3.1**	**6.9**	**2.3**	**36**	**19**	**45**	**1.2**	**10%**	**33%**	**72%**	**9**						**-4.0**	**56**	**73**	**-$3**

McAllister,Zach

Age: 25	Th: R	Role SP	Health	A	LIMA Plan	B
Ht: 6' 6"	Wt: 240	Type FB	PT/Exp	C	Rand Var	0
			Consist	B	MM	2205

6-8, 4.24 ERA with 110 Ks in 125 IP at CLE. There is a foundation here for something interesting: rising Dom and solid Ctl. Gopheritis was unlucky in 2H, so that figures to regress. At issue is whether he can do something about righties (.820 OBP). Risky, but possible sleeper... UP: 3.50 ERA

Yr	Tm	W	L	Sv	IP	K	ERA	xERA	WHIP	OBA	vL	vR	BF/G	Ctl	Dom	Cmd	G	L	F	hr/9	hr/f	H%	S%	GS	APC	DOM%	DIS%	Sv%	LI	RAR	BPV	BPX	R$
08																																	
09	aa	7	5	0	121	83	3.09	3.47	1.30	260			22.6	2.8	6.2	2.2				0.4		31%	76%							18.3	74	139	$8
10	aaa	9	12	0	150	84	5.82	5.94	1.63	323			24.7	2.6	5.0	1.9				1.1		35%	65%							-32.1	28	45	-$12
11	CLE *	12	4	0	172	120	3.99	4.31	1.38	292	421	256	25.0	1.9	6.3	3.2	43	27	30	0.6	5%	34%	71%	4	85	0%	50%			-0.9	84	126	$3
12	CLE *	11	10	0	189	152	3.96	4.51	1.36	274	243	299	23.9	2.7	7.3	2.7	41	19	40	1.1	12%	32%	75%	22	96	50%	18%			1.3	66	86	$4
1st Half		7	3	0	94	70	3.54	3.95	1.33	273	257	271	24.4	2.5	6.7	2.7	32	21	47	0.7	4%	32%	75%	5	102	40%	0%			5.5	78	102	$9
2nd Half		4	7	0	95	82	4.37	5.02	1.39	274	238	306	23.5	2.9	7.8	2.6	43	19	38	1.6	15%	31%	75%	17	95	53%	24%			-4.2	54	70	-$2
13	Proj	**11**	**10**	**0**	**189**	**139**	**4.06**	**4.37**	**1.38**	**280**	**259**	**309**	**24.0**	**2.5**	**6.6**	**2.6**	**39**	**20**	**42**	**1.0**	**8%**	**32%**	**73%**	**33**						**-0.9**	**68**	**88**	**$5**

McCarthy,Brandon

Age: 29	Th: R	Role SP	Health	F	LIMA Plan	B
Ht: 6' 7"	Wt: 200	Type Con	PT/Exp	C	Rand Var	-2
			Consist	C	MM	2101

Scary line drive off his head ended season in Sept, but the shoulder problem that put him on the DL in June is the long-term worry. Ctl is elite, but doesn't miss bats, so lucky 1H S% helped mask xERA issues. Hype the two years of ERA/WHIP, then let other owners deal with Health... DN: ERA over 4.00

Yr	Tm	W	L	Sv	IP	K	ERA	xERA	WHIP	OBA	vL	vR	BF/G	Ctl	Dom	Cmd	G	L	F	hr/9	hr/f	H%	S%	GS	APC	DOM%	DIS%	Sv%	LI	RAR	BPV	BPX	R$
08	TEX *	2	2	0	49	29	4.12	3.74	1.26	247	293	195	19.8	3.0	5.3	1.8	24	30	46	1.0	9%	27%	70%	5	75	40%	60%			1.2	45	85	$0
09	TEX *	7	5	0	119	82	4.85	4.47	1.41	266	264	246	22.9	3.5	6.2	1.8	39	19	42	1.1	10%	30%	68%	17	93	29%	29%			-7.8	44	82	$0
10	aaa	4	2	0	56	34	4.29	5.06	1.33	284			21.3	1.9	5.4	2.8				1.6		30%	74%							-1.4	40	65	-$1
11	OAK	9	9	0	171	123	3.32	3.46	1.13	258	256	260	27.6	1.3	6.5	4.9	47	21	32	0.6	6%	30%	71%	25	100	64%	4%			13.1	106	160	$13
12	OAK	8	6	0	111	73	3.24	4.20	1.25	267	288	245	26.1	1.9	5.9	3.0	41	24	35	0.8	8%	30%	77%	18	92	39%	17%			10.6	73	95	$6
1st Half		6	3	0	78	52	2.54	4.16	1.21	252	296	201	27.1	2.2	6.0	2.7	43	23	34	0.6	6%	29%	81%	12	94	42%	8%			14.2	70	91	$12
2nd Half		2	3	0	33	21	4.91	4.31	1.36	303	270	333	24.0	1.4	5.7	4.2	35	27	38	1.4	12%	33%	68%	6	88	33%	33%			-3.6	79	103	-$9
13	Proj	**7**	**7**	**0**	**116**	**76**	**3.90**	**4.10**	**1.27**	**275**	**274**	**276**	**23.9**	**1.8**	**5.9**	**3.3**	**41**	**23**	**36**	**1.0**	**10%**	**31%**	**72%**	**20**						**1.6**	**78**	**101**	**$4**

McDonald,James

Age: 28	Th: R	Role SP	Health	A	LIMA Plan	C+
Ht: 6' 4"	Wt: 205	Type Pwr FB	PT/Exp	B	Rand Var	0
			Consist	B	MM	2305

xERA tells us that terrific 1H was never as good as it looked, though still a step towards reclaiming minor league pedigree skills. 2H was a crash back down to earth, through its crust, near its molten core. Still young enough to have success, but has yet to show consistent Ctl needed to be a quality starter.

Yr	Tm	W	L	Sv	IP	K	ERA	xERA	WHIP	OBA	vL	vR	BF/G	Ctl	Dom	Cmd	G	L	F	hr/9	hr/f	H%	S%	GS	APC	DOM%	DIS%	Sv%	LI	RAR	BPV	BPX	R$
08	LA *	7	4	0	147	125	3.32	3.54	1.25	240	118	600	19.3	3.3	7.6	2.3	15	20	65	0.9	0%	29%	77%	0	24			0	0.24	18.2	75	140	$12
09	LA *	6	5	0	93	88	3.83	3.75	1.39	240	213	282	7.7	4.5	8.5	1.9	44	17	39	0.8	8%	30%	74%	4	25	0%	75%	0	0.91	5.6	74	139	$3
10	2 NL *	10	7	0	135	114	3.89	3.65	1.35	260	250	271	20.9	3.3	7.6	2.3	30	23	46	0.5	4%	32%	71%	12	81	42%	17%	0	0.86	3.1	84	135	$5
11	PIT	9	9	0	171	142	4.21	4.42	1.49	268	302	246	24.3	4.1	7.5	1.8	39	19	42	1.3	11%	31%	76%	31	94	39%	26%			-5.7	41	61	-$1
12	PIT	12	8	0	171	151	4.21	4.15	1.26	233	207	260	23.8	3.6	7.9	2.2	39	21	39	1.1	11%	28%	70%	29	93	52%	34%	0	0.75	-4.1	62	81	$6
1st Half		7	3	0	96	86	2.44	3.57	0.98	200	211	187	24.7	2.4	8.1	3.3	38	21	41	0.6	6%	25%	77%	15	97	67%	27%			18.7	95	124	$25
2nd Half		5	5	0	75	65	6.48	4.95	1.63	272	203	333	22.8	5.2	7.8	1.5	40	22	38	1.8	18%	30%	64%	14	89	36%	43%	0	0.72	-22.8	19	25	-$18
13	Proj	**12**	**10**	**0**	**189**	**163**	**3.94**	**4.32**	**1.36**	**253**	**234**	**269**	**23.5**	**3.7**	**7.8**	**2.1**	**38**	**21**	**41**	**1.1**	**10%**	**30%**	**75%**	**34**						**1.7**	**56**	**73**	**$8**

JOSH PALEY

Mcgee,Jake

Age: 26	Th: L	Role RP	Health	A	LIMA Plan B+
Ht: 6' 3"	Wt: 230	Type Pwr	PT/Exp	D	Rand Var -3
			Consist	D	MM 5510

Never a month with a BPV under 120, it's a travesty that he never got a shot at the ninth inning (thanks, Fernando Rodney). Signs that he can handle it: Electric Dom, reversed FB trend, embarrased RHBs all year. Nothing more than an ideal LIMA option for now, but there's certainly value in all those Ks.

Yr Tm	W	L	Sv	IP	K	ERA	xERA	WHIP	OBA	vL	vR	BF/G	Ctl	Dom	Cmd	G	L	F	hr/9	hr/f	H%	S%	GS	APC	DOM%	DIS%	Sv%	LI	RAR	BPV	BPX	R$
08 aa	6	4	0	78	57	4.47	3.84	1.40	247			21.8	4.2	6.6	1.6				0.7		29%	68%							-1.4	56	105	$0
09																																
10 TAM *	4	8	1	111	113	3.52	3.22	1.31	253	222	0	12.0	3.2	9.2	2.9	55	18	27	0.3	0%	34%	72%	0	10			100	0.31	7.6	112	182	$5
11 TAM *	9	4	9	61	58	3.75	4.67	1.38	272	164	400	4.2	2.9	8.6	2.9	33	18	49	1.3	13%	33%	78%	0	14			90	1.10	1.5	74	111	$5
12 TAM	5	2	0	55	73	1.95	2.48	0.80	168	259	98	3.1	1.8	11.9	6.6	44	19	37	0.5	7%	27%	78%	0	13			0	1.39	14.1	187	244	$10
1st Half	2	2	0	26	28	1.73	2.95	0.77	152	220	98	2.9	2.1	9.7	4.7	44	20	36	0.3	4%	22%	79%	0	12			0	1.23	7.3	140	182	$8
2nd Half	3	0	0	29	45	2.15	2.11	0.82	181	295	98	3.3	1.5	13.8	9.0	44	18	38	0.6	9%	31%	77%	0	14			0	1.55	6.8	229	298	$12
13 Proj	**5**	**2**	**3**	**51**	**58**	**2.92**	**3.06**	**1.08**	**221**	**345**	**128**	**4.2**	**2.5**	**10.2**	**4.1**	**44**	**19**	**37**	**0.7**	**8%**	**30%**	**75%**	**0**						**6.9**	**138**	**180**	**$6**

McPherson,Kyle

Age: 25	Th: R	Role SP	Health	A	LIMA Plan A
Ht: 6' 4"	Wt: 220	Type Con GB	PT/Exp	D	Rand Var 0
			Consist	B	MM 2201

0-2, 2.73 ERA in 26 IP at PIT. Promising debut from a rising prospect. Possesses stellar Ctl which he showcased in small MLB sample as both SP and RP. GB tilt also encouraging, but he'll need to repeat — and improve upon — it to be worthy of your end-game bid.

Yr Tm	W	L	Sv	IP	K	ERA	xERA	WHIP	OBA	vL	vR	BF/G	Ctl	Dom	Cmd	G	L	F	hr/9	hr/f	H%	S%	GS	APC	DOM%	DIS%	Sv%	LI	RAR	BPV	BPX	R$
08																																
09																																
10																																
11 aa	8	5	0	89	64	3.68	3.52	1.21	258			22.5	2.1	6.4	3.1				0.7		30%	71%							2.9	84	127	$4
12 PIT *	3	8	0	93	69	3.91	4.31	1.30	285	225	263	17.5	1.6	6.7	4.2	46	13	41	0.9	10%	33%	72%	3	44	33%	67%	0	0.51	1.2	99	129	-$1
1st Half	1	2	0	17	7	6.81	4.86	1.47	313	0	0	24.3	1.6	3.6	2.2				0.6	0%	34%	51%	0	0					-5.9	43	56	-$15
2nd Half	2	6	0	76	62	3.25	4.15	1.26	277	225	263	16.4	1.6	7.3	4.7	46	13	41	1.0	10%	33%	78%	3	44	33%	67%	0	0.51	7.3	112	146	$3
13 Proj	**7**	**9**	**0**	**118**	**79**	**4.33**	**4.29**	**1.31**	**280**	**255**	**298**	**23.3**	**1.9**	**6.1**	**3.1**	**46**	**13**	**41**	**0.8**	**6%**	**32%**	**68%**	**21**						**-4.5**	**81**	**105**	**$2**

Medlen,Kris

Age: 27	Th: R	Role SP	Health	F	LIMA Plan C+
Ht: 5' 10"	Wt: 190	Type	PT/Exp	C	Rand Var -5
			Consist	A	MM 4305

Hate to say we told you so. Finally inserted into ATL rotation in July and proceeded to shatter our lofty expectations. The H%-S%-hr/f trifecta helped, but pinpoint Ctl, healthy Dom, tons of GB testify to the stuff. Some regression is inevitable, but you shouldn't be afraid to go the extra buck for ace-level skills.

Yr Tm	W	L	Sv	IP	K	ERA	xERA	WHIP	OBA	vL	vR	BF/G	Ctl	Dom	Cmd	G	L	F	hr/9	hr/f	H%	S%	GS	APC	DOM%	DIS%	Sv%	LI	RAR	BPV	BPX	R$
08 aa	7	8	1	120	104	4.20	4.31	1.38	290			14.0	2.1	7.7	3.7				0.6		36%	70%							1.8	103	193	$4
09 ATL *	8	5	0	105	109	3.26	2.86	1.23	229	183	328	9.5	3.5	9.3	2.7	41	24	36	0.4	8%	31%	73%	4	30	25%	50%	0	0.70	13.8	108	203	$10
10 ATL	6	2	0	108	83	3.68	3.56	1.20	267	281	257	14.1	1.8	6.9	4.0	43	22	35	1.1	12%	30%	73%	14	51	50%	21%	0	0.84	5.3	98	159	$6
11 ATL	0	0	0	2	2	0.00	2.78	0.43	125	0	250	4.0	0.0	7.7	0.0	33	17	50	0.0	0%	18%	0%	0	12			0	3.05	1.1	150	225	-$3
12 ATL	10	1	1	138	120	1.57	2.98	0.91	208	208	207	10.4	1.5	7.8	5.2	53	19	28	0.4	6%	26%	85%	12	38	92%	0%	50	0.81	41.7	131	171	$29
1st Half	1	1	1	38	23	3.32	3.88	1.24	268	226	300	5.4	2.1	5.4	2.6	51	22	27	0.2	3%	31%	72%	0	20			50	0.81	3.3	69	90	-$7
2nd Half	9	0	0	100	97	0.90	2.68	0.79	184	202	163	16.8	1.3	8.7	6.9	55	17	29	0.5	7%	24%	93%	12	60	92%	0%	0	0.80	38.4	156	203	$42
13 Proj	**14**	**7**	**0**	**196**	**166**	**3.17**	**3.42**	**1.11**	**239**	**227**	**250**	**23.8**	**2.0**	**7.6**	**3.9**	**48**	**21**	**32**	**0.6**	**7%**	**29%**	**72%**	**32**						**20.4**	**109**	**142**	**$22**

Mejia,Jenrry

Age: 23	Th: R	Role RP	Health	A	LIMA Plan D
Ht: 6' 0"	Wt: 205	Type xGB	PT/Exp	D	Rand Var +1
			Consist	F	MM 2100

1-2, 5.63 ERA in 16 IP at NYM. Once-heralded prospect spent all of '11 and most of '12 in AAA, but seemingly still hasn't fully recovered from '10 MCL tear (Dom dropped from 9.2 to 5.2 between AA and AAA). Ctl improving, but Cmd says overall product remains uninspiring. Still young; check back in '14.

Yr Tm	W	L	Sv	IP	K	ERA	xERA	WHIP	OBA	vL	vR	BF/G	Ctl	Dom	Cmd	G	L	F	hr/9	hr/f	H%	S%	GS	APC	DOM%	DIS%	Sv%	LI	RAR	BPV	BPX	R$
08																																
09 aa	0	5	0	44	44	4.81	4.16	1.52	272			19.2	4.2	8.9	2.1				0.4		36%	67%							-2.6	86	162	-$4
10 NYM *	2	4	0	74	53	3.01	3.66	1.40	252	203	340	7.8	4.1	6.4	1.6	61	13	26	0.5	8%	30%	79%	3	22	0%	100%	0	0.79	9.8	62	100	$1
11 aaa	1	2	0	28	18	2.90	1.62	1.03	173			21.8	4.0	5.6	1.4				0.3		20%	71%							3.6	75	112	$0
12 NYM *	4	6	0	98	47	4.15	4.57	1.48	288	267	353	12.7	3.1	4.3	1.4	67	11	22	0.6	17%	31%	72%	3	60	33%	33%	0	0.57	-1.6	34	44	-$5
1st Half	0	1	0	31	16	4.49	4.60	1.42	274	0	0	10.9	3.2	4.5	1.4				1.1	0%	29%	71%	0	0					-1.8	25	33	-$9
2nd Half	4	5	0	67	31	3.99	4.51	1.52	295	267	353	13.8	3.0	4.2	1.4	67	11	22	0.4	17%	33%	73%	3	60	33%	33%	0	0.57	0.2	38	49	-$3
13 Proj	**1**	**3**	**0**	**51**	**33**	**4.41**	**4.15**	**1.46**	**273**	**220**	**312**	**10.9**	**3.7**	**5.8**	**1.6**	**65**	**12**	**24**	**0.6**	**9%**	**31%**	**70%**	**2**						**-2.4**	**48**	**62**	**-$3**

Melancon,Mark

Age: 28	Th: R	Role RP	Health	A	LIMA Plan A+
Ht: 6' 2"	Wt: 215	Type Pwr xGB	PT/Exp	C	Rand Var +5
			Consist	C	MM 4410

0-2, 6.20 ERA in 45 IP at BOS. Prematurely demoted in April, blew away AAA competition in May, returned in June only to have hr/f, S% wreak havoc on a solid skill set. Added respectable Ctl to already closer-worthy repertoire, solved LHBs in 2H. If opportunity visits him again... UP: 25 SV.

Yr Tm	W	L	Sv	IP	K	ERA	xERA	WHIP	OBA	vL	vR	BF/G	Ctl	Dom	Cmd	G	L	F	hr/9	hr/f	H%	S%	GS	APC	DOM%	DIS%	Sv%	LI	RAR	BPV	BPX	R$
08 a/a	7	1	3	70	58	2.78	2.28	0.99	210			8.6	2.2	7.5	3.5				0.7		25%	74%							13.2	111	208	$10
09 NYY *	4	1	3	69	55	4.00	2.95	1.18	233	276	161	6.2	2.9	7.1	2.4	62	14	24	0.6	0%	28%	66%	0	20			60	0.60	2.8	85	159	$4
10 2 TM *	9	1	7	82	72	3.91	5.18	1.65	293	167	280	5.6	4.3	7.9	1.8	46	17	37	0.8	9%	36%	78%	0	16			70	1.17	1.7	58	94	$2
11 HOU	8	4	20	74	66	2.78	3.22	1.22	234	243	228	4.4	3.1	8.0	2.5	57	22	21	0.6	11%	29%	79%	0	16			80	1.12	10.6	94	141	$14
12 BOS *	0	2	12	67	62	4.58	3.80	1.20	257	291	227	4.3	2.1	8.3	4.0	50	24	26	1.1	22%	31%	64%	0	18			92	0.62	-4.7	105	138	$2
1st Half	0	2	11	31	27	4.29	5.03	1.38	289	500	261	4.0	2.1	7.7	3.6	37	29	34	1.4	38%	33%	74%	0	15			92	0.45	-1.1	76	99	$4
2nd Half	0	0	1	35	35	4.84	2.68	1.05	225	220	216	4.7	2.0	8.9	4.4	55	21	23	0.8	13%	29%	53%	0	19			100	0.69	-3.6	132	172	$1
13 Proj	**3**	**2**	**5**	**58**	**52**	**3.95**	**3.30**	**1.25**	**252**	**257**	**248**	**4.7**	**2.7**	**8.1**	**3.0**	**56**	**22**	**23**	**0.8**	**14%**	**31%**	**70%**	**0**						**0.5**	**107**	**139**	**$3**

Mendoza,Luis

Age: 29	Th: R	Role SP	Health	A	LIMA Plan D
Ht: 6' 3"	Wt: 240	Type Con GB	PT/Exp	C	Rand Var 0
			Consist	C	MM 1003

Wasn't terrible...and that's saying a lot when you look at his history. 2H is where it all clicked, but even then he was only marginal. Dom, Ctl both mediocre, and while GB tendency offers a building block, it didn't help him all that much in '08 when he posted similar BPIs. Hard to see a path out of mediocrity.

Yr Tm	W	L	Sv	IP	K	ERA	xERA	WHIP	OBA	vL	vR	BF/G	Ctl	Dom	Cmd	G	L	F	hr/9	hr/f	H%	S%	GS	APC	DOM%	DIS%	Sv%	LI	RAR	BPV	BPX	R$
08 TEX *	5	11	1	100	51	7.82	6.53	1.85	346	336	350	13.7	3.2	4.6	1.5	50	21	29	0.7	10%	38%	55%	11	47	18%	73%	50	0.71	-43.0	22	41	-$17
09 TEX *	6	7	0	112	62	6.68	6.78	2.02	349	1000	0	20.9	4.6	5.0	1.1	0	40	60	0.5	33%	39%	65%	0	22			0	0.10	-32.7	22	41	-$19
10 KC *	10	10	0	136	45	5.53	6.04	1.63	327	429	467	21.6	2.4	3.0	1.2	35	20	45	1.1	44%	33%	68%	0	24			0	1.13	-24.3	0	0	-$10
11 KC *	14	5	2	159	66	2.50	3.74	1.42	266	200	222	19.2	3.5	3.7	1.1	44	24	31	0.3	0%	29%	82%	2	101	50%	0%			28.3	38	57	$11
12 KC	8	10	0	166	104	4.23	4.29	1.42	278	292	263	23.6	3.2	5.6	1.8	52	21	27	0.8	11%	31%	71%	25	84	44%	24%	0	0.79	-4.4	45	59	-$2
1st Half	3	4	0	68	35	4.50	4.67	1.51	280	311	246	21.0	4.0	4.6	1.2	58	19	23	0.5	8%	31%	70%	9	76	33%	33%	0	0.80	-4.1	12	16	-$9
2nd Half	5	6	0	98	69	4.04	4.05	1.35	278	279	276	25.9	2.7	6.3	2.4	48	22	30	1.0	12%	31%	73%	16	91	50%	19%			-0.3	68	89	$2
13 Proj	**9**	**12**	**0**	**174**	**96**	**4.39**	**4.64**	**1.50**	**288**	**293**	**284**	**21.1**	**3.2**	**4.9**	**1.5**	**51**	**21**	**28**	**0.8**	**9%**	**32%**	**72%**	**36**						**-8.0**	**32**	**41**	**-$3**

Mijares,Jose

Age: 28	Th: L	Role RP	Health	B	LIMA Plan C+
Ht: 6' 0"	Wt: 230	Type Pwr FB	PT/Exp	D	Rand Var -5
			Consist	D	MM 1400

Nice bounceback from '11 disaster. PRO: Dom spiked, re-established dominance of LHBs. CON: More Ks also led to more BBs in 2H, reduced FBs but LD says he was still hit hard, xERA dubious of ERA thanks to friendly S%. VERDICT: LOOGY with decent Dom upside, but only an asset in Holds formats.

Yr Tm	W	L	Sv	IP	K	ERA	xERA	WHIP	OBA	vL	vR	BF/G	Ctl	Dom	Cmd	G	L	F	hr/9	hr/f	H%	S%	GS	APC	DOM%	DIS%	Sv%	LI	RAR	BPV	BPX	R$
08 MIN *	1	2	2	26	19	2.39	2.76	1.09	227	143	50	4.8	2.3	6.8	2.9	39	14	46	0.7	0%	27%	81%	0	13			67	0.85	6.1	91	171	$1
09 MIN	2	2	0	62	55	2.34	4.12	1.18	224	155	283	3.6	3.4	8.0	2.4	38	12	51	1.0	8%	27%	86%	0	14			0	1.25	15.1	70	131	$5
10 MIN	1	1	0	33	28	3.31	4.21	1.32	268	268	268	3.0	2.5	7.7	3.1	31	14	55	1.1	7%	32%	79%	0	13			0	1.21	3.1	81	131	-$1
11 MIN	0	2	0	49	30	4.59	5.77	1.69	275	253	292	3.9	5.5	5.5	1.0	31	22	47	0.7	5%	31%	73%	0	16			0	1.14	-3.9	-41	-61	-$7
12 2 TM	3	2	0	56	57	2.56	3.93	1.26	238	211	276	3.1	3.4	9.1	2.7	35	26	39	0.5	5%	32%	81%	0	12			0	0.87	10.1	86	113	$3
1st Half	2	1	0	30	28	1.78	3.67	1.09	234	213	260	3.4	2.1	8.3	4.0	33	27	41	0.6	6%	29%	87%	0	14			0	0.85	8.4	104	135	$6
2nd Half	1	1	0	26	29	3.46	4.23	1.46	242	210	297	2.9	4.8	10.0	2.1	37	26	37	0.3	4%	34%	76%	0	11			0	0.88	1.8	65	85	-$1
13 Proj	**2**	**2**	**0**	**58**	**52**	**3.74**	**4.47**	**1.40**	**253**	**225**	**284**	**3.1**	**4.0**	**8.0**	**2.0**	**34**	**22**	**44**	**0.7**	**6%**	**31%**	**74%**	**0**						**2.0**	**49**	**64**	**-$1**

MATT GELFAND

Miley,Wade

Miley,Wade	Health	A	LIMA Plan	C
Age: 26 Th: L Role SP	PT/Exp	C	Rand Var	-1
Ht: 6' 0" Wt: 218 Type	Consist	A	MM	2205

Significant gains in both Ctl and Dom keyed this breakout, and 59/14 DOM/DIS split very impressive for a rookie. Was especially tough on LH, who have just 1 HR against him in 183 career AB. xERA, 2H GB dip give us slight pause in paying for a full repeat, but he appears to have bright future ahead of him.

Yr Tm	W	L	Sv	IP	K	ERA	xERA	WHIP	OBA	vL	vR	BF/G	Ctl	Dom	Cmd	G	L	F	hr/9	hr/f	H%	S%	GS	APC	DOM%	DIS%	Sv%	LI	RAR	BPV	BPX	R$
08																																
09																																
10 aa	5	2	0	73	51	2.72	4.26	1.43	267			23.8	3.7	6.3	1.7				0.8		31%	84%							12.2	52	84	$3
11 ARI *	12	5	0	170	107	4.42	4.47	1.44	279	391	289	24.1	3.1	5.7	1.8	46	24	30	0.8	15%	31%	70%	7	82	43%	29%	0	0.73	-9.9	47	71	-$1
12 ARI	16	11	0	195	144	3.33	3.87	1.18	255	200	270	25.2	1.7	6.7	3.9	43	23	34	0.6	7%	31%	73%	29	94	59%	14%	0	0.82	16.5	95	123	$17
1st Half	9	4	0	94	66	2.87	3.79	1.06	227	240	222	23.8	1.8	6.3	3.5	48	20	32	0.7	8%	27%	75%	13	86	69%	15%	0	0.85	13.3	90	117	$25
2nd Half	7	7	0	101	78	3.75	3.95	1.29	280	141	307	26.7	1.6	7.0	4.3	39	26	35	0.6	6%	34%	72%	16	102	50%	13%			3.3	100	130	$10
13 Proj	**14**	**8**	**0**	**189**	**132**	**3.70**	**4.12**	**1.32**	**270**	**251**	**274**	**24.3**	**2.5**	**6.3**	**2.5**	**44**	**24**	**32**	**0.8**	**9%**	**31%**	**74%**	**32**						**7.4**	**68**	**89**	**$10**

Miller,Andrew

Miller,Andrew	Health	B	LIMA Plan	C+
Age: 28 Th: L Role RP	PT/Exp	D	Rand Var	0
Ht: 6' 7" Wt: 210 Type Pwr	Consist	F	MM	2500

Move to pen started well: early Ctl, Cmd were much improved, backed by increased fastball velocity. But Ctl collapsed down stretch, and given previous struggles, can't assume he will dominate LH again. If Dom spike holds, could have some deep league value, but risk probably outweighs the reward.

Yr Tm	W	L	Sv	IP	K	ERA	xERA	WHIP	OBA	vL	vR	BF/G	Ctl	Dom	Cmd	G	L	F	hr/9	hr/f	H%	S%	GS	APC	DOM%	DIS%	Sv%	LI	RAR	BPV	BPX	R$
08 FLA	6	10	0	107	89	5.87	4.63	1.64	289	226	307	17.0	4.7	7.5	1.6	46	22	33	0.6	7%	35%	63%	20	67	30%	40%	0	0.93	-20.5	32	59	-$7
09 FLA *	4	7	0	98	77	5.26	4.70	1.65	270	309	261	18.2	5.5	7.1	1.3	48	22	30	0.6	9%	32%	68%	14	69	29%	36%	0	0.64	-11.3	52	97	-$6
10 FLA *	2	13	0	118	85	7.95	7.59	2.24	338	405	360	22.1	7.2	6.5	0.9	38	28	34	1.0	16%	39%	64%	7	72	0%	71%	0	0.60	-56.4	16	26	-$30
11 BOS *	9	6	0	131	98	4.52	4.59	1.62	263	312	298	19.3	5.5	6.7	1.2	45	23	31	0.7	12%	31%	72%	12	72	17%	42%	0	0.61	-9.4	47	71	-$6
12 BOS	3	2	0	40	51	3.35	3.35	1.19	194	149	263	3.2	4.5	11.4	2.6	43	23	34	0.7	9%	28%	73%	0	13			0	1.17	3.3	105	137	$1
1st Half	2	0	0	19	20	1.89	3.15	0.89	172	163	190	3.1	2.8	9.5	3.3	39	25	36	0.5	6%	23%	81%	0	12			0	1.18	5.0	110	143	$4
2nd Half	1	2	0	21	31	4.64	3.48	1.45	213	136	306	3.3	5.9	13.1	2.2	47	22	31	0.8	13%	34%	69%	0	14			0	1.15	-1.6	101	131	-$2
13 Proj	**3**	**3**	**0**	**51**	**52**	**4.65**	**4.27**	**1.52**	**248**	**200**	**284**	**5.6**	**5.3**	**9.2**	**1.7**	**44**	**24**	**33**	**0.7**	**9%**	**32%**	**70%**	**0**						**-4.0**	**44**	**57**	**-$3**

Miller,Jim

Miller,Jim	Health	A	LIMA Plan	D
Age: 31 Th: R Role RP	PT/Exp	D	Rand Var	-3
Ht: 6' 1" Wt: 200 Type Pwr FB	Consist	D	MM	1300

2-1, 2.59 ERA in 49 IP at OAK. First opportunity for more than a Sept callup, and while ERA was solid, skills tell different story. Cmd was subpar, FB% led to some HR issues (particularly on road), and Cmd dipped to 1.3 vs RH. Has 127 minor league saves, but unlikely to see many chances in majors.

Yr Tm	W	L	Sv	IP	K	ERA	xERA	WHIP	OBA	vL	vR	BF/G	Ctl	Dom	Cmd	G	L	F	hr/9	hr/f	H%	S%	GS	APC	DOM%	DIS%	Sv%	LI	RAR	BPV	BPX	R$
08 BAL *	3	8	11	88	81	3.98	3.85	1.36	257	333	250	5.7	3.5	8.3	2.4	48	26	26	0.7	0%	32%	72%	0	20			65	1.10	3.7	83	156	$6
09 aaa	4	4	17	65	44	4.05	5.57	1.68	322			5.4	3.0	6.1	2.0				0.6		37%	76%							2.2	50	94	$4
10 aaa	1	0	0	58	39	6.56	6.82	1.68	322			7.9	3.1	6.2	2.0				1.9		35%	65%							-17.6	11	19	-$9
11 COL *	8	5	24	79	56	4.92	5.65	1.65	323	167	118	5.0	2.8	6.4	2.3	26	21	53	0.8	0%	37%	71%	0	19			83	0.10	-9.5	53	80	$4
12 OAK *	2	4	6	68	60	2.78	3.44	1.30	230	136	283	5.7	4.1	7.9	1.9	35	21	44	0.8	10%	28%	82%	0	26			86	0.65	10.3	73	95	$4
1st Half	2	3	2	37	30	2.33	2.93	1.24	227	122	300	5.4	3.7	7.2	2.0	38	16	46	0.5	6%	28%	83%	0	24			100	0.95	7.8	80	104	$6
2nd Half	0	1	4	31	30	3.33	4.02	1.39	233	150	265	6.1	4.7	8.7	1.8	33	25	42	1.2	14%	28%	81%	0	28			80	0.29	2.6	64	83	$2
13 Proj	**2**	**2**	**0**	**44**	**35**	**4.06**	**4.64**	**1.47**	**276**	**177**	**356**	**5.8**	**3.6**	**7.3**	**2.0**	**35**	**22**	**44**	**1.0**	**8%**	**32%**	**75%**	**0**						**-0.2**	**47**	**61**	**-$3**

Miller,Shelby

Miller,Shelby	Health	A	LIMA Plan	B+
Age: 22 Th: R Role SP	PT/Exp	D	Rand Var	-1
Ht: 6' 3" Wt: 195 Type Pwr xFB	Consist	F	MM	3401

1-0, 1.32 ERA in 14 IP at STL. Top prospect got off to horrible start in AAA; Ctl and hr/9 were major issues. Turned things around, posting 57:4 K:BB in final eight starts. Will compete for rotation spot, armed with that strong Dom. Has ace potential, and if 2H skills spike is real, may be close to reaching it.

Yr Tm	W	L	Sv	IP	K	ERA	xERA	WHIP	OBA	vL	vR	BF/G	Ctl	Dom	Cmd	G	L	F	hr/9	hr/f	H%	S%	GS	APC	DOM%	DIS%	Sv%	LI	RAR	BPV	BPX	R$
08																																
09																																
10																																
11 aa	9	3	0	87	77	2.27	2.19	1.12	218			21.3	3.0	8.0	2.7				0.1		29%	79%							17.9	112	168	$11
12 STL *	12	10	0	150	153	4.54	4.47	1.37	267	167	194	19.1	3.1	9.1	2.9	42	15	42	1.2	0%	33%	70%	1	33	100%	0%	0	0.88	-9.7	82	107	$1
1st Half	4	6	0	71	69	5.85	6.26	1.69	304	0	0	21.3	4.1	8.8	2.1				1.7	0%	36%	69%	0	0					-16.0	41	53	-$13
2nd Half	8	4	0	79	84	3.37	2.82	1.09	230	167	194	17.2	2.2	9.5	4.3	42	15	42	0.8	0%	30%	71%	1	33	100%	0%	0	0.88	6.4	134	174	$14
13 Proj	**9**	**5**	**0**	**102**	**98**	**4.01**	**3.98**	**1.25**	**245**			**23.0**	**3.0**	**8.7**	**2.9**	**37**	**13**	**50**	**1.2**	**9%**	**30%**	**72%**	**18**						**0.1**	**92**	**119**	**$6**

Millwood,Kevin

Millwood,Kevin	Health	B	LIMA Plan	D
Age: 38 Th: R Role SP	PT/Exp	B	Rand Var	-1
Ht: 6' 4" Wt: 230 Type	Consist	C	MM	1101

Bumped up the GB% and Dom in 1H, with better than expected results. No surprise that 2H didn't go as well, as regression came home to roost. Cmd has been hovering around 2.0 benchmark, but age, recent track record suggest it isn't likely to get any better. His best days have scrolled out of this box.

Yr Tm	W	L	Sv	IP	K	ERA	xERA	WHIP	OBA	vL	vR	BF/G	Ctl	Dom	Cmd	G	L	F	hr/9	hr/f	H%	S%	GS	APC	DOM%	DIS%	Sv%	LI	RAR	BPV	BPX	R$
08 TEX	9	10	0	169	125	5.07	4.41	1.59	312	273	354	26.4	2.6	6.7	2.6	41	25	34	1.0	9%	37%	69%	29	93	48%	21%			-15.5	68	128	-$5
09 TEX	13	10	0	199	123	3.67	4.60	1.34	257	240	272	27.4	3.2	5.6	1.7	42	19	39	1.2	11%	28%	77%	31	106	45%	19%			16.0	33	63	$12
10 BAL	4	16	0	191	132	5.10	4.56	1.51	292	307	276	27.2	3.1	6.2	2.0	37	22	41	1.4	12%	32%	70%	31	104	26%	16%			-24.0	44	72	-$9
11 COL *	11	5	0	144	91	5.31	5.81	1.58	312	296	260	25.4	2.7	5.7	2.1	42	23	35	1.3	15%	34%	69%	9	93	44%	11%			-24.3	31	46	-$9
12 SEA	6	12	0	161	107	4.25	4.49	1.39	271	255	286	24.6	3.1	6.0	1.9	45	22	34	0.7	8%	31%	70%	28	93	43%	21%			-4.6	46	60	-$2
1st Half	3	6	0	83	62	4.00	4.29	1.36	253	248	257	23.9	3.6	6.7	1.9	49	20	31	0.4	5%	31%	70%	15	91	47%	27%			0.2	51	66	$0
2nd Half	3	6	0	78	45	4.52	4.69	1.43	290	261	320	25.5	2.7	5.2	2.0	40	24	36	1.0	10%	31%	71%	13	95	38%	15%			-4.8	40	52	-$5
13 Proj	**5**	**7**	**0**	**102**	**66**	**4.68**	**4.60**	**1.47**	**288**	**283**	**293**	**25.2**	**3.0**	**5.9**	**2.0**	**42**	**22**	**36**	**1.0**	**10%**	**32%**	**70%**	**17**						**-8.4**	**46**	**60**	**-$3**

Milone,Tommy

Milone,Tommy	Health	A	LIMA Plan	A
Age: 26 Th: L Role SP	PT/Exp	B	Rand Var	0
Ht: 6' 0" Wt: 205 Type Con	Consist	B	MM	3305

Very strong rookie season: Ctl was as good as advertised, Dom improved in 2H, and he posted a sub-4.00 ERA in every month. Still has some work to do, as low GB% led to 1.8 hr/9 on road. All in all, a solid debut, and while he doesn't possess #1 upside, probably has a few more seasons like '12 in him.

Yr Tm	W	L	Sv	IP	K	ERA	xERA	WHIP	OBA	vL	vR	BF/G	Ctl	Dom	Cmd	G	L	F	hr/9	hr/f	H%	S%	GS	APC	DOM%	DIS%	Sv%	LI	RAR	BPV	BPX	R$
08																																
09																																
10 aa	12	5	0	158	129	3.65	4.42	1.36	300			24.5	1.3	7.3	5.5				0.7		36%	74%							8.3	135	218	$8
11 WAS *	13	6	0	174	140	3.84	3.57	1.18	275	300	281	24.1	1.0	7.2	7.2	31	20	49	0.6	5%	33%	68%	5	82	20%	40%			2.1	176	264	$11
12 OAK	13	10	0	190	137	3.74	4.06	1.28	278	263	283	25.5	1.7	6.5	3.8	38	25	37	1.1	11%	31%	75%	31	98	52%	16%			6.4	87	113	$9
1st Half	8	6	0	101	63	3.73	4.30	1.19	250	230	256	26.0	2.1	5.6	2.6	39	24	37	1.3	13%	27%	75%	16	99	44%	13%			3.6	60	78	$14
2nd Half	5	4	0	89	74	3.76	3.79	1.38	308	290	316	25.0	1.2	7.5	6.2	37	25	38	0.9	8%	36%	75%	15	97	60%	20%			2.9	117	152	$3
13 Proj	**14**	**8**	**0**	**196**	**152**	**3.66**	**3.82**	**1.27**	**284**	**269**	**290**	**24.6**	**1.3**	**7.0**	**5.3**	**38**	**25**	**37**	**0.9**	**8%**	**33%**	**73%**	**33**						**8.5**	**106**	**138**	**$13**

Minor,Mike

Minor,Mike	Health	A	LIMA Plan	C+
Age: 25 Th: L Role SP	PT/Exp	B	Rand Var	-1
Ht: 6' 4" Wt: 205 Type Pwr FB	Consist	B	MM	2305

Strong 2011 2H created optimism, but 2012 got off to rocky start. Part of it was his doing (Ctl, FB%), but also had some bad luck (hr/f, S%). In the 2nd half, his Ctl improved dramatically and 11 of 15 starts were PQS-DOM. Sure, he was a little lucky, but if he keeps HR in check... UP: 3.50 ERA.

Yr Tm	W	L	Sv	IP	K	ERA	xERA	WHIP	OBA	vL	vR	BF/G	Ctl	Dom	Cmd	G	L	F	hr/9	hr/f	H%	S%	GS	APC	DOM%	DIS%	Sv%	LI	RAR	BPV	BPX	R$
08																																
09																																
10 ATL *	9	9	0	161	169	4.55	3.97	1.34	259	293	320	22.3	3.2	9.4	2.9	35	17	48	0.9	10%	33%	67%	8	85	50%	25%	0	0.71	-9.3	96	155	$4
11 ATL *	9	8	0	183	162	3.99	4.60	1.42	282	316	279	25.1	2.9	7.9	2.8	37	27	35	1.0	8%	34%	75%	15	92	27%	20%			-1.1	75	113	$2
12 ATL	11	10	0	179	145	4.12	4.14	1.15	232	239	230	24.3	2.8	7.3	2.6	35	21	44	1.3	12%	26%	69%	30	95	50%	17%			-2.2	68	89	$10
1st Half	4	6	0	86	72	6.20	4.70	1.47	271	267	272	24.9	4.0	7.6	1.9	35	20	45	1.9	16%	29%	62%	15	99	27%	27%			-23.1	42	55	-$10
2nd Half	7	4	0	94	73	2.21	3.63	0.86	193	214	186	23.6	1.7	7.0	4.1	36	22	43	0.8	7%	22%	79%	15	92	73%	7%			20.9	93	121	$29
13 Proj	**11**	**10**	**0**	**196**	**170**	**3.79**	**4.02**	**1.25**	**251**	**257**	**249**	**23.9**	**2.8**	**7.8**	**2.8**	**36**	**23**	**41**	**1.1**	**10%**	**30%**	**73%**	**33**						**5.5**	**79**	**103**	**$12**

BRIAN RUDD

Moore,Matt

Age: 24	Th: L	Role SP	Health	A	LIMA Plan	A
Ht: 6' 2"	Wt: 205	Type Pwr FB	PT/Exp	C	Rand Var	0
			Consist	F	MM	3505

Rookie campaign looks like a letdown if measured against those 2011 MLEs, but by most standards it was successful. Sudden spike in Ctl is problematic, and reminiscent of his pre-2011 work in lower minors. But elite Dom, well-managed workload and health all say "invest," and wait out the wildness.

Yr Tm	W	L	Sv	IP	K	ERA	xERA	WHIP	OBA	vL	vR	BF/G	Ctl	Dom	Cmd	G	L	F	hr/9	hr/f	H%	S%	GS	APC	DOM%	DIS%	Sv%	LI	RAR	BPV	BPX	R$
08																																
09																																
10																																
11 TAM *	13	3	0	164	200	2.05	2.05	0.98	201	222	250	20.8	2.5	11.0	4.4	43	19	38	0.6	13%	29%	83%	1	56	100%	0%	0	0.79	38.3	155	233	$29
12 TAM	11	11	0	177	175	3.81	4.22	1.35	238	243	237	24.5	4.1	8.9	2.2	37	20	43	0.9	9%	30%	74%	31	98	45%	23%			4.6	64	83	$7
1st Half	4	5	0	88	90	4.19	4.20	1.40	243	294	230	25.4	4.3	9.2	2.1	40	17	43	1.3	13%	30%	75%	15	102	33%	20%			-1.9	68	89	$3
2nd Half	7	6	0	89	85	3.43	4.23	1.30	233	202	244	23.6	3.9	8.6	2.2	35	22	43	0.5	5%	30%	74%	16	93	56%	25%			6.5	61	79	$11
13 Proj	13	8	0	181	195	3.31	3.66	1.20	224	222	225	25.0	3.4	9.7	2.8	37	20	43	1.0	10%	29%	76%	32						15.9	96	125	$18

Morales,Franklin

Age: 27	Th: L	Role RP	Health	D	LIMA Plan	C+
Ht: 6' 0"	Wt: 210	Type Pwr xFB	PT/Exp	D	Rand Var	0
			Consist	A	MM	1401

Flashed some elite skills in 1H, but was unable to sustain them. Shoulder fatigue that eventually ended his season may have fed his 2H deterioration. Durability concerns may be chronic at this point, but history of dominating LHBs says he can make a good living in middle relief if nothing else.

Yr Tm	W	L	Sv	IP	K	ERA	xERA	WHIP	OBA	vL	vR	BF/G	Ctl	Dom	Cmd	G	L	F	hr/9	hr/f	H%	S%	GS	APC	DOM%	DIS%	Sv%	LI	RAR	BPV	BPX	R$
08 COL *	11	7	0	136	76	5.68	5.25	1.70	269	200	295	23.6	6.0	5.1	0.8	40	20	40	1.1	6%	29%	68%	5	97	0%	40%			-22.8	17	33	-$8
09 COL *	5	4	7	81	70	4.17	4.44	1.50	261	205	265	7.3	4.5	7.8	1.7	27	23	50	0.9	7%	31%	74%	2	18	50%	50%	88	1.55	1.6	58	109	$3
10 COL *	3	4	4	59	53	4.49	4.48	1.55	230	171	293	4.4	6.3	8.2	1.3	39	14	47	1.3	13%	27%	74%	0	16			44	0.91	-3.0	47	77	-$1
11 2 TM	1	2	0	46	42	3.69	4.17	1.27	237	238	235	3.9	3.7	8.2	2.2	30	16	54	1.2	9%	28%	75%	0	15			0	0.94	1.4	55	83	-$1
12 BOS	3	4	1	76	76	3.77	3.96	1.23	224	184	245	8.8	3.5	9.0	2.5	40	19	41	1.3	13%	28%	75%	9	36	44%	33%	100	1.14	2.3	84	109	$2
1st Half	1	1	0	42	44	2.59	3.43	1.10	223	222	223	6.9	2.4	9.5	4.0	42	17	41	0.4	4%	31%	77%	3	27	100%	0%	0	1.36	7.3	127	165	$5
2nd Half	2	3	1	35	32	5.19	4.67	1.38	225	114	266	12.7	4.9	8.3	1.7	36	22	41	2.3	22%	23%	72%	6	55	17%	50%	100	0.67	-5.0	31	40	-$2
13 Proj	4	5	0	87	80	4.05	4.55	1.41	246	216	264	6.2	4.4	8.3	1.9	34	19	47	1.4	11%	29%	76%	0						-0.4	43	56	$0

Morrow,Brandon

Age: 28	Th: R	Role SP	Health	D	LIMA Plan	B
Ht: 6' 3"	Wt: 200	Type Pwr FB	PT/Exp	A	Rand Var	-3
			Consist	A	MM	3505

xERA and BPV tell us that, what looks like a breakout was just a correction of the poor fortune that had plagued him in 2010-11. Dom drop is of some concern, but oblique strain that cost him two months may have been a factor. Worth targeting at '12 skill levels; if Dom bounces back... UP: Cy Young contender.

Yr Tm	W	L	Sv	IP	K	ERA	xERA	WHIP	OBA	vL	vR	BF/G	Ctl	Dom	Cmd	G	L	F	hr/9	hr/f	H%	S%	GS	APC	DOM%	DIS%	Sv%	LI	RAR	BPV	BPX	R$
08 SEA *	4	6	10	95	105	3.59	2.92	1.19	188	198	149	6.7	4.8	9.9	2.1	33	16	51	1.1	13%	23%	74%	5	25	40%	40%	83	1.40	8.6	86	162	$11
09 SEA *	7	7	6	125	97	4.19	4.39	1.52	257	277	212	15.0	4.9	7.0	1.4	37	20	43	0.9	11%	30%	74%	10	48	20%	40%	75	0.95	2.1	50	94	$3
10 TOR	10	7	0	146	178	4.49	3.45	1.38	248	245	253	24.2	4.1	10.9	2.7	40	18	42	0.7	7%	35%	68%	26	97	58%	23%			-7.4	105	171	$4
11 TOR	11	11	0	179	203	4.72	3.54	1.29	237	220	260	25.9	3.5	10.2	2.9	36	22	42	1.1	10%	32%	65%	30	104	67%	23%			-17.1	104	156	$4
12 TOR	10	7	0	125	108	2.96	3.91	1.11	214	188	246	24.0	3.0	7.8	2.6	41	19	40	0.9	9%	26%	77%	21	94	48%	29%			16.2	79	104	$14
1st Half	7	4	0	78	67	3.01	3.77	1.00	194	194	195	23.5	2.8	7.8	2.8	41	19	40	0.8	8%	24%	73%	13	92	46%	23%			9.6	84	109	$20
2nd Half	3	3	0	47	41	2.87	4.15	1.30	246	178	315	24.8	3.3	7.9	2.4	41	19	40	1.0	9%	30%	82%	8	97	50%	38%			6.6	72	94	$3
13 Proj	14	9	0	189	190	3.71	3.74	1.23	235	213	262	20.5	3.3	9.1	2.8	39	20	41	1.0	10%	29%	73%	37						7.2	93	121	$15

Mortensen,Clayton

Age: 28	Th: R	Role RP	Health	A	LIMA Plan	D
Ht: 6' 4"	Wt: 185	Type Pwr	PT/Exp	D	Rand Var	-1
			Consist	F	MM	1200

1-1, 3.21 ERA in 42 IP at BOS. Somehow managed 0 BB/14 K in his first 15 big-league IP, but then crashed back to earth with 19 BB/26 K in next 27 IP. Improved Dom is enough to keep us from totally giving up on him, but long history of intolerable Cmd says we shouldn't hold out much hope, either.

Yr Tm	W	L	Sv	IP	K	ERA	xERA	WHIP	OBA	vL	vR	BF/G	Ctl	Dom	Cmd	G	L	F	hr/9	hr/f	H%	S%	GS	APC	DOM%	DIS%	Sv%	LI	RAR	BPV	BPX	R$
08 a/a	8	10	0	140	86	5.50	5.30	1.60	290			23.7	4.0	5.6	1.4				1.1		32%	67%							-20.3	27	51	-$7
09 2 TM *	11	12	0	168	94	5.42	5.28	1.57	300	317	338	24.6	3.2	5.0	1.6	52	21	27	1.0	19%	33%	66%	6	82	0%	50%	0	0.69	-22.8	28	52	-$7
10 OAK *	13	6	0	171	99	4.31	4.28	1.35	271	125	313	26.5	2.7	5.2	1.9	29	29	41	1.0	14%	30%	70%	1	95	100%	0%			-4.8	44	70	$4
11 COL *	4	12	0	122	70	6.36	6.57	1.74	321	281	240	18.0	3.7	5.2	1.4	53	14	34	1.6	15%	34%	66%	6	55	33%	17%	0	0.53	-36.4	5	7	-$18
12 BOS *	6	4	2	81	69	3.30	3.55	1.25	219	179	238	6.4	4.1	7.7	1.9	46	17	38	1.2	17%	25%	79%	0	27			67	0.70	7.1	60	78	$4
1st Half	4	2	2	41	31	2.67	2.54	1.03	199	160	179	7.2	3.0	6.9	2.3	50	13	38	1.0	13%	22%	80%	0	30			67	0.31	6.9	75	98	$10
2nd Half	2	2	0	39	37	3.97	4.59	1.49	239	190	268	5.8	5.4	8.5	1.6	43	19	38	1.4	19%	28%	79%	0	26			0	0.85	0.2	48	62	-$2
13 Proj	3	3	0	51	37	4.46	4.55	1.45	265	255	273	9.9	3.9	6.5	1.6	49	16	35	1.3	13%	29%	73%	0						-2.8	37	48	-$3

Moscoso,Guillermo

Age: 29	Th: R	Role RP	Health	A	LIMA Plan	D
Ht: 6' 1"	Wt: 200	Type xFB	PT/Exp	D	Rand Var	+5
			Consist	F	MM	0200

3-2, 6.12 ERA in 50 IP at COL. xFB profile moved to thin air with predictably disastrous results. In his defense, he did cut his FB rate to suit his new home. But those FBs turned into line drives, an approach that doesn't work well anywhere. Appalling RAR and R$ illustrate just how far he is from positive value.

Yr Tm	W	L	Sv	IP	K	ERA	xERA	WHIP	OBA	vL	vR	BF/G	Ctl	Dom	Cmd	G	L	F	hr/9	hr/f	H%	S%	GS	APC	DOM%	DIS%	Sv%	LI	RAR	BPV	BPX	R$
08 aa	3	1	0	35	39	3.68	2.96	1.04	222			22.3	2.1	10.2	4.9				1.1		29%	69%							2.7	140	263	$2
09 TEX *	8	5	0	126	88	4.15	3.90	1.39	279	412	205	17.2	2.7	6.3	2.3	33	18	49	0.4	5%	33%	69%	0	27			0	0.24	2.7	75	140	$3
10 TEX *	7	7	0	124	84	6.73	7.22	1.88	337	0	500	24.3	4.0	6.1	1.5	0	50	50	1.6	0%	37%	66%	0	26			0	0.03	-40.6	8	14	-$18
11 OAK *	11	13	0	174	114	3.61	3.22	1.17	233	225	197	21.7	2.8	5.9	2.1	27	18	56	0.9	6%	26%	72%	21	93	43%	29%	0	0.83	7.1	62	93	$11
12 COL *	11	8	0	148	106	6.99	7.25	1.82	348	304	333	16.8	2.8	6.5	2.3	35	25	40	1.5	12%	39%	63%	3	40	0%	67%	0	0.55	-54.4	26	33	-$29
1st Half	4	4	0	78	60	7.25	7.11	1.78	349	340	344	18.8	2.4	7.0	2.9	31	27	42	1.5	19%	40%	61%	2	51	0%	50%	0	0.46	-31.0	43	56	-$30
2nd Half	7	4	0	71	46	6.70	7.32	1.87	347	256	321	15.1	3.3	5.9	1.8	38	24	38	1.6	3%	38%	66%	1	31	0%	100%	0	0.62	-23.4	11	14	-$28
13 Proj	3	4	0	51	36	5.79	5.01	1.62	312	300	323	18.6	3.0	6.4	2.1	32	22	46	1.3	9%	35%	66%	10						-11.1	42	55	-$6

Motte,Jason

Age: 31	Th: R	Role RP	Health	A	LIMA Plan	C+
Ht: 6' 0"	Wt: 200	Type Pwr FB	PT/Exp	B	Rand Var	-1
			Consist	A	MM	5531

Carried his late/postseason 2011 success as closer right through 2012, even approaching Vintage Eck Territory in 2nd half. Other than lack of a GB tilt, this skill set encompasses pretty much everything you want in a closer, with multi-year stability to boot. An oasis in an otherwise cloudy closer marketplace.

Yr Tm	W	L	Sv	IP	K	ERA	xERA	WHIP	OBA	vL	vR	BF/G	Ctl	Dom	Cmd	G	L	F	hr/9	hr/f	H%	S%	GS	APC	DOM%	DIS%	Sv%	LI	RAR	BPV	BPX	R$
08 STL *	4	3	10	78	101	3.39	4.08	1.42	268	125	150	4.4	3.4	11.7	3.4	45	10	45	0.7	0%	39%	78%	0	14			71	1.91	8.9	122	229	$8
09 STL	4	4	0	57	54	4.76	4.15	1.41	264	341	214	3.5	3.7	8.6	2.3	38	17	45	1.6	14%	31%	71%	0	14			0	0.96	-3.1	72	134	-$1
10 STL	4	2	2	52	54	2.24	3.47	1.13	220	267	198	3.7	3.1	9.3	3.0	40	13	47	0.9	8%	28%	85%	0	15			67	1.20	11.9	102	164	$6
11 STL	5	2	9	68	63	2.25	3.19	0.96	202	270	162	3.4	2.1	8.3	3.9	44	18	39	0.3	3%	27%	76%	0	14			69	1.35	14.2	115	173	$12
12 STL	4	5	42	72	86	2.75	2.89	0.92	191	122	254	4.2	2.1	10.8	5.1	41	20	40	1.1	13%	25%	77%	0	17			86	1.43	11.2	155	202	$27
1st Half	3	3	16	35	34	3.38	3.47	1.01	193	134	269	4.4	3.1	8.8	2.8	44	17	38	1.3	15%	22%	73%	0	17			80	1.36	2.7	97	126	$22
2nd Half	1	2	26	37	52	2.17	2.43	0.83	188	107	244	4.0	1.2	12.5	10.4	37	22	41	1.0	11%	29%	81%	0	16			90	1.49	8.5	208	271	$31
13 Proj	4	4	40	70	78	2.63	3.10	1.00	208	195	218	3.7	2.3	10.0	4.3	41	18	41	0.9	9%	27%	78%	0						12.0	136	177	$25

Mujica,Edward

Age: 29	Th: R	Role RP	Health	A	LIMA Plan	A+
Ht: 6' 3"	Wt: 225	Type	PT/Exp	C	Rand Var	-1
			Consist	A	MM	4310

Adapt or die: has chopped his FB% since leaving PETCO, while maintaining pinpoint Ctl and sufficient Dom. The resulting skill profile doesn't quite spike BPV the same way, but it's still plenty viable. 2H was just plain awesome, and strongly suggests he can close if the opportunity arises. A LIMA gem.

Yr Tm	W	L	Sv	IP	K	ERA	xERA	WHIP	OBA	vL	vR	BF/G	Ctl	Dom	Cmd	G	L	F	hr/9	hr/f	H%	S%	GS	APC	DOM%	DIS%	Sv%	LI	RAR	BPV	BPX	R$
08 CLE *	3	4	4	65	50	6.38	5.59	1.61	311	277	318	5.6	3.0	6.9	2.3	30	23	46	1.0	8%	36%	60%	0	19			57	0.57	-16.4	52	97	-$5
09 SD	3	5	2	94	76	3.94	3.96	1.28	273	300	247	5.9	1.8	7.3	4.0	39	17	44	1.3	11%	32%	75%	4	22	0%	75%	67	0.84	4.4	99	186	$4
10 SD	2	1	0	70	72	3.62	2.82	0.93	226	202	243	4.5	0.8	9.3	12.0	45	13	42	1.8	18%	27%	73%	0	17			0	0.66	4.0	169	274	$6
11 FLA	9	6	0	76	63	2.96	3.15	1.03	233	220	245	4.4	1.7	7.5	4.5	48	18	34	0.8	10%	27%	75%	0	17			0	1.12	9.2	116	174	$9
12 2 NL	0	3	2	65	47	3.03	3.60	1.04	230	243	219	3.7	1.7	6.5	3.9	51	16	33	1.0	11%	26%	75%	0	13			25	1.21	7.9	101	132	$4
1st Half	0	3	2	34	18	4.46	4.46	1.22	250	281	221	4.1	2.4	4.7	2.0	50	15	35	1.3	13%	26%	68%	0	14			40	1.26	-1.9	49	64	-$2
2nd Half	0	0	0	31	29	1.45	2.75	0.84	207	196	217	3.3	0.9	8.4	9.7	52	17	31	0.6	8%	26%	88%	0	11			0	1.16	9.8	158	206	$10
13 Proj	3	3	2	68	56	3.13	3.37	1.04	236	233	238	4.0	1.5	7.4	4.9	48	17	35	1.0	11%	27%	75%	0						7.5	119	155	$6

RAY MURPHY

Myers,Brett

Age: 32	Th: R	Role SP	Health	B	LIMA Plan	B	
Ht: 6' 4"	Wt: 240	Type	PT/Exp	A	Rand Var	0	
			Consist	A	MM		3203

Another blow to the closer myth: Take any slightly above-average SP, confine him to the 9th inning, and he'll convert 90% of his save opps for you. If he stays in pen, expect similar performance, but figure his 2013 team will want to max his value by having him start. If so... UP: 15 Wins, 3.50 ERA.

Yr Tm	W	L	Sv	IP	K	ERA	xERA	WHIP	OBA	vL	vR	BF/G	Ctl	Dom	Cmd	G	L	F	hr/9	hr/f	H%	S%	GS	APC	DOM%	DIS%	Sv%	LI	RAR	BPV	BPX	R$
08 PHI *	11	15	0	210	180	4.51	4.63	1.38	269	235	293	26.8	3.1	7.7	2.5	47	21	32	1.3	16%	31%	71%	30	101	50%	23%			-4.8	61	115	$7
09 PHI	4	3	0	71	50	4.84	4.20	1.37	272	233	320	16.9	2.9	6.4	2.2	47	18	35	2.3	23%	27%	75%	10	64	30%	20%	0	0.75	-4.5	61	113	-$1
10 HOU	14	8	0	224	180	3.14	3.73	1.24	248	240	254	28.4	2.7	7.2	2.7	49	16	35	0.8	9%	30%	78%	33	105	61%	3%			25.9	86	139	$18
11 HOU	7	14	0	216	160	4.46	3.83	1.31	267	278	259	27.0	2.4	6.7	2.8	48	18	34	1.3	13%	30%	70%	33	98	52%	3%	0	0.75	-13.7	82	123	$1
12 2 TM	3	8	19	65	41	3.31	3.94	1.22	261	283	245	3.9	2.1	5.6	2.7	51	22	27	1.1	14%	28%	78%	0	14			90	1.36	5.7	75	98	$9
1st Half	0	3	17	27	19	3.71	3.84	1.31	280	316	240	3.9	1.7	6.4	3.8	52	20	28	1.4	16%	32%	77%	0	14			89	1.20	1.0	100	130	$10
2nd Half	3	5	2	39	22	3.03	4.01	1.16	247	245	247	3.9	2.3	5.1	2.2	50	24	26	0.9	13%	26%	78%	0	14			100	1.48	4.7	58	76	$8
13 Proj	**10**	**13**	**0**	**174**	**121**	**3.70**	**3.92**	**1.26**	**263**	**271**	**256**	**25.9**	**2.3**	**6.3**	**2.7**	**50**	**20**	**30**	**1.1**	**13%**	**29%**	**74%**	**27**						**6.8**	**78**	**101**	**$9**

Nathan,Joe

Age: 38	Th: R	Role RP	Health	F	LIMA Plan	C+	
Ht: 6' 4"	Wt: 225	Type Pwr	PT/Exp	C	Rand Var	0	
			Consist	C	MM		5530

In his second year back from 2010 TJ surgery, displayed skills that were essentially a carbon copy of his pre-injury form. If he was 10 years younger, we'd advise you to bid confidently, but age now becomes his biggest risk factor.

Yr Tm	W	L	Sv	IP	K	ERA	xERA	WHIP	OBA	vL	vR	BF/G	Ctl	Dom	Cmd	G	L	F	hr/9	hr/f	H%	S%	GS	APC	DOM%	DIS%	Sv%	LI	RAR	BPV	BPX	R$
08 MIN	1	2	39	68	74	1.33	2.88	0.90	179	167	192	3.8	2.4	9.8	4.1	47	19	33	0.7	9%	25%	91%	0	16			87	1.51	25.0	138	258	$27
09 MIN	2	2	47	69	89	2.10	2.94	0.93	171	160	181	3.9	2.9	11.7	4.0	41	12	47	0.9	10%	25%	84%	0	16			90	1.14	18.8	151	283	$30
10																																
11 MIN	2	1	14	45	43	4.84	3.83	1.16	222	198	247	4.0	2.8	8.7	3.1	35	18	47	1.4	11%	27%	62%	0	17			82	1.14	-4.9	93	140	$4
12 TEX	3	5	37	64	78	2.80	2.76	1.06	231	232	229	3.9	1.8	10.9	6.0	45	21	33	1.0	13%	32%	79%	0	16			93	1.10	9.7	170	222	$21
1st Half	0	2	18	34	42	1.87	2.50	0.89	213	210	220	3.8	1.1	11.2	10.5	40	26	34	0.5	7%	31%	82%	0	15			95	1.00	8.9	191	249	$23
2nd Half	3	3	19	31	36	3.82	3.05	1.24	250	262	236	4.0	2.6	10.6	4.0	51	17	32	1.5	19%	32%	76%	0	17			90	1.20	0.8	147	191	$18
13 Proj	**3**	**4**	**33**	**65**	**75**	**3.18**	**3.05**	**1.07**	**222**	**217**	**228**	**3.8**	**2.4**	**10.3**	**4.3**	**43**	**19**	**39**	**1.1**	**13%**	**29%**	**76%**	**0**						**6.8**	**142**	**185**	**$19**

Nicasio,Juan

Age: 26	Th: R	Role SP	Health	F	LIMA Plan	C+	
Ht: 6' 3"	Wt: 230	Type Pwr	PT/Exp	D	Rand Var	+5	
			Consist	A	MM		3403

Microfracture knee surgery in July ended his season, curtailing his comeback from a fractured vertebrae that ended 2011. Between injuries, he has demonstrated a promising high-Dom, GB-tilted profile that xERA likes. Poor results + injury history + latent skills = excellent end-game target... UP: sub-4.00 ERA

Yr Tm	W	L	Sv	IP	K	ERA	xERA	WHIP	OBA	vL	vR	BF/G	Ctl	Dom	Cmd	G	L	F	hr/9	hr/f	H%	S%	GS	APC	DOM%	DIS%	Sv%	LI	RAR	BPV	BPX	R$
08																																
09																																
10																																
11 COL *	9	5	0	128	106	3.53	3.75	1.24	265	313	205	23.7	2.0	7.4	3.7	46	22	32	0.8	11%	32%	74%	13	89	38%	23%			6.5	100	151	$7
12 COL	2	3	0	58	54	5.28	4.19	1.62	313	299	325	23.4	3.4	8.4	2.5	40	25	36	1.1	11%	37%	69%	11	93	45%	27%			-9.0	77	100	-$8
1st Half	2	3	0	58	54	5.28	4.19	1.62	313	299	325	23.4	3.4	8.4	2.5	40	25	36	1.1	11%	37%	69%	11	93	45%	27%			-9.0	76	99	-$8
2nd Half																																
13 Proj	**7**	**6**	**0**	**138**	**122**	**4.37**	**3.99**	**1.46**	**290**	**302**	**278**	**23.5**	**2.8**	**8.0**	**2.8**	**42**	**24**	**34**	**1.0**	**10%**	**35%**	**72%**	**25**						**-6.0**	**88**	**114**	**-$1**

Niemann,Jeff

Age: 30	Th: R	Role SP	Health	F	LIMA Plan	B+	
Ht: 6' 9"	Wt: 260	Type	PT/Exp	B	Rand Var	-1	
			Consist	A	MM		2303

Line drive off his leg essentially ended his season in May. Late-season return was curtailed by shoulder inflammation. Small-sample early-season work showed some growth in GB% that would nicely round out his skill set. If he can stay healthy... UP: 15 Wins, 3.25 ERA.

Yr Tm	W	L	Sv	IP	K	ERA	xERA	WHIP	OBA	vL	vR	BF/G	Ctl	Dom	Cmd	G	L	F	hr/9	hr/f	H%	S%	GS	APC	DOM%	DIS%	Sv%	LI	RAR	BPV	BPX	R$
08 TAM *	11	7	0	149	119	4.43	4.08	1.33	246	200	325	21.3	3.7	7.2	2.0	43	14	43	1.2	14%	28%	70%	2	56	50%	50%	0	0.56	-1.9	54	102	$6
09 TAM	13	6	0	181	125	3.94	4.38	1.35	266	274	258	24.8	2.9	6.2	2.1	41	20	39	0.8	8%	30%	73%	30	93	40%	30%	0	0.76	8.6	52	97	$10
10 TAM	12	8	0	174	131	4.39	4.09	1.26	242	244	239	24.4	3.1	6.8	2.1	44	16	39	1.3	12%	27%	69%	29	88	34%	14%	0	0.84	-6.7	59	95	$6
11 TAM	11	7	0	135	105	4.06	3.76	1.24	250	253	247	24.9	2.5	7.0	2.8	46	20	34	1.2	13%	29%	71%	23	93	61%	30%			-1.9	83	125	$6
12 TAM	2	3	0	38	34	3.08	3.53	1.11	213	280	119	19.5	2.8	8.1	2.8	51	19	30	0.5	6%	28%	73%	8	81	38%	25%			4.4	97	127	$0
1st Half	2	3	0	35	30	3.38	3.76	1.18	221	282	132	20.9	3.1	7.8	2.5	51	20	30	0.5	7%	28%	72%	7	86	43%	14%			2.7	85	111	$1
2nd Half	0	0	0	3	4	0.00	1.48	0.30	100	250	0	10.0	0.0	10.8	0.0	67	0	33	0.0	0%	16%	0%	1	45	0%	100%			1.7	239	311	-$4
13 Proj	**11**	**9**	**0**	**165**	**130**	**3.79**	**4.02**	**1.25**	**246**	**268**	**220**	**23.9**	**3.0**	**7.1**	**2.3**	**46**	**18**	**36**	**1.0**	**10%**	**29%**	**73%**	**28**						**4.7**	**70**	**91**	**$10**

Niese,Jon

Age: 26	Th: L	Role SP	Health	C	LIMA Plan	C+	
Ht: 6' 4"	Wt: 215	Type	PT/Exp	A	Rand Var	0	
			Consist	A	MM		3305

Ah, the wonders of regression: After hit/strand rates punished him in 2011, they corrected in 2012 and—presto!—his ERA snapped back to exactly the level that xERA said he deserved a year ago. Stable skill set doesn't suggest much room for further growth, but this is a fine level to establish a plateau.

Yr Tm	W	L	Sv	IP	K	ERA	xERA	WHIP	OBA	vL	vR	BF/G	Ctl	Dom	Cmd	G	L	F	hr/9	hr/f	H%	S%	GS	APC	DOM%	DIS%	Sv%	LI	RAR	BPV	BPX	R$
08 NYM *	12	9	0	178	137	3.83	4.10	1.43	273	353	326	23.6	3.3	6.9	2.1	44	23	33	0.6	13%	33%	73%	3	89	33%	67%			10.8	69	129	$8
09 NYM *	6	7	0	120	91	4.93	4.73	1.48	296	333	242	24.6	2.6	6.8	2.6	48	19	33	0.7	4%	35%	67%	5	80	20%	40%			-9.1	69	130	-$2
10 NYM	9	10	0	174	148	4.20	3.90	1.46	280	266	283	25.7	3.2	7.7	2.4	48	21	32	1.0	12%	33%	74%	30	98	40%	23%			-2.5	77	125	$1
11 NYM	11	11	0	157	138	4.40	3.52	1.41	284	259	291	25.7	2.5	7.9	3.1	51	21	28	0.8	10%	35%	70%	26	92	42%	15%	0	0.76	-9.0	103	155	$1
12 NYM	13	9	0	190	155	3.40	3.71	1.17	241	243	240	26.3	2.3	7.3	3.2	48	21	31	1.0	13%	28%	75%	30	101	70%	7%			14.3	95	124	$16
1st Half	6	3	0	89	85	3.55	3.53	1.27	246	263	242	24.9	3.0	8.6	2.8	51	22	28	1.3	19%	30%	78%	15	100	67%	13%			5.1	102	133	$14
2nd Half	7	6	0	102	70	3.28	3.85	1.08	236	230	238	27.7	1.7	6.2	3.7	47	21	33	0.8	9%	27%	72%	15	102	73%	0%			9.3	91	118	$19
13 Proj	**12**	**11**	**0**	**191**	**157**	**3.63**	**3.69**	**1.27**	**260**	**249**	**263**	**24.8**	**2.5**	**7.4**	**2.9**	**49**	**21**	**30**	**0.9**	**11%**	**31%**	**74%**	**31**						**9.2**	**92**	**120**	**$13**

Noesi,Hector

Age: 26	Th: R	Role RP	Health	A	LIMA Plan	D+	
Ht: 6' 3"	Wt: 200	Type	PT/Exp	D	Rand Var	+3	
			Consist	A	MM		1201

2-12, 5.82 ERA in 107 IP at SEA. Back in his 2010 MLEs, he flashed a viable skill set, highlighted by strong Cmd. In his 2011 MLB debut, the Ctl suffered, but at least he showed hints of a GB bias. Now the Dom is sub-par and FBs outnumber GBs. That leaves no reason to recommend him.

Yr Tm	W	L	Sv	IP	K	ERA	xERA	WHIP	OBA	vL	vR	BF/G	Ctl	Dom	Cmd	G	L	F	hr/9	hr/f	H%	S%	GS	APC	DOM%	DIS%	Sv%	LI	RAR	BPV	BPX	R$
08																																
09																																
10 a/a	9	5	0	117	84	4.28	4.34	1.33	287			24.4	1.8	6.4	3.6				0.8		33%	69%							-2.9	87	141	$3
11 NYY *	3	3	0	81	59	4.50	5.05	1.60	300	302	272	10.0	3.6	6.6	1.8	41	26	34	0.7	10%	35%	72%	2	32	0%	100%	0	0.80	-5.6	53	80	-$6
12 SEA *	4	18	0	171	115	5.81	5.27	1.48	286	278	253	22.3	3.2	6.0	1.9	37	18	45	1.4	14%	31%	63%	18	78	39%	33%	0	0.64	-38.0	31	41	-$17
1st Half	2	10	0	92	56	5.69	4.98	1.32	255	293	210	24.1	3.3	5.5	1.6	35	18	47	1.9	14%	25%	62%	16	91	44%	31%			-19.0	22	29	-$14
2nd Half	2	8	0	79	59	5.95	5.79	1.67	322	188	483	21.0	3.0	6.7	2.2	47	16	37	0.9	11%	37%	64%	2	43	0%	50%	0	0.29	-19.0	50	65	-$20
13 Proj	**4**	**7**	**0**	**102**	**72**	**5.11**	**4.61**	**1.52**	**296**	**259**	**335**	**15.5**	**3.1**	**6.4**	**2.1**	**42**	**20**	**38**	**1.0**	**9%**	**34%**	**68%**	**16**						**-13.7**	**52**	**67**	**-$6**

Nolasco,Ricky

Age: 30	Th: R	Role SP	Health	A	LIMA Plan	C+	
Ht: 6' 2"	Wt: 215	Type	PT/Exp	A	Rand Var	0	
			Consist	A	MM		3205

This was once a near-elite skill set just waiting for some hit/strand rate regression to facilitate a breakout. But while we were waiting for that regression, the skills deteriorated from elite to merely average. Without a significant Dom rebound, chances of ERA dipping below 4.00 are remote.

Yr Tm	W	L	Sv	IP	K	ERA	xERA	WHIP	OBA	vL	vR	BF/G	Ctl	Dom	Cmd	G	L	F	hr/9	hr/f	H%	S%	GS	APC	DOM%	DIS%	Sv%	LI	RAR	BPV	BPX	R$
08 FLA	15	8	0	212	186	3.52	3.66	1.10	239	238	239	25.5	1.8	7.9	4.4	39	19	42	1.2	11%	28%	73%	32	95	69%	19%	0	0.79	21.1	111	208	$24
09 FLA *	14	10	0	200	205	4.91	3.96	1.25	265	251	268	24.7	2.1	9.2	4.3	38	22	40	1.0	11%	33%	62%	31	98	58%	19%			-14.6	117	219	$11
10 FLA	14	9	0	158	147	4.51	3.57	1.28	273	283	263	25.6	1.9	8.4	4.5	40	19	41	1.4	12%	33%	69%	26	95	54%	23%			-8.4	118	191	$7
11 FLA	10	12	0	206	148	4.67	3.83	1.40	295	305	285	27.0	1.9	6.5	3.4	45	24	31	0.9	10%	34%	68%	33	97	48%	15%			-18.6	87	132	-$3
12 MIA	12	13	0	191	125	4.48	4.26	1.37	285	299	270	26.8	2.2	5.9	2.7	47	22	32	0.8	9%	32%	68%	31	96	39%	23%			-10.9	71	93	-$1
1st Half	6	6	0	90	54	4.78	4.51	1.36	275	267	286	26.1	2.7	5.4	2.0	48	20	33	1.0	10%	30%	66%	15	93	40%	20%			-8.5	50	65	-$2
2nd Half	6	7	0	101	71	4.20	4.06	1.37	294	332	259	27.5	1.8	6.3	3.6	46	23	31	0.7	8%	34%	70%	16	99	38%	25%			-2.3	90	117	$0
13 Proj	**12**	**11**	**0**	**182**	**136**	**4.24**	**3.97**	**1.34**	**284**	**296**	**272**	**25.7**	**2.0**	**6.7**	**3.3**	**44**	**22**	**34**	**0.9**	**10%**	**33%**	**70%**	**29**						**-4.9**	**88**	**115**	**$5**

RAY MURPHY

Norberto,Jordan

Age: 26 Th: L Role RP	Health C	LIMA Plan B	
Ht: 6' 0" Wt: 195 Type Pwr FB	PT/Exp D	Rand Var -5	
	Consist A	MM 2410	

In between two DL stints with left shoulder problems (one season-ending), he carved out a nice skill set that reached beyond that of a lefty specialist, as he held RH batters to a lower OPS than LH. That dual-side effectiveness, plus small-sample Ctl gains in 2nd half, suggest there's a capable bullpen asset here.

Yr	Tm	W	L	Sv	IP	K	ERA	xERA	WHIP	OBA	vL	vR	BF/G	Ctl	Dom	Cmd	G	L	F	hr/9	hr/f	H%	S%	GS	APC	DOM%	DIS%	Sv%	LI	RAR	BPV	BPX	R$
08																																	
09	aa	0	2	2	24	25	10.76	8.74	2.30	346			6.4	7.3	9.4	1.3				1.9		42%	53%							-18.8	10	20	-$10
10	ARI *	3	2	4	49	46	4.19	4.45	1.66	234	235	216	4.1	7.2	8.4	1.2	39	20	41	0.9	13%	29%	76%	0	13			50	0.74	-0.6	57	91	-$1
11	OAK *	6	2	2	64	57	4.34	4.06	1.58	264	333	294	5.3	5.1	8.1	1.6	39	30	30	0.2	0%	34%	71%	0	23			50	0.10	-3.1	76	115	-$2
12	OAK	4	1	1	52	46	2.77	4.07	1.13	200	225	184	5.4	3.8	8.0	2.1	46	12	42	0.9	8%	24%	80%	0	23			33	1.03	8.0	65	84	$4
1st Half		0	1	1	30	22	3.34	4.72	1.18	188	171	197	5.0	4.9	6.7	1.4	43	15	42	0.3	3%	23%	71%	0	21			50	1.14	2.5	10	13	$0
2nd Half		4	0	0	22	24	2.01	3.32	1.07	214	278	167	6.1	2.4	9.7	4.0	49	8	42	1.6	16%	26%	95%	0	25			0	0.86	5.5	136	177	$8
13	Proj	**4**	**3**	**3**	**58**	**54**	**3.75**	**4.29**	**1.36**	**233**	**276**	**204**	**5.1**	**4.5**	**8.3**	**1.8**	**47**	**11**	**42**	**0.8**	**7%**	**29%**	**74%**	**0**						**1.9**	**52**	**67**	**$1**

Norris,Bud

Age: 28 Th: R Role SP	Health B	LIMA Plan C	
Ht: 6' 0" Wt: 230 Type Pwr	PT/Exp A	Rand Var +1	
	Consist A	MM 2405	

ERA rose nearly a full run from 2011 despite carbon-copy skills; dip in S% drove the ERA spike. Third straight year of sub-4.10 xERA underscores the strength of the skill set—even in an unsupportive environment, the percentage play is to bet that those skills will win out... UP: 14 Wins, 3.60 ERA.

Yr	Tm	W	L	Sv	IP	K	ERA	xERA	WHIP	OBA	vL	vR	BF/G	Ctl	Dom	Cmd	G	L	F	hr/9	hr/f	H%	S%	GS	APC	DOM%	DIS%	Sv%	LI	RAR	BPV	BPX	R$
08	aa	3	8	0	80	73	4.38	5.26	1.58	301			18.5	3.3	8.2	2.4				0.9		37%	74%							-0.6	67	126	-$2
09	HOU *	10	12	0	176	150	3.70	4.47	1.50	270	200	323	25.3	4.1	7.7	1.9	37	20	43	0.8	13%	33%	77%	10	87	50%	10%	0	0.67	13.4	62	115	$6
10	HOU	9	10	0	154	158	4.92	4.02	1.48	256	241	269	25.3	4.5	9.3	2.1	43	18	39	1.1	11%	33%	69%	27	101	52%	30%			-15.9	66	106	-$2
11	HOU	6	11	0	186	176	3.77	3.80	1.33	250	280	220	25.6	3.4	8.5	2.5	40	21	39	1.2	12%	31%	76%	31	102	55%	13%			3.9	80	120	$6
12	HOU	7	13	0	168	165	4.65	4.09	1.37	254	263	245	25.3	3.5	8.8	2.5	39	21	40	1.2	12%	31%	69%	29	97	59%	21%			-13.2	81	105	-$2
1st Half		5	5	0	79	82	4.90	3.97	1.42	265	272	256	24.9	3.3	9.3	2.8	39	21	40	1.5	14%	33%	70%	14	96	57%	29%			-8.6	96	125	-$1
2nd Half		2	8	0	89	83	4.43	4.19	1.33	243	252	237	25.7	3.7	8.4	2.2	39	21	40	1.0	10%	30%	69%	15	98	60%	13%			-4.6	67	87	-$2
13	Proj	**8**	**15**	**0**	**203**	**196**	**4.08**	**4.07**	**1.39**	**259**	**262**	**255**	**24.2**	**3.7**	**8.7**	**2.4**	**40**	**21**	**40**	**1.1**	**11%**	**32%**	**74%**	**35**						**-1.7**	**75**	**97**	**$5**

Nova,Ivan

Age: 26 Th: R Role SP	Health A	LIMA Plan D+	
Ht: 6' 4" Wt: 225 Type	PT/Exp B	Rand Var +5	
	Consist A	MM 2203	

Under the cover of a disastrous ERA spike (particularly in 2nd half), he posted noteworthy Dom gains without sacrificing Ctl. The result is a heel turn from a pitcher who had been outpitching his skills, to one whose skills exceed his outward results. GB tilt says hr/9 problems should abate, if so... UP: 3.25 ERA.

Yr	Tm	W	L	Sv	IP	K	ERA	xERA	WHIP	OBA	vL	vR	BF/G	Ctl	Dom	Cmd	G	L	F	hr/9	hr/f	H%	S%	GS	APC	DOM%	DIS%	Sv%	LI	RAR	BPV	BPX	R$
08																																	
09	a/a	6	8	0	139	78	5.03	5.15	1.67	297			26.0	4.3	5.0	1.2				0.6		33%	69%							-12.1	31	59	-$8
10	NYY *	13	5	0	187	122	3.93	4.64	1.47	281	276	258	24.3	3.3	5.9	1.8	51	18	30	0.9	10%	32%	75%	7	67	43%	43%	0	0.91	3.5	46	74	$3
11	NYY *	17	6	0	181	113	3.79	4.03	1.34	264	240	275	24.3	2.9	5.6	1.9	53	18	29	0.9	8%	29%	74%	27	92	37%	19%	0	0.82	3.5	50	75	$8
12	NYY	12	8	0	170	153	5.02	3.96	1.47	288	272	303	26.7	3.0	8.1	2.7	45	22	32	1.5	17%	34%	70%	28	96	46%	21%			-21.1	89	116	-$6
1st Half		9	2	0	98	85	4.03	3.86	1.37	278	268	288	27.9	2.7	7.8	2.9	47	19	35	1.5	16%	32%	76%	15	99	53%	7%			-0.1	93	121	$6
2nd Half		3	6	0	72	68	6.38	4.09	1.60	301	277	323	25.4	3.4	8.5	2.5	43	27	30	1.5	18%	36%	62%	13	92	38%	38%			-20.9	83	108	-$22
13	Proj	**12**	**8**	**0**	**170**	**130**	**4.02**	**4.20**	**1.48**	**284**	**270**	**299**	**25.1**	**3.2**	**6.9**	**2.2**	**48**	**21**	**30**	**1.0**	**12%**	**33%**	**76%**	**29**						**0.0**	**64**	**83**	**$3**

O Day,Darren

Age: 30 Th: R Role RP	Health C	LIMA Plan B+	
Ht: 6' 4" Wt: 220 Type Pwr FB	PT/Exp D	Rand Var -4	
	Consist F	MM 4400	

Other than 2011 season that was derailed by a hip problem, this is now three really good relief seasons in four years. BA vR in those years underscores his utility as a matchup weapon, not that he's inept against LHers. A nice option in Holds leagues, or as a LIMA staff-filler.

Yr	Tm	W	L	Sv	IP	K	ERA	xERA	WHIP	OBA	vL	vR	BF/G	Ctl	Dom	Cmd	G	L	F	hr/9	hr/f	H%	S%	GS	APC	DOM%	DIS%	Sv%	LI	RAR	BPV	BPX	R$
08	LAA *	2	3	7	76	52	4.17	3.97	1.35	276	275	290	6.2	2.5	6.2	2.5	55	17	28	0.6	5%	32%	69%	0	22			70	0.29	1.5	73	136	$3
09	2 TM	2	1	2	59	56	1.84	3.48	1.01	199	239	180	3.4	2.8	8.6	3.1	41	17	42	0.5	5%	26%	84%	0	14			100	1.21	18.0	99	185	$8
10	TEX	6	2	0	62	45	2.03	3.58	0.89	196	229	181	3.3	1.7	6.5	3.8	37	21	42	0.7	7%	23%	82%	0	12			0	1.15	15.7	86	138	$9
11	TEX *	1	1	1	38	37	4.21	5.50	1.27	265	233	286	4.6	2.3	8.8	3.9	35	17	48	2.6	30%	28%	82%	0	17			100	0.47	-1.3	59	88	-$2
12	BAL	7	1	0	67	69	2.28	3.30	0.94	202	207	200	3.8	1.9	9.3	4.9	34	23	43	0.8	8%	26%	81%	0	15			0	1.10	14.3	128	167	$10
1st Half		4	0	0	34	34	2.38	3.25	0.97	226	244	215	4.1	1.3	9.0	6.8	34	24	43	0.8	8%	29%	80%	0	15			0	0.85	6.9	138	180	$11
2nd Half		3	1	0	33	35	2.18	3.36	0.91	178	167	184	3.6	2.5	9.5	3.9	34	23	43	0.8	9%	24%	81%	0	14			0	1.33	7.5	118	154	$10
13	Proj	**5**	**2**	**0**	**68**	**65**	**2.80**	**3.44**	**1.04**	**222**	**238**	**213**	**3.8**	**2.1**	**8.6**	**4.0**	**38**	**21**	**41**	**1.2**	**12%**	**26%**	**81%**	**0**						**10.2**	**113**	**147**	**$7**

O Flaherty,Eric

Age: 28 Th: L Role RP	Health A	LIMA Plan B+	
Ht: 6' 2" Wt: 220 Type Pwr xGB	PT/Exp D	Rand Var -5	
	Consist A	MM 4310	

Gave back some of 2011 skill spike, but career-best GB% helped sustain success. Death to LH batters (.305 OPS allowed). Given the overall pct. of his AB that end with a K or GB, it's very difficult for anyone to mount a rally on him. Relievers are generally volatile; this one's about as safe as they come.

Yr	Tm	W	L	Sv	IP	K	ERA	xERA	WHIP	OBA	vL	vR	BF/G	Ctl	Dom	Cmd	G	L	F	hr/9	hr/f	H%	S%	GS	APC	DOM%	DIS%	Sv%	LI	RAR	BPV	BPX	R$
08	SEA *	1	1	2	25	23	8.83	8.14	2.19	373	500	421	5.7	4.6	8.2	1.8	50	25	25	1.1	25%	45%	58%	0	23			100	1.06	-13.9	35	66	-$8
09	ATL	2	1	0	56	39	3.04	3.81	1.24	248	215	282	3.0	2.9	6.2	2.2	55	17	28	0.3	4%	29%	75%	0	12			0	1.07	8.9	68	126	$2
10	ATL	3	2	0	44	36	2.45	3.50	1.25	230	231	229	3.2	3.7	7.4	2.0	57	20	23	0.4	7%	28%	81%	0	12			0	1.15	8.8	68	110	$2
11	ATL	2	4	0	74	67	0.98	3.07	1.09	221	195	233	3.9	2.6	8.2	3.2	56	19	26	0.2	4%	29%	92%	0	15			0	1.23	26.9	112	168	$10
12	ATL	3	0	0	57	46	1.73	3.20	1.15	229	113	291	3.6	3.0	7.2	2.4	66	16	18	0.5	11%	28%	87%	0	13			0	1.24	16.2	93	122	$5
1st Half		1	0	0	28	23	3.18	3.63	1.38	269	108	358	3.8	3.5	7.3	2.1	63	14	23	1.0	16%	31%	81%	0	14			0	1.44	2.9	78	102	$0
2nd Half		2	0	0	29	23	0.31	2.80	0.93	188	118	224	3.4	2.5	7.1	2.9	69	19	12	0.0	0%	24%	96%	0	13			0	1.04	13.3	109	142	$11
13	Proj	**3**	**1**	**3**	**65**	**53**	**2.33**	**3.29**	**1.14**	**224**	**167**	**258**	**3.4**	**2.9**	**7.4**	**2.5**	**61**	**18**	**21**	**0.3**	**7%**	**28%**	**80%**	**0**						**13.5**	**93**	**121**	**$7**

Odorizzi,Jake

Age: 23 Th: R Role SP	Health A	LIMA Plan B	
Ht: 6' 2" Wt: 185 Type	PT/Exp D	Rand Var -1	
	Consist B	MM 2203	

0-1, 4.91 ERA in 7 IP at KC. Seemingly capped his development with a full season of strong work in high minors, including 107 IP at AAA. As MLEs show, doesn't profile as a high-Dom guy, but relies on Cmd to succeed. That can work, but limits margin for error and raises odds of a bumpy MLB transition.

Yr	Tm	W	L	Sv	IP	K	ERA	xERA	WHIP	OBA	vL	vR	BF/G	Ctl	Dom	Cmd	G	L	F	hr/9	hr/f	H%	S%	GS	APC	DOM%	DIS%	Sv%	LI	RAR	BPV	BPX	R$
08																																	
09																																	
10																																	
11	aa	5	3	0	69	45	4.97	4.56	1.32	266			23.7	2.7	5.9	2.2				1.4		28%	66%							-8.7	41	61	-$2
12	KC *	15	6	0	153	116	3.39	3.90	1.33	260	280	200	22.6	3.0	6.8	2.3	27	27	46	0.8	8%	30%	77%	2	76	0%	50%			11.8	68	88	$9
1st Half		9	2	0	81	71	3.41	3.57	1.28	261	0	0	22.0	2.5	8.0	3.1				0.6	0%	32%	74%	0	0					6.0	99	129	$15
2nd Half		6	4	0	72	45	3.37	4.22	1.38	259	280	200	23.3	3.6	5.6	1.6	27	27	46	1.0	8%	28%	79%	2	76	0%	50%			5.8	39	51	$2
13	Proj	**9**	**10**	**0**	**146**	**102**	**4.04**	**4.20**	**1.33**	**262**			**23.1**	**3.0**	**6.3**	**2.1**				**1.1**		**29%**	**73%**	**26**						**-0.4**	**53**	**69**	**$4**

Ogando,Alexi

Age: 29 Th: R Role SP	Health B	LIMA Plan B+	
Ht: 6' 4" Wt: 195 Type Pwr FB	PT/Exp C	Rand Var -1	
	Consist C	MM 3403	

Did everything TEX could ask in 2011 SP conversion, but then ended up without a rotation chair for all of 2012, despite SPs dropping like flies around him. His skills snapped right back to match prior bullpen work (2010); he's shown he can thrive in either role. SP in 2013? If so... UP: 3.25 ERA, 15 Wins.

Yr	Tm	W	L	Sv	IP	K	ERA	xERA	WHIP	OBA	vL	vR	BF/G	Ctl	Dom	Cmd	G	L	F	hr/9	hr/f	H%	S%	GS	APC	DOM%	DIS%	Sv%	LI	RAR	BPV	BPX	R$
08																																	
09																																	
10	TEX *	4	1	1	72	71	1.93	2.02	1.07	193	229	198	4.5	3.5	8.8	2.5	44	18	38	0.4	5%	25%	84%	0	16			20	1.02	19.2	109	177	$9
11	TEX	13	8	0	169	126	3.51	3.87	1.14	234	255	202	22.4	2.3	6.7	2.9	36	24	40	0.9	8%	28%	72%	29	88	62%	21%	0	0.74	8.9	73	110	$14
12	TEX	2	0	3	66	66	3.27	3.49	1.00	203	234	179	4.5	2.3	9.0	3.9	38	21	41	1.2	12%	25%	74%	1	18	0%	100%	50	1.20	6.0	115	151	$6
1st Half		1	0	1	35	35	2.08	3.16	0.81	175	211	143	4.6	1.8	9.1	5.0	37	20	43	0.5	5%	23%	77%	1	18	0%	100%	33	1.34	8.3	130	169	$9
2nd Half		1	0	2	31	31	4.60	3.86	1.21	231	260	211	4.4	2.9	8.9	3.1	38	22	40	2.0	19%	27%	71%	0	18			67	1.07	-2.2	99	129	$2
13	Proj	**12**	**6**	**0**	**148**	**134**	**3.55**	**3.73**	**1.15**	**235**	**265**	**208**	**22.0**	**2.5**	**8.2**	**3.2**	**38**	**22**	**40**	**1.1**	**11%**	**28%**	**73%**	**27**						**8.5**	**94**	**122**	**$14**

RAY MURPHY

Oliver,Darren

Oliver,Darren	Health	A	LIMA Plan	A
Age: 42 Th: L Role RP	PT/Exp	C	Rand Var	-5
Ht: 6' 2" Wt: 200 Type Pwr	Consist	A	MM	4400

There's precious little value here outside of Holds leagues or Sim formats. But let's take a moment to appreciate this extremely late peak: after zero triple-digit BPV seasons thru age 38, he's now popped off three straight seasons of closer-worthy skills starting at age 39. Even whiskey doesn't age this well.

Yr	Tm	W	L	Sv	IP	K	ERA	xERA	WHIP	OBA	vL	vR	BF/G	Ctl	Dom	Cmd	G	L	F	hr/9	hr/f	H%	S%	GS	APC	DOM%	DIS%	Sv%	LI	RAR	BPV	BPX	R$
08	LAA	7	1	0	72	48	2.88	3.88	1.15	254	229	271	5.4	2.0	6.0	3.0	47	15	38	0.6	6%	29%	77%	0	20			0	1.02	12.9	79	148	$7
09	LAA	5	1	0	73	65	2.71	3.60	1.14	237	263	217	4.7	2.7	8.0	3.0	44	14	41	0.6	6%	28%	78%	1	18	0%	100%	0	1.30	14.5	93	174	$7
10	TEX	1	2	1	62	65	2.48	2.85	1.10	242	200	281	3.8	2.2	9.5	4.3	48	20	32	0.6	8%	31%	80%	0	15			25	1.23	12.2	138	223	$5
11	TEX	5	5	2	51	44	2.29	3.53	1.14	236	227	243	3.5	1.9	7.8	4.0	38	29	33	0.5	6%	31%	82%	0	14			33	1.28	10.4	103	155	$5
12	TOR	3	4	2	57	52	2.06	3.33	1.02	214	234	196	3.6	2.4	8.3	3.5	44	22	34	0.5	6%	27%	82%	0	14			50	0.95	13.6	106	139	$7
1st Half		2	2	0	28	30	1.59	2.82	0.92	194	229	160	3.4	2.2	9.5	4.3	46	25	28	0.6	11%	25%	88%	0	14			0	1.07	8.5	136	177	$8
2nd Half		1	2	2	28	22	2.54	3.86	1.13	233	239	228	3.8	2.5	7.0	2.8	43	19	39	0.3	3%	28%	77%	0	14			67	0.81	5.2	78	102	$5
13	**Proj**	**3**	**4**	**0**	**58**	**52**	**2.62**	**3.45**	**1.09**	**229**	**228**	**229**	**3.6**	**2.3**	**8.1**	**3.6**	**43**	**23**	**34**	**0.5**	**6%**	**29%**	**77%**	**0**						**10.0**	**106**	**137**	**$5**

Ondrusek,Logan

Ondrusek,Logan	Health	A	LIMA Plan	F
Age: 28 Th: R Role RP	PT/Exp	D	Rand Var	-4
Ht: 6' 8" Wt: 230 Type Pwr	Consist	B	MM	0200

Two full MLB seasons, two sub-3.50 ERAs. Your next stable middle reliever? Quite the contrary. Three-year BPV and xERA trends scream "danger ahead;" gruesome 2H skills seal the deal. The fuse is lit, throw this one back on the waiver wire before it blows up in your hand.

Yr	Tm	W	L	Sv	IP	K	ERA	xERA	WHIP	OBA	vL	vR	BF/G	Ctl	Dom	Cmd	G	L	F	hr/9	hr/f	H%	S%	GS	APC	DOM%	DIS%	Sv%	LI	RAR	BPV	BPX	R$
08																																	
09	a/a	2	1	19	53	30	2.23	2.50	1.13	231			4.9	2.6	5.0	1.9				0.2		27%	80%							13.7	73	136	$12
10	CIN *	5	1	1	78	51	4.02	3.56	1.24	251	205	236	4.3	2.7	5.8	2.2	48	14	38	0.8	10%	28%	69%	0	15			25	1.06	0.6	62	100	$2
11	CIN	5	5	0	61	41	3.23	4.47	1.35	238	232	242	4.1	4.1	6.0	1.5	49	17	34	0.9	9%	27%	79%	0	15			0	1.26	5.4	24	37	$1
12	CIN	5	2	2	55	39	3.46	5.21	1.50	246	190	285	3.9	5.1	6.4	1.3	43	15	42	1.3	12%	27%	82%	0	15			50	1.46	3.8	-1	-2	-$1
1st Half		3	1	2	28	19	2.89	4.55	1.25	218	163	259	3.5	4.2	6.1	1.5	48	15	38	1.0	10%	24%	81%	0	13			67	1.41	3.9	23	30	$3
2nd Half		2	1	0	27	20	4.05	5.91	1.76	274	220	308	4.3	6.1	6.8	1.1	40	15	45	1.7	13%	30%	83%	0	16			0	1.51	-0.1	-25	-33	-$5
13	**Proj**	**5**	**2**	**0**	**58**	**40**	**4.35**	**4.84**	**1.42**	**249**	**214**	**270**	**4.0**	**4.3**	**6.1**	**1.4**	**46**	**16**	**39**	**1.1**	**10%**	**28%**	**72%**	**0**						**-2.4**	**17**	**22**	**-$1**

Oswalt,Roy

Oswalt,Roy	Health	C	LIMA Plan	B
Age: 35 Th: R Role RP	PT/Exp	B	Rand Var	+5
Ht: 6' 0" Wt: 190 Type	Consist	D	MM	3301

4-3, 5.80 ERA in 59 IP at TEX. In between back and forearm injuries, got absolutely smoked at MLB level. Elevated h% and hr/f punished him, skills say this wasn't that bad. But physical issues even after extended off-season say he may be washed up. There is rebound potential, but it's a high-risk bet.

Yr	Tm	W	L	Sv	IP	K	ERA	xERA	WHIP	OBA	vL	vR	BF/G	Ctl	Dom	Cmd	G	L	F	hr/9	hr/f	H%	S%	GS	APC	DOM%	DIS%	Sv%	LI	RAR	BPV	BPX	R$
08	HOU	17	10	0	209	165	3.54	3.52	1.18	253	262	243	26.9	2.0	7.1	3.5	50	20	29	1.0	13%	29%	74%	32	97	63%	9%			20.3	101	190	$21
09	HOU	8	6	0	181	138	4.12	3.84	1.24	265	279	252	25.2	2.1	6.8	3.3	43	21	36	0.9	10%	31%	69%	30	93	60%	10%			4.5	88	165	$10
10	2 NL	13	13	0	212	193	2.76	3.29	1.03	213	232	196	25.3	2.3	8.2	3.5	46	18	37	0.8	9%	26%	77%	32	97	72%	13%	0	0.79	34.3	109	176	$28
11	PHI	9	10	0	139	93	3.69	4.00	1.34	280	276	284	25.8	2.1	6.0	2.8	45	19	36	0.6	6%	32%	73%	23	94	52%	9%			4.3	74	111	$4
12	TEX *	5	4	0	74	68	6.31	6.50	1.63	335	306	331	15.8	1.9	8.3	4.3	45	24	32	1.5	19%	40%	64%	9	59	33%	33%	0	1.06	-21.1	83	108	-$12
1st Half		3	1	0	28	21	6.47	7.32	2.02	382	370	414	22.6	2.5	6.8	2.7	45	34	20	0.5	0%	45%	66%	2	109	100%	0%			-8.5	63	82	-$14
2nd Half		2	3	0	46	47	6.22	5.95	1.40	304	286	308	13.0	1.6	9.1	5.9	45	20	35	2.1	22%	35%	61%	7	52	14%	43%	0	1.10	-12.6	108	141	-$10
13	**Proj**	**5**	**5**	**0**	**80**	**67**	**4.08**	**3.89**	**1.44**	**300**	**302**	**298**	**19.3**	**2.1**	**7.5**	**3.6**	**45**	**20**	**35**	**1.1**	**11%**	**35%**	**75%**	**16**						**-0.6**	**103**	**134**	**$0**

Ottavino,Adam

Ottavino,Adam	Health	A	LIMA Plan	D+
Age: 27 Th: R Role RP	PT/Exp	D	Rand Var	+3
Ht: 6' 5" Wt: 230 Type Pwr	Consist	B	MM	2301

5-1, 4.56 ERA in 79 IP at COL. Before massive September fade, had found a home as first line of relief behind short-hooked COL SPs. He couldn't hold it together, but briefly showed a glimpse of the value proposition for COL MRs: vulture Win potential plus a lot of Ks. He's likely found a home in the bullpen.

Yr	Tm	W	L	Sv	IP	K	ERA	xERA	WHIP	OBA	vL	vR	BF/G	Ctl	Dom	Cmd	G	L	F	hr/9	hr/f	H%	S%	GS	APC	DOM%	DIS%	Sv%	LI	RAR	BPV	BPX	R$
08	aa	3	7	0	115	79	5.81	5.98	1.71	311			21.8	3.9	6.2	1.6				1.2		35%	67%							-21.2	27	52	-$10
09	aaa	7	12	0	144	97	5.64	5.15	1.70	286			24.1	5.1	6.0	1.2				0.7		33%	66%							-23.4	37	69	-$10
10	STL *	5	5	0	70	47	5.50	5.27	1.49	298	390	356	21.6	2.7	6.0	2.3	36	32	32	1.2	18%	33%	65%	3	84	0%	33%	0	0.53	-12.3	42	69	-$4
11	aaa	7	8	0	141	94	5.18	5.52	1.73	302			24.7	4.6	6.0	1.3				0.8		35%	70%							-21.5	35	52	-$13
12	COL *	5	1	0	99	99	4.39	4.54	1.45	268	286	232	6.4	3.8	9.1	2.4	48	26	26	1.0	16%	34%	72%	0	25			0	0.64	-4.5	75	98	-$3
1st Half		2	0	0	45	49	4.25	5.39	1.52	288	212	295	5.2	3.5	9.9	2.9	48	27	24	1.5	33%	36%	77%	0	18			0	0.55	-1.3	73	95	-$4
2nd Half		3	1	0	54	50	4.50	3.78	1.39	251	314	200	7.8	4.0	8.3	2.1	48	26	26	0.7	10%	31%	68%	0	32			0	0.71	-3.2	79	103	-$2
13	**Proj**	**4**	**3**	**0**	**73**	**63**	**4.27**	**4.09**	**1.55**	**284**	**309**	**267**	**7.4**	**3.9**	**7.9**	**2.0**	**48**	**26**	**26**	**0.9**	**13%**	**34%**	**74%**	**0**						**-2.2**	**63**	**81**	**-$3**

Padilla,Vicente

Padilla,Vicente	Health	F	LIMA Plan	C+
Age: 35 Th: R Role RP	PT/Exp	D	Rand Var	+5
Ht: 6' 0" Wt: 230 Type Pwr	Consist	A	MM	3400

Bounced back from lost 2011 by reclaiming full set of 2010 BPIs in Boston pen. Gopheritis remains his Achilles heel, keeping his ERA from diving down to a level commensurate with this kind of Cmd. That's a long-term problem that isn't going away, even if he defies that Health grade a little longer.

Yr	Tm	W	L	Sv	IP	K	ERA	xERA	WHIP	OBA	vL	vR	BF/G	Ctl	Dom	Cmd	G	L	F	hr/9	hr/f	H%	S%	GS	APC	DOM%	DIS%	Sv%	LI	RAR	BPV	BPX	R$
08	TEX	14	8	0	171	127	4.74	4.49	1.46	275	312	240	26.1	3.4	6.7	2.0	43	19	38	1.4	13%	31%	71%	29	100	24%	14%			-8.7	49	92	$3
09	2 TM	12	6	0	147	97	4.46	4.33	1.43	277	303	246	24.4	3.3	5.9	1.8	48	20	32	1.0	11%	31%	71%	25	94	32%	8%	0	0.75	-2.5	44	82	$3
10	LA	6	5	0	95	84	4.07	3.58	1.08	226	167	267	24.3	2.3	8.0	3.5	40	18	42	1.3	12%	26%	67%	16	92	50%	38%			0.1	100	162	$6
11	LA	0	0	3	9	9	4.15	3.24	1.38	226	462	56	4.0	5.2	9.3	1.8	67	10	24	0.0	0%	31%	67%	0	17			100	1.02	-0.2	73	110	-$2
12	BOS	4	1	1	50	51	4.50	3.69	1.48	298	280	314	3.9	2.7	9.2	3.4	44	19	37	1.3	13%	37%	73%	0	15			20	1.52	-3.0	114	149	-$3
1st Half		1	0	1	29	28	3.77	3.48	1.29	268	189	339	4.2	2.2	8.8	4.0	51	13	36	0.6	7%	35%	71%	0	16			50	1.36	0.9	128	167	-$2
2nd Half		3	1	0	21	23	5.48	3.98	1.73	337	400	283	3.6	3.4	9.7	2.9	34	28	38	2.1	22%	39%	75%	0	14			0	1.69	-3.9	96	125	-$5
13	**Proj**	**4**	**2**	**0**	**51**	**46**	**4.38**	**3.96**	**1.41**	**279**	**280**	**279**	**6.3**	**2.9**	**8.2**	**2.9**	**42**	**20**	**38**	**1.2**	**12%**	**33%**	**72%**	**0**						**-2.3**	**91**	**118**	**-$1**

Papelbon,Jonathan

Papelbon,Jonathan	Health	A	LIMA Plan	C+
Age: 32 Th: R Role RP	PT/Exp	A	Rand Var	-2
Ht: 6' 4" Wt: 225 Type Pwr FB	Consist	B	MM	5530

New league? Other than a couple more HR allowed, no problem. Now that Mariano Rivera has been dethroned, this may be the new gold standard for consistency among current closers: a more-than-worthy skill set, top-notch Health grade, and unquestioned grip on the role. These days, that's worth paying for.

Yr	Tm	W	L	Sv	IP	K	ERA	xERA	WHIP	OBA	vL	vR	BF/G	Ctl	Dom	Cmd	G	L	F	hr/9	hr/f	H%	S%	GS	APC	DOM%	DIS%	Sv%	LI	RAR	BPV	BPX	R$
08	BOS	5	4	41	69	77	2.34	2.64	0.95	223	235	210	4.1	1.0	10.0	9.6	49	20	31	0.5	7%	31%	77%	0	16			89	1.33	17.0	179	336	$27
09	BOS	1	1	38	68	76	1.85	3.79	1.15	213	187	242	4.3	3.2	10.1	3.2	27	21	52	0.7	5%	30%	88%	0	18			93	1.38	20.7	100	188	$23
10	BOS	5	7	37	67	76	3.90	3.63	1.27	226	255	189	4.4	3.8	10.2	2.7	38	18	44	0.9	9%	31%	72%	0	18			82	1.37	1.5	98	159	$18
11	BOS	4	1	31	64	87	2.94	2.45	0.93	207	156	261	4.0	1.4	12.2	8.7	38	21	41	0.4	5%	33%	68%	0	16			91	1.27	8.0	197	297	$20
12	PHI	5	6	38	70	92	2.44	2.83	1.06	216	208	224	4.1	2.3	11.8	5.1	41	18	40	1.0	12%	31%	83%	0	16			90	1.24	13.6	169	221	$24
1st Half		2	2	18	30	37	3.03	2.92	1.08	223	269	183	4.0	2.1	11.2	5.3	43	18	39	1.2	14%	31%	79%	0	16			95	1.16	3.6	166	216	$21
2nd Half		3	4	20	40	55	2.01	2.77	1.04	211	164	257	4.1	2.5	12.3	5.0	40	19	41	0.9	11%	31%	87%	0	17			87	1.30	10.0	173	225	$27
13	**Proj**	**4**	**4**	**41**	**65**	**83**	**2.74**	**2.84**	**1.06**	**222**	**208**	**236**	**3.9**	**2.3**	**11.5**	**5.0**	**40**	**19**	**41**	**0.8**	**9%**	**32%**	**78%**	**0**						**10.3**	**163**	**212**	**$24**

Parker,Jarrod

Parker,Jarrod	Health	A	LIMA Plan	C+
Age: 24 Th: R Role SP	PT/Exp	D	Rand Var	-1
Ht: 6' 1" Wt: 195 Type	Consist	A	MM	2205

13-8, 3.47 ERA in 181 IP at OAK. Very successful rookie season backed by worthy skills. 2H skill gains (Ctl dip coupled with GB uptick) show how he mastered on-the-job training; put it all together with a triple-digit September BPV. Lots of IP, but well-managed BF/G should mitigate sophomore burnout.

Yr	Tm	W	L	Sv	IP	K	ERA	xERA	WHIP	OBA	vL	vR	BF/G	Ctl	Dom	Cmd	G	L	F	hr/9	hr/f	H%	S%	GS	APC	DOM%	DIS%	Sv%	LI	RAR	BPV	BPX	R$
08																																	
09	aa	4	6	0	78	63	4.96	4.96	1.69	305			22.1	4.0	7.2	1.8				0.3		37%	69%							-6.2	66	124	-$5
10																																	
11	ARI *	11	8	0	136	95	4.10	3.50	1.33	251	143	250	21.0	3.5	6.3	1.8	35	6	59	0.5	0%	30%	69%	1	73	0%	0%			-2.6	65	98	$3
12	OAK *	14	8	0	202	158	3.35	3.43	1.28	250	247	248	25.1	3.1	7.0	2.3	44	26	30	0.6	7%	30%	75%	29	98	62%	10%			16.6	78	102	$14
1st Half		5	3	0	94	76	2.50	2.91	1.26	224	216	194	24.0	4.0	7.2	1.8	41	26	34	0.5	4%	27%	81%	12	98	67%	8%			17.7	78	102	$17
2nd Half		9	5	0	108	82	4.10	3.85	1.30	271	266	283	26.1	2.3	6.9	3.0	46	26	28	0.7	9%	32%	69%	17	97	59%	12%			-1.1	86	112	$10
13	**Proj**	**13**	**10**	**0**	**189**	**145**	**3.90**	**4.10**	**1.35**	**261**	**260**	**262**	**23.0**	**3.2**	**6.9**	**2.2**	**44**	**26**	**30**	**0.5**	**6%**	**31%**	**71%**	**34**						**2.8**	**62**	**80**	**$8**

RAY MURPHY

Parnell,Bobby

Age: 28	Th: R	Role RP	Health	B	LIMA Plan	A
Ht: 6' 4"	Wt: 200	Type Pwr xGB	PT/Exp	C	Rand Var	-3
			Consist	A	MM	4421

Made what would be described as the transition from thrower to pitcher: spiked Cmd by reducing both Ctl and Dom, and mixing in even more GBs. Net result was third straight year of BPV growth, reaching closer-worthy level. Intersection of those skills with opportunity may be at hand. If so... UP: 30 Sv

Yr Tm	W	L	Sv	IP	K	ERA	xERA	WHIP	OBA	vL	vR	BF/G	Ctl	Dom	Cmd	G	L	F	hr/9	hr/f	H%	S%	GS	APC	DOM%	DIS%	Sv%	LI	RAR	BPV	BPX	R$
08 NYM *	12	8	0	153	98	5.47	5.15	1.62	291	0	273	19.4	4.1	5.8	1.4	43	21	36	0.9	0%	33%	66%	0	16			0	0.28	-21.7	35	65	-$6
09 NYM	4	8	1	88	74	5.30	4.76	1.66	281	270	290	6.1	4.7	7.5	1.6	47	16	37	0.8	8%	35%	68%	8	24	25%	50%	20	0.92	-10.6	34	64	-$6
10 NYM *	1	2	4	76	67	3.78	3.99	1.41	276	327	276	5.0	3.0	7.9	2.6	56	26	18	0.5	5%	34%	73%	0	14			50	0.69	2.8	89	144	$1
11 NYM	4	6	6	59	64	3.64	3.61	1.47	258	239	270	4.5	4.1	9.7	2.4	51	17	32	0.6	8%	35%	76%	0	18			50	1.10	2.2	93	140	$2
12 NYM	5	4	7	69	61	2.49	3.28	1.24	249	235	261	3.9	2.6	8.0	3.1	62	17	22	0.5	9%	32%	81%	0	15			58	1.13	12.9	113	148	$8
1st Half	1	1	1	33	31	3.00	3.45	1.24	246	246	246	3.8	2.2	8.5	3.9	56	16	28	0.8	11%	33%	79%	0	14			25	1.11	4.1	128	167	$3
2nd Half	4	3	6	36	30	2.02	3.10	1.23	252	222	274	4.0	3.0	7.6	2.5	67	18	15	0.3	7%	31%	84%	0	16			75	1.15	8.8	99	129	$12
13 Proj	**5**	**5**	**18**	**73**	**66**	**3.22**	**3.50**	**1.36**	**261**	**251**	**269**	**4.3**	**3.3**	**8.2**	**2.5**	**57**	**18**	**24**	**0.5**	**9%**	**33%**	**77%**	**0**						**7.1**	**96**	**124**	**$10**

Parra,Manny

Age: 30	Th: L	Role RP	Health	F	LIMA Plan	D
Ht: 6' 3"	Wt: 203	Type Pwr	PT/Exp	C	Rand Var	+2
			Consist	A	MM	1400

Came back from 2011 elbow surgery with a new role in the bullpen, but the same old "throws hard with no idea where the ball is going" profile. Shoulder issues may have caused 2H skills decay, year-long elevated LD% and H% drove up ERA, but Dom+GB combo remains the basis of potential positive value.

Yr Tm	W	L	Sv	IP	K	ERA	xERA	WHIP	OBA	vL	vR	BF/G	Ctl	Dom	Cmd	G	L	F	hr/9	hr/f	H%	S%	GS	APC	DOM%	DIS%	Sv%	LI	RAR	BPV	BPX	R$
08 MIL	10	8	0	166	147	4.39	4.04	1.54	278	233	288	23.2	4.1	8.0	2.0	52	22	27	1.0	14%	34%	74%	29	88	45%	31%	0	0.72	-1.4	64	119	$2
09 MIL *	12	13	0	165	132	5.95	5.78	1.76	299	287	311	24.3	5.0	7.2	1.4	48	18	34	1.0	12%	35%	67%	27	95	30%	30%			-33.1	37	70	-$12
10 MIL	3	10	0	122	129	5.02	3.99	1.62	281	326	264	13.3	4.6	9.5	2.0	47	18	34	1.3	15%	35%	72%	16	51	19%	19%	0	0.60	-14.1	71	115	-$7
11																																
12 MIL	2	3	0	59	61	5.06	4.29	1.65	265	229	296	4.4	5.4	9.4	1.7	49	24	27	0.5	7%	36%	68%	0	17			0	0.79	-7.6	50	66	-$8
1st Half	0	2	0	36	39	4.54	3.60	1.51	273	206	333	5.2	3.8	9.8	2.6	50	24	25	0.3	4%	38%	68%	0	20			0	0.71	-2.3	103	134	-$7
2nd Half	2	1	0	23	22	5.87	5.55	1.87	253	268	240	3.6	7.8	8.6	1.1	47	24	29	0.8	10%	33%	68%	0	14			0	0.88	-5.3	-31	-40	-$9
13 Proj	**3**	**4**	**0**	**65**	**64**	**4.70**	**4.45**	**1.69**	**278**	**265**	**284**	**6.3**	**5.4**	**8.8**	**1.6**	**48**	**21**	**30**	**0.9**	**11%**	**35%**	**73%**	**0**						**-5.5**	**38**	**50**	**-$5**

Patton,Troy

Age: 27	Th: L	Role RP	Health	B	LIMA Plan	A
Ht: 6' 1"	Wt: 179	Type	PT/Exp	D	Rand Var	-2
			Consist	C	MM	3200

Moved the needle in the preferred direction on virtually every skill, and finally established dominance over LH hitters. He handles righties well too, so doesn't need to be confined to a specialist role. 2H LI shows how he gained Showalter's confidence. Should be a capable bullpen fixture going forward.

Yr Tm	W	L	Sv	IP	K	ERA	xERA	WHIP	OBA	vL	vR	BF/G	Ctl	Dom	Cmd	G	L	F	hr/9	hr/f	H%	S%	GS	APC	DOM%	DIS%	Sv%	LI	RAR	BPV	BPX	R$
08																																
09 a/a	7	5	0	108	58	5.77	6.90	1.68	324			24.3	2.9	4.8	1.6				2.0		33%	71%							-19.3	-7	-13	-$9
10 BAL *	8	11	0	137	72	5.60	5.85	1.61	312	333	0	23.3	3.0	4.7	1.6	50	0	50	1.3	0%	33%	67%	0	16			0	0.02	-25.6	16	26	-$10
11 BAL *	6	2	0	74	45	2.62	3.52	1.30	274	264	186	8.3	2.1	5.5	2.6	39	13	48	0.2	5%	32%	79%	0	23			0	0.87	12.1	80	120	$4
12 BAL	1	0	0	56	49	2.43	3.34	1.02	215	212	219	4.1	1.9	7.9	4.1	50	19	31	0.8	10%	27%	81%	0	15			0	1.03	10.9	118	154	$4
1st Half	1	0	0	37	35	3.13	3.24	0.99	210	191	229	4.8	1.9	8.4	4.4	48	20	32	0.7	9%	27%	71%	0	18			0	0.80	4.1	125	163	$5
2nd Half	0	0	0	18	14	0.98	3.57	1.09	225	244	192	3.3	2.0	6.9	3.5	55	16	29	1.0	13%	27%	100%	0	12			0	1.33	6.9	104	135	$3
13 Proj	**2**	**1**	**0**	**58**	**44**	**3.00**	**3.96**	**1.26**	**264**	**286**	**238**	**5.7**	**2.3**	**6.8**	**3.0**	**47**	**16**	**37**	**0.9**	**9%**	**31%**	**80%**	**0**						**7.3**	**86**	**111**	**$2**

Paulino,Felipe

Age: 29	Th: R	Role RP	Health	F	LIMA Plan	B+
Ht: 6' 2"	Wt: 270	Type Pwr	PT/Exp	C	Rand Var	-5
			Consist	A	MM	2401

Missed April with a sore elbow, then by June was shut down again and on his way to Tommy John surgery. Given that he was probably pitching hurt before surgery, fairly shocking that his skills were fully intact. Expect him to return in 2nd half of 2013; these skills are well worth waiting on.

Yr Tm	W	L	Sv	IP	K	ERA	xERA	WHIP	OBA	vL	vR	BF/G	Ctl	Dom	Cmd	G	L	F	hr/9	hr/f	H%	S%	GS	APC	DOM%	DIS%	Sv%	LI	RAR	BPV	BPX	R$
08																																
09 HOU *	5	12	0	132	117	5.70	6.08	1.70	304	354	286	19.9	4.2	7.9	1.9	42	19	39	1.4	17%	36%	69%	17	76	35%	35%	0	0.95	-22.5	38	71	-$10
10 HOU	1	9	0	92	83	5.11	4.40	1.54	270	306	248	21.6	4.5	8.1	1.8	42	16	42	0.4	4%	34%	65%	14	86	43%	14%	0	0.77	-11.6	45	72	-$6
11 2 TM	4	10	0	139	133	4.46	3.68	1.44	279	270	289	15.4	3.6	8.6	2.4	46	19	35	0.8	9%	34%	70%	20	62	50%	5%	0	0.87	-8.8	83	124	-$3
12 KC	3	1	0	38	39	1.67	3.69	1.22	223	190	273	22.3	3.6	9.3	2.6	45	19	37	0.7	8%	29%	91%	7	91	57%	14%			10.9	94	123	$2
1st Half	3	1	0	38	39	1.67	3.70	1.22	223	190	273	22.3	3.6	9.3	2.6	45	19	37	0.7	8%	29%	91%	7	91	57%	14%			10.9	94	122	$2
2nd Half																																
13 Proj	**3**	**5**	**0**	**73**	**69**	**4.04**	**4.12**	**1.43**	**263**	**261**	**264**	**19.5**	**3.9**	**8.6**	**2.2**	**44**	**18**	**39**	**0.7**	**7%**	**33%**	**73%**	**15**						**-0.2**	**71**	**92**	**-$1**

Pavano,Carl

Age: 37	Th: R	Role SP	Health	F	LIMA Plan	C
Ht: 6' 6"	Wt: 264	Type Con	PT/Exp	A	Rand Var	+5
			Consist	A	MM	2003

Shoulder injury, eventually diagnosed as just a bone bruise that required rest but not surgery, shut him down for good in mid-June. xERA shows he was doing his usual thing before injury, even while too many hits and HRs ruined his ERA. Best case, at 37, is that he comes back and replicates 2011.

Yr Tm	W	L	Sv	IP	K	ERA	xERA	WHIP	OBA	vL	vR	BF/G	Ctl	Dom	Cmd	G	L	F	hr/9	hr/f	H%	S%	GS	APC	DOM%	DIS%	Sv%	LI	RAR	BPV	BPX	R$
08 NYY	4	2	0	34	15	5.77	5.18	1.49	306	324	283	22.0	2.6	3.9	1.5	41	17	43	1.3	10%	31%	63%	7	81	0%	43%			-6.1	18	34	-$3
09 2 AL	14	12	0	199	147	5.10	3.99	1.37	294	271	317	25.9	1.8	6.6	3.8	43	19	37	1.2	11%	33%	65%	33	94	52%	18%			-19.2	93	174	$3
10 MIN	17	11	0	221	117	3.75	3.86	1.19	266	292	242	28.3	1.5	4.8	3.2	51	18	31	1.0	11%	29%	72%	32	98	56%	13%			9.1	74	120	$15
11 MIN	9	13	0	222	102	4.30	4.21	1.36	294	289	300	28.9	1.6	4.1	2.6	51	18	31	0.9	9%	31%	70%	33	103	27%	27%			-9.7	60	90	-$1
12 MIN	2	5	0	63	33	6.00	4.45	1.40	313	319	305	24.4	1.1	4.7	4.1	41	21	38	1.3	11%	33%	58%	11	83	36%	27%			-15.4	73	95	-$9
1st Half	2	5	0	63	33	6.00	4.45	1.40	313	319	305	24.4	1.1	4.7	4.1	41	21	38	1.3	11%	33%	58%	11	83	36%	27%			-15.4	73	95	-$9
2nd Half																																
13 Proj	**9**	**10**	**0**	**160**	**85**	**4.66**	**4.35**	**1.34**	**293**	**299**	**287**	**25.5**	**1.6**	**4.8**	**3.1**	**46**	**19**	**35**	**1.1**	**10%**	**31%**	**68%**	**26**						**-12.6**	**68**	**89**	**$0**

Peavy,Jake

Age: 32	Th: R	Role SP	Health	F	LIMA Plan	C+
Ht: 6' 1"	Wt: 195	Type FB	PT/Exp	B	Rand Var	0
			Consist	B	MM	3305

Last year in this space we called him "a very interesting investment if you can get him cheap," and he paid off in spades. Five-year stability of BPV underscores that this is a true skill level, not just a single nostalgic data point. Only blemish is the Health grade, which underscores the elevated risk level.

Yr Tm	W	L	Sv	IP	K	ERA	xERA	WHIP	OBA	vL	vR	BF/G	Ctl	Dom	Cmd	G	L	F	hr/9	hr/f	H%	S%	GS	APC	DOM%	DIS%	Sv%	LI	RAR	BPV	BPX	R$
08 SD	10	11	0	174	166	2.85	3.64	1.18	229	263	194	26.3	3.1	8.6	2.8	41	22	38	0.9	10%	28%	80%	27	106	63%	19%			31.6	91	171	$20
09 2 TM *	10	7	0	117	123	3.60	3.07	1.18	231	249	178	23.4	3.0	9.5	3.2	42	18	40	0.7	8%	30%	71%	16	98	75%	6%			10.4	110	205	$12
10 CHW	7	6	0	107	93	4.63	3.85	1.23	242	275	209	26.4	2.9	7.8	2.7	41	18	42	1.1	10%	29%	65%	17	101	59%	18%			-7.2	83	134	$3
11 CHW *	8	8	0	141	118	5.12	4.32	1.31	285	259	278	23.2	1.7	7.5	4.4	39	23	39	0.9	8%	34%	62%	18	98	67%	17%	0	0.81	-20.4	108	163	-$2
12 CHW	11	12	0	219	194	3.37	3.76	1.10	234	252	210	27.6	2.0	8.0	4.0	37	19	45	1.1	10%	28%	74%	32	109	75%	0%			17.4	104	136	$22
1st Half	6	5	0	113	101	2.96	3.66	0.99	215	254	163	27.6	1.9	8.1	4.2	35	18	47	0.9	8%	26%	74%	16	107	88%	0%			14.7	107	139	$30
2nd Half	5	7	0	106	93	3.81	3.86	1.20	254	250	259	27.5	2.1	7.9	3.7	38	19	42	1.4	12%	30%	74%	16	111	63%	0%			2.7	101	131	$14
13 Proj	**13**	**10**	**0**	**203**	**179**	**3.81**	**3.78**	**1.19**	**252**	**264**	**236**	**25.4**	**2.2**	**7.9**	**3.6**	**38**	**20**	**42**	**1.1**	**10%**	**30%**	**72%**	**32**						**5.2**	**100**	**130**	**$15**

Pelfrey,Mike

Age: 29	Th: R	Role SP	Health	F	LIMA Plan	D+
Ht: 6' 7"	Wt: 250	Type Con	PT/Exp	B	Rand Var	-5
			Consist	B	MM	2101

Season ended with Tommy John surgery on May 1. PRO: should be ready to return very early in 2013. CON: tiny 2012 sample aside, there is little redeeming value in this skill set. VERDICT: TJS has been known to add a few MPH to pitchers, but there's likely more help needed here. Pass.

Yr Tm	W	L	Sv	IP	K	ERA	xERA	WHIP	OBA	vL	vR	BF/G	Ctl	Dom	Cmd	G	L	F	hr/9	hr/f	H%	S%	GS	APC	DOM%	DIS%	Sv%	LI	RAR	BPV	BPX	R$
08 NYM	13	11	0	201	110	3.72	4.36	1.36	276	307	245	26.6	2.9	4.9	1.7	50	21	30	0.5	6%	30%	73%	32	104	34%	25%			14.9	39	74	$10
09 NYM	10	12	0	184	107	5.03	4.60	1.51	289	284	294	26.6	3.2	5.2	1.6	51	19	30	0.9	10%	32%	67%	31	102	35%	26%			-16.1	36	67	-$4
10 NYM	15	9	1	204	113	3.66	4.36	1.38	275	279	272	25.6	3.0	5.0	1.7	48	20	32	0.5	6%	30%	74%	33	100	45%	24%	100	0.82	10.5	35	56	$8
11 NYM	7	13	0	194	105	4.74	4.63	1.47	286	277	294	25.3	3.0	4.9	1.6	46	20	35	1.0	9%	31%	69%	33	95	30%	24%	0	0.75	-19.1	30	46	-$8
12 NYM	0	0	0	20	13	2.29	3.82	1.42	300	298	303	28.3	1.8	5.9	3.3	53	27	20	0.0	0%	36%	82%	3	102	33%	0%			4.2	89	116	-$3
1st Half	0	0	0	20	13	2.29	3.83	1.42	300	298	303	28.3	1.8	5.9	3.3	53	27	20	0.0	0%	36%	82%	3	102	33%	0%			4.2	89	116	-$3
2nd Half																																
13 Proj	**5**	**8**	**0**	**123**	**72**	**4.12**	**4.38**	**1.43**	**286**	**288**	**285**	**26.0**	**2.7**	**5.3**	**2.0**	**50**	**22**	**28**	**0.5**	**6%**	**32%**	**71%**	**20**						**-1.5**	**51**	**66**	**-$1**

RAY MURPHY

Peralta,Joel

Age: 37	Th: R	Role RP	Health	A	LIMA Plan	A
			PT/Exp	C	Rand Var	+1
Ht: 5' 11"	Wt: 205	Type Pwr xFB	Consist	B	MM	4510

A year ago, we tagged his elevated FB% as the only wart in this skill set. And in 2012 1H, he got burned by those FB clearing the fence too often. That eventually passed, and 2H was as good as ever. Skills-wise, whole year was an extension of this late peak. No reason to doubt his ability to extend it again.

Yr Tm	W	L	Sv	IP	K	ERA	xERA	WHIP	OBA	vL	vR	BF/G	Ctl	Dom	Cmd	G	L	F	hr/9	hr/f	H%	S%	GS	APC	DOM%	DIS%	Sv%	LI	RAR	BPV	BPX	R$
08 KC *	2	2	2	71	51	4.42	4.62	1.25	252	247	294	5.8	2.7	6.5	2.4	35	17	48	1.9	19%	26%	73%	0	21			67	0.49	-0.8	38	71	$1
09 COL *	6	3	4	61	44	4.36	4.68	1.47	277	348	216	4.5	3.5	6.5	1.8	25	26	49	1.0	8%	32%	72%	0	17			80	0.96	-0.3	47	89	$1
10 WAS *	3	0	20	82	76	1.83	2.25	0.97	212	212	145	4.7	1.9	8.3	4.5	26	18	56	0.7	7%	27%	86%	0	19			91	0.85	22.8	136	219	$19
11 TAM	3	4	6	68	61	2.93	3.65	0.92	188	155	218	3.6	2.4	8.1	3.4	27	16	57	0.9	7%	22%	73%	0	15			75	1.20	8.5	86	130	$9
12 TAM	2	6	2	67	84	3.63	3.18	0.99	200	173	229	3.4	2.3	11.3	4.9	30	18	52	1.2	11%	28%	68%	0	14			40	1.15	3.2	149	195	$6
1st Half	0	3	2	31	38	4.94	3.34	1.06	216	203	231	3.3	2.3	11.0	4.8	29	19	52	1.7	15%	28%	59%	0	14			40	1.13	-3.5	142	185	$0
2nd Half	2	3	0	36	46	2.50	3.05	0.92	186	143	227	3.6	2.3	11.5	5.1	31	17	52	0.8	7%	27%	77%	0	15			0	1.16	6.7	156	203	$10
13 Proj	**2**	**4**	**3**	**58**	**62**	**3.19**	**3.59**	**1.08**	**227**	**202**	**248**	**3.8**	**2.3**	**9.6**	**4.1**	**29**	**17**	**53**	**1.2**	**10%**	**28%**	**77%**	**0**						**5.9**	**117**	**152**	**$5**

Peralta,Wily

Age: 24	Th: R	Role SP	Health	A	LIMA Plan	D+
			PT/Exp	D	Rand Var	0
Ht: 6' 2"	Wt: 240	Type Pwr GB	Consist	D	MM	2303

2-1, 2.48 ERA in 29 IP at MIL. Spent most of year as starter in AAA, walking too many but striking out a batter per IP. Earned Sept callup, where he posted 3 PQS-DOM outings in five starts. While Ctl is a work in progress, big Dom plus GB tilt (if it holds in larger sample) will cover a few too many BBs. Keeper.

Yr Tm	W	L	Sv	IP	K	ERA	xERA	WHIP	OBA	vL	vR	BF/G	Ctl	Dom	Cmd	G	L	F	hr/9	hr/f	H%	S%	GS	APC	DOM%	DIS%	Sv%	LI	RAR	BPV	BPX	R$
08																																
09																																
10 aa	2	3	0	42	26	3.88	5.24	1.64	278			23.6	4.9	5.6	1.1				1.1		31%	80%							1.0	24	39	-$3
11 a/a	11	7	0	151	140	3.31	3.23	1.27	241			23.7	3.3	8.3	2.5				0.5		31%	75%							11.8	93	140	$10
12 MIL *	9	12	0	176	146	5.10	4.93	1.67	289	265	220	23.2	4.7	7.5	1.6	55	21	24	0.5	0%	35%	68%	5	76	60%	20%	0	0.66	-23.6	60	78	-$15
1st Half	3	8	0	78	59	7.18	5.92	1.92	314	667	500	21.8	5.7	6.7	1.2	75	25	0	0.5	0%	37%	60%	0	17			0	0.20	-30.5	41	53	-$33
2nd Half	6	4	0	97	87	3.43	4.08	1.46	268	239	208	24.5	3.9	8.1	2.1	54	21	25	0.5	0%	34%	77%	5	87	60%	20%			7.0	78	102	-$1
13 Proj	**9**	**9**	**0**	**145**	**121**	**4.17**	**4.10**	**1.51**	**270**	**289**	**252**	**23.5**	**4.2**	**7.5**	**1.8**	**54**	**21**	**25**	**0.7**	**10%**	**33%**	**73%**	**27**						**-2.8**	**54**	**70**	**$0**

Perez,Chris

Age: 28	Th: R	Role RP	Health	A	LIMA Plan	C
			PT/Exp	B	Rand Var	0
Ht: 6' 4"	Wt: 230	Type Pwr FB	Consist	B	MM	3430

Latest lesson in RP volatility: Compared to 2011, he regained the Dom that had mysteriously disappeared, spiked his Cmd, moderated his xFB profile... and his ERA actually went up! BPV column shows that, after nearly three years as closer, we can finally call him worthy of the role. Well, for now.

Yr Tm	W	L	Sv	IP	K	ERA	xERA	WHIP	OBA	vL	vR	BF/G	Ctl	Dom	Cmd	G	L	F	hr/9	hr/f	H%	S%	GS	APC	DOM%	DIS%	Sv%	LI	RAR	BPV	BPX	R$
08 STL *	4	4	18	67	73	3.49	3.55	1.31	222	220	231	4.1	4.5	9.8	2.2	39	20	41	1.0	11%	28%	77%	0	19			75	1.22	6.9	84	158	$11
09 2 TM	1	2	2	57	68	4.26	3.62	1.19	201	188	207	3.9	4.3	10.7	2.5	35	18	47	1.3	13%	26%	68%	0	16			40	1.02	0.4	91	171	$2
10 CLE	2	2	23	63	61	1.71	3.89	1.08	182	216	154	4.1	4.0	8.7	2.2	34	20	46	0.6	5%	24%	88%	0	17			85	1.53	18.4	61	98	$16
11 CLE	4	7	36	60	39	3.32	4.74	1.21	215	198	233	3.9	3.9	5.9	1.5	28	21	50	0.8	6%	24%	75%	0	15			90	1.68	4.6	6	9	$16
12 CLE	0	4	39	58	59	3.59	3.64	1.13	222	181	267	4.0	2.5	9.2	3.7	41	19	40	0.9	9%	29%	71%	0	16			91	1.23	3.0	117	153	$17
1st Half	0	1	23	29	30	2.76	3.54	1.02	207	196	218	3.9	2.1	9.2	4.3	41	17	42	0.3	3%	29%	72%	0	16			96	1.18	4.5	127	165	$22
2nd Half	0	3	16	28	29	4.45	3.75	1.24	236	167	320	4.1	2.9	9.2	3.2	40	22	38	1.6	16%	29%	70%	0	16			84	1.28	-1.5	107	139	$11
13 Proj	**3**	**4**	**40**	**58**	**54**	**3.36**	**3.93**	**1.16**	**220**	**194**	**246**	**3.8**	**3.3**	**8.4**	**2.5**	**36**	**20**	**44**	**1.1**	**10%**	**26%**	**76%**	**0**						**4.7**	**76**	**99**	**$19**

Perez,Martin

Age: 22	Th: L	Role SP	Health	A	LIMA Plan	D
			PT/Exp	D	Rand Var	0
Ht: 6' 0"	Wt: 180	Type GB	Consist	B	MM	1101

1-4, 5.45 ERA in 38 IP at TEX. One-time top prospect has seen his star diminish, along with his Dom, over past two years, with initial trial in TEX going about as poorly as you'd expect from a kid with a 1.2 Cmd. He's still young and left-handed, though, so he'll get plenty of chances yet. Patience.

Yr Tm	W	L	Sv	IP	K	ERA	xERA	WHIP	OBA	vL	vR	BF/G	Ctl	Dom	Cmd	G	L	F	hr/9	hr/f	H%	S%	GS	APC	DOM%	DIS%	Sv%	LI	RAR	BPV	BPX	R$
08																																
09 aa	1	3	0	21	13	6.13	6.01	1.65	337			18.8	1.9	5.7	2.9				0.9		38%	63%							-4.7	56	104	-$5
10 aa	5	8	0	100	90	7.35	6.52	1.82	319			19.3	4.5	8.1	1.8				1.3		38%	60%							-40.2	38	61	-$16
11 a/a	8	6	0	137	102	4.69	4.93	1.56	295			22.3	3.5	6.7	1.9				0.7		35%	70%							-12.6	55	83	-$6
12 TEX *	8	10	0	165	83	4.92	4.67	1.51	279	240	324	21.0	3.8	4.5	1.2	49	21	30	0.8	8%	30%	68%	6	55	0%	50%	0	0.75	-18.3	28	36	-$11
1st Half	6	5	0	90	47	5.39	4.41	1.47	270	333	333	22.8	3.9	4.7	1.2	48	29	24	0.8	20%	29%	63%	1	62	0%	0%	0	0.40	-15.3	31	40	-$9
2nd Half	2	5	0	75	36	4.34	4.93	1.56	290	227	322	19.2	3.7	4.3	1.2	49	20	31	0.8	6%	31%	73%	5	54	0%	60%	0	0.82	-3.0	24	31	-$12
13 Proj	**5**	**6**	**0**	**102**	**66**	**5.13**	**4.69**	**1.58**	**292**	**229**	**324**	**20.9**	**3.8**	**5.8**	**1.5**	**50**	**21**	**29**	**0.9**	**10%**	**33%**	**68%**	**22**						**-14.0**	**31**	**40**	**-$7**

Perkins,Glen

Age: 30	Th: L	Role RP	Health	A	LIMA Plan	B+
			PT/Exp	C	Rand Var	-2
Ht: 6' 0"	Wt: 204	Type Pwr	Consist	D	MM	4430

Successfully replicated the skills he displayed during his 2011 bullpen debut, and even kicked them up a notch. Long successful vL, he's now come up with answers vR, too. Worked his way into closer role in 2H and ran with it (8 Sept Sv). Should have leg up on that role for 2013, and BPV says he can succeed.

Yr Tm	W	L	Sv	IP	K	ERA	xERA	WHIP	OBA	vL	vR	BF/G	Ctl	Dom	Cmd	G	L	F	hr/9	hr/f	H%	S%	GS	APC	DOM%	DIS%	Sv%	LI	RAR	BPV	BPX	R$
08 MIN *	14	5	0	184	96	4.25	5.28	1.48	293	352	288	24.0	2.8	4.7	1.7	38	22	40	1.3	12%	31%	76%	26	91	31%	27%			1.6	20	38	$3
09 MIN	6	7	0	96	45	5.89	4.82	1.48	304	333	295	23.5	2.1	4.2	2.0	47	14	39	1.2	10%	32%	62%	17	82	35%	24%	0	0.74	-18.6	43	80	-$6
10 MIN *	5	10	0	146	87	6.78	6.71	1.82	349	241	386	17.3	2.7	5.4	2.0	50	22	28	1.0	14%	39%	62%	1	26	0%	100%	0	0.64	-48.5	30	48	-$22
11 MIN	4	4	2	62	65	2.48	3.07	1.23	244	222	259	3.9	3.1	9.5	3.1	50	21	29	0.3	4%	33%	80%	0	14			40	1.22	11.1	116	174	$5
12 MIN	3	1	16	70	78	2.56	3.10	1.04	222	192	241	4.0	2.0	10.0	4.9	42	19	39	1.0	12%	29%	82%	0	15			80	0.92	12.6	144	188	$14
1st Half	1	1	2	33	41	2.76	3.34	1.32	248	268	238	4.1	3.6	11.3	3.2	41	22	38	0.8	10%	35%	83%	0	16			50	0.92	5.1	125	163	$6
2nd Half	2	0	14	38	37	2.39	2.89	0.80	199	138	244	4.0	0.7	8.8	12.3	44	17	39	1.2	13%	24%	80%	0	14			88	0.92	7.6	162	211	$21
13 Proj	**3**	**2**	**35**	**65**	**62**	**3.00**	**3.54**	**1.23**	**256**	**228**	**271**	**4.5**	**2.4**	**8.5**	**3.6**	**45**	**19**	**36**	**1.0**	**11%**	**31%**	**80%**	**0**						**8.2**	**113**	**146**	**$18**

Pestano,Vinnie

Age: 28	Th: R	Role RP	Health	A	LIMA Plan	A
			PT/Exp	D	Rand Var	-3
Ht: 6' 0"	Wt: 200	Type Pwr FB	Consist	A	MM	4510

Third straight sub-3.00 ERA, but xERA wasn't quite as agreeable this time around. 2011 Dom spike now a bit of an outlier, and 2H return of FB bias is mildly concerning. But mostly these are quibbles; this is an enviable skill set. Just don't bank on another mid-2's ERA.

Yr Tm	W	L	Sv	IP	K	ERA	xERA	WHIP	OBA	vL	vR	BF/G	Ctl	Dom	Cmd	G	L	F	hr/9	hr/f	H%	S%	GS	APC	DOM%	DIS%	Sv%	LI	RAR	BPV	BPX	R$
08																																
09 aa	2	3	24	35	26	3.88	4.31	1.49	275			4.4	3.8	6.8	1.8				0.6		33%	74%							1.9	61	114	$8
10 CLE *	2	3	18	65	71	2.15	2.80	1.22	239	375	100	4.2	3.0	9.8	3.3	30	20	50	0.3	0%	33%	82%	0	20			90	0.39	15.4	128	207	$13
11 CLE	1	2	2	62	84	2.32	2.83	1.05	184	280	115	3.7	3.5	12.2	3.5	39	19	42	0.7	9%	28%	82%	0	15			33	1.22	12.4	142	214	$7
12 CLE	3	3	2	70	76	2.57	3.52	1.10	207	241	168	4.1	3.1	9.8	3.2	41	17	43	0.9	9%	27%	81%	0	17			40	1.54	12.5	112	146	$7
1st Half	3	0	0	31	36	2.03	3.37	1.03	171	218	125	3.8	3.8	10.5	2.8	44	17	39	0.6	7%	25%	83%	0	17			0	1.67	7.6	108	141	$9
2nd Half	0	3	2	39	40	3.00	3.64	1.15	235	256	206	4.3	2.5	9.2	3.6	39	16	45	1.2	10%	29%	80%	0	17			50	1.42	4.9	114	148	$6
13 Proj	**2**	**3**	**5**	**58**	**63**	**2.90**	**3.49**	**1.14**	**218**	**280**	**160**	**3.9**	**3.2**	**9.8**	**3.1**	**40**	**17**	**42**	**0.7**	**8%**	**29%**	**77%**	**0**						**8.0**	**108**	**140**	**$6**

Pettitte,Andy

Age: 41	Th: L	Role SP	Health	F	LIMA Plan	B
			PT/Exp	C	Rand Var	0
Ht: 6' 5"	Wt: 225	Type	Consist	B	MM	3201

Fractured fibula (on a comebacker) cost him most of the summer, but overall this was a more-than-credible return after a year away; Cmd cracked 3.0 level for first time since 2005. Durability questions will remain going forward, but there are very few pitchers posting triple-digit BPVs into their 40s.

Yr Tm	W	L	Sv	IP	K	ERA	xERA	WHIP	OBA	vL	vR	BF/G	Ctl	Dom	Cmd	G	L	F	hr/9	hr/f	H%	S%	GS	APC	DOM%	DIS%	Sv%	LI	RAR	BPV	BPX	R$
08 NYY	14	14	0	204	158	4.54	3.80	1.41	290	203	325	26.7	2.4	7.0	2.9	51	20	29	0.8	10%	34%	69%	33	99	45%	21%			-5.5	89	167	$6
09 NYY	14	8	0	195	148	4.16	4.36	1.38	259	282	249	26.1	3.5	6.8	1.9	43	19	38	0.9	9%	30%	72%	32	103	47%	16%			3.9	49	92	$9
10 NYY	11	3	0	129	101	3.28	3.89	1.27	257	186	283	25.5	2.9	7.0	2.5	44	18	38	0.9	9%	30%	77%	21	95	57%	24%			12.7	72	116	$9
11																																
12 NYY	5	4	0	75	69	2.87	3.29	1.14	232	202	245	25.3	2.5	8.2	3.3	56	15	29	1.0	13%	28%	79%	12	94	50%	17%			10.7	115	150	$6
1st Half	3	3	0	59	59	3.22	2.99	1.09	226	203	235	26.0	2.3	9.1	3.9	58	13	28	1.1	16%	28%	75%	9	97	67%	22%			5.8	137	178	$8
2nd Half	2	1	0	17	10	1.62	4.41	1.32	254	200	279	23.0	3.2	5.4	1.7	50	19	31	0.5	6%	29%	90%	3	86	0%	0%			4.9	38	49	-$2
13 Proj	**10**	**6**	**0**	**120**	**92**	**3.78**	**3.97**	**1.28**	**253**	**210**	**271**	**24.7**	**2.9**	**6.9**	**2.4**	**49**	**18**	**33**	**0.9**	**10%**	**29%**	**73%**	**20**						**3.5**	**73**	**95**	**$6**

RAY MURPHY

Phelps,David

Age: 26 Th: R Role RP	PT/Exp	D	Rand Var	-1
Ht: 6' 2" Wt: 200 Type Pwr	Consist	F	MM	2301
	Health	A	LIMA Plan	B

Concurrent rise of Dom and Ctl were a wash in terms of Cmd, but BPV loved this version. Swingman had slightly better skills out of pen, but credible as an SP as well. (Disregard the DIS%, many starts were short because he wasn't stretched out). Role ambiguity in March may create profit opportunity.

Yr	Tm	W	L	Sv	IP	K	ERA	xERA	WHIP	OBA	vL	vR	BF/G	Ctl	Dom	Cmd	G	L	F	hr/9	hr/f	H%	S%	GS	APC	DOM%	DIS%	Sv%	LI	RAR	BPV	BPX	R$
08																																	
09																																	
10	a/a	10	2	0	159	117	3.23	3.70	1.30	272			25.1	2.2	6.6	3.0				0.5		33%	75%							16.7	89	145	$10
11	aaa	6	6	0	107	72	4.51	6.23	1.64	326			26.6	2.5	6.1	2.4				1.4		36%	77%							-7.6	36	55	-$7
12	NYY	4	4	0	100	96	3.34	3.82	1.19	223	227	220	12.5	3.4	8.7	2.5	43	19	38	1.3	14%	27%	78%	11	51	45%	45%	0	0.83	8.3	84	110	$6
1st Half		1	3	0	37	34	3.16	3.99	1.32	250	286	221	11.4	3.4	8.3	2.4	46	19	36	1.5	16%	29%	84%	2	47	0%	100%	0	0.81	3.9	81	105	-$1
2nd Half		3	1	0	63	62	3.45	3.72	1.12	206	190	220	13.4	3.4	8.9	2.6	41	19	40	1.1	12%	25%	74%	9	54	56%	33%	0	0.84	4.4	86	112	$10
13	**Proj**	**5**	**4**	**0**	**102**	**84**	**3.74**	**4.14**	**1.37**	**271**	**277**	**266**	**16.8**	**2.9**	**7.4**	**2.5**	**43**	**19**	**38**	**1.2**	**11%**	**32%**	**77%**	**17**						**3.5**	**76**	**98**	**$2**

Pineda,Michael

Age: 24 Th: R Role SP	PT/Exp	C	Rand Var	0
Ht: 6' 7" Wt: 265 Type Pwr xFB	Consist	B	MM	2301
	Health	F	LIMA Plan	B+

Preseason surgery to a repair a torn labrum cost him 2012, and likely at least half of 2013. In projecting recovery, age and prior skill levels are on his side. But this is among the least recoverable of pitching injuries, so there are no guarantees. Don't count on any meaningful contribution until 2014, at least.

Yr	Tm	W	L	Sv	IP	K	ERA	xERA	WHIP	OBA	vL	vR	BF/G	Ctl	Dom	Cmd	G	L	F	hr/9	hr/f	H%	S%	GS	APC	DOM%	DIS%	Sv%	LI	RAR	BPV	BPX	R$
08																																	
09																																	
10	a/a	11	4	0	139	140	3.41	2.92	1.13	243			22.0	2.0	9.0	4.4				0.5		32%	70%							11.5	137	222	$13
11	SEA	9	10	0	171	173	3.74	3.50	1.10	211	237	184	24.9	2.9	9.1	3.1	36	19	45	0.9	9%	27%	69%	28	96	75%	11%			4.3	100	150	$13
12																																	
1st Half																																	
2nd Half																																	
13	**Proj**	**5**	**3**	**0**	**75**	**66**	**4.21**	**4.22**	**1.25**	**241**	**270**	**210**	**23.9**	**3.2**	**7.9**	**2.5**	**36**	**19**	**45**	**1.1**	**9%**	**28%**	**69%**	**13**						**-1.8**	**71**	**92**	**$2**

Pomeranz,Drew

Age: 24 Th: L Role RP	PT/Exp	D	Rand Var	+1
Ht: 6' 5" Wt: 240 Type Pwr	Consist	F	MM	2303
	Health	A	LIMA Plan	D+

2-9, 4.93 ERA in 97 IP at COL. Amid that carnage in COL, there were rays of hope: finally established a foothold at the 2.0 Cmd level in 2H, firming up his GB rate a the same time. There's a ton more work to do, and for 2013 the risk swamps the reward. But at least we have reason for longer-term optimism.

Yr	Tm	W	L	Sv	IP	K	ERA	xERA	WHIP	OBA	vL	vR	BF/G	Ctl	Dom	Cmd	G	L	F	hr/9	hr/f	H%	S%	GS	APC	DOM%	DIS%	Sv%	LI	RAR	BPV	BPX	R$
08																																	
09																																	
10																																	
11	COL *	3	2	0	42	32	3.35	2.06	1.03	215	222	279	18.1	2.3	6.8	2.9	47	26	26	0.3	0%	27%	66%	4	67	25%	25%			3.1	107	160	$2
12	COL *	6	13	0	147	122	4.25	5.06	1.57	283	169	287	20.2	4.1	7.5	1.8	44	20	36	1.0	14%	33%	75%	22	77	18%	64%			-4.3	50	66	-$7
1st Half		4	6	0	74	59	3.50	5.42	1.75	307	263	286	22.4	4.5	7.2	1.6	41	32	26	0.6	11%	37%	81%	5	83	40%	60%			4.7	53	69	-$6
2nd Half		2	7	0	74	63	5.01	4.65	1.40	257	141	288	18.3	3.8	7.7	2.0	45	16	39	1.5	14%	29%	68%	17	76	12%	65%			-9.0	48	62	-$8
13	**Proj**	**7**	**9**	**0**	**131**	**105**	**4.55**	**4.28**	**1.42**	**267**	**190**	**289**	**19.6**	**3.5**	**7.2**	**2.0**	**43**	**23**	**34**	**0.9**	**10%**	**32%**	**69%**	**27**						**-8.6**	**56**	**73**	**-$1**

Porcello,Rick

Age: 24 Th: R Role SP	PT/Exp	A	Rand Var	+3
Ht: 6' 6" Wt: 200 Type Con GB	Consist	A	MM	2105
	Health	A	LIMA Plan	D+

Upticks in Dom/Cmd hold promise, but Dom remains far below par. Normally, GBs would be a decent proxy for Ks, but he had DET's horrible defensive IF behind him. They caused the H% punishment; and without personnel changes we can't count on regression. In this case, expect ERA/xERA gap to persist.

Yr	Tm	W	L	Sv	IP	K	ERA	xERA	WHIP	OBA	vL	vR	BF/G	Ctl	Dom	Cmd	G	L	F	hr/9	hr/f	H%	S%	GS	APC	DOM%	DIS%	Sv%	LI	RAR	BPV	BPX	R$
08																																	
09	DET	14	9	0	171	89	3.96	4.31	1.34	267	281	248	23.2	2.7	4.7	1.7	54	17	29	1.2	14%	28%	75%	31	88	39%	32%			7.7	42	79	$9
10	DET *	11	14	0	191	100	4.76	4.47	1.38	286	303	272	25.8	2.2	4.7	2.1	50	18	32	0.8	10%	31%	66%	27	96	30%	19%			-16.0	45	72	-$1
11	DET	14	9	0	182	104	4.75	4.06	1.41	292	321	248	25.3	2.3	5.1	2.3	51	19	30	0.9	10%	32%	67%	31	92	29%	23%			-18.1	60	90	-$2
12	DET	10	12	0	176	107	4.59	4.19	1.53	310	325	294	25.3	2.2	5.5	2.4	53	24	23	0.8	12%	35%	71%	31	91	32%	26%			-12.6	69	90	-$9
1st Half		6	5	0	93	57	4.35	4.20	1.49	305	303	306	25.7	2.2	5.5	2.5	53	23	25	0.8	10%	34%	72%	16	93	44%	25%			-3.9	70	91	-$4
2nd Half		4	7	0	83	50	4.86	4.18	1.57	317	350	282	24.8	2.3	5.4	2.4	54	26	20	0.9	13%	36%	70%	15	90	20%	27%			-8.7	68	89	-$14
13	**Proj**	**11**	**12**	**0**	**181**	**104**	**4.63**	**4.25**	**1.46**	**300**	**320**	**276**	**24.7**	**2.3**	**5.2**	**2.2**	**52**	**21**	**26**	**0.9**	**11%**	**33%**	**70%**	**31**						**-13.6**	**62**	**80**	**-$2**

Price,David

Age: 27 Th: L Role SP	PT/Exp	A	Rand Var	-1
Ht: 6' 6" Wt: 220 Type Pwr	Consist	A	MM	4405
	Health	A	LIMA Plan	C

Carbon-copied his 2011 skills and threw in a GB% spike to create a masterful season. Results look a lot like 2010, but xERA much more supportive this time. Both in terms of skills and results, 2H was just about flawless, so it's not at all out on a limb to call for a full repeat in 2013. One of the best around.

Yr	Tm	W	L	Sv	IP	K	ERA	xERA	WHIP	OBA	vL	vR	BF/G	Ctl	Dom	Cmd	G	L	F	hr/9	hr/f	H%	S%	GS	APC	DOM%	DIS%	Sv%	LI	RAR	BPV	BPX	R$
08	TAM *	8	1	0	89	74	2.77	3.53	1.24	245	158	188	20.1	3.0	7.4	2.5	50	13	38	0.9	7%	29%	81%	1	47	0%	0%	0	0.74	17.1	78	146	$9
09	TAM *	11	11	0	163	131	4.54	4.31	1.38	249	236	242	22.1	4.0	7.3	1.8	41	19	39	1.2	11%	28%	71%	23	99	39%	26%			-4.3	49	92	$5
10	TAM	19	6	0	209	188	2.72	3.78	1.19	221	211	224	26.9	3.4	8.1	2.4	44	17	40	0.6	7%	28%	79%	31	105	68%	3%	0	0.77	35.0	76	123	$24
11	TAM	12	13	0	224	218	3.49	3.31	1.14	230	171	250	27.0	2.5	8.7	3.5	44	19	37	0.9	10%	29%	72%	34	109	62%	12%			12.5	111	167	$19
12	TAM	20	5	0	211	205	2.56	3.12	1.10	226	205	232	27.0	2.5	8.7	3.5	53	20	27	0.7	11%	29%	80%	31	107	74%	13%			37.9	120	157	$32
1st Half		11	4	0	105	97	2.92	3.36	1.22	242	209	252	26.6	3.0	8.3	2.8	54	20	25	0.8	12%	30%	79%	16	107	63%	19%			14.1	101	131	$30
2nd Half		9	1	0	106	108	2.20	2.91	0.98	209	200	212	27.4	2.0	9.1	4.5	52	19	29	0.6	9%	28%	80%	15	108	87%	7%			23.8	140	182	$35
13	**Proj**	**18**	**6**	**0**	**210**	**200**	**2.89**	**3.39**	**1.13**	**228**	**201**	**236**	**25.8**	**2.7**	**8.5**	**3.2**	**48**	**19**	**33**	**0.8**	**9%**	**29%**	**77%**	**32**						**29.3**	**107**	**139**	**$27**

Pryor,Stephen

Age: 23 Th: R Role RP	PT/Exp	F	Rand Var	-4
Ht: 6' 4" Wt: 245 Type Pwr xFB	Consist	F	MM	2500
	Health	A	LIMA Plan	B

3-1, 3.91 ERA in 23 IP at SEA. Here's what happens when the inconsistency of a young fireballer meets small sample sizes of the RP: in SEA in August, had 13 IP, 1 BB/13 K, 228 BPV. Then in September: 9 IP, 9 BB/7 K, -106 BPV. The elements of a closer are here, they just need to be harnessed.

Yr	Tm	W	L	Sv	IP	K	ERA	xERA	WHIP	OBA	vL	vR	BF/G	Ctl	Dom	Cmd	G	L	F	hr/9	hr/f	H%	S%	GS	APC	DOM%	DIS%	Sv%	LI	RAR	BPV	BPX	R$
08																																	
09																																	
10																																	
11	aa	2	1	6	23	24	1.29	0.11	0.73	132			4.7	2.7	9.7	3.6				0.0		20%	80%							7.4	162	244	$5
12	SEA *	4	1	10	59	66	1.86	2.75	1.20	201	243	260	4.5	4.4	10.1	2.3	37	18	45	0.8	18%	27%	89%	0	17			100	1.07	15.7	101	131	$10
1st Half		2	0	9	33	40	0.86	1.16	0.96	154	286	182	4.8	4.0	10.7	2.7	57	7	36	0.3	20%	23%	93%	0	16			100	1.30	13.0	136	177	$17
2nd Half		2	1	1	26	26	3.16	4.78	1.50	253	233	282	4.1	4.9	9.3	1.9	31	21	48	1.4	17%	31%	86%	0	16			100	1.00	2.7	58	76	$0
13	**Proj**	**4**	**1**	**0**	**51**	**55**	**3.28**	**4.20**	**1.30**	**218**	**195**	**236**	**4.4**	**4.6**	**9.8**	**2.1**	**31**	**21**	**48**	**0.9**	**8%**	**28%**	**78%**	**0**						**4.6**	**62**	**81**	**$2**

Putz,J.J.

Age: 36 Th: R Role RP	PT/Exp	B	Rand Var	0
Ht: 6' 5" Wt: 250 Type Pwr	Consist	A	MM	5530
	Health	D	LIMA Plan	B

Skills-wise, a terrific follow-up to 2011. Only disappointment was the diminished saves total. It seems that ARI has figured out that they need to keep his total IP in the fifties, and BF/G under 4, in order to keep him healthy. That lowered workload shaves his value a bit, but it's tough to dispute the results.

Yr	Tm	W	L	Sv	IP	K	ERA	xERA	WHIP	OBA	vL	vR	BF/G	Ctl	Dom	Cmd	G	L	F	hr/9	hr/f	H%	S%	GS	APC	DOM%	DIS%	Sv%	LI	RAR	BPV	BPX	R$
08	SEA	6	5	15	46	56	3.88	4.13	1.60	256	258	253	4.5	5.4	10.9	2.0	40	20	40	0.8	8%	36%	77%	0	18			65	1.24	2.5	67	126	$6
09	NYM	1	4	2	29	19	5.22	5.47	1.64	257	296	220	4.7	5.8	5.8	1.0	47	19	34	0.3	3%	31%	66%	0	18			50	1.16	-3.2	-27	-51	-$4
10	CHW	7	5	3	54	65	2.83	2.86	1.04	204	253	164	3.7	2.5	10.8	4.3	49	13	39	0.7	8%	30%	75%	0	13			43	1.27	8.3	155	250	$8
11	ARI	2	2	45	58	61	2.17	3.06	0.91	195	179	214	3.8	1.9	9.5	5.1	42	13	44	0.6	6%	27%	80%	0	14			92	1.37	12.7	140	211	$25
12	ARI	1	5	32	54	65	2.82	2.79	1.03	223	219	227	3.8	1.8	10.8	5.9	46	21	33	0.7	9%	32%	75%	0	14			86	1.07	8.0	169	220	$17
1st Half		1	4	14	25	28	5.04	3.36	1.20	245	241	250	4.1	2.2	10.1	4.7	41	19	40	1.4	14%	32%	62%	0	16			82	1.14	-3.2	143	186	$11
2nd Half		0	1	18	29	37	0.92	2.32	0.89	202	191	211	3.6	1.5	11.4	7.4	50	24	26	0.0	0%	31%	88%	0	13			90	1.01	11.2	191	249	$22
13	**Proj**	**3**	**4**	**38**	**58**	**68**	**3.11**	**2.91**	**1.05**	**220**	**221**	**220**	**3.7**	**2.3**	**10.5**	**4.6**	**45**	**18**	**37**	**0.6**	**8%**	**31%**	**72%**	**0**						**6.5**	**151**	**196**	**$20**

RAY MURPHY

Qualls,Chad

Age: 34	Th: R	Role: RP	Health	B	LIMA Plan: C
Ht: 6' 5"	Wt: 220	Type: Con xGB	PT/Exp	C	Rand Var: +3
			Consist	A	MM: 2100

Checked off three more MLB teams on his dance card, but since none of them play home games in PETCO, his ERA jumped again. Strong GB tilt is still in place, but now when balls get hit in the air, they go far. Once-elite Cmd has now fallen below 2.0, finishing his journey from valuable to value-less.

Yr	Tm	W	L	Sv	IP	K	ERA	xERA	WHIP	OBA	vL	vR	BF/G	Ctl	Dom	Cmd	G	L	F	hr/9	hr/f	H%	S%	GS	APC	DOM%	DIS%	Sv%	LI	RAR	BPV	BPX	R$
08	ARI	4	8	9	74	71	2.81	2.93	1.07	224	220	229	3.9	2.2	8.7	3.9	58	19	23	0.5	9%	29%	75%	0	14			53	1.32	13.8	133	249	$11
09	ARI	2	2	24	52	45	3.63	3.03	1.15	256	298	214	4.3	1.2	7.8	6.4	57	20	23	0.9	14%	32%	71%	0	15			83	1.24	4.4	142	267	$12
10	2 TM	3	4	12	59	49	7.32	4.08	1.80	340	392	292	4.0	3.2	7.5	2.3	55	17	28	1.1	12%	40%	59%	0	15			63	1.01	-23.6	81	131	-$5
11	SD	6	8	0	74	43	3.51	3.79	1.25	263	320	218	4.0	2.4	5.2	2.2	57	17	26	0.8	11%	28%	74%	0	14			0	1.22	4.0	63	95	$2
12	3 TM	2	1	0	52	27	5.33	4.47	1.47	297	337	268	3.9	2.4	4.6	1.9	55	19	26	1.2	15%	32%	66%	0	14			0	0.81	-8.5	52	67	-$7
1st Half		1	1	0	31	19	4.60	4.34	1.53	302	377	250	4.0	2.6	5.5	2.1	55	20	25	2.0	25%	32%	78%	0	14			0	1.06	-2.2	61	79	-$7
2nd Half		1	0	0	21	8	6.43	4.65	1.38	289	278	298	3.6	2.1	3.4	1.6	57	17	26	0.0	0%	32%	48%	0	14			0	0.47	-6.2	38	49	-$7
13	**Proj**	**2**	**2**	**0**	**44**	**26**	**5.15**	**4.13**	**1.41**	**289**	**324**	**261**	**3.8**	**2.4**	**5.4**	**2.2**	**56**	**18**	**26**	**0.8**	**11%**	**32%**	**64%**	**0**						**-6.1**	**65**	**85**	**-$4**

Quintana,Jose

Age: 24	Th: L	Role: SP	Health	A	LIMA Plan: C+
Ht: 6' 0"	Wt: 215	Type:	PT/Exp	D	Rand Var: 0
			Consist	F	MM: 1103

6-6, 3.76 ERA in 136 IP at CHW. There was no single hallmark skill here, but at least for 1H, he wrung the most out of a series of just-above-tolerance BPIs. He slipped off that tight rope in 2H, though, posting a skills profile that we just can't endorse. Being young and right-brained, he'll get more shots.

Yr	Tm	W	L	Sv	IP	K	ERA	xERA	WHIP	OBA	vL	vR	BF/G	Ctl	Dom	Cmd	G	L	F	hr/9	hr/f	H%	S%	GS	APC	DOM%	DIS%	Sv%	LI	RAR	BPV	BPX	R$
08																																	
09																																	
10																																	
11																																	
12	CHW *	7	9	0	185	117	3.65	4.03	1.35	268	252	284	22.7	2.8	5.7	2.0	47	22	31	0.7	11%	30%	74%	22	87	32%	32%	0	0.73	8.4	56	73	$4
1st Half		4	4	0	98	65	2.75	3.10	1.20	253	218	256	21.9	2.2	6.0	2.7	43	23	34	0.4	6%	30%	77%	7	76	43%	14%	0	0.73	15.3	84	109	$14
2nd Half		3	5	0	87	52	4.66	5.03	1.51	285	271	299	23.5	3.4	5.4	1.6	49	21	30	1.1	13%	31%	72%	15	93	27%	40%	0	0.73	-6.9	29	38	-$7
13	**Proj**	**6**	**9**	**0**	**174**	**109**	**4.31**	**4.41**	**1.38**	**272**	**249**	**282**	**22.9**	**2.9**	**5.6**	**1.9**	**47**	**22**	**31**	**0.9**	**10%**	**30%**	**70%**	**32**						**-6.3**	**47**	**61**	**$0**

Ramirez,Erasmo

Age: 23	Th: R	Role: SP	Health	C	LIMA Plan: B+
Ht: 5' 11"	Wt: 205	Type: Con	PT/Exp	D	Rand Var: 0
			Consist	C	MM: 3203

1-3, 3.36 ERA in 59 IP at SEA. Ctl specialist flashed interesting skills in between rides on the SEA-TAC shuttle, capped by an impressive MLB run in Sept: 27 IP, 9 ER, 5 BB/21 K. Not a terribly high ceiling, but well-established Ctl is a calling-card skill that spawns a good value proposition... UP: 3.50 ERA.

Yr	Tm	W	L	Sv	IP	K	ERA	xERA	WHIP	OBA	vL	vR	BF/G	Ctl	Dom	Cmd	G	L	F	hr/9	hr/f	H%	S%	GS	APC	DOM%	DIS%	Sv%	LI	RAR	BPV	BPX	R$
08																																	
09																																	
10																																	
11	a/a	10	8	0	153	106	4.45	4.24	1.34	291			24.4	1.7	6.3	3.7				0.7		34%	67%							-9.6	93	140	$0
12	SEA *	7	6	0	136	101	3.46	3.23	1.16	251	207	226	17.5	1.9	6.6	3.5	40	24	36	0.7	10%	30%	71%	8	55	50%	25%	0	0.76	9.3	99	129	$9
1st Half		3	4	0	68	51	3.34	3.41	1.15	254	233	236	15.1	1.8	6.8	3.8	43	26	31	0.8	14%	29%	74%	4	45	25%	50%	0	0.80	5.7	100	130	$9
2nd Half		4	2	0	68	49	3.58	3.01	1.16	249	176	216	20.8	2.0	6.5	3.3	37	22	41	0.5	6%	30%	69%	4	78	75%	0%	0	0.67	3.6	99	129	$9
13	**Proj**	**8**	**7**	**0**	**145**	**104**	**3.87**	**3.99**	**1.23**	**268**	**253**	**283**	**24.3**	**1.8**	**6.4**	**3.6**	**40**	**24**	**37**	**0.7**	**7%**	**31%**	**70%**	**24**						**2.7**	**85**	**110**	**$7**

Ramirez,Ramon

Age: 31	Th: R	Role: RP	Health	B	LIMA Plan: D
Ht: 5' 11"	Wt: 200	Type: Pwr	PT/Exp	C	Rand Var: -1
			Consist	C	MM: 1300

Skills-wise, was sailing along with a reasonable 2011 repeat until he pulled a hamstring in the Johan Santana no-hitter celebration. After DL stint, wheels came off completely in 2H. 2011 BPV/xERA now look like outliers, a.k.a. "one of these things is not like the other." Believe in '09, '10, '12: majority rule.

Yr	Tm	W	L	Sv	IP	K	ERA	xERA	WHIP	OBA	vL	vR	BF/G	Ctl	Dom	Cmd	G	L	F	hr/9	hr/f	H%	S%	GS	APC	DOM%	DIS%	Sv%	LI	RAR	BPV	BPX	R$
08	KC	3	2	1	72	70	2.64	3.72	1.23	222	300	153	4.2	3.9	8.8	2.3	46	19	35	0.3	3%	29%	78%	0	16			20	1.29	14.9	77	145	$6
09	BOS	7	4	0	70	52	2.84	4.82	1.33	233	244	220	4.3	4.1	6.7	1.6	35	18	48	0.9	7%	27%	83%	0	17			0	1.03	12.7	22	42	$5
10	2 TM	1	3	3	69	46	2.99	4.55	1.14	207	231	190	4.1	3.5	6.0	1.7	36	16	48	0.9	7%	23%	78%	0	16			100	0.78	9.3	27	43	$5
11	SF	3	3	4	69	66	2.62	3.38	1.17	216	250	203	4.3	3.4	8.7	2.5	50	17	33	0.4	5%	29%	78%	0	17			80	1.00	11.2	92	138	$7
12	NYM	3	4	1	64	52	4.24	4.74	1.46	247	273	224	4.8	4.9	7.4	1.5	47	14	40	0.6	6%	30%	71%	0	19			33	0.66	-1.8	24	31	-$3
1st Half		2	1	1	29	27	4.34	4.11	1.45	282	353	220	5.2	3.4	8.4	2.5	47	11	42	0.6	6%	35%	70%	0	20			33	0.87	-1.2	84	109	-$3
2nd Half		1	3	0	35	25	4.15	5.34	1.47	216	203	227	4.5	6.2	6.5	1.0	46	16	37	0.5	6%	26%	71%	0	18			0	0.50	-0.6	-27	-35	-$4
13	**Proj**	**2**	**3**	**0**	**59**	**48**	**3.95**	**4.42**	**1.36**	**237**	**266**	**216**	**4.4**	**4.3**	**7.5**	**1.7**	**45**	**16**	**39**	**0.6**	**6%**	**29%**	**71%**	**0**						**0.5**	**41**	**53**	**-$1**

Rapada,Clay

Age: 32	Th: L	Role: RP	Health	A	LIMA Plan: A
Ht: 6' 5"	Wt: 200	Type: Pwr	PT/Exp	D	Rand Var: -2
			Consist	F	MM: 3400

As literal an implementation of the LOOGY concept as you'll ever see: 70 appearances covering only 38 IP, microscopic BF/G. And enormous vL/vR splits (career: .493 OPS vL, 1.072 vR) tell us this is his optimal usage. Has a great chance to be the 21st century Tony Fossas.

Yr	Tm	W	L	Sv	IP	K	ERA	xERA	WHIP	OBA	vL	vR	BF/G	Ctl	Dom	Cmd	G	L	F	hr/9	hr/f	H%	S%	GS	APC	DOM%	DIS%	Sv%	LI	RAR	BPV	BPX	R$
08	DET *	3	1	2	56	49	3.53	4.33	1.58	273	237	250	4.7	4.7	7.8	1.7	51	22	27	0.4	0%	34%	77%	0	14			50	0.96	5.5	70	132	$0
09	DET *	4	2	5	49	37	4.25	6.33	1.92	343	333	250	5.2	4.1	6.8	1.7	50	8	42	0.4	20%	41%	77%	0	19			83	0.66	0.4	49	92	-$3
10	TEX *	1	2	2	68	49	2.64	2.32	1.15	198	53	385	4.3	4.1	6.5	1.6	32	12	56	0.4	14%	24%	78%	0	11			50	0.87	12.1	75	121	$5
11	BAL *	2	1	1	37	32	5.74	5.38	1.56	306	104	692	2.8	2.8	7.9	2.8	36	20	43	1.1	16%	37%	64%	0	9			50	1.05	-8.2	68	102	-$5
12	NYY	3	0	0	38	38	2.82	3.63	1.20	215	186	303	2.2	4.0	8.9	2.2	46	23	31	0.5	7%	28%	77%	0	9			0	0.85	5.7	77	100	$1
1st Half		2	0	0	23	20	2.70	4.22	1.11	169	143	238	2.6	5.0	7.7	1.5	45	19	36	0.4	5%	21%	76%	0	10			0	0.75	3.8	26	34	$2
2nd Half		1	0	0	15	18	3.00	2.81	1.33	276	239	417	1.9	2.4	10.8	4.5	47	29	24	0.6	11%	38%	79%	0	7			0	0.96	1.9	155	202	-$1
13	**Proj**	**3**	**1**	**0**	**44**	**41**	**3.68**	**3.76**	**1.36**	**256**	**223**	**368**	**2.6**	**3.5**	**8.4**	**2.4**	**46**	**25**	**29**	**0.6**	**8%**	**32%**	**74%**	**0**						**1.8**	**82**	**106**	**-$1**

Rauch,Jon

Age: 34	Th: R	Role: RP	Health	B	LIMA Plan: B+
Ht: 6' 11"	Wt: 290	Type: xFB	PT/Exp	C	Rand Var: -3
			Consist	A	MM: 2201

Journeyman played occasional backup closer in one of MLB's worst pens, with marginal results. Success vR might suggest continued utility as a specialist, except that success was driven by the fluky h%, esp. in 2H. Hasn't seen a sub-4.00 xERA since he turned 30. If he weren't tall, he'd be awfully generic.

Yr	Tm	W	L	Sv	IP	K	ERA	xERA	WHIP	OBA	vL	vR	BF/G	Ctl	Dom	Cmd	G	L	F	hr/9	hr/f	H%	S%	GS	APC	DOM%	DIS%	Sv%	LI	RAR	BPV	BPX	R$
08	2 NL	4	8	18	72	66	4.14	3.80	1.19	256	268	242	4.0	2.0	8.3	4.1	31	23	45	1.4	12%	30%	70%	0	16			75	1.19	1.6	104	195	$11
09	2 TM	7	3	2	70	49	3.60	4.54	1.33	262	237	282	4.0	3.0	6.3	2.1	36	20	44	0.8	6%	30%	75%	0	15			40	1.02	6.2	48	89	$4
10	MIN	3	1	21	58	46	3.12	4.04	1.30	268	288	248	4.2	2.2	7.2	3.3	38	18	44	0.5	4%	33%	76%	0	16			84	0.96	6.8	86	140	$10
11	TOR	5	4	11	52	36	4.85	4.50	1.35	269	267	272	4.2	2.4	6.2	2.6	35	16	50	1.9	13%	29%	71%	0	17			69	1.32	-5.8	60	90	$2
12	NYM	3	7	4	58	42	3.59	4.13	0.99	209	262	176	3.2	1.9	6.6	3.5	37	18	45	1.1	9%	24%	68%	0	13			50	1.08	3.0	82	108	$4
1st Half		3	7	1	30	20	4.20	4.38	1.17	244	288	209	3.6	1.8	6.0	3.3	37	22	40	0.9	8%	29%	66%	0	15			25	1.03	-0.7	75	98	$3
2nd Half		0	0	3	28	22	2.93	3.87	0.80	167	219	141	2.8	2.0	7.2	3.7	36	13	51	1.3	10%	18%	72%	0	11			75	1.13	3.7	90	117	$6
13	**Proj**	**4**	**6**	**1**	**73**	**54**	**4.03**	**4.17**	**1.17**	**249**	**280**	**225**	**3.4**	**2.1**	**6.7**	**3.2**	**36**	**17**	**47**	**1.2**	**10%**	**28%**	**70%**	**0**						**-0.1**	**77**	**100**	**$3**

Reed,Addison

Age: 24	Th: R	Role: RP	Health	A	LIMA Plan: A
Ht: 6' 4"	Wt: 220	Type: Pwr FB	PT/Exp	D	Rand Var: +2
			Consist	F	MM: 4530

CHW sprayed save opps all over the bullpen in April, until he notched first save on May 5 and seized the job. It wasn't all rainbows and unicorns from there, though: 2H hr/f problems were the culmination of a lot of hard contact against him. Nice Cmd show the makings of a reliable closer, but he's not there yet.

Yr	Tm	W	L	Sv	IP	K	ERA	xERA	WHIP	OBA	vL	vR	BF/G	Ctl	Dom	Cmd	G	L	F	hr/9	hr/f	H%	S%	GS	APC	DOM%	DIS%	Sv%	LI	RAR	BPV	BPX	R$
08																																	
09																																	
10																																	
11	CHW *	0	1	4	49	66	1.70	1.59	0.86	183	313	313	6.1	2.0	12.0	5.8	20	35	45	0.7	11%	27%	85%	0	23			67	0.13	13.6	193	290	$8
12	CHW	3	2	29	55	54	4.75	4.09	1.36	266	293	243	3.8	2.9	8.8	3.0	33	24	43	1.0	9%	34%	67%	0	15			88	1.53	-5.0	91	118	$8
1st Half		1	1	11	28	31	4.18	4.00	1.29	234	231	236	3.9	3.5	10.0	2.8	29	25	47	0.3	3%	33%	66%	0	15			92	1.80	-0.6	90	117	$8
2nd Half		2	1	18	27	23	5.33	4.18	1.44	299	362	250	3.8	2.3	7.7	3.3	37	24	39	1.7	15%	34%	68%	0	15			86	1.27	-4.4	90	117	$9
13	**Proj**	**2**	**2**	**30**	**58**	**62**	**4.03**	**3.46**	**1.17**	**240**	**269**	**215**	**4.3**	**2.5**	**9.7**	**3.9**	**33**	**24**	**42**	**1.0**	**10%**	**31%**	**68%**	**0**						**-0.1**	**118**	**153**	**$14**

RAY MURPHY

Resop,Chris

	Health	A	LIMA Plan	D+	
Age: 30 Th: R Role RP	PT/Exp	C	Rand Var	-1	
Ht: 6' 3" Wt: 225 Type Pwr	Consist	B	MM	2200	

While there were some positive changes to this skill set—improved Ctl, GB% growth—they are dwarfed by the negative impact of the Dom collapse. When your Dom gets cut in half, there's just no sweeping that under the rug. And it got worse month-over-month starting in June, so a recovery seems unlikely.

Yr	Tm	W	L	Sv	IP	K	ERA	xERA	WHIP	OBA	vL	vR	BF/G	Ctl	Dom	Cmd	G	L	F	hr/9	hr/f	H%	S%	GS	APC	DOM%	DIS%	Sv%	LI	RAR	BPV	BPX	R$
08	ATL *	2	1	0	36	31	3.96	4.02	1.56	246	192	268	6.4	5.8	7.6	1.3	51	18	31	0.5	12%	31%	74%	0	21			0	0.42	1.6	64	121	-$2
09																																	
10	2 NL *	6	3	0	107	98	3.07	3.06	1.29	226	281	140	11.0	4.2	8.2	2.0	34	28	38	0.5	5%	29%	77%	0	18			0	0.73	13.4	86	139	$7
11	PIT	5	4	1	70	79	4.39	3.68	1.48	269	255	277	4.1	3.9	10.2	2.6	37	25	38	1.0	11%	36%	73%	0	17			17	1.30	-3.9	94	141	-$1
12	PIT	1	4	1	74	46	3.91	4.66	1.43	276	237	302	5.4	2.9	5.6	1.9	50	15	34	0.7	7%	32%	74%	0	19			50	0.81	1.0	50	65	-$4
1st Half		0	3	1	38	27	3.76	5.29	1.59	275	274	276	6.2	4.0	6.3	1.6	45	12	43	1.2	9%	32%	80%	0	22			100	0.72	1.2	29	38	-$6
2nd Half		1	1	0	35	19	4.08	3.99	1.25	278	192	333	4.7	1.8	4.8	2.7	57	19	24	0.3	4%	31%	65%	0	16			0	0.89	-0.3	73	95	-$1
13	Proj	2	3	0	58	45	4.09	4.31	1.41	266	231	286	5.2	3.5	7.0	2.0	46	20	35	0.8	9%	31%	73%	0						-0.5	55	71	-$2

Reynolds,Matt

	Health	A	LIMA Plan	C+	
Age: 28 Th: L Role RP	PT/Exp	D	Rand Var	+4	
Ht: 6' 5" Wt: 240 Type Pwr	Consist	A	MM	3400	

Skill set is like a diamond that gets top grades for color and clarity, but has a giant crack in the middle. You can't appreciate the beauty of a 3.0 Cmd, or the increase in GBs, because of the glaring problem with HRs. As a RP, IP samples are small, so could still be a fluke. If so... UP: 3.50 ERA.

Yr	Tm	W	L	Sv	IP	K	ERA	xERA	WHIP	OBA	vL	vR	BF/G	Ctl	Dom	Cmd	G	L	F	hr/9	hr/f	H%	S%	GS	APC	DOM%	DIS%	Sv%	LI	RAR	BPV	BPX	R$
08																																	
09	aa	1	2	1	26	22	5.86	5.31	1.51	287			5.3	3.4	7.8	2.3				1.4		33%	64%							-4.9	49	92	-$4
10	COL *	2	3	7	73	67	2.65	3.00	1.18	241	152	179	4.1	2.5	8.3	3.3	41	23	36	0.5	13%	31%	79%	0	13			70	0.94	12.9	110	177	$8
11	COL	1	2	0	51	50	4.09	3.72	1.30	255	292	217	2.9	3.2	8.9	2.8	37	19	45	1.8	16%	29%	77%	0	12			0	1.25	-0.9	88	132	-$1
12	COL	3	1	0	57	51	4.40	3.92	1.43	291	269	311	3.5	2.7	8.0	3.0	43	25	32	1.7	20%	33%	76%	0	14			0	0.67	-2.7	93	121	-$4
1st Half		3	0	0	33	31	3.58	3.62	1.35	280	283	277	4.1	2.5	8.5	3.4	45	24	31	1.7	20%	32%	82%	0	17			0	0.48	1.8	110	143	$0
2nd Half		0	1	0	25	20	5.47	4.34	1.54	306	250	352	3.0	2.9	7.3	2.5	41	26	33	1.8	20%	34%	70%	0	11			0	0.84	-4.4	71	92	-$9
13	Proj	2	2	0	55	50	4.20	3.91	1.36	270	266	274	3.2	2.9	8.2	2.9	40	23	37	1.6	16%	31%	75%	0						-1.2	89	116	-$2

Richard,Clayton

	Health	C	LIMA Plan	C+	
Age: 29 Th: L Role SP	PT/Exp	A	Rand Var	+1	
Ht: 6' 5" Wt: 245 Type Con GB	Consist	A	MM	2005	

Entire career: 4.12 ERA in 721 IP. Career at PETCO Park: 2.82 ERA in 284 IP. When the workers show up to move the fences in this winter, they may discover that this guy has shackled himself to the fence somewhere around left-center field. And who could blame him? His non-PETCO career ERA is 5.05.

Yr	Tm	W	L	Sv	IP	K	ERA	xERA	WHIP	OBA	vL	vR	BF/G	Ctl	Dom	Cmd	G	L	F	hr/9	hr/f	H%	S%	GS	APC	DOM%	DIS%	Sv%	LI	RAR	BPV	BPX	R$
08	CHW *	14	11	0	175	99	4.21	3.84	1.27	275	274	320	21.8	1.8	5.1	2.8	50	23	27	0.6	11%	31%	67%	8	60	38%	63%	0	0.54	2.5	69	130	$9
09	2 TM	9	5	0	153	114	4.41	4.44	1.47	267	229	279	17.4	4.2	6.7	1.6	48	18	34	1.0	11%	30%	72%	26	69	31%	38%	0	0.74	-1.7	34	64	$2
10	SD	14	9	0	202	153	3.75	4.11	1.41	267	228	281	26.1	3.5	6.8	2.0	46	20	34	0.7	8%	31%	75%	33	97	52%	15%			8.2	53	86	$7
11	SD	5	9	0	100	53	3.88	4.49	1.42	272	261	276	23.7	3.4	4.8	1.4	50	18	32	0.7	8%	30%	74%	18	91	22%	33%			0.7	21	32	-$1
12	SD	14	14	0	219	107	3.99	4.17	1.23	267	241	275	27.6	1.7	4.4	2.5	54	18	28	1.3	15%	28%	72%	33	96	42%	15%			0.6	65	84	$8
1st Half		5	8	0	105	63	3.77	4.06	1.22	250	192	269	27.5	2.3	5.4	2.3	54	19	26	1.1	14%	27%	73%	16	97	56%	13%			3.2	67	87	$9
2nd Half		9	6	0	114	44	4.20	4.28	1.25	283	290	281	27.6	1.2	3.5	2.9	53	18	29	1.4	15%	28%	72%	17	95	29%	18%			-2.5	62	81	$7
13	Proj	12	15	0	210	115	4.32	4.36	1.35	275	253	282	25.0	2.5	4.9	2.0	51	19	30	1.0	11%	30%	70%	35						-7.9	51	66	$4

Richards,Garrett

	Health	A	LIMA Plan	D	
Age: 25 Th: R Role SP	PT/Exp	D	Rand Var	0	
Ht: 6' 3" Wt: 215 Type	Consist	B	MM	1103	

4-3, 4.69 ERA in 71 IP at LAA. Well-regarded prospect K'd over a batter per IP back in 2010 in A-ball, but failed to bring that skill to the high minors or to LAA. Without it, lefties are smashing him. But if he finds that Dom, he could develop quickly. Watch... from a safe distance.

Yr	Tm	W	L	Sv	IP	K	ERA	xERA	WHIP	OBA	vL	vR	BF/G	Ctl	Dom	Cmd	G	L	F	hr/9	hr/f	H%	S%	GS	APC	DOM%	DIS%	Sv%	LI	RAR	BPV	BPX	R$
08																																	
09																																	
10																																	
11	LAA *	12	4	0	157	96	3.94	3.89	1.30	262	367	200	22.3	2.7	5.5	2.1	43	28	28	0.8	31%	29%	71%	3	36	0%	67%	0	0.64	0.1	54	81	$5
12	LAA *	11	6	1	148	101	4.31	4.77	1.57	285	321	239	14.8	4.0	6.1	1.5	45	22	33	0.7	9%	33%	73%	9	40	22%	22%	33	0.95	-5.5	47	61	-$5
1st Half		7	3	0	88	65	3.61	4.47	1.55	274	276	233	24.1	4.4	6.6	1.5	41	23	35	0.6	6%	32%	78%	5	89	40%	20%	0	0.69	4.4	53	69	$1
2nd Half		4	3	1	60	36	5.35	5.14	1.59	302	377	242	9.4	3.4	5.4	1.6	48	20	31	0.8	12%	34%	66%	4	27	0%	25%	33	1.01	-9.8	39	51	-$14
13	Proj	10	8	0	160	102	4.49	4.62	1.46	280	324	238	24.2	3.3	5.8	1.7	46	22	33	0.8	8%	32%	70%	28						-9.3	37	48	-$1

Rivera,Mariano

	Health	F	LIMA Plan	B	
Age: 43 Th: R Role RP	PT/Exp	B	Rand Var	-4	
Ht: 6' 2" Wt: 195 Type Pwr GB	Consist	B	MM	4330	

Torn knee ligament in May ended his season, and maybe his 15-year run as the game's greatest closer. If he decides to come back, recovery from major knee surgery in his mid-40s is far from automatic. Then again, after all these years, we're still not sure he isn't a cyborg. So don't count him out.

Yr	Tm	W	L	Sv	IP	K	ERA	xERA	WHIP	OBA	vL	vR	BF/G	Ctl	Dom	Cmd	G	L	F	hr/9	hr/f	H%	S%	GS	APC	DOM%	DIS%	Sv%	LI	RAR	BPV	BPX	R$
08	NYY	6	5	39	71	77	1.40	2.32	0.67	165	147	183	4.0	0.8	9.8	12.8	55	15	31	0.5	8%	23%	84%	0	15			98	1.49	25.5	189	354	$32
09	NYY	3	3	44	66	72	1.76	2.62	0.90	197	182	211	3.9	1.6	9.8	6.0	51	22	27	0.9	15%	26%	89%	0	16			96	1.35	20.9	161	301	$29
10	NYY	3	3	33	60	45	1.80	3.19	0.83	183	214	155	3.8	1.7	6.8	4.1	51	15	33	0.3	4%	23%	79%	0	15			87	1.40	16.9	106	171	$22
11	NYY	1	2	44	61	60	1.91	2.71	0.90	215	240	191	3.6	1.2	8.8	7.5	47	20	33	0.4	6%	28%	81%	0	14			90	1.44	15.4	152	228	$25
12	NYY	1	1	5	8	8	2.16	3.34	0.96	200	154	235	3.6	2.2	8.6	4.0	45	14	41	0.0	0%	28%	75%	0	14			83	1.48	1.9	120	157	-$1
1st Half		1	1	5	8	8	2.16	3.34	0.96	200	154	235	3.6	2.2	8.6	4.0	45	14	41	0.0	0%	28%	75%	0	14			83	1.48	1.9	121	158	-$1
2nd Half																																	
13	Proj	2	2	28	48	42	2.88	3.38	1.12	235	241	229	3.9	2.3	7.9	3.4	50	19	31	0.6	8%	29%	76%	0						6.7	109	142	$14

Robertson,David

	Health	B	LIMA Plan	A+	
Age: 28 Th: R Role RP	PT/Exp	C	Rand Var	0	
Ht: 5' 11" Wt: 195 Type Pwr	Consist	B	MM	5520	

Another season of sterling skills, marred by one bad week: after Rivera got hurt in May, he blew his first save opp and then ended up on DL with an oblique strain, which opened the door for Soriano to seize the closer role. Don't buy the "he can't handle the 9th" narrative. If the door opens again... UP: 35 Sv.

Yr	Tm	W	L	Sv	IP	K	ERA	xERA	WHIP	OBA	vL	vR	BF/G	Ctl	Dom	Cmd	G	L	F	hr/9	hr/f	H%	S%	GS	APC	DOM%	DIS%	Sv%	LI	RAR	BPV	BPX	R$
08	NYY *	8	0	3	84	101	3.37	2.63	1.22	210	259	254	6.2	4.2	10.8	2.6	43	16	41	0.5	9%	30%	72%	0	23			75	0.64	9.9	118	222	$10
09	NYY	2	1	1	44	63	3.30	3.35	1.35	216	189	237	4.2	4.7	13.0	2.7	36	23	41	0.8	9%	35%	78%	0	19			100	0.67	5.5	120	224	$1
10	NYY	4	5	1	61	71	3.82	3.78	1.50	258	268	250	4.3	4.8	10.4	2.2	40	25	36	0.7	9%	35%	76%	0	18			33	1.12	2.0	75	121	$0
11	NYY	4	0	1	67	100	1.08	2.62	1.13	170	156	186	3.9	4.7	13.5	2.9	46	22	32	0.1	2%	31%	91%	0	17			25	1.38	23.5	139	210	$11
12	NYY	2	7	2	61	81	2.67	2.84	1.17	229	208	252	3.8	2.8	12.0	4.3	45	20	35	0.7	10%	34%	80%	0	15			40	1.15	10.1	163	213	$5
1st Half		0	2	1	21	35	2.57	2.48	1.14	208	200	216	3.9	3.4	15.0	4.4	42	16	42	0.9	11%	37%	82%	0	17			33	1.12	3.7	197	256	$0
2nd Half		2	5	1	40	46	2.72	3.06	1.18	240	213	271	3.8	2.5	10.4	4.2	46	21	33	0.7	9%	33%	80%	0	14			50	1.16	6.3	145	189	$7
13	Proj	3	4	11	58	79	2.50	2.95	1.22	220	205	236	3.9	3.8	12.3	3.2	44	21	36	0.6	8%	33%	81%	0						10.8	140	182	$9

Rodney,Fernando

	Health	B	LIMA Plan	D+	
Age: 36 Th: R Role RP	PT/Exp	B	Rand Var	-5	
Ht: 5' 11" Wt: 220 Type Pwr xGB	Consist	D	MM	4430	

Look at 2008-11 BPV column, and guess the next number in that series. Did you guess "152"? Didn't think so. To post a sub-1.00 ERA, you need to be both lucky and good: he got luck on h%, s%, hr/f, plus awesome BPV. Regression a given, but he can regress a long way and still close effectively.

Yr	Tm	W	L	Sv	IP	K	ERA	xERA	WHIP	OBA	vL	vR	BF/G	Ctl	Dom	Cmd	G	L	F	hr/9	hr/f	H%	S%	GS	APC	DOM%	DIS%	Sv%	LI	RAR	BPV	BPX	R$
08	DET	0	6	13	40	49	4.91	4.35	1.59	224	256	186	4.9	6.7	10.9	1.6	40	26	33	0.7	9%	32%	69%	0	20			68	1.40	-2.9	34	64	$2
09	DET	2	5	37	76	61	4.40	4.27	1.47	249	269	223	4.5	4.9	7.3	1.5	58	11	31	1.0	12%	29%	72%	0	19			97	1.08	-0.7	35	65	$14
10	LAA	4	3	14	68	53	4.24	4.37	1.54	263	273	254	4.3	4.6	7.0	1.5	50	20	30	0.5	6%	32%	72%	0	18			67	1.10	-1.3	29	47	$3
11	LAA	3	5	3	32	26	4.50	5.00	1.69	224	273	180	3.8	7.9	7.3	0.9	58	19	22	0.3	5%	28%	72%	0	16			43	1.69	-2.2	-45	-68	-$3
12	TAM	2	2	48	75	76	0.60	2.60	0.78	167	166	168	3.7	1.8	9.2	5.1	58	17	25	0.2	4%	23%	95%	0	15			96	1.24	31.4	152	198	$37
1st Half		2	1	22	35	35	1.04	2.67	0.75	172	164	182	3.6	1.3	9.1	7.0	49	23	28	0.3	4%	24%	88%	0	14			96	1.16	12.7	156	203	$35
2nd Half		0	1	26	40	41	0.23	2.53	0.80	162	167	155	3.8	2.3	9.2	4.1	66	13	22	0.2	5%	23%	100%	0	15			96	1.31	18.7	149	194	$38
13	Proj	3	4	38	58	54	2.81	3.30	1.11	206	219	191	3.7	3.4	8.4	2.5	57	18	25	0.4	6%	27%	74%	0						8.6	94	122	$20

RAY MURPHY

Rodriguez,Fernando

Age: 29	Th: R	Role RP	Health	A	LIMA Plan D+
			PT/Exp	D	Rand Var +3
Ht: 6' 3"	Wt: 235	Type Pwr FB	Consist	D	MM 2400

Amidst the wreckage that is the outward numbers, there are building blocks here: held on to 2011 Dom spike, and staked a claim at a tolerable Cmd. Then he really put it all together in 2H, with an eye-catching skill combination. FB% is a wart that might linger, but there's something brewing here.

Yr	Tm	W	L	Sv	IP	K	ERA	xERA	WHIP	OBA	vL	vR	BF/G	Ctl	Dom	Cmd	G	L	F	hr/9	hr/f	H%	S%	GS	APC	DOM%	DIS%	Sv%	LI	RAR	BPV	BPX	R$
08	aa	7	11	0	137	70	6.89	5.85	1.78	320			19.1	4.1	4.6	1.1				0.7		35%	60%							-43.2	21	40	-$17
09	LAA *	4	2	4	80	62	5.50	4.47	1.58	257	500	0	7.0	5.5	6.9	1.3	33	0	67	0.8	50%	30%	65%	0	34			80	0.09	-11.7	49	91	-$4
10	aaa	4	6	0	97	66	6.15	7.05	1.92	350			14.9	3.6	6.1	1.7				1.0		40%	69%							-24.8	26	42	-$14
11	HOU *	4	6	2	76	83	3.25	4.13	1.45	245	225	287	5.2	4.9	9.8	2.0	35	22	43	1.0	11%	32%	81%	0	20			100	0.97	6.5	78	118	$2
12	HOU	2	10	0	70	78	5.37	4.22	1.45	252	226	266	4.4	4.4	10.0	2.3	35	18	46	1.3	11%	33%	65%	0	18			0	1.28	-11.8	75	98	-$7
1st Half		1	7	0	29	29	6.28	4.82	1.47	236	243	233	4.0	5.0	9.1	1.8	30	21	49	1.6	13%	29%	59%	0	17			0	1.48	-8.0	37	48	-$10
2nd Half		1	3	0	42	49	4.75	3.83	1.44	263	214	288	4.6	3.9	10.6	2.7	39	16	45	1.1	10%	35%	69%	0	19			0	1.12	-3.8	103	134	-$4
13	Proj	**2**	**6**	**0**	**58**	**58**	**4.58**	**4.39**	**1.46**	**256**	**225**	**273**	**5.3**	**4.4**	**8.9**	**2.0**	**35**	**20**	**45**	**1.1**	**10%**	**32%**	**71%**	**0**						**-4.0**	**56**	**72**	**-$3**

Rodriguez,Francisco

Age: 31	Th: R	Role RP	Health	B	LIMA Plan C+
			PT/Exp	B	Rand Var +1
Ht: 6' 0"	Wt: 195	Type Pwr	Consist	A	MM 3510

More BBs and HRs, fewer GBs... and the 2010-11 rediscovery of closer-worthy skills ended, right as the MIL closer gig was sitting there for the taking. Still young enough to polish up the skill set again, and maybe even find a path to saves. Latest round of legal trouble could pose another obstacle, though.

Yr	Tm	W	L	Sv	IP	K	ERA	xERA	WHIP	OBA	vL	vR	BF/G	Ctl	Dom	Cmd	G	L	F	hr/9	hr/f	H%	S%	GS	APC	DOM%	DIS%	Sv%	LI	RAR	BPV	BPX	R$
08	LAA	2	3	62	68	77	2.24	3.69	1.29	216	227	205	3.8	4.5	10.1	2.3	42	20	38	0.5	6%	30%	85%	0	15			90	1.49	17.6	82	153	$31
09	NYM	3	6	35	68	73	3.71	4.27	1.31	203	185	223	4.2	5.0	9.7	1.9	35	19	46	0.9	9%	27%	74%	0	18			83	1.01	5.2	51	96	$17
10	NYM	4	2	25	57	67	2.20	3.20	1.15	213	245	188	4.5	3.3	10.5	3.2	42	19	39	0.5	5%	31%	83%	0	18			83	1.22	13.3	120	195	$16
11	2 NL	6	2	23	72	79	2.64	3.19	1.30	243	282	192	4.2	3.3	9.9	3.0	52	17	31	0.5	6%	34%	81%	0	16			79	1.37	11.5	120	181	$14
12	MIL	2	7	3	72	72	4.38	3.89	1.33	241	224	260	3.9	3.9	9.0	2.3	42	26	33	1.0	12%	30%	69%	0	16			30	1.15	-3.2	77	101	-$1
1st Half		0	4	1	34	32	3.97	3.80	1.41	273	225	328	3.9	3.2	8.5	2.7	43	27	29	0.8	10%	34%	73%	0	16			33	1.30	0.2	88	115	-$4
2nd Half		2	3	2	38	40	4.74	3.97	1.26	210	224	194	3.9	4.5	9.5	2.1	40	24	36	1.2	14%	26%	65%	0	15			29	1.00	-3.4	67	87	$1
13	Proj	**3**	**4**	**5**	**65**	**69**	**3.78**	**3.62**	**1.29**	**236**	**245**	**225**	**3.9**	**3.8**	**9.6**	**2.5**	**44**	**22**	**35**	**0.8**	**10%**	**31%**	**72%**	**0**						**1.9**	**93**	**120**	**$4**

Rodriguez,Henry

Age: 26	Th: R	Role RP	Health	D	LIMA Plan D
			PT/Exp	D	Rand Var +2
Ht: 6' 1"	Wt: 225	Type Pwr FB	Consist	C	MM 2500

Big Dom earned him some early-season save opps, before season was eventually scuttled by finger, back, and elbow injuries. Should be healthy for spring training, when he'll once again try to marry that big Dom with even marginal Ctl. If he does, he gets interesting in a hurry. Just don't hold your breath.

Yr	Tm	W	L	Sv	IP	K	ERA	xERA	WHIP	OBA	vL	vR	BF/G	Ctl	Dom	Cmd	G	L	F	hr/9	hr/f	H%	S%	GS	APC	DOM%	DIS%	Sv%	LI	RAR	BPV	BPX	R$
08	aa	2	7	0	41	36	7.49	6.44	2.25	313			14.8	8.7	7.9	0.9				0.2		39%	64%							-16.0	53	100	-$11
09	OAK *	2	1	4	48	64	5.89	4.68	1.75	251	429	100	5.4	7.2	12.1	1.7	54	15	31	0.7	0%	37%	65%	0	25			57	0.09	-9.2	91	171	-$4
10	OAK *	1	2	11	49	59	3.29	2.43	1.15	204	283	207	4.0	3.9	10.9	2.8	39	17	44	0.5	6%	29%	72%	0	18			79	0.44	4.8	124	200	$6
11	WAS	3	3	2	66	70	3.56	4.19	1.51	220	238	206	5.0	6.2	9.6	1.6	45	23	31	0.1	2%	32%	74%	0	21			40	0.73	3.1	29	44	$0
12	WAS	1	3	9	29	31	5.83	4.94	1.40	181	208	158	3.7	6.8	9.5	1.4	37	19	44	1.2	12%	22%	59%	0	16			75	1.05	-6.6	4	5	-$2
1st Half		1	3	9	21	23	5.14	4.59	1.29	176	200	154	3.8	6.0	9.9	1.6	35	19	46	1.3	13%	22%	63%	0	16			75	1.40	-2.9	28	36	$1
2nd Half		0	0	0	8	8	7.56	5.93	1.68	194	231	167	3.6	8.6	8.6	1.0	43	17	39	1.1	11%	24%	54%	0	16			0	0.29	-3.6	-56	-73	-$9
13	Proj	**1**	**3**	**0**	**36**	**41**	**4.71**	**4.30**	**1.46**	**221**	**245**	**201**	**4.6**	**5.9**	**10.2**	**1.7**	**39**	**21**	**40**	**0.7**	**8%**	**30%**	**68%**	**0**						**-3.1**	**40**	**52**	**-$3**

Rodriguez,Wandy

Age: 34	Th: L	Role SP	Health	B	LIMA Plan B
			PT/Exp	A	Rand Var 0
Ht: 5' 10"	Wt: 195	Type	Consist	A	MM 3305

Skills are largely stable, but four-year trend of Dom decline is getting disconcerting, with the effects seen in BPV trend. Did a reasonable job of compensating with better Ctl, but that's a more tenuous path to success. Expect some Dom recovery, but the luster on one of our favorites is starting to fade.

Yr	Tm	W	L	Sv	IP	K	ERA	xERA	WHIP	OBA	vL	vR	BF/G	Ctl	Dom	Cmd	G	L	F	hr/9	hr/f	H%	S%	GS	APC	DOM%	DIS%	Sv%	LI	RAR	BPV	BPX	R$
08	HOU	9	7	0	137	131	3.54	3.78	1.31	256	282	248	23.5	2.9	8.6	3.0	40	23	36	0.9	10%	32%	76%	25	91	44%	32%			13.3	95	178	$10
09	HOU	14	12	0	206	193	3.02	3.59	1.24	250	192	264	25.7	2.8	8.4	3.1	45	18	37	0.9	10%	31%	79%	33	102	67%	18%			33.0	101	188	$23
10	HOU	11	12	0	195	178	3.60	3.56	1.29	250	247	250	25.7	3.1	8.2	2.6	48	20	32	0.7	9%	31%	74%	32	100	66%	16%			11.5	89	144	$12
11	HOU	11	11	0	191	166	3.49	3.76	1.31	251	233	256	26.9	3.3	7.8	2.4	45	20	35	1.2	13%	30%	78%	30	105	57%	7%			10.7	76	114	$10
12	2 NL	12	13	0	206	139	3.76	4.19	1.27	255	255	255	25.7	2.5	6.1	2.5	48	20	32	0.9	10%	29%	73%	33	94	52%	15%	0	0.83	6.4	69	90	$9
1st Half		6	5	0	102	67	3.52	4.07	1.26	267	258	269	27.1	1.9	5.9	3.0	49	19	32	1.1	12%	30%	76%	16	97	50%	6%			6.3	81	105	$11
2nd Half		6	8	0	103	72	4.01	4.31	1.28	243	250	241	24.6	3.0	6.3	2.1	47	22	32	0.8	9%	29%	70%	17	92	53%	24%	0	0.87	0.1	58	76	$7
13	Proj	**11**	**12**	**0**	**189**	**149**	**3.88**	**3.95**	**1.28**	**256**	**250**	**257**	**24.9**	**2.8**	**7.1**	**2.5**	**47**	**20**	**33**	**0.9**	**11%**	**30%**	**72%**	**31**						**3.1**	**76**	**98**	**$10**

Roenicke,Josh

Age: 30	Th: R	Role RP	Health	A	LIMA Plan D
			PT/Exp	D	Rand Var -3
Ht: 6' 3"	Wt: 200	Type	Consist	A	MM 1101

Generates ground balls, but spent his 20s trying to cobble together a workable skill set around that one attribute, without success. Ctl was never a strength, once-promising Dom is now just a memory. xERA is very consistent, and makes a clear statement about his chances of repeating 2012 ERA. Avoid.

Yr	Tm	W	L	Sv	IP	K	ERA	xERA	WHIP	OBA	vL	vR	BF/G	Ctl	Dom	Cmd	G	L	F	hr/9	hr/f	H%	S%	GS	APC	DOM%	DIS%	Sv%	LI	RAR	BPV	BPX	R$
08	CIN *	6	2	13	64	63	3.91	5.07	1.64	291	600	300	4.6	4.3	8.9	2.0	22	44	33	0.8	0%	37%	77%	0	12			76	1.04	3.3	70	131	$5
09	2 TM *	1	0	12	59	58	4.48	4.65	1.60	300	351	190	5.1	3.5	8.9	2.5	49	22	30	0.3	8%	39%	70%	0	23			80	0.46	-1.2	93	173	$1
10	TOR *	10	1	1	78	60	3.96	4.64	1.53	274	219	250	6.6	4.2	6.9	1.6	51	14	35	0.8	5%	32%	76%	0	22			33	0.48	1.1	51	83	$1
11	COL *	1	4	0	70	41	4.32	4.63	1.48	276	158	268	5.2	3.6	5.3	1.5	45	19	36	0.9	6%	30%	72%	0	15			0	0.80	-3.3	35	53	-$4
12	COL	4	2	1	89	54	3.25	4.78	1.44	259	231	278	6.1	4.4	5.5	1.3	50	22	28	0.9	12%	28%	81%	0	23			33	0.70	8.4	9	11	$0
1st Half		3	0	0	47	32	2.66	4.64	1.48	253	274	237	5.9	5.1	6.1	1.2	52	24	24	0.6	9%	28%	84%	0	23			0	0.53	7.9	1	1	$2
2nd Half		1	2	1	41	22	3.92	4.93	1.40	266	175	317	6.2	3.5	4.8	1.4	48	19	32	1.3	13%	28%	77%	0	23			33	0.90	0.5	18	23	-$3
13	Proj	**3**	**2**	**0**	**73**	**48**	**4.40**	**4.62**	**1.48**	**268**	**285**	**256**	**5.7**	**4.0**	**5.9**	**1.5**	**49**	**21**	**29**	**0.9**	**11%**	**30%**	**72%**	**0**						**-3.4**	**25**	**33**	**-$3**

Rogers,Esmil

Age: 27	Th: R	Role RP	Health	C	LIMA Plan C+
			PT/Exp	D	Rand Var +4
Ht: 6' 1"	Wt: 190	Type Pwr	Consist	F	MM 3400

Continued to get hit hard early on, 2011-style. Then escaped COL for CLE, and suddenly developed control: 12 BB/54 K in 53 IP. Would want to see him do it again before jumping in with both feet, but if he now owns that 2H skill set, then he's a legitimate bullpen weapon.

Yr	Tm	W	L	Sv	IP	K	ERA	xERA	WHIP	OBA	vL	vR	BF/G	Ctl	Dom	Cmd	G	L	F	hr/9	hr/f	H%	S%	GS	APC	DOM%	DIS%	Sv%	LI	RAR	BPV	BPX	R$
08																																	
09	COL *	11	7	0	159	104	5.49	5.15	1.59	304	250	200	25.0	3.2	5.9	1.8	55	27	18	0.7	0%	35%	65%	1	80	0%	100%			-22.9	45	85	-$6
10	COL *	5	6	0	133	106	6.14	5.08	1.55	303	370	278	14.5	3.0	7.2	2.4	52	21	27	0.8	8%	36%	59%	8	45	13%	50%	0	0.85	-33.9	65	105	-$11
11	COL *	7	9	0	110	76	6.80	7.13	1.90	334	318	321	21.6	4.3	6.2	1.4	42	22	35	1.5	14%	37%	66%	13	84	46%	38%	0	0.63	-38.8	10	15	-$20
12	2 TM	3	3	0	79	83	4.69	3.66	1.44	269	248	288	5.2	3.4	9.5	2.8	47	23	30	0.8	10%	35%	68%	0	22			0	0.77	-6.6	103	135	-$4
1st Half		0	2	0	36	43	6.25	3.94	1.67	279	219	325	5.5	4.8	10.8	2.3	44	25	31	1.0	13%	39%	63%	0	24			0	0.73	-9.9	87	113	-$13
2nd Half		3	1	0	43	40	3.38	3.43	1.24	259	271	247	4.9	2.3	8.4	3.6	50	21	29	0.6	8%	33%	74%	0	20			0	0.82	3.4	117	152	$3
13	Proj	**3**	**3**	**0**	**69**	**62**	**3.99**	**3.88**	**1.43**	**275**	**272**	**277**	**7.8**	**3.2**	**8.2**	**2.5**	**46**	**22**	**31**	**0.8**	**10%**	**34%**	**74%**	**0**						**0.2**	**84**	**109**	**-$1**

Rogers,Mark

Age: 27	Th: R	Role SP	Health	A	LIMA Plan C+
			PT/Exp	D	Rand Var 0
Ht: 6' 2"	Wt: 226	Type Pwr FB	Consist	F	MM 1301

3-1, 3.92 ERA in 39 IP at MIL. Spent first half getting knocked around in Triple-A (shaking 2011 rust?), came to MIL in late July and had a very nice 7-start run (2.9 Cmd, 101 BPV). Injury history, multiple drug suspensions all speak to the risk here, but now we're starting to see upside too. Speculate.

Yr	Tm	W	L	Sv	IP	K	ERA	xERA	WHIP	OBA	vL	vR	BF/G	Ctl	Dom	Cmd	G	L	F	hr/9	hr/f	H%	S%	GS	APC	DOM%	DIS%	Sv%	LI	RAR	BPV	BPX	R$
08																																	
09																																	
10	MIL *	6	8	0	126	109	3.89	3.07	1.41	223	0	91	18.4	5.4	7.8	1.4	50	20	30	0.2	0%	29%	71%	2	37	50%	50%	0	0.46	2.9	81	131	$2
11	aaa	0	2	0	15	10	13.76	9.28	2.96	352			17.3	12.9	6.0	0.5				0.6		40%	50%							-18.2	12	19	-$12
12	MIL *	9	7	0	134	102	5.44	5.53	1.61	282	253	232	23.8	4.5	6.8	1.5	40	22	39	1.4	12%	32%	69%	7	96	57%	0%			-23.6	28	37	-$13
1st Half		3	5	0	71	41	7.29	7.55	1.94	322	0	0	24.3	5.4	5.2	1.0				2.0	0%	33%	66%	0	0					-28.8	-20	-26	-$29
2nd Half		6	2	0	63	61	3.35	3.18	1.24	230	253	232	23.3	3.6	8.7	2.4	40	22	39	0.7	12%	29%	75%	7	96	57%	0%			5.2	91	118	$6
13	Proj	**7**	**6**	**0**	**116**	**96**	**4.01**	**4.53**	**1.40**	**253**	**263**	**241**	**20.9**	**4.0**	**7.5**	**1.9**	**40**	**22**	**39**	**1.0**	**9%**	**30%**	**74%**	**23**						**0.1**	**44**	**57**	**$2**

RAY MURPHY

Romero,Ricky

Age: 28	Th: L	Role SP	Health A	LIMA Plan D	
Ht: 6' 0"	Wt: 220	Type Pwr GB	PT/Exp A	Rand Var +2	
			Consist B	MM 1203	

An across-the-board debacle of a season, with collapse fueled more by loss of skill than poor fortune, and amid allegedly good health. Only positive sign is that his GB% held up amid the carnage, so approach is intact. Expect a moderate rebound, but a full sub-4.00 recovery seems like a reach.

Yr	Tm	W	L	Sv	IP	K	ERA	xERA	WHIP	OBA	vL	vR	BF/G	Ctl	Dom	Cmd	G	L	F	hr/9	hr/f	H%	S%	GS	APC	DOM%	DIS%	Sv%	LI	RAR	BPV	BPX	R$
08	a/a	8	8	0	164	101	5.78	5.97	1.79	318			27.1	4.3	5.5	1.3				0.8		36%	68%							-29.4	27	51	-$14
09	TOR	13	9	0	178	141	4.30	4.02	1.52	284	297	278	26.6	4.0	7.1	1.8	54	19	27	0.9	13%	33%	74%	29	103	38%	21%			0.5	52	98	$3
10	TOR	14	9	0	210	174	3.73	3.60	1.29	242	276	231	27.6	3.5	7.5	2.1	55	18	27	0.6	9%	29%	72%	32	101	53%	9%			9.1	72	117	$12
11	TOR	15	11	0	225	178	2.92	3.54	1.14	216	269	194	28.7	3.2	7.1	2.2	55	14	31	1.0	13%	25%	80%	32	105	56%	9%			28.4	75	112	$23
12	TOR	9	14	0	181	124	5.77	4.97	1.67	282	310	268	25.9	5.2	6.2	1.2	53	20	26	1.0	14%	31%	66%	32	96	41%	25%			-39.1	1	1	-$22
1st Half		8	2	0	98	70	4.94	4.54	1.43	241	269	230	26.9	4.8	6.4	1.3	55	19	26	1.2	17%	27%	68%	16	101	50%	19%			-11.2	20	26	-$7
2nd Half		1	12	0	83	54	6.75	5.51	1.96	326	347	315	24.9	5.8	5.9	1.0	52	21	27	0.9	11%	36%	65%	16	92	31%	31%			-27.9	-20	-26	-$40
13	**Proj**	**10**	**11**	**0**	**174**	**127**	**4.55**	**4.48**	**1.52**	**267**	**302**	**251**	**26.2**	**4.4**	**6.6**	**1.5**	**54**	**18**	**28**	**0.9**	**12%**	**31%**	**72%**	**29**						**-11.4**	**31**	**40**	**-$2**

Romo,Sergio

Age: 30	Th: R	Role RP	Health B	LIMA Plan B	
Ht: 5' 10"	Wt: 185	Type Pwr	PT/Exp C	Rand Var -5	
			Consist B	MM 5530	

Still owns elite Cmd even after it got cut in half, and he's equally unhittable to lefties and righties. xERA tempers expectations for a repeat, but even a partial repeat has value at this level. In a pen full of question marks, has now demonstrated he can close, so all he needs is the role for... UP: 40 Sv.

Yr	Tm	W	L	Sv	IP	K	ERA	xERA	WHIP	OBA	vL	vR	BF/G	Ctl	Dom	Cmd	G	L	F	hr/9	hr/f	H%	S%	GS	APC	DOM%	DIS%	Sv%	LI	RAR	BPV	BPX	R$
08	SF *	4	4	11	67	62	3.06	1.84	0.94	195	83	176	4.5	2.3	8.4	3.6	33	14	53	0.5	7%	25%	68%	0	17			92	1.04	10.4	126	237	$12
09	SF	5	2	2	34	41	3.97	3.57	1.21	233	188	259	3.2	2.9	10.9	3.7	32	15	53	0.3	2%	35%	65%	0	13			100	1.20	1.5	127	237	$2
10	SF	5	3	0	62	70	2.18	3.16	0.97	204	241	185	3.6	2.0	10.2	5.0	35	14	51	0.9	8%	28%	83%	0	13			0	1.28	14.5	141	228	$9
11	SF	3	1	1	48	70	1.50	2.01	0.71	173	229	150	2.7	0.9	13.1	14.0	34	24	42	0.4	5%	29%	81%	0	10			50	1.39	14.5	223	335	$10
12	SF	4	2	14	55	63	1.79	2.65	0.85	185	167	192	3.1	1.6	10.2	6.3	49	21	30	0.8	12%	26%	86%	0	12			93	1.43	15.2	168	219	$15
1st Half		2	1	4	22	29	0.83	2.30	0.74	135	167	125	2.9	2.5	12.0	4.8	52	20	27	0.4	8%	22%	93%	0	11			100	1.75	8.5	180	234	$13
2nd Half		2	1	10	34	34	2.41	2.87	0.92	214	167	233	3.2	1.1	9.1	8.5	47	22	32	1.1	14%	27%	81%	0	12			91	1.22	6.7	159	207	$17
13	**Proj**	**4**	**2**	**25**	**58**	**70**	**2.25**	**2.59**	**0.85**	**193**	**199**	**190**	**3.0**	**1.6**	**10.9**	**6.7**	**41**	**20**	**38**	**0.7**	**8%**	**27%**	**77%**	**0**						**12.6**	**172**	**223**	**$19**

Rosenthal,Trevor

Age: 23	Th: R	Role SP	Health A	LIMA Plan A	
Ht: 6' 2"	Wt: 190	Type Pwr GB	PT/Exp F	Rand Var 0	
			Consist F	MM 3401	

0-2, 2.78 ERA in 22 IP at STL. Groomed to be a starter, he is taking the relief apprenticeship path to the job, with excellent results. 2H xERA and BPV show off his high ceiling. Super late-season relief work might trap him in the pen for another year. Or, this might be last chance to buy before value spikes.

Yr	Tm	W	L	Sv	IP	K	ERA	xERA	WHIP	OBA	vL	vR	BF/G	Ctl	Dom	Cmd	G	L	F	hr/9	hr/f	H%	S%	GS	APC	DOM%	DIS%	Sv%	LI	RAR	BPV	BPX	R$
08																																	
09																																	
10																																	
11																																	
12	STL *	8	8	0	132	114	3.03	2.38	1.09	206	143	200	13.2	3.2	7.8	2.4	54	13	33	0.5	11%	26%	73%	0	19			0	0.63	16.0	95	123	$14
1st Half		6	6	0	82	61	3.00	2.49	1.17	214	0	0	21.8	3.6	6.7	1.8				0.4	0%	26%	74%	0	0					10.3	80	104	$17
2nd Half		2	2	0	50	53	3.15	2.21	0.98	196	143	200	7.9	2.7	9.6	3.6	54	13	33	0.8	11%	25%	71%	0	19			0	0.63	5.3	125	163	$9
13	**Proj**	**5**	**5**	**0**	**102**	**95**	**3.92**	**3.66**	**1.16**	**225**	**183**	**257**	**27.2**	**3.1**	**8.4**	**2.7**	**49**	**14**	**37**	**0.7**	**7%**	**28%**	**67%**	**15**						**1.2**	**96**	**125**	**$6**

Ross,Robbie

Age: 24	Th: L	Role RP	Health A	LIMA Plan B+	
Ht: 5' 11"	Wt: 185	Type xGB	PT/Exp D	Rand Var -4	
			Consist A	MM 4300	

Prospect with nice skills who debuted in relief, but expected to return to SP role. Had very odd burst of Ctl problems July 30-August 15 (11 BB, 7 K in 5.1 IP), then rest of year 1 BB/10 K in 9 IP. Need to see more, but nice end-gamer in any role, with potential big profit if he starts.

Yr	Tm	W	L	Sv	IP	K	ERA	xERA	WHIP	OBA	vL	vR	BF/G	Ctl	Dom	Cmd	G	L	F	hr/9	hr/f	H%	S%	GS	APC	DOM%	DIS%	Sv%	LI	RAR	BPV	BPX	R$
08																																	
09																																	
10																																	
11	aa	1	1	0	38	30	3.14	4.01	1.12	260			25.0	1.2	7.1	5.9				1.5		29%	81%							3.8	125	189	$0
12	TEX	6	0	0	65	47	2.22	3.58	1.20	232	225	237	4.6	3.2	6.5	2.0	62	18	20	0.4	8%	28%	83%	0	18			0	0.97	14.4	71	93	$6
1st Half		6	0	0	42	26	1.08	3.17	0.96	221	242	205	5.2	1.7	5.6	3.3	64	16	20	0.4	8%	25%	92%	0	21			0	0.97	15.1	97	126	$14
2nd Half		0	0	0	23	21	4.24	4.37	1.63	250	200	288	3.9	5.8	8.1	1.4	59	22	19	0.4	8%	33%	73%	0	16			0	0.97	-0.7	26	34	-$9
13	**Proj**	**3**	**1**	**0**	**65**	**51**	**3.68**	**3.49**	**1.31**	**258**	**233**	**278**	**6.2**	**2.9**	**7.1**	**2.4**	**61**	**20**	**19**	**0.5**	**10%**	**31%**	**72%**	**0**						**2.7**	**87**	**114**	**$1**

Ross,Tyson

Age: 26	Th: R	Role RP	Health B	LIMA Plan D	
Ht: 6' 6"	Wt: 230	Type Pwr GB	PT/Exp D	Rand Var 0	
			Consist B	MM 1201	

2-11, 6.50 ERA in 73 IP at OAK. CON: Horrible Cmd is a chronic problem, and lefties hit like Miguel Cabrera against him (.974 OPS). PRO: 2H Dom and GB% give glimmer of hope that he's figuring things out, but buying into that requires a leap of faith that we can't recommend. Watch from a distance.

Yr	Tm	W	L	Sv	IP	K	ERA	xERA	WHIP	OBA	vL	vR	BF/G	Ctl	Dom	Cmd	G	L	F	hr/9	hr/f	H%	S%	GS	APC	DOM%	DIS%	Sv%	LI	RAR	BPV	BPX	R$
08																																	
09	aa	5	4	0	50	26	3.88	2.79	1.19	226			22.3	3.3	4.7	1.4				0.5		25%	67%							2.7	55	102	$2
10	OAK *	3	5	1	65	58	4.69	3.97	1.44	253	258	282	8.6	4.4	8.0	1.8	53	18	29	0.7	12%	31%	67%	2	27	0%	100%	50	0.58	-4.9	71	114	-$2
11	OAK *	6	5	0	73	53	5.23	5.24	1.68	301	250	254	18.2	4.2	6.5	1.6	48	22	30	0.6	3%	35%	68%	6	60	50%	33%	0	0.76	-11.6	47	71	-$7
12	OAK *	8	13	0	152	99	4.78	4.74	1.57	287	356	297	20.2	3.9	5.9	1.5	50	23	27	0.6	10%	33%	69%	13	72	23%	38%	0	0.97	-14.3	46	60	-$10
1st Half		4	9	0	84	44	5.37	5.28	1.63	300	354	277	23.4	3.7	4.7	1.3	49	24	27	0.8	12%	33%	67%	12	90	17%	42%			-14.1	24	31	-$15
2nd Half		4	4	0	67	55	4.03	4.00	1.49	269	368	385	17.1	4.1	7.3	1.8	53	22	25	0.4	0%	33%	72%	1	35	100%	0%	0	1.34	-0.1	72	94	-$4
13	**Proj**	**5**	**6**	**0**	**73**	**52**	**4.68**	**4.51**	**1.53**	**277**	**287**	**268**	**16.2**	**4.0**	**6.5**	**1.6**	**50**	**21**	**29**	**0.6**	**7%**	**33%**	**69%**	**12**						**-5.9**	**36**	**46**	**-$3**

Russell,James

Age: 27	Th: L	Role RP	Health A	LIMA Plan B+	
Ht: 6' 4"	Wt: 200	Type FB	PT/Exp C	Rand Var -2	
			Consist A	MM 2200	

His 2010 Cmd showed great promise, but has eroded from that peak even as ERA has been improving. Made some progress on reducing FB% in 2H, but turning them into LDs isn't really helpful. Doesn't even dominate vL. Continuing his trend of ERA improvement for a 5th year would be a major upset. Avoid.

Yr	Tm	W	L	Sv	IP	K	ERA	xERA	WHIP	OBA	vL	vR	BF/G	Ctl	Dom	Cmd	G	L	F	hr/9	hr/f	H%	S%	GS	APC	DOM%	DIS%	Sv%	LI	RAR	BPV	BPX	R$
08	aa	4	8	0	86	55	7.29	7.30	1.71	336			21.7	2.5	5.7	2.3				2.1		35%	61%							-31.6	6	12	-$12
09	a/a	5	6	0	103	61	5.29	6.10	1.65	325			12.4	2.6	5.3	2.0				1.2		35%	70%							-12.2	28	52	-$7
10	CHC	1	1	0	49	42	4.96	4.19	1.35	279	238	308	3.8	2.0	7.7	3.8	31	20	49	2.0	14%	31%	71%	0	15			0	0.94	-5.3	93	151	-$3
11	CHC	1	6	0	68	43	4.12	4.41	1.33	286	250	312	4.6	1.9	5.7	3.1	38	14	48	1.6	11%	30%	76%	5	17	0%	100%	0	0.89	-1.5	69	103	-$2
12	CHC	7	1	2	69	55	3.25	4.32	1.30	255	262	250	3.8	3.0	7.1	2.4	37	21	41	0.6	6%	31%	76%	0	15			40	0.98	6.6	63	82	$3
1st Half		2	0	1	37	30	2.45	4.62	1.28	239	216	253	4.0	3.4	7.4	2.1	33	18	49	1.0	8%	28%	86%	0	16			100	0.91	7.1	51	66	$4
2nd Half		5	1	1	33	25	4.13	3.98	1.32	272	308	247	3.6	2.5	6.9	2.8	42	26	33	0.3	3%	33%	67%	0	15			25	1.06	-0.5	77	100	$3
13	**Proj**	**4**	**3**	**0**	**65**	**48**	**4.13**	**4.38**	**1.35**	**277**	**265**	**285**	**4.2**	**2.5**	**6.7**	**2.7**	**37**	**19**	**44**	**1.1**	**9%**	**31%**	**73%**	**0**						**-0.9**	**69**	**90**	**$0**

Rzepczynski,Marc

Age: 27	Th: L	Role RP	Health A	LIMA Plan C	
Ht: 6' 1"	Wt: 205	Type Pwr xGB	PT/Exp D	Rand Var +5	
			Consist D	MM 3300	

"Scrabble" had a problem with G-O-P-H-E-R-I-T-I-S (two triple-word scores and double letter on the H for 180 points and 6.00 ERA). xERA, S% say 1H was never that bad. In 2H, Ctl and unlucky LD% drove up xERA, but he got back to mastery vL. Upside remains, as does history as a SP. And it's Zep-chin-ski.

Yr	Tm	W	L	Sv	IP	K	ERA	xERA	WHIP	OBA	vL	vR	BF/G	Ctl	Dom	Cmd	G	L	F	hr/9	hr/f	H%	S%	GS	APC	DOM%	DIS%	Sv%	LI	RAR	BPV	BPX	R$
08																																	
09	TOR *	11	9	0	149	151	3.43	4.12	1.50	267	220	226	23.9	4.3	9.1	2.1	51	20	28	0.5	15%	35%	77%	11	99	73%	18%			16.4	86	161	$8
10	TOR *	9	9	0	131	108	5.13	5.34	1.59	294	262	298	22.1	3.7	7.4	2.0	51	16	32	1.1	13%	34%	70%	12	77	33%	42%	0	0.83	-16.9	49	80	-$5
11	2 TM	2	6	0	62	61	3.34	2.96	1.23	223	163	275	3.6	3.8	8.9	2.3	65	15	20	0.4	9%	29%	73%	0	13			0	1.28	4.6	100	151	$2
12	STL	1	3	0	47	33	4.24	3.84	1.35	257	255	259	2.8	3.3	6.4	1.9	59	22	19	1.4	25%	28%	73%	0	11			0	1.31	-1.3	63	82	-$4
1st Half		1	3	0	27	18	6.00	3.92	1.56	303	279	333	3.2	3.0	6.0	2.0	64	18	19	2.0	35%	32%	67%	0	12			0	1.32	-6.6	69	90	-$8
2nd Half		0	0	0	20	15	1.83	3.74	1.07	186	212	162	2.4	3.7	6.9	1.9	51	29	20	0.5	9%	23%	85%	0	9			0	1.30	5.3	54	70	$2
13	**Proj**	**2**	**4**	**0**	**58**	**48**	**3.69**	**3.70**	**1.33**	**246**	**229**	**260**	**3.7**	**3.6**	**7.5**	**2.1**	**57**	**20**	**23**	**0.7**	**12%**	**30%**	**73%**	**0**						**2.3**	**72**	**93**	**$0**

JOSH PALEY

Sabathia,CC

Age: 32 Th: L Role SP | Health A | LIMA Plan C+
Ht: 6' 7" Wt: 290 Type Pwr | PT/Exp A | Rand Var 0
Consist A | MM 4405

Hit the DL twice (groin, elbow) and visited Dr. Andrews after the season, so longtime "PRO: durability" may be drifting to a "CON:". When healthy, skills are nearly bulletproof. Years of good GB%, strong Dom, elite Cmd. 2H Ctl represented new level of excellence. Check on spring health before investing.

Yr Tm	W	L	Sv	IP	K	ERA	xERA	WHIP	OBA	vL	vR	BF/G	Ctl	Dom	Cmd	G	L	F	hr/9	hr/f	H%	S%	GS	APC	DOM%	DIS%	Sv%	LI	RAR	BPV	BPX	R$
08 2 TM	17	10	0	253	251	2.70	3.16	1.11	237	205	247	29.2	2.1	8.9	4.3	47	22	32	0.7	9%	31%	78%	35	109	74%	9%			50.6	129	242	$36
09 NYY	19	8	0	230	197	3.37	3.71	1.15	232	198	242	27.6	2.6	7.7	2.9	43	20	37	0.7	7%	28%	72%	34	106	59%	9%			27.1	89	167	$28
10 NYY	21	7	0	238	197	3.18	3.56	1.19	239	261	232	28.5	2.8	7.5	2.7	51	15	34	0.8	9%	29%	76%	34	106	56%	3%			26.3	88	142	$24
11 NYY	19	8	0	237	230	3.00	3.19	1.23	255	207	273	29.8	2.3	8.7	3.8	47	23	30	0.6	8%	33%	77%	33	109	79%	0%			27.7	120	180	$23
12 NYY	15	6	0	200	197	3.38	3.29	1.14	238	227	241	29.8	2.0	8.9	4.5	48	21	31	1.0	13%	31%	74%	28	108	75%	4%			15.8	132	172	$21
1st Half	9	3	0	107	105	3.45	3.44	1.27	257	236	264	30.3	2.4	8.8	3.6	50	20	30	0.8	11%	33%	75%	15	112	73%	7%			7.5	121	158	$21
2nd Half	6	3	0	93	92	3.29	3.13	0.99	216	214	216	29.1	1.5	8.9	6.1	46	22	32	1.2	14%	28%	73%	13	104	77%	0%			8.3	145	189	$20
13 Proj	14	9	0	188	179	3.45	3.28	1.15	244	227	250	28.3	2.2	8.6	4.0	48	21	32	0.9	11%	30%	73%	26						13.2	122	158	$19

Salas,Fernando

Age: 28 Th: R Role RP | Health A | LIMA Plan C+
Ht: 6' 2" Wt: 200 Type Pwr FB | PT/Exp C | Rand Var 0
Consist A | MM 3400

1H wildness led to demotion to minors; it turns out that walks and line drives don't mix. Strong Dom remained intact all season and he regained most of Ctl in 2H. Has already shown he has the skills to close; just needs the opportunity.

Yr Tm	W	L	Sv	IP	K	ERA	xERA	WHIP	OBA	vL	vR	BF/G	Ctl	Dom	Cmd	G	L	F	hr/9	hr/f	H%	S%	GS	APC	DOM%	DIS%	Sv%	LI	RAR	BPV	BPX	R$
08 aa	7	3	25	74	82	4.06	3.98	1.18	256			4.9	1.9	10.0	5.3				1.4		32%	71%							2.4	134	251	$16
09 a/a	4	2	0	38	25	4.07	3.71	1.26	252			4.6	2.8	5.9	2.1				0.9		28%	70%							1.2	58	108	$0
10 STL *	1	0	19	66	64	3.74	3.19	1.21	232	250	235	4.4	3.2	8.7	2.7	33	18	48	0.8	10%	29%	71%	0	21			95	0.48	2.8	95	153	$9
11 STL	5	6	24	75	75	2.28	3.46	0.95	186	214	164	4.3	2.5	9.0	3.6	34	14	52	0.8	7%	24%	81%	0	17			80	1.45	15.4	106	159	$20
12 STL	1	4	0	59	60	4.30	4.13	1.41	251	270	239	3.9	4.1	9.2	2.2	38	24	38	0.8	8%	33%	71%	0	16			0	1.18	-2.0	70	91	-$4
1st Half	0	3	0	25	27	6.04	4.69	1.86	305	396	228	4.4	5.3	9.6	1.8	40	26	34	0.7	8%	40%	67%	0	18			0	1.25	-6.3	47	61	-$12
2nd Half	1	1	0	33	33	2.97	3.72	1.08	203	122	247	3.6	3.2	8.9	2.8	36	22	41	0.8	9%	26%	76%	0	14			0	1.12	4.3	87	113	$3
13 Proj	2	2	0	44	43	3.64	3.91	1.23	233	250	221	4.0	3.4	8.9	2.6	36	20	44	0.8	8%	30%	73%	0						2.0	83	108	$0

Sale,Chris

Age: 24 Th: L Role RP | Health A | LIMA Plan C+
Ht: 6' 6" Wt: 180 Type Pwr | PT/Exp B | Rand Var 0
Consist A | MM 4505

These are the skills of CC Sabathia, but eight years younger and 110 pounds fewer. CHW finally decided he was more useful as an SP, and he paid big dividends in 1H. Coughed up more HR and LD in 2H, which raised workload concerns. Sabathia-like durability is now the last hurdle to true stardom.

Yr Tm	W	L	Sv	IP	K	ERA	xERA	WHIP	OBA	vL	vR	BF/G	Ctl	Dom	Cmd	G	L	F	hr/9	hr/f	H%	S%	GS	APC	DOM%	DIS%	Sv%	LI	RAR	BPV	BPX	R$
08																																
09																																
10 CHW	2	1	4	23	32	1.93	2.64	1.07	185	290	120	4.4	3.9	12.3	3.2	51	12	37	0.8	11%	28%	87%	0	19			100	1.65	6.2	147	238	$3
11 CHW	2	2	8	71	79	2.79	3.02	1.11	203	208	199	5.0	3.4	10.0	2.9	50	18	32	0.8	11%	28%	78%	0	19			80	1.25	10.1	116	174	$9
12 CHW	17	8	0	192	192	3.05	3.28	1.14	235	233	236	25.7	2.4	9.0	3.8	45	23	32	0.9	12%	30%	77%	29	101	72%	7%	0	0.87	22.9	120	157	$24
1st Half	9	2	0	95	94	2.27	3.24	0.97	198	184	204	24.7	2.3	8.9	3.9	44	20	36	0.5	6%	26%	78%	14	98	86%	0%	0	0.94	20.6	121	158	$35
2nd Half	8	6	0	97	98	3.82	3.32	1.30	269	284	264	26.7	2.5	9.1	3.6	45	26	28	1.3	18%	33%	76%	15	103	60%	13%			2.4	120	156	$12
13 Proj	13	8	0	203	212	3.24	3.23	1.14	227	225	228	9.4	2.8	9.4	3.3	47	21	32	0.9	12%	29%	75%	0						19.5	118	154	$22

Samardzija,Jeff

Age: 28 Th: R Role RP | Health A | LIMA Plan C+
Ht: 6' 5" Wt: 225 Type Pwr | PT/Exp B | Rand Var +1
Consist B | MM 3405

PRO: Long-elusive Cmd seemingly fell out of the sky, and got better in 2H despite new high in IP; held righties to .636 OPS. CON: 2010 and 2011 remind us that this was completely uncharted territory for these skills. VERDICT: 2nd half xERA suggests... UP: sub-3.25 ERA

Yr Tm	W	L	Sv	IP	K	ERA	xERA	WHIP	OBA	vL	vR	BF/G	Ctl	Dom	Cmd	G	L	F	hr/9	hr/f	H%	S%	GS	APC	DOM%	DIS%	Sv%	LI	RAR	BPV	BPX	R$
08 CHC *	8	6	1	141	98	4.34	4.28	1.49	259	167	276	12.7	4.5	6.3	1.4	46	22	32	0.8	0%	30%	72%	0	19			25	0.83	-0.3	46	87	$1
09 CHC *	7	9	0	124	80	6.21	6.50	1.69	321	361	304	14.7	3.2	5.8	1.8	41	18	40	1.6	15%	35%	66%	2	30	0%	50%	0	0.58	-28.8	15	28	-$11
10 CHC *	13	5	0	131	91	5.45	4.47	1.57	244	103	367	13.7	6.0	6.3	1.0	30	17	52	1.0	11%	27%	66%	3	53	0%	67%	0	0.57	-22.0	37	60	-$5
11 CHC	8	4	0	88	87	2.97	4.12	1.30	200	208	195	5.1	5.1	8.9	1.7	41	18	41	0.5	5%	27%	78%	0	20			0	0.85	10.6	41	62	$6
12 CHC	9	13	0	175	180	3.81	3.46	1.22	240	241	239	25.8	2.9	9.3	3.2	45	22	33	1.0	13%	30%	72%	28	99	64%	11%			4.4	112	146	$10
1st Half	5	7	0	87	85	5.05	3.83	1.42	268	282	254	25.2	3.5	8.8	2.5	46	23	31	0.9	12%	33%	65%	15	96	60%	20%			-11.1	87	113	$0
2nd Half	4	6	0	87	95	2.58	3.10	1.02	211	200	222	26.5	2.3	9.8	4.3	43	22	35	1.1	14%	27%	82%	13	103	69%	0%			15.5	136	177	$21
13 Proj	12	14	0	203	191	3.65	3.90	1.27	236	244	229	11.0	3.6	8.5	2.4	43	20	37	0.9	10%	29%	74%	7						9.3	76	99	$14

Sanchez,Anibal

Age: 29 Th: R Role SP | Health C | LIMA Plan B+
Ht: 6' 0" Wt: 205 Type Pwr | PT/Exp A | Rand Var 0
Consist A | MM 3405

DET acquired him when MIA decided its fans were unworthy of watching competitive baseball. Once in DET, he spiked his Cmd but found that his GB ways didn't mix well with porous infielders, as H% demonstrates. A little better support with the leather is all that he needs for... UP: 3.25 ERA, 1.20 WHIP.

Yr Tm	W	L	Sv	IP	K	ERA	xERA	WHIP	OBA	vL	vR	BF/G	Ctl	Dom	Cmd	G	L	F	hr/9	hr/f	H%	S%	GS	APC	DOM%	DIS%	Sv%	LI	RAR	BPV	BPX	R$
08 FLA	2	5	0	52	50	5.57	4.39	1.57	267	340	188	24.1	4.7	8.7	1.9	40	27	32	1.2	14%	33%	66%	10	88	40%	20%			-8.0	48	90	-$4
09 FLA	4	8	0	86	71	3.87	4.72	1.51	253	231	276	23.9	4.8	7.4	1.5	42	20	38	1.0	10%	30%	78%	16	92	44%	31%			4.8	24	44	$0
10 FLA	13	12	0	195	157	3.55	4.06	1.34	257	262	252	26.3	3.2	7.2	2.2	45	17	38	0.5	5%	32%	73%	32	101	59%	16%			12.6	66	107	$10
11 FLA	8	9	0	196	202	3.67	3.38	1.28	250	243	257	25.9	2.9	9.3	3.2	44	20	36	0.9	10%	32%	74%	32	101	66%	16%			6.7	109	165	$10
12 2 TM	9	13	0	196	167	3.86	3.69	1.27	265	243	291	26.5	2.2	7.7	3.5	46	21	32	0.9	11%	32%	72%	31	99	68%	13%			3.6	103	134	$8
1st Half	4	6	0	96	87	3.94	3.63	1.22	244	217	275	26.5	2.8	8.2	2.9	49	19	33	0.8	10%	30%	69%	15	98	80%	13%			0.9	97	126	$9
2nd Half	5	7	0	100	80	3.79	3.75	1.31	283	265	304	26.4	1.6	7.2	4.4	45	24	32	1.0	11%	34%	74%	16	99	56%	13%			2.8	109	142	$7
13 Proj	12	9	0	189	168	3.61	3.78	1.31	263	254	273	25.2	2.7	8.0	2.9	45	21	34	0.9	10%	32%	75%	31						9.5	93	121	$11

Sanchez,Jonathan

Age: 30 Th: L Role SP | Health F | LIMA Plan F
Ht: 6' 0" Wt: 198 Type Pwr FB | PT/Exp B | Rand Var +5
Consist C | MM 0301

Biceps tendinitis plagued him most, if not all, of the season. COL acquired him mid-year in a Deal That Could Not Possibly End Well. Never a Ctl wizard, he'd now need a 15 k/9 to be viable. Lefties had .857 OPS vs him, so even a specialist role may not be possible. He'll be better because he can't be worse.

Yr Tm	W	L	Sv	IP	K	ERA	xERA	WHIP	OBA	vL	vR	BF/G	Ctl	Dom	Cmd	G	L	F	hr/9	hr/f	H%	S%	GS	APC	DOM%	DIS%	Sv%	LI	RAR	BPV	BPX	R$
08 SF	9	12	0	158	157	5.01	4.11	1.45	257	235	263	24.0	4.3	8.9	2.1	41	21	37	0.8	8%	33%	66%	29	98	45%	31%			-13.4	65	121	$1
09 SF	8	12	0	163	177	4.24	4.09	1.37	221	223	220	22.2	4.8	9.8	2.0	41	16	43	1.0	10%	29%	72%	29	89	41%	24%	0	0.75	1.6	64	119	$7
10 SF	13	9	0	193	205	3.07	3.80	1.23	204	181	210	23.9	4.5	9.5	2.1	41	15	44	1.0	10%	26%	79%	33	95	48%	18%	0	0.77	24.0	70	113	$18
11 SF	4	7	0	101	102	4.26	4.25	1.44	220	188	231	23.4	5.9	9.1	1.5	42	20	38	0.8	9%	28%	72%	19	92	37%	26%			-4.0	25	37	-$1
12 2 TM	1	9	0	65	45	8.07	6.71	2.09	314	258	333	21.8	7.4	6.3	0.8	40	19	42	1.5	12%	34%	62%	15	89	0%	67%			-32.4	-68	-89	-$23
1st Half	1	4	0	46	32	6.80	6.69	1.99	287	229	308	23.2	7.8	6.2	0.8	42	19	39	1.0	8%	32%	66%	10	96	0%	50%			-15.9	-78	-102	-$23
2nd Half	0	5	0	18	13	11.29	6.79	2.35	375	333	387	19.0	6.4	6.4	1.0	35	19	46	2.9	19%	38%	54%	5	77	0%	100%			-16.4	-45	-59	-$22
13 Proj	6	12	0	116	100	5.18	5.14	1.66	267	230	278	20.6	5.7	7.8	1.4	40	19	42	1.5	14%	31%	73%	25						-16.7	5	6	-$8

Santana,Ervin

Age: 30 Th: R Role SP | Health A | LIMA Plan C
Ht: 6' 2" Wt: 185 Type | PT/Exp A | Rand Var +2
Consist A | MM 2205

Pitchers that give up two home runs per game don't last long. Those bombs plus poor Cmd caused 1H mess. Ctl returned in 2H, giving hitters even juicier pitches, resulting in a nearly identical mess. hr/f will regress, but four years of average BPVs tell us that there is now decidedly more risk than reward here.

Yr Tm	W	L	Sv	IP	K	ERA	xERA	WHIP	OBA	vL	vR	BF/G	Ctl	Dom	Cmd	G	L	F	hr/9	hr/f	H%	S%	GS	APC	DOM%	DIS%	Sv%	LI	RAR	BPV	BPX	R$
08 LAA	16	7	0	219	214	3.49	3.48	1.12	237	240	234	28.0	1.9	8.8	4.6	39	20	42	0.9	9%	30%	72%	32	107	75%	0%			22.4	123	231	$26
09 LAA	8	8	0	140	107	5.03	4.44	1.47	288	323	248	25.6	3.0	6.9	2.3	38	20	42	1.5	13%	32%	70%	23	96	48%	22%	0	0.78	-12.1	58	109	-$2
10 LAA	17	10	0	223	169	3.92	4.26	1.32	259	271	246	28.9	3.0	6.8	2.3	35	22	43	1.1	9%	30%	74%	33	108	55%	6%			4.3	56	91	$11
11 LAA	11	12	0	229	178	3.38	3.86	1.22	241	245	237	28.8	2.8	7.0	2.5	44	19	38	1.0	10%	28%	76%	33	105	58%	6%			15.7	72	108	$15
12 LAA	9	13	0	178	133	5.16	4.36	1.27	239	262	213	25.5	3.1	6.7	2.2	43	20	37	2.0	19%	25%	66%	30	95	47%	23%			-25.1	59	77	-$2
1st Half	4	8	0	102	73	5.12	4.36	1.30	240	251	227	27.3	3.4	6.4	1.9	48	19	33	1.7	18%	26%	66%	16	102	38%	25%			-13.8	49	64	-$3
2nd Half	5	5	0	76	60	5.21	4.37	1.22	238	278	196	23.4	2.6	7.1	2.7	37	20	43	2.4	19%	25%	67%	14	88	57%	21%			-11.2	73	95	-$1
13 Proj	11	11	0	189	146	4.45	4.17	1.26	250	270	228	25.4	2.9	7.0	2.4	41	20	40	1.6	15%	27%	71%	30						-10.0	67	87	$7

JOSH PALEY

Santana,Johan

Age: 34 Th: L Role SP	Health	F	LIMA Plan	C+	
Ht: 6' 0" Wt: 210 Type Pwr FB	PT/Exp	B	Rand Var	+1	
	Consist	A	MM	2303	

Came back from missing 2011 with a very representative skill set, which of course culminated with no-hitter. But ankle, shoulder, and eventually back problems shelved him shortly after the no-no, and remind us that Health is a skill too, and it's not in evidence here. Caveat emptor.

Yr Tm	W	L	Sv	IP	K	ERA	xERA	WHIP	OBA	vL	vR	BF/G	Ctl	Dom	Cmd	G	L	F	hr/9	hr/f	H%	S%	GS	APC	DOM%	DIS%	Sv%	LI	RAR	BPV	BPX	R$
08 NYM	16	7	0	234	206	2.53	3.68	1.15	232	247	227	28.4	2.4	7.9	3.3	41	22	36	0.9	9%	29%	83%	34	106	79%	3%			51.7	96	180	$32
09 NYM	13	9	0	167	146	3.13	4.04	1.21	244	267	235	28.0	2.5	7.9	3.2	36	17	48	1.1	9%	30%	79%	25	103	56%	4%			24.5	89	166	$18
10 NYM	11	9	0	199	144	2.98	4.13	1.18	240	273	229	28.2	2.5	6.5	2.6	35	20	45	0.7	6%	28%	77%	29	104	62%	3%			26.9	63	102	$18
11																																
12 NYM	6	9	0	117	111	4.85	4.12	1.33	258	281	251	23.8	3.0	8.5	2.8	33	24	43	1.3	12%	31%	67%	21	92	57%	19%			-12.0	84	109	-$2
1st Half	6	4	0	98	93	2.76	3.89	1.09	207	207	207	24.7	3.0	8.5	2.8	32	24	44	0.8	8%	26%	79%	16	97	75%	6%			15.3	82	107	$6
2nd Half	0	5	0	19	18	15.63	5.32	2.58	448	469	438	20.8	2.8	8.5	3.0	35	24	41	3.8	25%	50%	39%	5	78	0%	60%			-27.2	90	117	-$45
13 Proj	**9**	**11**	**0**	**131**	**114**	**3.95**	**4.13**	**1.35**	**272**	**301**	**260**	**22.6**	**2.7**	**7.9**	**2.9**	**35**	**22**	**43**	**1.4**	**12%**	**32%**	**76%**	**24**						**1.1**	**82**	**107**	**$5**

Santiago,Hector

Age: 25 Th: L Role RP	Health	A	LIMA Plan	C+	
Ht: 6' 0" Wt: 210 Type Pwr FB	PT/Exp	D	Rand Var	-2	
	Consist	A	MM	2400	

Opened season as surprise closer, but too many BBs and HRs ended experiment quickly. Began a new experiment in Sept/Oct, where in 4 GS (19 IP) he had 26/11 K/BB, 4 ER, and 24/19 GB/FB. Any pitcher with his Dom must be taken seriously. High risk until he cuts the BBs down, but high reward too.

Yr Tm	W	L	Sv	IP	K	ERA	xERA	WHIP	OBA	vL	vR	BF/G	Ctl	Dom	Cmd	G	L	F	hr/9	hr/f	H%	S%	GS	APC	DOM%	DIS%	Sv%	LI	RAR	BPV	BPX	R$
08																																
09																																
10																																
11 CHW *	7	5	0	89	66	4.34	4.06	1.50	257	0	111	22.5	4.7	6.7	1.4	60	13	27	0.6	0%	31%	71%	0	33			0	0.43	-4.4	57	86	-$2
12 CHW	4	1	4	70	79	3.33	4.12	1.34	211	211	211	7.3	5.1	10.1	2.0	38	20	42	1.3	14%	27%	81%	4	32	50%	50%	67	0.83	6.0	60	78	$3
1st Half	2	1	4	27	32	4.61	4.33	1.50	259	320	207	5.0	4.3	10.5	2.5	29	20	51	2.3	18%	32%	79%	0	22			67	0.90	-2.0	81	105	-$1
2nd Half	2	0	0	43	47	2.51	3.98	1.23	176	119	213	10.6	5.7	9.8	1.7	45	21	34	0.6	9%	24%	82%	4	48	50%	50%	0	0.72	8.0	48	62	$6
13 Proj	**4**	**2**	**0**	**58**	**56**	**3.78**	**4.40**	**1.41**	**234**	**235**	**233**	**9.5**	**4.9**	**8.8**	**1.8**	**39**	**20**	**41**	**1.3**	**13%**	**28%**	**78%**	**0**						**1.7**	**42**	**54**	**$0**

Santos,Sergio

Age: 29 Th: R Role RP	Health	F	LIMA Plan	B	
Ht: 6' 3" Wt: 240 Type Pwr	PT/Exp	C	Rand Var	+5	
	Consist	F	MM	4510	

Torn labrum shut him down before we could find out if he could sustain 2011's skill gains; eventually required surgery in July. He's supposed to be near 100% for spring training. Won't likely be named the closer right away, but if his skills are intact he could climb back into the mix in-season.

Yr Tm	W	L	Sv	IP	K	ERA	xERA	WHIP	OBA	vL	vR	BF/G	Ctl	Dom	Cmd	G	L	F	hr/9	hr/f	H%	S%	GS	APC	DOM%	DIS%	Sv%	LI	RAR	BPV	BPX	R$
08																																
09																																
10 CHW	2	2	1	52	56	2.96	3.92	1.53	261	207	298	4.2	4.5	9.8	2.2	43	21	36	0.3	4%	36%	81%	0	16			33	1.03	7.1	74	120	$0
11 CHW	4	5	30	63	92	3.55	2.74	1.11	181	234	130	4.1	4.1	13.1	3.2	43	18	39	0.9	11%	29%	70%	0	16			83	1.31	3.0	145	218	$16
12 TOR	0	1	2	5	4	9.00	5.61	2.00	316	182	500	4.0	7.2	7.2	1.0	50	25	25	1.8	25%	33%	56%	0	17			50	1.52	-3.1	-37	-48	-$5
1st Half	0	1	2	5	4	9.00	5.61	2.00	316	182	500	4.0	7.2	7.2	1.0	50	25	25	1.8	25%	33%	56%	0	17			50	1.52	-3.1	-37	-48	-$5
2nd Half																																
13 Proj	**3**	**4**	**8**	**58**	**71**	**3.78**	**3.45**	**1.27**	**221**	**230**	**213**	**4.0**	**4.3**	**11.0**	**2.6**	**43**	**19**	**38**	**1.0**	**12%**	**30%**	**73%**	**0**						**1.7**	**103**	**133**	**$5**

Saunders,Joe

Age: 32 Th: L Role SP	Health	A	LIMA Plan	B	
Ht: 6' 3" Wt: 210 Type Con	PT/Exp	A	Rand Var	0	
	Consist	A	MM	1103	

Should BPV spike get us interested in this innings-eater? Dom growth is nice, but only brings him up to mediocrity. Ctl was elite, especially in 2H, but he'll never be above average as an SP since he has to face righties, and he has a staggering OPS split (.451 vL, .849 vR). Our interest level remains tepid.

Yr Tm	W	L	Sv	IP	K	ERA	xERA	WHIP	OBA	vL	vR	BF/G	Ctl	Dom	Cmd	G	L	F	hr/9	hr/f	H%	S%	GS	APC	DOM%	DIS%	Sv%	LI	RAR	BPV	BPX	R$
08 LAA	17	7	0	198	103	3.41	4.39	1.21	253	260	250	26.0	2.4	4.7	1.9	47	15	38	1.0	9%	27%	75%	31	97	32%	16%			22.3	44	83	$18
09 LAA	16	7	0	186	101	4.60	4.72	1.43	279	257	287	26.0	3.1	4.9	1.6	47	17	36	1.4	13%	29%	72%	31	97	23%	23%			-6.3	29	55	$4
10 2 TM	9	17	0	203	114	4.47	4.56	1.46	291	259	301	26.7	2.8	5.0	1.8	44	19	37	1.1	10%	31%	72%	33	100	42%	24%			-9.8	36	59	-$2
11 ARI	12	13	0	212	108	3.69	4.37	1.31	266	212	281	26.5	2.8	4.6	1.6	44	21	35	1.2	12%	27%	77%	33	97	24%	3%			6.5	28	42	$7
12 2 TM	9	13	0	175	112	4.07	4.33	1.34	281	199	307	26.6	2.0	5.8	2.9	43	21	36	1.1	10%	31%	73%	28	97	54%	11%			-1.2	71	92	$2
1st Half	4	5	0	81	53	3.44	4.45	1.38	284	224	302	26.7	2.3	5.9	2.5	43	18	38	1.0	9%	32%	79%	13	98	69%	15%			5.7	64	83	$3
2nd Half	5	8	0	94	59	4.61	4.24	1.30	279	178	311	26.5	1.7	5.7	3.3	43	24	34	1.2	11%	31%	67%	15	96	40%	7%			-6.9	76	99	$0
13 Proj	**9**	**11**	**0**	**160**	**93**	**4.18**	**4.47**	**1.34**	**277**	**215**	**295**	**26.1**	**2.4**	**5.3**	**2.2**	**44**	**21**	**36**	**1.1**	**11%**	**30%**	**72%**	**25**						**-3.2**	**52**	**67**	**$3**

Scheppers,Tanner

Age: 26 Th: R Role RP	Health	A	LIMA Plan	C	
Ht: 6' 4" Wt: 220 Type Pwr	PT/Exp	F	Rand Var	+2	
	Consist	C	MM	2300	

1-1, 4.45 ERA in 32 IP at TEX. Once thought to be a future saves source, there has been no need to rush him... which is good news, since the skills haven't reached a commensurate level yet. 104 BPV in TEX speaks to his progress, though. Next step: hold those skills amid looming H% reversion.

Yr Tm	W	L	Sv	IP	K	ERA	xERA	WHIP	OBA	vL	vR	BF/G	Ctl	Dom	Cmd	G	L	F	hr/9	hr/f	H%	S%	GS	APC	DOM%	DIS%	Sv%	LI	RAR	BPV	BPX	R$
08																																
09																																
10 a/a	1	3	6	80	75	6.01	5.36	1.63	306			9.9	3.5	8.4	2.4				0.8		38%	63%							-19.1	70	113	-$6
11 a/a	4	1	2	44	35	4.31	4.17	1.56	276			6.8	4.4	7.2	1.7				0.2		34%	71%							-2.0	70	106	-$2
12 TEX *	2	3	12	63	54	4.32	5.56	1.51	315	302	369	4.2	1.9	7.7	4.1	43	20	37	1.2	15%	37%	75%	0	14			80	0.95	-2.4	88	115	$0
1st Half	1	2	10	39	30	5.68	5.48	1.46	315	300	391	4.9	1.4	7.0	4.9	38	15	47	1.3	19%	36%	63%	0	19			77	0.55	-8.0	98	128	$0
2nd Half	1	1	2	25	24	2.19	5.60	1.58	315	303	361	3.4	2.6	8.8	3.4	45	23	32	1.1	13%	39%	92%	0	13			100	1.07	5.6	84	109	$0
13 Proj	**3**	**2**	**0**	**51**	**44**	**4.18**	**4.04**	**1.41**	**275**	**245**	**292**	**4.9**	**3.1**	**7.8**	**2.5**	**45**	**23**	**32**	**0.8**	**8%**	**34%**	**71%**	**0**						**-1.0**	**80**	**104**	**-$2**

Scherzer,Max

Age: 28 Th: R Role SP	Health	A	LIMA Plan	B+	
Ht: 6' 3" Wt: 220 Type Pwr	PT/Exp	A	Rand Var	+3	
	Consist	A	MM	4505	

Posted a 7.77 ERA in April and a 3.14 mark from May 1 on. 2H showed us the stud we have been waiting for, correcting unlucky hr/9 and S%, and shredding opponents down the stretch. Late-season ankle/shoulder injuries a minor concern, but these are Verlander-level skills, so... UP: sub-3.00 ERA.

Yr Tm	W	L	Sv	IP	K	ERA	xERA	WHIP	OBA	vL	vR	BF/G	Ctl	Dom	Cmd	G	L	F	hr/9	hr/f	H%	S%	GS	APC	DOM%	DIS%	Sv%	LI	RAR	BPV	BPX	R$
08 ARI *	1	5	0	109	129	2.95	2.74	1.18	219	319	167	15.0	3.5	10.6	3.0	41	28	31	0.6	12%	31%	76%	7	58	43%	14%	0	0.51	18.5	122	228	$10
09 ARI	9	11	0	170	174	4.12	3.81	1.34	253	265	239	24.7	3.3	9.2	2.8	42	18	40	1.1	10%	32%	72%	30	102	50%	20%			4.2	96	179	$9
10 DET *	14	11	0	211	197	3.30	3.22	1.19	231	239	250	25.6	3.1	8.4	2.7	40	20	40	0.9	10%	29%	75%	31	106	65%	13%			20.2	91	147	$19
11 DET	15	9	0	195	174	4.43	3.76	1.35	272	281	262	25.2	2.6	8.0	3.1	40	20	39	1.3	13%	32%	71%	33	101	52%	9%			-11.7	93	139	$4
12 DET	16	7	0	188	231	3.74	3.33	1.27	250	292	201	24.6	2.9	11.1	3.9	36	22	41	1.1	12%	34%	75%	32	102	63%	19%			6.3	136	177	$14
1st Half	7	5	0	90	114	4.98	3.39	1.43	274	310	229	24.7	3.2	11.4	3.6	38	23	38	1.4	15%	37%	69%	16	103	56%	25%			-10.7	135	176	$4
2nd Half	9	2	0	97	117	2.59	3.27	1.13	227	274	174	24.5	2.6	10.8	4.2	35	21	44	0.8	8%	32%	81%	16	102	69%	13%			17.1	137	178	$24
13 Proj	**17**	**7**	**0**	**203**	**226**	**3.37**	**3.37**	**1.21**	**242**	**268**	**212**	**23.3**	**2.8**	**10.0**	**3.6**	**39**	**21**	**39**	**1.0**	**11%**	**32%**	**76%**	**35**						**16.1**	**122**	**159**	**$21**

Scribner,Evan

Age: 27 Th: R Role RP	Health	A	LIMA Plan	C+	
Ht: 6' 3" Wt: 190 Type Pwr	PT/Exp	D	Rand Var	-1	
	Consist	B	MM	3300	

2-0, 2.55 ERA in 35 IP at OAK. PRO: Cmd, xERA fully supports ERA; keeps ball in park; owns righties. CON: Lefties pounded him (.834 OPS); yet to match 2010 skills at any level above AA; and he's not young for a prospect. VERDICT: Per BPX, a slight-above-average middle reliever.

Yr Tm	W	L	Sv	IP	K	ERA	xERA	WHIP	OBA	vL	vR	BF/G	Ctl	Dom	Cmd	G	L	F	hr/9	hr/f	H%	S%	GS	APC	DOM%	DIS%	Sv%	LI	RAR	BPV	BPX	R$
08																																
09 aa	8	4	21	70	68	3.19	3.01	1.20	246			4.9	2.5	8.7	3.5				0.4		32%	73%							9.8	118	221	$16
10 aa	4	5	16	66	69	3.02	3.11	1.14	241			4.6	2.2	9.4	4.3				0.8		31%	76%							8.7	130	211	$12
11 SD *	2	3	10	43	33	4.89	3.88	1.39	269	379	226	4.7	3.1	6.9	2.2	39	22	39	0.5	5%	32%	63%	0	23			91	0.13	-5.0	74	111	$1
12 OAK *	5	0	9	71	60	2.95	3.00	1.16	230	278	183	5.0	2.8	7.6	2.7	38	25	38	0.7	5%	28%	77%	0	20			100	0.46	9.3	90	117	$9
1st Half	3	0	9	40	35	2.96	2.72	1.07	219	0	182	5.4	2.5	7.8	3.1	10	20	70	0.8	0%	26%	76%	0	24			100	0.42	5.3	99	129	$14
2nd Half	2	0	0	31	25	2.93	3.34	1.27	245	300	183	4.6	3.2	7.3	2.3	41	25	34	0.6	6%	30%	78%	0	19			0	0.46	4.1	80	104	$2
13 Proj	**2**	**1**	**0**	**36**	**31**	**3.44**	**3.88**	**1.23**	**245**	**318**	**194**	**4.8**	**2.8**	**7.8**	**2.8**	**41**	**25**	**34**	**0.6**	**6%**	**30%**	**73%**	**0**						**2.6**	**83**	**107**	**$0**

JOSH PALEY

Shaw,Bryan

Age: 25 Th: R Role RP	Health A	LIMA Plan D+	
Ht: 6' 1" Wt: 210 Type xGB	PT/Exp D	Rand Var -1	
	Consist C	MM	2200

Followed up nice 2011 with a good 1H, with improved skills even if ERA was unsupported. However, it's how he finished that is scary: Sep+Oct: 6 BB, 2K in 12 IP. No reports of injury, perhaps he tired. High GB% is a start, but we need to see it combined with Cmd before investing.

Yr	Tm	W	L	Sv	IP	K	ERA	xERA	WHIP	OBA	vL	vR	BF/G	Ctl	Dom	Cmd	G	L	F	hr/9	hr/f	H%	S%	GS	APC	DOM%	DIS%	Sv%	LI	RAR	BPV	BPX	R$
08																																	
09																																	
10	aa	4	9	2	101	62	5.72	5.06	1.67	303			13.8	4.0	5.5	1.4				0.4		35%	64%							-20.6	43	70	-$9
11	ARI *	5	1	16	67	49	2.56	3.44	1.19	244	244	292	4.2	2.5	6.6	2.6	60	22	18	0.9	13%	28%	83%	0	15			94	0.58	11.3	73	110	$11
12	ARI	1	6	2	59	41	3.49	4.09	1.42	273	333	211	3.9	3.6	6.2	1.7	56	21	23	0.6	10%	31%	76%	0	15			50	0.78	3.9	48	62	-$2
1st Half		1	3	2	32	26	2.81	3.56	1.25	256	292	212	3.7	2.8	7.3	2.6	55	20	25	0.8	13%	30%	81%	0	14			67	0.95	4.8	89	116	$2
2nd Half		0	3	0	27	15	4.28	4.80	1.61	291	391	211	4.2	4.6	4.9	1.1	58	22	20	0.3	6%	32%	72%	0	15			0	0.57	-0.9	0	0	-$6
13	Proj	**2**	**3**	**0**	**44**	**29**	**3.80**	**4.08**	**1.40**	**266**	**332**	**202**	**4.6**	**3.4**	**6.1**	**1.8**	**57**	**21**	**22**	**0.7**	**11%**	**31%**	**74%**	**0**						**1.1**	**51**	**67**	**-$2**

Sheets,Ben

Age: 34 Th: R Role SP	Health	LIMA Plan	
Ht: 6' 1" Wt: 220 Type	PT/Exp	Rand Var	
	Consist	MM	

Supposedly retiring as shoulder inflammation is the latest thing to send him to the sidelines. Career numbers of 3.78/1.22 despite torn flexor tendon (elbow) problems that cost him more than two whole seasons. He still has value if he decides to unhang them up.

Yr	Tm	W	L	Sv	IP	K	ERA	xERA	WHIP	OBA	vL	vR	BF/G	Ctl	Dom	Cmd	G	L	F	hr/9	hr/f	H%	S%	GS	APC	DOM%	DIS%	Sv%	LI	RAR	BPV	BPX	R$
08	MIL	13	9	0	198	158	3.09	3.89	1.15	241	256	226	26.2	2.1	7.2	3.4	41	18	41	0.8	7%	29%	76%	31	99	65%	6%			30.3	90	170	$22
09																																	
10	OAK	4	9	0	119	84	4.53	4.33	1.39	267	255	278	25.6	3.2	6.3	2.0	44	16	39	1.4	12%	29%	72%	20	98	45%	10%			-6.6	48	78	-$1
11																																	
12	ATL	4	4	0	49	35	3.47	4.12	1.32	275	265	292	23.0	2.4	6.4	2.7	41	27	32	1.1	12%	31%	78%	9	85	56%	22%			3.3	70	91	-$1
1st Half																																	
2nd Half		4	4	0	49	35	3.47	4.12	1.32	275	265	292	23.0	2.4	6.4	2.7	41	27	32	1.1	12%	31%	78%	9	85	56%	22%			3.4	70	91	-$1
13	Proj																																

Shields,James

Age: 31 Th: R Role SP	Health A	LIMA Plan C+	
Ht: 6' 4" Wt: 215 Type Pwr	PT/Exp A	Rand Var +1	
	Consist A	MM	4405

Enjoyed his best skills year to date, buoyed by monster 2H Dom and Ctl. He was not as lucky in S% or H% as he was in 2011, so his surface numbers dipped a bit. But this is an elite skill set, with growth in GB% the latest addition to the arsenal. Treat 2012 as his floor; UP: 2011

Yr	Tm	W	L	Sv	IP	K	ERA	xERA	WHIP	OBA	vL	vR	BF/G	Ctl	Dom	Cmd	G	L	F	hr/9	hr/f	H%	S%	GS	APC	DOM%	DIS%	Sv%	LI	RAR	BPV	BPX	R$
08	TAM	14	8	0	215	160	3.56	3.71	1.15	254	255	253	26.6	1.7	6.7	4.0	46	16	37	1.0	10%	29%	73%	33	95	58%	9%			20.3	99	186	$21
09	TAM	11	12	0	220	167	4.14	4.01	1.32	275	272	279	28.2	2.1	6.8	3.2	42	20	37	1.2	11%	32%	73%	33	101	55%	6%			5.0	86	160	$10
10	TAM	13	15	0	203	187	5.18	3.79	1.46	294	286	304	26.4	2.3	8.3	3.7	41	20	38	1.5	14%	35%	68%	33	99	48%	18%	0	0.81	-27.6	107	173	-$2
11	TAM	16	12	0	249	225	2.82	3.21	1.04	217	219	215	29.5	2.3	8.1	3.5	46	18	35	0.9	11%	26%	78%	33	108	67%	9%			34.7	107	161	$32
12	TAM	15	10	0	228	223	3.52	3.25	1.17	239	232	248	28.6	2.3	8.8	3.8	52	19	29	1.0	13%	30%	73%	33	110	70%	6%			13.9	127	165	$21
1st Half		7	5	0	105	99	4.04	3.61	1.40	273	252	297	28.8	2.8	8.5	3.1	54	19	28	1.0	13%	34%	74%	16	111	63%	6%			-0.3	111	145	$9
2nd Half		8	5	0	123	124	3.07	2.95	0.97	208	213	202	28.5	1.9	9.1	4.8	51	19	30	1.0	13%	26%	73%	17	108	76%	6%			14.3	141	184	$31
13	Proj	**16**	**8**	**0**	**210**	**201**	**3.17**	**3.28**	**1.15**	**242**	**238**	**247**	**27.3**	**2.2**	**8.6**	**3.8**	**49**	**19**	**32**	**0.9**	**12%**	**30%**	**76%**	**31**						**22.0**	**121**	**158**	**$23**

Simon,Alfredo

Age: 32 Th: R Role RP	Health D	LIMA Plan B	
Ht: 6' 6" Wt: 260 Type Pwr	PT/Exp D	Rand Var -3	
	Consist B	MM	2200

PRO: Improved Dom and GB%. CON: 2H suggests that Dom was an outlier; hr/f was lucky (particularly given his home park); has always been hittable, lacks the top-notch Ctl needed to overcome that. VERDICT: 2010 saves are gone, probably never to return.

Yr	Tm	W	L	Sv	IP	K	ERA	xERA	WHIP	OBA	vL	vR	BF/G	Ctl	Dom	Cmd	G	L	F	hr/9	hr/f	H%	S%	GS	APC	DOM%	DIS%	Sv%	LI	RAR	BPV	BPX	R$
08	BAL *	7	2	0	94	72	3.72	3.78	1.21	247	243	412	19.9	2.6	6.9	2.7	62	9	30	1.2	29%	28%	74%	1	51	100%	0%	0	0.52	7.1	68	128	$6
09	BAL	0	1	0	6	3	9.95	5.80	1.58	308	333	273	14.0	2.8	4.3	1.5	22	17	61	7.1	36%	17%	60%	2	58	0%	50%			-4.4	0	0	-$5
10	BAL *	5	3	17	66	47	4.23	5.45	1.53	283	269	284	5.4	3.7	6.4	1.7	47	19	34	1.5	18%	31%	78%	0	17			81	1.16	-1.2	26	43	$5
11	BAL *	5	9	0	134	97	4.85	4.86	1.47	283	282	287	21.2	3.2	6.6	2.1	43	20	37	1.1	11%	32%	69%	16	83	44%	38%	0	0.84	-15.0	48	72	-$6
12	CIN	3	2	1	61	52	2.66	3.81	1.43	275	267	283	7.5	3.2	7.7	2.4	54	21	25	0.3	4%	34%	81%	0	28			100	0.61	10.2	82	108	$1
1st Half		0	1	0	30	30	1.78	3.46	1.32	263	196	323	6.9	2.7	8.9	3.3	51	20	30	0.3	4%	35%	87%	0	26			0	0.45	8.4	117	152	$1
2nd Half		3	1	1	31	22	3.52	4.18	1.53	288	333	241	8.1	3.8	6.5	1.7	57	22	20	0.3	5%	34%	76%	0	30			100	0.79	1.9	48	62	$1
13	Proj	**3**	**2**	**0**	**58**	**45**	**3.63**	**4.15**	**1.44**	**276**	**275**	**277**	**8.8**	**3.3**	**7.0**	**2.1**	**49**	**20**	**30**	**0.8**	**9%**	**33%**	**76%**	**0**						**2.8**	**64**	**83**	**-$1**

Sipp,Tony

Age: 29 Th: L Role RP	Health A	LIMA Plan D+	
Ht: 6' 0" Wt: 190 Type Pwr xFB	PT/Exp C	Rand Var 0	
	Consist A	MM	2400

2009-11 ERAs were all propped up by favorable S%; when that finally reverted, his world came crashing down. Dom remains good despite decline, but Ctl needs to improve before he can have plus value. .823 OPS vR means his best role is LOOGY.

Yr	Tm	W	L	Sv	IP	K	ERA	xERA	WHIP	OBA	vL	vR	BF/G	Ctl	Dom	Cmd	G	L	F	hr/9	hr/f	H%	S%	GS	APC	DOM%	DIS%	Sv%	LI	RAR	BPV	BPX	R$
08	aa	0	3	1	22	26	5.06	5.60	1.46	279			5.8	3.3	11.0	3.3				2.0		35%	73%							-2.0	75	140	-$3
09	CLE *	3	0	1	57	66	3.44	3.75	1.39	229	208	179	4.1	5.0	10.4	2.1	35	14	51	1.0	11%	30%	79%	0	16			100	1.03	6.2	87	162	$2
10	CLE	2	2	1	63	69	4.14	4.30	1.38	218	212	223	3.8	5.6	9.9	1.8	31	14	55	1.7	14%	25%	77%	0	16			33	1.15	-0.5	36	58	$0
11	CLE	6	3	0	62	57	3.03	4.16	1.11	201	229	180	3.6	3.5	8.2	2.4	26	14	60	1.4	10%	23%	81%	0	15			0	1.25	7.0	59	88	$5
12	CLE	1	2	1	55	51	4.42	4.27	1.27	228	209	250	3.7	3.8	8.3	2.2	33	25	42	1.5	14%	27%	70%	0	15			50	0.91	-2.7	60	78	-$2
1st Half		0	2	1	25	28	6.39	4.06	1.38	253	176	333	3.7	3.6	9.9	2.8	27	29	44	2.1	19%	30%	59%	0	15			100	1.08	-7.4	88	115	-$7
2nd Half		1	0	0	30	23	2.73	4.46	1.18	206	237	167	3.7	3.9	7.0	1.8	38	22	40	0.9	9%	24%	81%	0	15			0	0.76	4.7	35	46	$2
13	Proj	**2**	**1**	**0**	**44**	**42**	**3.82**	**4.29**	**1.25**	**221**	**221**	**220**	**3.7**	**4.1**	**8.7**	**2.1**	**31**	**19**	**49**	**1.4**	**12%**	**26%**	**76%**	**0**						**1.0**	**55**	**71**	**$0**

Skaggs,Tyler

Age: 21 Th: L Role SP	Health A	LIMA Plan A	
Ht: 6' 3" Wt: 197 Type Pwr xFB	PT/Exp D	Rand Var 0	
	Consist C	MM	2401

1-3, 5.83 ERA in 29 IP at ARI. Definition of "inauspicious beginning": gave up one HR in each of his six major league starts. Righties mauled him with .863 OPS; success vL is a 19 AB sample. #40 pick overall in 2009, he has a good minors pedigree, and this is the growth phase of his career. Be patient.

Yr	Tm	W	L	Sv	IP	K	ERA	xERA	WHIP	OBA	vL	vR	BF/G	Ctl	Dom	Cmd	G	L	F	hr/9	hr/f	H%	S%	GS	APC	DOM%	DIS%	Sv%	LI	RAR	BPV	BPX	R$
08																																	
09																																	
10																																	
11	aa	4	1	0	58	64	2.68	2.59	1.06	227			22.4	2.1	10.0	4.8				0.6		31%	77%							9.0	151	227	$5
12	ARI *	10	9	0	152	121	3.55	4.01	1.28	258	167	273	22.2	2.7	7.2	2.6	34	18	48	1.1	13%	30%	76%	6	87	33%	50%			8.6	70	91	$7
1st Half		5	4	0	70	61	3.46	4.32	1.32	268	0	0	22.2	2.6	7.9	3.0				1.2	0%	32%	79%	0	0					4.8	77	100	$10
2nd Half		5	5	0	82	60	4.04	4.19	1.33	261	167	273	22.7	3.0	6.6	2.2	34	18	48	1.1	13%	30%	73%	6	87	33%	50%			-0.3	55	72	$5
13	Proj	**5**	**8**	**0**	**116**	**107**	**4.13**	**4.11**	**1.27**	**259**	**168**	**275**	**22.7**	**2.6**	**8.3**	**3.2**	**34**	**18**	**48**	**1.3**	**10%**	**31%**	**72%**	**21**						**-1.6**	**92**	**119**	**$3**

Smith,Joe

Age: 29 Th: R Role RP	Health B	LIMA Plan C+	
Ht: 6' 2" Wt: 205 Type Pwr xGB	PT/Exp D	Rand Var -2	
	Consist A	MM	3200

PRO: Case study for how high GB% helps to prevent HR; hitters have yet to solve him from either side.
CON: Two years of ERA outpacing xERA in a big way; insufficient Cmd.
VERDICT: xERA says to set ERA expectation in 3.50 range rather than sub-3.00.

Yr	Tm	W	L	Sv	IP	K	ERA	xERA	WHIP	OBA	vL	vR	BF/G	Ctl	Dom	Cmd	G	L	F	hr/9	hr/f	H%	S%	GS	APC	DOM%	DIS%	Sv%	LI	RAR	BPV	BPX	R$
08	NYM	6	3	0	63	52	3.55	3.69	1.29	220	320	192	3.3	4.4	7.4	1.7	63	20	18	0.6	13%	27%	73%	0	13			0	1.32	6.0	55	103	$3
09	CLE	0	0	0	34	30	3.44	3.61	1.26	236	355	198	3.8	3.4	7.9	2.3	55	17	28	1.1	15%	28%	77%	0	15			0	1.20	3.7	83	155	-$1
10	CLE *	4	3	2	63	47	3.24	3.16	1.33	218	342	160	3.6	4.9	6.7	1.4	56	16	28	0.6	13%	26%	77%	0	12			50	1.13	6.5	63	103	$3
11	CLE	3	3	0	67	45	2.01	3.48	1.09	217	152	248	3.8	2.8	6.0	2.1	57	20	23	0.1	2%	26%	81%	0	14			0	1.05	15.9	68	102	$6
12	CLE	7	4	0	67	53	2.96	3.72	1.16	213	218	209	3.9	3.4	7.1	2.1	58	17	25	0.5	8%	26%	76%	0	15			0	1.22	8.8	73	96	$5
1st Half		5	2	0	34	29	3.44	3.63	1.26	234	239	231	3.9	3.7	7.7	2.1	58	18	24	0.5	9%	29%	73%	0	15			0	1.50	2.4	74	96	$6
2nd Half		2	2	0	33	24	2.45	3.82	1.06	192	200	186	3.9	3.0	6.5	2.2	58	16	26	0.5	8%	24%	79%	0	15			0	0.93	6.4	73	95	$5
13	Proj	**3**	**2**	**0**	**44**	**33**	**3.39**	**3.80**	**1.24**	**233**	**243**	**227**	**3.7**	**3.5**	**6.8**	**2.0**	**58**	**18**	**25**	**0.5**	**7%**	**28%**	**73%**	**0**						**3.4**	**64**	**83**	**$1**

JOSH PALEY

Smith,Will

Age: 23	Th: L	Role SP	Health	A	LIMA Plan	D
Ht: 6' 5"	Wt: 240	Type Con	PT/Exp	D	Rand Var	+1
			Consist	D	MM	1101

6-9, 5.32 ERA in 90 IP at KC. Took lumps in first MLB action but did have moments, as DOM/DIS attests. Still, scant evidence he'll start missing more bats (especially LH) soon. Gave up 7+ hits in each of last seven starts, thus the ugly WHIP. For now, probably best to monitor progress from afar.

Yr	Tm	W	L	Sv	IP	K	ERA	xERA	WHIP	OBA	vL	vR	BF/G	Ctl	Dom	Cmd	G	L	F	hr/9	hr/f	H%	S%	GS	APC	DOM%	DIS%	Sv%	LI	RAR	BPV	BPX	R$
08																																	
09																																	
10	a/a	3	6	0	72	41	6.18	6.49	1.79	337			25.4	3.2	5.2	1.6				1.0		37%	66%							-18.6	22	35	-$10
11	aa	13	9	0	161	90	4.10	4.31	1.40	287			25.2	2.4	5.0	2.1				0.6		32%	71%							-3.1	53	80	$2
12	KC *	10	13	0	179	119	4.57	5.29	1.55	306	356	295	25.3	2.7	6.0	2.2	42	23	35	0.9	11%	35%	72%	16	88	50%	44%			-12.4	48	62	-$9
1st Half		3	6	0	84	51	5.15	5.96	1.58	320	217	351	24.5	2.3	5.5	2.4	49	20	31	1.4	38%	35%	71%	3	77	33%	67%			-11.7	34	44	-$15
2nd Half		7	7	0	96	68	4.07	4.64	1.52	294	397	286	25.9	3.1	6.4	2.1	41	24	36	0.6	7%	35%	73%	13	91	54%	38%			-0.6	61	79	-$3
13	**Proj**	**6**	**7**	**0**	**102**	**63**	**4.59**	**4.73**	**1.48**	**295**	**372**	**267**	**25.0**	**2.7**	**5.5**	**2.1**	**41**	**24**	**36**	**1.1**	**9%**	**32%**	**71%**	**17**						**-7.2**	**46**	**60**	**-$3**

Smyly,Drew

Age: 24	Th: L	Role SP	Health	B	LIMA Plan	B+
Ht: 6' 3"	Wt: 190	Type Pwr FB	PT/Exp	F	Rand Var	0
			Consist	F	MM	3403

4-3, 3.99 ERA in 99 IP at DET. Holding own before July intercostal strain; once off DL, Anibal Sanchez left no room at the inn. Could be bargain given strong skills (91 BPV, 3.86 xERA in MLB) masked by role changes, minor injuries. Monitor how role evolves in off-season. If SP... UP: 14 Wins, 3.50 ERA.

Yr	Tm	W	L	Sv	IP	K	ERA	xERA	WHIP	OBA	vL	vR	BF/G	Ctl	Dom	Cmd	G	L	F	hr/9	hr/f	H%	S%	GS	APC	DOM%	DIS%	Sv%	LI	RAR	BPV	BPX	R$
08																																	
09																																	
10																																	
11	aa	4	3	0	46	44	1.35	2.00	1.06	211			22.2	2.8	8.7	3.1				0.2		28%	88%							14.6	124	187	$6
12	DET *	4	5	0	117	114	4.50	4.38	1.36	264	224	258	16.3	3.1	8.8	2.8	40	19	41	1.2	10%	32%	70%	18	76	56%	33%	0	0.83	-7.0	79	102	-$2
1st Half		2	4	0	72	64	5.01	5.02	1.40	280	259	275	20.3	2.7	8.0	2.9	37	21	42	1.5	13%	33%	69%	13	89	46%	38%			-8.8	63	82	-$5
2nd Half		2	1	0	45	50	3.70	3.30	1.29	237	143	218	12.3	3.8	10.0	2.7	46	14	40	0.6	3%	32%	72%	5	59	80%	20%	0	0.89	1.8	104	135	$2
13	**Proj**	**10**	**8**	**0**	**145**	**144**	**3.81**	**3.69**	**1.22**	**237**	**200**	**253**	**23.8**	**3.1**	**9.0**	**2.9**	**43**	**17**	**41**	**0.9**	**9%**	**30%**	**71%**	**25**						**3.8**	**98**	**127**	**$10**

Soria,Joakim

Age: 29	Th: R	Role RP	Health	F	LIMA Plan	B+
Ht: 6' 3"	Wt: 200	Type Pwr	PT/Exp	C	Rand Var	0
			Consist	A	MM	4530

Reportedly on track for spring return after missing entire 2012 season due to April TJ surgery. If he returns to KC, Royals have luxury to ease him back into closer role, given Holland's success. But if skills return to pre-injury form, no reason for anyone else not to hand him ball in ninth.

Yr	Tm	W	L	Sv	IP	K	ERA	xERA	WHIP	OBA	vL	vR	BF/G	Ctl	Dom	Cmd	G	L	F	hr/9	hr/f	H%	S%	GS	APC	DOM%	DIS%	Sv%	LI	RAR	BPV	BPX	R$
08	KC	2	3	42	67	66	1.60	3.23	0.86	169	167	171	4.1	2.5	8.8	3.5	45	14	41	0.7	7%	22%	87%	0	17			93	1.31	22.6	113	212	$28
09	KC	3	2	30	53	69	2.21	3.05	1.13	219	224	213	4.7	2.7	11.7	4.3	40	18	42	0.8	9%	33%	85%	0	19			91	1.52	13.8	156	291	$18
10	KC	1	2	43	66	71	1.78	3.00	1.05	216	231	196	4.1	2.2	9.7	4.4	48	17	35	0.5	7%	30%	86%	0	17			93	1.28	18.6	142	230	$25
11	KC	5	5	28	60	60	4.03	3.49	1.28	259	242	277	4.3	2.5	9.0	3.5	40	21	39	1.0	10%	32%	71%	0	17			80	1.32	-0.6	111	166	$12
12																																	
1st Half																																	
2nd Half																																	
13	**Proj**	**3**	**3**	**25**	**51**	**52**	**3.29**	**3.51**	**1.16**	**229**	**228**	**230**	**4.2**	**2.9**	**9.2**	**3.2**	**42**	**18**	**40**	**0.8**	**9%**	**29%**	**74%**	**0**						**4.6**	**107**	**140**	**$13**

Soriano,Rafael

Age: 33	Th: R	Role RP	Health	D	LIMA Plan	C
Ht: 6' 1"	Wt: 230	Type Pwr FB	PT/Exp	B	Rand Var	-5
			Consist	A	MM	3531

A credible Mariano impression, but he'll never match Rivera's Ctl, GB tilt. Charmed life with hr/f ended in 2H, but he compensated by cranking up other skills to closer-worthy levels, putting quick halt to atypical RHB struggles. Health willing, this free agent can close wherever he lands.

Yr	Tm	W	L	Sv	IP	K	ERA	xERA	WHIP	OBA	vL	vR	BF/G	Ctl	Dom	Cmd	G	L	F	hr/9	hr/f	H%	S%	GS	APC	DOM%	DIS%	Sv%	LI	RAR	BPV	BPX	R$
08	ATL	0	1	3	14	16	2.57	4.33	1.14	149	222	103	4.1	5.8	10.3	1.8	23	16	61	0.6	5%	20%	80%	0	17			75	1.05	3.0	30	56	$0
09	ATL	1	6	27	76	102	2.97	3.10	1.06	194	258	138	4.0	3.2	12.1	3.8	31	21	48	0.7	7%	30%	74%	0	16			87	1.16	12.6	141	263	$19
10	TAM	3	2	45	62	57	1.73	3.45	0.80	163	196	132	3.7	2.0	8.2	4.1	33	16	52	0.6	5%	21%	83%	0	14			94	1.44	18.0	105	169	$28
11	NYY	2	3	2	39	36	4.12	4.09	1.30	229	302	173	3.9	4.1	8.2	2.0	35	20	44	0.9	8%	28%	70%	0	16			40	1.14	-0.9	50	75	-$1
12	NYY	2	1	42	68	69	2.26	3.77	1.17	217	221	214	4.0	3.2	9.2	2.9	36	24	40	0.8	8%	29%	85%	0	16			91	1.27	14.6	93	121	$23
1st Half		2	0	17	29	26	1.84	4.32	1.43	259	235	292	4.0	3.7	8.0	2.2	38	27	35	0.0	0%	35%	86%	0	16			94	1.14	7.9	60	78	$19
2nd Half		0	1	25	38	43	2.58	3.38	0.97	183	206	159	4.1	2.8	10.1	3.6	34	22	44	1.4	14%	23%	84%	0	16			89	1.37	6.8	117	152	$26
13	**Proj**	**3**	**3**	**35**	**73**	**74**	**3.10**	**3.71**	**1.13**	**214**	**243**	**184**	**3.8**	**3.2**	**9.1**	**2.8**	**34**	**22**	**44**	**0.8**	**8%**	**27%**	**75%**	**0**						**8.2**	**89**	**116**	**$20**

Stammen,Craig

Age: 29	Th: R	Role RP	Health	A	LIMA Plan	B
Ht: 6' 3"	Wt: 200	Type Pwr	PT/Exp	C	Rand Var	-5
			Consist	D	MM	2300

Dom continued progress, leading to success as RP, but H%, S% luck helped, too. Season BPV misleading: after 29/6 K/BB in April-May, Ctl rose and Cmd dipped under 2.0, leading to lesser role. Might be worth speculative bid as SP, where he pitched in minors. Otherwise, not too interesting.

Yr	Tm	W	L	Sv	IP	K	ERA	xERA	WHIP	OBA	vL	vR	BF/G	Ctl	Dom	Cmd	G	L	F	hr/9	hr/f	H%	S%	GS	APC	DOM%	DIS%	Sv%	LI	RAR	BPV	BPX	R$
08	a/a	4	5	0	81	53	5.84	4.86	1.57	303			23.8	3.1	5.9	1.9				0.5		35%	61%							-15.2	55	103	-$6
09	WAS *	8	9	0	146	59	4.37	4.28	1.27	271	290	247	22.9	2.0	3.6	1.8	47	21	32	1.2	12%	28%	69%	19	83	32%	32%			-0.8	26	49	$4
10	WAS *	6	4	0	148	93	4.85	4.89	1.47	294	291	301	16.7	2.7	5.6	2.1	51	23	26	0.9	12%	33%	68%	19	60	37%	32%	0	0.59	-14.0	46	75	-$4
11	WAS *	11	8	0	152	108	5.72	6.05	1.64	323	67	105	21.2	2.7	6.4	2.4	52	14	33	1.2	0%	36%	67%	0	21			0	1.55	-33.4	41	62	-$13
12	WAS	6	1	1	88	87	2.34	3.80	1.20	215	198	224	6.3	3.7	8.9	2.4	45	20	35	0.7	8%	28%	84%	0	23			50	0.92	18.2	84	109	$9
1st Half		3	1	0	43	42	1.48	3.64	1.20	215	220	212	6.0	3.6	8.9	2.5	49	22	29	0.4	6%	29%	90%	0	22			0	1.10	13.4	90	117	$11
2nd Half		3	0	1	46	45	3.15	3.94	1.20	214	177	236	6.6	3.7	8.9	2.4	41	19	40	1.0	10%	27%	78%	0	25			100	0.74	4.9	78	102	$8
13	**Proj**	**3**	**1**	**0**	**51**	**41**	**3.92**	**4.02**	**1.37**	**266**	**263**	**268**	**9.5**	**3.2**	**7.4**	**2.3**	**47**	**21**	**32**	**0.9**	**10%**	**32%**	**74%**	**0**						**0.6**	**72**	**93**	**-$1**

Stauffer,Tim

Age: 31	Th: R	Role RP	Health	F	LIMA Plan	D+
Ht: 6' 1"	Wt: 225	Type	PT/Exp	C	Rand Var	+5
			Consist	B	MM	2201

Lost season wasn't a total surprise, given his history of arm issues. Made one start in between triceps injury, elbow woes that eventually led to August surgery. Free agent this winter, expected to be ready for spring training. Despite extreme injury history, skills make him worth keeping on radar.

Yr	Tm	W	L	Sv	IP	K	ERA	xERA	WHIP	OBA	vL	vR	BF/G	Ctl	Dom	Cmd	G	L	F	hr/9	hr/f	H%	S%	GS	APC	DOM%	DIS%	Sv%	LI	RAR	BPV	BPX	R$
08																																	
09	SD *	7	8	1	115	76	3.16	3.54	1.28	244	239	279	15.7	3.3	6.0	1.8	44	20	36	0.8	10%	28%	78%	14	90	36%	36%			16.5	57	106	$9
10	SD *	6	5	0	100	67	2.41	3.01	1.24	247	197	236	10.7	2.8	6.0	2.1	55	15	31	0.3	4%	29%	80%	7	38	57%	29%	0	0.74	20.6	79	127	$8
11	SD	9	12	0	186	128	3.73	3.71	1.25	258	276	239	25.1	2.6	6.2	2.4	52	20	28	1.0	13%	29%	73%	31	97	45%	16%			4.8	72	109	$8
12	SD	0	0	0	5	5	5.40	4.47	2.00	333	286	429	24.0	5.4	9.0	1.7	53	20	27	1.8	25%	40%	78%	1	91	0%	0%			-0.9	47	62	-$5
1st Half		0	0	0	5	5	5.40	4.47	2.00	333	286	429	24.0	5.4	9.0	1.7	53	20	27	1.8	25%	40%	78%	1	91	0%	0%			-0.9	48	62	-$5
2nd Half																																	
13	**Proj**	**5**	**5**	**0**	**87**	**59**	**3.47**	**4.15**	**1.26**	**249**	**244**	**255**	**15.9**	**2.9**	**6.1**	**2.1**	**49**	**19**	**32**	**0.9**	**10%**	**28%**	**76%**	**13**						**5.8**	**57**	**74**	**$3**

Storen,Drew

Age: 25	Th: R	Role RP	Health	D	LIMA Plan	A
Ht: 6' 2"	Wt: 190	Type Pwr	PT/Exp	C	Rand Var	-5
			Consist	A	MM	4331

It took most of year, but worked way back from injury into share of closer role in Sept., when skills (14/0 K/BB in 13 IP) warranted it. Superior GB% should keep challengers at bay, so long as he can stay off DL (and get past playoff meltdown). Pass off LHB struggles to small sample, but keep an eye on it.

Yr	Tm	W	L	Sv	IP	K	ERA	xERA	WHIP	OBA	vL	vR	BF/G	Ctl	Dom	Cmd	G	L	F	hr/9	hr/f	H%	S%	GS	APC	DOM%	DIS%	Sv%	LI	RAR	BPV	BPX	R$
08																																	
09																																	
10	WAS *	4	4	9	72	64	3.07	2.99	1.21	234	247	238	4.3	3.1	8.1	2.6	40	20	40	0.5	5%	30%	75%	0	17			82	1.25	9.0	95	154	$8
11	WAS	6	3	43	75	74	2.75	3.16	1.02	204	198	209	4.2	2.4	8.8	3.7	47	17	35	1.0	11%	26%	78%	0	15			90	1.42	11.1	120	180	$25
12	WAS	3	1	4	30	24	2.37	3.33	0.99	210	289	164	3.1	2.4	7.1	3.0	54	18	28	0.0	0%	26%	73%	0	11			80	1.21	6.1	96	125	$3
1st Half																																	
2nd Half		3	1	4	30	24	2.37	3.33	0.99	210	289	164	3.1	2.4	7.1	3.0	54	18	28	0.0	0%	26%	73%	0	11			80	1.21	6.1	96	125	$3
13	**Proj**	**6**	**3**	**33**	**73**	**64**	**2.77**	**3.55**	**1.09**	**218**	**243**	**202**	**3.7**	**2.7**	**7.9**	**3.0**	**46**	**19**	**35**	**0.4**	**5%**	**28%**	**75%**	**0**						**11.2**	**94**	**123**	**$21**

KRIS OLSON

Straily,Dan

			Health	A	LIMA Plan	B+
Age: 24	Th: R	Role SP	PT/Exp	D	Rand Var	+2
Ht: 6' 2"	Wt: 215	Type Pwr xFB	Consist	F	MM	2403

2-1, 3.89 ERA in 39 IP at OAK. Minor-league K leader rocketed from AA to majors by Aug. First 7 MLB starts had ups, downs (2 PQS-5, 3 PQS-0). Survived xFB profile in minors; home park should help hr/f to turn, but 2H H%, S% luck due to head other way. Given 4.77 MLB xERA, temper short-term hopes.

Yr Tm	W	L	Sv	IP	K	ERA	xERA	WHIP	OBA	vL	vR	BF/G	Ctl	Dom	Cmd	G	L	F	hr/9	hr/f	H%	S%	GS	APC	DOM%	DIS%	Sv%	LI	RAR	BPV	BPX	R$
08																																
09																																
10																																
11																																
12 OAK *	11	8	0	191	193	3.17	2.96	1.11	224	271	215	23.5	2.7	9.1	3.4	30	15	55	0.9	17%	28%	75%	7	96	29%	43%			19.9	109	142	$21
1st Half	4	5	0	98	105	3.34	2.82	1.14	234	0	0	24.3	2.5	9.6	3.8				0.6	0%	31%	71%	0	0					8.2	129	168	$20
2nd Half	7	3	0	93	88	2.99	3.07	1.08	213	271	215	22.7	2.9	8.5	3.0	30	15	55	1.2	17%	25%	79%	7	96	29%	43%			11.7	88	115	$23
13 Proj	9	6	0	145	139	3.92	4.12	1.23	243	279	221	24.1	2.9	8.6	3.0	34	15	51	1.4	10%	29%	74%	24						1.6	88	115	$9

Strasburg,Stephen

			Health	F	LIMA Plan	B
Age: 24	Th: R	Role SP	PT/Exp	C	Rand Var	0
Ht: 6' 4"	Wt: 220	Type Pwr	Consist	A	MM	5505

Shook off rust of late '11 cameo to post a stellar, if artificially shortened, year. Skills approached pre-TJS form and elite at any rate. LHB found some success, but little to quibble with here. Sub-3.00 ERA only better H% luck away. No more coddling, please!

Yr Tm	W	L	Sv	IP	K	ERA	xERA	WHIP	OBA	vL	vR	BF/G	Ctl	Dom	Cmd	G	L	F	hr/9	hr/f	H%	S%	GS	APC	DOM%	DIS%	Sv%	LI	RAR	BPV	BPX	R$
08																																
09																																
10 WAS *	12	5	0	123	147	2.33	2.02	0.99	209	241	207	20.4	2.2	10.7	4.9	48	21	32	0.4	10%	30%	78%	12	89	58%	17%			26.6	167	271	$20
11 WAS	1	1	0	24	24	1.50	2.65	0.71	179	125	227	17.6	0.8	9.0	12.0	38	25	38	0.0	0%	26%	76%	5	66	60%	40%			7.2	158	237	$2
12 WAS	15	6	0	159	197	3.16	2.97	1.15	230	271	185	23.3	2.7	11.1	4.1	44	23	33	0.8	11%	32%	76%	28	93	71%	14%			16.7	149	194	$19
1st Half	9	3	0	93	122	2.81	2.72	1.08	217	236	196	23.3	2.6	11.8	4.5	44	23	33	0.6	8%	32%	76%	16	94	81%	13%			13.9	164	214	$29
2nd Half	6	3	0	66	75	3.66	3.33	1.27	248	316	169	23.3	2.8	10.2	3.6	44	23	33	1.2	15%	33%	76%	12	93	58%	17%			2.9	129	168	$5
13 Proj	19	8	0	201	242	2.92	2.86	1.11	227	266	190	21.7	2.5	10.8	4.3	46	22	32	0.7	10%	31%	76%	36						27.3	150	195	$29

Street,Huston

			Health	F	LIMA Plan	B
Age: 29	Th: R	Role RP	PT/Exp	B	Rand Var	-5
Ht: 6' 0"	Wt: 190	Type Pwr FB	Consist	A	MM	5530

When on field, skills on par with any RP in game. But "F" health grade says you'll have to deal with DL stint or three. Lucky H%, S% helped forge sub-2.00 ERA, but he had a hand, too, with best Dom, GB rate in years. Given skills, only worry should be about the ever-present injury risk.

Yr Tm	W	L	Sv	IP	K	ERA	xERA	WHIP	OBA	vL	vR	BF/G	Ctl	Dom	Cmd	G	L	F	hr/9	hr/f	H%	S%	GS	APC	DOM%	DIS%	Sv%	LI	RAR	BPV	BPX	R$
08 OAK	7	5	18	70	69	3.73	3.81	1.21	229	200	250	4.6	3.5	8.9	2.6	36	22	42	0.8	8%	29%	71%	0	18			72	1.24	5.1	80	150	$13
09 COL	4	1	35	62	70	3.06	3.00	0.91	194	167	217	3.8	1.9	10.2	5.4	38	19	43	1.0	11%	26%	71%	0	14			95	1.04	9.6	149	278	$23
10 COL	4	4	20	47	45	3.61	3.44	1.06	225	208	238	4.3	2.1	8.6	4.1	37	16	48	1.0	8%	28%	69%	0	16			80	1.22	2.7	113	182	$11
11 COL	1	4	29	58	55	3.86	3.34	1.22	276	284	270	3.9	1.4	8.5	6.1	35	24	41	1.5	14%	32%	75%	0	15			88	1.18	0.6	128	193	$11
12 SD	2	1	23	39	47	1.85	2.75	0.72	130	127	132	3.6	2.5	10.8	4.3	42	20	38	0.5	6%	19%	77%	0	15			96	1.19	10.4	147	191	$15
1st Half	1	0	11	20	26	1.35	2.66	0.70	119	167	65	3.5	2.7	11.7	4.3	38	24	38	0.0	0%	21%	79%	0	15			100	1.18	6.6	154	200	$16
2nd Half	1	1	12	19	21	2.37	2.87	0.74	141	74	189	3.7	2.4	9.9	4.2	45	17	38	0.9	13%	18%	75%	0	14			92	1.21	3.9	138	180	$15
13 Proj	3	3	28	51	55	2.83	3.07	0.93	196	180	209	3.7	2.2	9.7	4.4	39	20	41	0.9	10%	25%	74%	0						7.5	133	172	$16

Strop,Pedro

			Health	A	LIMA Plan	B
Age: 28	Th: R	Role RP	PT/Exp	D	Rand Var	-5
Ht: 6' 0"	Wt: 215	Type Pwr xGB	Consist	A	MM	3410

Stats improving. Skills? Not so much. Ctl rising, Dom and Cmd waning. Fortunate H%, S% caught up to him in 2H. Stellar GB rate helped earn him high-leverage opportunities. Ability to hang on to such a role will likely hinge on reigning in those walks, and he's offered scant evidence that's going to happen.

Yr Tm	W	L	Sv	IP	K	ERA	xERA	WHIP	OBA	vL	vR	BF/G	Ctl	Dom	Cmd	G	L	F	hr/9	hr/f	H%	S%	GS	APC	DOM%	DIS%	Sv%	LI	RAR	BPV	BPX	R$
08																																
09 TEX *	6	6	5	71	60	6.73	4.82	1.68	285	154	308	5.9	4.9	7.6	1.5	41	35	24	0.5	0%	35%	57%	0	18			50	0.11	-21.1	61	114	-$5
10 TEX *	1	2	13	53	56	3.91	4.25	1.52	269	368	357	4.3	4.4	9.6	2.2	31	28	42	0.5	13%	36%	74%	0	16			76	1.22	1.1	88	143	$3
11 2 AL *	6	5	11	70	63	3.42	4.33	1.58	279	176	214	4.9	4.4	8.1	1.8	56	20	24	0.3	0%	36%	78%	0	16			73	1.12	4.5	77	116	$4
12 BAL	5	2	3	66	58	2.44	3.80	1.34	217	252	184	4.0	5.0	7.9	1.6	64	16	20	0.3	6%	28%	82%	0	16			30	1.25	12.9	48	63	$5
1st Half	4	2	3	36	31	1.25	3.35	1.11	172	207	141	4.4	4.8	7.8	1.6	70	16	14	0.3	8%	22%	90%	0	17			50	1.33	12.3	59	77	$12
2nd Half	1	0	0	30	27	3.86	4.33	1.62	263	298	230	3.8	5.3	8.0	1.5	59	16	26	0.3	4%	34%	75%	0	15			0	1.18	0.6	37	48	-$4
13 Proj	4	3	3	58	53	3.50	3.82	1.50	255	294	218	4.3	4.8	8.2	1.7	63	16	21	0.3	6%	33%	76%	0						3.7	59	76	$1

Stults,Eric

			Health	B	LIMA Plan	D
Age: 33	Th: L	Role RP	PT/Exp	D	Rand Var	-2
Ht: 6' 0"	Wt: 225	Type	Consist	F	MM	1101

8-3, 2.91 in 99 IP at CHW and SD. A late bloomer? Not exactly, says 4.42 MLB xERA. Cmd marginal, and he benefited from favorable H%, S%. GB rate is decent, but hr/f likely to rise. Would perhaps be better cast as LOOGY. Let someone else bet on a repeat.

Yr Tm	W	L	Sv	IP	K	ERA	xERA	WHIP	OBA	vL	vR	BF/G	Ctl	Dom	Cmd	G	L	F	hr/9	hr/f	H%	S%	GS	APC	DOM%	DIS%	Sv%	LI	RAR	BPV	BPX	R$
08 LA *	9	10	0	156	110	4.00	4.90	1.44	285	314	233	24.7	2.9	6.3	2.2	38	22	41	1.2	12%	32%	76%	7	89	43%	43%			6.3	47	88	$4
09 LA *	9	7	0	114	64	5.58	6.01	1.81	327	262	270	24.0	4.0	5.0	1.3	35	17	48	0.7	4%	36%	69%	10	88	50%	30%			-17.7	26	50	-$10
10																																
11 COL *	4	4	1	80	55	4.81	5.63	1.45	299	158	276	5.9	2.2	6.1	2.8	28	15	58	1.7	17%	32%	73%	0	32			20	0.39	-8.5	39	59	-$4
12 2 TM *	9	4	0	134	83	2.91	3.38	1.27	254	161	278	20.4	2.8	5.5	2.0	40	26	34	0.5	6%	29%	78%	15	76	60%	0%	0	0.67	18.3	65	85	$9
1st Half	2	3	0	60	33	2.76	3.58	1.31	252	208	261	22.4	3.3	5.0	1.5	49	25	26	0.6	15%	28%	81%	5	78	20%	0%	0	0.64	9.3	48	62	$4
2nd Half	7	1	0	75	50	3.03	3.19	1.24	255	145	286	18.9	2.4	6.0	2.5	37	26	37	0.4	4%	30%	75%	10	75	80%	0%	0	0.68	9.1	81	105	$13
13 Proj	6	7	0	124	79	4.26	4.67	1.41	280	241	292	17.1	2.8	5.7	2.0	39	22	39	1.2	11%	31%	74%	22						-3.7	44	57	$0

Swarzak,Anthony

			Health	B	LIMA Plan	D
Age: 27	Th: R	Role RP	PT/Exp	C	Rand Var	+1
Ht: 6' 4"	Wt: 209	Type Con	Consist	C	MM	0100

Progress has ground to a glacial pace. Picked up some Dom, but traded some Ctl to do so. Induced a few more GB, but FB were more damaging, particularly in 2H. Early season starting nod didn't go well. Unless something drastically changes, more mop-up duty likely in store.

Yr Tm	W	L	Sv	IP	K	ERA	xERA	WHIP	OBA	vL	vR	BF/G	Ctl	Dom	Cmd	G	L	F	hr/9	hr/f	H%	S%	GS	APC	DOM%	DIS%	Sv%	LI	RAR	BPV	BPX	R$
08 a/a	8	8	0	147	88	5.11	5.49	1.60	312			24.0	2.9	5.4	1.9				0.9		35%	69%							-14.3	36	67	-$6
09 MIN *	7	12	0	139	72	5.01	5.26	1.52	303	331	292	24.1	2.7	4.7	1.7	36	19	45	1.1	13%	32%	69%	12	88	8%	50%			-11.8	27	51	-$4
10 aaa	5	12	0	112	54	7.11	6.62	1.82	342			23.6	3.2	4.3	1.4				1.0		37%	60%							-41.8	12	19	-$18
11 MIN *	6	8	0	134	75	4.43	4.45	1.39	288	253	301	17.1	2.2	5.0	2.2	38	20	42	0.8	6%	32%	69%	11	62	64%	27%	0	0.69	-8.1	50	76	-$2
12 MIN	3	6	0	97	62	5.03	4.56	1.42	284	254	309	9.4	2.9	5.8	2.0	43	21	35	1.4	13%	30%	68%	5	33	0%	40%	0	0.77	-12.1	47	61	-$7
1st Half	1	4	0	57	33	4.58	4.50	1.32	279	263	293	10.2	2.4	5.2	2.2	42	19	39	1.1	10%	29%	68%	4	36	0%	50%	0	0.50	-4.0	50	65	-$6
2nd Half	2	2	0	40	29	5.67	4.64	1.56	291	243	330	8.5	3.6	6.6	1.8	45	24	31	1.8	20%	31%	69%	1	30	0%	0%	0	1.07	-8.1	43	56	-$9
13 Proj	2	3	0	51	31	5.11	4.82	1.51	296	274	318	12.4	2.9	5.4	1.9	41	21	38	1.2	10%	32%	68%	4						-6.9	39	50	-$5

Takahashi,Hisanori

			Health	A	LIMA Plan	C+
Age: 38	Th: L	Role RP	PT/Exp	C	Rand Var	+5
Ht: 5' 10"	Wt: 175	Type Pwr FB	Consist	A	MM	3400

Triple-digit BPV, sub-4.00 xERA say shame on LAA for losing faith, using him in low-leverage spots then waiving him. When S% turns, could be a decent MLB RP, especially given Dom resurgence, but dalliances with starting gig likely done.

Yr Tm	W	L	Sv	IP	K	ERA	xERA	WHIP	OBA	vL	vR	BF/G	Ctl	Dom	Cmd	G	L	F	hr/9	hr/f	H%	S%	GS	APC	DOM%	DIS%	Sv%	LI	RAR	BPV	BPX	R$
08 for	8	5	0	122	89	5.13	5.57	1.42	284			22.5	2.7	6.6	2.4				2.0		30%	71%							-12.1	29	55	-$1
09 for	10	6	0	144	120	3.65	5.17	1.41	280			24.3	2.8	7.5	2.7				1.7		31%	82%							12.0	50	94	$7
10 NYM	10	6	8	122	114	3.61	3.93	1.30	252	217	264	9.7	3.2	8.4	2.7	38	16	45	1.0	8%	31%	75%	12	39	50%	25%	100	1.08	7.0	82	132	$10
11 LAA	4	3	2	68	52	3.44	4.02	1.22	232	261	206	4.6	3.3	6.9	2.1	41	22	37	0.9	10%	27%	75%	0	18			40	1.37	4.2	54	80	$3
12 2 TM	0	3	0	50	52	5.54	3.81	1.25	251	234	273	4.2	2.5	9.3	3.7	37	17	46	1.4	12%	31%	58%	0	16			0	0.64	-9.5	115	150	-$5
1st Half	0	2	0	27	24	4.33	3.78	1.15	248	254	237	4.2	2.0	8.0	4.0	38	18	44	1.3	12%	29%	67%	0	17			0	0.74	-1.1	106	138	-$4
2nd Half	0	1	0	23	28	6.94	3.83	1.37	255	205	300	4.1	3.1	10.8	3.5	36	15	48	1.5	13%	35%	50%	0	15			0	0.53	-8.4	125	163	-$7
13 Proj	2	3	0	66	63	4.11	3.91	1.28	254	246	261	5.0	2.9	8.5	2.9	39	18	43	1.3	12%	30%	72%	0						-0.8	92	119	$0

KRIS OLSON

Tazawa,Junichi

Age: 27 Th: R Role RP	Health F	LIMA Plan A+	
Ht: 5' 11" Wt: 180 Type Pwr xGB	PT/Exp F	Rand Var -2	
	Consist D	MM 4410	

1-1, 1.43 ERA in 44 IP at BOS. Lost amid Red Sox drama was breakout of former SP two years past TJ surgery. Return to health, role change helped fastball velocity hit new heights. Take a closer look at that Vintage Eck 2H and then try to argue he wouldn't be a dark horse for saves, if need arose.

Yr	Tm	W	L	Sv	IP	K	ERA	xERA	WHIP	OBA	vL	vR	BF/G	Ctl	Dom	Cmd	G	L	F	hr/9	hr/f	H%	S%	GS	APC	DOM%	DIS%	Sv%	LI	RAR	BPV	BPX	R$
08																																	
09	BOS *	11	10	0	135	90	4.40	4.65	1.42	287	323	440	22.0	2.6	6.0	2.3	25	23	53	0.9	7%	32%	71%	4	83	25%	50%	0	0.94	-1.3	55	102	$3
10																																	
11	BOS *	4	3	0	40	41	5.02	4.68	1.38	280	500	125	8.9	2.5	9.1	3.6	13	0	88	1.2	14%	35%	66%	0	18			0	0.21	-5.4	93	139	-$2
12	BOS *	4	3	5	86	89	2.53	3.06	1.22	250	234	222	5.6	2.5	9.3	3.7	49	24	27	0.4	3%	33%	80%	0	18			63	0.82	15.9	128	167	$9
1st Half		3	2	3	42	39	3.66	4.23	1.49	275	100	267	7.0	3.8	8.4	2.2	38	29	33	0.5	0%	35%	76%	0	21			50	0.21	1.9	81	105	$4
2nd Half		1	1	2	44	50	1.43	1.89	0.95	224	259	214	4.6	1.3	10.2	8.1	51	23	26	0.2	4%	32%	85%	0	17			100	0.92	14.0	236	307	$14
13	**Proj**	**4**	**3**	**1**	**58**	**57**	**3.61**	**3.27**	**1.28**	**264**	**295**	**244**	**7.3**	**2.4**	**8.8**	**3.7**	**51**	**23**	**26**	**0.7**	**9%**	**34%**	**73%**	**0**						**2.9**	**124**	**161**	**$2**

Teaford,Everett

Age: 29 Th: L Role RP	Health A	LIMA Plan D	
Ht: 6' 0" Wt: 165 Type	PT/Exp D	Rand Var 0	
	Consist B	MM 1101	

1-4, 4.99 ERA in 61 IP at KC. Flicker of promise seen late in '11 snuffed out by Dom, Cmd regression, continued struggles with HR. Drop in FB velocity may have led to increase in hard-hit balls, OBA, especially vs. LHB. Auditions as SP haven't been long ones, yet we've seen enough.

Yr	Tm	W	L	Sv	IP	K	ERA	xERA	WHIP	OBA	vL	vR	BF/G	Ctl	Dom	Cmd	G	L	F	hr/9	hr/f	H%	S%	GS	APC	DOM%	DIS%	Sv%	LI	RAR	BPV	BPX	R$
08																																	
09	aa	3	7	0	81	32	6.17	6.01	1.69	307			22.8	3.9	3.6	0.9				1.3		31%	65%							-18.5	-5	-10	-$10
10	a/a	14	4	0	104	89	4.51	4.51	1.45	285			15.8	2.9	7.7	2.7				0.8		35%	69%							-5.6	78	126	$2
11	KC *	5	3	1	79	53	3.57	3.50	1.12	221	197	253	7.4	2.9	6.0	2.1	45	24	32	1.5	20%	23%	76%	3	26	67%	33%	50	0.65	3.7	47	70	$5
12	KC *	5	4	0	94	53	3.69	4.46	1.34	267	300	275	15.7	2.8	5.1	1.8	44	20	36	1.2	15%	28%	77%	5	58	0%	60%	0	0.63	3.7	33	43	$0
1st Half		4	1	0	49	27	2.52	3.43	1.27	241	320	219	18.2	3.4	5.0	1.5	55	13	32	0.7	13%	26%	83%	2	76	0%	50%	0	0.62	9.0	46	60	$6
2nd Half		1	3	0	45	26	4.96	5.52	1.41	293	292	291	13.7	2.2	5.2	2.4	40	22	37	1.8	16%	30%	71%	3	53	0%	67%	0	0.63	-5.3	23	30	-$7
13	**Proj**	**5**	**3**	**0**	**73**	**45**	**4.19**	**4.42**	**1.34**	**266**	**268**	**265**	**12.6**	**2.8**	**5.6**	**2.0**	**46**	**21**	**34**	**1.3**	**13%**	**29%**	**73%**	**6**						**-1.5**	**47**	**61**	**$0**

Teheran,Julio

Age: 22 Th: R Role SP	Health A	LIMA Plan D	
Ht: 6' 2" Wt: 175 Type FB	PT/Exp D	Rand Var -1	
	Consist C	MM 1200	

0-0, 5.68 ERA in 6 IP at ATL. Second tour of AAA-Gwinnett went nowhere near as smoothly as the first, as he yielded more hits and struck out fewer batters. Will likely have to demonstrate a new mastery of AAA before he gets another big-league shot, but too young to give up on completely.

Yr	Tm	W	L	Sv	IP	K	ERA	xERA	WHIP	OBA	vL	vR	BF/G	Ctl	Dom	Cmd	G	L	F	hr/9	hr/f	H%	S%	GS	APC	DOM%	DIS%	Sv%	LI	RAR	BPV	BPX	R$
08																																	
09																																	
10	aa	3	2	0	40	35	3.71	2.57	1.17	215			22.8	3.6	7.9	2.2				0.4		27%	68%							1.8	92	150	$1
11	ATL *	16	4	0	164	122	3.19	3.39	1.28	252	340	172	22.5	3.0	6.7	2.2	30	24	46	0.5	13%	30%	76%	3	70	0%	67%	0	0.72	15.2	76	115	$13
12	ATL *	7	9	0	137	92	5.45	5.08	1.48	294	125	267	21.1	2.7	6.0	2.2	22	33	44	1.1	0%	33%	64%	1	50	0%	100%	0	0.71	-24.2	45	59	-$11
1st Half		5	5	0	72	51	5.02	4.96	1.47	284	167	273	20.7	3.2	6.3	2.0	8	42	50	1.2	0%	32%	68%	1	74	0%	100%			-9.0	43	56	-$6
2nd Half		2	4	0	65	41	5.92	5.16	1.48	304	0	250	21.5	2.2	5.7	2.6	50	17	33	1.0	0%	34%	60%	0	25			0	0.68	-15.3	51	66	-$15
13	**Proj**	**3**	**2**	**0**	**44**	**31**	**4.47**	**4.62**	**1.36**	**270**			**21.8**	**2.9**	**6.5**	**2.2**	**32**	**23**	**45**	**1.2**	**10%**	**30%**	**71%**	**8**						**-2.4**	**48**	**63**	**-$2**

Thatcher,Joe

Age: 31 Th: L Role RP	Health F	LIMA Plan B	
Ht: 6' 2" Wt: 230 Type Pwr	PT/Exp D	Rand Var 0	
	Consist D	MM 4500	

Replaced '11 shoulder woes with knee issue that cost him a little over a month and required off-season surgery. If they can rebuild him, should be able to resume status as top-notch LOOGY. But given extreme struggles against RHB, unlikely to be anything more than that.

Yr	Tm	W	L	Sv	IP	K	ERA	xERA	WHIP	OBA	vL	vR	BF/G	Ctl	Dom	Cmd	G	L	F	hr/9	hr/f	H%	S%	GS	APC	DOM%	DIS%	Sv%	LI	RAR	BPV	BPX	R$
08	SD *	5	6	3	65	53	5.06	5.59	1.67	316	414	370	4.7	3.3	7.4	2.2	41	25	34	0.8	13%	38%	70%	0	20			38	1.13	-5.9	59	111	-$3
09	SD *	2	2	1	64	73	2.63	3.19	1.28	245	182	267	3.7	3.3	10.2	3.1	44	18	38	0.4	5%	34%	80%	0	16			33	0.95	13.3	120	225	$4
10	SD	1	0	0	35	45	1.29	2.51	0.86	185	197	172	2.1	1.8	11.6	6.4	41	21	38	0.3	3%	29%	86%	0	9			0	1.08	12.1	179	289	$5
11	SD	0	0	0	10	9	4.50	4.81	1.50	216	158	278	2.4	6.3	8.1	1.3	38	19	42	0.9	9%	27%	71%	0	10			0	1.07	-0.7	-8	-12	-$4
12	SD	1	4	1	32	39	3.41	3.58	1.39	250	175	333	2.6	4.0	11.1	2.8	43	19	38	0.6	6%	36%	76%	0	10			100	1.39	2.4	113	148	-$2
1st Half		0	2	0	20	21	3.10	3.71	1.23	234	147	302	2.9	3.1	9.3	3.0	45	13	42	0.4	4%	32%	75%	0	10			0	1.27	2.3	107	139	-$2
2nd Half		1	2	1	11	18	3.97	3.33	1.68	279	207	429	2.2	5.6	14.3	2.6	38	31	31	0.8	13%	44%	78%	0	9			100	1.53	0.1	124	161	-$2
13	**Proj**	**1**	**2**	**0**	**36**	**39**	**3.37**	**3.42**	**1.24**	**245**	**194**	**291**	**3.0**	**2.9**	**9.8**	**3.4**	**44**	**17**	**39**	**0.5**	**5%**	**33%**	**73%**	**0**						**2.9**	**119**	**155**	**$0**

Thayer,Dale

Age: 32 Th: R Role RP	Health A	LIMA Plan B+	
Ht: 6' 0" Wt: 195 Type	PT/Exp D	Rand Var -1	
	Consist D	MM 2210	

Surprised with 5-for-5 blitz when May save chances came; skills say it wasn't the worst idea a manager ever had. After June-July swoon, rebounded with BPV of 132, 134 in Aug/Sept. 2H Dom slipped back below ideal closer level. He'd need planets to align again to see more saves, but a useful reliever.

Yr	Tm	W	L	Sv	IP	K	ERA	xERA	WHIP	OBA	vL	vR	BF/G	Ctl	Dom	Cmd	G	L	F	hr/9	hr/f	H%	S%	GS	APC	DOM%	DIS%	Sv%	LI	RAR	BPV	BPX	R$
08	aaa	3	1	9	68	58	3.58	5.43	1.74	323			6.0	3.6	7.7	2.2				0.3		40%	79%							6.2	72	136	$1
09	TAM *	2	5	18	77	41	3.46	5.01	1.49	308	208	382	5.4	2.1	4.8	2.2	30	16	54	0.8	11%	34%	79%	0	21			75	0.17	8.2	46	85	$6
10	TAM *	4	1	3	62	43	5.15	6.76	1.97	349	500	556	6.3	4.1	6.3	1.5	50	30	20	0.6	50%	40%	74%	0	53			75	0.37	-8.2	36	58	-$7
11	NYM *	4	6	21	81	52	3.22	3.56	1.16	255	500	222	5.0	1.7	5.8	3.3	44	28	28	1.0	0%	28%	76%	0	14			81	0.59	7.3	79	119	$13
12	SD	2	2	7	58	47	3.43	3.78	1.13	248	253	244	3.7	1.9	7.3	3.9	41	21	38	0.6	6%	30%	70%	0	15			70	1.15	4.1	100	131	$4
1st Half		1	2	5	22	20	5.24	3.67	1.30	287	317	261	3.9	1.6	8.1	5.0	43	21	37	1.2	12%	34%	62%	0	17			83	1.04	-3.4	122	159	-$1
2nd Half		1	0	2	35	27	2.29	3.85	1.02	221	200	234	3.5	2.0	6.9	3.4	40	21	39	0.3	3%	27%	77%	0	14			50	1.21	7.5	87	113	$7
13	**Proj**	**2**	**2**	**3**	**58**	**43**	**3.65**	**4.13**	**1.31**	**273**	**279**	**268**	**4.4**	**2.3**	**6.7**	**2.9**	**41**	**21**	**38**	**0.7**	**7%**	**32%**	**73%**	**0**						**2.6**	**78**	**101**	**$1**

Thornburg,Tyler

Age: 24 Th: R Role RP	Health A	LIMA Plan A	
Ht: 6' 0" Wt: 190 Type Pwr GB	PT/Exp F	Rand Var +5	
	Consist F	MM 3401	

0-0, 4.50 ERA in 22 IP in MIL. Unceremoniously welcomed with 4 HR in debut. Three more went yard in next two games, but work in minors suggests more hr/f fluke than chronic issue. On plus side, showed ability to carry Dom into MLB. Bullpen may be home long term, but intriguing enough to keep eye on.

Yr	Tm	W	L	Sv	IP	K	ERA	xERA	WHIP	OBA	vL	vR	BF/G	Ctl	Dom	Cmd	G	L	F	hr/9	hr/f	H%	S%	GS	APC	DOM%	DIS%	Sv%	LI	RAR	BPV	BPX	R$
08																																	
09																																	
10																																	
11																																	
12	MIL *	10	4	0	135	116	4.00	4.25	1.34	263	268	289	19.3	3.1	7.8	2.5	42	20	38	1.1	32%	31%	74%	3	48	0%	100%	0	0.42	0.2	70	91	$3
1st Half		8	1	0	80	63	3.96	3.84	1.23	245	200	375	23.2	2.8	7.0	2.5	32	11	58	1.2	36%	28%	72%	1	93	0%	100%			0.6	64	83	$10
2nd Half		2	3	0	54	54	4.03	4.76	1.51	286	278	241	15.7	3.4	8.9	2.6	47	23	30	0.9	29%	36%	75%	2	41	0%	100%	0	0.37	-0.1	80	104	-$7
13	**Proj**	**7**	**4**	**0**	**116**	**106**	**3.95**	**3.88**	**1.41**	**272**	**289**	**251**	**18.0**	**3.2**	**8.2**	**2.6**	**47**	**23**	**30**	**1.0**	**11%**	**33%**	**75%**	**22**						**0.9**	**86**	**111**	**$2**

Thornton,Matt

Age: 36 Th: L Role RP	Health A	LIMA Plan A+	
Ht: 6' 6" Wt: 240 Type Pwr GB	PT/Exp C	Rand Var 0	
	Consist A	MM 4410	

That sound you heard? Window closing on his chance to seize full-time closer role. New mgr, similar usage. Dom slip (year over year and in 2H) a bit concerning given his age. Still, a rock solid Cmd/GB profile. Something to be said about knowing what you get: solid ERA and a few situational save scraps.

Yr	Tm	W	L	Sv	IP	K	ERA	xERA	WHIP	OBA	vL	vR	BF/G	Ctl	Dom	Cmd	G	L	F	hr/9	hr/f	H%	S%	GS	APC	DOM%	DIS%	Sv%	LI	RAR	BPV	BPX	R$
08	CHW	5	3	1	67	77	2.67	2.75	1.00	196	170	218	3.6	2.5	10.3	4.1	53	20	27	0.7	11%	28%	76%	0	14			17	1.21	13.7	148	277	$9
09	CHW	6	3	4	72	87	2.74	2.90	1.08	217	208	223	4.2	2.5	10.8	4.4	46	17	36	0.6	8%	31%	77%	0	17			44	1.46	14.1	152	284	$11
10	CHW	5	4	8	61	81	2.67	2.66	1.01	191	175	203	3.9	3.0	12.0	4.1	40	23	37	0.4	6%	30%	74%	0	16			80	1.38	10.5	154	249	$11
11	CHW	2	5	3	60	63	3.32	3.32	1.36	255	260	252	4.2	3.2	9.5	3.0	49	24	27	0.5	7%	35%	76%	0	17			43	1.28	4.6	113	169	$2
12	CHW	4	10	3	65	53	3.46	3.45	1.23	257	256	258	3.6	2.4	7.3	3.1	54	20	26	0.6	8%	31%	72%	0	14			43	1.43	4.4	101	131	$3
1st Half		2	5	1	33	30	3.24	3.45	1.32	262	227	297	3.7	2.7	8.1	3.0	56	20	25	0.5	8%	33%	76%	0	14			25	1.12	3.2	107	139	$2
2nd Half		2	5	2	32	23	3.69	3.45	1.14	252	291	217	3.5	2.0	6.5	3.3	53	21	26	0.6	8%	29%	68%	0	13			67	1.76	1.3	95	124	$3
13	**Proj**	**4**	**7**	**3**	**65**	**64**	**3.53**	**3.27**	**1.20**	**243**	**245**	**242**	**3.7**	**2.6**	**8.8**	**3.4**	**50**	**22**	**28**	**0.5**	**7%**	**32%**	**71%**	**0**						**3.9**	**116**	**150**	**$4**

KRIS OLSON

Tillman,Chris

Age: 25	Th: R	Role SP	Health A	LIMA Plan C+
Ht: 6' 5"	Wt: 210	Type Pwr FB	PT/Exp C	Rand Var 0
			Consist D	MM 2303

9-3, 2.93 ERA in 86 IP at BAL. Suddenly found his way out of the woods, guided by velocity gains, newfound control and great progress vL. MLB xERA doesn't buy that he's a sub-4.00 ERA pitcher just yet, but the skills say he's right on the cusp. UP: 3.75 ERA.

Yr	Tm	W	L	Sv	IP	K	ERA	xERA	WHIP	OBA	vL	vR	BF/G	Ctl	Dom	Cmd	G	L	F	hr/9	hr/f	H%	S%	GS	APC	DOM%	DIS%	Sv%	LI	RAR	BPV	BPX	R$
08	aa	11	4	0	136	132	3.91	4.06	1.42	254			20.6	4.1	8.7	2.1				0.8		32%	74%							7.0	76	142	$7
09	BAL *	10	11	0	162	122	4.37	4.85	1.42	283	254	341	22.9	2.8	6.8	2.4	37	18	45	1.2	15%	32%	73%	12	97	0%	33%			-1.1	53	99	$3
10	BAL *	13	12	0	175	111	4.56	4.61	1.41	275	274	238	23.1	3.1	5.7	1.8	43	22	36	1.1	15%	30%	70%	11	87	18%	55%			-10.4	40	65	$1
11	BAL *	6	11	0	138	91	5.94	6.08	1.65	298	300	302	22.1	4.1	5.9	1.4	37	18	45	1.6	5%	32%	68%	13	90	31%	54%			-34.1	12	18	-$15
12	BAL *	17	12	0	179	142	3.95	3.87	1.29	256	216	192	22.9	2.9	7.2	2.5	35	21	44	0.9	11%	30%	72%	15	96	60%	20%			1.5	72	93	$9
1st Half		8	8	0	89	75	5.04	4.86	1.55	297	0	0	24.4	3.2	7.5	2.3				0.7	0%	36%	67%	0	0					-11.3	69	90	$1
2nd Half		9	4	0	89	68	3.21	3.14	1.08	219	216	192	21.8	2.6	6.8	2.6	35	21	44	1.2	11%	24%	77%	15	96	60%	20%			8.9	70	91	$18
13	**Proj**	**12**	**11**	**0**	**160**	**129**	**4.05**	**4.32**	**1.35**	**263**	**264**	**263**	**22.3**	**3.1**	**7.2**	**2.3**	**38**	**20**	**41**	**1.2**	**10%**	**30%**	**74%**	**30**						**-0.7**	**63**	**82**	**$6**

Torres,Alexander

Age: 25	Th: L	Role RP	Health A	LIMA Plan F
Ht: 5' 10"	Wt: 175	Type Pwr	PT/Exp D	Rand Var +5
			Consist C	MM 1400

1-1, 3.38 ERA in 8 IP at TAM. A power arm with Rick Ankiel-like accuracy, broad sides of barns would be decidedly safe in his presence. Move to bullpen didn't solve those woes, neither did late-season callup to TAM (7 BB in 8 IP). Elite Dom holds our attention, but he's very much a project at this point.

Yr	Tm	W	L	Sv	IP	K	ERA	xERA	WHIP	OBA	vL	vR	BF/G	Ctl	Dom	Cmd	G	L	F	hr/9	hr/f	H%	S%	GS	APC	DOM%	DIS%	Sv%	LI	RAR	BPV	BPX	R$
08																																	
09	aa	3	3	0	35	28	3.65	4.32	1.66	265			22.2	5.8	7.2	1.2				0.3		33%	77%							2.9	63	118	-$2
10	aa	11	6	0	143	129	4.14	4.64	1.59	279			23.3	4.5	8.2	1.8				0.6		35%	74%							-1.1	69	111	$0
11	TAM *	10	8	0	154	141	3.47	4.31	1.60	268	200	313	22.0	5.1	8.2	1.6	59	23	18	0.4	0%	34%	78%	0	40			0	0.71	8.9	72	108	$1
12	aaa	3	7	0	69	75	8.53	6.31	2.09	294			13.0	8.2	9.8	1.2				0.8		39%	57%							-38.4	56	73	-$23
1st Half		3	3	0	48	52	7.61	6.16	2.08	290			12.5	8.4	9.7	1.2				0.8		38%	62%							-21.4	57	74	-$23
2nd Half		0	4	0	21	23	10.68	6.55	2.11	304			14.5	7.9	10.1	1.3				0.9		40%	46%							-17.0	55	72	-$23
13	**Proj**	**1**	**3**	**0**	**27**	**27**	**5.00**	**4.70**	**1.66**	**249**			**16.1**	**6.6**	**8.9**	**1.4**	**49**	**20**	**31**	**1.0**	**12%**	**31%**	**71%**	**5**						**-3.3**	**11**	**14**	**-$4**

Torres,Carlos

Age: 30	Th: R	Role RP	Health A	LIMA Plan D
Ht: 6' 1"	Wt: 190	Type Pwr	PT/Exp D	Rand Var -1
			Consist A	MM 1200

5-3, 5.26 ERA in 53 IP at COL. Its been two years since we last saw him, and it doesn't seem like much progress has been made. Decent GB tilt, but there's little evidence that it's a permanent part of his skill set. Ctl still horrible, and he still has yet to scrape together a 2.0 Cmd. Next.

Yr	Tm	W	L	Sv	IP	K	ERA	xERA	WHIP	OBA	vL	vR	BF/G	Ctl	Dom	Cmd	G	L	F	hr/9	hr/f	H%	S%	GS	APC	DOM%	DIS%	Sv%	LI	RAR	BPV	BPX	R$
08	a/a	9	5	0	121	89	4.99	4.88	1.56	295			18.3	3.5	6.6	1.9				0.7		35%	68%							-9.9	56	104	-$2
09	CHW *	11	6	1	156	125	4.09	4.44	1.57	266	264	308	22.1	4.9	7.2	1.5	38	18	45	0.6	13%	32%	74%	5	61	40%	40%	100	0.54	4.5	56	105	$3
10	CHW *	9	10	0	174	123	4.93	5.02	1.60	272	400	355	24.0	4.9	6.3	1.3	29	35	37	1.1	11%	31%	71%	1	54	0%	0%	0	0.24	-18.3	34	55	-$7
11																																	
12	COL *	10	7	0	114	83	5.06	4.81	1.57	282	225	279	11.1	4.2	6.5	1.6	44	27	29	0.8	5%	33%	68%	0	29			0	0.60	-14.7	48	62	-$8
1st Half		5	4	0	66	43	4.92	5.85	1.71	303	125	333	17.6	4.4	5.8	1.3	47	35	18	1.2	33%	34%	74%	0	24			0	0.17	-7.4	22	29	-$9
2nd Half		5	3	0	48	40	5.25	3.31	1.38	251	236	273	7.2	3.9	7.5	1.9	43	26	30	0.2	2%	32%	59%	0	30			0	0.67	-7.3	84	109	-$6
13	**Proj**	**3**	**2**	**0**	**36**	**27**	**4.90**	**4.67**	**1.55**	**274**	**251**	**290**	**13.4**	**4.4**	**6.8**	**1.5**	**48**	**29**	**33**	**0.7**	**8%**	**32%**	**68%**	**4**						**-3.9**	**29**	**38**	**-$4**

Turner,Jacob

Age: 22	Th: R	Role SP	Health A	LIMA Plan B
Ht: 6' 5"	Wt: 210	Type FB	PT/Exp D	Rand Var +1
			Consist A	MM 1103

2-5, 4.42 ERA in 55 IP at DET/MIA. Former 1st rounder showed flashes in Sept. (2.63 ERA), but it was mostly H%/S%-induced. Height and mid-90s fastball suggests strikeouts should come, but there is little sign of them yet, which tempers our short-term interest. Still raw...check back in a year.

Yr	Tm	W	L	Sv	IP	K	ERA	xERA	WHIP	OBA	vL	vR	BF/G	Ctl	Dom	Cmd	G	L	F	hr/9	hr/f	H%	S%	GS	APC	DOM%	DIS%	Sv%	LI	RAR	BPV	BPX	R$
08																																	
09																																	
10																																	
11	DET *	4	6	0	144	102	4.34	3.82	1.27	264	400	241	25.5	2.3	6.4	2.8	41	20	39	0.8	17%	30%	67%	3	80	33%	67%			-7.1	74	112	$1
12	2 TM *	8	7	0	145	85	3.62	3.71	1.30	250	189	274	23.9	3.2	5.3	1.6	45	19	36	0.8	14%	28%	74%	10	90	40%	10%			7.1	47	62	$5
1st Half		3	1	0	53	28	3.58	3.42	1.41	242	333	125	24.9	4.6	4.8	1.0	53	20	27	0.3	0%	27%	74%	1	94	0%	0%			2.8	48	62	-$2
2nd Half		5	6	0	92	57	3.64	3.84	1.24	255	174	284	23.3	2.5	5.5	2.3	44	19	36	1.1	15%	28%	74%	9	89	44%	11%			4.3	53	69	$8
13	**Proj**	**6**	**6**	**0**	**138**	**87**	**4.08**	**4.49**	**1.33**	**263**	**194**	**317**	**24.8**	**2.9**	**5.7**	**1.9**	**49**	**21**	**40**	**1.1**	**10%**	**29%**	**73%**	**23**						**-1.1**	**50**	**65**	**$2**

Uehara,Koji

Age: 38	Th: R	Role RP	Health F	LIMA Plan A
Ht: 6' 1"	Wt: 190	Type Pwr xFB	PT/Exp D	Rand Var -5
			Consist A	MM 5500

Strained lat cut IP in half, but still managed his third straight 150+ BPV. If FB% didn't hurt him in Arlington, it's probably time we stopped mentioning it as a detriment, right? Maybe, but H%/S% regression, second straight year of -5 Rand Var still loom. Pay for sub-3.00 ERA, not sub-2.00.

Yr	Tm	W	L	Sv	IP	K	ERA	xERA	WHIP	OBA	vL	vR	BF/G	Ctl	Dom	Cmd	G	L	F	hr/9	hr/f	H%	S%	GS	APC	DOM%	DIS%	Sv%	LI	RAR	BPV	BPX	R$
08	for	6	5	1	90	68	4.72	5.00	1.29	276			14.2	2.0	6.8	3.4				1.8		30%	70%							-4.4	58	110	$2
09	BAL	2	4	0	67	48	4.05	4.38	1.25	270	273	266	23.3	1.6	6.5	4.0	30	17	53	0.9	6%	31%	70%	12	88	33%	17%			2.2	81	151	$1
10	BAL	1	2	13	44	55	2.86	2.98	0.95	220	263	185	4.1	1.0	11.3	11.0	24	18	58	1.0	8%	32%	76%	0	16			87	1.23	6.6	177	286	$9
11	2 AL	2	3	0	65	85	2.35	2.56	0.72	164	130	197	3.7	1.2	11.8	9.4	32	14	53	1.5	14%	22%	83%	0	14			0	1.06	12.7	188	283	$10
12	TEX	0	0	1	36	43	1.75	2.67	0.64	160	188	125	3.5	0.8	10.8	14.3	33	17	51	1.0	10%	21%	84%	0	14			100	0.66	10.1	184	240	$5
1st Half		0	0	0	21	22	2.11	3.06	0.70	171	179	162	4.0	0.8	9.3	11.0	35	16	49	1.3	11%	21%	83%	0	15			0	0.39	5.0	157	204	$4
2nd Half		0	0	1	15	21	1.23	2.16	0.55	143	200	53	3.0	0.6	12.9	21.0	29	18	54	0.6	7%	23%	86%	0	12			100	0.97	5.0	222	289	$7
13	**Proj**	**1**	**2**	**0**	**44**	**46**	**2.90**	**3.20**	**0.91**	**216**	**228**	**205**	**4.8**	**1.2**	**9.6**	**8.0**	**30**	**17**	**54**	**1.3**	**10%**	**27%**	**76%**	**0**						**6.0**	**148**	**192**	**$3**

Valdes,Raul

Age: 35	Th: L	Role RP	Health C	LIMA Plan B
Ht: 5' 11"	Wt: 190	Type Pwr xFB	PT/Exp D	Rand Var 0
			Consist F	MM 3400

3-2, 2.90 ERA in 31 IP at PHI. Where did THIS come from? Pitched sporadically thanks to injuries (hip, meniscus), but was integral cog in PHI bullpen when healthy. Age plus lack of pedigree suggest this was more fluke than late-career revival. He's merely a fringe LIMA play for now.

Yr	Tm	W	L	Sv	IP	K	ERA	xERA	WHIP	OBA	vL	vR	BF/G	Ctl	Dom	Cmd	G	L	F	hr/9	hr/f	H%	S%	GS	APC	DOM%	DIS%	Sv%	LI	RAR	BPV	BPX	R$
08																																	
09																																	
10	NYM *	5	4	1	95	83	4.41	4.57	1.46	274	330	216	8.6	3.5	7.9	2.2	34	18	48	1.0	8%	33%	72%	1	28	0%	0%	33	0.86	-3.9	66	106	-$1
11	2 TM *	7	3	0	76	63	5.95	6.47	1.64	329	296	286	7.5	2.3	7.5	3.2	31	28	41	1.6	8%	38%	67%	0	19			0	0.75	-18.7	54	81	-$8
12	PHI *	4	4	3	61	65	3.45	3.01	1.00	238	149	183	5.4	1.1	9.6	8.8	24	26	50	1.1	8%	30%	70%	1	17	0%	100%	75	0.96	4.2	219	286	$6
1st Half		3	3	3	46	48	3.80	3.67	1.10	259	160	175	6.4	1.1	9.3	8.8	20	30	50	1.2	9%	32%	70%	1	21	0%	100%	75	0.80	1.3	208	271	$8
2nd Half		1	1	0	15	18	2.40	0.91	0.69	165	136	200	3.5	1.2	10.6	8.9	29	21	50	0.6	7%	23%	68%	0	14			0	1.13	3.0	254	331	$0
13	**Proj**	**2**	**2**	**0**	**29**	**29**	**4.20**	**3.74**	**1.21**	**262**	**294**	**242**	**5.7**	**1.9**	**8.9**	**4.8**	**28**	**23**	**49**	**1.1**	**9%**	**32%**	**68%**	**0**						**-0.7**	**116**	**150**	**-$1**

Valverde,Jose

Age: 35	Th: R	Role RP	Health A	LIMA Plan D+
Ht: 6' 4"	Wt: 254	Type Pwr FB	PT/Exp A	Rand Var -3
			Consist B	MM 1230

Couldn't repeat Sv% perfection, and there's a laundry list of ominous signs that say the worst is yet to come: LHBs are figuring him out, Dom took a severe dip, FB% continues to rise, miniscule hr/f has to rise. BPV trend sums it up: try to contain evil cackle if someone drafts him as a top-tier closer again.

Yr	Tm	W	L	Sv	IP	K	ERA	xERA	WHIP	OBA	vL	vR	BF/G	Ctl	Dom	Cmd	G	L	F	hr/9	hr/f	H%	S%	GS	APC	DOM%	DIS%	Sv%	LI	RAR	BPV	BPX	R$
08	HOU	6	3	44	72	83	3.38	3.41	1.18	225	190	252	4.1	2.9	10.4	3.6	39	20	41	1.3	13%	30%	77%	0	17			86	1.10	8.4	126	237	$25
09	HOU	4	2	25	54	56	2.33	3.67	1.13	207	281	144	4.2	3.5	9.3	2.7	41	13	46	0.8	8%	27%	84%	0	17			86	1.06	13.2	93	173	$16
10	DET	2	4	26	63	63	3.00	3.51	1.16	184	165	204	4.3	4.6	9.0	2.0	55	13	32	0.7	10%	24%	76%	0	17			90	0.95	8.4	72	116	$14
11	DET	2	4	49	72	69	2.24	3.85	1.19	198	230	158	4.0	4.2	8.6	2.0	43	16	41	0.6	6%	26%	84%	0	16			100	1.10	15.2	61	92	$25
12	DET	3	4	35	69	48	3.78	4.78	1.25	229	257	193	4.1	3.5	6.3	1.8	34	22	44	0.4	3%	28%	69%	0	16			88	0.98	2.0	30	39	$14
1st Half		3	2	14	31	21	3.77	5.44	1.39	226	262	185	4.3	4.9	6.1	1.2	34	20	46	0.6	5%	27%	73%	0	17			82	1.14	0.9	-11	-14	$13
2nd Half		0	2	21	38	27	3.79	4.29	1.13	231	253	200	4.0	2.4	6.4	2.7	34	23	43	0.2	2%	29%	64%	0	15			91	0.85	1.1	63	82	$16
13	**Proj**	**3**	**4**	**33**	**65**	**50**	**4.01**	**4.45**	**1.28**	**234**	**258**	**206**	**4.0**	**3.8**	**6.9**	**1.8**	**40**	**19**	**41**	**1.0**	**9%**	**27%**	**71%**	**0**						**0.0**	**41**	**53**	**$13**

MATT GELFAND

Vargas,Jason

Age: 30 Th: L Role SP	Health B	LIMA Plan C
Ht: 6' 0" Wt: 215 Type Con FB	PT/Exp A	Rand Var -1
	Consist A	MM 1105

Barely noticeable steps in the right direction: Shut down LHBs in 2H, GB% creeping upwards, other skills stable. That said, sub-4 ERAs in even years both H%-fueled, so he's really been the same mediocre pitcher four years running. He'll eat up innings, but let xERA guide your bidding.

Yr Tm	W	L	Sv	IP	K	ERA	xERA	WHIP	OBA	vL	vR	BF/G	Ctl	Dom	Cmd	G	L	F	hr/9	hr/f	H%	S%	GS	APC	DOM%	DIS%	Sv%	LI	RAR	BPV	BPX	R$
08																																
09 SEA *	7	9	0	143	92	4.40	4.51	1.34	274	290	277	18.6	2.5	5.8	2.3	37	21	42	1.2	13%	30%	71%	14	64	14%	43%	0	0.86	-1.4	48	91	$3
10 SEA	9	12	0	193	116	3.78	4.57	1.25	251	200	268	26.2	2.5	5.4	2.1	36	17	47	0.8	6%	28%	72%	31	97	39%	13%			7.0	43	70	$9
11 SEA	10	13	0	201	131	4.25	4.43	1.31	260	278	255	26.8	2.6	5.9	2.2	36	20	44	1.0	8%	30%	70%	32	102	50%	22%			-7.7	48	73	$3
12 SEA	14	11	0	217	141	3.85	4.31	1.18	245	239	247	26.9	2.3	5.8	2.6	40	19	40	1.4	13%	26%	74%	33	102	48%	21%			4.4	62	80	$13
1st Half	7	7	0	109	74	4.54	4.30	1.19	248	287	236	26.1	2.4	6.1	2.6	40	18	42	1.7	15%	26%	69%	17	100	47%	18%			-7.1	63	82	$10
2nd Half	7	4	0	108	67	3.16	4.33	1.16	242	196	258	27.8	2.2	5.6	2.6	40	21	39	1.2	11%	27%	79%	16	103	50%	25%			11.5	60	78	$17
13 Proj	11	11	0	203	130	4.15	4.46	1.26	261	252	264	25.2	2.4	5.7	2.4	38	19	42	1.2	10%	28%	71%	33						-3.3	55	71	$8

Venters,Jonny

Age: 28 Th: L Role RP	Health A	LIMA Plan B
Ht: 6' 3" Wt: 195 Type Pwr xGB	PT/Exp C	Rand Var +5
	Consist A	MM 5500

"Down" year exacerbated by fluky 1H where ridiculous H% and hr/f actually caused much more pain. High GB% mitigated the damage somewhat, and then things corrected in 2H. Skills-wise, he was as strong as ever, as elite Dom continues to offset Ctl issues. A return to 30+ holds likely.

Yr Tm	W	L	Sv	IP	K	ERA	xERA	WHIP	OBA	vL	vR	BF/G	Ctl	Dom	Cmd	G	L	F	hr/9	hr/f	H%	S%	GS	APC	DOM%	DIS%	Sv%	LI	RAR	BPV	BPX	R$
08																																
09 a/a	8	11	0	157	83	5.71	5.59	1.80	308			24.9	4.9	4.8	1.0				0.6		34%	67%							-26.7	25	46	-$14
10 ATL	4	4	1	83	95	1.95	2.71	1.20	204	198	207	4.4	4.2	10.1	2.4	68	15	17	0.1	3%	30%	83%	0	17			20	1.05	21.8	113	183	$9
11 ATL	6	2	5	88	96	1.84	2.57	1.09	176	127	194	4.2	4.4	9.8	2.2	73	14	14	0.2	7%	25%	83%	0	16			56	1.28	22.8	109	164	$14
12 ATL	5	4	0	59	69	3.22	3.06	1.52	270	250	281	4.0	4.3	10.6	2.5	63	21	16	0.9	24%	36%	82%	0	15			0	0.97	5.7	116	151	-$1
1st Half	3	3	0	30	41	3.86	3.01	1.78	312	311	312	3.9	4.7	12.2	2.6	59	25	16	1.5	38%	43%	84%	0	15			0	1.08	0.6	128	167	-$2
2nd Half	2	1	0	28	28	2.54	3.09	1.24	221	171	246	4.1	3.8	8.9	2.3	67	17	16	0.3	8%	30%	79%	0	14			0	0.84	5.2	102	133	$1
13 Proj	5	3	0	65	69	2.86	3.05	1.36	238	212	250	4.4	4.3	9.5	2.2	68	17	15	0.4	10%	32%	79%	0						9.3	101	131	$3

Veras,Jose

Age: 32 Th: R Role RP	Health A	LIMA Plan C
Ht: 6' 6" Wt: 235 Type Pwr	PT/Exp D	Rand Var 0
	Consist A	MM 3500

Despite year-long MIL bullpen turmoil, never got a shot in the big chair, as Ctl kept him out of high-leverage situations (see LI). High Dom is a nice start, but it doesn't work in isolation (see Ctl). And at age 32, we're getting past the window for a new skill to emerge here.

Yr Tm	W	L	Sv	IP	K	ERA	xERA	WHIP	OBA	vL	vR	BF/G	Ctl	Dom	Cmd	G	L	F	hr/9	hr/f	H%	S%	GS	APC	DOM%	DIS%	Sv%	LI	RAR	BPV	BPX	R$
08 NYY	5	3	0	58	63	3.59	3.99	1.40	239	217	254	4.2	4.5	9.8	2.2	41	18	41	1.1	11%	31%	78%	0	17			0	0.76	5.2	74	138	$2
09 2 AL	4	3	0	50	40	5.19	4.99	1.39	225	259	198	4.8	5.0	7.2	1.4	36	16	47	1.4	12%	25%	66%	0	19			0	0.70	-5.4	8	14	-$2
10 FLA *	4	4	2	77	83	4.53	4.47	1.57	256	155	221	4.7	5.4	9.7	1.8	40	23	37	0.8	12%	33%	72%	0	17			50	1.22	-4.3	74	120	-$2
11 PIT	2	4	1	71	79	3.80	3.77	1.24	206	184	220	3.9	4.3	10.0	2.3	37	18	45	0.8	7%	28%	71%	0	16			13	1.26	1.2	79	119	$2
12 MIL	5	4	1	67	79	3.63	3.99	1.51	239	260	220	4.2	5.4	10.6	2.0	44	25	31	0.7	9%	34%	77%	0	18			50	0.91	3.2	68	89	-$1
1st Half	3	3	1	33	37	3.82	4.60	1.76	265	250	281	4.5	6.3	10.1	1.6	42	30	28	0.3	4%	38%	77%	0	19			50	1.02	0.8	32	42	-$2
2nd Half	2	1	0	34	42	3.44	3.44	1.26	211	273	162	3.9	4.5	11.1	2.5	46	18	35	1.1	14%	29%	77%	0	17			0	0.81	2.4	103	134	$1
13 Proj	4	4	0	65	74	3.87	3.95	1.42	235	241	229	4.0	5.0	10.2	2.0	41	21	37	0.8	9%	31%	74%	0						1.2	68	88	$0

Verlander,Justin

Age: 30 Th: R Role SP	Health A	LIMA Plan C
Ht: 6' 6" Wt: 225 Type Pwr	PT/Exp A	Rand Var -2
	Consist A	MM 4405

A virtual carbon-copy of 2011 Cy Young effort. We said last year that he's not a true sub-3 ERA pitcher, and xERA still agrees, but that's a nitpick. At 220+ IP for four straight years, the only real concern is how long his seemingly-rubber arm can hold up, and no signs of trouble there yet.

Yr Tm	W	L	Sv	IP	K	ERA	xERA	WHIP	OBA	vL	vR	BF/G	Ctl	Dom	Cmd	G	L	F	hr/9	hr/f	H%	S%	GS	APC	DOM%	DIS%	Sv%	LI	RAR	BPV	BPX	R$
08 DET	11	17	0	201	163	4.84	4.52	1.40	254	254	254	26.7	3.9	7.3	1.9	40	18	42	0.8	7%	30%	66%	33	107	48%	18%			-12.7	44	83	$3
09 DET	19	9	0	240	269	3.45	3.31	1.18	243	248	237	28.1	2.4	10.1	4.3	36	21	43	0.8	7%	33%	73%	35	112	77%	6%			25.8	132	247	$29
10 DET	18	9	0	224	219	3.37	3.54	1.16	228	230	225	28.0	2.8	8.8	3.1	41	19	40	0.6	6%	30%	72%	33	114	70%	3%			19.6	100	162	$23
11 DET	24	5	0	251	250	2.40	3.12	0.92	192	174	215	28.5	2.0	9.0	4.4	40	18	42	0.9	9%	25%	79%	34	116	88%	0%			47.7	124	187	$45
12 DET	17	8	0	238	239	2.64	3.34	1.06	217	213	222	29.0	2.3	9.0	4.0	42	22	36	0.7	8%	29%	78%	33	114	79%	3%			40.3	121	158	$36
1st Half	8	5	0	124	121	2.69	3.37	0.98	204	202	206	28.6	2.1	8.8	4.2	39	22	38	0.7	8%	26%	76%	17	113	82%	6%			20.2	119	155	$40
2nd Half	9	3	0	115	118	2.59	3.31	1.14	231	225	238	29.4	2.4	9.3	3.8	45	22	33	0.7	9%	31%	80%	16	116	75%	0%			20.2	124	161	$32
13 Proj	18	8	0	232	231	3.03	3.36	1.07	222	216	230	27.6	2.4	9.0	3.7	41	20	38	0.7	8%	28%	74%	33						28.2	116	151	$31

Villanueva,Carlos

Age: 29 Th: R Role SP	Health A	LIMA Plan B+
Ht: 6' 2" Wt: 235 Type Pwr FB	PT/Exp C	Rand Var +2
	Consist B	MM 2403

92 BPV in 15 2H starts suggests he could become another bullpen-to-rotation success story. But SP durability is a question, and unless he cures his gopheritis, all bets are off. Cmd, xERA speak to upside, but the first step is lowering that 2H FB% trend. If he flips it back to 1H...UP: 3.75 ERA.

Yr Tm	W	L	Sv	IP	K	ERA	xERA	WHIP	OBA	vL	vR	BF/G	Ctl	Dom	Cmd	G	L	F	hr/9	hr/f	H%	S%	GS	APC	DOM%	DIS%	Sv%	LI	RAR	BPV	BPX	R$
08 MIL	4	7	1	108	93	4.07	3.80	1.31	266	227	300	9.9	2.5	7.7	3.1	47	19	35	1.5	16%	31%	75%	9	38	11%	22%	100	1.02	3.4	97	182	$4
09 MIL	4	10	3	96	83	5.34	4.20	1.43	268	257	278	6.6	3.3	7.8	2.4	40	23	37	1.2	12%	32%	65%	6	25	17%	50%	38	0.80	-12.1	69	130	-$2
10 MIL	2	0	1	53	67	4.61	3.36	1.33	238	232	243	4.6	3.8	11.4	3.0	34	27	39	1.2	13%	33%	68%	0	18			25	0.98	-3.5	117	189	$0
11 TOR	6	4	0	107	68	4.04	4.41	1.26	251	259	241	13.8	2.7	5.7	2.1	36	22	43	0.9	8%	28%	70%	13	53	46%	23%	0	0.75	-1.3	44	67	$2
12 TOR	7	7	0	125	122	4.16	3.98	1.27	242	239	246	13.7	3.3	8.8	2.7	37	19	44	1.7	15%	28%	74%	16	53	63%	19%	0	0.79	-2.3	84	109	$3
1st Half	2	0	0	38	42	3.52	4.01	1.43	231	197	260	7.3	5.2	9.9	1.9	48	18	34	1.2	14%	30%	80%	1	28	0%	0%	0	0.80	2.3	64	83	-$3
2nd Half	5	7	0	87	80	4.45	3.95	1.20	248	256	239	23.5	2.5	8.3	3.3	32	20	48	1.9	16%	27%	71%	15	91	67%	20%			-4.6	92	120	$6
13 Proj	11	9	0	174	162	4.06	4.02	1.30	248	244	252	23.4	3.3	8.4	2.5	37	21	41	1.3	13%	29%	74%	31						-0.8	77	100	$8

Villarreal,Brayan

Age: 26 Th: R Role RP	Health A	LIMA Plan C+
Ht: 6' 0" Wt: 170 Type Pwr xFB	PT/Exp D	Rand Var -4
	Consist D	MM 1400

Fared well enough in 1H when H%/S% cooperated, but when luck faded, so did he. FB tilt suggests hr/f may be next shoe to drop. And 22% H% vL says he's no lefty specialist, either. Not to mention rising Ctl and 2H Dom decline. We're picking up a real negative vibe here...

Yr Tm	W	L	Sv	IP	K	ERA	xERA	WHIP	OBA	vL	vR	BF/G	Ctl	Dom	Cmd	G	L	F	hr/9	hr/f	H%	S%	GS	APC	DOM%	DIS%	Sv%	LI	RAR	BPV	BPX	R$
08																																
09																																
10 aa	0	4	0	44	38	4.31	4.26	1.31	254			22.5	3.2	7.8	2.5				1.3		29%	71%							-1.3	63	102	-$2
11 DET *	4	6	0	82	46	6.52	5.66	1.69	300	375	273	11.2	4.3	5.0	1.2	42	24	34	1.1	18%	32%	62%	0	20			0	0.88	-26.0	17	26	-$13
12 DET	3	5	0	55	66	2.63	3.85	1.21	201	190	206	4.5	4.6	10.9	2.4	30	20	49	0.5	5%	28%	79%	0	19			0	0.85	9.3	79	103	$3
1st Half	3	1	0	25	36	1.44	3.00	0.92	151	174	143	4.7	3.6	13.0	3.6	29	20	51	0.7	8%	24%	90%	0	21			0	0.81	7.9	143	186	$9
2nd Half	0	4	0	30	30	3.64	4.66	1.45	243	200	270	4.4	5.5	9.1	1.7	31	21	48	0.3	3%	31%	74%	0	17			0	0.87	1.4	26	34	-$2
13 Proj	2	5	0	58	53	4.14	4.64	1.41	247	229	256	6.7	4.4	8.3	1.9	30	20	49	1.0	8%	30%	73%	0						-0.9	40	51	-$1

Vizcaino,Arodys

Age: 22 Th: R Role RP	Health F	LIMA Plan C+
Ht: 6' 0" Wt: 190 Type Pwr	PT/Exp F	Rand Var 0
	Consist F	MM 2410

March TJS cancelled his 2012 campaign, should be ready for Opening Day. Formidable 5-pitch repertoire remains, although role is uncertain following trade to CHC. Rising Ctl (2.2, 3.3, 4.7 from high-A to MLB) is a concern, but given Cubs' unstable bullpen, a relief role could be his quickest path to fantasy value.

Yr Tm	W	L	Sv	IP	K	ERA	xERA	WHIP	OBA	vL	vR	BF/G	Ctl	Dom	Cmd	G	L	F	hr/9	hr/f	H%	S%	GS	APC	DOM%	DIS%	Sv%	LI	RAR	BPV	BPX	R$
08																																
09																																
10																																
11 ATL *	4	4	0	74	74	4.04	3.58	1.32	255	286	205	9.0	3.2	9.0	2.8	35	17	48	0.6	4%	33%	69%	0	19			0	1.28	-0.9	99	148	$1
12																																
1st Half																																
2nd Half																																
13 Proj	3	3	4	44	43	4.41	4.23	1.44	272			8.4	3.5	8.9	2.5				0.7		35%	70%	0						-2.1	87	113	-$1

MATT GELFAND

Vogelsong,Ryan

Age: 35 Th: R Role SP	Health	A	LIMA Plan	C
Ht: 6' 4" Wt: 215 Type Pwr	PT/Exp	B	Rand Var	-1
	Consist	C	MM	2305

A worthy follow-up to 2011's luck-enhanced breakout. When H%/S% finally failed him in 2H, he displayed some encouraging skills growth (see: Dom, Cmd), offering hope that this rebirth can sustain a bit longer. While xERA still isn't fully convinced, there won't likely be too much more regression.

Yr Tm	W	L	Sv	IP	K	ERA	xERA	WHIP	OBA	vL	vR	BF/G	Ctl	Dom	Cmd	G	L	F	hr/9	hr/f	H%	S%	GS	APC	DOM%	DIS%	Sv%	LI	RAR	BPV	BPX	R$
08																																
09																																
10 aaa	3	8	1	95	80	5.41	6.48	1.99	322			13.9	5.9	7.5	1.3				0.8		39%	73%							-15.7	40	64	-$12
11 SF	13	7	0	180	139	2.71	3.86	1.25	244	258	233	25.1	3.1	7.0	2.3	46	20	34	0.8	8%	29%	81%	28	98	61%	7%	0	0.75	27.4	67	100	$16
12 SF	14	9	0	190	158	3.37	4.00	1.23	242	254	230	25.4	2.9	7.5	2.5	44	18	38	0.8	8%	29%	75%	31	99	61%	13%			15.1	78	101	$15
1st Half	7	3	0	97	67	2.23	4.29	1.15	223	221	225	28.2	3.1	6.2	2.0	44	16	40	0.6	5%	26%	83%	14	107	57%	0%			21.3	51	66	$24
2nd Half	7	6	0	93	91	4.55	3.72	1.31	261	282	237	23.1	2.8	8.8	3.1	43	21	36	1.1	11%	32%	68%	17	92	65%	24%			-6.1	104	135	$6
13 Proj	**12**	**9**	**0**	**181**	**150**	**3.81**	**4.02**	**1.32**	**258**	**273**	**245**	**21.3**	**3.0**	**7.5**	**2.5**	**44**	**19**	**36**	**0.9**	**9%**	**31%**	**73%**	**35**						**4.5**	**75**	**98**	**$9**

Volquez,Edinson

Age: 29 Th: R Role SP	Health	D	LIMA Plan	B
Ht: 6' 0" Wt: 225 Type Pwr GB	PT/Exp	C	Rand Var	0
	Consist	B	MM	2405

Another season of porous Ctl left many bats on shoulders, trivializing PETCO's spacious dimensions. Dom/GB combo still intriguing, but DOM/DIS (esp 2H) says he's too volatile. If the promise of 2008 (and his last season of 2.0+ Cmd) seems like eons ago... well, it's because it is.

Yr Tm	W	L	Sv	IP	K	ERA	xERA	WHIP	OBA	vL	vR	BF/G	Ctl	Dom	Cmd	G	L	F	hr/9	hr/f	H%	S%	GS	APC	DOM%	DIS%	Sv%	LI	RAR	BPV	BPX	R$
08 CIN	17	6	0	196	206	3.21	3.71	1.33	232	249	214	25.4	4.3	9.5	2.2	46	20	34	0.6	8%	31%	77%	32	103	66%	9%	0	0.82	26.8	79	148	$20
09 CIN	4	2	0	50	47	4.35	4.38	1.33	191	202	181	24.2	5.8	8.5	1.5	45	21	34	1.1	14%	23%	70%	9	94	44%	33%			-0.2	20	37	$0
10 CIN *	7	3	0	86	84	3.82	3.55	1.36	231	229	273	22.4	4.6	8.8	1.9	54	15	31	0.8	12%	29%	73%	12	92	50%	33%			2.7	79	127	$3
11 CIN *	9	9	0	196	168	4.49	4.64	1.49	261	274	249	25.6	4.4	7.7	1.7	52	18	30	1.2	21%	31%	73%	20	98	35%	20%			-13.2	51	77	-$3
12 SD	11	11	0	183	174	4.14	4.19	1.45	236	230	240	25.1	5.2	8.6	1.7	51	21	28	0.7	10%	30%	72%	32	101	44%	25%			-2.8	44	57	$1
1st Half	5	7	0	100	88	3.68	4.49	1.40	222	224	219	25.4	5.4	7.9	1.5	48	18	33	0.7	9%	27%	75%	17	102	47%	12%			4.2	23	30	$5
2nd Half	6	4	0	82	86	4.70	3.84	1.52	252	238	261	24.7	4.9	9.4	1.9	53	25	22	0.7	12%	34%	69%	15	99	40%	40%			-6.9	68	89	-$4
13 Proj	**10**	**11**	**0**	**181**	**172**	**4.22**	**4.06**	**1.44**	**243**	**240**	**245**	**24.2**	**4.9**	**8.6**	**1.8**	**51**	**20**	**29**	**0.7**	**10%**	**31%**	**72%**	**32**						**-4.5**	**52**	**68**	**$3**

Volstad,Chris

Age: 26 Th: R Role SP	Health	A	LIMA Plan	D
Ht: 6' 8" Wt: 230 Type GB	PT/Exp	C	Rand Var	+5
	Consist	B	MM	1101

3-12, 6.31 in 111 IP at CHC. Mid-summer demotion may not have been completely justified (see BPV, H%/S%), but his BPIs were merely pedestrian, and 2H hr/f, Dom drop sealed his fate. Chronic gopheritis compounds risk. There is natural regression in a 6+ ERA, but the upside is still just xERA.

Yr Tm	W	L	Sv	IP	K	ERA	xERA	WHIP	OBA	vL	vR	BF/G	Ctl	Dom	Cmd	G	L	F	hr/9	hr/f	H%	S%	GS	APC	DOM%	DIS%	Sv%	LI	RAR	BPV	BPX	R$
08 FLA *	10	8	0	175	102	3.44	3.40	1.37	259	243	236	24.5	3.4	5.3	1.5	53	18	29	0.2	4%	30%	73%	14	87	36%	14%	0	0.75	19.0	62	116	$9
09 FLA	9	13	0	159	107	5.21	4.34	1.43	278	255	302	23.5	3.3	6.1	1.8	49	17	34	1.6	17%	29%	68%	29	89	34%	38%			-17.4	46	86	-$2
10 FLA *	13	9	0	192	114	4.49	4.33	1.41	271	292	263	24.6	3.3	5.3	1.6	48	18	34	0.8	9%	30%	69%	30	94	33%	23%			-9.6	42	68	$1
11 FLA *	6	14	0	184	128	4.85	4.93	1.45	287	305	273	24.5	2.8	6.3	2.2	52	20	28	1.2	16%	32%	69%	29	90	38%	21%			-20.7	47	70	-$7
12 CHC *	6	17	0	183	102	6.26	5.95	1.65	317	283	322	24.8	3.1	5.0	1.6	49	23	28	1.2	15%	34%	63%	21	90	33%	29%			-50.5	21	27	-$27
1st Half	2	9	0	92	57	6.27	5.55	1.62	319	270	326	25.4	2.7	5.6	2.0	49	20	31	0.8	7%	36%	60%	8	87	38%	13%			-25.5	42	55	-$27
2nd Half	4	8	0	91	46	6.24	6.29	1.69	315	292	319	24.1	3.5	4.5	1.3	50	24	26	1.5	20%	33%	65%	13	92	31%	38%			-25.0	1	1	-$27
13 Proj	**4**	**8**	**0**	**102**	**61**	**5.44**	**4.59**	**1.54**	**298**	**292**	**304**	**24.5**	**3.1**	**5.4**	**1.7**	**50**	**21**	**29**	**1.1**	**13%**	**33%**	**66%**	**18**						**-17.9**	**41**	**54**	**-$8**

Wainwright,Adam

Age: 31 Th: R Role SP	Health	F	LIMA Plan	B+
Ht: 6' 7" Wt: 230 Type Pwr GB	PT/Exp	A	Rand Var	0
	Consist	A	MM	4405

ERA says he took a half-season to shake off TJS rust, but skills say he was sharp all year. Dom held up, and luck corrected in 2H to restore ace status (see: DOM/DIS). One quibble—lost 3 MPH from his fastball—which probably caps Dom, so we wouldn't pay for full 2009-10 recovery, but repeat is likely.

Yr Tm	W	L	Sv	IP	K	ERA	xERA	WHIP	OBA	vL	vR	BF/G	Ctl	Dom	Cmd	G	L	F	hr/9	hr/f	H%	S%	GS	APC	DOM%	DIS%	Sv%	LI	RAR	BPV	BPX	R$
08 STL	11	3	0	132	91	3.20	3.99	1.18	245	264	234	27.2	2.3	6.2	2.7	46	19	35	0.8	8%	28%	76%	20	98	55%	5%			18.2	73	137	$13
09 STL	19	8	0	233	212	2.63	3.45	1.21	244	275	217	28.5	2.5	8.2	3.2	51	19	30	0.7	8%	31%	81%	34	106	65%	0%			48.7	108	201	$31
10 STL	20	11	0	230	213	2.42	3.06	1.05	224	226	222	27.6	2.2	8.3	3.8	52	18	31	0.6	8%	28%	79%	33	102	82%	3%			47.1	121	195	$34
11																																
12 STL	14	13	0	199	184	3.94	3.39	1.25	259	261	256	26.0	2.4	8.3	3.5	51	23	26	0.7	10%	32%	69%	32	97	69%	13%			1.8	115	151	$11
1st Half	6	8	0	97	91	4.75	3.42	1.34	272	263	281	25.8	2.6	8.5	3.3	53	23	24	0.9	14%	34%	66%	16	97	56%	19%			-8.7	113	147	$4
2nd Half	8	5	0	102	93	3.18	3.35	1.16	245	259	236	26.1	2.1	8.2	3.9	49	23	28	0.4	6%	31%	73%	16	96	81%	6%			10.6	117	152	$18
13 Proj	**16**	**10**	**0**	**199**	**178**	**3.31**	**3.37**	**1.18**	**246**	**256**	**238**	**26.1**	**2.3**	**8.1**	**3.5**	**50**	**21**	**29**	**0.7**	**10%**	**30%**	**74%**	**30**						**17.2**	**111**	**145**	**$20**

Walden,Jordan

Age: 25 Th: R Role RP	Health	B	LIMA Plan	B
Ht: 6' 5" Wt: 235 Type Pwr	PT/Exp	C	Rand Var	0
	Consist	B	MM	4510

Ousted from closer chair after one month due to ongoing Ctl issues; then neck, bicep injuries shelved him for 6 weeks. Rediscovered closer skills upon return, but small sample keeps us skeptical that 2H Ctl is for real. With already elite Dom on the rise, he's at least made a case for LIMA-worthiness.

Yr Tm	W	L	Sv	IP	K	ERA	xERA	WHIP	OBA	vL	vR	BF/G	Ctl	Dom	Cmd	G	L	F	hr/9	hr/f	H%	S%	GS	APC	DOM%	DIS%	Sv%	LI	RAR	BPV	BPX	R$
08																																
09 aa	1	5	0	60	48	7.00	6.55	1.94	338			22.0	4.5	7.2	1.6				0.7		40%	62%							-19.8	42	79	-$12
10 LAA *	1	2	9	65	57	3.33	4.16	1.50	274	214	233	4.7	4.0	7.9	2.0	60	23	17	0.4	17%	34%	78%	0	17			64	1.00	6.0	78	126	$3
11 LAA	5	5	32	60	67	2.98	3.40	1.24	223	227	218	4.1	3.9	10.0	2.6	45	18	37	0.4	5%	31%	76%	0	18			76	1.70	7.1	98	148	$17
12 LAA	3	2	1	39	48	3.46	3.70	1.36	229	171	286	3.8	4.2	11.1	2.7	40	25	36	0.7	8%	34%	76%	0	16			50	0.61	2.7	105	137	-$1
1st Half	2	2	1	24	28	3.00	4.28	1.46	217	170	267	4.0	5.6	10.5	1.9	38	26	35	0.4	4%	32%	79%	0	17			50	0.71	3.0	54	70	$0
2nd Half	1	0	0	15	20	4.20	2.91	1.20	246	172	313	3.6	1.8	12.0	6.7	41	22	37	1.2	13%	37%	69%	0	15			0	0.46	-0.3	187	243	-$2
13 Proj	**4**	**3**	**3**	**58**	**65**	**3.50**	**3.53**	**1.30**	**239**	**202**	**278**	**4.1**	**3.7**	**10.1**	**2.7**	**42**	**21**	**36**	**0.8**	**10%**	**32%**	**75%**	**0**						**3.7**	**102**	**133**	**$3**

Walters,P.J.

Age: 28 Th: R Role SP	Health	C	LIMA Plan	D
Ht: 6' 4" Wt: 215 Type	PT/Exp	D	Rand Var	+3
	Consist	B	MM	1201

2-5, 5.69 ERA in 62 IP at MIN. Lost two months to shoulder inflammation and displayed passable skills upon return in Sept. (57 BPV). Ctl issues from minors still present, though, and slight GB tilt isn't enough to effectively complement weak (and poorly trending) Dom. Not much to get excited about here.

Yr Tm	W	L	Sv	IP	K	ERA	xERA	WHIP	OBA	vL	vR	BF/G	Ctl	Dom	Cmd	G	L	F	hr/9	hr/f	H%	S%	GS	APC	DOM%	DIS%	Sv%	LI	RAR	BPV	BPX	R$
08 a/a	10	6	0	158	128	4.99	5.07	1.53	281			23.7	3.9	7.3	1.9				1.2		33%	70%							-12.9	47	89	-$2
09 STL *	8	10	0	137	106	5.88	5.25	1.62	304	355	263	21.0	3.5	7.0	2.0	46	18	36	0.8	30%	36%	63%	1	39	0%	100%	0	0.39	-26.2	54	102	-$8
10 STL *	10	5	0	139	107	4.39	4.34	1.35	274	264	286	22.2	2.5	7.0	2.7	43	15	42	1.0	13%	32%	70%	3	69	67%	33%	0	0.39	-5.4	69	112	$3
11 2 TM *	8	7	0	137	96	5.02	5.07	1.58	293	143	182	20.8	3.7	6.3	1.7	36	29	36	0.9	20%	34%	69%	0	20			0	0.23	-18.3	44	66	-$8
12 MIN *	5	8	0	120	78	5.57	6.15	1.63	316	318	261	20.5	2.9	5.9	2.0	41	26	33	1.5	18%	34%	69%	12	85	33%	33%			-23.0	25	33	-$15
1st Half	5	3	0	70	42	4.57	5.51	1.50	299	311	288	23.3	2.7	5.4	2.0	45	27	28	1.5	21%	32%	74%	7	82	29%	43%			-4.8	27	35	-$7
2nd Half	0	5	0	50	36	6.97	6.97	1.81	339	327	224	17.8	3.3	6.5	2.0	34	26	40	1.5	15%	38%	63%	5	88	40%	20%			-18.2	23	30	-$25
13 Proj	**4**	**5**	**0**	**81**	**55**	**5.27**	**4.80**	**1.60**	**306**	**325**	**287**	**20.5**	**3.2**	**6.1**	**1.9**	**41**	**22**	**38**	**1.2**	**10%**	**34%**	**69%**	**17**						**-12.5**	**43**	**56**	**-$7**

Wang,Chien-Ming

Age: 33 Th: R Role SP	Health	F	LIMA Plan	D
Ht: 6' 4" Wt: 225 Type Con GB	PT/Exp	D	Rand Var	+5
	Consist	F	MM	1000

2-3, 6.68 ERA in 32 IP at WAS. Hasn't eclipsed 100 IP since '07, and we've been repeating the same narrative since then: Ground balls, low Dom, injuries, yada, yada, yada...can we close the book on this story already? A return to the DL more likely than a return to relevance.

Yr Tm	W	L	Sv	IP	K	ERA	xERA	WHIP	OBA	vL	vR	BF/G	Ctl	Dom	Cmd	G	L	F	hr/9	hr/f	H%	S%	GS	APC	DOM%	DIS%	Sv%	LI	RAR	BPV	BPX	R$
08 NYY	8	2	0	95	54	4.07	4.22	1.32	249	261	238	26.8	3.3	5.1	1.5	55	22	23	0.4	6%	29%	68%	15	94	33%	13%			2.9	36	67	$4
09 NYY	1	6	0	42	29	9.64	4.86	2.02	365	394	329	17.2	4.1	6.2	1.5	53	20	27	1.5	17%	40%	51%	9	62	0%	67%	0	0.63	-27.6	33	62	-$14
10																																
11 WAS *	6	4	0	84	34	4.17	4.71	1.34	291	368	186	23.3	1.6	3.6	2.2	53	18	28	1.1	13%	30%	72%	11	82	18%	27%			-2.4	31	46	-$1
12 WAS *	5	8	0	98	44	7.69	7.82	1.95	369	413	343	21.3	2.8	4.0	1.5	53	18	29	1.4	14%	39%	61%	5	57	0%	80%	0	0.82	-44.6	-5	-7	-$28
1st Half	4	3	0	44	18	6.80	7.59	2.04	362	407	341	21.5	3.9	3.6	0.9	51	17	32	1.1	14%	38%	67%	4	60	0%	75%	0	0.82	-15.2	-9	-12	-$22
2nd Half	1	5	0	54	26	8.40	7.91	1.88	373	444	346	21.1	1.8	4.4	2.4	58	21	21	1.6	14%	39%	56%	1	48	0%	100%	0	0.83	-29.2	9	12	-$33
13 Proj	**2**	**3**	**0**	**44**	**21**	**5.08**	**4.69**	**1.56**	**309**	**348**	**266**	**20.4**	**2.7**	**4.4**	**1.6**	**53**	**19**	**28**	**1.1**	**12%**	**33%**	**69%**	**9**						**-5.7**	**38**	**49**	**-$5**

MATT GELFAND

Watson,Tony

Watson,Tony		Health	A	LIMA Plan	B+
Age: 28	Th: L Role RP	PT/Exp	D	Rand Var	-2
Ht: 6' 4"	Wt: 210 Type Pwr FB	Consist	A	MM	3400

Revised his repertoire, went with sinker/slider almost exclusively. Induced more GB as a result, and posted impressive 9.9 Dom after rough April. vR column doesn't show it, but he was tougher on RH hitters than in 2011, as Cmd jumped from 1.3 to 2.3 vs them. New approach appears to be a keeper.

Yr Tm	W	L	Sv	IP	K	ERA	xERA	WHIP	OBA	vL	vR	BF/G	Ctl	Dom	Cmd	G	L	F	hr/9	hr/f	H%	S%	GS	APC	DOM%	DIS%	Sv%	LI	RAR	BPV	BPX	R$
08																																
09 aa	0	3	0	15	11	10.01	8.83	2.39	373			16.0	6.4	6.5	1.0				1.3		42%	57%							-10.8	3	6	-$9
10 aa	6	4	2	111	81	3.27	3.14	1.09	237			12.8	2.0	6.5	3.3				0.9		27%	74%							11.1	88	143	$10
11 PIT *	5	5	0	75	63	3.47	3.42	1.25	228	279	193	4.4	3.7	7.5	2.0	32	24	44	1.0	13%	27%	76%	0	15			0	1.28	4.4	68	102	$3
12 PIT	5	2	0	53	53	3.38	3.85	1.13	198	183	213	3.2	3.9	8.9	2.3	40	18	42	0.8	9%	25%	73%	0	13			0	1.21	4.2	74	97	$3
1st Half	4	0	0	25	21	3.96	4.16	1.24	233	292	167	2.9	3.6	7.6	2.1	39	20	41	1.1	11%	27%	71%	0	12			0	1.39	0.2	56	73	$2
2nd Half	1	2	0	28	32	2.86	3.57	1.02	165	67	250	3.5	4.1	10.2	2.5	42	15	43	0.6	7%	23%	74%	0	14			0	1.03	4.0	91	118	$3
13 Proj	**3**	**2**	**0**	**44**	**40**	**3.35**	**4.00**	**1.15**	**212**	**215**	**211**	**4.0**	**3.5**	**8.2**	**2.3**	**37**	**20**	**43**	**0.9**	**9%**	**26%**	**74%**	**0**						**3.6**	**67**	**87**	**$2**

Weaver,Jered

Weaver,Jered		Health	A	LIMA Plan	C
Age: 30	Th: R Role SP	PT/Exp	A	Rand Var	-4
Ht: 6' 7"	Wt: 210 Type xFB	Consist	A	MM	3305

Continues to be stingy with the free passes, but there are warning signs: H% can't stay that low; Dom dipped further and Cmd followed (especially in 2H); 6+ K in five of first six starts, but just four more times all year. Someone will pay for ~20 W/sub-3 ERA, but BPIs suggest those are unlikely repeats.

Yr Tm	W	L	Sv	IP	K	ERA	xERA	WHIP	OBA	vL	vR	BF/G	Ctl	Dom	Cmd	G	L	F	hr/9	hr/f	H%	S%	GS	APC	DOM%	DIS%	Sv%	LI	RAR	BPV	BPX	R$
08 LAA	11	10	0	177	152	4.33	4.16	1.28	254	243	266	24.8	2.8	7.7	2.8	33	21	46	1.0	8%	31%	69%	30	101	57%	17%			-0.1	76	143	$9
09 LAA	16	8	0	211	174	3.75	4.31	1.24	246	276	208	26.7	2.8	7.4	2.6	31	19	50	1.1	8%	29%	74%	33	103	58%	15%			14.8	67	125	$18
10 LAA	13	12	0	224	233	3.01	3.41	1.07	222	223	220	26.6	2.2	9.3	4.3	36	16	48	0.9	8%	29%	76%	34	109	79%	6%			29.6	124	200	$27
11 LAA	18	8	0	236	198	2.41	3.69	1.01	212	216	208	28.1	2.1	7.6	3.5	32	19	49	0.8	6%	26%	80%	33	114	79%	6%			44.7	88	133	$35
12 LAA	20	5	0	189	142	2.81	3.96	1.02	214	199	235	24.6	2.1	6.8	3.2	36	21	43	1.0	9%	25%	77%	30	95	60%	17%			27.9	78	102	$29
1st Half	8	1	0	82	66	2.31	3.71	0.92	193	169	236	24.2	2.0	7.3	3.7	37	22	41	0.6	5%	24%	77%	13	95	62%	15%			17.2	92	120	$31
2nd Half	12	4	0	107	76	3.20	4.15	1.09	230	227	234	24.9	2.3	6.4	2.8	36	20	44	1.3	11%	25%	77%	17	95	59%	18%			10.8	67	87	$28
13 Proj	**18**	**7**	**0**	**203**	**167**	**3.01**	**3.92**	**1.10**	**233**	**227**	**240**	**25.5**	**2.2**	**7.4**	**3.3**	**35**	**20**	**46**	**1.1**	**9%**	**27%**	**78%**	**31**						**25.2**	**86**	**112**	**$26**

Webb,Ryan

Webb,Ryan		Health	B	LIMA Plan	D+
Age: 27	Th: R Role RP	PT/Exp	D	Rand Var	0
Ht: 6' 6"	Wt: 214 Type xGB	Consist	A	MM	3201

Some of those GB turned into LD, resulting in inflated H%. Still did a nice job of keeping the ball down, though, and once again kept nearly all FB in the park. Has no out pitch vL, as shown by career 1.5 Cmd, .300 BA against. That flaw, plus lack of Dom, will prevent him from taking on a greater role.

Yr Tm	W	L	Sv	IP	K	ERA	xERA	WHIP	OBA	vL	vR	BF/G	Ctl	Dom	Cmd	G	L	F	hr/9	hr/f	H%	S%	GS	APC	DOM%	DIS%	Sv%	LI	RAR	BPV	BPX	R$
08 aa	9	8	0	130	78	5.26	5.51	1.63	320			23.2	2.8	5.4	2.0				0.7		36%	68%							-15.0	43	80	-$6
09 SD *	9	2	2	75	56	4.23	4.99	1.57	302	250	278	5.3	3.2	6.7	2.1	57	18	25	0.7	14%	36%	74%	0	16			50	0.88	0.8	59	110	$1
10 SD *	4	1	1	80	64	2.37	3.11	1.26	255	333	239	4.6	2.7	7.2	2.7	62	21	17	0.2	3%	32%	81%	0	18			33	0.80	16.8	97	158	$6
11 FLA	2	4	0	51	31	3.20	3.87	1.34	255	276	238	4.0	3.6	5.5	1.6	61	17	22	0.4	6%	29%	76%	0	14			0	1.15	4.7	42	63	$0
12 MIA	4	3	0	60	44	4.03	4.09	1.52	295	314	282	4.2	3.0	6.6	2.2	52	27	21	0.3	5%	36%	72%	0	16			0	1.03	-0.1	68	88	-$4
1st Half	3	1	0	34	24	5.08	3.94	1.28	262	350	186	4.2	2.4	6.4	2.7	46	29	25	0.5	7%	31%	59%	0	16			0	1.10	-4.4	75	98	-$3
2nd Half	1	2	0	27	20	2.70	4.25	1.84	333	262	375	4.1	3.7	6.8	1.8	58	25	17	0.0	0%	41%	84%	0	16			0	0.96	4.3	57	74	-$5
13 Proj	**4**	**4**	**0**	**73**	**51**	**3.83**	**3.98**	**1.49**	**288**	**298**	**280**	**4.3**	**3.2**	**6.4**	**2.0**	**57**	**22**	**20**	**0.4**	**7%**	**34%**	**74%**	**0**						**1.7**	**64**	**83**	**-$1**

Werner,Andrew

Werner,Andrew		Health	A	LIMA Plan	C+
Age: 26	Th: L Role SP	PT/Exp	D	Rand Var	+2
Ht: 6' 2"	Wt: 215 Type xGB	Consist	F	MM	3301

2-3, 5.58 ERA in 40 IP at SD. In first season above Class A, flashed improved Dom while maintaining solid Ctl. Started MLB career with four straight quality starts, but ERA was 10.13 in last four. Doesn't project to have much upside, but combination of GB%, Ctl, PETCO could help make him serviceable.

Yr Tm	W	L	Sv	IP	K	ERA	xERA	WHIP	OBA	vL	vR	BF/G	Ctl	Dom	Cmd	G	L	F	hr/9	hr/f	H%	S%	GS	APC	DOM%	DIS%	Sv%	LI	RAR	BPV	BPX	R$
08																																
09																																
10																																
11																																
12 SD *	7	13	0	167	128	4.16	4.23	1.39	285	205	316	23.4	2.4	6.9	2.9	53	15	32	0.6	13%	34%	70%	8	83	38%	38%			-3.0	82	107	-$1
1st Half	2	8	0	80	54	3.88	4.63	1.50	301	0	0	24.6	2.6	6.1	2.4				0.5	0%	35%	74%	0	0					1.3	66	86	-$4
2nd Half	5	5	0	87	74	4.66	4.07	1.35	278	205	316	22.7	2.4	7.7	3.2	53	15	32	0.7	13%	34%	65%	8	83	38%	38%			-6.9	93	121	$1
13 Proj	**5**	**9**	**0**	**116**	**91**	**4.33**	**3.97**	**1.41**	**287**	**206**	**318**	**23.4**	**2.5**	**7.0**	**2.9**	**53**	**15**	**32**	**0.6**	**6%**	**34%**	**69%**	**21**						**-4.5**	**91**	**118**	**-$1**

Westbrook,Jake

Westbrook,Jake		Health	D	LIMA Plan	B
Age: 35	Th: R Role SP	PT/Exp	A	Rand Var	0
Ht: 6' 3"	Wt: 210 Type Con xGB	Consist	A	MM	2105

GB tilt remains consistent, and skills were strong as ever until late-season Sept oblique strain and fade. Showed previous year's struggles vR were a H% related aberration. Solid hr/9, Ctl limits his downside risk, but he's also long past the point of growth. 1H is probably best-case scenario from here on out.

Yr Tm	W	L	Sv	IP	K	ERA	xERA	WHIP	OBA	vL	vR	BF/G	Ctl	Dom	Cmd	G	L	F	hr/9	hr/f	H%	S%	GS	APC	DOM%	DIS%	Sv%	LI	RAR	BPV	BPX	R$
08 CLE	1	2	0	35	19	3.12	3.79	1.15	256	238	273	27.8	1.8	4.9	2.7	55	17	28	1.3	17%	26%	80%	5	101	20%	0%			5.2	73	136	$0
09																																
10 2 TM	10	11	0	203	128	4.22	3.94	1.34	262	268	256	26.1	3.0	5.7	1.9	56	17	26	0.9	12%	29%	70%	33	101	36%	18%			-3.5	55	89	$4
11 STL	12	9	0	183	104	4.66	4.23	1.53	290	260	316	24.5	3.6	5.1	1.4	59	18	23	0.8	11%	32%	70%	33	93	27%	36%			-16.3	32	48	-$6
12 STL	13	11	0	175	106	3.97	4.02	1.39	282	297	269	26.8	2.7	5.5	2.0	58	21	21	0.6	10%	32%	72%	28	96	39%	21%			1.0	62	81	$2
1st Half	6	6	0	93	59	3.77	3.87	1.32	268	283	253	26.3	2.4	5.7	2.4	58	21	21	0.7	11%	31%	72%	15	97	53%	20%			2.8	74	96	$6
2nd Half	7	5	0	82	47	4.19	4.20	1.47	298	316	285	27.4	3.0	5.2	1.7	58	21	21	0.6	9%	32%	71%	13	94	23%	23%			-1.7	49	64	-$2
13 Proj	**12**	**11**	**0**	**189**	**111**	**4.12**	**4.14**	**1.40**	**277**	**276**	**278**	**25.8**	**2.9**	**5.3**	**1.8**	**58**	**19**	**23**	**0.8**	**11%**	**31%**	**72%**	**31**						**-2.4**	**53**	**69**	**$3**

Wheeler,Zack

Wheeler,Zack		Health	A	LIMA Plan	C+
Age: 23	Th: R Role SP	PT/Exp	F	Rand Var	+1
Ht: 6' 4"	Wt: 185 Type Pwr	Consist	F	MM	2301

Displayed strong Dom while keeping ball down, and in the park, while improving Ctl for second straight season. Has ace-level ceiling; should get the call by the Mets at some point in 2013, perhaps early. Ctl still a work in progress, but as a power arm in a good park, odds are good for quick value.

Yr Tm	W	L	Sv	IP	K	ERA	xERA	WHIP	OBA	vL	vR	BF/G	Ctl	Dom	Cmd	G	L	F	hr/9	hr/f	H%	S%	GS	APC	DOM%	DIS%	Sv%	LI	RAR	BPV	BPX	R$
08																																
09																																
10																																
11																																
12 a/a	12	8	0	149	124	3.30	2.43	1.16	222			23.7	3.2	7.5	2.4				0.2		28%	70%							13.2	99	129	$14
1st Half	7	4	0	85	69	2.81	1.99	1.10	208			23.9	3.3	7.2	2.2				0.1		27%	72%							12.7	100	130	$21
2nd Half	5	4	0	64	55	4.00	3.03	1.24	242			23.5	3.0	7.8	2.6				0.4		31%	66%							0.1	96	125	$5
13 Proj	**7**	**5**	**0**	**87**	**73**	**3.82**	**4.02**	**1.23**	**240**			**23.9**	**3.1**	**7.6**	**2.5**	**43**	**17**	**40**	**0.8**	**8%**	**29%**	**71%**	**15**						**2.1**	**74**	**96**	**$4**

White,Alex

White,Alex		Health	C	LIMA Plan	D
Age: 24	Th: R Role SP	PT/Exp	D	Rand Var	+2
Ht: 6' 3"	Wt: 215 Type GB	Consist	B	MM	1103

2-9, 5.51 ERA in 98 IP at COL. Two of first three starts were PQS-5s, but it was all downhill from there. Ability to keep ball on ground is a plus at Coors, and provides a glimmer of hope. But sub-1.0 Cmd vL, and against everyone on road, shows how much work he has left before becoming roster-worthy.

Yr Tm	W	L	Sv	IP	K	ERA	xERA	WHIP	OBA	vL	vR	BF/G	Ctl	Dom	Cmd	G	L	F	hr/9	hr/f	H%	S%	GS	APC	DOM%	DIS%	Sv%	LI	RAR	BPV	BPX	R$
08																																
09																																
10 aa	8	7	0	107	66	2.44	3.10	1.16	245			23.6	2.2	5.5	2.5				0.6		28%	81%							21.6	74	120	$11
11 2 TM *	5	5	0	91	67	4.73	4.83	1.35	264	325	292	21.1	3.0	6.6	2.2	46	14	40	1.7	22%	28%	71%	10	91	20%	50%			-8.9	38	57	-$2
12 COL *	5	13	0	159	99	4.94	4.89	1.55	280	285	291	20.4	4.1	5.6	1.4	54	21	24	0.9	16%	31%	69%	20	78	10%	70%	0	0.72	-18.2	33	44	-$12
1st Half	3	9	0	80	54	5.48	5.00	1.56	290	316	284	22.0	3.6	6.1	1.7	55	24	21	0.9	22%	33%	65%	10	90	20%	50%			-14.5	42	55	-$14
2nd Half	2	4	0	78	45	4.39	4.73	1.55	268	247	299	19.0	4.7	5.1	1.1	53	19	29	1.0	11%	29%	74%	10	69	0%	90%	0	0.67	-3.6	27	35	-$10
13 Proj	**6**	**9**	**0**	**138**	**90**	**4.43**	**4.45**	**1.42**	**268**	**268**	**267**	**20.9**	**3.5**	**5.9**	**1.7**	**51**	**18**	**31**	**1.1**	**13%**	**30%**	**72%**	**28**						**-7.0**	**41**	**53**	**-$1**

BRIAN RUDD

Wieland,Joe

Age: 23	Th: R	Role SP	Health F	LIMA Plan C
Ht: 6' 3"	Wt: 195	Type FB	PT/Exp F	Rand Var +2
			Consist D	MM 2300

Injuries in SD rotation opened door for April callup, but it wasn't long before he suffered an injury of his own. Eventually underwent Tommy John surgery in July, which will sideline him for much of 2013. With strong skills, youth, and pitcher-friendly park on his side, still makes for an intriguing keeper target.

Yr	Tm	W	L	Sv	IP	K	ERA	xERA	WHIP	OBA	vL	vR	BF/G	Ctl	Dom	Cmd	G	L	F	hr/9	hr/f	H%	S%	GS	APC	DOM%	DIS%	Sv%	LI	RAR	BPV	BPX	R$
08																																	
09																																	
10																																	
11	aa	7	1	0	70	49	1.66	2.18	1.05	226			22.6	2.0	6.4	3.2				0.2		27%	84%							19.7	108	163	$10
12	SD	0	4	0	28	24	4.55	4.12	1.27	245	250	241	23.8	2.9	7.8	2.7	41	20	39	1.6	16%	28%	70%	5	93	60%	20%			-1.8	80	105	-$4
1st Half		0	4	0	28	24	4.55	4.13	1.27	245	250	241	23.8	2.9	7.8	2.7	41	20	39	1.6	16%	28%	70%	5	93	60%	20%			-1.8	80	104	-$4
2nd Half																																	
13	**Proj**	**2**	**5**	**0**	**58**	**46**	**4.18**	**4.13**	**1.27**	**258**	**263**	**253**	**23.1**	**2.6**	**7.2**	**2.8**	**40**	**20**	**39**	**1.1**	**9%**	**30%**	**70%**	**10**						**-1.1**	**78**	**101**	**$0**

Wilhelmsen,Tom

Age: 29	Th: R	Role RP	Health A	LIMA Plan D+
Ht: 6' 6"	Wt: 230	Type Pwr	PT/Exp C	Rand Var -3
			Consist D	MM 2431

Elite skills in 1H helped him claim closer role, and he never looked back. But despite save totals, skills slipped in 2H. Strong chance of entering season as closer, but lack of proven track record, '11 BPIs are each cause for some concern. Hence, he's a risky option at a volatile position.

Yr	Tm	W	L	Sv	IP	K	ERA	xERA	WHIP	OBA	vL	vR	BF/G	Ctl	Dom	Cmd	G	L	F	hr/9	hr/f	H%	S%	GS	APC	DOM%	DIS%	Sv%	LI	RAR	BPV	BPX	R$
08																																	
09																																	
10																																	
11	SEA *	6	5	0	93	62	5.55	5.13	1.58	287	200	220	10.5	4.0	6.0	1.5	34	21	45	1.0	5%	32%	66%	0	20			0	0.59	-18.5	34	51	-$8
12	SEA	4	3	29	79	87	2.50	3.38	1.11	202	223	181	4.5	3.3	9.9	3.0	48	16	35	0.6	7%	28%	80%	0	17			85	1.38	14.9	115	150	$20
1st Half		3	1	6	41	50	2.63	3.02	1.12	226	241	211	4.7	2.4	11.0	4.5	45	20	36	0.7	8%	33%	79%	0	17			86	1.23	7.0	155	202	$17
2nd Half		1	2	23	38	37	2.35	3.78	1.10	175	203	147	4.2	4.2	8.7	2.1	52	13	35	0.5	6%	24%	80%	0	16			85	1.53	7.9	72	94	$24
13	**Proj**	**4**	**3**	**35**	**73**	**66**	**3.47**	**4.06**	**1.30**	**239**	**250**	**228**	**5.7**	**3.7**	**8.2**	**2.2**	**43**	**18**	**39**	**0.7**	**7%**	**30%**	**75%**	**0**						**4.9**	**68**	**88**	**$17**

Williams,Jerome

Age: 31	Th: R	Role RP	Health B	LIMA Plan B+
Ht: 6' 3"	Wt: 240	Type Con GB	PT/Exp C	Rand Var +2
			Consist C	MM 2101

Spent 1st half in rotation, where he displayed respectable BPIs, mediocre results. Later moved to pen, where he flashed impressive 4.3 Cmd. GB% is solid, and Cmd uptick intriguing. But future role is unclear, and with long history of medicocrity, taking another step up at his age is unlikely.

Yr	Tm	W	L	Sv	IP	K	ERA	xERA	WHIP	OBA	vL	vR	BF/G	Ctl	Dom	Cmd	G	L	F	hr/9	hr/f	H%	S%	GS	APC	DOM%	DIS%	Sv%	LI	RAR	BPV	BPX	R$
08	aaa	2	2	0	26	17	2.16	3.81	1.34	259			10.8	3.1	5.9	1.9				0.7		30%	87%							6.9	58	109	$0
09	aaa	5	6	0	102	39	6.83	6.87	1.83	331			17.5	3.9	3.4	0.9				1.4		34%	64%							-31.5	-15	-28	-$16
10																																	
11	LAA *	11	2	0	118	72	3.95	4.87	1.40	289	235	305	23.7	2.3	5.5	2.4	50	16	34	1.2	13%	32%	76%	6	68	50%	17%	0	0.82	-0.1	45	68	$2
12	LAA	6	8	1	138	98	4.58	3.81	1.26	263	263	264	17.9	2.3	6.4	2.8	54	18	28	1.1	14%	30%	66%	15	64	40%	20%	100	0.67	-9.5	86	112	$0
1st Half		6	5	0	83	56	4.46	4.06	1.38	273	281	265	27.2	2.8	6.1	2.2	56	18	26	0.8	10%	31%	68%	12	96	50%	17%	0	0.83	-4.6	67	87	$2
2nd Half		0	3	1	55	42	4.75	3.44	1.09	248	233	262	11.5	1.5	6.9	4.7	50	19	31	1.6	20%	27%	62%	3	42	0%	33%	100	0.56	-4.9	112	146	-$3
13	**Proj**	**6**	**5**	**0**	**116**	**74**	**4.65**	**4.16**	**1.37**	**281**	**264**	**299**	**17.6**	**2.4**	**5.7**	**2.4**	**52**	**18**	**31**	**1.1**	**12%**	**31%**	**68%**	**21**						**-9.1**	**68**	**88**	**-$1**

Wilson,Brian

Age: 31	Th: R	Role RP	Health F	LIMA Plan C+
Ht: 6' 2"	Wt: 205	Type Pwr	PT/Exp B	Rand Var +5
			Consist F	MM 3420

Elbow soreness sidelined him in late 2011, and when it was still sore in March, it raised a red flag. Made just two appearances before landing on DL, undergoing TJ surgery. Expected to be ready for spring training and would certainly be in the saves mix. But whether he can regain '09-'10 skills remains to be seen.

Yr	Tm	W	L	Sv	IP	K	ERA	xERA	WHIP	OBA	vL	vR	BF/G	Ctl	Dom	Cmd	G	L	F	hr/9	hr/f	H%	S%	GS	APC	DOM%	DIS%	Sv%	LI	RAR	BPV	BPX	R$
08	SF	3	2	41	62	67	4.62	3.58	1.44	263	202	320	4.3	4.0	9.7	2.4	52	19	30	1.0	14%	34%	70%	0	19			87	1.66	-2.3	95	178	$16
09	SF	5	6	38	72	83	2.74	3.31	1.20	223	189	255	4.5	3.4	10.3	3.1	46	18	36	0.4	4%	32%	77%	0	19			84	1.73	14.1	119	223	$23
10	SF	3	3	48	75	93	1.81	2.98	1.18	220	206	231	4.4	3.1	11.2	3.6	49	13	38	0.4	4%	33%	86%	0	19			91	1.50	20.9	144	233	$28
11	SF	6	4	36	55	54	3.11	3.89	1.47	240	223	257	4.3	5.1	8.8	1.7	53	17	30	0.3	4%	32%	78%	0	18			88	1.54	5.7	53	80	$16
12	SF	0	0	1	2	2	9.00	7.70	3.00	400	333	429	6.0	9.0	9.0	1.0	25	38	38	0.0	0%	52%	67%	0	28			100	0.39	-1.2	-78	-102	-$5
1st Half		0	0	1	2	2	9.00	7.71	3.00	400	333	429	6.0	9.0	9.0	1.0	25	38	38	0.0	0%	52%	67%	0	28			100	0.39	-1.2	-78	-102	-$5
2nd Half																																	
13	**Proj**	**3**	**3**	**23**	**44**	**43**	**3.36**	**3.75**	**1.32**	**237**	**208**	**265**	**4.2**	**3.9**	**8.9**	**2.3**	**49**	**17**	**34**	**0.5**	**6%**	**31%**	**74%**	**0**						**3.5**	**82**	**106**	**$10**

Wilson,C.J.

Age: 32	Th: L	Role SP	Health A	LIMA Plan B
Ht: 6' 1"	Wt: 210	Type Pwr	PT/Exp A	Rand Var 0
			Consist B	MM 3305

Good fortune in 1H hid the fact he had given back Ctl gains of '11. When h%, hr/f shot up in 2H, so did ERA. But look past the ups and downs, the huge ERA splits, and BPIs are a near carbon copy of '10. Assuming he's fully recovered from October elbow surgery, expect something close to a repeat in '13.

Yr	Tm	W	L	Sv	IP	K	ERA	xERA	WHIP	OBA	vL	vR	BF/G	Ctl	Dom	Cmd	G	L	F	hr/9	hr/f	H%	S%	GS	APC	DOM%	DIS%	Sv%	LI	RAR	BPV	BPX	R$
08	TEX	2	2	24	46	41	6.02	4.67	1.64	268	265	269	4.3	5.2	8.0	1.5	49	16	35	1.6	16%	31%	66%	0	18			86	1.36	-9.7	29	54	$5
09	TEX	5	6	14	74	84	2.81	3.21	1.33	234	206	249	4.4	3.9	10.3	2.6	55	20	25	0.4	6%	34%	79%	0	18			78	1.12	13.7	112	210	$12
10	TEX	15	8	0	204	170	3.35	3.91	1.25	217	144	236	25.8	4.1	7.5	1.8	49	17	34	0.4	5%	27%	73%	33	104	45%	12%			18.3	51	83	$16
11	TEX	16	7	0	223	206	2.94	3.35	1.19	232	251	227	26.9	3.0	8.3	2.8	49	19	32	0.6	8%	29%	77%	34	106	59%	15%			27.6	96	144	$23
12	LAA	13	10	0	202	173	3.83	4.10	1.34	239	217	246	25.4	4.0	7.7	1.9	50	20	30	0.8	11%	29%	74%	34	101	47%	12%			4.7	57	75	$8
1st Half		9	4	0	99	81	2.36	3.87	1.15	205	172	216	25.4	3.7	7.3	2.0	53	18	29	0.5	6%	25%	81%	16	100	56%	13%			20.4	62	81	$26
2nd Half		4	6	0	103	92	5.24	4.33	1.53	269	264	271	25.5	4.4	8.0	1.8	48	21	30	1.2	15%	32%	68%	18	102	39%	11%			-15.6	53	69	-$11
13	**Proj**	**13**	**9**	**0**	**203**	**180**	**3.72**	**3.91**	**1.32**	**240**	**224**	**245**	**25.5**	**3.9**	**8.0**	**2.1**	**50**	**19**	**31**	**0.8**	**10%**	**29%**	**74%**	**33**						**7.3**	**67**	**87**	**$12**

Wood,Travis

Age: 26	Th: L	Role SP	Health A	LIMA Plan B
Ht: 5' 11"	Wt: 175	Type FB	PT/Exp C	Rand Var +1
			Consist C	MM 1203

6-13, 4.27 ERA in 156 IP at CHC. PRO: Stifled LH (.614 OPS against), 2H Cmd growth. CON: High FB rate will continue to lead to issues with the long ball. Still young enough to put it all together, but at least for the short-term, looks like someone to play the matchups with in pitcher-friendly parks.

Yr	Tm	W	L	Sv	IP	K	ERA	xERA	WHIP	OBA	vL	vR	BF/G	Ctl	Dom	Cmd	G	L	F	hr/9	hr/f	H%	S%	GS	APC	DOM%	DIS%	Sv%	LI	RAR	BPV	BPX	R$
08	aa	4	9	0	80	50	8.19	6.37	1.86	309			22.0	5.4	5.6	1.1				1.2		34%	55%							-38.1	13	24	-$15
09	a/a	13	5	0	168	119	2.25	2.77	1.18	231			24.8	3.0	6.4	2.1				0.4		27%	82%							42.8	80	149	$23
10	CIN *	10	10	0	203	171	3.54	3.27	1.15	242	136	240	24.4	2.2	7.6	3.4	31	21	48	0.9	6%	29%	72%	17	95	59%	12%			13.4	98	158	$16
11	CIN *	8	9	0	158	116	5.26	5.21	1.56	299	316	287	21.7	3.2	6.6	2.0	32	22	45	1.0	7%	34%	67%	18	81	33%	22%	0	0.79	-25.7	49	73	-$10
12	CHC *	9	16	0	197	151	4.50	4.27	1.29	253	195	241	24.6	3.0	6.9	2.3	34	22	44	1.4	13%	28%	70%	26	96	46%	15%			-11.7	52	68	$2
1st Half		5	6	0	90	67	4.37	4.62	1.39	270	127	263	25.2	3.1	6.7	2.1	40	27	33	1.3	16%	30%	72%	8	94	50%	13%			-3.9	48	62	$0
2nd Half		4	10	0	108	84	4.60	3.94	1.20	238	254	234	24.0	2.8	7.0	2.5	32	20	48	1.5	12%	26%	67%	18	97	44%	17%			-7.7	56	73	$3
13	**Proj**	**8**	**12**	**0**	**174**	**132**	**4.63**	**4.52**	**1.35**	**265**	**233**	**273**	**23.6**	**3.0**	**6.8**	**2.3**	**33**	**22**	**44**	**1.1**	**9%**	**30%**	**68%**	**31**						**-13.1**	**53**	**68**	**$1**

Worley,Vance

Age: 25	Th: R	Role SP	Health B	LIMA Plan C
Ht: 6' 2"	Wt: 230	Type Pwr	PT/Exp C	Rand Var +1
			Consist B	MM 2303

Success from '11 carried over into 1H, and GB spike was encouraging. But Dom, GB%, h% took turn for worse in 2H, and led to elbow surgery in Sept. He is expected to be healthy by March. 2H fade, injury could depress value, making him a potential bargain.

Yr	Tm	W	L	Sv	IP	K	ERA	xERA	WHIP	OBA	vL	vR	BF/G	Ctl	Dom	Cmd	G	L	F	hr/9	hr/f	H%	S%	GS	APC	DOM%	DIS%	Sv%	LI	RAR	BPV	BPX	R$
08																																	
09	aa	7	12	0	153	87	6.48	5.39	1.53	301			24.7	2.9	5.1	1.8				1.2		33%	58%							-40.9	28	52	-$12
10	PHI *	11	8	0	171	112	3.79	4.40	1.41	284	100	240	22.6	2.6	5.9	2.3	45	15	39	0.8	8%	32%	74%	2	41	0%	0%	0	0.40	6.1	58	94	$5
11	PHI *	16	5	0	182	161	2.99	3.39	1.23	243	201	272	21.7	2.9	7.9	2.7	39	24	37	0.8	7%	30%	79%	21	87	71%	14%	0	0.80	21.5	88	133	$17
12	PHI	6	9	0	133	107	4.20	4.18	1.51	296	312	280	25.7	3.2	7.2	2.3	46	24	30	0.8	10%	35%	74%	23	95	39%	22%			-3.0	68	89	-$5
1st Half		4	4	0	74	66	2.92	3.55	1.26	247	259	234	25.7	3.0	8.0	2.6	51	24	25	1.0	15%	30%	81%	12	98	67%	8%			10.0	91	118	$7
2nd Half		2	5	0	59	41	5.80	4.99	1.83	350	381	323	25.6	3.4	6.3	1.9	41	24	35	0.6	6%	40%	67%	11	92	9%	36%			-13.0	41	53	-$20
13	**Proj**	**10**	**10**	**0**	**174**	**143**	**3.77**	**4.11**	**1.42**	**277**	**274**	**279**	**23.4**	**3.0**	**7.4**	**2.4**	**43**	**24**	**33**	**0.8**	**9%**	**33%**	**75%**	**31**						**5.3**	**72**	**93**	**$5**

BRIAN RUDD

Wright,Jamey

Age: 38 Th: R Role RP	Health A	LIMA Plan D	
	PT/Exp C	Rand Var 0	
Ht: 6'6" Wt: 235 Type Pwr xGB	Consist A	MM 3200	

Career-best GB%, Dom would be intriguing, but for his age. 2H much more in line with history than 1H, as that 1H Dom came out of nowhere. Still hasn't posted a 2.0 Cmd in 11-year career, so while xERA confirms he's earned back-to-back sub-4.00 ERA's, high number of walks are sure to do damage.

Yr	Tm	W	L	Sv	IP	K	ERA	xERA	WHIP	OBA	vL	vR	BF/G	Ctl	Dom	Cmd	G	L	F	hr/9	hr/f	H%	S%	GS	APC	DOM%	DIS%	Sv%	LI	RAR	BPV	BPX	R$
08	TEX	8	7	0	84	60	5.12	3.97	1.52	283	286	280	5.1	3.7	6.4	1.7	61	20	19	0.5	10%	33%	65%	0	19			0	1.19	-8.3	53	100	-$2
09	KC	3	5	0	79	60	4.33	4.27	1.48	247	200	285	5.4	5.0	6.8	1.4	59	17	24	0.9	14%	29%	72%	0	21			0	0.98	-0.1	25	46	-$2
10	2 AL	1	3	0	58	28	4.17	4.38	1.37	256	227	280	5.4	3.9	4.3	1.1	61	14	25	0.5	6%	28%	69%	0	20			0	1.02	-0.6	13	20	-$2
11	SEA	2	3	1	68	48	3.16	3.80	1.33	246	226	266	4.8	4.0	6.3	1.6	58	17	24	0.8	13%	28%	79%	0	18			20	1.02	6.6	43	65	$1
12	LA	5	3	0	68	54	3.72	3.70	1.51	270	252	283	4.6	4.0	7.2	1.8	67	21	12	0.3	8%	34%	74%	0	17			0	0.75	2.4	67	87	-$2
1st Half		3	2	0	34	34	4.01	3.24	1.46	254	230	275	5.6	4.3	9.1	2.1	67	21	12	0.3	9%	34%	71%	0	21			0	0.65	0.0	93	121	-$1
2nd Half		2	1	0	34	20	3.44	4.18	1.56	285	278	289	4.0	3.7	5.3	1.4	67	21	12	0.3	7%	33%	77%	0	14			0	0.81	2.4	40	52	-$4
13	Proj	**3**	**3**	**0**	**65**	**46**	**4.14**	**3.98**	**1.45**	**263**	**243**	**279**	**4.6**	**4.0**	**6.3**	**1.6**	**63**	**19**	**18**	**0.5**	**9%**	**31%**	**71%**	**0**						**-1.0**	**48**	**62**	**-$2**

Wright,Wesley

Age: 28 Th: L Role RP	Health A	LIMA Plan B+	
	PT/Exp D	Rand Var 0	
Ht: 5'11" Wt: 180 Type Pwr	Consist D	MM 3310	

From 2008-10, put up ugly 5.33 ERA and 1.6 hr/9. Since his recall in late '11, has served as LOOGY, and results have been better. LH have just .478 OPS against him in 163 PA, and he's inducing a ton of GB. Probably won't see many save opps, but had 19 holds in '12, and the ratios should remain strong.

Yr	Tm	W	L	Sv	IP	K	ERA	xERA	WHIP	OBA	vL	vR	BF/G	Ctl	Dom	Cmd	G	L	F	hr/9	hr/f	H%	S%	GS	APC	DOM%	DIS%	Sv%	LI	RAR	BPV	BPX	R$
08	HOU	4	3	1	56	57	5.01	4.45	1.42	214	207	220	3.5	5.5	9.2	1.7	40	21	39	1.3	14%	27%	68%	0	14			100	0.95	-4.7	35	67	-$1
09	HOU *	5	5	0	64	62	5.07	5.31	1.63	276	359	265	4.6	5.0	8.8	1.8	43	23	34	1.3	20%	34%	72%	0	17			0	0.71	-5.9	52	97	-$3
10	HOU *	5	3	0	103	63	5.36	5.70	1.64	298	206	316	15.8	4.0	5.5	1.4	44	20	37	1.3	16%	32%	70%	4	40	25%	50%	0	0.31	-16.2	20	32	-$8
11	HOU *	3	1	2	77	53	2.18	2.81	1.16	221	38	385	5.1	3.3	6.2	1.9	57	11	32	0.6	11%	26%	84%	0	8			67	1.96	16.8	69	104	$7
12	HOU	2	2	1	52	54	3.27	3.17	1.18	226	198	269	2.9	2.9	9.3	3.2	55	22	24	0.7	12%	30%	74%	0	11			50	1.10	4.8	121	158	$1
1st Half		0	1	0	22	22	3.63	3.56	1.34	250	182	364	2.5	3.2	8.9	2.8	52	23	26	1.2	18%	32%	78%	0	9			0	1.25	1.1	102	133	-$4
2nd Half		2	1	1	30	32	3.00	2.88	1.07	207	212	200	3.3	2.7	9.6	3.6	58	21	22	0.3	6%	29%	71%	0	13			50	0.94	3.8	136	177	$6
13	Proj	**3**	**2**	**5**	**58**	**51**	**3.49**	**3.77**	**1.28**	**242**	**212**	**268**	**3.8**	**3.4**	**7.9**	**2.3**	**49**	**21**	**30**	**0.8**	**10%**	**30%**	**75%**	**0**						**3.8**	**78**	**101**	**$3**

Young,Chris

Age: 34 Th: R Role SP	Health F	LIMA Plan F	
	PT/Exp D	Rand Var -1	
Ht: 6'10" Wt: 260 Type xFB	Consist B	MM 0203	

Returned in June following May '11 shoulder surgery, and recorded most IP since '07. Dom came around after slow start, but LH hit him hard and FB% always an issue. He's kept ERA well below xERA for most of his career, but BPIs suggest caution, and next DL stint probably right around the corner.

Yr	Tm	W	L	Sv	IP	K	ERA	xERA	WHIP	OBA	vL	vR	BF/G	Ctl	Dom	Cmd	G	L	F	hr/9	hr/f	H%	S%	GS	APC	DOM%	DIS%	Sv%	LI	RAR	BPV	BPX	R$
08	SD	7	6	0	102	93	3.96	4.64	1.29	221	259	189	24.1	4.2	8.2	1.9	22	25	53	1.1	9%	27%	73%	18	97	61%	17%			4.6	33	62	$6
09	SD	4	6	0	76	50	5.21	5.46	1.45	246	210	297	24.0	4.7	5.9	1.3	30	18	52	1.4	10%	26%	67%	14	93	43%	36%			-8.3	-13	-25	-$3
10	SD	2	0	0	20	15	0.90	4.89	1.05	143	167	130	20.5	5.0	6.8	1.4	29	16	55	0.5	3%	18%	95%	4	77	50%	25%			7.8	-5	-8	$1
11	NYM	1	0	0	24	22	1.88	4.29	0.96	146	104	206	23.8	4.1	8.3	2.0	19	15	66	1.1	8%	16%	90%	4	99	50%	25%			6.1	34	51	$1
12	NYM	4	9	0	115	80	4.15	5.07	1.35	269	278	261	24.7	2.8	6.3	2.2	22	20	58	1.3	8%	30%	73%	20	92	50%	20%			-1.9	37	48	-$2
1st Half		2	1	0	30	18	3.30	5.20	1.40	281	271	290	26.2	2.4	5.4	2.3	29	16	55	0.3	2%	33%	76%	5	94	40%	0%			2.7	39	51	-$4
2nd Half		2	8	0	85	62	4.45	5.02	1.33	265	281	250	24.1	3.0	6.6	2.2	20	21	59	1.6	10%	28%	72%	15	92	53%	27%			-4.5	36	47	-$1
13	Proj	**7**	**10**	**0**	**137**	**97**	**4.41**	**5.12**	**1.38**	**256**	**249**	**264**	**23.7**	**3.7**	**6.3**	**1.7**	**26**	**20**	**55**	**1.2**	**8%**	**28%**	**71%**	**24**						**-6.7**	**19**	**25**	**$0**

Zambrano,Carlos

Age: 32 Th: R Role RP	Health B	LIMA Plan F	
	PT/Exp B	Rand Var -1	
Ht: 6'5" Wt: 270 Type Pwr	Consist A	MM 1201	

After 9-start run that included no PQS-DOM starts and a 7.62 ERA, was moved to bullpen in July. He's now had seven straight years with a sub-2.0 Cmd, and has more BB than K vs LH over last two. It would take dramatic turnaround to make him a useful starter, and nobody needs a ratio-killing reliever.

Yr	Tm	W	L	Sv	IP	K	ERA	xERA	WHIP	OBA	vL	vR	BF/G	Ctl	Dom	Cmd	G	L	F	hr/9	hr/f	H%	S%	GS	APC	DOM%	DIS%	Sv%	LI	RAR	BPV	BPX	R$
08	CHC	14	6	0	189	130	3.91	4.32	1.29	241	235	247	26.5	3.4	6.2	1.8	47	18	35	0.9	9%	28%	72%	30	101	47%	17%			9.6	44	82	$12
09	CHC	9	7	0	169	152	3.77	4.15	1.38	246	258	235	26.2	4.1	8.1	1.9	45	18	37	0.5	6%	31%	73%	28	102	54%	18%			11.4	56	106	$9
10	CHC	11	6	0	130	117	3.33	4.27	1.45	246	279	221	15.9	4.8	8.1	1.7	44	20	37	0.5	5%	31%	77%	20	63	45%	20%	0	0.93	12.0	39	63	$6
11	CHC	9	7	0	146	101	4.82	4.37	1.44	277	289	268	26.4	3.5	6.2	1.8	42	21	37	1.2	11%	30%	69%	24	103	33%	21%			-15.8	39	58	-$4
12	MIA	7	10	0	132	95	4.49	4.83	1.50	251	244	257	16.9	5.1	6.5	1.3	49	23	28	0.6	8%	29%	70%	20	66	40%	15%	0	0.81	-7.7	6	7	-$5
1st Half		4	6	0	90	68	4.12	4.44	1.35	230	235	224	25.6	4.7	6.8	1.4	50	21	29	0.7	10%	27%	70%	15	99	53%	13%			-1.1	24	31	-$1
2nd Half		3	4	0	43	27	5.27	5.70	1.80	290	267	309	10.4	5.9	5.7	1.0	47	26	28	0.4	5%	33%	69%	5	40	0%	20%	0	0.85	-6.6	-32	-42	-$15
13	Proj	**6**	**6**	**0**	**94**	**69**	**4.68**	**4.79**	**1.52**	**262**	**262**	**262**	**15.9**	**4.7**	**6.6**	**1.4**	**46**	**22**	**32**	**0.7**	**8%**	**31%**	**69%**	**15**						**-7.8**	**16**	**20**	**-$3**

Ziegler,Brad

Age: 33 Th: R Role RP	Health A	LIMA Plan B	
	PT/Exp C	Rand Var -1	
Ht: 6'4" Wt: 212 Type xGB	Consist B	MM 4100	

Still can't solve LH (.872 career OPS vs), but has RH in his pocket (.531). Recent usage has been ideal, as 68% of batters faced in past three years have been RH. Dom dropped, but ridiculously low FB% compensated. Extreme splits make it unlikely he claims closer role, but he's still a solid LIMA target.

Yr	Tm	W	L	Sv	IP	K	ERA	xERA	WHIP	OBA	vL	vR	BF/G	Ctl	Dom	Cmd	G	L	F	hr/9	hr/f	H%	S%	GS	APC	DOM%	DIS%	Sv%	LI	RAR	BPV	BPX	R$
08	OAK *	5	0	19	84	44	0.88	2.21	1.09	216	280	198	5.0	2.8	4.7	1.7	65	16	19	0.2	6%	25%	93%	0	18			83	1.31	35.7	69	130	$21
09	OAK	2	4	7	73	54	3.07	3.71	1.50	293	336	265	4.5	3.4	6.6	1.9	62	18	20	0.2	4%	34%	79%	0	17			70	0.88	11.3	67	124	$3
10	OAK	3	7	0	61	41	3.26	4.14	1.35	241	317	213	4.0	4.2	6.1	1.5	54	19	27	0.6	8%	28%	77%	0	14			0	1.14	6.1	29	47	$1
11	2 TM	3	2	1	58	44	2.16	3.05	1.23	245	373	188	3.6	2.9	6.8	2.3	69	18	13	0.0	0%	31%	81%	0	13			50	0.96	12.8	90	135	$4
12	ARI	6	1	0	69	42	2.49	3.02	1.09	228	268	211	3.4	2.8	5.5	2.0	76	17	8	0.3	13%	26%	77%	0	12			0	0.93	12.9	79	103	$7
1st Half		4	1	0	31	20	2.30	3.17	1.21	248	259	244	3.5	3.2	5.7	1.8	72	22	6	0.0	0%	28%	79%	0	13			0	0.87	6.6	68	89	$6
2nd Half		2	0	0	37	22	2.65	2.91	0.99	211	273	179	3.4	2.4	5.3	2.2	79	12	9	0.5	20%	23%	74%	0	12			0	0.98	6.3	87	113	$7
13	Proj	**5**	**2**	**0**	**68**	**45**	**3.01**	**3.38**	**1.18**	**230**	**298**	**200**	**3.7**	**3.0**	**5.9**	**2.0**	**70**	**17**	**13**	**0.3**	**7%**	**27%**	**73%**	**0**						**8.4**	**72**	**94**	**$4**

Zimmermann,Jordan

Age: 27 Th: R Role SP	Health D	LIMA Plan C+	
	PT/Exp B	Rand Var -2	
Ht: 6'2" Wt: 220 Type	Consist A	MM 3305	

Went with GB-heavy approach in 1H, then allowed more FB but took Dom up a notch in 2H. Both proved effective, and the bottom line was similar to '11. It wasn't until 25th start that he had first PQS-DISaster. Don't count on another sub-3.00 ERA, but consistency, elite Ctl make him a reliable not-quite-ace.

Yr	Tm	W	L	Sv	IP	K	ERA	xERA	WHIP	OBA	vL	vR	BF/G	Ctl	Dom	Cmd	G	L	F	hr/9	hr/f	H%	S%	GS	APC	DOM%	DIS%	Sv%	LI	RAR	BPV	BPX	R$
08	aa	7	2	0	107	86	3.71	3.62	1.29	249			21.9	3.2	7.3	2.3				0.8		30%	73%							8.0	73	138	$6
09	WAS	3	5	0	91	92	4.63	3.51	1.36	271	279	263	24.4	2.9	9.1	3.2	44	24	32	1.0	12%	34%	68%	16	98	56%	6%			-3.5	108	202	$0
10	WAS *	2	2	0	53	39	3.13	3.30	1.08	220	276	238	17.1	2.6	6.7	2.6	49	13	38	1.4	22%	24%	79%	7	79	43%	57%			6.2	64	104	$3
11	WAS	8	11	0	161	124	3.18	3.71	1.15	251	252	251	25.5	1.7	6.9	4.0	39	19	42	0.7	6%	30%	74%	26	95	62%	8%			15.2	95	143	$13
12	WAS	12	8	0	196	153	2.94	3.77	1.17	251	234	268	25.2	2.0	7.0	3.6	43	23	33	0.8	9%	30%	78%	32	97	56%	6%			25.9	94	123	$20
1st Half		4	6	0	97	65	2.77	3.80	1.15	251	240	263	26.6	1.8	6.0	3.3	50	21	29	1.0	13%	28%	81%	15	96	53%	0%			14.9	86	112	$18
2nd Half		8	2	0	98	88	3.11	3.73	1.19	251	228	272	23.9	2.1	8.1	3.8	36	26	38	0.6	6%	31%	75%	17	97	59%	12%			11.0	102	133	$21
13	Proj	**14**	**9**	**0**	**209**	**166**	**3.16**	**3.79**	**1.18**	**251**	**246**	**256**	**24.9**	**2.1**	**7.2**	**3.4**	**42**	**21**	**37**	**0.9**	**9%**	**30%**	**76%**	**34**						**22.0**	**92**	**120**	**$20**

Zito,Barry

Age: 35 Th: L Role SP	Health D	LIMA Plan C+	
	PT/Exp B	Rand Var -1	
Ht: 6'2" Wt: 205 Type FB	Consist B	MM 1103	

Ended season with 3.03 ERA, 3.2 Cmd in Sept-Oct, then strong post-season. But before that, it was four PQS-DISasters in Aug and another year of lousy BPIs. Career best splits vs LH probably won't repeat, nor will the 15 wins. Still just one positive RAR since signing mega-deal. No more miracles in '13.

Yr	Tm	W	L	Sv	IP	K	ERA	xERA	WHIP	OBA	vL	vR	BF/G	Ctl	Dom	Cmd	G	L	F	hr/9	hr/f	H%	S%	GS	APC	DOM%	DIS%	Sv%	LI	RAR	BPV	BPX	R$
08	SF	10	17	0	180	120	5.15	5.44	1.60	270	213	285	25.6	5.1	6.0	1.2	36	23	41	0.8	7%	30%	68%	32	100	28%	34%			-18.3	-16	-29	-$5
09	SF	10	13	0	192	154	4.03	4.37	1.35	250	230	256	24.8	3.8	7.2	1.9	38	22	40	1.0	9%	29%	73%	33	97	48%	24%			6.9	43	81	$9
10	SF	9	14	0	199	150	4.15	4.49	1.34	250	232	255	24.9	3.8	6.8	1.8	36	19	45	0.9	7%	28%	71%	33	96	42%	33%	0	0.82	-1.8	34	54	$5
11	SF *	5	4	0	71	45	5.07	4.01	1.28	237	294	248	18.3	3.6	5.6	1.5	40	22	38	1.4	16%	25%	64%	9	67	22%	33%	0	0.54	-9.9	33	49	-$2
12	SF	15	8	0	184	114	4.15	4.89	1.39	263	209	281	25.0	3.4	5.6	1.6	40	20	40	1.0	9%	29%	72%	32	96	34%	28%			-3.1	26	34	$2
1st Half		6	6	0	94	52	3.84	5.30	1.40	244	202	257	25.5	4.3	5.0	1.2	43	17	40	1.1	9%	26%	76%	16	98	44%	31%			2.0	-6	-8	$3
2nd Half		9	2	0	91	62	4.47	4.48	1.38	282	215	305	24.4	2.5	6.2	2.5	38	23	39	0.9	8%	32%	69%	16	94	25%	25%			-5.0	60	78	$1
13	Proj	**12**	**8**	**0**	**160**	**105**	**4.45**	**4.74**	**1.36**	**256**	**225**	**265**	**22.5**	**3.5**	**5.9**	**1.7**	**39**	**21**	**40**	**1.1**	**9%**	**28%**	**70%**	**30**						**-8.6**	**28**	**37**	**$3**

BRIAN RUDD

Offseason Injury Report

by Rick Wilton

There's always a good bit of uncertainty in providing injury status updates during the early off-season. Until rehabbers report to spring training and offer some concrete evidence of their condition, the best we can do is to separate players into two groups: those injury situations that should not linger into 2013, and those injuries that are of higher risk.

In each case, we list the player, injury and prognosis for 2013. For those injured players whose status is likely to affect 2013 playing time and/or performance, we add a risk factor to help guide early draft decisions.

First, the injured players most likely to be ready to go by spring training 2013:

David Aardsma (RHP, SEA)

Injury: Tommy John surgery, July 2011
Prognosis: He has taken longer than most to recover from TJS. Expected to be ready at the start of spring training.

Scott Baker (RHP, MIN)

Injury Tommy John surgery, April 2012
Prognosis: He should be ready for the season very close to the start of the season.

Kyle Blanks (OF, SD)

Injury: Surgery to repair a torn labrum, left shoulder, April 2012
Prognosis: Labrum surgery for position players is iffy, though the recovery track record is much better than pitchers. Recovery will slow his development, though he shouldn't start the year on the DL.

Carlos Carrasco (RHP, CLE)

Injury: Tommy John surgery, August 2010
Prognosis: It will be a year and a half since his surgery on Opening Day and he should be ready.

Carl Crawford (OF, LA)

Injury: Tommy John surgery, left elbow, August 2012
Prognosis: The Dodgers believe he'll be ready right around the opener and his work ethic should make that happen.

John Danks (RHP, CHW)

Injury: Left shoulder clean-up surgery in August 2012; there was no labrum damage
Prognosis: A slow start may be in order but he should not need a stint on the DL.

Sergio Escalona (LHP, HOU)

Injury: Tommy John surgery, April 2012
Prognosis: Likely to need a few weeks in extended spring training to get ready for 2013.

Matt Gamel (1B, MIL)

Injury: Surgery to repair torn right anterior cruciate ligament (ACL)
Prognosis: Expected to be ready at the start of spring training without any restrictions.

Dillon Gee (RHP, NYM)

Injury: Surgery to remove blood clot from his right arm, August 2012
Prognosis: Angiogram after the surgery gave a clean bill of health. Should be at full strength when pitchers report to spring training.

Alex Gonzalez (SS, MIL)

Injury: Surgery to repair torn right anterior cruciate ligament (ACL), May 2012
Prognosis: Almost made it back by the end of the season and will be at full strength at the start of spring training.

J.A. Happ (LHP, TOR)

Injury: Fractured right foot September 2012
Prognosis: Team says he'll be ready when pitchers report in February.

Nick Hundley (C, SD)

Injury: Surgery for torn meniscus, right knee, August 2012
Prognosis: He'll be ready when catchers report to spring training.

Nick Markakis (OF, BAL)

Injury: Fractured left thumb and follow-up surgery (with pins), September 2012
Prognosis: Orioles said he would have played in the World Series if they had made it. OK for spring training.

Jason Marquis (RHP, SD)

Injury: Fractured left hand, August 2012
Prognosis: He will be 100% by the start of spring training.

Brandon McCarthy (RHP, CHA)

Injury: Skull fracture, September 2012
Prognosis: Expected to be recovered by the start of spring training.

Will Middlebrooks (3B, BOS)

Injury: Fractured right hand
Prognosis: Expected be 100% by the start of spring training.

Logan Morrison (OF, MIA)

Injury: Right knee surgery, September 2012
Prognosis: If he avoids setbacks the Marlins believe he'll be ready at the start of spring training.

Chris Narveson (LHP, MIL)

Injury: Surgery to repair small damage to his labrum and rotator cuff, May 2012
Prognosis: A solid rehab into the fall has him likely to be ready for the start of spring training.

Juan Nicasio (RHP, COL)

Injury: Microfracture surgery on the underside of his left patella (kneecap)
Prognosis: The surgery location means he should bounce back over the off-season and be ready for the start of spring training.

Carl Pavano (RHP, MIN)
Injury: Bruised humerus (upper arm bone), right arm
Prognosis: He avoided a fracture and the need for surgery. Pavano will be ready at the start of spring training.

Rafael Perez (LHP, CLE)
Injury: Arthroscopic debridement surgery, left shoulder, September 2012
Prognosis: Cleanup procedure will have him ready by March 1.

Nolan Reimold (OF, BAL)
Injury: Herniated disc, cervical spine, June 2012
Prognosis: The pinched nerve in his neck cleared up after the surgery and he'll be 100% by the start of spring games.

Mariano Rivera (RHP, NYY)
Injury: Surgery to repair a torn ACL, June 2012
Prognosis: Looks like he'll have the green light at the start of spring training.

Daniel Schlereth (LHP, DET)
Injury: Recovery from surgery on left shoulder – April 2012
Prognosis: He was pitching in the minors by the end of the season. He'll be 100% by January 1st.

Joakim Soria (RHP, KC)
Injury: Tommy John surgery, April 2012
Prognosis: He was throwing before the end of the season and he'll be ready once pitchers and catchers report in February.

Ian Stewart (3B, CHC)
Injury: Left wrist surgery, July 2012
Prognosis: Enough time to get his hand and wrist strength back.

Troy Tulowitzki (SS, COL)
Injury: Recovery from a groin injury
Prognosis: Playing in minor league rehab games at the end of the season but was not activated in September. Will be ready for opening of spring training.

Kyle Weiland (RHP, HOU)
Injury: Shoulder surgery (May 2012), and setback with infection
Prognosis: Expect him to be ready at the start of spring training.

Brian Wilson (RHP, SF)
Injury: Tommy John surgery, April 2012
Prognosis: He's on the fast track to recovery and the Giants believe he'll be ready for Opening Day 2013.

Injured players whose health status is still in question for the beginning of 2013:

Lance Berkman (1B, STL)
Injury: Continuing left knee problems
Prognosis: Unless he can shake the left knee problems, Berkman may struggle to stay healthy in 2013.
2013 risk factor: High

Joey Devine (P, OAK)
Injury: Recovery from second Tommy John surgery, April 2012
Prognosis: He'll start the season on the DL. The big question is whether his elbow will hold up
2013 risk factor: Medium

Kyle Drabek (P, TOR)
Injury: Tommy John surgery, June 2012
Prognosis: He won't be back until after the break in 2013.
2013 risk factor: High

Neftali Feliz (P, TEX)
Injury: Tommy John surgery, August 2012
Prognosis: Likely to return as a reliever sometime in August.
2013 risk factor: Medium

Rafael Furcal (SS, STL)
Injury: Torn ulnar collateral ligament, right elbow, August 2012
Prognosis: He avoided surgery but will need a solid rehab to be able to start the 2013 season on time.
2013 risk factor: High

Freddy Galvis (2B, PHI)
Injury: Pars fracture in lumbar region of his back
Prognosis: This type of fracture is tricky to project return dates from, though he played winter ball in Venezuela.
2013 risk factor: High

Jaime Garcia (LHP, STL)
Injury: Strained rotator cuff, September 2012 (no surgery as of October 2012)
Prognosis: They say he'll be ready for spring training. We doubt it, as three doctors recommended surgery, but Dr. James Andrews said it wasn't needed.
2013 risk factor: High

Matt Garza (RHP, CHC)
Injury: Stress reaction, right elbow, August 2012
Prognosis: Garza says he'll be ready for spring training. Stress reaction injuries, though, can linger or surface again.
2013 risk factor: High

Derek Jeter (SS, NYY)
Injury: Fractured left ankle
Prognosis: Because of his age, position played and injury he's a good candidate to start the year on the DL. It could be May before he's ready.
2013 risk factor: Medium

Matt Kemp (OF, LA)
Injury: Left shoulder surgery, October 2012
Prognosis: A torn labrum that needed to be re-attached is still a very serious injury even if it's his non-throwing shoulder. He may not be back until May-June 2013.
2013 risk factor: Medium

Colby Lewis (P, TEX)
Injury: Torn flexor tendon surgery, July 2012
Prognosis: Some of his recovery will roll over into the season. Look for a post All-Star break return.
2013 risk factor: Medium

Cory Luebke (LHP, SD)
Injury: Tommy John surgery, late May 2012
Prognosis: If he has an uneventful recovery he should post a solid second half of the season.
2013 risk factor: Low

Nick Masset (RHP, CIN)
Injury: Shoulder surgery, September 2012
Prognosis: He'll need a chunk of time to recover. We may not see him pitch until the middle of the season.
2013 risk factor: Medium

Brian McCann (C, ATL)
Injury: Surgery to reduce partial subluxations of his right shoulder
Prognosis: A good candidate to start the year on the DL.
2013 risk factor: Medium

Kyle McClellan (RHP, STL)
Injury: Torn labrum right shoulder, July 2012
Prognosis: Don't look for him to be ready at the start of the season. Extended spring training; likely miss at least the first month.
2013 risk factor: Medium

Dustin McGowan (P, TOR)
Injury: Recovery from shoulder surgery, August 2012
Prognosis: He may need some extra time to build up his shoulder strength after spring training.
2013 risk factor: Medium

Charlie Morton (RHP, PIT)
Injury: Tommy John surgery, June 2012
Prognosis: He'll be out for at least the first half.
2013 risk factor: Medium

Mike Pelfrey (RHP, NYM)
Injury: Tommy John surgery, April 2012
Prognosis: If he stays on a 12 month recovery period he will be ready to pitch very early in the season.
2013 risk factor: Low

Michael Pineda (RHP, NYY)
Injury: Labrum surgery, April 2012
Prognosis: Labrum surgery for a power pitcher this young is never a good thing. He could miss the first few months.
2013 risk factor: Medium

Sergio Santos (RHP, TOR)
Injury: Frayed labrum, right shoulder, surgery July 2012
Prognosis: Though the damage was not as extensive as first feared, he's likely to miss the first month of the season.
2013 risk factor: Medium

Grady Sizemore (OF, CLE)
Injury: Back surgery, March 2012
Prognosis: By season's end he still wasn't ready. With his injury history we could see him start the year on the DL.
2013 risk factor: Extreme

Tim Stauffer (RHP, SD)
Injury: Flexor tendon injury, spring of 2012
Prognosis: Should have been ready by the end of the season but because he didn't have surgery, could have more problems in 2013.
2013 risk factor: High

Randy Wolf (LHP, FA)
Injury: Torn UCL, left elbow
Prognosis: Tommy John surgery expected; if so, out for 2013.
2013 risk factor: Extreme

C.J. Wilson (LHP, LAA)
Injury: Elbow surgery, October 2012
Prognosis: Surgery this late usually leads to the pitcher starting the year on the DL. He could be back by May 2013.
2013 risk factor: Medium

Vance Worley (RHP, PHI)
Injury: Right elbow surgery, September 2012
Prognosis: Surgery was to remove bone chips; expected to be ready for spring but is a candidate for a slow start.
2013 risk factor: Low

5-Year Injury Log

The following chart details the disabled list stints for all players during the past five years. For each injury, the number of days the player missed during the season is listed. A few DL stints are for fewer than 15 days; these are cases when a player was placed on the DL prior to Opening Day (only in-season time lost is listed).
Abbreviations:
Lt = left
Rt = right
fx = fractured
R/C = rotator cuff
str = strained
surg = surgery
TJS = Tommy John (ulnar collateral ligament reconstruction) surgery
x 2 = two occurrences of the same injury
x 3 = three occurrences of the same injury

FIVE-YEAR INJURY LOG

Batters	Yr	Days	Injury
Allen,Brandon	12	27	Strained RT quad
Almonte,Erick	11	38	Concussion
Alvarez,Pedro	11	66	Rt. quadriceps tightness
Andino,Robert	12	15	Subluxation of LT shoulder
Ankiel,Rick	09	19	Bruised shoulder
	10	80	Strained RT quadriceps
	11	37	Rt. wrist sprain
	12	10	Quad injury
Arencibia,JP	12	43	Fractured RT hand
Avila,Alex	12	15	Strained RT hamstring
Aviles,Mike	09	134	Strained RT forearm
Aybar,Erick	08	28	Dislocated RT pinkie finger
	11	17	Strained LT oblique muscle
	12	15	Fractured RT toe
Baker,Jeff	09	66	Sprained LT hand
	11	14	Lt. groin strain
Baker,John	10	143	Strained RT elbow
	11	158	Recovery from TJS
Barajas,Rod	10	26	Strained LT oblique muscle
	11	25	Sprained RT ankle
Barmes,Clint	11	29	Lt. hand fracture
Barney,Darwin	11	15	Lt. knee sprain
Bartlett,Jason	08	20	Sprained RT knee
	09	21	Sprained LT ankle
	10	17	Strained RT hamstring
	12	140	Strained RT knee
Barton,Daric	08	17	Strained neck
	09	25	Strained RT hamstring
	11	27	Torn labrum in RT shoulder
	12	4	Sprained RT shoulder
Bautista,Jose	12	77	Inflam RT wrist/Surgery on RT wrist
Baxter,Mike	11	126	Torn ligament in LT thumb
	12	58	Displaced RT collarbone
Bay,Jason	10	69	Post concussion syndrome
	11	21	Strained LT rib cage
	12	67	Non-displaced Rib+ Concussionx2
Belt,Brandon	11	44	Hairline LT wrist fracture
Beltran,Carlos	09	78	Bone bruise, RT knee
	10	102	Recovery from surgery - RT knee
	11	15	Strained RT hand
Beltre,Adrian	09	69	Surgery - RT Shldr; bruised testicle
	11	40	Strained LT hamstring
Berkman,Lance	09	20	Strained LT calf
	10	32	Sprained ankle;LT knee surg
	12	108	Rt. knee inflam x2 + LT calf str
Bernadina,Roger	09	169	Fractured RT ankle
Betancourt,Yuniesky	09	20	Strained RT hamstring x 2
	12	30	Sprained RT ankle
Betemit,Wilson	08	34	Strained RT hamstring
	12	21	Injured RT wrist
Blackmon,Charlie	11	83	Fractured LT foot
	12	135	Turf toe
Blanco,Andres	09	28	Strained LT calf
	11	46	Stress reaction-back; Inflam - back
Blanco,Henry	09	24	Strained RT hamstring
	12	59	Sprained LT thumb

FIVE-YEAR INJURY LOG

Batters	Yr	Days	Injury
Blanks,Kyle	09	37	Strained arch-Rt. foot
	10	138	Strained RT elbow
	11	26	Recovery from TJS
	12	173	Labrum tear LT shoulder
Bloomquist,Willie	08	51	Strained RT hamstring
	11	23	Strained RT hamstring
	12	23	Strained lower back
Blum,Geoff	09	15	Strained LT hamstring
	10	32	Bone chips RT elbow
	11	144	Rt. knee surgery
	12	76	Strained LT oblique
Boesch,Brennan	11	20	Torn ligament in RT thumb
Bonifaco,Emilio	12	112	Sprained LT thumb x2; spr. RT knee
Borbon,Julio	11	20	Inflam - LT hamstring
Bourgeois,Jason	11	50	Strained LT oblique
Bourjos,Peter	11	15	Tight RT hamstring
	12	15	Sore RT wrist
Brantley,Michael	11	34	Inflam in RT wrist
Bruce,Jay	09	64	Fractured RT wrist
Buck,John	09	36	Herniated disc – lower back
	10	15	Laceration – RT thumb
Buck,Travis	08	20	Shin splints
	09	15	Strained LT oblique
	10	100	Strained RT oblique
	12	128	Rt. Achilles tendinitis
Burrell,Pat	09	32	Strained neck
	11	47	Bone spur in RT foot
Burriss,Emmanuel	09	34	Fractured LT toe
	10	82	Fractured - LT foot
Byrd,Marlon	08	27	Inflam LT knee
	11	40	Facial fractures
Cabrera,Asdrubal	09	26	AC Joint sprain – LT shoulder
	10	63	Fractured LT forearm
Cabrera,Everth	09	60	Fractured hamate bone - LT hand
	10	49	Strained RT hamstring x 2
Cain,Lorenzo	12	89	Strained LT groin
Cairo,Miguel	12	22	Strained LT hamstring
Carp,Mike	12	91	Strained RT shoulder x2; RT groin
Carpenter,Matt	12	30	Rt. oblique strain
Carroll,Brett	08	100	Separated RT shoulder
	10	10	Strained LT oblique
Carroll,Jamey	09	36	Fractured LT hand
Casilla,Alexi	08	23	Torn ligament RT thumb
	10	51	Bone spur in RT elbow
	11	62	Strained RT hamstring
Castillo,Welington	12	71	MCL sprain in RT knee
Castro,Jason	11	182	Rt. knee surgery
	12	36	Rt. knee swelling
Castro,Ramon	08	56	Strained RT hamstring x 2
	10	29	Contusion - RT heel
	11	81	Fractured RT hand and index finger
Cedeno,Ronny	11	20	Concussion
	12	46	Lt. intercostal strain+str RT calf
Cervelli,Francisco	11	50	Fractured LT foot; Concussion
Cespedes,Yoenis	12	25	Strained muscle in LT hand

FIVE-YEAR INJURY LOG

Batters	Yr	Days	Injury
Chavez,Endy	09	107	Torn ACL – RT knee
	12	50	Strained intercostal muscle
Chavez,Eric	08	155	Inflam of RT shoulder; Back spasms
	09	163	Strained RT forearm/elbow
	10	135	Neck spasms
	11	81	Broken LT foot
	12	8	Concussion
Chirinos,Robinson	12	182	Concussion
Chisenhall,Lonnie	12	71	Fractured RT ulna
Choo,Shin-Soo	08	61	Recovery from surgery on LT elbow
	10	20	Sprained RT thumb
	11	71	Fract. LT thumb; Strain LT oblique
Christian,Justin	12	15	Sprained LT wrist
Clevenger,Steve	12	33	Strained RT oblique
Coghlan,Chris	10	69	Torn meniscus – LT knee
	11	104	Lt. knee Inflam
Colvin,Tyler	10	13	Chest puncture wound
Cooper,David	12	42	Strained back
Cora,Alex	08	25	Sore RT elbow
	09	68	Torn lig. RT thmb; Surg. LT/RT thmb
Corona,Reegie	11	183	Fractured RT elbow
Cousins,Scott	11	108	Lower back strain
Cowgill,Collin	12	24	Sprained LT ankle
Cozart,Zack	11	67	Hyperextended LT elbow
Craig,Allen	11	78	Lt. groin strain
	12	43	Surg recovery; LT hamstring strain
Crawford,Carl	08	47	Dislocated RT index finger
	11	30	Strained LT hamstring
	12	148	Recovery from LT wrist surgery+ TJS
Crisp,Coco	09	114	Sore RT shoulder
	10	77	Fx finger; ribcage muscle
	12	18	Infected ear/sinus
Crowe,Trevor	09	18	Strained RT oblique
	11	160	Recov. from surgery - RT shoulder
Cruz,Nelson	09	16	sprained LT ankle
	10	56	Strained RT & LT hammy
	11	34	Strained RT quad; Strained LT ham.
Cuddyer,Michael	08	96	Dislocted RT fing; Fx LT foot, LT fing.
	12	61	Rt. oblique strainx2
Damon,Johnny	08	14	Sprained A/C joint RT shoulder
d'Arnaud,Chase	11	29	Fractured little finger on RT hand
Darnell,James	12	139	Rt. shoulder subluxation
Davis,Chris	11	22	Strained RT shoulder
Davis,Ike	11	141	Lt. ankle sprain and bone bruise
Davis,Rajai	11	64	Sore RT ankle; Torn LT hamstring
De Aza,Alejandro	08	184	High ankle sprain LT ankle
	12	15	Bruised LT ribs
DeJesus,David	10	72	Torn ligament – RT thumb
Denorfia,Chris	08	73	Lower back stiffness
	11	35	Strained RT hamstring
DeRosa,Mark	09	17	Sprained LT wrist
	10	147	Neuritis - LT wrist
	11	91	Sore LT wrist
	12	85	Lt. abdominal strain+ oblique str
Desmond,Ian	12	26	Torn LT oblique

FIVE-YEAR INJURY LOG

Batters	Yr	Days	Injury
Diaz,Matt	08	119	Strained ligament LT knee
	10	45	Infected RT thumb
	12	75	Rt. thumb contusion
Dickerson,Chris	09	52	Bruised RT R/C; sprained LT ankle
	10	101	Fractured hamate bone - RT hand
Dirks,Andy	12	61	Tendinitis in RT Achilles tendon
Dobbs,Greg	09	25	Strained RT calf
Donald,Jason	11	29	Fractured LT hand
Doumit,Ryan	08	23	Fractured tip of LT thumb
	09	80	Fractured scaphoid bone RT wrist
	10	16	Concussion
	11	135	Lt. ankle sprain
Drew,Stephen	09	17	Strained LT hamstring
	11	70	Fract. RT ankle
	12	83	Recovering from RT ankle surgery
Ellis,Mark	08	9	Torn labrum - RT shoulder
	09	60	Strained LT calf
	10	31	Strained LT hamstring
	11	15	Strained RT hamstring
	12	46	Sprained LT leg
Ellsbury,Jacoby	10	158	Fractured ribs x 3
	12	90	Subluxation of RT shoulder
Encarnacion,Edwin	09	81	Fract. LT wrist; LT knee soreness
	10	48	Sprained RT wrist & shoulder
Escobar,Yunel	10	15	Strained LT adductor
	11	9	Inflam - LT elbow
Ethier,Andre	10	16	Fractured pinkie finger – RT hand
	12	15	Strained LT oblique
Figgins,Chone	08	37	Strained RT hamstring x 2
	11	33	Strained RT hip flexor
Flaherty,Ryan	12	16	Tonsilitis
Flores,Jesus	08	15	Sprained LT ankle
	09	139	Torn labrum & bruised RT shoulder
	10	182	Recov. from surgery - RT shoulder
Fontenot,Mike	11	43	Lt. groin strain
Ford,Darren	11	28	Lt. ankle sprain
Forsythe,Logan	12	60	Lt. foot fracture
Fowler,Dexter	09	15	Bruised LT knee
	11	40	Lt. abdominal strain
Francisco,Ben	12	35	Strained LT hamstring
Francisco,Juan	11	31	Lt. calf strain
Freese,David	10	97	Sprained RT ankle
	11	56	Broken hamate bone in LT hand
Fukudome,Kosuke	12	122	Strained RT oblique
Fuld,Sam	12	110	Surgery - RT wrist
Furcal,Rafael	08	141	Back surgery 7/08
	10	58	Strained lower back; LT hammy
	11	70	Broken LT thumb
	12	34	Rt. elbow strain
Galvis,Freddy	12	119	Fracture of L4-5 vertebra
Gamel,Mat	10	61	Torn RT lat muscle
	12	155	Torn RT ACL
Gardner,Brett	09	43	Fractured LT thumb
	12	164	Sore RT elbow
Gentry,Craig	10	34	Fractured RT wrist
	11	14	Concussion

FIVE-YEAR INJURY LOG

Batters	Yr	Days	Injury
Getz,Chris	09	20	Strained RT oblique
	10	15	Tight RT oblique muscle
	12	89	Bruised ribs+str LT leg+fx LT thumb
Giambi,Jason	09	18	Strained RT quad
	11	17	Strained LT quadriceps
	12	42	Viral syndrome
Gimenez,Chris	11	64	Strained LT oblique muscle
Gimenez,Hector	11	173	Rt. knee surgery
Gomez,Carlos	10	36	Concussion; Strained RT hip
	11	42	Fractured LT clavicle
	12	15	Strained LT hamstring
Gomez,Hector	12	182	Groin strain
Gonzalez,Alex	08	184	Compress fx LT lower leg/surgery
	09	35	Bone chips - RT elbow
	12	151	Rt. knee injury
Gonzalez,Carlos	11	37	Strained RT wrist
Gonzalez,Marwin	12	38	Bruised RT heel
Gordon,Alex	08	20	Torn RT quadriceps
	09	91	Torn labrum - RT hip / surgery
	10	13	Fractured tip of RT thumb
Gordon,Dee	11	22	Bruised RT shoulder
	12	68	Torn RT thumb ligament
Grandal,Yasmani	12	17	Strained RT oblique
Granderson,Curtis	08	24	Fractured 3rd metacarpal, RT Hand
	10	26	Strained LT groin
Green,Nick	12	52	Sprained LT thumb
Greene,Tyler	10	16	Bruised RT hand
Guerrero,Vladimir	09	64	Torn RT pectoral; sore LT knee
	11	15	Fracture in RT hand
Guillen,Carlos	09	80	Inflam RT shoulder
	10	97	Lt hammy; RT calf; LT knee
	11	127	Recov. fr LT knee surg; Sore LT wrist
Gutierrez,Franklin	11	71	Gastritis; Strained LT oblique
	12	128	Concussion + torn RT pec muscle
Guyer,Brandon	12	144	Strained LT shoulder
Gwynn Jr.,Tony	08	19	Strained LT hamstring
	10	25	Fractured hamate bone – RT hand
Hafner,Travis	08	102	Strained RT shoulder
	09	26	Sore and weak RT shoulder
	10	17	Sore RT shoulder
	11	50	Strained RT oblique; Strain RT foot
	12	82	Inflamed lower back+sore RT knee
Hairston Jr.,Jerry	08	50	Strain RT ham x 2; Fract. LT thumb
	10	15	Sprained RT elbow
	11	18	Rt. wrist fracture
	12	71	Lt. hip Inflam+ LT hammy str
Hairston,Scott	08	32	Torn ligament - LT thumb
	09	20	Strained LT biceps
	10	17	Strained LT hamstring
	11	36	Lt. oblique strain
Hall,Bill	11	17	Deep laceration of LT leg
Hamilton,Josh	09	52	Strained ribcage; abdominal wall
	11	40	Fractured RT humerus
Hanigan,Ryan	09	16	Concussion
	10	41	Fractured LT thumb

FIVE-YEAR INJURY LOG

Batters	Yr	Days	Injury
Hannahan,Jack	10	26	Strained RT groin
	12	19	Strained LT calf
Hardy,J.J.	10	46	Sore LT wrist
	11	30	Strained LT oblique muscle
Harris,Willie	09	15	Strained LT oblique
Hart,Corey	09	37	Appendicitis
	11	27	Lt. oblique strain
Hawpe,Brad	08	16	Strained RT hamstring
	10	15	Strained LT quad muscle
	11	102	Strained RT middle finger
Hayes,Brett	10	15	Bruised LT wrist
Headley,Chase	11	43	Fractured LT pinkie finger
Heisey,Chris	11	26	Strained LT oblique
Helton,Todd	08	71	Sore lower back
	10	29	Stiff lower back
	12	77	Rt. hip labrum tear+ hip Inflam
Hermida,Jeremy	08	9	Tight LT hamstring
	10	42	Fractured ribs
	12	160	Strained RT hip flexor
Hernandez,Diory	10	81	Torn capsule - LT shoulder surgery
Hernandez,Ramon	09	64	Lt. knee surgery
	10	17	Inflam – RT knee
	12	50	Lt. hand strain
Herrera,Jonathan	11	23	Rt. index finger fracture
	12	45	Infection in LT wrist+ RT hammy str.
Heyward,Jason	10	18	Bone bruise – LT thumb
	11	23	Sore RT shoulder
Hicks,Brandon	10	13	Fractured RT index finger
Hill,Aaron	08	123	Post concussion syndrome
	10	15	Strained RT hamstring
	11	18	Sore RT hamstring
Holliday,Matt	08	16	Strained LT hamstring
	11	15	Lt. quadriceps strain
Howard,Ryan	10	19	Sprained LT ankle
	12	93	Recov. Fr. LT Achilles tendon surg.
Hudson,Orlando	08	51	Dislocated LT wrist
	10	33	Stained RT oblique; sore LT wrist
	11	39	Rt. hamstring strain
	12	16	Contusion in LT foot
Huff,Aubrey	12	94	Anxiety disorder+rt knee spr x 2
Hundley,Nick	09	55	Bruised LT wrist
	11	71	Rt. oblique strain; Str RT elbow
	12	49	Torn meniscus in RT knee
Hunter,Torii	09	39	Strained RT adductor
Iannetta,Chris	09	16	Strained RT hamstring
	12	80	Fractured RT wrist
Ibanez,Raul	09	22	Strained LT groin
Infante,Omar	08	54	Strain LT hamstring; Fract. LT hand
	09	82	Fract 5th metacarpal – LT hand
	11	15	Fractured RT middle finger
Inge,Brandon	08	17	Strained LT oblique
	10	15	Fractured LT hand
	11	22	Mononucleosis
	12	68	Str. RT shouldx2+str groin x2
Ishikawa,Travis	12	28	Lt. rib-cage strain

FIVE-YEAR INJURY LOG

Batters	Yr	Days	Injury
Izturis,Cesar	08	15	Strained RT hamstring
	09	37	Appendicitis
	11	136	Irritation, ulnar nerve, RT hand numbness; Strained groin
	12	27	Strained LT hamstring
Izturis,Maicer	08	61	Strain back; torn thumb ligament
	10	85	Inflam RT shouldx2; Str. LT forearm
Jackson,Austin	12	15	Strained abdominal
Jackson,Conor	09	146	Valley fever
	10	108	Strained RT ham x 2; Ab strain
Jaso,John	11	39	Stained RT oblique muscle
Jay,Jon	12	38	Sprained RT shoulder
Jennings,Desmond	12	24	Sprained LT knee
Jeter,Derek	11	20	Strained RT calf
Johnson,Chris	10	20	Strained intercostal muscle
Johnson,Elliot	11	19	Sprained LT knee
Johnson,Kelly	09	20	Tendinitis - RT wrist
Johnson,Nick	12	98	Sprained RT wrist
Johnson,Reed	08	15	Lower back spasms
	09	68	Fractured LT foot; back spasms
	10	26	Lower back spasms
	11	15	Lower back spasms
Johnson,Rob	12	50	Torn ligament in LT thumb
Jones,Adam	08	29	Fractured LT foot
	09	33	Sprained LT ankle
Jones,Andruw	08	82	Tendinitis - RT patellar tendon
	09	15	Strained LT hamstring
Jones,Chipper	08	15	Strained LT hamstring
	10	53	Torn ACL – LT knee
	11	16	Torn meniscus in RT knee
	12	23	LT knee meniscus tear+ bruise calf
Joyce,Matt	10	57	Strained RT elbow
	12	27	Tightness in lower back
Kalish,Ryan	11	4	Herniated cervical disc
Kearns,Austin	08	78	Stress fx LT foot; surgery RT elbow
	09	62	Bruised RT thumb
	12	15	Rt. hamstring strain
Kemp,Matt	12	58	Strained LT hamstring
Kendrick,Howie	08	78	Strained LT hamstring x 2
	11	15	Strained RT hamstring
Kennedy,Adam	12	38	Strained RT groin
Keppinger,Jeff	08	39	Fractured LT patellar
	10	15	Fractured big to – LT foot
	11	57	Lt. foot surgery
	12	34	Broken RT big toe
Kinsler,Ian	08	43	Sports hernia
	09	16	Strained LT hamstring
	10	61	Sprained RT ankle; Stra. LT groin
Kipnis,Jason	11	23	Strained RT hamstring
Konerko,Paul	08	23	Strained LT oblique
	12	9	Concussion
Kotchman,Casey	09	15	Bruised RT lower leg
Kotsay,Mark	08	36	Strained lower back
	09	58	Recov. from herniated disc surgery
	12	33	Lower back strain+rt calf str

FIVE-YEAR INJURY LOG

Batters	Yr	Days	Injury
Kottaras,George	09	33	Strained lower back
Kubel,Jason	11	52	Strained LT foot
Laird,Gerald	08	35	Strained LT hamstring
	11	45	Rt. index finger fracture
LaPorta,Matt	11	18	Sprained RT ankle
LaRoche,Adam	08	17	Rt. intercostal strain
	11	130	Torn labrum in LT shoulder
Lawrie,Brett	11	8	Fractured RT middle finger
	12	34	Strained RT oblique
Lee,Carlos	08	51	Fractured LT pink finger
	12	15	Stained LT hamstring
Lee,Derek	11	18	Strained LT oblique muscle
Lewis,Fred	10	11	Strain intercostal muscle - LT side
	11	35	Strained RT oblique
Lillibridge,Brent	11	20	Fract. metacarpal bone in RT hand
Lind,Adam	11	27	Soreness - lower back
	12	31	Strained mid-back
Lobaton,Jose	11	46	Sprained LT knee
	12	45	Sore RT shoulder
Longoria,Evan	08	29	Fractured RT hand
	11	30	Strained LT oblique muscle
	12	98	Torn LT hamstring
Lopez,Felipe	10	21	Strained RT elbow
Lowrie,Jed	09	119	Fractured and strained LT wrist
	10	108	Mononucleosis
	11	52	Sore LT shoulder
	12	66	Rt. ankle + RT thumb sprains
Lucroy,Jonathan	11	12	Fractured RT pinkie finger
	12	58	Rt. hand fracture
Ludwick,Ryan	09	15	Strained RT hamstring
	10	28	Strained LT calf muscle
	11	15	Mid-back muscle spasms
Maldonado,Carlos	12	127	Strained lower back
Markakis,Nick	12	40	Fractured RT hand
Marrero,Chris	12	184	Torn LT hamstring
Marte,Starling	12	19	Strained RT oblique
Martin,Russell	10	60	Torn labrum – RT hip
Martinez,Fernando	09	93	Inflam behind RT knee
	12	9	Concussion
Martinez,Michael	12	65	Rt. foot fracture
Martinez,Victor	08	78	Surgery - RT elbow
	10	28	Fractured LT thumb
	11	15	Strained RT groin
	12	183	Recovery from surgery - LT knee
Mathis,Jeff	10	58	Fractured RT wrist
Matsui,Hideki	08	56	Inflam LT knee
Mauer,Joe	09	26	Inflamed RT sacroiliac joint
	11	79	Bilateral leg weakness; Pneumonia
Maxwell,Justin	11	28	Recovery from TJS
	12	17	Loose bodies in LT ankle
Maybin,Cameron	11	16	Rt. knee Inflam
McCann,Brian	09	15	Lt. eye infection
	11	19	Strained LT oblique
McDonald,Darnell	11	19	Strained LT quad muscle
	12	24	Strained RT oblique

FIVE-YEAR INJURY LOG

Batters	Yr	Days	Injury
McDonald,John	08	31	Sprained RT ankle
	11	21	Strained RT hamstring
	12	29	Strained LT oblique
McLouth,Nate	09	19	Strained-Lt. hamstring
	10	41	Post concussion syndrome
	11	89	Lt. oblique strain
Mesoraco,Devin	12	8	Concussion
Middlebrooks,Wil	12	54	Fractured RT wrist
Miles,Aaron	09	60	Strained RT shoulder; RT elbow
Molina,Jose	09	61	Strained LT hamstring
Montero,Miguel	08	24	Fractured index finger RT hand
	10	62	Torn meniscus - RT knee
Moore,Adam	10	40	Sublexed LT fibula
	11	175	Surgery to repair RT meniscus
Moore,Jeremy	12	182	Recovering from LT hip surgery
Morales,Kendrys	11	183	Recovery from surgeries - LT ankle
Morel,Brent	12	75	Strained back
Moreland,Mitch	12	40	Strained LT hamstring
Morgan,Nyjer	09	38	Fractured LT hand
	10	15	Strained RT hip flexor
	11	36	Deep thigh bruise
Morneau,Justin	10	87	Concussion
	11	80	Strain LT wrist; Post conc. synd.
	12	15	Sore RT wrist
Morrison,Logan	11	22	Lt. foot strain
	12	67	Rt. knee Inflam
Morse,Michael	10	35	Strained LT calf
	12	58	Strained RT lat
Moss,Brandon	08	21	Appendectomy
Murphy,Daniel	10	50	Sprained RT knee
	11	52	Torn ligament in LT knee
Murphy,David	08	54	Sprain RT post. cruciate ligament
Murphy,Donnie	08	32	Inflam RT elbow
	10	31	Dislocated RT wrist
	11	128	Rt. wrist Inflam
	12	15	Lt. hamstring strain
Nady,Xavier	09	172	Torn ligament - RT elbow
	11	47	Fractured LT hand
	12	69	Rt. wrist tendonitis
Napoli,Mike	08	32	Inflam RT shoulder
	11	22	Strained LT oblique muscle
	12	35	Strained LT quadriceps
Nava,Daniel	12	40	Sprained LT wristx2
Navarro,Dioner	08	17	Lacerat., two fingers on RT Hand
	11	26	Rt. oblique strain
Negron,Kristopher	12	34	Rt. knee injury
Nelson,Chris	09	27	Torn ligament – RT wrist
	12	37	Irreg. heartbeat+ LT wrist Inflam
Nieves,Wil	12	31	Turf toe in RT foot
Nishioka,Tsuyoshi	11	85	Fract. LT fibula; Strain RT oblique
Nix,Jayson	09	26	Strained RT quad muscle
	11	23	Contusion - LT shin
Nix,Laynce	09	15	Herniated disc-cervical spine
	10	23	Sprained RT ankle
	12	73	Strained RT elbow
Olivo,Miguel	12	23	Strained RT groin

FIVE-YEAR INJURY LOG

Batters	Yr	Days	Injury
Ordonez,Magglio	08	18	Strained RT oblique
	10	70	Fractured RT ankle
	11	33	Weakness in RT ankle
Ortiz,David	08	54	Torn tendon sheath - LT wrist
	12	78	Strained RT achilles tendonx2
Pagan,Angel	08	140	Bruised labrum LT shoulder
	09	80	Strained RT groin; RT elbow surgery
	11	35	Pulled LT oblique
Parrino,Andy	12	24	Injured RT hand
Patterson,Corey	11	11	Concussion
Patterson,Eric	10	16	Strained neck
	11	10	Strained LT hamstring
Paul,Xavier	09	137	Skin infection - LT leg
Paulino,Ronny	11	19	Anemia
Pearce,Steve	10	131	Sprained RT ankle
	11	91	Rt. calf strain
Pedroia,Dustin	10	97	Fx LT navicular bone; sore LT foot
	12	15	Sprained RT thumb
Pena,Brayan	08	18	Lower back strain
Pena,Carlos	08	23	Fractured index finger LT hand
	09	27	Fractured LT index and ring finger
	10	15	Plantar Fasciitis - RT foot
Pena,Ramiro	11	50	Appendicitis
Pennington,Cliff	12	18	Tendinitis in LT elbow
Perez,Salvador	12	78	Surgery for torn LT meniscus
Phillips,Brandon	08	18	Fractured RT index finger & surgery
Pie,Felix	10	81	Strained LT shoulder
Pierre,Juan	08	25	Sprain LT med. collateral ligament
Pierzynski,A.J.	11	20	Bruised LT wrist
Pina,Manuel	12	149	Surgery on RT knee
Plouffe,Trevor	12	23	Bruised RT thumb
Polanco,Placido	10	21	Bone spur –Rt. elbow
	11	40	Lower back Inflam
	12	57	Lower back Inflamx2
Posada,Jorge	08	108	Torn RT subscapularis muscle
	09	24	Strained RT hamstring
	10	16	Stress fracture – RT foot
Posey,Buster	11	126	Fract. LT fibula and torn ankle lig.
Prado,Martin	08	59	Sprained LT thumb
	10	17	Fractured RT pinky finger
	11	37	Staph infection in RT calf
Presley,Alex	11	33	Lt. hand contusion
	12	12	Concussion
Pujols,Albert	08	15	Strained LT calf
	11	15	Fractured LT forearm
Punto,Nick	08	40	Strained LT hamstring x 2
	09	15	Strained RT groin
	10	55	Strained LT hammy; hip flexor
	11	99	Sports hernia surgery
Quentin,Carlos	09	55	Plantar Fasciitis – LT foot
	11	22	Sprained LT shoulder
	12	54	Rt. knee surgery
Quintanilla,Omar	08	20	Concussion
Quintero,Humberto	09	17	Strained RT shoulder
	11	39	High RT ankle sprain
Raburn,Ryan	12	52	Sprain RT thumb; Strain RT quad

FIVE-YEAR INJURY LOG

Batters	Yr	Days	Injury
Ramirez,Aramis	09	58	Dislocated LT shoulder
Ramirez,Hanley	11	72	Lt. back strain
Ramirez,Manny	10	65	Strained RT calf x 2; RT hammy
Ramos,Wilson	12	144	Torn RT knee ligament
Ransom,Cody	09	60	Strained RT quad muscle
Rasmus,Colby	11	23	Jammed RT wrist
Reimold,Nolan	09	17	Tendinitis – LT Achilles tendon
	12	156	Surgery for herniated disk
Renteria,Edgar	10	57	Strained RT groin; hammy; biceps
Repko,Jason	11	36	Strain RT quad; Bursitis-LT should.
	12	62	Separation of RT shoulder
Reyes,Jose	09	137	Tendinitis RT calf
	10	6	Recovery from hyperthyroidism
	11	37	Lt. hamstring strain
Reynolds,Mark	12	17	Strained LT oblique
Rivera,Juan	12	148	Torn LT hamstring
Roberts,Brian	10	104	Strained ab muscle; sore back
	11	135	Concussion
	12	162	Surg.-torn RT hip labrum+concuss.
Rodriguez,Alex	08	19	Grade 2 strain of RT quad muscle
	09	33	Surg. to repair torn labrum - RT hip
	10	15	Strained LT calf
	11	44	Torn meniscus in RT knee
	12	40	Broken LT hand
Rodriguez,Luis	09	28	Sprained LT ankle
Rodriguez,Sean	12	15	Fractured RT hand
Rohlinger,Ryan	10	30	Strained LT hamstring
Rolen,Scott	08	41	Fract. finger; Inflam RT shoulder
	09	15	Postconcussion syndrome
	11	91	Lt. shoulder strain
	12	37	Strained LT shoulder
Rollins,Jimmy	08	19	Sprained RT ankle
	10	65	Strained RT calf x 2
	11	17	Rt. groin strain
Romine,Austin	12	182	Strained lower back
Rosales,Adam	10	29	Stress fracture – RT ankle
	11	67	Fractured RT foot
Ross,Cody	11	21	Rt. calf strain
	12	31	Fractured bone in LT foot
Ross,David	08	24	Back Spasms
	09	12	Strained LT groin
Rowand,Aaron	10	15	Fractured check bone
Ruggiano,Justin	11	22	Bursitis in LT knee
Ruiz,Carlos	09	21	Strained RT oblique
	10	21	Concussion
	11	15	Lower back Inflam
	12	35	Plantar fasciitis in LT foot
Ryan,Brendan	08	24	Strained ribcage
	09	15	Strained LT hamstring
	11	15	Sprained LT shoulder
Saltalamacchia,Jarrod	09	18	Numbness, fatigue-Rt. arm
	10	35	Strained upper back; infected leg
Sanchez,Angel	08	28	Sprained finger LT hand
Sanchez,Freddy	09	20	Strained LT shoulder
	10	45	Recov, from surgery - LT shoulder
	12	182	Recov. from surgery - RT shoulder

FIVE-YEAR INJURY LOG

Batters	Yr	Days	Injury
Sanchez,Hector	12	15	Lt. knee sprain
Sandoval,Pablo	11	45	Broken hamate bone in RT hand
	12	56	Strained LT hamstring+ Fx RT hand
Santana,Carlos	12	10	Concussion
Santiago,Ramon	08	33	Separated LT shoulder
Schafer,Jordan	09	30	Rehab from surgery – RT wrist
	10	43	Recovery from surgery - LT wrist
	11	26	Chip fracture in LT middle finger
	12	25	Shoulder
Schierholtz,Nate	09	16	Strained LT hip
	11	38	Hairline fracture in RT foot
	12	19	Fractured RT great toe
Schneider,Brian	09	42	Strained back muscle
	10	15	Strained RT Achilles
	11	43	Straing LT hamstring
	12	77	Strain LT hamstring+ spr RT Ankle
Schumaker,Skip	11	37	Rt. triceps strain
	12	36	Rt. hammy strain+torn RT oblique
Scott,Luke	09	16	Strained LT shoulder
	10	18	Strained LT hamstring
	11	86	Bruise-RT knee; Strain RT should.
	12	50	Str RT oblique+back spasms
Scutaro,Marco	11	30	Strained LT oblique muscle
Sellers,Justin	12	134	Bulging disc in lower back
Shoppach,Kelly	10	54	Sprained RT knee
Simmons,Andrelton	12	63	Non-displaced fract. RT hand
Sizemore,Grady	09	54	Inflamed LT elbow; torn ab. wall
	10	139	Bone brse–LT knee;microfrac surg.
	11	77	Recv.. LT knee surg.; Bruise RT Knee
	12	183	Recovery from back surgery
Sizemore,Scott	12	182	Recovery from torn ACL surgery
Smith,Seth	12	18	Strained LT hamstring
Smoak,Justin	11	20	Fracture of the nose
Snider,Travis	10	63	Sprained RT wrist
Snyder,Chris	08	19	Lt. testicular fracture
	09	81	Strained lower back x 2
	11	126	Sore lower back
Sogard,Eric	12	58	Strained back/sprained ankle
Solano,Jhonatan	12	78	Lt. oblique strain
Soriano,Alfonso	08	56	Fx LT hand; Strain RT calf
	09	31	Surgery – LT knee
	11	15	Lt. quadriceps strain
Soto,Geovany	09	90	Strained LT oblique
	10	30	Sprain RT shoulder; Shoulder Surg.
	11	18	Lt. groin strain
	12	30	Torn LT meniscus
Span,Denard	09	15	Rt. ear infection
	11	91	Concussion; Migraine headaches
	12	15	Strained RT sternoclavicular joint
Spilborghs,Ryan	08	54	Strained LT oblique
	11	45	Plantar fascitis in RT foot
Stairs,Matt	10	24	Sore RT knee
Stanton,Giancarlo	12	30	Arthroscopic RT knee surgery
Stewart,Ian	10	28	Strained RT oblique
	12	113	Sore LT wrist
Stubbs,Drew	12	19	Strained LT oblique

FIVE-YEAR INJURY LOG

Batters	Yr	Days	Injury
Suzuki,Ichiro	09	10	Bleeding ulcer
Suzuki,Kurt	10	22	Intercostal strain
Sweeney,Ryan	08	29	Sprained thumb; Bruised LT foot
	09	15	Sprained LT knee
	10	83	Pending surg. for patella tendinitis
	12	93	Concussion+toe+fx LT hand
Tabata,Jose	11	100	Rt. hand contusion; Str LT quad
Teagarden,Taylor	12	100	Strained back
Teahen,Mark	10	73	Fractured RT middle finger
	11	24	Strained RT oblique muscle
Tejada,Miguel	11	28	Lower abdominal strain
Tejada,Ruben	12	48	Strained RT quadriceps
Thames,Marcus	09	46	Strained RT oblique
	10	21	Strained RT hamstring
	11	34	Rt. quad strain
Theriot,Ryan	12	15	Rt. elbow Inflam
Thole,Josh	12	24	Concussion
Thomas,Brad	11	141	Rt. elbow surgery
Thome,Jim	11	45	Strain LT oblique; Strain LT quad
	12	92	Strained lower back, Back spasms
Tolbert,Matt	08	109	Torn ligament LT thumb
	10	45	Sprained RT middle finger
Torrealba,Yorvit	08	31	Torn Meniscus - LT knee/surgery
Torres,Andres	09	59	Strained LT hamstring x 2
	11	45	Strained LT Achilles Tendon
	12	24	Lt. calf strain
Tracy,Chad	12	65	Rt. adductor strain
Treanor,Matt	08	28	Strained LT hip
	09	166	Torn labrum - RT hip
	10	30	Sprained RT knee
	11	32	Concussion
Tulowitzki,Troy	08	67	Torn tendon RT quad; Cut LT hand
	10	39	Fractured LT wrist
	12	126	Strained LT groin muscle
Turner,Justin	12	18	Sprained RT ankle
Upton,B.J.	09	8	Recov. Fr. labrum surg. - RT should.
	12	15	Soreness in lower back
Upton,Justin	08	55	Strained LT oblique muscle
	09	20	Strained RT oblique
Uribe,Juan	08	15	Strained LT hamstring
	11	83	Lt. hip flexor muscle strain
	12	28	Lt. wrist injury
Utley,Chase	10	49	Sprained RT thumb
	11	53	Rt. knee tendinitis
	12	84	Worn cartilage behind LT kneecap
Velez,Eugenio	10	18	Concussion
Venable,Will	10	19	Lower back pain
Viciedo,Dayan	11	6	Fractured RT thumb
Victorino,Shane	08	16	Strained RT calf
	10	15	Strained LT abdominal muscle
	11	30	Rt. hamstring str; Sprain LT thumb
Vizquel,Omar	08	40	Surgery LT knee
Votto,Joey	09	24	Stress-related issue
	12	50	Torn medial meniscus in LT knee

FIVE-YEAR INJURY LOG

Batters	Yr	Days	Injury
Weeks,Rickie	08	15	Sprained LT knee
	09	140	Torn sheath LT wrist.
	11	42	Sprained LT ankle
Wells,Vernon	08	59	Fract. LT wrist; Strain LT hamstring
	11	28	Strained RT groin
	12	67	Torn ligament in RT thumb
Werth,Jayson	08	15	Strained RT oblique
	12	87	Broken LT wrist
Whiteside,Eli	11	7	Concussion
Wieters,Matt	10	15	Strained RT hamstring
Wigginton,Ty	08	26	Fractured thumb LT hand
	11	16	Lt. oblique strain
Willingham,Josh	08	57	Back spasms
	10	48	Surgery – LT knee
	11	19	Strained LT achilles tendon
Willits,Reggie	08	17	Concussion
	10	10	Strained RT hamstring
	11	13	Strained LT calf
Wilson,Bobby	10	22	Bruised ankle; concussion
	12	13	Concussion
Wilson,Jack	08	51	Strained LT calf
	09	17	Sprained LT index finger
	10	101	Fract RT hand; Strain RT hamstring
	11	15	Bruised LT heel
	12	82	Dislocated RT pinky finger
Wise,DeWayne	08	15	Strained LT adductor
	09	61	Sep. RT shoulder; strained A/C joint
Wood,Brandon	10	22	Rt. Hip flexor strain
Wright,David	09	15	Concussion
	11	67	Lower back stress fracture
Youkilis,Kevin	09	15	Strained LT oblique
	10	61	Sprained RT thumb
	11	16	Sore back; Bursitis RT hip
	12	23	Strained lower back
Young,Chris	12	30	Rt. shoulder contusion
Young,Delmon	09	10	Recovery from elbow surgery
	11	39	Strain LT oblique; Sprain RT ankle
Young,Eric	10	77	Stress Fracture; RT tibia
	12	45	Lt. intercostal muscle strain
Zimmerman,Ryan	08	57	Torn labrum - LT shoulder
	11	65	Lt. abdominal strain
	12	17	Sore RT shoulder

FIVE-YEAR INJURY LOG

Pitchers	Yr	Days	Injury
Aardsma,David	08	40	Strained RT groin
	11	182	Recov. from surgery-left hip; TJS
	12	173	Recovery from TJS
Abad,Fernando	11	88	Left shoulder tendinitis
	12	20	Right intercostal strain
Accardo,Jeremy	08	143	Tightness RT forearm
Aceves,Alfredo	10	147	Herniated disk in lower back
Acosta,Manny	08	49	Strained RT hamstring
Adams,Mike	09	90	Labrum surg-RT should+strain
	10	26	Strained LT oblique
Affeldt,Jeremy	10	28	Torn LT oblique muscle
	12	15	Sprained RT knee
Albers,Matt	08	96	Torn labrum - pitching shoulder
	11	15	Sore RT lat muscle
Alburquerque,Al	11	39	Inflam - RT elbow; Concussion
	12	141	Recov. fr. surg. - RT elbow
Anderson,Brett	10	90	Left elbow Inflam x 2
	11	115	Soreness in LT elbow
	12	137	Recovery from TJS
Arias,Alberto	09	42	Strained RT hamstring
	10	182	Impingement - RT shoulder
	11	182	Right shoulder surgery
Arredondo,Jose	11	60	Right shoulder Inflam
Arrieta,Jake	11	59	Bone spur in RT elbow
Ascanio,Jose	09	54	Tendinitis - RT shoulder
	10	182	Recov. fr. surg. - RT shoulder
	11	41	Right elbow tightness
Atchison,Scott	12	60	Tightness In RT forearm
Augenstein,Bryan	11	169	Right groin strain
Ayala,Luis	11	28	Strained lat muscle
Badenhop,Burke	08	100	Tendinitis RT shoulder
	09	30	Strained RT trapezius muscle
Baez,Danys	08	184	TJS 9/2007
	10	15	Back spasms
Bailey,Andrew	10	32	Right intercostal strain
	11	59	Strained RT forearm
	12	132	Right thumb surgery
Bailey,Homer	10	83	Inflam – RT shoulder
	11	66	Right shoulder impingement
Baker,Scott	08	32	Strained RT groin
	09	10	Stiffness - RT shoulder
	11	58	Strained RT flexor muscle
	12	182	TJS - RT elbow
Balfour,Grant	10	34	Strained intercostal muscle
	11	15	Strained RT oblique muscle
Barrera,Henry	10	101	Recovery from TJS 6/09
	11	183	Sprained RT elbow
Bass,Anthony	12	72	Right shoulder Inflam
Bastardo,Antonio	09	69	Strained RT shoulder
	10	29	Ulnar Neuritis – LT elbow
Batista,Miguel	12	16	Lower back strain
Beachy,Brandon	11	39	Left oblique strain
	12	109	TJS
Beato,Pedro	11	15	Right elbow tendinitis
	12	92	Right shoulder stiffness
Beckett,Josh	08	32	Back spasms; Sore pitching elbow
	10	65	Strained lower back
	12	18	Inflam in RT shoulder

FIVE-YEAR INJURY LOG

Pitchers	Yr	Days	Injury
Bedard,Erik	08	102	Torn labrum surgery; Sore hip
	09	100	Inflamed LT shoulder x 2
	10	182	Recov. fr. surg. on LT shoulder
	11	31	Sprained LT knee
Beimel,Joe	09	15	Strained LT hip flexor
	11	48	Sore LT elbow
Belisle,Matt	08	44	Sore RT knee; sore RT forearm
Beltre,Omar	10	30	Sprained RT ankle
	11	182	Recov. fr. surg. - back
Benoit,Joaquin	08	34	Soreness - RT shoulder
	09	183	Recov. from R/C surg. - RT shoulder
Bergesen,Brad	09	66	Contusion - LT leg
Berken,Jason	10	51	Inflam – RT shoulder
	11	25	Strained RT forearm
Betances,Dellin	12	15	Right shoulder Inflam
Betancourt,Rafael	09	38	Strained RT groin
	10	15	Strained RT groin
Billingsley,Chad	10	16	Strained RT groin
	12	46	Right elbow pain
Blackburn,Nick	11	38	Strained RT forearm
	12	18	Strained LT quad
Blanton,Joe	10	29	Strained LT oblique
	11	127	Impingement in RT elbow
Braddock,Zach	11	32	Sleep disorder
Braden,Dallas	09	65	Infection - LT foot
	10	27	Sore LT elbow
	11	165	Surg. - torn capsule in LT shoulder
	12	182	Recov. fr. surg. - LT shoulder
Bray,Bill	12	78	Lumbar strain+ LT groin str
Britton,Zach	11	17	Strained LT shoulder
	12	62	Left shoulder impingement
Broxton,Jonathan	11	148	Sore RT elbow
Bruney,Brian	08	97	Lisfranc injury RT foot
	09	54	Strained RT elbow x 2
	12	101	Inflam in LT hip
Buchholz,Clay	08	18	Broken fingernail RT hand
	10	24	Strained LT hamstring
	11	103	Strained lower back
	12	24	Gastro-intestinal problem
Buchholz,Taylor	09	183	Sprained UCL - RT elbow
	10	129	Sore back; RT elbow
	11	122	Right shoulder fatigue
Bulger,Jason	10	80	Sore RT shoulder
Burnett,AJ	12	17	Fractured RT orbital bone
Burton,Jared	08	45	Strained RT lat muscle
	09	16	Fatigue – RT shoulder
	11	135	Arthroscopic surg-RT shoulder
Byrdak,Tim	10	20	Strained RT hamstring
	12	62	Left shoulder soreness
Cabral,Cesar	12	182	Fractured LT elbow
Cahill,Trevor	10	16	Stress reaction - LT scapula
Capps,Matt	08	54	Bursitis - pitching shoulder
	12	88	Irritation of RT rotator cuff
Capuano,Chris	08	184	TJS 5/08
Carignan,Andrew	12	120	TJS - RT elbow
Carlson,Jesse	11	182	Surgery - torn LT rotator cuff
Hernandez, Roberto	08	63	Strained LT hip
(aka Fausto Carmona)	11	15	Strained RT quad muscle

FIVE-YEAR INJURY LOG

Pitchers	Yr	Days	Injury
Carpenter,Chris	08	184	TJS recov; Compress nerve RT arm
	09	35	Strained LT ribcage muscle
	12	171	Nerve irritation in RT shoulder
	12	182	Recov. fr. surg.-bone spur RT elbow
Carrasco,Carlos	11	16	Inflam - RT elbow
	12	183	Recovery from TJS
Carrasco,DJ	12	32	Right ankle sprain
Cashner,Andrew	11	150	Right rotator cuff strain
	12	59	Strained RT latissimus dorsi
Casilla,Santiago	08	33	Sore RT elbow
	09	15	Sprain RT lat. collateral ligament
	11	57	Sore RT elbow
Cassevah,Bobby	12	22	Inflam in RT shoulder
Castillo,Alberto	11	33	Left shoulder tendinitis
Castillo,Lendy	12	87	Left groin strain
Ceda,Jose	12	184	TJS
Chacin,Jhoulys	12	111	Right shoulder Inflam
Chamberlain,Joba	08	26	Tendinitis - RT rotator cuff
	11	115	TJS
	12	117	Dislocated RT ankle
Chapman,Aroldis	11	39	Left shoulder Inflam
Chen,Bruce	09	17	Torn LT oblique muscle
	11	49	Strained LT lat muscle
Choate,Randy	08	102	Fractured finger LT hand
	11	44	Left elbow Inflam
Cobb,Alex	11	53	Surgery - rib cage
Coello,Robert	12	101	Strained RT elbow
Coffey,Todd	10	21	Bruised RT thumb
	11	15	Left calf strain
	12	109	Right knee Inflam+TJS
Coke,Phil	11	15	Bone bruise in RT foot
Collmenter,Josh	12	22	Ulcers
Colon,Bartolo	08	82	Strained oblique
	09	99	Inflamed RT knee; RT elbow
	11	20	Strained LT hamstring
	12	15	Strained RT oblique
Contreras,Jose	08	74	Ruptured Achilles; Strain RT elbow
	11	135	Right elbow strain
	12	136	Right elbow strain
Cook,Aaron	09	34	Strained RT shoulder
	10	54	Turf toe; Fx RT fibula
	11	69	Broken finger on RT hand
	12	49	Laceration of LT knee
Cordero,Francisco	12	63	Right foot sesamoiditis
Correia,Kevin	08	48	Strained LT intercostals
	11	40	Strained LT oblique
Cortes,Dan	11	15	Bruised LT ankle
Crain,Jesse	09	16	Inflamed RT shoulder
	12	51	Strained RT shoulder+ LT oblique
Crotta,Michael	11	141	Right posterior elbow Inflam
Cruz,Juan	08	27	Strained LT oblique
	09	48	Strained RT shoulder
	11	15	Strained RT groin
	12	22	Right shoulder Inflam
Cruz,Rhiner	12	15	Sprained RT ankle
Cueto,Johnny	09	15	Inflam RT shoulder
	11	39	Right biceps/triceps irritation
Daley,Matt	09	18	Sprained LT foot
	10	87	Inflam – RT shoulder
	11	120	Right shoulder Inflam

FIVE-YEAR INJURY LOG

Pitchers	Yr	Days	Injury
Danks,John	11	24	Strained RT oblique muscle
	12	137	Surgery - strained LT shoulder
Davies,Kyle	11	111	Inflam R/C; Impingement RT should.
Davis,Wade	10	18	Strained RT shoulder
	11	15	Strained RT forearm
De Fratus,Justin	12	152	Right elbow sprain
De La Rosa,Jorge	10	74	Torn tendon – LT middle finger
	11	127	TJS
	12	168	TJS
De La Rosa,Rubby	11	59	TJS
De Vries,Cole	12	20	Fractured Rib
Del Rosario,Enerio	11	27	Strained RT shoulder
Demel,Sam	11	38	Right shoulder tendinitis
Dempster,Ryan	09	25	Fractured RT big toe
	12	37	Right quad strain, Tight RT lat.
Detwiler,Ross	10	110	Rt hip strain; hip cartilage
Devine,Joey	08	67	Inflam - RT elbow setback 7/08
	09	183	Sprained RT elbow
	10	182	Recov. fr. surg. - RT elbow
	11	2	Strained rhomboid- RT shoulder
	12	182	TJS - RT elbow
DiFelice,Mark	09	21	Strained RT shoulder
Dotel,Octavio	11	8	Sore LT hamstring
	12	16	Inflam in RT elbow
Doubront,Felix	11	8	Inflam - LT forearm
	12	15	Contusion in RT knee
Downs,Scott	09	43	Bruised LT toe; sprained LT toe
	11	27	Fx LT big toe; Gastrointestinal virus
	12	21	Strained LT shoulder
Drabek,Kyle	12	112	TJS
Drake,Oliver	12	8	Tendinitis in RT shoulder
Duchscherer,Justin	08	62	Strain RT hip;Strain RT biceps tend.
	09	183	Recov. fr. surg. on RT elbow
	10	156	Left Hip Inflam x 2
	11	182	Strained LT hip
Duffy,Danny	12	143	TJS
Duke,Zach	10	25	Strained LT elbow
	11	58	Broken LT hand
Dumatrait,Phil	08	95	Sore pitching shoulder/ surgery
	09	138	Inflam LT shoulder
Durbin,Chad	09	19	Strained lat muscle
	10	21	Strained RT hamstring
Elbert,Scott	12	62	Left elbow Inflamx2
Escalona,Edgmer	11	20	Right rotator cuff strain
	12	27	Right elbow Inflam
Escalona,Sergio	11	33	Left elbow tendinitis
	12	183	TJS
Estrada,Marco	10	124	Right shoulder fatigue
	12	33	Right quadriceps strain
Eyre,Willie	09	64	Tightness RT groin
Farina,Alan	12	183	Recovery from TJS
Farnsworth,Kyle	12	86	Strained RT elbow
Feldman,Scott	10	16	Bone bruise – RT knee
	11	105	Recov. fr. surg. - RT knee
Feliciano,Pedro	11	183	Strained LT rotator cuff
	12	182	Recov. fr. surg. - RT shoulder
Feliz,Neftali	11	15	Inflam - RT shoulder
	12	136	TJS - RT elbow
Fish,Robert	12	183	Left elbow tendinitis

FIVE-YEAR INJURY LOG

Pitchers	Yr	Days	Injury
Fister, Doug	10	24	Right shoulder fatigue
	12	47	Strained LT side
Floyd, Gavin	12	31	Strain RT elbow flex+ tend RT Elbow
Francis, Jeff	08	38	Inflam - pitching shoulder
	09	183	Recov. fr. labrum surg. - LT shoulder
	10	73	Soreness – LT shoulder x 2
Francisco, Frank	09	53	Tendntis RT should. x 2; pneumonia
	10	36	Strained RT lat muscle
	11	19	Sore RT pectoral
	12	42	Left oblique strain
Frasor, Jason	12	48	Tightness In RT forearm
Friedrich, Christian	12	67	Stress fract-RT side of lower spine
Frieri, Ernesto	11	15	Back problem
Fuentes, Brian	10	178	Mid-back strain
Fulchino, Jeff	10	34	Tendinitis - RT elbow
Furbush, Charlie	12	30	Strained LT triceps muscle
Gallardo, Yovani	08	165	Two knee surgeries
	10	17	Strained oblique muscle
Garcia, Freddy	11	20	Lacerated RT index finger
Garcia, Jaime	09	137	Sore LT elbow
	12	74	Left shoulder strain
Garland, Jon	11	133	Left oblique strain
Garza, Matt	08	16	Inflamed radial nerve in RT arm
	11	13	Right elbow bone contusion
	12	68	Right elbow stress reaction
Gaudin, Chad	08	14	Left hip surgery
	11	156	Right shoulder Inflam
Gee, Dillon	12	88	Damaged artery in RT shoulder
Gonzalez, Mike	08	80	TJS 6/2008
	10	102	Strained LT shoulder
Gorzelanny, Tom	08	19	Irritated LT middle finger
	11	26	Left elbow Inflam
Grabow, John	10	15	Tendinitis - LT knee
Green, Sean	10	126	Strained RT ribcage
Gregerson, Luke	09	28	Strained RT shoulder
	11	28	Left oblique strain
Greinke, Zack	11	35	Fractured LT rib
Griffin, AJ	12	27	Strained RT shoulder
Grilli, Jason	09	20	Inflam-right elbow
Guerra, Javy	12	63	Strained LT oblique+ RT knee Inflam
Guerrier, Matt	12	133	Right elbow tendinitis
Guthrie, Jeremy	08	21	Impingement - RT rotator cuff
	12	22	Right shoulder sprain
Gutierrez, Juan	10	15	Inflam – RT shoulder
	11	127	Right shoulder Inflam
Halladay, Roy	09	15	Right groin strain
	12	50	Right back strain
Hamels, Cole	11	16	Left shoulder Inflam
Hammel, Jason	10	18	Strained RT groin
	12	54	Injured RT knee
Hanrahan, Joel	10	8	Strained flexor tendon - RT forearm
Hanson, Tommy	11	68	Right shoulder tendinitis x2
	12	17	Lower back strain
Happ, J.A.	10	81	Strained LT forearm
	12	30	Fractured RT foot
Harang, Aaron	08	28	Strained pitching forearm
	09	45	Appendectomy
	10	61	Lower back spasms
	11	29	Sore RT foot

FIVE-YEAR INJURY LOG

Pitchers	Yr	Days	Injury
Harden, Rich	08	37	Strained RT subscapularis muscle
	09	26	Strained lower back
	10	64	Tendinitis RT should.; Strain LT glut.
	11	92	Strained RT shoulder
Haren, Dan	12	18	Stiff lower back
Harrison, Matt	09	125	Inflamed LT elbow; shoulder
	10	22	Left biceps tendinitis
Hawkins, LaTroy	09	16	Shingles
	10	136	Rt shoulder weakness x 2
	11	22	Right shoulder surgery
	12	33	Fractured RT pinkie finger
Hawksworth, Blake	11	26	Strained RT groin
	12	183	Right elbow surgery
Heilman, Aaron	11	20	Right shoulder tendinitis
Hellickson, Jeremy	12	15	Fatigued RT shoulder
Hensley, Clay	08	68	Strained RT shoulder
	10	20	Strained LT neck muscle
	11	62	Left rib contusion
	12	15	Right groin strain
Hernandez, David	10	33	Sprained LT ankle
Hernandez, Felix	08	16	Sprained LT ankle
Herndon, David	12	157	TJS
Hill, Rich	08	30	Lower back soreness
	09	110	Inflamed RT shoulder; LT elbow
	11	119	Sprained LT elbow
	12	107	TJS recov.+Soreness in LT forearm
Hochevar, Luke	08	41	Ribcage contusion
	10	83	Strained RT elbow
Holland, Derek	10	62	Left rotator cuff Inflam
	12	31	Fatigued LT shoulder
Holland, Greg	12	21	Stress reaction in LT ribs
Howell, J.P.	10	182	Strained LT shoulder
	11	50	Recov. fr. surg. - LT labrum
Hudson, Daniel	12	137	Right shoulder impingement +TJS
Hudson, Tim	08	65	Torn RT ulnar collateral ligament
	09	150	Recovery from TJS
	12	25	Recovering from back surgery
Huff, David	12	18	Strained RT hamstring
Hughes, Phil	08	90	Fractured rib
	11	82	Tired arm
Humber, Philip	11	15	Facial Contusion
	12	30	Strained RT elbow
Hunter, Tommy	10	24	Strained LT oblique
	11	92	Stained RT groin
Hurley, Eric	08	91	Strain LT hammy; sore RT shoulder
	09	183	Torn rotator cuff - RT shoulder
	10	182	Recov. fr. surg. x 2 - LT wrist
	11	159	Concussion
Hutchison, Drew	12	110	TJS - RT elbow
Igarashi, Ryota	10	32	Strained LT hamstring
Isringhausen, Jason	08	73	Torn flexor tendon; Lac. RT hand
	09	155	Torn UCL RT elbow; surgery
Jakubauskas, Chris	10	115	Concussion
James, Chuck	08	10	Torn rotator cuff
Jansen, Kenley	11	49	Right shoulder Inflam
Janssen, Casey	08	184	Torn labrum - RT shoulder
	09	66	Sore RT shoulder x 2
	11	34	Sore RT forearm

FIVE-YEAR INJURY LOG

Pitchers	Yr	Days	Injury
Jenks,Bobby	08	18	Bursitis - LT scapula area
	11	132	Strain RT biceps; Tightness in back
	12	183	Recov. fr. surg. - back
Jepsen,Kevin	09	15	Lower back spasms
Jimenez,Cesar	09	183	Tendinitis LT biceps tendon
Jimenez,Ubaldo	11	17	Cuticle cut on RT thumb
Johnson,Jim	08	29	Impingement - RT shoulder
	10	91	Small tear in RT elbow
Johnson,Josh	08	102	TJS 8/2007
	11	135	Right shoulder Inflam
Jurrjens,Jair	10	61	Strained LT hamstring
	11	28	Sore RT torso; Sore RT knee
	12	64	Strained RT groin
Karstens,Jeff	08	50	Strained RT groin
	09	22	Strained lower back
	12	68	Sore RT shoulder
Kazmir,Scott	08	35	Strained LT elbow
	09	37	Strained RT quadriceps
	10	36	Strain RT hammy;Fatigue LT should.
	11	178	Lower back stiffness
Kelley,Shawn	09	58	Strained LT oblique
	10	109	Right elbow Inflam
	11	132	Recov. fr. surg. - RT elbow
Kennedy,Ian	08	26	Strain RT lat, bursitis RT shoulder
Kimball,Cole	11	111	Right shoulder Inflam
	12	184	Rehab from RT shoulder surgery
Kinney,Josh	08	156	2 setbacks from TJ Surgery
Kintzler,Brandon	11	147	Right triceps tendonitis
	12	151	Sore RT forearm
Kohn,Michael	12	182	Right forearm strain
Kuo,Hong-Chih	09	85	Sore LT elbow
	10	18	Sore LT shoulder
	11	56	Left low back strain
Kuroda,Hiroki	08	19	Tendinitis - RT shoulder
	09	72	Strained LT oblique; concussion
Lackey,John	08	44	Grade 2 strain, RT triceps
	09	41	Inflam - RT elbow
	11	24	Strained RT elbow
	12	182	TJS - RT elbow
Laffey,Aaron	09	46	Strained RT oblique
	10	42	Fatigued – LT shoulder
Latos,Mat	10	15	Strained LT oblique
	11	11	Strained RT shoulder
Leake,Mike	10	15	Fatigue – RT shoulder
LeCure,Sam	11	30	Right forearm strain
Lee,Cliff	10	26	Strained RT abdominal muscle
	12	20	Left oblique strain
Leroux,Chris	09	22	Inflamed RT shoulder
	10	30	Strained RT elbow
	11	25	Strained LT calf
	12	151	Strained RT pectoral muscle
Lester,Jon	11	19	Strained lower LT lat muscle
Lewis,Colby	12	101	Surg. torn tendon RT elbow
Lewis,Rommie	10	18	Inflam - LT shoulder
Lidge,Brad	08	6	Surgery RT knee
	09	19	Sprained RT knee
	10	47	Inflam RT elbow/surgery;Recov. RT knee
	11	113	Right posterior rotator cuff strain
	12	46	Abdominal wall strain

FIVE-YEAR INJURY LOG

Pitchers	Yr	Days	Injury
Lilly,Ted	09	27	Inflam LT shoulder; surgery LT knee
	10	20	Recov. fr. surg. - LT shoulder
	12	143	Left shoulder inflam.; str neck
Lincoln,Brad	11	11	Bruised RT arm
Lindstrom,Matt	09	37	Strained RT elbow
	10	15	Back spasms
	11	16	Nerve injury in upper RT arm
	12	47	Torn ligament in RT middle finger
Linebrink,Scott	08	40	Inflamed subscapularis muscle
	11	15	Lower back strain
	12	184	Right shoulder capsulitis
Liriano,Francisco	09	22	Left arm fatigue
	09	174	Strained RT forearm
	11	36	Inflam LT should.; Strain LT should.
Litsch,Jesse	10	128	TJS recovery; Torn labrum RT hip
	11	60	Impingement in RT shoulder
	12	183	Surgery to repair RT biceps tendon
Lohse,Kyle	09	54	Strained RT forearm; LT groin
	10	84	Exertional compartment syndrome- right forearm
Lopez,Wilton	11	19	Irritation-ulnar nerve RT elbow
	12	28	Sprained RT elbow
Loux,Shane	12	62	Neck strain
Lowe,Mark	10	148	Herniated lumbar disc
	12	45	Strained RT intercostal muscle
Luebke,Cory	12	159	TJS
Lynn,Lance	11	50	Left oblique strain
Lyon,Brandon	11	142	Partially rotator cuff tear
Madson,Ryan	10	70	Fractured RT toe + surgery
	11	26	Right hand contusion
	12	183	TJS
Magnuson,Trystan	11	44	Tendinitis in RT shoulder
Maholm,Paul	11	42	Left shoulder strain
Maloney,Matt	11	87	Left oblique strain
Marcum,Shaun	08	33	Strained pitching elbow
	09	183	Recovery from TJS 9/08
	10	16	Inflam – RT elbow
	12	70	Right elbow tightness
Marmol,Carlos	12	16	Strained RT hamstring
Marquez,Jeff	11	101	Inflam - RT shoulder
Marquis,Jason	10	111	Debris in RT elbow
	11	44	Fractured RT fibula
	12	43	Fractured LT wrist
Marte,Damaso	09	117	Tendinitis – LT shoulder
	10	87	Inflam – LT shoulder
	11	183	Recov. fr. surg. - LT shoulder
Marte,Luis	12	51	Strained LT hamstring
Masset,Nick	09	15	Strained LT oblique
	12	182	Sore RT shoulder
Mateo,Marcos	11	86	Right elbow soreness
	12	183	Sore RT elbow
Mathieson,Scott	08	184	Setbacks from TJ Surgery
	10	27	Strained back
Matsuzaka,Daisuke	08	24	Strained rotator cuff - RT shoulder
	09	124	Weak and strained RT shoulder
	10	44	Strained neck; RT forearm
	11	135	Sprained RT elbow
	12	121	TJS recovery+trained RT upper trap

FIVE-YEAR INJURY LOG

Pitchers	Yr	Days	Injury
Mattheus, Ryan	11	25	Right shoulder strain
	12	27	Plantar fascia strain in LT foot
Matusz, Brian	11	59	Strained LT intecostal muscle
Mazzaro, Vin	09	27	Tendinitis – RT shoulder
McCarthy, Brandon	08	146	Inflam RT Forearm/setback 4/08
	09	88	Stress fracture – RT scapula
	10	66	Recovery from shoulder surgery
	11	45	Stress reaction in RT scapula
	12	95	Strained RT shoulderx2 + skull Fx
McClellan, Kyle	11	15	Left hip flexor strain
	12	139	Right elbow strain
McGowan, Dustin	08	83	Frayed labrum, surgery 7/08
	09	183	Recov. Fr. labrum surg.-RT shoulder
	10	182	Sore RT shoulder
	11	158	Recov. fr. surg. - RT shoulder
	12	183	RT Plant. Fasciitis+RT should. surg.
Medlen, Kris	10	59	Partial tear of UCL- RT elbow
	11	178	Recovery from TJS
Meek, Evan	09	54	Strained LT oblique
	11	116	Right shoulder tendinitis
Mendoza, Luis	08	59	Inflam RT shoulder, Blister RT hand
Mickolio, Kam	09	28	Inflam RT shoulder
Mijares, Jose	10	58	Strained LT knee; blured vision
	11	15	Strained LT elbow
Miller, Andrew	08	49	Tendinitis in RT patellar tendon
	09	25	Strained RT oblique
	12	32	Strained LT hamstring
Millwood, Kevin	08	40	Strained RT groin x 2
	10	16	Strained RT forearm
Mitre, Sergio	08	184	Strained RT Forearm
	10	49	Strained LT oblique
	11	75	Tendinitis in RT shoulder
Morales, Franklin	09	51	Strained LT shoulder
	10	27	Left shoulder weakness
	11	33	Strained LT forearm
	12	41	Fatigue in LT shoulder
Morrow, Brandon	09	15	Tendinitis – RT triceps
	11	21	Inflam - RT forearm
	12	74	Strained LT oblique
Morton, Charlie	09	7	Strained LT oblique
	10	35	Right shoulder weakness
	12	137	Recovering from RT hip surgery+TJS
Moscoso, Guillermo	10	4	Blister - RT index finger
Moseley, Dustin	08	22	Forearm stiffness pitching arm
	09	170	Irritation - RT elbow
	11	60	Left shoulder strain
	12	179	Strained RT shoulder
Mota, Guillermo	09	15	Ingrown toenail
	10	15	IT band syndrome
Motte, Jason	10	27	Sprained RT shoulder
Moylan, Peter	08	171	Soreness RT Elbow, TJS 5/08
	11	143	Back surgery
Mujica, Edward	12	18	Fractured RT pinky toe
Myers, Brett	09	98	Torn and frayed labrum - RT hip
Narveson, Chris	11	15	Left thumb laceration
	12	171	Left rotator cuff tear
Nathan, Joe	10	182	TJS - RT elbow
	11	31	Strained RT flexor muscle

FIVE-YEAR INJURY LOG

Pitchers	Yr	Days	Injury
Neshek, Pat	08	145	Partially torn UCL - RT elbow
	09	185	Recovery from TJS
	10	37	Inflamed RT middle finger
Nicasio, Juan	11	54	Neck surgery
	12	123	Strained LT knee
Niemann, Jeff	10	21	Strained RT shoulder
	11	45	Stiff back
	12	109	Fractured RT fibula
Niese, Jonathon	09	60	Torn RT hamstring tendon
	10	19	Strained RT hamstring
	11	36	Intercostal strain of the RT side
Nolasco, Ricky	10	35	Torn meniscus – RT knee
Norberto, Jordan	12	68	Str + tendinitis in LT shoulder
Norris, Bud	10	35	Biceps tendinitis – RT shoulder
	12	16	Left knee sprain
Nova, Ivan	12	17	Inflam in RT rotator cuff
Oviedo, Juan Carlos	08	54	Strained RT lat muscle
	12	73	TJS
O'Day, Darren	11	85	Torn labrm RT hip+Inflam RT should.
O'Flaherty, Eric	10	41	Viral infection
Ogando, Alexi	12	35	Strained RT groin
Ohlendorf, Ross	10	68	Strained RT lat; sore back
	11	136	Right shoulder strain
Ohman, Will	09	130	Inflam – LT shoulder
Okajima, Hideki	10	22	Strained RT hamstring
Oliver, Darren	09	11	Strained LT triceps
Olsen, Scott	09	129	Tendinitis/torn labrum RT shoulder
	10	68	Tightness LT shoulder
	11	182	Left shoulder Inflam
Ondrusek, Logan	11	18	Strained RT forearm
O'Sullivan, Sean	11	31	Tendinitis In RT biceps
Oswalt, Roy	08	16	Strained LT abductor muscle
	09	19	Lower back pain
	11	63	Lower back Inflam
Outman, Josh	09	107	Sprained LT elbow
	10	182	Recov. fr. surg. - LT elbow
	12	37	Strained oblique
Owings, Micah	09	24	Tightness - RT shoulder
	12	161	Right elbow surgery
Padilla, Vicente	08	30	Strain LT hamstring; Strained neck
	09	16	Strained deltoid - RT shoulder
	10	75	Sore RT foreram; herniated disc
	11	161	Right elbow surgery
	12	15	Strained RT bicep
Parker, Blake	12	112	RT elbow stress react+bone bruise
Parnell, Bobby	11	40	Circulatory issues RT middle finger
Parra, Manny	11	183	Facet joint injury in RT back
Patton, Troy	08	184	Torn labrum
	12	39	Sprained RT ankle
Paulino, Felipe	08	184	Pinched nerve upper RT arm
	09	19	Strained RT groin
	10	83	Right shoulder tendinitis
	12	149	TJS - LT elbow
Pavano, Carl	08	145	TJS 8/2007
	12	124	Strained RT shoulder
Peavy, Jake	08	28	Strained RT elbow
	09	101	Strained tendon - RT ankle
	10	88	Detached lat in RT shoulder
	11	57	Recov. Fr. surg. RT should.+ strained adductor muscle

FIVE-YEAR INJURY LOG

Pitchers	Yr	Days	Injury
Pelfrey,Mike	12	165	TJS
Pena,Tony	11	124	Tendinitis In RT elbow
Penny,Brad	08	95	Inflam RT shoulder
	10	134	Strained upper back
	12	18	Right shoulder impingement
Perez,Luis	12	87	TJS - LT elbow
Perez,Rafael	12	161	Strained LT lat/ankle injury
Perkins,Glen	09	52	Inflam LT shoulder; elbow
	11	26	Strained RT oblique muscle
Perry,Ryan	10	26	Tendinitis upper RT biceps
	11	15	Infected eye
Pettitte,Andy	12	83	Fractured fibula in LT ankle
Pineda,Michael	12	182	Surgery torn labrum RT shoulder
Pineiro,Joel	08	36	Sore RT shoulder; Sore RT groin
	10	55	Strained LT oblique
	11	29	Right shoulder tightness
Pomeranz,Stuart	12	131	Strained LT oblique
Proctor,Scott	08	71	Tendinitis pitching elbow
	09	183	Sore RT elbow
Purcey,David	10	19	Strained ligaments – RT foot
Putz,J.J.	08	57	Costochndritis+Hyperext. RT elbow
	09	122	Bone chips - RT elbow
	10	15	Tendinitis – RT knee
	11	27	Right elbow tendinitis
Qualls,Chad	09	35	Dislocated kneecap - LT leg
	12	15	Irritation of LT toe
Ramirez,Elvin	11	183	Sore RT shoulder
Ramirez,Erasmo	12	62	Strained RT elbow flexor
Ramirez,Ramon	12	24	Hamstring strain
Rapada,Clay	08	18	Biceps tendinitis LT arm
Rauch,Jon	11	33	Appendicitis; Torn cartilge RT knee
Ray,Chris	08	184	TJS
	09	25	Biceps tendinitis - RT arm
	10	16	Strained RT ribcage muscle
	11	61	Strained RT shoulder
Resop,Chris	10	49	Strained LT oblique
Reyes,Dennys	10	16	Strained LT elbow
Reyes,Jo-Jo	09	56	Strained LT hamstring
	10	33	Strained RT knee
Reynolds,Greg	09	34	Sore RT shoulder
	10	70	Bruised RT elbow
Richard,Clayton	11	86	Strained LT shoulder
Richards,Garrett	11	21	Right adductor strain
Richmond,Scott	09	28	Tendinitis – RT shoulder
	10	78	Impingement - RT shoulder
Rivera,Mariano	12	153	Torn ACL in RT knee
Robertson,David	12	33	Strained LT oblique
Robles,Maricio	11	74	Recov. fr. surg. - LT shoulder
Rodney,Fernando	08	78	Tendinitis RT shoulder
	11	39	Strained upper back
Rodriguez,Francisco	11	142	Inflam - RT shoulder
Rodriguez,Henry	11	28	Right arm injury
	12	91	Low back strain+ RT index finger
Rodriguez,Wandy	08	38	Strained LT groin
	11	21	Fluid in LT elbow
Rogers,Esmil	11	84	Right lat strain
Romero,J.C.	09	70	Strained LT forearm
	10	18	Recov. fr. surg. on LT elbow
	11	15	Right calf strain
Romero,Ricky	09	22	Strained LT oblique

FIVE-YEAR INJURY LOG

Pitchers	Yr	Days	Injury
Romo,Sergio	09	54	Sprained RT elbow
	11	18	Right elbow Inflam
Rosario,Sandy	12	110	Right quad strain
Ross,Robbie	12	20	Sore LT forearm
Ross,Tyson	11	66	Strained LT oblique muscle
Runzler,Dan	10	54	Dislocated LT knee
	12	153	Strained lat muscle
Rzepczynski,Marc	10	45	Fractured middle finger - LT hand
Sabathia,CC	12	15	Sore LT elbow+ strain abductor
Saito,Takashi	08	31	Sprained pitching elbow
	10	18	Left hamstring strain
	11	88	Left hamstring strain
	12	126	Strained LT hamstring+ calf str
Sanches,Brian	10	22	Strained RT hamstring
	11	26	Right elbow strain
Sanchez,Anibal	08	123	Labrum surgery - RT Shoulder
	09	104	Sprained RT shoulder x 2
Sanchez,Eduardo	11	92	Right shoulder strain
Sanchez,Jonathan	08	20	Strained LT shoulder
	11	80	LT biceps tendinitis; Spr LT ankle
	12	61	Left bicep tendinitis
Sanit,Amauri	11	110	Inflam - RT elbow
Santana,Ervin	09	60	Spr MCL RT elbow+inflam triceps
Santana,Johan	09	45	Bone spurs-left elbow
	11	182	Left sholder surgery
	12	70	Inflam of lower back+ spr RT ankle
Santos,Sergio	12	166	Surgery torn labrum in RT shoulder
Saunders,Joe	09	18	Tightness - LT shoulder
	12	15	LT shoulder strain
Scherzer,Max	09	9	Sore RT shoulder
Schlereth,Daniel	12	166	Tendinitis in LT shoulder
Scribner,Evan	11	27	Right shoulder strain
Septimo,Leyson	12	18	Inflam in LT biceps
Sheets,Ben	12	25	Right shoulder Inflam
Sherrill,George	08	26	Inflam LT shoulder
	10	15	Back tightness
	11	30	Left elbow Inflam
	12	177	TJS - LT elbow
Simon,Alfredo	09	173	Soreness RT elbow
	10	21	Strained LT hamstring
	11	16	Strained RT hamstring
Slaten,Doug	08	25	Strained RT knee
	11	89	Left elbow ulnar neuritis
Slowey,Kevin	08	25	Strained biceps RT arm
	09	95	Strained RT wrist
	10	15	Strained RT triceps
	11	94	Sore RT biceps; Abdominal strain
Smith,Joe	09	66	Sprained LT knee; sore RT R/C
	11	15	Abdominal strain
Smith,Jordan	12	182	Sore RT elbow
Smyly,Drew	12	37	Strain RT intercostal+ fing. blister
Sonnanstine,Andy	10	16	Strained LT hamstring
Soria,Joakim	09	25	Strained rotator cuff – RT shoulder
	12	182	Recovering from TJS
Soriano,Rafael	08	154	Inflam RT elbow x 2
	11	76	Inflam - RT elbow
Sosa,Henry	09	61	Torn muscle-right shoulder

FIVE-YEAR INJURY LOG

Pitchers	Yr	Days	Injury
Stauffer,Tim	08	184	Torn Labrum/surgery 5/08
	10	52	Appendectomy
	12	182	Right elbow sprain
Stetter,Mitch	11	137	Left hip injury
Storen,Drew	12	106	Elbow injury
Strasburg,Stephen	10	61	Stiff RT shoulder; TJS surgery 9/10
	11	160	Recovery from TJS
Street,Huston	10	79	Strained RT shoulder
	11	17	Right triceps strain
	12	72	Strained LT calf+ LT lat str
Stults,Eric	09	31	Sprained LT thumb
	12	48	Strained LT latissimus dorsi
Stutes,Michael	12	26	Right shoulder Inflam
Surkamp,Eric	12	182	TJS
Swarzak,Anthony	12	33	Strained RT rotator cuff
Talbot,Mitch	10	15	Strained back
	11	125	Strain RT elbow; Strain lower back
Tallet,Brian	08	19	Fractured toe - RT foot
	10	44	Sore LT forearm
	11	56	Strained RT intercostal muscle
Tazawa,Junichi	09	14	Strained LT groin
	10	182	TJS out for 2010
	11	88	Recovery from TJS
Teaford,Everett	12	25	Strained lower abdominal
Tejeda,Robinson	09	30	Tendinitis – RT rotator cuff
	10	30	Tendinitis – RT biceps
	11	36	Inflam - RT shoulder
Texeira,Kanekoa	10	27	Strained RT elbow
Thatcher,Joe	10	18	STrained LT shoulder
	11	125	Left shoulder surgery
	12	37	Mid-back strain
Thompson,Rich	10	20	Inflam – RT shoulder
Thornton,Matt	10	16	Inflam LT forearm
Tobin,Mason	11	162	TJS
Tomko,Brett	08	49	Strained RT elbow
Tomlin,Josh	11	35	Soreness in RT elbow
	12	72	Inflam in RT elbow+rt wrist
Uehara,Koji	09	121	Tndntis RT elbow+strain LT hammy
	10	70	Strained LT hammy; RT elbow
	12	77	Strained RT lat
Valdes,Raul	12	62	Torn meniscus RT knee+Str RT hip
Valverde,Jose	09	47	Strained RT calf
VandenHurk,Rick	09	60	Sore RT elbow
Vargas,Jason	08	184	Left hip surgery 3/08
Venters,Jonny	12	16	Left elbow impingement
Villanueva,Carlos	11	27	Strained RT forearm
Vizcaino,Arodys	12	183	TJS
Vogelsong,Ryan	12	10	Strained lower back
Volquez,Edinson	09	140	Inflam nerve RT elb.; back spasms
	10	104	Recovery from TJS 8/09
Wada,Tsuyoshi	12	182	TJS - RT elbow
Wade,Cory	08	19	Inflam RT shoulder
	09	40	Strained & bursitis - RT shoulder
	10	88	Surg.-frayed labrum, R/C
Wainwright,Adam	08	75	Sprained middle finger - RT hand
	11	182	TJS
Wakefield,Tim	08	18	Soreness - pitching shoulder
	09	48	Lower back strain
Walden,Jordan	12	41	Strained RT bicep
Walters,PJ	12	79	Inflam in RT shoulder

Pitchers	Yr	Days	Injury
Wang,Chien-Ming	08	106	Lisfranc sprn, torn tendon - RT foot
	09	125	Strain RT shoulder; weak hip
	10	182	Recov. fr. surg. - RT shoulder
	11	121	Recovery from RT shoulder surgery
	12	113	Strained LT hamstring+rt hip str
Weaver,Jered	12	22	Strained lower back
Webb,Brandon	09	176	Bursitis - RT shoulder
	10	182	Recovery from 8/09 shoulder surg.
	11	183	Recov. fr. surg. - RT shoulder
Webb,Ryan	11	51	Right shoulder Inflam
Weiland,Kyle	12	162	Right shoulder bursitis
Wells,Randy	11	50	Right forearm strain
Westbrook,Jake	08	162	TJS 06/08
	09	183	Recovery from TJ Surgery
Wheeler,Dan	11	15	Strained LT calf
White,Alex	11	94	Soreness in RT middle finger
Wieland,Joe	12	150	TJS
Williams,Jerome	12	35	Respir. infection+str LT hamstring
Willis,Dontrelle	08	38	Hyperextended RT Knee
	09	152	Anxiety disorder
Wilson,Brian	11	35	Str LT oblique; Inflam LT elbow
	12	174	TJS
Wilson,C.J.	08	53	Bone spurs - LT elbow, surgery
Withrow,Chris	12	32	Right shoulder strain
Wolf,Randy	12	11	TJS 10/2012
Wood,Blake	12	182	TJS - RT elbow
Wood,Kerry	08	22	Blister on pitching hand
	10	52	Strained back; RT index finger
	11	22	Blister on RT index finger
	12	19	Right shoulder fatigue
Worley,Vance	12	54	Loose bodies in RT elbow+ Inflam
Wright,Wesley	09	20	Strained LT shoulder
Wuertz,Michael	10	29	Tendinitis - RT shoulder
	11	53	Strain LT hammy; Tndnts RT thumb
Young,Chris	08	89	Strain RT forearm; nasal fractures
	09	112	Inflam RT shoulder
	10	164	Inflam - RT shoulder
	11	165	Right biceps tendinitis
Zagurski,Mike	08	184	TJS 4/08
	09	183	Recovery from TJ Surgery
Zambrano,Carlos	08	15	Strained RT shoulder
	09	42	Strain LT hamstring; strained back
	11	15	Lower back soreness
Zimmermann,Jordan	09	78	Right elbow soreness
	10	119	Recovery from TJS
Zito,Barry	11	110	Right foot sprain
Zumaya,Joel	08	130	Recov. fr. surg. on RT shoulder
	09	96	Sore RT shoulder x 2
	10	96	Fract. olecranon process-RT elbow
	11	183	Recov. fr. surg. - RT elbow

Top 100 Impact Prospects for 2013

by Rob Gordon and Jeremy Deloney

The following minor league prospects are expected to be the ones who will have the most impact during the 2013 season.

Matt Adams (1B, STL) had a chance to take over the 1B job in St. Louis when Lance Berkman was sidelined with a knee injury, but a slow start and an elbow injury resulted in a lost season. The 24-year-old Adams has big-time power, but needs to prove he can stay healthy and is limited to playing 1B.

Lars Anderson (1B, CLE) was acquired from the Red Sox at the trade deadline, and now has a better shot at playing time. He only hit .250/.353/.396 with 9 HR in Triple-A, but the sweet-swinging lefty exhibits above average bat speed and solid hitting ability to go along with sufficient glove work.

Chris Archer (RHP, TAM) features a low- to mid-90s fastball with plenty of movement and a terrific slider that misses bats. After posting a 3.66 ERA, 9.8 Dom, and .216 oppBA in Triple-A, Archer struck out 36 in 29 innings at TAM. He'll get a shot at the Rays rotation in '13.

Oswaldo Arcia (OF, MIN) elevated his prospect stock by hitting .320/.388/.539 with 17 HR between High-A and Double-A. He combines a mature approach with pure hitting ability and should be able to hit 25+ HR annually. While he doesn't run particularly well, his strong arm is an asset in right field.

Nolan Arenado (3B, COL) struggled to duplicate his 2011 breakout at Double-A Tulsa, but is still just 21 and has plenty of time to develop. He continues to improve defensively and the Rockies don't have many other viable options. A strong spring could land him the starting job.

Cody Asche (3B, PHI) has good offensive upside and the Phillies don't have a lot of good in-house options at 3B. Asche had a nice breakout this year, hitting .324/.369/.481 with 33 doubles and 12 home runs between High-A and Double-A. If the Phillies retool in 2013, Asche could see extended action at the hot corner.

Phillippe Aumont (RHP, PHI) could be on the verge of becoming an effective big league reliever, though he still struggles with control (34 BB/59 K in 44.1 IP at Triple-A). Aumont features a good mid-90s heater and a sharp power curve. When he is on, he can dominate and has the potential to move into the closer role down the road.

Trevor Bauer (RHP, ARI) struggled in his MLB debut, but he still has front of the rotation stuff. Bauer showed solid command and control in college but struggled with inconsistent control and mechanics in ARI. If the control re-emerges this spring he could be poised for a significant breakout in 2013.

Jackie Bradley (OF, BOS) crushed High-A and Double-A to the tune of .315/.430/.482 with 9 HR, 24 SB, and 87 walks. The 22-year-old has keen instincts for the game and while he may never become a pure power hitter, but his plus speed and plate discipline work well in tandem.

Rob Brantly (C, MIA) has a short, compact LH stroke that produces plenty of line drives but not many home runs. He is a work in progress behind the plate, but he is athletic and moves well. Brantly will enter 2013 as the Marlins starter and he could put up solid numbers at a thin position.

Bryce Brentz (OF, BOS) enjoyed a solid campaign at Double-A, batting .296/.355/.478. The 23-year-old right-handed hitter needs to improve his free-swinging ways, but his plus bat speed and power project well. He also has the ideal arm strength to patrol right field, though he doesn't run particularly well.

Gary Brown (OF, SF) has decent plate discipline, good pop, with a strong arm and plus range in CF. Long-term, he profiles as a true top-of-the-order hitter with excellent SB potential.

Dylan Bundy (RHP, BAL) was the most talked about prospect in baseball in '12, and for good reason. After thriving on three levels in the minors and posting a 2.08 ERA, 2.4 Ctl, and 10.3 Dom, the 19-year-old appeared in two games for the Orioles. With a 93-98 mph fastball and plus curveball, Bundy has the goods to front a rotation very quickly.

Edwar Cabrera (RHP, COL) continues to put up good numbers despite the lack of overpowering stuff. He dominated Double-A and Triple-A, but struggled in two outings with the Rockies. Cabrera doesn't have a lot of upside and should be used cautiously, but should see plenty of action in 2013.

Carter Capps (RHP, SEA) quickly reached SEA by posting a 1.26 ERA, 2.1 Ctl, and 12.9 Dom in Double-A. The hard-throwing 22-year-old found success in the majors with his high-90s fastball and improving curveball. He should make an impact in '13 out of the bullpen.

Alex Castellanos (UT, LA) is a scrappy player with a professional approach at the plate. He struggled when the Dodgers brought him to the majors, but he can play 2B, 3B, RF, and LF. Castellanos isn't likely to start, but his position flexibility, speed, and potent bat add up to nice bench potential.

Nick Castellanos (3B/RF, DET) hit .405 in High-A before a Double-A promotion and mid-season position switch to right field. He possesses ideal hitting ability with power to all fields and exceptional hand-eye coordination. Still just 20 years old, he'll need to improve his outfield play before he makes the majors.

Tony Cingrani (LHP, CIN) has a good 92-94 mph fastball, a change, and an average slider from a deceptive motion. Some scouts still see him as a reliever, but it is hard to argue with the results as a starter—13-6 with a 1.73 ERA, 58 BB/252 K over two seasons. Cingrani looked very good in three late-season outings with the Reds, striking out 9 in 5 innings of work.

Gerrit Cole (RHP, PIT) had a very impressive professional debut, going 9-7 with a 2.80 ERA. He throws a plus 94-97 mph fastball, a nasty hard slider, a power curve, and an improving change-up. Cole runs into trouble when he leaves the ball up in the zone, but has the potential to be a true #1 starter.

Alex Colome (RHP, TAM) often gets overlooked, but he has consistently dominated minor league hitters. He pounds the plate with a 90-95 mph sinker, and his hard curveball and slider both can register strikeouts. Command is the key and he needs to polish his mechanics in order to throw consistent strikes.

Christian Colon (SS/2B, KC) doesn't have the overwhelming talent one expects from the fourth overall pick in the draft (2010), but he maximizes his average tools. He is fundamentally sound and has an extreme contact approach. An excellent defender, he'll likely slide over to 2B in the big leagues.

Daniel Corcino (RHP, CIN) draws comparisons to Johnny Cueto because of his 5'11" stature, and sports a plus 92-95 mph fastball, slider, and improved change-up. He struggles with control at times, but can be unhittable and gives CIN another power arm.

Jarred Cosart (RHP, HOU) had a quietly successful season between Double-A and Triple-A as a 22-year-old. Once he polishes his arsenal and finds consistency with his mechanics, he could become a dynamite starter for the Astros. His mid-90s fastball and hard curveball are both plus offerings.

Zack Cox (3B, MIA) should get an extended look in 2013. He has shown the ability to hit for BA, but lacks the power needed at 3B and strikes out too frequently. He does have good hands and a strong arm and might be MIA's best option at the hot corner.

Casey Crosby (LHP, DET) didn't fare well in three starts with in 2012 (9.49 ERA), but with good size, a plus 92-96 mph fastball, and terrific curveball, he possesses ideal traits for a frontline lefty starter. He needs to throw more strikes and continue to show improvement with his change-up.

Charlie Culberson (2B, COL) was traded from the Giants in July, and it seemed to spark him, as he hit .336 for Colorado Springs. Culberson is a solid defender with a good bat, but little power. He will likely be in the mix for action at 2B in 2013.

James Darnell (OF, SD) suffered a shoulder injury in May that caused him to miss the rest of the season. When healthy, Darnell hits for power and average with good plate discipline. Unfortunately he is below average defensively and doesn't run well. In PETCO, that isn't a good combination.

Travis d'Arnaud (C, TOR) tore a knee ligament in June, and missed the rest of the season. He finished at .333/.380/.595 with 16 HR in 279 AB in Triple-A. With his improved defense, he could become one of the better all-around catchers in baseball.

Matt Davidson (3B, ARI) has good raw power and continues to make progress defensively. He now profiles as the ARI 3B of the future. Davidson whiffs too much to hit for average—he hit .261 at Double-A—but he is willing to draw a walk and should reach the majors by the middle of 2013.

Justin De Fratus (RHP, PHI) is one of the better relief prospects in the minors. He attacks hitters with a 92-95 mph sinking fastball and a plus, sweeping slider that is a true out pitch. He missed some time with an elbow injury, but was healthy by the end of the year and should earn a role in the Phillies pen in 2013.

Matt Den Dekker (OF, NYM) started hot in Double-A, but struggled in Triple-A. He's a gap hitter, but has the speed and range to handle CF. Because of his lack of power and streakiness, he profiles better as a 4th OF, but does have above-average speed.

Adam Eaton (OF, ARI) continues to put up impressive numbers—a combined line of .355/.456/.510 in three seasons. At 5'8", he doesn't have much power, but he gets on base and runs. Eaton has the inside track playing time after the Chris Young trade.

Robbie Erlin (LHP, SD) missed most of the season with a sore elbow, and though not overpowering, he locates his low-90s fastball about as well as any player in the minors. In four minor league seasons, Erlin has a 2.64 ERA with 50 BB/368 K in 327 IP.

Jeurys Familia (RHP, NYM) struggled with control for much of 2012, and though he has a plus mid-90s fastball and a decent slider, he lacks a quality change-up. With Zach Wheeler and Matt Harvey competing for rotation spots, Familia could be moved to the pen where his power arsenal might work more effectively.

Nick Franklin (2B/SS, SEA) is expected to battle for a job soon. The 21-year-old batted .322/.394/.502 with 4 HR in Double-A before being elevated to Triple-A in late June. He split time between 2B and SS and could play either in SEA. Switch-hitting, smooth-swinging middle infielders are always in demand.

Avisail Garcia (OF, DET) is blessed with bat speed, all-fields power, and good speed and has exciting potential. Despite an approach that results in few walks and plenty of strikeouts, his hitting tool and terrific defense could lead to a starting job in DET.

Kyle Gibson (RHP, MIN) is recovering from Tommy John surgery (Sept. '11) and can register strikeouts and induce ground-balls with his low-90s sinking fastball and slider. He could play a prominent role in MIN rotation or bullpen early in the season.

Sonny Gray (RHP, OAK) spent most of the season at Double-A where he was 6-9 with a 4.14 ERA, 3.5 Ctl, and 5.9 Dom in 26 starts. He has a pure fastball/curveball combination and though he has a tendency to nibble at the corners, his stuff is too good to ignore. Potentially could be a late-innings reliever in OAK.

Grant Green (UT, OAK) was drafted as a SS, but has also played CF, LF, 3B and 2B the past two seasons. The 25-year-old can still hit—.296/.338/.458 with 15 HR and 13 SB in Triple-A. He exhibits a smooth swing from the right side and makes such easy contact that he should hit for a high BA.

Brandon Guyer (OF, TAM) had a torn labrum in late May and missed the rest of the season. At 27, he will soon need to capitalize on his opportunities. He's a versatile and well-rounded prospect with the ability to hit for a high BA with moderate power and above average speed. He can also play all three outfield positions.

Jedd Gyorko (3B, SD) put together yet another impressive season, hitting .311/.373/.547 with 28 doubles and 30 home runs. He remains one of the best pure hitters in the minors, but below-average defense at 3B is his hurdle. With Chase Headley firmly ensconced at 3B in SD, Gyorko will need to find a new position.

Billy Hamilton (SS/OF, CIN) broke the 30-year-old minor league SB record (155 SB in 132 games). He continues to make strides at the plate, walking 86 times and notching 159 hits for an OB% of .410. Though moving to the OF could stall his development, he has the speed to lead the league in SB someday.

Heath Hembree (RHP, SF) struggled in his first stint in the PCL, but has a good mid-90s fastball and a plus slider. He is being groomed as a future closer and has 56 saves since 2010. He will need to improve his control before he's ready for MLB.

Aaron Hicks (OF, MIN) regained his prospect status by hitting .286/.384/.460 with 13 HR and 32 SB in Double-A as a 22-year-old. While he doesn't make consistent contact yet, he has a patient approach and plus speed. Few outfield prospects can match his strong defense and plus-plus arm.

L.J. Hoes (OF, BAL) was up in September and is a pure hitter in a solid but unspectacular package. His power is below average, but a mature approach and balanced, level swing should lead to a decent BA and good OB numbers. He plays average defense in the corners.

Danny Hultzen (LHP, SEA) dominated Double-A with a 1.19 ERA and 9.4 Dom, but fell apart in Triple-A (5.92 ERA, 8.0 Ctl). He has a potent 88-94 mph fastball, above average slider, and devastating change-up to combat hitters and he should battle for a rotation spot in spring training.

Donnie Joseph (LHP, KC) is a career reliever who could fit nicely at the back end of the KC bullpen. Between Double-A and Triple-A, he posted a 2.33 ERA, 3.9 Ctl, and 11.2 Dom. He has a max-effort delivery that results in inconsistent command, but its deception allows his 90-95 mph fastball looks sneaky quick.

Brett Jackson (OF, CHC) looked overmatched when the Cubs called him up in August (.175 with 59 strikeouts in 120 AB). Long-term, Jackson has the potential to hit 20 home runs and steal 20 bases, but he will need to improve his plate discipline first. The retooling Cubs should give Jackson plenty of playing time in 2013.

Casey Kelly (RHP, SD) went 2-3 with an ugly 6.21 ERA in his MLB debut after elbow inflammation issues. He should be 100% by spring, has good stuff and should get a chance to win a spot in the Padres starting rotation.

Hak-Ju Lee (SS, TAM) doesn't project to hit for much power, but his defense and speed stand out. The 22-year-old has at least 32 SB in each full season as a pro and that could increase as he learns to become more patient at the plate. He's a fairly good hitter and he could hit loads of doubles and triples.

Charlie Leesman (LHP, CHW) has flown under the radar even after a successful season at Triple-A. The 25-year-old went 12-10 with a 2.47 ERA, 3.5 Ctl, and 6.9 Dom in 26 starts. He doesn't throw particularly hard—86-90 mph—but his plus change-up sets him apart. He has an excellent feel for pitching.

Jhan Marinez (RHP, CHW) was among the most dominant relievers in the minors in '12, posting a 2.86 ERA and 9.3 Dom at Triple-A. He throws with quick, loose arm action from a low ¾ slot to generate a crisp 92-97 mph fastball. He complements it with a hard slider that, though inconsistent, registers strikeouts.

Nick Maronde (LHP, LAA) reached the majors quickly as a RP after being selected in the third round of 2011. LAA is likely to move him back to the rotation, where his 89-95 mph fastball and improved slider are bigger assets. His command is his best attribute and he rarely walks batters.

Chris Marrero (1B, WAS) was limited to 180 AB after hamstring issues in winter ball, hitting .272/.351/.391 with 11 doubles and 3 home runs. He has shown solid power and he is still just 24 years old.

Leonys Martin (OF, TEX) saw action with TEX in 2011, but began the '12 season in Triple-A where he ended up hitting .359/.422/.610 with 12 HR and 10 SB in 231 AB. Not only can he hit, but he is a solid defender with good range and a strong arm.

Carlos Martinez (RHP, STL) put together a solid season with excellent stuff—a plus mid-90s fastball, slider, and change-up. But he missed time with shoulder tendinitis, and his funky delivery

leads many to believe he'll ultimately end up in the bullpen. STL has shown, though, that they can get the most out of their prospects.

Trevor May (RHP, PHI) has an ideal power pitching frame (6'5" 214), but too many free passes plagued him in 2012. He struck out 151 batters in 149.1 IP, but he also walked 78. He throws a 90-95 mph sinking fastball and mixes in a decent change-up and a slider, but needs to sharpen his control before his MLB debut.

Kyle McPherson (RHP, PIT) throws strikes and maintained solid control in the majors, going 0-2 with a 2.73 ERA, 7 BB/21 K in 26.3 IP. With a low-90s fastball, a good change-up, and an improved curve, the 24-year-old should be able to secure a spot in PIT's starting rotation.

Shelby Miller (RHP, STL) got off to a slow start, but with a mechanical adjustment, he zipped through the 2nd half (7-2, 2.88 ERA). He walked 43 in 77.1 IP in the first half, but gave up just 7 BB after the break, striking out 70. He attacks hitters with a mid-90s fastball, a power curve, and a decent change.

Mark Montgomery (RHP, NYY) continues to exceed expectations with dominant relief work. Between High-A and Double-A, the 22-year-old went 7-2 with a 1.54 ERA, 3.1 Ctl, and 13.8 Dom. He possesses an outstanding slider that punishes hitters, and he offers good velocity (89-95 mph fastball) despite his 5'11" frame.

Mike Montgomery (LHP, KC) had a disastrous time in Triple-A, then was demoted to Double-A where things got worse (6.07 ERA and 6.7 Dom combined). However, he still has a solid arsenal, highlighted by his quick 90-95 mph fastball and nasty curveball. Command and inefficiency have been the issues.

Hunter Morris (1B, MIL) put up huge offensive numbers in 2012, hitting .303/.357/.563 with 40 doubles and 28 home runs. Unlike most power hitting 1B, Morris is a slick defender and if the Brewers decide to move Corey Hart back to RF, Morris could get a chance to earn regular playing time.

Wil Myers (OF, KC) was phenomenal between Double-A and Triple-A. He batted .314/.387/.600 with 37 HR with improved outfield defense. It would be hard to envision KC not making room in the everyday lineup for him and he's likely to enter the '13 season on the top line of most prospect lists.

Jake Odorizzi (RHP, KC) posted a 3.03 ERA, 3.1 Ctl, and 8.4 Dom in Double-A and Triple-A. He uses a 89-95 mph fastball to get ahead in the count, three solid secondary pitches, and an exceptional feel for pitching. With a deceiving four-pitch mix and plus command, he is good enough to succeed without a high Dom.

Andrew Oliver (LHP, DET) suffered through a dismal season in Triple-A (5-9, 4.88 ERA, 6.7 Ctl). He was marginally better after a late-season move to the bullpen, but lefties with plus velocity and above average breaking balls are in high demand.

Mike Olt (3B, TEX) hit .288/.398/.579 with 28 HR in only 354 minor-league AB. His powerful right-handed stroke emerged and he shortened his swing when he was behind in the count. He could stand to make more contact, but his power is undeniable. He's also evolving into a plus defender with clean feet and a strong arm.

Rudy Owens (LHP, HOU) finished the season with a 3.48 ERA, 2.2 Ctl, and 6.0 Dom in Triple-A. He won't miss many bats with his 87-92 mph fastball and average curveball, but he exhibits uncanny command. The margin for error is slim, but he knows how to sequence pitches and retire hitters.

Chris Owings (SS, ARI) finally had a breakout season many expected when he was selected 41st overall in '09. He has a quick bat, above-average power, and plays solid defense. If he can be more selective, he has some nice long-term potential.

James Paxton (LHP, SEA) certainly could polish his command and control (4.6 bb/9), but he improved despite missing time with an injury. He runs his fastball to the mid-to-high 90s and he complements it with a plus curveball, and could either start or relieve in '13 because of his power repertoire.

Brad Peacock (RHP, OAK) found it difficult to live up to his breakout season in '11 as he was lit up with a 6.01 ERA and 4.4 Ctl. Some of the carnage was a result of the hitter-friendly environments of the Triple-A PCL. Regardless, he throws hard and has a legitimate swing-and-miss curveball (9.3 Dom).

Wily Peralta (RHP, MIL) made a mid-season adjustment that led to a late-season MLB promotion after a rough start. Once in the majors, Peralta looked like a different player (2-1, 2.86 ERA, 23 K in 29 IP). He needs to reduce his walk rate to have sustained success, but his future is more promising than it was a year ago.

Eury Perez (OF, WAS) puts the bat on the ball and might be the fastest player in the organization. He has almost no power (career high 4 HR in 2008), but possesses good hand-eye coordination, and good range with a strong arm in CF. He projects as a 4th or 5th OF, but has enough speed (51 SB) to give him value.

Martin Perez (LHP, TEX) has long tantalized with his above average repertoire and durability, but hasn't put together a good season since '09. In 2012, the 21-year-old reached the majors and started six games for TEX. His pure stuff is still quite good and his youth works to his advantage. He posted a 4.25 ERA, 4.0 Ctl, and 4.9 Dom in Triple-A.

A.J. Pollock (OF, ARI) is a solid 4th OF type who can do a bit of everything. Pollock doesn't have enough power to be an everyday player, but did hit .318 at Triple-A and has the speed and on-base ability to make him a potential asset.

Jurickson Profar (SS, TEX) was just 19 when he made his major league debut in September. There are no glaring weaknesses in his overall game and he's a standout with the glove. Add in a mature approach to the game and well above average instincts and you have a future perennial All-Star.

Anthony Rendon (3B, WAS) broke his ankle and was limited to just 133 AB in 2012. When healthy, Rendon is one of the best pure hitters in the minors and saw much needed playing time in the Arizona Fall League. Rendon is blocked at 3B, but could move to 2B or the OF in order to get his bat in the Nationals lineup.

Mark Rogers (RHP, MIL) managed to log a career high 134.1 IP while going 3-1 with a 3.92 ERA for the Brewers before being shut down in September. Rogers has a mid-90s fastball that tops out at 97 mph and a plus 12-6 curveball. If the 25-year-old righty can stay healthy and throw strikes, he has the stuff to succeed.

Bruce Rondon (RHP, DET) was exceptional on three levels in '12, going 2-1 with a 1.53 ERA, 4.4 Ctl, and 11.2 Dom. He improved his ability to throw consistent strikes and he's learned

to harness his arm strength. He can now focus on his secondary pitches, including a very hard slider.

Trevor Rosenthal (RHP, STL) doesn't get as much attention as he should. The 6'2" right-hander has a plus mid-90s fastball, a good curve, and a decent change-up. He attacks the strike zone and has good movement on all of his offerings. Rosenthal will be a part of the Cardinals staff in some capacity in 2013.

Darin Ruf (1B/OF, PHI) put on amazing offensive display in August—.367, 19 HRs and 31 RBI in 29 games. The 26-year-old does have good power, but is well below average in the OF and will have to mash regularly to earn consistent playing time. Given AB, he'd had plenty of fantasy value, but the jury is still out.

Carlos Sanchez (SS/2B, CHW) enjoyed a surprise breakout in 2012. He only hit 1 HR, but he batted .323/.378/.403 with 26 SB. He makes easy contact with a compact stroke while offering above average quickness and speed. He split time between 2B and SS and could easily play either position in the big leagues.

Tony Sanchez (C, PIT) is a former 1st-round pick who spent most of the season at Triple-A. Sanchez is okay behind the plate and makes consistent contact, but lacks power. He's hit for average in the past, so there is still some hope he will develop into an above-average offensive catcher.

Logan Schafer (OF, MIL) profiles as a solid 4th OF type who made his major league debut in 2012, hitting .304/.320/.522 in 23 AB. Schafer can do a bit of everything on the field and has the tools to play all three OF positions, but lacks the power needed to be an everyday regular.

Tyler Skaggs (LHP, ARI) has a plus 12-6 curveball and a good low-90s fastball. He keeps hitters off-balance with deception and movement. He is probably a lock for an ARI rotation spot and could be under-valued because of his 5.83 ERA. He doesn't have the same upside as Trevor Bauer but he is also likely to be less volatile.

Jonathan Singleton (1B, HOU) is one of the better offensive prospects in baseball with well above average power and a professional approach that results in a very high OBP. He'll continue to rack up strikeouts until he improves against breaking balls, but the power is legitimate.

George Springer (OF, HOU) was a first round pick in '11 and hit .302/.383/.526 with 24 HR and 32 SB in his first full season as a pro. While some of his success can likely be attributed to his home environment in the High-A California League, his bat will play anywhere due to his vicious bat speed. Not only can he hit for power, he has the athleticism and defensive abilities to play CF.

Dan Straily (RHP, OAK) was arguably the biggest surprise of any pitching prospect in baseball in '12, rising to make seven starts with OAK and registering a 3.89 ERA. His natural stuff isn't overly exciting, but he gets hitters out by sequencing his pitches and locating them impeccably in constructive parts of the strike zone.

Oscar Taveras (OF, STL) has developed into one of the better offensive prospects in baseball. He has an aggressive approach at the plate, but makes consistent contact and can drive the ball out to all parts. Taveras is only an average defender, but he's now won three consecutive league MVP awards and could force his way into the Cardinals lineup by mid-season.

Julio Teheran (RHP, ATL) struggled with control and consistency in 2012. He flashed signs of dominance, but too often found the middle of the plate and had a .289 oppBA. Teheran is still only 20 and will likely get plenty of chances in 2013, but for now he remains a high-risk/high-reward hurler.

Tyler Thornburg (RHP, MIL) had a solid season of growth in 2012 and should be able to secure a spot in the Brewers starting rotation this spring. He isn't physically imposing, but features a nice low-90s fastball with some good deception, a curve, and a decent change-up. He should settle in as a solid mid-rotation starter.

Scott Van Slyke (1B, LA) has proven he can dominate PCL pitching (.982 OPS), but struggled in limited MLB action (.167/.196/.315 in 54 AB). He has solid power, is below average defensively, but can play 1B, RF, and LF and could earn a bench role in 2013.

Josh Vitters (3B, CHC) had a disastrous MLB debut, hitting .121 with 77 strikeouts in 126 AB. He's still young enough that he should get another chance to grab the starting 3B job. Vitters has good hand-eye coordination but needs to be more selective at the plate. He has good power, but might struggle to hit for average.

Taijuan Walker (RHP, SEA), pitching most of the year as a 19-year-old in Double-A, had a 4.69 ERA, 3.6 Ctl, and 8.4 Dom. His electric 92-98 mph fastball is among the minors' best and he also brings a terrific curveball and change-up to the table. His ceiling is as high as any pitching prospect in baseball.

Adam Warren (RHP, NYY) was roughed up in a spot start with the Yankees (6 ER in 2.1 innings), but he continues to impress with his command and pitchability. He may be short on strikeouts, but he gets the job done with his deep arsenal and ability to deceive hitters with his quick fastball and average secondary pitches.

Ryan Wheeler (3B, ARI) put up impressive numbers in the hitter-friendly PCL—.351/.388/.572—but struggled in extended action in the majors. Wheeler is below average defensively, but should have enough offense to get a second chance in 2013.

Tim Wheeler (OF, COL) suffered a hand injury in April and never really looked 100% in 2012. Wheeler hit just 2 home runs in 379 AB in the hitter-friendly PCL. He has decent speed and the arm to handle RF in the majors, but has little long-term value if his power doesn't return quickly. Wheeler could win a 4th OF spot this spring, which should give him some value.

Zack Wheeler (RHP, NYM) is one of the best pitching prospects in the NL. In 2012, he cut his walk rate and finished the year at 12-8 with a 3.26 ERA, 59 BB/148 K in 149 IP. Wheeler will likely start the season in the minors, but he gives the Mets the power arm they need to solidify their starting rotation.

Joe Wieland (RHP, SD) secured a spot in the Padres starting rotation last spring, but suffered an elbow injury and had Tommy John surgery in July. Prior to the injury, Wieland was 0-4 with a 4.55 ERA and 9 BB/24 K in 27.2 IP. Wieland won't be ready to start the season, but should be set to go by the All-Star break and would be a good end-game pick.

Kolten Wong (2B, STL) has quickly developed into one of the best 2B prospects in baseball. The Cardinals skipped Wong over High-A in 2012 and he responded with a solid season for Double-A Springfield, hitting .287/.348/.405 with 23 doubles, 9 home runs, and 21 SB. Wong uses a short, compact left-handed stroke and gets surprising power from his 5'9" frame. Wong has decent speed, good range, and soft hands and should be ready for the majors by the 2nd half of 2013.

Mike Zunino (C, SEA) found a way to exceed expectations even after being selected with the third overall pick in the '12 draft. He hit .360/.447/.689 with 13 HR between short-season ball and Double-A. The 21-year-old impressed all with his solid all-around package of tools, particularly his power and his ability to make consistent, hard contact. He'll contend for the starting catching job in spring training.

• • •

The chart on the following page ranks the Top 100 Impact Prospects for 2013, along with BaseballHQ.com's rating system grade and projected Mayberry Scores. The rating system grade consists of two parts:

Player Potential Rating (1-10) representing a player's upside potential

   10 - Hall of Fame-type player
   9 - Elite player
   8 - Solid regular
   7 - Average regular
   6 - Platoon player
   5 - Major League reserve player
   4 - Top minor league player
   3 - Average minor league player
   2 - Minor league reserve player
   1 - Minor league roster filler

Probability Rating (A-E) representing the player's realistic chances of achieving their potential

   A - 90% probability of reaching potential
   B - 70% probability of reaching potential
   C - 50% probability of reaching potential
   D - 30% probability of reaching potential
   E - 10% probability of reaching potential

This grading system is used thoughout BaseballHQ.com in our daily minor-league coverage and offseason organizational reports.

Top 100 Impact Prospects for 2013

RANK/BATTER/POS, TM	RATING	POWER	SPEED	BATAVG	PT '13	RANK/BATTER/POS, TM	RATING	POWER	SPEED	BATAVG	PT '13
RANK/PITCHER/POS, TM	RATING	ERA	DOM	SAVES	PT '13	RANK/PITCHER/POS, TM	RATING	ERA	DOM	SAVES	PT '13
1. Wil Myers (OF, KC)	9B	5	2	4	3	51. Grant Green (INF/OF, OAK)	8B	2	3	3	3
2. Tyler Skaggs (LHP, ARI)	9C	3	3	2	3	52. Christian Colon (INF, KC)	7B	2	3	3	1
3. Dan Straily (RHP, OAK)	8C	3	2	0	3	53. James Darnell (OF, SD)	8D	2	1	3	2
4. Jake Odorizzi (RHP, KC)	8B	3	2	0	3	54. Phillippe Aumont (RHP, PHI)	8C	2	3	3	2
5. Shelby Miller (RHP, STL)	9C	3	4	2	3	55. Josh Vitters (3B, CHC)	8E	2	1	2	3
6. Trevor Bauer (RHP, ARI)	9C	4	4	1	3	56. Ryan Wheeler (3B, ARI)	8D	2	1	3	2
7. Jurickson Profar (SS, TEX)	9B	2	4	3	3	57. Nick Maronde (LHP, LAA)	8C	3	3	2	3
8. Zack Wheeler (RHP, NYM)	9C	3	4	1	3	58. Tim Wheeler (OF, COL)	8D	3	2	2	2
9. Travis d'Arnaud (C, TOR)	8A	4	1	3	3	59. Zack Cox (3B, MIA)	8D	1	1	3	2
10. Dylan Bundy (RHP, BAL)	10C	3	4	1	3	60. Bruce Rondon (RHP, DET)	8B	2	4	3	2
11. Gerrit Cole (RHP, PIT)	9C	3	4	1	3	61. Edwar Cabrera (RHP, COL)	8D	2	3	1	2
12. Julio Teheran (RHP, ATL)	9D	2	3	2	3	62. Chris Owings (SS, ARI)	8D	2	2	2	2
13. Casey Kelly (RHP, SD)	9D	3	3	1	3	63. Tony Sanchez (C, PIT)	7C	1	2	3	2
14. Brett Jackson (OF, CHC)	8C	3	4	2	4	64. A.J. Pollock (OF, ARI)	7B	2	2	2	1
15. Wily Peralta (RHP, MIL)	9C	3	3	1	3	65. Charlie Culberson (2B, COL)	7C	1	2	2	1
16. Tyler Thornburg (RHP, MIL)	8B	3	3	1	2	66. Hak-Ju Lee (SS, TAM)	8B	0	4	3	1
17. Avisail Garcia (OF, DET)	9E	3	3	2	3	67. Matt Davidson (3B, ARI)	8D	4	1	2	2
18. Danny Hultzen (LHP, SEA)	9C	3	3	0	3	68. Darin Ruf (1B/OF, PHI)	8D	3	2	3	1
19. Kyle Gibson (RHP, MIN)	8D	2	2	1	3	69. Daniel Corcino (RHP, CIN)	9D	3	3	1	1
20. Jeurys Familia (RHP, NYM)	9D	3	3	3	2	70. George Springer (OF, HOU)	9C	3	3	3	1
21. Jonathan Singleton (1B, HOU)	9C	4	1	3	1	71. Mike Zunino (C, SEA)	9C	4	1	3	3
22. Billy Hamilton (SS/OF, CIN)	9D	1	5	3	2	72. Gary Brown (OF, SF)	9C	2	4	3	1
23. Rob Brantly (C, MIA)	7B	2	1	3	3	73. Sonny Gray (RHP, OAK)	8C	3	2	0	1
24. Nolan Arenado (3B, COL)	9D	3	1	3	3	74. Lars Anderson (1B, CLE)	7C	2	1	3	1
25. Martin Perez (LHP, TEX)	9D	2	2	0	3	75. Trevor May (RHP, PHI)	9D	2	4	2	1
26. Jedd Gyorko (3B, SD)	8B	3	1	3	2	76. Oswaldo Arcia (OF, MIN)	9D	3	1	3	1
27. Mike Olt (3B, TEX)	9C	4	1	3	3	77. Brad Peacock (RHP, OAK)	8D	2	3	0	1
28. Carlos Martinez (RHP, STL)	9D	3	3	2	2	78. Andy Oliver (LHP, DET)	8D	1	3	1	1
29. Tony Cingrani (LHP, CIN)	9D	3	4	1	2	79. Matt den Dekker (OF, NYM)	8D	1	2	3	2
30. Robbie Erlin (LHP, SD)	8B	4	2	1	2	80. Casey Crosby (LHP, DET)	9D	2	3	0	1
31. Matt Adams (1B, STL)	8D	3	1	3	2	81. Eury Perez (OF, WAS)	7A	1	4	3	2
32. Trevor Rosenthal (RHP, STL)	9D	2	4	2	3	82. Hunter Morris (1B, MIL)	7B	3	1	2	1
33. Chris Archer (RHP, TAM)	9E	2	3	0	1	83. Chris Marrero (1B, WAS)	8D	3	1	3	2
34. Leonys Martin (OF, TEX)	8C	2	4	3	1	84. Logan Schafer (OF, MIL)	7B	1	2	3	1
35. Nick Franklin (2B/SS, SEA)	8B	2	4	4	3	85. Alex Castellanos (OF, LA)	7B	1	2	3	er
36. Oscar Taveras (OF, STL)	9C	4	1	4	1	86. Justin De Fratus (RHP, PHI)	7B	2	3	2	2
37. Anthony Rendon (3B, WAS)	9D	3	1	3	2	87. Mike Montgomery (LHP, KC)	8D	2	2	0	1
38. Kyle McPherson (RHP, PIT)	8C	2	2	1	3	88. Scott Van Slyke (1B, LA)	7C	3	1	2	2
39. Mark Rogers (RHP, MIL)	8D	2	3	0	2	89. Heath Hembree (RHP, SF)	8C	2	4	3	2
40. Adam Eaton (OF, ARI)	8C	1	4	3	2	90. L.J. Hoes (OF, BAL)	7B	1	3	3	1
41. James Paxton (LHP, SEA)	9D	2	4	1	3	91. Adam Warren (RHP, NYY)	7B	2	2	1	1
42. Joe Wieland (RHP, SD)	8C	3	2	1	3	92. Mark Montgomery (RHP, NYY)	7A	3	3	1	1
43. Taijuan Walker (RHP, SEA)	9B	2	4	0	1	93. Alex Colome (RHP, TAM)	8C	2	3	0	1
44. Rudy Owens (LHP, HOU)	7C	3	1	0	1	94. Brandon Guyer (OF, TAM)	8C	3	3	3	1
45. Nick Castellanos (3B/OF, DET)	9C	2	2	4	1	95. Charlie Leesman (LHP, CHW)	7C	3	1	0	1
46. Jackie Bradley (OF, BOS)	8B	1	4	4	1	96. Carlos Sanchez (INF, CHW)	8C	0	3	4	3
47. Kolten Wong (2B, STL)	8C	1	2	4	2	97. Jhan Marinez (RHP, CHW)	9D	3	3	1	1
48. Bryce Brentz (OF, BOS)	8C	4	1	2	1	98. Donnie Joseph (LHP, KC)	7C	2	3	1	1
49. Jarred Cosart (RHP, HOU)	9D	2	3	2	1	99. Carter Capps (RHP, SEA)	8C	3	4	2	1
50. Aaron Hicks (OF, MIN)	8B	2	4	2	1	100. Cody Asche (3B, PHI)	8D	2	2	3	1

Top Japanese Players for 2013 and Beyond

by Tom Muhall

2012 was a banner year for Japanese imports. Yu Darvish was almost everything promised, with room for growth. Chen Wei-yin was a capable SP in a hitter's park and Hisashi Iwakuma had a strong second half. Those who had Norichika Aoki on their farm team or risked a few bucks or a low-round selection were rewarded with a $25 player. This year you may have to dig a little deeper for those hidden gems.

Kyuji Fujikawa (RHP, Hanshin Tigers) is at the end of his restrictive free-agency period and rumors are strong that he intends to fulfill his longtime dream to play in MLB. Considered by many to be the best closer in Japan, he pitches in a relatively large stadium which should help his transition. If he starts off in middle relief, he could be a cheap source of saves.
Probable ETA: 2013

Yusei Kikuchi (LHP, Seibu Lions) drew interest from several MLB teams when it looked like he might pass up the Japanese draft to sign in 2009. Instead, he stayed home, but has had trouble fulfilling his promise until 2012. He's still years away from international free agency, and his team is unlikely to let go of what they see as an emerging star.
Possible ETA: 2014

Chang-Yong Lim (RHP, Yakult Swallows) was long considered among the best closers in Japan and was nearing free agency when he underwent his second Tommy John surgery in July. He'll be 38 years old in 2014. The side-winding Korean is known as "Mr. Zero" due to his stingy ERA, but unless "cool nicknames" is a category in your league, scratch him off your list.
Probable ETA: Never

Hiroyuki Nakajima (SS, Seibu Lions) was posted before the 2012 season but could not come to terms with the Yankees, his only option. This year he's an unrestricted international free agent, although the struggles of Tsuyoshi Nishioka and other Japanese infielders may limit interest. Nakajima is that rare Japanese MIF who has a little power to complement his speed and solid BA. Good defensively, he may have to move to 2B but he could also be an outstanding utility player. The perennial All Star may have 15/15 potential in the right park. This year's Aoki? A-OK!
Probable ETA: Almost certainly 2013

Shohei Otani (RHP, Hanamaki Higashi High School) is still a high school student and is the longest of long shots. However, if your league has an extended farm system, he could be an interesting final selection. Allegedly, he has hit 100 mph, and though normally we regard a report like that as noise, Dodgers' Assistant GM Logan White compared him to Clayton Kershaw and called Otani one of the best prospects in the world. If the Dodgers are that interested, maybe we should be, too.
Possible ETA in MLB minors: 2013

Toshiya Sugiuchi (LHP, Yomiuri Giants) has exceptional command of his pitches and has more international experience than almost any player. He now has two sub-2.00 ERA seasons in a row (though see the caveat below about pitching stats). Despite the skewed statistics, the former MVP and Sawamura Award

winner could be a capable MLB pitcher. Worthy of a reserve spot if he does not sign in 2013.
Possible ETA: 2013 or 2014

Kensuke Tanaka (2B, Hokkaido Nippon Ham Fighters) is yet another good defender with a high BA and some speed. Tanaka has no power but can hit to all fields and utilize his speed to get on base. However, an elbow injury caused him to miss the last two months of the 2012 season. At best, he probably projects as a bench player or even pinch-runner.
Possible ETA: 2013

Takashi Toritani (SS, Hanshin Tigers) has reached international free agency and is rumored to be interested in MLB. Unfortunately, after three strong years with a high BA and double digit SB, he struggled offensively in 2012. Toritani throws right and bats left, and can beat a pitcher to both sides of the field. He is a solid defender but will almost certainly have to move to 2B or accept a utility role. Toritani is not as good as Nakajima, so he would be a gamble for any MLB team signing him.
Probable ETA: 2013 or 2014

Hideaki Wakui (SP, Seibu Lions) previously indicated a desire to play in MLB. But at age 27, the former Sawamura Award winner would have to be posted—though it's possible since the team is still stinging from his rare request for (and even rarer win in) arbitration. After an 0-3 start on the heels of an embarrassing magazine article about his private life, he was demoted to the bullpen where he regained his velocity and thrived. His transition to MLB could be tough since he possesses only an average fastball, although it is complemented by an array of solid off-pitches and dependable control.
Possible ETA: 2014

Caveat about pitching stats: Japan instituted a new ball in 2011 which has lower-elasticity rubber surrounding the cork. The new design has limited offense and almost certainly inflated pitching stats. Exercise some caution when analyzing pitching stats and look for possible signs of optimism in subpar hitting stats.

Ryu Hyun-jin (LHP, Hanwha Eagles, Korean League) was posted this fall and the Dodgers were confirmed as the top bidder. Ryu is 25 years old with a low-90s fastball and an array of off-speed pitches, including a change-up and slider. At 6-2, 215, he has good size, though as with many Asian pitchers, workload is a concern. He has extensive international experience (2008 Olympics, 2009 World Baseball Classic) and has dominated the Korean League throughout his seven-year career. Baseball in Korea, though, is a notch lower than Japanese baseball, so expect an adjustment period. Assuming LA signs him, his future is an average back-of-the-rotation MLB starter rather than a star. An inital assignment to the minors would not be surprising.
Possible ETA: 2013
—*T.M.*

MAJOR LEAGUE EQUIVALENTS

In his 1985 *Baseball Abstract*, Bill James introduced the concept of major league equivalencies. His assertion was that, with the proper adjustments, a minor leaguer's statistics could be converted to an equivalent major league level performance with a great deal of accuracy.

Because of wide variations in the level of play among different minor leagues, it is difficult to get a true reading on a player's potential. For instance, a .300 batting average achieved in the high-offense Pacific Coast League is not nearly as much of an accomplishment as a similar level in the Eastern League. MLEs normalize these types of variances, for all statistical categories.

The actual MLEs are not projections. They represent how a player's previous performance might look at the major league level. However, the MLE stat line can be used in forecasting future performance in just the same way as a major league stat line would.

The model we use contains a few variations to James' version and updates all of the minor league and ballpark factors. In addition, we designed a module to convert pitching statistics, which is something James did not originally do.

Players are listed if they spent at least part of 2011 or 2012 in Triple-A or Double-A and had at least 100 AB or 30 IP within those two levels (players who split a season at both levels are indicated as a/a). Major league and Single-A (and lower) stats are excluded. Each player is listed in the organization with which they finished the season.

These charts also provide the unique perspective of looking at two years' worth of data. These are only short-term trends, for sure. But even here we can find small indications of players improving their skills, or struggling, as they rise through more difficult levels of competition. Since players—especially those with any modicum of talent—are promoted rapidly through major league systems, a two-year scan is often all we get to spot any trends. Five-year trends do appear in the *Minor League Baseball Analyst*.

Used correctly, MLEs are excellent indicators of potential. But, just like we cannot take traditional major league statistics at face value, the same goes for MLEs. The underlying measures of base skill—contact rates, pitching command ratios, BPV, etc.—are far more accurate in evaluating future talent than raw home runs, batting averages or ERAs. This year's chart format focuses more on those underlying gauges.

Here are some things to look for as you scan these charts:

Target players who...
- had a full season's worth of playing time in AA and then another full year in AAA
- had consistent playing time from one year to the next
- improved their base skills as they were promoted

Raise the warning flag for players who...
- were stuck at the same level both years, or regressed
- displayed marked changes in playing time from one year to the next
- showed large drops in BPIs from one year to the next

BATTER	yr	b	age	pos	lvl	org	ab	hr	sb	ba	bb%	ct%	px	sx	bpv
Abraham,Adam	12	R	25	1B	aa	CLE	379	11	2	231	9%	76%	115	59	34
Abreu,Miguel	11	R	27	OF	a/a	BAL	34	0	3	97	8%	76%	0	103	-47
	12	R	28	SS	aa	PHI	378	3	4	220	1%	89%	41	60	13
Abreu,Tony	11	B	27	2B	aaa	ARI	483	5	6	214	3%	78%	66	84	-1
Acosta,Mayobanex	12	R	25	C	a/a	TAM	112	4	0	207	9%	77%	108	25	21
Adair,Travis	11	L	24	OF	aa	TEX	126	2	1	209	4%	84%	53	86	14
	12	L	25	2B	aa	BAL	122	1	1	138	6%	81%	23	49	-31
Adams,David	12	R	25	2B	aa	NYY	327	7	2	263	8%	81%	86	42	26
Adams,Matt	11	L	23	1B	aa	STL	463	18	0	234	5%	78%	109	37	21
	12	L	24	1B	aaa	STL	258	12	2	272	4%	74%	149	48	42
Adams,Ryan	11	R	24	2B	aaa	BAL	377	8	4	250	6%	70%	121	75	12
	12	R	25	2B	aaa	BAL	232	4	2	201	9%	71%	99	45	-2
Adduci,James	11	L	26	OF	aa	CHC	237	3	14	251	7%	83%	65	118	37
	12	L	27	OF	a/a	CHC	399	5	13	242	8%	73%	69	94	-5
Adrianza,Ehire	12	B	23	SS	aa	SF	451	2	14	203	7%	78%	61	116	12
Adrianza,Ehire Enrique	12	B	23	SS	aa	SF	451	2	14	203	7%	78%	61	116	12
Aliotti,Anthony	12	L	25	1B	aa	OAK	455	7	0	238	10%	66%	88	37	-33
Allen,Brandon	11	L	25	1B	aaa	OAK	344	13	5	236	12%	64%	154	100	35
	12	L	26	OF	aaa	TAM	122	3	0	214	2%	68%	116	61	-9
Almonte,Abraham	12	B	23	OF	aa	NYY	319	4	24	246	9%	80%	68	129	31
Almonte,Denny	12	B	24	OF	aa	SEA	434	10	22	218	10%	63%	101	112	-12
Almonte,Zoilo	11	B	22	OF	aa	NYY	175	3	3	227	6%	72%	92	81	2
	12	B	23	OF	aa	NYY	419	19	12	250	5%	73%	129	88	33
Amarista,Alexi	11	L	22	2B	aaa	LAA	363	3	10	238	4%	83%	68	96	23
	12	L	23	2B	aaa	SD	126	1	3	220	2%	88%	52	109	35
Anderson,Bryan	11	L	25	C	aaa	STL	335	5	1	222	7%	73%	74	28	-23
	12	L	26	C	aaa	STL	347	4	0	176	7%	70%	50	30	-56
Anderson,Lars	11	L	24	1B	aaa	BOS	491	11	4	244	12%	73%	111	68	27
	12	L	25	1B	aaa	CLE	396	6	1	207	11%	69%	95	49	-12
Anderson,Leslie	11	L	29	1B	aaa	TAM	462	9	1	211	3%	83%	67	29	3
	12	L	30	OF	aaa	TAM	444	10	0	234	4%	83%	64	27	2
Angle,Matt	11	L	26	OF	aaa	BAL	424	3	20	229	8%	76%	44	120	-8
	12	L	27	OF	aaa	LA	393	3	8	219	6%	74%	51	86	-26
Anna,Dean	11	L	25	2B	aa	SD	198	1	2	192	13%	88%	73	88	65
	12	L	26	2B	aa	SD	425	7	4	210	11%	77%	58	76	2
Antonelli,Matthew	11	R	26	3B	a/a	WAS	315	6	5	251	10%	78%	93	73	30
	12	R	27	2B	aaa	NYY	154	2	1	165	11%	75%	47	62	-19
Apodaca,Juan	11	R	25	C	aa	CLE	86	0	1	159	8%	67%	36	47	-71
	12	R	26	C	a/a	CHC	213	1	1	240	12%	78%	72	23	1
Arbelo,Yazy	12	L	24	1B	aa	ARI	183	5	0	183	8%	59%	104	15	-56
Arcia,Oswaldo Celestino	12	L	21	OF	aa	MIN	262	7	2	302	8%	75%	133	109	56
Arenado,Nolan	12	R	21	3B	aa	COL	516	12	0	287	6%	89%	94	26	53
Arnal,Cristo	11	R	26	2B	aa	CLE	225	0	4	156	5%	83%	18	63	-23
Asche,Cody	12	L	22	3B	aa	PHI	263	8	1	269	6%	76%	125	70	41
Ashley,Nevin	11	R	27	C	a/a	TAM	380	6	1	204	7%	69%	69	51	-38
	12	R	28	C	aaa	TAM	110	4	1	192	9%	71%	107	75	13
Aubrey,Michael	11	L	29	DH	aaa	WAS	228	8	0	212	9%	84%	92	22	35
Avery,Xavier	11	L	21	OF	aa	BAL	557	4	32	246	7%	71%	73	109	-10
	12	L	22	OF	aaa	BAL	390	8	20	226	10%	72%	78	124	9
Baez,Alberys	11	R	23	3B	aa	LA	105	1	1	173	6%	70%	130	57	15
	12	R	24	3B	aa	LA	273	3	4	184	8%	73%	69	99	-2
Bailey,Adam	11	L	23	OF	aa	HOU	93	2	0	274	2%	76%	107	30	4
	12	L	24	OF	a/a	HOU	139	1	1	198	4%	77%	89	44	3
Bailey,Dwayne	11	R	25	2B	a/a	LAA	129	0	1	211	8%	65%	55	69	-56
Bailli,Kenen	12	L	27	OF	a/a	TOR	160	1	3	251	3%	77%	63	87	-6
Baisley,Jeffrey	11	R	29	3B	aaa	LAA	538	11	3	213	4%	79%	77	62	7
	12	R	30	3B	aaa	CHW	318	8	0	206	7%	74%	93	50	3
Bantz,Brandon	11	R	24	C	aa	SEA	236	1	0	180	10%	72%	39	31	-49
	12	R	25	C	aaa	SEA	109	1	1	177	3%	68%	74	48	-45
Barfield,Jeremy	11	R	23	OF	aa	OAK	495	7	1	211	6%	79%	68	50	-1
	12	R	24	OF	aa	OAK	482	9	1	225	5%	80%	75	46	6
Barnes,Brandon	11	R	25	OF	a/a	HOU	432	11	7	194	6%	69%	111	95	10
	12	R	26	OF	a/a	HOU	399	8	14	254	6%	72%	117	97	23
Barnhart,Tucker	12	B	21	C	aa	CIN	130	2	1	190	7%	82%	55	60	5
Barton,Daric	11	L	26	1B	aaa	OAK	61	0	0	148	13%	68%	28	34	-67
	12	L	27	1B	aaa	OAK	259	5	5	193	15%	74%	80	92	20
Bates,Aaron	11	R	27	DH	aaa	MIN	358	5	1	256	10%	70%	83	35	-23
	12	R	28	1B	aaa	STL	139	0	0	156	9%	68%	40	17	-70
Becker,Joseph	11	R	26	3B	aaa	LA	187	2	0	223	4%	74%	59	45	-34
	12	R	27	2B	a/a	LA	155	1	1	169	7%	83%	31	63	-9
Beckham,Tim	11	R	21	SS	a/a	TAM	524	9	14	239	6%	75%	86	118	16
	12	R	22	SS	aaa	TAM	285	5	5	227	8%	72%	64	87	-17
Bell,Bubba	11	L	29	OF	a/a	NYM	209	1	8	163	4%	80%	47	88	-5
Bell,Josh	11	B	25	3B	aaa	BAL	395	16	3	219	7%	66%	114	74	-5
	12	B	26	3B	aaa	ARI	360	8	2	226	6%	74%	100	58	7
Bellows,Kyle	11	R	23	3B	aa	CLE	432	2	5	205	6%	83%	56	72	12
	12	R	24	3B	aa	CLE	202	4	3	221	11%	77%	79	54	10
Belnome,Vince	11	L	23	2B	aa	SD	267	11	0	270	12%	73%	141	43	44
	12	L	24	DH	aaa	SD	258	3	3	211	11%	65%	62	58	-48
Beltre,Engel	11	L	22	OF	aa	TEX	437	1	12	211	5%	76%	48	130	-9
	12	L	23	OF	aa	TEX	564	12	28	244	4%	78%	85	146	33
Benson,Joe	11	R	23	OF	aa	MIN	400	10	10	242	9%	69%	125	94	27
	12	R	24	OF	a/a	MIN	236	4	6	159	8%	67%	76	107	-21
Beresford,James	12	L	23	SS	aa	MIN	369	0	2	237	7%	84%	31	58	-5
Bermudez,Ronald	11	R	23	OF	a/a	BOS	252	2	0	248	3%	79%	86	47	8
	12	R	24	OF	a/a	BOS	201	2	4	234	3%	78%	67	84	0
Berry,Quintin	11	L	27	OF	a/a	CIN	338	4	27	220	9%	68%	68	118	-19
	12	L	28	OF	aaa	DET	159	0	14	217	9%	66%	44	91	-55

BATTER	yr	b	age	pos	lvl	org	ab	hr	sb	ba	bb%	ct%	px	sx	bpv
Bertram,Michael	11	L	27	DH	aa	DET	267	3	1	207	8%	67%	94	37	-27
Bethancourt,Christian	12	R	21	C	aa	ATL	268	2	7	224	3%	81%	28	82	-18
Bianchi,Jeff	11	R	25	2B	aa	KC	444	1	14	215	6%	79%	51	100	-1
	12	R	26	SS	a/a	MIL	326	4	11	274	6%	78%	65	77	1
Bianucci,Michael	11	R	25	DH	aa	TEX	535	24	4	210	5%	72%	136	66	28
	12	R	26	1B	aaa	TEX	325	11	1	220	3%	72%	93	38	-16
Bigley,Evan	11	R	24	OF	aa	MIN	487	4	4	210	5%	75%	81	67	-4
	12	R	25	OF	a/a	MIN	487	10	3	214	4%	71%	91	63	-13
Bishop,Rawley	11	R	26	1B	aa	DET	455	7	12	218	7%	73%	81	71	-3
	12	R	27	3B	a/a	DET	431	6	11	195	7%	71%	70	76	-21
Blackmon,Charlie	11	L	25	OF	aaa	COL	243	6	6	261	4%	84%	103	94	56
	12	L	26	OF	aaa	COL	228	3	6	246	7%	79%	95	129	47
Blackwood,Jacob	12	R	27	OF	aa	SD	283	3	4	164	3%	70%	51	77	-51
Bloxom,Justin	12	B	24	1B	aa	WAS	243	7	0	220	6%	71%	98	36	-14
Boggs,Brandon	11	B	28	OF	aaa	MIL	270	6	2	181	11%	61%	119	51	-22
	12	B	29	OF	aaa	PIT	409	6	4	206	10%	65%	92	84	-18
Bolivar,Domnit	11	R	22	2B	aa	STL	47	1	1	240	4%	81%	64	73	7
	12	R	23	SS	aa	MIL	207	3	4	175	6%	73%	48	50	-42
Bond,Brock	11	B	26	2B	aaa	SF	57	0	1	187	7%	83%	32	98	2
	12	B	27	2B	aaa	SF	337	1	2	256	8%	85%	36	59	3
Bonilla,Leury	11	R	26	OF	a/a	SEA	146	0	3	171	5%	75%	12	111	-45
	12	R	27	3B	a/a	SEA	257	1	3	204	5%	70%	48	87	-43
Borbon,Julio	11	L	25	OF	a/a	TEX	135	0	11	245	7%	81%	81	161	52
	12	L	26	OF	aaa	TEX	533	8	13	252	4%	85%	62	101	32
Borchering,Robert	12	B	22	3B	aa	HOU	172	5	1	139	5%	60%	91	55	-60
Bortnick,Tyler	12	R	25	2B	a/a	ARI	480	4	18	202	7%	79%	67	119	23
Bour,Justin	12	L	24	1B	aa	CHC	506	14	3	247	9%	74%	106	42	14
Bourgeois,Jason	11	R	29	OF	a/a	HOU	28	0	1	272	2%	95%	84	128	93
	12	R	30	OF	aaa	KC	222	2	4	180	5%	87%	34	93	14
Bowker,John	11	L	28	OF	aaa	PIT	421	10	1	241	4%	80%	91	39	13
Bowman,Shawn	11	R	27	3B	a/a	ATL	200	6	1	211	4%	63%	97	56	-45
	12	R	28	3B	a/a	MIA	421	7	1	191	5%	65%	77	29	-59
Bradley,Jackie	12	L	22	OF	aa	BOS	229	5	7	260	11%	77%	110	94	50
Brantly,Rob	12	L	23	C	a/a	MIA	362	4	0	260	4%	84%	66	27	8
Brenly,Michael	12	R	26	C	aa	CHC	269	5	1	189	7%	74%	68	26	-25
Brentz,Bryce	12	R	24	OF	a/a	BOS	473	13	6	267	6%	68%	123	58	4
Brewer,Daniel	11	R	24	OF	a/a	NYY	186	0	9	236	7%	65%	69	106	-36
	12	R	25	OF	aa	NYY	104	1	2	188	5%	73%	47	38	-49
Brignac,Reid	11	L	25	SS	aaa	TAM	39	1	0	194	12%	82%	89	105	56
	12	L	26	SS	aaa	TAM	346	6	2	188	9%	72%	67	64	-18
Britton,Buck	11	L	25	3B	a/a	BAL	262	3	4	250	6%	83%	83	96	40
	12	L	26	OF	a/a	BAL	387	8	4	248	7%	81%	77	52	18
Brown,Andrew	11	R	27	OF	aaa	STL	359	12	3	215	10%	64%	105	70	-18
	12	R	28	OF	aaa	COL	390	15	2	240	5%	70%	149	75	33
Brown,Corey	11	L	26	OF	aaa	WAS	396	11	3	195	8%	61%	112	64	-28
	12	L	27	OF	aaa	WAS	484	18	13	234	8%	66%	128	116	20
Brown,Domonic	11	L	24	OF	aaa	PHI	138	2	10	229	14%	73%	74	83	5
	12	L	25	OF	aaa	PHI	220	4	3	251	6%	78%	87	82	19
Brown,Dusty	11	R	29	C	aaa	PIT	172	5	0	218	8%	76%	125	19	26
	12	R	30	C	aaa	TEX	141	3	0	166	12%	70%	101	14	-12
Brown,Gary	12	R	24	OF	aa	SF	538	6	29	250	6%	82%	70	104	28
Brown,Jordan	11	L	28	OF	aaa	MIL	425	7	1	235	3%	86%	79	48	28
	12	L	29	OF	aaa	MIL	359	6	1	242	4%	82%	72	43	10
Brown,Kelson	12	R	25	3B	aa	PIT	138	1	2	251	7%	82%	55	78	11
Buchholz,Alexander	12	R	25	3B	aa	TEX	301	6	3	218	5%	80%	69	81	11
Burgess,Michael	12	L	24	OF	aa	CHC	332	8	0	226	10%	79%	94	29	19
Burriss,Emmanuel	11	B	26	2B	aaa	SF	175	1	15	226	7%	87%	44	117	32
	12	B	27	2B	aaa	SF	106	0	3	210	6%	86%	54	100	31
Buss,Nicholas	12	L	26	OF	aa	LA	492	6	14	223	5%	83%	65	109	29
Butler,Daniel	11	R	25	C	a/a	BOS	69	1	0	191	9%	79%	85	10	5
	12	R	26	C	a/a	BOS	320	7	0	218	9%	78%	93	39	17
Butler,Joey	11	R	25	OF	a/a	TEX	470	11	10	264	7%	63%	120	104	-5
	12	R	26	OF	aaa	TEX	493	15	4	239	10%	70%	106	56	4
Cabrera,Everth	11	B	25	SS	aaa	SD	246	1	17	212	7%	79%	50	135	12
	12	B	26	SS	aaa	SD	144	0	10	250	6%	74%	50	127	-11
Cabrera,Ramon	12	B	23	C	a/a	PIT	389	2	0	251	8%	88%	57	40	28
Cabrera,Willie	11	R	25	OF	a/a	ATL	395	4	2	213	5%	88%	45	65	21
Calhoun,Kole	12	L	25	OF	aaa	LAA	410	9	8	229	6%	74%	99	105	22
Camp,Matt	11	L	27	SS	a/a	CHC	252	0	2	149	6%	84%	37	64	-2
Campana,Tony	11	L	25	OF	aaa	CHC	120	0	5	271	3%	77%	63	131	5
	12	L	26	OF	aaa	CHC	143	1	12	228	6%	72%	25	121	-44
Campbell,Eric	11	R	26	3B	aa	CIN	257	8	0	204	4%	78%	105	26	16
	11	R	24	3B	aa	NYM	405	3	4	184	8%	79%	55	69	-1
Campbell,Eric	12	R	25	1B	aa	NYM	394	7	8	231	10%	78%	77	71	15
	12	R	27	2B	aa	SEA	200	4	3	201	9%	79%	68	53	4
Canzler,Russ	11	R	25	OF	aaa	TAM	474	14	4	264	10%	67%	144	80	30
	12	R	26	OF	aaa	CLE	487	15	1	215	6%	69%	127	53	7
Cardenas,Adrian	11	L	24	OF	aaa	OAK	491	3	9	254	6%	86%	57	80	30
	12	L	25	2B	aaa	CHC	243	2	4	251	9%	85%	88	88	55
Carp,Mike	11	L	25	OF	aaa	SEA	251	12	4	257	7%	74%	130	59	33
	12	L	26	DH	aaa	SEA	139	1	1	168	6%	72%	59	39	-41
Carrera,Ezequiel	11	L	24	OF	aaa	CLE	328	1	27	244	8%	81%	33	138	12
	12	L	25	OF	aaa	CLE	394	4	19	246	5%	82%	62	126	28
Carrithers,Alden	11	L	27	2B	aa	CHW	359	0	14	226	11%	88%	42	113	45
	12	L	28	OF	aa	ATL	165	0	7	256	14%	84%	25	68	6
Carroll,Sawyer	11	L	25	OF	aa	SD	460	11	8	206	9%	74%	96	101	21
	12	L	26	OF	aaa	SD	372	5	6	195	7%	76%	59	87	-6

BATTER	yr	b	age	pos	lvl	org	ab	hr	sb	ba	bb%	ct%	px	sx	bpv
Carter,Chris	11	R	25	1B	aaa	OAK	296	11	3	214	9%	65%	139	80	15
	12	R	26	1B	aaa	OAK	276	7	3	216	9%	67%	113	74	-1
Castellanos,Alex	11	R	25	OF	aa	LA	475	16	10	259	5%	70%	139	125	43
	12	R	26	2B	aaa	LA	344	10	10	245	7%	69%	121	104	21
Castellanos,Nick	12	R	20	OF	aa	DET	322	6	4	244	3%	76%	71	67	-10
Castillo,Angel	11	R	22	OF	a/a	LAA	365	4	13	178	5%	67%	59	105	-41
	12	R	23	OF	aa	LAA	273	5	7	164	7%	65%	72	100	-37
Castillo,Welington	11	R	24	C	aaa	CHC	227	10	0	228	5%	71%	113	22	-8
	12	R	25	C	a/a	CHC	157	6	0	225	12%	70%	102	20	-5
Castillo,Wilkin	11	B	27	C	aaa	ATL	279	4	4	214	2%	79%	58	53	-15
	12	B	28	C	aaa	COL	233	3	2	195	2%	85%	47	75	7
Castro,Leandro	12	R	23	OF	aa	PHI	478	8	10	251	3%	83%	84	75	31
Cates,Chris	11	B	26	SS	aa	MIN	200	0	0	163	5%	87%	28	48	-4
Catricala,Vincent	11	R	23	OF	aa	SEA	239	8	8	300	8%	76%	175	116	98
	12	R	24	3B	aaa	SEA	463	7	3	181	5%	77%	61	57	-13
Cavan,Ryan	12	B	25	2B	aa	SF	426	8	3	200	6%	76%	61	58	-16
Cavazos-Galvez,Brian	11	R	24	1B	aa	LA	411	10	9	227	2%	82%	96	99	41
	12	R	25	OF	a/a	LA	256	7	4	236	3%	81%	90	93	31
Centeno,Juan	12	L	23	C	aa	NYM	281	0	1	230	6%	83%	34	56	-10
Cerda,Matthew	12	L	22	3B	aa	CHC	259	2	3	244	15%	75%	56	78	1
Cervelli,Francisco	12	R	26	C	aaa	NYY	354	2	5	206	8%	73%	47	80	-29
Cesario,James	11	L	26	2B	aa	COL	252	3	3	267	5%	80%	58	63	-1
	12	L	27	2B	a/a	COL	269	4	1	205	3%	80%	64	56	-4
Chalk,Bradley	11	L	25	OF	aa	PIT	266	0	3	208	7%	82%	34	88	-4
Chambers,Adron	11	L	25	OF	aaa	STL	426	6	15	220	8%	75%	69	102	5
	12	L	26	OF	aaa	STL	357	2	9	255	10%	73%	50	83	-22
Chang,Ray	11	R	28	SS	a/a	MIN	256	2	1	209	5%	81%	59	35	-8
	12	R	29	3B	aaa	MIN	266	0	2	192	5%	82%	22	47	-28
Chavez,Johermyn	11	R	22	OF	aa	SEA	439	10	5	187	9%	68%	87	67	-21
	12	R	23	OF	aa	SEA	246	7	2	206	12%	71%	96	65	5
Chen,Chun-Hsiu	11	R	23	C	aa	CLE	413	13	2	234	8%	67%	129	69	11
	12	R	24	1B	aa	CLE	399	4	5	282	11%	72%	93	68	6
Chiang,Chih-Hsien	11	L	23	OF	aa	SEA	451	14	6	258	5%	76%	143	95	60
	12	L	24	OF	a/a	SEA	449	5	2	207	4%	79%	63	51	-8
Chirinos,Robinson	11	R	27	C	aaa	TAM	282	4	1	206	7%	70%	72	38	-37
Chisenhall,Lonnie	11	L	23	3B	aaa	CLE	255	5	0	232	8%	79%	96	68	32
	12	L	24	3B	aaa	CLE	118	3	0	268	2%	79%	123	26	27
Choice,Michael	12	R	23	OF	aa	OAK	359	7	4	242	7%	72%	75	84	-13
Christian,Jason	11	L	24	2B	aa	OAK	128	1	3	222	5%	70%	71	102	-18
	12	L	25	SS	aa	ATL	155	0	2	188	10%	76%	20	77	-37
Ciriaco,Audy	11	R	24	SS	a/a	DET	444	4	4	225	2%	81%	72	105	18
	12	R	25	3B	aaa	DET	348	9	13	190	4%	76%	80	89	6
Ciriaco,Juan	12	R	29	OF	a/a	SF	243	4	7	181	7%	78%	54	98	0
Ciriaco,Pedro	11	R	26	SS	aaa	PIT	277	1	9	189	1%	80%	35	114	-12
	12	R	27	SS	aaa	BOS	276	3	11	260	2%	79%	64	105	4
Clark,Matthew	11	L	25	OF	aaa	SD	462	12	0	206	7%	67%	94	25	-31
	12	L	26	1B	aaa	SD	445	13	0	214	8%	67%	105	41	-17
Clemens,Koby	11	R	25	1B	aaa	HOU	384	12	3	192	8%	64%	122	63	-9
	12	R	26	DH	aa	TOR	124	4	4	186	9%	56%	165	101	6
Clevlen,Brent	11	R	28	OF	a/a	PHI	202	7	4	236	9%	61%	144	73	3
	12	R	29	OF	a/a	ARI	300	8	4	222	7%	63%	130	110	4
Cline,Matthew	11	R	26	SS	aa	MIL	274	2	2	195	9%	76%	53	82	-9
	12	R	27	3B	aa	MIL	111	1	0	131	6%	81%	24	31	-32
Coghlan,Chris	11	L	26	OF	a/a	MIA	72	1	2	181	10%	90%	57	78	52
	12	L	27	OF	aaa	MIA	317	5	7	226	10%	83%	73	87	38
Colabello,Chris	12	R	29	1B	aa	MIN	496	12	0	220	6%	76%	98	36	8
Coleman,Dustin	11	R	24	SS	aaa	OAK	36	0	0	271	2%	53%	99	59	-85
	12	R	25	SS	aa	OAK	427	10	6	162	7%	50%	114	92	-68
Colon,Christian	11	R	22	SS	aa	KC	491	5	13	226	6%	89%	41	88	30
	12	R	23	SS	a/a	KC	290	4	9	260	8%	90%	50	79	40
Conger,Hank	11	B	23	C	aaa	LAA	100	3	0	241	7%	79%	85	17	6
	12	B	24	C	aaa	LAA	264	6	1	233	4%	78%	86	56	9
Conley,Kyle	12	R	25	OF	aa	STL	159	6	0	180	8%	64%	119	27	-22
Constanza,Jose	11	L	28	OF	aaa	ATL	333	1	17	252	5%	84%	15	110	-5
	12	L	29	OF	aaa	ATL	344	1	9	239	7%	83%	28	94	0
Contreras,Anthony	11	L	28	2B	a/a	SD	373	3	2	160	4%	73%	52	57	-37
	12	L	29	2B	aaa	SD	407	4	4	193	2%	79%	62	79	-4
Cook,David	11	R	30	OF	a/a	CIN	365	5	4	179	9%	61%	98	55	-41
Coon,Bradley	11	L	29	OF	a/a	LA	283	0	8	187	9%	74%	53	98	-11
	12	L	30	OF	aa	TAM	278	1	9	170	10%	73%	38	94	-28
Cooper,David	11	L	24	1B	aaa	TOR	467	6	1	291	8%	89%	98	28	60
	12	L	25	1B	aaa	TOR	261	7	0	255	8%	84%	118	37	61
Copeland,Ben	11	L	28	OF	a/a	CLE	230	4	6	203	6%	75%	95	100	21
	12	L	29	OF	a/a	CLE	181	2	9	155	4%	74%	62	138	-4
Costanzo,Mike	11	L	28	3B	a/a	CIN	408	9	2	189	7%	60%	114	69	-31
	12	L	29	3B	a/a	CIN	343	10	0	212	10%	66%	105	30	-20
Cousins,Scott	12	L	27	OF	aaa	MIA	233	5	10	236	7%	69%	87	106	-4
Cowgill,Collin	11	R	25	OF	aaa	ARI	395	7	17	277	6%	81%	91	133	50
	12	R	26	OF	aaa	OAK	260	2	5	196	5%	76%	67	80	-5
Cox,Zack	11	L	22	3B	aa	STL	352	6	0	234	5%	78%	71	30	-10
	12	L	23	3B	a/a	MIA	394	7	1	219	4%	74%	94	45	-3
Crabbe,Callix	11	B	28	2B	aa	TOR	220	6	7	211	9%	84%	75	78	38
Crowe,Trevor	11	B	28	OF	aaa	CLE	20	0	1	76	3%	82%	0	94	-36
	12	B	29	OF	a/a	LAA	310	2	12	209	7%	78%	58	104	7
Crumbliss,Conner	12	L	25	OF	aa	OAK	470	7	17	210	16%	75%	69	111	23
Cruz,Luis	11	R	27	SS	aaa	TEX	275	6	1	213	2%	83%	78	49	15
	12	R	28	SS	aaa	LA	289	4	1	227	2%	85%	94	55	37
Culberson,Charlie	12	R	23	2B	aaa	COL	476	8	9	226	3%	79%	81	105	20
Cunningham,Jarek	12	R	23	2B	aa	PIT	359	5	2	194	8%	68%	82	73	-23
Cunningham,Todd	12	B	23	OF	aa	ATL	466	2	20	279	7%	87%	53	121	44
Curry,Matthew	11	L	23	1B	aa	PIT	302	5	1	214	8%	69%	90	69	-14
	12	L	24	1B	a/a	PIT	401	8	3	254	8%	71%	125	75	26
Curry,Ryan	11	R	26	2B	aa	MIA	369	5	3	191	5%	81%	68	73	13
Curtis,Colin	12	L	27	OF	aaa	NYY	250	1	9	179	9%	74%	52	93	-15
Curtis,Jermaine	11	R	24	OF	aa	STL	276	3	0	245	8%	87%	51	42	19
	12	R	25	3B	a/a	STL	397	1	4	253	10%	84%	39	67	8
Cusick,Matthew	11	L	25	2B	aa	LAA	207	3	2	221	13%	84%	48	62	23
Cutler,Charles	11	L	25	C	aa	STL	204	3	0	254	6%	83%	56	55	9
	12	L	26	C	aa	PIT	152	1	1	251	9%	88%	59	86	44
D Arnaud,Chase	11	R	24	SS	aaa	PIT	288	3	15	227	6%	80%	65	140	28
	12	R	25	SS	aaa	PIT	381	5	28	219	7%	74%	83	148	22
D Arnaud,Travis	11	R	22	C	aa	TOR	424	19	3	290	6%	74%	160	64	57
	12	R	23	C	aaa	TOR	279	12	1	284	4%	75%	140	50	39
Danks,Jordan	11	L	25	OF	aaa	CHW	463	13	14	222	10%	60%	129	111	-3
	12	L	26	OF	aaa	CHW	218	8	5	278	16%	63%	152	67	28
Darnell,James	11	R	24	3B	a/a	SD	422	14	1	234	10%	77%	109	46	30
	12	R	25	3B	aaa	SD	116	4	1	199	9%	73%	101	50	6
Davidson,Matthew	12	R	21	3B	aa	ARI	486	19	2	245	10%	73%	129	59	33
Davis,Blake	11	L	28	OF	aaa	BAL	232	4	4	227	4%	76%	48	83	-22
	12	L	29	SS	aaa	BAL	355	3	5	206	5%	79%	54	86	-3
Davis,Brad	11	R	29	C	aaa	MIA	344	3	1	191	5%	70%	66	44	-44
	12	R	30	C	aaa	DET	199	1	3	151	5%	72%	59	89	-26
Davis,Kentrail	12	L	24	OF	aa	MIL	438	6	15	241	9%	68%	89	104	-6
Davis,Khristopher	11	R	24	OF	aa	MIL	124	2	0	180	6%	78%	77	36	0
	12	R	25	OF	a/a	MIL	241	10	2	303	12%	70%	156	44	44
Davis,Lars	11	L	26	C	aa	COL	149	4	0	213	10%	72%	79	25	-18
	12	L	27	C	aa	COL	307	8	1	257	5%	73%	81	29	-22
De Jesus,Ivan	11	R	24	2B	aaa	LA	387	5	2	233	6%	79%	58	55	-7
	12	R	25	2B	aaa	BOS	250	2	2	276	5%	75%	75	81	-5
De Los Santos,Estarling	12	B	25	SS	aa	MIN	287	1	6	183	4%	77%	36	89	-27
de San Miguel,Allan	11	R	23	C	aa	MIN	42	0	0	160	5%	61%	51	40	-92
	12	R	24	C	a/a	BAL	114	3	1	196	9%	67%	131	61	13
Decker,Cody	11	R	24	1B	aa	SD	177	8	0	183	4%	59%	167	74	4
	12	R	25	OF	a/a	SD	453	18	1	192	10%	65%	130	33	-5
Decker,Jaff	11	L	21	OF	aa	SD	496	13	11	192	14%	66%	110	87	9
	12	L	22	OF	aa	SD	147	2	5	154	18%	71%	54	116	1
Delarosa,Anderson	11	R	27	C	aa	MIL	184	4	0	193	3%	72%	85	48	-21
	12	R	28	C	aa	MIL	224	5	0	182	4%	70%	78	37	-36
Den Dekker,Matthew	11	L	24	OF	aa	NYM	272	8	9	179	6%	62%	113	126	-8
	12	L	25	OF	a/a	NYM	533	13	16	213	5%	67%	104	128	-1
Dening,Mitchell	11	L	23	OF	aa	BOS	264	4	2	193	7%	73%	79	78	-3
Denker,Travis	11	R	26	3B	aa	LA	233	7	4	227	9%	77%	102	60	26
	12	R	27	1B	aa	LA	206	3	3	183	7%	72%	77	58	-18
Dent,Ryan	11	R	22	SS	aa	BOS	170	1	5	186	7%	72%	83	75	-9
	12	R	23	2B	a/a	BOS	280	2	3	220	8%	75%	40	64	-30
Derba,Nicholas	11	R	26	C	a/a	STL	150	1	0	138	8%	65%	48	39	-72
	12	R	27	C	a/a	STL	192	1	0	127	7%	66%	38	24	-84
DeWitt,Blake	12	L	27	OF	aaa	CHC	102	0	0	98	8%	73%	22	11	-68
Diaz,Argenis	11	R	24	SS	aaa	DET	340	0	2	249	9%	81%	47	62	-2
	12	R	25	SS	aaa	DET	356	0	9	216	5%	80%	26	61	-28
Diaz,Jonathan	11	B	26	2B	a/a	TOR	282	1	6	207	9%	73%	52	56	-31
	12	B	27	2B	a/a	TOR	457	3	12	174	10%	77%	35	94	-13
Diaz,Juan	11	B	23	SS	aa	CLE	522	7	8	229	6%	75%	73	90	1
	12	B	24	SS	a/a	CLE	443	10	1	234	5%	71%	105	55	-3
Diaz,Robinzon	11	R	28	C	a/a	TEX	198	5	0	250	3%	93%	50	33	28
	12	R	29	C	aaa	TEX	183	3	1	223	2%	93%	64	69	51
Dickerson,Chris	11	L	29	OF	aaa	NYY	212	2	14	194	10%	63%	66	115	-38
	12	L	30	OF	aaa	NYY	266	6	12	247	12%	65%	128	123	25
Dickerson,Corey	12	L	23	OF	aa	COL	266	13	6	271	5%	81%	139	100	77
Dietrich,Derek	12	L	23	2B	aa	TAM	133	3	0	235	4%	69%	97	75	-14
Dinkelman,Brian	11	L	28	OF	aaa	MIN	469	2	5	192	6%	76%	55	64	-18
	12	L	29	DH	aaa	MIN	246	3	4	201	7%	77%	67	85	3
Dolenc,Mark	11	R	27	OF	aa	MIN	418	2	11	209	5%	64%	53	92	-63
	12	R	28	OF	aa	MIN	113	1	3	132	2%	57%	21	76	-125
Dominguez,Chris	11	R	25	3B	aa	SF	295	5	1	210	2%	69%	112	73	-5
	12	R	26	OF	a/a	SF	362	3	3	190	2%	68%	66	51	-55
Dominguez,Jeffrey	12	B	26	2B	a/a	MIA	333	3	6	193	5%	74%	63	78	-16
Dominguez,Matt	11	R	22	3B	a/a	MIA	340	8	0	211	6%	83%	79	43	21
	12	R	23	3B	aaa	HOU	447	6	0	210	5%	87%	58	21	10
Donald,Jason	11	R	27	SS	a/a	CLE	203	3	6	245	7%	77%	74	79	6
Donaldson,Josh	11	R	26	C	aaa	OAK	444	10	8	199	7%	72%	94	77	3
	12	R	27	3B	aaa	OAK	209	8	3	257	7%	79%	108	79	43
Dorn,Daniel	11	L	27	1B	aaa	CIN	448	14	1	197	5%	63%	129	47	-17
	12	L	28	1B	aaa	DET	393	10	4	201	8%	67%	106	67	-7
Douglas,Brandon	11	R	26	2B	aa	DET	499	2	16	232	3%	87%	55	114	35
	12	R	27	2B	aa	DET	471	2	10	216	6%	82%	47	89	5
Dozier,Brian	11	R	24	SS	aa	MIN	311	4	8	269	6%	83%	94	120	58
	12	R	25	SS	aaa	MIN	181	1	2	202	6%	79%	67	67	2
Drennen,John	11	L	25	OF	aa	CLE	284	5	1	206	11%	77%	91	66	22
Duarte,Jose	12	R	27	OF	a/a	MIA	205	2	3	186	11%	80%	39	44	-12
Duncan,Eric	11	L	27	OF	aa	STL	351	12	2	194	4%	72%	107	56	2
	12	L	28	3B	aa	KC	187	2	2	215	3%	71%	60	86	-32
Dunigan,Joseph	11	L	25	DH	aa	SEA	172	5	3	174	11%	43%	191	82	-29
	12	L	26	DH	aa	SEA	426	20	12	212	7%	49%	199	108	4

BATTER	yr	b	age	pos	lvl	org	ab	hr	sb	ba	bb%	ct%	px	sx	bpv
Durango,Luis	11	B	25	OF	aaa	HOU	331	0	19	211	8%	81%	20	134	-4
	12	B	26	OF	aaa	ATL	499	0	33	234	7%	78%	26	114	-18
Durham,Miles	11	R	28	OF	a/a	PIT	376	3	6	174	5%	64%	76	105	-42
	12	R	29	OF	a/a	PIT	177	1	6	183	6%	66%	83	119	-20
Dykstra,Allan	11	L	24	1B	aa	NYM	390	14	1	204	11%	62%	129	39	-15
	12	L	25	1B	aa	NYM	191	5	1	203	17%	61%	100	40	-30
Easley,Edward	11	R	26	C	aa	ARI	289	3	1	224	7%	79%	62	32	-9
	12	R	27	C	aa	ARI	204	1	1	219	10%	82%	38	23	-12
Eaton,Adam	11	L	23	OF	aa	ARI	212	3	7	268	9%	82%	68	110	34
	12	L	24	OF	a/a	ARI	528	5	30	323	7%	83%	91	124	59
Elmore,Jake	11	R	24	2B	aa	ARI	381	2	10	231	9%	81%	54	74	8
	12	R	25	SS	aaa	ARI	419	1	19	278	9%	85%	68	129	52
Emaus,Brad	11	R	25	2B	aaa	COL	163	5	2	241	6%	83%	101	74	49
	12	R	26	2B	aaa	NYM	203	3	1	156	7%	83%	50	32	-3
Erickson,Gorman	11	B	23	C	aa	LA	142	5	1	230	5%	82%	101	35	33
	12	B	24	C	aa	LA	274	2	1	200	11%	77%	61	34	-10
Erickson,Gorman Charles	11	B	23	C	aa	LA	142	5	1	230	5%	82%	101	35	33
	12	B	24	C	aa	LA	274	2	1	200	11%	77%	61	34	-10
Escobar,Eduardo	11	B	22	SS	aaa	CHW	489	4	11	242	5%	76%	63	91	-7
	12	B	23	3B	aaa	MIN	138	1	3	199	5%	80%	44	128	3
Espino,Damaso	11	B	28	C	aaa	LA	202	2	1	200	4%	81%	35	53	-22
	11	R	28	C	aaa	LA	202	2	1	200	4%	81%	35	53	-22
Espino,Damaso	12	B	29	C	a/a	CHW	236	0	1	213	7%	83%	24	29	-25
Exposito,Luis	11	R	24	C	aaa	BOS	330	6	0	223	6%	74%	89	22	-14
	12	R	25	C	aaa	BAL	215	6	0	239	7%	81%	92	44	26
Fairley,Wendell	11	L	23	OF	aa	SF	98	0	2	241	6%	69%	50	105	-37
	12	L	24	OF	aa	SF	109	0	1	198	9%	66%	47	29	-70
Falu,Irving	11	B	28	OF	aaa	KC	385	1	14	239	6%	85%	41	116	22
	12	B	29	3B	aaa	KC	365	4	13	250	5%	86%	61	104	35
Farrell,Jeremy	11	R	25	3B	aa	PIT	312	4	3	221	6%	73%	76	67	-13
	12	R	26	3B	a/a	PIT	327	3	2	186	7%	70%	62	54	-38
Farris,Eric	11	R	25	2B	aaa	MIL	538	4	14	218	4%	84%	54	96	18
	12	R	26	2B	aaa	MIL	483	6	27	241	4%	86%	51	95	23
Federowicz,Tim	11	R	24	C	a/a	LA	422	9	1	224	6%	77%	87	35	2
	12	R	25	C	aaa	LA	412	7	0	222	7%	73%	91	36	-8
Fedroff,Tim	11	L	24	OF	a/a	CLE	490	2	8	269	9%	83%	63	81	26
	12	L	25	OF	a/a	CLE	468	9	11	273	9%	81%	84	112	44
Felix,Jose	11	R	23	C	aa	TEX	263	2	1	202	3%	89%	45	47	14
	12	R	24	C	aa	TEX	292	6	2	234	1%	91%	60	66	36
Fellhauer,Joshua	11	L	23	OF	aa	CIN	72	0	1	228	9%	71%	36	54	-52
	12	L	24	OF	aa	CIN	338	4	5	284	12%	82%	68	70	28
Fernandez,Jair	11	R	25	C	a/a	MIN	126	1	1	183	10%	64%	94	44	-35
	12	R	26	C	a/a	HOU	194	4	0	205	5%	76%	74	28	-17
Field,Tommy	11	R	24	2B	aa	COL	472	13	6	238	7%	76%	96	76	18
	12	R	25	SS	aaa	COL	435	5	2	201	5%	81%	82	90	29
Fields,Daniel	12	L	21	OF	aa	DET	106	2	7	241	9%	80%	56	83	8
Figueroa,Cole	11	L	24	2B	aa	TAM	410	4	7	236	9%	88%	58	100	49
	12	L	25	3B	a/a	TAM	397	4	3	245	8%	91%	60	70	49
Fletcher,Scott	12	R	24	OF	aa	KC	254	7	5	222	4%	59%	114	95	-34
Fleury,Mark	12	L	24	C	aa	CIN	187	1	1	143	14%	56%	72	49	-72
Flores,David	11	R	25	3B	aa	HOU	227	4	0	161	5%	81%	54	28	-11
Flores,Wilmer	12	R	21	3B	aa	NYM	251	7	0	261	6%	87%	92	49	50
Florimon Jr.,Pedro	11	B	25	SS	aa	BAL	454	7	12	236	8%	72%	92	84	5
	12	B	26	SS	a/a	MIN	424	3	11	218	6%	68%	62	81	-41
Ford,Darren	11	R	26	OF	a/a	SF	157	1	11	196	5%	64%	48	100	-64
	12	R	27	OF	aaa	SEA	304	2	17	204	5%	74%	58	105	-15
Ford,Joshua	11	R	28	C	aa	ARI	306	5	0	208	6%	62%	100	40	-48
Fox,Adam	11	R	30	3B	a/a	WAS	233	4	2	162	4%	73%	84	86	-4
Franklin,Nick	11	B	20	SS	aa	SEA	83	2	4	296	6%	75%	85	127	22
	12	B	21	SS	a/a	SEA	472	9	10	244	8%	74%	102	107	28
Frazier,Jeff	11	R	29	OF	aaa	WAS	371	7	1	175	6%	83%	72	28	9
	12	R	30	OF	aaa	CHC	148	1	0	170	3%	77%	52	18	-36
Freiman,Nathan	12	R	26	1B	aa	SD	516	16	0	232	7%	76%	97	32	9
Frey,Evan	11	L	25	OF	a/a	ARI	464	1	14	208	8%	79%	47	114	5
	12	L	26	OF	a/a	ARI	464	1	22	204	8%	81%	36	108	6
Friday,Brian	11	R	26	2B	aaa	PIT	223	2	4	194	9%	74%	74	80	-3
	12	R	27	2B	aaa	ATL	282	1	7	166	8%	75%	47	92	-18
Fryer,Eric	11	R	26	C	a/a	PIT	231	5	3	226	10%	75%	80	93	16
	12	R	27	C	aaa	PIT	162	0	1	169	4%	74%	36	45	-52
Fuentes,Reymond	12	L	21	OF	aa	SD	473	3	28	184	8%	68%	56	123	-28
Fuller,Clayton	11	B	24	OF	aa	LAA	277	6	8	215	6%	72%	77	91	-8
Gac,Ian	12	R	27	1B	aa	ATL	255	5	3	201	9%	59%	155	59	-4
Gale,Rocky	11	R	23	C	a/a	SD	35	0	0	88	0%	87%	35	85	2
	12	R	24	C	a/a	SD	128	0	0	132	3%	78%	33	39	-39
Gallagher,Jim	11	L	26	1B	aaa	CHW	472	6	5	206	10%	79%	92	75	33
	12	L	27	OF	a/a	CHW	320	2	5	193	9%	76%	53	73	-13
Galvez,Jonathan	12	R	21	2B	aa	SD	312	4	10	249	8%	74%	83	98	9
Gamel,Mat	11	L	26	1B	aaa	MIL	493	20	1	246	6%	79%	114	44	33
Garcia,Adonis	12	R	27	OF	aa	NYY	118	3	1	237	3%	82%	117	59	46
Garcia,Avisail	12	R	21	OF	aa	DET	215	5	7	289	3%	82%	81	115	33
Garcia,Drew	11	B	25	2B	a/a	CHW	491	9	2	187	7%	61%	120	65	-25
	12	B	26	2B	a/a	CHW	498	5	4	215	6%	75%	71	71	-9
Garcia,Greg	12	L	23	SS	aa	STL	412	7	8	241	13%	77%	70	84	20
Garcia,Jose	11	R	23	2B	a/a	STL	363	3	14	260	5%	80%	53	78	-2
	12	R	24	3B	a/a	STL	304	3	8	215	5%	75%	46	74	-27
Garcia,Leury	12	B	21	2B	aa	TEX	377	2	25	280	5%	79%	62	149	20
Gardenhire,Toby	11	B	29	SS	aaa	MIN	332	2	1	190	4%	83%	43	32	-16

BATTER	yr	b	age	pos	lvl	org	ab	hr	sb	ba	bb%	ct%	px	sx	bpv
Garner,Cole	12	R	28	OF	aaa	NYY	236	5	2	209	5%	61%	98	63	-46
Gartrell,Maurice	11	R	27	OF	aaa	ATL	454	19	3	213	7%	68%	148	52	20
	12	R	28	OF	aaa	ATL	418	13	7	192	8%	62%	113	86	-18
Gattis,Evan	12	R	26	OF	aa	ATL	182	7	1	217	8%	81%	128	80	67
Gennett,Scooter	12	L	22	2B	aa	MIL	533	4	9	267	4%	85%	60	74	21
Gentile,Zach	12	L	26	2B	aa	BOS	133	0	2	212	6%	84%	44	63	2
Giavotella,Johnny	11	R	24	2B	aaa	KC	453	6	6	288	6%	86%	81	68	43
	12	R	25	2B	aaa	KC	362	6	5	267	8%	87%	67	78	45
Gibson,Derrik	12	R	23	SS	aa	BOS	405	0	12	210	8%	75%	38	91	-23
Gil,Jose	11	R	25	C	a/a	NYY	264	5	2	220	9%	81%	89	40	26
	12	R	26	C	a/a	NYY	253	5	5	179	7%	78%	69	63	1
Gil,Leonardo	12	R	25	3B	aa	OAK	211	1	2	229	7%	64%	42	79	-72
Gillaspie,Conor	11	L	24	3B	aaa	SF	428	6	6	235	9%	78%	75	72	13
	12	L	25	3B	aaa	SF	413	8	0	222	6%	84%	66	45	18
Gillespie,Cole	11	R	27	OF	aaa	ARI	484	6	12	223	8%	77%	75	124	21
	12	R	28	OF	aaa	ARI	441	7	6	230	7%	77%	92	78	21
Gillies,Tyson	12	L	24	OF	aa	PHI	276	3	6	262	5%	78%	76	134	25
Gilmore,Jonny	11	R	23	DH	aa	CHW	180	3	0	255	8%	79%	93	32	21
	12	R	24	DH	aa	CHW	122	0	0	152	7%	59%	52	44	-94
Gimenez,Chris	11	R	29	C	aaa	SEA	49	1	0	179	7%	63%	39	47	-85
	12	R	30	C	aaa	TAM	261	7	0	235	8%	71%	91	25	-18
Gimenez,Hector	11	B	29	1B	aa	LA	231	7	0	210	6%	74%	124	37	21
	12	B	30	C	aaa	CHW	375	12	2	209	8%	69%	114	54	0
Gindl,Caleb	11	L	23	OF	aaa	MIL	472	11	4	259	9%	77%	90	72	20
	12	L	24	OF	aaa	MIL	452	10	3	231	6%	75%	99	78	16
Glenn,Brad	12	R	25	OF	aa	TOR	423	16	6	207	5%	66%	136	56	3
Goebbert,Jacob	11	L	24	OF	a/a	HOU	378	5	1	250	6%	80%	86	54	17
	12	L	25	OF	a/a	HOU	398	6	3	235	9%	81%	78	85	30
Goedert,Jared	11	R	26	3B	a/a	CLE	313	13	0	224	9%	74%	131	22	27
	12	R	27	3B	a/a	CLE	450	14	0	257	8%	75%	103	34	11
Goins,Ryan	12	L	24	SS	aa	TOR	546	6	12	257	6%	84%	70	84	30
Golson,Greg	11	R	26	OF	aaa	NYY	384	8	12	229	6%	68%	74	122	-16
	12	R	27	OF	aaa	CHW	449	6	16	235	3%	68%	93	145	0
Gomes,Yan	11	R	24	C	a/a	TOR	290	10	0	206	6%	68%	130	31	-1
	12	R	25	C	aaa	TOR	305	9	3	267	5%	71%	137	57	24
Gomez,Mauro	11	R	27	1B	aaa	ATL	506	18	5	249	6%	68%	135	71	13
	12	R	28	1B	aaa	BOS	387	17	1	263	6%	73%	162	47	49
Gonzalez,Elevys	12	B	23	2B	aa	PIT	148	2	1	175	7%	71%	62	51	-36
Gonzalez,Jose	12	R	25	C	aa	COL	174	1	1	215	5%	76%	46	47	-34
Goodwin,Brian	12	L	22	OF	aa	WAS	166	4	2	203	8%	68%	98	65	-11
Gose,Anthony	11	L	21	OF	aa	TOR	509	15	59	239	9%	67%	115	166	31
	12	L	22	OF	aaa	TOR	420	4	24	247	7%	73%	78	149	15
Gosewisch,James	11	R	28	C	aa	PHI	369	9	3	190	4%	79%	80	41	2
Gosewisch,Tuffy	11	R	28	C	aa	PHI	369	9	3	190	4%	79%	80	41	2
Gosselin,Phil	12	R	24	2B	aa	ATL	484	2	10	212	7%	78%	50	89	-3
Gotay,Ruben	11	B	29	2B	aaa	ATL	449	6	8	191	9%	77%	50	83	-10
Gran,Paul	11	R	25	3B	aa	MIA	292	4	6	209	8%	69%	103	111	10
	12	R	26	2B	aa	MIA	368	3	7	196	9%	66%	65	91	-38
Grandal,Yasmani	11	B	23	C	a/a	CIN	168	3	0	267	7%	72%	124	25	12
	12	B	24	C	aaa	SD	194	4	0	260	12%	77%	99	30	24
Green,Grant	11	R	24	SS	aa	OAK	530	6	4	235	5%	73%	75	51	-20
	12	R	25	OF	aaa	OAK	524	9	9	236	4%	83%	73	87	25
Green,Taylor	11	L	25	3B	a/a	MIL	431	17	1	281	8%	79%	139	38	57
	12	L	26	3B	aaa	MIL	282	6	1	230	7%	75%	85	18	-8
Greene,Brodie	12	R	25	2B	aa	CIN	435	3	10	215	8%	81%	54	87	12
Greene,Jonathan	11	R	26	OF	aa	TEX	487	15	4	246	4%	62%	126	51	-24
Greene,Justin	11	R	26	OF	a/a	CHW	411	10	10	220	7%	55%	140	102	-19
	12	R	27	OF	a/a	CHW	320	7	20	213	9%	67%	95	125	1
Greene,Kyle	11	L	25	3B	a/a	ARI	157	1	0	170	8%	56%	81	31	-85
	12	L	26	1B	aa	ARI	123	1	0	180	5%	53%	55	78	-109
Gregorius,Didi	11	L	21	SS	aa	CIN	148	2	2	230	4%	81%	61	93	11
	12	L	22	SS	a/a	CIN	501	6	3	245	6%	82%	69	87	26
Grossman,Robert	12	B	23	OF	aa	HOU	485	8	9	226	10%	71%	87	92	5
Guez,Ben	11	R	24	OF	a/a	DET	443	5	9	251	6%	77%	98	104	30
	12	R	25	OF	a/a	DET	370	7	12	250	10%	72%	102	118	27
Gutierrez,Chris	11	R	27	SS	a/a	MIA	408	0	3	171	12%	73%	40	73	-28
	12	R	28	SS	a/a	MIA	430	3	4	189	8%	75%	55	50	-24
Guzman,Joel	12	R	28	1B	aa	CIN	236	6	1	218	7%	77%	75	29	-7
Gyorko,Jedd	11	R	23	3B	aa	SD	236	5	1	231	8%	74%	77	48	-9
	12	R	24	3B	a/a	SD	499	20	4	245	7%	76%	107	42	20
Ha,Jae-Hoon	11	R	21	OF	aa	CHC	226	2	5	251	4%	86%	74	79	38
	12	R	22	OF	aa	CHC	465	5	9	249	8%	78%	74	83	13
Haerther,Casey	12	R	25	DH	aa	LAA	487	8	1	236	2%	85%	58	34	2
Hagerty,Jason	11	B	24	C	aa	SD	130	1	0	180	7%	63%	61	60	-66
	12	B	25	C	aa	SD	246	5	0	194	10%	74%	70	21	-18
Hague,Matt	11	R	26	1B	aaa	PIT	534	8	3	255	6%	86%	80	55	37
	12	R	27	3B	aaa	PIT	367	3	2	236	5%	85%	38	46	-5
Hallberg,Marcus	11	R	26	2B	a/a	ARI	430	4	1	226	5%	93%	62	55	51
Halton,Sean	11	R	24	1B	aa	MIL	439	6	5	259	5%	78%	102	59	23
	12	R	25	1B	aaa	MIL	358	14	0	238	9%	73%	131	43	30
Hamilton,Billy	12	B	22	SS	aa	CIN	175	1	45	271	15%	73%	55	174	22
Hamilton,Mark	11	L	27	1B	aaa	STL	252	1	0	266	10%	78%	86	29	13
	12	L	28	OF	aaa	STL	303	9	1	171	10%	66%	90	33	-33
Hanson,Nate	11	R	24	1B	aa	MIN	202	1	1	198	5%	85%	62	54	18
	12	R	25	2B	aa	MIN	351	5	2	234	3%	87%	55	50	14
Hanzawa,Troy	11	R	26	SS	aa	PHI	26	0	0	60	5%	86%	0	202	19
	12	R	27	SS	aa	PHI	413	0	3	199	5%	80%	41	83	-12

BATTER	yr	b	age	pos	lvl	org	ab	hr	sb	ba	bb%	ct%	px	sx	bpv
Harbin,Taylor	11	R	25	SS	aa	ARI	481	6	5	226	5%	81%	61	60	2
	12	R	26	2B	aaa	ARI	478	3	10	239	2%	87%	74	98	43
Harrilchak,Cory	11	L	24	OF	aa	ATL	429	5	7	221	7%	80%	74	74	17
	12	L	25	OF	a/a	ATL	148	0	7	139	9%	73%	55	82	-20
Hassan,Alexander	11	R	23	OF	aa	BOS	454	9	6	259	11%	81%	104	63	49
	12	R	24	OF	aaa	BOS	312	5	1	236	12%	75%	71	29	-6
Haveman,Brandon	11	L	25	OF	a/a	SEA	246	3	5	198	5%	72%	62	108	-18
Havens,Reese	11	L	25	2B	aa	NYM	211	4	1	216	8%	67%	102	72	-10
	12	L	26	2B	aa	NYM	325	7	1	162	11%	59%	86	33	-59
Haydel,Lee	11	L	24	OF	aa	MIL	449	0	13	236	6%	74%	31	93	-39
	12	L	25	OF	aa	MIL	282	2	8	242	7%	75%	27	85	-39
Hazelbaker,Jeremy	11	L	24	OF	aa	BOS	354	8	25	230	8%	67%	108	127	8
	12	L	25	OF	a/a	BOS	466	15	29	245	6%	71%	119	138	32
Head,Jerad	11	R	29	OF	aaa	CLE	422	16	2	217	4%	70%	130	57	11
	12	R	30	OF	aaa	DET	295	8	6	206	6%	73%	95	81	8
Head,Miles	12	R	21	3B	aa	OAK	213	4	0	239	6%	61%	89	61	-54
Hechavarria,Adeiny	11	R	22	SS	a/a	TOR	572	6	14	229	4%	81%	70	103	19
	12	R	23	SS	aaa	TOR	443	4	6	263	6%	77%	63	100	3
Hee,Jonathan	11	R	26	1B	aa	BOS	331	3	2	230	6%	70%	94	47	-17
	12	R	27	2B	a/a	BOS	218	1	2	211	6%	75%	66	42	-21
Heether,Adam	11	R	29	OF	a/a	OAK	424	8	4	171	8%	72%	72	66	-15
	12	R	30	OF	a/a	LAA	222	4	3	154	7%	72%	56	67	-34
Heid,Andrew	12	L	25	OF	a/a	LAA	118	1	4	171	8%	82%	27	72	-9
Henriquez,Ralph	11	B	24	C	a/a	SEA	271	1	0	176	4%	79%	46	35	-25
	12	B	25	C	a/a	SEA	159	2	2	183	4%	71%	71	55	-33
Henry,Jordan	11	L	23	OF	aa	CLE	454	0	28	227	11%	82%	16	106	-4
	12	L	24	OF	aa	CLE	248	0	7	254	11%	86%	22	76	8
Henry,Justin	11	L	26	OF	a/a	DET	395	0	17	266	11%	84%	62	113	45
	12	L	27	OF	aaa	DET	476	1	16	249	8%	84%	31	100	8
Henson,Bobby	11	R	24	OF	aaa	BAL	449	3	7	217	7%	76%	50	82	-18
	12	R	25	OF	a/a	LA	156	3	1	213	10%	60%	106	58	-37
Hernandez,Anderson	11	B	29	2B	aaa	HOU	510	4	13	226	6%	80%	54	84	4
	12	B	30	2B	aaa	PIT	369	1	2	212	3%	81%	29	76	-20
Hernandez,Brian	12	R	24	3B	aa	LAA	233	1	2	220	8%	72%	44	35	-48
Hernandez,Cesar	12	B	22	2B	a/a	PHI	532	2	18	266	5%	84%	65	115	33
Hernandez,Diory	11	R	27	3B	aaa	ATL	273	4	2	163	2%	79%	59	51	-15
	12	R	28	3B	aaa	CHC	202	1	1	172	4%	80%	45	51	-19
Hernandez,Gorkys	11	R	24	OF	aaa	PIT	424	1	16	244	6%	77%	69	119	12
	12	R	25	OF	aaa	PIT	237	2	11	224	10%	71%	60	113	-12
Herrera,Elian	11	B	26	2B	aa	LA	378	2	22	218	9%	67%	61	124	-25
	12	B	27	SS	aaa	LA	273	2	6	249	3%	78%	76	114	15
Herrmann,Chris	11	L	24	C	aa	MIN	337	4	6	216	12%	77%	68	96	18
	12	L	25	C	aa	MIN	490	7	2	234	8%	79%	64	60	5
Hester,John	11	R	28	C	aaa	BAL	317	5	0	203	6%	70%	64	13	-52
	12	R	29	C	aaa	LAA	126	2	0	159	5%	59%	101	61	-53
Hicks,Aaron	12	B	23	OF	aa	MIN	472	9	26	255	12%	73%	93	144	35
Hicks,Brandon	11	R	26	SS	aaa	ATL	361	14	6	210	8%	54%	142	77	-30
	12	R	27	SS	aaa	OAK	328	11	3	183	9%	56%	161	88	-2
Hill,Steven	11	R	26	1B	a/a	STL	148	8	1	211	5%	67%	137	37	1
	12	R	27	1B	aaa	STL	301	11	0	203	6%	70%	106	39	-10
Hinze,Kody	11	R	24	1B	aa	HOU	199	5	0	232	8%	73%	77	22	-24
	12	R	25	DH	aa	HOU	260	8	1	171	8%	63%	86	32	-53
Hissey,Peter	12	L	22	OF	aa	BOS	236	1	13	240	6%	79%	66	93	10
Hodges,Wes	11	R	27	1B	a/a	SF	379	6	0	202	3%	68%	83	36	-42
	12	R	28	1B	aa	SF	139	2	1	220	3%	77%	89	62	5
Hoes,LJ	11	R	21	OF	aa	BAL	344	6	14	292	10%	83%	72	81	35
	12	R	22	OF	a/a	BAL	513	5	17	267	10%	84%	58	101	35
Hoffmann,Jaime	11	R	27	OF	aaa	LA	475	12	8	208	5%	73%	84	79	-8
	12	R	28	OF	aaa	BAL	366	9	7	214	10%	76%	88	77	20
Hoffpauir,Jarrett	11	R	28	2B	aaa	SD	306	2	1	185	6%	84%	67	57	20
	12	R	29	2B	aaa	WAS	336	2	3	218	6%	85%	45	73	12
Holaday,Bryan	11	R	24	C	aa	DET	330	5	5	207	6%	75%	76	59	-9
	12	R	25	C	aaa	DET	250	2	2	205	6%	81%	49	49	-8
Holcomb,Darin	11	R	26	3B	aa	COL	272	3	1	225	6%	81%	77	42	14
Hollimon,Michael	11	B	29	OF	a/a	MIN	450	11	7	173	9%	67%	92	108	-7
	12	B	30	3B	aaa	MIN	166	3	1	174	9%	62%	90	84	-35
Holt,Brock	11	L	23	2B	aa	PIT	511	1	14	257	7%	83%	64	107	30
	12	L	24	SS	a/a	PIT	477	2	13	308	8%	87%	65	87	42
Holt,Tyler	12	R	23	OF	aa	CLE	216	0	12	233	9%	79%	27	115	-7
Hood,Destin	12	R	22	OF	aa	WAS	355	3	5	223	5%	74%	70	96	-8
Horton,Joshua	11	L	25	3B	a/a	OAK	95	1	1	163	5%	85%	32	47	-8
	12	L	26	2B	a/a	OAK	471	6	3	221	7%	70%	78	62	-24
Howell,Jeffery	11	R	28	C	aa	BOS	38	1	0	252	2%	58%	159	77	-13
	12	R	29	C	a/a	WAS	101	0	0	177	3%	77%	22	34	-56
Hoying,Jared	12	L	23	OF	aa	TEX	247	4	7	254	6%	79%	58	109	7
Hudson,Kyle	11	L	24	OF	a/a	BAL	337	0	27	268	9%	74%	32	112	-24
	12	L	25	OF	aaa	PHI	406	0	18	229	8%	79%	14	90	-28
Huffman,Chad	11	R	26	OF	aaa	CLE	431	9	4	200	10%	71%	106	73	11
	12	R	27	OF	aaa	CLE	234	4	1	225	6%	70%	112	42	-4
Hughes,Luke	11	R	27	2B	aaa	MIN	117	3	1	185	6%	82%	81	86	31
	12	R	28	2B	a/a	TOR	235	4	2	207	8%	63%	107	89	-19
Hughes,Rhyne	11	L	28	DH	aaa	BAL	342	12	2	201	7%	61%	152	70	2
	12	L	29	1B	aa	BAL	266	10	3	218	9%	65%	134	66	10
Hulett,Tug	11	L	28	3B	aaa	WAS	346	4	5	224	8%	77%	84	64	11
	12	L	29	3B	a/a	PHI	283	3	3	227	8%	74%	60	79	-14
Hunter,Cedric	11	L	23	OF	aaa	SD	282	1	5	187	6%	90%	48	91	38
	12	L	24	OF	aaa	STL	355	3	5	220	9%	86%	54	62	26
Ibarra,Walter	12	B	25	SS	aa	NYY	156	1	2	234	2%	80%	89	79	22

BATTER	yr	b	age	pos	lvl	org	ab	hr	sb	ba	bb%	ct%	px	sx	bpv
Iglesias,Jose	11	R	21	SS	aaa	BOS	357	1	10	227	5%	83%	29	75	-11
	12	R	22	SS	aaa	BOS	353	1	10	255	6%	86%	28	89	8
Iorg,Cale	11	R	26	SS	a/a	DET	396	5	10	163	3%	70%	71	92	-29
	12	R	27	2B	aaa	DET	134	1	1	128	3%	62%	68	84	-66
Iribarren,Hernan	12	L	28	OF	aaa	COL	381	1	11	233	6%	82%	43	101	5
Ivany,Devin	11	R	29	C	aa	WAS	156	2	2	180	5%	72%	69	58	-28
	12	R	30	C	aa	WAS	156	2	1	164	4%	78%	58	76	-9
Jackson,Anthony	11	B	27	OF	aa	LA	44	1	1	209	6%	72%	28	53	-61
	12	B	28	OF	aa	LA	129	0	9	188	7%	77%	25	135	-15
Jackson,Brett	11	L	23	OF	a/a	CHC	431	14	14	229	10%	64%	130	111	15
	12	L	24	OF	aaa	CHC	407	11	19	219	8%	56%	149	142	3
Jackson,Justin	11	R	23	OF	aa	TOR	85	1	2	193	7%	66%	109	109	-1
	12	R	24	OF	aa	TOR	204	0	9	200	8%	66%	49	124	-42
Jackson,Ryan	11	R	23	SS	aa	STL	533	6	1	217	5%	80%	70	53	6
	12	R	24	SS	aaa	STL	445	7	1	223	7%	81%	63	49	4
James,Jiwan	12	B	23	OF	aa	PHI	381	5	6	217	4%	66%	70	102	-38
Jaramillo,Jason	11	B	29	C	aaa	PIT	134	1	1	212	8%	80%	55	30	-8
Jefferies,Jacob	12	L	25	C	a/a	MIA	148	1	0	184	7%	82%	48	42	-5
Jenkins,Ryan	12	R	25	C	aa	KC	129	0	0	205	3%	76%	58	20	-35
Jensen,Kyle	11	R	23	OF	aa	MIA	80	3	1	208	6%	68%	102	90	-7
	12	R	24	OF	aa	MIA	445	17	1	197	11%	59%	135	55	-17
Jeroloman,Brian	11	L	26	C	aaa	TOR	271	1	2	177	7%	67%	38	35	-74
	12	L	27	C	aa	TOR	113	0	2	158	9%	73%	0	42	-76
Jimenez,Antonio	12	R	22	C	aa	TOR	105	2	2	237	4%	85%	64	92	30
Jimenez,Luis	11	R	23	3B	aa	LAA	490	15	13	256	4%	84%	114	78	60
	11	L	29	DH	a/a	SEA	385	9	2	209	9%	74%	77	60	-4
Jimenez,Luis	12	R	24	3B	aaa	LAA	485	10	11	244	3%	83%	88	85	35
	12	L	30	DH	aaa	SEA	471	12	2	221	8%	71%	96	47	-6
Johnson,Cody	11	L	23	DH	aa	NYY	297	14	1	202	5%	49%	198	51	-17
	12	L	24	DH	aa	NYY	221	14	0	218	10%	55%	209	27	16
Johnson,Jamie	11	L	24	OF	aa	DET	534	3	11	238	10%	81%	67	89	28
	12	L	25	OF	a/a	DET	463	2	11	235	9%	88%	35	79	22
Johnson,Joshua	11	B	25	SS	aa	WAS	447	6	16	209	10%	77%	75	99	21
	12	B	26	SS	a/a	WAS	272	1	6	212	10%	85%	41	73	17
Jones,Brandon	11	L	28	OF	aa	MIL	230	3	1	189	9%	67%	84	71	-23
Jones,Corey	12	L	25	3B	aa	DET	235	2	2	207	4%	79%	69	64	0
Joseph,Caleb	11	R	25	C	aa	BAL	375	6	4	227	8%	82%	61	60	13
	12	R	26	C	a/a	BAL	347	10	2	222	7%	77%	100	56	21
Joseph,Corban	11	L	23	2B	aa	NYY	499	5	3	244	9%	77%	92	85	26
	12	L	24	2B	a/a	NYY	413	14	0	243	12%	81%	108	34	46
Joseph,Tommy	12	R	21	C	aa	PHI	404	9	0	231	6%	74%	91	18	-11
Ka aihue,Kila	11	L	27	DH	aaa	KC	323	6	1	214	10%	70%	90	27	-15
	12	L	28	DH	aaa	OAK	254	9	1	187	10%	70%	112	36	1
Kaczrowski,Daniel	11	R	24	3B	aa	ARI	181	1	1	206	4%	89%	36	48	8
	12	R	25	OF	a/a	ARI	201	1	5	182	9%	88%	26	53	9
Kahaulelio,Jacob	11	R	26	3B	aa	CIN	276	3	1	167	6%	77%	58	70	-12
Kalish,Ryan	11	L	23	OF	aaa	BOS	86	0	3	199	7%	75%	73	76	-2
	12	L	24	OF	a/a	BOS	120	3	6	237	10%	72%	98	76	10
Kang,Kyeong	11	L	23	OF	aa	TAM	316	8	4	222	11%	69%	101	93	9
	12	L	24	DH	aa	TAM	345	11	3	207	10%	55%	142	95	-17
Kazmar,Sean	11	R	27	SS	aaa	SEA	462	2	4	177	4%	81%	50	60	-9
	12	R	28	SS	a/a	NYM	224	3	0	160	4%	80%	53	60	-10
Kelly,Tyler	12	B	24	3B	a/a	BAL	208	2	2	271	9%	84%	64	69	25
Kennelly,Matt	11	R	22	C	a/a	ATL	263	2	0	232	9%	72%	53	26	-44
	12	R	23	C	aa	ATL	197	1	3	227	8%	85%	59	67	26
Kennelly,Timothy	11	R	25	C	aa	PHI	181	2	4	177	4%	72%	74	100	-14
	12	R	26	3B	a/a	PHI	236	3	2	201	3%	76%	56	69	-21
Khoury,Ryan	11	R	27	3B	a/a	BOS	262	3	4	204	10%	73%	80	105	9
Kieschnick,Roger	11	L	24	OF	aa	SF	459	12	11	224	6%	70%	107	116	13
	12	L	25	OF	aaa	SF	222	9	0	243	7%	63%	152	87	15
King,Stephen	11	R	24	3B	aa	WAS	258	4	2	165	8%	60%	85	49	-59
	12	R	25	3B	aa	WAS	124	0	1	158	3%	62%	23	82	-100
Kiniry,Rian	11	L	25	OF	a/a	LAA	143	1	6	213	6%	76%	45	83	-20
	12	L	26	OF	aa	LAA	169	1	7	118	7%	68%	48	148	-28
Kjeldgaard,Riley	11	R	25	OF	aa	MIL	203	5	1	229	6%	61%	109	60	-36
	12	R	26	OF	aa	MIL	158	6	1	197	12%	67%	130	35	9
Kleinknecht,Barrett	12	R	24	SS	aa	ATL	128	0	2	190	8%	79%	68	59	7
Kobernus,Jeff	12	R	24	2B	aa	WAS	330	1	33	247	4%	81%	32	121	-4
Komatsu,Erik	11	L	24	OF	aa	WAS	448	6	17	243	10%	84%	65	77	32
	12	L	25	OF	aaa	WAS	104	2	2	229	8%	86%	61	54	27
Kozma,Pete	11	R	23	SS	aaa	STL	398	2	1	175	6%	75%	47	61	-31
	12	R	24	2B	aaa	STL	448	7	5	189	6%	81%	55	74	6
Krauss,Marc	11	L	24	OF	aa	ARI	433	11	1	210	9%	68%	123	82	16
	12	L	25	OF	a/a	HOU	432	14	5	215	11%	68%	125	70	17
Kreke,Jordan	11	R	24	2B	aa	ATL	354	2	1	179	4%	75%	43	54	-41
	12	R	25	3B	a/a	HOU	181	1	7	166	2%	65%	50	131	-54
Kroeger,Josh	11	L	29	OF	aaa	MIA	282	6	5	202	7%	85%	73	59	34
	12	L	30	OF	aaa	ATL	334	7	2	197	7%	78%	83	39	8
Krum,Austin	11	L	25	OF	a/a	NYY	502	2	22	217	9%	77%	48	117	0
Kruml,Raymond	11	L	26	OF	a/a	NYY	491	4	31	237	6%	72%	53	135	-17
	12	L	27	OF	a/a	STL	102	1	5	158	5%	62%	47	79	-78
Kuhn,Tyler	11	L	25	3B	a/a	CHW	505	1	12	287	7%	81%	69	105	28
	12	L	26	OF	aaa	ARI	489	4	4	210	3%	81%	62	81	5
Ladendorf,Tyler	11	R	23	2B	a/a	OAK	451	4	4	182	7%	76%	53	72	-15
	12	R	24	2B	aa	OAK	416	6	5	198	7%	75%	66	71	-10
Lagares,Juan	11	R	22	OF	aa	NYM	162	2	8	302	2%	80%	79	120	25
	12	R	23	OF	aa	NYM	499	3	17	228	5%	79%	60	113	12

BATTER	yr	b	age	pos	lvl	org	ab	hr	sb	ba	bb%	ct%	px	sx	bpv
Laird,Brandon	11	R	24	3B	aaa	NYY	462	16	0	236	3%	80%	106	22	19
	12	R	25	3B	aaa	NYY	503	13	1	219	5%	77%	95	40	7
Lake,Junior	11	R	21	SS	aa	CHC	242	5	14	220	4%	73%	79	141	8
	12	R	22	SS	aa	CHC	405	8	17	255	7%	72%	101	100	13
Lalli,Blake	11	L	28	1B	aa	CHC	349	6	1	222	7%	79%	78	37	5
	12	L	29	1B	aaa	OAK	316	5	0	184	4%	77%	68	26	-21
LaMarre,Ryan	12	R	24	OF	aa	CIN	482	5	26	238	10%	72%	63	108	-9
LaPorta,Matt	12	R	27	1B	aaa	CLE	375	13	0	209	8%	74%	101	35	3
Larish,Jeff	11	L	29	1B	aaa	PHI	254	10	1	189	9%	58%	141	46	-24
	12	L	30	OF	aaa	PIT	181	1	0	142	11%	57%	94	54	-54
Lasater,Ben	11	R	27	1B	aa	MIA	348	7	0	228	6%	68%	106	39	-17
	12	R	28	1B	a/a	MIA	209	3	1	228	6%	69%	77	35	-38
Latimore,Quincy	11	R	22	OF	aa	PIT	457	12	6	214	5%	69%	122	62	4
	12	R	23	OF	aa	PIT	413	12	8	225	7%	74%	107	78	19
Lavarnway,Ryan	11	R	24	C	a/a	BOS	435	23	1	256	9%	72%	154	31	42
	12	R	25	C	aaa	BOS	319	6	1	267	9%	78%	95	42	21
Lawson,Matthew	11	R	26	2B	aa	CLE	90	1	0	225	7%	71%	76	64	-20
	12	R	27	2B	aa	CLE	196	1	6	281	9%	82%	85	89	41
Lee,Hak-Ju	11	L	21	SS	aa	TAM	100	1	4	169	8%	76%	54	145	8
	12	L	22	SS	aa	TAM	475	3	30	233	8%	76%	55	147	10
Lehmann,Daniel	11	R	26	C	a/a	MIN	192	1	0	189	6%	82%	55	34	-5
	12	R	27	C	a/a	MIN	135	0	0	152	12%	76%	47	28	-22
LeMahieu,DJ	11	R	23	3B	a/a	CHC	414	4	6	269	4%	86%	57	69	22
	12	R	24	2B	aaa	COL	255	1	8	265	5%	88%	49	79	26
Lemmerman,Jacob	11	R	22	SS	aa	LA	77	1	1	198	7%	69%	111	54	-5
	12	R	23	SS	aa	LA	373	6	6	203	10%	72%	99	90	16
Lennerton,Jordan	12	L	26	1B	aa	DET	495	15	2	223	10%	68%	122	39	3
Leon,Sandy	12	B	23	C	a/a	WAS	187	2	1	288	8%	84%	92	34	37
Leonard,Joe	12	R	24	3B	aa	ATL	426	7	5	231	9%	76%	76	77	7
Lerud,Steven	11	L	27	C	aa	BAL	228	4	0	163	6%	56%	88	50	-75
	12	L	28	C	aa	PHI	102	0	0	183	8%	57%	70	22	-91
Liberto,Michael	12	R	24	3B	aa	KC	101	0	2	207	8%	69%	18	59	-74
Liddi,Alex	11	R	23	3B	aaa	SEA	559	18	3	198	7%	63%	123	84	-9
	12	R	24	3B	aaa	SEA	296	7	6	215	6%	69%	100	79	-7
Liles,Nicholas	12	R	25	OF	aa	SF	259	0	5	229	7%	81%	22	83	-17
Limonta,Johan	11	L	28	OF	a/a	SEA	423	9	2	227	7%	74%	75	39	-16
	12	L	29	OF	aaa	SEA	147	2	1	199	4%	73%	64	53	-30
Lin,Che-Hsuan	11	R	23	OF	a/a	BOS	466	1	22	222	9%	85%	40	110	24
	12	R	24	OF	aaa	BOS	396	2	12	228	8%	82%	40	101	8
Linares,Donell	11	R	28	3B	aa	ATL	412	5	0	213	6%	86%	47	30	6
Linares,J.C.	11	R	27	OF	aaa	BOS	60	2	0	203	5%	77%	155	89	69
	12	R	28	OF	a/a	BOS	412	11	0	267	5%	81%	104	39	30
Linares,Juan Carlos	11	R	27	OF	aaa	BOS	60	2	0	203	5%	77%	155	89	69
Lind,Adam	12	L	29	1B	a/a	TOR	136	6	1	315	8%	71%	145	32	26
Linton,Ollie	11	L	25	OF	aa	ARI	334	2	14	240	8%	73%	47	113	-18
Lipkin,Ryan	12	R	25	C	a/a	OAK	202	3	1	152	2%	75%	56	38	-39
Liriano,Rymer	12	R	21	OF	aa	SD	183	2	8	214	8%	69%	80	119	-7
Lisson,Mario	11	R	27	3B	aa	KC	283	9	10	230	7%	66%	133	95	15
	12	R	28	1B	aa	KC	376	7	14	196	8%	74%	87	92	10
Locke,Andrew	11	R	28	OF	aaa	HOU	375	8	6	203	6%	77%	92	68	15
	12	R	29	OF	aa	HOU	261	5	1	221	5%	76%	81	47	-6
Loewen,Adam	11	L	27	OF	aaa	TOR	520	10	6	227	6%	66%	123	68	-1
	12	L	28	1B	aaa	NYM	207	6	3	162	9%	67%	86	64	-22
Lollis,Ryan	12	L	26	OF	a/a	SF	175	2	1	242	8%	82%	59	65	12
Loman,Seth	11	L	26	DH	aa	CHW	427	17	4	234	8%	65%	137	45	2
	12	L	27	DH	a/a	CHW	424	14	0	230	8%	72%	104	39	2
Long,Matt	11	L	24	OF	aa	LAA	71	2	7	243	8%	84%	99	151	79
	12	L	25	2B	a/a	LAA	444	9	17	229	7%	76%	88	120	28
Lopez,Roberto	11	R	26	OF	a/a	LAA	361	8	1	207	6%	80%	102	34	26
	12	R	27	OF	aa	LAA	524	13	4	213	6%	84%	86	46	32
Lough,David	11	L	25	OF	aaa	KC	456	6	10	269	5%	88%	79	122	64
	12	L	26	OF	aaa	KC	491	6	17	225	3%	85%	61	138	38
Lozada,Jose	12	B	27	SS	aa	WAS	286	4	1	198	6%	77%	54	53	-18
Lucas,Edward	11	R	29	SS	a/a	ATL	421	7	3	180	7%	65%	76	70	-42
	12	R	30	SS	aaa	LAA	412	7	3	181	4%	74%	63	61	-27
Luna,Aaron	11	R	24	OF	a/a	STL	255	6	3	205	8%	72%	79	70	-9
Luna,Omar	11	R	25	2B	aaa	TAM	172	0	1	167	1%	85%	17	54	-26
	12	R	26	3B	aa	TAM	470	2	14	259	6%	89%	39	91	28
Lutz,Donald	12	L	23	OF	aa	CIN	149	5	1	224	7%	76%	88	57	8
Lutz,Zach	11	R	25	3B	aaa	NYM	220	8	0	231	8%	63%	131	32	-15
	12	R	26	3B	aaa	NYM	244	7	0	227	11%	63%	118	33	-18
Lyerly,Robert	11	L	24	1B	aa	NYY	272	4	2	213	4%	62%	93	73	-47
Machado,Manny	12	R	20	SS	aa	BAL	402	10	11	249	9%	82%	99	102	57
Macri,Matthew	11	R	29	3B	aaa	COL	374	7	0	190	4%	76%	83	48	-6
Maggi,Andrew	12	R	23	SS	aa	PIT	179	0	4	196	7%	76%	27	113	-22
Mahoney,Joseph	11	L	24	1B	aa	BAL	315	10	6	263	6%	71%	147	104	46
	12	L	25	1B	aaa	BAL	491	9	3	238	5%	78%	80	51	6
Mahoney,Kevin	12	L	25	3B	aa	NYY	318	10	3	213	8%	74%	97	78	14
Mahtook,Mikie	12	R	23	OF	aa	TAM	153	3	3	215	5%	77%	92	79	18
Maier,Mitch	12	L	30	OF	aaa	KC	132	2	1	214	9%	71%	59	76	-27
Maldonado,Brahiam	11	R	26	OF	aa	NYM	477	19	6	163	5%	64%	118	90	-10
	12	R	27	OF	aa	LA	243	5	3	198	4%	74%	79	84	-5
Maldonado,Martin	11	R	25	C	a/a	MIL	342	8	1	236	7%	73%	92	38	-8
	12	R	26	C	aaa	MIL	121	3	0	167	5%	63%	103	27	-44
Malo,Jonathan	11	R	28	3B	a/a	NYM	235	2	1	159	5%	73%	42	87	-37
Mangini,Matt	11	L	26	1B	aaa	SEA	232	1	2	247	6%	74%	40	54	-41
	12	L	27	3B	a/a	ARI	341	3	1	217	6%	68%	70	29	-50
Manriquez,Salomon	11	R	29	C	a/a	NYM	265	4	1	188	4%	80%	66	35	-6

BATTER	yr	b	age	pos	lvl	org	ab	hr	sb	ba	bb%	ct%	px	sx	bpv
Manzella,Tommy	11	R	28	SS	aaa	ARI	422	4	6	164	5%	63%	62	82	-63
Marisnick,Jake	12	R	21	OF	aa	TOR	223	2	12	218	4%	78%	69	134	17
Marrero,Chris	11	R	23	1B	aaa	WAS	483	11	2	267	8%	78%	95	34	18
	12	R	24	1B	a/a	WAS	149	1	0	216	7%	77%	58	41	-16
Marrero,Christian	11	L	25	1B	aa	CHW	420	11	8	254	11%	80%	103	102	59
	12	L	26	1B	a/a	PIT	259	5	5	202	11%	76%	84	63	12
Marte,Alfredo	11	R	22	OF	aa	ARI	43	1	1	205	6%	75%	53	39	-32
	12	R	23	OF	aa	ARI	398	16	5	269	6%	80%	125	77	58
Marte,Andy	11	R	28	3B	aaa	PIT	287	5	1	157	6%	76%	70	49	-12
Marte,Jefry	12	R	21	3B	aa	NYM	462	7	7	208	7%	82%	59	86	18
Marte,Starling	11	R	23	OF	aa	PIT	536	9	19	297	3%	80%	100	122	46
	12	R	24	OF	aaa	PIT	388	9	17	256	5%	75%	113	139	46
Martin,Dustin	11	L	27	OF	aaa	MIN	490	10	7	214	7%	74%	89	78	6
	12	L	28	OF	a/a	NYM	315	5	8	203	8%	69%	83	110	-5
Martin,Leonys	11	L	23	OF	a/a	TEX	287	3	13	259	6%	88%	67	110	53
	12	L	24	OF	aaa	TEX	231	10	7	314	7%	81%	132	86	72
Martinez,Fernando	11	L	23	OF	aaa	NYM	223	6	0	210	6%	70%	96	29	-20
	12	L	24	OF	aaa	HOU	341	9	1	255	4%	70%	108	53	-6
Martinez,Francisco	11	R	21	3B	aa	SEA	477	8	8	256	4%	75%	79	111	6
	12	R	22	3B	aa	SEA	352	2	25	207	10%	73%	52	121	-9
Martinez,Jose	11	R	23	OF	aa	CHW	200	1	4	265	6%	86%	63	68	28
	12	R	24	OF	aa	CHW	436	4	5	212	7%	76%	46	58	-23
Martinez,Jose	12	R	26	2B	a/a	HOU	498	9	3	226	5%	88%	60	75	34
Martinez,Jose Gregorio	12	R	26	2B	a/a	HOU	498	9	3	226	5%	88%	60	75	34
Martinez,Luis	11	R	26	C	aaa	SD	198	1	1	226	5%	69%	74	55	-37
	12	R	27	C	aaa	TEX	215	1	0	217	7%	76%	73	46	-9
Martinez,Michael	12	B	30	SS	aaa	PHI	107	2	2	214	6%	86%	57	89	30
Martinez,Osvaldo	11	R	23	SS	aaa	MIA	339	2	7	199	4%	81%	44	84	-5
	12	R	24	SS	aaa	LA	316	0	2	153	3%	82%	28	49	-25
Maruszak,Addison	11	R	25	1B	a/a	NYY	352	6	2	209	11%	77%	88	43	14
	12	R	26	SS	aa	NYY	416	14	4	233	6%	78%	101	47	21
Mastroianni,Darin	11	R	26	OF	a/a	TOR	488	2	22	215	8%	80%	62	137	30
	12	R	27	OF	a/a	MIN	113	0	11	236	6%	74%	36	144	-20
Matthes,Kent	12	R	25	OF	aa	COL	336	16	5	203	5%	75%	135	89	47
Mattison,Kevin	11	L	26	OF	aa	MIA	503	5	25	208	8%	70%	71	143	-4
	12	L	27	OF	aaa	MIA	482	8	19	190	6%	63%	87	127	-24
Matulia,John	11	L	25	OF	a/a	TAM	321	9	2	194	5%	71%	93	85	-3
May,Lucas	11	R	27	C	aaa	ARI	248	5	1	171	6%	68%	95	57	-20
	12	R	28	C	aaa	NYM	256	2	1	151	3%	65%	81	86	-44
Mayora,Daniel	11	R	26	3B	a/a	TAM	459	6	6	232	6%	78%	80	99	19
	12	R	27	3B	aa	SF	495	3	11	238	6%	81%	50	61	-3
Mayorson,Manuel	11	R	28	2B	aaa	TOR	335	2	9	226	5%	90%	40	73	26
	12	R	29	3B	a/a	WAS	163	0	0	186	2%	93%	18	49	4
McBride,Matt	11	R	26	1B	a/a	COL	372	9	2	219	5%	83%	99	68	44
	12	R	27	OF	aaa	COL	439	7	0	275	2%	88%	95	57	50
McCann,James	12	R	22	C	aa	DET	220	2	2	179	3%	79%	56	43	-18
McClure,Alex	12	R	23	SS	aa	KC	193	1	5	190	3%	67%	43	92	-62
Mcconnell,Christopher	11	R	26	SS	a/a	WAS	358	2	5	162	5%	75%	59	75	-19
	12	R	27	SS	a/a	WAS	141	0	1	144	4%	70%	41	73	-54
McDade,Michael	11	B	22	1B	aa	TOR	484	14	0	260	5%	76%	125	34	26
	12	B	23	1B	a/a	TOR	449	14	1	248	8%	76%	89	35	1
McElroy,Brad	12	L	26	OF	aa	TOR	148	1	8	163	4%	71%	22	78	-64
McGuiness,Christopher	12	L	24	1B	aa	TEX	456	20	0	242	11%	75%	124	17	27
McOwen,James	11	L	26	OF	aa	SEA	257	3	7	209	5%	76%	57	87	-13
Means,Andrew	12	R	26	OF	aa	CIN	156	3	3	211	8%	78%	53	78	-4
Mejia,Ernesto	11	R	26	1B	aa	ATL	499	18	3	236	8%	61%	153	52	0
	12	R	27	1B	aaa	ATL	514	17	7	234	5%	67%	114	62	-9
Melker,Adam	12	L	24	OF	aa	STL	352	7	4	231	7%	76%	65	64	-9
Mendonca,Thomas	11	L	23	3B	aa	TEX	504	21	0	251	5%	66%	147	49	9
	12	L	24	3B	a/a	TEX	332	10	0	200	4%	61%	95	24	-64
Meneses,Heiker	11	R	20	SS	aa	BOS	83	0	2	246	3%	68%	42	74	-63
	12	R	21	2B	a/a	BOS	127	1	1	187	8%	73%	26	66	-50
Mercado,Orlando	11	R	26	C	a/a	LAA	219	3	1	208	6%	80%	57	24	-13
Mercer,Jordy	11	R	25	SS	a/a	PIT	491	14	7	214	5%	83%	96	81	44
	12	R	26	SS	aaa	PIT	209	3	2	245	7%	76%	83	63	6
Mertins,Kurt	11	R	25	3B	a/a	KC	235	2	3	215	7%	73%	63	78	-19
	12	R	26	3B	a/a	KC	131	1	1	185	4%	84%	31	64	-13
Mesa,Melky	11	R	24	OF	aa	NYY	386	8	14	218	7%	63%	117	110	-7
	12	R	25	OF	a/a	NYY	458	20	17	229	6%	71%	131	109	34
Miclat,Gregory	11	B	24	2B	aa	BAL	421	2	42	254	10%	75%	48	146	5
	12	B	25	SS	aaa	TEX	109	1	4	230	7%	71%	92	76	-3
Milledge,Lastings	11	R	26	OF	aaa	CHW	444	11	21	250	8%	83%	84	98	44
Miller,Bradley	12	L	23	SS	aa	SEA	147	3	4	289	12%	79%	85	90	39
Miller,Jai	11	R	26	OF	aaa	OAK	410	19	10	210	8%	46%	224	130	19
	12	R	27	OF	a/a	BAL	312	10	4	164	10%	41%	173	64	-59
Milligan,Adam	12	L	24	OF	aa	ATL	102	1	0	153	6%	57%	71	5	-99
Mills,Beau	11	L	25	1B	a/a	CLE	349	13	0	245	7%	80%	118	33	41
	12	L	26	1B	a/a	CIN	333	14	2	207	6%	74%	120	38	18
Minicozzi,Mark	12	R	29	1B	aa	SF	282	6	1	229	8%	71%	93	32	-13
Miranda,Juan	11	L	28	1B	aa	ARI	105	3	0	161	8%	57%	103	62	-52
	12	L	29	1B	aaa	TAM	150	1	1	140	10%	64%	58	49	-62
Miranda,Sergio	11	B	24	2B	aa	MIL	356	0	1	232	6%	86%	39	53	7
Mitchell,Derrick	11	R	24	OF	aa	PHI	476	14	15	223	6%	73%	103	87	15
	12	R	25	OF	aaa	PHI	238	6	7	190	6%	74%	82	67	-3
Mitchell,Jared	12	L	24	OF	a/a	CHW	455	10	17	210	13%	54%	142	127	-4
Mitchell,Jermaine	11	L	27	OF	a/a	OAK	536	9	18	256	10%	73%	96	119	28
	12	L	28	OF	aaa	OAK	409	3	10	189	8%	67%	65	126	-23

BATTER	yr	b	age	pos	lvl	org	ab	hr	sb	ba	bb%	ct%	px	sx	bpv
Mitchell,Michael	11	R	26	OF	aa	COL	224	2	10	179	6%	74%	60	118	-5
	12	R	27	OF	aa	COL	462	4	17	212	3%	77%	47	101	-14
Mitchell,Russ	11	R	26	3B	aaa	LA	336	9	1	202	7%	77%	94	50	14
	12	R	27	1B	aa	SF	220	1	0	161	12%	67%	68	30	-43
Mittelstaedt,Tom	12	L	24	3B	aa	MIL	122	3	2	164	14%	65%	110	55	-6
Molina,Gustavo	11	R	29	C	aaa	NYY	162	4	0	206	3%	72%	71	2	-47
	12	R	30	C	a/a	NYY	132	5	0	154	3%	71%	100	13	-26
Monell,Johnny	11	L	25	C	aa	SF	385	7	0	214	9%	72%	96	33	-6
	12	L	26	C	aa	SF	323	8	2	221	9%	69%	128	51	16
Montz,Luke	11	R	28	C	aa	MIA	395	13	5	203	11%	70%	119	63	17
	12	R	29	1B	aaa	MIA	370	18	1	163	8%	65%	125	31	-12
Moore,Adam	12	R	28	C	aaa	KC	201	3	1	197	6%	77%	75	48	-3
Moore,Jeremy	11	L	24	OF	aaa	LAA	426	10	14	233	3%	68%	116	137	15
Moore,Scott	11	L	28	3B	aaa	CHC	363	5	2	216	7%	72%	74	68	-16
	12	L	29	3B	aaa	HOU	245	6	2	232	8%	72%	125	55	23
Moore,Tyler	11	R	24	1B	aa	WAS	519	25	2	237	4%	71%	162	67	43
	12	R	25	1B	aaa	WAS	101	7	1	263	8%	71%	183	57	65
Morales,Jose	12	B	29	C	aaa	PIT	158	1	0	212	10%	74%	42	30	-40
Morel,Brent	12	R	25	3B	aaa	CHW	124	1	0	170	6%	73%	42	31	-51
Morris,Hunter	12	L	24	1B	aa	MIL	522	24	2	268	6%	74%	154	65	52
Morrison,Christopher	12	L	22	OF	aa	TAM	405	2	16	241	7%	76%	59	133	5
Morrison,Erik	12	R	27	3B	aa	CHW	295	5	1	219	5%	76%	60	47	-23
Mount,Ryan	11	L	25	2B	aa	LAA	161	4	7	281	9%	72%	116	102	29
	12	L	26	OF	aa	LAA	254	4	2	200	6%	74%	72	55	-18
Mujica,Yadil	11	L	26	SS	aa	NYY	172	1	2	193	6%	85%	25	59	-8
	12	L	27	SS	a/a	NYY	226	1	1	199	6%	84%	33	46	-12
Muren,Andrew	12	L	24	OF	aa	HOU	110	1	4	244	5%	81%	64	117	21
Murphy,John	12	R	21	C	aa	NYY	147	4	0	212	8%	77%	115	55	35
Murton,Luke	12	R	26	1B	aa	NYY	466	22	0	211	7%	70%	124	29	4
Mustelier,Ronnier	12	R	28	OF	a/a	NYY	449	13	7	255	5%	81%	89	71	31
Myers,D'Arby	12	R	24	OF	aa	PHI	121	2	5	262	4%	81%	63	88	9
Myers,Wil	11	R	21	OF	aa	KC	354	5	7	225	10%	74%	90	75	14
	12	R	22	OF	a/a	KC	522	25	5	279	8%	72%	143	90	46
Navarro Jr,Efren	11	L	25	1B	aaa	LAA	492	8	3	245	5%	81%	83	63	21
	12	L	26	1B	aaa	LAA	528	4	2	222	4%	84%	56	51	5
Navarro,Oswaldo	11	R	27	3B	aaa	HOU	315	1	2	209	8%	82%	40	41	-10
	12	R	28	SS	a/a	NYM	175	2	0	177	6%	73%	48	42	-41
Navarro,Reynaldo	11	B	22	3B	aa	KC	188	1	4	239	5%	85%	40	68	6
	12	B	23	2B	a/a	KC	460	3	7	224	6%	89%	40	82	25
Navarro,Yamaico	11	R	24	SS	aaa	KC	220	4	4	224	7%	79%	88	102	32
	12	R	25	3B	aaa	PIT	222	7	7	243	10%	80%	109	112	63
Neal,Thomas	11	R	24	OF	aaa	CLE	256	1	6	247	4%	75%	68	101	-7
	12	R	25	OF	aa	CLE	405	10	11	281	9%	80%	91	85	38
Negron,Kristopher	11	R	25	SS	aaa	CIN	417	7	8	178	4%	71%	72	112	-15
	12	R	26	OF	aaa	CIN	284	5	12	179	5%	67%	79	112	-21
Negrych,James	11	L	26	2B	aa	MIA	398	3	8	241	8%	84%	53	63	15
	12	L	27	2B	a/a	WAS	281	6	1	221	10%	83%	63	34	14
Nelson,Daniel	11	B	27	3B	a/a	ATL	321	4	1	226	7%	80%	58	62	0
Nick,David	12	R	22	2B	aa	ARI	458	4	10	231	5%	80%	62	85	7
Nicol,Sean	12	R	26	3B	aa	WAS	242	2	2	215	5%	74%	60	71	-22
Nina,Angelys	12	R	24	2B	aa	COL	412	6	8	258	5%	83%	65	78	21
Nommensen,Brett	12	L	26	OF	aa	TAM	157	2	1	206	11%	74%	74	40	-8
Noonan,Nick	11	L	22	SS	a/a	SF	297	3	2	190	8%	77%	48	45	-22
	12	L	23	SS	aaa	SF	490	6	5	246	5%	80%	63	66	3
Noriega,Gabriel	11	B	21	SS	aa	SEA	93	0	1	208	3%	76%	38	48	-46
	12	B	22	SS	aa	SEA	269	0	2	190	6%	74%	13	48	-66
Norris,Derek	11	R	22	C	aa	WAS	334	17	11	190	15%	63%	164	105	49
	12	R	23	C	aaa	OAK	218	6	4	223	7%	78%	100	96	37
Nunez,Eduardo	12	R	25	SS	aaa	NYY	163	2	12	195	3%	80%	36	105	-9
Nunez,Luis	11	R	25	2B	aaa	NYY	256	2	2	206	4%	85%	54	59	13
	12	R	26	2B	aa	LA	405	8	16	211	7%	84%	78	111	48
Ochinko,Sean	12	R	25	C	aa	TOR	216	7	0	229	3%	78%	96	39	9
Oeltjen,Trent	11	L	28	OF	aaa	LA	180	4	4	235	7%	63%	124	85	-7
	12	L	29	OF	aaa	LA	402	7	8	202	4%	65%	86	100	-30
Oester,Jake	11	R	25	3B	aa	CHW	167	1	1	184	7%	64%	72	29	-60
	12	R	26	3B	aa	CHW	124	0	0	170	10%	64%	60	24	-65
Olt,Mike	12	R	24	3B	aa	TEX	354	25	3	262	12%	69%	176	61	62
O'Malley,Shawn	11	B	24	2B	aa	TAM	308	1	18	230	9%	78%	37	130	0
	12	B	25	SS	a/a	TAM	337	1	14	201	7%	74%	36	137	-16
Orlando,Paulo	11	R	26	OF	a/a	KC	354	3	9	224	4%	79%	76	127	26
	12	R	27	OF	aa	KC	420	4	15	228	5%	84%	48	94	15
Orloff,Ben	12	R	25	SS	aa	HOU	122	0	2	241	4%	94%	31	78	35
Ortiz,Ryan	11	R	24	C	aa	OAK	152	1	1	189	9%	69%	40	48	-58
	12	R	25	C	aa	OAK	144	1	0	134	10%	67%	53	60	-49
Osuna,Renny	11	R	26	SS	aa	TEX	520	8	14	248	5%	86%	60	78	28
	12	R	27	2B	aa	LAA	476	2	15	214	6%	87%	43	93	23
Overbeck,Cody	11	R	25	1B	a/a	PHI	459	19	1	234	5%	68%	117	31	-13
	12	R	26	1B	aaa	PHI	458	11	0	212	6%	71%	101	41	-9
Owings,Christopher	12	R	21	SS	aa	ARI	297	5	3	247	3%	75%	70	87	-9
Ozga,Travis	11	B	25	3B	aa	NYM	34	0	0	151	4%	83%	0	-10	-61
	12	B	26	1B	aa	NYM	139	3	1	129	7%	75%	55	54	-23
Padron,Jorge	11	L	25	1B	aa	BOS	243	3	1	207	6%	90%	45	40	21
Padron,Raul	11	L	27	1B	aa	CLE	200	2	1	185	6%	71%	80	63	-21
Pagnozzi,Matt	11	R	29	C	aaa	COL	178	2	0	191	4%	72%	78	57	-22
	12	R	30	C	aaa	CLE	245	4	0	167	8%	63%	80	19	-61
Pahuta,Tim	11	L	28	3B	aa	WAS	246	11	1	209	5%	64%	141	42	-8
	12	L	29	1B	aa	WAS	421	11	1	177	6%	69%	99	67	-9

BATTER	yr	b	age	pos	lvl	org	ab	hr	sb	ba	bb%	ct%	px	sx	bpv
Paiml,Gregory	12	R	28	SS	a/a	CHW	246	0	4	165	6%	61%	42	85	-83
Paredes,Jimmy	11	B	23	2B	aa	HOU	385	7	20	228	3%	75%	91	134	20
	12	B	24	2B	aaa	HOU	507	9	24	259	3%	76%	81	125	14
Parker,Stephen	11	L	24	3B	a/a	OAK	529	6	1	232	9%	75%	72	42	-12
	12	L	25	3B	aaa	OAK	328	4	3	204	6%	66%	73	95	-35
Parmelee,Chris	11	L	23	1B	aa	MIN	530	8	0	245	9%	80%	80	50	19
	12	L	24	1B	aaa	MIN	228	13	1	299	16%	74%	165	47	77
Parraz,Jordan	11	R	27	OF	aaa	NYY	443	8	4	245	7%	76%	95	82	20
	12	R	28	OF	aaa	ATL	142	1	4	217	7%	71%	62	84	-24
Parrino,Andy	11	B	26	SS	a/a	SD	305	7	3	229	8%	72%	96	73	4
	12	B	27	SS	aaa	SD	235	1	3	240	7%	72%	84	93	-1
Pastornicky,Tyler	11	R	22	SS	a/a	ATL	459	6	22	281	5%	89%	50	107	40
	12	R	23	SS	aaa	ATL	153	1	2	229	5%	84%	83	65	35
Patterson,Eric	11	L	28	OF	aaa	SD	190	1	2	167	3%	79%	63	104	6
	12	L	29	OF	aaa	DET	221	1	9	192	11%	68%	42	95	-40
Patterson,Ryan	12	R	29	OF	aa	MIA	168	2	2	185	4%	81%	65	67	7
Paul,Xavier	12	L	27	OF	aaa	CIN	238	7	6	270	6%	76%	111	76	28
Paulk,Michael	11	L	27	OF	aaa	COL	288	3	0	240	5%	81%	71	47	7
Paulsen,Benjamin	11	L	24	1B	aa	COL	547	14	1	212	5%	74%	102	56	7
	12	L	25	1B	aa	COL	436	12	1	238	6%	73%	95	55	-2
Peacock,Brian	12	R	28	C	a/a	CIN	148	2	0	207	5%	63%	66	29	-76
Pearce,Steve	11	R	28	3B	aaa	PIT	30	2	0	206	0%	65%	199	35	31
	12	R	29	1B	aaa	NYY	192	9	2	254	10%	78%	132	50	56
Pedroza,Jaime	11	B	25	2B	aa	LA	268	4	6	199	9%	67%	93	75	-16
	12	B	26	SS	aa	ATL	109	3	1	160	7%	61%	112	65	-29
Peguero,Carlos	11	L	24	OF	aaa	SEA	240	8	5	241	4%	57%	143	102	-18
	12	L	25	OF	aaa	SEA	281	14	1	223	7%	54%	161	53	-24
Peguero,Francisco	11	R	23	OF	aa	SF	285	4	7	280	1%	82%	75	120	30
	12	R	24	OF	aaa	SF	449	3	1	222	2%	79%	59	77	-9
Pena,Francisco	12	R	23	C	aa	NYM	126	2	1	157	9%	78%	70	44	2
Pena,Ramiro	11	B	26	SS	a/a	NYY	216	4	2	236	7%	81%	74	60	15
	12	B	27	SS	aaa	NYY	360	2	1	212	7%	75%	41	50	-35
Perales,Daniel	11	L	26	OF	a/a	TOR	293	4	5	212	4%	82%	69	87	19
	12	L	27	OF	aaa	TOR	262	4	3	215	3%	80%	78	76	15
Perez,Audry	11	R	23	C	aa	STL	230	5	0	202	1%	86%	76	26	16
	12	R	24	C	aa	STL	312	3	0	218	1%	79%	45	32	-34
Perez,Darwin	11	B	22	SS	aa	LAA	424	2	20	231	12%	74%	49	116	-3
	12	B	23	SS	aa	LAA	407	5	13	192	9%	74%	57	99	-11
Perez,Eury	12	R	22	OF	a/a	WAS	510	0	38	283	2%	84%	32	107	-2
Perez,Felix	11	L	27	OF	a/a	CIN	361	3	5	194	3%	81%	51	86	-1
	12	L	28	OF	aaa	CIN	392	3	4	237	4%	80%	59	48	-10
Perez,Fernando	11	B	28	OF	aaa	NYM	364	3	16	159	8%	66%	52	133	-35
Perez,Juan	11	R	25	OF	aa	SF	457	3	18	223	5%	76%	78	144	20
	12	R	26	OF	aa	SF	483	8	15	262	4%	79%	78	96	17
Perez,Nelson	11	L	24	OF	aa	CHC	237	6	1	209	6%	58%	139	53	-27
	12	L	25	OF	aa	CHC	127	4	1	176	7%	68%	112	90	7
Perez,Roberto	12	R	24	C	aa	CLE	283	1	0	193	13%	74%	63	46	-12
Perez,Rossmel	12	L	23	C	aa	ARI	263	0	3	244	9%	92%	29	42	25
Perez,Yordanys	12	B	28	OF	a/a	CIN	195	3	0	173	3%	74%	59	37	-37
Pertusati,Daniel	12	R	22	OF	aa	MIA	120	3	1	269	9%	80%	91	86	37
Petersen,Bryan	11	L	25	OF	aaa	MIA	248	7	4	277	9%	80%	108	50	41
	12	L	26	OF	aaa	MIA	243	2	6	264	6%	79%	43	89	-10
Peterson,Shane	11	L	23	OF	a/a	OAK	394	6	9	226	9%	78%	80	102	26
	12	L	24	OF	a/a	OAK	288	6	9	271	15%	68%	107	107	20
Petit,Gregorio	12	R	28	SS	aaa	CLE	377	7	1	202	5%	75%	79	38	-12
Pettit,Chris	11	R	27	OF	a/a	LAA	455	7	12	137	7%	67%	72	104	-28
	12	R	28	OF	a/a	COL	291	5	5	232	6%	67%	111	101	1
Phegley,Joshua	11	R	23	C	a/a	CHW	443	9	1	217	6%	80%	84	50	14
	12	R	24	C	aaa	CHW	394	6	3	242	5%	82%	70	60	14
Phelps,Cord	11	B	24	2B	aaa	CLE	378	10	2	251	9%	73%	118	56	24
	12	B	25	2B	aaa	CLE	503	11	7	230	9%	78%	94	74	31
Phillips,Patrick	12	B	26	OF	a/a	CIN	186	2	4	161	4%	68%	55	56	-57
Phipps,Denis	11	R	26	OF	a/a	CIN	463	9	9	278	6%	67%	116	99	2
	12	R	27	OF	aaa	CIN	357	12	3	178	6%	65%	111	52	-23
Pie,Felix	11	L	26	OF	aaa	BAL	24	0	2	210	8%	81%	92	178	69
	12	L	27	OF	aaa	ATL	333	4	11	226	5%	83%	85	126	47
Pill,Brett	11	R	27	1B	aaa	SF	536	14	4	231	3%	87%	87	58	43
	12	R	28	1B	aaa	SF	246	6	0	211	3%	81%	92	36	17
Pina,Manny	11	R	24	C	a/a	KC	218	3	0	199	10%	80%	77	30	13
	12	R	25	C	aa	KC	131	3	0	218	12%	80%	58	0	-9
Pirela,Jose	11	R	22	SS	aa	NYY	468	7	7	216	4%	80%	70	78	9
	12	R	23	2B	aa	NYY	317	7	7	263	6%	83%	86	96	45
Plagman,Tony	12	L	25	OF	aa	DET	393	10	8	194	5%	72%	108	90	15
Pollock IV,A.J.	11	R	24	OF	aa	ARI	550	6	25	266	5%	82%	87	126	49
	12	R	25	OF	aaa	ARI	428	2	12	252	4%	86%	52	88	21
Pounds,Bryan	11	R	26	3B	a/a	DET	427	7	2	231	8%	70%	96	46	-12
	12	R	27	3B	a/a	DET	207	5	2	155	6%	73%	77	96	-3
Powell,Landon	11	B	29	C	aaa	OAK	46	1	0	203	9%	74%	22	20	-61
	12	B	30	C	aaa	HOU	239	5	0	178	8%	69%	56	22	-56
Poythress,Richard	11	R	24	1B	aa	SEA	450	8	2	223	8%	78%	86	50	14
	12	R	25	1B	aa	SEA	303	5	3	262	13%	87%	75	56	51
Prades,Yem	12	R	24	OF	aa	KC	495	5	11	235	2%	75%	76	106	-2
Presley,Alex	11	L	26	OF	aaa	PIT	342	6	16	277	6%	82%	77	115	38
	12	L	27	OF	aaa	PIT	153	4	5	257	11%	81%	69	115	36
Pridie,Jason	11	L	28	OF	aaa	NYM	59	2	1	135	3%	75%	75	72	-8
	12	L	29	OF	aaa	PHI	178	4	3	239	6%	73%	81	86	-3
Prince,Jared	12	R	26	OF	aa	TEX	385	10	0	201	4%	84%	67	26	8
Prince,Joshua	12	R	24	OF	aa	MIL	505	6	32	220	11%	75%	72	108	14

BATTER	yr	b	age	pos	lvl	org	ab	hr	sb	ba	bb%	ct%	px	sx	bpv
Profar,Jurickson	12	B	19	SS	aa	TEX	480	14	14	279	11%	84%	102	112	74
Puckett,Cody	11	R	24	2B	aa	CIN	339	11	7	199	5%	72%	130	72	27
	12	R	25	OF	a/a	CIN	433	14	7	202	8%	68%	97	81	-9
Rahl,Christopher	11	R	28	OF	aa	WAS	429	4	18	226	4%	72%	81	140	4
	12	R	29	OF	aa	WAS	330	9	19	229	4%	69%	99	125	1
Ramirez,Carlos	12	R	24	C	aa	LAA	275	2	3	179	9%	78%	47	72	-10
Ramirez,Max	11	R	27	C	aaa	SF	266	7	0	204	4%	72%	96	33	-13
Ramirez,Wilkin	11	R	26	OF	aaa	ATL	288	8	15	223	4%	70%	113	124	20
	12	R	27	OF	a/a	MIN	419	13	7	237	4%	69%	108	82	-2
Rapoport,James	11	L	26	OF	a/a	STL	402	2	4	181	10%	86%	19	54	-5
Recker,Anthony	11	R	28	C	aaa	OAK	345	9	4	210	9%	69%	111	61	6
	12	R	29	C	a/a	CHC	222	7	2	201	8%	63%	98	43	-39
Retherford,Chris	11	R	26	3B	aa	DET	128	1	0	165	5%	82%	56	14	-10
	12	R	27	3B	aa	LA	148	2	1	200	5%	84%	58	67	12
Reyes,Raul	11	L	25	OF	a/a	NYM	422	10	4	213	4%	69%	102	80	-8
	12	L	26	OF	a/a	NYM	302	5	1	190	8%	66%	62	54	-54
Rhinehart,William	11	L	27	OF	a/a	CIN	391	19	1	217	8%	71%	139	51	30
	12	L	28	OF	a/a	CIN	312	7	1	183	7%	71%	84	40	-22
Rhymes,Will	11	L	28	2B	aaa	DET	405	2	10	251	8%	87%	46	87	26
	12	L	29	2B	aaa	TAM	172	3	1	197	7%	86%	53	73	23
Richardson,Antoan	11	B	28	OF	a/a	ATL	275	1	12	222	14%	69%	33	91	-42
	12	B	29	OF	a/a	BAL	315	1	20	216	13%	74%	22	132	-17
Ridling,Rebel	11	R	25	1B	aa	CHC	433	14	4	256	7%	76%	114	55	26
	12	R	26	OF	aa	CHC	226	6	1	159	9%	72%	77	54	-17
Rike,Brian	11	L	26	OF	aa	COL	250	9	1	211	6%	57%	155	27	-28
Rincon,Edinson	12	R	22	3B	aa	SD	494	7	1	246	4%	81%	68	19	-5
Rivera,Rene	11	R	28	C	aaa	MIN	149	3	0	211	5%	78%	100	16	8
	12	R	29	C	aaa	MIN	288	7	0	178	7%	73%	81	34	-15
Rivero,Carlos	11	R	23	3B	a/a	PHI	518	13	4	238	6%	76%	112	57	23
	12	R	24	3B	aaa	WAS	455	8	5	265	5%	79%	80	51	7
Rizzo,Anthony	11	L	22	1B	aaa	SD	356	15	4	251	7%	69%	161	55	38
	12	L	23	1B	aaa	CHC	257	18	1	300	6%	77%	175	60	81
Rizzotti,Matthew	11	L	26	1B	aa	PHI	499	17	3	239	10%	70%	130	45	18
	12	L	27	DH	a/a	OAK	321	4	1	205	7%	70%	88	26	-27
Roberts,Brandon	11	L	27	OF	aaa	MIN	255	1	10	216	4%	81%	41	95	-6
	12	L	28	OF	aaa	COL	238	0	7	217	5%	88%	49	106	33
Robertson,Daniel	11	R	26	OF	aa	SD	438	3	14	215	8%	85%	54	122	39
	12	R	27	OF	aaa	SD	490	1	12	220	6%	84%	44	86	13
Robinson,Christopher	11	R	27	C	aaa	CHC	225	1	1	236	2%	82%	51	35	-17
	12	R	28	C	aaa	BAL	177	0	0	194	6%	82%	49	60	-1
Robinson,Clint	11	L	26	1B	aaa	KC	503	14	1	264	7%	80%	102	38	28
	12	L	27	1B	aaa	KC	487	8	1	229	10%	84%	77	35	30
Robinson,Derrick	11	B	24	OF	aa	KC	419	1	40	213	7%	77%	19	118	-24
	12	B	25	OF	aaa	KC	422	1	16	221	7%	78%	33	107	-14
Robinson,Trayvon	11	B	24	OF	aaa	SEA	377	15	6	219	7%	58%	126	88	-23
	12	B	25	OF	aaa	SEA	340	6	13	206	7%	69%	78	98	-18
Rockett,Michael	11	R	24	OF	aa	DET	134	1	2	232	2%	76%	52	91	-19
	12	R	25	OF	aa	DET	171	3	2	208	1%	68%	80	119	-22
Rodriguez,Guilder	11	B	28	SS	a/a	TEX	421	0	11	212	7%	85%	22	87	-1
	12	B	29	2B	a/a	TEX	265	0	9	169	8%	84%	5	69	-20
Rodriguez,Henry	11	B	21	2B	aa	CIN	278	4	13	257	6%	82%	78	93	34
	12	B	22	3B	a/a	CIN	345	5	7	261	4%	83%	57	65	6
Rodriguez,Josh	11	R	27	2B	a/a	PIT	295	5	3	208	6%	75%	46	48	-34
	12	R	28	SS	a/a	NYM	471	9	6	200	7%	73%	81	67	-9
Rodriguez,Julio	12	R	23	C	aa	KC	201	1	0	207	3%	84%	40	29	-18
Rodriguez,Reynaldo	11	R	25	1B	aa	BOS	186	5	4	215	3%	70%	139	88	28
	12	R	26	1B	a/a	BOS	370	12	5	221	7%	71%	144	86	43
Rohan,Gregory	12	R	26	3B	a/a	CHC	202	7	0	228	6%	78%	109	15	19
Rohlfing,Danny	11	R	22	C	aa	MIN	166	0	1	214	5%	78%	36	44	-32
	12	R	23	C	aa	MIN	163	0	0	224	3%	75%	69	53	-20
Rohlinger,Ryan	11	R	28	SS	aaa	COL	364	5	1	175	7%	81%	66	65	12
	12	R	29	3B	a/a	CLE	366	6	1	186	9%	79%	53	38	-8
Rojas,Carlos	11	R	27	SS	a/a	BAL	313	0	2	170	7%	75%	22	38	-55
	12	R	28	2B	a/a	CLE	163	0	0	157	7%	77%	14	26	-58
Rojas,Miguel	11	R	22	SS	aa	CIN	239	0	8	217	4%	81%	19	66	-28
	12	R	23	SS	a/a	CIN	272	1	2	177	6%	86%	16	39	-15
Roling,Kiel	12	R	25	1B	aa	COL	268	12	1	246	6%	70%	138	36	14
Romak,Jamie	11	R	26	1B	aa	KC	439	14	4	199	8%	77%	96	66	22
	12	R	27	OF	a/a	STL	389	6	4	202	7%	73%	73	81	-8
Romero,Alex	11	L	28	OF	a/a	MIA	409	4	5	231	6%	85%	59	72	23
Romero,Deibinson	11	R	25	3B	aa	MIN	414	7	1	208	6%	74%	89	49	-4
	12	R	26	3B	aa	MIN	469	13	2	219	9%	76%	86	44	6
Romero,Niuman	11	B	26	2B	a/a	NYM	238	0	6	170	6%	71%	19	79	-64
	12	B	27	SS	aa	DET	523	6	14	245	7%	86%	61	92	34
Romero,Stefen	12	R	24	2B	aa	SEA	216	10	5	307	6%	79%	142	108	77
Romine,Andrew	11	L	26	SS	aaa	LAA	381	2	14	211	7%	72%	33	97	-41
	12	L	27	SS	aaa	LAA	351	2	14	210	4%	84%	38	115	9
Roof,Jonathan	12	R	23	OF	aaa	SD	120	0	1	195	8%	81%	11	47	-35
Roof,Shawn	11	R	27	OF	aa	DET	152	0	4	224	5%	85%	29	81	-1
	12	R	28	2B	aa	MIN	117	0	4	169	4%	78%	19	107	-31
Rosales,Adam	11	R	28	SS	aaa	OAK	147	2	1	195	5%	72%	53	70	-37
Rosario,Alberto	11	R	24	C	aa	LAA	290	2	4	196	6%	84%	31	75	-1
	12	R	25	C	a/a	LAA	240	1	4	178	3%	76%	41	55	-38
Ruf,Darin	12	R	26	1B	aa	PHI	489	28	1	262	9%	75%	153	45	55
Ruggiano,Justin	11	R	29	OF	aaa	TAM	168	5	8	232	8%	67%	129	109	22
	12	R	30	OF	aaa	HOU	117	3	3	234	8%	72%	132	78	36
Ruiz,Jose	11	L	26	1B	a/a	TEX	466	11	3	222	6%	81%	96	50	31
Russell,Kyle	12	L	26	OF	a/a	LA	247	7	3	194	10%	64%	124	62	-3
Russo,Kevin	11	R	27	2B	aaa	NYY	450	4	10	231	6%	73%	61	99	-17
	12	R	28	OF	aaa	NYY	402	0	11	227	8%	78%	43	93	-8
Rutledge,Josh	12	R	23	SS	aa	COL	356	13	12	301	3%	80%	132	114	70
Saladino,Tyler	12	R	23	SS	a/a	CHW	467	4	32	211	13%	74%	52	127	3
Sammons,Clint	11	R	28	C	aaa	MIA	23	2	0	119	10%	40%	234	37	-19
	12	R	29	C	aaa	MIA	138	4	0	140	3%	63%	71	15	-78
Sams,Kalian	12	R	26	OF	aa	SEA	256	9	11	203	7%	61%	126	139	2
Samson,Nathan	11	R	24	2B	aa	CHC	276	4	4	198	5%	82%	76	98	32
	12	R	25	3B	a/a	CHC	260	2	3	230	5%	84%	45	60	1
Sanchez,Angel	12	R	29	SS	aaa	HOU	344	3	4	232	6%	90%	36	51	20
Sanchez,Carlos	12	B	20	SS	a/a	CHW	158	0	6	324	6%	80%	65	87	13
Sanchez,Jorge	11	R	23	C	aa	PIT	402	4	4	213	8%	80%	47	55	-6
	12	R	24	C	a/a	PIT	347	6	1	221	9%	76%	96	45	13
Sanchez,Juan	12	R	25	OF	a/a	MIL	132	1	0	154	5%	78%	41	24	-37
Sanchez,Karexon	11	B	24	2B	aa	CLE	350	7	13	192	8%	67%	80	104	-17
Sands,Jerry	11	R	24	OF	aaa	LA	370	16	2	207	5%	72%	130	68	26
	12	R	25	OF	aaa	LA	452	15	1	224	7%	72%	94	55	-6
Santos,Adalberto	12	R	25	OF	aa	PIT	238	2	14	296	9%	82%	55	94	21
Sappelt,Dave	11	R	24	OF	aaa	CIN	297	6	3	268	7%	85%	78	66	36
	12	R	25	OF	aaa	CHC	500	5	11	221	5%	83%	58	78	13
Sardinha,Bronson	11	L	28	OF	aa	COL	275	7	4	243	9%	79%	90	53	23
Satin,Josh	11	R	27	3B	a/a	NYM	483	9	2	237	9%	68%	108	53	-4
	12	R	28	1B	aaa	NYM	441	10	2	206	11%	69%	84	43	-19
Savastano,Scott	11	R	25	2B	aa	SEA	368	7	2	232	9%	79%	95	56	29
	12	R	26	1B	aaa	SEA	224	1	1	197	6%	68%	70	71	-39
Savastano,Scott Allen	11	R	25	2B	aa	SEA	368	7	2	232	9%	79%	95	56	29
	12	R	26	1B	aaa	SEA	224	1	1	197	6%	68%	70	71	-39
Schaeffer,Warren	11	R	26	3B	a/a	COL	173	0	1	148	4%	72%	53	55	-42
	12	R	27	SS	aa	COL	228	1	2	168	3%	73%	35	57	-53
Schafer,Logan	11	L	25	OF	a/a	MIL	359	4	11	261	6%	85%	74	109	48
	12	L	26	OF	aaa	MIL	464	9	12	236	5%	81%	82	119	37
Schimpf,Ryan	12	L	24	3B	aa	TOR	111	7	2	249	14%	67%	188	53	64
Schmidt,Konrad	11	R	27	C	aaa	ARI	346	5	1	205	3%	76%	83	50	-6
	12	R	28	C	aaa	ARI	332	4	1	204	4%	74%	75	39	-23
Schoop,Jonathan	12	R	21	2B	aa	BAL	485	12	4	224	7%	78%	84	57	12
Schoop,Sharlon	11	R	24	SS	aa	SF	207	3	2	190	7%	79%	58	58	-6
	12	R	25	1B	aa	KC	165	5	1	224	7%	72%	86	36	-15
Scram,Deik	11	L	27	OF	a/a	DET	258	6	2	214	13%	65%	124	96	15
Scruggs,Xavier	12	R	25	1B	aa	STL	452	14	6	187	9%	62%	122	65	-17
Segedin,Robert	12	R	24	OF	aa	NYY	165	3	0	163	6%	78%	55	25	-24
Segura,Jean	12	R	22	SS	aa	MIL	404	6	31	278	5%	83%	59	123	29
Seratelli,Anthony	11	B	28	1B	aa	KC	440	5	23	221	10%	75%	55	134	6
	12	B	29	3B	aaa	KC	384	9	9	225	7%	70%	86	93	-7
Sexton,Gregory	11	R	26	3B	aa	TAM	194	3	0	174	5%	82%	41	40	-13
	12	R	27	3B	aa	TAM	247	4	0	185	9%	80%	80	23	13
Shaffer,Jacob	11	L	24	OF	aa	SEA	442	8	6	242	5%	77%	83	88	14
	12	L	25	OF	aa	STL	260	3	2	212	6%	79%	63	43	-8
Shaw,Travis	12	L	22	1B	aa	BOS	110	2	1	222	14%	68%	174	36	49
Shelby III,John	11	R	26	OF	a/a	TAM	418	11	5	198	3%	71%	101	105	5
Sheridan,Michael	12	L	25	1B	aa	TAM	465	7	2	204	6%	82%	68	70	19
Shoemaker,Brady	12	R	25	OF	aa	CHW	189	3	2	214	16%	62%	103	54	-17
Shuck,J.B.	11	L	24	OF	aaa	HOU	354	0	14	251	10%	90%	35	113	44
	12	L	25	OF	aaa	HOU	315	0	8	236	7%	92%	27	80	31
Sierra,Luis	11	L	24	C	aa	CHW	42	0	0	229	11%	86%	52	97	39
	12	L	25	C	aa	CHW	219	0	0	202	8%	80%	47	47	-9
Sierra,Moises	11	R	23	OF	aa	TOR	495	16	13	252	6%	79%	95	92	33
	12	R	24	OF	aaa	TOR	377	12	5	238	6%	73%	94	58	0
Silverio,Alfredo	11	R	24	OF	aa	LA	533	11	8	251	4%	80%	116	114	57
Simmons,Andrelton	12	R	23	SS	aa	ATL	174	2	8	264	9%	87%	67	117	56
Simunic,Andrew	11	R	26	OF	a/a	HOU	96	0	2	147	10%	64%	38	116	-59
	12	R	27	3B	a/a	HOU	400	1	10	223	5%	78%	27	78	-31
Singleton,Jonathan	12	L	21	1B	aa	HOU	461	16	5	250	12%	68%	128	84	27
Singleton,Steven	11	L	26	2B	a/a	PHI	404	5	4	231	3%	85%	85	63	33
Skipworth,Kyle	11	L	21	C	aa	MIA	396	7	0	177	6%	61%	77	37	-69
	12	L	22	C	aa	MIA	420	15	1	187	7%	63%	116	63	-21
Smith,Blake	12	L	25	OF	aa	LA	461	10	11	224	9%	66%	106	87	-3
Smith,Bryson	12	R	24	OF	aa	CIN	153	1	3	280	2%	83%	58	111	16
Smith,Corey	11	R	29	3B	a/a	LA	399	6	3	181	4%	67%	62	77	-49
	12	R	30	3B	aa	CHW	259	6	1	216	6%	78%	94	48	15
Smith,Curt	12	R	26	1B	aa	MIA	268	6	2	213	6%	74%	94	77	7
Smith,Marquez	11	R	26	3B	aaa	CHC	259	4	0	212	5%	71%	92	58	-12
	12	R	27	3B	aa	BOS	280	6	1	254	6%	78%	106	53	27
Smith,Timothy	11	L	25	OF	aa	KC	238	6	6	259	5%	82%	92	93	44
	12	L	26	OF	aa	ATL	165	2	2	235	6%	81%	46	74	-4
Smolinski,Jacob	11	R	22	OF	aa	MIA	396	5	4	208	10%	84%	68	40	26
	12	R	23	OF	aa	MIA	408	5	7	224	14%	80%	71	84	31
Snider,Travis	11	L	23	OF	aaa	TOR	248	3	7	264	6%	79%	95	103	36
	12	L	24	OF	aaa	TOR	209	9	1	279	10%	76%	138	44	49
Sobolewski,Mark	11	R	25	3B	aa	TOR	400	7	0	236	6%	72%	79	26	-29
	12	R	26	3B	a/a	TOR	454	15	2	203	3%	74%	96	62	0
Sogard,Eric	11	L	25	SS	aaa	OAK	315	3	9	236	8%	87%	55	92	37
	12	L	26	2B	aaa	OAK	157	3	7	261	9%	86%	58	105	44
Solano,Donovan	11	R	24	2B	a/a	STL	330	2	1	209	4%	82%	72	39	8
	12	R	25	2B	aaa	MIA	141	0	3	219	5%	78%	42	81	-19
Solarte,Yangervis	11	B	24	2B	aa	MIN	459	4	4	278	4%	90%	76	62	51
	12	B	25	2B	aaa	TEX	518	9	2	243	5%	90%	60	40	34

BATTER	yr	b	age	pos	lvl	org	ab	hr	sb	ba	bb%	ct%	px	sx	bpv
Solis,Ali	11	R	24	C	a/a	SD	293	3	0	190	3%	67%	73	36	-57
	12	R	25	C	aa	SD	329	4	1	224	3%	71%	86	36	-30
Soto,Elliot	12	R	23	SS	aa	CHC	209	0	2	198	9%	76%	31	75	-27
Soto,Neftali	11	R	22	1B	a/a	CIN	396	25	0	243	5%	72%	163	54	46
	12	R	23	1B	aaa	CIN	465	12	2	214	6%	72%	101	38	-6
Spears,Nate	11	L	26	2B	aaa	BOS	315	6	10	219	11%	75%	99	105	33
	12	L	27	3B	aaa	BOS	346	7	2	207	9%	71%	92	74	-2
Spencer,Matthew	11	L	25	OF	a/a	CHC	391	9	4	195	6%	72%	94	71	-1
Spidale,Michael	11	R	29	OF	aa	PHI	494	3	13	248	4%	87%	36	80	8
	12	R	30	OF	a/a	PHI	269	1	5	221	2%	89%	28	61	3
Spina,Michael	11	R	25	1B	aa	OAK	483	6	1	223	9%	72%	85	51	-7
	12	R	26	DH	aa	OAK	256	4	0	137	8%	65%	73	35	-54
Spring,Matthew	11	R	27	C	a/a	BOS	84	3	0	212	7%	55%	230	24	27
	12	R	28	C	a/a	BOS	207	5	1	170	8%	55%	109	25	-69
Statia,Hainley	11	B	25	SS	aa	MIL	297	2	2	236	8%	85%	60	81	30
	12	B	26	SS	a/a	MIL	342	0	5	215	7%	80%	35	55	-17
Stavinoha,Nick	11	R	29	1B	aaa	STL	533	16	3	194	5%	76%	95	61	10
Steele,Thomas	11	R	25	OF	aa	HOU	415	8	13	174	2%	67%	82	121	-22
	12	R	26	OF	aa	SD	155	1	4	154	4%	65%	49	113	-58
Stoneburner,Davis	11	R	26	2B	aa	TEX	438	7	13	228	6%	77%	88	109	24
	12	R	27	2B	aa	CLE	313	0	11	169	6%	72%	56	105	-23
Strausborger,Ryan	12	R	24	OF	aa	TEX	433	5	20	225	6%	75%	73	156	19
Strieby,Ryan	11	R	26	1B	aaa	DET	487	15	4	215	9%	60%	127	50	-23
	12	R	27	1B	a/a	ARI	445	10	1	155	7%	62%	91	47	-47
Stromsmoe,Skyler	11	B	27	SS	aa	SF	195	1	2	229	10%	76%	43	65	-22
	12	B	28	OF	aaa	SF	229	2	8	184	7%	74%	60	82	-14
Sucre,Jesus	11	R	23	C	aa	SEA	221	1	0	184	4%	90%	31	29	3
	12	R	24	C	aa	SEA	321	1	1	239	5%	86%	29	31	-13
Sulentic,Matthew	11	L	24	OF	aa	OAK	493	4	17	219	6%	77%	51	83	-10
Susdorf,Stephen	11	L	25	OF	aa	PHI	242	4	5	283	7%	76%	103	79	27
	12	L	26	OF	a/a	PHI	377	2	5	240	7%	82%	63	60	12
Sutil,Wladimir	11	R	27	SS	a/a	HOU	264	1	10	209	6%	87%	37	78	14
	12	R	28	SS	a/a	ARI	270	1	3	171	6%	87%	43	60	13
Suttle,Bradley	11	B	25	3B	aa	NYY	326	8	3	182	9%	62%	121	98	-5
Sutton,Drew	11	B	28	2B	aaa	BOS	166	4	0	251	8%	72%	121	50	21
	12	B	29	2B	aaa	PIT	158	0	2	192	10%	77%	61	85	4
Swauger,Christopher	11	L	25	OF	aa	STL	363	7	1	222	4%	78%	61	49	-16
	12	L	26	OF	a/a	STL	357	8	1	229	5%	75%	70	53	-16
Sweeney,Matthew	11	L	23	1B	aa	TAM	266	5	1	127	9%	61%	87	50	-52
Swift,James	12	R	25	OF	a/a	LAA	226	2	2	190	4%	67%	51	55	-66
Szczur,Matthew	12	R	23	OF	aa	CHC	143	2	3	189	7%	78%	80	134	32
Tabata,Jose	11	R	23	OF	aaa	PIT	33	0	0	295	10%	87%	144	60	105
	12	R	24	OF	aaa	PIT	158	0	4	266	5%	87%	43	70	13
Tartamella,Travis	11	R	24	C	aa	STL	46	0	0	114	4%	68%	31	72	-71
	12	R	25	C	aa	STL	132	1	0	127	2%	68%	48	23	-76
Taveras,Oscar	12	L	20	OF	aa	STL	477	17	8	287	7%	87%	117	104	90
Taylor,Beau	12	L	22	C	aa	OAK	120	0	0	201	7%	66%	40	28	-78
Taylor,Michael	11	R	26	OF	aaa	OAK	349	10	9	207	8%	72%	89	64	-5
	12	R	27	OF	aaa	OAK	449	7	12	218	11%	70%	86	85	0
Tejeda,Oscar	11	R	22	2B	aa	BOS	457	4	10	225	4%	76%	67	73	-9
	12	R	23	OF	aa	PIT	400	6	4	226	5%	78%	80	65	8
Tekotte,Blake	11	L	24	OF	aa	SD	414	12	26	224	11%	68%	120	107	23
	12	L	25	OF	aaa	SD	321	5	6	181	4%	64%	90	82	-38
Tenbrink,Nathaniel	11	L	25	3B	aa	SEA	211	4	8	178	11%	65%	104	130	8
	12	L	26	3B	aa	SEA	152	6	4	238	12%	54%	182	119	23
Terdoslavich,Joseph	12	B	24	1B	a/a	ATL	492	7	6	225	7%	73%	79	91	0
Testa,Carlo	12	L	26	OF	aa	KC	364	10	9	203	7%	66%	103	108	-4
Thames,Eric	11	L	25	OF	aaa	TOR	210	4	3	278	6%	76%	147	93	63
	12	L	26	OF	aaa	TOR	197	4	1	264	8%	74%	109	66	19
Thomas,Anthony	11	R	25	2B	a/a	BOS	298	6	10	191	5%	70%	103	100	3
	12	R	26	2B	aaa	BOS	223	8	9	213	7%	67%	119	123	16
Thomas,Clete	11	L	28	OF	aaa	DET	367	9	15	203	6%	58%	104	103	-39
	12	L	29	OF	aaa	MIN	393	8	11	184	5%	66%	100	116	-11
Thomas,Mark	12	R	24	C	aa	TAM	311	4	3	216	7%	71%	83	87	-9
Thorman,Scott	11	L	29	DH	aaa	DET	388	9	7	189	5%	75%	67	67	-14
Tolbert,Matt	11	B	29	SS	aaa	MIN	59	0	3	105	10%	77%	25	128	-11
	12	B	30	SS	aaa	CHC	329	1	6	179	6%	74%	40	68	-36
Tolisano,John	11	B	23	OF	aa	TOR	339	12	6	201	10%	67%	145	73	27
	12	B	24	OF	aa	TOR	436	10	16	222	9%	78%	96	97	39
Tolleson,Steve	11	R	28	3B	aaa	SD	487	4	13	181	7%	74%	56	87	-19
	12	R	29	SS	aaa	BAL	162	1	2	228	10%	76%	47	39	-26
Torres,Tim	11	B	28	OF	a/a	MIA	222	1	7	194	7%	67%	47	72	-56
	12	B	29	OF	aa	COL	292	3	11	192	10%	66%	74	104	-24
Tosoni,Rene	11	L	25	OF	aaa	MIN	275	4	3	188	5%	72%	74	61	-23
	12	L	26	OF	a/a	MIN	289	2	3	182	7%	78%	44	42	-23
Tovar,Wilfredo	12	R	21	SS	aa	NYM	193	0	2	209	4%	88%	44	79	21
Towles,J.R.	11	R	27	C	aaa	HOU	105	2	2	217	10%	87%	57	61	34
	12	R	28	C	aaa	MIN	168	1	2	174	5%	74%	75	72	-10
Tripp,Brandon	12	L	27	OF	aa	PHI	228	4	1	214	4%	72%	74	65	-24
Triunfel,Carlos	11	R	21	SS	a/a	SEA	506	4	4	234	4%	80%	61	55	-6
	12	R	22	SS	aaa	SEA	496	7	2	215	3%	79%	72	67	2
Tuiasosopo,Matt	11	R	25	1B	aaa	SEA	439	8	6	164	9%	62%	87	98	-31
	12	R	26	3B	aaa	NYM	418	9	2	181	8%	67%	66	34	-51
Valaika,Chris	11	R	26	2B	aaa	CIN	417	5	1	212	3%	81%	54	30	-15
	12	R	27	2B	aaa	CIN	291	5	1	179	4%	73%	70	62	-23
Valbuena,Luis	11	L	26	SS	aaa	CLE	420	12	4	247	7%	73%	99	51	2
	12	L	27	SS	aaa	CHC	211	6	1	242	8%	71%	116	55	12

BATTER	yr	b	age	pos	lvl	org	ab	hr	sb	ba	bb%	ct%	px	sx	bpv
Valdespin,Jordany	12	L	25	2B	aaa	NYM	151	4	8	221	5%	83%	50	97	13
Valdez,Jesus	11	R	27	OF	a/a	WAS	499	9	3	220	4%	78%	75	44	-4
	12	R	28	OF	a/a	WAS	426	7	1	226	3%	81%	76	66	11
Valdez,Jeudy	12	R	23	SS	aa	SD	462	8	10	184	4%	68%	83	90	-26
Valle,Sebastian	12	R	22	C	a/a	PHI	388	14	0	229	3%	68%	110	26	-26
Van Kirk,Brian	12	R	27	OF	aa	TOR	399	6	9	226	7%	78%	78	59	10
Van Ostrand,James	11	R	27	1B	aa	HOU	346	8	2	239	7%	81%	86	43	23
	12	R	28	OF	aa	WAS	271	7	0	250	4%	85%	71	24	15
Van Slyke,Scott	11	R	25	OF	aa	LA	457	14	4	281	9%	74%	144	64	49
	12	R	26	OF	aaa	LA	358	11	3	244	7%	78%	117	52	36
Van Stratten,Nick	11	R	26	OF	aa	KC	208	3	6	192	5%	85%	66	118	39
	12	R	27	OF	aa	KC	134	0	2	236	2%	84%	44	90	6
Vazquez,Jorge	11	R	29	1B	aaa	NYY	455	28	0	216	5%	55%	196	20	-5
Velez,Eugenio	11	B	29	2B	aaa	LA	218	1	3	231	2%	78%	60	73	-13
Vidal,David	12	R	23	3B	aa	CIN	335	11	0	212	7%	70%	118	40	2
Villar,Jonathan	11	B	20	SS	aa	HOU	324	8	10	204	6%	66%	103	106	-6
	12	B	21	SS	aa	HOU	326	9	29	228	7%	70%	71	125	-8
Vitek,Kolbrin	12	R	23	3B	aa	BOS	186	1	0	229	4%	73%	84	36	-20
Vitters,Josh	11	R	22	3B	aa	CHC	449	11	3	249	4%	87%	87	51	41
	12	R	23	3B	aaa	CHC	415	13	4	263	5%	79%	114	60	38
Vogt,Stephen	11	L	27	C	a/a	TAM	510	12	3	236	4%	80%	100	79	36
	12	L	28	C	aaa	TAM	349	6	1	214	8%	78%	75	67	9
Wallace,Brett	11	L	25	1B	aaa	HOU	104	1	1	295	9%	67%	106	38	-14
	12	L	26	3B	aaa	HOU	310	11	0	233	5%	65%	111	30	-30
Wallace,Christopher	11	R	23	C	aa	HOU	123	4	1	205	6%	62%	111	39	-38
	12	R	24	C	a/a	HOU	236	4	2	207	6%	66%	94	50	-33
Wallach,Matthew	11	L	25	C	aa	LA	186	2	2	197	12%	81%	63	50	16
	12	L	26	C	aa	LA	168	3	2	190	9%	75%	44	47	-28
Walters,Zachary	12	B	23	SS	a/a	WAS	262	6	1	235	4%	73%	101	80	6
Ward,Brian	12	R	27	C	aa	BAL	161	1	3	176	9%	82%	29	58	-9
Waring,Brandon	11	R	25	3B	aa	BAL	406	19	0	197	6%	65%	153	58	15
	12	R	26	3B	a/a	BAL	419	20	2	224	8%	61%	169	64	18
Wates,Austin	12	R	24	OF	aa	HOU	359	5	12	255	6%	77%	67	100	4
Watkins,Logan	12	L	23	2B	aa	CHC	488	7	22	254	11%	78%	76	140	39
Watts,Kristopher	11	L	27	C	a/a	PIT	230	2	0	189	8%	79%	59	38	-6
	12	L	28	C	a/a	WAS	133	1	0	137	9%	77%	49	13	-30
Webb,Donnie	11	B	25	OF	a/a	CLE	292	1	11	173	7%	72%	48	112	-21
	12	B	26	OF	aa	MIA	285	5	5	200	11%	66%	88	110	-8
Weeks,Joel	11	L	27	SS	aa	SF	39	0	0	147	5%	72%	23	37	-69
	12	L	28	C	aa	SF	146	1	0	192	8%	71%	41	28	-56
Weems,Beamer	11	B	24	SS	aa	SD	272	6	0	191	7%	69%	97	48	-14
	12	B	25	SS	aaa	SD	245	3	0	179	5%	71%	59	37	-46
Weglarz,Nick	11	L	24	OF	aa	CLE	134	2	0	156	18%	64%	101	43	-12
	12	L	25	OF	aa	CLE	368	12	3	213	12%	57%	142	44	-20
Weisenburger,Adam	12	R	24	C	aa	MIL	139	2	0	161	8%	70%	42	32	-58
Welch,Stefan	12	L	24	3B	aa	PIT	214	4	2	234	10%	71%	87	71	-4
Welty,Ronnie	11	R	23	OF	aa	BAL	390	12	9	211	10%	66%	124	92	11
	12	R	24	OF	aa	BAL	140	7	1	251	2%	70%	167	89	45
Wheeler,Ryan	11	L	23	3B	aa	ARI	480	12	2	258	6%	76%	104	52	19
	12	L	24	3B	aaa	ARI	362	9	2	288	4%	78%	109	65	30
Wheeler,Timothy	11	L	23	OF	aa	COL	561	26	14	259	7%	74%	140	101	52
	12	L	24	OF	aaa	COL	379	1	4	256	4%	80%	69	79	11
Wheeler,Zelous	11	R	24	3B	a/a	MIL	279	7	5	230	9%	76%	118	76	41
	12	R	25	3B	a/a	BAL	386	12	4	236	8%	79%	94	66	30
Whittleman,John	12	L	25	1B	aa	KC	305	10	1	183	14%	60%	133	45	-9
Widlansky,Robert	11	L	27	DH	a/a	BAL	437	8	1	220	4%	81%	79	18	2
	12	L	28	DH	aa	BAL	469	6	8	253	9%	81%	75	65	22
Wiley,Keenan	12	L	25	OF	aa	ATL	372	1	12	203	8%	74%	39	87	-29
Wilkins,Andrew	12	L	24	1B	aa	CHW	435	15	5	207	11%	75%	113	55	29
Williams,Jackson	11	R	25	C	a/a	SF	178	3	0	152	8%	70%	52	36	-49
	12	R	26	C	aaa	SF	295	6	0	190	3%	74%	79	33	-22
Williams,Kenny	11	B	25	OF	aa	CHW	318	3	4	167	8%	69%	59	81	-36
	12	B	26	OF	aa	CHW	260	3	4	206	7%	74%	86	83	6
Wilson,Mike	11	R	28	OF	aaa	SEA	335	9	3	232	7%	64%	120	56	-13
	12	R	29	OF	aaa	SEA	230	7	1	169	9%	63%	107	55	-25
Wilson,Steffan	11	R	25	3B	aa	MIL	419	5	3	198	6%	74%	58	59	-24
Wimberly,Corey	11	B	28	2B	aaa	PIT	172	0	10	188	3%	87%	30	123	18
	12	B	29	DH	aaa	NYM	133	1	5	214	7%	86%	29	119	17
Wise,Jeremy	12	R	26	1B	aa	LA	418	7	1	229	10%	64%	126	41	-7
Witherspoon,Travis	12	R	23	OF	aa	LAA	208	5	8	181	9%	72%	89	109	10
Wong,Kolten	12	L	22	2B	aa	STL	523	6	16	249	6%	84%	58	100	29
Worth,Danny	11	R	26	3B	aaa	DET	309	6	10	218	8%	69%	109	124	17
	12	R	27	2B	aaa	DET	216	4	7	217	9%	69%	99	97	5
Wright,Ty	11	R	26	OF	a/a	CHC	267	5	1	255	7%	81%	80	56	19
	12	R	27	OF	a/a	CHC	244	4	2	238	5%	77%	91	51	10
Wrigley,Henry	11	R	25	1B	aa	TAM	468	12	2	221	3%	81%	100	60	32
	12	R	26	1B	a/a	TAM	476	15	2	229	5%	74%	117	49	15
Ynoa,Rafael	12	B	25	SS	aa	LA	421	0	18	234	9%	81%	47	98	10
Young,Matt	11	L	29	OF	aaa	ATL	366	1	12	214	10%	79%	43	106	5
	12	L	30	OF	aaa	STL	336	1	12	176	12%	69%	30	103	-40
Zaneski,Zach	12	R	26	C	aa	TEX	209	3	0	244	7%	78%	84	39	9
Zapata,Pedro	12	R	25	OF	aa	NYM	334	2	11	164	4%	63%	43	132	-62
Zawadzki,Lance	11	B	26	SS	aaa	KC	326	5	10	190	5%	74%	77	135	8
	12	B	27	2B	aaa	STL	192	2	3	171	3%	74%	46	76	-35
Zazueta,Amadeo	11	B	25	SS	aa	SD	53	1	1	221	0%	79%	48	78	-21
	12	B	26	SS	aaa	SD	115	0	0	132	1%	79%	28	49	-43
Zuanich,Michael	11	R	25	DH	aa	COL	88	4	1	224	6%	72%	127	47	17

PITCHER	yr	t	age	lvl	org	ip	era	whip	bf/g	ctl	dom	cmd	hr/9	h%	s%	bpv
Abreu,Erick	11	R	28	a/a	HOU	128	5.29	1.46	14.8	2.3	6.2	2.8	1.7	32	69	39
	12	R	29	aa	HOU	76	4.85	1.43	9.0	3.1	6.0	1.9	1.7	29	72	24
Abreu,Juan	11	R	26	aaa	HOU	58	2.44	1.42	5.1	5.3	9.7	1.8	0.8	30	87	81
	12	R	27	aaa	TOR	49	7.52	1.91	5.5	6.6	8.6	1.3	2.6	32	66	-2
Adcock,Nathan	12	R	24	aaa	KC	99	5.98	1.58	23.0	2.6	4.3	1.6	0.4	35	60	41
Additon,Nicholas	11	L	24	a/a	STL	158	3.73	1.27	23.1	2.9	6.0	2.0	1.0	28	74	54
	12	L	25	aaa	STL	87	4.96	1.66	24.4	4.3	6.7	1.6	0.9	34	71	41
Aguasviva,Geison	12	L	25	aa	LA	64	3.04	1.21	5.2	3.9	4.6	1.2	0.5	24	75	50
Albaladejo,Jonathan	12	R	30	aaa	ARI	57	4.00	1.36	4.8	3.7	6.9	1.9	1.3	28	75	47
Albers,Andrew	11	L	26	aa	MIN	43	3.25	1.33	13.8	1.5	5.6	3.8	0.0	35	73	109
	12	L	27	aa	MIN	98	4.76	1.52	22.5	1.2	5.1	4.3	0.7	37	69	90
Alderson,Tim	11	R	23	aa	PIT	74	4.90	1.43	7.5	3.2	5.5	1.7	0.7	31	66	47
	12	R	24	a/a	PIT	89	5.44	1.59	14.0	2.9	5.2	1.8	0.9	34	66	36
Allen,Cody	12	R	24	a/a	CLE	39	2.52	0.95	5.1	2.1	8.5	4.1	1.0	25	79	122
Alvarez,Jose	11	L	22	aa	MIA	66	5.57	1.62	24.3	2.9	5.3	1.8	1.1	35	67	31
	12	L	23	aa	MIA	136	5.00	1.37	22.9	1.8	3.9	2.2	0.5	32	62	50
Ambriz,Hector	12	R	28	aaa	HOU	57	3.61	1.61	6.7	4.4	5.2	1.2	0.6	32	78	36
Ames,Steven	11	R	23	aa	LA	33	2.51	1.34	4.8	2.7	9.6	3.5	0.7	35	84	110
	12	R	24	aa	LA	63	1.84	1.14	4.6	1.8	8.5	4.7	0.3	33	85	146
Anderson,Chase	12	R	25	aa	ARI	104	3.73	1.32	20.5	2.2	6.7	3.0	0.9	32	75	75
Antigua,Jeffry	12	L	22	aa	CHC	40	4.60	1.50	8.6	3.0	7.8	2.6	1.5	34	74	52
Antonini,Michael	11	L	26	aa	LA	148	4.33	1.52	23.8	2.4	6.3	2.6	1.1	35	74	53
	12	L	27	aaa	LA	87	5.33	1.69	13.0	3.6	4.6	1.3	1.5	33	72	2
Anundsen,Evan	12	R	24	aa	MIL	119	5.89	1.71	19.2	3.6	4.3	1.2	0.8	34	65	19
Arbiso,Cory	11	R	25	aa	NYY	83	6.66	1.99	9.9	3.2	4.5	1.4	0.6	40	65	21
	12	R	26	aa	NYY	32	4.40	1.87	19.0	3.7	3.9	1.1	1.5	35	81	-13
Archer,Chris	11	R	23	a/a	TAM	147	4.36	1.63	24.3	4.9	6.9	1.4	0.6	33	73	51
	12	R	24	aaa	TAM	128	4.18	1.35	21.4	4.3	8.3	1.9	0.4	30	68	85
Arenas,Orangel	11	R	22	aa	LAA	149	5.24	1.59	26.2	2.3	3.5	1.5	0.8	34	67	21
	12	R	23	aa	LAA	140	6.71	1.80	24.0	2.8	4.4	1.6	1.2	37	63	8
Arguelles,Noel	12	L	22	aa	KC	119	7.39	1.90	22.5	4.9	3.7	0.8	0.8	35	60	3
Arias,Jonathan	12	R	24	aa	SEA	33	3.79	1.26	6.2	5.5	5.4	1.0	1.5	18	77	26
Aristil,Jonnathan	11	R	25	a/a	HOU	121	6.49	1.72	17.8	4.7	7.2	1.5	1.6	34	65	23
	12	R	26	a/a	HOU	46	6.13	1.67	7.1	2.7	7.5	2.8	1.8	37	67	40
Arnesen,Erik	11	R	27	a/a	WAS	144	3.32	1.37	20.8	1.7	6.5	3.7	0.7	34	77	93
	12	R	28	aaa	WAS	64	4.61	1.64	8.6	3.1	4.8	1.5	1.0	34	74	23
Arrieta,Jake	12	R	26	aaa	BAL	56	5.82	1.63	24.9	5.0	6.8	1.3	0.7	32	63	48
Arroyo,Spencer	12	L	24	aa	CHW	69	5.61	1.81	26.5	4.6	4.1	0.9	1.2	33	71	0
Atkins,Mitch	11	R	26	a/a	BAL	121	6.69	1.63	25.6	3.8	5.4	1.4	1.2	33	59	22
	12	R	27	aaa	WAS	118	6.20	1.73	19.2	3.0	5.2	1.7	1.1	36	65	24
Augenstein,Bryan	11	R	25	aaa	STL	36	4.22	1.44	5.8	3.0	7.1	2.4	1.1	33	74	58
	12	R	26	aaa	TAM	43	4.28	1.48	8.0	2.6	6.8	2.6	0.4	36	70	79
Aumont,Phillippe	11	R	22	a/a	PHI	54	3.10	1.37	5.2	4.1	11.4	2.8	0.4	36	77	122
	12	R	23	aaa	PHI	44	5.51	1.71	4.9	7.2	10.2	1.4	0.7	33	68	75
Avery,James	11	R	27	aa	CIN	140	5.03	1.70	23.4	3.4	3.9	1.1	1.2	33	73	1
	12	R	28	aa	DET	158	6.32	1.87	27.5	3.3	4.7	1.4	0.9	38	66	16
Avilan,Luis	11	L	22	aa	ATL	105	4.82	1.46	12.5	2.9	5.9	2.0	0.8	33	67	51
	12	L	23	aa	ATL	61	3.99	1.47	16.5	4.7	7.0	1.5	1.1	29	76	44
Axelrod,Dylan	11	R	26	a/a	CHW	151	3.63	1.33	24.1	2.5	6.5	2.6	0.3	33	71	86
	12	R	27	aaa	CHW	97	4.30	1.53	26.4	3.7	6.9	1.9	1.2	33	75	44
Baker,Brian	11	R	28	aaa	TAM	105	8.17	1.78	19.3	3.8	5.1	1.3	1.6	34	54	1
	12	R	29	a/a	MIL	122	5.62	1.85	21.2	4.7	5.4	1.1	1.5	34	73	4
Baker,Nathaniel	12	L	25	aa	PIT	107	6.30	1.71	14.6	5.0	5.0	1.0	0.8	32	63	23
Balcom-Miller,Christo	11	R	22	aa	BOS	82	5.60	1.74	23.5	3.3	7.0	2.1	0.4	39	66	64
	12	R	23	aa	BOS	86	5.86	1.71	14.9	5.3	5.4	1.0	1.1	31	67	19
Balester,Collin	11	R	25	aaa	WAS	39	5.32	1.79	6.5	3.4	8.3	2.5	0.5	42	69	74
	12	R	26	aaa	DET	47	4.70	1.26	6.2	2.4	6.6	2.7	1.5	28	68	54
Ballard,Michael	11	L	27	a/a	BAL	159	5.27	1.45	25.2	1.9	6.4	3.4	1.5	34	67	61
	12	L	28	aa	WAS	65	5.75	1.88	25.3	2.5	5.7	2.3	1.7	39	73	14
Banuelos,Manuel	12	L	21	aaa	NYY	24	5.49	1.80	18.5	3.8	7.1	1.9	1.0	39	70	42
Banwart,Travis	11	R	25	aaa	OAK	150	4.77	1.35	23.1	2.7	6.0	2.2	1.1	30	67	49
	12	R	26	aaa	OAK	129	4.16	1.44	17.1	2.6	5.6	2.2	0.9	32	73	48
Bard,Daniel	12	R	27	aaa	BOS	32	10.32	2.32	5.3	9.3	6.9	0.7	0.7	37	52	28
Barnes,Scott	11	L	24	a/a	CLE	99	4.07	1.35	22.9	3.3	8.1	2.5	1.1	31	73	70
	12	L	25	aaa	CLE	52	4.54	1.25	6.8	3.9	9.4	2.4	0.2	31	61	112
Barnese,Nicholas	11	R	22	aa	TAM	117	3.79	1.41	20.7	3.9	6.1	1.6	0.5	30	73	57
	12	R	23	aa	TAM	57	6.33	1.69	19.6	3.8	4.1	1.1	0.8	33	62	17
Bascom,Timothy	11	R	26	aa	BAL	130	4.34	1.40	18.9	2.6	5.9	2.3	0.8	32	70	59
	12	R	27	a/a	BAL	135	5.96	1.68	22.5	4.1	5.1	1.2	0.9	33	65	24
Bass,Brian	11	R	29	aaa	PHI	158	5.41	1.85	26.4	3.7	4.5	1.2	1.0	36	72	11
	12	R	30	aaa	HOU	78	6.03	2.03	22.2	4.0	4.0	1.0	1.1	38	71	-5
Batista,Frank	12	R	23	a/a	CHC	60	3.15	1.31	5.1	3.8	5.6	1.5	1.1	26	81	37
Bauer,Trevor	11	R	20	aa	ARI	17	8.11	1.704	18.85	3.9	12.4	3.2	1.1	44	51	101
	12	R	21	a/a	ARI	130	2.54	1.289	24.35	3.8	9.4	2.5	0.6	31	82	98
Baumann,George	11	L	24	aa	KC	72	4.69	1.505	12.03	3.4	6.7	2.0	1.0	33	71	50
	12	L	25	aa	KC	59	5.05	1.525	8.012	5.2	6.9	1.3	1.1	29	68	42
Bawcom,Logan	12	R	24	aa	SEA	49	3.04	1.562	5.505	6.1	8.2	1.3	0.4	30	81	72
Bay,Ronald	11	R	28	aaa	LAA	160	5.27	1.689	25.71	2.2	4.1	1.9	1.2	36	71	14
	12	R	29	aaa	SD	117	4.75	1.604	20.65	2.3	4.4	1.9	0.8	35	71	34
Bayne,Cameron	11	R	23	a/a	CHW	22	6.73	2.278	28.04	7.0	3.2	0.5	1.1	36	71	-18
	12	R	24	aa	CHW	106	7.86	1.982	25.53	5.5	3.6	0.7	1.4	33	61	-17
Beard,Hayden	12	R	27	aa	SD	119	6.26	1.76	17.63	3.2	4.2	1.3	0.8	36	64	17
Beato,Pedro	12	R	26	aaa	BOS	42	5.23	1.417	6.355	3.6	5.7	1.6	1.9	27	69	14
Beavan,Blake	11	R	22	aaa	SEA	93	3.63	1.372	24.36	1.6	5.6	3.4	0.7	34	75	81
	12	R	23	aaa	SEA	38	2.53	1.281	25.98	2.0	3.2	1.6	0.6	29	82	35
Beck,Chad	11	R	26	a/a	TOR	137	5.14	1.672	20.46	3.5	5.0	1.4	1.0	34	71	22
	12	R	27	aaa	TOR	48	1.45	1.206	4.494	2.4	3.6	1.5	0.4	27	90	45

PITCHER	yr	t	age	lvl	org	ip	era	whip	bf/g	ctl	dom	cmd	hr/9	h%	s%	bpv
Beeler,Dallas	12	R	23	aa	CHC	136	5.20	1.79	23.2	3.3	3.9	1.2	0.8	36	71	11
Belfiore,Michael	12	L	24	aa	BAL	47	3.43	1.50	7.3	4.0	7.7	1.9	0.5	34	77	74
Beliveau,Jeff	11	L	24	aa	CHC	57	2.15	0.96	5.3	2.1	9.0	4.4	1.2	25	87	125
	12	L	25	aaa	CHC	44	4.55	1.58	5.2	3.8	8.6	2.3	0.9	36	73	69
Bell,Chadwick	12	L	23	a/a	TEX	131	4.47	1.42	20.6	3.5	5.5	1.6	0.7	30	69	46
Bell,Trevor	11	R	25	aaa	LAA	56	5.96	1.53	22.2	1.9	6.4	3.4	1.4	36	63	60
	12	R	26	aaa	LAA	37	8.14	2.40	19.3	5.4	3.7	0.7	1.5	40	67	-31
Below,Duane	12	L	27	aaa	DET	17	8.22	2.48	23.0	6.7	2.7	0.4	1.8	38	69	-51
Berg,Jeremy	11	R	25	a/a	LAA	74	4.88	1.52	6.1	3.2	5.7	1.8	0.4	34	66	57
	12	R	26	a/a	LAA	74	4.28	1.41	6.5	2.3	7.1	3.1	1.0	34	72	75
Berger,Eric	11	L	25	a/a	CLE	71	4.86	1.67	7.6	4.6	8.9	1.9	0.8	37	71	67
	12	L	26	a/a	CLE	111	6.74	1.61	15.9	3.2	6.4	2.0	1.7	34	61	23
Bergesen,Brad	11	R	26	aaa	BAL	22	2.11	1.17	29.2	3.5	5.7	1.7	0.5	25	84	65
	12	R	27	aaa	ARI	84	3.99	1.48	15.7	2.4	3.6	1.5	1.0	31	76	17
Berken,Jason	11	R	28	aaa	BAL	18	4.73	1.86	16.8	3.9	6.0	1.5	0.7	39	75	36
	12	R	29	aaa	BAL	144	5.43	1.87	26.0	2.9	4.5	1.5	1.0	38	72	14
Betances,Dellin	11	R	23	a/a	NYY	126	4.77	1.55	22.1	5.3	8.5	1.6	0.9	32	70	63
	12	R	24	a/a	NYY	131	8.20	2.12	24.0	7.2	7.0	1.0	1.2	37	61	18
Bibens-Dirkx,Austin	11	R	26	a/a	CHC	130	6.46	1.62	19.9	2.8	5.0	1.8	1.5	34	62	15
	12	R	27	a/a	COL	70	8.73	2.04	8.8	4.3	5.9	1.4	1.3	40	56	10
Billings,Bruce	11	R	26	aaa	OAK	77	4.69	1.60	7.7	4.0	6.8	1.7	0.5	35	70	59
	12	R	27	a/a	OAK	139	4.52	1.42	21.8	2.9	6.2	2.1	0.9	32	70	53
Black,Victor	12	R	24	aa	PIT	60	2.08	1.28	4.8	4.4	9.9	2.3	0.3	31	84	109
Blackburn,Nick	12	R	30	aaa	MIN	37	3.88	1.84	24.4	2.6	2.0	0.7	0.6	36	79	-5
Blazek,Michael	11	R	22	a/a	STL	146	4.84	1.51	24.3	4.1	7.1	1.7	1.2	31	71	43
	12	R	23	a/a	STL	83	4.69	1.29	8.2	3.8	7.6	2.0	1.1	27	66	62
Bleier,Richard	11	L	24	aa	TEX	101	7.02	1.83	14.7	1.5	3.9	2.6	0.6	40	59	41
	12	L	25	aa	TEX	32	5.38	1.57	6.4	2.2	3.7	1.7	1.2	33	68	13
Bochy,Brett	12	R	25	aa	SF	53	3.39	1.03	5.0	3.2	9.5	3.0	0.6	26	67	120
Bolsinger,Michael	12	R	24	aa	ARI	78	4.89	1.76	23.7	4.5	6.1	1.4	0.7	36	72	37
Bonilla,Lisalberto	12	R	22	aa	PHI	33	1.86	1.24	6.4	4.5	10.9	2.4	0.3	31	86	122
Boscan,Wilfredo	11	R	22	aa	TEX	22	8.38	1.92	20.9	3.3	5.1	1.5	2.6	36	60	-30
	12	R	23	aa	TEX	98	4.92	1.43	12.3	2.7	6.6	2.4	1.2	32	68	52
Bowden,Michael	11	R	25	aaa	BOS	53	3.82	1.40	5.4	3.3	8.4	2.5	1.0	33	76	73
	12	R	26	aaa	CHC	33	3.29	1.24	5.8	5.0	7.7	1.5	0.6	24	75	76
Boxberger,Brad	11	R	23	a/a	CIN	62	2.13	0.98	4.3	3.8	11.7	3.1	0.6	24	81	138
	12	R	24	aaa	SD	43	2.48	1.28	4.8	3.7	11.2	3.0	0.0	36	78	138
Brach,Brett	11	R	23	a/a	CLE	33	5.03	1.54	24.0	3.7	3.7	1.0	1.4	29	71	0
	12	R	24	aa	CLE	94	4.95	1.80	22.8	3.6	3.9	1.1	0.9	35	73	8
Brackman,Andrew	12	R	27	aaa	CIN	17	12.48	2.27	17.7	9.0	5.4	0.6	2.0	32	43	-22
Bramhall,Bobby	12	L	27	a/a	MIA	62	4.24	1.40	9.0	3.3	6.9	2.1	0.6	32	70	68
Brasier,Ryan	11	R	24	a/a	LAA	52	3.09	1.33	4.3	3.7	7.4	2.0	0.5	30	77	78
	12	R	25	aaa	LAA	60	4.21	1.53	4.7	3.3	6.6	2.0	0.1	36	70	75
Brewer,Charles	11	R	23	aa	ARI	52	2.91	1.37	19.9	3.1	6.9	2.2	0.4	32	79	79
	12	R	24	a/a	ARI	151	6.38	1.67	25.1	2.0	5.7	2.8	1.7	36	65	29
Brigham,Jacob	11	R	23	aa	TEX	114	5.52	1.58	14.4	4.5	7.3	1.6	1.3	32	67	38
	12	R	24	aa	CHC	128	5.92	1.65	24.8	3.7	7.0	1.9	1.7	34	68	25
Britton,Drake	12	L	23	aa	BOS	85	4.94	1.69	23.9	4.2	6.8	1.6	0.4	36	69	58
Britton,Zach	11	L	24	a/a	BAL	17	5.56	1.41	17.6	1.7	7.9	4.7	2.1	34	67	79
	12	L	25	a/a	BAL	63	5.43	1.49	24.8	3.4	5.4	1.6	0.9	31	64	37
Broadway,Michael	12	R	25	aa	SD	40	6.82	1.76	5.5	3.0	8.7	2.9	0.8	42	60	76
Broderick,Brian	11	R	25	aaa	STL	91	5.27	1.69	18.6	2.1	3.6	1.7	0.9	36	70	17
	12	R	26	a/a	WAS	108	8.09	2.09	18.9	3.1	4.4	1.4	1.5	40	62	-12
Bromberg,David	11	R	24	aa	MIN	37	6.52	1.88	21.7	3.5	4.6	1.3	0.6	38	64	22
	12	R	25	a/a	MIN	92	4.44	1.63	12.4	4.7	6.6	1.4	0.5	34	72	53
Brooks,Richard	11	R	27	aa	NYM	82	4.07	1.45	6.6	2.2	4.8	2.2	0.6	33	72	52
	12	R	28	aaa	COL	32	10.66	2.35	11.8	5.6	4.0	0.7	2.1	39	55	-43
Brown,Brooks	11	R	26	aaa	DET	94	7.01	1.72	25.0	2.7	4.8	1.8	1.1	36	59	22
	12	R	27	aaa	DET	112	6.47	1.96	18.4	5.0	4.9	1.0	1.0	36	67	7
Browning,Barret	11	L	27	aaa	LAA	66	4.58	1.60	5.9	4.5	5.0	1.1	0.6	31	71	34
	12	L	28	aaa	STL	42	2.01	1.27	4.9	4.2	6.2	1.5	0.2	27	84	72
Brummett,Tyson	11	R	27	a/a	PHI	126	6.24	1.76	15.5	3.0	5.2	1.7	1.4	36	67	11
	12	R	28	a/a	PHI	90	4.35	1.43	8.7	3.3	6.4	1.9	0.5	32	69	64
Bruney,Brian	11	R	29	aaa	CHW	21	1.88	1.34	4.5	5.1	10.1	2.0	0.0	31	84	114
	12	R	30	aaa	CHW	37	2.70	1.32	6.1	4.3	6.9	1.6	0.4	28	80	72
Bryson,Robert	11	R	24	aa	CLE	21	3.64	1.51	5.8	5.2	8.0	1.6	0.4	32	76	73
	12	R	25	aa	CLE	65	3.62	1.59	6.7	6.5	8.5	1.3	0.7	30	78	67
Buchanan,David	12	R	23	aa	PHI	72	4.47	1.45	25.8	2.8	4.3	1.5	0.9	31	71	27
Buchanan,Jake	12	R	23	a/a	HOU	142	5.46	1.62	21.0	2.2	4.8	2.2	0.7	36	66	43
Buchter,Ryan	12	L	25	a/a	ATL	49	3.32	1.58	4.9	6.9	8.4	1.2	0.4	29	79	74
Buckel,Cody	12	R	20	aa	TEX	69	4.72	1.26	21.7	3.0	7.6	2.5	1.2	29	65	68
Buckner,Billy	11	R	28	aaa	COL	109	5.78	1.80	21.9	4.0	4.7	1.2	1.0	35	68	14
	12	R	29	a/a	BOS	153	5.56	1.66	25.37	3.7	4.8	1.3	1.4	32	69	7
Bullock,William	11	R	23	a/a	ATL	51	5.04	1.48	4.271	6.0	10.2	1.7	0.4	32	64	97
	12	R	24	a/a	ATL	60	7.54	2.18	7.458	8.6	8.6	1.0	1.1	37	65	34
Bundy,Robert	11	R	21	aa	BAL	15	12.21	2.68	16.49	6.6	6.7	1.0	2.3	45	54	-33
	12	R	22	aa	BAL	81	7.22	1.77	21.79	3.7	6.0	1.6	0.9	37	58	34
Burgos,Hiram	12	R	25	a/a	MIL	130	2.86	1.34	25.7	3.2	6.5	2.0	0.6	31	80	67
Burke,Greg	11	R	29	aaa	SD	79	4.94	1.81	5.715	4.4	6.8	1.5	0.7	38	73	44
	12	R	30	a/a	BAL	65	2.23	1.24	5.964	2.4	5.0	2.1	0.2	29	81	71
Burns,Cory	11	R	24	aa	CLE	60	2.60	1.18	4.423	2.3	8.8	3.8	0.5	32	79	123
	12	R	25	aaa	SD	66	2.94	1.02	4.692	2.2	9.1	4.1	0.1	30	69	149
Buschmann,Matthew	11	R	27	a/a	SD	134	5.68	1.72	19.04	3.4	5.0	1.5	0.8	36	67	28
	12	R	28	a/a	TAM	151	4.94	1.59	25.65	3.4	5.5	1.6	1.0	33	70	33
Butler,Joshua	12	R	28	a/a	MIL	26	5.92	1.92	12.49	5.1	3.5	0.7	1.3	33	71	-14
Butler,Keith	12	R	23	aa	STL	59	2.92	1.35	4.585	3.4	7.5	2.2	0.7	31	80	75
Byrd,Darren	11	R	25	aa	MIL	64	3.52	1.58	6.871	4.7	5.9	1.3	0.3	32	77	52
	12	R	26	aa	MIL	73	3.28	1.50	6.313	4.8	7.2	1.5	0.3	32	78	69

PITCHER	yr	t	age	lvl	org	ip	era	whip	bf/g	ctl	dom	cmd	hr/9	h%	s%	bpv
Cabrera,Alberto	11	R	23	a/a	CHC	137	6.29	1.885	23.07	4.6	5.6	1.2	0.9	37	67	20
	12	R	24	a/a	CHC	55	3.72	1.508	6.612	2.4	10.0	4.2	1.1	40	79	110
Cabrera,Daniel	12	R	31	aaa	ARI	126	4.78	1.522	23.79	3.0	4.3	1.4	0.7	32	68	32
Cabrera,Edwar	12	L	25	a/a	COL	130	3.99	1.146	24.49	2.6	6.4	2.5	2.0	23	76	40
Capps,Carter	12	R	22	a/a	SEA	51	1.31	1.064	5.112	2.0	11.9	5.9	0.3	35	89	194
Caridad,Esmailin	11	R	28	a/a	CHC	46	9.13	2.282	7.571	6.0	5.9	1.0	1.3	41	59	1
	12	R	29	aaa	CHC	65	3.88	1.51	6.429	4.5	6.7	1.5	0.7	31	75	53
Carpenter,Drew	11	R	26	aaa	PHI	60	2.38	1.192	7.119	1.8	7.8	4.3	0.4	33	81	130
	12	R	27	a/a	NYM	84	3.47	1.511	11.78	2.2	5.8	2.6	1.2	34	82	47
Carraway,Andrew	11	R	25	aa	SEA	138	4.22	1.216	19.84	1.7	5.9	3.5	0.6	31	65	93
	12	R	26	a/a	SEA	150	4.82	1.435	23.64	2.3	5.1	2.2	1.0	32	68	43
Carreno,Joel	11	R	24	aa	TOR	135	4.37	1.417	23.77	4.7	8.6	1.8	1.0	29	71	66
	12	R	25	a/a	TOR	90	6.88	1.707	15.09	4.6	7.3	1.6	1.3	34	60	35
Carroll,Scott	11	R	27	aaa	CIN	145	6.57	1.89	27.38	3.1	4.2	1.4	0.9	38	65	10
	12	R	28	a/a	CHW	92	6.39	1.799	12.18	4.5	5.0	1.1	1.5	34	66	2
Carson,Robert	11	L	22	aa	NYM	128	4.68	1.564	22.5	3.3	5.3	1.6	0.8	33	71	37
	12	L	23	a/a	NYM	51	3.80	1.615	5.553	3.3	7.5	2.2	0.5	37	76	71
Carter,Anthony	11	R	25	a/a	CHW	62	7.71	1.913	6.21	5.4	7.6	1.4	1.2	38	59	31
	12	R	26	aaa	CHW	63	6.73	1.927	7.628	4.0	6.4	1.6	1.3	39	66	19
Cassevah,Bobby	11	R	26	aaa	LAA	21	4.51	1.584	5.22	3.9	4.0	1.0	0.7	31	72	21
	12	R	27	aaa	LAA	46	6.25	1.812	4.878	3.5	4.2	1.2	0.5	37	64	23
Castillo,Fabio	11	R	22	aa	TEX	52	7.67	1.706	5.64	4.0	5.3	1.3	1.3	33	55	14
	12	R	23	a/a	TEX	56	4.34	1.411	6.769	4.3	5.4	1.2	0.6	28	69	45
Castillo,Richard	11	R	22	aa	STL	44	3.64	1.742	8.363	3.7	7.3	2.0	0.6	39	80	59
	12	R	23	aa	STL	110	4.03	1.531	25.19	2.6	4.5	1.7	0.6	34	74	39
Castro,Fabio	11	L	26	aaa	SEA	79	3.22	1.345	13.77	3.5	6.1	1.7	0.8	29	78	53
	12	L	27	a/a	OAK	125	6.41	1.922	21.22	5.1	5.7	1.1	0.8	37	66	23
Castro,Simon	11	R	23	a/a	SD	115	4.77	1.373	21.92	2.4	6.5	2.7	0.8	33	65	73
	12	R	24	a/a	CHW	115	5.01	1.549	25.12	2.5	5.9	2.4	0.6	36	67	60
Cecil,Brett	11	L	25	aaa	TOR	79	4.92	1.446	27.96	2.5	6.0	2.4	1.6	32	71	36
	12	L	26	a/a	TOR	82	3.52	1.409	23.21	2.4	5.9	2.5	0.4	34	75	74
Cedeno,Juan	12	L	29	aaa	NYY	64	4.03	1.776	5.55	3.5	5.9	1.7	1.1	37	80	28
Cedeno,Xavier	12	L	26	aaa	HOU	28	2.28	1.366	5.264	2.8	6.6	2.4	0.0	34	81	90
Chaffee,Ryan	12	R	24	aa	LAA	43	3.54	1.333	4.826	5.9	9.7	1.6	0.7	25	75	87
Chapman,Jaye	11	R	24	a/a	ATL	68	2.90	1.209	5.294	4.1	8.7	2.1	0.8	26	79	85
	12	R	25	a/a	CHC	65	4.91	1.624	5.778	5.3	8.1	1.5	0.5	34	69	68
Chapman,Kevin	11	L	23	aa	KC	40	5.42	1.527	6.897	4.6	9.2	2.0	1.0	34	65	70
	12	L	24	aa	HOU	58	2.76	1.441	5.043	4.7	7.7	1.6	0.3	31	81	78
Chatwood,Tyler	11	R	22	aaa	LAA	16	4.53	1.874	18.78	5.3	5.3	1.0	0.9	35	77	19
	12	R	23	a/a	COL	61	5.88	1.752	21.57	3.9	6.2	1.6	0.8	37	66	39
Chavez,Jesse	11	R	28	aaa	KC	58	4.51	1.622	5.692	2.7	6.1	2.3	0.9	36	74	49
	12	R	29	aaa	OAK	105	4.36	1.349	20.85	2.0	6.2	3.0	0.8	33	69	74
Christiani,Nick	11	R	24	a/a	CIN	61	4.08	1.42	4.907	2.8	5.1	1.8	0.3	32	70	58
	12	R	25	aaa	CIN	73	4.05	1.775	6.183	3.7	3.6	1.0	0.6	35	78	14
Cingrani,Tony	12	L	23	aa	CIN	89	2.81	1.26	22.78	4.2	8.8	2.1	0.9	27	82	80
Cisco,Michael	11	R	24	aa	PHI	62	1.81	1.168	8.573	4.1	6.2	1.5	0.9	22	91	56
	12	R	25	a/a	PHI	75	2.29	1.43	7.969	3.3	5.7	1.7	0.8	31	88	45
Cisnero,Jose	12	R	23	a/a	HOU	148	3.63	1.408	22.4	3.5	7.8	2.2	0.5	33	74	81
Claiborne,Preston	12	R	24	a/a	NYY	82	3.77	1.402	6.925	4.2	7.0	1.7	0.4	30	73	69
Clark,Zachary	11	R	28	aa	BAL	139	7.29	1.901	27.27	3.1	3.9	1.3	1.0	38	61	3
	12	R	29	a/a	BAL	168	4.02	1.574	26.31	3.3	3.8	1.1	0.7	32	75	22
Clay,Caleb	11	R	23	aa	BOS	59	8.50	1.918	9.984	5.0	6.8	1.4	1.4	37	55	18
	12	R	24	aa	BOS	66	6.25	1.717	8.851	2.7	6.8	2.5	1.9	37	68	24
Clemens,Paul	11	R	23	a/a	HOU	144	3.90	1.358	23.14	3.6	6.7	1.9	0.7	30	72	62
	12	R	24	a/a	HOU	143	5.79	1.655	23.76	2.5	5.6	2.2	1.4	36	67	28
Cleto,Maikel	11	R	22	a/a	STL	106	3.80	1.379	22.19	4.2	7.4	1.8	0.5	30	72	72
	12	R	23	aaa	STL	54	5.61	1.42	5.056	3.6	9.3	2.6	0.6	35	59	94
Cloyd,Tyler	11	R	24	aa	PHI	107	3.17	1.21	23.88	1.3	7.0	5.6	0.6	33	75	140
	12	R	25	a/a	PHI	167	2.88	1.179	25.68	2.3	5.0	2.1	1.0	26	80	52
Cobb,Alex	11	R	24	aaa	TAM	67	2.12	1.253	22.86	2.1	7.9	3.8	0.5	33	85	113
	12	R	25	aaa	TAM	41	4.83	1.669	23.19	3.9	7.9	2.0	0.2	38	69	77
Cochran,Thomas	11	L	29	aaa	CIN	89	4.54	1.538	14.31	4.7	5.2	1.1	1.0	29	73	26
	12	L	30	aaa	PHI	127	5.89	1.817	23.62	6.0	5.6	0.9	1.0	32	68	21
Coello,Robert	11	R	27	a/a	CHC	116	4.66	1.462	14.61	3.8	6.6	1.7	1.0	31	70	48
	12	R	28	aaa	TOR	42	3.40	1.307	9.122	3.9	7.1	1.8	0.9	27	77	60
Cohoon,Mark	11	L	24	a/a	NYM	146	5.34	1.643	24.19	3.1	4.7	1.5	1.0	34	69	22
	12	L	25	a/a	NYM	155	4.50	1.372	25.93	1.8	4.0	2.2	0.8	31	68	43
Cole,Gerrit	12	R	22	a/a	PIT	65	3.73	1.421	21.2	3.2	7.5	2.3	0.3	34	72	86
Coleman,Casey	11	R	24	aaa	CHC	74	3.53	1.248	25.09	2.5	5.4	2.2	1.2	27	77	46
	12	R	25	aaa	CHC	58	5.08	1.505	19.29	4.0	6.6	1.6	0.7	32	66	54
Colla,Michael	11	R	25	aa	PIT	134	4.60	1.341	19.18	2.7	5.6	2.1	1.4	29	70	36
	12	R	26	aa	PIT	96	4.93	1.538	11.31	2.7	5.3	2.0	1.2	33	70	32
Colome,Alexander	11	R	22	a/a	TAM	52	4.18	1.308	23.85	4.4	4.7	1.1	0.8	24	69	38
	12	R	23	a/a	TAM	92	3.82	1.428	22.91	4.0	7.6	1.9	0.3	32	72	80
Colon,Roman	11	R	32	aaa	LA	30	4.42	1.411	4.649	1.9	3.8	2.0	1.2	31	72	22
	12	R	33	aaa	KC	67	3.77	1.682	7.541	4.1	5.6	1.4	0.9	34	80	29
Colvin,Brody	12	R	22	aa	PHI	33	12.50	2.138	23.14	6.1	3.8	0.6	1.7	35	38	-29
Cooper,Patrick	12	R	23	aa	DET	109	6.13	1.563	20.84	2.8	4.8	1.7	1.1	33	61	27
Corbin,Patrick	11	L	22	aa	ARI	160	4.65	1.403	26.04	2.1	6.8	3.3	0.9	34	68	80
	12	L	23	a/a	ARI	79	3.07	1.355	25.48	2.4	7.6	3.1	0.5	34	78	97
Corcino,Daniel	12	R	22	aa	CIN	143	3.92	1.388	23.2	4.2	7.0	1.6	0.7	29	73	60
Cordier,Erik	12	R	26	a/a	ATL	29	8.18	2.44	11.6	8.7	5.4	0.6	0.3	39	64	21
Cosart,Jarred	11	R	21	aa	HOU	36	4.58	1.245	21.1	2.9	4.8	1.7	0.9	27	64	42
	12	R	22	a/a	HOU	115	3.17	1.364	22.85	3.6	6.4	1.8	0.2	31	76	73
Crabbe,Timothy	12	R	24	aa	CIN	86	6.64	1.984	23.04	7.4	8.2	1.1	1.3	35	68	31
Crawford,Evan	11	L	25	aa	TOR	51	4.39	1.64	5.054	3.9	9.1	2.3	0.7	38	74	78
	12	L	26	a/a	TOR	32	7.11	1.983	5.244	4.1	5.8	1.4	0.7	40	62	29

PITCHER	yr	t	age	lvl	org	ip	era	whip	bf/g	ctl	dom	cmd	hr/9	h%	s%	bpv
Crosby,Casey	12	L	24	aaa	DET	126	4.96	1.57	25.07	4.7	6.4	1.4	0.9	31	70	39
Cruz,Joseph	11	R	23	aa	TAM	47	8.66	2.09	20.98	3.5	6.9	2.0	1.4	43	58	21
	12	R	24	aa	TAM	78	5.19	1.59	19.21	6.1	6.2	1.0	0.8	28	68	41
Cumpton,Brandon	12	R	24	aa	PIT	152	4.84	1.47	24.2	2.7	4.1	1.5	0.6	32	66	35
Daley Jr.,Gary	11	R	26	a/a	OAK	115	5.74	1.76	23.93	4.3	5.0	1.2	0.5	35	66	33
	12	R	27	aa	OAK	118	6.06	1.95	16.57	5.8	4.8	0.8	0.7	35	68	17
Daly,Matthew	11	R	25	aa	TOR	36	8.19	2.15	6.176	7.4	6.0	0.8	0.6	37	60	25
	12	R	26	aa	TOR	70	5.98	1.79	6.839	4.9	5.3	1.1	1.3	33	69	8
Darnell,Logan	11	L	22	aa	MIN	31	5.74	1.43	26.05	1.1	5.0	4.6	0.7	35	59	96
	12	L	23	aa	MIN	156	5.91	1.70	25.2	2.7	4.7	1.7	1.2	36	67	18
Davis,Doug	11	L	36	aaa	CHW	56	4.00	1.63	24.74	2.5	6.3	2.5	0.5	38	75	66
	12	L	37	aaa	KC	106	5.69	1.84	24.78	3.5	5.2	1.5	1.0	37	70	20
Davis,Erik	11	R	25	aa	WAS	94	5.98	1.84	21.88	3.9	7.0	1.8	1.0	39	68	39
	12	R	26	a/a	WAS	73	3.42	1.46	6.508	2.5	7.0	2.8	0.9	35	79	72
De Fratus,Justin	12	R	25	aaa	PHI	22	3.36	1.01	4.883	1.4	7.5	5.5	1.0	27	71	138
de la Cruz,Frankie	11	R	27	aaa	MIL	137	4.22	1.55	23.96	4.2	6.6	1.6	1.0	32	75	43
	12	R	28	aaa	CHC	95	4.75	1.87	16.43	6.1	4.1	0.7	0.7	32	75	15
De La Cruz,Kelvin	11	L	23	aa	CLE	86	5.05	1.60	16.53	6.0	8.4	1.4	0.3	32	66	75
	12	L	24	aa	DET	115	6.02	1.60	17	3.9	5.7	1.5	1.4	32	64	21
De La Rosa,Dane	11	R	28	aaa	TAM	70	3.95	1.50	5.837	3.5	8.3	2.4	1.1	34	77	65
	12	R	29	aaa	TAM	68	3.56	1.35	5.23	6.1	8.8	1.4	0.3	26	73	90
De la Rosa,Eury	12	L	22	aa	ARI	63	3.49	1.12	4.704	2.4	8.3	3.5	0.5	30	69	117
De La Rosa,Wilkins	11	L	26	a/a	LA	28	2.74	1.76	5.831	6.0	7.2	1.2	0.0	35	83	67
	12	L	27	aa	CIN	43	3.60	1.81	4.363	6.5	6.8	1.0	0.9	32	82	34
De La Rossa,Wilkins	11	L	26	a/a	LA	28	2.74	1.76	5.831	6.0	7.2	1.2	0.0	35	83	67
	12	L	27	aa	CIN	43	3.60	1.81	4.363	6.5	6.8	1.0	0.9	32	82	34
De La Torre,Jose	11	R	26	aaa	NYM	20	0.98	1.35	5.304	5.1	5.8	1.1	0.0	26	92	70
	12	R	27	a/a	BOS	74	4.07	1.38	6.765	3.3	6.9	2.1	0.3	32	69	78
De Los Santos,Fautinc	11	R	25	a/a	OAK	29	2.26	1.52	5.47	4.8	9.3	1.9	0.3	35	85	91
	12	R	26	aaa	MIL	50	7.44	2.07	6.229	4.0	8.9	2.2	0.5	46	62	69
De los Santos,Frank	11	L	24	aa	TAM	79	3.72	1.39	10.04	2.5	4.6	1.9	0.3	32	72	56
	12	L	25	a/a	TAM	81	2.45	1.41	6.711	2.8	4.7	1.7	0.3	32	83	52
De Los Santos,Miguel	11	L	23	aa	TEX	28	9.88	1.75	21.31	5.6	9.9	1.8	1.6	35	41	46
	12	L	24	aa	TEX	59	6.98	1.76	10.33	5.7	8.5	1.5	1.7	33	63	30
Deduno,Samuel	11	R	28	aaa	SD	105	3.33	1.50	11.37	4.7	5.8	1.2	0.1	31	76	61
	12	R	29	aaa	MIN	42	3.04	1.48	20.05	5.6	7.2	1.3	0.5	29	80	65
Del Rosario,Enerio	12	R	27	aaa	HOU	41	5.12	1.62	5.099	4.2	3.1	0.7	1.1	29	70	-1
Delaney,Rob	11	R	27	aaa	TAM	68	2.25	1.17	5.291	2.4	6.0	2.6	0.4	29	82	83
	12	R	28	aaa	MIA	63	2.93	1.48	6.161	3.0	5.0	1.7	0.3	33	80	53
Delcarmen,Manny	11	R	29	aaa	TEX	39	6.75	2.08	7.284	3.8	5.5	1.4	1.2	41	68	9
	12	R	30	aaa	NYY	57	6.41	2.24	7.397	6.9	6.8	1.0	1.2	39	73	11
Delgado,Randall	11	R	21	a/a	ATL	139	4.28	1.45	23.72	3.5	7.9	2.2	0.9	33	72	66
	12	R	22	aaa	ATL	44	4.38	1.60	24.47	4.1	9.2	2.3	1.2	36	76	65
DeMark,Mike	11	R	28	a/a	ARI	36	1.91	1.11	4.163	2.2	9.0	4.1	0.5	31	85	133
	12	R	29	aaa	ARI	69	4.54	1.65	5.786	2.6	6.1	2.3	0.7	37	73	56
Demel,Sam	12	R	27	aaa	ARI	66	4.21	1.32	4.905	2.8	7.8	2.8	1.4	30	73	64
Demny,Paul	12	R	23	aa	WAS	124	6.53	1.75	20.19	4.2	5.8	1.4	1.0	35	63	25
Dennick,Ryan	12	L	25	aa	KC	74	5.66	1.46	10.56	3.8	6.8	1.8	1.1	31	62	47
DeVries,Cole	11	R	26	a/a	MIN	90	3.97	1.45	8.536	2.4	5.9	2.5	0.7	34	73	64
	12	R	27	aaa	MIN	70	5.93	1.53	25.36	1.4	4.9	3.4	1.0	36	61	62
Diamond,Scott	11	L	25	aaa	MIN	123	6.66	1.81	24.75	2.7	5.3	1.9	0.8	39	62	35
	12	L	26	aaa	MIN	35	3.45	1.48	24.86	2.0	5.3	2.6	0.3	36	76	72
Diaz,Jose	11	R	27	a/a	BAL	45	3.59	1.72	4.227	4.7	7.4	1.6	0.8	36	81	48
	12	R	28	aaa	PIT	45	5.07	1.73	4.99	4.2	5.3	1.2	0.7	34	71	30
Dickson,Brandon	11	R	27	aaa	STL	157	4.31	1.44	25.78	1.9	5.5	2.9	1.1	33	73	54
	12	R	28	aaa	STL	141	4.23	1.48	26.45	1.9	5.0	2.7	1.0	34	74	48
Dodson,Stephen	11	R	26	aa	COL	62	4.40	1.50	6.416	3.7	5.2	1.4	1.3	30	75	20
	12	R	27	aaa	COL	38	4.94	2.01	6.124	3.6	3.8	1.0	0.0	40	73	27
Doran,Robert	12	R	23	aa	HOU	54	4.96	1.48	23.2	2.5	6.2	2.5	1.0	34	68	55
Downs,Darin	12	L	28	aaa	DET	29	2.90	1.39	4.944	2.7	7.4	2.8	0.0	35	77	101
Doyle,John	11	R	26	aa	CHW	100	4.38	1.41	28.22	2.4	5.4	2.3	1.0	32	71	47
	12	R	27	aaa	CHW	76	4.23	1.23	25.79	2.7	6.8	2.5	0.9	29	67	70
Dubee,Michael	11	R	25	a/a	PIT	69	4.61	1.68	6.602	2.8	5.3	1.9	0.5	37	72	45
	12	R	26	aaa	TOR	55	5.38	1.98	6.329	5.1	7.0	1.4	1.1	39	74	27
Dunning,Jake	12	R	24	aa	SF	68	5.38	1.65	6.913	3.0	5.9	2.0	0.3	37	65	59
Dwyer,Christopher	11	L	23	aa	KC	140	6.13	1.50	22.44	4.8	6.6	1.4	0.8	30	58	49
	12	L	24	a/a	KC	136	6.70	1.76	23.95	4.5	5.5	1.2	1.4	33	63	10
Dyer,Shane	11	R	23	aa	TAM	157	4.60	1.56	24.55	2.4	3.3	1.4	0.6	33	70	23
	12	R	24	a/a	TAM	108	5.02	1.60	14.92	3.1	4.2	1.3	0.5	34	68	31
Dyson,Sam	12	R	24	aa	TOR	45	3.02	1.34	5.719	3.1	3.7	1.2	0.5	28	78	35
Edgin,Josh	12	L	26	a/a	NYM	43	3.88	1.47	4.53	4.0	7.2	1.8	0.2	33	72	77
Edlefsen,Steve	11	R	26	aaa	SF	41	5.39	1.69	5.826	3.7	5.1	1.4	0.3	35	66	41
	12	R	27	aaa	SF	38	3.97	1.42	4.607	4.1	5.4	1.3	0.6	29	73	46
Egan,Patrick	11	R	27	a/a	BAL	64	5.79	2.01	7.723	4.2	4.7	1.1	0.6	39	70	19
	12	R	28	a/a	BAL	67	2.46	1.38	7.207	2.0	5.3	2.7	0.2	34	81	80
Egbert,Jack	11	R	28	a/a	NYM	46	3.45	1.35	13.71	3.1	4.0	1.3	0.8	28	77	30
	12	R	29	aaa	NYM	40	6.26	1.65	6.619	2.1	4.4	2.1	0.9	36	62	30
Eitel,Derek	12	R	25	aa	ARI	150	5.71	1.72	25.28	3.2	4.4	1.4	1.2	34	69	7
Ekstrom,Mike	11	R	28	aaa	TAM	68	5.36	1.80	6.866	4.1	6.6	1.6	0.7	38	70	43
	12	R	29	aaa	COL	57	3.06	1.35	5.533	3.0	6.3	2.1	0.0	32	75	83
Elarton,Scott	12	R	36	aaa	PHI	136	8.06	2.09	25.75	4.3	4.3	1.0	1.2	39	61	-6
Ely,John	11	R	25	aaa	LA	144	4.93	1.45	24.66	2.3	5.0	2.2	1.0	33	67	43
	12	R	26	aaa	LA	169	2.92	1.11	24.53	1.7	7.0	4.1	0.8	29	77	111
Enright,Barry	11	R	25	aaa	ARI	123	4.69	1.35	24.35	2.7	5.1	1.9	1.2	29	68	34
	12	R	26	aaa	LAA	163	4.78	1.45	24.02	3.6	4.5	1.2	1.1	29	69	22
Eovaldi,Nathan	11	R	21	aa	LA	103	2.58	1.14	20.42	3.5	7.5	2.2	0.2	27	77	96
	12	R	22	aa	LA	35	3.48	1.29	16	3.1	6.7	2.1	0.5	30	73	74

PITCHER	yr	t	age	lvl	org	ip	era	whip	bf/g	ctl	dom	cmd	hr/9	h%	s%	bpv
Erlin,Robert	11	L	21	aa	SD	93	3.23	1.171	21.76	1.0	8.2	8.3	0.8	34	75	199
	12	L	22	aa	SD	52	2.95	1.316	19.68	2.3	11.2	4.8	0.9	38	81	143
Escalona,Edgmer	11	R	25	aaa	COL	40	2.85	1.139	4.619	2.2	6.9	3.2	0.8	28	79	90
	12	R	26	aaa	COL	40	3.31	1.49	5.388	3.8	6.7	1.8	0.5	33	78	62
Espino,Paolo	11	R	24	a/a	CLE	120	3.26	1.173	14.13	1.9	7.4	4.0	0.8	30	75	106
	12	R	25	a/a	CLE	123	4.12	1.548	22.39	2.9	6.6	2.3	0.7	35	74	61
Evans,Bryan	11	R	24	aa	MIA	37	3.67	1.641	20.82	4.7	5.4	1.2	0.2	33	76	48
	12	R	25	aa	MIA	135	5.74	1.653	20.87	4.5	5.2	1.2	0.9	32	65	27
Eveland,Dana	11	L	28	aaa	LA	154	3.86	1.367	25.79	3.1	4.8	1.5	0.5	30	72	47
	12	L	29	aaa	BAL	84	4.32	1.76	27.48	3.6	4.3	1.2	0.7	35	76	21
Everts,Clinton	11	R	27	a/a	TOR	64	3.87	1.418	5.507	4.0	7.6	1.9	0.8	31	74	66
	12	R	28	a/a	TOR	80	4.18	1.724	7.45	5.3	6.6	1.3	0.3	35	74	55
Familia,Jeurys	11	R	22	aa	NYM	88	3.33	1.308	21.29	3.1	8.3	2.7	0.9	31	77	84
	12	R	23	aaa	NYM	137	4.82	1.599	21.62	4.3	6.9	1.6	0.5	34	69	59
Farquhar,Daniel	11	R	24	aaa	TOR	60	3.73	1.499	4.773	2.8	6.6	2.4	0.5	35	75	69
	12	R	25	a/a	SEA	68	3.01	1.142	6.123	2.9	7.9	2.8	0.4	29	73	103
Faulk,Kenny	12	L	25	aa	DET	58	5.66	1.77	6.617	5.1	8.3	1.6	0.9	37	68	53
Feierabend,Ryan	11	L	26	aaa	PHI	132	7.24	1.729	21.44	3.1	5.0	1.6	1.7	35	60	3
	12	L	27	aaa	CIN	35	8.54	2.127	24.5	4.8	5.1	1.1	3.6	35	68	-73
Fernandez,Anthony	12	L	22	aa	SEA	76	4.06	1.446	24.94	2.9	5.9	2.0	0.7	32	73	53
Fick,Chuckie	11	R	26	aaa	STL	70	2.46	1.236	5.282	4.8	6.1	1.3	0.2	24	79	72
	12	R	27	aaa	HOU	46	5.20	1.568	4.294	2.8	3.6	1.3	1.2	32	69	7
Fields,Joshua	11	R	26	a/a	BOS	56	4.81	1.629	6.595	7.1	8.0	1.1	0.7	28	71	59
	12	R	27	a/a	BOS	58	2.92	1.21	5.597	3.1	9.3	2.9	0.8	30	79	102
Fien,Casey	11	R	28	aaa	HOU	24	5.60	1.719	5.26	3.1	6.9	2.2	2.9	34	78	-9
	12	R	29	aaa	MIN	46	6.11	1.491	6.009	3.2	6.0	1.9	1.1	32	59	40
Fiers,Mike	11	R	26	a/a	MIL	126	2.11	1.055	14.36	2.6	7.7	2.9	0.9	25	86	94
	12	R	27	aaa	MIL	55	5.80	1.484	23.67	3.3	6.4	1.9	1.2	32	62	40
Fife,Stephen	11	R	25	aa	LA	137	3.96	1.504	23.7	3.2	5.1	1.6	0.6	33	74	44
	12	R	26	aaa	LA	135	4.25	1.486	23.31	2.6	4.9	1.9	0.7	33	72	44
Figueroa,Pedro	12	L	27	aaa	OAK	45	2.89	1.316	5.773	3.7	6.4	1.7	0.2	29	77	75
Fisher,Carlos	11	R	28	aaa	CIN	40	4.18	1.434	5.361	4.3	6.9	1.6	1.1	29	74	46
	12	R	29	aaa	CIN	66	6.11	2.077	6.247	8.7	6.6	0.8	1.1	32	71	21
Fitzgerald,Justin	11	R	25	aa	SF	146	4.40	1.588	23.89	3.4	5.6	1.6	0.4	34	71	49
	12	R	26	aa	SF	165	4.41	1.423	24.95	3.5	5.7	1.6	0.5	31	68	55
Flande,Yohan	11	L	25	aaa	ATL	137	5.06	1.657	18.59	2.7	5.7	2.1	0.7	37	69	49
	12	L	26	aaa	ATL	148	4.94	1.602	22.51	3.5	5.3	1.5	0.7	34	69	38
Flannery,Ryan	12	R	26	aa	NYY	45	5.23	1.864	5.739	6.2	4.7	0.8	0.0	34	69	40
Fleet,Austin	12	R	25	aa	SF	56	5.14	1.977	6.591	3.5	7.1	2.0	0.0	44	71	68
Fleming,Marquis	11	R	25	a/a	TAM	83	3.87	1.343	8.002	4.6	9.5	2.1	0.5	30	71	93
	12	R	26	a/a	TAM	76	5.31	1.608	7.042	5.3	7.5	1.4	1.0	31	68	46
Flores,Adalberto	11	R	25	aa	TEX	81	4.26	1.575	8.718	4.5	6.9	1.5	0.7	33	74	51
	12	R	26	a/a	HOU	65	7.92	1.876	6.137	3.5	6.1	1.8	1.9	37	60	2
Flynn,Brian	12	L	22	aa	MIA	50	5.01	1.561	24.34	2.8	5.4	2.0	0.7	35	68	47
Fornataro,Eric	12	R	24	aa	STL	68	2.62	1.154	4.718	2.3	4.5	2.0	0.1	28	76	71
Fox,Matt	12	R	30	a/a	SEA	20	6.69	1.76	18.63	3.5	4.1	1.2	0.5	36	60	24
Fraser,Ryan	12	R	24	aa	NYM	34	3.70	1.301	5.337	3.2	5.4	1.7	0.3	29	70	64
Frazier,Parker	12	R	24	aa	COL	167	5.96	1.708	28.01	2.5	3.9	1.6	1.6	34	69	-5
Freeman,Justin	11	R	25	aa	CIN	60	5.38	1.732	5.058	3.6	7.0	2.0	1.5	36	73	27
	12	R	26	aa	CIN	68	4.12	1.193	4.788	2.4	7.3	3.1	1.3	28	70	74
Freeman,Sam	11	L	24	aa	STL	59	2.68	1.318	4.722	3.9	6.5	1.7	0.5	28	81	65
	12	L	25	a/a	STL	48	2.08	1.217	4.582	3.1	5.9	1.9	0.7	27	86	63
French,Luke	11	L	26	aaa	SEA	146	5.56	1.748	25.71	3.4	4.2	1.2	1.4	34	71	-2
	12	L	27	a/a	MIN	130	5.99	1.691	20.95	4.4	4.0	0.9	1.1	31	65	6
Frias,Marcos	12	R	24	aa	WAS	65	5.89	1.843	6.482	4.2	7.1	1.7	0.5	40	66	54
Friedrich,Christian	11	L	24	aa	COL	133	6.08	1.694	24.08	2.9	5.4	1.8	1.7	35	68	10
	12	L	25	aaa	COL	30	3.33	0.995	22.89	1.2	6.2	5.3	0.3	28	65	146
Friend,Justin	11	R	25	aa	PHI	29	3.92	1.418	4.286	2.5	7.8	3.1	0.3	36	71	100
	12	R	26	a/a	PHI	54	1.73	1.367	4.521	3.2	7.2	2.2	0.2	33	87	86
Fujikawa,Kyuji	11	R	0	for	JPN	51	1.53	0.843	3.336	2.8	13.4	4.7	0.6	26	86	185
	12	R	0	for	JPN	47	1.66	1.168	3.921	3.6	10.5	3.0	0.3	31	87	127
Gailey,Frank	11	L	26	aa	TOR	30	7.63	1.734	7.191	3.6	5.6	1.6	1.6	35	57	10
	12	L	27	a/a	PHI	30	6.05	2.064	5.366	4.0	6.2	1.5	0.7	42	70	29
Galarraga,Armando	11	R	29	aaa	ARI	23	9.12	2.116	23.04	6.2	4.5	0.7	3.2	32	63	-65
	12	R	30	aaa	HOU	44	4.47	1.416	20.55	3.8	4.8	1.3	1.5	27	74	13
Gallagher,Sean	11	R	26	aaa	PIT	132	6.26	1.689	20.53	4.5	5.0	1.1	1.1	32	63	17
	12	R	27	aaa	CIN	139	6.23	1.769	24.53	5.2	4.3	0.8	1.5	30	67	-6
Gamboa,Eduardo	11	R	27	aa	BAL	74	4.36	1.248	14.27	1.6	4.7	2.8	1.2	29	69	51
	12	R	28	a/a	BAL	109	5.48	1.715	18.25	2.1	4.9	2.4	0.9	38	69	38
Garate,Victor	11	L	27	aaa	MIA	56	2.91	1.513	5.677	5.7	7.3	1.3	0.7	29	83	57
	12	L	28	aaa	MIL	39	10.44	2.336	6.993	5.8	7.2	1.2	1.2	44	53	13
Garcia,Christian	12	R	27	a/a	WAS	52	1.11	1.072	4.526	3.0	8.6	2.8	0.0	28	89	124
Garcia,Ramon	11	L	27	a/a	DET	105	5.64	1.611	14.06	2.7	4.8	1.8	1.3	34	67	18
	12	L	28	a/a	DET	159	6.37	1.723	24.96	2.5	4.2	1.7	1.4	35	65	6
Gardner,Joe	11	R	23	aa	COL	134	5.13	1.599	23.63	3.7	4.4	1.2	0.6	33	67	30
	12	R	24	aa	COL	138	6.18	1.556	21.62	2.9	5.0	1.7	1.4	32	62	20
Garrison,Steve	11	L	25	aa	NYY	76	7.58	1.916	21.08	2.6	4.4	1.7	1.9	38	63	-13
	12	L	26	a/a	SEA	125	5.96	1.645	23.19	1.8	3.5	1.9	1.4	35	66	7
Gast,John	11	L	22	aa	STL	79	3.47	1.327	25.31	3.3	5.2	1.6	0.7	28	75	48
	12	L	23	a/a	STL	161	4.33	1.425	24.36	3.0	6.0	2.0	0.7	32	70	55
Gaub,John	11	L	26	aaa	CHC	55	3.45	1.527	4.811	6.3	9.7	1.5	0.9	29	80	72
	12	L	27	aaa	STL	53	6.15	1.699	4.463	4.8	7.4	1.5	0.8	35	63	50
Gayhart,Jared	11	R	25	aa	DET	67	4.08	1.415	7.631	3.5	6.1	1.7	1.2	29	75	40
	12	R	26	aa	DET	92	5.86	1.589	11.63	3.4	7.4	2.1	1.2	35	65	47
Gearrin,Cory	11	R	25	aaa	ATL	50	2.27	1.437	6.082	3.8	9.0	2.4	0.0	36	82	106
	12	R	26	aaa	ATL	55	2.71	1.34	5.831	3.8	8.9	2.4	0.0	33	78	109
Geer,Josh	12	R	29	a/a	SD	160	5.79	1.746	26.09	2.2	4.6	2.1	0.8	38	67	32

PITCHER	yr	t	age	lvl	org	ip	era	whip	bf/g	ctl	dom	cmd	hr/9	h%	s%	bpv
Geltz,Steve	12	R	25	a/a	LAA	59	3.41	1.14	5.077	3.0	8.7	2.9	0.6	28	71	105
Germano,Justin	11	R	29	aaa	CLE	49	5.32	1.37	12.84	0.8	5.3	6.6	1.0	34	62	134
	12	R	30	aaa	BOS	105	3.73	1.25	25.11	1.3	4.5	3.3	1.7	28	79	44
Germen,Gonzalez	12	R	25	a/a	NYM	127	4.96	1.44	25.67	2.3	5.6	2.4	0.8	33	65	57
Gilliam,Robert	12	R	25	aa	WAS	85	7.96	1.76	19.4	3.9	6.3	1.6	1.1	36	54	29
Gilmartin,Sean	12	L	22	a/a	ATL	157	4.39	1.32	24.06	2.2	5.7	2.6	0.9	31	68	62
Gleason,Sean	12	R	27	a/a	BAL	43	8.42	2.16	10.63	3.5	5.3	1.5	1.7	42	62	-10
Gloor,Christopher	12	L	25	aa	SF	106	3.77	1.44	14.06	2.6	5.2	2.0	0.7	32	75	50
Godfrey,Graham	11	R	27	a/a	OAK	111	2.81	1.26	22.7	2.6	6.1	2.4	0.4	30	78	77
	12	R	28	aaa	OAK	104	3.72	1.37	21.8	2.4	4.0	1.7	0.7	30	74	39
Gomes,Brandon	11	R	27	aaa	TAM	25	1.29	1.09	4.959	2.6	11.3	4.3	0.4	33	90	158
	12	R	28	aaa	TAM	55	3.85	1.25	5.636	2.4	9.2	3.8	0.9	33	72	111
Gomez,Jeanmar	11	R	23	aaa	CLE	138	2.82	1.33	27.18	3.1	5.9	1.9	0.5	30	80	64
	12	R	24	aaa	CLE	69	4.93	1.45	26.91	2.1	5.8	2.7	0.7	34	66	64
Gonzalez,Edgar	11	R	28	aaa	COL	133	4.79	1.55	22.4	2.6	4.2	1.6	0.9	33	70	26
	12	R	29	aaa	HOU	60	4.68	1.39	14.76	2.0	5.5	2.8	0.8	33	67	64
Gonzalez,Miguel	11	R	27	a/a	BOS	52	7.70	1.84	15.05	4.0	6.7	1.7	1.0	38	57	34
	12	R	28	aaa	BAL	45	2.44	0.93	11.97	2.4	8.0	3.4	0.3	25	74	126
Gorgen,Matthew	12	R	25	a/a	ARI	62	3.27	1.38	5.425	3.5	8.3	2.4	0.6	33	77	84
Gorgen,Scott	12	R	25	a/a	STL	129	4.53	1.49	19.24	4.1	6.7	1.6	0.6	32	70	56
Gorski,Darin	12	L	25	aa	NYM	140	4.35	1.36	23.37	3.1	6.0	2.0	1.3	29	72	41
Graham,Caleb	12	R	25	a/a	LAA	59	3.26	1.15	4.753	2.7	8.3	3.1	0.8	29	74	101
Graham,J.R.	12	R	22	aa	ATL	45	3.85	1.26	20.56	3.4	7.4	2.2	0.4	30	69	85
Gray,Sonny	11	R	22	aa	OAK	20	0.44	1.05	15.48	2.5	7.1	2.9	0.0	28	95	115
	12	R	23	a/a	OAK	152	4.48	1.48	24.23	3.3	5.1	1.5	0.4	32	69	48
Greenwood,Nick	11	L	24	a/a	STL	79	4.20	1.33	5.485	2.2	5.0	2.2	0.8	30	70	53
	12	L	25	aaa	STL	78	4.80	1.55	6.933	2.7	4.4	1.6	0.6	34	69	35
Griffin,A.J.	11	R	23	a/a	OAK	38	5.91	1.56	23.78	2.9	5.7	2.0	1.4	33	64	29
	12	R	24	a/a	OAK	102	3.03	1.02	23.06	1.6	6.8	4.4	0.6	28	71	124
Griffith,Nevin	11	R	22	aa	CHW	108	7.55	2.06	21.14	8.9	6.3	0.7	0.9	32	62	27
	12	R	23	aa	CHW	55	7.88	2.08	8.366	10.2	5.9	0.6	0.4	29	59	40
Grimm,Justin	12	R	24	a/a	TEX	135	3.51	1.32	22.28	2.1	5.5	2.6	0.4	32	73	74
Grube,Jarrett	11	R	30	a/a	SEA	144	4.24	1.34	21.42	2.5	5.8	2.3	0.8	31	70	58
	12	R	31	a/a	LAA	92	7.61	2.04	18.62	2.7	6.0	2.2	1.1	43	62	29
Guerra,Deolis	11	R	22	aa	MIN	95	5.76	1.41	10.85	2.5	7.7	3.1	0.9	35	58	84
	12	R	23	a/a	MIN	70	4.95	1.37	8.152	2.9	7.6	2.7	0.9	33	64	76
Guilmet,Preston	12	R	25	aa	CLE	53	3.31	1.25	4.288	2.4	7.1	2.9	0.8	30	76	83
Gustafson,Timothy	11	R	27	aa	CIN	97	5.18	1.61	13.81	4.2	4.4	1.0	1.1	30	69	13
	12	R	28	a/a	CIN	132	7.44	1.96	19.71	4.5	4.9	1.1	1.6	36	64	-10
Guzman,Jose	12	R	25	aa	OAK	54	5.11	1.54	6.925	3.4	6.8	2.0	0.5	35	65	65
Hacker,Eric	11	R	28	aaa	MIN	136	7.80	1.89	24.6	3.7	4.9	1.3	1.2	37	58	7
	12	R	29	aaa	SF	150	4.40	1.45	24.67	2.6	4.6	1.8	0.7	32	70	43
Hale,David	12	R	25	aa	ATL	146	4.86	1.50	23.33	4.5	6.4	1.4	0.8	30	68	48
Hall,Shaeffer	11	L	24	a/a	NYY	157	5.35	1.69	26.2	2.4	4.7	2.0	1.2	36	70	22
	12	L	25	aa	NYY	164	4.73	1.60	26.88	2.4	4.4	1.8	1.1	34	73	22
Hamburger,Mark	11	R	24	a/a	TEX	82	3.94	1.21	7.898	2.8	6.1	2.2	1.1	27	71	58
	12	R	25	aaa	HOU	78	6.08	1.83	8.478	3.8	6.0	1.6	1.2	37	68	22
Hamren,Erik	11	R	25	a/a	SD	52	0.92	0.99	5.653	2.4	7.4	3.0	0.1	26	91	119
	12	R	26	a/a	SD	62	3.86	1.58	4.706	5.0	9.1	1.8	0.5	35	75	80
Hand,Brad	11	L	21	aa	MIA	109	3.51	1.31	23.64	4.0	5.1	1.3	0.8	26	75	43
	12	L	22	aaa	MIA	148	4.52	1.47	23.58	4.6	7.4	1.6	0.8	30	70	57
Hand,Donovan	11	R	25	a/a	MIL	66	3.77	1.73	6.289	3.0	5.0	1.7	0.9	36	80	27
	12	R	26	aaa	MIL	80	4.93	1.63	8.063	2.2	5.0	2.2	1.0	36	71	37
Hankins,Derek	11	R	28	a/a	TEX	110	7.24	1.89	17.92	3.7	4.2	1.1	2.4	34	67	-36
	12	R	29	aaa	TEX	83	6.55	1.96	11.33	3.6	3.9	1.1	1.6	37	69	-19
Hardy,Blaine	11	L	24	a/a	KC	69	4.35	1.57	7.176	4.5	6.7	1.5	1.0	31	75	40
	12	L	25	a/a	KC	75	4.03	1.73	8.577	3.7	5.4	1.4	1.0	35	79	24
Harman,Casey	12	L	23	aa	CHC	55	5.99	1.66	7.284	1.9	5.9	3.2	1.9	36	68	33
Harris,Tyrelle	11	R	25	a/a	CHC	37	2.31	1.66	9.288	6.7	5.9	0.9	0.7	28	89	38
	12	R	26	a/a	CHC	61	5.37	1.70	12.46	4.2	5.3	1.3	0.7	34	68	32
Harris,Will	12	R	28	a/a	COL	52	2.90	1.16	4.708	2.5	8.2	3.2	0.5	30	76	109
Harvey,Kris	11	R	27	aa	MIA	32	7.74	1.85	6.293	4.5	5.0	1.1	1.6	34	59	-4
	12	R	28	aa	PIT	55	4.53	1.78	8.11	4.9	5.3	1.1	0.8	34	75	25
Harvey,Matt	11	R	22	aa	NYM	60	4.33	1.32	20.56	2.9	8.1	2.7	0.5	33	66	94
	12	R	23	aaa	NYM	110	3.75	1.33	22.8	3.5	7.5	2.1	0.7	30	73	75
Hatcher,Chris	11	R	26	aa	MIA	47	2.15	1.20	4.536	3.8	8.6	2.2	0.4	28	83	100
	12	R	27	aaa	MIA	47	0.96	1.22	5.132	3.2	6.7	2.1	0.2	29	93	86
Hatley,Marcus	11	R	23	aa	CHC	29	5.16	1.52	5.717	3.4	5.3	1.6	0.6	32	65	42
	12	R	24	a/a	CHC	60	5.54	1.48	6.48	4.6	7.9	1.7	0.5	32	61	72
Haviland,Shawn	11	R	26	aa	OAK	144	7.61	1.89	25.09	2.6	5.6	2.1	1.3	40	60	20
	12	R	27	aa	OAK	120	5.69	1.65	17.3	3.8	6.2	1.6	0.8	35	65	41
Hayes,Andrew	12	R	25	aa	CIN	63	4.72	1.72	5.131	6.0	7.5	1.3	0.6	33	72	55
Heath,Deunte	11	R	26	aaa	CHW	103	6.01	1.93	16.25	6.6	8.5	1.3	1.5	36	71	29
	12	R	27	aaa	CHW	67	2.21	1.32	7.713	3.5	8.0	2.3	0.8	31	88	77
Heckathorn,Kyle	11	R	23	aa	MIL	36	8.21	1.86	24.28	4.2	5.2	1.2	1.9	34	57	-12
	12	R	24	aa	MIL	119	5.76	1.57	14.98	3.0	5.7	1.9	0.6	35	62	50
Hefner,Jeremy	11	R	25	aaa	SD	157	3.95	1.42	23.84	3.1	5.9	1.9	0.8	31	74	51
	12	R	26	aaa	NYM	62	3.01	1.16	24.55	1.4	4.2	3.0	0.6	29	75	73
Heidenreich,Matthew	12	R	21	aa	HOU	53	4.59	1.50	20.67	1.9	5.3	2.9	0.5	36	68	70
Hellweg,John	12	R	24	aa	MIL	140	3.99	1.57	21.9	5.0	5.8	1.1	0.6	30	75	43
Hembree,Heath	11	R	22	aa	SF	29	3.33	1.22	4.137	3.9	9.3	2.4	0.3	30	72	108
	12	R	23	aaa	SF	38	4.55	1.24	3.961	4.1	7.3	1.8	0.4	27	61	81
Henderson,Jim	11	R	29	a/a	MIL	61	5.20	1.47	6.232	5.0	7.8	1.5	1.4	28	68	44
	12	R	30	aaa	MIL	48	2.34	1.54	5.978	4.9	7.9	1.6	0.5	33	86	69
Hendriks,Liam	11	R	22	a/a	MIN	139	3.61	1.20	22.42	1.3	6.1	4.7	0.3	32	68	129
	12	R	23	aaa	MIN	106	2.74	1.11	26.12	2.5	5.8	2.4	0.4	27	76	81
Henry,Bryan	11	R	26	aa	ARI	99	5.59	1.72	14	3.0	4.9	1.6	1.5	35	71	6
	12	R	27	a/a	ARI	79	5.79	1.81	12.14	2.4	3.3	1.4	1.9	35	73	-23

PITCHER	yr	t	age	lvl	org	ip	era	whip	bf/g	ctl	dom	cmd	hr/9	h%	s%	bpv
Hensley,Steven	11	R	25	aa	SEA	96	5.31	1.758	23.05	3.7	5.2	1.4	0.9	36	71	23
	12	R	26	a/a	SEA	71	5.63	1.556	7.028	5.2	6.2	1.2	1.0	29	64	35
Hermsen,BJ	12	R	23	aa	MIN	140	3.75	1.355	26.5	1.6	4.0	2.5	0.7	32	74	52
Hernandez,Carlos	11	L	24	a/a	OAK	152	5.37	1.615	24.97	2.4	5.9	2.5	0.9	37	67	50
	12	L	25	a/a	OAK	102	5.59	1.619	14.65	2.6	5.9	2.2	1.2	36	67	37
Hernandez,Chris	12	L	24	a/a	BOS	146	4.45	1.586	24.8	3.5	4.5	1.3	0.8	32	73	26
Hernandez,Fernando	11	R	27	a/a	NYY	37	8.52	2.598	5.896	4.8	8.2	1.7	2.1	49	70	-8
	12	R	28	aa	TOR	106	6.01	1.9	13.85	2.8	5.6	2.0	0.9	40	69	31
Hernandez,Gaby	11	R	25	aaa	ARI	141	5.98	1.758	24.83	4.1	4.8	1.2	1.4	33	68	2
	12	R	26	aa	ARI	65	8.36	1.842	21.53	3.7	6.3	1.7	1.9	37	56	5
Hernandez,Moises	11	R	27	aa	SEA	72	7.52	2.004	8.683	3.9	4.5	1.1	1.3	38	63	-4
	12	R	28	aa	SEA	50	9.26	2.375	8.117	6.6	2.4	0.4	1.1	37	60	-28
Hernandez,Pedro	11	L	22	a/a	SD	59	3.52	1.305	18.83	2.1	6.9	3.2	0.7	32	75	87
	12	L	23	a/a	MIN	103	4.00	1.458	23.19	2.0	4.8	2.4	0.7	34	73	53
Herrmann,Frank	12	R	28	aaa	CLE	53	5.83	1.648	5.602	2.7	7.5	2.8	1.4	37	67	51
Heston,Chris	12	R	24	aa	SF	149	2.94	1.29	24.44	2.5	6.8	2.7	0.1	33	76	97
Heyer,Craig	11	R	26	aa	NYY	147	5.92	1.685	23.6	2.6	3.6	1.4	0.8	35	64	17
	12	R	27	a/a	NYY	74	7.77	1.919	13.49	3.5	4.4	1.3	1.0	38	59	6
Hill,Shawn	12	R	31	aaa	TOR	90	5.29	1.823	27.76	2.3	3.9	1.7	1.1	38	73	8
Hinton,Robert	11	R	27	a/a	MIL	62	2.87	1.38	6.056	3.5	7.8	2.2	1.1	31	85	62
	12	R	28	aa	BAL	59	4.38	1.561	6.341	2.3	6.8	2.9	0.8	37	73	70
Hirschfeld,Steven	11	R	26	aa	MIN	128	4.17	1.387	17.95	3.1	5.0	1.6	0.6	30	70	46
	12	R	27	a/a	MIN	146	6.48	1.849	24.29	2.5	4.5	1.8	1.2	38	66	11
Hoey,Jim	11	R	29	aaa	MIN	42	5.01	1.53	5.58	5.1	5.9	1.2	1.3	28	70	24
	12	R	30	aaa	TOR	61	5.39	1.917	6.248	6.6	5.0	0.8	0.8	33	72	16
Hoffman,Matthew	11	L	23	a/a	DET	63	4.16	1.493	5.406	3.5	5.4	1.5	0.5	32	72	49
	12	L	24	aaa	DET	46	4.56	1.745	4.919	3.1	4.9	1.6	0.9	36	75	26
Holder,Trevor	12	R	25	aa	WAS	52	4.72	1.466	22.43	1.9	3.1	1.7	0.6	33	67	29
Hollands,Mario	12	L	24	a/a	PHI	60	7.11	1.945	23.83	4.2	4.8	1.1	1.4	37	65	-3
Hollingsworth,Ethan	11	R	24	a/a	OAK	105	3.83	1.464	23.75	2.2	5.3	2.4	0.7	34	75	55
	12	R	25	a/a	KC	103	5.60	1.701	13.65	2.7	4.5	1.7	0.7	37	66	31
Holmberg,David	12	L	21	aa	ARI	95	4.38	1.482	27.24	2.1	5.5	2.6	0.9	34	72	55
Holt,Bradley	11	R	25	aa	NYM	94	4.64	1.401	11.63	4.9	5.6	1.1	0.6	26	66	48
	12	R	26	a/a	NYM	53	4.48	1.738	5.368	5.2	5.9	1.1	0.5	34	74	41
Hooker,James	11	R	22	aa	STL	58	4.19	1.22	21.42	2.4	5.1	2.1	0.9	28	67	54
	12	R	23	aa	STL	48	4.62	1.526	5.639	3.2	6.8	2.1	0.8	34	71	57
Hoover,J.J.	11	R	24	a/a	ATL	106	3.06	1.213	9.91	3.4	8.5	2.5	0.4	29	75	99
	12	R	25	aaa	CIN	37	1.47	0.813	4.48	3.0	11.1	3.7	0.3	22	83	161
Horst,Jeremy	11	L	26	aaa	CIN	51	3.35	1.227	5.771	2.5	6.0	2.3	0.4	29	72	77
	12	L	27	aaa	PHI	38	2.97	1.99	7.092	4.8	5.9	1.2	0.9	38	88	21
House,T.J.	12	L	23	aa	CLE	124	5.29	1.479	23.24	3.3	5.5	1.7	0.6	32	63	49
Houston,Daniel	11	R	25	aa	COL	78	5.30	1.601	26.53	2.1	4.5	2.1	0.9	35	67	34
	12	R	26	aa	COL	161	6.07	1.77	27.43	2.5	4.0	1.6	1.5	36	68	-2
Huff,David	11	L	27	aaa	CLE	107	4.66	1.538	25.9	2.6	4.3	1.6	0.9	33	71	28
	12	L	28	a/a	CLE	138	6.45	1.728	25.1	2.5	4.1	1.6	2.0	34	67	-15
Hughes,Dusty	11	L	29	aaa	MIN	57	5.61	1.723	5.987	4.3	7.9	1.8	1.0	37	68	50
	12	L	30	aaa	ATL	65	4.37	1.957	5.78	5.7	5.7	1.0	0.3	37	77	37
Hultzen,Danny	12	L	23	a/a	SEA	124	3.33	1.367	20.77	5.4	8.8	1.6	0.3	29	75	91
Hunt,Leroy	12	R	25	aa	CHW	55	5.48	1.941	9.084	6.4	4.4	0.7	0.4	34	70	22
Hunter,Brett	11	R	24	a/a	OAK	30	4.33	1.593	5.237	4.9	7.4	1.5	0.8	33	74	54
	12	R	25	aa	OAK	56	5.11	1.644	5.953	5.1	8.0	1.6	1.1	33	71	49
Hunter,Tommy	11	R	25	a/a	TEX	31	5.92	1.657	15.26	1.2	4.8	4.0	1.1	38	65	64
	12	R	26	a/a	BAL	29	4.13	1.205	23.62	2.0	4.8	2.4	0.8	28	67	58
Huntzinger,Brock	11	R	23	aa	BOS	124	7.02	1.752	22.68	2.9	7.5	2.6	1.6	39	62	38
	12	R	24	aa	BOS	74	5.48	1.43	7.862	3.2	5.9	1.8	0.6	32	60	56
Hurley,Eric	11	R	26	aaa	TEX	84	6.27	1.908	24.92	3.9	3.7	1.0	1.2	36	68	-9
	12	R	27	aaa	MIN	112	9.30	1.986	23.34	4.0	5.0	1.2	1.4	38	52	-2
Hyatt,Austin	11	R	25	aa	PHI	154	4.48	1.339	22.92	2.9	8.2	2.8	1.3	31	70	73
	12	R	26	a/a	PHI	142	6.86	1.739	23.92	3.6	5.6	1.6	1.8	34	64	2
Hyde,Lee	11	L	26	aaa	WAS	38	7.10	1.963	4.327	6.2	6.9	1.1	1.4	35	65	17
	12	L	27	a/a	NYY	44	5.28	1.694	4.054	5.6	6.9	1.2	0.6	33	68	50
Hynes,Colt	11	L	26	a/a	SD	84	3.85	1.535	5.481	3.0	4.7	1.6	0.2	34	73	52
	12	L	27	aaa	SD	127	5.64	1.856	19.74	2.1	4.3	2.1	0.6	40	69	32
Hynick,Brandon	11	R	26	a/a	CIN	119	5.90	1.546	16.76	3.1	5.0	1.6	1.2	32	63	24
	12	R	27	a/a	COL	102	4.33	1.527	26.08	2.3	4.2	1.8	1.0	33	74	26
Ibarra,Edgar	12	L	23	aa	MIN	34	7.16	1.791	6.468	4.0	6.3	1.6	1.5	36	61	16
Infante,Gregory	11	R	24	a/a	CHW	64	3.29	1.589	6.103	4.6	6.6	1.4	1.0	32	83	41
	12	R	25	a/a	CHW	33	4.73	1.702	7.107	5.2	4.8	0.9	0.4	32	71	35
Inman,Jeffrey	12	R	25	aa	PIT	52	4.93	1.438	7.333	3.4	4.8	1.4	0.4	31	64	47
Inman,Will	11	R	24	aaa	SD	117	4.78	1.532	12.12	3.8	8.0	2.1	0.8	35	69	68
	12	R	25	aaa	BOS	48	3.14	1.685	6.222	6.9	9.0	1.3	0.7	32	83	67
Irwin,Phillip	11	R	24	aa	PIT	87	4.64	1.332	24.17	1.0	5.5	5.4	1.0	34	67	113
	12	R	25	a/a	PIT	125	3.74	1.34	23.7	1.8	6.1	3.4	0.6	33	73	86
Jackson,Jay	11	R	24	aaa	CHC	147	5.16	1.571	24.77	2.6	4.9	1.9	0.6	35	66	45
	12	R	25	aaa	CHC	86	7.68	1.924	11.07	4.6	6.4	1.4	1.6	37	61	8
Jackson,Matthew	12	R	25	a/a	SD	53	2.89	1.062	22.86	1.2	5.8	4.9	0.4	29	73	130
Jackson,Randy	11	R	24	aaa	CHC	147	5.16	1.571	24.77	2.6	4.9	1.9	0.6	35	66	45
	12	R	25	aaa	CHC	86	7.68	1.924	11.07	4.6	6.4	1.4	1.6	37	61	8
Jackson,Zach	11	L	28	aaa	TEX	152	6.50	1.856	25.39	3.5	3.4	1.0	1.5	35	67	-19
	12	L	29	aaa	TEX	158	6.79	1.96	28.03	4.0	3.0	0.8	1.4	35	67	-23
Jacobson,Brett	11	R	25	aa	MIN	101	4.99	1.529	11.52	5.1	5.7	1.1	0.7	29	67	41
	12	R	26	aa	COL	47	12.53	2.841	11.49	12.0	5.0	0.4	1.6	37	54	-24
Jeffress,Jeremy	11	R	24	a/a	KC	56	6.08	1.883	10.47	6.3	5.7	0.9	1.0	33	68	19
	12	R	25	a/a	KC	59	5.64	1.455	6.675	4.0	7.6	1.9	0.6	32	60	70
Jenkins,Chad	11	R	24	aa	TOR	100	5.29	1.393	26.42	2.5	5.6	2.2	0.9	32	62	52
	12	R	25	aa	TOR	114	6.42	1.833	26.6	2.6	3.7	1.4	1.7	36	68	-14
Jennings,Dan	11	L	24	a/a	MIA	56	5.50	1.648	5.593	4.5	7.4	1.7	0.5	35	65	60
	12	L	25	aaa	MIA	52	3.76	1.424	5.221	3.0	6.8	2.3	0.3	34	73	77

PITCHER	yr	t	age	lvl	org	ip	era	whip	bf/g	ctl	dom	cmd	hr/9	h%	s%	bpv
Jimenez,Cesar	11	L	27	aaa	SEA	71	3.67	1.50	7.141	4.2	8.4	2.0	0.3	35	75	85
	12	L	28	aaa	SEA	40	6.27	1.97	8.405	4.4	6.6	1.5	0.6	40	67	38
Jimenez,Jose	12	L	25	a/a	SEA	29	6.01	1.80	6.383	4.2	9.0	2.2	0.6	41	65	72
Johnson,Blake	11	R	26	a/a	COL	77	5.95	1.70	8.134	3.5	4.5	1.3	0.8	35	64	23
	12	R	27	a/a	LA	72	5.10	1.48	7.34	3.4	5.3	1.6	1.0	31	67	34
Johnson,Kevin	12	R	24	a/a	LAA	63	4.04	1.50	4.889	2.2	3.7	1.7	1.0	32	76	21
Johnson,Kristofer	11	L	27	aaa	BOS	21	18.41	2.95	14.91	3.0	4.0	1.4	3.9	48	36	-104
	12	L	28	a/a	PIT	102	4.43	1.64	12.95	4.1	4.7	1.2	1.1	32	75	17
Johnson,Steve	11	R	24	a/a	BAL	146	5.40	1.60	23.86	3.9	6.1	1.6	1.1	33	68	33
	12	R	25	aaa	BAL	91	4.05	1.29	19.77	3.3	6.7	2.0	1.0	28	71	60
Jokisch,Eric	11	L	22	aa	CHC	15	4.47	1.70	23.09	5.1	7.6	1.5	0.0	36	71	75
	12	L	23	aa	CHC	105	3.58	1.28	23.91	2.9	4.6	1.6	0.7	27	73	44
Jones,Beau	11	L	25	a/a	TEX	68	3.91	1.51	6.887	3.9	6.1	1.5	1.3	30	79	29
	12	L	26	a/a	OAK	46	6.35	1.71	4.959	6.4	5.7	0.9	1.1	29	63	23
Jones,Chris	12	L	24	aa	ATL	60	4.92	1.70	6.031	3.0	7.8	2.6	0.2	41	69	86
Joseph,Don	11	L	24	aa	CIN	58	6.96	1.70	4.623	4.3	8.6	2.0	1.2	37	59	51
	12	L	25	a/a	KC	70	2.70	1.36	5.299	3.9	8.8	2.2	0.2	33	80	98
Judy,Josh	11	R	25	aaa	CLE	52	3.59	1.45	4.443	4.3	8.4	2.0	0.9	32	78	70
	12	R	26	aaa	CIN	57	8.65	2.00	6.834	5.0	7.2	1.4	1.2	39	56	25
Jurrjens,Jair	12	R	26	aaa	ATL	72	5.84	1.51	22.37	2.1	4.0	1.9	1.3	32	63	18
Kaminska,Kyle	11	R	23	aa	MIA	17	3.94	1.25	9.89	2.1	5.4	2.6	0.5	30	68	74
	12	R	24	a/a	PIT	66	6.12	1.74	8.099	1.3	5.9	4.7	1.3	40	67	76
Keating,Patrick	11	R	24	aa	KC	38	6.83	1.54	5.716	2.8	8.3	3.0	1.9	35	59	50
	12	R	25	aa	KC	41	5.87	1.60	5.709	4.1	6.6	1.6	1.5	32	66	26
Keck,Jonathon	12	L	24	aa	KC	42	4.85	1.72	6.861	5.8	7.1	1.2	0.4	34	71	56
Kehrt,Jeremy	11	R	26	a/a	BOS	93	5.81	1.74	14.67	2.9	3.9	1.4	1.5	34	70	-6
	12	R	27	a/a	BOS	113	6.24	1.86	19.64	2.9	4.2	1.5	1.1	38	67	7
Kelly,Casey	12	R	23	a/a	SD	29	3.02	0.92	21.47	0.9	8.9	9.9	0.2	30	66	264
Kelly,Joe	11	R	23	aa	STL	59	4.33	1.53	23.44	3.4	6.5	1.9	0.8	34	72	54
	12	R	24	aaa	STL	72	3.05	1.42	25.59	2.6	4.6	1.8	0.2	32	77	56
Kelly,Kenneth	12	R	24	aa	TAM	88	3.80	1.37	11.56	2.8	5.3	1.9	0.4	31	72	59
Kelly,Ryan	12	R	25	a/a	SD	55	3.28	1.36	5.109	2.8	7.1	2.6	0.3	34	75	89
Keuchel,Dallas	11	L	23	a/a	HOU	164	4.22	1.31	25.04	2.0	4.3	2.2	0.8	30	69	48
	12	L	24	aaa	HOU	92	3.74	1.23	23.38	1.8	4.1	2.3	0.4	29	69	61
Kickham,Mike	12	L	24	aa	SF	151	4.00	1.47	23.09	4.6	6.9	1.5	0.5	30	73	61
Kintzler,Brandon	12	R	28	a/a	MIL	47	3.80	1.50	5.241	3.0	4.6	1.5	0.2	33	73	49
Kirkman,Michael	11	L	25	aaa	TEX	73	5.59	1.85	12.62	4.5	8.1	1.8	0.8	39	70	51
	12	L	26	aaa	TEX	48	6.45	1.86	14.98	6.2	6.9	1.1	1.2	34	66	25
Kloess,Brandon	11	R	27	a/a	CHW	41	1.53	0.94	8.495	1.9	7.0	3.6	0.6	24	89	113
	12	R	28	a/a	CHW	74	3.83	1.63	8.861	4.7	6.8	1.4	0.2	35	75	64
Kluber,Corey	11	R	25	aaa	CLE	151	6.40	1.63	24.84	4.2	6.9	1.7	1.1	34	61	39
	12	R	26	aaa	CLE	125	4.18	1.52	25.93	3.6	7.3	2.0	0.6	34	73	65
Koehler,Tom	11	R	25	aaa	MIA	150	5.09	1.56	23.53	4.7	5.6	1.2	0.9	30	68	33
	12	R	26	aaa	MIA	151	5.12	1.67	23.37	4.0	6.5	1.6	0.9	35	70	41
Kontos,George	11	R	26	aaa	NYY	89	3.79	1.39	9.399	3.0	7.2	2.4	1.8	30	82	39
	12	R	27	aaa	SF	32	1.79	1.06	5.341	1.9	5.8	3.1	0.2	27	83	101
Kopp,David	11	R	26	a/a	STL	74	6.02	1.69	10.77	3.6	4.6	1.3	1.3	33	66	8
	12	R	27	aa	DET	32	8.00	2.16	9.467	4.4	5.0	1.1	1.6	40	64	-14
Koronis,Alexander	12	R	24	aa	TAM	39	4.65	1.58	7.203	6.7	7.2	1.1	0.5	28	69	61
Kown,Andrew	11	R	29	aaa	SF	137	4.56	1.54	23.83	3.3	5.1	1.5	0.8	32	71	34
	12	R	30	aaa	SF	119	6.20	1.75	23.63	3.4	3.7	1.1	1.0	34	65	6
Kroenke,Zach	11	L	27	aaa	ARI	128	5.54	1.78	25.68	3.2	3.9	1.2	0.9	36	69	12
	12	L	28	aaa	ARI	119	6.00	1.73	16.91	2.6	3.4	1.3	0.9	35	65	8
Kunz,Edward	11	R	25	aa	SD	73	4.27	1.51	6.103	4.1	2.8	0.7	0.4	29	71	20
	12	R	26	a/a	SD	87	5.91	1.72	10.44	4.1	3.4	0.8	0.6	33	64	12
Kurcz,Aaron	12	R	22	aa	BOS	50	3.95	1.53	7.556	4.9	11.0	2.2	0.8	36	76	92
Kussmaul,Ryan	12	R	26	a/a	CHW	58	1.90	1.24	6.204	4.5	7.8	1.7	0.7	25	88	77
Lafferty,Brendan	11	L	25	aa	KC	25	4.89	1.60	10.05	2.5	5.6	2.2	1.0	36	71	42
	12	L	26	aa	KC	60	5.98	1.81	6.493	6.3	8.1	1.3	1.4	33	69	33
Laffey,Aaron	12	L	27	aaa	TOR	64	5.01	1.71	26.2	2.8	4.3	1.5	0.9	35	72	19
LaFromboise,Robert	11	L	25	aa	SEA	61	3.57	1.58	5.473	3.7	6.7	1.8	0.9	34	80	48
	12	L	26	a/a	SEA	66	1.58	1.13	5.569	3.0	7.9	2.6	0.1	29	86	110
Lamm,Mark	12	R	24	aa	ATL	60	4.95	1.63	5.311	3.2	6.8	2.1	0.5	37	69	64
Landis,Kyle	12	R	26	a/a	CLE	69	4.67	1.44	6.997	1.9	5.9	3.0	0.9	34	69	68
Langwell,Matt	11	R	25	a/a	CLE	69	3.63	1.48	6.145	3.7	7.6	2.0	0.7	33	77	68
	12	R	26	a/a	CLE	69	3.50	1.46	7.034	3.7	8.4	2.2	0.0	36	73	98
Lanigan,Robert	11	R	24	aa	MIN	154	4.77	1.57	24.97	2.3	4.9	2.1	0.7	35	69	46
	12	R	25	a/a	MIN	71	5.44	1.61	7.109	2.8	5.0	1.8	0.8	35	66	36
Lannan,John	12	L	28	aaa	WAS	149	5.60	1.75	28.29	3.2	3.8	1.2	1.2	35	70	2
Lara,Robert	12	R	26	aa	SD	53	3.54	1.66	6.602	5.5	6.8	1.2	0.5	33	79	54
Latimer,William	12	L	27	a/a	BOS	59	7.37	1.89	10.24	3.7	5.1	1.4	1.7	36	63	-7
Layne,Tom	11	L	27	a/a	ARI	139	6.13	1.76	18.25	3.9	3.5	0.9	1.0	33	65	2
	12	L	28	a/a	SD	78	6.82	1.86	8.654	4.9	6.4	1.3	1.0	36	63	26
Leach,Brent	12	L	30	a/a	ATL	65	6.51	2.11	11.44	5.6	6.0	1.1	1.2	39	70	10
LeBlanc,Wade	11	L	27	aaa	SD	107	3.57	1.25	25.55	2.2	6.3	2.9	0.5	31	71	87
	12	L	28	aaa	MIA	99	4.79	1.39	25.96	2.1	6.3	3.0	1.0	33	67	69
Lee,Zach	12	R	21	aa	LA	66	4.74	1.46	21.61	2.8	6.1	2.2	0.8	33	68	55
Leesman,Charles	11	L	24	aa	CHW	152	5.22	1.83	26.15	5.7	5.8	1.0	0.3	35	70	42
	12	L	25	aaa	CHW	135	3.53	1.70	23.47	4.3	5.8	1.4	0.8	34	81	34
Lehman,Patrick	11	R	25	aa	WAS	34	4.63	0.89	4.352	1.1	7.1	6.7	0.6	26	46	177
	12	R	26	a/a	WAS	51	3.78	1.47	4.865	3.4	5.2	1.5	0.8	31	76	38
Leon,Alex	12	R	24	a/a	OAK	51	2.07	1.26	6.55	3.1	7.3	2.3	0.6	30	87	80
Leon,Arcenio	11	R	25	a/a	HOU	67	5.19	1.89	6.543	6.4	8.2	1.3	0.4	37	71	59
	12	R	26	aa	HOU	64	4.79	1.58	6.368	4.6	6.6	1.4	0.9	32	71	43
Leon,Arnold	12	R	24	a/a	OAK	51	2.07	1.26	6.55	3.1	7.3	2.3	0.6	30	87	80
Leroux,Chris	11	R	27	a/a	PIT	68	3.54	1.36	7.681	2.9	6.1	2.1	0.4	32	74	69
	12	R	28	aaa	PIT	64	4.38	1.32	12.55	2.2	5.7	2.6	1.0	30	69	57
Leverton,James	12	L	26	aa	MIA	56	4.23	1.45	10.47	3.6	6.7	1.9	0.7	32	71	61

PITCHER	yr	t	age	lvl	org	ip	era	whip	bf/g	ctl	dom	cmd	hr/9	h%	s%	bpv
Lewis,Jensen	11	R	27	aaa	CLE	28	6.19	2.273	6.482	5.0	5.5	1.1	1.3	42	75	-5
	12	R	28	aaa	ARI	57	3.87	1.346	4.54	3.1	5.1	1.7	1.1	28	75	36
Liberatore,Adam	12	L	25	a/a	TAM	73	2.86	1.506	6.445	3.5	4.9	1.4	0.5	32	82	42
Lindsay,Shane	11	R	26	a/a	CHW	70	2.93	1.588	6.2	9.1	9.5	1.0	0.4	23	82	89
	12	R	27	aaa	CHW	31	11.86	2.942	7.362	16.6	7.8	0.5	0.9	34	57	28
Link,Jon	11	R	27	aaa	LA	68	3.64	1.376	5.284	3.7	6.5	1.8	0.6	30	74	62
	12	R	28	a/a	MIA	36	3.61	1.591	4.916	3.8	5.4	1.4	0.5	33	78	42
Lively,Mitchell	11	R	26	aa	SF	22	4.72	1.707	5.533	3.8	6.2	1.6	0.0	38	69	64
	12	R	27	aaa	SF	78	3.13	1.209	6.715	2.5	6.2	2.5	0.5	29	75	80
Lobstein,Kyle	12	L	23	aa	TAM	144	4.50	1.531	23.21	4.1	7.0	1.7	0.7	33	71	55
Locke,Jeff	11	L	24	a/a	PIT	153	4.41	1.433	23.29	3.2	6.4	2.0	0.6	32	69	62
	12	L	25	aaa	PIT	142	3.27	1.411	24.97	2.9	6.4	2.2	0.6	33	78	65
Lollis,Matthew	12	R	22	a/a	SD	42	5.85	1.601	6.876	3.6	8.2	2.3	1.0	36	64	62
Loop,Derrick	11	L	28	aa	PHI	34	6.58	1.71	8.107	4.3	6.5	1.5	1.8	33	65	10
	12	L	29	aaa	LA	103	4.76	1.482	13.07	3.6	4.3	1.2	0.8	30	69	26
Lorin,Brett	12	R	25	aa	ARI	103	8.36	1.869	16.6	3.2	4.9	1.5	1.3	38	54	9
Lotzkar,Kyle	12	R	23	aa	CIN	86	6.92	1.728	21.81	5.8	8.6	1.5	1.7	32	62	32
Loup,Aaron	12	L	25	aa	TOR	45	3.60	1.563	5.371	2.9	7.1	2.4	1.0	36	80	57
Loux,Barret	12	R	23	aa	TEX	127	4.55	1.478	21.83	3.1	5.8	1.9	1.0	32	71	42
Lowe,Johnnie	11	R	26	aa	CHW	69	4.94	1.637	10.25	5.5	4.7	0.9	1.1	28	72	15
	12	R	27	a/a	MIL	86	6.00	1.911	13.56	6.0	5.0	0.8	1.5	32	71	-2
Lueke,Josh	11	R	27	aaa	SEA	42	2.50	1.103	5.536	2.4	6.1	2.5	0.2	28	76	94
	12	R	28	aaa	TAM	68	6.97	1.822	7.479	2.4	7.3	3.0	0.9	42	61	65
Lugo,Jose	11	L	27	a/a	ATL	105	3.48	1.607	14.13	4.7	5.3	1.1	0.5	32	78	41
	12	L	28	a/a	ATL	125	6.17	1.893	18.41	5.1	6.1	1.2	0.7	37	67	30
Lyles,Jordan	11	R	21	aaa	HOU	62	3.67	1.318	21.49	2.2	5.4	2.4	0.6	31	73	66
	12	R	22	aaa	HOU	41	3.26	1.176	23.22	1.5	6.4	4.2	0.4	31	72	117
Lyons,Tyler	12	L	24	a/a	STL	153	4.46	1.376	23.73	2.2	6.9	3.2	0.8	34	68	82
Mabee,Henry	12	R	27	aa	CHW	34	1.03	1.367	8.457	3.8	5.3	1.4	0.4	29	94	55
Machi,Jean	12	R	30	aaa	SF	57	4.40	1.704	4.837	2.7	5.2	1.9	1.0	36	76	29
Maday,Daryl	11	R	26	a/a	SF	131	5.19	1.629	20.76	3.0	5.5	1.8	1.1	35	70	31
	12	R	27	aa	SF	84	4.35	1.458	8.357	1.9	6.1	3.3	0.9	35	72	73
Magill,Matthew	12	R	23	aa	LA	146	4.32	1.375	23.61	3.6	8.7	2.4	0.5	33	68	92
Magnuson,Trystan	11	R	26	aaa	OAK	45	3.13	1.248	6.148	3.7	7.4	2.0	0.7	27	77	75
	12	R	27	aa	TOR	32	2.64	1.263	5.28	2.2	5.3	2.5	0.4	31	79	74
Maine,Scott	11	L	26	aaa	CHC	51	3.71	1.278	5.536	4.3	10.0	2.4	0.5	31	71	105
	12	L	27	aaa	CLE	36	3.25	1.127	4.78	3.3	5.6	1.7	0.3	25	70	74
Maloney,Matt	12	L	28	aaa	MIN	24	13.54	2.837	16.97	3.0	4.5	1.5	2.1	49	51	-43
Mandel,Jeff	11	R	26	a/a	WAS	62	4.56	1.756	5.943	2.6	5.9	2.2	0.8	39	75	44
	12	R	27	a/a	WAS	149	4.50	1.506	21.53	2.2	3.9	1.7	0.7	33	70	32
Maness,Michael	12	R	24	aa	STL	124	3.58	1.167	24.65	0.7	5.0	7.5	0.8	31	72	161
Manno,Chris	12	L	24	aa	CIN	50	6.10	1.734	4.554	4.3	7.8	1.8	1.2	36	66	41
Manship,Jeff	11	R	26	aaa	MIN	25	5.28	1.319	9.407	1.5	5.9	3.9	1.4	32	63	72
	12	R	27	aaa	MIN	80	3.95	1.746	16.67	4.4	4.5	1.0	0.6	34	78	23
Marbry,Michael	12	R	28	aa	COL	65	6.82	1.761	6.077	3.5	3.5	1.0	2.4	31	67	-41
Marimon,Sugar	12	R	24	aa	KC	67	5.51	1.592	24.51	4.0	3.9	1.0	1.2	30	67	6
Marinez,Jhan	11	R	23	aa	MIA	58	3.80	1.597	4.575	6.5	9.7	1.5	0.9	31	79	69
	12	R	24	aaa	CHW	63	4.01	1.353	6.572	5.2	8.0	1.5	1.0	26	73	61
Mariot,Michael	12	R	24	a/a	KC	122	3.79	1.356	15.4	2.4	4.9	2.0	0.8	31	74	48
Marks,Justin	12	L	24	a/a	KC	87	5.30	1.584	21.29	4.2	6.0	1.4	0.8	32	66	42
Maronde,Nick	12	L	23	aa	LAA	32	4.26	1.524	20.07	0.9	4.9	5.8	0.3	38	71	129
Marquez,Jeff	11	R	27	a/a	NYY	68	4.85	1.495	24.33	2.8	4.8	1.7	1.4	31	71	20
	12	R	28	aaa	COL	79	7.93	2.19	20.92	4.3	3.8	0.9	1.5	39	65	-25
Marshall,Brett	12	R	22	aa	NYY	158	4.27	1.432	24.94	3.1	5.8	1.9	1.1	31	73	41
Marshall,Evan	12	R	22	aa	ARI	49	4.31	1.622	5.147	2.9	4.3	1.5	0.4	35	73	36
Martin,Blake	11	L	25	aa	MIN	61	6.83	2.112	13.6	8.5	5.4	0.6	0.5	33	66	26
	12	L	26	aa	MIN	77	5.80	1.612	8.751	4.4	6.7	1.5	0.8	33	64	46
Martin,Christopher	12	R	26	aa	BOS	76	6.33	1.66	14.87	2.3	6.0	2.6	0.6	38	60	61
Martin,David	11	L	25	aa	MIN	61	6.83	2.112	13.6	8.5	5.4	0.6	0.5	33	66	26
	12	L	26	aa	MIN	77	5.80	1.612	8.751	4.4	6.7	1.5	0.8	33	64	46
Martin,Ethan	11	R	22	aa	LA	40	3.99	1.427	8.157	5.7	8.3	1.5	0.6	28	72	73
	12	R	23	aa	PHI	158	4.03	1.34	24.29	4.5	7.2	1.6	0.5	28	69	71
Martin,J.D.	11	R	28	aaa	WAS	108	5.13	1.4	15.15	1.5	4.4	3.0	1.7	31	69	32
	12	R	29	aaa	MIA	130	7.81	1.812	20.76	1.4	4.6	3.3	1.3	39	57	38
Martin,Rafael	11	R	27	aa	WAS	36	2.31	1.174	4.452	2.4	8.4	3.5	0.3	32	80	122
	12	R	28	a/a	WAS	35	9.58	2.058	6.039	6.3	5.6	0.9	1.9	34	54	-15
Martinez,Carlos	12	R	21	aa	STL	71	3.02	1.211	19.17	2.7	6.3	2.4	0.6	28	77	74
Martinez,Joe	11	R	28	aaa	CLE	118	4.98	1.677	15.16	2.4	5.9	2.5	0.9	38	71	49
	12	R	29	aaa	ARI	155	5.84	1.858	26.91	2.8	4.2	1.5	0.9	38	69	15
Martis,Shairon	11	R	24	aa	WAS	133	3.73	1.37	24.23	2.6	7.9	3.1	0.7	34	74	91
	12	R	25	a/a	MIN	139	6.49	1.549	20.99	3.1	4.5	1.5	1.4	31	59	12
Mathis,Doug	11	R	28	aaa	OAK	86	4.70	1.717	23.04	4.3	5.2	1.2	0.6	34	72	33
	12	R	29	aaa	BOS	102	6.52	2.005	25.82	3.8	3.8	1.0	1.4	37	69	-15
Matusz,Brian	11	L	24	a/a	BAL	61	4.01	1.41	25.66	3.1	5.1	1.7	0.8	30	73	43
	12	L	25	aaa	BAL	47	5.98	1.517	20.38	3.1	4.9	1.6	0.5	33	59	42
Maurer,Brandon	12	R	22	aa	SEA	138	3.92	1.471	24.61	3.3	6.9	2.1	0.3	34	72	77
May,Trevor	12	R	23	aa	PHI	150	5.64	1.563	23.43	4.6	7.8	1.7	1.4	31	67	40
Maya,Yunesky	11	R	30	aaa	WAS	130	6.76	1.579	25.93	2.1	4.8	2.3	1.2	35	57	31
	12	R	31	aaa	WAS	167	5.24	1.499	25.76	2.3	3.4	1.5	1.3	31	68	5
Mazzaro,Vin	11	R	25	aaa	KC	124	4.84	1.77	25.8	4.3	6.1	1.4	0.6	36	72	40
	12	R	26	aaa	KC	67	4.09	1.485	13.11	2.7	6.4	2.3	0.5	35	72	69
Mazzoni,Cory	12	R	23	aa	NYM	81	4.66	1.422	24.44	2.0	5.1	2.5	1.0	33	69	51
McAllister,Zach	11	R	24	aaa	CLE	155	3.74	1.324	25.64	1.8	6.2	3.5	0.6	33	72	90
	12	R	25	aaa	CLE	63	3.40	1.363	24.09	2.7	6.0	2.2	0.7	31	77	62
McBryde,Jeremy	12	R	25	aa	SD	53	3.83	1.233	4.383	2.8	9.4	3.4	0.5	33	68	119
McClendon,Mike	11	R	26	aaa	MIL	59	3.59	1.485	6.646	2.9	6.0	2.1	0.3	34	75	67
	12	R	27	aaa	MIL	43	5.49	1.635	5.805	4.2	4.5	1.1	0.5	32	65	30

PITCHER	yr	t	age	lvl	org	ip	era	whip	bf/g	ctl	dom	cmd	hr/9	h%	s%	bpv
McCoy,Patrick	12	L	24	aa	WAS	58	4.52	1.61	5.163	2.7	7.4	2.8	1.6	36	77	47
McCully,Nicholas	12	R	24	aa	CHW	55	5.80	1.70	15.54	5.7	5.9	1.0	1.0	31	67	26
McCurry,Cole	11	L	26	a/a	BAL	73	3.49	1.46	8.64	4.1	6.8	1.7	0.7	31	77	59
	12	L	27	a/a	ATL	80	7.25	1.80	11.98	4.9	4.5	0.9	0.8	34	58	17
McCutchen,Daniel	12	R	30	aaa	PIT	63	4.35	1.41	7.45	2.3	5.4	2.3	0.5	33	69	62
McFarland,T.J.	11	L	22	aa	CLE	137	4.57	1.51	23.77	3.2	5.8	1.8	0.6	33	69	52
	12	L	23	a/a	CLE	163	4.84	1.49	26.05	2.5	4.5	1.8	0.6	33	67	43
McGregor,Scott	12	R	26	aa	STL	59	7.83	1.77	22.58	2.9	3.6	1.2	1.6	35	56	-12
McGuire,Deck	11	R	22	aa	TOR	21	5.36	1.45	22.08	3.0	8.4	2.8	2.1	32	70	44
	12	R	23	aa	TOR	144	7.30	1.75	23.51	3.9	5.2	1.3	1.7	34	60	1
McHugh,Collin	11	R	24	aa	NYM	93	2.79	1.17	20.71	2.7	7.8	2.8	0.2	30	75	109
	12	R	25	a/a	NYM	148	3.13	1.21	23.93	2.6	6.5	2.5	0.7	29	76	75
McKiernan,Eddie	11	R	22	aa	LAA	140	6.11	1.47	22.2	1.9	5.2	2.7	1.5	33	61	34
	12	R	23	a/a	LAA	115	6.77	1.67	16.72	2.9	5.0	1.8	1.0	35	59	26
McNutt,Kenneth	11	R	22	aa	CHC	95	4.94	1.76	18.94	3.6	5.3	1.5	0.5	37	71	38
	12	R	23	aa	CHC	95	5.23	1.63	12.43	4.4	5.3	1.2	1.3	31	71	15
McPherson,Kyle	11	R	24	aa	PIT	89	3.68	1.21	22.53	2.1	6.4	3.1	0.7	30	71	84
	12	R	25	a/a	PIT	67	4.37	1.34	23.25	1.3	6.5	5.1	0.9	34	69	115
McSwain,Matt	11	R	26	aa	PIT	67	4.77	1.36	8.742	2.4	2.9	1.2	1.6	27	70	-6
	12	R	27	aa	OAK	71	7.40	2.20	11.81	4.9	4.8	1.0	0.5	41	64	16
Meadows,Dan	11	L	24	a/a	MIL	77	2.91	1.17	7.519	2.6	7.4	2.8	0.6	29	77	92
	12	L	25	a/a	MIL	70	5.29	1.55	6.647	4.4	5.3	1.2	0.9	30	66	29
Medina,Yoervis	11	R	23	aa	SEA	25	5.17	1.37	26.2	3.2	5.4	1.7	1.7	27	67	19
	12	R	24	aa	SEA	69	4.14	1.63	6.71	4.9	8.7	1.8	0.7	35	75	68
Medina,Yoervis Jose	11	R	23	aa	SEA	25	5.17	1.37	26.2	3.2	5.4	1.7	1.7	27	67	19
	12	R	24	aa	SEA	69	4.14	1.63	6.71	4.9	8.7	1.8	0.7	35	75	68
Mejia,Jenrry	11	R	22	aaa	NYM	28	2.90	1.03	21.82	4.0	5.6	1.4	0.3	20	71	75
	12	R	23	a/a	NYM	82	3.86	1.42	12.37	2.7	4.3	1.6	0.5	31	73	41
Merklinger,Daniel	11	L	26	aa	MIL	158	4.99	1.56	24.74	3.5	6.2	1.8	1.2	33	71	35
	12	L	27	a/a	COL	69	7.97	2.09	12.61	8.3	6.4	0.8	1.6	32	63	2
Meyer,Matt	11	L	26	a/a	LAA	31	2.85	1.48	4.646	6.8	9.6	1.4	0.3	28	80	93
	12	L	27	aaa	LAA	42	6.30	2.15	4.059	8.4	6.4	0.8	0.6	35	69	32
Mikolas,Miles	11	R	23	aa	SD	32	1.59	1.09	4.521	1.6	6.7	4.2	0.0	31	84	134
	12	R	24	a/a	SD	32	3.03	1.52	4.784	3.0	6.9	2.3	0.2	36	79	78
Miller,Aaron	12	L	25	aa	LA	121	5.34	1.71	22.01	5.2	6.6	1.3	0.8	33	69	40
Miller,Adam	11	R	27	aa	CLE	33	8.24	2.16	7.148	4.7	5.3	1.1	0.0	42	58	37
	12	R	28	a/a	NYY	49	6.89	2.27	19.18	3.6	2.5	0.7	0.5	42	68	-11
Miller,Shelby	11	R	21	aa	STL	87	2.27	1.12	21.32	3.0	8.0	2.7	0.1	29	79	112
	12	R	22	aaa	STL	137	4.86	1.41	21.42	3.2	9.0	2.9	1.3	33	69	75
Mills,Brad	11	L	26	aaa	TOR	157	3.83	1.31	27.08	2.0	6.3	3.1	1.1	31	74	70
	12	L	27	aaa	LAA	109	5.90	1.69	23.4	3.1	4.3	1.4	1.0	34	65	16
Miner,Zach	11	R	29	a/a	KC	67	6.50	1.78	13.34	4.1	4.2	1.0	1.2	34	64	2
	12	R	30	a/a	DET	38	3.95	1.60	6.993	5.9	2.8	0.5	0.9	25	77	6
Mitchell,D.J.	11	R	24	aaa	NYY	161	4.41	1.63	25.67	3.9	5.1	1.3	0.8	33	74	29
	12	R	25	aaa	SEA	134	4.34	1.36	24.4	3.1	6.0	1.9	0.7	30	68	58
Mock,Garrett	11	R	28	a/a	WAS	36	10.23	2.07	9.771	7.1	6.8	1.0	1.5	35	49	8
	12	R	29	aaa	HOU	62	4.06	1.66	5.882	4.1	7.5	1.8	0.9	36	78	51
Molina,Nestor	11	R	22	aa	TOR	22	0.50	0.72	15.57	0.8	11.9	14.6	0.0	30	92	395
	12	R	23	a/a	CHW	127	5.82	1.79	25.39	2.2	5.5	2.5	0.9	40	67	44
Molleken,Dustin	11	R	27	a/a	COL	46	5.50	1.42	5.459	1.9	6.0	3.1	1.5	32	65	50
	12	R	28	aaa	COL	49	6.13	1.82	5.648	3.5	4.8	1.4	1.1	36	67	11
Montgomery,Michael	11	L	22	aaa	KC	151	5.63	1.54	23.47	3.9	6.4	1.7	0.8	33	63	49
	12	L	23	a/a	KC	150	6.77	1.74	25.27	3.7	5.4	1.5	1.3	35	62	15
Moran,Brian	11	L	23	aa	SEA	61	5.08	1.45	5.758	3.2	8.3	2.6	1.3	33	68	65
	12	L	24	a/a	SEA	69	2.92	1.13	5.768	2.4	9.4	3.9	0.9	30	78	120
Moran,Gary	12	R	27	aa	ATL	161	3.92	1.50	23.95	2.6	5.2	2.0	0.5	34	74	54
Morgan,Adam	12	L	22	aa	PHI	36	4.01	1.35	24.81	2.7	6.4	2.4	0.5	32	70	73
Morillo,Juan	12	R	29	a/a	PHI	59	7.43	2.13	7.302	9.7	7.7	0.8	0.4	34	63	51
Morris,Bryan	11	R	24	aa	PIT	78	4.07	1.50	9.625	3.8	5.8	1.5	0.2	33	71	59
	12	R	25	aaa	PIT	81	3.52	1.37	7.384	2.0	6.7	3.4	1.0	33	78	78
Morrison,Michael	12	R	25	aa	DET	63	3.93	1.52	6.837	5.8	8.0	1.4	1.0	28	77	56
Mortensen,Clayton	11	R	26	aaa	COL	64	8.64	2.09	20.96	3.7	5.7	1.5	1.7	41	60	-5
	12	R	27	a/a	BOS	39	3.39	1.29	6.355	4.2	6.4	1.5	0.9	26	77	54
Moscoso,Guillermo	11	R	28	aaa	OAK	46	4.27	1.39	21.65	3.2	7.8	2.4	0.5	33	69	84
	12	R	29	aaa	COL	98	7.43	1.87	25.65	2.5	5.4	2.1	1.6	39	62	12
Moskos,Daniel	11	L	25	aaa	PIT	42	4.11	1.38	5.876	2.3	4.7	2.0	0.4	32	69	56
	12	L	26	aaa	CHW	34	6.14	2.30	5.666	7.3	6.9	1.0	0.8	41	73	23
Mulvey,Kevin	12	R	27	aa	NYM	19	6.35	1.87	6.981	6.0	4.9	0.8	1.0	33	66	13
Munson,Kevin	12	R	23	aa	ARI	53	7.87	1.73	5.477	4.6	9.1	2.0	0.6	39	51	73
Murata,Toru	12	R	27	a/a	CLE	73	3.85	1.45	12.05	2.8	6.1	2.2	0.3	34	72	72
Murphy,Bill	12	L	31	aaa	TOR	101	5.13	1.81	16.66	4.4	3.9	0.9	0.7	34	72	12
Murphy,Timothy	12	L	25	aa	TEX	83	8.63	1.99	12.43	3.7	4.2	1.1	1.1	38	55	0
Musick,Wesley	12	L	26	a/a	HOU	42	3.61	1.44	19.71	3.1	5.1	1.6	0.2	32	73	57
Neal,Zachary	12	R	24	aa	MIA	69	4.59	1.49	14.1	1.7	4.9	2.9	0.5	35	68	66
Neil,Matthew	12	R	26	aa	MIA	92	6.02	1.60	21.49	1.9	5.1	2.8	1.1	36	63	44
Nelo,Hector	12	R	26	aa	WAS	53	3.48	1.58	4.931	5.0	8.3	1.6	0.8	33	80	62
Nelson,Jimmy	12	R	23	aa	MIL	46	4.65	1.67	20.64	7.4	7.2	1.0	0.5	28	71	59
Newby,Kyler	11	R	26	a/a	ARI	118	4.44	1.47	13.36	3.1	5.9	1.9	1.0	32	72	44
	12	R	27	a/a	BAL	56	3.30	1.32	5.423	3.9	9.0	2.3	0.2	32	74	103
Ni,Fu-Te	12	L	30	aaa	DET	24	6.37	2.19	16.93	6.0	3.8	0.6	2.4	34	77	-50
Nieve,Fernando	11	R	29	aaa	HOU	15	9.10	2.50	27.21	3.1	7.6	2.4	0.0	52	60	64
	12	R	30	aaa	LA	119	5.89	1.82	22.16	2.7	5.9	2.2	1.3	39	69	28
Noesi,Hector	11	R	24	aaa	NYY	25	4.55	1.82	19.09	3.7	5.1	1.4	0.0	39	72	48
	12	R	25	aaa	SEA	64	5.80	1.67	26.27	3.0	6.6	2.2	0.9	37	65	50
Nunez,Jhonny	11	R	26	aaa	CHW	47	6.39	1.60	7.215	4.1	7.9	1.9	1.9	32	64	28
	12	R	27	aaa	TAM	37	8.01	2.21	8.453	6.6	5.6	0.8	2.1	36	67	-25
Nuno,Vidal	12	L	25	aa	NYY	114	3.16	1.42	24.17	2.3	6.3	2.7	1.1	33	82	60

PITCHER	yr	t	age	lvl	org	ip	era	whip	bf/g	ctl	dom	cmd	hr/9	h%	s%	bpv
O Connor,Mike	11	L	31	aaa	NYM	60	6.24	1.738	7.051	3.0	7.0	2.4	1.1	39	65	46
	12	L	32	aaa	NYY	109	5.41	1.773	16.1	2.8	5.7	2.0	1.8	37	74	11
O Sullivan,Sean	11	R	24	aaa	KC	75	4.65	1.476	22.91	1.9	5.3	2.8	0.6	35	68	64
	12	R	25	aaa	TOR	143	4.48	1.491	19.84	2.8	3.7	1.3	0.7	31	70	24
Oberholtzer,Brett	11	L	22	aa	HOU	155	3.93	1.278	23.53	2.7	6.2	2.3	0.5	30	69	74
	12	L	23	a/a	HOU	167	4.29	1.384	25.02	2.0	6.4	3.3	1.2	33	73	67
Obispo,Wirfin	12	R	28	a/a	CIN	96	4.14	1.336	11.4	4.6	6.6	1.4	1.0	25	72	48
O'Brien,Michael	12	R	22	aa	NYY	105	5.09	1.577	23.08	3.4	5.3	1.5	0.8	33	68	37
Odorizzi,Jake	11	R	21	aa	KC	69	4.97	1.317	23.68	2.7	5.9	2.2	1.4	28	66	41
	12	R	22	a/a	KC	145	3.31	1.313	23.1	2.9	6.9	2.4	0.8	31	77	71
Oliver,Andrew	11	L	24	aaa	DET	147	6.03	1.77	25.95	5.0	7.0	1.4	1.0	35	66	34
	12	L	25	aaa	DET	118	6.17	1.813	19.53	6.9	6.7	1.0	0.6	32	65	43
Oliveros,Lester	11	R	23	a/a	MIN	48	4.53	1.57	6.197	3.8	9.1	2.4	1.3	36	75	62
	12	R	24	a/a	MIN	48	2.98	1.149	5.995	2.9	7.8	2.7	0.4	29	74	102
Olson,Garrett	11	L	28	aaa	PIT	86	3.90	1.504	15.43	5.2	4.6	0.9	0.8	26	76	27
	12	L	29	aaa	NYM	122	5.38	1.755	16.46	4.0	5.7	1.4	0.9	36	70	30
Omogrosso,Brian	11	R	27	a/a	CHW	65	4.18	1.635	6.93	4.1	8.0	2.0	0.6	37	75	67
	12	R	28	aaa	CHW	47	6.98	1.578	6.309	3.0	8.9	2.9	0.9	38	54	81
Oramas,Juan	11	L	21	a/a	SD	108	2.87	1.149	21.5	2.1	8.1	3.9	0.7	30	78	113
	12	L	22	aa	SD	35	6.43	1.59	19.48	3.9	7.6	1.9	1.1	34	59	52
Ortega,Jose	11	R	23	aaa	DET	50	7.90	1.972	7.26	4.8	6.4	1.3	1.4	38	60	12
	12	R	24	aaa	DET	63	7.10	2.244	7.052	7.3	7.8	1.1	0.6	41	67	38
Ortega,Yonata	11	R	25	aa	ARI	18	3.00	1.074	4.914	5.5	7.4	1.3	1.1	14	78	66
	12	R	26	aa	ARI	52	9.18	2.174	6.223	7.3	6.9	0.9	1.7	36	58	0
Ortiz,Jonathan	11	R	26	aa	OAK	65	4.32	1.441	6.594	3.3	6.7	2.0	0.9	32	71	57
	12	R	27	aa	OAK	62	4.45	1.417	5.079	2.8	5.7	2.1	1.0	31	71	46
Ortiz,Joseph	12	L	22	a/a	TEX	63	2.59	1.18	4.915	1.3	6.2	4.8	1.4	29	87	95
Otero,Dan	11	R	26	a/a	SF	74	2.52	1.244	5.37	1.3	7.4	5.8	0.4	35	81	151
	12	R	27	aaa	SF	62	3.04	1.387	5.435	1.1	5.1	4.6	0.5	35	79	106
Ottavino,Adam	12	R	27	aaa	COL	20	3.71	1.681	6.809	3.3	8.4	2.6	1.1	39	81	62
Outman,Josh	11	L	27	aaa	OAK	78	4.20	1.724	20.94	5.5	6.6	1.2	0.7	33	76	41
	12	L	28	a/a	COL	71	4.93	1.668	20.01	4.3	6.5	1.5	0.7	35	71	45
Owen,Dylan	11	R	25	a/a	NYM	124	4.55	1.455	18.33	3.4	5.5	1.6	1.3	30	72	28
	12	R	26	aaa	NYM	76	6.81	1.76	12.43	4.8	3.3	0.7	1.5	30	63	-17
Owens,Rudy	11	L	24	aaa	PIT	112	5.92	1.596	23.62	2.5	4.4	1.8	0.8	35	62	31
	12	L	25	aaa	HOU	163	3.41	1.23	24.45	2.0	4.9	2.5	1.0	28	76	54
Oye,Matthew	12	R	26	aa	LAA	112	5.22	1.659	14.8	3.5	4.8	1.4	1.0	34	70	21
Packer,Matt	11	L	24	aa	CLE	169	5.30	1.414	26.56	1.8	5.7	3.2	0.9	34	63	69
	12	L	25	a/a	CLE	53	5.52	1.763	26.99	2.6	4.8	1.8	1.5	36	72	10
Paduch,Jim	11	R	29	a/a	TAM	98	6.34	1.807	25.28	3.7	5.5	1.5	1.3	36	66	14
	12	R	30	a/a	TAM	120	7.12	1.874	19.43	3.6	4.2	1.2	1.1	36	62	2
Parisi,Michael	11	R	28	aaa	LA	55	4.58	1.414	26.03	4.4	4.5	1.0	1.2	25	70	19
	12	R	29	aaa	LA	43	2.66	1.244	19.42	2.2	5.8	2.7	0.4	31	79	82
Parker,Blake	12	R	27	aaa	CHC	24	4.18	1.092	4.409	2.5	6.5	2.6	1.3	24	66	65
Parker,Jarrod	12	R	24	aaa	OAK	21	2.26	1.428	21.95	2.5	7.7	3.1	0.8	35	88	86
Partch,Curtis	11	R	24	aa	CIN	39	6.94	1.807	25.78	2.8	6.4	2.3	0.7	40	60	52
	12	R	25	aa	CIN	70	6.55	1.862	7.317	4.7	6.8	1.5	1.2	37	66	24
Paterson,Joe	12	L	26	aaa	ARI	43	4.21	1.372	3.785	3.1	6.5	2.1	1.4	30	74	44
Patterson,John	12	R	25	aa	LA	70	3.68	1.621	6.645	4.1	7.4	1.8	0.3	36	76	70
Paukovits,Bryan	12	R	25	aa	KC	56	6.14	1.931	9.119	4.5	5.7	1.3	0.6	38	67	29
Pauley,David	12	R	29	aaa	SEA	59	2.68	1.499	12.81	2.4	4.9	2.0	1.0	33	87	35
Paxton,James	11	L	23	aa	SEA	39	2.04	1.123	21.97	3.0	10.5	3.5	0.4	31	83	134
	12	L	24	aa	SEA	106	3.88	1.628	22.52	4.9	8.1	1.6	0.5	35	76	69
Peacock,Brad	11	R	23	a/a	WAS	147	2.84	1.068	22.81	2.7	8.9	3.3	0.6	28	75	116
	12	R	24	aaa	OAK	135	6.23	1.649	21.5	4.2	7.9	1.8	0.9	36	62	54
Pease,Dustin	12	L	27	aa	SD	64	4.42	1.525	5.348	3.8	6.4	1.7	1.0	32	73	42
Peavey,Greg	12	R	24	aa	NYM	144	5.40	1.523	25.02	2.1	4.2	2.0	1.1	33	66	26
Pena,Ariel	12	R	23	aa	MIL	147	4.67	1.497	24.35	4.1	7.5	1.8	1.3	31	73	44
Pena,Hassan	11	R	26	a/a	WAS	63	5.77	1.384	5.635	2.0	6.9	3.4	0.8	34	57	85
	12	R	27	aaa	WAS	57	4.86	1.555	5.903	3.6	4.3	1.2	1.1	31	71	14
Pena,Tony	11	R	30	aaa	BOS	116	5.49	1.899	16.64	3.3	3.7	1.1	0.7	37	71	8
	12	R	31	aaa	BOS	91	7.37	2.063	13.89	3.6	4.5	1.2	1.5	39	65	-10
Pendleton,Lance	11	R	28	aaa	NYY	67	4.70	1.622	16.45	3.9	4.6	1.2	1.5	31	76	3
	12	R	29	aaa	TAM	129	6.14	1.83	23.07	4.2	5.5	1.3	1.1	36	67	17
Peralta,Wily	11	R	22	a/a	MIL	151	3.31	1.266	23.68	3.3	8.3	2.5	0.5	31	75	93
	12	R	23	aaa	MIL	147	5.62	1.756	23.97	4.9	7.5	1.5	0.6	36	67	53
Perdomo,Luis	11	R	27	aaa	SD	72	4.48	1.789	5.082	5.3	5.2	1.0	0.5	34	75	32
	12	R	28	a/a	MIN	73	3.49	1.296	6.646	3.1	6.3	2.1	0.5	30	73	70
Perez,Kelvin	12	R	27	a/a	NYY	86	2.14	1.455	7.63	4.8	6.5	1.4	0.4	29	87	60
Perez,Martin	11	L	20	a/a	TEX	137	4.69	1.563	22.29	3.5	6.7	1.9	0.7	35	70	55
	12	L	21	aaa	TEX	127	4.76	1.476	24.8	3.8	4.1	1.1	0.8	29	68	23
Perez,Sergio	11	R	27	aaa	HOU	110	4.85	1.817	23.18	4.0	4.6	1.1	1.3	35	76	4
	12	R	28	aaa	HOU	75	4.75	1.674	8.464	4.4	5.5	1.2	1.0	33	73	26
Perry,Ryan	11	R	24	aaa	DET	33	3.88	1.162	6.503	2.5	6.6	2.6	0.3	29	65	92
	12	R	25	a/a	WAS	85	3.79	1.387	14.9	3.0	5.0	1.6	0.4	31	72	55
Petit,Yusmeiro	12	R	28	aaa	SF	167	3.70	1.434	25.32	1.9	6.3	3.4	0.7	35	75	83
Petricka,Jacob	12	R	24	aa	CHW	58	6.68	1.965	27.59	6.2	3.6	0.6	1.4	32	68	-15
Petrini,Christopher	12	L	25	aa	BAL	69	3.22	1.347	11.92	2.9	7.0	2.4	0.2	33	74	89
Pettibone,Jonathan	12	R	22	a/a	PHI	160	3.71	1.344	25.57	2.7	5.6	2.0	0.6	31	73	60
Pettit,Jacob	12	L	26	aa	BAL	124	4.85	1.311	21.29	1.8	4.9	2.7	1.4	29	67	41
Phillips,Zach	11	L	25	aaa	BAL	58	5.07	1.776	5.704	4.5	5.5	1.2	0.6	36	71	34
	12	L	26	aaa	BAL	54	4.59	1.807	5.95	4.1	5.8	1.4	0.2	38	73	48
Piazza,Michael	11	R	25	aa	LAA	30	4.06	1.752	6.935	5.8	6.0	1.0	1.3	31	81	17
	12	R	26	aa	LAA	107	4.80	1.454	11.73	3.2	6.0	1.9	0.7	32	67	53
Pimentel,Carlos	11	R	22	aa	TEX	142	5.71	1.592	22.43	5.1	5.8	1.1	1.2	29	66	24
	12	R	23	aa	TEX	88	3.34	1.414	10.68	5.6	7.6	1.4	0.6	27	77	69
Pimentel,Elisaul	12	R	24	aa	KC	54	7.40	1.771	14.58	3.6	5.3	1.5	1.1	36	58	19

PITCHER	yr	t	age	lvl	org	ip	era	whip	bf/g	ctl	dom	cmd	hr/9	h%	s%	bpv
Pimentel,Stolmy	12	R	22	aa	BOS	116	5.97	1.55	22.96	3.3	5.7	1.7	0.8	33	61	43
Pino,Johan	11	R	28	a/a	TOR	99	4.89	1.31	10.44	1.5	7.5	5.0	1.6	33	67	100
Pino,Yohan	11	R	28	a/a	TOR	99	4.89	1.31	10.44	1.5	7.5	5.0	1.6	33	67	100
	12	R	29	a/a	TOR	143	6.08	1.58	22.5	2.2	5.7	2.6	1.4	35	63	37
Pomeranz,Drew	11	L	23	aa	COL	24	1.79	0.82	17.48	2.2	7.2	3.2	0.5	20	81	118
	12	L	24	a/a	COL	51	2.95	1.76	23.18	3.9	6.9	1.8	0.5	38	84	56
Pope,Ryan	11	R	25	a/a	NYY	41	8.91	1.79	5.209	2.9	7.3	2.5	1.2	40	48	45
	12	R	26	aa	NYY	64	6.11	1.87	6.531	2.2	7.3	3.3	1.6	42	70	49
Portice,Eammon	12	R	27	aa	LA	27	6.26	1.73	7.231	4.2	6.0	1.4	2.6	31	72	-20
Portillo,Adys	12	R	21	aa	SD	35	7.20	1.69	19.72	6.2	6.1	1.0	0.8	30	56	35
Poveda,Omar	11	R	24	aa	MIA	156	4.69	1.42	24.58	3.2	5.5	1.8	0.8	31	68	45
	12	R	25	a/a	MIA	131	5.84	1.81	23.4	4.2	6.3	1.5	1.1	37	69	27
Price,Bryan	11	R	25	aa	CLE	52	3.51	1.46	7.906	2.7	4.7	1.7	0.9	31	79	32
	12	R	26	a/a	CLE	70	5.12	1.61	7.721	3.3	6.5	2.0	1.1	35	70	40
Pryor,Stephen	11	R	22	aa	SEA	23	1.29	0.73	4.733	2.7	9.7	3.6	0.0	20	80	162
	12	R	23	a/a	SEA	36	0.55	0.99	5.077	4.0	9.8	2.5	0.0	24	94	133
Pucetas,Kevin	11	R	27	aaa	KC	107	5.86	1.66	14.49	3.3	4.2	1.3	1.4	32	67	1
	12	R	28	a/a	WAS	105	4.87	1.44	15.37	1.9	4.6	2.4	1.0	32	68	41
Pugh,Bruce	11	R	23	aa	MIN	18	9.80	2.00	6.801	7.5	8.6	1.2	1.7	35	50	23
	12	R	24	aa	MIN	42	1.78	1.28	5.548	5.0	8.4	1.7	0.4	26	88	88
Purcey,David	12	L	30	aaa	PHI	58	6.51	2.05	5.972	6.2	7.3	1.2	0.4	39	66	45
Putkonen,Luke	11	R	25	aa	DET	52	9.16	1.95	22.7	3.8	3.1	0.8	1.5	36	52	-24
	12	R	26	aaa	DET	57	6.35	1.83	10.97	3.2	5.6	1.8	0.5	39	63	40
Putnam,Zach	11	R	24	aaa	CLE	69	4.12	1.32	6.493	2.9	7.4	2.5	0.8	31	70	77
	12	R	25	aaa	COL	61	4.60	1.79	5.71	3.9	5.5	1.4	0.8	36	75	28
Quintana,Jose	12	L	23	aa	CHW	49	3.32	1.33	22.45	2.9	6.7	2.3	0.2	32	74	84
Quirarte,Edwin	11	R	25	aa	SF	46	6.82	2.02	6.406	4.0	6.1	1.5	0.6	41	65	34
	12	R	26	aa	SF	45	4.35	1.48	4.996	3.0	3.8	1.3	0.2	32	68	40
Raley,Brooks	11	L	23	aa	CHC	136	4.69	1.70	23.72	2.9	4.5	1.5	1.1	35	75	15
	12	L	24	a/a	CHC	131	4.29	1.51	25.7	2.9	5.6	2.0	0.7	34	72	50
Ramirez,Edgar	11	R	28	aa	NYM	31	3.67	1.30	7.514	2.8	4.7	1.7	0.8	28	74	42
	12	R	29	a/a	NYM	49	5.36	1.49	6.64	3.2	4.1	1.3	1.0	30	65	20
Ramirez,Elvin	12	R	25	a/a	NYM	55	2.29	1.21	5.413	4.9	7.3	1.5	0.3	24	81	82
Ramirez,Erasmo	11	R	21	a/a	SEA	153	4.45	1.34	24.45	1.7	6.3	3.7	0.7	34	67	93
	12	R	22	aaa	SEA	77	3.54	1.27	21.1	1.9	6.1	3.2	0.5	32	72	90
Ramirez,J.C.	11	R	23	aa	PHI	144	5.02	1.48	23.81	3.3	4.8	1.4	1.0	30	67	28
	12	R	24	a/a	PHI	67	5.00	1.46	6.406	4.3	5.8	1.4	0.9	29	67	39
Ramirez,Neil	11	R	22	a/a	TEX	93	3.66	1.34	16.18	4.0	8.8	2.2	0.8	30	74	82
	12	R	23	a/a	TEX	123	7.70	1.57	19.33	3.5	6.4	1.8	1.7	32	52	23
Ramos,A.J.	12	R	26	aa	MIA	69	1.82	0.98	4.743	3.1	9.3	3.0	0.4	25	83	125
Ramos,Cesar	12	L	28	aaa	TAM	62	4.71	1.43	10.55	2.5	5.2	2.1	1.6	30	73	23
Ranaudo,Anthony	12	R	23	aa	BOS	38	8.88	2.06	20.42	6.7	5.4	0.8	1.1	35	55	8
Rasmus,Cory	12	R	25	aa	ATL	59	4.75	1.52	5.092	5.3	8.0	1.5	0.5	31	68	69
Rasmussen,Robert	12	L	23	aa	HOU	54	4.93	1.44	21.06	2.8	6.3	2.3	1.0	33	67	54
Ray,Chris	12	R	30	aaa	OAK	42	3.76	1.76	4.928	5.4	5.8	1.1	0.4	34	78	41
Ray,Jason	12	R	28	a/a	SD	53	3.97	1.60	4.809	3.9	8.5	2.2	1.0	36	78	62
Ray,Robert	11	R	27	a/a	TOR	67	7.69	1.64	24.8	3.3	6.3	1.9	2.0	33	55	12
	12	R	28	aaa	MIA	54	4.46	1.55	7.203	3.8	5.7	1.5	0.9	32	73	37
Redmond,Todd	11	R	26	aaa	ATL	170	3.77	1.40	25.59	2.7	6.2	2.3	1.1	31	77	51
	12	R	27	aaa	CIN	149	4.60	1.53	24.85	2.5	6.5	2.6	1.4	34	74	45
Reed,Chris	12	L	22	aa	LA	35	5.46	1.50	12.71	4.8	6.4	1.3	0.5	30	62	55
Reed,Evan	12	R	26	a/a	MIA	67	5.82	1.65	6.015	4.0	7.4	1.9	0.4	37	62	67
Reichard,Andy	12	R	28	aa	SF	37	8.08	1.91	14.45	3.9	3.8	1.0	2.0	34	60	-32
Reid,Ryan	11	R	26	a/a	TAM	71	5.73	1.68	9.179	2.8	6.4	2.3	1.1	37	67	43
	12	R	27	aaa	TAM	79	4.29	1.51	7.472	3.3	7.1	2.1	1.0	34	74	55
Reifer,Adam	12	R	26	aaa	STL	64	5.45	1.46	4.748	2.9	4.8	1.7	1.4	30	65	19
Reineke,Chad	11	R	29	aaa	CIN	127	4.90	1.77	23.26	3.1	4.1	1.4	1.2	35	75	5
	12	R	30	aaa	CIN	152	6.12	1.83	26.15	3.0	4.8	1.6	1.3	37	68	9
Remenowsky,Dan	11	R	25	a/a	CHW	67	4.59	1.36	6.391	3.5	8.8	2.5	0.9	32	68	82
	12	R	26	a/a	CHW	67	3.66	1.38	7.812	4.4	8.3	1.9	0.8	30	75	74
Reyes,Jo-Jo	12	L	28	aaa	PIT	54	3.76	1.51	13.75	2.4	5.1	2.1	1.0	33	78	39
Reyes,Jorge	11	R	24	aa	SD	113	3.03	1.29	14.03	2.3	6.8	2.9	0.4	32	76	92
	12	R	25	aaa	SD	152	4.78	1.61	19.8	2.6	5.0	1.9	0.7	36	70	41
Reynolds,Greg	11	R	26	aaa	COL	110	6.24	1.77	26.52	2.4	4.0	1.7	0.8	38	64	21
	12	R	27	aaa	TEX	163	6.65	1.87	28.32	2.8	2.8	1.0	1.6	36	67	-25
Rhee,Dae-Eun	12	R	23	aa	CHC	142	5.90	1.74	24.06	3.3	4.2	1.2	1.3	34	68	2
Rhoderick,Kevin	11	R	23	aa	CHC	57	3.85	1.38	5.316	5.8	7.8	1.3	0.3	26	71	78
	12	R	24	aa	CHC	58	6.26	1.87	6.149	7.8	6.9	0.9	0.9	31	66	35
Rice,Jason	12	R	26	aaa	ATL	19	3.96	2.09	5.728	7.5	7.1	0.9	0.0	38	79	56
Rice,Scott	11	L	30	aa	LA	51	2.28	1.36	6.223	3.1	5.5	1.8	0.6	30	85	55
	12	L	31	aaa	LA	59	4.35	1.45	4.689	3.2	5.2	1.6	0.4	32	69	53
Richards,Garrett	11	R	23	aa	LAA	143	3.76	1.26	26.55	2.5	5.5	2.2	0.7	29	71	62
	12	R	24	aaa	LAA	77	3.97	1.57	24.14	3.6	6.3	1.7	0.5	34	74	56
Richmond,Scott	11	R	32	aaa	TOR	113	7.58	2.00	20.96	4.4	5.2	1.2	1.9	37	65	-17
	12	R	33	aaa	TOR	135	6.58	1.81	23.11	3.0	5.6	1.8	1.6	37	66	10
Rienzo,Andre	12	R	24	a/a	CHW	78	3.90	1.46	23.97	4.7	8.1	1.7	0.3	32	72	81
Riordan,Cory	11	R	25	a/a	COL	149	5.53	1.47	22.88	1.4	4.8	3.4	1.4	34	65	50
	12	R	26	a/a	COL	95	5.84	1.53	12.48	1.8	4.7	2.7	1.2	34	63	40
Rivas,Amaury	11	R	26	aaa	MIL	151	5.02	1.66	24.09	4.8	5.3	1.1	0.9	31	70	27
	12	R	27	aaa	MIL	67	6.88	1.88	6.301	4.8	4.2	0.9	1.2	34	64	-2
Roark,Tanner	11	R	25	aa	WAS	117	5.87	1.61	24.69	3.0	5.6	1.9	0.9	35	63	39
	12	R	26	aaa	WAS	148	5.47	1.64	23.51	2.9	6.1	2.1	1.0	36	67	43
Robertson,Tyler	12	L	25	aaa	MIN	29	4.90	1.60	3.837	4.4	8.3	1.9	0.7	35	69	69
Robinson,Dakota	12	L	24	aa	LAA	50	7.50	1.93	5.523	4.5	5.7	1.3	1.5	37	62	5
Robles,Mauricio	11	L	22	a/a	SEA	20	6.28	1.69	15.05	8.9	5.7	0.6	1.4	20	65	20
	12	L	23	a/a	SEA	72	6.31	1.76	7.627	7.8	7.7	1.0	0.6	29	62	56
Robowski,Ryan	12	L	24	a/a	DET	55	4.46	1.28	7.007	2.6	6.2	2.3	0.9	29	67	62
Rodebaugh,Ryan	12	R	23	aa	TEX	52	3.20	1.25	5.685	1.8	8.8	4.7	0.9	34	78	125

PITCHER	yr	t	age	lvl	org	ip	era	whip	bf/g	ctl	dom	cmd	hr/9	h%	s%	bpv
Rodriguez,Aneury	12	R	25	aaa	HOU	93	6.47	1.928	15.17	4.0	6.0	1.5	0.9	39	66	27
Rodriguez,Armando	12	R	24	a/a	NYM	77	3.32	1.137	8.706	2.5	7.4	3.0	1.5	26	79	72
Rodriguez,Francisco	12	R	29	aaa	LAA	51	6.69	1.89	6.005	5.4	3.7	0.7	1.0	33	64	-1
Rodriguez,Julio	12	R	22	aa	PHI	134	4.80	1.548	20.18	4.9	8.0	1.6	1.0	31	71	55
Rodriguez,Santos	12	L	24	a/a	CHW	71	3.79	1.252	6.915	5.2	7.5	1.5	1.0	22	73	61
Rodriguez,Wilmin	11	L	26	a/a	SF	64	4.74	1.735	7.326	3.9	4.8	1.2	0.5	35	72	32
	12	L	27	aaa	SF	62	6.20	2.09	8.272	4.3	3.9	0.9	0.9	39	70	-2
Roemer,Wesley	11	R	25	a/a	ARI	164	4.48	1.433	24.91	2.3	5.1	2.2	0.9	32	70	45
	12	R	26	aa	LA	53	3.35	1.466	9.815	3.0	6.2	2.1	0.6	34	78	62
Rogers,Chad	12	R	23	aa	CIN	32	2.64	1.231	21.38	1.8	5.6	3.1	1.1	29	85	67
Rogers,Mark	11	R	25	aaa	MIL	15	13.76	2.963	17.35	12.9	6.0	0.5	0.6	40	50	12
	12	R	26	aaa	MIL	95	6.06	1.747	24.19	5.1	5.7	1.1	1.5	32	68	8
Romanski,Joshua	11	L	25	aa	NYY	18	2.60	1.736	6.191	3.3	5.7	1.7	1.4	36	91	20
	12	L	26	aa	NYY	29	6.54	1.887	11.38	3.1	4.9	1.6	0.9	39	65	21
Rondon,Bruce	12	R	22	a/a	DET	30	1.43	1.278	4.053	4.7	8.0	1.7	0.6	26	93	78
Rondon,Francisco	12	L	24	a/a	NYY	66	5.38	1.735	7.157	5.8	8.1	1.4	1.1	33	70	44
Rondon,Jorge	11	R	23	aa	STL	37	7.93	1.91	4.772	7.1	6.1	0.9	0.7	33	56	32
	12	R	24	a/a	STL	49	3.77	1.413	4.509	4.4	7.5	1.7	0.3	31	72	77
Ronick,Ari	12	L	26	aa	SF	36	10.85	2.191	5.201	5.6	4.6	0.8	1.4	38	48	-14
Rosario,Adrian	12	R	23	aa	NYM	29	6.09	2.179	5.64	8.1	6.8	0.8	0.3	38	70	42
Rosenbaum,Daniel	11	L	24	aa	WAS	39	2.80	1.078	25.55	2.5	5.0	2.0	0.0	26	71	83
	12	L	25	aa	WAS	155	4.91	1.513	25.89	2.2	4.5	2.0	0.5	34	66	47
Rosenberg,B.J.	11	R	26	aa	PHI	109	5.09	1.59	12.36	3.2	6.8	2.1	1.0	35	69	49
	12	R	27	a/a	PHI	62	2.51	1.42	10.52	2.9	8.3	2.9	0.9	35	86	82
Rosenthal,Trevor	12	R	22	a/a	STL	109	3.08	1.128	21.52	3.3	7.3	2.2	0.5	26	73	88
Ross,Tyson	11	R	24	aaa	OAK	37	7.67	2.079	19.96	5.1	7.1	1.4	1.0	41	62	26
	12	R	25	aaa	OAK	78	3.16	1.335	21.7	3.3	6.1	1.9	0.4	30	76	67
Rowland-Smith,Ryan	11	L	28	aaa	HOU	105	7.22	1.906	22.48	3.7	5.8	1.6	1.5	38	64	7
	12	L	29	aaa	CHC	78	5.04	1.82	12.01	5.4	5.3	1.0	0.8	34	73	22
Ruffin,Chance	11	R	23	a/a	DET	49	2.45	1.318	4.577	4.0	9.0	2.3	0.6	31	84	91
	12	R	24	aaa	SEA	71	5.93	1.591	6.234	4.2	6.0	1.4	0.9	32	62	38
Rusin,Chris	11	L	25	a/a	CHC	139	4.22	1.409	22.56	1.9	5.0	2.6	0.8	33	71	55
	12	L	26	a/a	CHC	143	5.57	1.632	24.54	3.6	4.7	1.3	1.2	32	68	13
Russell,Adam	11	R	28	aaa	TAM	17	5.23	1.765	5.196	6.8	5.7	0.8	1.2	29	72	20
	12	R	29	a/a	LAA	50	8.57	2.363	5.889	6.6	6.6	1.0	0.4	43	61	30
Russell,Andrew	12	R	28	a/a	ATL	64	2.74	1.434	5.041	4.4	4.8	1.1	0.3	29	81	47
Salazar,Danny	12	R	22	aa	CLE	34	2.41	1.113	22.29	2.2	5.3	2.4	0.3	27	78	81
Sampson,Keyvius	12	R	21	aa	SD	122	5.00	1.359	19.66	4.0	8.2	2.0	0.7	31	63	78
Sanabia,Alex	11	R	23	aaa	MIA	22	7.76	1.813	25.1	1.2	4.6	3.8	1.3	40	57	48
	12	R	24	aaa	MIA	89	4.77	1.478	22.42	2.6	5.3	2.1	1.1	32	70	38
Sanchez,Jesus	11	R	24	aa	MIL	99	5.73	1.688	14.88	4.4	5.1	1.2	1.3	32	68	11
	12	R	25	a/a	MIL	72	2.04	1.279	5.65	3.0	6.7	2.3	0.3	31	85	84
Sanchez,Romulo	12	R	28	aaa	TAM	51	7.87	1.787	6.956	3.9	6.1	1.6	1.7	35	57	7
Savage,William	11	R	27	aa	LA	141	4.36	1.407	23.9	1.7	4.3	2.6	0.8	33	70	52
	12	R	28	aaa	LA	142	5.34	1.626	20.99	2.3	3.2	1.4	1.0	34	68	7
Scahill,Rob	11	R	24	aa	COL	161	4.77	1.572	26.13	3.4	4.5	1.3	0.8	32	70	26
	12	R	25	aaa	COL	152	6.30	1.722	23.81	4.3	7.2	1.7	0.7	37	62	50
Schenk,Neil	11	L	25	aa	TAM	67	4.03	1.527	6.332	5.6	5.5	1.0	0.6	27	74	40
	12	L	26	aa	TAM	61	3.32	1.518	6.266	3.0	5.0	1.7	1.1	32	82	29
Scheppers,Tanner	11	R	24	a/a	TEX	44	4.31	1.559	6.829	4.4	7.2	1.7	0.2	34	71	70
	12	R	25	aaa	TEX	31	4.19	1.27	4.696	1.2	7.0	5.8	0.7	34	68	140
Schlitter,Brian	12	R	27	aa	CHC	42	4.01	1.592	6.39	2.7	7.3	2.8	0.5	38	75	78
Schmidt,Joshua	11	R	29	a/a	NYY	66	3.38	1.397	6.505	4.1	7.7	1.9	0.8	30	78	65
	12	R	30	a/a	MIA	55	4.82	1.82	5.971	7.0	6.7	1.0	0.4	32	72	50
Schmidt,Nick	12	L	27	a/a	COL	147	5.93	1.686	25.48	3.1	5.4	1.7	1.2	35	66	23
Scholl,Christian	11	R	24	aa	LAA	85	2.83	1.098	10.45	2.4	5.8	2.5	0.8	26	78	71
	12	R	25	aa	LAA	40	8.67	1.97	5.806	2.2	6.8	3.1	1.9	42	57	29
Schugel,Andrew	12	R	23	aa	LAA	140	3.68	1.39	21.88	3.6	5.9	1.6	0.7	30	74	53
Schwinden,Chris	11	R	25	a/a	NYM	149	3.99	1.322	21.99	2.7	6.6	2.5	0.8	31	71	69
	12	R	26	aaa	NYM	129	3.93	1.453	21.2	2.5	5.4	2.1	0.8	33	75	49
Scribner,Evan	11	R	26	aaa	SD	29	3.82	1.297	4.215	3.4	7.1	2.1	0.4	30	70	79
	12	R	27	aaa	OAK	36	3.35	1.127	5.414	2.6	7.6	2.9	0.9	27	74	89
Searle,Ryan	11	R	22	aa	CHC	85	3.81	1.527	16	4.4	6.1	1.4	0.4	32	75	53
	12	R	23	a/a	CHC	31	3.74	1.525	13.47	3.8	5.4	1.4	0.6	32	76	42
Seaton,Ross	11	R	22	aa	HOU	155	5.13	1.389	23.3	2.5	5.0	2.0	1.0	31	64	39
	12	R	23	a/a	HOU	169	3.86	1.303	24.07	1.8	5.4	2.9	1.0	31	73	64
Seddon,Chris	11	L	28	aaa	SEA	149	5.81	1.728	24.26	4.0	5.7	1.4	1.0	35	67	28
	12	L	29	aaa	CLE	123	4.29	1.377	25.81	2.1	5.9	2.7	1.3	32	73	53
Segovia,Zack	11	R	28	aaa	MIL	63	4.43	1.917	6.667	5.6	5.6	1.0	0.9	35	79	19
	12	R	29	aa	DET	65	8.19	2.059	26.29	3.4	3.0	0.9	1.9	37	62	-39
Seidel,RJ	11	R	24	aa	MIL	31	6.85	1.669	15.3	3.6	6.5	1.8	2.0	33	63	10
	12	R	25	aa	MIL	67	4.14	1.588	7.61	4.4	5.9	1.3	1.0	31	76	34
Sena,Jandy	12	R	23	a/a	SEA	61	4.05	1.459	7.417	3.4	4.5	1.3	0.6	31	72	38
Septimo,Leyson	11	L	26	aa	CHW	56	7.17	1.855	6.088	8.0	8.0	1.0	0.5	32	59	59
	12	L	27	aaa	CHW	34	1.96	1.375	6.001	6.8	9.1	1.3	0.4	24	87	89
Serrano,Mark	12	R	27	aa	CIN	93	5.72	1.64	10.15	3.3	7.3	2.2	1.5	35	68	36
Severino,Atahualpa	11	L	27	aaa	WAS	32	5.75	2.17	4.562	6.7	8.1	1.2	0.7	41	73	42
	12	L	28	aaa	WAS	48	3.67	1.763	4.782	7.1	5.9	0.8	1.1	28	83	23
Sexton,Timothy	11	R	24	aaa	LA	79	5.54	1.711	23.76	2.2	3.8	1.7	1.1	36	69	13
	12	R	25	a/a	COL	35	6.38	1.537	6.354	2.2	6.7	3.1	1.0	36	58	65
Shirek,Charles	11	R	26	aa	CHW	88	5.24	1.724	16.73	3.5	4.8	1.4	0.9	35	70	23
	12	R	27	aaa	CHW	170	5.46	1.572	26.72	2.0	5.0	2.5	1.5	34	69	29
Shoemaker,Matthew	11	R	25	a/a	LAA	177	3.39	1.259	26.79	2.3	5.8	2.5	1.0	29	77	61
	12	R	26	aaa	LAA	177	5.67	1.636	27.14	2.1	5.0	2.4	1.1	36	67	35
Shreve,Colby	12	R	24	aa	PHI	43	5.19	1.739	7.001	5.3	5.1	1.0	0.5	33	69	34
Shuman,Scott	12	R	24	aa	TAM	35	9.97	2.363	6.196	11.9	11.9	1.0	0.8	39	55	70
Siegrist,Kevin	12	L	23	aa	STL	32	3.88	1.148	16.04	2.5	6.3	2.5	1.0	27	69	70
Simmons,James	12	R	26	a/a	OAK	63	3.18	1.296	6.684	3.2	5.8	1.8	0.5	29	76	61

PITCHER	yr	t	age	lvl	org	ip	era	whip	bf/g	ctl	dom	cmd	hr/9	h%	s%	bpv
Simons,Zachary	11	R	24	a/a	MIA	57	6.13	1.63	7.2	5.5	5.7	1.0	1.9	27	67	1
	12	R	25	a/a	COL	58	4.66	1.63	6.143	4.8	5.6	1.2	1.5	30	76	13
Simpson,Jesse	11	R	24	aa	STL	23	4.91	1.38	5.288	2.5	5.5	2.2	1.4	30	68	35
	12	R	25	aa	STL	31	6.09	1.56	5.279	2.7	7.2	2.7	1.0	36	61	61
Sinclair,Taylor	12	L	27	a/a	ARI	37	7.16	1.82	6.137	5.2	2.6	0.5	1.1	31	60	-12
Sisk,Brandon	11	L	26	a/a	KC	61	2.91	1.13	5.85	3.5	6.6	1.9	0.4	25	74	80
	12	L	27	aaa	KC	67	2.93	1.52	5.844	4.4	7.3	1.7	1.0	31	85	50
Skaggs,Tyler	11	L	20	aa	ARI	58	2.68	1.06	22.38	2.1	10.0	4.8	0.6	31	77	151
	12	L	21	a/a	ARI	122	3.01	1.24	22.58	2.4	7.4	3.0	0.9	30	79	85
Slama,Anthony	11	R	27	aaa	MIN	37	3.65	1.36	5.73	4.2	7.9	1.9	1.0	29	76	64
	12	R	28	aaa	MIN	36	1.72	1.50	5.069	5.1	10.4	2.0	0.3	35	89	102
Smith,Eric	12	R	24	aa	ARI	42	5.48	1.76	6.416	6.1	4.0	0.7	0.3	31	67	30
Smith,Greg	11	L	28	aaa	BOS	82	6.74	1.92	22.78	4.3	4.2	1.0	1.6	35	67	-14
	12	L	29	a/a	LAA	173	4.95	1.56	27.14	2.5	4.1	1.6	1.3	33	71	12
Smith,Jordan	11	R	25	aaa	CIN	26	3.59	1.45	4.68	3.1	3.7	1.2	0.8	30	77	22
	12	R	26	aaa	CIN	57	5.90	1.72	5.047	2.7	4.6	1.7	0.4	37	64	40
Smith,Murphy	12	R	25	aa	OAK	140	5.47	1.81	24	3.7	4.4	1.2	0.5	37	68	26
Smith,Will	11	L	22	aa	KC	161	4.10	1.40	25.2	2.4	5.0	2.1	0.6	32	71	53
	12	L	23	aaa	KC	90	3.83	1.48	25.73	2.1	6.0	2.9	0.7	35	75	70
Smyth,Paul	11	R	24	aa	OAK	65	4.99	1.54	7.081	3.9	6.9	1.8	0.9	33	69	49
	12	R	25	aa	OAK	69	4.57	1.54	6.867	3.2	5.7	1.8	1.0	33	72	38
Snow,Forrest	11	R	22	aaa	SEA	35	4.36	1.14	15.55	2.2	8.3	3.9	0.7	30	62	116
	12	R	24	a/a	SEA	118	7.08	1.81	17.03	5.2	6.6	1.3	0.7	36	59	38
Snyder,Benjamin	11	L	26	aa	TEX	119	5.07	1.56	13	2.5	3.9	1.6	1.5	32	72	2
	12	L	27	aaa	TEX	86	5.25	1.53	8.692	3.0	5.1	1.7	1.5	31	69	17
Socolovich,Miguel	11	R	25	a/a	CHW	55	4.54	1.61	7.168	5.2	9.7	1.8	0.5	36	71	85
	12	R	26	aaa	CHC	55	2.53	1.04	6.886	2.4	7.4	3.1	0.9	25	81	93
Sogard,Alexander	12	L	25	aa	HOU	54	4.13	1.69	7.336	4.1	4.9	1.2	0.5	34	75	33
Solano,Javier	11	R	21	aa	LA	33	2.98	1.37	7.199	3.8	6.5	1.7	0.2	30	77	72
	12	R	22	aa	LA	63	3.08	1.27	6.753	2.3	7.4	3.3	0.6	32	77	97
Sosa,Henry	11	R	26	a/a	HOU	89	4.94	1.63	13.72	3.2	6.3	2.0	0.5	37	69	56
	12	R	27	aaa	HOU	32	5.23	1.60	23.33	2.8	4.7	1.7	0.6	35	66	40
Soto,Giovanni	12	L	21	aa	CLE	121	5.07	1.48	23.74	3.7	6.5	1.8	0.8	32	66	51
Souza,Justin	11	R	26	a/a	OAK	63	3.95	1.13	6.217	1.9	5.6	3.0	1.3	26	70	64
	12	R	27	aaa	OAK	58	7.59	2.04	7.78	2.9	3.2	1.1	1.7	38	65	-30
Spence,Josh	11	L	23	aa	SD	47	1.63	0.85	4.961	2.0	7.1	3.6	0.6	22	85	118
	12	L	24	aaa	SD	49	3.86	1.37	6.67	3.4	5.7	1.7	0.6	30	72	56
Spoone,Chorye	11	R	26	a/a	BAL	122	6.04	1.87	18.44	5.3	4.6	0.9	0.6	34	66	21
	12	R	27	a/a	TOR	64	4.13	1.77	6.963	7.3	4.7	0.6	0.7	28	77	26
Spruill,Ezekiel	11	R	22	aa	ATL	45	3.34	1.42	27.23	3.2	2.8	0.9	0.6	29	77	19
	12	R	23	aa	ATL	162	4.54	1.43	25.47	2.6	5.1	1.9	0.5	33	67	55
St Clair,Allen	11	L	25	aa	LA	50	3.21	1.18	4.796	2.2	6.7	3.1	0.2	31	71	104
	12	L	26	aaa	LA	81	3.87	1.42	8.336	2.9	3.1	1.1	0.4	30	72	29
Stange,Daniel	11	R	26	aaa	ARI	37	5.65	1.81	6.792	5.8	5.6	1.0	1.3	32	71	12
	12	R	27	a/a	SD	58	4.41	1.51	4.892	3.2	8.5	2.6	0.4	37	70	92
Stevens,Jeff	11	R	28	a/a	CHC	65	5.99	1.80	7.148	4.1	7.1	1.7	0.9	38	67	46
	12	R	29	a/a	NYM	50	4.86	1.89	5.89	5.0	5.4	1.1	1.0	36	76	17
Stevenson,Jason	11	L	30	a/a	SF	18	4.64	1.80	28.23	3.6	5.8	1.6	1.9	35	81	0
	12	L	31	a/a	SF	139	7.70	1.94	23.7	3.5	3.9	1.1	1.6	37	62	-18
Stewart,Zach	11	R	25	a/a	CHW	101	5.55	1.74	26.98	2.9	6.0	2.1	0.7	38	68	46
	12	R	26	aaa	BOS	59	5.66	1.53	23.47	2.4	5.0	2.1	1.1	34	64	34
Stilson,John	12	R	22	aa	TOR	50	6.14	1.69	13.28	4.1	7.0	1.7	1.3	35	65	33
Stinson,Josh	11	R	23	a/a	NYM	109	5.88	1.58	11.98	3.6	4.8	1.3	0.6	33	61	35
	12	R	24	aaa	MIL	145	3.83	1.85	23.41	4.6	4.8	1.1	0.5	36	79	26
Stoffel,Jason	11	R	23	aa	HOU	48	4.54	1.63	4.24	4.3	8.1	1.9	0.7	36	73	64
	12	R	24	aa	HOU	58	2.44	1.03	3.986	2.4	7.5	3.2	0.5	26	78	110
Stoneburner,Graham	11	R	24	aa	NYY	58	5.20	1.82	24.63	3.3	4.6	1.4	0.6	38	71	25
	12	R	25	aa	NYY	38	6.47	1.75	8.598	2.3	5.4	2.3	1.9	36	67	8
Storey,Mickey	11	R	25	a/a	HOU	67	4.28	1.61	5.964	3.2	6.5	2.0	0.8	36	75	51
	12	R	26	aaa	HOU	65	3.05	1.24	6.94	1.8	8.1	4.4	1.1	32	80	110
Stowell,Bryce	11	R	25	aa	CLE	19	2.34	1.28	6.104	4.8	10.6	2.2	0.5	30	83	107
	12	R	26	aa	CLE	29	5.27	1.37	4.858	3.1	10.8	3.5	1.9	33	68	83
Straily,Dan	12	R	24	a/a	OAK	152	2.98	1.06	23.58	2.4	9.5	3.9	0.5	29	72	136
Strickland,Hunter	12	R	24	aa	PIT	41	5.76	1.75	8.217	3.1	5.4	1.8	1.2	37	69	23
Struck,Nicholas	11	R	22	a/a	CHC	97	4.17	1.53	23.5	2.4	5.1	2.1	0.2	36	71	63
	12	R	23	aa	CHC	156	3.90	1.34	23.12	2.6	6.0	2.3	0.9	30	73	57
Sturdevant,Tyler	11	R	26	a/a	CLE	34	4.27	1.62	7.124	3.1	8.1	2.6	0.6	39	74	79
	12	R	27	a/a	CLE	30	7.13	2.08	6.061	3.9	5.9	1.5	2.0	40	70	-13
Sulbaran,Juan	12	R	23	aa	KC	131	5.59	1.74	23.82	5.2	7.6	1.4	1.6	33	71	26
Sullivan,Joshua	11	R	27	aa	COL	118	7.24	1.79	21.69	4.5	4.9	1.1	1.9	32	63	-14
	12	R	28	aa	COL	62	4.68	1.79	4.761	4.4	6.5	1.5	0.8	37	74	40
Tanner,Clayton	11	L	24	a/a	CIN	123	4.47	1.37	22.35	2.6	5.8	2.2	1.0	31	70	51
	12	L	25	a/a	SF	59	7.21	1.84	6.508	3.9	5.2	1.3	0.4	38	58	34
Tatusko,Ryan	12	R	26	a/a	WAS	87	6.69	2.10	12.18	4.7	5.4	1.2	0.4	41	66	29
	12	R	27	aa	WAS	82	4.56	1.52	13.23	4.0	6.4	1.6	0.5	33	69	57
Taylor,Andrew	11	L	25	aa	LAA	112	6.40	1.99	18.58	5.9	4.8	0.8	1.2	34	69	2
	12	L	26	a/a	LAA	59	4.88	1.60	4.922	3.8	6.8	1.8	1.1	34	72	42
Taylor,Graham	11	L	27	aa	MIA	99	4.74	1.75	21.55	2.4	4.4	1.9	1.3	37	76	12
	12	L	28	aa	MIA	147	5.23	1.73	25.77	2.4	4.0	1.6	1.2	36	72	10
Tazawa,Junichi	11	R	25	a/a	BOS	37	4.95	1.38	9.808	2.5	8.9	3.6	1.1	35	66	95
	12	R	26	aaa	BOS	42	3.66	1.49	7.296	4.0	9.4	2.3	0.5	36	76	90
Teaford,Everett	11	L	27	aaa	KC	35	3.93	1.11	8.59	2.9	6.3	2.2	1.2	23	69	58
	12	L	28	aaa	KC	33	1.29	1.13	18.62	2.3	5.0	2.2	0.5	26	92	67
Teheran,Julio	11	R	20	aaa	ATL	145	2.94	1.26	23.59	2.9	7.0	2.4	0.3	31	76	88
	12	R	21	aaa	ATL	131	5.43	1.50	21.77	2.8	6.0	2.1	1.2	33	65	41
Tepera,Dennis	12	R	25	aa	TOR	74	6.27	1.87	21.79	4.7	5.7	1.2	0.6	37	65	32
Tepesch,Nicholas	12	R	24	aa	TEX	90	5.73	1.63	25.12	2.8	5.4	1.9	1.4	34	67	23

PITCHER	yr	t	age	lvl	org	ip	era	whip	bf/g	ctl	dom	cmd	hr/9	h%	s%	bpv
Texeira,Kanekoa	11	R	25	a/a	NYY	26	14.12	3.075	6.305	5.1	4.2	0.8	2.5	49	54	-70
	12	R	26	aaa	CIN	56	3.36	1.511	7.175	4.5	4.5	1.0	0.4	29	78	39
Thielbar,Caleb	12	L	25	a/a	MIN	65	3.63	1.411	6.742	2.8	6.4	2.3	0.8	32	76	61
Thomas,Justin	11	L	27	aaa	PIT	69	4.87	1.525	4.782	3.2	5.6	1.7	0.6	33	67	50
	12	L	28	aaa	NYY	63	4.83	1.503	7.967	3.4	5.8	1.7	0.6	33	67	50
Thomas,Kevin	11	R	25	aa	STL	94	5.81	1.669	12.74	4.4	5.5	1.3	0.9	33	65	30
	12	R	26	aa	STL	73	4.90	1.357	6.807	2.8	7.0	2.5	1.1	31	66	61
Thompson,Aaron	11	L	24	a/a	PIT	103	5.65	1.665	13.95	2.5	4.2	1.7	0.5	36	65	33
	12	L	25	aa	MIN	86	6.35	1.845	18.24	2.4	3.8	1.6	0.9	38	65	12
Thompson,Daryl	11	R	26	a/a	CIN	137	4.75	1.54	23.03	2.6	6.5	2.5	1.3	34	73	45
	12	R	27	aaa	MIN	42	6.40	2.099	22.95	6.0	4.9	0.8	0.7	37	69	14
Thompson,Jacob	12	R	23	aa	TAM	125	6.15	1.864	23.36	3.9	5.6	1.5	0.8	38	67	26
Thompson,Rich	12	R	28	aaa	OAK	62	3.77	1.263	5.503	3.5	6.5	1.9	1.0	27	73	57
Thornburg,Tyler	12	R	24	a/a	MIL	113	3.90	1.331	22.27	3.1	7.7	2.5	0.7	32	71	82
Tillman,Chris	11	R	23	aaa	BAL	76	6.29	1.659	22.79	4.4	5.3	1.2	2.4	29	69	-19
	12	R	24	a/a	BAL	93	4.89	1.513	23.62	3.2	7.4	2.3	0.6	35	67	71
Todd,Jesse	11	R	25	aaa	STL	55	6.36	1.703	4.848	3.6	6.0	1.6	0.8	36	62	37
	12	R	26	aaa	STL	66	4.84	1.708	6.39	3.0	7.8	2.6	0.7	40	72	69
Torra,Matthew	11	R	27	aaa	TAM	147	6.12	1.671	25.45	2.0	3.5	1.7	1.3	35	65	5
	12	R	28	aaa	TAM	147	5.11	1.434	24.05	1.7	3.7	2.2	1.7	30	69	11
Torres,Alexander	11	L	24	aaa	TAM	146	3.48	1.586	23.88	5.0	8.1	1.6	0.4	34	78	71
	12	L	25	aaa	TAM	69	8.53	2.09	13.03	8.2	9.8	1.2	0.8	39	57	56
Torres,Carlos	12	R	30	aaa	COL	61	4.88	1.711	19.74	4.0	6.0	1.5	1.1	35	74	27
Troncoso,Ramon	11	R	28	aaa	LA	57	4.45	1.477	6.998	3.6	4.9	1.4	1.0	30	72	28
	12	R	29	aaa	LA	59	6.52	1.848	6.155	3.7	4.5	1.2	0.8	37	64	16
Tufts,Tyler	11	R	25	aa	TEX	56	4.15	1.616	6.332	1.2	5.8	4.8	0.4	40	74	108
	12	R	26	a/a	TEX	30	7.37	1.762	7.315	2.3	3.4	1.5	1.6	35	60	-11
Turner,Jacob	11	R	20	a/a	DET	131	3.94	1.227	26.51	2.2	6.5	2.9	0.7	30	69	82
	12	R	21	aaa	MIA	90	3.13	1.36	25.08	3.6	4.9	1.4	0.4	29	77	51
Turpen,Daniel	11	R	25	aa	COL	60	6.00	1.867	5.827	5.5	3.8	0.7	1.0	32	68	2
	12	R	26	a/a	MIN	72	5.61	1.73	7.122	5.2	7.3	1.4	0.6	35	67	51
Urquidez,Jason	11	R	29	aaa	ARI	54	6.20	1.773	5.942	3.4	6.2	1.8	1.1	37	66	32
	12	R	30	aa	BOS	47	4.36	1.808	12.89	2.5	5.0	2.0	0.8	39	77	34
Uviedo,Ronald	11	R	25	a/a	TOR	74	4.93	1.478	6.332	3.3	8.3	2.5	1.0	34	68	70
	12	R	26	a/a	TOR	64	3.54	1.474	5.943	3.9	7.1	1.8	0.7	32	77	62
Valdez,Jose	11	R	28	aaa	HOU	21	6.60	1.786	4.759	4.1	8.8	2.1	1.9	38	67	30
	12	R	29	aaa	HOU	44	5.30	1.685	4.277	2.5	9.2	3.7	1.1	42	70	89
Van Mil,Loek	11	R	27	aa	LAA	66	2.65	1.373	9.271	3.4	4.9	1.4	0.6	29	83	43
	12	R	28	a/a	CLE	65	4.28	1.542	6.88	3.5	5.2	1.5	0.6	32	73	40
VanAllen,Cory	11	L	27	aa	WAS	58	3.26	1.46	5.251	3.6	8.4	2.3	1.1	33	82	66
	12	L	28	a/a	WAS	32	8.15	2.044	5.559	6.2	6.2	1.0	1.0	37	59	18
VandenHurk,Rick	11	R	26	aaa	BAL	154	5.72	1.398	25.04	2.5	4.9	2.0	1.7	29	63	18
	12	R	27	aaa	PIT	123	4.02	1.476	25.23	2.8	6.0	2.2	0.7	34	74	57
Varvaro,Anthony	11	R	27	aaa	ATL	59	3.82	1.448	6.627	5.9	8.4	1.4	0.5	28	74	76
	12	R	28	aaa	ATL	44	2.74	1.666	6.026	5.3	7.5	1.4	0.2	35	83	68
Vasquez,Anthony	11	L	25	a/a	SEA	154	3.54	1.452	27.35	2.1	4.5	2.2	0.6	33	76	50
	12	L	26	aaa	SEA	61	6.75	1.777	25.35	3.1	3.8	1.2	0.5	36	60	21
Vasquez,Esmerling	11	R	28	aaa	ARI	28	5.95	1.721	5.462	6.3	6.4	1.0	0.9	30	65	35
	12	R	29	aaa	MIN	100	3.95	1.443	13.8	4.1	6.5	1.6	0.8	30	74	50
Vasquez,Luis	12	R	26	a/a	LA	53	7.82	1.994	5.933	5.9	5.3	0.9	0.3	37	57	31
Veal,Donnie	12	L	28	aaa	CHW	52	3.18	1.637	6.621	5.2	8.3	1.6	0.0	36	78	84
Ventura,Yordano	12	R	21	aa	KC	29	5.25	1.294	20.11	3.9	6.4	1.7	0.3	28	56	73
Verdugo,Ryan	11	L	24	aa	SF	130	5.34	1.518	22.62	4.3	7.7	1.8	1.0	32	66	55
	12	L	25	aaa	KC	137	4.15	1.422	21.47	4.3	6.1	1.4	1.1	28	74	37
Vessella,Thomas	12	L	27	aa	SF	53	5.74	1.765	5.749	5.3	6.0	1.1	0.4	35	66	44
Villanueva,Elih	11	R	25	aaa	MIA	165	5.48	1.665	26.43	3.2	4.6	1.4	1.1	34	68	17
	12	R	26	aaa	MIA	113	4.79	1.702	15.97	3.9	5.3	1.4	0.9	34	73	26
Villar,Henry	11	R	24	a/a	HOU	76	5.69	1.603	8.003	3.3	4.8	1.5	1.4	32	67	11
	12	R	25	aa	HOU	50	5.01	1.263	8.167	1.4	4.5	3.2	1.5	29	64	48
Villarreal,Pedro	11	R	24	aa	CIN	92	4.43	1.268	22.04	1.8	5.6	3.1	1.1	30	68	66
	12	R	25	a/a	CIN	149	5.63	1.583	25.18	2.5	5.4	2.2	0.9	35	64	44
Vincent,Nick	11	R	25	aa	SD	79	2.25	0.976	4.563	2.2	8.6	3.8	0.6	26	79	129
	12	R	26	a/a	SD	31	4.70	1.441	4.172	3.2	8.1	2.5	0.5	35	66	87
Viola,Pedro	11	L	28	aa	BAL	40	2.98	1.253	4.039	3.4	6.8	2.0	0.7	28	78	70
	12	L	29	a/a	BAL	47	6.85	1.611	5.826	5.0	9.3	1.8	1.9	32	61	38
Volstad,Chris	11	R	25	aaa	MIA	18	4.53	1.673	27.45	4.4	5.6	1.3	0.4	34	72	44
	12	R	26	aaa	CHC	71	6.18	1.709	26.92	2.5	5.2	2.1	1.0	37	64	33
Wade,Cory	11	R	28	aaa	NYY	38	1.78	1.469	7.474	1.7	6.2	3.6	1.5	34	98	61
	12	R	29	aaa	NYY	32	3.26	1.272	7.622	3.1	4.2	1.4	1.3	25	81	21
Wagner,Neil	11	R	27	a/a	OAK	66	3.54	1.351	5.534	3.2	9.4	2.9	0.2	35	72	113
	12	R	28	aaa	SD	63	5.90	1.74	6.212	3.4	6.4	1.9	0.4	39	64	57
Waite,Rob	11	R	24	aa	DET	75	5.40	1.717	8.507	3.4	6.0	1.8	0.8	37	68	41
	12	R	25	a/a	DET	78	5.95	1.745	8.685	3.6	3.9	1.1	0.8	34	65	13
Waldrop,Kyle	11	R	26	aaa	MIN	79	4.74	1.514	6.115	2.2	3.9	1.8	0.8	33	69	31
	12	R	27	aaa	MIN	35	4.54	1.694	6.583	3.8	3.2	0.8	0.3	34	72	21
Walker,Taijuan	12	R	20	aa	SEA	127	5.57	1.489	21.83	3.6	7.8	2.2	0.9	34	62	66
Wall,Josh	11	R	24	aa	LA	69	4.07	1.475	5.782	3.2	6.2	1.9	0.7	33	73	54
	12	R	25	aaa	LA	54	4.05	1.264	3.985	2.9	7.1	2.5	0.9	29	70	71
Walters,P.J.	11	R	26	aaa	TOR	132	4.94	1.594	24.34	3.6	6.2	1.7	0.8	34	70	44
	12	R	27	aaa	MIN	58	5.45	1.755	19.06	2.6	5.6	2.1	1.2	38	71	30
Warren,Adam	11	R	24	aaa	NYY	152	5.00	1.576	24.8	3.5	5.4	1.5	1.1	32	70	27
	12	R	25	aaa	NYY	153	4.87	1.672	26.38	3.0	5.1	1.7	0.9	36	72	30
Watts,Dakota	11	R	24	aa	MIN	34	8.44	1.88	7.016	4.8	6.0	1.2	0.7	37	52	33
	12	R	25	aa	MIN	34	3.25	1.583	6.176	4.5	5.8	1.3	0.3	33	79	54
Weathers,Casey	12	R	27	aa	CHC	34	8.85	2.693	6.046	15.9	6.0	0.4	0.7	28	65	29
Weathers,Casey McG	11	R	26	aa	COL	46	6.75	1.966	4.967	10.0	7.1	0.7	0.8	27	65	43
Webb,Travis	11	L	27	a/a	CIN	70	4.96	1.621	8.441	4.7	9.0	1.9	0.9	35	70	67
	11	L	27	a/a	CIN	70	4.96	1.621	8.441	4.7	9.0	1.9	0.9	35	70	67

PITCHER	yr	t	age	lvl	org	ip	era	whip	bf/g	ctl	dom	cmd	hr/9	h%	s%	bpv
Weber,Thad	11	R	27	aaa	DET	151	7.71	1.84	26.12	3.2	4.9	1.6	2.0	36	61	-13
	12	R	28	aaa	SD	147	4.24	1.33	24.41	2.1	5.4	2.5	0.9	31	70	59
Webster,Allen	11	R	21	aa	LA	91	4.96	1.48	21.75	3.1	6.3	2.0	0.6	34	66	60
	12	R	22	aa	BOS	131	5.02	1.68	20.27	4.3	7.6	1.8	0.2	38	68	73
Weinhardt,Robbie	11	R	26	a/a	DET	61	6.97	1.72	6.969	3.8	6.2	1.6	1.0	36	59	32
	12	R	27	aa	DET	66	3.56	1.50	6.479	3.8	5.7	1.5	1.0	31	79	37
Welker,Duke	12	R	26	a/a	PIT	55	3.05	1.44	5.709	4.3	6.0	1.4	0.2	30	78	64
Werner,Andrew	12	L	25	a/a	SD	126	3.71	1.37	24.08	2.2	6.6	3.0	0.4	34	72	88
Wesson,Jared	12	L	26	aa	DET	119	7.54	1.93	23.54	4.5	4.8	1.1	1.5	36	62	-4
Westcott,Craig	12	R	26	aa	SF	165	5.60	1.76	27	3.3	2.9	0.9	0.4	35	66	14
Whatcott,Jordan	12	R	27	aa	PHI	71	5.57	1.91	8.885	4.3	5.0	1.1	0.9	37	71	15
Wheeler,Zack	12	R	22	a/a	NYM	149	3.30	1.16	23.7	3.2	7.5	2.4	0.2	28	70	99
White,Alex	11	R	23	a/a	COL	40	1.80	0.90	18.58	1.2	6.8	5.5	0.5	26	82	156
	12	R	24	aaa	COL	61	4.03	1.35	22.98	3.3	5.2	1.6	0.5	29	70	53
Whitley,Chase	11	R	22	aa	NYY	43	4.04	1.68	10.1	4.1	6.7	1.6	1.6	34	82	21
	12	R	23	a/a	NYY	84	3.86	1.20	7.877	3.0	6.5	2.2	1.0	26	71	63
Wickswat,Matt	12	L	26	aa	CHW	53	12.34	3.02	14.73	12.2	4.8	0.4	0.7	41	56	-3
Wilk,Adam	11	L	24	aaa	DET	103	4.15	1.37	23.87	1.2	5.3	4.2	1.5	32	75	70
	12	L	25	aaa	DET	150	3.49	1.18	24.95	1.7	6.0	3.5	0.9	29	73	86
Williamson,Joseph	11	R	25	a/a	COL	89	4.55	1.64	14.11	3.8	6.4	1.7	1.1	34	75	35
	12	R	26	a/a	COL	56	4.26	1.82	5.683	5.2	7.8	1.5	0.4	38	76	59
Wilson,Alex	11	R	25	a/a	BOS	133	3.99	1.46	22.75	3.1	6.7	2.2	0.8	33	74	61
	12	R	26	aaa	BOS	73	5.33	1.86	8.506	4.5	7.6	1.7	0.5	40	70	57
Wilson,Justin	11	L	24	aaa	PIT	124	4.84	1.64	18.49	4.7	5.3	1.1	0.9	31	71	28
	12	L	25	aaa	PIT	136	4.99	1.33	19.43	4.6	7.0	1.5	0.9	26	63	57
Wise,Brendan	11	R	25	a/a	DET	64	3.55	1.73	5.46	4.3	4.4	1.0	0.5	34	80	27
	12	R	26	aaa	MIN	53	7.49	2.54	9.73	4.7	4.6	1.0	0.5	46	69	3
Withrow,Chris	11	R	22	aa	LA	129	4.17	1.41	21.74	4.6	7.9	1.7	0.5	30	70	75
	12	R	23	aa	LA	60	5.35	1.55	11.91	5.2	8.1	1.6	0.5	33	64	72
Wojciechowski,Asher	12	R	24	aa	HOU	44	2.38	1.05	21.12	2.7	5.9	2.2	0.0	26	75	94
Wolf,Ross	11	R	29	aaa	HOU	74	5.68	1.77	6.039	3.5	5.1	1.4	0.6	37	67	33
	12	R	30	a/a	TEX	62	4.49	1.57	5.478	2.6	5.9	2.3	1.1	35	74	44
Wood,Tim	11	R	29	aaa	TEX	49	4.22	1.36	4.659	3.0	4.5	1.5	0.5	30	68	46
	12	R	30	aaa	PIT	70	3.19	1.45	5.533	3.4	5.9	1.7	0.5	32	78	58
Wood,Travis	11	L	24	aaa	CIN	52	6.10	1.71	23.7	2.9	6.8	2.4	1.2	38	65	44
	12	L	25	aaa	CHC	41	5.35	1.62	26.22	2.5	6.9	2.8	1.2	37	69	54
Woodall,Bryan	11	R	25	aa	ARI	66	4.03	1.47	5.639	2.4	7.5	3.1	0.8	36	74	82
	12	R	26	a/a	ARI	67	7.27	1.86	6.532	3.3	6.7	2.0	0.9	40	60	42
Woods,Coty	12	R	24	a/a	COL	56	4.09	1.63	4.107	3.2	5.9	1.9	1.0	35	78	35
Wooten,Robert	11	R	26	aa	MIL	43	4.11	1.52	5.147	3.4	7.1	2.1	0.7	34	74	61
	12	R	27	a/a	MIL	73	4.32	1.49	5.547	3.1	6.9	2.2	0.8	34	72	61
Wright,Justin	12	L	23	aa	STL	61	4.77	1.48	5.215	4.0	8.0	2.0	0.8	33	68	68
Wright,Matthew	12	L	25	aa	TOR	52	5.12	1.27	7.931	3.3	8.3	2.5	2.0	27	67	50
Wright,Mike	12	R	22	aa	BAL	62	5.68	1.53	22.61	2.4	5.5	2.3	1.2	34	64	40
Wright,Steven	11	R	27	a/a	CLE	49	7.56	1.90	25.86	5.4	5.2	1.0	1.6	33	61	-3
	12	R	28	a/a	BOS	142	3.97	1.61	25.12	5.1	5.7	1.1	0.7	31	77	36
Yan,Johan	11	R	23	aa	TEX	27	0.41	1.13	5.547	3.1	4.9	1.6	0.0	26	96	74
	12	R	24	a/a	TEX	52	4.98	1.71	5.229	5.1	5.0	1.0	1.1	31	73	14
Yates,Kirby	12	R	25	aa	TAM	68	3.05	1.38	5.717	5.1	10.3	2.0	0.5	31	79	98
Zagone,Richard	11	L	25	aa	BAL	97	6.62	1.83	23.66	3.3	4.2	1.3	1.9	35	68	-18
	12	L	26	a/a	BAL	87	5.01	1.42	24.59	3.7	4.4	1.2	0.8	28	65	29
Zaleski,Matthew	11	R	30	a/a	CHW	139	6.13	1.69	25.14	4.4	5.5	1.2	1.2	33	65	19
	12	R	31	a/a	CHW	140	5.50	1.90	24.5	4.7	4.1	0.9	1.3	34	73	-6
Zeid,Joshua	11	R	24	aa	HOU	80	6.70	1.55	9.938	3.5	6.8	1.9	1.6	32	58	32

This section provides rankings of projected skills indicators for 2013. Rather than take shots in the dark predicting league leaders in the exact number of home runs, or stolen bases, or strikeouts, the Forecaster's Leaderboards focus on the component elements of each skill.

For batters, we've ranked the top players in terms of pure power, speed, and batting average skill, breaking each down in a number of different ways to provide more insight. For pitchers, we rank some of the key base skills, differentiating between starters and relievers, and provide a few interesting cuts that might uncover some late round sleepers.

These are clearly not exhaustive lists of sorts and filters. If there is another cut you'd like to see, drop me a note and I'll consider it for next year's book. Also note that the database at BaseballHQ.com allows you to construct your own custom sorts and filters. Finally, remember that these are just tools. Some players will appear on multiple lists—even mutually exclusive lists—so you have to assess what makes most sense and make decisions for your specific application.

Power

Top PX, 400+ AB: Top power skills among projected full-time players.

Top PX, –300 AB: Top power skills among projected part-time players. Possible end-game options are here.

Position Scarcity: A quick scan to see which positions have deeper power options than others.

Top PX, ct% over 85%: Top power skills among the top contact hitters. Best pure power options here.

Top PX, ct% under 75%: Top power skills among the worst contact hitters. These are free-swingers who might be prone to streakiness or lower batting averages.

Top PX, FB% over 40%: Top power skills among the most extreme fly ball hitters. Most likely to convert their power into home runs.

Top PX, FB% under 35%: Top power skills among those with lesser fly ball tendencies. There may be more downside to their home run potential.

Speed

Top Spd, 400+ AB: Top speed skills among projected full-time players.

Top Spd, –300 AB: Top speed skills among projected part-time players. Possible end-game options are here.

Position Scarcity: A quick scan to see which positions have deeper speed options than others.

Top Spd, OB% over .350: Top speed skills among those who get on base most often. Best opportunities for stolen bases here.

Top Spd, OB% under .310: Top speed skills among those who have trouble getting on base. These names may bear watching if they can improve their on base ability.

Top Spd, SBO% over 20%: Top speed skills among those who get the green light most often. Most likely to convert their speed into stolen bases.

Top Spd, SBO% under 15%: Top speed skills among those who are currently not getting the green light. There may be sleeper SBs here if given more opportunities to run.

Batting Average

Top ct%, 400+ AB: Top contact skills among projected full-time players. Contact does not always convert to higher BAs, but is still strongly correlated.

Top ct%, -300 AB: Top contact skills among projected part-time players. Possible end-gamers here.

Low ct%, 400+ AB: The poorest contact skills among projected full-time players. Potential BA killers.

Top ct%, bb% over 10%: Top contact skills among the most patient hitters. Best batting average upside here.

Top ct%, bb% under 6%: Top contact skills among the least patient hitters. These are free-swingers who might be prone to streakiness or lower batting averages.

Top ct%, GB% over 50%: Top contact skills among the most extreme ground ball hitters. A ground ball has a higher chance of becoming a hit than a non-HR fly ball so there may be some batting average upside here.

Top ct%, GB% under 40%: Top contact skills from those with lesser ground ball tendencies. These players make contact but hit more fly balls, which tend to convert to hits at a lower rate than GB.

Pitching Skills

Top Command: Leaders in projected K/BB rates.

Top Control: Leaders in fewest projected walks allowed.

Top Dominance: Leaders in projected strikeout rate.

Top Ground Ball Rate: GB pitchers tend to have lower ERAs (and higher WHIP) than fly ball pitchers.

Top Fly Ball Rate: FB pitchers tend to have higher ERAs (and lower WHIP) than ground ball pitchers.

High GB, Low Dom: GB pitchers tend to have lower K rates, but these are the most extreme examples.

High GB, High Dom: The best at dominating hitters and keeping the ball down. These are the pitchers who keep runners off the bases and batted balls in the park, a skills combination that is the most valuable a pitcher can own.

Lowest xERA: Leaders in projected skills-based ERA.

Top BPV: Two lists of top skilled pitchers. For starters, those projected to be rotation regulars (180+ IP) and fringe starters with skill (<150 IP). For relievers, those projected to be frontline closers (10+ saves) and high-skilled bullpen fillers (<9 saves).

Risk Management

These lists include players who've accumulated the most days on the disabled list over the past five years (Grade "F" in Health) and whose performance was the most consistent over the past three years. Also listed are the most reliable batters and pitchers overall, with a focus on positional and skills reliability. As a reminder, reliability in this context is not tied to skill level; it is a gauge of which players manage to accumulate playing time and post consistent output from year to year, whether that output is good or bad.

LIMA Plan

These are the players ranked as B or better for those employing the LIMA Plan, set up in a grid by position. A full description of this plan appears in the Encyclopedia.

Portfolio3 Plan

Players are sorted and ranked based on how they fit into the three draft tiers of the Portfolio3 Plan. A full description of this plan appears in the Encyclopedia.

Random Variance

These charts list +/- 3, 4 and 5 Rand Var scores for players with a minimum of 300 AB or 100 IP. The scores identify players who, in 2011, posted outlying levels of meaures that are prone to regression. A full description appears in the Batters and Pitchers introductory pages.

BATTER SKILLS RANKING - POWER

TOP PX, 400+ AB

NAME	POS	PX
Stanton,Giancarlo	9	220
Dunn,Adam	0 3	177
Reynolds,Mark	3	176
Votto,Joey	3	172
Bruce,Jay	9	170
Hamilton,Josh	7 8	169
Granderson,Curtis	8	168
Carter,Chris	3	161
Davis,Chris	0 3 9	161
Willingham,Josh	0 7	161
Braun,Ryan	7	158
Kemp,Matt	8	158
Saltalamacchia,Jarrod	2	158
Davis,Ike	3	157
Bautista,Jose	9	155
Longoria,Evan	0 5	155
Kubel,Jason	7	154
Maxwell,Justin	7 8 9	154
Upton,B.J.	8	153
Cabrera,Miguel	5	152
Soriano,Alfonso	7	152
Cruz,Nelson	9	152
Goldschmidt,Paul	3	152
Hart,Corey	3 9	151
Arencibia,J.P.	2	151
Encarnacion,Edwin	0 3	151
Colvin,Tyler	3 8 9	149
Scott,Luke	0	149
Howard,Ryan	3	148
Frazier,Todd	3 5	147
Pujols,Albert	0 3	145
Ortiz,David	0	143
Quentin,Carlos	7	143
Jones,Garrett	3 9	142
Craig,Allen	3 9	141
Heyward,Jason	9	140
Ruggiano,Justin	7 8	140
Holliday,Matt	7	139
Fielder,Prince	3	139
Tulowitzki,Troy	6	139

TOP PX, 300 or fewer AB

NAME	POS	PX
Flowers,Tyler	2	172
Moss,Brandon	3	158
Gomes,Jonny	0 7	153
Shoppach,Kelly	2	151
Thome,Jim	0	151
Jones,Andruw	7 9	149
Moore,Tyler	7	145
Francisco,Juan	5	141
D Arnaud,Travis	2	140
Ross,David	2	140
Gomes,Yan	3	139
Nix,Laynce	7	138
Kottaras,George	2	137
Ransom,Cody	5 6	135
Kratz,Erik	2	128
Liddi,Alex	5	126
Ankiel,Rick	8	125
McKenry,Michael	2	125
LaHair,Bryan	3 9	124
Berkman,Lance	3	122
Duncan,Shelley	7	122
Guzman,Jesus	7	122
Moore,Scott	5	122

POSITIONAL SCARCITY

NAME	POS	PX
Dunn,Adam	DH	177
Davis,Chris	2	161
Willingham,Josh	3	161
Longoria,Evan	4	155
Gomes,Jonny	5	153
Encarnacion,Edwin	6	151
Napoli,Mike	CA	182
Flowers,Tyler	2	172
Saltalamacchia,Jarrod	3	158
Arencibia,J.P.	4	151
Shoppach,Kelly	5	151
D Arnaud,Travis	6	140
Ross,David	7	140
Kottaras,George	8	137
Napoli,Mike	1B	182
Dunn,Adam	2	177
Reynolds,Mark	3	176
Votto,Joey	4	172
Carter,Chris	5	161
Davis,Chris	6	161
Moss,Brandon	7	158
Davis,Ike	8	157
Goldschmidt,Paul	9	152
Hart,Corey	10	151
Cano,Robinson	2B	137
Zobrist,Ben	2	129
Weeks,Rickie	3	126
Espinosa,Danny	4	125
Uggla,Dan	5	124
Hill,Aaron	6	122
Flaherty,Ryan	7	117
Raburn,Ryan	8	117
Longoria,Evan	3B	155
Cabrera,Miguel	2	152
Frazier,Todd	3	147
Francisco,Juan	4	141
Alvarez,Pedro	5	137
Beltre,Adrian	6	135
Ransom,Cody	7	135
Zimmerman,Ryan	8	129
Ramirez,Aramis	9	128
Youkilis,Kevin	10	127
Tulowitzki,Troy	SS	139
Ransom,Cody	2	135
Zobrist,Ben	3	129
Rutledge,Josh	4	127
Espinosa,Danny	5	125
Desmond,Ian	6	114
Lowrie,Jed	7	112
Ramirez,Hanley	8	106
Stanton,Giancarlo	OF	220
Bruce,Jay	2	170
Hamilton,Josh	3	169
Granderson,Curtis	4	168
Davis,Chris	5	161
Willingham,Josh	6	161
Braun,Ryan	7	158
Kemp,Matt	8	158
Bautista,Jose	9	155
Kubel,Jason	10	154
Maxwell,Justin	11	154
Upton,B.J.	12	153
Gomes,Jonny	13	153
Soriano,Alfonso	14	152
Cruz,Nelson	15	152
Hart,Corey	16	151

TOP PX, ct% over 85%

NAME	Ct%	PX
Pujols,Albert	88	145
Cano,Robinson	86	137
Beltre,Adrian	87	135
Hill,Aaron	86	122
Taveras,Oscar	89	115
Ruiz,Carlos	87	111
Pedroia,Dustin	89	109
Kinsler,Ian	87	106
Markakis,Nick	88	105
Martinez,Victor	89	95
Perez,Salvador	90	95
Molina,Yadier	90	93
Rollins,Jimmy	87	93
Cabrera,Melky	86	92
Victorino,Shane	87	90
Phillips,Brandon	86	89
Crisp,Coco	86	89
Prado,Martin	88	89
Betancourt,Yuniesky	88	88
Murphy,Daniel	86	88
Castro,Starlin	86	87
Reyes,Jose	91	86
Rivera,Juan	87	85
Aoki,Norichika	90	84
Lee,Carlos	90	82
Pacheco,Jordan	87	82
Pierzynski,A.J.	87	81
Ellsbury,Jacoby	87	81
Aybar,Erick	88	80
Mauer,Joe	86	79
Turner,Justin	86	79
Hairston,Jerry	87	77
Loney,James	87	76
Brantley,Michael	88	75
Ramirez,Alexei	87	74
Amarista,Alexi	86	73
Infante,Omar	88	73
Young,Michael	87	72
Cairo,Miguel	86	69
Kotsay,Mark	89	69

TOP PX, ct% under 75%

NAME	Ct%	PX
Stanton,Giancarlo	66	220
Napoli,Mike	69	182
Dunn,Adam	61	177
Reynolds,Mark	63	176
Flowers,Tyler	59	172
Bruce,Jay	73	170
Granderson,Curtis	70	168
Carter,Chris	65	161
Davis,Chris	67	161
Willingham,Josh	73	161
Kemp,Matt	74	158
Moss,Brandon	68	158
Saltalamacchia,Jarrod	69	158
Davis,Ike	73	157
Kubel,Jason	73	154
Maxwell,Justin	61	154
Upton,B.J.	71	153
Gomes,Jonny	66	153
Soriano,Alfonso	74	152
Goldschmidt,Paul	73	152
Arencibia,J.P.	71	151
Shoppach,Kelly	60	151
Thome,Jim	65	151

Top PX, FB% over 40%

NAME	FB%	PX
Stanton,Giancarlo	41	220
Napoli,Mike	43	182
Dunn,Adam	46	177
Reynolds,Mark	46	176
Bruce,Jay	46	170
Granderson,Curtis	46	168
Carter,Chris	48	161
Willingham,Josh	45	161
Moss,Brandon	42	158
Saltalamacchia,Jarrod	45	158
Davis,Ike	41	157
Bautista,Jose	48	155
Longoria,Evan	42	155
Kubel,Jason	43	154
Maxwell,Justin	43	154
Upton,B.J.	41	153
Gomes,Jonny	50	153
Soriano,Alfonso	48	152
Cruz,Nelson	42	152
Arencibia,J.P.	49	151
Encarnacion,Edwin	48	151
Shoppach,Kelly	46	151
Colvin,Tyler	41	149
Jones,Andruw	46	149
Scott,Luke	42	149
Hairston,Scott	50	143
Quentin,Carlos	49	143
Jones,Garrett	42	142
Ross,David	43	140
Wells,Casper	44	139
Young,Chris	48	137
Teixeira,Mark	42	135
Beltre,Adrian	41	135
Ransom,Cody	44	135
Saunders,Michael	41	134
Upton,Justin	41	134
Joyce,Matt	44	133
LaRoche,Adam	43	133
Ross,Cody	43	130
Ludwick,Ryan	43	130

Top PX, FB% under 35%

NAME	FB%	PX
Votto,Joey	34	172
Thome,Jim	30	151
Howard,Ryan	32	148
Francisco,Juan	32	141
Cano,Robinson	29	137
Gonzalez,Carlos	32	137
Alvarez,Pedro	34	137
Morse,Michael	30	134
Cuddyer,Michael	31	131
Harper,Bryce	33	131
Fowler,Dexter	34	130
Morales,Kendrys	33	130
Jackson,Brett	34	129
Rutledge,Josh	32	127
Jones,Adam	33	125
Middlebrooks,Will	34	125
Choo,Shin-Soo	32	123
Butler,Billy	32	122
Headley,Chase	33	121
Viciedo,Dayan	33	119
Ethier,Andre	34	118
Posey,Buster	30	117
Montero,Jesus	33	114

BATTER SKILLS RANKING - SPEED

TOP Spd, 400+ AB

NAME	POS	Spd
Jackson,Austin	8	172
Bourjos,Peter	8	171
Segura,Jean	6	170
Marte,Starling	7	163
Fowler,Dexter	8	160
Ciriaco,Pedro	5	156
Gardner,Brett	7	156
Bonifacio,Emilio	8	154
Jennings,Desmond	7 8	153
Simmons,Andrelton	6	147
Trout,Mike	7 8	147
Revere,Ben	8 9	146
Escobar,Alcides	6	144
Stubbs,Drew	8	143
Weeks,Jemile	4	142
Bourn,Michael	8	141
Castro,Starlin	6	140
Reyes,Jose	6	139
Maybin,Cameron	8	138
Gomez,Carlos	8	136
Venable,Will	8 9	135
Cain,Lorenzo	8	131
Pagan,Angel	8	131
Ackley,Dustin	4	130
Eaton,Adam	8	130
Machado,Manny	5	129
McCutchen,Andrew	8	128
Suzuki,Ichiro	7 9	128
Aoki,Norichika	9	127
Infante,Omar	4	127
Victorino,Shane	7 8	127
Hechavarria,Adeiny	5	126
Andrus,Elvis	6	125
Rutledge,Josh	6	125
Crawford,Carl	7	124
Cabrera,Everth	6	123
Altuve,Jose	4	122
Cabrera,Melky	7	122
Barney,Darwin	4	118
Upton,Justin	9	118

TOP Spd, 300 or fewer AB

NAME	POS	Spd
Mastroianni,Darin	7 9	158
Arias,Joaquin	5 6	145
Gordon,Dee	6	143
Campana,Tony	8	139
Gentry,Craig	8	135
Escobar,Eduardo	5	132
Robinson,Shane	8	132
Morgan,Nyjer	8 9	131
Hernandez,Gorkys	8	130
Presley,Alex	7	128
LeMahieu,DJ	4	126
Pastornicky,Tyler	6	125
Garcia,Avisail	9	124
Berry,Quintin	7 8	123
Rhymes,Will	4	119
Greene,Tyler	4 6	118
Harrison,Josh	4 6	118
Kawasaki,Munenori	6	118
Profar,Jurickson	4	118
Hudson,Orlando	4 5	117
Podsednik,Scott	7 8	115
Johnson,Elliot	6	114
Johnson,Reed	7 8 9	114

POSITIONAL SCARCITY

NAME	POS	Spd
Jeter,Derek	DH	109
Cespedes,Yoenis	2	105
Young,Michael	3	99
Smith,Seth	4	91
Gomes,Jonny	5	90
Mauer,Joe	6	87
Hundley,Nick	CA	112
Marson,Lou	2	108
Lucroy,Jonathan	3	105
Grandal,Yasmani	4	101
Norris,Derek	5	97
Cruz,Tony	6	96
D Arnaud,Travis	7	95
Ellis,A.J.	8	90
Olt,Mike	1B	116
Colvin,Tyler	2	111
Frazier,Todd	3	108
Lillibridge,Brent	4	108
Belt,Brandon	5	103
Hart,Corey	6	99
Young,Michael	7	99
Carpenter,Matt	8	98
Cuddyer,Michael	9	96
Gomez,Mauro	10	95
Weeks,Jemile	2B	142
Ackley,Dustin	2	130
Infante,Omar	3	127
Carroll,Jamey	4	126
LeMahieu,DJ	5	126
Forsythe,Logan	6	125
Lombardozzi,Steve	7	124
Amarista,Alexi	8	123
Ciriaco,Pedro	3B	156
Arias,Joaquin	2	145
Escobar,Eduardo	3	132
Machado,Manny	4	129
Carroll,Jamey	5	126
Hechavarria,Adeiny	6	126
Descalso,Daniel	7	122
Hudson,Orlando	8	117
Lawrie,Brett	9	116
Prado,Martin	10	112
Segura,Jean	SS	170
Simmons,Andrelton	2	147
Arias,Joaquin	3	145
Escobar,Alcides	4	144
Gordon,Dee	5	143
Castro,Starlin	6	140
Reyes,Jose	7	139
Nunez,Eduardo	8	136
Jackson,Austin	OF	172
Bourjos,Peter	2	171
Dyson,Jarrod	3	170
Marte,Starling	4	163
Fowler,Dexter	5	160
Mastroianni,Darin	6	158
Gardner,Brett	7	156
Bonifacio,Emilio	8	154
Jennings,Desmond	9	153
Gose,Anthony	10	148
Trout,Mike	11	147
Revere,Ben	12	146
Pierre,Juan	13	145
Young Jr.,Eric	14	145
Stubbs,Drew	15	143
Bourn,Michael	16	141

TOP Spd, OBP over .350

NAME	OBP	Spd
Jackson,Austin	352	172
Fowler,Dexter	367	160
Trout,Mike	359	147
Reyes,Jose	355	139
McCutchen,Andrew	376	128
Upton,Justin	356	118
Prado,Martin	352	112
Tulowitzki,Troy	367	106
Werth,Jayson	366	106
Kemp,Matt	364	102
Murphy,David	359	101
Pedroia,Dustin	366	101
Braun,Ryan	380	99
Zobrist,Ben	366	96
Utley,Chase	354	93
Markakis,Nick	362	92
Bautista,Jose	378	91
Headley,Chase	363	87
Mauer,Joe	392	87
Gonzalez,Carlos	360	86
Youkilis,Kevin	373	85
Ethier,Andre	362	83
Jaso,John	371	82
Longoria,Evan	365	81
Holliday,Matt	377	80
Zimmerman,Ryan	357	80
Wright,David	371	77
Beltran,Carlos	356	76
Berkman,Lance	400	76
Choo,Shin-Soo	361	76
Posey,Buster	376	76
Cano,Robinson	362	75
Goldschmidt,Paul	358	75
Gordon,Alex	354	75
Abreu,Bobby	354	74
Montero,Miguel	351	74
Napoli,Mike	353	74
Santana,Carlos	378	72
Avila,Alex	354	72
Swisher,Nick	363	69

TOP Spd, OBP under .310

NAME	OBP	Spd
Bourjos,Peter	293	171
Marte,Starling	283	163
Ciriaco,Pedro	285	156
Gose,Anthony	302	148
Arias,Joaquin	275	145
Escobar,Alcides	308	144
Gordon,Dee	279	143
Stubbs,Drew	295	143
Weeks,Jemile	303	142
Campana,Tony	291	139
Gomez,Carlos	286	136
Nunez,Eduardo	301	136
Gentry,Craig	293	135
Escobar,Eduardo	270	132
Robinson,Shane	290	132
Morgan,Nyjer	308	131
Hernandez,Gorkys	280	130
Machado,Manny	302	129
Presley,Alex	309	128
Wells,Casper	308	127
Hechavarria,Adeiny	279	126
Rutledge,Josh	303	125
Dozier,Brian	280	124

Top Spd, SBO% over 20%

NAME	SBO%	Spd
Dyson,Jarrod	45%	170
Segura,Jean	31%	170
Marte,Starling	38%	163
Mastroianni,Darin	44%	158
Ciriaco,Pedro	34%	156
Gardner,Brett	37%	156
Bonifacio,Emilio	34%	154
Jennings,Desmond	24%	153
Gose,Anthony	44%	148
Trout,Mike	28%	147
Revere,Ben	31%	146
Pierre,Juan	34%	145
Young Jr.,Eric	31%	145
Escobar,Alcides	24%	144
Gordon,Dee	44%	143
Stubbs,Drew	30%	143
Bourn,Michael	33%	141
Campana,Tony	62%	139
Reyes,Jose	28%	139
Maybin,Cameron	26%	138
Gomez,Carlos	42%	136
Nunez,Eduardo	37%	136
Gentry,Craig	31%	135
Venable,Will	28%	135
Morgan,Nyjer	25%	131
Pagan,Angel	25%	131
Eaton,Adam	23%	130
Hernandez,Gorkys	26%	130
Presley,Alex	21%	128
Victorino,Shane	25%	127
Andrus,Elvis	21%	125
Bloomquist,Willie	25%	124
Crawford,Carl	29%	124
Berry,Quintin	33%	123
Cabrera,Everth	38%	123
Altuve,Jose	32%	122
Davis,Rajai	50%	122
Paredes,Jimmy	31%	122
Blanco,Gregor	25%	120
Greene,Tyler	24%	118

Top Spd, SBO% under 15%

NAME	SBO%	Spd
Simmons,Andrelton	8%	147
Arias,Joaquin	10%	145
Escobar,Eduardo	12%	132
Robinson,Shane	13%	132
Ackley,Dustin	9%	130
Machado,Manny	11%	129
Infante,Omar	12%	127
Wells,Casper	10%	127
Carroll,Jamey	7%	126
Hechavarria,Adeiny	13%	126
Forsythe,Logan	13%	125
Lombardozzi,Steve	14%	124
Cabrera,Melky	7%	122
Descalso,Daniel	7%	122
Barney,Darwin	6%	118
Profar,Jurickson	12%	118
Drew,Stephen	5%	117
Hudson,Orlando	12%	117
Cozart,Zack	9%	116
Dirks,Andy	11%	116
Heisey,Chris	11%	116
Olt,Mike	5%	116
Reddick,Josh	8%	115

BATTER SKILLS RANKING - BATTING AVERAGE

TOP ct%, 400+ AB

NAME	Ct%	BA
Scutaro,Marco	91	289
Reyes,Jose	91	300
Aoki,Norichika	90	284
Lee,Carlos	90	268
Molina,Yadier	90	303
Perez,Salvador	90	294
Revere,Ben	90	280
Suzuki,Ichiro	90	282
Callaspo,Alberto	89	268
Kotchman,Casey	89	251
Martinez,Victor	89	296
Pedroia,Dustin	89	299
Aybar,Erick	88	286
Barney,Darwin	88	258
Brantley,Michael	88	278
Markakis,Nick	88	297
Altuve,Jose	88	289
Hanigan,Ryan	88	258
Infante,Omar	88	283
Prado,Martin	88	299
Pujols,Albert	88	291
Kinsler,Ian	87	261
Pierzynski,A.J.	87	279
Ramirez,Alexei	87	272
Beltre,Adrian	87	309
Ellsbury,Jacoby	87	280
Escobar,Yunel	87	266
Furcal,Rafael	87	261
Loney,James	87	283
Pacheco,Jordan	87	280
Rollins,Jimmy	87	253
Ruiz,Carlos	87	293
Span,Denard	87	276
Victorino,Shane	87	266
Young,Michael	87	296
Cano,Robinson	86	310
Castro,Starlin	86	292
Jeter,Derek	86	277
Phillips,Brandon	86	283
Cabrera,Melky	86	285

TOP ct%, 300 or fewer AB

NAME	Ct%	BA
Izturis,Cesar	91	254
Frandsen,Kevin	89	255
Getz,Chris	89	263
Kotsay,Mark	89	257
Taveras,Oscar	89	286
Theriot,Ryan	88	273
Betancourt,Yuniesky	88	243
Pena,Brayan	88	253
Chavez,Endy	87	229
Hairston,Jerry	87	261
Harrison,Josh	87	251
Izturis,Maicer	87	266
Rhymes,Will	87	236
Rivera,Juan	87	249
Damon,Johnny	86	254
Cairo,Miguel	86	227
Cruz,Luis	86	245
Gonzalez,Marwin	86	242
Kawasaki,Munenori	86	245
Turner,Justin	86	261
Arias,Joaquin	85	248
Burriss,Emmanuel	85	219
Casilla,Alexi	85	251

LOW ct%, 400+ AB

NAME	Ct%	POS
Dunn,Adam	61	211
Maxwell,Justin	61	234
Reynolds,Mark	63	231
Carter,Chris	65	233
Stanton,Giancarlo	66	274
Alvarez,Pedro	67	241
Davis,Chris	67	257
Howard,Ryan	67	243
Stubbs,Drew	67	230
Ruggiano,Justin	69	253
Saltalamacchia,Jarrod	69	231
Wallace,Brett	69	256
Espinosa,Danny	70	226
Granderson,Curtis	70	243
Upton,B.J.	71	245
Arencibia,J.P.	71	231
Johnson,Kelly	71	233
Martinez,Fernando	71	235
Saunders,Michael	71	234
Uggla,Dan	71	235
Belt,Brandon	72	263
Colvin,Tyler	72	252
Bruce,Jay	73	266
Kubel,Jason	73	260
Davis,Ike	73	268
Fowler,Dexter	73	278
Goldschmidt,Paul	73	276
Jackson,Austin	73	284
Johnson,Chris	73	260
Middlebrooks,Will	73	271
Rasmus,Colby	73	242
Snider,Travis	73	260
Weeks,Rickie	73	261
Willingham,Josh	73	256
Soriano,Alfonso	74	256
Swisher,Nick	74	268
Trumbo,Mark	74	256
Cabrera,Everth	74	232
Frazier,Todd	74	260
Kemp,Matt	74	297
Marte,Starling	74	251
Hart,Corey	75	277
Ross,Cody	75	260
Young,Chris	75	238
Cain,Lorenzo	75	265
Choo,Shin-Soo	75	281
Donaldson,Josh	75	244
Gomez,Carlos	75	247
Headley,Chase	75	282
Joyce,Matt	75	245
LaRoche,Adam	75	268
Scott,Luke	75	243
Venable,Will	75	252
Bourn,Michael	76	272
Maybin,Cameron	76	267
Montero,Miguel	76	271
Smoak,Justin	76	245
Bourjos,Peter	76	239
Freese,David	76	281
Hamilton,Josh	76	282
Heyward,Jason	76	266
Ludwick,Ryan	76	264
Morse,Michael	76	290
Rodriguez,Alex	76	265
Rosario,Wilin	76	256
Trout,Mike	76	286

TOP ct%, bb% over 10%

NAME	bb%	Ct%
Hanigan,Ryan	12	88
Mauer,Joe	13	86
Utley,Chase	12	85
Cabrera,Miguel	12	84
Huff,Aubrey	12	84
Jaso,John	14	84
Konerko,Paul	11	83
Encarnacion,Edwin	11	83
Profar,Jurickson	11	83
Fielder,Prince	14	82
Helton,Todd	14	82
Teixeira,Mark	12	81
Gardner,Brett	11	81
Zobrist,Ben	14	80
Beltran,Carlos	11	80
Berkman,Lance	16	80
Martin,Russell	11	80
Ortiz,David	15	80
Holliday,Matt	11	79
Santana,Carlos	16	79
Bautista,Jose	16	79
Carpenter,Matt	11	79
McCutchen,Andrew	11	79
McLouth,Nate	11	79
Morrison,Logan	11	79
Punto,Nick	13	79
Ellis,A.J.	12	78
Longoria,Evan	12	78
Votto,Joey	18	78
Youkilis,Kevin	13	78
Abreu,Bobby	14	77
Barton,Daric	15	77
Gordon,Alex	11	77
Nava,Daniel	11	77
Wright,David	12	77
Montero,Miguel	11	76
Smoak,Justin	11	76
Grandal,Yasmani	11	76
Heyward,Jason	11	76
Marson,Lou	13	76

TOP ct%, bb% under 6%

NAME	bb%	Ct%
Izturis,Cesar	3	91
Perez,Salvador	3	90
Revere,Ben	5	90
Suzuki,Ichiro	5	90
Frandsen,Kevin	4	89
Aybar,Erick	5	88
Barney,Darwin	5	88
Altuve,Jose	5	88
Betancourt,Yuniesky	3	88
Infante,Omar	5	88
Pena,Brayan	5	88
Pierzynski,A.J.	5	87
Ramirez,Alexei	5	87
Chavez,Endy	5	87
Harrison,Josh	4	87
Pacheco,Jordan	4	87
Amarista,Alexi	4	86
Cairo,Miguel	5	86
Cruz,Luis	3	86
Gonzalez,Marwin	5	86
Lombardozzi,Steve	5	86
Escobar,Alcides	5	85
Arias,Joaquin	4	85

Top ct%, GB% over 50%

NAME	GB%	Ct%
Pierre,Juan	56	93
Polanco,Placido	52	93
Aoki,Norichika	56	90
Revere,Ben	68	90
Suzuki,Ichiro	55	90
Frandsen,Kevin	55	89
Kotchman,Casey	55	89
Theriot,Ryan	52	88
Altuve,Jose	52	88
Hanigan,Ryan	51	88
Chavez,Endy	54	87
Escobar,Yunel	55	87
Furcal,Rafael	52	87
Span,Denard	53	87
Jeter,Derek	62	86
Gonzalez,Marwin	54	86
Kawasaki,Munenori	64	86
Mauer,Joe	52	86
Simmons,Andrelton	58	86
Andrus,Elvis	58	85
Carroll,Jamey	53	85
Escobar,Alcides	52	85
Burriss,Emmanuel	60	85
Casilla,Alexi	54	85
Andrus,Elvis	58	85
Carroll,Jamey	53	85
Denorfia,Chris	60	84
Hernandez,Ramon	52	84
Herrera,Jonathan	52	84
Jay,Jon	56	84
Pastornicky,Tyler	63	84
Denorfia,Chris	60	84
Hernandez,Ramon	52	84
Herrera,Jonathan	52	84
Clevenger,Steve	53	83
Dominguez,Matt	54	83
Eaton,Adam	59	83
Hosmer,Eric	52	83
Iglesias,Jose	59	83
Clevenger,Steve	53	83

Top ct%, GB% under 40%

NAME	GB%	Ct%
Lee,Carlos	39	90
Kinsler,Ian	37	87
Beltre,Adrian	39	87
Hairston,Jerry	36	87
Cruz,Luis	38	86
Hill,Aaron	36	86
McDonald,John	39	85
Ramirez,Aramis	36	85
Stewart,Chris	34	85
Utley,Chase	39	85
Cooper,David	30	84
Pagan,Angel	39	84
Encarnacion,Edwin	34	83
Janish,Paul	36	83
Quentin,Carlos	35	83
Roberts,Brian	37	83
McCann,Brian	39	82
Dirks,Andy	37	82
Rolen,Scott	39	82
Seager,Kyle	34	82
Lowrie,Jed	32	81
Morneau,Justin	39	81
Moustakas,Mike	36	81

PITCHER SKILLS RANKINGS - Starting Pitchers

Top Command (k/bb)

NAME	Cmd
Lee,Cliff	6.8
Milone,Tommy	5.3
Halladay,Roy	4.7
Strasburg,Stephen	4.3
Hamels,Cole	4.1
Sabathia,CC	4.0
Haren,Dan	4.0
Medlen,Kris	3.9
Blanton,Joe	3.8
Shields,James	3.8
Greinke,Zack	3.8
Verlander,Justin	3.7
Ramirez,Erasmo	3.6
Bumgarner,Madison	3.6
Peavy,Jake	3.6
Scherzer,Max	3.6
Oswalt,Roy	3.6
Baker,Scott	3.5
Fister,Doug	3.5
Wainwright,Adam	3.5
Hernandez,Felix	3.5
Estrada,Marco	3.5
Corbin,Patrick	3.4
Carpenter,Chris	3.4
Zimmermann,Jordan	3.4
Kershaw,Clayton	3.4
Collmenter,Josh	3.4
Lewis,Colby	3.3
McCarthy,Brandon	3.3
Nolasco,Ricky	3.3
Kuroda,Hiroki	3.3

Top Control (bb/9)

NAME	Ctl
Milone,Tommy	1.3
Lee,Cliff	1.3
Beavan,Blake	1.4
Pavano,Carl	1.6
Halladay,Roy	1.7
McCarthy,Brandon	1.8
Ramirez,Erasmo	1.8
Haren,Dan	1.8
Karstens,Jeff	1.8
Germano,Justin	1.9
Cloyd,Tyler	1.9
McPherson,Kyle	1.9
Fister,Doug	1.9
Hunter,Tommy	1.9
Carpenter,Chris	2.0
Nolasco,Ricky	2.0
Lohse,Kyle	2.0
Blanton,Joe	2.0
Medlen,Kris	2.0
Arroyo,Bronson	2.0
Buehrle,Mark	2.0
Corbin,Patrick	2.1
Francis,Jeff	2.1
Anderson,Brett	2.1
Hendriks,Liam	2.1
Kuroda,Hiroki	2.1
Zimmermann,Jordan	2.1
Hamels,Cole	2.1
Oswalt,Roy	2.1
Collmenter,Josh	2.1
Baker,Scott	2.2

Top Dominance (k/9)

NAME	Dom
Strasburg,Stephen	10.8
Darvish,Yu	10.0
Scherzer,Max	10.0
Moore,Matt	9.7
Lincecum,Tim	9.3
Kershaw,Clayton	9.3
Bauer,Trevor	9.2
Morrow,Brandon	9.1
Gallardo,Yovani	9.1
Beachy,Brandon	9.1
Hultzen,Danny	9.0
Smyly,Drew	9.0
Verlander,Justin	9.0
Torres,Alexander	8.9
Liriano,Francisco	8.9
Hanson,Tommy	8.8
Gonzalez,Gio	8.8
Greinke,Zack	8.8
Bedard,Erik	8.7
Miller,Shelby	8.7
Norris,Bud	8.7
Hamels,Cole	8.7
de la Rosa,Jorge	8.6
Straily,Dan	8.6
Harvey,Matt	8.6
Volquez,Edinson	8.6
Sabathia,CC	8.6
Shields,James	8.6
Lee,Cliff	8.6
Paulino,Felipe	8.6
Price,David	8.5

Top Ground Ball Rate

NAME	GB
Deduno,Samuel	58
Lowe,Derek	58
Britton,Zach	58
Hudson,Tim	58
Westbrook,Jake	58
Cahill,Trevor	58
Harrell,Lucas	58
Cook,Aaron	57
Cobb,Alex	57
Hernandez,Roberto	56
Kelly,Casey	56
Anderson,Brett	56
Masterson,Justin	56
Archer,Chris	55
Alvarez,Henderson	55
Lannan,John	54
Peralta,Wily	54
Garcia,Jaime	54
Romero,Ricky	54
Wang,Chien-Ming	53
Chatwood,Tyler	53
Marquis,Jason	53
Werner,Andrew	53
Iwakuma,Hisashi	53
Carrasco,Carlos	52
Keuchel,Dallas	52
Porcello,Rick	52
Burnett,A.J.	52
Williams,Jerome	52
Adcock,Nathan	51
White,Alex	51

Top Fly Ball Rate

NAME	FB
Young,Chris	55
Johnson,Steve	52
Bundy,Dylan	51
Straily,Dan	51
Miller,Shelby	50
Cloyd,Tyler	49
Skaggs,Tyler	48
Lewis,Colby	46
Matsuzaka,Daisuke	46
Lilly,Ted	46
Chen,Bruce	46
Hughes,Phil	46
Weaver,Jered	46
Moscoso,Guillermo	46
Collmenter,Josh	46
Matusz,Brian	45
Teheran,Julio	45
Baker,Scott	45
Pineda,Michael	45
Estrada,Marco	45
DeVries,Cole	44
Hultzen,Danny	44
Wood,Travis	44
LeBlanc,Wade	44
Duffy,Danny	43
Santana,Johan	43
Moore,Matt	43
Beachy,Brandon	43
Cecil,Brett	42
Sanchez,Jonathan	42
Harang,Aaron	42

High GB, Low Dom

NAME	GB	Dom
Lowe,Derek	58	5.1
Hudson,Tim	58	5.6
Westbrook,Jake	58	5.3
Cook,Aaron	57	3.3
Hernandez,Roberto	56	5.3
Alvarez,Henderson	55	4.8
Lannan,John	54	4.5
Wang,Chien-Ming	53	4.4
Chatwood,Tyler	53	5.3
Marquis,Jason	53	5.7
Keuchel,Dallas	52	4.3
Porcello,Rick	52	5.2
Williams,Jerome	52	5.7
Adcock,Nathan	51	5.0
White,Alex	51	5.9
Diamond,Scott	51	5.1
Mendoza,Luis	51	4.9
Richard,Clayton	51	4.9
Perez,Martin	50	5.8
Volstad,Chris	50	5.4
Pelfrey,Mike	50	5.3
Gomez,Jeanmar	49	5.6
Turner,Jacob	49	5.7
Francis,Jeff	48	5.6
Correia,Kevin	48	5.2
Feldman,Scott	48	5.9
Blackburn,Nick	47	3.8
Detwiler,Ross	47	5.7
Quintana,Jose	47	5.6
Harrison,Matt	47	5.6
Germano,Justin	46	5.5

High GB, High Dom

NAME	GB	Dom
Cahill,Trevor	58	7.0
Cobb,Alex	57	7.4
Kelly,Casey	56	7.0
Archer,Chris	55	8.1
Peralta,Wily	54	7.5
Garcia,Jaime	54	7.3
Werner,Andrew	53	7.0
Burnett,A.J.	52	8.0
Volquez,Edinson	51	8.6
Hernandez,Felix	51	8.5
Wilson,C.J.	50	8.0
Wainwright,Adam	50	8.1
Lester,Jon	50	7.7
Torres,Alexander	49	8.9
Rosenthal,Trevor	49	8.4
Gee,Dillon	49	7.6
Hammel,Jason	49	7.7
Niese,Jon	49	7.4
Shields,James	48	8.6
Lynn,Lance	49	8.1
Cole,Gerrit	48	7.7
De La Rosa,Rubby	48	8.1
Halladay,Roy	48	7.9
Sabathia,CC	48	8.6
Medlen,Kris	48	7.6
Gonzalez,Gio	48	8.8
Price,David	48	8.5
Dickey,R.A.	48	7.1
Billingsley,Chad	47	7.5
Delgado,Randall	47	7.8
Johnson,Josh	47	8.1

Lowest xERA

NAME	xERA
Strasburg,Stephen	2.86
Lee,Cliff	3.16
Kershaw,Clayton	3.27
Hernandez,Felix	3.27
Sabathia,CC	3.28
Shields,James	3.28
Hamels,Cole	3.30
Halladay,Roy	3.32
Greinke,Zack	3.32
Verlander,Justin	3.36
Wainwright,Adam	3.37
Scherzer,Max	3.37
Darvish,Yu	3.38
Price,David	3.39
Medlen,Kris	3.42
Anderson,Brett	3.51
Bumgarner,Madison	3.55
Gallardo,Yovani	3.55
Cobb,Alex	3.57
Beachy,Brandon	3.57
Johnson,Josh	3.59
Garcia,Jaime	3.61
Lincecum,Tim	3.64
Latos,Mat	3.65
Rosenthal,Trevor	3.66
Moore,Matt	3.66
Garza,Matt	3.66
Kuroda,Hiroki	3.66
Blanton,Joe	3.68
Smyly,Drew	3.69
Niese,Jon	3.69

Top BPV, 180+ IP

NAME	BPV
Strasburg,Stephen	150
Lee,Cliff	143
Sabathia,CC	122
Scherzer,Max	122
Hamels,Cole	122
Shields,James	121
Greinke,Zack	121
Hernandez,Felix	117
Verlander,Justin	116
Kershaw,Clayton	115
Wainwright,Adam	111
Medlen,Kris	109
Blanton,Joe	107
Bumgarner,Madison	107
Price,David	107
Milone,Tommy	106
Darvish,Yu	102
Haren,Dan	100
Peavy,Jake	100
Gallardo,Yovani	99
Garza,Matt	97
Moore,Matt	96
Kuroda,Hiroki	96
Latos,Mat	96
Fister,Doug	95
Morrow,Brandon	93
Sanchez,Anibal	93
Niese,Jon	92
Zimmermann,Jordan	92
Dickey,R.A.	92
Lincecum,Tim	90

Top BPV, <150 IP

NAME	BPV
Beachy,Brandon	104
Oswalt,Roy	103
Anderson,Brett	99
Smyly,Drew	98
Rosenthal,Trevor	96
Corbin,Patrick	96
Ogando,Alexi	94
Carpenter,Chris	93
Miller,Shelby	92
Skaggs,Tyler	92
Baker,Scott	91
Lewis,Colby	91
Werner,Andrew	91
Nicasio,Juan	88
Straily,Dan	88
Hudson,Daniel	87
Lynn,Lance	87
Thornburg,Tyler	86
Ramirez,Erasmo	85
Luebke,Cory	84
Kelly,Casey	84
Collmenter,Josh	84
Hutchison,Drew	83
Santana,Johan	82
McPherson,Kyle	81
Wieland,Joe	78
McCarthy,Brandon	78
Billingsley,Chad	77
Carrasco,Carlos	77
Phelps,David	76
Bedard,Erik	75

PITCHER SKILLS RANKINGS - Relief Pitchers

Top Command (k/bb)

NAME	Cmd
Uehara,Koji	8.0
Romo,Sergio	6.7
Kimbrel,Craig	5.2
Lopez,Wilton	5.1
Papelbon,Jonathan	5.0
Mujica,Edward	4.9
Valdes,Raul	4.8
Doolittle,Sean	4.7
Putz,J.J.	4.6
Street,Huston	4.4
Betancourt,Rafael	4.3
Nathan,Joe	4.3
Motte,Jason	4.3
Janssen,Casey	4.2
Mcgee,Jake	4.1
Marshall,Sean	4.1
Peralta,Joel	4.1
O Day,Darren	4.0
Reed,Addison	3.9
Belisle,Matt	3.8
Dotel,Octavio	3.7
Tazawa,Junichi	3.7
Herrera,Kelvin	3.7
Oliver,Darren	3.6
Perkins,Glen	3.6
Lincoln,Brad	3.5
Jansen,Kenley	3.5
Benoit,Joaquin	3.5
Thatcher,Joe	3.4
Rivera,Mariano	3.4
Capps,Carter	3.4

Top Control (bb/9)

NAME	Ctl
Uehara,Koji	1.2
Lopez,Wilton	1.4
Mujica,Edward	1.5
Romo,Sergio	1.6
Capps,Matt	1.8
Valdes,Raul	1.9
Betancourt,Rafael	2.0
Belisle,Matt	2.0
Janssen,Casey	2.1
O Day,Darren	2.1
Rauch,Jon	2.1
Street,Huston	2.2
Martinez,Cristhian	2.2
Herrera,Kelvin	2.2
Atchison,Scott	2.3
Rivera,Mariano	2.3
Johnson,Jim	2.3
Lincoln,Brad	2.3
Oliver,Darren	2.3
Patton,Troy	2.3
Peralta,Joel	2.3
Putz,J.J.	2.3
Thayer,Dale	2.3
Papelbon,Jonathan	2.3
Motte,Jason	2.3
Hernandez,Livan	2.3
Qualls,Chad	2.4
Badenhop,Burke	2.4
Doolittle,Sean	2.4
Tazawa,Junichi	2.4
Nathan,Joe	2.4

Top Dominance (k/9)

NAME	Dom
Kimbrel,Craig	15.0
Chapman,Aroldis	13.3
Jansen,Kenley	13.1
Bastardo,Antonio	12.4
Robertson,David	12.3
Marmol,Carlos	11.9
Frieri,Ernesto	11.5
Grilli,Jason	11.5
Brothers,Rex	11.5
Papelbon,Jonathan	11.5
Axford,John	11.3
Doolittle,Sean	11.2
Alburquerque,Al	11.0
Santos,Sergio	11.0
Hernandez,David	10.9
Romo,Sergio	10.9
Delabar,Steve	10.7
Holland,Greg	10.6
Fujikawa,Kyuji	10.6
Putz,J.J.	10.5
Collins,Tim	10.5
Gonzalez,Michael	10.4
Capps,Carter	10.4
Coleman,Louis	10.3
Nathan,Joe	10.3
Clippard,Tyler	10.3
Rodriguez,Henry	10.2
Mcgee,Jake	10.2
Brach,Brad	10.2
Veras,Jose	10.2
Diekman,Jake	10.1

Top Ground Ball Rate

NAME	GB
Ziegler,Brad	70
Venters,Jonny	68
Mejia,Jenrry	65
Strop,Pedro	63
Wright,Jamey	63
Alburquerque,Al	62
Choate,Randy	62
Belisario,Ronald	62
Lopez,Javier	61
O Flaherty,Eric	61
Ross,Robbie	61
Downs,Scott	60
Eppley,Cody	60
Affeldt,Jeremy	60
Johnson,Jim	60
Hughes,Jared	60
Loe,Kameron	59
Smith,Joe	58
Aumont,Phillippe	58
Shaw,Bryan	57
Rodney,Fernando	57
Rzepczynski,Marc	57
Parnell,Bobby	57
Webb,Ryan	57
Qualls,Chad	56
Melancon,Mark	56
League,Brandon	56
Hawkins,LaTroy	55
Badenhop,Burke	55
Lopez,Wilton	55
Burnett,Sean	55

Top Fly Ball Rate

NAME	FB
Coleman,Louis	57
Clippard,Tyler	57
Doolittle,Sean	55
Frieri,Ernesto	55
Uehara,Koji	54
Bastardo,Antonio	53
Peralta,Joel	53
Bowden,Michael	52
Kelley,Shawn	51
Fien,Casey	51
Feliz,Neftali	49
Valdes,Raul	49
Sipp,Tony	49
Villarreal,Brayan	49
Jansen,Kenley	49
Pryor,Stephen	48
Betancourt,Rafael	48
Cruz,Juan	47
Hernandez,David	47
Rauch,Jon	47
Morales,Franklin	47
Fuentes,Brian	46
Dotel,Octavio	46
Benoit,Joaquin	46
Bailey,Andrew	45
Crain,Jesse	45
Rodriguez,Fernando	45
Brach,Brad	45
Miller,Jim	44
Salas,Fernando	44
Mijares,Jose	44

High GB, Low Dom

NAME	GB	Dom
Ziegler,Brad	70	5.9
Mejia,Jenrry	65	5.8
Johnson,Jim	60	5.5
Hughes,Jared	60	5.8
Qualls,Chad	56	5.4
Hawkins,LaTroy	55	4.8
Camp,Shawn	51	5.6
Laffey,Aaron	50	4.5
Burnett,Alex	50	5.6
Mattheus,Ryan	49	5.6
Roenicke,Josh	49	5.9
Duensing,Brian	47	5.7
Ayala,Luis	47	5.9
Carpenter,David	46	5.8
Corpas,Manuel	46	5.6
Accardo,Jeremy	42	5.4
Capps,Matt	42	5.7
Swarzak,Anthony	41	5.4
Hernandez,Livan	41	5.6

High GB, High Dom

NAME	GB	Dom
Venters,Jonny	68	9.5
Strop,Pedro	63	8.2
Alburquerque,Al	62	11.0
Choate,Randy	62	8.1
Belisario,Ronald	62	7.4
O Flaherty,Eric	61	7.4
Ross,Robbie	61	7.1
Affeldt,Jeremy	60	8.1
Aumont,Phillippe	58	9.8
Rodney,Fernando	57	8.4
Rzepczynski,Marc	57	7.5
Parnell,Bobby	57	8.2
Melancon,Mark	56	8.1
Lopez,Wilton	55	7.2
Burnett,Sean	55	7.9
Herrera,Kelvin	55	8.1
Marshall,Sean	54	10.1
Cishek,Steve	54	9.0
Albers,Matt	53	7.2
Crow,Aaron	53	8.7
Casilla,Santiago	52	7.9
Kontos,George	52	7.5
Howell,J.P.	51	8.2
Broxton,Jonathan	51	8.6
Tazawa,Junichi	51	8.8
Rivera,Mariano	50	7.9
Familia,Jeurys	50	7.5
Thornton,Matt	50	8.8
Cashner,Andrew	50	7.9
Hensley,Clay	49	7.1
Wilson,Brian	49	8.9

Lowest xERA

NAME	xERA
Kimbrel,Craig	1.95
Romo,Sergio	2.59
Chapman,Aroldis	2.59
Marshall,Sean	2.81
Papelbon,Jonathan	2.84
Putz,J.J.	2.91
Robertson,David	2.95
Jansen,Kenley	2.97
Nathan,Joe	3.05
Venters,Jonny	3.05
Mcgee,Jake	3.06
Street,Huston	3.07
Motte,Jason	3.10
Herrera,Kelvin	3.11
Lopez,Wilton	3.19
Uehara,Koji	3.20
Fujikawa,Kyuji	3.22
Sale,Chris	3.23
Janssen,Casey	3.24
Tazawa,Junichi	3.27
Thornton,Matt	3.27
O Flaherty,Eric	3.29
Melancon,Mark	3.30
Rodney,Fernando	3.30
Axford,John	3.30
Doolittle,Sean	3.33
Mujica,Edward	3.37
Rivera,Mariano	3.38
Ziegler,Brad	3.38
Bastardo,Antonio	3.39
Grilli,Jason	3.39

Top BPV, 10+ Saves

NAME	BPV
Kimbrel,Craig	216
Romo,Sergio	172
Papelbon,Jonathan	163
Chapman,Aroldis	157
Putz,J.J.	151
Jansen,Kenley	143
Nathan,Joe	142
Robertson,David	140
Motte,Jason	136
Street,Huston	133
Lopez,Wilton	125
Janssen,Casey	123
Reed,Addison	118
Perkins,Glen	113
Betancourt,Rafael	112
Madson,Ryan	109
Rivera,Mariano	109
Axford,John	108
Soria,Joakim	107
Brothers,Rex	106
Gregerson,Luke	105
Holland,Greg	101
Broxton,Jonathan	100
Frieri,Ernesto	96
Clippard,Tyler	96
Cook,Ryan	96
Parnell,Bobby	96
Cishek,Steve	95
Rodney,Fernando	94
Storen,Drew	94
Balfour,Grant	92

Top BPV, 9- Saves

NAME	BPV
Doolittle,Sean	150
Uehara,Koji	148
Marshall,Sean	148
Mcgee,Jake	138
Tazawa,Junichi	124
Dotel,Octavio	121
Capps,Carter	121
Herrera,Kelvin	121
Thatcher,Joe	119
Mujica,Edward	119
Grilli,Jason	118
Benoit,Joaquin	118
Sale,Chris	118
Bastardo,Antonio	117
Peralta,Joel	117
Valdes,Raul	116
Thornton,Matt	116
O Day,Darren	113
Chamberlain,Joba	112
Hernandez,David	111
Belisle,Matt	110
Pestano,Vinnie	108
Melancon,Mark	107
Oliver,Darren	106
Furbush,Charlie	106
Lincoln,Brad	105
Santos,Sergio	103
Brach,Brad	103
Burnett,Sean	103
Walden,Jordan	102
Gonzalez,Michael	101

RISK MANAGEMENT

GRADE "F" in HEALTH

Pitchers	Pitchers
Alburquerque,Al	Thatcher,Joe
Anderson,Brett	Uehara,Koji
Bailey,Andrew	Vizcaino,Arodys
Baker,Scott	Wainwright,Adam
Beachy,Brandon	Wang,Chien-Ming
Bedard,Erik	Wieland,Joe
Blanton,Joe	Wilson,Brian
Buchholz,Clay	Young,Chris
Carpenter,Chris	
Carrasco,Carlos	
Cashner,Andrew	**Batters**
Chamberlain,Joba	Baker,John
Cook,Aaron	Baxter,Mike
Danks,John	Bay,Jason
de la Rosa,Jorge	Berkman,Lance
Duffy,Danny	Blackmon,Charlie
Feliz,Neftali	Castro,Jason
Francis,Jeff	Chavez,Eric
Gaudin,Chad	Crawford,Carl
Hawkins,LaTroy	Crisp,Coco
Howell,J.P.	Darnell,James
Hudson,Daniel	Diaz,Matt
Johnson,Josh	Drew,Stephen
Jurrjens,Jair	Ellsbury,Jacoby
Kelley,Shawn	Furcal,Rafael
Lackey,John	Gamel,Mat
Lilly,Ted	Gardner,Brett
Lowe,Mark	Gutierrez,Franklin
Luebke,Cory	Helton,Todd
Lyon,Brandon	Hundley,Nick
Madson,Ryan	Izturis,Cesar
Marcum,Shaun	Longoria,Evan
Marquis,Jason	Lowrie,Jed
Matsuzaka,Daisuke	Martinez,Victor
McCarthy,Brandon	Morales,Kendrys
Medlen,Kris	Morneau,Justin
Nathan,Joe	Morse,Michael
Nicasio,Juan	Nady,Xavier
Niemann,Jeff	Pearce,Steve
Padilla,Vicente	Punto,Nick
Parra,Manny	Ramos,Wilson
Paulino,Felipe	Reimold,Nolan
Pavano,Carl	Rivera,Juan
Peavy,Jake	Roberts,Brian
Pelfrey,Mike	Rolen,Scott
Pettitte,Andy	Scott,Luke
Pineda,Michael	Sizemore,Grady
Rivera,Mariano	Sizemore,Scott
Sanchez,Jonathan	Snyder,Chris
Santana,Johan	Stewart,Ian
Sheets,Ben	Sweeney,Ryan
Soria,Joakim	Thome,Jim
Santos,Sergio	Tulowitzki,Troy
Stauffer,Tim	Utley,Chase
Strasburg,Stephen	
Street,Huston	
Tazawa,Junichi	

Highest Reliability Grades - Health / Experience / Consistency (Min. Grade = BBB)

CA	POS	Rel
Suzuki,Kurt	2	ABA
McCann,Brian	2	ABB
Montero,Jesus	20	ABB
Pierzynski,A.J.	2	ABB
Santana,Carlos	203	ABB
Wieters,Matt	2	ABB
Montero,Miguel	2	BBA

1B/DH	POS	Rel
Swisher,Nick	39	AAA
Teixeira,Mark	3	AAA
Butler,Billy	03	AAB
Konerko,Paul	03	AAB
Reynolds,Mark	3	AAB
Alonso,Yonder	3	ABA
Freeman,Freddie	3	ABA
Wigginton,Ty	35	ABA
Montero,Jesus	20	ABB
Santana,Carlos	203	ABB
Gomez,Mauro	3	ABB
Ibanez,Raul	07	ABB
Jones,Garrett	39	ABB
Smoak,Justin	3	ABB
Trumbo,Mark	079	ABB
Hart,Corey	39	BAA
Jeter,Derek	06	BAB
Lind,Adam	03	BBB
Young,Delmon	07	BBB

2B	POS	Rel
Espinosa,Danny	46	AAA
Cano,Robinson	4	AAB
Kendrick,Howie	4	AAB
Phillips,Brandon	4	AAB
Walker,Neil	4	AAB
Zobrist,Ben	469	AAB
Carroll,Jamey	456	ABA
Giavotella,Johnny	4	ABA
Kipnis,Jason	4	ABA
Theriot,Ryan	4	ABA
Barney,Darwin	4	ABB
Beckham,Gordon	4	ABB
Pennington,Cliff	46	ABB
Kinsler,Ian	4	BAB
Scutaro,Marco	46	BAB

SS	POS	Rel
Espinosa,Danny	46	AAA
Castro,Starlin	6	AAA
Zobrist,Ben	469	AAB
Andrus,Elvis	6	AAB
Escobar,Alcides	6	AAB
Ramirez,Alexei	6	AAB
Carroll,Jamey	456	ABA
Pennington,Cliff	46	ABB
Ryan,Brendan	6	ABB
Jeter,Derek	06	BAB
Scutaro,Marco	46	BAB
Aybar,Erick	6	BAB
Cabrera,Asdrubal	6	BAB
Cozart,Zack	6	BBA
Barmes,Clint	6	BBB

3B	POS	Rel
Cabrera,Miguel	5	AAB
Wigginton,Ty	35	ABA
Carroll,Jamey	456	ABA
Liddi,Alex	5	ABA

OF	POS	Rel
Swisher,Nick	39	AAA
Bourn,Michael	8	AAA
Holliday,Matt	7	AAA
Jones,Adam	8	AAA
Upton,B.J.	8	AAA
Zobrist,Ben	469	AAB
Bruce,Jay	9	AAB
Gonzalez,Carlos	7	AAB
Hunter,Torii	9	AAB
Pierre,Juan	7	AAB
Ibanez,Raul	07	ABB
Jones,Garrett	39	ABB
Trumbo,Mark	079	ABB
Abreu,Bobby	7	ABB
Brantley,Michael	8	ABB
Damon,Johnny	7	ABB
Jennings,Desmond	78	ABB
Maybin,Cameron	8	ABB
Reddick,Josh	9	ABB
Thames,Eric	79	ABB
Hart,Corey	39	BAA
Ethier,Andre	9	BAA
Young,Chris	8	BAA
Markakis,Nick	9	BAB
Young,Delmon	07	BBB
Kubel,Jason	7	BBB
Ross,Cody	79	BBB
Soriano,Alfonso	7	BBB
Stanton,Giancarlo	9	BBB

RP		Rel
Axford,John	AAA	AAA
Hernandez,Livan	AAA	AAA
Bell,Heath	AAB	AAB
Davis,Wade	AAB	AAB
Marmol,Carlos	AAB	AAB
Papelbon,Jonathan	AAB	AAB
Valverde,Jose	AAB	AAB
Duensing,Brian	ABA	AAB
Johnson,Jim	ABA	AAB
Motte,Jason	ABA	ABA
Sale,Chris	ABA	ABA
Clippard,Tyler	ABB	ABA
Hanrahan,Joel	ABB	ABB
Kimbrel,Craig	ABB	ABB
League,Brandon	ABB	ABB
Perez,Chris	ABB	ABB
Samardzija,Jeff	ABB	ABB
Gorzelanny,Tom	BBA	ABB
Rodriguez,Francisco	BBA	BBA

SP	Rel
Arroyo,Bronson	AAA
Buehrle,Mark	AAA
Burnett,A.J.	AAA
Cahill,Trevor	AAA
Cain,Matt	AAA
Capuano,Chris	AAA
Gonzalez,Gio	AAA
Hamels,Cole	AAA
Haren,Dan	AAA
Hernandez,Felix	AAA
Iwakuma,Hisashi	AAA
Jackson,Edwin	AAA
Kendrick,Kyle	AAA
Kershaw,Clayton	AAA
Latos,Mat	AAA
Leake,Mike	AAA
Lester,Jon	AAA
Lincecum,Tim	AAA
Masterson,Justin	AAA
Nolasco,Ricky	AAA
Porcello,Rick	AAA
Price,David	AAA
Sabathia,CC	AAA
Santana,Ervin	AAA
Saunders,Joe	AAA
Scherzer,Max	AAA
Shields,James	AAA
Verlander,Justin	AAA
Weaver,Jered	AAA
Bumgarner,Madison	AAB
Dickey,R.A.	AAB
Greinke,Zack	AAB
Hellickson,Jeremy	AAB
Jimenez,Ubaldo	AAB
Kennedy,Ian	AAB
Lowe,Derek	AAB
Romero,Ricky	AAB
Wilson,C.J.	AAB
Cecil,Brett	ABA
Garcia,Freddy	ABA
Nova,Ivan	ABA
Hernandez,Roberto	ABB
McDonald,James	ABB
Milone,Tommy	ABB
Minor,Mike	ABB
Billingsley,Chad	BAA
Correia,Kevin	BAA
Cueto,Johnny	BAA
Dempster,Ryan	BAA
Floyd,Gavin	BAA
Gallardo,Yovani	BAA
Guthrie,Jeremy	BAA
Hochevar,Luke	BAA
Kuroda,Hiroki	BAA
Lee,Cliff	BAA
Maholm,Paul	BAA
Myers,Brett	BAA
Norris,Bud	BAA
Rodriguez,Wandy	BAA
Vargas,Jason	BAA
Liriano,Francisco	BAB

RISK MANAGEMENT

GRADE "A" in CONSISTENCY

Pitchers (min 120 IP)	Pitchers (min 120 IP)
Arroyo,Bronson	Chen,Bruce
Buehrle,Mark	Zimmermann,Jordan
Burnett,A.J.	Buchholz,Clay
Cahill,Trevor	Carpenter,Chris
Cain,Matt	Johnson,Josh
Capuano,Chris	Lilly,Ted
Gonzalez,Gio	Marcum,Shaun
Hamels,Cole	Pavano,Carl
Haren,Dan	Wainwright,Adam
Hernandez,Felix	Blanton,Joe
Iwakuma,Hisashi	Lackey,John
Jackson,Edwin	Niemann,Jeff
Kendrick,Kyle	Santana,Johan
Kershaw,Clayton	Anderson,Brett
Latos,Mat	Medlen,Kris
Leake,Mike	Strasburg,Stephen
Lester,Jon	Nicasio,Juan
Lincecum,Tim	
Masterson,Justin	**Batters (min 400 AB)**
Nolasco,Ricky	Alonso,Yonder
Porcello,Rick	Altuve,Jose
Price,David	Arencibia,J.P.
Sabathia,CC	Bourn,Michael
Santana,Ervin	Castro,Starlin
Saunders,Joe	Chisenhall,Lonnie
Scherzer,Max	Cozart,Zack
Shields,James	Dominguez,Matt
Verlander,Justin	Espinosa,Danny
Weaver,Jered	Ethier,Andre
Sale,Chris	Freeman,Freddie
Nova,Ivan	Freese,David
Beavan,Blake	Goldschmidt,Paul
Collmenter,Josh	Hanigan,Ryan
Miley,Wade	Hart,Corey
Deduno,Samuel	Holliday,Matt
Corbin,Patrick	Jay,Jon
Harvey,Matt	Jones,Adam
Keuchel,Dallas	Kipnis,Jason
Lyles,Jordan	Martin,Russell
Parker,Jarrod	Martinez,Victor
Turner,Jacob	McLouth,Nate
Correia,Kevin	Montero,Miguel
Cueto,Johnny	Quentin,Carlos
Dempster,Ryan	Revere,Ben
Floyd,Gavin	Rodriguez,Alex
Gallardo,Yovani	Rollins,Jimmy
Guthrie,Jeremy	Saltalamacchia,Jarrod
Hochevar,Luke	Seager,Kyle
Kuroda,Hiroki	Swisher,Nick
Lee,Cliff	Teixeira,Mark
Maholm,Paul	Upton,B.J.
Myers,Brett	Young,Chris
Norris,Bud	
Rodriguez,Wandy	
Vargas,Jason	
Estrada,Marco	
Lynn,Lance	
Laffey,Aaron	
Fister,Doug	
Halladay,Roy	
Holland,Derek	
Niese,Jon	
Richard,Clayton	
Sanchez,Anibal	
Garcia,Jaime	
Britton,Zach	
Hudson,Tim	
Morrow,Brandon	
Westbrook,Jake	
Bailey,Homer	

TOP COMBINATION OF SKILLS AND RELIABILITY
Maximum of one "C" in Reliability Grade

BATTING POWER

PX 120+	PX	Rel
Stanton,Giancarlo	220	BBB
Reynolds,Mark	176	AAB
Bruce,Jay	170	AAB
Granderson,Curtis	168	AAC
Carter,Chris	161	ACB
Braun,Ryan	158	AAC
Saltalamacchia,J.	158	ACA
Kubel,Jason	154	BBB
Upton,B.J.	153	AAA
Cabrera,Miguel	152	AAB
Soriano,Alfonso	152	BBB
Arencibia,J.P.	151	BCA
Hart,Corey	151	BAA
Frazier,Todd	147	ACB
Pujols,Albert	145	AAC
Jones,Garrett	142	ABB
Fielder,Prince	139	AAC
Holliday,Matt	139	AAA
Swisher,Nick	138	AAA
Cano,Robinson	137	AAB
Gonzalez,Carlos	137	AAB
Young,Chris	137	BAA
Trumbo,Mark	136	ABB
Beltre,Adrian	135	CAB
McCutchen,Andrew	135	AAC
Teixeira,Mark	135	AAA
Upton,Justin	134	AAC
Cuddyer,Michael	131	CBB
Cespedes,Yoenis	130	ACB
Fowler,Dexter	130	BBC
Ross,Cody	130	BBB
Freeman,Freddie	129	ABA
Zimmerman,Ryan	129	CAB
Zobrist,Ben	129	AAB
Ramirez,Aramis	128	BAC
Santana,Carlos	128	ABB
Reddick,Josh	127	ABB
Moreland,Mitch	126	BCB
Wieters,Matt	126	ABB
Espinosa,Danny	125	AAA
Jones,Adam	125	AAA
Wright,David	125	BAC
Uggla,Dan	124	AAC
Butler,Billy	122	AAB
Headley,Chase	121	BAC

RUNNER SPEED

Spd 100+	SX	Rel
Fowler,Dexter	160	BBC
Jennings,Desmond	153	ABB
Revere,Ben	146	ACA
Escobar,Alcides	144	AAB
Stubbs,Drew	143	AAC
Bourn,Michael	141	AAA
Castro,Starlin	140	AAA
Maybin,Cameron	138	ABB
Venable,Will	135	ACB
Ackley,Dustin	130	AAC
McCutchen,Andrew	128	AAC
Suzuki,Ichiro	128	AAC
Infante,Omar	127	CAB
Hechavarria,Adeiny	126	ACB
Andrus,Elvis	125	AAB
Barney,Darwin	118	ABB
Upton,Justin	118	AAC
De Aza,Alejandro	117	ACB
Aybar,Erick	116	BAB
Cozart,Zack	116	BBA
Upton,B.J.	116	AAA
Reddick,Josh	115	ABB
Ramirez,Alexei	114	AAB
Granderson,Curtis	113	AAC
Jeter,Derek	109	BAB
Espinosa,Danny	108	AAA
Frazier,Todd	108	ACB
Jay,Jon	106	BCA
Cespedes,Yoenis	105	ACB
Kipnis,Jason	104	ABA
Rasmus,Colby	104	AAC
Tejada,Ruben	104	BCB
Brantley,Michael	103	ABB
Jones,Adam	101	AAA
Pedroia,Dustin	101	CAB
Scutaro,Marco	101	BAB

OVERALL PITCHING SKILL

BPV over 80	BPV	Rel
Kimbrel,Craig	216	ABB
Romo,Sergio	172	BCB
Papelbon,Jonathan	163	AAB
Chapman,Aroldis	157	BCB
Marshall,Sean	148	ACA
Lee,Cliff	143	BAA
Jansen,Kenley	143	BCB
Robertson,David	140	BCB
Motte,Jason	136	ABA
Lopez,Wilton	125	BCA
Hamels,Cole	122	AAA
Sabathia,CC	122	AAA
Scherzer,Max	122	AAA
Halladay,Roy	122	CAA
Shields,James	121	AAA
Greinke,Zack	121	AAB
Dotel,Octavio	121	BCA
Mujica,Edward	119	ACA
Sale,Chris	118	ABA
Hernandez,Felix	117	AAA
Peralta,Joel	117	ACB
Verlander,Justin	116	AAA
Thornton,Matt	116	ACA
Kershaw,Clayton	115	AAA
Betancourt,Rafael	112	BCB
Hernandez,David	111	ACB
Belisle,Matt	110	ACA
Axford,John	108	AAA
Price,David	107	AAA
Bumgarner,Madison	107	AAB
Milone,Tommy	106	ABB
Oliver,Darren	106	ACA
Lincoln,Brad	105	ACB
Darvish,Yu	102	AAC
Walden,Jordan	102	BCB
Venters,Jonny	101	ACA
Haren,Dan	100	AAA
Estrada,Marco	100	BCA
Gallardo,Yovani	99	BAA
Davis,Wade	99	AAB
Garza,Matt	97	CAB
Latos,Mat	96	AAA
Kuroda,Hiroki	96	BAA
Garcia,Jaime	96	CBA
Parnell,Bobby	96	BCA
Clippard,Tyler	96	ABB
Fister,Doug	95	CAA
Lecure,Sam	95	ACB
Sanchez,Anibal	93	CAA
Rodriguez,Francisco	93	BBA
Niese,Jon	92	CAA
Dickey,R.A.	92	AAB
Takahashi,Hisanori	92	ACA
Balfour,Grant	92	BCA
Lincecum,Tim	90	AAA
Nolasco,Ricky	88	AAA
Kennedy,Ian	88	AAB
Affeldt,Jeremy	88	BCA
Capuano,Chris	87	AAA
Dempster,Ryan	87	BAA
Lynn,Lance	87	BCA
Weaver,Jered	86	AAA
Burnett,A.J.	85	AAA
Cain,Matt	85	AAA
Beckett,Josh	85	CAB
Hanson,Tommy	85	CAB
Gee,Dillon	85	CBB
Collmenter,Josh	84	ACA
Hanrahan,Joel	84	ABB
Cueto,Johnny	83	BAA
Salas,Fernando	83	ACA
Gonzalez,Gio	81	AAA
Iwakuma,Hisashi	81	AAA
Jackson,Edwin	81	AAA

LIMA Plan Targets

LIMA	1B	3B	2B	SS	CA	DH	OF
A	Encarnacion,Edwin			Tulowitzki,Troy			
B+	Cuddyer,Michael Santana,Carlos	Beltre,Adrian Ramirez,Aramis	Hill,Aaron Kinsler,Ian Utley,Chase Zobrist,Ben	Rollins,Jimmy Zobrist,Ben	Santana,Carlos		Cespedes,Yoenis Victorino,Shane
B	Craig,Allen Davis,Ike Fielder,Prince Frazier,Todd Freeman,Freddie Goldschmidt,Paul Gonzalez,Adrian Hart,Corey Hosmer,Eric Konerko,Paul Morneau,Justin Teixeira,Mark	Frazier,Todd Longoria,Evan Machado,Manny Prado,Martin Zimmerman,Ryan	Infante,Omar Scutaro,Marco	Scutaro,Marco	Molina,Yadier Ruiz,Carlos Wieters,Matt		Cabrera,Melky Hamilton,Josh Holliday,Matt Kubel,Jason Prado,Martin Quentin,Carlos Soriano,Alfonso Willingham,Josh

LIMA	STARTING PITCHERS			RELIEF PITCHERS			
A+	Corbin,Patrick Halladay,Roy			Adams,Mike Belisle,Matt Brach,Brad Brothers,Rex	Burnett,Sean Capps,Carter Doolittle,Sean Dotel,Octavio	Grilli,Jason Lecure,Sam Melancon,Mark Mujica,Edward	Robertson,David Tazawa,Junichi Thornton,Matt
A	Garcia,Jaime Luebke,Cory Lyles,Jordan McPherson,Kyle	Milone,Tommy Moore,Matt Rosenthal,Trevor Thornburg,Tyler		Affeldt,Jeremy Cashner,Andrew Cishek,Steve Collins,Tim Crain,Jesse Crow,Aaron	Davis,Wade Francisco,Frank Hernandez,David Herrera,Kelvin Kontos,George Logan,Boone	Madson,Ryan Marshall,Sean Martinez,Cristhian Oliver,Darren Parnell,Bobby Patton,Troy	Pestano,Vinnie Reed,Addison Storen,Drew
B+	Anderson,Brett Archer,Chris Bauer,Trevor Beachy,Brandon Cobb,Alex Darvish,Yu	Fister,Doug Floyd,Gavin Hendriks,Liam Iwakuma,Hisashi Jackson,Edwin Johnson,Josh	Niemann,Jeff Ramirez,Erasmo Sanchez,Anibal Scherzer,Max Smyly,Drew Wainwright,Adam	Axford,John Bell,Heath Breslow,Craig Broxton,Jonathan Gregerson,Luke	Holland,Greg Hughes,Jared Jepsen,Kevin Lopez,Wilton Lyon,Brandon	Mcgee,Jake O Flaherty,Eric Perkins,Glen Ross,Robbie Soria,Joakim	Thayer,Dale Watson,Tony Wright,Wesley
B	Billingsley,Chad Buchholz,Clay Cahill,Trevor Cloyd,Tyler Dempster,Ryan Eovaldi,Nathan Fiers,Mike	Greinke,Zack Hammel,Jason Harvey,Matt Karstens,Jeff Lackey,John Latos,Mat Lynn,Lance	McAllister,Zach McCarthy,Brandon Morrow,Brandon Pettitte,Andy Rodriguez,Wandy Strasburg,Stephen Wilson,C.J.	Bastardo,Antonio Belisario,Ronald Blevins,Jerry Boggs,Mitchell Clippard,Tyler	Cook,Ryan Frieri,Ernesto Gorzelanny,Tom Janssen,Casey League,Brandon	Pryor,Stephen Putz,J.J. Rivera,Mariano Romo,Sergio Santos,Sergio	Street,Huston Venters,Jonny Walden,Jordan Ziegler,Brad

BATTERS
Contact rate of at least 80%
Walk rate of at least 10%
PX or Spd level of at least 100
Regular playing time
Projected Rotisserie value between $10 and $30

PITCHERS
Command ratio (K/BB) of 2.0 or better.
Strikeout rate of 5.6 or better.
Expected home run rate of 1.0 or less.
2012 Rotisserie value less than $20

PORTFOLIO 3 PLAN

TIER 1

High Skill, Low Risk			Filters:	BBB	80	one of 100	100	
BATTERS	Age	Bats	Pos	REL	ct%	PX	Spd	R$
Cabrera,Miguel	30	R	5	AAB	84	152	66	$42
Cano,Robinson	30	L	4	AAB	86	137	75	$32
Butler,Billy	27	R	03	AAB	84	122	49	$28
Jones,Adam	27	R	9	AAA	80	125	101	$26
Kinsler,Ian	31	R	4	BAB	87	106	99	$25
Markakis,Nick	29	L	8	BAB	88	105	92	$25
Aybar,Erick	29	B	6	BAB	88	80	116	$24
Castro,Starlin	23	R	6	AAA	86	87	140	$24
Andrus,Elvis	24	R	6	AAB	85	54	125	$23
Zobrist,Ben	32	B	846	AAB	80	129	96	$23
Escobar,Alcides	26	R	6	AAB	85	60	144	$21
Teixeira,Mark	33	B	3	AAA	81	135	62	$21
Cabrera,Asdrubal	27	B	6	BAB	82	104	84	$20
Konerko,Paul	37	R	30	AAB	83	112	61	$20
Ramirez,Alexei	31	R	6	AAB	87	74	114	$20
Wieters,Matt	27	B	2	ABB	80	126	59	$20
Pierre,Juan	35	L	7	AAB	93	33	145	$19
Scutaro,Marco	37	R	46	BAB	91	68	101	$19
Walker,Neil	27	B	4	AAB	80	105	85	$18
Alonso,Yonder	26	L	3	ABA	81	112	52	$16
Montero,Jesus	23	R	02	ABB	80	114	64	$16
Brantley,Michael	26	L	9	ABB	88	75	103	$15
Jeter,Derek	39	R	60	BAB	86	63	109	$15
Cozart,Zack	27	R	6	BBA	80	103	116	$11
McCann,Brian	29	L	2	ABB	82	105	53	$11
Barney,Darwin	27	R	4	ABB	88	54	118	$10
Ibanez,Raul	41	L	70	ABB	81	128	73	$10

TIER 2

Mod Skill, Low Risk			Filters:	BBB	80	one of 100	100	<$20
BATTERS	Age	Bats	Pos	REL	ct%	PX	Spd	R$
Kipnis,Jason*	26	L	4	ABA	79	103	104	$21
Maybin,Cameron*	26	R	9	ABB	76	84	138	$21
Ethier,Andre	31	L	8	BAA	79	118	83	$19
Kendrick,Howie	29	R	4	AAB	80	93	91	$19
Santana,Carlos	27	B	203	ABB	79	128	72	$19
Swisher,Nick	32	B	83	AAA	74	138	69	$19
Freeman,Freddie	23	L	3	ABA	77	129	75	$18
Kubel,Jason	31	L	7	BBB	73	154	59	$18
Soriano,Alfonso	37	R	7	BBB	74	152	78	$18
Trumbo,Mark	27	R	780	ABB	74	136	83	$18
Reddick,Josh	26	L	8	ABB	77	127	115	$17
Young,Delmon	27	R	07	BBB	82	99	64	$17
Ross,Cody	32	R	87	BBB	75	130	75	$16
Smoak,Justin	26	B	3	ABB	76	107	65	$10

TIER 2

Mod Skill, Low Risk			Filters:	BBB	50	<$20
PITCHERS	Age	Thrw	REL	BPV	R$	
League,Brandon	30	R	ABB	71	$16	
Hellickson,Jeremy	26	R	AAB	58	$13	
Cahill,Trevor	25	R	AAA	74	$13	
Wilson,C.J.	32	L	AAB	67	$12	
Marmol,Carlos	30	R	AAB	52	$10	
Arroyo,Bronson	36	R	AAA	65	$9	
Buehrle,Mark	34	L	AAA	62	$9	
Maholm,Paul	31	L	BAA	65	$9	
Floyd,Gavin	30	R	BAA	73	$9	
Vargas,Jason	30	L	BAA	55	$8	
Kendrick,Kyle	28	R	AAA	52	$8	

TIER 1

High Skill, Low Risk		Filters:	BBB	75	
PITCHERS	Age	Thrw	REL	BPV	R$
Kershaw,Clayton	25	L	AAA	115	$33
Verlander,Justin	30	R	AAA	116	$31
Hamels,Cole	29	L	AAA	122	$29
Kimbrel,Craig	25	R	ABB	216	$28
Price,David	27	L	AAA	107	$27
Weaver,Jered	30	R	AAA	86	$26
Lee,Cliff	34	L	BAA	143	$26
Cain,Matt	28	R	AAA	85	$25
Motte,Jason	31	R	ABA	136	$25
Hernandez,Felix	27	R	AAA	117	$24
Papelbon,Jonathan	32	R	AAB	163	$24
Shields,James	31	R	AAA	121	$23
Cueto,Johnny	27	R	BAA	83	$22
Sale,Chris	24	L	ABA	118	$22
Gonzalez,Gio	27	L	AAA	81	$21
Latos,Mat	25	R	AAA	96	$21
Scherzer,Max	28	R	AAA	122	$21
Dickey,R.A.	38	R	AAB	92	$20
Bumgarner,Madison	23	L	AAB	107	$20
Greinke,Zack	29	R	AAB	121	$20
Axford,John	30	R	AAA	108	$20
Sabathia,CC	32	L	AAA	122	$19
Perez,Chris	28	R	ABB	76	$19
Gallardo,Yovani	27	R	BAA	99	$17
Hanrahan,Joel	31	R	ABB	84	$17
Johnson,Jim	30	R	ABA	76	$17
Kuroda,Hiroki	38	R	BAA	96	$16
Kennedy,Ian	28	R	AAB	88	$14
Samardzija,Jeff	28	R	ABB	76	$14
Milone,Tommy	26	L	ABB	106	$13
Haren,Dan	32	R	AAA	100	$13
Minor,Mike	25	L	ABB	79	$12
Dempster,Ryan	36	R	BAA	87	$11
Lester,Jon	29	L	AAA	78	$11
Clippard,Tyler	28	R	ABB	96	$11
Iwakuma,Hisashi	32	R	AAA	81	$10
Rodriguez,Wandy	34	L	BAA	76	$10
Lincecum,Tim	29	R	AAA	90	$10
Capuano,Chris	34	L	AAA	87	$9
Myers,Brett	32	R	BAA	78	$9
Burnett,A.J.	36	R	AAA	85	$9
Jackson,Edwin	29	R	AAA	81	$8
Davis,Wade	27	R	AAB	99	$6
Nolasco,Ricky	30	R	AAA	88	$5
Norris,Bud	28	R	BAA	75	$5
Leake,Mike	25	R	AAA	75	$5
Rodriguez,Francisco	31	R	BBA	93	$4
Billingsley,Chad	28	R	BAA	77	$2

TIER 2, cont.

Mod Skill, Low Risk		Filters:	BBB	50	<$20
PITCHERS	Age	Thrw	REL	BPV	R$
McDonald,James	28	R	ABB	56	$8
Santana,Ervin	30	R	AAA	67	$7
Bell,Heath	35	R	AAB	70	$6
Saunders,Joe	32	L	AAA	52	$3
Nova,Ivan	26	R	ABA	64	$3
Gorzelanny,Tom	30	L	BBA	59	$2
Jimenez,Ubaldo	29	R	AAB	58	$1
Masterson,Justin	28	R	AAA	63	$1

PORTFOLIO 3 PLAN

TIER 3

						one of			
High Skill, High Risk			Filters:	N/A	80	100	100	<$10	
BATTERS	Age	Bats	Pos	REL	Ct%	PX	Spd	R$	
Carrera,Ezequiel	26	L	7	ACA	81	58	112	$9	
Casilla,Alexi	28	B	4	CDB	85	65	102	$9	
Francoeur,Jeff	29	R	8	AAD	80	101	93	$9	
Gordon,Dee	25	L	6	CCC	82	37	143	$9	
Lombardozzi,Steve	24	B	47	ADB	86	60	124	$9	
Morgan,Nyjer	32	L	98	CCF	80	54	131	$9	
Simmons,Andrelton	23	R	6	CFF	86	57	147	$9	
Dozier,Brian	26	R	6	AFC	81	83	124	$8	
Getz,Chris	29	L	4	DDA	89	45	112	$8	
Presley,Alex	27	L	7	BCB	81	94	128	$8	
Rolen,Scott	38	R	5	FCD	82	113	80	$8	
Wells,Vernon	34	R	7	DBC	84	108	74	$8	
Amarista,Alexi	24	L	47	ADB	86	73	123	$7	
Profar,Jurickson	20	B	4	AFF	83	108	118	$7	
Sanchez,Gaby	29	R	3	ABC	81	101	65	$7	
Garcia,Avisail	22	R	8	AFF	83	56	124	$6	
Gentry,Craig	29	R	9	AFB	81	55	135	$6	
LeMahieu,DJ	24	R	4	ADB	85	55	126	$6	
Arias,Joaquin	28	R	56	AFD	85	77	145	$5	
Mesoraco,Devin	25	R	2	ADC	80	107	68	$5	
Pastornicky,Tyler	23	R	6	ADB	84	56	125	$5	
Blackmon,Charlie	27	L	8	FDB	84	71	100	$4	
Descalso,Daniel	26	L	465	ACB	81	63	122	$4	
Solano,Donovan	25	R	4	ADB	81	54	110	$4	
Cooper,David	26	L	3	BCB	84	121	76	$3	
Hudson,Orlando	35	B	45	CCB	80	89	117	$3	
Podsednik,Scott	37	L	79	BDC	80	55	115	$3	
Chavez,Endy	35	L	78	CFF	87	59	103	$2	
Gwynn,Tony	30	L	97	ADC	80	47	106	$2	
Harrison,Josh	25	R	46	BCA	87	63	118	$2	
Herrera,Jonathan	28	B	6	CDA	84	43	104	$2	
Iglesias,Jose	23	R	6	ADB	83	51	101	$2	
Izturis,Cesar	33	B	6	FFC	91	57	102	$2	
Kawasaki,Munenori	32	L	6	ACC	86	41	118	$2	
Pill,Brett	28	R	3	ACA	84	108	82	$2	
Robinson,Shane	28	R	9	AFB	83	76	132	$2	
Kelly,Don	33	L	8	AFB	81	47	107	$1	
Santiago,Ramon	33	B	46	ADC	83	54	104	$1	

TIER 3

High Skill, High Risk		Filters:	N/A	75	<$10
PITCHERS	Age	Thrw	REL	BPV	R$
Vogelsong,Ryan	35	R	ABC	75	$9
Garcia,Jaime	26	L	CBA	96	$9
Harvey,Matt	24	R	ADA	80	$9
Gee,Dillon	27	R	CBB	85	$9
Hanson,Tommy	26	R	CAB	85	$9
Straily,Dan	24	R	ADF	88	$9
Herrera,Kelvin	23	R	ADC	121	$9
Robertson,David	28	R	BCB	140	$9
Luebke,Cory	28	L	FCB	84	$8
Beckett,Josh	33	R	CAB	85	$8
Carpenter,Chris	38	R	FAA	93	$8
Villanueva,Carlos	29	R	ACB	77	$8
Benoit,Joaquin	35	R	DCA	118	$8
Francisco,Frank	33	R	DCB	91	$8
Collmenter,Josh	27	R	ACA	84	$7
Estrada,Marco	29	R	BCA	100	$7
Hammel,Jason	30	R	CAC	78	$7
Lynn,Lance	26	R	BCA	87	$7
Ramirez,Erasmo	23	R	CDC	85	$7
Cobb,Alex	25	R	BDB	92	$7
O Flaherty,Eric	28	L	ADA	93	$7
Broxton,Jonathan	29	R	DCD	100	$7

TIER 3 (Cont.)

High Skill, High Risk		Filters:	N/A	75	<$10
PITCHERS	Age	Thrw	REL	BPV	R$
Fujikawa,Kyuji	32	R	ABF	98	$7
O Day,Darren	30	R	CDF	113	$7
Belisario,Ronald	30	R	ADB	76	$7
Hernandez,David	28	R	ACB	111	$7
Madson,Ryan	32	R	FCA	109	$7
Marshall,Sean	30	L	ACA	148	$7
Brothers,Rex	25	L	ADA	106	$7
Miller,Shelby	22	R	ADF	92	$6
Rosenthal,Trevor	23	R	AFF	96	$6
Beachy,Brandon	26	R	FCA	104	$6
Mcgee,Jake	26	L	ADD	138	$6
Pestano,Vinnie	28	R	ADA	108	$6
Mujica,Edward	29	R	ACA	119	$6
Bauer,Trevor	22	R	ADF	75	$5
Santana,Johan	34	L	FBA	82	$5
Blanton,Joe	32	R	FBA	107	$5
Oliver,Darren	42	L	ACA	106	$5
Lewis,Colby	33	R	DAA	91	$5
Peralta,Joel	37	R	ACB	117	$5
McCarthy,Brandon	29	R	FCC	78	$4
Cashner,Andrew	26	R	FDA	90	$4
de la Rosa,Jorge	32	L	FCC	75	$4
Crain,Jesse	31	R	CCA	81	$4
Furbush,Charlie	27	L	BDD	106	$4
Burnett,Sean	30	L	ACC	103	$4
Doolittle,Sean	26	L	AFF	150	$4
Dotel,Octavio	39	R	BCA	121	$4
Grilli,Jason	36	R	ADB	118	$4
Thornton,Matt	36	L	ACA	116	$4
Skaggs,Tyler	21	L	ADC	92	$3
Lyles,Jordan	22	R	ADA	81	$3
Uehara,Koji	38	R	FDA	148	$3
Affeldt,Jeremy	34	L	BCA	88	$3
Rauch,Jon	34	R	BCA	77	$3
Adams,Mike	34	R	CCB	99	$3
Capps,Matt	29	R	DBA	75	$3
Lecure,Sam	29	R	ACB	95	$3
Brach,Brad	27	R	ADC	103	$3
Walden,Jordan	25	R	BCB	102	$3
Wright,Wesley	28	L	ADD	78	$3
Belisle,Matt	33	R	ACA	110	$3
Delabar,Steve	29	R	ADB	98	$3
Bastardo,Antonio	27	L	ADA	117	$3
Melancon,Mark	28	R	ACC	107	$3
Phelps,David	26	R	ADF	76	$2
Carrasco,Carlos	26	R	FCA	77	$2
McPherson,Kyle	25	R	ADB	81	$2
Corbin,Patrick	23	L	ADA	96	$2
Thornburg,Tyler	24	R	AFF	86	$2
Capps,Carter	22	R	AFF	121	$2
Kontos,George	28	R	ADD	87	$2
Patton,Troy	27	L	BDC	86	$2
Tazawa,Junichi	27	R	FFD	124	$2
Farnsworth,Kyle	37	R	DCB	92	$2
Baker,Scott	31	R	FBA	91	$2
Collins,Tim	23	L	ADF	80	$2
Crow,Aaron	26	R	ADC	87	$2
Ross,Robbie	24	L	ADA	87	$1
Breslow,Craig	32	L	ACB	75	$1
Kelley,Shawn	29	R	FDC	87	$1
Lyon,Brandon	33	R	FCD	75	$1
Thayer,Dale	32	R	ADD	78	$1
Logan,Boone	28	L	ADA	89	$1
Martinez,Cristhian	31	R	ADB	91	$1
Loe,Kameron	31	R	ACC	93	$1

*Tier 2 players should generally be less than $20. If you're going to spend more than $20, be aware of the added risk.

**Tier 3 players should generally be less than $10. If you're going to spend more than $10, be aware of the added risk.

RANDOM VARIANCE - Rebounds/Corrections

Rebounds/Improvements

BATTERS	POS	+
Bautista,Jose	9	+5
Bay,Jason	7	+5
Davis,Ike	3	+5
Huff,Aubrey	3	+5
Hundley,Nick	2	+5
Ibanez,Raul	70	+5
Soto,Geovany	2	+5
Amarista,Alexi	47	+4
Hosmer,Eric	3	+4
Kotchman,Casey	3	+4
Martin,Russell	2	+4
McCann,Brian	2	+4
Loney,James	3	+3
Morrison,Logan	37	+3
Pennington,Cliff	46	+3
Ryan,Brendan	6	+3
Sanchez,Gaby	3	+3
Scott,Luke	0	+3
Stewart,Ian	5	+3
Teixeira,Mark	3	+3
Torres,Andres	8	+3
Youkilis,Kevin	35	+3
Young,Chris	8	+3

Corrections/Declines

BATTERS	POS	-
Cabrera,Melky	7	-5
Colvin,Tyler	389	-5
Dirks,Andy	79	-5
Ellis,A.J.	2	-5
Fowler,Dexter	8	-5
Hunter,Torii	9	-5
Keppinger,Jeff	345	-5
Lucroy,Jonathan	2	-5
Martinez,Fernando	7	-5
McCutchen,Andrew	8	-5
Montero,Miguel	2	-5
Pacheco,Jordan	35	-5
Posey,Buster	23	-5
Solano,Donovan	4	-5
Young Jr.,Eric	8	-5

Corrections/Declines

BATTERS	POS	-
Blanco,Gregor	789	-4
Bloomquist,Willie	6	-4
Castillo,Welington	2	-4
Cespedes,Yoenis	780	-4
Ciriaco,Pedro	5	-4
Hechavarria,Adeiny	5	-4
Hill,Aaron	4	-4
Jackson,Austin	8	-4
Johnson,Chris	5	-4
Rios,Alex	9	-4
Ruggiano,Justin	78	-4
Tejada,Ruben	6	-4
Trout,Mike	78	-4
Trumbo,Mark	790	-4
Belt,Brandon	3	-3
Beltre,Adrian	50	-3
Braun,Ryan	7	-3
Butler,Billy	30	-3
Cabrera,Everth	6	-3
Carter,Chris	3	-3
Dobbs,Greg	57	-3
Eaton,Adam	8	-3
Escobar,Alcides	6	-3
Freese,David	5	-3
Gardner,Brett	7	-3
Headley,Chase	5	-3
Jay,Jon	8	-3
Jeter,Derek	60	-3
Kemp,Matt	8	-3
Martinez,Victor	0	-3
Mauer,Joe	230	-3
Molina,Yadier	2	-3
Murphy,David	7	-3
Ramos,Wilson	2	-3
Reimold,Nolan	7	-3
Ruiz,Carlos	2	-3
Votto,Joey	3	-3
Walker,Neil	4	-3
Werth,Jayson	9	-3

Rebounds/Improvements

PITCHERS	+
Arrieta,Jake	+5
de la Rosa,Jorge	+5
Hochevar,Luke	+5
Kelly,Casey	+5
Nicasio,Juan	+5
Nova,Ivan	+5
Pavano,Carl	+5
Sanchez,Jonathan	+5
Thornburg,Tyler	+5
Volstad,Chris	+5
Feldman,Scott	+4
Gomez,Jeanmar	+4
Matsuzaka,Daisuke	+4
Alvarez,Henderson	+3
Blanton,Joe	+3
Cashner,Andrew	+3
Deduno,Samuel	+3
Doubront,Felix	+3
Jurrjens,Jair	+3
Leake,Mike	+3
Lincecum,Tim	+3
Liriano,Francisco	+3
Noesi,Hector	+3
Porcello,Rick	+3
Scherzer,Max	+3

Corrections/Declines

PITCHERS	-
Lilly,Ted	-5
Medlen,Kris	-5
Pelfrey,Mike	-5
Hellickson,Jeremy	-4
Luebke,Cory	-4
Weaver,Jered	-4
Cain,Matt	-3
Morrow,Brandon	-3

Batters minimum 300 AB. Pitchers minimum 100 IP.

Universal Draft Grid

Most publications and websites provide cheat sheets with ranked player lists for different fantasy draft formats. The biggest problem with these tools was that they perpetuated the myth that players can be ranked in a linear fashion.

Since rankings are based on highly variable projections, it is foolhardy to draw conclusions that a $24 player is better than a $23 player is better than a $22 player. Yes, a first round pick is better than a 10th round pick, but within most rounds, all players are pretty much interchangeable commodities.

But typical cheat sheets don't reflect that reality. Auction sheets rank players by dollar value. Snake draft sheets rank players within round, accounting for position and categorical scarcity. But just as ADPs have a ridiculously low success rate, these cheat sheets are similarly flawed.

We have a tool at BaseballHQ.com called the Rotisserie Grid. It is a chart—that can be customized to your league parameters—which organizes players into pockets of skill, by position. It is one of the most popular tools on the site. One of the best features of this grid is that its design provides immediate insight into position scarcity.

So in the *Forecaster*, we recently transitioned to this format as a sort of Universal Draft Grid.

How to use the chart

Across the top of the grid, players are sorted by position. First and third base, and Second and shortstop are presented side-by-side for easy reference when considering corner and middle infielders, respectively.

The vertical axis separates each group of players into tiers based on potential fantasy impact. At the top are the Elite players; at the bottom are the Fringe players.

Auction leagues: The tiers in the grid represent rough breakpoints for dollar values. Elite players could be considered those that are purchased for $30 and up. Each subsequent tier is a step down of approximately $5.

Snake drafters: Tiers can be used to rank players similarly, though most tiers will encompass more than one round. Any focus on position scarcity will bump some players up a bit. For instance, with the dearth of Elite shortstops and the wealth of Elite outfielders, one might opt to draft Troy Tulowitzki (from the Gold tier) before the Elite level Carlos Gonzalez. The reason we target scarce positions early is that there will be plenty of solid outfielders and starting pitchers later on.

To build the best foundation, you should come out of the first 10 rounds with all your middle infielders, all your corner infielders, one outfielder, at least one catcher and two pitchers (at least one closer).

The players are listed at the position where they both qualify and provide the most fantasy value. Additional position eligibility (20 games) is listed in parentheses. Listings in bold are players with high reliability grades (minimum "B" across the board).

Each player is presented with his 7-character Mayberry score. The first four digits (all on a 0-5 scale) represent skill: power, speed, batting average and playing time for batters; ERA, dominance, saves potential and playing time for pitchers. The last four alpha characters are the reliability grade (A-F): health, experience and consistency.

Within each tier, players are sorted by the first character of their Mayberry score. This means that batters are sorted by power; pitchers by ERA potential. If you need to prospect for the best skill sets among players in a given tier, target those with 4s and 5s in whatever skill you need.

CAVEATS and DISCLAIMERS

The placement of players in tiers does not represent average draft positions (ADP) or average auction values (AAV). It represents where each player's true value may lie. It is the variance between this true value and the ADP/AAV market values—or better, the value that your league-mates place on each player—where you will find your potential for profit or loss.

That means **you cannot take this chart right into your draft with you.** You have to compare these rankings with your ADPs and AAVs, and build your draft list from there. In other words, if we project Carl Crawford as a "Gold" level pick but you know the other owners (or your ADPs) see him as a fourth-rounder, you can probably wait to pick him up in round 3. If you are in an auction league with owners who overvalue Yankees and Derek Jeter (projected at $20) gets bid past $25, you will likely take a loss should you decide to chase the bidding.

Finally, this chart is intended as a preliminary look based on current factors. For Draft Day, you will need to make your own adjustments based upon many different criteria that will impact the world between now and then. Daily updates appear online at BaseballHQ.com. A free projections update is available in March at **http://www.baseballhq.com/content/ron-shandlers-baseball-forecaster-2013**

Universal Draft Grid

TIER	FIRST BASE		THIRD BASE		SECOND BASE		SHORTSTOP	
Elite	Votto,Joey	(5155 BAD)	**Cabrera,Miguel**	**(4155 AAB)**	**Cano,Robinson**	**(4155 AAB)**	Reyes,Jose	(2535 CAF)
	Pujols,Albert	(4155 AAC)			Pedroia,Dustin	(3345 CAB)		
Gold	Goldschmidt,Paul	(4225 ADA)	Zimmerman,Ryan	(4235 CAB)	Hill,Aaron	(4235 BAD)	Tulowitzki,Troy	(4245 FCC)
	Gonzalez,Adrian	(4145 AAF)	Ramirez,Aramis	(4235 BAC)	**Kinsler,Ian**	**(3325 BAB)**	Desmond,Ian	(3425 AAD)
	Encarnacion,Edwin	(4135 CBC)	Headley,Chase	(4225 BAC)	Altuve,Jose	(1535 ADA)	Ramirez,Hanley (3)	(3225 BBD)
	Fielder,Prince	(4045 AAC)	Wright,David	(4225 BAC)			Rollins,Jimmy	(2325 CAA)
	Butler,Billy	**(4045 AAB)**	Beltre,Adrian	(4145 CAB)				
			Prado,Martin (O)	(2335 BAF)				
Stars	Craig,Allen (O)	(4245 CDC)	Middlebrooks,Will	(4215 BFD)	Weeks,Rickie	(4315 DAB)	**Zobrist,Ben (2O)**	**(4235 AAB)**
	Hart,Corey (O)	**(4235 BAA)**	Longoria,Evan	(4135 FBB)	**Kipnis,Jason**	**(3425 ABA)**		
	Teixeira,Mark	**(4135 AAA)**	Lawrie,Brett	(3425 BBF)	**Phillips,Brandon**	**(2235 AAB)**		
	Morales,Kendrys	(4035 FFB)	Sandoval,Pablo	(3035 DBF)				
	Konerko,Paul	**(3035 AAB)**	Young,Michael (1)	(1235 AAF)				
Regulars	Davis,Chris	(5115 ACD)	Frazier,Todd (1)	(4325 ACB)	Utley,Chase	(3335 FCB)	Rutledge,Josh	(4535 AFF)
	Reynolds,Mark	**(5105 CAB)**	Youkilis,Kevin (1)	(4225 CBF)	**Walker,Neil**	**(3125 ABA)**	Nakajima,Hiroyuki	(2323 ACB)
	Cuddyer,Michael (O)	(4245 CBB)	Machado,Manny	(3415 AFF)	**Kendrick,Howie**	**(2335 AAB)**	**Jeter,Derek**	**(1235 BAB)**
	Jones,Garrett (O)	**(4225 ABB)**	Rodriguez,Alex	(3215 DBA)	Murphy,Daniel	(2245 DCD)	**Scutaro,Marco (2)**	**(1235 BAB)**
	Freeman,Freddie	**(4135 ABA)**	Freese,David	(3125 DCA)	Infante,Omar	(1425 CAB)		
	LaRoche,Adam	(4115 DBF)	Seager,Kyle	(2125 ACA)				
	Davis,Ike	(4025 DCF)						
	Swisher,Nick (O)	**(4025 AAA)**						
	Belt,Brandon	(3315 BDF)						
	Morneau,Justin	(3225 FCF)						
	Morrison,Logan (O)	(3125 CCB)						
	Rizzo,Anthony	(3125 ACD)						
	Alonso,Yonder	**(3035 ABA)**						
	Hosmer,Eric	(2235 ACF)						
Mid-Level	Carter,Chris	(5105 ACB)	Plouffe,Trevor	(4115 ACC)	Uggla,Dan	(4105 AAC)	**Espinosa,Danny (2)**	**(4405 AAA)**
	Dunn,Adam	(5005 AAF)	Alvarez,Pedro	(4105 BBF)	Johnson,Kelly	(3305 AAC)	**Cozart,Zack**	**(3425 BBA)**
	Colvin,Tyler (O)	(4315 ACF)	Betemit,Wilson	(4103 BCB)	Ackley,Dustin	(2415 AAC)	Lowrie,Jed	(3215 FDF)
	Mayberry,John (O)	(4213 ACC)	Chisenhall,Lonnie	(3225 CCA)	Roberts,Ryan (3)	(2203 ABD)	Peralta,Jhonny	(3015 AAD)
	Berkman,Lance	(4123 FCF)	Johnson,Chris	(3215 ACD)	Weeks,Jemile	(1505 ACD)	Hardy,J.J.	(2115 BBC)
	Howard,Ryan	(4115 DBC)	Moustakas,Mike	(3115 ABC)	**Barney,Darwin**	**(1325 ABB)**	Nunez,Eduardo	(1513 ADB)
	Moreland,Mitch	(4025 BCB)	Pacheco,Jordan (1)	(2245 ADF)	**Giavotella,Johnny**	**(1223 ABA)**	Cabrera,Everth	(1505 BDB)
	Parmelee,Chris	(4025 ACC)	Donaldson,Josh	(2115 ACB)			Bloomquist,Willie	(1423 CDA)
	Smoak,Justin	**(3205 ABB)**	Ciriaco,Pedro	(1515 ADC)			Furcal,Rafael	(1225 FCD)
	Lind,Adam	**(3115 BBB)**	Callaspo,Alberto	(1125 ABC)			Escobar,Yunel	(1225 AAD)
	Wallace,Brett	(3005 ACB)					Tejada,Ruben	(0215 BCB)
	Lee,Carlos	(2025 BAC)						
	Loney,James	(1035 AAC)						
Bench	Olt,Mike	(4303 AFF)	**Liddi,Alex**	**(4203 ABA)**	Greene,Tyler (S)	(3501 ADB)	Greene,Tyler (2)	(3501 ADB)
	Moss,Brandon	(4013 ACC)	Francisco,Juan	(4013 ADA)	Profar,Jurickson	(3421 AFF)	Drew,Stephen	(3215 FCC)
	Pena,Carlos	(4005 BAD)	Sizemore,Scott	(3303 FDB)	Nelson,Chris (3)	(3223 DDC)	Dozier,Brian	(2413 AFC)
	Gamel,Mat	(3213 FDB)	Rolen,Scott	(3123 FCD)	Hudson,Orlando (3)	(2421 CCB)	Rodriguez,Sean (23)	(2301 ACB)
	Gomez,Mauro	**(3203 ABB)**	Chavez,Eric	(3013 FFC)	Forsythe,Logan	(2403 CDB)	Simmons,Andrelton	(1525 CFF)
	Sanchez,Gaby	(3113 ABC)	Carpenter,Matt (1)	(2123 BCD)	**Beckham,Gordon**	**(2115 ABB)**	Arias,Joaquin (3)	(1523 AFD)
	Adams,Matt	(3103 ADC)	Wheeler,Ryan	(2123 ADA)	Casilla,Alexi	(1423 CDB)	Lillibridge,Brent (1O)	(1501 AFF)
	Carp,Mike (O)	(3013 DDF)	**Wigginton,Ty (1)**	**(2113 ABA)**	Lombardozzi,Steve (O)	(1423 ADB)	Pastornicky,Tyler	(1431 ADB)
	Helton,Todd	(2111 FCD)	Hechavarria,Adeiny	(1305 ACB)	LeMahieu,DJ	(1421 ADB)	Izturis,Maicer (23)	(1321 CDB)
	Huff,Aubrey	(2023 DCF)	Dobbs,Greg (O)	(1123 ADB)	Amarista,Alexi (O)	(1413 ADB)	**Pennington,Cliff (2)**	**(1303 ABB)**
	Kotchman,Casey	(1125 ABF)			Punto,Nick (3)	(1311 FFC)	Aviles,Mike	(1213 CCA)
					Pennington,Cliff (S)	**(1303 ABB)**	Crawford,Brandon	(1115 ADC)
					Ellis,Mark	(1213 DBC)	Gordon,Dee	(0513 CCC)
					Keppinger,Jeff (1S)	(1133 DCD)	**Carroll,Jamey (23)**	**(0323 ABA)**
					Turner,Justin	(1131 ADA)		
					Hairston,Jerry (3)	(1123 DCB)		
					Schumaker,Skip	(1123 CCA)		
					Getz,Chris	(0423 DDA)		
					Theriot,Ryan	**(0321 ABA)**		
Fringe	Gomes,Yan	(4201 AFC)	Moore,Scott	(4111 ADB)	Raburn,Ryan (O)	(3201 BDD)	Ransom,Cody (3)	(4101 ADA)
	LaHair,Bryan (O)	(4101 ACB)	Stewart,Ian	(4103 FDC)	Flaherty,Ryan	(3101 AFB)	Johnson,Elliot	(2401 ADC)
	Cooper,David	(4031 BCB)	Murphy,Donnie	(3201 DFF)	Betancourt,Yuniesky	(2021 BCA)	Cedeno,Ronny (2)	(2111 CCA)
	Baker,Jeff (O)	(3321 BFB)	Nix,Jayson	(3201 ADC)	Solano,Donovan	(1413 ADB)	Harrison,Josh (2)	(1411 BCA)
	Pill,Brett	(3121 ACA)	Inge,Brandon	(3001 DCC)	Roberts,Brian	(1301 FFD)	**Ryan,Brendan**	**(1403 ABB)**
	Ishikawa,Travis	(3111 AFF)	Donald,Jason	(2311 ADB)	Galvis,Freddy	(1211 DCB)	Izturis,Cesar	(1331 FFC)
	Overbay,Lyle	(3111 ACB)	Lopez,Jose	(2111 ACA)	Andino,Robert	(1203 ABC)	Descalso,Daniel (23)	(1313 ACB)
	Downs,Matt	(3101 AFF)	Vitters,Josh	(2103 ACB)	Rhymes,Will	(0311 ACB)	Iglesias,Jose	(1301 ADB)
	Hinske,Eric	(3001 AFC)	Dominguez,Matt	(2025 ACA)	Burriss,Emmanuel	(0301 AFA)	Sogard,Eric	(1211 BDA)
	Rivera,Juan (O)	(2021 FCA)	McGehee,Casey (1)	(2011 ABC)			Santiago,Ramon (2)	(1201 ADC)
	LaPorta,Matt	(2003 AFC)	Valencia,Danny	(2011 ABC)			Florimon Jr.,Pedro	(1201 ADC)
	Cairo,Miguel	(1311 BFD)	Uribe,Juan	(2001 DDC)			Parrino,Andy	(1201 ADA)
	Barton,Daric	(1201 BCD)	Hannahan,Jack	(2001 ADC)			Gonzalez,Marwin	(1121 BDA)
			Valbuena,Luis	(2001 ACA)			**Barmes,Clint**	**(1103 BBB)**
			Herrera,Elian (O)	(1311 ACB)			Janish,Paul	(1101 ADC)
			Kennedy,Adam	(1211 BDB)			McDonald,John	(1011 CFC)
			Frandsen,Kevin	(1121 BDB)			Quintanilla,Omar (2)	(1001 AFB)
			Castellanos,Nick	(1101 AFF)			Cruz,Luis (3)	(1001 ACB)
			Escobar,Eduardo	(0401 ADA)			Kawasaki,Munenori	(0431 ACC)
			Polanco,Placido	(0223 DBB)			Valdez,Wilson (2)	(0221 ADC)
							Herrera,Jonathan	(0211 CDA)

Universal Draft Grid

TIER	CATCHER		DH		OUTFIELD			
Elite					Trout,Mike	(4525 ADF)	Kemp,Matt	(4335 BAF)
					Braun,Ryan	(4445 AAC)	**Gonzalez,Carlos**	**(4335 AAB)**
					McCutchen,Andrew	(4435 AAC)		
Gold					Hamilton,Josh	(5235 BAD)	Crawford,Carl	(3535 FCF)
					Bruce,Jay	**(5225 AAB)**	Rios,Alex	(3435 AAF)
					Stanton,Giancarlo	**(5135 BBB)**	Pence,Hunter	(3325 AAF)
					Upton,B.J.	**(4515 AAA)**	**Markakis,Nick**	**(3245 BAB)**
					Harper,Bryce	(4435 AFC)	Aoki,Norichika	(2545 ABF)
					Upton,Justin	(4425 AAC)	Crisp,Coco	(2535 FCC)
					Cespedes,Yoenis	(4335 ACB)	Pagan,Angel	(2525 DAC)
					Jones,Adam	**(4335 AAA)**	Victorino,Shane	(2525 BAD)
					Heyward,Jason	(4325 AAD)	Ellsbury,Jacoby	(2435 FCF)
					Choo,Shin-Soo	(4225 CAD)	**Bourn,Michael**	**(1515 AAA)**
					Holliday,Matt	**(4135 AAA)**	Revere,Ben	(0535 ACA)
Stars	**Wieters,Matt**	**(4125 ABB)**	Ortiz,David	(4045 DBC)	Granderson,Curtis	(5315 AAC)	De Aza,Alejandro	(3425 ACB)
	Posey,Buster (1)	(3135 DCF)			Willingham,Josh	(5125 CBC)	Murphy,David	(3335 AAD)
	Molina,Yadier	(2145 ABD)			Fowler,Dexter	(4525 BBC)	**Jennings,Desmond**	**(2515 ABB)**
	Mauer,Joe (1)	(1145 CBF)			Bautista,Jose	(4225 CAF)	**Maybin,Cameron**	**(2515 ABB)**
					Beltran,Carlos	(4135 DBD)	Davis,Rajai	(2513 BBC)
					Cruz,Nelson	(4135 CBC)	Cabrera,Melky	(2435 AAD)
					Gordon,Alex	(4125 BAD)	Suzuki,Ichiro	(1535 AAC)
					Morse,Michael	(4025 FCC)	Gardner,Brett	(1515 FCB)
					Jackson,Austin	(3515 AAD)	Bonifacio,Emilio	(0505 DCD)
					Gomez,Carlos	(3505 CDB)		
Regulars	Napoli,Mike (1)	(5123 CCF)	Martinez,Victor	(2235 FCA)	Werth,Jayson	(4415 DBF)	**Ethier,Andre**	**(3135 BAA)**
	Santana,Carlos (1)	**(4125 ABB)**			Maxwell,Justin	(4405 BDC)	Viciedo,Dayan	(3025 ACB)
	Lucroy,Jonathan	(3335 CCD)			Ruggiano,Justin	(4315 ADC)	Cain,Lorenzo	(2515 CDB)
	Ruiz,Carlos	(3145 CCF)			**Reddick,Josh**	**(4315 ABB)**	Eaton,Adam	(2435 AFD)
	Montero,Jesus	**(3035 ABB)**			**Soriano,Alfonso**	**(4225 BBB)**	Dirks,Andy	(2425 CCC)
	Montero,Miguel	**(3015 BBA)**			**Ross,Cody**	**(4115 BBB)**	**Hunter,Torii**	**(2115 AAB)**
	Perez,Salvador	(2055 CFC)			**Trumbo,Mark**	**(4115 ABB)**	**Young,Delmon**	**(2025 BBB)**
					Quentin,Carlos	(4035 DCA)	Young Jr.,Eric	(1513 DDD)
					Ludwick,Ryan	(4025 BBD)	Dyson,Jarrod	(1503 ADB)
					Kubel,Jason	**(4025 BBB)**	Span,Denard	(1435 DBB)
					Marte,Starling	(3525 ADB)	Jay,Jon	(1335 BCA)
					Venable,Will	(3515 ACB)	**Brantley,Michael**	**(1235 ABB)**
					Stubbs,Drew	(3505 AAC)	**Pierre,Juan**	**(0533 AAB)**
Mid-Level	Rosario,Wilin	(4115 ACF)	Scott,Luke	(4125 FCD)	Heisey,Chris	(4413 ADC)	Myers,Wil	(3203 ADF)
	Arencibia,J.P.	(4105 BCA)			Saunders,Michael	(4405 ACC)	Snider,Travis	(3115 BDC)
	Saltalamacchia,Jarrod	(4015 ACA)			Reimold,Nolan	(4323 FDF)	Bourjos,Peter	(2505 ACC)
	McCann,Brian	**(3113 ABB)**			**Ibanez,Raul**	**(4233 ABB)**	Denorfia,Chris	(2433 BDB)
	Doumit,Ryan	(3025 DCB)			**Young,Chris**	**(4215 BAA)**	Parra,Gerardo	(2323 ACC)
	Martin,Russell	(3025 BCA)			Hairston,Scott	(4213 CDB)	Valdespin,Jordany	(2303 ADB)
	Grandal,Yasmani	(3015 AFC)			Gomes,Jonny	(4203 ACC)	DeJesus,David	(2225 BBD)
	Ramos,Wilson	(3013 FDC)			Joyce,Matt	(4115 CCC)	Brown,Domonic	(2115 ADB)
	Jaso,John	(2233 BDF)			Taveras,Oscar	(3331 AFF)	Gose,Anthony	(1503 ADB)
	Pierzynski,A.J.	**(2025 ABB)**			Martin,Leonys	(3253 AFD)	Bernadina,Roger	(1411 CDD)
					Boesch,Brennan	(3215 ABC)	Campana,Tony	(0511 ADB)
					Rasmus,Colby	(3205 AAC)		
Bench	Flowers,Tyler	(5101 AFC)	Hafner,Travis	(3013 DCA)	Jackson,Brett	(4403 ACA)	Schierholtz,Nate	(2223 BDB)
	D Arnaud,Travis	(4121 AFB)			Moore,Tyler	(4311 ADD)	Diaz,Matt	(2221 FFB)
	Avila,Alex	(4113 ACF)			Wells,Casper	(4303 ADC)	Baxter,Mike	(2203 FFD)
	Kottaras,George	(4011 AFA)			Smith,Seth	(4223 ACC)	Sierra,Moises	(2103 ADA)
	Soto,Geovany	(3113 DCD)			**Thames,Eric**	**(4213 ABB)**	Martinez,J.D.	(2015 ADC)
	Olivo,Miguel	(3103 BCC)			Guzman,Jesus	(4123 ACA)	Morgan,Nyjer	(1513 CCF)
	Lavarnway,Ryan	(3103 ADC)			Martinez,Fernando	(4005 ADB)	Gentry,Craig	(1513 AFB)
	Mesoraco,Devin	(3013 ADC)			Sizemore,Grady	(4003 FFC)	Mastroianni,Darin	(1511 ACC)
	Castillo,Welington	(3003 CFB)			Wise,DeWayne	(3401 BFC)	Blanco,Gregor	(1503 ADD)
	Iannetta,Chris	(3003 CDB)			Wells,Vernon	(3223 DBC)	Berry,Quintin	(1501 ACB)
	Castro,Jason	(2123 FFD)			Francoeur,Jeff	(3213 AAD)	Carrera,Ezequiel	(1413 ACA)
	Brantly,Rob	(2023 AFF)			Duda,Lucas	(3103 ACD)	Torres,Andres	(1403 DCC)
	Ellis,A.J.	(2005 ADC)			Presley,Alex	(2433 BCB)	Paredes,Jimmy	(1403 ADA)
	Suzuki,Kurt	**(1113 ABA)**			McLouth,Nate	(2315 DDA)	Tabata,Jose	(1333 BCB)
	Hanigan,Ryan	(0215 BDA)			Bay,Jason	(2303 FCC)	Kalish,Ryan	(1303 AFF)
					Gutierrez,Franklin	(2303 FCC)	Garcia,Avisail	(1301 AFF)
					Johnson,Reed	(2223 CFD)	Sweeney,Ryan	(1111 FDA)
Fringe	Shoppach,Kelly	(4301 BFC)	Thome,Jim	(4101 FDF)	Ankiel,Rick	(4101 DDA)	Schafer,Jordan	(1501 BDC)
	Kratz,Erik	(4011 AFB)			Jones,Andruw	(4101 ADD)	Robinson,Shane	(1501 AFB)
	McKenry,Michael	(4003 ADC)			Nix,Laynce	(4011 DFB)	**Damon,Johnny**	**(1411 ABB)**
	Ross,David	(4001 AFB)			Duncan,Shelley	(4001 ADA)	Podsednik,Scott	(1401 BDC)
	Norris,Derek	(3303 AFB)			Darnell,James	(3201 FDB)	Hernandez,Gorkys	(1401 ACA)
	Barajas,Rod	(3103 BDB)			Sutton,Drew	(3101 AFD)	Chavez,Endy	(1321 CFF)
	Buck,John	(3003 ACC)			Canzler,Russ	(3101 ACC)	Blackmon,Charlie	(1311 FDB)
	Maldonado,Martin	(3001 ADA)			Francisco,Ben	(2211 BFB)	Cowgill,Collin	(1311 ACC)
	Molina,Jose	(2111 BFC)			**Abreu,Bobby**	**(2211 ABB)**	Bogusevic,Brian	(1301 ACB)
	Conger,Hank	(2101 ADA)			Nieuwenhuis,Kirk	(2201 ACB)	Mather,Joe	(1201 ACA)
	Hernandez,Ramon	(2021 DDC)			Robinson,Trayvon	(2201 ACB)	Petersen,Bryan	(1201 ACF)
	Hundley,Nick	(2003 FDF)			Nady,Xavier	(2200 FFB)	Kotsay,Mark	(1021 CDB)
	Snyder,Chris	(2001 FFD)			Nava,Daniel	(2103 BCB)	Gwynn,Tony	(0401 ADC)
	Flores,Jesus	(2001 AFA)			Pearce,Steve	(2101 FFF)	Figgins,Chone	(0301 BCC)
	Thole,Josh	(1013 ADB)			Kearns,Austin	(2001 CDF)	Kelly,Don	(0300 AFB)

Universal Draft Grid

TIER	STARTING PITCHERS				RELIEF PITCHERS			
Elite	Kershaw,Clayton	(4505 AAA)						
	Verlander,Justin	(4405 AAA)						
Gold	Strasburg,Stephen	(5505 FCA)	Price,David	(4405 AAA)	Motte,Jason	(5531 ABA)		
	Lee,Cliff	(5405 BAA)	Cain,Matt	(3305 AAA)	Chapman,Aroldis	(5530 BCB)		
	Hamels,Cole	(4405 AAA)	Weaver,Jered	(3305 AAA)	Kimbrel,Craig	(5530 ABB)		
Stars	Sale,Chris	(4505 ABA)	Medlen,Kris	(4305 FCA)	Putz,J.J.	(5530 DBA)	Storen,Drew	(4331 DCA)
	Darvish,Yu	(4505 AAC)	Bumgarner,Madison	(4305 AAB)	Jansen,Kenley	(5530 BCB)	Soriano,Rafael	(3531 DBA)
	Scherzer,Max	(4505 AAA)	Gonzalez,Gio	(3405 AAA)	Papelbon,Jonathan	(5530 BAA)		
	Wainwright,Adam	(4405 FAA)	Latos,Mat	(3405 AAA)	Axford,John	(4531 AAA)		
	Greinke,Zack	(4405 AAB)	Zimmermann,Jordan	(3305 DBA)	Janssen,Casey	(4430 DCA)		
	Hernandez,Felix	(4405 AAA)	Dickey,R.A.	(3305 AAB)	Rodney,Fernando	(4430 BBD)		
	Shields,James	(4405 AAA)	Cueto,Johnny	(3205 BAA)				
Regulars	Gallardo,Yovani	(4505 BAA)			Nathan,Joe	(5530 FCC)	Perkins,Glen	(4430 ACD)
	Sabathia,CC	(4405 AAA)			Street,Huston	(5530 FBA)	Cook,Ryan	(4421 ADC)
	Halladay,Roy	(4303 CAA)			Romo,Sergio	(5530 BCB)	Hanrahan,Joel	(3531 ABB)
	Morrow,Brandon	(3505 DAA)			Lopez,Wilton	(5330 BCA)	Balfour,Grant	(3530 BCA)
	Moore,Matt	(3505 ACF)			Cishek,Steve	(4531 ADB)	Betancourt,Rafael	(3430 BCB)
	Peavy,Jake	(3305 FBB)			Holland,Greg	(4530 ADD)	Perez,Chris	(3430 ABB)
	Kuroda,Hiroki	(3205 BAA)			Frieri,Ernesto	(4530 ACD)	League,Brandon	(3231 ABB)
Mid-Level	Johnson,Josh	(4403 FAA)	Lester,Jon	(3305 AAA)	Soria,Joakim	(4530 FCA)		
	Anderson,Brett	(4203 FCA)	Fister,Doug	(3205 CAA)	Reed,Addison	(4530 ADF)		
	Lincecum,Tim	(3505 AAA)	Cahill,Trevor	(3205 CAA)	Gregerson,Luke	(4421 BCC)		
	Garza,Matt	(3405 CAB)	Iwakuma,Hisashi	(3203 AAA)	Parnell,Bobby	(4421 BCA)		
	Sanchez,Anibal	(3405 CAA)	Hudson,Tim	(3105 DAA)	Rivera,Mariano	(4330 FBA)		
	Dempster,Ryan	(3405 BAA)	Holland,Derek	(2305 CAA)	Clippard,Tyler	(3521 ABB)		
	Samardzija,Jeff	(3405 ABB)	Minor,Mike	(2305 ABB)	Marmol,Carlos	(3520 AAB)		
	Smyly,Drew	(3403 BFF)	Niemann,Jeff	(2303 FBA)	Wilson,Brian	(3420 FBF)		
	Ogando,Alexi	(3403 BCC)	Lilly,Ted	(2303 FAA)	Wilson,C.J.	(3305 AAB)		
	Fiers,Mike	(3403 ADC)	Marcum,Shaun	(2303 FAA)	Bailey,Andrew	(2430 FCB)		
	Bailey,Homer	(3305 DBA)	Buchholz,Clay	(2205 FAA)	Valverde,Jose	(1230 AAB)		
	Niese,Jon	(3305 CAA)	Miley,Wade	(2205 ACA)				
	Rodriguez,Wandy	(3305 BAA)	Hellickson,Jeremy	(2205 AAB)				
	Milone,Tommy	(3305 ABB)	Lohse,Kyle	(2105 CAC)				
	Kennedy,Ian	(3305 AAB)	Harrison,Matt	(2105 CAB)				
	Haren,Dan	(3305 AAA)						
Bench	Beachy,Brandon	(4501 FCA)	Villanueva,Carlos	(2403 ACB)	Robertson,David	(5520 BCB)		
	Cobb,Alex	(4303 BDB)	Floyd,Gavin	(2305 BAA)	Mcgee,Jake	(5510 ADD)		
	Bauer,Trevor	(3501 ADF)	Vogelsong,Ryan	(2305 ABC)	Marshall,Sean	(5510 ACA)		
	Hanson,Tommy	(3403 CAB)	McDonald,James	(2305 ABB)	Herrera,Kelvin	(5411 ADC)		
	Lynn,Lance	(3403 BCA)	Santana,Johan	(2303 FBA)	Brothers,Rex	(4520 ADA)		
	Harvey,Matt	(3403 ADA)	Hughes,Phil	(2303 CAB)	Benoit,Joaquin	(4511 DCA)		
	Rosenthal,Trevor	(3401 AFF)	Worley,Vance	(2303 BCB)	Santos,Sergio	(4510 FCF)		
	Miller,Shelby	(3401 ADF)	Tillman,Chris	(2303 ACD)	Pestano,Vinnie	(4510 ADA)		
	Blanton,Joe	(3305 FBA)	Collmenter,Josh	(2301 ACA)	Hernandez,David	(4510 ACB)		
	Burnett,A.J.	(3305 AAA)	Danks,John	(2205 FAB)	Peralta,Joel	(4510 ACB)		
	Capuano,Chris	(3305 AAA)	Maholm,Paul	(2205 BAA)	Fujikawa,Kyuji	(4501 ABF)		
	Jackson,Edwin	(3305 AAA)	Parker,Jarrod	(2205 ADA)	Davis,Wade	(4501 AAB)		
	Gee,Dillon	(3303 CBB)	McAllister,Zach	(2205 ACB)	Madson,Ryan	(4420 FCA)		
	Garcia,Jaime	(3303 CBA)	Harrell,Lucas	(2205 ABC)	Broxton,Jonathan	(4420 DCD)		
	Hammel,Jason	(3303 CAC)	Chen,Wei-Yin	(2205 AAC)	O Day,Darren	(4400 CDF)		
	Beckett,Josh	(3303 CAB)	Santana,Ervin	(2205 AAA)	Oliver,Darren	(4400 ACA)		
	Luebke,Cory	(3301 FCB)	Griffin,A.J.	(2203 ADF)	Belisario,Ronald	(4311 ADB)		
	Lewis,Colby	(3301 DAA)	Eovaldi,Nathan	(2203 ADD)	O Flaherty,Eric	(4310 ADA)		
	Nolasco,Ricky	(3205 AAA)	Arroyo,Bronson	(2105 AAA)	Mujica,Edward	(4310 ACA)		
	Carpenter,Chris	(3203 FAA)	Buehrle,Mark	(2105 AAA)	Francisco,Frank	(3521 DCB)		
	Ramirez,Erasmo	(3203 CDC)	Leake,Mike	(2105 AAA)	Estrada,Marco	(3403 BCA)		
	Myers,Brett	(3203 BAA)	Karstens,Jeff	(2103 CCC)	Bell,Heath	(3321 AAB)		
	Pettitte,Andy	(3201 FCB)	Kendrick,Kyle	(2103 AAA)	Burton,Jared	(3310 DDF)		
	Happ,J.A.	(2405 CCB)	Cloyd,Tyler	(1201 ADA)	Casilla,Santiago	(3310 CCA)		
	Norris,Bud	(2405 BAA)	Vargas,Jason	(1105 BAA)	Aceves,Alfredo	(2311 DCB)		
	Straily,Dan	(2403 ADF)	Beavan,Blake	(1003 ACA)				
Fringe	de la Rosa,Jorge	(3401 FCC)	McPherson,Kyle	(2201 ADB)	Uehara,Koji	(5500 FDA)	Veras,Jose	(3500 ADA)
	De La Rosa,Rubby	(3401 BFF)	Westbrook,Jake	(2105 DAA)	Venters,Jonny	(5500 ACA)	Farnsworth,Kyle	(3410 DCB)
	Thornburg,Tyler	(3401 AFF)	Hendriks,Liam	(2103 ADB)	Walden,Jordan	(4510 BCB)	Crow,Aaron	(3410 ADC)
	Corbin,Patrick	(3303 ADA)	Diamond,Scott	(2103 ACD)	Doolittle,Sean	(4510 AFF)	Strop,Pedro	(3410 ADA)
	Baker,Scott	(3301 FBA)	McCarthy,Brandon	(2101 FCC)	Grilli,Jason	(4510 ADB)	Howell,J.P.	(3400 FDA)
	Oswalt,Roy	(3301 CBD)	Richard,Clayton	(2005 CAA)	Thatcher,Joe	(4500 FDD)	Adams,Mike	(3400 CCB)
	Billingsley,Chad	(3301 BAA)	Pavano,Carl	(2003 FAA)	Alburquerque,Al	(4500 FDC)	Watson,Tony	(3400 ADA)
	Masterson,Justin	(3205 AAA)	Alvarez,Henderson	(2003 ACD)	Chamberlain,Joba	(4500 FDB)	Breslow,Craig	(3400 BDD)
	Volquez,Edinson	(2405 DCB)	Rogers,Mark	(1301 ADF)	Dotel,Octavio	(4500 BCA)	Lecure,Sam	(3400 ACB)
	Doubront,Felix	(2403 ACC)	Chacin,Jhoulys	(1203 DCC)	Capps,Carter	(4500 AFF)	Lincoln,Brad	(3400 ACB)
	Duffy,Danny	(2401 FDB)	Chen,Bruce	(1203 DBA)	Brach,Brad	(4500 ADC)	Salas,Fernando	(3400 ACA)
	Archer,Chris	(2401 ADD)	Harang,Aaron	(1203 DAB)	Delabar,Steve	(4500 ADB)	Takahashi,Hisanori	(3400 ACA)
	Skaggs,Tyler	(2401 ADC)	Gonzalez,Miguel	(1203 ADF)	Bastardo,Antonio	(4500 ADA)	Belisle,Matt	(3311 ACA)
	Jimenez,Ubaldo	(2305 AAB)	Wood,Travis	(1203 ACC)	Tazawa,Junichi	(4410 FFD)	Kontos,George	(3310 ADD)
	Peralta,Wily	(2303 ADD)	LeBlanc,Wade	(1201 ACB)	Affeldt,Jeremy	(4410 BCA)	Wright,Wesley	(3310 ADD)
	Pineda,Michael	(2301 FCB)	Guthrie,Jeremy	(1105 BAA)	Melancon,Mark	(4410 ACC)	Martinez,Cristhian	(3301 ADB)
	Wheeler,Zack	(2301 AFF)	Zito,Barry	(1103 DBB)	Thornton,Matt	(4410 ACA)	Lindstrom,Matt	(3300 DCA)
	Phelps,David	(2301 ADF)	Detwiler,Ross	(1103 CCB)	Furbush,Charlie	(4400 BDD)	Rzepczynski,Marc	(3300 ADD)
	Wieland,Joe	(2300 FFD)	Correia,Kevin	(1103 BAA)	Burnett,Sean	(4311 ACC)	Scribner,Evan	(3300 ADB)
	Hudson,Daniel	(2300 FBA)	Quintana,Jose	(1103 ADF)	Cashner,Andrew	(4301 FDA)	Lopez,Javier	(3210 ADA)
	Lackey,John	(2205 FBA)	Turner,Jacob	(1103 ADF)	Ross,Robbie	(4300 ADA)	Boggs,Mitchell	(3210 ACA)
	Odorizzi,Jake	(2203 ADB)	Saunders,Joe	(1103 AAA)	Loe,Kameron	(4210 ACC)	Atchison,Scott	(3200 CDA)
	Nova,Ivan	(2203 ABA)	Johnson,Steve	(0301 ADC)	Ziegler,Brad	(4100 ACB)	Patton,Troy	(3200 BDC)
	Carrasco,Carlos	(2201 CCA)	Young,Chris	(0203 FDB)	Crain,Jesse	(3510 CCA)	Badenhop,Burke	(3200 BDA)
	Bass,Anthony	(2201 CDC)			Rodriguez,Francisco	(3510 BBA)	Smith,Joe	(3200 BDA)
	Kelly,Joe	(2201 ADB)			Frasor,Jason	(3500 BDA)	Hughes,Jared	(3110 ADB)
					Collins,Tim	(3500 ADF)	Pryor,Stephen	(2500 AFF)
					Logan,Boone	(3500 ADA)	Norberto,Jordan	(2410 CDA)

Universal Draft Grid

TIER	STARTING PITCHERS				RELIEF PITCHERS			
Fringe (cont'd)					Kelley,Shawn	(2400 FDC)	Stauffer,Tim	(2201 FCB)
					Arredondo,Jose	(2400 BDB)	Rauch,Jon	(2201 BCA)
					Lindblom,Josh	(2400 ADF)	Avilan,Luis	(2200 ADC)
					Jones,Nate	(2400 ADB)	Russell,James	(2200 ACA)
					Santiago,Hector	(2400 ADA)	Capps,Matt	(2110 DBA)
					Sipp,Tony	(2400 ACA)	Ayala,Luis	(2101 BDD)
					Jepsen,Kevin	(2310 ADF)	Mattheus,Ryan	(2101 BDD)
					Gorzelanny,Tom	**(2301 BBA)**	Morales,Franklin	(1401 DDA)
					Lyon,Brandon	(2300 FCD)	Bundy,Dylan	(1201 AFF)
					Albers,Matt	(2300 BCA)	Fien,Casey	(1200 ADF)
					Blevins,Jerry	(2300 ADB)	Stults,Eric	(1101 BDF)
					Thayer,Dale	(2210 ADD)	Teaford,Everett	(1101 ADB)
Below Fringe	Nicasio,Juan	(3403 FDA)	Teheran,Julio	(1200 ADC)	Choate,Randy	(4400 BDB)	Cruz,Juan	(1400 BDA)
	Bedard,Erik	(3400 FCB)	White,Alex	(1103 CDB)	Aumont,Phillippe	(3510 AFD)	Villarreal,Brayan	(1400 ADD)
	Werner,Andrew	(3301 ADF)	Richards,Garrett	(1103 ADB)	Gonzalez,Michael	(3500 CDA)	Kirkman,Michael	(1400 ADC)
	Kelly,Casey	(3301 ADC)	Gomez,Jeanmar	(1103 ACC)	Padilla,Vicente	(3400 FDA)	Torres,Alexander	(1400 ADC)
	Hutchison,Drew	(3300 DFF)	Millwood,Kevin	(1101 BBC)	Rogers,Esmil	(3400 CDF)	Bard,Daniel	(1310 ACD)
	Liriano,Francisco	**(2403 BAB)**	**Colon,Bartolo**	**(1101 BBA)**	Valdes,Raul	(3400 CDF)	Gaudin,Chad	(1300 FDD)
	Paulino,Felipe	(2401 FCA)	Smith,Will	(1101 ADD)	Rapada,Clay	(3400 ADF)	Feliz,Neftali	(1300 FBB)
	Pomeranz,Drew	(2303 ADF)	Perez,Martin	(1101 ADB)	Reynolds,Matt	(3400 ADA)	Hensley,Clay	(1300 DCB)
	Delgado,Randall	(2301 ADB)	Volstad,Chris	(1101 ACB)	Webb,Ryan	(3201 BDA)	Fuentes,Brian	(1300 DCA)
	Cole,Gerrit	(2300 AFF)	**Hernandez,Roberto**	**(1101 ABB)**	Downs,Scott	(3200 CCA)	Ramirez,Ramon	(1300 BCC)
	Hochevar,Luke	**(2205 BAA)**	Drabek,Kyle	(1100 DCF)	Eppley,Cody	(3200 ADC)	Miller,Jim	(1300 ADD)
	Britton,Zach	(2203 CDA)	Hefner,Jeremy	(1100 ADA)	Wright,Jamey	(3200 ACA)	Bowden,Michael	(1300 ADB)
	Friedrich,Christian	(2201 CDB)	Keuchel,Dallas	(1003 ADA)	Rodriguez,Henry	(2500 DDC)	Cedeno,Xavier	(1300 ADB)
	Garcia,Freddy	**(2201 ABA)**	Mendoza,Luis	(1003 ACC)	Miller,Andrew	(2500 BDF)	Isringhausen,Jason	(1300 ADA)
	Porcello,Rick	**(2105 AAA)**	Hunter,Tommy	(1001 CDB)	Diekman,Jake	(2500 AFA)	Deduno,Samuel	(1203 ADA)
	Francis,Jeff	(2103 FBB)	Lannan,John	(1001 ABC)	Coleman,Louis	(2500 ADB)	Ross,Tyson	(1201 BDB)
	Marquis,Jason	(2101 FCB)	Wang,Chien-Ming	(1000 FDF)	Vizcaino,Arodys	(2410 FFF)	Humber,Philip	(1201 BBC)
	Pelfrey,Mike	(2101 FBB)	Hultzen,Danny	(0401 AFF)	Luetge,Lucas	(2410 ADC)	**Zambrano,Carlos**	**(1201 BBA)**
	Feldman,Scott	(2101 DCA)	Sanchez,Jonathan	(0301 FBC)	Coke,Phil	(2410 ACA)	Blackley,Travis	(1201 ADD)
	Williams,Jerome	(2101 BCC)	Matsuzaka,Daisuke	(0201 FDC)	Elbert,Scott	(2400 CDB)	Noesi,Hector	(1201 ADA)
	Kluber,Corey	(1303 ACB)	Moscoso,Guillermo	(0200 ADF)	Rodriguez,Fernando	(2400 ADD)	Matusz,Brian	(1200 BCF)
	Arrieta,Jake	(1301 BCA)	Chatwood,Tyler	(0101 ADB)	Familia,Jeurys	(2310 ADB)	Dillard,Tim	(1200 ADF)
	Romero,Ricky	**(1203 AAB)**	Cook,Aaron	(0001 FCB)	Ottavino,Adam	(2301 ADB)	Dolis,Rafael	(1200 ADF)
	Walters,P.J.	(1201 CDB)	Jurrjens,Jair	(0001 FBC)	Lowe,Mark	(2300 FDB)	Mortensen,Clayton	(1200 ADF)
	Cecil,Brett	**(1201 ABA)**	Blackburn,Nick	(0001 BCD)	Abad,Fernando	(2300 DDC)	Axelrod,Dylan	(1200 ADD)
					Guerra,Javy	(2300 CDF)	Cruz,Rhiner	(1200 ADD)
					Durbin,Chad	(2300 BCA)	Marte,Victor	(1200 ADD)
					Scheppers,Tanner	(2300 AFC)	Layne,Tom	(1200 ADB)
					Acosta,Manny	(2300 ADA)	Torres,Carlos	(1200 ADA)
					Stammen,Craig	(2300 ACD)	DeVries,Cole	(1103 ADC)
					Simon,Alfredo	(2200 DDB)	Roenicke,Josh	(1101 ADA)
					Shaw,Bryan	(2200 ADC)	**Hernandez,Livan**	**(1101 AAA)**
					Resop,Chris	(2200 ACB)	Carpenter,David	(1100 AFF)
					Qualls,Chad	(2100 BCA)	Adcock,Nathan	(1100 ADB)
					Mejia,Jenrry	(2100 ADF)	Burnett,Alex	(1100 ADB)
					Germano,Justin	(2100 ADB)	Corpas,Manuel	(1100 ADB)
					Camp,Shawn	(2100 ACA)	**Lowe,Derek**	**(1100 AAB)**
					Duensing,Brian	**(2100 ABA)**	Ondrusek,Logan	(0200 ADB)
					Hawkins,LaTroy	(2000 FDA)	Swarzak,Anthony	(0100 BCC)
					Dunn,Mike	(1500 ADC)	Accardo,Jeremy	(0100 ADB)
					Parra,Manny	(1400 FCA)	Laffey,Aaron	(0003 BDA)
					Mijares,Jose	(1400 BDD)	Below,Duane	(0000 ADC)

Rotisserie 500

This is a modified Rotisserie format that incorporates some of the rules variations discussed in the Encyclopedia, and adds a few more. Its intent is to resolve several incongruities in the original game. The format has proven very popular in trial leagues.

1. Stat categories: Roto500 uses a modified 4x4 format. It keeps **HR, SB, Wins, Strikeouts** and **ERA. On base average** replaces batting average as a more accurate measure of that element of skill. **Runs Produced** (R + RBI – HR) combines runs and RBI into one category, thereby reducing the impact of situation-dependent stats (from 40% to 25%). A new relief pitcher stat (**Saves + Holds – Blown Saves**) provides value to more members of the bullpen.

Perhaps the biggest change is the elimination of WHIP. While WHIP is a good category in its own right, few fantasy leaguers use it to manage their pitching staffs. Its elimination allows us to have a single ratio category on each of the batting and pitching sides, and a balance that has always been missing in Rotisserie.

Despite scaling back to eight categories, Roto500 captures just as much performance, if not more. In addition, with fewer moving parts, it becomes easier to manage your roster, which in turn provides more control over running your team.

2. Valuing of players: Within an individual league, there are several different "currencies" that measure the value of a player. For the active roster in an auction league, the currency is a $260 budget. For the reserve roster, the currency is snake picks. For free agents, the currency might be FAAB dollars or first owner to the computer.

Roto500 suggests that we should use a common currency to value and roster players no matter how we acquire them. After all, a player is a player is a player. Dylan Bundy shouldn't be valued using one unit of measure if he's drafted, another if he's a reserve pick and yet another if he's FAABed. There should be a standard, consistent unit of measure used for all players, for every aspect of the game.

In Roto500, that unit of measure is dollars, and this is used for every aspect of player acquisition, all season long. Every owner gets a $500 budget at the beginning of the season. This goes to pay for everything - the draft roster, reserves and free agents acquired during the season.

There is no $260 limit for the draft. This means you have to decide how you are going to budget your money. If you spend $260 on your active roster, that will leave you $240 for reserve

players and free agents. You can opt to stock up with the very best players for your active roster - perhaps $300 worth, or more - but that will limit your options for reserves and free agents. If you excel at in-season management, perhaps you draft a $200 team, or less, and leave yourself with more money during the season. Each owner has to decide how he is going to play it.

3. Selection of players: Roto500 starts as a 12-team mixed league with 23 man active rosters and 17-man reserves. (While this is the recommended player pool, Roto500 can also be played as an AL-only or NL-only league, with a shallower reserve list.)

Each player has a pre-set list price, calculated as the average of his end-of-season values from the past two years (rounded up, if necessary). Seasons in which a player maintained his rookie eligibility are valued at $10. Negative valued years revert to $0, but every player must have a list price for the upcoming season of at least $1. **The following pages contain the Roto500 price list for 2013 drafts.**

The draft is conducted as a standard snake draft. Players are selected one-by-one, but as owners fill their rosters, they use up some portion of their $500 budget. When a player is selected, it is possible for another owner to open an auction in an attempt to purchase that player above list price. Any owner can initiate such an auction by simply announcing a higher bid once that player is selected. At that point, it becomes an open auction for that player. High bid wins that player and the final bid becomes the player's new list price for the season. Getting outbid for a player you selected means that you lose your pick in that round. The only way to mitigate that loss is to win an auction on a player someone else has selected.

Each owner can purchase a maximum of eight players in this fashion, three during the first five rounds and five more during the rest of the draft. During any draft, there would be a maximum of 96 players auctioned off to a dollar amount above list price.

The draft continues for 40 rounds, with the only positional requirement that all 23 active spots have eligible players selected by the end of the draft. Reserve rosters constitute each team's bench as well as its disabled list. In-season free agents are acquired using a traditional FAAB bidding process. Minimum bid is $1; maximum bid is whatever amount keeps an owner under the $500 cap. A player's winning bid becomes his list price for the remainder of the season. Players may be dropped during the season and their salary deducted from the team total, but the sum of all 40 salaries must never exceed $500.

ROTISSERIE 500 — 2013 Draft - List Prices — Batters

BATTERS	'11	'12	R$
Braun,Ryan	40	41	41
Cabrera,Miguel	40	38	39
Fielder,Prince	35	29	32
Kemp,Matt	48	15	32
McCutchen,Andrew	24	36	30
Votto,Joey	35	24	30
Granderson,Curtis	37	21	29
Trout,Mike	10	46	28
Bautista,Jose	44	11	28
Bourn,Michael	25	23	24
Cano,Robinson	22	26	24
Pedroia,Dustin	33	15	24
Gonzalez,Carlos	23	24	24
Reyes,Jose	25	22	24
Hamilton,Josh	17	29	23
Pujols,Albert	27	19	23
Gonzalez,Adrian	32	13	23
Upton,Justin	26	19	23
Zobrist,Ben	22	23	23
Gordon,Alex	26	18	22
Kinsler,Ian	29	15	22
Beltran,Carlos	20	21	21
Holliday,Matt	17	24	21
Ortiz,David	25	16	21
Ellsbury,Jacoby	39	0	20
Encarnacion,Edwin	7	32	20
Headley,Chase	7	32	20
Cabrera,Melky	20	18	19
Konerko,Paul	24	14	19
Beltre,Adrian	15	22	19
Butler,Billy	16	21	19
Ramirez,Aramis	16	21	19
Stanton,Giancarlo	18	19	19
Upton,B.J.	21	16	19
Wright,David	9	28	19
Swisher,Nick	19	17	18
Bruce,Jay	18	17	18
Pence,Hunter	22	11	17
Willingham,Josh	12	21	17
Santana,Carlos	17	14	16
Andrus,Elvis	18	12	15
Victorino,Shane	17	13	15
Crisp,Coco	15	14	15
Jackson,Austin	8	21	15
Jones,Adam	11	18	15
Teixeira,Mark	20	9	15
Berkman,Lance	28	0	14
Castro,Starlin	15	13	14
Hunter,Torii	12	16	14
Jeter,Derek	12	16	14
Cespedes,Yoenis	10	17	14
Hart,Corey	14	13	14
Napoli,Mike	22	5	14
Pagan,Angel	11	16	14
Phillips,Brandon	17	10	14
Posey,Buster	0	27	14
Fowler,Dexter	10	16	13
Harper,Bryce	10	16	13
Aoki,Norichika	10	15	13
Freeman,Freddie	11	14	13
Hill,Aaron	3	22	13
Mauer,Joe	0	25	13
Molina,Yadier	7	18	13
Cabrera,Asdrubal	16	8	12
Montero,Miguel	10	14	12
Tulowitzki,Troy	24	0	12
Young,Michael	22	1	12
Cruz,Nelson	11	11	11
Longoria,Evan	18	4	11
Zimmerman,Ryan	5	17	11
Choo,Shin-Soo	1	20	11
Ethier,Andre	9	12	11
Heyward,Jason	1	20	11
Ramirez,Hanley	6	15	11
Rios,Alex	0	21	11
Uggla,Dan	10	11	11
Adams,Matt	10	10	10
Brantly,Rob	10	10	10
Canzler,Russ	10	10	10
Darnell,James	10	10	10
Dominguez,Matt	10	10	10
Eaton,Adam	10	10	10

BATTERS	'11	'12	R$
Garcia,Avisail	10	10	10
Goldschmidt,Paul	0	20	10
Gomez,Mauro	10	10	10
Hechavarria,Adeiny	10	10	10
Iglesias,Jose	10	10	10
Kawasaki,Munenori	10	10	10
Olt,Mike	10	10	10
Profar,Jurickson	10	10	10
Reynolds,Mark	14	6	10
Rodriguez,Alex	9	11	10
Vitters,Josh	10	10	10
Weeks,Rickie	10	10	10
Wheeler,Ryan	10	10	10
Bonifacio,Emilio	19	0	10
Desmond,Ian	3	16	10
Markakis,Nick	13	6	10
Suzuki,Ichiro	11	8	10
Avila,Alex	17	1	9
Dunn,Adam	0	18	9
Gardner,Brett	18	0	9
Howard,Ryan	18	0	9
Kipnis,Jason	0	18	9
Maybin,Cameron	14	4	9
Pena,Carlos	15	3	9
Pierre,Juan	8	10	9
Stubbs,Drew	15	3	9
Walker,Neil	10	8	9
Jones,Chipper	8	9	9
Joyce,Matt	13	4	9
LaRoche,Adam	0	17	9
Morse,Michael	16	1	9
Murphy,David	3	14	9
Prado,Martin	0	17	9
Trumbo,Mark	7	10	9
Aybar,Erick	11	5	8
Cuddyer,Michael	13	3	8
Francoeur,Jeff	16	0	8
Kendrick,Howie	11	5	8
Lee,Carlos	12	4	8
Scutaro,Marco	5	11	8
Young,Chris	16	0	8
Craig,Allen	1	14	8
Espinosa,Danny	8	7	8
Freese,David	1	14	8
Hosmer,Eric	11	4	8
Revere,Ben	4	11	8
Roberts,Ryan	15	0	8
Sandoval,Pablo	11	4	8
Soriano,Alfonso	2	13	8
Wieters,Matt	7	8	8
Youkilis,Kevin	12	3	8
De Aza,Alejandro	1	13	7
Jennings,Desmond	4	10	7
Altuve,Jose	0	13	7
Kubel,Jason	1	12	7
Werth,Jayson	10	3	7
Abreu,Bobby	12	0	7
Escobar,Alcides	1	11	6
Gomez,Carlos	0	12	6
Helton,Todd	12	0	6
Jones,Garrett	3	9	6
Reddick,Josh	0	12	6
Ruiz,Carlos	2	10	6
Sanchez,Gaby	12	0	6
Venable,Will	4	8	6
Brantley,Michael	3	8	6
Damon,Johnny	11	0	6
Davis,Chris	0	11	6
Davis,Rajai	0	11	6
Parra,Gerardo	8	3	6
Peralta,Jhonny	11	0	6
Smith,Seth	10	1	6
Baxter,Mike	10	0	6
Berry,Quintin	10	0	5
Carter,Chris	10	0	5
Castillo,Welington	10	0	5
Ciriaco,Pedro	10	0	5
Clevenger,Steve	10	0	5
Constanza,Jose	10	0	5
Cooper,David	10	0	5
Cowgill,Collin	10	0	5
Danks,Jordan	10	0	5

BATTERS	'11	'12	R$
Donaldson,Josh	10	0	5
Dozier,Brian	10	0	5
Escobar,Eduardo	10	0	5
Escobar,Yunel	10	0	5
Florimon Jr.,Pedro	10	0	5
Galvis,Freddy	10	0	5
Gomes,Yan	10	0	5
Gonzalez,Marwin	10	0	5
Gose,Anthony	10	0	5
Grandal,Yasmani	10	0	5
Green,Taylor	10	0	5
Hernandez,Gorkys	10	0	5
Herrera,Elian	10	0	5
Jackson,Brett	10	0	5
Jay,Jon	2	8	5
Johnson,Kelly	6	4	5
Kalish,Ryan	10	0	5
Liddi,Alex	10	0	5
Lobaton,Jose	10	0	5
Machado,Manny	10	0	5
Maldonado,Martin	10	0	5
Marte,Starling	10	0	5
Martin,Leonys	10	0	5
Mastroianni,Darin	10	0	5
McCann,Brian	10	0	5
Mesoraco,Devin	10	0	5
Middlebrooks,Will	10	0	5
Montero,Jesus	10	0	5
Moore,Scott	10	0	5
Moore,Tyler	10	0	5
Navarro,Yamaico	10	0	5
Nieuwenhuis,Kirk	10	0	5
Norris,Derek	10	0	5
Pastornicky,Tyler	10	0	5
Pill,Brett	10	0	5
Ross,Cody	2	8	5
Rutledge,Josh	10	0	5
Sanchez,Hector	10	0	5
Sappelt,Dave	10	0	5
Segura,Jean	10	0	5
Sierra,Moises	10	0	5
Simmons,Andrelton	10	0	5
Snyder,Brandon	10	0	5
Sogard,Eric	10	0	5
Solano,Donovan	10	0	5
Solano,Jhonatan	10	0	5
Valdespin,Jordany	10	0	5
Cozart,Zack	10	0	5
Lombardozzi,Steve	10	0	5
Nickeas,Mike	10	0	5
Parmelee,Chris	10	0	5
Parrino,Andy	10	0	5
Robinson,Trayvon	10	0	5
Callaspo,Alberto	7	2	5
Ludwick,Ryan	1	8	5
Murphy,Daniel	4	5	5
Ramirez,Alexei	8	1	5
Alvarez,Pedro	0	8	4
Cabrera,Everth	0	8	4
Hardy,J.J.	8	0	4
Iannetta,Chris	8	0	4
Saunders,Michael	0	8	4
Seager,Kyle	0	8	4
Utley,Chase	4	4	4
Belt,Brandon	0	7	4
Boesch,Brennan	7	0	4
Bourjos,Peter	7	0	4
Davis,Ike	0	7	4
Pierzynski,A.J.	0	7	4
Rosario,Wilin	0	7	4
Span,Denard	0	7	4
Bay,Jason	6	0	3
Blanco,Gregor	0	6	3
Colvin,Tyler	0	6	3
DeJesus,David	0	6	3
Jaso,John	0	6	3
Kotchman,Casey	6	0	3
Loney,James	6	0	3
Martin,Russell	0	6	3
Morneau,Justin	0	6	3
Morrison,Logan	6	0	3
Quentin,Carlos	5	1	3

BATTERS	'11	'12	R$
Ruggiano,Justin	0	6	3
Ellis,A.J.	0	5	3
Frazier,Todd	0	5	3
Gomes,Jonny	0	5	3
Hudson,Orlando	5	0	3
Lucroy,Jonathan	0	5	3
Alonso,Yonder	0	4	2
Denorfia,Chris	0	4	2
Johnson,Chris	0	4	2
Lawrie,Brett	0	4	2
Lind,Adam	4	0	2
Morales,Kendrys	0	4	2
Moss,Brandon	0	4	2
Pennington,Cliff	4	0	2
Weeks,Jemile	4	0	2
Carroll,Jamey	1	2	2
Furcal,Rafael	0	3	2
Hafner,Travis	3	0	2
Infante,Omar	0	3	2
Matsui,Hideki	3	0	2
Mayberry,John	3	0	2
Morgan,Nyjer	3	0	2
Rivera,Juan	3	0	2
Tabata,Jose	3	0	2
Thome,Jim	3	0	2
Thompson,Rich	3	0	2
Ackley,Dustin	1	1	1
Amarista,Alexi	0	1	1
Andino,Robert	2	0	1
Arencibia,J.P.	0	0	1
Arias,Joaquin	0	0	1
Barney,Darwin	0	0	1
Beckham,Gordon	0	0	1
Bernadina,Roger	0	0	1
Brown,Domonic	0	0	1
Cain,Lorenzo	0	0	1
Carpenter,Matt	0	1	1
Carrera,Ezequiel	0	0	1
Casilla,Alexi	0	0	1
Chisenhall,Lonnie	0	0	1
Crawford,Brandon	0	0	1
Crawford,Carl	2	0	1
Cruz,Luis	0	0	1
Cruz,Tony	0	0	1
Dirks,Andy	0	2	1
Doumit,Ryan	0	2	1
Duda,Lucas	2	0	1
Dyson,Jarrod	0	2	1
Forsythe,Logan	0	0	1
Francisco,Juan	0	0	1
Gamel,Mat	0	0	1
Gentry,Craig	0	0	1
Giavotella,Johnny	0	0	1
Gordon,Dee	0	0	1
Greene,Tyler	0	0	1
Gutierrez,Franklin	0	0	1
Guzman,Jesus	2	0	1
Hundley,Nick	0	0	1
Ibanez,Raul	2	0	1
Keppinger,Jeff	0	2	1
Kratz,Erik	0	0	1
LaHair,Bryan	0	1	1
LaPorta,Matt	0	0	1
Lavarnway,Ryan	0	0	1
Lowrie,Jed	0	0	1
Martinez,Fernando	0	0	1
Martinez,J.D.	0	0	1
Morel,Brent	0	0	1
Moreland,Mitch	2	0	1
Moustakas,Mike	0	1	1
Nelson,Chris	0	2	1
Nunez,Eduardo	1	0	1
Pacheco,Jordan	0	2	1
Paredes,Jimmy	0	0	1
Plouffe,Trevor	0	0	1
Rasmus,Colby	1	1	1
Reimold,Nolan	1	0	1
Rizzo,Anthony	0	1	1
Robinson,Shane	0	0	1
Saltalamacchia,Jarrod	0	0	1
Schafer,Jordan	0	0	1
Viciedo,Dayan	0	2	1

ROTISSERIE 500   2013 Draft - List Prices   Pitchers

PITCHERS	'11	'12	R$	PITCHERS	'11	'12	R$	PITCHERS	'11	'12	R$	PITCHERS	'11	'12	R$
Verlander,Justin	40	35	38	Iwakuma,Hisashi	10	4	7	Valdes,Raul	10	0	5	Capps,Matt	0	0	1
Kershaw,Clayton	38	32	35	Motte,Jason	6	8	7	Villarreal,Brayan	10	0	5	Cecil,Brett	0	0	1
Weaver,Jered	30	24	27	Adams,Mike	13	0	7	Walters,P.J.	10	0	5	Chatwood,Tyler	0	0	1
Gonzalez,Gio	18	30	24	Axford,John	13	0	7	Wieland,Joe	10	0	5	Chen,Bruce	0	0	1
Hamels,Cole	21	25	23	Diamond,Scott	10	3	7	Aceves,Alfredo	9	0	5	Cobb,Alex	0	0	1
Price,David	12	34	23	Harrell,Lucas	10	3	7	Dempster,Ryan	0	9	5	Collins,Tim	0	0	1
Lee,Cliff	32	13	23	Johnson,Jim	5	8	7	Frieri,Ernesto	0	9	5	Collmenter,Josh	2	0	1
Cain,Matt	17	27	22	Peavy,Jake	0	13	7	Jansen,Kenley	0	9	5	Colon,Bartolo	0	2	1
Shields,James	26	17	22	Strop,Pedro	10	3	7	Pestano,Vinnie	2	7	5	Correia,Kevin	0	0	1
Sabathia,CC	26	16	21	Balfour,Grant	4	8	6	Soriano,Rafael	0	9	5	Davis,Wade	0	0	1
Dickey,R.A.	6	35	21	Burton,Jared	10	2	6	Wilhelmsen,Tom	0	9	5	De La Rosa,Rubby	0	0	1
Cueto,Johnny	12	28	20	Hudson,Daniel	12	0	6	Bailey,Homer	0	8	4	Drabek,Kyle	0	0	1
Hernandez,Felix	15	23	19	Jones,Nate	10	2	6	Boggs,Mitchell	0	8	4	Duensing,Brian	0	0	1
Kimbrel,Craig	15	19	17	Lester,Jon	12	0	6	Buehrle,Mark	4	4	4	Eovaldi,Nathan	0	0	1
Halladay,Roy	33	0	17	Lynn,Lance	0	12	6	Garcia,Jaime	8	0	4	Estrada,Marco	0	0	1
Kennedy,Ian	26	6	16	Valverde,Jose	12	0	6	Harang,Aaron	5	3	4	Feldman,Scott	0	0	1
Bumgarner,Madison	14	17	16	Chen,Wei-Yin	10	1	6	Hernandez,David	4	4	4	Feliz,Neftali	1	0	1
Kuroda,Hiroki	14	16	15	Darvish,Yu	0	11	6	Jurrjens,Jair	8	0	4	Floyd,Gavin	0	0	1
Gallardo,Yovani	15	14	15	Garza,Matt	11	0	6	Marcum,Shaun	8	0	4	Garcia,Freddy	1	0	1
Lohse,Kyle	7	21	14	Holland,Greg	6	5	6	Putz,J.J.	8	0	4	Gee,Dillon	0	0	1
Wilson,C.J.	22	6	14	Masterson,Justin	11	0	6	Rivera,Mariano	8	0	4	Grilli,Jason	0	2	1
Vogelsong,Ryan	15	12	14	Niese,Jonathon	0	11	6	Worley,Vance	8	0	4	Guthrie,Jeremy	0	0	1
Greinke,Zack	10	16	13	Rodriguez,Wandy	7	4	6	Belisario,Ronald	0	7	4	Hammel,Jason	0	0	1
Medlen,Kris	0	25	13	Ross,Robbie	10	1	6	Downs,Scott	7	0	4	Happ,J.A.	0	0	1
Harrison,Matt	8	16	12	Storen,Drew	11	0	6	Morrow,Brandon	0	7	4	Hochevar,Luke	0	0	1
Miley,Wade	10	14	12	Avilan,Luis	10	0	5	Salas,Fernando	7	0	4	Howell,J.P.	0	0	1
Sale,Chris	2	22	12	Axelrod,Dylan	10	0	5	Samardzija,Jeff	4	3	4	Humber,Philip	0	0	1
Lincecum,Tim	22	0	11	Blackley,Travis	10	0	5	Sanchez,Anibal	5	2	4	Hunter,Tommy	0	0	1
Rodney,Fernando	0	22	11	Bowden,Michael	10	0	5	Bell,Heath	6	0	3	Janssen,Casey	0	0	1
Cook,Ryan	10	11	11	Brach,Brad	10	0	5	Cahill,Trevor	0	6	3	Jimenez,Ubaldo	0	0	1
Hudson,Tim	15	6	11	Capps,Carter	10	0	5	Capuano,Chris	0	6	3	Johnson,Josh	0	1	1
Allen,Cody	10	10	10	Carpenter,Chris	10	0	5	Casilla,Santiago	0	6	3	Karstens,Jeff	1	0	1
Archer,Chris	10	10	10	Carpenter,Chris	10	0	5	Cordero,Francisco	6	0	3	Kendrick,Kyle	0	0	1
Aumont,Phillippe	10	10	10	Carpenter,David	10	0	5	Crain,Jesse	6	0	3	Laffey,Aaron	0	0	1
Bauer,Trevor	10	10	10	Cedeno,Xavier	10	0	5	Holland,Derek	6	0	3	League,Brandon	1	0	1
Bundy,Dylan	10	10	10	Cruz,Rhiner	10	0	5	Maholm,Paul	0	6	3	Leake,Mike	1	0	1
Chapman,Aroldis	0	20	10	Deduno,Samuel	10	0	5	Ogando,Alexi	6	0	3	Lewis,Colby	0	0	1
Cingrani,Tony	10	10	10	Delabar,Steve	10	0	5	Stammen,Craig	0	6	3	Lincoln,Brad	0	0	1
Cloyd,Tyler	10	10	10	Delgado,Randall	10	0	5	Wainwright,Adam	0	6	3	Lindblom,Josh	0	0	1
Familia,Jeurys	10	10	10	DeVries,Cole	10	0	5	Bastardo,Antonio	5	0	3	Liriano,Francisco	0	0	1
Fife,Stephen	10	10	10	Diekman,Jake	10	0	5	Chacin,Jhoulys	5	0	3	Locke,Jeff	0	0	1
Hellickson,Jeremy	11	9	10	Dolis,Rafael	10	0	5	Gregerson,Luke	0	5	3	Lowe,Derek	0	0	1
Johnson,Steve	10	10	10	Doolittle,Sean	10	0	5	Mcgee,Jake	0	5	3	Lyles,Jordan	0	0	1
Kelly,Casey	10	10	10	Doubront,Felix	10	0	5	Melancon,Mark	5	0	3	Marquis,Jason	0	0	1
Kluber,Corey	10	10	10	Fien,Casey	10	0	5	Nathan,Joe	0	5	3	Mattheus,Ryan	0	0	1
Latos,Mat	7	13	10	Fiers,Mike	10	0	5	O Day,Darren	0	5	3	McDonald,James	0	0	1
Layne,Tom	10	10	10	Friedrich,Christian	10	0	5	Perkins,Glen	1	4	3	Mijares,Jose	0	0	1
McPherson,Kyle	10	10	10	Gonzalez,Michael	10	0	5	Wolf,Randy	5	0	3	Millwood,Kevin	0	0	1
Miller,Shelby	10	10	10	Gonzalez,Miguel	10	0	5	Beachy,Brandon	2	2	2	Minor,Mike	0	0	1
Odorizzi,Jake	10	10	10	Griffin,A.J.	10	0	5	Broxton,Jonathan	0	4	2	Morales,Franklin	0	0	1
Peralta,Wily	10	10	10	Harvey,Matt	10	0	5	Cishek,Steve	0	4	2	Myers,Brett	0	0	1
Perez,Martin	10	10	10	Hefner,Jeremy	10	0	5	Detwiler,Ross	0	4	2	Nicasio,Juan	0	0	1
Pryor,Stephen	10	10	10	Hendriks,Liam	10	0	5	Hanson,Tommy	4	0	2	Noesi,Hector	0	0	1
Rogers,Mark	10	10	10	Hughes,Jared	10	0	5	Jackson,Edwin	4	0	2	Nolasco,Ricky	0	0	1
Rosenthal,Trevor	10	10	10	Hutchison,Drew	10	0	5	Lopez,Wilton	0	4	2	Norris,Bud	1	0	1
Rusin,Chris	10	10	10	Kelly,Joe	10	0	5	Luebke,Cory	4	0	2	Oswalt,Roy	0	0	1
Savery,Joe	10	10	10	Keuchel,Dallas	10	0	5	McCarthy,Brandon	4	0	2	Patton,Troy	0	0	1
Skaggs,Tyler	10	10	10	Kontos,George	10	0	5	Nova,Ivan	4	0	2	Peralta,Joel	1	1	1
Straily,Dan	10	10	10	Luetge,Lucas	10	0	5	Vargas,Jason	0	4	2	Perez,Chris	1	0	1
Teheran,Julio	10	10	10	Marte,Victor	10	0	5	Wilson,Brian	4	0	2	Porcello,Rick	0	0	1
Thornburg,Tyler	10	10	10	McAllister,Zach	10	0	5	Arroyo,Bronson	0	3	2	Richard,Clayton	0	0	1
Vincent,Nick	10	10	10	Mejia,Jenrry	10	0	5	Benoit,Joaquin	2	1	2	Rodriguez,Fernando	0	0	1
Werner,Andrew	10	10	10	Norberto,Jordan	10	0	5	Billingsley,Chad	0	3	2	Santana,Johan	0	0	1
Zimmermann,Jordan	4	16	10	Ottavino,Adam	10	0	5	Farnsworth,Kyle	3	0	2	Santos,Sergio	2	0	1
Fister,Doug	14	5	10	Phelps,David	10	0	5	Hughes,Phil	0	3	2	Saunders,Joe	2	0	1
Romero,Ricky	19	0	10	Pomeranz,Drew	10	0	5	Mujica,Edward	3	0	2	Shaw,Bryan	0	0	1
Haren,Dan	18	0	9	Quintana,Jose	10	0	5	Parnell,Bobby	0	3	2	Sipp,Tony	2	0	1
Marshall,Sean	12	6	9	Ramirez,Erasmo	10	0	5	Uehara,Koji	3	0	2	Smith,Joe	0	1	1
Parker,Jarrod	10	8	9	Reed,Addison	10	0	5	Walden,Jordan	3	0	2	Stults,Eric	0	0	1
Robertson,David	15	3	9	Richards,Garrett	10	0	5	Alvarez,Henderson	0	0	1	Thornton,Matt	0	0	1
Strasburg,Stephen	0	18	9	Rodriguez,Francisco	10	0	5	Arredondo,Jose	0	0	1	Tomlin,Josh	0	0	1
Herrera,Kelvin	10	7	9	Ross,Tyson	10	0	5	Arrieta,Jake	0	0	1	Villanueva,Carlos	0	0	1
Venters,Jonny	17	0	9	Santana,Ervin	10	0	5	Atchison,Scott	0	0	1	Volquez,Edinson	0	0	1
Beckett,Josh	16	0	8	Santiago,Hector	10	0	5	Bard,Daniel	1	0	1	Volstad,Chris	0	0	1
O Flaherty,Eric	11	5	8	Scheppers,Tanner	10	0	5	Bass,Anthony	0	0	1	Webb,Ryan	0	0	1
Papelbon,Jonathan	5	11	8	Scribner,Evan	10	0	5	Beavan,Blake	0	0	1	Westbrook,Jake	0	0	1
Scherzer,Max	1	15	8	Smith,Will	10	0	5	Betancourt,Rafael	1	0	1	White,Alex	0	0	1
Clippard,Tyler	13	2	8	Smyly,Drew	10	0	5	Blanton,Joe	0	0	1	Williams,Jerome	0	0	1
Milone,Tommy	10	5	8	Tazawa,Junichi	10	0	5	Blevins,Jerry	0	1	1	Wood,Travis	0	0	1
Moore,Matt	10	5	8	Thayer,Dale	10	0	5	Brothers,Rex	0	0	1	Young,Chris	0	0	1
Romo,Sergio	5	10	8	Torres,Carlos	10	0	5	Buchholz,Clay	0	0	1	Ziegler,Brad	0	1	1
Hanrahan,Joel	8	6	7	Turner,Jacob	10	0	5	Burnett,Sean	0	2	1	Zito,Barry	0	0	1

Simulation League Cheat Sheet   Using Runs Above Replacement creates a more real-world ranking of player value, which serves simulation gamers well. Batters and pitchers are integrated, and value break-points are delineated.

SIMULATION LEAGUE DRAFT   TOP 500+

NAME	POS	RAR	NAME	POS	RAR	NAME	POS	RAR	NAME	POS	RAR
Cabrera,Miguel	5	74.1	Latos,Mat	P	17.4	Jones,Adam	8	9.9	Rivera,Mariano	P	6.7
Votto,Joey	3	59.1	Wainwright,Adam	P	17.2	Casilla,Santiago	P	9.8	Soriano,Alfonso	7	6.6
Braun,Ryan	7	58.8	Gordon,Alex	7	17.1	Hellickson,Jeremy	P	9.8	Holland,Greg	P	6.5
Cano,Robinson	4	47.7	Gonzalez,Adrian	3	17.0	Konerko,Paul	3	9.8	Putz,J.J.	P	6.5
Tulowitzki,Troy	6	42.4	Prado,Martin	57	16.6	Burton,Jared	P	9.7	Capps,Carter	P	6.4
Kershaw,Clayton	P	39.9	Kimbrel,Craig	P	16.4	Fister,Doug	P	9.7	Garcia,Jaime	P	6.4
Fielder,Prince	3	38.1	Ethier,Andre	9	16.3	Fujikawa,Kyuji	P	9.7	McCann,Brian	2	6.4
Holliday,Matt	7	35.7	Morse,Michael	79	16.3	Kuroda,Hiroki	P	9.7	Pence,Hunter	9	6.4
Pedroia,Dustin	4	35.2	Scherzer,Max	P	16.1	Avila,Alex	2	9.5	Profar,Jurickson	4	6.3
Posey,Buster	23	34.1	Moore,Matt	P	15.9	Morales,Kendrys	3	9.5	Hernandez,David	P	6.2
Beltre,Adrian	5	33.6	Weeks,Rickie	4	15.9	Sanchez,Anibal	P	9.5	Hudson,Tim	P	6.2
McCutchen,Andrew	8	33.5	Lucroy,Jonathan	2	15.8	Morrison,Logan	37	9.4	Jaso,John	2	6.2
Kemp,Matt	8	32.9	Lowrie,Jed	6	15.6	Samardzija,Jeff	P	9.3	Peralta,Jhonny	6	6.2
Butler,Billy	3	31.7	Cabrera,Asdrubal	6	15.4	Venters,Jonny	P	9.3	Cruz,Nelson	9	6.1
Stanton,Giancarlo	9	31.1	Werth,Jayson	9	15.2	Niese,Jon	P	9.2	Hammel,Jason	P	6.0
Reyes,Jose	6	30.6	Kinsler,Ian	4	14.8	Jansen,Kenley	P	9.0	Uehara,Koji	P	6.0
Hamels,Cole	P	30.4	Cook,Ryan	P	14.6	Hart,Corey	39	8.9	Drew,Stephen	6	5.9
Ortiz,David	0	30.1	Darvish,Yu	P	14.6	Lopez,Wilton	P	8.9	Kennedy,Ian	P	5.9
Trout,Mike	78	29.7	Zobrist,Ben	469	14.6	Cabrera,Melky	7	8.8	Lopez,Javier	P	5.9
Encarnacion,Edwin	3	29.4	Craig,Allen	39	14.5	Freese,David	5	8.7	Peralta,Joel	P	5.9
Price,David	P	29.3	Chapman,Aroldis	P	14.1	Nakajima,Hiroyuki	6	8.6	Infante,Omar	4	5.8
Longoria,Evan	5	28.4	Montero,Miguel	2	14.1	Rodney,Fernando	P	8.6	Stauffer,Tim	P	5.8
Zimmerman,Ryan	5	28.3	Beltran,Carlos	9	14.0	Scutaro,Marco	46	8.6	Lecure,Sam	P	5.6
Verlander,Justin	P	28.2	Murphy,David	7	14.0	Balfour,Grant	P	8.5	Lilly,Ted	P	5.6
Gonzalez,Carlos	7	27.9	Kubel,Jason	7	13.6	Garza,Matt	P	8.5	Pagan,Angel	8	5.6
Hill,Aaron	4	27.6	O Flaherty,Eric	P	13.5	Milone,Tommy	P	8.5	Minor,Mike	P	5.5
Pujols,Albert	3	27.6	Rutledge,Josh	6	13.5	Ogando,Alexi	P	8.5	Belisario,Ronald	P	5.3
Strasburg,Stephen	P	27.3	Heyward,Jason	9	13.3	Ziegler,Brad	P	8.4	Gorzelanny,Tom	P	5.3
Mauer,Joe	23	26.8	Choo,Shin-Soo	9	13.2	Cishek,Steve	P	8.3	Worley,Vance	P	5.3
Santana,Carlos	23	26.6	Sabathia,CC	P	13.2	Frazier,Todd	35	8.3	Benoit,Joaquin	P	5.2
Wright,David	5	25.9	Goldschmidt,Paul	3	13.1	Perkins,Glen	P	8.2	Brach,Brad	P	5.2
Cueto,Johnny	P	25.8	Greinke,Zack	P	13.1	Soriano,Rafael	P	8.2	Furbush,Charlie	P	5.2
Ramirez,Aramis	5	25.7	Aybar,Erick	6	12.8	Lohse,Kyle	P	8.1	Lindstrom,Matt	P	5.2
Molina,Yadier	2	25.4	Cahill,Trevor	P	12.8	Beachy,Brandon	P	8.0	Peavy,Jake	P	5.2
Hamilton,Josh	78	25.2	Martinez,Victor	0	12.8	Berkman,Lance	3	8.0	Dirks,Andy	79	5.1
Weaver,Jered	P	25.2	Murphy,Daniel	4	12.7	Pestano,Vinnie	P	8.0	Iannetta,Chris	2	5.1
Cain,Matt	P	24.5	Perez,Salvador	2	12.7	Davis,Wade	P	7.8	Taveras,Oscar	9	5.1
Bautista,Jose	9	23.4	Jackson,Austin	8	12.6	Janssen,Casey	P	7.8	Grilli,Jason	P	5.0
Youkilis,Kevin	35	22.7	Romo,Sergio	P	12.6	Crisp,Coco	8	7.7	Betancourt,Rafael	P	4.9
Hernandez,Felix	P	22.6	Swisher,Nick	39	12.5	Lawrie,Brett	5	7.7	Kontos,George	P	4.9
Headley,Chase	5	22.3	Gallardo,Yovani	P	12.4	Ludwick,Ryan	7	7.7	Teixeira,Mark	3	4.9
Napoli,Mike	23	22.0	Doumit,Ryan	2	12.3	Frieri,Ernesto	P	7.5	Wilhelmsen,Tom	P	4.9
Shields,James	P	22.0	Rollins,Jimmy	6	12.2	Mujica,Edward	P	7.5	Brothers,Rex	P	4.8
Zimmermann,Jordan	P	22.0	Anderson,Brett	P	12.1	Street,Huston	P	7.5	D Arnaud,Travis	2	4.8
Ruiz,Carlos	2	21.7	Granderson,Curtis	8	12.1	Kipnis,Jason	4	7.4	Hanrahan,Joel	P	4.8
Wieters,Matt	2	21.5	Motte,Jason	P	12.0	Miley,Wade	P	7.4	Niemann,Jeff	P	4.7
Cespedes,Yoenis	78	21.3	Herrera,Kelvin	P	11.9	Patton,Troy	P	7.3	Perez,Chris	P	4.7
Dickey,R.A.	P	21.2	Johnson,Josh	P	11.9	Wilson,C.J.	P	7.3	Carpenter,Chris	P	4.6
Lee,Cliff	P	20.5	Quentin,Carlos	7	11.7	Broxton,Jonathan	P	7.2	Pryor,Stephen	P	4.6
Gonzalez,Gio	P	20.4	Gregerson,Luke	P	11.4	Morrow,Brandon	P	7.2	Ross,David	2	4.6
Medlen,Kris	P	20.4	Storen,Drew	P	11.2	Parnell,Bobby	P	7.1	Soria,Joakim	P	4.6
Markakis,Nick	9	19.6	Robertson,David	P	10.8	Crain,Jesse	P	7.0	Vogelsong,Ryan	P	4.5
Sale,Chris	P	19.5	Phillips,Brandon	4	10.7	Luebke,Cory	P	7.0	Pierzynski,A.J.	2	4.4
Castro,Starlin	6	19.1	Halladay,Roy	P	10.5	Affeldt,Jeremy	P	6.9	Altuve,Jose	4	4.3
Sandoval,Pablo	5	19.0	Crawford,Carl	7	10.4	Mcgee,Jake	P	6.9	Breslow,Craig	P	4.3
Bumgarner,Madison	P	18.8	Papelbon,Jonathan	P	10.3	Ramirez,Hanley	56	6.9	Jeter,Derek	6	4.3
Utley,Chase	4	18.4	O Day,Darren	P	10.2	Harrison,Matt	P	6.8	LaRoche,Adam	3	4.3
Willingham,Josh	7	18.4	Marshall,Sean	P	10.1	Kendrick,Howie	4	6.8	Andrus,Elvis	6	4.2
Desmond,Ian	6	18.1	Walker,Neil	4	10.1	Myers,Brett	P	6.8	League,Brandon	P	4.2
Fowler,Dexter	8	17.9	Davis,Ike	3	10.0	Nathan,Joe	P	6.8	Middlebrooks,Will	5	4.1
Upton,Justin	9	17.9	Iwakuma,Hisashi	P	10.0	Rodriguez,Alex	5	6.8	Upton,B.J.	8	4.1
Bruce,Jay	9	17.7	Oliver,Darren	P	10.0	Clippard,Tyler	P	6.7	Montero,Jesus	2	4.0
Harper,Bryce	89	17.6	Burnett,Sean	P	9.9	Cuddyer,Michael	39	6.7	Adams,Mike	P	3.9

SIMULATION LEAGUE DRAFT — TOP 500+

NAME	POS	RAR	NAME	POS	RAR	NAME	POS	RAR	NAME	POS	RAR
Cloyd,Tyler	P	3.9	Karstens,Jeff	P	2.3	Collmenter,Josh	P	1.1	Morales,Franklin	P	-0.4
Kottaras,George	2	3.9	Martin,Russell	2	2.3	Fiers,Mike	P	1.1	Odorizzi,Jake	P	-0.4
Thornton,Matt	P	3.9	Rzepczynski,Marc	P	2.3	Hanson,Tommy	P	1.1	Trumbo,Mark	79	-0.4
Delabar,Steve	P	3.8	Saltalamacchia,Jarrod	2	2.3	Keppinger,Jeff	345	1.1	Johnson,Steve	P	-0.5
Madson,Ryan	P	3.8	Dempster,Ryan	P	2.2	Lowe,Mark	P	1.1	Nix,Laynce	7	-0.5
Smyly,Drew	P	3.8	Maholm,Paul	P	2.2	Santana,Johan	P	1.1	Parra,Gerardo	78	-0.5
Thome,Jim	0	3.8	Bundy,Dylan	P	2.1	Segura,Jean	6	1.1	Resop,Chris	P	-0.5
Wright,Wesley	P	3.8	Danks,John	P	2.1	Shaw,Bryan	P	1.1	Schumaker,Skip	4	-0.5
Ayala,Luis	P	3.7	Floyd,Gavin	P	2.1	Lyon,Brandon	P	1.0	Carpenter,David	P	-0.6
Boggs,Mitchell	P	3.7	Jones,Nate	P	2.1	Sipp,Tony	P	1.0	Estrada,Marco	P	-0.6
Johnson,Jim	P	3.7	Morneau,Justin	3	2.1	Alburquerque,Al	P	0.9	Kelly,Joe	P	-0.6
Ramos,Wilson	2	3.7	Ramirez,Alexei	6	2.1	Darnell,James	7	0.9	Oswalt,Roy	P	-0.6
Strop,Pedro	P	3.7	Wheeler,Zack	P	2.1	Gee,Dillon	P	0.9	Sizemore,Scott	5	-0.6
Walden,Jordan	P	3.7	Atchison,Scott	P	2.0	Thornburg,Tyler	P	0.9	Coleman,Louis	P	-0.7
Axford,John	P	3.6	Billingsley,Chad	P	2.0	Viciedo,Dayan	7	0.8	Kennedy,Adam	5	-0.7
Marcum,Shaun	P	3.6	Crow,Aaron	P	2.0	Frasor,Jason	P	0.7	Thames,Eric	79	-0.7
Watson,Tony	P	3.6	De La Rosa,Rubby	P	2.0	Cashner,Andrew	P	0.6	Tillman,Chris	P	-0.7
Doolittle,Sean	P	3.5	Flowers,Tyler	2	2.0	Elbert,Scott	P	0.6	Valdes,Raul	P	-0.7
Pettitte,Andy	P	3.5	Hairston,Scott	79	2.0	Ellis,A.J.	2	0.6	Acosta,Manny	P	-0.8
Phelps,David	P	3.5	Howell,J.P.	P	2.0	Gonzalez,Michael	P	0.6	Beckett,Josh	P	-0.8
Wilson,Brian	P	3.5	Mijares,Jose	P	2.0	Lincoln,Brad	P	0.6	Harang,Aaron	P	-0.8
Reimold,Nolan	7	3.4	Salas,Fernando	P	2.0	Soto,Geovany	2	0.6	Nunez,Eduardo	6	-0.8
Smith,Joe	P	3.4	Cobb,Alex	P	1.9	Stammen,Craig	P	0.6	Takahashi,Hisanori	P	-0.8
Archer,Chris	P	3.3	Norberto,Jordan	P	1.9	Escobar,Alcides	6	0.5	Villanueva,Carlos	P	-0.8
Kelley,Shawn	P	3.3	Rodriguez,Francisco	P	1.9	Furcal,Rafael	6	0.5	Grandal,Yasmani	2	-0.9
Kendrick,Kyle	P	3.3	Chamberlain,Joba	P	1.8	Heisey,Chris	78	0.5	McAllister,Zach	P	-0.9
Uggla,Dan	4	3.3	Eovaldi,Nathan	P	1.8	Melancon,Mark	P	0.5	Mesoraco,Devin	2	-0.9
Badenhop,Burke	P	3.2	Jackson,Edwin	P	1.8	Ramirez,Ramon	P	0.5	Russell,James	P	-0.9
Betemit,Wilson	5	3.2	Marmol,Carlos	P	1.8	Smith,Seth	7	0.5	Villarreal,Brayan	P	-0.9
Haren,Dan	P	3.2	Rapada,Clay	P	1.8	Fien,Casey	P	0.4	Baker,Scott	P	-1.0
Lincecum,Tim	P	3.2	Young Jr.,Eric	8	1.8	Holland,Derek	P	0.4	Cruz,Juan	P	-1.0
Lewis,Colby	P	3.1	McDonald,James	P	1.7	Nelson,Chris	45	0.4	Helton,Todd	3	-1.0
Rodriguez,Wandy	P	3.1	Rosario,Wilin	2	1.7	Bernadina,Roger	78	0.3	Scheppers,Tanner	P	-1.0
Albers,Matt	P	2.9	Santiago,Hector	P	1.7	Buehrle,Mark	P	0.3	Wright,Jamey	P	-1.0
Avilan,Luis	P	2.9	Santos,Sergio	P	1.7	Capps,Matt	P	0.3	Axelrod,Dylan	P	-1.1
Capuano,Chris	P	2.9	Webb,Ryan	P	1.7	Ellsbury,Jacoby	8	0.3	Bloomquist,Willie	6	-1.1
Dotel,Octavio	P	2.9	Collins,Tim	P	1.6	Feliz,Neftali	P	0.3	Gardner,Brett	7	-1.1
Hardy,J.J.	6	2.9	Downs,Scott	P	1.6	Freeman,Freddie	3	0.3	Rios,Alex	9	-1.1
Ibanez,Raul	7	2.9	Eaton,Adam	8	1.6	Loe,Kameron	P	0.2	Scott,Luke	0	-1.1
Lindblom,Josh	P	2.9	Eppley,Cody	P	1.6	Rogers,Esmil	P	0.2	Turner,Jacob	P	-1.1
Tazawa,Junichi	P	2.9	Gomes,Jonny	7	1.6	Detwiler,Ross	P	0.1	Wieland,Joe	P	-1.1
Thatcher,Joe	P	2.9	McCarthy,Brandon	P	1.6	Hawkins,LaTroy	P	0.1	de la Rosa,Jorge	P	-1.2
Bell,Heath	P	2.8	Straily,Dan	P	1.6	Miller,Shelby	P	0.1	Duffy,Danny	P	-1.2
Buchholz,Clay	P	2.8	Burnett,A.J.	P	1.5	Rogers,Mark	P	0.1	Reynolds,Matt	P	-1.2
Lester,Jon	P	2.8	Escobar,Yunel	6	1.5	Rolen,Scott	5	0.1	Abreu,Bobby	7	-1.3
Mattheus,Ryan	P	2.8	Harvey,Matt	P	1.5	Bass,Anthony	P	0.0	Accardo,Jeremy	P	-1.3
Parker,Jarrod	P	2.8	Belisle,Matt	P	1.4	Nova,Ivan	P	0.0	Arencibia,J.P.	2	-1.3
Simon,Alfredo	P	2.8	Davis,Chris	39	1.4	Roberts,Brian	4	0.0	Pacheco,Jordan	35	-1.3
Bauer,Trevor	P	2.7	Young,Michael	35	1.4	Valverde,Jose	P	0.0	Moore,Tyler	7	-1.4
Harrell,Lucas	P	2.7	Aoki,Norichika	9	1.3	Coke,Phil	P	-0.1	Martin,Leonys	8	-1.5
Ramirez,Erasmo	P	2.7	Bastardo,Antonio	P	1.3	Francisco,Frank	P	-0.1	McKenry,Michael	2	-1.5
Ross,Robbie	P	2.7	Bowden,Michael	P	1.3	Hefner,Jeremy	P	-0.1	Pelfrey,Mike	P	-1.5
Arredondo,Jose	P	2.6	Diekman,Jake	P	1.3	Rauch,Jon	P	-0.1	Teaford,Everett	P	-1.5
Bailey,Homer	P	2.6	Guzman,Jesus	7	1.3	Reed,Addison	P	-0.1	Hafner,Travis	0	-1.6
Farnsworth,Kyle	P	2.6	Logan,Boone	P	1.3	Dunn,Mike	P	-0.2	Jones,Andruw	79	-1.6
Scribner,Evan	P	2.6	Martinez,Cristhian	P	1.3	Lavarnway,Ryan	2	-0.2	Joyce,Matt	79	-1.6
Thayer,Dale	P	2.6	Griffin,A.J.	P	1.2	Miller,Jim	P	-0.2	Parmelee,Chris	3	-1.6
Choate,Randy	P	2.5	Guerra,Javy	P	1.2	Paulino,Felipe	P	-0.2	Skaggs,Tyler	P	-1.6
Victorino,Shane	78	2.5	Hughes,Jared	P	1.2	Diamond,Scott	P	-0.3	Brantly,Rob	2	-1.7
Lynn,Lance	P	2.4	Jepsen,Kevin	P	1.2	Camp,Shawn	P	-0.4	Cooper,David	3	-1.7
Blevins,Jerry	P	2.3	Rosenthal,Trevor	P	1.2	Carrasco,Carlos	P	-0.4	Norris,Bud	P	-1.7
Chavez,Eric	5	2.3	Veras,Jose	P	1.2	Durbin,Chad	P	-0.4	Wells,Casper	79	-1.7
Chen,Wei-Yin	P	2.3	Bailey,Andrew	P	1.1	Luetge,Lucas	P	-0.4	Alvarez,Pedro	5	-1.8

2013 FANTASY BASEBALL WINNERS RESOURCE GUIDE

orders.baseballhq.com

10 REASONS

why <u>winners</u> rely on BASEBALL HQ PRODUCTS for fantasy baseball information

1 **NO OTHER RESOURCE** provides you with more vital intelligence to help you win. Compare the <u>depth</u> of our offerings in these pages with any other information product or service.

2 **NO OTHER RESOURCE** provides more <u>exclusive</u> information, like cutting-edge component skills analyses, revolutionary strategies like the LIMA Plan, and innovative gaming formats like Rotisserie 500. *You won't find these anywhere else on the internet, guaranteed.*

3 **NO OTHER RESOURCE** has as long and consistent a <u>track record of success</u> in top national competitions... Our writers and readers have achieved 33 first place finishes, plus another 28 second and third place finishes since 1997. *No other resource comes remotely close.*

4 **NO OTHER RESOURCE** has as consistent a track record in <u>projecting impact performances</u>. In 2012, our readers had surprises like Everth Cabrera, Chris Davis, Edwin Encarnacion, Dexter Fowler, Yadier Molina, Trevor Plouffe, Wilin Rosario, Carlos Ruiz, Homer Bailey, A.J. Burnett, R.A. Dickey, Casey Janssen, Kris Medlen, Brandon Morrow, Jake Peavy, Max Scherzer and Chris Tillman on their teams, *and dozens more.*

5 **NO OTHER RESOURCE** is supported by more than 50 <u>top writers and analysts</u> — all paid professionals and proven winners, not weekend hobbyists or corporate staffers.

6 **NO OTHER RESOURCE** has a <u>wider scope</u>, providing valuable information not only for Rotisserie, but for alternative formats like simulations, salary cap contests, online games, points, head-to-head, dynasty leagues and others.

7 **NO OTHER RESOURCE** is as <u>highly regarded by its peers in the industry</u>. Baseball HQ is the *only* three-time winner of the Fantasy Sports Trade Association's "Best Fantasy Baseball Online Content" award and Ron Shandler has won two lifetime achievement awards.

8 **NO OTHER RESOURCE** is as <u>highly regarded *outside* of the fantasy industry</u>. Many Major League general managers are regular customers. We were advisors to the St. Louis Cardinals in 2004 and our former Minor League Director is now a scout for the organization.

9 **NO OTHER RESOURCE** has been <u>creating fantasy baseball winners for as long as we have</u>. Our 27 years of stability *guarantees your investment.*

10 Year after year, more than 90% of our customers report that Baseball HQ products and services have helped them improve their performance in their fantasy leagues. <u>That's the bottom line</u>.

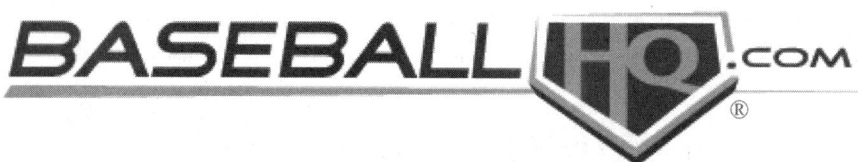

 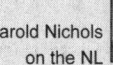 
 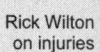 

2013 MINOR LEAGUE BASEBALL ANALYST

By Rob Gordon and Jeremy Deloney

The **Minor League Baseball Analyst** is the first book to integrate sabermetrics and scouting. For baseball analysts and those who play in fantasy leagues with farm systems, the *Analyst* is the perfect complement to the *Baseball Forecaster* and is designed exactly for your needs:

- *Stats and Sabermetrics...* Over three dozen categories for 1000 minor leaguers, including batter skills ratings, pitch repertoires and more
- *Performance Trends...* spanning each player's last five minor league stops, complete with leading indicators
- *Scouting reports...* for all players, including expected major league debuts, potential major league roles and more
- *Major League Equivalents...* Five year scans for every player
- *Mega-Lists...* The Top 100 of 2013, retrospective looks at the Top 100s of 2005-2012, organizational Top 15s, top prospects by position, power and speed prospects, and more
- *Additional Reports...* on international prospects, fantasy implications and more...
- *Player Potential Ratings...* Baseball HQ's exclusive system that evaluates each player's upside potential and chances of achieving that potential.

The *Analyst* was founded by Deric McKamey, a Bill James disciple and graduate of Major League Baseball's scout school. Deric is now a scout for the St. Louis Cardinals.

Available January 2013

BOOKS

Art McGee's
HOW TO VALUE PLAYERS FOR ROTISSERIE® BASEBALL

Learn how to calculate the best player values for your draft or auction! Art McGee applies concepts from economics, finance, and statistics to develop a pricing method that far surpasses any other published. His method is highly sophisticated, yet McGee explains it in terms that any fantasy baseball owner can understand and apply.

In the 2nd Edition...
- Discover the power of Standings Gain Points (SGP)
- Learn how to adjust values for position scarcity, injury risk and future potential
- Set up your own pricing spreadsheet, as simple or sophisticated as you want
- Make better decisions on trades, free agents, and long-term contracts
- Apply these methods even if your league uses non-standard categories or has a non-standard number of teams
- PLUS... 10 additional essays to expand your knowledge base.

2013 CHEATER'S BOOKMARK

BATTING STATISTICS — BENCHMARKS

Abbrv	Term	Formula / Desc.	BAD UNDER	'12 LG AVG AL	'12 LG AVG NL	BEST OVER
Avg	Batting Average	h/ab	235	256	261	290
xBA	Expected Batting Average	See glossary		269	271	
OB	On Base Average	(h+bb)/(ab+bb)	290	317	323	350
Slg	Slugging Average	total bases/ab	350	412	414	475
OPS	On Base plus Slugging	OB+Slg	650	729	737	800
bb%	Walk Rate	bb/(ab+bb)	5%	8%	8%	10%
ct%	Contact Rate	(ab-k) / ab	75%	79%	79%	85%
Eye	Batting Eye	bb/k	0.40	0.42	0.43	0.80
PX	Power Index	Normalized power skills	80	100	100	120
Spd	Statistically Scouted Speed	Normalized speed skills	80	100	100	120
SBO	Stolen Base Opportunity %	(sb+cs)/(singles+bb)		10%	11%	
G/F	Groundball/Flyball Ratio	gb / fb		1.3	1.3	
G	Ground Ball Per Cent	gb / balls in play		44%	45%	
L	Line Drive Per Cent	ld / balls in play		21%	21%	
F	Fly Ball Per Cent	fb / balls in play		35%	34%	
BPV	Base Performance Value	See glossary	25	43	43	50
RC/G	Runs Created per Game	See glossary	3.00	4.47	4.59	6.00
RAR	Runs Above Replacement	See glossary	0.0			15.0

PITCHING STATISTICS — BENCHMARKS

Abbrv	Term	Formula / Desc.	BAD OVER	'12 LG AVG AL	'12 LG AVG NL	BEST UNDER
ERA	Earned Run Average	er*9/ip	4.75	4.09	3.95	3.00
xERA	Expected ERA	See glossary		3.84	3.74	
WHIP	Baserunners per Inning	(h+bb)/ip	1.50	1.31	1.31	1.15
BF/G	Batters Faced per Game	((ip*2.82)+h+bb)/g	28.0			
PC	Pitch Counts per Start		120	95	94	
OBA	Opposition Batting Avg	Opp. h/ab	290	255	254	240
OOB	Opposition On Base Avg	Opp. (h+bb)/(ab+bb)	350	315	316	290
BABIP	BatAvg on balls in play	(h-hr)/((ip*2.82)+h-k-hr)		296	303	
Ctl	Control Rate	bb*9/ip		3.0	3.1	2.8
hr/9	Homerun Rate	hr*9/ip		1.1	1.0	1.0
hr/f	Homerun per Fly ball	hr/fb		12%	11%	10%
S%	Strand Rate	(h+bb-er)/(h+bb-hr)		72%	72%	
DIS%	PQS Disaster Rate	% GS that are PQS 0/1		24%	21%	20%

Abbrv	Term	Formula / Desc.	BAD UNDER	'12 LG AVG AL	'12 LG AVG NL	BEST OVER
RAR	Runs Above Replacement	See glossary	-0.0			+25.0
Dom	Dominance Rate	k*9/ip		7.4	7.7	7.0
Cmd	Command Ratio	k/bb		2.5	2.5	2.5
G/F	Groundball/Flyball Ratio	gb / fb		1.28	1.37	
BPV	Base Performance Value	See glossary	50	74	79	100
DOM%	PQS Dominance Rate	% GS that are PQS 4/5		45%	50%	50%
Sv%	Saves Conversion Rate	(saves / save opps)		72%	68%	80%
REff%	Relief Effectiveness Rate	See glossary		67%	67%	80%

NOTES